The **RED-HOT** Book of
Spanish Slang
and **Idioms**

Other titles by the same authors

Streetwise Spanish

Streetwise Spanish, CD edition

Streetwise Spanish Dictionary/Thesaurus

Tune Up Your Spanish

The RED-HOT Book of Spanish Slang and Idioms

5,000 Expressions to Spice Up Your Spanish

Mary McVey Gill & Brenda Wegmann

New York   Chicago   San Francisco   Lisbon   London   Madrid   Mexico City
Milan   New Delhi   San Juan   Seoul   Singapore   Sydney   Toronto

The McGraw-Hill Companies

Library of Congress Cataloging-in-Publication Data

Gill, Mary McVey.
    The red-hot book of Spanish slang and idioms : 5,000 expressions to spice up your
Spanish / by Mary McVey Gill & Brenda Wegmann.
        p.   cm.
    ISBN 0-07-143301-5 (alk. paper)
    1. Spanish language—Slang.   I. Wegmann, Brenda, 1941–   II. Title.

    PC4971.G547   2006
    467—dc22   2006044904

1 2 3 4 5 6 7 8 9 10 11 12 13 14 15 16 17 18 19   FGR/FGR   0 9 8 7 6

ISBN-13: 978-0-07-143301-3
ISBN-10:   0-07-143301-5

All illustrations by Luc Nisset
Interior design by Terry Stone

McGraw-Hill books are available at special quantity discounts to use as premiums and
sales promotions, or for use in corporate training programs. For more information, please
write to the Director of Special Sales, Professional Publishing, McGraw-Hill, Two Penn
Plaza, New York, NY 10121-2298. Or contact your local bookstore.

This book is printed on acid-free paper.

Contents

Preface

You're walking down the street and you hear **¡Qu'húbole!** or **¡Qué padre!** or **¿Qué onda?** but you never learned these expressions and can't find them in a dictionary. Later on that day, you want to tell some Spanish-speaking friends that you think the gift they gave you was "cool"; you know it can't possibly be **fresco**, which applies to temperature, but what is the word to use? You'll find the answer in *The Red-Hot Book of Spanish Slang and Idioms: 5,000 Expressions to Spice Up Your Spanish*. It has both a Spanish-English and an English-Spanish component.

Spanish–English

Whether you are listening to people talk, watching a Spanish-language movie, listening to the radio, or reading an interview of Antonio Banderas or Salma Hayek, the book you are holding in your hand will be a great companion. In addition to slang and idioms that are universal, it includes common regional slang. Country codes, or references, are given so that you know just where each expression is used.

English–Spanish

You're writing an e-mail to a friend and you want to know how to say "That's a drag!" or "What a downer!" in Spanish. Or you're calling a Spanish-speaking friend to accept an invitation to a party or invite that person to your house, but beforehand you want to know how to say "Super!" or "Awesome!" The English-Spanish section of *The Red-Hot Book of Spanish Slang and Idioms* is just the ticket to give your Spanish the **chispa** or *spark* that it needs.

Typical Entries

Here is a typical entry in the Spanish-English section:

creerse la última Coca-Cola en el de- ← Spanish word/expression
sierto (to think one is the last Coca-Cola ← literal translation in parentheses
in the desert) to think one is hot stuff, ← actual definition
God's gift *Mex, DR, PR, ES, Nic, Pan, Col* ◆ ← countries/regions used
Carmen se ve muy bonita, ¿no? Su vestido ← example
es de París. —¡Pero es tan engreída! Se cree
la última Coca-Cola en el desierto. Carmen
looks very pretty, doesn't she? Her dress is from ← translation
Paris. —But she's so stuck-up! She thinks she's
God's gift.

Definite articles indicate gender of nouns. Feminine forms of nouns are given in parentheses:

definite article(s)   feminine ending
↙   ↙
el/la **cuate(-a)** good friend, pal *Mex, C. Am.*
◆ *Paco es un buen cuate. Paco is a good pal.*

The feminine ending is typically added after dropping **-o** or **-e**; for example, the feminine form of **el cuate** is **la cuata.** If no feminine ending is given, the noun is invariable (it is the same in the feminine as in the masculine): **el/la hincha** (fan, sports enthusiast). When an expression requires a specific verb form in the second person (*you* in English), the **tú** form is normally used rather than **usted,** since slang is primarily informal. Notes referring to register (level of formality) or to specific country variations are given in parentheses.

Here is a typical entry in the English-Spanish section:

English word/expression   English meaning/synonym
↓   ↓
to be **flabbergasted** **1.** (astounded) **quedarse** ← Spanish equivalent(s)
boquiabierto(-a) (to be left open-mouthed) ← literal translation(s) in parentheses
L. Am., Sp; **quedarse frío(-a)** (**helado**[-a]))
(to end up cold [frozen]) *L. Am., Sp;* ← countries/regions used
quedarse con la cara cuadrada (to be left
with the face square) *Mex;* **alucinar (en co-**
lores) (to hallucinate [in color]) *Sp* ◆ *Susana* ← example(s)
was flabbergasted when I told her I'd gotten
married. **Susana se quedó boquiabierta** ← translation(s)
cuando le dije que me había casado.

While no attempt was made to sanitize the language by eliminating off-color expressions, words considered vulgar are marked with the word *vulgar* in parentheses and some very strong terms have been avoided.

Native Readers

Native readers from many different Spanish-speaking countries helped to create the final manuscript. Each word or expression is accompanied by a list of abbreviations representing the countries and regions in which the word or expression is used. Where there is regional variation in the use of a particular expression, a note is made, preceded by the abbreviation RVAR.

Abbreviations

Country/Regional Abbreviations

Arg	Argentina
Bol	Bolivia
C. Am.	Central America
Ch	Chile
Col	Colombia
CR	Costa Rica
DR	Dominican Republic
Ec	Ecuador
ES	El Salvador
G	Guatemala
Hond	Honduras
L. Am.	Latin America
Mex	Mexico
Nic	Nicaragua
Pan	Panama
Para	Paraguay
PR	Puerto Rico
S. Cone	Southern Cone (Argentina, Chile, Paraguay, Uruguay)

S. Am.	South America
Sp	Spain
U	Uruguay
Ven	Venezuela

(Caribbean, Cuba, Florida, Peru, and Chicano are not abbreviated.)

The country abbreviations for any specific entry are listed roughly from north to south, with Spain following the Southern Cone countries. The Caribbean refers to Cuba, Puerto Rico, the Dominican Republic, some smaller islands, and certain coastal regions of Central America, Colombia, and Venuzuela.

Grammatical Abbreviations

adj	adjective
inf	infinitive
n	noun

Acknowledgments

We would like to thank Christopher Brown, our editor at McGraw-Hill, for his constant support, good cheer, advice, superb editorial work, and insight from the inception of the project throughout its development. Without him, this book would not have been possible. Thanks also to Nancy Hall of McGraw-Hill for her very competent handling of the production of the project, to Elizabeth Millán for excellent copyediting, and to Luc Nisset for delightful drawings. Deep appreciation to the following native readers who read through the manuscript and gave us many comments and suggestions: Adriana de Álvarez, Anna Colom, Sofía Domínguez de Málvarez, Dolores Fernández, Pilar Hernández, Llanca Letelier, Yolanda Magaña, Fernando Moscoso, Anna Elisa Ordóñez, Elka Scheker, and Andreu Veá-Baro.

A special thank you to the following people for contributing many colorful expressions from their native countries and answering our endless questions about usage and meaning: María Elena Alvarado, Ingrid de la Barra, Cristina Cantú, Myriam Castillo, Teresa Castro-Albaracín, Lucy Flores, Nidia González Araya, Sylvia Henríquez Rivas, Iván H. Jiménez Williams, Naldo Lombardi, Gilda Mesa de Yi, Francisco Montaño, Gerardo Montaño, Ofelia Romero, Teresa Rubio, Luciana Sacchi, Armando Sánchez Lona, Hugo Sánchez Lona, Susana Singer, Cristina Stricker de Márquez, and María Teresa Varese.

Spanish-English Dictionary

de **abajo** down below, underneath; downstairs *L. Am., Sp* ◆ *Viven en el piso de abajo. They live downstairs.*

abajo →**ir abajo**

abatatarse (to get sweet potatoed) to blow it, get flustered and make mistakes; from **batata**, sweet potato *Para, U, Arg* ◆ *Había mucha gente en la entrevista y me abataté y no contesté la pregunta correctamente.* There were a lot of people at the interview and I blew it and didn't answer the question correctly.

abierto(-a) de par en par wide open *L. Am., Sp* ◆ *¿Por qué dejaste la puerta abierta de par en par? Why did you leave the door wide open?*

abriles →**tener abriles**

abrir su corazón a alguien to open one's heart to someone *Mex, DR, U, Arg, Sp* ◆ *Finalmente Ana le abrió su corazón. Finally, Ana opened her heart to him.*

en un **abrir y cerrar de ojos** (in an opening and closing of the eyes) in the blink of an eye *L. Am., Sp* ◆ *Se tomaron las decisiones en un abrir y cerrar de ojos. They made the decisions in the blink of an eye.*

abrirse 1. (to open) to leave, go off *CR, S. Cone, Sp* ◆ *Fabio se abrió temprano porque estaba cansado, así que no supimos nada de su viaje. Fabio took off early because he was tired, so we never found out anything about his trip.* **2.** (to open) to break up (a relationship, business or social) *S. Cone* ◆ *Después de la muerte de su hijo, se abrieron. After the death of their son, they broke up.*

en **absoluto** →**no... en absoluto**

aburrirse como una ostra (to be bored as an oyster) to be or get very bored *Mex, DR, Ven, Peru, Ch, Arg, Sp* ◆ *Esta fiesta fue un desastre. Nos aburrimos como una ostra. That party was a disaster. We were bored stiff.*

abusado(-a) (abused) sharp as a tack, clever *Mex* ◆ *Paco es muy abusado, abusadísimo. Paco is very clever, extremely sharp.*

el/la **abusador(-a)** opportunist, mooch *S. Cone* ◆ *Elena es una abusadora, y ha aprovechado de la bondad de su esposo.* Elena is a mooch, and she has abused her husband's good will.

el/la **abusivo(-a)** (abusive) someone who takes advantage of others, mooch; wolf *Mex, C. Am.* ◆ *Carmen se comió toda la comida. ¡Qué abusiva! Carmen ate all the food. What a mooch! ◆ Cuando pasé junto a él, me tocó, el muy abusivo. When I passed near him, he touched me (inappropriately), the wolf.*

el **abusón, la abusona** mooch, someone who takes advantage of others, sponge *Mex, Sp* ◆ *El muy abusón se acabó la comida de los demás, sin ser invitado a la fiesta. The mooch finished up everyone else's food without having been invited to the party.*

acabar (to finish) to come sexually (vulgar) *Mex, C. Am., S. Cone* ◆ *Me inspiraste, chica. Acabé tres veces. You inspired me, dear. I came three times.*

acabar bien (mal) (to end well [badly]) to have a happy (sad) ending *L. Am., Sp* ◆ *¿Cómo acabó la película? —Acabó bien. Se casaron los dos amantes. How did the film end? —It had a happy ending. The two lovers got married.*

acabar de (hacer algo) to have just (done something) *L. Am., Sp* ◆ *Acabo de graduarme de la universidad. I've just graduated from college.*

acalorado(-a) (heated up) someone who gets upset easily, excitable, a hothead, temperamental *U, Arg, Sp* ◆ *Yo soy un acalorado, un verdadero fosforito. I'm a hothead, a real hothead (little match).*

el/la **acartonado(-a)** (cardboard-like) snob, stiff and unsociable person; pretentious person *Arg* ◆ *Ese señor ni saluda; es un acartonado. That man doesn't even say hello; he's* *very standoffish.* ◆ *Esa señora tan paqueta es una acartonada; desprecia a todos.* That nicely dressed lady is a snob; she looks down on everyone.

acasito used instead of **acá**, meaning here *Mex, Peru, Bol* ◆ *Ven acasito, mi amor.* Come here, dear.

acaso →**por si acaso**

el **aceite** →**como el aceite y el vinagre**

acelerado fast (not waiting very long before pressing for sex) *Mex, G, ES, Sp* ◆ *Salí con Fernando por primera y última vez. ¡Qué acelerado!* I went out with Fernando for the first and last time. He's so fast!

acelerado(-a) 1. (sped up) high on alcohol or stoned on drugs *Mex, PR, G, Col, Sp* ◆ *Ese loco parece acelerado.* That dude seems stoned. **2.** (sped up) jittery from caffeine *Mex, PR, G, Col, Ch, Sp* ◆ *Tomé tres cafés y ahora estoy acelerada.* I had three coffees and now I'm jittery.

acerca de about *L. Am., Sp* ◆ *Escribió un artículo acerca de Gabriel García Márquez.* He wrote an article about Gabriel García Márquez.

ser de **acero (bronce)** (to be of steel [bronze]) to be made of steel, tough, inflexible, strong *Mex, U, Arg, Sp* ◆ *Claudia parece ser de acero. No se inmuta bajo ninguna circunstancia.* Claudia seems to be made of steel. She doesn't get perturbed under any circumstances.

achacoso(-a) person who complains a lot about health problems or imagines he or she is sick all the time, hypochondriac *Mex, DR, PR, Ch, U, Arg* ◆ *Es joven para ser tan achacoso.* He's young to be such a hypochondriac.

el/la **achanchado(-a)** (pigged out) slacker, loafer, underachiever *Arg, U* ◆ *Mira a Mariano. Ya casi ni trabaja. Está totalmente achanchado.* Just look at Mariano. He hardly works anymore. He's a total slacker. ◆ *Ese muchacho no te conviene; es un achanchado.* That boy is no good for you; he's a slacker.

el/la **achantado(-a)** (hidden, lying low, submitting) person with no ambition, loser, slacker *Hond, Nic, CR, Ven* ◆ *Mi sobrino es un achantado. No le gusta trabajar y tampoco quiere estudiar.* My nephew is a slacker.

He doesn't like to work and he doesn't want to study either.

achantar to scare, frighten, stifle *Nic, Sp* ◆ *A mí tus chantajes no me achantan.* Your blackmail threats don't scare me. ◆ *Esto a mí no me va a achantar.* This won't stifle me one bit.

achantarse to put a lid on it, stifle it, comply and be quiet about something *Sp* ◆ *Se achantó en la reunión y no dijo nada.* He (She) put a lid on it at the meeting and didn't say anything. ◆ *Nos achantamos cuando vimos tanto lujo.* We were intimidated (silenced) when we saw so much luxury.

¡Acharál, ¡Charál What a shame! *CR* ◆ *¿Así que no puedes ir con nosotros al partido? ¡Acharál* So you can't go to the game with us? Too bad!

achatado(-a) (pug-nosed, with nose cut off) so-so, mediocre, blah, without personality *Arg* ◆ *A Marianita no le gusta ni ir al cine; es tan achatada.* Marianita doesn't even like to go to the movies; she's so dull.

achicarse (to get small) to get scared and back down, chicken out *S. Cone, Sp* ◆ *Te voy a proponer un asunto pero sospecho que te vas a achicar.* I'm going to make you a proposition but I suspect that you will chicken out. ◆ *Por favor, señora, ¡no se me achique!* (Arg) Please, lady, don't cop out on me! ◆ *No te achiques por esa gente y plántales cara.* (Sp) Don't back down because of those people and just face up to them.

achicopalarse to be down, sad, depressed *Mex, ES, Nic* ◆ *¡Ánimo! No te achicopales, 'mano.* Hang in there! Don't let yourself get down, pal.

acho word used to introduce a request, short form of **muchacho**; can also begin a conversation *PR* ◆ *Acho 'mano, ¡cuánto tiempo que no te veía!* Hey, bro', I haven't seen you in a long time! ◆ *Acho, ¿me prestas ese lápiz?* Hey, will you lend me that pencil?

estar **achuchado(-a)** to be scared stiff *U, Para, Arg* ◆ *Los obreros están achuchados pensando que perderán el trabajo.* The workers are scared stiff thinking they'll lose their jobs.

una **achurada** →**dar una achurada**

acostarse con las gallinas: Me acuesto con las gallinas, a las siete de la noche.
I go to bed with the chickens, at seven at night.

ácido(-a) (acidic) disagreeable (person), sourpuss *PR,G, Col, Sp* ◆ *¡Qué ácida eres! What a sourpuss you are!*

ser un **acojonado** (to be without balls) to be a coward, timid (vulgar) *Sp* ◆ *Felipe es un acojonado. Me dijo que iba a hablar con el jefe, pero no lo hizo. Felipe doesn't have any balls. He told me he was going to speak with the boss, but he didn't do it.*

estar **acojonado(-a)** (to be without balls) to be scared shitless (vulgar) *PR, Sp* ◆ *Estábamos acojonados, sin saber qué hacer. We were scared shitless, not knowing what to do.*

el **acomodo 1.** connection in government, business, or with powerful people *U, Arg* ◆ *Cecilia entró a trabajar en ese banco porque tiene un buen acomodo. Cecilia got a job at that bank because she has connections.* **2.** bribe *Arg* ◆ *Juan recibió un acomodo cuando trabajaba en la aduana. Juan took a bribe when he worked at the customs office.*

Lo (La/Le) **acompaño en su dolor (en sus sentimientos). Te acompaño en tu dolor.** (I accompany you in your pain.) I feel for you. Please accept my condolences. *L. Am., Sp* ◆ *Elena, me dijeron que falleció tu padre. Te acompaño en tu dolor. Elena, they told me that your father passed away. Please accept my sympathy.*

el **acordeón** (accordion) crib sheet (because it's folded) *Mex, Cuba, G, U* (RVAR *Sp:* **chuleta**) ◆ *Llevó un acordeón a la clase de matemáticas. He took a crib sheet to math class.*

acostarse con las gallinas (to go to bed with the chickens) to go to bed early *L. Am., Sp* ◆ *Me acuesto con las gallinas, a las diez de la noche. I go to bed early, at ten o'clock.*

acto →hacer acto de presencia

acto seguido right afterwards *L. Am., Sp* ◆ *Me pagaron ayer y acto seguido fui a la joyería y compré el anillo. They paid me yesterday and right afterwards I went to the jewelry store and bought the ring.*

en la **actualidad** at the present time *L. Am., Sp* ◆ *En la actualidad la mayoría de las mujeres trabaja fuera del hogar. At the present* *time, the majority of women work outside the home.*

adelante →**más adelante**

Adelante con la cruz. (Forward with the cross.) Hang in there. Let's not give up. (expresses resolve to proceed in spite of difficulties) *most of L. Am., Sp* ♦ *Adelante con la cruz si quieres terminar tu carrera este año. Hang in there if you want to finish your studies (get your degree) this year.*

además de in addition to *L. Am., Sp* ♦ *Además de ser muy buen mozo, es inteligente y simpático. In addition to being very handsome, he is intelligent and nice.*

¿(A)dónde vamos a parar? (Where are we going to end up?) What will become of us? (expresses worry about unforeseen developments) *Mex, DR, ES, S. Cone, Sp* ♦ *¿Cómo vamos a resolver esta crisis? ¿Adónde vamos a parar? How are we going to resolve this crisis? Where are we going to end up?*

afanado(-a) zealously, with enthusiasm *Mex, DR, G, ES* ♦ *Me puse a trabajar bien afanada. I started working really hard (with enthusiasm).*

el/la **afanador(a)** con artist, scam, person or company involved in illegal or shady deals *U, Arg* ♦ *Esa compañía es una afanadora. Compré mercadería por la Red, les di mi número de la tarjeta de crédito, me han cobrado, pero aún no recibí la mercadería después de dos meses. That company is a scam. I bought merchandise on the Net, gave them my credit-card number, they charged me, but I still haven't received the merchandise after two months.*

afanar (to take advantage of someone; from Lunfardo, Buenos Aires slang) to steal, swindle, or mug, without violence *Cuba, Peru, U, Arg, Sp* ♦ *El gobierno afanó el dinero del pueblo y compró autos para los políticos. The government stole money from the people and bought cars for the politicians.*

el **afano total** rip-off *U, Arg* ♦ *Este suéter cuesta carísimo; es un afano total. This sweater is really expensive; it's a total rip-off.*

aflojar (to loosen up) to give up (on), back down, give in *Mex, ES, CR, Col, Peru, S. Cone, Sp* ♦ *No aflojes; dale duro. Don't cave in; hang tough.*

aflojar el billete (to loosen the bill) used like **aflojar la bolsa**, to loosen up and spend money *Mex, Ch* ♦ *Para salir de ese apuro, tuvo que aflojar el billete. To get out of that jam, he (she) had to loosen up and spend money.*

aflojar la bolsa to loosen the purse strings *Mex, Sp* (RVar U: **el bolsillo**) ♦ *Afloja el bolsillo, viejo; queremos ir a bailar con las chicas. Loosen the purse strings, Dad; we want to go dancing with the girls.*

aflojar la cuerda (to loosen the cord) to take a breather, loosen up (discipline) *Mex, Sp* ♦ *El entrenador tuvo que aflojar la cuerda porque los jugadores estaban furiosos con el régimen de disciplina. The coach had to loosen up because the players were angry about the discipline.*

aflojar las riendas (to loosen the reins) to loosen up (discipline) *Mex, DR, U, Sp* ♦ *Los padres de Mónica no le aflojan las riendas porque no confían en ella. Monica's parents won't loosen up with her because they don't trust her.*

el/la **agachado(-a)** (bent over) doormat, pushover, submissive person *Mex* ♦ *Lo acepta todo; es un agachado. He accepts everything; he's a doormat.*

agallas →**tener agallas**

agandallar to take over, snatch *Mex* ♦ *Vio la billetera y la agandalló. He saw the wallet and snatched it.*

agarrado(-a) (grabbed) stingy, tight-fisted *most of L. Am., Sp* ♦ *No me quiso llevar a cenar porque es bien agarrado. He refused to take me to dinner because he's very stingy.* ♦ *Ese señor es más agarrado que la hiedra de la roca. That man is stingier (tighter) than the ivy on the rock.*

agarrar el avión (to grab the plane) to go on a (drug/alcohol) trip *Mex, ES* ♦ *Ya supiste de Julián; volvió a agarrar el avión. You heard about Julián; he started using drugs (or drinking) again.*

agarrar el hilo (to grasp the thread) to get the point *Mex, ES, Col, Ch* ♦ *Agarraron el hilo de la conversación inmediatamente. They got the point of the conversation immediately.*

agarrar la onda (to grasp the sound wave) to get it, get with it *Mex, G, ES, Col, Ch* ◆ *Llegamos tarde pero pudimos agarrar la onda de la discusión.* We got here late but we were able to get with the discussion.

agarrar su patín (to grab your skate) to take off, sometimes to go find your path (opportunity) in life *Mex, ES* ◆ *Manuel no me escuchó y agarró su patín.* Manuel didn't listen to me and took off.

agarrar viaje (to grab a journey) to accept an invitation or proposal, go for it *U, Arg* ◆ *Me propuso un negocio y agarré viaje.* He (She) made me a business proposition and I went for it.

agarrar viento en la camiseta (to grab wind in the T-shirt) to get carried away *U, Arg* ◆ *Le dimos permiso para salir con sus amigos a bailar, pero ella agarró viento en la camiseta y no regresó a casa en todo el fin de semana.* We gave her permission to go out with her friends to dance, but she got carried away and didn't come home the whole weekend.

agarrarse (to hang onto oneself) to prepare oneself, get ready for a shock or surprise, *Mex, DR, PR, ES, S. Cone, Sp* ◆ *Agárrate. ¿Adivina quién me llamó anoche?* Prepare yourself. Guess who called me last night?

agarrarse a los faldones de alguien to cling to someone's skirts, accept his or her protection or help *Mex, Sp* ◆ *Siempre se agarra a los faldones de su madre. Este chico nunca prosperará.* He always clings to his mother's skirts. This kid will never be successful.

agarrarse a un clavo ardiendo (to cling to a burning nail) to grasp at straws *L. Am., Sp* ◆ *Están tan desesperados por el hambre que se agarran a un clavo ardiendo. Hacen lo que les pidas.* They're so desperate from hunger that they're grasping at straws. They do whatever you ask them.

agarrarse una chinche (to grab oneself a bedbug) to get very angry, blow a gasket *U, Arg* ◆ *María se quedó plantada y se agarró una chinche. María* got stood up and she blew a gasket.

agitarse to get agitated, upset, worked up *Mex, DR, G, ES, Col* ◆ *No te agites. No es para tanto.* Don't get upset. It's no big deal.

su **agosto** →hacer su agosto

agrado: ser de mi (tu, etc.) agrado to be to one's liking *L. Am., Sp* ◆ *Esperamos que este regalo sea de tu agrado, querida.* We hope this gift is to your liking, dear.

el/la **agrandado(-a)** (made larger) big snob, self-important, person with a big ego *ES, U, Arg* ◆ *Ese tipo es un agrandado; vive diciendo tonterías y haciéndose el importante.* That guy is a big snob; he goes around talking nonsense and acting like he's important.

agringado(-a) "Americanized," having become like a gringo *Chicano, Mex, DR, C. Am., Col* ◆ *Marcos ha venido bien agringado; ya no quiere comer la comida de nosotros.* Marcos came back acting like a gringo; he doesn't want to eat our food anymore.

el **agua** →como el agua y el aceite; echar agua en el mar; estar como agua para (pa') chocolate; estar como pez en el agua; hacerle agua la boca; No tiene agua para beber y quiere bañarse.; por debajo del agua; sacar agua de las piedras

¡Agua sucia! (Dirty water!) Watch out! There's trouble! *Mex, Col* ◆ *¡Agua sucia! Cambiemos de tema.* Watch out! Let's change the topic.

Al **agua, patos.** (To the water, ducks.) Let's go to it. Take the plunge. *Mex, DR, ES, S. Cone, Sp* (RVAR *S. Cone:* **pato**, not **patos**) ◆ *No perdamos más tiempo. ¡Al agua, patos!* Let's not lose any more time. (Time's a-wastin'!) Take the plunge!

aguacate (aguacatón, aguacatudo[-a]) (avocado) dope; dumb, stupid *PR, G, ES, CR* ◆ *No te metas con él, que es aguacatón.* Don't get involved with him; he's an idiot.

aguado(-a) (watery, watered-down) simple, with no charm, down, tired or weak *Mex, DR, G, Nic, CR, Col, Para* ◆ *Ese Martín, siempre haragán y aguado.* That Martín, always lazy and weak.

el **aguafiestas** (party water, maybe implying someone who pours water over something to ruin it) party pooper; feminine form: **el/una aguafiestas** *L. Am., Sp* ◆ *Como no quería ser aguafiestas, fui con ellos.* Since I didn't want to be a party pooper, I went with them.

aguaitar, estar al aguaite to be on one's toes, watching out for something *Pan, Ec, Peru, Ch* ◆ *Aguaítame las ollas, que no se queme la comida. Watch the pots for me, so that the food doesn't burn.* ◆ *Estáte al aguaite de la casa, que se queda sola. Keep an eye on the house because there's no one there.*

aguantar el chaparrón (to put up with the rain shower) to wait it out, get through something difficult but necessary, take your medicine, face the music *S. Cone, Sp* ◆ *Aguantaron el chaparrón que les cayó de su jefe de forma muy profesional. They took their medicine from their boss in a very professional manner.*

aguantar el nublado (el nubarrón) (to put up with the cloudiness) to wait it out, wait patiently until someone (usually a superior) is no longer angry *Sp* ◆ *Beatriz aguantó el nublado de sus padres porque sabía que tenían razón. Beatriz waited out her parents' anger patiently because she knew they were right.*

aguantar la respiración to hold one's breath *L. Am., Sp* ◆ *Cuando ya no podía aguantar la respiración, la buceadora subió. When she could no longer hold her breath, the scuba diver came up.*

¡Aguas! (Waters!) Watch out! *Mex, G, ES, Col* ◆ *¡Aguas! Llegó el capataz. Watch out! The foreman has arrived.*

águila →**ponerse águila**

agüitado(-a) down, tired, low *Mex, C. Am.* ◆ *Pobre Carlos. Le quitaron la novia y anda agüitado. Poor Carlos. They stole his girlfriend (took her away) and he's down.*

agüitarse to be down, tired, low *Mex, C. Am.* ◆ *No te agüites, 'mana. Vamos a conseguir el dinero. Don't get down, dear. We'll get the money.*

Ahí muere. (It dies there.) No go. No way. Absolutely not, period. *Mex, ES* (RVar *Ch*: **Ahí murió el payaso.** The clown died there.) ◆ *No voy a la reunión; me quedo en casa. Ahí muere. I'm not going to the meeting; I'm staying at home. And that's that.*

ahí nomasito (over there no farther) very near *ES, Nic, CR, Peru, Bol* (RVar *U, Arg:* **ahí nomás**) ◆ *Ponlo ahí nomasito. Put it right over there.*

Ahí nos vidrios. (We'll see each other there; but **vidrios**, pieces of glass, instead of **vemos**.) See you. *Mex, C. Am., Ven, Ec, Peru* (RVar *Mex, Ec:* also, **Los vidrios.**) ◆ *Bueno, más tarde voy a la fiesta. Ahí nos vidrios. Well, I'll go to the party later on. See you there.*

estar **ahogado(-a)** (to be drowned) to be drunk (also, **ahogado[-a] hasta el gorro**) *Mex, ES* ◆ *Carlos estaba ahogado de borracho. Carlos was totally drunk.*

ahogarse en un vaso de agua (to drown in a glass of water) to sweat the small stuff, worry about something unimportant *L. Am., Sp* ◆ *No te preocupes. No te ahogues en un vaso de agua. Don't worry. Don't sweat the small stuff.*

Ahora caigo. (Now I fall.) Now I get it. *L. Am., Sp* ◆ *Ahora caigo. Quieres romper conmigo. Now I get it. You want to break up with me.*

de **ahora en adelante** (from now on forward) from now on *L. Am., Sp* ◆ *De ahora en adelante, compraré los boletos con más anticipación. From now on, I'll buy the tickets more in advance.*

ahora más que nunca now more than ever *L. Am., Sp* ◆ *Necesitamos la paz ahora más que nunca. We need peace now more than ever.*

ahora mismo right now, right away *L. Am., Sp* ◆ *Miguelito, ídame el dinero ahora mismo! Miguelito, give me the money right now!*

ahorcarse (to hang oneself) to take the ball and chain, get hitched (married) (like **echarse la soga al cuello**) *Mex, CR, U* ◆ *Adela y Beto decidieron ahorcarse el próximo verano. Adela and Beto decided to take the plunge next summer.*

ahorita (diminutive of **ahora**) right now; sometimes used to mean in a little while or maybe later *L. Am. (not Cuba, S. Cone)* ◆ *Ahorita voy a limpiar la cocina. I'm going to clean the kitchen right now.*

al **aire libre** in the open air *L. Am., Sp* ◆ *La comida sabe mejor al aire libre, ¿no? Food tastes better outdoors, doesn't it?*

ajá uh-huh *L. Am., Sp* ◆ *¿Estás listo? —Ajá, casi casi. Are you ready? —Uh-huh, just about.*

ser **ajeno(-a) a algo** to be unaware of or to distance oneself from something *L. Am., Sp* ◆ *No se puede ser ajeno a la lucha para los derechos civiles en ese país.* It's impossible to be unaware of the struggle for civil rights in that country.

el **ajetreo** a lot of work; also, **ajetrear** *Mex, ES, U, Arg* ◆ *Ay, ¡qué ajetreo! Ya vienen los invitados y no tengo la comida lista.* Oh, what a lot of work! The guests are arriving now and I don't have the food ready.

estar en el **ajo** (to be in the garlic) to be in the know *Mex, Sp* ◆ *Bien saben lo que está pasando. Están en el ajo.* They know what's happening. They're in the know.

ajumarse to get drunk *Cuba, DR, PR* (RVar *ES, CR:* **jumarse**) ◆ *A mi tío Felipe siempre le da con ajumarse en las fiestas de Año Nuevo.* My Uncle Felipe always goes and gets blasted at New Year's Eve parties.

alas →**dar alas**

el/la **alborotado(-a)** (made upset) troublemaker, someone who upsets others *Mex, DR, ES, Arg* ◆ *Miguel es un alborotado; siempre molesta a sus compañeros en el trabajo.* Miguel is a troublemaker; he always bothers his coworkers.

alborotar el gallinero (to stir up the henhouse) to upset the apple cart, get people riled up *Mex, Ch, Sp* ◆ *La profesora alborotó el gallinero y luego no nos dio apoyo.* The professor upset the apple cart (got us all riled up) and then didn't support us.

alborotar las avispas (el panal) (to stir up the wasps [honeycomb]) to upset the apple cart, get people riled up *Mex, ES, CR, Ch, Sp* ◆ *Juana siempre anda alborotando las avispas.* Juana is always stirring up trouble.

alburear to talk with double meaning, confuse in a teasing way *Mex, ES, CR* ◆ *Me albureó y al final no entendí nada.* He (She) confused me with double meanings and in the end I didn't understand anything.

el/la **alcahuete(-a)** (procurer, pimp) person who spoils or pampers someone, gives in to their wishes or goes along with them *Mex, DR, PR, C. Am., Col, Ec, Ch, Sp* (RVar also, teacher's pet in *Col*) ◆ *Mi colega es un alcahuete del jefe; por eso tiene excelentes informes.* My coworker is a brown noser to the boss; that's why he gets such good evaluations.

◆ *Sus padres son unos alcahuetes y por esta razón el niño es intolerable.* His parents spoil him and for that reason the boy is unbearable.

alcahuetear (to procure, pimp) to give in or go along (with something) *Mex, DR, ES, Col, Ch* ◆ *No le alcahuetées eso. Ese niño es un malcriado porque sus padres le alcahuetean todo.* Don't go along with him and give him that. That boy is a spoiled brat because his parents give in to him on everything.

alcanzarle (el dinero, el tiempo, etc.) (to reach, extend) to be enough (money, time, etc.) *L. Am., Sp* ◆ *¿Te alcanzó el dinero? —Sí, me alcanzó.* Did you have enough money? —Yes, I had enough.

¡Ale, ale! Step on it! *Mex* ◆ *¡Vámonos! ¡Ale, ale! Let's go! Step on it!*

alegrar: ¡Cuánto me alegro! How happy I am! *L. Am., Sp* ◆ *¿Tu mamá salió del hospital? ¡Cuánto me alegro!* Your mom got out of the hospital? I'm so happy!

alegrarle la vida to cheer up, make happy *L. Am., Sp* ◆ *Siempre me alegras la vida, amiga.* You always cheer me up, my friend.

estar **alegre como unas castañuelas** (to be happy as castanets) to be happy as a lark *Mex, Sp* ◆ *Estos niños siempre están alegres como unas castañuelas.* These kids are always as happy as a lark.

alegría: ¡Qué alegría! (What happiness!) How terrific! *L. Am., Sp* ◆ *¡Qué alegría verte!* I'm so happy to see you!

algodón (cotton, sounds like **algo**) vague evasive answers to indiscreet questions *Mex* ◆ *¿Qué tienes en la mano? —Algodón.* What do you have in your hand? —Nothing.

algodones →**tener entre algodones**

alhaja: ¡Buena alhaja! What a gem! *L. Am., Sp* ◆ *Fernando es un cero a la izquierda. —Sí, ¡buena alhaja!* Fernando is a total jerk. —Yes, he's a real gem!

aliento →**sin aliento**

¡Allí está el detalle! (There's the detail!) That's the point! (a saying popularized by the actor Cantinflas) *Mex, DR, S. Cone* ◆ *No sé porque estás enojada. —Ahí está el detalle: no entiendes mis problemas.* I don't know why you're mad. —That's the point: you don't understand my problems.

alma →**como alma que lleva el diablo; tener a alguien en el alma; tener alma de acero**

mi **alma** (my soul) darling, dear *L. Am.* ◆ *Mi alma, ¡qué bonita estás con ese vestido nuevo! Darling, how beautiful you look with that new dress!*

un **almíbar** →**estar hecho(-a) un almíbar**

Aló. Hello (answering the telephone). *most of L. Am.* ◆ *Aló, familia Rosales. Hello, [this is] the Rosales family.*

alocado(-a) (turned crazy) nutty, crazy for action, unpredictable *L. Am., Sp* ◆ *Nadie confía en él porque es muy alocado. Nobody trusts him because he's really crazy.*

alrededor de about *L. Am., Sp* ◆ *Estuve en Tejas alrededor de tres meses. I was in Texas for about three months.*

a **altas horas** late *L. Am., Sp* ◆ *Llegué a altas horas de la noche y por eso no te llamé. I got back late at night and so I didn't call you.*

alternativa →**no tener alternativa**

alto →**írsele por alto**

en lo **alto de** at the top of *L. Am., Sp* ◆ *Hay una vista muy bonita en lo alto de la montaña. There's a very beautiful view at the top of the mountain.*

estar a la **altura de** to be up to, equal to, capable of *L. Am., Sp* ◆ *Temo no estar a la altura de sus expectativas. I'm afraid of not being up to his expectations.*

a estas **alturas** at this advanced point or stage *L. Am., Sp* ◆ *¿Quieres cambiar el plan a estas alturas? ¡No lo creo! You want to change the plan at this time? I don't believe it!* ◆ *A estas alturas no importa lo que piensen. At this point it doesn't matter what they think.*

alucinante impressive, awesome *Sp* ◆ *La nueva aspiradora es alucinante. Funciona ella sola sin que nadie la pase. Es un robot. The new vacuum cleaner is awesome. It works all by itself without anyone operating it. It's a robot.*

alucinar to be surprising, to be impressive; to be surprised or impressed *parts of Mex, Sp* (RVar *Mex*: also, to dislike, as **Alucino a mi suegra.** I dislike my mother-in-law.) ◆ *Alucina lo bien que habla este niño. It's surprising how well this boy talks.* ◆ *Me alucinó la película. The film impressed me.* ◆ *Cuando oí la noticia, aluciné en colores. When I heard the news, I was amazed.*

alzado(-a) (raised up) in heat, horny *Mex, U, Arg* ◆ *Ese hombre está alzado; quiere ligarse. That guy is horny; he wants to pick up a woman.* ◆ *Tu gata está alzada, lista para aparearse. Your cat is in heat, ready to be mated.*

el/la **alzado(-a)** (raised up) snob, pretentious, arrogant person *Mex, U, Arg* ◆ *Esmeralda es una alzada; no le viene nadie bien. Esmeralda is a snob; she doesn't like anybody.*

alzar vuelo (to take flight) to leave, take off *Mex, DR, PR, ES* ◆ *Adrián apenas tuvo dinero y alzó vuelo. Adrián hardly had any money and he took off.*

alzarse con el santo y la limosna (to make off with the saint and the alms) to make off with it all, take everything, one's own and others' *DR, PR, CR* (RVar *CR*: **quedarse sin el santo y sin la limosna,** to be left with nothing, often when two things were possible and neither was obtained) ◆ *Cristián se nos fue ayer y se alzó con el santo y la limosna. Cristián left yesterday and made off with it all.*

al **amanecer** at dawn *L. Am., Sp* ◆ *Mamá tiene que salir a trabajar al amanecer. Mom has to leave for work at dawn.*

amarrado(-a) (tied) hitched, married *Chicano, Mex, DR, G, ES, Col* ◆ *Es muy joven para estar amarrado. He's very young to be hitched already.*

amarrarse los pantalones (to tie up or tighten one's pants) to make one's authority felt *CR, ES, Ch* ◆ *Tienes que amarrarte bien los pantalones con esa mujer. You really have to put your foot down with that woman.*

el **amarrete** (one who ties things up) tightwad, stingy person *Bol, S. Cone* ◆ *Nadie tolera a los amarretes. Nobody likes tightwads.*

¡Amigo! (Friend!) used to get a stranger's attention *Mex, G, ES, DR* ◆ *¡Eh, amigo! ¿Qué hora es? Hey, my man! What time is it?*

amigos →**tener cara de pocos amigos**

los **amigos (las amigas) del alma** (friends of the soul) bosom buddies, pals *L. Am., Sp* ◆ *Todos los amigos del alma estuvieron junto a Martina en su graduación. All her*

9

bosom buddies were with Martina at her graduation.

amilanarse to back down, chicken out *G, S. Cone, Sp* ◆ *A último momento me amilané y decidí retirar mi candidatura para diputada.* At the last minute I chickened out and decided to withdraw my candidacy for representative.

amolado(-a) (ground, sharpened) worn to a frazzle, ruined, exhausted *Mex, C. Am.* ◆ *Te dejaron bien amolado.* They left you totally worn out.

el **amor** →Hasta aquí llegó mi (el) amor.

mi **amor** my love *L. Am., Sp* ◆ *¿A qué horas regresas, mi amor?* What time will you be back, my love?

mi **amorciano** (my Martian love, used instead of **mi amorcito**, sounds like **amor** and **marciano**, Martian) my darling, my love (used mostly by women) *Mex* ◆ *Mi amorciano me regaló flores este fin de semana.* My sweetie pie gave me flowers this weekend.

mi **amorcito** (little love) sweetheart *L. Am., Sp* ◆ *Mi amorcito siempre llega tarde.* My sweetheart is always late.

estar **amormado(-a)** →tener un muermo, estar amormado(-a)

amoroso(-a) →¡Qué amoroso(-a)!

los **amos del cotarro** (the masters of the **cotarro**, the bank of a ravine or a shelter for vagrants) the people in charge, the ones with the power *Sp* ◆ *Como son los dueños del negocio, son los amos del cotarro.* Since they are the owners of the business, they rule.

amuermar to bore, put to sleep *Sp* ◆ *Ese tipo amuerma a cualquiera.* That guy puts anyone to sleep.

analfabestia (used instead of **analfabeta**, illiterate; **bestia** means beast) lowlife, ignorant and proud of it *Mex, Col* ◆ *Pasaron unos analfabestias en una caminoneta.* Some lowlifes went by in a truck.

¡Anda la hostia (leche, osa, puta)! (Go the host [milk, bear, whore]!) Damn! (expressions of surprise; all are vulgar and sometimes can also express annoyance) *Sp* ◆ *¡Anda la hostia! Perdí mi cartera.* Goddammit! I lost my wallet.

¡Ándale! (¡Ándate!) Right! That's it! *Chicano, Mex, Col* ◆ *Ándale, pues. Así se toca*

la marimba. That's it. That's how you play the marimba.

Andando. (Walking.) Make tracks. Step on it. *Mex, Sp* ◆ *Andando, muchachos; tenemos un largo camino a la montaña.* Step on it, guys; we have a long road to the mountain.

andando los años as the years go (went) by *L. Am., Sp* ◆ *Andando los años, es fácil perder el contacto con los amigos.* As the years go by, it's easy to lose contact with friends.

andar a palos to be at blows, always fighting *Mex, U, Sp* ◆ *Germán y Dora casi no se hablan porque andan a palos constantemente.* Germán and Dora hardly speak to each other because they are always fighting.

andar cacheteando la banqueta (to go along with one's cheek on the sidewalk) to be drunk *Mex* ◆ *Paco andaba cacheteando la banqueta después de tomar tres tequilas.* Paco was drunk after drinking three tequilas.

andar como bola sin manija (to walk like a ball without a string) to be going around in circles, any which way *Para, U, Arg* ◆ *Mañana salgo para España, así que hoy ando como bola sin manija.* Tomorrow I leave for Spain, so today I'm going around in circles.

andar como perro y gato (to walk like dog and cat) to be like cats and dogs, enemies (also, **ser como perro y gato**) *Mex, DR, ES, Ch, U, Sp* (RVar *Sp:* also, **como el perro y el gato**) ◆ *Estos niños se pelean todo el día; son como perro y gato. Estoy cansada de sus peleas.* These kids fight all day; they're like cats and dogs. I'm tired of their fights.

andar con las hilachas colgando (to go with threads hanging) to be dressed in rags *S. Cone* ◆ *No entiendo qué problemas tienen mis sobrinos. Andan con las hilachas colgando como si no tuvieran ropa para ponerse.* I don't know what kind of problems my nieces and nephews have. They're dressed in rags as though they didn't have any clothes to wear.

andar con ojo (to go with eye) to be always cautious and suspicious *Sp* ◆ *Ándate con ojo... ese vendedor no es de fiar.* Watch out . . . that salesman is not to be trusted.

andar con pies de plomo (to walk with lead feet) to move slowly, with caution; to drag one's feet *L. Am., Sp* ◆ *Decidieron comprar una casa, pero andan con pies de plomo.* They decided to buy a house, but they're dragging their feet.

andar de boca en boca (to go from mouth to mouth) to travel by word of mouth, be common knowledge, all over town *L. Am., Sp* ◆ *Escuchamos los comentarios que andan de boca en boca sobre el fraude en las elecciones.* We heard the commentaries that travel by word of mouth about the election fraud. ◆ *La noticia del accidente anda de boca en boca.* The news about the accident is all over town.

andar de buenas to be in a good mood *L. Am., Sp* ◆ *Esta mañana todos andamos de buenas.* This morning we are all in a good mood.

andar de malas to be in a bad mood *L. Am., Sp* ◆ *Después de tres días de lluvia, todo el mundo anda de malas.* After three days of rain, everyone is in a bad mood.

andar de maleta (to walk with a suitcase) to be in a bad mood *Ch* ◆ *No le hables a Sergio. Anda de maleta hoy.* Don't talk to Sergio. He's in a rotten mood today.

andar de novios to be engaged; also, to go steady in a serious way *L. Am.* ◆ *Felipe y Carmen andan de novios.* Felipe and Carmen are going steady (engaged).

andar haciendo eses (to go around making *s*'s) to be drunk *Mex, S. Cone, Sp* ◆ *Vi a tu tío ayer saliendo del bar y caminaba haciendo eses.* I saw your uncle yesterday coming out of the bar and he was stumbling drunk.

andar mosca (to go fly) to be upset *PR, Sp* ◆ *Andaba un poco mosca.* He (She) was a little bit upset.

andar(se) por las ramas (to go around the branches) to beat around the bush *L. Am., Sp* ◆ *Este muchacho no se anda por las ramas. Dice directamente lo que piensa y no se entretiene.* This guy doesn't beat around the bush. He says exactly what he thinks and doesn't hold back.

andar quebrado(-a) to be broke *Mex* ◆ *Mario anda quebrado. No puede pagar sus cuentas.* Mario is broke. He can't pay his bills.

andar/ir/marchar sobre ruedas (to go on wheels) to be going great *Mex, DR, PR,* *ES, Nic, Col, Ch, Sp* ◆ *Todo anda (marcha) sobre ruedas.* Everything is going great.

andar tras sus huesos (to go after his or her bones) to be out to get, on the prowl for or chasing *Mex, ES* ◆ *Esa chava es muy creída. Piensa que todos los chicos andan tras sus huesos.* That girl is very stuck-up. She thinks all the guys are after her.

andarse con rodeos (to go around and around) to beat around the bush *L. Am., Sp* ◆ *No te andes con rodeos. Dime la verdad.* Don't beat around the bush. Tell me the truth.

ángel →**tener ángel**

los **ángeles** →**como los ángeles**

anillo →**como anillo al dedo**

en el **año catapún** (in the year **catapún**) ages ago, a long time ago *Sp* ◆ *Esa canción es del año catapún.* That song is from ages ago.

en el **año de la pera** (in the year of the pear) ages ago, a long time ago *Ven, Peru, Ch, Sp* ◆ *¿Ves esta foto del colegio? Es del año de la pera.* See this picture from school? It's from the Stone Age.

al **anochecer** at nightfall *L. Am., Sp* ◆ *Al anochecer, salí a mirar las estrellas.* At nightfall, I went out to look at the stars.

de **antemano** ahead of time, in advance *L. Am., Sp* ◆ *Encargaron el pastel de antemano.* They ordered the cake in advance.

la **antena** →**poner la antena**

antes hoy que mañana the sooner the better *L. Am., Sp* ◆ *Si piensas comprar la casa, antes hoy que mañana.* If you're thinking of buying the house, the sooner the better.

con **anticipación** in advance, ahead of time *L. Am., Sp* ◆ *Hoy en día hay que llegar al aeropuerto con anticipación.* These days you have to get to the airport ahead of time.

antojado(-a) (antojao[-a]) bent or intent on; (n.) person who wants something *Mex, PR, G, Col* ◆ *Estos niños son muy antojados y siempre quieren golosinas.* These kids are always after something (craving something), and they always want candy.

el **antro** dive, seedy bar or club *Mex, U, Arg, Sp* ◆ *¿Vamos a tomar un trago aquí? —No en ese antro; no me gusta ese lugar.* Shall we have a drink here? —Not in that dive; I don't like that place.

añicos →hacerse añicos; hecho(-a) pedazos, añicos

Apaga y vámonos. (Turn off and let's go.) It's all over. Let's beat it! (said when something comes to an end or something crazy or scandalous happens) *L. Am., Sp* ◆ *Adivina quien llegó. ¡Felipe, borracho! —Apaga y vámonos que siempre se pone pesado cuando está así.* Guess who came. Felipe, drunk! —Let's beat it because he's always a drag when he's like that.

apalancarse to stay in one place without moving, settle down or in *Sp* ◆ *Me apalanqué en su casa y no salimos por la noche.* I settled down at their (his, her) house and we didn't go out in the evening. ◆ *No te apalanques en el sillón; ponte a hacer las tareas.* Don't get settled down in the easy chair; start doing your chores.

apantallar to toot one's own horn, impress or surprise *Mex, DR, ES, Col* ◆ *Hugo aprendió unas palabras de francés y las usa para apantallar a las chicas.* Hugo learned a few words of French and uses them to impress girls.

apañar (to seize) to have sex (vulgar) *Mex*

aparte de aside from *L. Am., Sp* ◆ *No conozco a nadie aquí, aparte de mi amigo Juan.* I don't know anyone here, aside from my friend Juan.

apearse del burro (to get off the burro) to back down *Sp* ◆ *Finalmente cuando vio el informe se apeó del burro.* Finally when he saw the report he backed down.

apendejarse to back down, lose one's nerve *Mex, Cuba, DR, PR, Col* ◆ *Se apendejaron cuando supieron que para comenzar un nuevo negocio necesitarían mucho dinero y muchas horas de trabajo.* They lost their nerve when they found out that they'd need a great deal of money and hours of work to start a new business.

apetecerle (to provoke a desire or yearning, be appealing or appetizing) to like or feel like *Sp* ◆ *Me apetece bailar.* I feel like dancing.

apiolarse to be a go-getter, be clever and try hard to get something, wheel and deal *Mex, Arg* ◆ *Esos comerciantes se están apiolando.* Those businesspeople are really wheeling and dealing.

aplastar la oreja (to flatten the ear) to get some shut-eye, sleep *Mex* ◆ *Estábamos cansadísimos. Llegamos al hotel y aplastamos la oreja antes de la cena.* We were very tired. We got to the hotel and got some shut-eye before dinner.

aplatanado(-a) lazy, slow; settled in *Mex, DR, PR, Sp* (RVar *Sp:* sleepy) ◆ *¡Qué aburrimiento! Me pasé todo el fin de semana aplatanado en casa.* How boring (What boredom)! I spent the whole weekend lazing around at home.

aplatanarse to get bummed out, beaten down by troubles, beaten down (also, **aplatanado[-a]**) *Mex, Col* ◆ *Marcos se ha aplatanado y ya no hace nada.* Marcos has gotten bummed out and he no longer does anything.

aplicar (la) retirada (to apply [the] retreat) to scram, beat it, leave *U, Arg* ◆ *Cuando vimos los tanques y la policía marchando hacia la universidad, aplicamos la retirada.* When we saw the tanks and the police going toward the university, we beat it.

apolillar (to moth) to hit the sack, sleep, go to sleep (from **polilla**, moth) *U, Arg* ◆ *Estoy cansado; me voy a apolillar.* I'm tired; I'm going to go to sleep.

aprender en cabeza ajena (to learn in another's head, usually used in the negative) to learn from someone else's experience *DR, U, Sp* ◆ *Nadie aprende en cabeza ajena.* Nobody learns from the experience of others.

apretada (tight) tight-assed, proud, prissy (woman) *Mex, ES* ◆ *Silvia siempre se hace del rogar; es bien apretada.* Silvia always plays hard to get; she's very tight-assed (not vulgar in Spanish).

apretarse el cinturón to tighten one's belt (economically) *Mex, DR, PR, ES, S. Cone, Sp* (RVar *Mex:* also, **amarrarse el cinturón**) ◆ *Con esta crisis económica, todos tenemos que apretarnos el cinturón.* With this economic crisis, we all have to tighten our belts.

aprobar un examen to pass a test, exam *L. Am., Sp* ◆ *¿Aprobaste el examen de química?* Did you pass the chemistry test?

aprovechado(-a) opportunistic; (n) mooch *L. Am., Sp* (RVar *S. Cone:* **aprovechador [-a]**) ◆ *Es un aprovechado; siempre está comiendo en mi casa y nunca trae nada.*

He's a mooch; he's always eating at my house and he never brings anything.

aprovecharse de to take advantage of *L. Am., Sp* ♦ *Se aprovecharon de la situación y ganaron un dineral. They took advantage of the situation and made a lot of money.*

apuntarse to join in, do something with others *most of L. Am., Sp* ♦ *¿Van al concierto de Gloria Estefan? —Me apunto. Are you going to the Gloria Estefan concert? —Count me in.*

el **apunte** →**llevarle el apunte (llevar de apunte)**

un **apuro** →**sacarle a alguien de un apuro**

en **aquel entonces** back then, at that time, way back when *L. Am., Sp* ♦ *En aquel entonces los adolescentes no tenían acceso a las drogas. At that time adolescents didn't have access to drugs.*

Aquí nomás. ([I'm] Just here.) Same as usual. Nothing new. *Mex, C. Am.* ♦ *¿Cómo están tus nietos? —Aquí nomás. How are your grandchildren? —Same as usual.*

Aquí pasándola. (Por aquí pasándola.) (Passing it here.) Just getting along, so-so. Same as usual. *Mex, ES, Col, U, Arg* ♦ *¿Te sientes mejor de salud? —Aquí pasándola. Do you feel better (health-wise)? —So-so.*

arar en el mar (to plough in the sea) to take coals to Newcastle, do something useless *Mex, DR, PR* ♦ *Es la tercera vez hoy que limpio la cocina. Es como arar en el mar. This is the third time I've cleaned the kitchen today. It's a lost cause.*

Está que **arde.** (It's burning.) It's at fever pitch and getting worse and worse. *L. Am., Sp* ♦ *La situación en mi casa está que arde. Mis padres no se hablan. The situation in my house is getting worse and worse. My parents don't speak to each other.*

estar **ardido(-a) (mordido[-a])** (to be burned [bitten]) to be angry, mad, hot under the collar *Mex, G, CR, Col* ♦ *Ella me tiene ardida después de lo que dijo de mí. She's got me hot under the collar after what she said about me.*

armado(-a) hasta los dientes armed to the teeth *L. Am., Sp* ♦ *Vino a la reunión armada hasta los dientes con todos sus argumentos preparados y convenció al directorio. She came to the meeting armed to the teeth with all her arguments prepared and convinced the board of directors.*

armar gresca (to make a din or brawl) to cause a big fuss or fight *S. Cone, Sp* ♦ *A la salida del partido de fútbol, se armó gresca entre los aficionados de los dos equipos. As they were leaving the soccer game, the fans from both teams had a big brawl.*

armar la de San Quentín (to make that of Saint Quentín) to cause a fuss *Mex, Ch, Sp* (RVar *Mex:* **un sanquentín**; also, **armarle un sanquentín**, to give hell to) ♦ *El papá de la novia le armó un sanquintín al novio. (Mex) The bride's father gave the groom hell.*

armar mitote (to make a big myth) to create a fuss; to make trouble *Mex* ♦ *En un ratito se armó un mitote y ni vimos quien lo empezó. In a short time, a huge ruckus was created and we didn't even see who started it.*

armar o tener una bronca to have a fight, raise a fuss *L. Am., Sp* ♦ *Tuvieron tal bronca que las voces se oían desde la calle. They had such a big argument that their voices were heard out in the street.* ♦ *Armaron una bronca tan fuerte que los vecinos llamaron a la policía. They raised such a big fuss that the neighbors called the police.*

armar un cristo (to make a Christ) to make a scene, create a big mess or problem *Sp* ♦ *Ese cliente armó un cristo en la sala de espera. Estaba enfadado por el error en la factura. That client made a scene in the waiting room. He was angry about the error on the bill.*

armar un escándalo (to make a scandal) to make a scene *L. Am., Sp* ♦ *La niña armó un escándalo en la clínica y no permitió que el doctor la examinara. The girl made a scene at the clinic and didn't allow the doctor to examine her.*

armar un jaleo to make a scene, commotion *Mex, Sp* ♦ *Unos borrachos armaron un jaleo en la discoteca. Some drunks made a scene at the disco.*

armar un molote (to make a bunch) to cause a huge mess, make a scene *DR, C. Am.* ♦ *Sólo llegaron esos sinvergüenzas y armaron un molote. Those creeps only just got there and they made a big scene.*

armar un revuelo to make a commotion, scene *U, Arg, Sp* ♦ *Hubo una manifestación* *de estudiantes. Llegó la policía y se armó un revuelo cerca del colegio.* There was a student demonstration. The police came and there was a big commotion near the school.

armarla to cheat *Mex, Sp* ◆ *Daniel me la armó.* Daniel pulled one over on me.

armarse la gorda (to make the fat one) to have a ruckus or upheaval created, to have all hell break loose *L. Am., Sp* ◆ *Cuando supo que su novio salía con su mejor amiga, se armó la gorda.* When she found out that her boyfriend was going out with her best friend, all hell broke loose.

armar(se) un taco to make a mess, cause a scene, get balled up *Sp* ◆ *Qué lío tienen en el cuarto. ¡Han armado un buen taco!* What a mess they have in their room. They've really made a mess!

arrancado(-a) (torn out) broke, penniless *Cuba, DR, Nic, Col* (RVar *CR:* angry) ◆ *Estoy totalmente arrancada.* I am totally broke.

arrancarle a alguien el alma (to tear out one's soul) to break someone's heart, cause great pain *Mex, ES, Sp* ◆ *Me arrancó el alma ver a esos niños trabajando.* It broke my heart to see those children working.

arrancarle a alguien la vida (to tear out one's life) to break someone's heart, cause great pain *Mex, ES* ◆ *La guerra le ha arrancado la vida a muchas familias.* The war has caused great pain to many families.

arrastrando la cobija (dragging the blanket) dragging along, just getting by *Mex, ES, Col* ◆ *Andrés llegó de su viaje arrastrando la cobija, pero sus padres lo ayudaron.* Andrés came back from his trip just getting by, but his parents helped him out.

arrebatado(-a) (carried away) nutty, crazy, high on drugs or alcohol *Cuba, DR, PR, G* ◆ *Esos tipos de la esquina siempre andan arrebata'os. ¡Qué fuerte!* Those guys from the corner are always high on something. What a way to act!

arrecharse (to get horns like an animal) to get very angry, lose it *Nic, Ven, Ec* ◆ *Cuando esa chica me insultó, me arreché.* When that girl insulted me, I lost it. ◆ *Hombre, ¡no te arreches! No es para tanto.* Man, don't hit the roof! It's no big deal.

arreglar el pastel (to fix the cake) to patch things up *S. Cone* ◆ *La organización del congreso fue un desastre; al final arreglaron el pastel con disculpas y devolvieron parte del dinero a los participantes.* The organization of the conference was a disaster; in the end, they patched things up with apologies and returned part of the participants' money.

arreglárselas (to arrange them) to manage, be competent, able to do something (often something tricky) *DR, ES, S. Cone, Sp* ◆ *Me las arreglé para convencerla.* I managed to convince her. ◆ *Se las arregló para conquistarlo.* She managed to win him over.

arremangarse to put up with, submit, give in *Arg* ◆ *Ni modo. Tuve que aguantar ese regaño. Me tuve que arremangar.* No way. I had to accept being dumped on (literally, that dressing-down, scolding). I had to put up with it.

arrevesado(-a) nutty, crazy *DR, ES, CR, U* ◆ *No puedes confiar en ella; es muy arrevesada.* You can't trust her; she's really nutty.

de **arriba** on top, above; upstairs *L. Am., Sp* ◆ *Está en el estante de arriba.* It's on the top shelf.

de **arriba abajo** from top to bottom, from head to foot *L. Am., Sp* ◆ *Me miraron de arriba abajo.* They looked me over from head to foot. ◆ *El árabe se lee de arriba abajo y de derecha a izquierda.* Arabic is read from top to bottom and from right to left.

¡Arriba el son! (Up with **son** [Cuban music]!) expression used to help create a festive mood *Mex, Col* ◆ *Vamos a bailar, chica. ¡Arriba el son!* Let's dance, honey. What great music! (Hurray for the son beat!)

¡Arriba, abajo, al centro y p'adentro! (Up, down, to the center, and inside!) Down the hatch! (a toast, sometimes shortened to **¡Al centro y p'adentro!**) *L. Am., Sp* ◆ *Vamos a brindar. ¡Arriba, abajo, al centro y p'adentro!* Let's make a toast. Down the hatch with great dispatch!

Arrieros somos que en el camino andamos. (We are muleteers and we go down the road.) You'll get yours. Someday we'll meet and we'll be in the same situation. (reply after someone has criticized another, putting them in their place) *Mex, ES, Ch* ◆ *Trabajamos mucho más que Edgar en ese* *proyecto por la misma plata, pero arrieros somos y en el camino andamos.* We worked much harder than Edgar on that project for the same pay, but time will tell: what goes around comes around.

arrimado(-a) opportunistic (from **arrimarse al sol que más calienta**) *Mex, DR, PR, G, Nic, CR, Col* ◆ *Sabemos que Lorenzo es un arrimado y estará con su familia hasta que obtenga sus propósitos.* We know that Lorenzo is a mooch and will be with his family until he gets what he wants.

arrimarse al sol que más calienta (to put oneself by the sun that heats the most) to serve and flatter the most powerful, go with the winner *Mex, Sp* ◆ *Elena es muy oportunista; siempre se arrima al sol que más calienta.* Elena is very opportunistic; she always goes with the winner.

el **arroz con bicicleta** (rice with a bicycle) absurdity, crazy situation *Florida, PR, Col* ◆ *El arroz con bicicleta que tenemos en los servicios de salud aquí nos afecta a todos.* The crazy situation we have with health services here affects us all.

Ese **arroz ya se coció.** (That rice has already been cooked.) It's in the bag. (said when something one has tried to get has come through [e.g., a favor]) *Mex, ES* ◆ *Lo que planeaste va por buen camino. Ese arroz ya se coció.* What you planned is going well. It's in the bag.

arroz →**¡Que si quieres arroz, Catalina!**

arrugarse 1. (to wrinkle up, get wrinkled) to put up with, accept *U, Arg* ◆ *Me la tuve que tragar; tuve que arrugarme.* I had to swallow it; I had to put up with it. **2.** (to wrinkle up, get wrinkled) to give in or up *Sp* ◆ *Los jugadores se arrugaron y perdieron el partido.* The players gave up and lost the game.

arruinar el estofado (to spoil the stew) to ruin the plan, mess things up *U, Arg* ◆ *Yo lo tenía todo arreglado y esa mujer me arruinó el estofado.* I had it all set up and that woman ruined my whole plan.

arte →**no tener arte ni parte; por arte de birlibirloque**

ser el **as de la baraja** (to be the ace of the deck) to make oneself scarce *most of L. Am.* ◆ *Felipe se ha desaparecido. Es el as de la baraja.* Felipe has disappeared. He's made himself scarce.

el **asaltacunas** (cradle assaulter) cradle robber, person who goes out with someone much younger *Mex, Sp* ◆ *Rolando estaba muy enamorado de Silvia, aunque sus amigos le decían asaltacunas.* Rolando was very much in love with Silvia, although his friends said he was robbing the cradle.

ser un **asco** to be gross, something disgusting; to be worthless *Mex, U, Arg, Sp* ◆ *Este televisor es un asco. Siempre con interferencias.* This television is worthless. There is always interference.

un **asco** →**dar asco; estar hecho(-a) un asco**

estar en **ascuas** (to be on embers) to be on edge, on pins and needles, anxiously awaiting something *Mex, ES, Nic, S. Cone, Sp* ◆ *Estaba en ascuas hasta que me dieron la noticia.* I was on pins and needles until they gave me the news.

estar **asfixiado(-a)** (to be asphyxiated) to be broke *Mex, Sp* ◆ *No podré seguir estudiando; estoy asfixiado.* I won't be able to continue studying; I'm broke.

así como así just like that *L. Am., Sp* ◆ *No puedo decidirme así como así.* I can't decide just like that.

Así me (te, nos) luce el pelo. (That way my [your, our] hair looks good.) expression used to tell that one is wasting time or not taking advantage of an opportunity *Sp*

¡Así se hace! Way to go! That's the way to do it! *L. Am., Sp* ◆ *Terminaré mi carrera este año. —Te felicito, ¡así se hace!* I'll finish my studies (degree) this year. —Congratulations, way to go!

asomarse to show up *L. Am.* ◆ *El arquitecto se asomó en el lugar de construcción para estar seguro que todos estábamos trabajando.* The architect showed up at the construction site to make sure that all of us were working.

asomo →**Ni por asomo.**

en las **astas del toro** (at the horns of the bull) in hot water, a dangerous position (usually used with **dejar**) *Mex, Sp* ◆ *Nos dejaron en las astas del toro.* They left us up the creek without a paddle.

Está el **asunto feo.** (It's an ugly business.) It's awful. *L. Am., Sp* ◆ *¿Qué piensas de todos los cambios ambientales de los últimos veinte años? —Está el asunto feo. What do you think of all the environmental changes in the last twenty years? —It's awful.*

asustón, asustona scaredy-cat *Chicano, Mex* ◆ *Claudia tiene miedo de todo. ¡Qué asustona! Claudia is afraid of everything. What a scaredy-cat!*

Atácame un pulmón. (Attack my lung.) Give me a nail (cigarette or joint) for my coffin. *Mex*

el **ataque de caspa** (dandruff attack) fit, tantrum *S. Cone* ◆ *Tuvo un ataque de caspa porque nos faltaba un documento. He (She) had a fit because we were missing a document.*

atar cabos (to tie ends) to put two and two together *L. Am., Sp* ◆ *Atando cabos, adiviné que eran primos. Putting two and two together, I guessed that they were cousins.*

atenido(-a) laid back, letting others do things *Mex, ES, CR* ◆ *Ese cipote es muy atenido; no le gusta hacer nada. That kid is very laid back; he doesn't like to do anything.*

Atente a pan y no comas queso. (Rely on bread and don't eat cheese.) Be happy with what you've got, be content with one thing and don't wish for something else. *Mex, PR*

atole →**dar atole con el dedo a alguien**

el **atolladero** drag, mess, quagmire, bad situation *ES, CR, Ch, Sp* ◆ *Estoy preocupado. No sé cómo vamos a salir de este atolladero en que nos ha metido Juan. Realmente es una situación muy complicada. I'm worried. I don't know how we're going to get out of this quagmire that Juan has gotten us into. It's really a very complicated situation.*

el/la **atorrante** tramp, bum *Peru, S. Cone* ◆ *No tiene dinero porque es un atorrante. He doesn't have money because he's a bum.*

atracar (to hold up, waylay) to rip off, overcharge, take advantage of someone money-wise *Mex, DR, CR* ◆ *En esa tienda me atracaron cuando compré mi bicicleta. In that store they ripped me off when I bought my bicycle.*

un **atracón** →**darse un atracón**

estar **atrasado(-a)** to be behind (in work, payments, etc.) *L. Am., Sp.* ◆ *Estoy atrasado en el trabajo. I'm behind in my work.*

atrás →**echar (para) atrás**

ser un **atraso a la cultura** (to be a setback for the culture) to be old-fashioned, out of date, retro *Col* ◆ *¡Qué atraso a la cultura! How retro!*

atravesado(-a) (crossed) off one's rocker, crazy *Mex, Nic, CR, Col* ◆ *¿Levantarnos a las cinco? ¿Estás atravesado? Get up at five? Are you off your rocker?*

atreverse →**no atreverse a decir «esta boca es mía»**

aumentar (subir) de peso to gain weight *L. Am., Sp* ◆ *¡Híjole! He aumentado de peso. Yikes! I've gained weight.*

aumentar el doble to double *L. Am., Sp* ◆ *El precio de la gasolina ha aumentado el doble. The price of gasoline has doubled.*

aunque truene y relampaguée (even if it thunders and there is lightning) no matter what, come hell or high water *Mex, ES, S. Cone* ◆ *Aunque truene y relampaguée, vamos a viajar. Come hell or high water, we're going to travel.*

¡Aupa! Go! (at a sports event) *Sp* ◆ *¡Aupa, Armstrong! A ver si ganas la carrera. Go, Armstrong! Let's see if you win the race.*

autostop →**hacer (viajar por) autostop**

¡Ave María! Good heavens!, expression of surprise or other emotion, said mainly by people who are religious *Mex, PR, G, CR, Col, Sp* ◆ *¡Ave María! Qué alegría verte. No sabía que habías regresado de tu viaje. Good heavens! What a pleasure to see you. I didn't know you had returned from your trip.*

en una **avemaría** (in the time it takes to say **Ave María**) in a jiffy, an instant *L. Am., Sp* ◆ *Nos alistamos en una avemaría. We got ready in a jiffy.*

aventado(-a) (thrown out) thrown into a course of action, risking oneself; (n.) daredevil, risk taker *Mex, G, ES, Nic, Col, Peru* ◆ *Aurelio es aventado y aceptó el desafío de sus amigos. Aurelio is a daredevil and accepted his friends' challenge (dare).*

aventarse to take risks, throw oneself into action *Mex, DR, ES, Nic, Peru* ◆ *Cuando empezó la fiesta, se aventó a bailar. When the* *party began, he (she) threw herself out on the dance floor.*

un **aventón** →**dar (pedir) un aventón**

la **aventura** (adventure) love affair, fling *L. Am., Sp* ◆ *Tuve una aventura fantástica en Sevilla. I had a great fling (love affair) in Sevilla.*

el/la **aviador(-a)** (aviator) someone who is paid for a job but doesn't really work *Mex* ◆ *El jefe tiene de aviadores a dos primos suyos. The boss has two of his cousins on the payroll for doing nothing.*

avispado(-a) (wasped) on the ball, sharp as a tack, clever *L. Am., Sp* ◆ *Ivana es muy avispada. Ivana is sharp as a tack.* ◆ *Esta niña es muy avispada para su edad. This girl is very clever for her age.*

¡Ay, bendito! (Blessed one!) Bless my soul!, Good heavens!, expression of sympathy *PR* ◆ *¡Ay, bendito! ¿Qué vas a hacer? Good heavens! What are you going to do?*

ayotes →**dar calabazas (ayotes)**

estar en **ayunas** (to be fasting) to be in the dark, unaware *Mex, S. Cone, Sp* (RVar *Mex:* also said of a woman who has just had a baby and stays at home for a while) ◆ *María estaba en ayunas. Pues no había caído. María was completely in the dark. She hadn't figured it out.*

al **azar** at random, by chance *L. Am., Sp* ◆ *Me seleccionaron al azar... ¡qué suerte! They chose me at random . . . what luck!*

el **azote del barrio** (whip of the neighborhood) person who commits crimes and repeatedly makes trouble, scourge of the neighborhood *Mex, Ven* ◆ *La comunidad colaboró para identificar a un grupo que era el azote del barrio. The community collaborated to identify a group that was the scourge of the neighborhood.*

azurumbado(-a) confused *Nic, CR, Col* (RVar *ES, Nic:* **zurumbo[-a]**) ◆ *Quedé azurumbada de oírlo hablar tan rápido. I was confused from hearing him speak so quickly.*

la **baba** →**tirar (salírsele) la baba (por litros)**

la **babosada** stupidity, nonsensical thing or action; worthless object *most of L. Am.* ◆ *Es una babosada. ¿Hay alguien tan idiota que vaya a creer eso?* It's nonsense. Is there anyone so stupid as to believe that?

baboso(-a) (drooling) dumb, stupid *most of L. Am.* ◆ *¡Qué baboso mi hermano!* How dumb my brother is!

el **bacalao** (codfish) very thin, skinny person, string bean *Florida, PR, Col, U* ◆ *No sé qué se cree esa tipa si no es más que un bacalao. ¡Parece anoréxica!* I don't know why that girl thinks she's hot stuff when she's nothing but a beanpole. She looks anorexic!

bacán super, great *Cuba, Col, Ec, Peru, S. Cone* ◆ *¿Viste a Antonio Banderas? ¡Bacán!* You saw Antonio Banderas? Super!

el **bacán** (controller of a woman who earns money for him; from Lunfardo, Buenos Aires slang) **1.** shallow glamour boy, jerk (implies someone with money also) *S. Cone* ◆ *Mira que hombre tan bacán; tiene un Mercedes Benz último modelo.* Look at that shallow glamour boy; he has the newest model Mercedes Benz. **2.** player, successful player, achiever *S. Cone* ◆ *Ese hombre es un bacán; consigue todo lo que quiere.* That guy is a successful player; he gets everything he wants.

bacano(-a) good, excellent, generous (people or things) *DR, Col* ◆ *El concierto estuvo bien bacano.* The concert was great.

la **bachata** (a type of music) party, fun *Cuba, DR* ◆ *¡Cómo le gusta a Alejandro la bachata!* How Alejandro likes partying!

bachatear to relax, joke around *Cuba, PR* ◆ *Siempre estás bachateando.* You're always joking (fooling) around.

el **bache** (pothole) hassle, disappointment, obstacle, something that gets in the way of success *Mex, DR, ES* ◆ *No pude terminar mi carrera; la tensión fue un bache grande.* I wasn't able to finished my studies; stress was a big obstacle.

ser una **bacteria en el horizonte** (to be a bacterium on the horizon) to be the low man on the totem pole, be of no consequence *Sp* ◆ *No contraten a ese cantante; es una bacteria en el horizonte.* Don't hire that singer; he's of no consequence.

bailar a alguien (to dance someone) to rip someone off, deceive *Mex, G, ES* ◆ *Me bailaron con ese producto porque era de otra marca.* They ripped me off with that product because it was another brand name.

bailar al son que le tocan (to dance to the sound that is played) to go along with others, do whatever is appropriate, play the game *L. Am., Sp* ◆ *Esteban siempre baila al son que le tocan.* Esteban always goes along with the others and plays the game.

bailar de coronilla (to dance on one's head) to work like a dog, do something very diligently *L. Am., Sp* ◆ *Tuvimos que bailar de coronilla antes de la auditoría.* We had to work like dogs before the audit.

bailar en la cuerda floja (to dance on the tightrope) to try to do many things at once or try to please more than one person; have too many irons in the fire *L. Am., Sp* ◆ *Está bailando en la cuerda floja. Es muy posible que lo despidan.* He has too many irons in the fire. It's very possible that they'll fire him.

el **bailongo** dance, dancing party *U, Arg* ◆ *¡Vamos ya al bailongo!* Let's go to the dance now!

bajado(-a) del cielo (brought down from heaven) perfect, excellent, heavenly *Mex, DR, PR, ES, Sp* ◆ *Parece bajado del cielo. Este empleado ha llegado a la empresa en el momento en que más lo necesitábamos.* It's as though he were sent from heaven. This employee has come to the company right when we most needed him.

Bájale. (Lower it.) Don't exaggerate. Get off it. *Mex, ES, Col*

Bájale de crema a tus tacos. (Lower or decrease the cream in your tacos.) Get off

bailar en la cuerda floja: Está bailando en la cuerda floja.
He has too many irons in the fire.

it. *Mex, Col* ◆ *¿No te gusta nada en esta tienda? Bájale de crema a tus tacos. You don't like anything in this store? Get off it.*

Bájale de huevos a tu licuado. (Lower or decrease the eggs in your blended drink.) Get off it. *Mex, ES, Col*

bajar a todos los santos (to get all the saints down—as if to pray to all of them at once) to go all out, try everything in times of trouble *Mex, ES* ◆ *¡Qué problema más grande! Vamos a bajar a todos los santos para tratar de resolverlo. What a big problem! We're going to go all out to try to solve it.*

bajar de peso to lose weight *L. Am., Sp* ◆ *¿Has bajado de peso? Te ves muy delgada. Have you lost weight? You look very slim.*

bajar el volumen (to lower the volume) to take it easy, cool down *Mex, Col* ◆ *Baja el volumen, querida. Busquemos una solución al problema. Cool down, darling. Let's find (literally, look for) a solution to the problem.*

bajar la caña (to lower the reed, pole) to charge an excessive price, rip (someone) off *U, Arg* ◆ *En aquel restaurante nos bajaron la caña. They ripped us off at that restaurant.*

bajar las orejas (to lower the ears) to give in during a dispute or response *Sp* ◆ *Finalmente, cuando vio que todos estaban en su contra, bajó las orejas. Finally, when he saw that everyone was against him, he gave in.*

bajar un archivo to download a file *L. Am., Sp* ◆ *Bajemos el archivo otra vez. Let's download the file again.*

bajarle a alguien los humos (to lower someone's airs) to put someone in his or her place *Mex, DR, PR, S. Cone, Sp* ◆ *La señora le bajó los humos al funcionario mal educado. The lady took that rude bureaucrat down a peg or two.*

bajarle el copete (to take down his or her crest or hairpiece) to take him or her off a high horse, take down a peg *S. Cone* ◆ *Le bajé el copete a Juan porque me habló como si fuera un criminal. I took Juan off his high horse because he spoke to me like I was a criminal.*

bajarse del burro (to get off the donkey) to back down, give in *Mex, Col, Ec, Peru* ◆ *No seas terco. Bájate del burro.* Don't be stubborn. Give in.

lo **bajini (bajo)** →**por lo bajini (bajo)**

bajo llave under lock and key *L. Am., Sp* ◆ *En esa casa, tienen el alcohol bajo llave.* In that house, they have the alcohol under lock and key.

el **bajón** (big down) bad feeling, downer (including one caused by drugs), funk, bummer *Mex, DR, PR, ES, S. Cone, Sp* (see illustration, page 295) ◆ *Pedro tiene un gran bajón porque fracasó en sus exámenes finales.* Pedro is in a big funk because he failed his final exams.

bajoneado(-a) bummed out, down and depressed *S. Cone* ◆ *Joaquín y Claudia andan bajoneados porque extrañan su país de origen.* Joaquín and Claudia are bummed out because they miss their native country.

bala →**ir hecho(-a) bala**

balconear a alguien (to balcony someone) to embarrass someone in front of others or put someone on the spot by asking an indiscreet question or getting the person to do something compromising *Mex, ES* ◆ *La reportera balconeó al señor delante de sus colegas.* The reporter embarrassed the gentleman in front of his colleagues.

balconearse (to balcony oneself) to strut one's stuff (generally used to refer to women) *Mex* ◆ *Esa chica se puso una minifalda porque le gusta balconearse.* That chick put on a miniskirt because she likes to strut her stuff.

de **balde** free of charge *most of L. Am (not U, Arg), Sp* ◆ *Este viaje me ha salido de balde.* This trip was free for me.

en **balde** (in bucket) for nothing, in vain *L. Am., Sp* ◆ *Después del incendio, en balde trataron de recuperar las fotos.* After the fire, they tried to recover the pictures in vain.

la **ballena** (whale) very corpulent person, cow *Mex, G, ES, Col* ◆ *Este vestido será para una ballena.* This dress must be for a cow.

balurdo(-a) weird, in poor taste, boring, tacky *Ven* (RVar *Nic, Ec:* **balurde**) ◆ *La película no fue interesante; fue balurde.* The movie wasn't interesting; it was dull.

bambalán, bambalana dumb, stupid *PR* ◆ *Pobre Marisa. Está viviendo con ese bambalán de Pedro.* Poor Marisa. She's living with that idiot Pedro.

banca →**tener banca**

bancar →**no bancarle a alguien**

bancar(se) to put up with, cope *U, Arg* (RVar *Arg:* also, to bankroll, support financially) ◆ *Me la tuve que tragar; tuve que bancarme.* I had to swallow it; I had to put up with it. ◆ *Mientras estuve estudiando mis padres me bancaron.* While I was studying my parents bankrolled me.

estar de **bandera** (to be of flag) to be attractive, gorgeous *Sp* ◆ *Esas tías están de bandera, ¿no?* Those girls are gorgeous, aren't they?

bañarse →**mandar a alguien a bañarse**

el/la **baquiano(-a)** person who seems to be from the neighborhood, local yokel, local expert in something *S. Cone* ◆ *Pregúntale a ese baquiano la dirección. Debe ser de estos lugares.* Ask that local yokel for the address. He must be from around here.

barajar (to shuffle) to lay it out, explain *Mex, DR, PR, C. Am., Col* ◆ *No entiendo; barájame eso (barájamela más despacio).* I don't understand; lay it out for me (lay it out more slowly for me).

las **baratijas** baubles, trifles, claptrap *L. Am., Sp* ◆ *Tu cómoda está llena de baratijas.* Your nightstand (commode, small chest of drawers) is full of baubles.

la **barba** →**hacer la barba**

ser un **barbaján** to be coarse, rude, a lowlife (masculine only) *Mex, Cuba* ◆ *Felipe es tan tosco, tan grosero. —Sí, es un barbaján.* Felipe is so coarse, so rude. —Yes, he's a lowlife.

el **barbarazo** Don Juan, two-timer, someone who goes after someone else's woman *Mex, PR, Col* ◆ *Ahí está María llorando por Juan otra vez. —Ella se lo busca andando con ese barbarazo.* There's María crying about Juan again. —She's bringing it on herself going around with that two-timer.

barbaridad →**¡Qué barbaridad!**

la **barbaridad** (barbarity) tons, large amount *L. Am., Sp* ◆ *Fuimos a Miami y compramos una barbaridad de cosas.* We went to Miami and bought a whole bunch of things.

bárbaro →¡Qué bárbaro!

bárbaro(-a) (barbarous) super (good or bad), abnormal, unusual, exceptional; badly done *L. Am., Sp* ◆ *Nos reunamos en la playa. –¡Bárbaro! Let's get together at the beach. —Super!*

barbero(-a) sucking up *Mex* ◆ *Pasé el examen de química por estar barbero con la maestra. I passed the chemistry exam by sucking up to the teacher.*

el **barco, el barcazo** (ship) pushover, parent who never says no or professor who passes everyone or gives good grades *Mex, Hond* ◆ *No estudio mucho porque mis profesores son barcos. I don't study much because my professors are pushovers.*

la **barra** (bar) group of friends *U, Arg* ◆ *Anoche fui al cine con mi barra. Last night I went to the movies with the gang.*

la **barrabasada** huge mistake, big mess-up *Mex, DR, Col, S. Cone, Sp* ◆ *La barrabasada fue enorme; no hubo solución. The mess-up was colossal; there was no solution for it.*

barrigón, barrigona potbellied; **barrigona** pregnant *L. Am., Sp* ◆ *Roberta está barrigona porque está embarazada. Roberta is potbellied because she's pregnant.* ◆ *Estoy haciendo ejercicios porque estoy barrigona. I'm doing exercises because I have a paunch.*

de **barril** (from the barrel) draft (beer) *L. Am., Sp* ◆ *Una cerveza, por favor. De barril. A beer, please. Draft.*

el **barrio** →irse para el (al) otro barrio (mundo)

el **barullo** noisy fuss or mess, uproar *CR, U, Arg, Sp* ◆ *Por favor, ¡no armen tanto barullo! Please, don't make such a hullabaloo!*

la **basca, basquilla** group of good friends *Sp* ◆ *Los sábados salgo con la basca del barrio. I go out on Saturdays with the neighborhood crowd.*

bastar de to be enough *L. Am., Sp* ◆ *¡Basta ya de tonterías! That's enough nonsense!*

basto(-a) raunchy, tacky, vulgar *Sp* ◆ *Es más basto que matar un cerdo a besos. It's tackier than a seascape painted on velvet (literally, killing a pig with kisses).*

el **batacazo** bad blow or black and blue mark *U, Arg, Sp* ◆ *Se dio un batacazo. He (She) got bruised (a black and blue mark).*

la **bataclana** floozie, woman who acts on the stage wearing very little clothing; vulgar-looking woman wearing scanty or cheap-looking clothing *S. Cone* ◆ *Mirá esa mina mal vestida; parece una bataclana. Look at that badly dressed girl; she looks like a floozie.*

el/la **batata** (sweet potato) loser, idiot *Para, Arg* ◆ *Ese señor es un batata. That man is a fool.* ◆

la **batuta** →llevar la batuta

el **bayú** party, get-together *PR* ◆ *Tremendo bayú se armó en casa de René anoche. ¿Por qué no fuiste? There was a great party at René's house last night. Why didn't you go?*

baza →meter baza

be →por hache o por be

beber como una esponja to drink like a sponge *Sp* ◆ *Manolo bebe como una esponja y tiene problemas de salud. Manolo drinks like a sponge and has health problems.*

el **bembé** party *Caribbean* ◆ *Sin planearlo llegaron los muchachos y se formó un bembé fantástico. The guys (and girls) showed up on the spur of the moment (literally, without planning) and there was an all-out bash.*

la **bendición** →echar la bendición

bendito(-a) (blessed) sometimes used ironically for the opposite *L. Am.* ◆ *¡Ese bendito coche! That darn (blessed) car!*

el **berenjenal** (eggplant patch) mess, disorder, fix *Mex, PR, S. Cone, Sp* ◆ *Te has metido en un berenjenal al aceptar su propuesta. You've gotten into a mess by accepting his (her, their) offer.*

berreta cheap, low quality; used to describe things or people *U, Arg* ◆ *No compres esa bolsa, que es muy berreta. Don't buy that purse because it looks very cheap.* ◆ *Ese señor es muy berreta. That guy is very lowbrow.*

un **berrinche** →hacer un berrinche

berros →mandar a alguien a buscar berros; ~ a freír buñuelos; ~ espárragos; ~ papas

besar con la lengua (to kiss with the tongue) to french-kiss; also, **beso de lengua**, a french kiss *L. Am., Sp* ◆ *Fernando trató de besarme con la lengua, y no me gustó. Fernando tried to french-kiss me, and I didn't like it.*

Lo (La) besó el diablo. (The devil kissed him [her].) He [She] was tripped up, fell down and tripped. *Mex, ES* ◆ *Ten cuidado como andas, chico, o vas a besar el diablo. Watch where you're walking, kiddo, or you're going to bonk your head.*

besos y abrazos (kisses and hugs) hugs and kisses (common ending for a letter, e-mail or phone conversation to a friend or relative) *L. Am., Sp* ◆ *Besos y abrazos para toda la familia. Hugs and kisses to your whole family.*

los **besotes** (big sloppy kisses) smooches (common ending for a letter, e-mail or phone conversation) *Mex, C. Am., most of S. Am.* ◆ *Besotes para todos ustedes. Hugs and kisses (literally, Smooches) to all of you.*

lo **bestia** →hacer algo a lo bestia

ser **bestia** (to be a beast, animal) to be rude, a boor, someone with bad manners *L. Am., Sp* ◆ *No seas bestia. Don't be crude.*

bestial amazing (good or bad), great, tremendous *Mex, DR, PR, Col, Peru, U, Arg, Sp* ◆ *Fue una película bestial. It was an amazing film.*

besuquearse to smooch *DR, PR, C. Am., S. Cone, Sp* ◆ *Elisa y su novio se estaban besuqueando cuando llegó su padre. Elisa and her boyfriend were necking when her father came in.*

el **besuqueo** necking, smooching, repeated kissing *L. Am., Sp* ◆ *Estoy harta de tanto besuqueo de mi madre. I'm sick of so much smooching from my mother.*

la **biblia en verso** (the Bible in verse) huge amount of knowledge or material, too much to digest *Sp* ◆ *De esa materia, Julia sabe la biblia en verso. Julia knows a ton about that subject.*

bicho →¿Qué bicho te ha picado?

el/la **bicho(-a)** (bug, beast) kid *ES, Sp* (RVAR *Sp*: implies naughtiness) ◆ *Es un bicho; no para de tocar cosas. He's a kid; he never stops touching things.*

ser un **bicho raro** (to be a strange bug, beast) to be an oddball *Mex, S. Cone, Sp* ◆ *Esa persona es un bicho raro. That person is an oddball.*

la **bici** (short for bicicleta) bike *L. Am., Sp* ◆ *Le robaron la bici en la escuela. They stole her bike at school.*

bien →más bien

bien educado(-a) well brought up, polite *L. Am., Sp* ◆ *Es un niño muy bien educado. He's a very well-brought-up child.*

la **bienvenida** →dar la bienvenida

el **billete** →tener el billete largo

birlibirloque →por arte de birlibirloque

la **birra** beer, brewsky *DR, Hond, CR, Col, Ven, Sp* ◆ *Pedí birras para todos. I ordered beers for everyone.*

la **birria** beer, brewsky *Mex, PR, G, Nic* ◆ *Dame una birria. Give me a beer.*

el/la **birriondo(-a)** letch, dirty old man (woman) *Mex, G, ES* ◆ *A ese señor no se le quita lo birriondo. Es un birriondo total. You can't get the letchery out of that man. He's a total letch.*

el **bisnes** business (from English) *ES, Nic* ◆ *Juan está trabajando en el bisnes de su padre. Juan is working at his father's business.*

el **bizcocho 1.** (biscuit) sexy, hot, good-looking person, usually a woman (also, **bizcochito**) *Mex, PR, Col* ◆ *¡Qué bizcocho! What a babe!* **2.** (biscuit) female organ (vulgar) *Chicano, Mex*

blanca →no tener blanca; sin blanca

estar en **blanco** (to be blank) to have not eaten, be half-starved *Mex, Cuba, G* (RVAR *Mex:* also, to have not slept) ◆ *Desde anoche ando en blanco, sin probar bocado. I haven't eaten since last night, not even a bite (literally, without having tasted a mouthful).*

el **blanco** →dar en el blanco

el/la **blandengue** (soft and squishy) person who can be easily influenced and who likes to help others; softie *Mex, DR, Arg, Sp* ◆ *No se puede ser tan blandengue cuando se defiende una postura; uno debe mantenerse firme. You can't be such a softie when you want to defend your position; you have to remain firm.*

un **bledo** →no valer un bledo

bobo(-a) silly, foolish *L. Am., Sp* ◆ *¿Eres boba? Piensa en lo que vas a hacer. Are you foolish (stupid)? Think about what you're going to do.*

la **boca** →hacerle agua la boca; meterse en la boca del lobo

boca abajo (arriba) (mouth down, up) face down (up) *L. Am., Sp* ◆ *El niño casi siempre duerme boca arriba.* The child almost always sleeps face up.

En **boca cerrada no entran moscas.** (In a closed mouth flies don't enter.) Loose lips sink ships. Talking can get you into trouble. *L. Am., Sp* ◆ *Piensa antes de hablar. En boca cerrada no entran moscas.* Think before talking. Loose lips sink ships.

bocachón, bocachona (big mouth) with a big mouth, blabbermouth *U, Arg* ◆ *Cuídate de Angelina; es muy bocachona.* Watch out with Angelina; she's a real blabbermouth.

ser un **bocazas** (to be a big mouth) to be a blabbermouth *Sp* ◆ *Eres un bocazas. ¿Por qué le dijiste a mi padre que salgo con Mónica?* You're a blabbermouth. Why did you tell my father that I'm going out with Mónica?

el **bochinche** blowup, dispute among several people, usually noisy; fuss *DR, PR, C. Am., Col, Ven, S. Cone* (RVar *ES:* **buchinche**) ◆ *Se armó un bochinche en la calle anoche.* There was a noisy argument in the street last night. ◆ *No me gusta contarle nada a Luisa. ¡Siempre forma un bochinche!* I don't like to tell Luisa anything. She always makes such a fuss!

bochinchero(-a) argumentative; troublemaker *DR, PR, ES, Nic, Ven, Bol, Ch* (RVar *Ven:* also, party animal; *Pan, Col:* **bochinchoso**, gossiping troublemaker) ◆ *Marta es una bochinchera.* Marta is a troublemaker.

el **bocho** →hacerse el bocho

el **bocón, la bocona** big mouth, blabbermouth, gossip *Mex, PR, ES, Nic, CR, Col, Arg* ◆ *No seas bocón.* Don't be a blabbermouth.

el **bodrio** stupid, boring thing or person, bore, drag *S. Cone, Sp* ◆ *Esta película es un bodrio.* This film is a bore. ◆ *Ese señor es aburridísimo, un bodrio.* That gentleman is totally boring, a drag.

en **boga** to be in vogue, popular *L. Am., Sp* ◆ *Las películas de Pedro Almodóvar están en boga en toda Europa.* The films of Pedro Almodóvar are popular all over Europe.

bola →dar bola a alguien; hacerse bolas; tener bolas; tener las bolas bien puestas; tener las bolas llenas

la **bola** 1. (ball) gossip, rumor *G, Cuba, DR, ES, CR, U, Arg* ◆ *¿Tú crees de verdad que ella dijo eso? A lo mejor es una bola.* You really believe that she said that? It's probably just a piece of gossip. ◆ *La bola se regó por toda la oficina.* The rumor went around the whole office. **2.** (ball) bunch *Mex, ES* ◆ *Es una bola de idiotas.* They're a bunch of idiots.

bolá →¿Qué bolá?

en **bolas** (in balls) bare-assed, naked (somewhat vulgar, used for males or females) *Nic, U, Arg, Sp* ◆ *Fuimos a la playa, y había mucha gente en bolas.* We went to the beach, and there were many bare-assed people.

las **bolas** balls; testicles (vulgar) *S. Cone*

de **boleto** (of ticket) on the fly, fast or while doing something else *Mex* ◆ *Nos veremos de boleto antes de que salga el avión.* We'll see each other on the fly before the plane leaves.

el **boleto** →dar el boleto

el **boli** (short for **bolígrafo**) pen *L. Am. (not S. Cone)* ◆ *¿Dónde está mi boli? Recién la vi sobre el escritorio.* Where is my pen? I saw it a little while ago on the desk.

el **boliche** nightclub for dancing; dive *U, Arg* ◆ *El viernes fui con los amigos a un boliche.* Friday I went with some friends to a club.

el/la **bolillo(-a)** (bread roll) anglo, white *Chicano, Mex* ◆ *Usted no parece chicana; parece bolilla.* You don't look Chicano; you look anglo.

el **bollo** (bread roll) female organ (vulgar) *Cuba, PR, ES, Nic, Col*

estar **bolo(-a)** to be wasted, drunk *C. Am.* ◆ *Ruperto llegó a su casa bolo, y su esposa no lo dejó entrar.* Ruperto came home wasted, and his wife wouldn't let him in. ◆ *¿Estás bolo o qué?* Are you bombed or what?

bolsear (to purse) to steal, pick pockets *Mex, C. Am.* ◆ *Sólo se suben a los buses a bolsear a las personas.* They just get on buses to pick people's pockets.

bolsillo →tener en el bolsillo a alguien; tener bolsillos alegres

el/la **boludo(-a)** (big balled) idiot, lazy dope, stupid jerk, deadhead (vulgar) *Nic, CR, S. Cone* ◆ *El gobernador es un boludo que no* *sabe hacer nada.* The governor is a stupid jerk who doesn't know how to do anything.

estar **bomba** (to be bomb) to be gorgeous, really hot (a woman) *DR, U, Sp* (RVar *U, Arg:* **ser una bomba**) ◆ *Mira, esa mujer está bomba (es una bomba).* Look, that woman is really hot.

la **bomba, el bombazo** (bomb) surprising piece of news, news flash *Mex, DR, G, ES, Sp* ◆ *El asunto de Juan y Teresa ha sido una bomba; nadie sabía que salían juntos.* The thing about Juan and Teresa was a bombshell; no one knew that they were going out together. ◆ *Agárrate, que tengo un bombazo. Adivina quién salió embarazada.* Hang on—I've got a news flash. Guess who got pregnant.

bombo →**dar bombo a alguien**

a **bombo y platillo** (at drum and saucer) with a lot of fanfare; often said when news is broadcast far and wide (also: **con bombos y platillos**) *L. Am., Sp* ◆ *A bombo y platillo las noticias llegaron desde España hasta México.* The news arrived from Spain to Mexico with a lot of fanfare. ◆ *Con bombos y platillos festejaron la llegada de su primera hija.* With a lot of fanfare they celebrated the arrival of their first daughter.

bombón →**¡Qué bombón y yo con diabetes!**

el **bonche 1.** bash, party, celebration; also, mess or disorder *Mex, DR, ES, Nic, Ven, Bol* ◆ *Ana tiene un bonchecito (bonche) en su casa esta noche.* Ana's having a little party at her house tonight. **2.** bunch, group (from English) *Mex, PR* ◆ *Tengo un bonche de ropita que ya no le queda a mi hija.* I have a bunch of clothes that my daughter can no longer wear.

la **bondad** →**tener la bondad de**

boquiabierto(-a) (open-mouthed) flabbergasted, amazed *L. Am., Sp* ◆ *Susana se quedó boquiabierta cuando le dije que me había casado.* Susana was dumbfounded when I told her I'd gotten married.

el/la **boquisabroso(-a)** person who loves food *Mex, Col* ◆ *Yo soy un boquisabroso. Me encanta probar comidas exóticas.* I'm a gourmand. I love trying exotic foods.

borde →**ponerse borde**

borde rude, vulgar; stupid *Sp* ◆ *No nos imaginamos que Leticia fuera tan borde.* We never imagined that Leticia would be so rude.

borrar (to erase) to kill, wipe out *Chicano, Mex* ◆ *¿Paco está muerto? —Se dice que lo borraron porque sabía demasiado del crimen.* Paco is dead? —People say they wiped him out because he knew too much about the crime.

borrar a algo (a alguien) del mapa (to wipe something [someone] off the map) to forget about something (someone), wash one's hands of *Mex, DR, ES, S. Cone, Sp* ◆ *Borra eso del mapa.* Wash your hands of all that. ◆ *Después de lo que me hizo, lo voy a borrar del mapa.* After what he did to me, I'm going to erase him from my mind.

borrarse, borrarse del mapa (to wipe oneself off the map) to take off, get out of a situation, leave or disappear from it quickly *Mex, ES, S. Cone, Sp* ◆ *¡Bórrense! Viene la policía.* Scram! The police are coming. ◆ *Se borraron olímpicamente.* They took off in grand style.

la **botana** appetizer(s), munchies, snacks *Mex* ◆ *Nos quitamos la mochila y disfrutamos de la botana.* We took off our backpacks and enjoyed the snacks.

botar la bola (pelota), botarla (to throw away the ball) to go too far, go over the top, do or say something extraordinary or ridiculous *Mex, Cuba, DR, PR* ◆ *Martín es un tonto, ¡pero Rafaelito botó la bola!* Martín is a fool, but Rafaelito went over the top (took the cake)!

botar la canica (la bola) (to throw the marble [ball]) to lose one's marbles, go crazy *Mex* ◆ *Se botó la canica y empezó a cantar en el entierro.* He (She) went loopy and began to sing at the funeral. ◆ *A mi perro se le botó la canica de estar tan viejo.* My dog lost his marbles from being so old.

botarse to outdo oneself (dressing well, doing things well, looking good); to have something special *DR, PR* (RVar *CR, Col:* to treat someone, invite and pay) ◆ *Bótate.* You look great. ◆ *¡Qué fiestón! Esta vez se botaron los Martínez.* What a super party! This time the Martínezes have outdone themselves. ◆ *Qué cuero de novia se bota Miguel.* What a gorgeous bride Miguel has.

borrarse del mapa: No sé dónde están; se borraron del mapa.
I don't know where they are; they took off (disappeared).

las **botas** →ponerse las botas

estar con las **botas puestas** (to have one's boots on) to be on the way out, about to take off or ready for a trip *Mex, Sp* ◆ *Los Almeda están con las botas puestas; salen mañana para Argentina.* The Almedas are about to take off; they're leaving tomorrow for Argentina.

en el **bote** →tener en el bote

estar en el **bote** (to be in the jar, container) to be in the clinker (jail) *Mex, Cuba, C. Am.* ◆ *Felipe está en el bote; le dieron cinco meses.* Felipe is in the clinker; they gave him five months.

la **botella** (bottle) what is memorized (as for an exam, in the short term; also, **botellar**) *DR, PR* ◆ *Mario es inteligentísimo; se sabe todas las fórmulas químicas. —¡Bah! Eso es una botella; mañana se le olvida.* Mario is very intelligent; he knows all the chemical formulas. —Bah! That's just crammed-in stuff; tomorrow he'll forget it.

botellas →no es soplar y hacer botellas

el **botero** large or robust person (from the Colombian artist Fernando Botero, whose figures are rotund) *Col* ◆ *Dios mío, si no dejo de comer, seré un botero.* Good Lord, if I don't stop eating, I'll be a like a Botero figure.

el **boyo** punch, hit *U, Arg* ◆ *Portáte bien o te voy a dar un boyo.* Behave yourself or I'm going to give you a smack.

a la **brava** 1. without refinement, sloppily, using force (also, **a la mala**) *Mex, G, ES, Sp* ◆ *José abrió la puerta sin utilizar la llave; la abrió a la brava.* José opened the door without using the key; he opened it by force. ◆ *¡Qué tipo tan mal educado! Se metió en la fila a la brava.* What a rude guy! He forced himself in line in front of everyone. **2.** by force, against one's will (like **a la fuerza**) *Chicano, Mex, DR, PR, ES, CR, Col, Sp* ◆ *Terminé el trabajo, pero lo hice a la brava.* I finished the work, but I did it because I had to (not wanting to).

bravo(-a) angry *L. Am., Sp* ◆ *Se puso bravo cuando le acusaron de ese robo. He got mad*

25

when they accused him of that robbery. ◆ *¿Por qué andas tan brava? Why are you so upset?*

el **brazo** →**no dar el brazo a torcer**

a **brazo partido** (to a broken arm) to the max, the limit (describing how hard someone is working) *L. Am., Sp* ◆ *Trabajamos a brazo partido para el candidato de nuestro partido. We worked to the max for our party's candidate.*

con los **brazos abiertos** with open arms *L. Am., Sp* ◆ *Mis tíos me recibieron con los brazos abiertos. My aunt and uncle welcomed me with open arms.*

con los **brazos cruzados** (with arms crossed) twiddling one's thumbs, idle, doing nothing (also, **de brazos cruzados**) *L. Am., Sp* ◆ *En vez de ayudarme, Pablo se queda allí con los brazos cruzados. Instead of helping me, Pablo's there twiddling his thumbs.*

en los **brazos de Morfeo** in the arms of Morpheus, asleep *L. Am., Sp* ◆ *Ahora que el bebé está en los brazos de Morfeo, voy a descansar también. Now that the baby is in the arms of Morpheus, I'm going to rest also.*

brecha →**hacer brecha**

la **breva** stogie, cigar *Mex, Cuba, Pan, Peru* ◆ *¿Compraste una breva? Did you buy a stogie?*

en **breve** shortly, soon; in brief *L. Am., Sp* ◆ *En breve publicarán un informe sobre el incidente. Shortly they'll publish a report about the incident.*

el/la **briago(-a)** drunkard *Mex, C. Am.* ◆ *Pobre Leonor; su esposo es un briago. Poor Leonor; her husband is a drunkard.*

brillar por su ausencia to be conspicuous (shine) by its absence *L. Am., Sp* ◆ *Todos esperábamos las explicaciones del gerente, pero éste brilló por su ausencia, y salimos de la reunión muy defraudados. We were all waiting for an explanation from the manager, but he was conspicuous by his absence, and we left the meeting feeling cheated.*

brindar por las otras (cervezas que vienen) to toast the others (the other beers to come) *Mex, ES, Col* ◆ *Brindemos por las otras (cervezas que vienen). Let's drink to the drinks we're going to have.*

bróder (from English "brother") friend, pal *ES, Nic, Ven* ◆ *¡Hola, bróder! ¿Qué tal? Hi, bro! How are things?*

en **broma** as a joke, in jest *L. Am., Sp* ◆ *Lo hizo en broma; no te pongas tan serio. He did it as a joke; don't act so serious.*

bromas →**no estar para bromas**

el/la **broncudo(-a)** someone who gets in fights, troublemaker *Mex, ES* ◆ *Ese señor es un broncudo. That man is a troublemaker.*

bronquear(se) to fight, fuss, argue, get upset with *Mex, Col, Peru, U, Arg* ◆ *No me gusta bronquear. I don't like to argue.*◆ *Si me trata mal, me voy a bronquear con él. If he treats me badly, I'm going to get upset with him.*

bruto(-a) (brutish) stupid; rude *L. Am., Sp* ◆ *Nadie la tolera porque es una bruta. Nobody can stand her because she's so rude.*

el **buay** guy *Pan* ◆ *¿Qué dijo el buay? ¿Que vayamos recto? What did the guy say? That we go straight (down that way)?*

buche →**echarle algo al buche (al pico)**

de **buen (mal) gusto** in good (bad) taste *L. Am., Sp* ◆ *Rafael contó un chiste de muy mal gusto. Rafael told a joke that was in very bad taste.*

de **buen humor** in a good mood *L. Am., Sp* ◆ *Hoy abuelito está de muy buen humor; se levantó temprano y tiene mucha energía. Today Grandpa is in a very good mood; he got up early and has a lot of energy.*

ser un **buen partido** to be a good match (for marriage) *L. Am., Sp* ◆ *Debes casarte con Julián. Es un buen partido. You should marry Julián. He's a good match.*

con **buen pie** (with good foot) on the right foot, happily, with good fortune *Mex, DR, PR, Ch* ◆ *Hoy me levanté con buen pie. Estoy contento. Today I started the day on the right foot. I'm happy.*

¡Buen viaje! Have a good trip! also: Good riddance! (for people or things) *Mex, U, Arg, Sp* ◆ *¿Que no quiere ir al club con nosotras? ¡Buen viaje! So she doesn't want to go to the club with us? Good riddance!*

¡Buena alhaja! (Good gem!) What a gem! *L. Am., Sp* ◆ *Fernando es un cero a la izquierda. —Sí, ¡buena alhaja! Fernando is a total jerk. —Yes, he's a real gem!*

de **buena (mala) gana** gladly (grudgingly) *L. Am., Sp* ◆ *De buena gana tomaría vacaciones, pero no tengo dinero.* I'd gladly take a vacation, but I don't have the money. ◆ *Terminamos el trabajo de mala gana.* We finished the job grudgingly.

buena (mala) noticia good (bad) news *L. Am., Sp* ◆ *¿Jaime y Juliana se van a casar? ¡Qué buena noticia!* Jaime and Juliana are getting married? What good news!

a la **buena de Dios** (at the good [will] of God) without a plan, without preparation, by the seat of one's pants *DR, ES, Nic, CR, S. Cone, Sp* ◆ *Coge el abrigo. No salgas a la calle a la buena de Dios. (Sp)* Grab your coat. Don't go out on the street unprepared. ◆ *Ésos son pobres; viven a la buena de Dios (sin planes ni dinero).* Those folks are really poor; they live from one day to the next (without plans or money). ◆ *Voy a viajar a Chile a la buena de Dios.* I'm going to Chile by the seat of my pants.

en **(buena) forma** in (good) shape *L. Am., Sp* ◆ *Don César está en buena forma para su edad.* Don César is in good shape for his age.

buena gente (good people) nice, kind person or people *L. Am., Sp* ◆ *Lola es muy buena gente.* Lola is a nice person.

buena nota (good note) all right, good, great, cool (people or things) *CR, Ven* (RVAR *Ven:* also, high on drugs) ◆ *Mi tío es muy buena nota.* My uncle is a cool guy.

buena onda (good sound wave) good deal or thing; good idea *L. Am., Sp* ◆ *Fernando es muy buena onda.* Fernando is a good guy.

Buenas. (Good. As a shortened response to **Buenas tardes/noches**.) Good afternoon/evening. *L. Am., Sp* ◆ *Buenas tardes, don Carlos. —Buenas, María.* —Good evening, Carlos. —Good evening, María.

las **buenas** →**por las buenas o por las malas**

estar de **buenas** to be in a good mood *L. Am., Sp* ◆ *Esta mañana todos estamos de buenas.* This morning we are all in a good mood.

de **buenas a primeras** (from good ones to first ones) from the beginning, at first sight, right away or on the spur of the moment *L. Am., Sp* ◆ *De buenas a primeras nos hicimos amigas.* Right from the start we became friends.

el/la **buenas peras** (good pears) simpleton, fool *Bol, Ch* ◆ *Traté de explicárselo, pero no le cayó. Tú sabes, Juan es buenas peras.* I tried to explain it to him, but he didn't get it. You know, Juan is not too bright.

estar de **buenas pulgas** (to be of good fleas) to be in a good mood (also, **andar de** or **tener**) *ES, CR, Col, Ch, Arg, Sp* ◆ *Hoy anda de buenas pulgas.* Today he (she) is in a good mood.

estar **buenísima** (to be very good) to be very hot, good in bed (said about women) *Mex, DR, PR, ES, Ven, Ch* (RVAR *Sp:* to be stacked) ◆ *Esa chica está buenísima.* That girl is a hot number.

bueno →**más bueno que el pan**

De lo **bueno, poco.** (Of the good, a little.) All good things in moderation. *L. Am., Sp* ◆ *¿Te sirvo más postre? —No, gracias. De lo bueno, poco.* Can I serve you more dessert? —No, thank you. All good things in moderation.

Bueno. (Good.) Hello (answering the telephone). *Mex* ◆ *Bueno, ¿quién habla?* Hello. May I ask who's speaking?

Bueno... (Good.) Uh . . . , Well . . . *L. Am., Sp* ◆ *Bueno, estoy de acuerdo.* Well, I agree.

la **buenona** good-looking woman, babe *Mex, Cuba, G, Hond, Pan, Col, Ch, Para, Sp* (RVAR *Ch:* hot, good in bed [vulgar]) ◆ *Mi vecina es una buenona.* My neighbor is a babe.

los «**Buenos días**» →**no dar ni los «Buenos días»**

la **buenota** (adj. or n.) stacked (woman), woman with a good figure *Chicano, Mex, ES, Pan, Ec, Para* ◆ *Esa chava está buenota.* That chick is stacked.

el **buey** →**güey**

bufear to clown around, have a good time; to tease *DR, Col* ◆ *Siempre estás bufeando. Habla en serio.* You're always clowning around. Talk seriously.

el **bufeo** good time, joking around *Mex, DR* ◆ *Jorgito, deja el bufeo, que estoy hablando en serio.* Jorgito, stop clowning around because I'm serious about what I'm saying.

el **buga** car, wheels *Sp* ◆ *Dejé el buga cerca de la plaza.* I left my wheels near the square.

el **buitre** 1. (vulture) opportunist, operator *Mex, PR, Col, Ven, U, Arg, Sp* ◆ *No le demos información a ese buitre; la usará para su propio beneficio.* Let's not give that operator any information; he'll use it for his own gain. 2. (vulture) wolf, womanizer *Mex, PR, Col, Ven, U, Sp* ◆ *Franco es un buitre; no es buena persona.* Franco is a womanizer; he's not a good person.

el **bullín** hotel or apartment where people go to have sex *U, Arg* ◆ *Óscar y sus hermanos tienen un bullín y allí van con sus novias o amantes a acostarse.* Óscar and his brothers have an apartment and they go there with their girlfriends or lovers to have sex.

el **bululú** noisy, moving crowd *Ven* (RVAR *Col:* **bololó**) ◆ *Se está formando un bululú.* A big crowd of people is forming.

buñuelos ➝**mandar a alguien a freír buñuelos**

el **buqui** kid, young person *Chicano* ◆ *Los buquis están en la calle.* The kids are in the street.

el **burdel** (bordello) mess *U, Arg* ◆ *Por favor, muchachos, limpien el apartamento; esto es un burdel.* Please, guys, clean up the apartment; this is a mess.

burdo(-a) (coarse) in poor taste, rude *Mex, CR, Col* ◆ *Y ese burdo, ¿de dónde salió?* And that rude guy, where did he come from?

burguesito(-a) (bourgeois) stuck-up, pretentious, snooty *Mex, G, Col, U, Arg* ◆ *Mis primos son unos pobres burguesitos, pero se creen muy intelectuales.* My cousins are poor snobs, but they think they're intellectuals.

burlarse de to make fun of *L. Am., Sp* ◆ *No te burles de Mario ... es mi amigo.* Don't make fun of Mario . . . he's my friend.

en un **burro** ➝**no ver ni tres en un burro**

El **burro delante, para que no se espante.** (The burro first, so he isn't frightened, doesn't get startled.) Said to (or about) someone who goes first or names himself or herself first; often just: **El burro delante.** Age before beauty. *Mex, DR, ES, Ch, U, Arg, Sp* (RVAR *U:* **el burro primero**) ◆ *Yo fui con mis amigos al cine. Como siempre Alejandro, el burro delante para que no se espante. I* went with my friends to the movies. As always Alejandro charged ahead of everyone.

la **burundanga** something confusing, mess *Mex, Cuba, PR* ◆ *Mañana tengo que pagar los impuestos y estoy muy desorganizada. ¡Qué burundanga!* Tomorrow I have to pay my taxes and I'm very disorganized. What a confusing mess!

el/la **buscapleitos** troublemaker *L. Am., Sp* ◆ *Ese buscapleitos me tiene hasta la coronilla.* I've had it up to here with that troublemaker.

buscar berros ➝**mandar a alguien a buscar berros**

buscar chichis a las culebras (to look for breasts on a snake) to look for the impossible or for something one can never find *Mex* ◆ *Termina de leer el informe y no busques chichis a las culebras.* Finish reading the report and don't waste time looking for something you'll never find.

buscar una aguja en un pajar to look for a needle in a haystack *L. Am., Sp* ◆ *No insistas. Encontrar tu anillo en el estadio donde hay cien mil personas es como buscar una aguja en un pajar.* Don't persist with that. Finding your ring in the stadium where there are more than a hundred thousand people is like looking for a needle in a haystack.

buscarle las pulgas a alguien (to look for someone's fleas) to provoke or irritate someone *Mex, Cuba, Sp* ◆ *No me busques las pulgas hoy. No estoy para bromas.* Don't bug me today. I'm in no mood for jokes.

(**no**) **buscarle pelos a la sopa** (to [not] look for hairs in the soup) to (not) look for problems, (not) make excuses *Mex* ◆ *No le busques pelos a la sopa. Tienes que terminar ese trabajo.* Don't look for problems (make excuses); you have to finish that work.

buscarle tres (cinco) pies al gato (to look for three [five] feet on the cat) to get involved in something that can be harmful; to look for solutions or reasons that make no sense; to sweat the small stuff *L. Am., Sp* (RVAR *Ch, U:* **buscarle la quinta pata al gato**) ◆ *¿Para qué buscarle tres pies al gato si tiene cuatro?* Why sweat the small stuff? (Literally, Why look for three feet on the cat if it has four?)

buscárselo(-la) (to look for it) to bring something on oneself *L. Am, Sp* ◆ *No te que-*

jes porque te insultaron. Te la buscaste. Don't complain because they insulted you. You brought it on yourself.

el **buscón, la buscona** 1. (searcher) someone who is looking for a fight, troublemaker *Mex, DR, PR* ◆ *Mira ahora si encontró lo que quería ese buscón.* Let's see if that troublemaker got what he was looking for. 2. (searcher) opportunist, operator *Mex, DR, PR, Col, Sp* ◆ *Cerca del departamento de tránsito, hay unos buscones que por unos pesos te renuevan la licencia de conducir.*

Near the transportation department, there are some opportunists who will renew your driver's license for a few pesos.

buzo (diver) smart, alert, on the ball *Mex, G, Hond, ES* ◆ *Si te pones buzo, lo logras.* If you're on the ball, you'll manage (achieve) it. ◆ *Jaime Ernesto ya se puso buzo para los negocios.* ◆ *Jaime Ernesto became sharp at business.*

el **buzón** (mailbox) mouth, kisser *Mex, Cuba* ◆ *Cierra el buzón. Shut your trap.*

C

estar en sus **cabales** to be in one's right mind *L. Am., Sp* ◆ *Desde que se divorció, Paco no está en sus cabales.* Since he divorced, Paco is not in his right mind.

el **caballo** (horse) heroin (also, **la farlopa, el jaco**) *Sp* ◆ *A ese tío le gusta meterse caballo.* That guy likes to take heroin.

caber ➞no caber duda; no caber en sí de contento; no caber una cosa en el pecho

cabeza ➞dar cráneo (cabeza); echar de cabeza; meter cabeza; meterse algo en la cabeza; no dejar títere con cabeza; tener el santo de cabeza; tener la cabeza hueca; tener la cabeza llena de humos

la **cabeza de cebolla** (onion head) someone with gray hair *Mex, ES* ◆ *Soy cabeza de cebolla pero con tallo verde.* I'm a gray-headed senior (onion head) but with the fire of youth (a green stem).

el/la **cabeza de chorlito** (head of golden plover [a small bird]) birdbrain, scatterbrain *L. Am., Sp* ◆ *Este tipo es un cabeza de chorlito. ¿Cómo se le puede ocurrir hacer algo así?* That guy is a birdbrain. How could he even think of doing something like that?

cabezón, cabezona (bighead) hardheaded, stubborn *Florida, Mex, DR, PR, G, Col, S. Cone, Sp* ◆ *No seas cabezón. Escucha lo que te dice tu médico.* Don't be so stubborn. Listen to what your doctor tells you.

cabezota (bigheaded) stubborn, bull-headed *Sp* ◆ *Si sigues siendo tan cabezota, acabarás mal.* If you persist in being so bull-headed, you'll come to a bad end.

cabida ➞dar cabida

con **cables** ➞tener (andar con) cables pelados

a **cabo** ➞llevar a cabo

de **cabo a rabo** from top to bottom, from beginning to end, completely *L. Am., Sp* ◆ *Leí el libro de cabo a rabo.* I read the book from beginning to end.

al **cabo de un rato** after a while *L. Am., Sp* ◆ *Esteban se fue pero al cabo de un rato regresó con el dinero en la mano.* Esteban left but after a while he came back with the money in his hand.

cabos sueltos loose ends *L. Am., Sp* ◆ *No me gustó esa telenovela porque quedaron muchos cabos sueltos.* I didn't like that soap opera because there were too many loose ends.

cabreado(-a) horny; angry (slightly vulgar) *Mex, CR, Col, Sp* ◆ *Ando cabreado desde que mi mujer me abandonó.* I've been horny ever since my woman (or wife) left me. ◆ *Está muy cabreado por la putada que le hiciste. (Sp)* He's very angry because of the dirty trick you played on him.

cabrear(se) (to act like a goat) to make angry (become angry) (vulgar) *CR, Ec, Ch, Arg, Sp* ◆ *No te cabrées, chico. Es sólo una broma.* Don't get all pissed off, man. It's just a joke.

el **cabreo monumental** huge outburst of anger *Sp* ◆ *El violinista cogió un cabreo monumental cuando se canceló el concierto.* The violinist threw a major tantrum when the concert was cancelled.

el/la **cabrito(-a)** (little goat, kid) kid *Ch* ◆ *¿Dónde están las cabritas?* Where are the (female) kids?

cabrón, cabrona (big goat) unbearable (person); damn, a bitch of (plus a noun) (vulgar) *most of L. Am., Sp* ◆ *La cabrona máquina no funciona.* The damn machine doesn't work. ◆ *No se puede contigo. Está cabrón.* You're impossible. (Nothing can be done with you.) It's a bitch of a situation. ◆ *¡Qué enfermedad más cabrona!* What a bitch of an illness!

el **cabrón, la cabrona** (big goat) son of a bitch, sometimes used with affection among males (bitch) (vulgar) *most of L. Am., Sp (not Arg., U)* ◆ *No le hablemos a esa cabrona.* Let's not speak to that bitch. ◆ *¡Qué gusto de* *encontrarte aquí, cabrón! What a pleasure to find you here, you SOB!*

la **cabronada** dirty trick, cheap shot, evil action *Mex, PR, G, Col, Sp* ◆ *¿Te robaron la cartera? ¡Qué cabronada! They stole your wallet? What a cheap shot!*

la **caca de la vaca** (cow dung) crap, scumbag, something of poor quality or someone not trustworthy, often used in negation (vulgar) *Sp* ◆ *Sobre la compra de otro coche, ¡caca de la vaca! Y no hablemos más de eso. About buying another car, what crap! And let's not talk about it any more.*

cacahuete →no valer ni cacahuete

un **cacao** →tener un cacao mental

cacarear (to cackle like a hen) to boast loudly *Arg* ◆ *Es tan orgulloso. Le encanta cacarear. He's so proud. He loves to toot his own horn.*

cacarear y no poner huevo (to cackle and not lay an egg) to promise something and not fulfill it *Mex, ES, Sp* ◆ *Ese diputado cacarea y no pone huevo. That politician talks a good game but doesn't deliver.*

la **cachapera** (from **cachapa**, corn bread) lesbian, dike, bisexual woman (pejorative) *PR, Ven*

cachar to catch the drift, get it *most of L. Am.* (RVar *Ch, Peru:* also, to have sex) ◆ *¿Cachas? (¿Cachaste?) —No cacho, amigo. Get it? (Did you get it?) —I don't get it, pal.*

el **cacharro** **1.** jalopy, old car *Mex, DR, PR, Col, U, Arg, Sp* ◆ *Este cacharro cualquier día nos deja tirados en medio de la carretera. This jalopy is going to leave us out in the middle of the highway some day.* **2.** piece of junk, worthless object *Mex, DR, PR, Col, U, Arg, Sp* ◆ *No sé como funciona aún este cacharro; pronto tendremos que reemplazarlo. I don't know how this old piece of junk is still working; we'll have to replace it soon.*

el **cache** person or thing that is pretentious and in bad taste (something chintzy, nouveau riche) *Arg* ◆ *La casa de mi prima me pareció un cache. My cousin's house struck me as very chintzy.* ◆ *Ese muchacho me pareció un cache. That boy seemed vulgar (tacky) to me.*

estar de la **cachetada** to be in a bad way, bad; to suck *Mex, Col* ◆ *Este color está de la ca-*

chetada. This color is way bad. ◆ *¿No tienes la llave? Esto está de la cachetada. You don't have the key? This sucks.*

el **cachimbazo** blow, smack *G, ES, Nic, CR* (RVar *Nic:* vulgar) ◆ *Emilio se subió a la escalera y se dio un cachimbazo. Emilio climbed up the ladder and hit himself on the head (literally, gave himself a smack or hit).*

ser **cachimbón, cachimbona** to be good at everything, competent *Mex, G, ES* ◆ *Ese chico es bien cachimbón para trabajar con madera. That guy is super at working with wood.*

el **cachito** (little catch) little bit *most of L. Am., Sp* ◆ *Dame un cachito de canela, porfa. Give me a little bit of cinnamon, please.* ◆ *Espera un cachito. (Ch) Wait a bit.*

los **cachivaches** junk, trinkets, things of little value *L. Am., Sp* ◆ *En esa tienda sólo se venden cachivaches. In that store they sell only junk (trinkets, odds and ends).*

cachondear to make out, indulge in foreplay (vulgar) *Mex, ES* ◆ *Hugo y su novia llegan al cine sólo a cachondear. Hugo and his girlfriend only go to the movies to make out.*

cachondearse (de alguien) to make fun of or tease (someone, vulgar) *Sp* ◆ *Te estás cachondeando de mí, ¿verdad? You're making fun of me, right?*

de **cachondeo** →irse de cachondeo

el **cachondeo** (horning around) petting, foreplay (vulgar) *Mex, ES, Sp* ◆ *¿Qué es el amor, mi cielo, sin un poquito de cachondeo? What's love, my darling, without a little fooling around?*

cachondeo(s) →Sin cachondeo(s).

ser un **cachondo mental** to be wild and crazy, funny; also, to be obsessed with sex (vulgar) *Sp* ◆ *Soy un cachondo mental y lo paso muy bien. I'm wild and crazy and I have a good time.*

estar **cachondo(-a)** to be horny, sexually excited, hot (vulgar) (also, **poner a alguien cachondo**) *Mex, ES, Sp* ◆ *Está muy cachondo. He's very horny.* ◆ *Me pones siempre muy cachondo. You always make me hot. A Eduardo le gustan los bailes cachondos. Eduardo likes sexy dances.*

ser **cachondo(-a)** to be damn amusing, wild and crazy (vulgar) *Mex, Sp* ◆ *Vendrá gente* *muy cachonda y lo pasaremos bien. (Mex)* Some wild and crazy people will be coming and we'll have a good time. ◆ *Jaime es un cachondo total. (Sp)* Jaime is a real wild man.

los **cachos** →**ponerle los cachos a alguien**

cada hijo de vecino (each neighbor's son) everybody (and his uncle) *Mex, Sp* ◆ *Cada hijo de vecino debería ayudar a proteger el medio ambiente.* Everybody should help protect the environment.

a **cada instante** every other minute, constantly *L. Am., Sp* ◆ *A cada instante se le ocurre una buena idea.* He (She) is constantly coming up with good ideas.

Cada loco con su tema. (Every crazy person with his or her subject.) It's his (her) hobbyhorse. He's (She's) running it into the ground. (expression usually used when someone is too insistent about something) *L. Am., Sp* ◆ *Dejémoslo que hable; cada loco con su tema.* Let's let him talk; it's his hobby horse.

cada muerte de un obispo (each death of a bishop) once in a blue moon *CR, Col, Peru, S. Cone* ◆ *Escucho música rock cada muerte de un obispo.* I listen to rock music once in a blue moon.

Cada oveja con su pareja. (Every sheep with its partner.) In twos. All paired up. Everyone with a partner. *L. Am., Sp* ◆ *Navegamos en el Caribe por tres días, y cada oveja fue con su pareja.* We sailed in the Caribbean for three days, and all of us paired up.

Cada quien se rasque con sus propias uñas. (Each person should scratch himself or herself with his or her own fingernails.) Everyone for himself or herself, being alone or without support. *Mex, ES, Ch* ◆ *No hay transporte al congreso. Nos han dicho que cada quien se rasque con sus propias uñas.* There's no transportation to the conference. They told us everyone for himself or herself.

a **cada rato** all the time, frequently *L. Am., Sp* ◆ *Me pides la hora a cada rato. ¿Por qué no llevas reloj?* You keep asking me what time it is all the time. Why don't you wear a watch?

Se me **caen las medias (los calzones).** (My stockings [underpants] are falling down.) I'm excited, surprised (usually by a good-looking person). *parts of L. Am.* ◆ *Es tan guapo que se me caen las medias cuando lo miro.* He's so handsome that my heart beats faster when I look at him.

caer (to fall) to drop by, visit *L. Am.* ◆ *Más tarde te caigo.* Later I'll drop in on you. ◆ *A Raúl le cayeron sus amigos cuando no tenía nada preparado.* Raul's friends popped in on him when he had nothing prepared.

estar al **caer** (to be to fall) to be about to arrive *Sp* ◆ *Mi cumpleaños está al caer.* My birthday is just around the corner.

caer como bomba to fall like a bomb(shell); to arrive as a surprise, generally unpleasant *Mex, DR, PR, G, ES, S. Cone, Sp* ◆ *La noticia (La comida) me cayó como bomba.* The news (food) hit me like a bombshell.

caer con (to fall with) to pay up *Mex* ◆ *Cáele con la lana.* Fork over the dough.

caer de cajón (to fall like a drawer) to go without saying, be obvious (also, **ser de cajón**) *Mex, Hond, Nic, Ven, Ec, Peru, S. Cone, Sp* ◆ *Cae de cajón que Gloria está enamorada de Héctor.* It goes without saying that Gloria is in love with Hector.

caer de madre a alguien (to fall of mother to someone) to strike someone as worthless, be scorned by someone (vulgar) *Mex* ◆ *Le cae de madre al que no tenga valor de ir.* Anybody not brave enough to go is a worthless scumbag.

caer el veinte (to have the twenty [meaning twenty-cent coin] fall, as into the telephone) to get it, understand *Mex* ◆ *Ya me cayó el veinte.* Now I get the message.

caer en el chiste (to fall into the joke) to get it, wise up, figure out the reason that someone is saying or doing something *Mex, Sp* ◆ *Caímos en el chiste al ver las estadísticas de la fábrica.* We wised up when we saw the statistics from the factory.

caer en la cuenta (to fall into the account) to become aware of something or finally get it, have something dawn on one *Mex, DR, PR, U, Arg, Sp* ◆ *Cuando vi su foto, caí en la cuenta de que lo conocía desde hacía muchos años.* When I saw his photo, it dawned on me (I figured out) that I had known him for many years.

caer en la trampa (en la red) to fall into the trap (the net) *Mex, DR, ES, S. Cone, Sp*

caerle gordo: Ese hombre me cae gordo. No lo tolero.
That man is a pain. I can't stand him.

(RVar *Ch:* **trampa** only) ◆ *Cayeron en la trampa y compraron un auto robado.* They *fell into the trap and bought a stolen car.*

caer (irse) en picada to fall off sharply *L. Am., Sp* ◆ *El año pasado el negocio empezó a caer en picada.* Last year the business *started to fall off sharply.*

caer parado(-a) (to fall standing up) to land on one's feet, get out of a bad situation with no harmful consequences *DR, ES, S. Cone* ◆ *En la oficina Mario metió la pata pero pudo solucionar el problema. ¡Qué suerte! Cayó parado.* At work Mario made a big mistake but managed to solve the problem. What luck! He landed on his feet.

caerle bien (mal) una persona (to fall well [badly] on someone) to be likeable (not likeable, used like **gustar**) *L. Am., Sp* ◆ *Esteban es muy antipático; me cae muy mal. Esteban is very unpleasant; I don't like him.* ◆ *Creo que no le caigo bien a la maestra. I don't think the teacher likes me.*

caerle como piedra (plomo) (to fall on someone like stone [lead]) to be a pain, not

be tolerable to, hit like a ton of bricks *S. Cone* ◆ *Lo que leímos en el periódico nos cayó como piedra.* What we read in the newspaper hit us like a ton of bricks.

caerle de la patada (pedrada) (to fall on someone like the kick [blow with a stone]) to be a pain, not be tolerable to) *Mex, Ch* ◆ *Su mamá me cae de la patada. I can't stand his mom.*

caerle en el hígado (to fall to one's liver) to be intolerable, distasteful to (also, **caerle en los huevos**, vulgar) *Mex, ES* ◆ *Me cae en el hígado ir a trabajar lejos. I hate working far away.*

caerle gordo(-a) (to fall fat on someone) to be a pain, be intolerable to (also, **caerle pesado[-a]**) *L. Am., Sp* ◆ *Ese hombre me cae gordo. That man is a pain in the neck. (I can't stand that man.)*

caerse con todo el equipo (to fall with the whole team or equipment) to wash out, fail totally *Mex, Sp* ◆ *El estafador se cayó con todo el equipo. Finalmente fue descubierto, y ahora está en la cárcel. The con* man messed up royally. Finally he was found out, and now he's in jail.

caerse de la mata (to fall out of the bush or shrub) to find out something everyone else already knows, wise up *Cuba, DR, PR, Col* ◆ *¿Te caíste de la mata?* Did you (finally) wise up?

caerse del mecate (to fall off the cord) to wise up, realize one has been deceived *Mex* ◆ *Por fin Juan se cayó del mecate. Ahora se da cuenta del problema.* Finally Juan wised up. Now he realizes what the problem is.

caerse del susto (to fall from the fright) to be scared stiff *most of L. Am., Sp* (RVAR *Arg, Sp: more common, darse un susto de muerte*) ◆ *Paco se cayó del susto al enterarse de lo que había pasado.* Paco was scared stiff when he found out what had happened.

caerse por acá (ahí) (to fall by here [there]) to drop in here (there) *L. Am.* ◆ *Dejé mi paraguas en el colegio de Luz. Este lunes nos dejamos caer por ahí.* I left my umbrella at Luz' school. This Monday we'll drop in there.

caérsele a alguien el alma a los pies (to have one's soul fall to one's feet) to lose heart *DR, Ch, U, Sp* ◆ *Se nos cayó el alma a los pies al verlos tan tristes.* We lost heart seeing them so sad.

caérsele a alguien el mundo encima (to have the world fall on one) to have something terrible happen, have the world crumbling around one *Mex, DR, PR, ES, S. Cone, Sp* ◆ *¡Pobre doña Altagracia! Se le está cayendo el mundo encima. Primero murió don Danilo y ahora se le enfermó Altagracita.* Poor Doña Altagracia! Her world is crumbling around her. First Don Danilo died and now little Altagracita is sick.

caérsele a alguien la baba (to have drool falling) to be go wild (for), drool over (someone or something, be drooling with admiration *Mex, ES, S. Cone* ◆ *Se me cayó la baba cuando ella salió en esa minifalda (cuando vi mis calificaciones).* I went wild when she came out in that miniskirt. ◆ *Se le cayó la baba cuando vio a ese muchacho.* She was drooling with admiration when she saw that guy.

caérsele a alguien la casa encima (to have the house fall on one) to have the world crumbling around one, have something terrible happen *Mex, DR, S. Cone, Sp* ◆ *Con todos los problemas familiares y económicos, se les ha caído la casa encima.* With all their family and economic problems, the world is crumbling around them.

caérsele las alas (to have one's wings fall) to get discouraged *L. Am., Sp* ◆ *Se me cayeron las alas al oír la crítica.* I got discouraged when I heard the critique.

caérsele un tornillo (to have a screw fall out) to have a screw loose *Mex, ES, CR, Col, Sp* ◆ *Se te cayó un tornillo.* You have a screw loose.

el **cafiche** pimp *S. Cone* ◆ *Ese cafiche explota a varias mujeres.* That pimp is exploiting several women.

cafre 1. rude, lacking in respect *G, Sp* ◆ *Javier es tan cafre que ni siquiera fue al entierro de su tía.* Javier's so rude he didn't even go to his aunt's funeral. 2. stupid, incompetent *Mex, Cuba, PR, Col* ◆ *Maneja el coche como cafre.* He (She) drives the car like a maniac (incompetently).

la **cafrería** junk, claptrap, useless stuff (similar to **porquería**) *Mex, PR* ◆ *En esta maleta sólo hay cafrería.* There is only claptrap in this suitcase.

los **cafres del volante** (jerks at the wheel) maniac drivers *Mex, Col* ◆ *Los cafres del volante causaron un accidente en el centro.* The maniac drivers caused an accident downtown.

cagada →¡Qué gran cagada!

la **cagada** (shit) dirty trick, piece of crap, betrayal (vulgar) *L. Am., Sp* ◆ *Ana me hizo una gran cagada; trató de salir con mi novio.* Ana played a hell of a dirty trick on me; she tried to go out with my boyfriend.

estar **cagado(-a)** (to be pooped) to be scared stiff, scared shitless (vulgar) *S. Cone, Sp* (RVAR *S. Cone:* also, to be screwed, messed up) ◆ *Angelina llegó tarde y estaba cagada porque sus padres estaban furiosos.* Angelina arrived late and she was scared shitless because her parents were furious. ◆ *Estoy cagada.* I'm screwed.

cagando →Ni cagando.

cagar (to shit on) **1.** to mess (someone) up by abusing, lying to, or cheating on that person or by being unfaithful; to give (someone) the shaft (vulgar) *S. Cone* ◆ *No fueron responsables y cagaron toda la situación. They were not responsible and they screwed up the whole situation.* ◆ *Cagué mi matrimonio por salir con otras mujeres. I screwed up my marriage by going out with other women.* **2.** to insult, ream out, rip apart, give (someone) a lot of shit (vulgar) *Mex, Col, S. Cone* ◆ *Me cagaron en la oficina. They gave me a lot of shit at the office.*

cagarla (to shit on it) to f**k up, make a mistake, blow it (vulgar) (sometimes used without **la**) *L. Am., Sp* ◆ *La cagué invitándolo a la fiesta porque estuvo tan pesado como siempre. I screwed up by inviting him to the party because he was just as much of a jerk as always.*

cagarse de la risa (to shit from laughter) to laugh one's ass off, die laughing (also, **cagado de la risa**) (vulgar) *Mex, ES, Ven, S. Cone* ◆ *Nos cagamos de la risa escuchando sus historias. We laughed our asses off hearing his stories.*

un **cagazo** →darse un cagazo

¡Me **cago en Dios!** (I shit on God!) strong expletive implying sacrilege, something like God dammit to hell! (vulgar) *Sp* ◆ *¿Otra vez suben los impuestos? ¡Me cago en Dios! They're raising the taxes again? Goddammit to hell!*

¡Me **cago en la puta (diez, leche)!** (I shit on the whore [ten, milk]!) expression of anger (vulgar) *Sp* ◆ *¡Me cago en la puta! Olvidé mi reloj en el gimnasio. Goddamnit to hell! I forgot my watch at the gym.*

¡Me **cago en tu madre (en la madre que te parió, en tus muertos)!** (I shit on your mother [that gave birth to you, on your dead]!) F**k you! *PR, Sp* (RVar *Sp*: also, **cagarse en su padre**) (vulgar) ◆ *Ese profesor me ha vuelto a suspender. ¡Me cago en su madre (padre)! That teacher has flunked me again. F**k him!*

el **cagón, la cagona** (big shitter) damn scaredy-cat, chicken (vulgar) *U, Arg, Sp* (RVar *Sp*: also, **cagado[-a]**) (vulgar) ◆ *No seas cagona, pídele aumento a tu jefe. Don't*

be a damn scaredy-cat; ask your boss for a raise.

a la **caída del sol** at sunset *L. Am., Sp* ◆ *El Gran Cañón está muy bonito a la caída del sol. The Grand Canyon is very pretty at sunset.*

caído(-a) →como caído(-a) de las nubes

caído(-a) de la cuna (fallen from the cradle) clueless, not right in the head (because of being dropped from the cradle), easily taken advantage of *U, Arg* ◆ *¿Piensas que soy una caída de la cuna, para creer tus mentiras? Do you think I was born yesterday, and that I'll believe your lies?*

caído(-a) del cielo (fallen from the sky) out of the blue, describing a windfall, boon *Mex, ES, S. Cone* ◆ *El dinero me vino como caído del cielo. Me cayó del cielo. The money was a real windfall. It came out of nowhere.*

caído(-a) del nido (fallen out of the nest) wet behind the ears, naive, clueless *L. Am.* ◆ *Te lo expliqué cien veces, pero ni cuenta te diste. Pareces como caído del nido. I explained it to you a hundred times, but you didn't get it. You seem clueless.*

me **caigo** →Estoy que me caigo.

el **caimán** (alligator) wolf, Don Juan *Mex, Col* ◆ *Ahí viene el caimán de la familia. Here comes the Don Juan of the family.*

la **caja tonta** (idiot box) boob tube, television *Mex, Sp* ◆ *No paso mucho tiempo frente a la caja tonta. I don't spend much time in front of the boob tube.*

la **cajetilla** dandy, braggart *Arg* ◆ *Jacinto es una cajetilla, muy creído. Jacinto is a dandy, very stuck up.*

a **cal y canto** (lime and stone, stone masonry) strong, thick, tightly *Mex, Sp* ◆ *Nuria tiene un acento catalán a cal y canto. Nuria has a thick Catalonian accent.* ◆ *La tienda estaba cerrada a cal y canto. The store was closed tightly.*

la **calabaza** (pumpkin) failing grade, F *Sp* ◆ *Saqué dos calabazas: en matemáticas y literatura. I got two rotten grades: in math and literature.*

¡Calabaza! (Pumpkin!) The party's over! Time to go! (from the phrase **¡Calabaza, calabaza, cada uno [or cada quien] para su casa!**) *ES, Ch*

calabazas →dar calabazas (ayotes)

la **calaca** death, Grim Reaper *Mex, ES* ◆ *Si no se cuida la salud, se lo va a llevar la calaca.* If you don't take care of your health, the Grim Reaper will take you.

el **calambre** (cramp) anxiety attack *Mex, Col* ◆ *Le dio un calambre en el hospital.* He had an anxiety attack at the hospital.

a **caldo** →poner a caldo

la **calentadita** (little heating up) little "workover" (beating or sexual play) *Mex, ES, Col, U* ◆ *Beatriz y Rolando estaban de calentadita en el jardín cuando llegaron los padres y se pusieron furiosos.* Beatriz and Rolando were all hot for each other in the garden when their parents arrived and were enraged. ◆ *Dijeron que buscaban a un tipo para darle una calentadita.* They said they were looking for a guy to give him a little workover.

calentar →no calentar el asiento

calentar(se) to heat up (become heated) with anger or sexual desire; to anger (become angry); to turn on (often has sexual overtones) *L. Am., Sp* ◆ *Esa mujer me calienta mucho.* That woman really turns me on.

el **calentón, la calentona** (big hot one) person who is easily aroused sexually; hothead *U, Arg* ◆ *Me gusta esa mujer porque es calentona.* I like that woman because she is easily turned on.

una **calentura** →tener una calentura

el **caliche** street slang (n.); of the street (adj., also, **calichera**) *Mex, ES* ◆ *Es habla caliche.* It's street slang.

caliente (hot) fast (sexually), passionate, excited *L. Am., Sp* ◆ *Vamos a hacer el amor, muñeca; estoy caliente.* Let's make love, doll; I'm hot for you.

el **callejón sin salida** dead-end situation; problem or conflict that is difficult or impossible to resolve *L. Am., Sp* ◆ *No sé qué hacer; estoy en un callejón sin salida.* I don't know what to do; I'm in a dead-end situation.

el **callo** →dar el callo

con **calma** calmly *L. Am., Sp* ◆ *¡Hombre! Toma las cosas con calma.* Take things calmly.

la **calva** (the bald one) death, Grim Reaper *Cuba, G, ES, Col* ◆ *Tengo miedo. Soñé con la calva toda la noche.* I'm afraid. I dreamt of the Grim Reaper all night.

a **calzón quitado** (with underwear removed) openly, frankly *L. Am.* ◆ *A calzón quitado le dije que no lo quería ver más en mi casa.* I told him frankly that I didn't want to see him again in my home.

el **calzonazos** (oversized pants) man who is pushed around by his wife or girlfriend or overly attached to his mother, henpecked man, wimp, mama's boy *Ch, Sp* ◆ *El muy calzonazos pensó que podría asustarnos.* The wimp thought he could scare us.

los **calzones** →tener bien puestos los calzones

el **calzonudo** (oversized pants) man who is pushed around by his wife or girlfriend or overly attached to his mother, henpecked man, wimp, mama's boy *Mex, ES, Peru, Ch, Arg* ◆ *No me extraña que se haya casado con esa sargenta; siempre ha sido un calzonudo.* It doesn't surprise me that he married that bossy woman; he's always been a mama's boy.

calzonudo(-a) (in oversized pants) lazy (like **huevón**) *ES, CR, Col, Ch* ◆ *Es un haragán calzonudo; se levanta bien tarde.* He's a slacker; he gets up really late.

la **cama** →hacerle la cama a alguien

cambiar de canal (to change the channel) to change pace, subject, activity; to shift gears (figuratively) *Mex, DR, ES, Col* ◆ *El ministro cambió de canal para no hablar del tema de los impuestos.* The minister (secretary) shifted gears so as not to talk about the subject of taxes.

cambiar de chaqueta (casaca) (to change jacket [coat]) to leave a group, political party, etc., and go to a different one, be a turncoat *L. Am., Sp* (RVar *Sp* and *Ch*: also, **cambiar de camisa**) ◆ *¿Te has fijado cuántas veces cambió de casaca ese político en los últimos quince años?* Have you noticed how often that politician has changed sides (or parties) in the last fifteen years?

cambiar de idea to change one's mind, have a different idea *L. Am., Sp* ◆ *Iban a ir a Toledo, pero cambiaron de idea.* They were going to go to Toledo, but they changed their minds.

cambiar el chip: Necesita cambiar el chip para tener éxito.
He needs to change his mindset to be successful.

cambiar de opinión to change one's mind or opinion *L. Am., Sp* ◆ *Pensaba que podía confiar en Felipe, pero he cambiado de opinión. I thought I could trust Felipe, but now I've changed my mind.*

cambiar de tema to change the subject *L. Am., Sp* ◆ *Cambiando de tema, ¿has leído el periódico hoy? Changing the subject, have you read the newspaper today?*

cambiar el agua a los peces (to change the fishes' water) to make a pit stop, see a man about a dog (euphemism for to urinate) *Cuba, DR, PR, Col, U, Arg* (RVAR *CR:* **cambiar el agua al pájaro;** *U, Arg:* **cambiar el agua a las aceitunas;** *Ven, Sp:* **cambiar el agua al canario**) ◆ *Un momento. Tengo que cambiar el agua a los peces. Wait a minute. I have to make a pit stop.*

cambiar el cassette (to change the cassette) to change the subject *U, Ch* ◆ *¿Podemos cambiar de cassette? Hablemos de algo más divertido. Can we change the subject? Let's talk about something more fun.*

cambiar el chip (to change one's [computer] chip) to change one's mindset, way of thinking *Mex, Sp* ◆ *Ustedes tienen que cambiar el chip si quieren tener éxito. You have to change your way of thinking if you want to succeed.*

camellar (to camel) to work *Mex, ES, Nic, CR, Col, Ec* ◆ *Después de buscar trabajo durante mucho tiempo, Ariel ya está camellando. After looking for work for a long time, Ariel is now working.*

el **camello** (camel) work, job *Mex, ES, Col, Ec* ◆ *Ese camello me parece aburrido. That job sounds boring to me.*

en **camisa** →**meterse en camisa de once varas**

con la **camiseta puesta** (with the T-shirt on) fired up, describing a real fan, enthusiast *S. Cone* ◆ *Con la camiseta puesta, Ernesto trabajó día y noche para el candidato de su partido político. All fired up, Ernesto worked day and night for the candidate of his political party.*

el **camorrero** troublemaker, instigator of conflicts *S. Cone* ◆ *Martín es muy camorrero y siempre termina peleando con alguien. Martín is a real troublemaker, and he always ends up fighting with someone.*

camote →**hacerse camote; poner como camote a alguien**

el **camote** (sweet potato) mess, trouble *Mex* (RVAR *CR:* also, fight or fit) ◆ *No tenía los papeles que necesitaba y me metí en un camote. I didn't have the papers that I needed and I got into a bind.* ◆ *Resolver el problema de la inmigración es un camote. Solving the immigration problem is a mess.*

campana →**hacer campana**

el **campo** →**más del campo que las amapolas**

la **cana 1.** jail, the clinker *Cuba, Ec, Peru, Col, Ch, U* ◆ *Humberto pasó la noche en la cana. Humberto spent the night in jail.* **2.** cops, police *Arg* ◆ *Se lo llevó la cana porque robó dinero de la caja. The cops took him away because he robbed money from the cash register.*

el/la **canalla** (from canine, dog) scoundrel, creep (a bit old-fashioned in *Sp*) *L. Am., Sp* ◆ *Se comportó como un canalla. ¡Qué sinvergüenza! He acted like a scoundrel. What a creep!*

la **canallada** cheap shot, dirty trick, evil action *most of L. Am.* ◆ *Joaquín me hizo una canallada con mi hermana. Joaquín played a dirty trick on me with my sister.*

En la **cancha se ven los gallos.** (It's in the ring that we see the roosters.) Actions speak louder than words. *Ch, U* ◆ *El nuevo jefe dice que sabe aumentar la productividad, pero en la cancha se ven los gallos. The new boss says he knows how to increase productivity, but actions speak louder than words.*

un **candado** →**poner un candado a la boca**

la **candela** (candle) fiery woman *Cuba, DR, PR, Col* ◆ *Margarita es candela. Margarita is a hot number.*

ser **canela fina** (to be fine cinnamon) to be fine, of great worth *Mex, G, ES, Peru, Sp* ◆ *Esta música es canela fina. This music is fine.* ◆ *Su biografía es canela fina. His (Her) biography is terrific.*

el/la **canguro** (kangaroo) babysitter *Sp* ◆ *Soy la canguro; la señora no está en casa. I'm the babysitter; the lady of the house isn't home.*

la **canilla** (long bone of leg or arm) leg, skinny leg *Cuba, DR, G, Nic, CR, Col, Ch* ◆ *Ella anda en minifaldas exhibiendo las canillas como si tuviera piernas. She goes around in miniskirts showing off those toothpicks as if she had legs.*

una **canita** →**echar una canita al aire**

la **cañona** ditching, standing up of someone, used like **bomba**, with **tirar** *DR, PR* ◆ *¿Por qué me tiraron cañona anoche (ustedes)? Why did you ditch me last night?*

Canta. (Sing.) Tell me, do tell. *Sp* ◆ *Canta, canta toda la historia de tu viaje. Tell me, do tell the whole story of your trip.*

una **cantaleta** →**dar una cantaleta**

el/la **cantamañanas** flake, person who doesn't have much responsibility or who is unreliable, a dreamer who doesn't get things done *Sp* ◆ *Ese tipo es un cantamañanas. No hagas nunca caso de su palabra. Es realmente un incumplidor. That guy is a real flake. Never pay attention to what he says. He never gets anything done.*

cantar (to sing) to squeal, denounce, inform *L. Am., Sp* ◆ *Por más que lo golpearon no cantó. No matter how much they beat him, he didn't squeal.*

cantar →**¿Hay alguien que canta aquí? Porque hay uno que está tocando.**

cantar a alguien las cuarenta (to sing the forty to someone) to tell it like it is, speak one's mind clearly, tell an unpleasant truth *Ec, Peru, Ch, Arg, Sp* (RVAR *U:* **cantar las cuarentas**) ◆ *Le canté las cuarenta cuando lo vi. I gave him a piece of my mind when I saw him.*

cantar como una almeja (to sing like a clam) to call attention to oneself and look ridiculous *Sp* ◆ *Cantaba como una almeja con ese vestido estrafalario. She stood out like a sore thumb with that outlandish dress.*

cantar la justa (la pura) (to sing the just [the pure]) to speak frankly, tell it like it is *U, Arg* ◆ *Vilma nos cantó la justa sobre la situación política. Vilma told us the truth about the political situation.*

cantar victoria (to sing victory) to brag about or rejoice in a triumph, bring out the champagne *L. Am., Sp* ◆ *No cantemos victoria todavía. Let's not bring out the champagne yet.*

cantarle a alguien la cartilla (el salmo) (to sing someone the primer [psalm]) to set someone straight, read the riot act, lay down the law *Mex, Ch, Sp* ◆ *Josefina le cantó la cartilla a su amante. Josefina laid down the law to her lover.* ◆ *El director les cantó la cartilla a los gerentes en su primer día en la empresa. Están todos bastante asustados. The director read the managers the riot act on his first day at the business. They are all scared.*

el **cante** →dar el cante

cantidad a whole lot (used as an adverb in slang) *Mex, ES, Ch, Sp* ◆ *Mola cantidad. (Sp) It really rocks (literally, It pleases a lot, from the verb* **molar***).* ◆ *He comido cantidad. I've eaten a lot.*

la **cantinflada (cantinflear)** (a cantinflas thing, to cantinflas) nonsense or hot air (to speak a lot of nonsense or hot air without saying anything, the way the Mexican actor Cantinflas did in his satirical movies) *L. Am.* ◆ *Gerardo sólo habló cantinfladas. Gerardo only talked nonsense.*

el **canuto** joint, marijuana cigarette *Mex, Sp* ◆ *Fumó un canuto en el metro aunque está prohibido. He smoked a joint in the subway although it's forbidden.*

caña →meterle caña; bajar la caña

la **caña** (cane) beer, brewsky *Sp* ◆ *¿Qué le pongo? —Una caña. What do you want? (literally, what shall I put before you?) —A beer.*

capar (to neuter, castrate) to punish, to kill (figuratively) *Mex, Col, U, Arg* ◆ *Me van a capar en la casa si no paso el examen. They're going to kill me at home if I don't pass the exam.*

ser **capaz de dormir a un muerto** (to be capable of putting a dead person to sleep) to be very boring (people) *Mex, Sp* ◆ *Ese profesor es capaz de dormir a un muerto. That prof is so dull he could put the dead to sleep.*

la **capirucha** good old capital *Mex, ES* (RVAR *Mex:* Mexico City; *ES:* San Salvador) ◆ *En la capirucha encontré el material necesario para mi tesis. In the capital (city) I found the necessary material for my thesis.*

ser **capítulo aparte** (to be a separate chapter) to be another kettle of fish, different topic *Mex, DR, S. Cone, Sp* ◆ *Ese tema es capítulo aparte. Vamos a dejarlo para más tarde. That topic is another kettle of fish. Let's leave it for later.*

un **capote** →echar un capote (echar la capa)

captar la onda (to capture the sound wave) to get it, pick up or understand something insinuated *Mex, DR* ◆ *Capté la onda de lo que decía Marita, pero no le contesté. I picked up what Marita was implying, but I didn't answer her.*

cara →echar algo en cara; la jeta/la cara; no quedar títere con cara (cabeza); no tener cara; ponerse la cara como un chile; por su cara bonita; por su linda cara; tener el santo de cara; tener mucha cara; tener una cara de teléfono ocupado

cara a cara face to face *L. Am., Sp* ◆ *Vamos a hablar cara a cara, no por teléfono. Let's talk face to face, not on the telephone.*

el/la **cara de culo** (ass face) asshole (vulgar) *ES, U, Arg, Sp* ◆ *¿Por qué tienes esa cara de culo? Why do you have that asshole look on your face?* ◆ *El gerente es un cara de culo. The manager is an asshole.*

el/la **cara de limón** (lemon face) unpleasant or annoyed appearance, sourpuss *Mex, ES, U* ◆ *Marieta siempre anda con cara de limón. Marieta always looks like a sourpuss.*

el/la **cara de perro** (dog face) hostile appearance, crab *Mex, PR, U, Sp* ◆ *No me atreví a hablarle al policía porque tenía una cara de perro terrible. I didn't dare talk to the police officer because he had a horribly fierce expression (looked like a crab).*

el/la **cara dura** (hard face) pushy person, someone with a lot of nerve or chutzpah; someone who doesn't pay attention to criticism *PR, ES, S. Cone, Sp* (RVAR *U:* also, **cara rota**) ◆ *Miguel es un cara dura. A pesar de haber tratado mal a su suegro, ahora vive en su casa y usa su auto. Miguel has a lot of chutzpah. In spite of having treated his father-in-law badly, he now lives in his house and uses his car.*

la **cara larga** (long face) sad appearance *Mex, DR, ES, Col, Ch, U, Sp* ◆ *Sonia entró a la habitación y vio que su madre tenía la cara larga. Sonia came into the room and saw that her mother looked sad.*

¡Caracoles! (snails) Darn it! euphemism for **¡Carajo!** *Mex, DR, Col, U, Arg, Sp* ◆ *¡Caracoles! No recuerdo dónde puse los documentos del abogado. Darn it! I don't remember where I put the documents from the lawyer.*

carácter →**tener buen carácter; tener mal carácter**

el/la **carajillo(-a)** (diminutive of **carajo**, vulgar) boy (girl), adolescent, young person *Nic, CR* ◆ *El carajillo anda en la escuela. The boy's at school right now.*

el/la **carajito(-a)** (diminutive of **carajo**, vulgar) boy (girl), adolescent, young person *DR, Ven* ◆ *Esa carajita siempre está pidiendo dinero. That darn girl is always asking for money.*

del **carajo** (of the male organ) super, damn fantastic, great(ly) (vulgar) *DR, PR, Col, Ven* ◆ *Esa muchacha es del carajo. That girl is damn fantastic.* ◆ *Hay que divertirse del carajo. (PR) We have to have a damn good time.*

el **carajo** →**irse al (para el) carajo; mandar a alguien al carajo; no valer un carajo**

¡Carajo! (male organ) Damn!, common expression of anger (has lost its original vulgar meaning in most places and in some, like S. Cone, it is not vulgar) *L. Am., Sp* ◆ *¡Carajo! Me olvidé de llamar a mi suegra para el día de su cumpleaños. Debe estar muy enojada. Damn! I forgot to call my mother-in-law for her birthday. She must be really mad.*

el/la **carajo(-a)** (male organ) so-and-so, unknown person (pejorative) *DR, ES, Nic, CR, Col* (RVAR *ES:* used like **tonto** but can be used for unknown person without being too strong; also, **carajito** for affection) ◆ *¿Quién es ese carajo (esa caraja) que va por allá? (CR) Who's that guy (girl) going that way?* ◆ *¡Cuidado, carajo! (ES) Be careful, you jerk!*

ser **carajo(-a)** (to be male organ) to be not too damn likely, be difficult (vulgar) *Mex* ◆ *Es muy carajo que nuestro equipo llegue al campeonato. It's not too damn likely that our team'll make it to the championship.*

¡Caramba! Jeez! Darn it! (euphemism for **¡Carajo!**, vulgar) *L. Am., Sp* ◆ *¡Caramba! Has tenido mucho éxito con tu nuevo libro. Wow! You've had good luck with your new book.*

la **carambada** trinket, thing of little value; nonsense *ES, Nic, CR, Col* ◆ *¡Qué carambada más cara! What an expensive piece of junk!* ◆ *Deja de hablar carambadas. Stop talking nonsense.*

de **carambola** (billiard term referring to a lucky play) by a stroke of luck *DR, ES, Nic, Ch, U* ◆ *De carambola encontramos a Alicia en el aeropuerto antes de que abordara su avión. By a stroke of luck we found Alicia in the airport before she boarded her plane.*

ser un **caramelo** (to be a caramel) to be a sweetie, nice, kind *Mex, Cuba, G, Col* ◆ *La nueva novia de Hernando es un caramelito. Hernando's new girlfriend is a real sweetie.*

¡Caray! (euphemism for **¡Carajo!**) Jeez! Darn it! *Mex, Cuba, DR, PR, Col, Sp* ◆ *¡Caray! ¿Por qué las cosas no me salen bien? Darn! Why don't things turn out well for me?*

la **carcacha** old car, jalopy, old piece of junk *Mex, DR, G, ES, Col* ◆ *Ya es hora de que cambies esa carcacha por un carro nuevo. It's time for you to trade in that piece of junk for a new car.*

ser un **cardo borriquero** (to be a cotton thistle) to be an ugly duckling (used for people) *Sp* ◆ *Ese niño es un cardo borriquero. That kid is an ugly duckling.*

carecer de to be without (something), not have (something), lack *L. Am., Sp* ◆ *Mi tía es muy buena gente pero carece de sentido común. My aunt is a very good person but she doesn't have any common sense.*

un **careto** →**tener un careto**

la **carga** →**llevarle la carga**

cargar 1. (to load) to tease, make fun of *U, Arg* ◆ *¡Me estás cargando! You must be kidding!* **2.** (to load) to make a pass at, hit on, come on to *U, Arg* ◆ *Me cargó toda la noche. He hit on me all evening.*

cargar con el mochuelo (to carry the **mochuelo**, a nocturnal bird of prey) to do the dirty work, get the job no one else wants

L. Am., Sp (RVar *Sp, Ch:* also, **cargar con el muerto,** carry the dead person) ◆ *Finalmente el primero que pasó cargó con el mochuelo. Finally the first one that passed by had to do the dirty work.*

cargar el arpa (to carry the harp) to go along with a couple on a date, be a fifth wheel *Mex, Ec* ◆ *Por favor no traigas a tu hermana a cargar el arpa cuando salgamos mañana. Please don't bring your sister along as a fifth wheel when we go out tomorrow.*

cargo →hacerse cargo de

a **cargo de** in charge of, with the responsibility *L. Am., Sp* ◆ *Laura está a cargo de los boletos. Laura is in charge of the tickets.*

el/la **carmelita** mulatto *Cuba, Col* ◆ *¿Has escuchado a esa carmelita en la clase de filosofía? Es muy inteligente. Have you listened to the mulatto girl in the philosophy class? She's very intelligent.*

el **carnaval** bash, fun time (like carnival, Mardi Gras) *Mex, ES, CR, Col* (RVar *ES:* a big street dance) ◆ *Una vez que la fiesta comenzó, ésta se convirtió en carnaval. Once the party began, it turned into a real bash.*

carne →no ser carne ni pescado; poner toda la carne en el asador

carne de gallina goosebumps *L. Am., Sp* ◆ *Se me pone la carne de gallina cuando pienso en esa película. I get goosebumps when I think about that movie.*

de **carne y hueso** (of flesh and bone) flesh and blood *L. Am., Sp* ◆ *Este trabajo es demasiado pesado para mí. Sólo soy de carne y hueso. This work is too hard for me. I'm only flesh and blood.*

en **carnes** (in flesh) in the raw, naked *Sp* ◆ *La puerta del baño estaba abierta; entré y Jacinto estaba en carnes, afeitándose. The bathroom door was open; I went in and Jacinto was naked, shaving.*

el **carrazo** nice big car *Mex, ES, CR, Col* ◆ *Alejo compró un carrazo. Alejo bought a nice big car.*

carretas →No voy a tragar carros y carretas.

carrete →dar carrete a alguien

el **carro** car *Mex, C. Am., Peru, Arg* ◆ *Nuestro carro estaba en el taller, pero un amigo nos*

dio un aventón. Our car was in the shop, but a friend gave us a ride.

carros →No voy a tragar carros y carretas.

carros y carretas (cars and carts) hassles, obstacles or problems (that one puts up with patiently) *Mex, Sp* ◆ *Néstor ha tenido que aguantar carros y carretas en su trabajo porque tiene tres niños y necesita el dinero. Néstor has had to put up with hassles in his job because he has three kids and needs the money.*

carroza (carriage) old, mature, over the hill; sometimes describing someone middle-aged who tries to be young *Mex, Sp* ◆ *Aunque tenga 25 años, se comporta como una carroza. Even though he's 25, he acts like an old fogey.*

a **carta cabal** just so, exactly, right; irreproachably or impeccably *Mex, DR, Ch, U, Arg, Sp* ◆ *El proyecto fue terminado a carta cabal. The project was finished impeccably.*

las **cartas** →poner las cartas sobre la mesa

la **casa** →echar/tirar la casa por la ventana

La **casa es chica, el corazón grande.** (The house is small, the heart large.) My humble home is yours. Make yourself at home. (similar to the expression **Estás en tu casa.**) *S. Cone* ◆ *Quédense con nosotros. La casa es chica, el corazón grande. Stay with us. Make yourself at home.*

la **casaca** (coat) false arguments, baloney *G, ES* ◆ *No me des casaca. Don't give me that baloney.* ◆ *No le creas, que es casaca. Don't believe him (her). It's a crock.*

el **casado** (married man) plate of rice, beans, meat or fish, and salad *CR* ◆ *Tengo hambre. Un casado y una cerveza, por favor. I'm hungry. I'll have a "married man combo" and a beer, please.*

casarse →no casarse con nadie

casarse de penalti (to get married as a penalty) to have a shotgun wedding *Mex, Col, Sp* ◆ *Se casó de penalti con su novia a la edad de diecisiete años. He had a shotgun wedding with his girlfriend at the age of seventeen.*

casarse por detrás de la iglesia (to get married behind the church) to go off or live together without getting married *U* (RVar *Ch:* **detrás de la puerta**, behind the door;

ES: detrás del palo, behind the tree) ◆ *Después de andar de novios por varios años decidieron casarse por detrás de la iglesia. After going out for a number of years they decided to move in together without getting married.*

casarse por el sindicato de las prisas (to get married by the syndicate of haste) to have a shotgun wedding, get married hastily because the woman is pregnant *Sp* ◆ *Mi sobrina es muy joven, pero se casó por el sindicato de las prisas. My niece is really young, but she had a shotgun wedding.*

el **cascabel** →poner el cascabel al gato

un **cascajo** →estar hecho(-a) un cascajo

la **cascarita** informal ball game *Mex* ◆ *Se echaron una cascarita en la calle. They started a pickup ball game in the street.*

el **cascarón, la cascarona** (thick rind or bark) old man, old woman *Mex, PR* ◆ *Vivo con unos cascarones muy simpáticos. I live with some really sweet old folks.*

de sus **casillas** →sacar a alguien de sus casillas (de quicio)

caso →hacer caso; hacer caso omiso

un **casquete** →echar un casquete

casquivano(-a) feather-brained, silly *L. Am., Sp* ◆ *¡Qué casquivana! No sé dónde puse las llaves. What a feather-brain! I don't know where I put the keys.*

las **castañas** →sacar las castañas del fuego

el **castigador** (punisher) lady-killer, stud, guy who thinks women are attracted to him *Chicano, Mex, DR, PR, Col* ◆ *Juan es un castigador; me tiene loca. Juan is a lady-killer; he has me going crazy.*

la **castigadora** (punisher) woman with an attractive body *DR, PR, Col* ◆ *Esa mujer es una castigadora. That woman is hot.*

Castígame. (Punish me.) said when an attractive member of the opposite sex goes by *Mex, DR, PR, Col* ◆ *Castígame, preciosa, y déjame que te acompañe. Oh, break my heart, gorgeous, and let me walk along with you.*

castillos →hacer castillos de naipes; hacer castillos en el aire

casualidad →por pura casualidad

catar el melón (to inspect the melon) to sound or feel someone or something out *Sp* ◆ *Ojalá haya tiempo suficiente para catar el melón. I hope there will be time to sound things out.*

catear (to search) to flunk, wash out, fail *Sp* ◆ *¿Qué tal la clase de física? —Me han cateado otra vez. How's the physics class? —They flunked me again.*

catire(-a) fair-headed or fair-complexioned *Col, Ven, Peru, Bol* (RVar *Ec:* **catiro[-a]**) ◆ *Tu vecino catire no es muy amable. Your light-complexioned neighbor is not very friendly.*

catrín chic, elegant *Mex, C. Am.* ◆ *¡Qué catrín te ves! How elegant (well-dressed, chic) you look!*

a **causa de** because of *L. Am., Sp* ◆ *No quiero asistir a la boda de mi ex-novia a causa de las malas lenguas. I don't want to attend my ex-girlfriend's wedding because of the nosy gossips.*

cayendo el muerto y soltando el llanto (the dead person falling and the scream being let out) like a shot, fast, right away *Mex, ES* ◆ *¿Me vas a pagar cuando termine el trabajo? ¿El mismo día? —Sí, cayendo el muerto y soltando el llanto. Are you going to pay me when I finish the work? The same day? —Yes, right away.*

el **cazo** →meter el cazo

de la **Ceca a la Meca** (from Ceca to Mecca) from pillar to post *Mex, DR, PR, ES, Ch, Sp* ◆ *Me mandaron de la Ceca a la Meca. They sent me from pillar to post.*

ceja →estar hasta las cejas; meterse algo entre ceja y ceja; tener algo entre ceja y ceja

cemento armado →tener cara de cemento armado

el **cepillo** →estar hasta el cepillo

el/la **cerdo(-a)** (pig) person who is dirty or who has loose morals *Sp* ◆ *Es un cerdo; se lava una vez al mes. He's a pig; he washes himself once a month.* ◆ *Es un cerdo; se fue sin pagar. He's a swine; he left without paying.*

cerebro →hacer cerebro

el **cero a la izquierda** (zero to the left) worthless, no good, a nobody *L. Am., Sp* ◆

¡Qué mujeriego! Ese chico es un cero a la izquierda. *What a playboy! That guy is a total loser.* ◆ *En la clase nadie le habla; lo tratan como un cero a la izquierda. No one in class talks to him; they treat him like a nobody.*

el **cerote** (turd) asshole (vulgar) *C. Am.* ◆ *No seas cerote; acompáñanos al partido de fútbol. Don't be an asshole; come with us to the soccer game.*

cerrado(-a) 1. (closed) clammed up, not admitting anything, taciturn; *G, Col, U, Arg, Sp* ◆ *Marilú es muy cerrada y nunca nos habló durante la excursión. Marilú is very taciturn and never spoke to us during the excursion.* **2.** (closed) introverted *Sp* ◆ *A Teresita le cuesta hacer amigos porque es muy cerrada. It's hard for Teresita to make friends because she's very introverted.* **3.** (closed) closed-minded *L. Am., Sp* ◆ *No me gusta hablar de esos temas con Felipe porque es muy cerrado y terminamos peleados. I don't like to talk to Felipe about those topics because he's very close-minded and we end up not speaking to each other (literally, having fought).*

cerrado(-a) →**más cerrado(-a) que un huevo de gallina (un tubo de radio)**

cerrar con llave (to close with key) to lock *L. Am., Sp* ◆ *¿Cerraste la puerta con llave? Did you lock the door?*

cerrar el paraguas (to close the umbrella) to kick the bucket, die *CR* ◆ *Gertrudis cerró el paraguas después de una larga enfermedad. Gertrudis kicked the bucket after a long illness.*

cerrar el pico (to close the beak) to shut one's trap, put a lid on it, be quiet *Mex, DR, PR, U, Arg, Sp* ◆ *Cierra el pico, que los niños están escuchando. Shut up (Close your mouth); the children are listening.*

cerrarle una puerta y abrirle otra to have one door (opportunity) close and another open *Mex, ES, Sp* ◆ *Las circunstancias económicas le cerraron una puerta, pero le abrieron otra muy interesante. The economic circumstances closed one door for him but opened another interesting one.*

la **cháchara** chatter, gab session *Mex, DR, Sp* (RVar *Mex:* trinket) ◆ *Llegué tarde porque en la oficina teníamos una cháchara muy entretenida. I got here (there) late because in the office we had a very entertaining gab session.* ◆ *Íbamos de cháchara y se nos pasó el tiempo volando. (Sp) We were talking away and the time flew by.* ◆ *Allí venden puras chácharas. (Mex) They sell nothing but claptrap there.*

chachi interesting, good, super *Sp* ◆ *Vamos a pasarlo chachi. Me encanta poder ir a esta fiesta. We're going to have a super time. I'm delighted to be able to go to this party.*

la **chacra** (Quechua word) country cottage *Peru, Bol, S. Cone* ◆ *Mis tíos han plantado en la chacra varias hectáreas de árboles frutales. My aunt and uncle have planted several acres of fruit trees at the country cottage.*

la **chafa** low-quality or fake item; (adj.) **chafo(-a)** cheap *Mex, G, ES* ◆ *¿Esto un Rolex? No, es una chafa. This a Rolex? No, it's a fake.* ◆ *El novio de Mariela le regaló un perfume chafa. Mariela's boyfriend gave her a cheap perfume.*

¡Chale! Wow! No way!, expression of surprise, like **caray** or **caramba**; often negative or indicating disbelief *Chicano, Mex* ◆ *¡Chale! No te creo. Wow! I don't believe you.*

a **chaleco** (at vest) by force, against one's will *Mex* ◆ *Tenía que pasar el examen a chaleco. I had to pass the test no matter what.*

la **chamacada** group of young people *Mex* ◆ *Había una chamacada en la calle. There was a group of kids in the street.*

el/la **chamaco(-a)** young person (also, **chamaquito[-a]**) *Chicano, Mex, Cuba, PR, ES, CR* ◆ *Los chamacos fueron al campo con sus abuelos. The young people went to the country with their grandparents.*

la **chamba** work, job *Mex, C. Am., Col, Ven, Ec, Peru* ◆ *Gerardo consiguió una buena chamba. Gerardo got a good job.*

chambear (chambiar) to work *Mex, C. Am., Col, Ven, Ec, Peru* ◆ *No puedo ir a la playa; tengo que chambear. I can't go to the beach; I have to work.*

el **chambre** gossip *ES* ◆ *María ya viene con el chambre. Here comes María already with the gossip.*

chambroso(-a) gossipy, given to gossip *Mex, ES* ◆ *A Gloria hay que tenerle un poco de* *miedo; es bien chambrosa. You have to be a little afraid of Gloria; she's a real gossip.*

el/la **chamo(-a)** guy (girl) *Col, Ven* (RVAR *Cuba:* **la chama** only) ◆ *Los chamos fueron al cine. The kids went to the movies.*

chamullar to sweet-talk, talk at length trying to persuade *Peru, Ch, Arg* ◆ *Le chamullé al vendedor para que me bajara el precio. I sweet-talked the salesman so he would lower the price for me.*

el **chamullo** sweet talk, fib, story *Peru, Ch, Arg* ◆ *Ese tipo es el rey del chamullo. That guy is the king of sweet talk.*

el **chance** 1. break, chance (from English) *most of L. Am.* ◆ *Dame otro chance; te prometo que esta vez no te voy a fallar. Give me another chance; I promise you that this time I won't let you down.* 2. work, job *Mex, G* ◆ *El chance no le gusta, pero el salario es bueno. He doesn't like the work, but the salary is good.*

chancho →**como chancho en misa**

el **chanchullo** (piggish) rip-off; faked or rigged deal, rigged elections, or jacked-up prices *Mex, DR, PR, CR, Peru, Bol, Ch, Sp* ◆ *Está investigando un gran chanchullo de dinero. He (She) is investigating a big money scam.*

chancla →**estar hasta las chanclas; meterle la chancla al pedal**

¡Chanclas! (Old shoes!) Wow! (expression of surprise) *Mex, ES* ◆ *¡Chanclas! ¿Estás embarazada? Wow! You're pregnant?*

el **chanclazo** (blow or hit with a **chancleta**, sandal, from killing bugs with the sandal) boogie, dance (old term) *Chicano, Mex* ◆ *¿Quieres dar un chanclazo? Do you want to boogie?*

chanclear to boogie, dance (old term) *Chicano, Mex* ◆ *Es un salón de baile donde se iba a chanclear. It's a dance hall where people went to boogie.*

la **chancleta** (sandal) recently born female baby, said with affection *DR, PR, S. Cone* ◆ *¡Qué lindo! ¡Fue una chancleta! How lovely! It was a little girl!*

¡Chanfle! Good grief! Wow! expression of surprise *Mex, Col* ◆ *¡Chanfle! ¡Qué casa más grande! Wow! What a big house!*

el **chante** digs, home *Mex, ES, Nic, CR, Pan* (RVAR *ES:* **chanti;** *Pan:* **chantín**) ◆ *Mi chante está lejos del centro. My digs are far from downtown.*

la **chanza** break, chance (from the English "chance") *Chicano, Mex, Hond, Col* ◆ *Dame chanza. Quiero explicártelo. Give me a chance. I want to explain it to you.*

Chao, mano(-a). (from the Italian "ciao") Bye, friend. *Mex, DR, PR, Col* ◆ *Hora de ir al trabajo. Chao, manas. Time to go to work. 'Bye, gals (friends).*

Chao, pesca'o. (Bye, fish.) comic way of saying good-bye, like See you later, alligator! *Ven*

chapado(-a) a la antigua old-fashioned *L. Am., Sp* ◆ *Es un hombre chapado a la antigua. He's an old-fashioned kind of man.*

chaparro(-a) short (of stature) *Mex, parts of Caribbean, C. Am., Col* ◆ *Ernesto es muy chaparro; todas sus hermanas son más altas que él. Ernesto is very short; all of his sisters are taller than he is.*

el **chapín,** la **chapina** Guatemalan *most of L. Am.* ◆ *¿Cómo se llama el chapín? What's the Guatemalan guy's name?*

chapuzas →**hacer algunas chapuzas**

una **chaqueta** →**hacerse una chaqueta**

la **charanga** party, dance *ES, CR, Col* ◆ *Fuimos a una charanga en casa de Lola. We went to a party at Lola's house.*

una **charola** →**ponerle algo en (una) charola de plata**

charro(-a) (relating to cowboys) old-fashioned, out of it, ridiculous *Mex, PR, Col* (RVAR *Col except Medellín,* where it means great, good) ◆ *Qué gustos tan charros tiene ella. What poor taste she has.*

Chasgracias. Thanks, short for **Muchas gracias.** *L. Am., Sp* ◆ *Chasgracias, hermano. Thanks, brother.*

chatear to chat on the Internet *parts of L. Am.* ◆ *Todos los sábados a mediodía chateo con mi hermana. Every Saturday at noon I chat with my sister on the Internet.*

chato(-a) (pug-nosed) affectionate nickname *most of L. Am., Sp* ◆ *Chata, regresa pronto. Te extraño. Sweetie, come back soon. I miss you.*

Chau, chau. (from the Italian "ciao") Bye-bye. *S. Cone* ◆ *Nos vemos esta noche. Chau, chau. See you tonight. Bye-bye.*

la **chavala** girl *Mex, C. Am., Sp (where it is a bit old-fashioned)* ◆ *¿Quién es esa chavala con Enrique? Who's that girl with Enrique?*

el **chavalo** guy, boy *Chicano, Mex, C. Am.* ◆ *Mi chavalo nunca viene a la casa antes de las seis. My guy never gets home before 6:00.*

la **chaveta** head, noggin *Mex, DR, PR, ES* ◆ *Se me fue la chaveta. I lost my head.*

el/la **chavito(-a)** diminutive of **chavo(-a)** *Chicano, Mex, G, ES* ◆ *La chavita de mi amiga es muy estudiosa. My friend's little girl is very studious.*

la **chaviza** young folk (opposite of **momiza**, fogies) *Mex, Col* ◆ *La chaviza anda toda alborotada porque les cerraron la disco. The young folks are all upset because they closed the disco.*

el **chavo** small coin *Cuba, PR* ◆ *¿Tú tienes chavos? Se me quedó la cartera en casa. Do you have any money? I left my wallet at home.*

el/la **chavo(-a)** boy (girl) *Chicano, Mex, G, ES, Col* (RVAR *Nic:* **los chavos** are **los novios**, boyfriend and girlfriend) ◆ *No conozco a ese chavo. I don't know that boy.*

chayote (vegetable with prickly skin) bothersome, uncomfortable, troubling *Mex, PR* ◆ *El ambiente en la oficina está chayote en estos días. The environment at the office is uncomfortable these days.*

el **chayote** (vegetable with prickly skin) bribe *Mex* ◆ *Con un buen chayote todo se arregla. Everything can be solved with a good bribe.*

che friend, pal, used in direct address *U, Arg* (RVAR *Ch:* an Argentinian) ◆ *¡Hola, che! (Arg) Hi, friend!* ◆ *Vino un che a la fiesta. (Ch) An Argentinian came to the party.*

la **chela** (blond, light) light-colored beer *Mex, ES, Ec, Peru, Bol* ◆ *Vamos a tomar una chela. Let's have a beer.*

chele blue-eyed, fair-complexioned (also, green-eyed) (from the Mayan word "chel," blue). *ES, Nic, CR* (RVAR in *Nic* the feminine is **chela**) ◆ *Tengo un nieto chele. I have a blue-eyed grandson.*

el **chele** cent *DR, Sp* ◆ *Lo siento. No tengo ni un chele encima. I'm sorry. I don't have a penny on me.*

chelo(-a) fair, blue-eyed (from the Mayan word "chel," blue) *Mex* ◆ *Los amigos de Silvia temen que ella se enamore de un chelo en Tejas y luego no vuelva a su país. Silvia's friends are afraid that she'll fall in love with a blue-eyed (fair) guy in Texas and then won't go back to her country.*

el **chen chen** money, dough *Pan* ◆ *Ese viejo siempre tiene chen chen. That guy always has dough.*

de **chepa** luckily, by pure luck or chance *DR, PR, CR, Col* ◆ *Encontré tu casa de pura chepa pues tenía la dirección equivocada. I found your house by pure chance because I had the wrong address.* ◆ *De chepa pasó los exámenes finales. By sheer luck he passed his final exams.*

Chepa la bola. Who knows? *Mex* ◆ *¿Me va a llamar o no? Chepa la bola. Is he (she) going to call me or not? Only God knows!*

chequear, checar to check (from English) *Mex, DR, PR, C. Am., Ven, Ch, Sp* (RVAR *Mex:* **checar**) ◆ *Mi esposo me trae bien chequadita ahora que tengo mi celular. (Mex) My husband keeps tabs on me now that I have my cell phone.* ◆ *¿A qué hora sale el autobús? —No sé, vamos a chequear. (ES) What time does the bus leave? —I don't know. Let's check.*

el **chesco** (shortened form of **refresco**) soda, soft drink *Mex* ◆ *Pedí dos tacos y un chesco. I ordered two tacos and a soft drink.*

la **cheve** beer, brewsky *Mex, G, ES* ◆ *¿Quieres una cheve? Do you want a beer?*

chévere great, fantastic *most of L. Am.; most common in Caribbean, Col, Ven* ◆ *¿Vamos a un concierto de Carlos Vives? ¡Qué chévere! Es cheverísimo. We're going to a Carlos Vives concert? How cool! He's really awesome.*

el/la **chibolo(-a)** (ball) boy (girl), kid *Peru* ◆ *¿Dónde están los chibolos? Where are the kids?*

chicato(-a) wearing glasses, blind (as a bat) *Peru, U, Arg* ◆ *Nelda es chicata, y a pesar de usar lentes, ve poco. Nelda is blind as a bat, and although she uses glasses, she sees very little.*

chicha →**no ser ni chicha ni limonada**

los **chicharrones** (pork rinds served as a side dish, used because it sounds like chichis) female breasts *Mex*

los **chiches** knickknacks, trinkets, small toys *S. Cone* ◆ *El cuarto de los niños está lleno de chiches. The kids' room is full of knick-knacks.*

el/la **chichí** baby *Mex, DR, Hond, ES, CR* ◆ *¿Dónde está mi chichí? Where's my baby?*

los **chichis** (from Náhuatl, "to suckle") breasts *Mex*

chicho(-a) good, nice, great *Mex* ◆ *Se cree muy chicho. He thinks he's really cool.*

el **chicle** (chewing gum) person who sticks like glue, annoying person *Mex, Cuba, DR, PR, G* ◆ *Vámonos de aquí que ya llegó Tomás. —Ay, ¡ese chicle! Si nos ve, no se nos despega. Let's get out of here because Tomás has already arrived. —Oh, that pest! If he sees us, he'll stick to us like glue.*

chicles →**Ni chicles.**

¡Chicles, muéganos y palomitas! (Chewing gum, caramel-covered candies, and popcorn!) Jeez Louise! exclamation of great surprise *Mex, Col*

al **chico rato, al ratón** in a little while (that may never come), an indefinite time *Mex, Col* ◆ *Nos vemos al ratón. See you in a while.* ◆ *¡Y que se va apareciendo al chico rato! And he (she) finally making an appearance (appearing late)!*

chico(-a) (guy, girl; used in direct address) friend, pal *Caribbean* ◆ *No es para tanto, chico. Things aren't really that bad, my dear.*

el/la **chico(-a) bien** rich kid, young man (woman) from a well-off family *Mex, DR, U, Arg, Sp* ◆ *Sólo chicos bien fueron invitados al estreno del club. Only rich kids were invited to the opening night of the club.*

chido(-a) great, super (perhaps from **chingón** or from **chic**) *Chicano, Mex, ES* ◆ *¿Qué es lo chido? Lo que vale la pena, lo divertido, lo congruente con la moda. What is considered "in"? Whatever is worth the trouble, whatever is fun, whatever is in step with the latest fad.*

chiflado(-a) off one's rocker, crazy; foolish; like mad *L. Am., Sp* ◆ *Estás chiflado. You're soft in the head.*

chiflar to be crazy about, love *Mex, Sp* ◆ *Me chifla bailar. I love to dance.*

chiflar el mono (the monkey whistles) to be cold (weather) *Mex, Cuba* ◆ *Anoche chifló el mono, ¿no? ¡Qué frío! Last night it was freezing, wasn't it? What cold weather!*

la **chifles** →**No la chifles que va cantada.**

el/la **chilango(-a)** person from Mexico City *Mex* ◆ *¿Dónde está el Castillo de Chapultepec? —No eres chilanga, ¿verdad? Where is Chapultepec Castle? —You're not from the capital, are you?*

chile →**ponerse la cara como un chile**

el **chile** (chili pepper) male organ (vulgar) *Mex, ES*

ser un **chile de todos los moles** (to be a chili pepper for all sauces) to be a good egg, be everywhere and good at everything, always helpful *Mex* ◆ *Miriam es un chile de todos los moles; siempre podemos contar con ella. Miriam is a good egg; we can always count on her.*

la **chilla** poverty; **en la quinta chilla** in the worst poverty *Mex* ◆ *De niña, mi abuela vivía en la quinta chilla. As a girl, my grandmother lived in the worst poverty.*

chillar to squeal (inform on); to complain, cry, whine *Chicano, Mex, G, Col, U* ◆ *Fui a la oficina de impuestos y chillé y chillé hasta que escucharon y me devolvieron mi dinero. I went to the tax office and I whined and complained until they gave me back my money.* ◆ *Niños, no chillen tanto; me duele la cabeza. Children, don't whine so much; I've got a headache.*

chillar goma(s), chillarla (to burn rubber) to take off quickly *Mex, PR* ◆ *Antonio salió furioso, chillando gomas. Antonio left hopping mad, in a big rush.*

chillón, chillona crybaby, complainer *Chicano, Mex, G, ES, Col, Sp* (RVar *Sp:* person who yells a lot) ◆ *¡Tan grandote y tan chillón! Such a big kid and such a crybaby (whiner)!*

el/la **chilpayate(-a)** kid, young person *Mex* ◆ *Sandra está con los chilpayates; Pedro fue a Oaxaca. Sandra is with the kids; Pedro went to Oaxaca.*

en las **chimbambas** in the boonies, far away, on the outskirts *DR, PR, Sp* (RVar *Cuba:*

quimbambas) ◆ *Tienen una casa en las chimbambas.* They have a house out in the boonies.

¡Chin chin! (imitating the sound of glass clinking) Cheers! *parts of L. Am., Sp* ◆ *¡Chin chin y que seas muy feliz! Cheers and may you be very happy!*

¡Chin! ¡Chihuahua! Darn! Wow! euphemisms for **chinga'o**, screwed *Mex* ◆ *¡Chin! ¡Qué linda casa tienen! Wow! What a gorgeous house you (all) have!*

el/la **chinchudo(-a)** (big ugly bedbug) person who gets angry easily, hothead, person with a short fuse *U, Arg* ◆ *Juan es muy chinchudo. Juan is a real hothead.*

chinear to carry (usually a baby); also, to pamper *C. Am.* ◆ *Su papá la llevaba chineada. Her dad was carrying her in his arms.*

estar de la **chingada** (to be of the **chingada**, a woman who has been violated) to be in deep trouble, screwed (vulgar) *Mex, G, ES, Col* (RVAR *Mex:* also, **estar de la fregada**, less strong) ◆ *¿Van a cancelar la reunión? ¡Esto está de la chingada! They're going to cancel the meeting? This sucks!*

la **chingada** →**irse a la chingada; mandar a alguien a la chingada**

la **chingadera** thingamajig, worthless thing, bad thing, trick, bad or swear word (vulgar) *Chicano, Mex, G, ES* ◆ *Esa chingadera, ¿qué es? What's that piece of crap? ◆ No digas chingaderas. Don't say bad things (like that).*

chingado(-a) (chinga'o[-a]) (ripped, torn, broken) screwed (vulgar) *Mex, Cuba, PR, C. Am., Col* ◆ *Estoy chingado. No sé qué hacer. I'm screwed. I don't know what to do.*

chingar (to rip, tear) to screw, screw around or up; to have sex (equivalent of the F-word) (vulgar) *Mex, Cuba, PR, C. Am., Col* (RVAR *PR:* to have sex, only) ◆ *Vete a chingar a otra parte. Go somewhere else to screw around. ◆ No me chingues; necesito dinero. Don't f**k with me; I need money.*

chingarse (to get screwed) to suffer or work like hell (vulgar) *Mex, ES, Col* (RVAR *Ch:* to get frustrated or disappointed, not vulgar; *Sp:* to break down, as a machine) ◆ *Yo me chingo trabajando día y noche. I wear myself out working night and day. ◆ Si quieres* ganar la vida, tienes que chingarte. *If you want to earn a living, you have to work damn hard.* ◆ *Yo creía que tendría ese puesto y me chingué. (Ch) I believed that I'd get that job and I got screwed. ◆ Mi auto se chingó. (Sp) My car went all to hell (broke down).*

el **chingo** a damn large amount, a shitload (vulgar) *Mex, C. Am.* ◆ *Había (un) chingo de gente allí. There was a shitload of people there.*

ser un(a) **chingón (chingona)** to be good at something (vulgar) *Chicano, Mex, C. Am.* ◆ *Juan es un chingón para la música. Juan is damn good at music. ◆ Ella es una chingona para las matemáticas. She's a damn whiz in mathematics.*

chingón, chingona annoying or bothersome (vulgar) *Chicano, Mex, C. Am.* ◆ *Valentín no quiere hacer negocios con los clientes chingones. Valentín doesn't want to do business with annoying clients.*

estar en **chino** (to be in Chinese) to be incomprehensible *Mex, DR, CR, Col, Peru, Bol, Ch, Arg, Sp* ◆ *Este libro parece que está en chino. No entiendo ni jota. This book looks like it's in Greek. I don't understand squat.*

el **chiquilín, la chiquilina** kid, young person *U, Arg* ◆ *Los chiquilines terminaron las clases y se fueron a la playa. The kids finished class and went to the beach.*

chiquitico(-a) very, very tiny *Cuba, CR, Col, Ven* ◆ *Sofía tiene manos y pies chiquiticos. Sofía has very small hands and feet.*

el **chiquitín, la chiquitina** kid, small child *most of L. Am., Sp* ◆ *Vamos a llevar a los chiquitines al parque. Let's take the kids to the park.*

el **chirimbolo** doohickey, thingamabob *Mex, Cuba, Col, U, Arg* ◆ *¿Por qué hay tantos chirimbolos en esta casa? Why are there so many thingamabobs in this house?*

la **chirimoya** (type of fruit) head, noggin *Mex, ES, CR* ◆ *Tito se cayó de un árbol y se lastimó la chirimoya. Tito fell down from a tree and hurt his noggin.*

chiripa →**por chiripa**

estar en **chirona** to be in the clinker (jail) *Mex, most of C. Am., Peru, Sp* ◆ *Es triste pensar que estos jóvenes se han pasado la mayor parte de sus vidas en chirona. It's sad to* *think that those young people have passed the greater part of their lives in the clinker.*

¡Chis! exclamation of annoyance, disgust *Mex, G, ES* ♦ *¡Chis! No jodas. Jeez! Don't bug me.*

los **chismorreos** gossip *most of L. Am., Sp* ♦ *¿Qué yo salgo con Enrique? ¡Puros chismorreos! So I'm going out with Enrique? Pure gossip!*

la **chispa** (spark) smarts, intelligence, astuteness *Mex, DR, ES, CR, Col* ♦ *Julio tiene chispa para trabajar (para los negocios). Julio es muy chispa. Julio is good at work (astute in business). Julio is very sharp.*

chispas →**echar chispas**

¡Chispas! (Sparks!) Wow! expression of surprise *Mex, Col* ♦ *¡Chispas! No tengo mis llaves. Darn! I don't have my keys.*

chiste →**no tener chiste; sin chiste; tener cara de chiste**

el **chiste colorado (rojo)** (red joke) off-color joke *L. Am., Sp* (RVAR more common in *Mex, ES, Ch* than **chiste verde**) ♦ *Manolito contó un chiste colorado e hizo ruborizar a sus padres. Manolito told a dirty joke and made his parents blush.*

el **chiste pelado** (peeled joke) off-color joke *Mex* ♦ *No cuentes chistes pelados, que no me gustan para nada. Don't tell dirty jokes; I don't like them at all.*

el **chiste verde** (green joke) off-color joke *L. Am., Sp* ♦ *Cuenta buenos chistes aunque algunos son verdes y no son apropiados cuando hay niños. He (She) tells good jokes although some are off-color and not appropriate when children are around.*

la **chiva** trinket, thing of little value *Mex* ♦ *Levanto mis chivas y me voy. I'll pick up my stuff and go.*

el **chivato** traitor, fink, person who rats on others *Mex, Cuba, DR, Sp* (RVAR *Cuba, DR*: also, CHIVA) ♦ *Si mi hermano se entera de que llegue tarde, estoy frita. Es un chivato y seguro me chivatea con papi. If my brother finds out I'm coming late, I'm toast. He's a fink, and for sure he'll fink on me to Dad.*

chiveado(-a) inhibited, sheepish, timid, embarrassed *Mex, ES* ♦ *¿Qué pasa con tu hermano? —Está chiveado y no quiere hablar porque allí está el patrón. What's wrong with*

your brother? —He's embarrassed and doesn't want to talk because there's the boss over there.

chivearse to act sheepish, embarrassed or timid *Mex, G, ES* ♦ *Cuando le pidieron que cantara, se chiveó. When they asked him to sing, he acted sheepish.*

chiviar to gamble, play dice *Mex, C. Am.* ♦ *A abuelito le gusta chiviar. Grandpa likes to gamble.*

el **chivo 1.** (kid goat) die; dice game *Mex, G, Hond, ES* ♦ *¿De quiénes son estos chivos? Whose dice are these?* **2.** (kid goat) womanizer; man who lives off women *C. Am., Col* (RVAR *Nic*: cuckold) ♦ *Esa mujer mantiene a su chivo. That woman supports her guy.*

el **chivo loco** →**hacerse el chivo loco**

¡Chócala! (Hit it!) Put it here! (said in greeting before a handshake) *Mex, DR, PR, Col, U, Sp* ♦ *¡Chócala, mi hermano! ¿Cómo estás? Put 'er here, bro'! How're you doing?*

chochear to be a bit senile, forgetful because of age, have senior moments *Mex, S. Cone, Sp* ♦ *No preste atención a lo que diga don Santiago. Chochea y no sabe lo que dice. Don't pay attention to what Don Santiago says. He has senile moments and doesn't know what he's saying.*

el **chocho** (round sweet) female organ (vulgar) *Mex, Cuba, Nic, Sp* (RVAR *PR*: **la chocha, el bicho**)

chocho(-a) doting, proud (like a grandparent); gaga *Mex, DR, PR, CR, Col, S. Cone* (RVAR *U, Arg*: no implication of senility) ♦ *Está chocho con su nieta. He's gaga over his granddaughter.* ♦ *Ya está chochita. She's bit gaga.*

chocolate →**estar como agua para (pa')chocolate**

el **chocolate** (chocolate) hashish *Sp* ♦ *Lo arrestaron por vender chocolate en una plaza pública. They arrested him for selling hashish in a public square.*

Chogusto. (short for **Mucho gusto.**) Glad to meet you. *parts of L. Am.*

el **chollo** break, lucky stroke; bargain, something very cheap *Sp* ♦ *Mira qué chollo ha tenido esta chica; acaba de terminar la carrera y ya ha encontrado un trabajo. Look what a lucky break this girl has had; she just* *finished her studies and she's already found a job.*

ser un **chollo** to be a steal, a bargain *Sp* ◆ *El comprar este coche fue un chollo; es una oferta irrepetible. Buying that car was a steal; it's an offer that won't be repeated.*

chorearse to lose patience, get angry (a bit vulgar) *Ch* ◆ *Te choreaste sin motivos. You got all pissed off for no reason.*

el **chorizo** (sausage) male organ (vulgar) *Mex, Cuba, G, ES, U*

choro(-a) ballsy, brave, daring, admirable *Bol, Ch* ◆ *El marido de la Mónica la dejó, pero no importa. Ella trabaja, mantiene la casa y viste bien a sus tres hijas. ¡Es una mujer muy chora! Mónica's husband left her but it doesn't matter. She works, takes care of the house, and dresses her three daughters very well. What a ballsy gal!*

las **chorradas** stupidities, nonsense, pieces of junk *Sp* ◆ *No me gusta lo que dijo Felipe porque son sólo unas chorradas. I don't like what Felipe said because it's only nonsense.* ◆ *¡Qué chorradas hace Pedro! What stupid things Pedro does!*

el **chorro** (stream) large amount, tons *Mex, ES* ◆ *Gastó un chorro de dinero. He spent gobs of money.* ◆ *Falta un chorro para las elecciones. There's a ton of time before the elections.*

chorrocientos(-as) gazillion, many, an uncountable number *Mex, ES* ◆ *¿Cuánto vale? Umm... como chorrocientos. How much is it? Hmmm . . . about a gazillion.*

chotear (to make fun of) to tease, make someone look ridiculous (like **vacilar** in *Mex*), make fun of *Mex, Cuba, CR* ◆ *Felipe me choteó. Felipe made me look like a fool.*

la **choza** (hut, shanty) digs, house, home *Mex, G, ES, CR, Col, Para, U, Arg* ◆ *Voy a mi choza ahora. I'm going home now.*

¡Chuchas! (female organ) Crap! (very common, vulgar) *Ch* ◆ *¡Chuchas! Perdí mi pasaporte. Crap! I lost my passport.*

la **chuchería 1.** (from **chuches**, candy) fast food, junk food *DR, PR, ES, Sp* ◆ *Me llené con puras chucherías y ahora no tengo hambre. I filled up on junk food and now I'm not hungry.* **2.** (from **chuches**, candy) trinket, something of little value but cute *DR,*

PR, Ch, U, Sp ◆ *No me quiero gastar mucho dinero para el cumpleaños de Claudia; sólo le quiero comprar una chuchería. I don't want to spend a lot of money for Claudia's birthday; I just want to buy her a little trinket.*

el **chucho 1.** peso *Mex (central)* ◆ *Con unos chuchos más y la hacemos. With a few more pesos, we'll have it.* **2.** pooch, dog *Mex, ES* ◆ *El ladrón entró por la ventana, y el chucho lo atacó. The robber came in the window, and the pooch attacked him.*

chueco(-a) crooked *Mex, DR, ES, Col, Ch* (RVAR ALSO, TRAITOR IN *Mex, Ch*) ◆ *Juegan chueco. They play crooked.*

chulis darling, my dear (between women) *Mex, ES* ◆ *Chulis, platícanos, ¿cómo te fue con tu nueva conquista? Darling, tell us, how did it go with your new conquest (romance)?*

el **chulo** man who lives off women *DR, PR, Pan, Col, Ven, Sp* (RVAR *Ch:* lout) ◆ *Felipe es un chulo; nunca trabaja. Felipe lives off his woman (women); he never works.*

chulo(-a) cute, good *Florida, Mex, DR, PR, G, Sp* ◆ *Me encanta el vestido de Sandra. ¡Está superchulo! I adore Sandra's dress. It's super cute!*

el **chunche** thingamajig *C. Am.* ◆ *Dame ese chunche allí. Give me that thingamajig there.*

chungo(-a) bad, inappropriate, deteriorated *Mex, Sp* ◆ *Tengo un trabajo muy chungo. I have a crummy job.* ◆ *Estos zapatos están un poco chungos. These shoes are a little down at the heel.*

estar **chupado(-a)** (to be sucked) to be a piece of cake, easy *Sp* ◆ *Los deberes de hoy están chupados. En cinco minutos los tendré terminados. Today's homework is a piece of cake. I'll be finished with it in five minutes.*

el/la **chupamedia(s)** (stocking sucker) suck-up, person who does anything to please people in authority, brownnoser (also, **chupar media**) *Peru, Bol, S. Cone* ◆ *Agustín le chupa las medias al director. Agustín really sucks up to the director.*

chupar to drink booze, alcohol *L. Am., Sp* (RVAR SLIGHTLY VULGAR IN *C. Am.*) ◆ *En la fiesta, todos chuparon hasta el amanecer. At the party, everyone drank until dawn.*

el **chuparrosa, chupaflor** (hummingbird) gay, homosexual *Chicano, Mex* ◆ *¿Paco es chuparrosa? No lo sabía. Paco is gay? I didn't know it.*

chuparse →**no chuparse el dedo**

el/la **chupatintas** (ink sucker) paper-pusher, drudge *Mex, Ch, Sp* ◆ *Desde que la ascendieron, es una chupatintas. Ever since they promoted her, she's a paper-pusher.*

el **chupe 1.** small alcoholic drink *Mex* ◆ *¿Por qué no llegaste a la fiesta? Hubo chupe hasta para lavar el patio. Why didn't you come to the party? There were enough drinks to wash the patio.* **2.** dish *Pan, Ec, Peru, Bol, Ch, Arg* ◆ *El chupe de camarones es delicioso. The shrimp dish is delicious.*

el **chupito** small alcoholic drink *Sp* ◆ *¿Salimos esta noche? Vamos a tomarnos un chupito. Shall we go out this evening? Let's go have a little drink.*

el **churro** (fritter, long doughnut) **1.** attractive male, hunk *Peru, S. Cone* ◆ *Juan es un churro bárbaro. Juan is a real hunk.* **2.** joint, marijuana cigarette *Mex* ◆ *Paco fumó un churro y comió cuatro tamales. Paco smoked a joint and ate four tamales.*

chute nosy, putting one's nose into everything *Mex, ES* (RVAR *G:* shute) ◆ *Jorge es bien chute; se mete en todo. Jorge is a real busybody; he sticks his nose into everybody's business.*

el **chute** shot (injection) of heroin or other drugs *Sp* ◆ *Enrique necesitaba tres chutes al día de heroína. Enrique needed three shots of heroin a day.*

a **ciegas** blindly *L. Am., Sp* ◆ *Obedecieron a ciegas, sin hacer preguntas. They obeyed blindly, without asking questions.*

en el **cielo** →**poner en el cielo a alguien**

(mi) **cielo** ([my] heaven) sweetheart, darling *L. Am., Sp* ◆ *Cielo, ¿cuándo vamos a cenar? Darling, when are we going to have supper?*

¡Cielo verde! (Green sky!) Holy smoke!, used to express that something is surprising or unusual *PR* ◆ *¡Cielo verde! ¿Qué hacen los García aquí? Holy smoke! What are the Garcías doing here?*

estar con **cien (diez) ojos** (to be with one hundred [ten] eyes) to be warned, alert, suspicious *U, Arg, Sp* ◆ *En este barrio hay que estar con cien ojos para que no te roben. In this neighborhood you have to be on the lookout so you don't get robbed.*

a **ciencia cierta** (for certain knowledge) for sure *L. Am., Sp* ◆ *No hay duda. Lo sabemos a ciencia cierta. No doubt about it. We know it for sure.*

ciento y la madre (one hundred and the mother) in droves, tons, abundance of people *Sp* ◆ *Eran ciento y la madre; al final desistimos en enfrentarnos con ellos y nos fuimos. There were a zillion of them; finally we stopped confronting them and left.*

ciertas hierbas (certain herbs) a certain someone (used jokingly to avoid naming a person) *Col* ◆ *Ciertas hierbas no limpió su cuarto. A certain someone didn't clean up his (her) room.*

cinco →**no tener ni cinco**

cincuentón, cincuentona fiftyish (the **-ón** is an augmentative, emphasizing age) *L. Am., Sp* ◆ *Agustina es cincuentona, pero parece mucho más joven, y siempre está muy activa. Agustina is fiftyish, but she looks much younger, and she's always very active.*

de **cine** good, super (used like **de película**) *Sp* ◆ *La fiesta fue de cine. Estaba todo perfectamente organizado. The party was great. Everything was perfectly organized.*

en **cintura** →**meter/poner en cintura**

el/la **cipote(-a) 1.** kid, young person *G, Hond, ES, Nic* ◆ *¿Están aquí los cipotes? —No, están en la escuela. Are the kids here? —Nope, they're at school.* **2.** prick, jerk *Sp*

el **cirio** (candle) upheaval; mess *Sp* ◆ *Vaya cirio se montó cuando se salió el agua de la lavadora. What a mess there was when the water came out of the washing machine.*

en **claro** →**poner en claro; sacar en claro**

Claro, y los chanchos vuelan. (Right, and pigs fly.) Right, and that's likely. (sarcastic) *parts of L. Am.* ◆ *¿Te parece que vamos a ganar el concurso? —Claro, y los chanchos vuelan. You think we're going to win the contest? —Yeah, right, like that's really gonna happen.*

una **clavada** →**dar una clavada; darse una clavada**

clavado(-a) (nailed) stuck *Mex, Col, U, Arg* ◆ *Estoy clavada aquí, cocinando. I'm stuck* *here, cooking.* ◆ *Nos tienen clavados estudiando. They have us stuck studying.*

clavar (to nail) to have sex with, screw *Mex, Cuba, PR, G, ES, Col, U* (RVAR *U:* **clavarse;** *Mex:* **clavado** can mean in love) ◆ *Anoche mi novio me clavó por primera vez. Last night my boyfriend made love to me for the first time.*

clavar (to nail) to rip off, swindle *Mex, Cuba, DR, G, CR, S. Cone, Sp* ◆ *A esos turistas los clavaron con una estatua taína; ¡creen que es una pieza original! They conned those tourists with a Taino statue; they think it's an original work of art!*

clavar el pico (to nail the beak) to go out like a light, fall asleep *Mex, CR, Col, U* ◆ *El niño fue a su cuarto y clavó el pico de inmediato. The child went to his room and fell asleep immediately.*

clavarse 1. (to be nailed) to buckle down to study, cram *Mex, Col* ◆ *Luis se clavaba estudiando día y noche y por eso pudo graduarse. Luis buckled down to study day and night and that's why he was able to graduate.* **2.** (to be nailed) to flunk (as on an exam), to get nailed, to get involved in a bad situation or problem *Mex, PR, U* ◆ *Confié en una amiga, y me clavé. I trusted a friend, and I got nailed.*

el **clavo** (nail) drag, problem, embarrassment *G, ES, Nic, CR, S. Cone* ◆ *Tengo un clavo, un problema muy grande. I have a problem, a very big problem.* ◆ *¡Qué clavo! How embarrassing!* ◆ *Mi auto es un clavo: necesita muchos arreglos. My car is a problem; it needs a lot of repairs.*

el **clavo** →**dar en el clavo**

Un **clavo saca otro clavo.** (One nail takes out another nail.) One problem overshadows another, making it less important, sometimes used in reference to love affairs (a new love makes you forget an old one). One problem is solved. *Mex, DR, PR, ES, S. Cone, Sp* ◆ *Julio acaba de romper con Susi y ahora está con Diana. —Bueno, dicen que un clavo saca otro clavo. Julio just broke up with Susi and now he's with Diana. —Well, they say that one thing overshadows another.* ◆ *Tuve que pedirles dinero a mis padres para pagar las cuentas. Ahora les debo dinero. Pero un clavo saca otro clavo. I had to ask my par-*

ents for money to pay the bills. Now I owe them money. But one problem is solved.

clic →**hacer clic**

cliquear to click (e.g., on a key, from English) *parts of L. Am.* ◆ *Mira, hay que cliquear aquí. Look, you have to click here.*

co →**sin co**

coba →**dar coba; darse coba**

cochambroso(-a) messy, like a slob, in ruins; dirty (usually referring to the mind, with reference to sex, except in *Sp*) *Mex, DR, PR, ES, Col, Sp* ◆ *Mi amiga tiene la mente bien cochambrosa. My friend has a very dirty mind.*

el **coche** →**ir en el coche de San Fernando**

la **cochinada** (pig act) dirty trick, crappy cheap shot *L. Am., Sp* ◆ *¡Qué cochinadas hacen! What dirty tricks they play!*

los **cochos** folks, parents *Peru* (RVAR *Col, Ec:* **cuchos**) ◆ *¿Dónde están tus cochos, niño? Where are your folks, kid?*

coco →**darle al coco; meter el coco; tener buen coco; tener mucho coco**

el **coco** (coconut) head, noggin *L. Am., Sp* (RVAR *Ch:* also, **testicle**) ◆ *Me duele el coco. My head aches.*

ser (un) **coco** (to be a coconut) to be a brain, smart, intelligent (feminine is also **coco**) *most of L. Am. (not S. Cone)* ◆ *Marisa es bien coco. Pedro es un coco. Marisa is a smart cookie. Pedro is a smart cookie.*

cocodrilo →**como cocodrilo en fábrica de carteras**

el **cocotazo** blow to the head (the **coco**, coconut) *Chicano, Cuba, DR, PR, Col* ◆ *Su mamá le dio un cocotazo para callarlo. His mom gave him a little smackeroo on the head to quiet him down.*

codo(-a) (elbow) stingy *Chicano, Mex, DR, PR, C. Am.* (RVAR *ES:* invariable as an adj.) ◆ *Paula es bien coda; tiene dinero pero nunca quiere gastarlo. Paula is very stingy; she has money but she never wants to spend it.* ◆ *Marcos no puso dinero para la colecta; es un codo. Marcos didn't put any money in the kitty; he's a tightwad.*

codos →**hacer codos**

coger (to take, catch, grab) to have sex (vulgar) *most of L. Am. (not Ch)* ◆ *Después del* *cine cogimos en el auto. After the movie we had sex in the car.*

coger una trompa (to grab an elephant's trunk) to tie one on, get blasted, go on a bender *Sp* ◆ *Cogieron una trompa que les tuve que llevar al hospital. They got so blasted I had to take them to the hospital.*

el **cogote** →**estar hasta el cogote**

la **coima** bribe (also, **el coimero**, person on the take, accepting bribes) *Peru, S. Cone* ◆ *La policía paró a Jorge por exceso de velocidad. En lugar de darle la boleta, le pidieron una coima. The police stopped Jorge for speeding. Instead of giving him a ticket, they asked for a bribe.*

cojo(-a) →**no ser cojo(-a) ni manco(-a)**

de los **cojones** (of the testicles) awful, damn (vulgar) *Mex, Sp* ◆ *¿De dónde viene esa musiquita de los cojones? Where is that godawful music coming from?*

los **cojones** testicles (vulgar) *parts of L. Am., Sp*

los **cojones** →**estar hasta los cojones; (no) salirle a alguien algo de los cojones (huevos); tener los cojones bien puestos; tener los cojones por corbata; tener más cojones que nadie**

¡Cojones! (Testicles!) Damn! common expletive used for anger, surprise (vulgar) *Cuba, Sp* ◆ *¡Cojones! Me han robado la computadora. Damn! Someone's stolen my computer.*

cojonudo(-a) 1. ballsy, brave (vulgar, from **cojones**, testicles) *Mex, Cuba, Col, Sp* ◆ *Eres una tía cojonuda. You're a ballsy chick.* **2.** damn fantastic, admirable (vulgar) *Sp* ◆ *Esa comida fue cojonuda. That meal was damn incredible.*

cola →**hacer cola**

el/la colado(-a) (passed through a sieve) party or gate crasher, someone who shows up uninvited or gets in somewhere *L. Am., Sp* (RVar *Sp:* also, **estar colado[-a]** to be in love) ◆ *Como no tenían boletos, se colaron en el concierto. Son unos colados. Since they didn't have tickets, they crashed the concert. They're gate crashers.*

colarse (to be filtered or strained) to cut in line, squeeze in or through, crash *L. Am., Sp* ◆ *Se coló al estadio y no pagó la entrada.*

He (She) sneaked into the stadium and didn't pay the entrance fee.

el **cole** (short for **colegio**) school *parts of L. Am., Sp* ◆ *Virginia camina a su cole. Virginia walks to her school.*

colgado(-a) (hung, suspended) high on alcohol or drugs *Sp* ◆ *Cuando está colgado, no hay quien lo aguante. When he's wasted, nobody can stand him.*

estar **colgado(-a)** (to be hung, suspended) **1.** to be left hanging, stood up *Mex, ES, U, Arg, Sp* ◆ *Estoy colgado esperando la llamada de mi novia. I've been left hanging waiting for my girlfriend's call.* **2.** to have a crush on, be in love *Mex, G, Sp* ◆ *Marta está colgada por un chico de Córdoba. Marta is in love with a guy from Córdoba.*

colgado(-a) del cuello (hung by the neck) in a bind, usually economic *Mex, ES* ◆ *La sequía nos ha dejado colgados del cuello. The drought has left us in a bind.*

colgar la toalla to throw in (hang up) the towel *Mex, U, Arg* ◆ *Si no gano en ésta, cuelgo la toalla. If I don't win this one, I'll throw in the towel.*

colgar los guantes (to hang up the gloves) to kick the bucket, die *ES, Nic, Sp* (RVar *Sp:* to retire) ◆ *Anoche su bisabuela colgó los guantes. Last night his great-grandmother kicked the bucket.*

colgar los tenis (to hang up one's tennis shoes) to kick the bucket, die *Mex, DR, C. Am., Peru* (see illustration, page 346) ◆ *El perrito de Caty colgó los tenis. Caty's little dog gave up the ghost.*

colgarse 1. (to hang, be suspended) to be hung up *Mex, ES* ◆ *Se colgó una hora en el teléfono. He (She) was hung up on the telephone for an hour.* ◆ *Me colgué una hora allí. I was hung up there for an hour.* **2.** (to hang, be suspended) to be behind in something (e.g., work) *Mex, Col* ◆ *Rosario se colgó en el pago del alquiler. Rosario got behind in her rent payments.*

colmarle a alguien de to shower someone with *L. Am., Sp* ◆ *Me colmaron de besos y abrazos. They showered me with hugs and kisses.*

colmillo →**tener colmillo**

el **colmo** →**¡Esto es el colmo!**

ser el **colmo** (to be the culmination) to be the height, too much, the last straw *L. Am., Sp* ◆ *Vino a la fiesta con otro hombre mientras su esposo estaba en casa con los hijos. ¡Esto es el colmo!* She came to the party with another man while her husband was home with the children. This is too much!

colocarse (con) (to place oneself) to get high, stoned; drunk, plastered *Mex, Sp* (RVAR *Sp:* **colocarse con**) ◆ *Me coloqué con dos cervezas. (Sp)* I got high on two beers.

el **colocón** drunkenness *Sp* ◆ *Del colocón que llevaban, no conocían ni a sus amigos.* Because of the drunken stupor they were in, they didn't even know their own friends.

una **coma** →**sin faltar una coma (jota)**

El **comal le dijo a la olla: ¡Mira qué tiznada estás!** (The comal [a flat pan for cooking tortillas] said to the pot: Look how charred you are!) The pot calls the kettle black, meaning that both are alike but one puts the other down *Mex, ES* ◆ *¿Crees que yo estoy gastando demasiada plata? El comal le dijo a la olla: ¡Mira qué tiznada estás!* You think that I'm spending too much money? Ha, like the pot's calling the kettle black!

el **comelibros** (book eater) bookworm *most of L. Am., Sp* ◆ *No salimos este fin de semana porque mi novio es un comelibros y estaba estudiando para sus exámenes.* We didn't go out this weekend because my boyfriend is a bookworm and he was studying for his exams.

el/la **comemierda** (shit-eater) proud or stupid person, snob; fake (vulgar) *Mex, Cuba, DR, PR, G, ES, Nic, Col, Sp* ◆ *No soporto al primo de Lucy. Es tremendo comemierda; se cree mejor que todo el mundo.* I can't stand Lucy's cousin. He's a shithead; he thinks he's better than everyone else.

comer a dos carrillos (to eat with two cheeks) to serve two masters, work for two (often opposing) people or ideas; to eat like a horse *U, Sp* ◆ *No se puede comer a dos carrillos; tienes que escoger.* You can't serve two masters; you have to choose. ◆ *Mi hijo mayor come a dos carrillos.* My older son eats like a horse.

comer como chancho (to eat like a pig) to eat fast and in a sloppy way *ES, Nic, S. Cone* ◆ *Comimos como chanchos en nuestras vacaciones.* We ate like pigs on our vacation.

comer como niño Dios (to eat like a child of God, meaning a child from the orphanage) to eat fast, wolf down food hungrily (or it can mean the opposite, to eat with too much care as though from the orphanage) *Mex, ES, Nic* ◆ *Rafael comió como niño Dios y se fue.* Rafael wolfed down his food and left.

comer delante de los pobres (to eat in front of the poor) to show off in front of less fortunate people *S. Cone* ◆ *Cuando Pedro regresó de su cita, nos hablaba de su novia hasta que le dije, "Deja de comer delante de los pobres".* When Pedro came back from his date, he talked about his girlfriend until I said to him, "Don't show off in front of the less fortunate."

comer el coco a alguien (to eat someone's coconut, meaning head) to brainwash, sweet-talk, influence or convince someone *DR, PR, U, Sp* ◆ *Le comieron el coco a Paula e ingresó en esa secta.* They brainwashed (convinced) Paula and she joined that cult. ◆ *Para de comerme el coco y déjame en paz.* Stop hammering away at me and leave me in peace.

comer el sanduche antes del recreo (to eat the sandwich before recess) to jump the gun, enjoy something before it should be enjoyed, usually with a sexual overtone *PR* ◆ *¡No me digas! ¿Se comió el sanduche antes del recreo?* Don't tell me! They jumped the gun (started the honeymoon before the wedding)?

comer en el mismo plato (to eat out of the same plate) to be bosom buddies, on very friendly terms *Mex, G, ES, Ch* ◆ *Julio y Berta comen en el mismo plato.* Julio y Berta are bosom buddies.

comer la torta antes de la fiesta (to eat the cake before the party) to jump the gun, enjoy something before it should be enjoyed, usually with a sexual overtone *ES* ◆ *La novia está embarazada. Parece que comieron la torta antes de la fiesta.* The bride is pregnant. Looks like they jumped the gun.

A **comer se ha dicho.** (To eat it has been said.) Let's eat. *L. Am., Sp* ◆ *La comida está lista. A comer se ha dicho.* The food is ready. Let's eat.

comer vivo(-a) a alguien (to eat someone alive) to rip someone apart, criticize, treat badly *Mex, DR, ES, S. Cone, Sp* ◆ *Ya estoy harto de ese trabajo. Mi jefe me comió vivo solamente porque olvidé unos documentos en casa.* I've had it with that job. My boss ripped me apart just because I forgot and left some documents at home.

Comer y callar. (Eat and be quiet.) Beggars can't be choosers, said when someone is benefiting from someone else and should not speak against them *most of L. Am., Sp* ◆ *¿Qué importa que esta cabaña sea chica? Comer y callar.* Who cares that this cabin is small? Beggars can't be choosers.

comerse con los ojos to devour with one's eyes *L. Am., Sp* ◆ *Laura estaba guapísima; todos los hombres se la comían con los ojos.* Laura looked gorgeous; all the men were devouring her with their eyes (they couldn't take their eyes off of her).

comerse el coco (to eat the head) to fixate on, worry or be preoccupied *Mex, Sp* (RVAR *Sp*: also, **comerse el tarro, comerse la olla**) ◆ *No te comas el coco; vamos a conseguir el dinero.* Don't worry; we're going to get the money.

comerse un cable (to eat a cable) to get by on a shoestring, be in a tight spot (economically) *Cuba, DR, PR, Pan* ◆ *Llevo tres meses sin trabajo, así que andamos comiéndonos un cable.* I've been out of work for three months, so we're in a tight spot financially.

cometer un error to make a mistake *L. Am., Sp* ◆ *Nadie quería decir que el jefe había cometido el error.* No one wanted to say that the boss had made the mistake.

cometer una burrada (to commit a drove of donkeys) to make a gaffe, mistake *L. Am., Sp* ◆ *Cometimos una burrada al no explicar claramente nuestra posición en este asunto.* We made a big gaffe in not clearly explaining our position on this issue.

la **comida chatarra** (scrap-metal food) junk food, fast food *Mex, Col, Ch, U* ◆ *Durante el fin de semana no cociné; solo comimos comida chatarra.* Over the weekend, I didn't cook; we just ate fast food.

Comida hecha, amistad deshecha. (Meal finished, friendship ended.) said when someone eats and runs *most of L. Am., Sp* ◆ *Desgraciadamente, tenemos que irnos ahora. Comida hecha, amistad deshecha.* Unfortunately we have to go now. Eat and run!

comilón, comilona eating like a horse, gluttonous *L. Am., Sp* ◆ *¡Tomás es tan comilón!* Tomás eats like a horse!

¿Cómo? (What? How?) Excuse me? What (did you say)? *L. Am., Sp* ◆ *Mami, me voy a vivir con mi novio. —¿Cómo?* Mom, I'm going to live with my boyfriend. —Excuse me?

¿Cómo (lo) diría? How should I put it (say this)? *L. Am., Sp* ◆ *¿Qué piensas de mi decisión? —Bueno, ¿cómo lo diría? Pienso que eres muy joven para casarte.* What do you think of my decision? —Well, how should I put it? I think you are too young to get married.

como a un santo cristo un par de pistolas (like a couple of pistols for a statue of Christ) phrase indicating that something is not appropriate with respect to something else *Sp* ◆ *Ese sombrero le queda a Daniel como a un santo cristo un par de pistolas.* That hat sticks out like a sore thumb on Daniel.

estar **como agua para (pa') chocolate** (to be like water for chocolate) to be at the boiling point because of either anger or passion *Mex, CR* ◆ *Cuando Miguel llegó a la casa, su esposa estaba como agua para chocolate.* When Miguel got home, his wife was ready to explode.

como alma que lleva el diablo (like a soul that the devil takes) like a bat out of hell, with great agitation or speed *Mex, DR, ES, CR, S. Cone, Sp* ◆ *Oye, niño, tienes que manejar más despacio. Ayer te vi por la (Avenida) Lincoln como alma que lleva el diablo.* Listen (child), you have to drive more slowly. Yesterday I saw you on Lincoln Avenue speeding like the devil.

como anillo al dedo (like a ring on the finger) fitting, opportune, perfectly *L. Am., Sp* ◆ *El abrigo le sentó como anillo al dedo. Qué bien le queda.* The coat fit him (her) perfectly. How well it fits.

ser **como arroz blanco** (to be like white rice) to be everywhere, get around *most of L. Am.* ◆ *Eres como arroz blanco; te veo hasta en la sopa.* You really get around; we've got to *stop meeting like this (literally, I see you even in the soup).*

como caído(-a) de las nubes (like fallen from the clouds) out of the blue, unexpected *Mex, Sp* ◆ *Tu visita me cae de las nubes. Necesitaba hablar con alguien. Your visit comes out of the blue. I needed to talk to someone.*

como chancho en misa (like a pig in mass) out of place *Ec, Ch* ◆ *Me sentía como chancho en misa en ese hotel de lujo. I felt like I stuck out like a sore thumb in that fancy hotel.*

como cocodrilo en fábrica de carteras (like a crocodile in a wallet factory) nervous as a cat *PR* ◆ *Tengo una entrevista de trabajo y me siento como cocodrilo en fábrica de carteras. I have a job interview and I feel really uptight.*

¿Cómo cree(s)? How can you think that? If you say so. (disclaimer after a compliment) *L. Am., Sp* ◆ *Te ves tan jovencita. —¿Cómo crees? How young you look! —How can you think that?*

como de costumbre (as is the custom) as usual *L. Am., Sp* ◆ *Fuimos al restaurante de la esquina, como de costumbre. We went to the restaurant on the corner, as usual.*

Como dijo Herodes, te jodes. (As Herod said, you're screwed.) You're screwed. (phrase of resignation, vulgar) *Mex, DR, Sp*

como Dios manda (as God commands) in the proper way, perfectly, as it should be *L. Am., Sp* ◆ *Lo vamos a hacer como Dios manda. We're going to do it good and proper (as it should be done).*

¿Cómo diré? How shall I put it (say this)? *most of L. Am. (not S. Cone)* ◆ *¿Te vas el otro fin de semana? —Pues, no sé. Tuvimos un problema. ¿Cómo diré? Quizás vamos a postergar el viaje. Are you going next weekend? —Well, I don't know. We had a problem. How shall I put it? Maybe we'll postpone the trip.*

como dos gotas de agua (like two drops of water) like two peas in a pod *L. Am., Sp* ◆ *Paco y su amigo Miguelito son como dos gotas de agua. Paco and his friend Miguelito are like two peas in a pod.*

como dos y dos son cuatro (like two and two are four) as sure as shootin', as we're standing here *L. Am., Sp* ◆ *¿Estás segura de lo que dices? —Por supuesto, como que dos y dos son cuatro. Are you sure of what you're saying? —As sure as we're standing here.*

como el aceite y el vinagre (like oil and vinegar) like oil and water, said of two people who don't get along *Mex, Caribbean, Col, U, Arg* ◆ *Estos dos grupos son como el aceite y el vinagre; no se mezclan y siempre se pelean. Those two groups are like oil and water; they don't mix and they always fight.*

como el agua y el aceite (like water and oil) like oil and water, said of two people who don't get along *Mex, G, ES, Ch* ◆ *Juan y su hermano son como el agua y el aceite; no se llevan bien. Juan and his brother are like oil and water; they don't get along.*

estar **como energúmeno** (to be like one possessed) to be hysterical *Mex, ES, Ch, U, Arg* (RVAR *U, Arg*, **ponerse como un...**) ◆ *Nunca podemos arreglar nuestros problemas porque él se pone como un energúmeno y se va. (U) We can never resolve our problems because he has a fit, and then he leaves.* ◆ *Estás como energúmeno. Tranquilízate. You're hysterical. Calm down.*

como entierro de pobre (like a poor person's funeral) with no ado, like a shot, quickly *ES, CR, Col* ◆ *Este año se fue como entierro de pobre. This year went by like a shot.*

¿Cómo está la movida? How's the action? *parts of L. Am.*

como gallina en corral ajeno (like a hen in someone else's or a different pen) in a poorly adjusted way, like a fish out of water *Col, Peru, Ch* ◆ *Vi a Maruja en el parlamento, y estaba como gallina en corral ajeno. I saw Maruja in the parliament, and she was like a fish out of water.*

como gallo en patio ajeno (like a rooster in someone else's or a different patio) totally lost, like a fish out of water *ES, Nic, CR, Pan* ◆ *Desde que Paco llegó a Estados Unidos, se ha sentido como gallo en patio ajeno. Since Paco came to the United States, he's felt like a fish out of water.*

estar **como la mona** (to be like the she-monkey) to be under the weather, feeling really bad (physically or mentally) *Ch, U* ♦ *¿Por qué estás tan callado? —Estoy como la mona.* Why are you so quiet? —I'm under the weather.

¿Cómo lo llevas? (How do you carry it?) How are things? What's up? *Mex, Sp*

como los ángeles (like the angels) very good, excellent, heavenly *Mex, DR, Sp* ♦ *Mi hija canta muy bien. Como los ángeles.* My daughter sings very well. Heavenly.

como nalga de lavandera (like a washerwoman's buttock) very cold, (cold) as a witch's tit *Nic* ♦ *Después de muchas caídas en la nieve, Patricia se sentía como nalga de lavandera.* After many falls in the snow, Patricia felt really cold.

como niño con juguete nuevo (like a kid with a new toy) like a kid in a candy store, happy *Mex, ES, U, Arg* ♦ *Alejandro compró una camioneta y está como niño con juguete nuevo.* Alejandro bought a pickup truck, and he's like a kid in a candy store.

como niño con zapatos nuevos (like a kid with new shoes) like a kid in a candy store, happy *Mex, DR, ES, Ch, U, Sp* ♦ *Le aumentaron el sueldo. Está como niño con zapatos nuevos.* They gave him a raise. He's like a kid in a candy store.

estar **como nunca** (to be like never) to look better than ever *L. Am., Sp* ♦ *Estás como nunca, Marisol.* You look better than ever, Marisol.

ser **como payaso de circo** (to be like a circus clown) to be a cutup, silly *Mex, ES* ♦ *Roberto es como payaso de circo; nos hace reír a todos.* Roberto is a cutup; he makes us all laugh.

como perro en canoa (like a dog in a canoe) nervous as a cat *PR* (RVar *U:* **como perro en bote**) ♦ *Estaba asustada, como perro en canoa.* She was scared, nervous as a cat.

como perros y gatos (like dogs and cats) like cats and dogs, enemies *Mex, ES, Col, Peru, Ch* ♦ *Los recién casados se peleaban como perros y gatos día y noche.* The newlyweds were fighting like cats and dogs day and night.

estar **como pez en el agua** (to be like a fish in water) to be in one's element, enjoy comforts and conveniences *L. Am., Sp* ♦ *Me siento muy contento; aquí estoy como pez en el agua.* I feel very content; I'm really in my element here.

¿Cómo que...? What do you mean . . . ? *parts of L. Am., Sp* ♦ *¿Cómo que perdiste el dinero?* What do you mean you lost the money?

como quien dice as if to say *L. Am., Sp* ♦ *Hizo un gesto como quien dice "¡Huácala!"* He made a face as if to say "Yuck!"

Como quiera(s). As you like. If you want. *L. Am., Sp* ♦ *¿Comamos en aquel restaurán? —Como quieras.* Shall we eat at that restaurant? —If you want.

como sardina en lata (like a sardine in a can) crowded or packed *L. Am., Sp* (RVar *Sp:* also, **como una lata de sardinas**) ♦ *Este autobús está muy lleno. Estamos como sardina en lata.* This bus is very full. We're like sardines in a can.

como si nada (as if nothing) just like that, without giving the matter any importance, like you don't have a care in the world *L. Am., Sp* ♦ *Escuchó las malas noticias como si nada.* He heard the bad news as though he didn't have a care in the world.

¿Cómo te ha ido? (How has it gone for you?) How's it going? *L. Am., Sp* ♦ *¿Cómo te ha ido? ¿Cuándo llegaste del campo?* How's it going? When did you get back from the country?

¿Cómo te va? (How's it going for you?) How are you? *L. Am., Sp* ♦ *¿Cómo te va? Hace mucho que no te veo.* How are you? I haven't seen you in a long time.

estar **como todos los diablos** to be beside oneself (like all the devils), in a very bad mood *Mex, G, CR* ♦ *Es difícil trabajar contigo hoy; estás como todos los diablos.* It's difficult to work with you today; you're in a very bad mood.

como un (el) culo (like an [the] ass) ugly, unpleasant (vulgar) *Cuba, Col, S. Cone* ♦ *Ese tipo me cae como un culo.* I think that guy is an ass. ♦ *Esa falda le queda como un culo.* That skirt looks like hell on her.

estar **como un león (de bravo)** (to be like a lion [angry]) to be very angry *Mex, G, U* ◆ *No pude hablar con Hernán porque está como un león de bravo. I couldn't speak with Hernán because he's angry as can be.*

como un rayo (like a lightning bolt) quick as lightning, lightning fast *ES, Nic, CR, U, Ch, Sp* ◆ *Es rápido como un rayo. He's lightning fast.* ◆ *Pasaste a mi lado como un rayo, y no me viste. You passed by my side quick as lightning, and you didn't see me.*

estar **como un tanque (como un tren)** (to be like a tank [like a train]) to be a hunk, attractive, strong *Mex, Sp* ◆ *Elvira dice que su novio está como un tanque. Elvira says that her boyfriend is a hunk.*

estar **como una cuba** (to be like a cask) to be drunk *U, Arg, Sp* ◆ *Cuando terminó la fiesta, todo el mundo estaba como una cuba. When the party ended, everybody was drunk.*

como una fiera (like a wild one) like a wild animal trying to defend her young *L. Am., Sp* ◆ *La mamá defendió a sus hijos como una fiera cuando la vecina los estaba atacando. The mother defended her children like a wild animal when the neighbor was attacking them.*

estar **como una regadera** (to be like a watering can) to have one's mind like a sieve, forget things *Sp* ◆ *Esta mujer está como una regadera. No pierdas el tiempo discutiendo con ella. This woman has a mind like a sieve. Don't waste time arguing with her.*

estar **como una reina** (to be like a queen) to look beautiful *L. Am., Sp* ◆ *Está (usted) como una reina. You look like a queen.*

estar **como unas pascuas** (to be like Easter) to be happy as a lark *Sp* ◆ *Claudio estaba como unas pascuas después que le leyeron su ensayo en público. Claudio was as happy as a lark after they read his essay in public.*

el **compa** close male friend (from **compadre**) *L. Am.* (RVar *Ch:* **cumpa**) ◆ *Oye, compa, ven aquí, que tengo algo que contarte. Hey, pal, come here; I have something to tell you.*

el **compadrito** (little pal) dude, young hustler *Arg* ◆ *Daniel es el compadrito del barrio. Daniel is the young hustler of the neighborhood.*

el **compi** (short for **compinche**) pal *Mex, Peru, Sp* ◆ *Jorge es mi compi de trabajo. Jorge is my pal at work (coworker).*

el **compinche** (accomplice) friend, pal *L. Am.* ◆ *Soy bien compinche con Fernando. I'm really close friends with Fernando.*

de **compras** →**ir de compras**

la **compu** short for **la computadora** *L. Am.* ◆ *La compu de la oficina no funcionó esta mañana, y no pudimos terminar las estadísticas. The office computer didn't work this morning, and we could not finish the statistics.*

de **común acuerdo** by mutual agreement *L. Am., Sp* ◆ *De común acuerdo, ya no hablamos de política. By mutual agreement, we no longer talk politics.*

común y corriente regular, ordinary *L. Am., Sp* ◆ *Aunque es famoso, se porta como un tipo común y corriente. Although he's famous, he acts like a regular guy.*

la **concha 1.** (shell) shamelessness, insolence, nerve *Mex, Nic, CR, Pan, Ec, Peru* ◆ *¡Qué concha la tuya... me debes plata y no me has pagado! What nerve you have . . . you owe me money and you haven't paid me!* **2.** (shell) female organ (vulgar) *S. Cone* ◆ *Esa mujer tiene una concha de oro; los hombres le pagan mucho por acostarse con ella. That woman has a golden pussy; men pay lots of money to sleep with her.*

la **concha de tu madre** (your mother's shell, referring to female organ) son of a bitch (to friend or foe, as an insult or term of endearment, vulgar) *S. Cone* ◆ *La concha de tu madre, hombre, siempre eres el mismo estúpido. Son of a bitch, man, you're still the same idiot as always.*

conchudo(-a) (hard-shelled) brassy, thick-skinned; (n.) person without shame, thick-skinned and insensitive; con man; brassy or pushy female *Mex, C. Am., Col, Ven, Ec, Peru, Bol* (RVar vulgar, very pejorative in *U, Arg*) ◆ *Trinidad es tan conchuda que aunque la rechazan, ella regresa. Trinidad is so thick-skinned that even though they reject her, she comes back.*

el **conecte** connection *Mex, ES, Nic* ◆ *Tengo un conecte en el gobierno. Ahorita lo llamo. I have a connection in the government. I'll call him now.*

consultar con la almohada: Va a consultar con la almohada sobre el problema.
He's going to sleep on the problem.

conexiones →**tener conexiones**

de **confianza** trustworthy *L. Am., Sp* ◆ *No conozco a Raúl. ¿Es una persona de confianza? I don't know Raúl. Is he a trustworthy person?*

conformarse con to make the most of or resign oneself to, put up with *L. Am., Sp* ◆ *Hay que conformarse con lo que tienes... así es la vida. You have to make the most of what you have . . . that's life.*

confundir la gimnasia con la magnesia (to confuse gymnastics with magnesia) to confuse two very different things, mix apples and oranges *Mex, Sp* ◆ *Estás confundiendo la gimnasia con la magnesia. No se puede comparar una casa en Madrid con una casa en el campo. You're mixing apples and oranges. You can't compare a house in Madrid with a house in the country.*

Lo (La) **conocen en su casa.** (They know him [her] in his [her] own home.) unknown person, describing someone who goes to a party or meeting and no one knows who he or she is (used ironically, as if to say, "Well, at least he must be known in his own home!") *Mex, Ch* (RVar *Sp:* **A ése no lo conocen, ni en su casa.**)

conocer a alguien desde su (la) cuna to know someone from infancy (literally, from their cradle) *most of L. Am., Sp* ◆ *Conozco a Carlos y Beto desde la cuna. I've known Carlos and Beto from infancy.*

conocer como la palma de la mano to know like the back (literally, palm) of one's hand *L. Am., Sp* ◆ *Conozco la capital como la palma de la mano. I know the capital like the back of my hand.*

a **consecuencia de** because of, as a consequence of *L. Am., Sp* ◆ *Tres personas murierion a consecuencia de las altas temperaturas. Three people died because of the high temperatures.*

consejos →**dar consejos**

consultar con la almohada (to consult with the pillow) to sleep on it, wait and think things over (RVar ALSO, **hablar con la almohada**) *L. Am., Sp* ◆ *Antes de tomar una decisión, voy a consultar con la almohada.*

Before making a decision, I'm going to sleep on it.

al **contado** with cash *L. Am., Sp* ◆ *¿Cómo vas a pagar? ¿Al contado?* How are you going to pay? Cash?

contar batallitas (to recount small battles) to tell "war stories," stories of one's life *Sp* ◆ *Tu abuelo siempre nos está contando batallitas de su juventud.* Your grandpa is always telling us the stories of his youth.

contar con to count on *L. Am., Sp* ◆ *No podemos contar con su ayuda.* We can't count on his (her, their) help.

contener el aliento to hold one's breath *L. Am., Sp* ◆ *Ya no pude contener el aliento.* I could no longer hold my breath.

Contigo ni a China me voy. (I'm not even going to China with you.) You're impossible. I want nothing to do with you. *Mex, ES, Col* ◆ *Ya basta. No insistas. Contigo ni a China me voy.* Enough already. Don't insist. I want nothing to do with you.

Contigo ni a la vuelta de la esquina. (I'm not even going down to the corner with you.) You're impossible. I want nothing to do with you. *S. Cone* ◆ *¿Vamos al teatro mañana? —No, contigo ni a la vuelta de la esquina.* Shall we go to the theater tomorrow? —No, I want nothing to do with you.

Contigo ni el saludo. (With you not even the greeting.) You're impossible, used humorously after being refused when an invitation was made, meaning that the other person is being unfriendly *Mex, G, ES, Col* ◆ *¿Así que otra vez no tienes tiempo para vernos? Contigo ni el saludo.* So once again you don't have time for us? You're impossible! We're writing you off.

a **continuación** immediately following, after(ward) *L. Am., Sp* ◆ *A continuación se ven las notas.* See the notes immediately following.

contra viento y marea (against wind and tides) come what may, come hell or high water *L. Am., Sp* ◆ *Voy a luchar contra viento y marea para conseguir el papel en la película.* I'm going to struggle to get the role in the film come hell or high water.

a **contrapelo** (against the natural direction, the way the hair or fur grows) against one's

will or against the norm *DR, Ch, U, Sp* ◆ *Te están haciendo ese favor a contrapelo. Seguro que van a querer una contraprestación.* They're doing that favor for you grudgingly. For sure they'll want a payback.

la **contraria (contra)** →**llevar la contraria (contra)**

el **contrario** →**por el contrario**

al **contrario** on the contrary *L. Am., Sp* ◆ *No estoy de buen humor; al contrario, me siento algo deprimida.* I'm not in a good mood; on the contrary, I feel a bit depressed.

Contreras →**¡Qué no te enteras, Contreras!**

convenirle (algo) to be convenient, suitable *L. Am., Sp* ◆ *No me conviene esa fecha.* That date isn't convenient for me.

convertirse en to turn into, become *L. Am., Sp* ◆ *¿No apoyas a ninguno de los candidatos? Te vas a convertir en anarquista.* You're not supporting any of the candidates? You're going to turn into an anarchist.

de **coña** →**Ni de coña.**

estar de **coña** to be shitting (someone), just joking (vulgar) *Sp* ◆ *¿Estás de coña? ¿Cómo piensas que me voy a creer que has ganado dos millones?* Are you shitting me? Do you think I'm going to believe that you won (or earned) two million (euros)?

estar de **coña** to look damn good on, fit well (vulgar) *Sp* ◆ *Este vestido te está de coña.* This dress looks damn good on you.

ser la **coña** to be too much, unusual, strange (people) (vulgar) *Sp* ◆ *¡Eres la coña! Nunca sé si estás hablando en serio o en broma.* You're too damn much! I never know if you're talking seriously or in jest.

¡Coña! Damn! (from **coño**, vulgar) *Sp* ◆ *Vaya coña tener que ir al cine con Jaime.* Damn my luck to have to go to the movies with Jaime.

el **coñazo** (blow, from **coño**, vulgar) drag, something bothersome or bad; also, hard time (vulgar) *Sp* ◆ *¡Qué coñazo! No recibí las entradas a tiempo.* What a bitch of a problem! I didn't get the tickets on time.

el **coño de su madre** (his [her] mother's female organ) real son of a bitch (vulgar) *DR, PR, Ven* ◆ *Ese coño de su madre salió sin pagar la cuenta.* That S.O.B. left without paying the bill.

¡Coño! (reference to female organ) Damn! interjection of anger, surprise, pain (vulgar, especially in L. Am.) *Mex, Caribbean, Col, Sp* ◆ *¡Coño! ¡Qué suerte has tenido! ¡Qué guapa que estás!* Damn! What luck you've had! How gorgeous you look!

copado(-a), recopado(-a) (cupped, trophied) overwhelmed (usually with joy or a positive emotion), happy, fantastic *Arg* ◆ *¡Qué lindo regalo! Estoy copada.* What a lovely gift! I'm overwhelmed. ◆ *Han llegado los nietos, y los abuelos están copados.* The grandchildren have arrived, and their grandparents are in heaven. ◆ *¿Cómo estás, Naldo? —¡Recopado!* How are you, Naldo? —Fantastic!

la **coperacha** kitty, pool of money used to buy something collectively *Mex, G, ES* ◆ *Para comprar la comida, hacemos una coperacha entre todos.* To buy the food, everyone puts money in a kitty.

el **copete** ➞ **estar hasta el copete**

copetudo(-a) (crested, referring to the **copete**, crest or crown) highfalutin', stuck-up *ES, S. Cone* ◆ *Es buena persona aunque un poco copetuda.* She's a good person although a bit stuck up.

una **copia** ➞ **sacar una copia**

la **copucha** piece of gossip *Ch* ◆ *Amiga, ¡te cuento una copucha! Conocí a la amante de Gustavo y es más fea que el diablo.* My dear, do I have a piece of gossip for you! I met Gustavo's lover and she is as ugly as sin.

copuchar (to puff up cheeks) to gossip (also, **copuchear**) *Bol, Ch* ◆ *Estaban allí copuchando toda la tarde.* You guys were there gossiping the whole afternoon.

el/la **copuchento(-a)** gossip, person who gossips *Bol, Ch* ◆ *Mira, esos hombres son más copuchentos que sus esposas. No pierden nada.* Look, those guys are bigger gossips than their wives. They don't miss a thing!

el **coraje** (courage) anger *parts of L. Am., Sp* ◆ *Me da coraje que me engañen.* It makes me mad that I'm being taken advantage of.

un **coraje** ➞ **hacer un coraje**

corazón (heart) darling *L. Am., Sp* ◆ *Corazón, hazme un favor.* Darling, do me a favor.

corazón ➞ **hacer de tripas corazón; tener un corazón de oro; tener un corazón de piedra**

con el **corazón en la mano** (with one's heart in one's hand) with one's heart on one's sleeve, frankly and sincerely *L. Am., Sp* ◆ *Con el corazón en la mano, les dije lo que sabía de su padre.* Frankly and sincerely, I told them what I knew of their father.

con el **corazón en un puño** (with the heart in a fist) stressed out, in a situation of anxiety or depression *most of L. Am., Sp* ◆ *Está con el corazón en un puño esperando los resultados de sus exámenes.* He's all tied up in knots waiting for his exam results.

el **corillo** group, social gathering; **corillo bacanal**, party *PR* ◆ *Vamos a la fiesta con el corillo de Luis, que son unos muchachos cheverísimos.* Let's go to the party with Luis's group; they're a great bunch of guys (and girls).

el/la **cornudo(-a)** cuckold *L. Am., Sp* ◆ *Aldo sabe que es un cornudo, y no le importa porque él también tiene una amante.* Aldo knows he's a cuckold, and it doesn't matter to him because he also has a lover.

la **coronilla** ➞ **estar hasta la coronilla**

el **corre-corre** (run-run) rat race, mess *Mex, DR, PR* ◆ *No me gusta el corre-corre de la ciudad.* I don't like the rat race in the city. ◆ *Cuando llegó la policía, se armó un corre-corre en la discoteca.* When the police arrived, there was a big hullabaloo in the discoteque.

¡Córrele! Go for it! (transformation of **ándale**) *Mex, ES, Col* ◆ *¡Córrele, Daniela, no te avergüences!* Go for it, Daniela, don't be embarrassed!

correr (to run) to kick (someone) out, run off or fire *Mex, C. Am., U, Arg* ◆ *Lo corrieron porque no trabajaba bien.* They fired him because he wasn't working well. ◆ *Los corrieron de la casa porque hacían mucha bulla.* They kicked them out of the house because they made too much of a ruckus.

correr peligro (to run danger) to be in danger *L. Am., Sp* ◆ *Los que van en esos barcos corren mucho peligro.* Those who go in those boats are in great danger.

correrse to come sexually (vulgar) *Sp*

correrse que (to be run that) to be said, rumored that *Mex, Cuba, G, Sp* ◆ *Se corre que tiene novia.* There's a rumor going around that he has a girlfriend.

corresponderle (to correspond to one) to be one's turn *L. Am., Sp* ◆ *A Juan le corresponde cocinar hoy.* It's Juan's turn to cook today.

la **corriente** →**ir (nadar) contra la corriente**

ser una **corriente** to be coarse, rude, a dope (for women) *Mex* ◆ *Esa mujer es una corriente. No le hagas caso.* That woman is very coarse. Don't pay attention to her.

estar al **corriente de** (to be at the running total of) to be up to date on *L. Am., Sp* ◆ *¿Necesitas más información sobre la propuesta? —No, gracias, estoy al corriente.* Do you need more information about the proposal? —No, thank you, I'm up to date.

corriente y moliente run of the mill, everyday, normal *Mex, Sp* ◆ *Aunque es un actor famoso, es una persona corriente y moliente.* Even though he's a famous actor, he's a regular guy.

la **corta** →**hacer la corta (la grande)**

a la **corta o a la larga** (in the short or the long) sooner or later *L. Am., Sp* ◆ *A la corta o a la larga sabrán la verdad.* Sooner or later they will know the truth.

¡Corta! ¡Corta! (Cut! Cut!) Put a lid on it! Stop! Cut it out! *Mex, PR*

cortado(-a) por (con) el mismo patrón (cut by [with] the same pattern) cut from the same cloth, very similar, chip off the old block *Mex, Sp* ◆ *Sin duda son de la familia; están cortados con el mismo patrón.* Obviously they're from the family; they're cut from the same cloth.

cortado(-a) por la misma tijera (cut by the same scissors) cut from the same cloth, very similar, chip off the old block *Mex, DR, PR, ES, S. Cone, Sp* ◆ *Realmente se nota que son familiares. Están cortados por la misma tijera.* You really notice that they're relatives. They're cut from the same cloth.

¡Córtala! (Cut it!) Put a lid on it! Cut it out! *Mex, ES, S. Cone* ◆ *Córtala. No es necesario seguir con esta discusión absurda.* Put a lid on it. There's no point going on with this absurd discussion.

cortante (cutting) short, abrupt, giving short answers only *Mex, G, ES, Col, Ch, Arg, Sp* ◆ *Estaba hablando con ella, pero es bien cortante.* I was talking to her, but she's very abrupt.

cortar 1. (to cut) to hang up (the phone) *L. Am., Sp* ◆ *Tengo que cortar. Mamá quiere usar el teléfono.* I have to hang up. Mom wants to use the phone. **2.** to cut off (a relationship), drop *Mex, G, U, Sp* ◆ *Corté a Mario. Me tenía cansado con sus problemas.* I dropped Mario. I was sick and tired of hearing about his problems.

cortar de raíz (to cut the root) to nip in the bud *L. Am., Sp* ◆ *Mira, m'hija, es mejor que cortes esas relaciones de raíz.* Look, my dear, it's best that you nip that relationship in the bud.

cortar el hilo (to cut the thread) to cut off, interrupt a conversation or other thing, make someone lose their train of thought *Mex, DR, S. Cone* ◆ *No me cortes el hilo porque me pierdo la historia. Es muy complicada.* Don't make me lose my train of thought because I'll forget (lose) the story. It's very complicated.

cortar el rollo (to cut the roll) to cut the jive, talk *Mex, Sp* ◆ *Corta el rollo y págame lo que me debes.* Cut the jive and pay me what you owe me.

cortar por lo sano to make a clean break *L. Am., Sp* ◆ *Nos mudamos al sur para cortar por lo sano.* We moved to the south to make a clean break.

cortarle las alas to clip one's wings *L. Am., Sp* ◆ *Dejamos que Jaime fuera a Europa porque no nos pareció bueno cortarle las alas.* We let Jaime go to Europe because we didn't think it was advantageous to clip his wings.

cortarse, sentirse cortado(-a) (to cut oneself off, to feel cut off) to be shy, embarrassed *S. Cone, Sp* ◆ *No te cortes; pide lo que quieras.* Don't be timid; ask for what you want. ◆ *Me corté (Me quedé cortada) cuando me hizo esa pregunta tan personal.* I felt embarrassed when he (she) asked me that very personal question. ◆ *Me siento muy cortada cuando Juan está delante.* I feel shy when Juan is around.

corte →**dar corte**

ser de **corto alcance** (to be of short reach) to be narrow-minded, conventional *Ch* ◆ *No esperamos mucho del secretario porque es de corto alcance. We don't expect much from the secretary because he is narrow-minded.*

corto(-a) →**más corto(-a) que las mangas de un chaleco**

ser **corto(-a) de genio** (to be short on brilliance) to be a wimp, timid *Peru, Ch* ◆ *Mi hijo es corto de genio y no sabe defenderse. My son is timid and doesn't know how to defend himself.*

a corto plazo, a la corta in the short run *L. Am., Sp* ◆ *A corto plazo, los efectos no serán graves. In the short run, the effects will not be serious.*

un **cortón** →**dar un cortón a alguien**

la **cosa** (thing) can be a euphemism for male or female organ *parts of L. Am., Sp* ◆ *Dicen que Nicolás tiene una cosa muy grande. They say that Nicolás has a really big thing.*

la **cosa grandototota** (great big thing) humongous thing *Mex, ES, Nic, U, Arg* ◆ *La idea del divorcio es una cosa grandototota. The idea of divorce is a humongous thing.*

las **cosas para picar** (things to pick at) munchies, appetizers *Ch, U, Sp* ◆ *Elisa preparó las cosas para picar. Elisa prepared the appetizers.*

el **coscolino** dirty old man, letch *Mex, ES* (RVar *Mex:* also, **la coscolina**) ◆ *Ese viejito es un coscolino. That old guy is a letch.*

ser **coser y cantar** (to be sew and sing) to be child's play, a cinch *L. Am., Sp* ◆ *Para ti que sabes tanto, este trabajo será coser y cantar. For you who knows so much, this job will be child's play.*

la **costa** →**Hay moros en la costa.**

costar más que un hijo tonto (to cost more than a foolish son) to cost a fortune, said when someone keeps showing up to eat or costs someone money excessively *Mex, U, Sp* (RVar *Arg: ... bobo*) ◆ *La matrícula de este master me costará más que un hijo tonto. ¿Cómo se puede pagar tanto? The registration for that master's degree will cost me a fortune. How can anyone pay that much?*

costar un huevo y la mitad de otro (to cost an egg, meaning testicle, and a half) to cost a fortune or a lot of effort (vulgar) *Mex,* *G, ES, Sp* (RVar *S. Cone:* **costar un huevo**) ◆ *Este coche costó un huevo. This car cost a fortune.*

costar un ojo de la cara (to cost an eye of the face) to cost an arm and a leg *L. Am., Sp* ◆ *No puedes comprar ese abrigo. Es muy bonito, pero cuesta un ojo de la cara. You can't buy that coat. It's pretty, but it costs an arm and a leg.*

costar un pastón to cost a fortune (augmentative of **pasta**, meaning money) *Sp* ◆ *Esta moto me costó un pastón. This motorcycle cost me a fortune.*

costumbre →**como de costumbre**

el/la **cotilla** gossip, person who gossips *Sp* ◆ *Eres realmente un cotilla. ¿Cómo puedes estar mirando dentro de mi bolso y después contárselo a tus amigos? You're a real gossip. How can you look in my purse and then tell your friends about it?*

la **cotorra** (parrot) chatterbox, someone who talks a lot *L. Am., Sp* ◆ *Durante la cena, Sonia habló como una cotorra sobre su viaje. During dinner, Sonia spoke non-stop about her trip.*

cotorrear 1. to jabber away *Mex, DR, PR, G, Col, U, Arg, Sp* ◆ *Después de muchos años, nos encontramos con mis amigas en el café; cotorreamos por horas contándonos nuestras vidas. After many years, my friends and I met at a café; we jabbered away for hours telling each other about our lives.* **2.** to jive, feed a line *Chicano, Mex, ES, Col* ◆ *Me estaba cotorreando, pero no le hice caso. He was jive-talking me, but I didn't pay any attention to him.*

el **cotorreo** gab session *Mex, DR, ES, Col* ◆ *Estuvieron en un constante cotorreo anoche y no dejaron dormir a nadie. They were in a constant gab session last night and didn't let anyone sleep.*

los **coyoles** (fruits of a kind of palm tree) testicles (vulgar) *C. Am.*

el **coyote** (coyote) someone who takes people across the U.S. border; also, an intermediary to get things (sometimes illegally or below cost) *Mex, C. Am.* ◆ *El coyote que la traía la abandonó. La dejó tirada. The coyote who brought her abandoned her. He left her by the wayside.* ◆ *Le pagaron a un coyote para que les consiguiera los docu-*

mentos. They paid an intermediary to get the documents for them.

cranear to rack one's brain, think a lot *G, Col, Ec, Ch* ◆ *Estoy aquí craneando, pero no veo ninguna solución. I'm here racking my brain, but I don't see any solution.*

cráneo →**dar cráneo (cabeza)**

con **creces** and then some, plus more *L. Am., Sp* ◆ *Pagamos la deuda con creces. We paid the debt and then some.*

a **crédito** on credit *L. Am., Sp* ◆ *Compraron el auto a crédito. They bought the car on credit.*

creer que el dinero se encuentra debajo de las piedras (to believe that money is found underneath rocks) to think that money is easy to get, that money grows on trees *U, Sp* ◆ *La familia de Isabel siempre le pide mucho dinero. Ellos creen que el dinero se encuentra debajo de las piedras aquí en Norteamérica. Isabel's family always asks her for lots of money. They think money grows on trees here in North America.*

creerse (to believe oneself) to feel superior (without reason), be proud or pretentious, stuck-up *L. Am., Sp* ◆ *Juanita se cree mucho. Juanita is very stuck-up.* ◆ *No te creas. Don't kid yourself. Don't be so full of yourself.*

creerse el (la) muy muy (to think one is the very very) to think one is hot stuff *Mex, C. Am., Col* ◆ *Hablamos con Alicia en la exposición de arte. Se cree la muy muy. We spoke with Alicia at the art exhibit. She thinks she's hot stuff.*

creerse el hoyo del queque (to think one is the hole in the center of the cake) to have a very high opinion of oneself, think one is the center of the universe *Ch* ◆ *El señor Brown se cree el hoyo del queque del laboratorio. Mr. Brown thinks he's the center of the universe in the laboratory.*

creerse el ombligo del mundo (to think one is the belly button of the world) to think one is hot stuff *Sp* ◆ *No me gusta trabajar con Daniel porque se cree el ombligo del mundo y hay que escucharlo. I don't like to work with Daniel because he thinks he's hot stuff and you have to listen to him.*

creerse la divina garza (to think one is the divine heron) to think one is hot stuff *most of L. Am.* ◆ *Elena se cree la divina garza. Es muy egoísta. Elena thinks she's God's gift to humanity. She's very selfish.*

creerse la divina pomada (to think one is the divine cream) to think one is hot stuff *L. Am.* ◆ *Ese extranjero se cree la divina pomada y espera que lo admiremos. That foreigner thinks he's hot stuff and expects us to admire him.*

creerse la gran caca (to think one is the great poop) to think one is a big deal (vulgar) *Chicano, Mex, G, Col* ◆ *En la empresa donde Ricardo trabaja hay gente que se cree la gran caca. In the company where Ricardo works there are people who think they are hot shit.*

creerse la gran cosa (to think one is the big thing) to think one is a big deal, hot stuff (also, **cosota**) *Mex, DR, G, U, Arg, Sp* ◆ *No soporto a Raquel. Es una engreída; se cree la gran cosa. I can't stand Raquel. She's very conceited; she thinks she's hot stuff.*

creerse la última chupada del mango (to think one is the last suck on the mango) to think one is hot stuff *Mex* (RVAR *S. Cone:* **del mate,** of the mate, a strong tea) ◆ *Esmeralda se cree la última chupada del mango desde que se casó. Esmeralda thinks she's hot stuff since she got married.*

creerse la última Coca-Cola en el desierto (to think one is the last Coca-Cola in the desert) to think one is hot stuff, God's gift *Mex, DR, PR, ES, Nic, Pan, Col* ◆ *Carmen se ve muy bonita, ¿no? Su vestido es de París. —¡Pero es tan engreída! Se cree la última Coca-Cola en el desierto. Carmen looks very pretty, doesn't she? Her dress is from Paris. —But she's so stuck-up! She thinks she's God's gift.*

creído(-a) (believed) stuck-up *Mex, G, ES, Ch, U, Arg, Sp* ◆ *Tu hemana es muy creída, y ni siquiera me habla en el colegio. Your sister is very stuck-up, and she doesn't even speak to me at school.*

la **crema y nata** (cream and cream at the top of the milk) upper crust, highest social class *L. Am., Sp* ◆ *A esa boda va a ir gente de pura crema y nata. Only really upper-class people are going to go to that wedding.* ◆ *A* *la inauguración del teatro acudió toda la crema y nata de la sociedad dominicana. The upper crust of Dominican society attended the dedication of the theater.*

estar en la **cresta de la ola** (to be on the crest of the wave) to be riding high, at one's high point *Sp* ◆ *Esta cantante está en la cresta de la ola en este momento. This singer is riding high at this moment.*

el/la **cretino(-a)** (cretin) idiot *L. Am., Sp* ◆ *Ese cretino no sabe nada. That idiot doesn't know anything.*

criado(-a) a puro machete (raised by pure machete) badly raised or brought up *Mex, ES* ◆ *Qué mal educado ese chavo. Parece que fue criado a puro machete. How rude that kid is. It looks like he was brought up in a barn.*

criar margaritas to push up (grow) daisies, that is, to be dead *Mex, Sp* ◆ *Si no fuera por ti, estaría criando margaritas ahora. If it weren't for you, I'd be pushing up daisies now.*

la **criatura** (creature) baby *L. Am., Sp* ◆ *Esta criatura es muy hermosa e inteligente. This little one (baby) is very cute and intelligent.*

la **cruda** (rawness) hangover *Mex, C. Am.* ◆ *Al día siguiente de la fiesta tenía una cruda tremenda y no pude trabajar. The day after the party I had a horrible hangover and couldn't work.*

crudo →**tenerlo crudo**

estar **crudo(-a)** (to be raw) to be hung over *Mex, C. Am.* ◆ *Tomé tres tequilas anoche y estoy crudo. I drank three tequillas last night and I'm hung over.*

cruz →**hacerle la cruz a alguien; ¡Qué cruz!**

cruzado(-a) (crossed) high (on drugs or alcohol) *Mex* ◆ *Llegó cruzado a casa y se durmió. He came home high (drunk) and fell asleep.*

cruzar el charco (to cross the puddle) to cross a sea, usually to go to America or to the United States *Mex, Cuba, DR, PR, Sp* (RVar *U, Arg:* to go over the Uruguay River or Río de la Plata) ◆ *Por fin nos vamos a Europa. Tenía ganas de cruzar el charco. Finally we're going to Europe. I've been wanting to cross the pond.*

cruzarse los cables (to have one's cables crossed) to be off one's rocker, crazy *L. Am., Sp* ◆ *¿Cómo que vas a comprar otra computadora? ¿Se te cruzaron los cables? What's this about you buying another computer? Have you lost your marbles?*

el/la **cuadernícola** grind, very serious student who studies a lot; from **cuaderno**, notebook most of *L. Am.* ◆ *Es otro chiste sobre un cuadernícola. It's another joke about a grind.*

cuadrado 1. (square) corpulent, with a nice build (man) *Mex, G, ES, Sp* (RVar *U:* a very heavy person) ◆ *Hace mucho deporte y está cuadrado. He plays a lot of sports and has a nice build.* **2.** (square) hooked up with, going steady with *Col* ◆ *Juan está cuadrado con Marisa; llevan un año cuadrados. Juan is going steady with Marisa; they've been going together for a year.*

cuadrar (to square) to suit; to agree with *L. Am.* ◆ *No me cuadra el color de este vestido. I don't like the color of this dress (it doesn't look good on me).*

cuadrar con alguien to agree, make a deal, square things with someone *Mex, Cuba, Col* (RVar ALSO, IN *Cuba;* **cuadrar la caja con,** to make peace with) ◆ *Cuadramos con el jefe para salir temprano hoy. We squared things with the boss to leave early today.*

la **cuadratura del círculo** (the squareness of the circle) the impossibility or overcomplication of something *Mex, Sp* ◆ *Quieren demostrar la cuadratura del círculo. No entiendo cómo pueden insistir en algo que es imposible. They want to square the circle. I don't understand how they can insist on something that's impossible.*

de **cuando en cuando** (from when in when) from time to time *L. Am., Sp* ◆ *De cuando en cuando veo a los García. From time to time I see the Garcías.*

cuando Franco era cabo (corneta) (when Franco was a corporal [a trumpet player]) ages ago, a long time ago *Sp* ◆ *Nos conocimos cuando Franco era cabo y aún me quedaba pelo en la cabeza. We met a long time ago when Franco was a corporal and I still had hair on my head.*

¿Cuándo hemos comido en el mismo plato? (When have we eaten from the same plate?) Since when are we bosom buddies? *Mex, G, ES* ◆ *¿Cómo? ¿Ir de vacaciones juntos? ¿Cuándo hemos comido en el mismo plato? What? Go on vacation together? Since when are we such bosom buddies?*

cuando la rana eche pelos (when the frog sprouts hair) the twelfth of never, when hell freezes over *L. Am.* ◆ *¿Enrique te va a llamar? —Sí, cuando la rana eche pelos. Is Enrique going to call you? —Yes, when hell freezes over.*

cuando menos se piensa when one least expects it *L. Am., Sp* ◆ *El hijo de Lupe vive en Europa pero se asoma a su casa cuando menos se piensa. Lupe's son lives in Europe but shows up at her house when she least expects it.*

cuanto antes as soon as possible *L. Am., Sp* ◆ *La llamaré cuanto antes. I'll call her as soon as possible.*

¡Cuánto me alegro! How happy I am! *L. Am., Sp* ◆ *¿Vienes a la fiesta? ¡Cuánto me alegro! You're coming to the party? How happy I am!*

cuarta ➞**meter cuarta**

cuartel ➞**dar cuartel**

un **cuarto** ➞**no tener un cuarto**

el **cuarto de discusión** chat room; often, **el foro** *L. Am., Sp* (RVAR *Mex:* **el chat**) ◆ *Si te interesa ese tema, debes entrar en el cuarto de discusión. If you're interested in that topic, you should go in the chat room.*

el/la **cuate(-a)** good friend, pal *Mex, C. Am.* ◆ *Paco es un buen cuate. Paco is a good pal.*

cuatrapear to get all messed or mixed up; to turn out badly *Mex* ◆ *Todo se me cuatrapeó. Everything went wrong.*

el/la **cuatrojos** (four-eyes) four-eyes, person with glasses *L. Am.* ◆ *Me puse lentes de contacto para que no me dijeran cuatrojos. I put on contact lenses so they wouldn't call me four-eyes.*

una **cuba** ➞**estar como una cuba**

cubrirse de mierda (to cover oneself with shit) to dishonor oneself (vulgar) *Mex, Sp* ◆ *Gerónimo es muy deshonesto y se ha cubierto de mierda. Gerónimo is very dishonest and he's screwed himself (vulgar).*

la **cuca** (sedge; a sweet) female organ (vulgar) *DR, G, ES, Col, Ven*

la **cucha** ➞**irse a la cucha**

cuchara ➞**meter a alguien con cuchara una cosa; meter la cuchara**

cuchi-cuchi ➞**hacer cuchi-cuchi**

cuenta ➞**darse cuenta de; más de la cuenta; por su (propia) cuenta; tener en cuenta**

Cuenta conmigo. (Count with me.) You can count on me. *L. Am., Sp* ◆ *Necesitamos voluntarios. —Cuenta conmigo. We need volunteers. —You can count on me.*

cuentiar to sweet-talk; to butter up *Mex, G, ES, CR, Col* (RVAR *CR:* **cuentear**) ◆ *Ese hombre me estaba cuentiando, pero no le hice caso... lo mandé a volar. That man was sweet-talking me, but I didn't pay any attention to him . . . I told him to get lost (literally, told him to fly off).*

cuento ➞**no hacer el cuento; ¡Qué cuento!**

el **cuento chino** (Chinese story) big lie, fishy story *Mex, Nic, U, Arg, Sp* ◆ *Dime la verdad. No me vengas con cuentos chinos. Tell me the truth. Don't come to me with fishy stories.*

el **cuento de viejas** old wives' tale *most of L. Am., Sp* ◆ *¿Que el martes 13 es día de mala suerte? No, no, son cuentos de viejas. Tuesday (for English speakers, Friday) the thirteenth is a day of bad luck? No, no, those are old wives' tales.*

cuerda ➞**dar cuerda; por debajo de cuerda (bajo cuerda); tener mucha cuerda**

cuerno ➞**irse al cuerno; mandar a alguien al cuerno, a la eme; poner sobre los cuernos de la luna; ponerle los cuernos a alguien; tener cuernos**

el **cuero 1.** (skin, leather) girl, woman; pretty woman (a bit vulgar, RVAR especially *Ch*, where it can be a come-on) *ES, Col, Ec, Peru, Ch* ◆ *Tomás sale con un cuero de la capital. Tomás is going out with a chick from the capital.* **2.** attractive man or woman, fox, hunk *Mex* ◆ *¿Ya viste ese cuero? Did you see that good-looking guy (girl)?* **3.** easy woman (vulgar) *Cuba, DR, PR, Col* ◆ *En la escuela Martica tiene fama de cuero. At school Martica has a reputation for being easy.* **4.** (hide, leather) male organ (vulgar) *Chicano, Cuba, Col*

el **cuero** →**sacarle el cuero a alguien**

en **cueros** (in skins) in the raw, naked *Mex, DR, G, Sp* ◆ *Miguelito se puso en cueros en la playa.* Miguelito got naked at the beach.

cuesta abajo (arriba) downhill (uphill) *L. Am., Sp* ◆ *Tuve que caminar dos kilómetros cuesta arriba y estoy muy cansada.* I had to walk two kilometers uphill and I'm very tired.

cueste lo que cueste (cost whatever it may cost) come what may, no matter what *L. Am., Sp* ◆ *Cueste lo que cueste, tenemos que luchar por un mundo sin contaminación.* No matter what, we need to fight for a world without pollution.

la **cuestión** (issue, theme) thingamajig, whatchamacallit *DR, ES, Nic, Ch, U* ◆ *¿De qué cuestión estabas hablando?* What thingamajig were you talking about?

La **cuestión es que...** The thing is that . . . *L. Am., Sp* ◆ *La cuestión es que no sabemos dónde se encuentra el niño.* The thing is that we don't know where the boy is.

la **cueva** (cave) crib, teenagers' word for home *Mex, Col* ◆ *Tenemos que regresar a la cueva antes de la medianoche.* We need to get back to the crib before midnight.

Cuidado con la liebre. (Be careful of the hare.) Be careful (of the enemy). *Mex, ES, Col* ◆ *Cuidado con la liebre; la policía está cerca.* Be careful; the police are close by.

Cuídame el changarro. (Take care of my stand [at a market].) Take my place for a few minutes. *Mex, ES* ◆ *La gente va a llegar pronto y tengo que salir por refrescos. Cuídame el changarro un momento.* People are coming soon and I have to go get some soft drinks. Take my place for a minute.

cuidarse mucho to take good care, take care of oneself *L. Am., Sp* ◆ *Cuídate mucho, mamá.* Take good care of yourself, mom.

cul laidback, calm; super (from the English "cool") *Mex, DR* ◆ *Esa película fue muy cul.* That film was very cool.

culear to have sex (vulgar) *ES, Nic, CR, Ec, Ch*

el **culebrón** (big snake) soap opera *CR, Ven, Bol, Ch, Arg, Sp* ◆ *Estoy totalmente engan-*chado al culebrón mexicano de las cuatro de la tarde. I am completely hooked on the Mexican soap opera at four o'clock in the afternoon.

el/la **culero(-a)** lazy, uncooperative person, person who takes no initiative (vulgar, referring to **culo**; can also mean pedofile or homosexual, but not usually; commonly used in masculine) *Chicano, Mex, C. Am.* ◆ *Esos culeros no hicieron nada para ayudarnos.* Those assholes did nothing to help us.

el **culito** (small ass) piece of ass, hot chick, girl, woman (vulgar, like piece of ass) *Mex, G, Ven*

el **culo** ass (vulgar) *L. Am., Sp* ◆ *No tiene culo; por eso los pantalones le caen mal.* She has no ass; that's why pants look bad on her.

un **culo** →**como un (el) culo; hacer algo con el culo; ir de culo**

en el **culo del mundo** (in the world's ass) far away, in some damn godforsaken spot (vulgar) *PR, Nic, Ven, U, Arg, Sp* ◆ *Marcelino vive en el culo del mundo; para llegar allí tenemos que tomar varios autobuses.* Marcelino lives in some damn godforsaken spot; we have to take several buses to get there.

la **culpa** →**echar la culpa; tener la culpa**

la **cuña** (prop, wedge) connection (social, political, etc.) *S. Cone* ◆ *Aquí todo se arregla con cuñas.* Everything is arranged through connections here. ◆ *Tienen cuñas allí.* They have connections there.

el/la **curda** drunk (from Lunfardo, Buenos Aires slang) *Cuba, Ven, U, Arg* (RVar invariable in *Cuba, Arg* but **curdo** is used in *Ven* for masculine form; drunkenness) ◆ *Salimos del bar en curda.* We left the bar completely pickled. ◆ *Es un(a) curda. (Arg)* He (She) is a drunk.

una **curda** →**ponerse (estar) en curda, tener una curda**

el/la **currante** working guy/girl, rank and file *Sp* ◆ *Sólo soy un currante; díselo a mi jefe.* I'm just a worker; tell (it to) my boss.

currar to work *Sp* ◆ *¿En qué curras?* What kind of work do you do? ◆ *"Si te toca la lotería, el currar se va a acabar."* "If you win the lottery, work is going to end." (saying) el **curro** work, job *Sp* ◆ *Ahora tengo un buen curro.* *I have a good job now.*

cursi corny, too sentimental, often referring to someone who uses overly sweet or sentimental language *L. Am., Sp* ◆ *Tesoro divino de mi alma y corazón, ¿quieres ir a cenar?* *—Por favor, no seas tan cursi.* *Divine treasure of my soul and heart, do you want to go out for dinner? —Please don't be so sappy.*

curvas →¡Qué curvas y yo sin freno!

cutre poor, of low quality *Sp* ◆ *Es un bar muy cutre.* *It's a bar for down and outers.*

Le da el pie y le toma la mano. You give him or her an inch (literally, your foot) and he or she takes a mile (literally, your hand). *L. Am., Sp* (RVAR *Mex:* more common, **Le das la mano y se toma el pie.** Also, **Te dan la mano y quieres el pie.**)

Le da la mano y se agarra hasta el codo. (You give him or her a hand and he or she takes even the elbow.) Give him (her) an inch and he'll (she'll) take a mile. *ES, S. Cone, Sp* (RVAR *Mex:* **... y se toma el pie**) ◆ *Don Gervasio le dio la mano a sus nietos, y éstos se agarraron hasta el codo. Don Gervasio gave his grandchildren an inch and they took a mile.*

dabuten, dabuti very good, great *Sp* ◆ *Aquí todo va dabuten. Everything's going great here.* ◆ *Este vino está dabuti.* ◆ *This wine is super.*

dado →**poner como dado**

dale que dale on and on, over and over again, phrase that expresses repetition *L. Am., Sp* ◆ *Aquí estoy, dale que dale a la cocina. Here I am, working away in the kitchen.* ◆ *Ya me cansé de que siempre estés dale que dale al piano. I'm tired of you always banging away at the piano.*

Dame cinco dedos. Give me five (fingers). *Mex* ◆ *¡Hola, muchachos! Dame cinco dedos. Hi, boys! Give me five.*

Dame. Give me. (implies Give me five.) *Mex, Col*

daño: (no) hacer daño to (not) harm, hurt *L. Am., Sp* ◆ *No hace daño llamar. It doesn't hurt to call.*

dar a to face, be on *L. Am., Sp* ◆ *El hotel da a la plaza central. The hotel is on (facing) the main square.*

dar a alguien con la puerta en las narices (to slam the door on someone's nostrils) to refuse someone something, slam the door on him (her) *Mex, ES, S. Cone, Sp* ◆ *Fui al consulado para pedir los documentos, pero me dieron con la puerta en las narices. I went to the consulate to ask for the documents, but they turned me down.*

dar a entender (to give to understand) to lead to believe or think (something) *L. Am., Sp* ◆ *Tu mamá me dio a entender que estabas de vacaciones. Your mom led me to believe that you were on vacation.*

dar a luz (to give to light) to give birth *L. Am., Sp* ◆ *Mi esposa dio a luz hoy a las tres de la mañana. My wife gave birth today at three in the morning.* ◆ *Ayer Elena dio a luz a una nena. Elena had a baby girl yesterday.*

dar alas (to give wings) to stimulate, inspire; to lead on *Mex, DR, S. Cone, Sp* ◆ *No le sigas dando alas a Marcelo. Don't keep leading Marcelo on.*

dar asco (to give nausea) to make (someone) sick to his or her stomach, disgust *L. Am., Sp* ◆ *Esa carne me da asco. That meat makes me sick to my stomach (disgusts me).*

dar atole con el dedo a alguien (to give someone **atole** [a cornmeal drink] with the finger) to deceive someone, pull the wool over his or her eyes *Mex, CR* (RVAR *CR:* **dar atolillo**) ◆ *El jefe me prometió un aumento pero no me lo dio; me dio atole con el dedo. The boss promised me a raise but didn't give it to me; he pulled the wool over my eyes.*

dar bola a alguien (to give someone the ball) to pay attention to someone *CR, S. Cone* (RVAR *CR, U, Arg:* also, **dar pelota**) ◆ *Traté de explicar la situación, pero no me dieron bola. I tried to explain the situation, but they didn't give me the time of day.*

dar bombo a alguien (to give someone drum, fanfare) to praise someone to the skies, with exaggeration *Mex, DR, U* ◆ *Yo no sé por qué le dan tanto bombo a esa cantante... ¡tan mal que canta! I don't know why they praise that singer so highly . . . she sings so badly.*

dar cabida (to give space) to make room *L. Am., Sp* (RVAR *Mex, ES:* also, to turn on, tease a man sexually, said of women) ◆ *Va-*

mos a darle cabida; no te preocupes. We're going to make room; don't worry.

dar calabazas (ayotes) (to give pumpkins [squash]) to stand (someone) up, jilt *L. Am., Sp* (RVAR *Sp:* also, to fail someone [on an exam]; *C. Am.:* also, to make jealous) ◆ *Pobre Martín. Su novia le dio calabazas. Poor Martín. His girlfriend jilted him.*

dar carrete a alguien (to give someone a reel, coil) to put someone off, make them wait or keep them dangling; used like **dar cuerda** *Sp* ◆ *Ella le da carrete y le sigue hablando, pero él le dice que tiene que ir a trabajar. She strings him along and keeps talking to him, but he says he has to go to work.*

dar coba (to give flattery, tales) to flatter, usually to gain something, butter up, suck up *most of L. Am., Sp* ◆ *A Rolando lo nombraron vicepresidente del banco y lo único que sabe hacer es dar coba al presidente. They made Rolando vice president of the bank, and all he knows how to do is suck up to the president.*

dar consejos to give advice, advise *L. Am., Sp* ◆ *¿Qué consejos me das? What do you advise (me to do)?*

dar corte (to give cut) to be embarrassed or ashamed *DR, PR, Sp* ◆ *Me da corte hablar en público. I find it embarrassing to speak in public.*

dar cráneo (cabeza) (to give cranium, skull [head]) to rack one's brain, think a lot *Mex, PR* ◆ *El ingeniero le dio mucho cráneo a la construcción del puente. The engineer racked his brain over the construction of the bridge.*

dar cuartel (to give quarters, barracks) to help someone, give someone a break *L. Am., Sp* ◆ *Les vamos a dar cuartel a estos chicos porque siempre se han comportado bien. We're going to give these kids a break because they've always behaved well.*

dar cuerda (to give string) to string someone along, often in a provocative or annoying way or to butter up, sweet-talk *L. Am., Sp* (see illustration, page 408) ◆ *Carlos me iba dando cuerda para que le contara lo que realmente pasó. Carlos was buttering me up so that I would tell him what really happened.* ◆ *Deja de darle cuerda a Luis, que tú sabes cómo se pone. Stop jive-talking Luis; you know how he gets.*

dar diente con diente (to have teeth hitting each other) to be very cold or to be afraid, when teeth chatter *L. Am., Sp* ◆ *Vi una sombra a través de la ventana, y di diente con diente del susto. Resultó que era mi gato. I saw a shadow in the window, and my teeth chattered with fear. It turned out to be my cat.*

dar el boleto (to give the ticket) to give (someone) his or her walking papers *Mex, ES, U* (RVAR *Sp:* **dar la boleta**) ◆ *Mónica le dio el boleto a su novio. Mónica gave her boyfriend his walking papers.*

dar el callo (to give callus) to work one's fingers to the bone *Sp* ◆ *Aunque pensábamos que Jorge no trabajaba, dio el callo tanto o más que los demás. Although we thought that Jorge didn't work, he worked his fingers to the bone as much as or more than anyone else.*

dar el cante (to give flamenco singing) to call attention to oneself and look ridiculous *Sp* ◆ *Carlos iba dando el cante con ese sombrero de color rojo. Carlos was calling attention to himself and looked ridiculous with that red hat.*

dar el pésame (to give the "it weighs on me") to give condolences, express one's sympathy in times of death or misfortune *L. Am., Sp* ◆ *Tenemos que ir a dar el pésame a la señora García y su familia. We have to go give our condolences to Mrs. García and her family.*

dar en el blanco to hit the target, to get or be right *L. Am., Sp* ◆ *Diste en el blanco, amigo: necesito un préstamo. You got that right, my friend: I need a loan.*

dar en el clavo to hit the nail on the head, figure out or be right about something *L. Am., Sp* ◆ *¡Eso es! Diste en el clavo. That's right! You hit the nail on the head.*

dar en la madre (romper/partir la madre) (to give in the mother [to break the mother]) to hit hard, hurt someone where he or she is vulnerable *Chicano, Mex, C. Am., Col* ◆ *Si no te callas, te voy a romper (partir) la madre. If you don't shut up, I'm going to beat the living daylights out of you.* ◆ *Le dieron en la madre. They gave it to him (her) where it hurts.*

dar en la torre (to give in the tower) to knock (someone's) block off, fix (someone) good, hurt someone where he or she is vulnerable *Mex, C. Am.* ◆ *Me dieron en la torre. They knocked my block off.*

dar (un) esquinazo (to hit someone with a corner) to steer clear of, go out of one's way so as not to encounter (someone) *Arg, Sp* ◆ *Mi amigo me dio un esquinazo. My friend went out of his way to avoid me.* ◆ *Vi a ese profesor tan pesado en la calle, pero le di esquinazo. I saw that jerk of a professor walking down the street, but I gave him the cold shoulder.*

dar entrada (to give entrance) to flirt *Mex* ◆ *Lilián le daba entrada al novio de su amiga. Lilián was flirting with her friend's boyfriend.*

dar frente a to face *L. Am., Sp* ◆ *La catedral da frente al parque. The cathedral faces the park.*

dar fruto to bear (literally, give) fruit *L. Am., Sp* ◆ *Pensamos que en tres meses nuestros esfuerzos empezarán a dar fruto. We think that in three months our efforts will begin to bear fruit.*

dar (pasar) gato por liebre (to give cat for rabbit) to deceive someone, giving them something inferior, give (someone) a lemon *L. Am., Sp* (see illustration, page 314) ◆ *La cámara que compré el lunes ya se estropeó; creo que me dieron gato por liebre. The camera I bought Monday is already broken; I think I got a pig in a poke.*

dar hielo (to give ice) to treat coldly, not pay attention to someone, give the cold shoulder *Mex, Cuba, DR, Ch* (RVAR *DR:* **hacer el hielo;** *Ch:* **poner al hielo;** *Mex:* **hacer a alguien la ley del hielo**) ◆ *Yo fui a saludarlo muy simpática y el tipo me hizo un hielo... yo no sé qué le hice. (DR) I went up to greet him very nicely and the guy gave me the cold shoulder . . . I don't know what I did to him.*

dar igual, dar lo mismo (to give the same) to be all the same to, be indifferent *L. Am., Sp* ◆ *Me da igual (lo mismo) ir a la fiesta que no ir. Going to the party or not is all the same to me.*

dar la bienvenida to welcome *L. Am., Sp* ◆ *Miren, aquí llegan los Montaño. ¡Vamos a darles la bienvenida! Look, here comes the Montaño family. Let's welcome them!*

dar la enhorabuena to offer congratulations *L. Am., Sp* ◆ *Todos le dieron la enhorabuena al novio. Everyone congratulated the groom.*

dar la nota (to give the note) to stand out in a bad way *Bol, U, Arg, Sp* ◆ *Le gusta llamar la atención y siempre da la nota. He (She) likes to attract attention and always sticks out like a sore thumb.*

dar la nota alta (to give the high note) to stand out, often in a bad way *DR, Nic, Ch* ◆ *Decidió no dejar su trabajo de maestro porque en la literatura estaba claro que no iba a dar la nota alta. He decided not to leave his teaching job because it was clear that in literature he wasn't going to stand out.*

dar la puntilla (to give the dagger) to finish off, be the ruin of someone *Sp* ◆ *Sus insultos al gerente fue lo que le acabó de dar la puntilla. Está despedido. His insults to the manager were what led to his ruin (finished him off). He's fired.*

dar la última pincelada (to give the last brush stroke) to put on the finishing touch, to perfect *Sp* ◆ *Anoche dimos la última pincelada al proyecto; mañana lo presentamos en público. Last night we put the finishing touch on the project; tomorrow we present it in public.*

dar la vuelta a la tortilla (to turn over the omelette) to turn the tables *Ch, Sp* ◆ *Rosario ha dado la vuelta a la tortilla y ahora es ella la que manda en esa casa. Rosario has turned the tables and now she's the one who gives the orders in that house.*

dar lata (to give tin can) to give someone a hard time; to annoy; to bore by talking a lot *L. Am., Sp* (RVAR *Sp:* **dar la lata**) ◆ *Estos vecinos no paran de darnos la lata con la música. Cada noche igual. These neighbors never stop annoying us with their music. Every night the same thing.*

dar leña (to give wood) to beat up, hit *Cuba, DR, PR, U, Sp* ◆ *Ese bestia le dio mucha leña a su mujer y la tuvieron que ingresar en el hospital. That animal beat his wife senseless and they had to take her to the hospital.*

dar(se) manija (to give [oneself] a crank, pull with a string) to fire up, inspire enthusiasm (get fired up or enthusiastic about) *U,*

Arg ◆ *¡No te des manija!* Don't get carried away! ◆ *No le des más manija a ese muchacho, que se va a terminar enamorando de ti.* Don't go getting that boy all worked up. He's going to wind up falling in love with you. ◆ *La manija que le dio el presidente a su discurso fue exagerada.* The enthusiasm that the president put into his speech was exaggerated.

dar marcha (to give march) to give energy, a lift *Sp* ◆ *Esa música me da mucha marcha.* That music gives me a real lift.

dar marcha atrás to back up; to back off or down on *L. Am., Sp* ◆ *El camionero dio marcha atrás y topó con la pared.* The truck driver backed up and ran into the wall. ◆ *El gobierno dio marcha atrás en su plan de cerrar la clínica.* The government backed down on its plans to close the clinic.

dar pasaporte a alguien 1. (to give someone passport) to give someone his or her walking papers, break off with someone *Mex, ES, Sp* ◆ *Le dimos pasaporte a la secretaria porque no estaba haciendo su trabajo.* We gave the secretary her walking papers because she wasn't doing her job. **2.** (to give someone passport) to kill off, wipe out, knock off *Mex, ES, Sp* ◆ *Si te sigue jodiendo, le van a dar pasaporte.* If he keeps screwing you around, they're going to knock him off.

dar picones (to give scratches) to provoke, antagonize, rile up, excite *Mex, ES* (RVAR *ES:* also, **dar chile**) ◆ *En la fiesta mi ex-novia me daba picones.* At the party my ex-girlfriend was bugging (provoking) me.

dar (un) plantón (to give [a] planting) to stand (someone) up; also, **plante** *L. Am., Sp* (RVAR *Ch, Arg:* **pegarse un plantón**) ◆ *Me dio un plantón porque le surgió un problema en el último momento.* He (She) stood me up because something came up at the last minute. ◆ *No me des plantón.* Don't stand me up.

dar (pedir) pon to give (ask for) a ride *PR, Col, Sp* ◆ *Otra vez se me dañó el carro. Tengo que pedirle pon al vecino. (PR)* The car is out of commission (damaged) again. I have to ask the neighbor for a ride.

dar saltos de alegría (to give jumps of happiness) to jump for joy *L. Am., Sp* ◆ *Con la* noticia que le dieron sobre su hija, Susana daba saltos de alegría.* When they gave her the news about her daughter, Susana was jumping for joy.

dar tiempo al tiempo (to give time to time) to give something enough time, be patient, wait for an opportunity *Mex, DR, PR, ES, Ch* ◆ *Dale tiempo al tiempo y verás cómo se resuelven las cosas.* Give it some time and you'll see that things will work out.

dar (pedir) un aventón to give (ask for) a ride *Mex, ES, Nic* ◆ *Mi amiga me dio un aventón porque mi carro está en el taller.* My friend gave me a ride because my car is in the shop.

dar un cortón a alguien to cut someone down to size in a sharp reply *Mex* (RVAR *Sp:* **dar un corte**) ◆ *Julio le dio un cortón muy feo.* Julio cut him (her) down in an ugly way.

dar un examen (to give an exam) to take a test *L. Am., Sp* ◆ *Ayer me tocó dar un examen de matemáticas.* Yesterday I had to take a math test.

dar un golpe (to give a hit) to make a hit, steal or rob *Mex, ES, U, Sp* ◆ *Dos asaltantes dieron un golpe en el banco y se llevaron mucho dinero.* Two robbers made a hit on the bank and got away with a great deal of money.

dar (pedir) un jalón to give (ask for) a ride *ES, CR, Peru* (RVAR *CR:* **ir al jalón**, to hitchhike) ◆ *Me dieron un jalón al centro.* They gave me a ride downtown.

dar un paseo to take a walk or ride *L. Am., Sp* ◆ *Dimos un paseo por la playa.* We took a walk along the beach.

dar un paso to take a step *L. Am., Sp* ◆ *Hoy Tomasito dio su primer paso.* Today Tomasito took his first step.

dar un toque (to give a touch) to give notice *Sp* ◆ *Nos dieron un toque de que debíamos evacuar el edificio.* They gave us notice that we should evacuate the building.

dar una achurada (to eviscerate) to give (someone) a scolding or dirty deal, chew out *U, Arg* ◆ *A Juan le dieron una achurada tremenda en la oficina.* They gave Juan a heck of a dirty deal at the office.

dar una cantaleta to give a sermon, repeat something ad nauseam, lecture at *Mex, DR, C. Am., Col, Peru* ◆ *La jefa nos dio una can-*

taleta y sabíamos que tenía razón. The boss lectured at us, and we knew she was right.

dar una clavada (to give a nailing) to charge more than what is proper or right, rip off *DR, Arg, Sp* ◆ *En ese restaurante me dieron una clavada. That restaurant was a real rip-off for me.*

dar una mano to give (someone) a hand; also, **echar una mano** *Mex, Cuba, DR, PR, G, S. Cone, Sp* (RVAR *Sp:* **echar una mano** only) ◆ *Necesito ayuda, ¿Puedes darme una mano? I need help. Can you give me a hand?*

dar una patada to (give a) kick *L. Am., Sp* ◆ *El niño, enojado, le dio una patada al pobre gato. The child was angry and kicked the poor cat.*

dar una puñalada por la espalda to stab in the back *L. Am., Sp* ◆ *No podía creer que mi hermana saliera con mi ex-marido. ¡Qué puñalada me dio por la espalda! I couldn't believe that my sister was going out with my ex-husband. What a stab in the back (she gave me)!*

dar una vuelta to go for a walk or ride *L. Am., Sp* ◆ *Dieron una vuelta en su nuevo Mercedes. They went for a ride in their new Mercedes.*

dar vuelta a la página (to turn the page) to put some unpleasant experience from the past behind you and go forward, turn over a new leaf *ES, CR, S. Cone, Sp* (RVAR *Sp:* also, **pasar o girar página**) ◆ *Es mejor olvidarnos de ese asunto y dar vuelta a la página. It's better to forget that affair and let bygones be bygones (put the whole thing behind us).*

darle (duro) (to give to it [hard]) to apply oneself, give it one's all *Mex, DR, C. Am., S. Cone* ◆ *¿Cómo te va? –Aquí, dándole (dándole duro). How's it going? —I'm here, at it.* ◆ *¡Dale duro! Go for it! Give it all you've got!*

darle a alguien el punto (to give someone the point) to feel like (doing something), get in a mood (**punto** means attitude, state of mind, mood) *Sp* ◆ *El otro día me dio el punto y mandé a mi jefe a freír espárragos. The other day I got in a mood and told my boss to go jump in the lake.*

darle a alguien la gana (to give someone the desire) to feel like or have a yen (to do

something) *L. Am., Sp* ◆ *Lo hice porque me dio la gana. I did it because I felt like it.*

darle a alguien la real gana (to give someone the royal desire) to want to do something with or without a reason; to do exactly what one pleases *Mex, S. Cone, Sp* ◆ *Alberto siempre hace lo que le da la real gana. Alberto always does exactly what he pleases.*

darle a alguien la regalada gana (to give someone the gifted desire) to want to do something with or without a reason; to do whatever one pleases *Mex, ES* ◆ *Me fui a la playa toda la tarde porque se me dio la regalada gana. I went to the beach the whole afternoon just because I felt like it.*

darle al coco (to give to the coconut, head) to rack one's brain, think, study *Mex, Sp* ◆ *Le tuvimos que dar al coco para poder resolver el problema que el profesor nos planteó en clase. We had to rack our brains to be able to solve the problem the professor gave us in class.*

darle con la puerta en las narices (to slam the door on one's nostrils) to slam the door in one's face, turn down *L. Am., Sp* ◆ *Cuando les pedí un aumento, me dieron con la puerta en las narices. When I asked them for a raise, they slammed the door in my face (turned me down).*

darle la mano a alguien (to give someone your hand) to shake hands *L. Am., Sp* ◆ *Le dio la mano al gerente. He (She) shook hands with the manager.*

darle lástima a alguien to make someone sad, make someone feel pity *L. Am., Sp* ◆ *Me da lástima ver a mi hija tan deprimida. It makes me sad to see my daughter so depressed.*

darle mala espina (to give one bad thorn) to give one a bad feeling (about someone or something) *L. Am., Sp* ◆ *Me da mala espina que todavía no han llegado. It gives me a bad feeling that they still haven't gotten here (arrived).*

darle mate (to give kill) to kill off, finish *Mex* ◆ *Vamos a darle mate al pastel. Let's finish off the cake.*

darle palo (to give someone stick) to be a pain, be disagreeable to, not want to *Sp* ◆ *Me da palo salir con él, pero tengo que ir. I hate* *going out with him (Going out with him is a pain), but I have to go.*

darle/meterle caña (to give/put cane to it) to lay it on, give it a lot of effort *Sp* ◆ *Métele caña al acelerador, que vas muy despacio. Floor it (apply more effort to the accelerator); you're going very slowly.* ◆ *Dale más caña, que no llegaremos nunca. Speed it up, or we'll never get there.*

darse (to give up): see **darse por vencido**

darse (agarrarse) una rabieta to have a fit, tantrum *L. Am., Sp* ◆ *A Marta le dio una rabieta porque no había chocolate en casa. Marta threw a fit because there wasn't any chocolate in the house.*

darse coba (to give oneself flattery) to be full of oneself, brag, put on airs *Mex, DR, CR, Sp* ◆ *Ese tipo es un engreído; todo el día se la pasa dándose coba. That guy is stuck-up; he spends all day tooting his own horn.*

darse cuenta de to realize *L. Am., Sp* ◆ *Hoy es el primero de mayo: ¿te das cuenta? Today's the first of May: do you realize that?*

darse el lote (to give each other the lot) to hug and kiss *Sp* ◆ *Se estaban dando el lote cuando de repente aparecieron sus abuelos. They were making out when suddenly his (her) grandparents appeared.*

darse el piro to escape, go off (like **pirotécnica**, fireworks) *Sp* ◆ *Cuando los ladrones vieron a la policía, intentaron darse el piro pero fueron alcanzados. When the thieves saw the police, they tried to escape but they were overtaken.*

darse en el queso (to give it to oneself in the cheese) to smack oneself, hit oneself in the face *Mex* ◆ *Me caí y me di en el queso. I fell down and smacked myself in the chops.*

darse la buena (gran) vida (to give oneself the good [great] life) to live it up, enjoy oneself *Mex, DR, PR, S. Cone* (RVar *Sp*: **darse la vida padre**) ◆ *Yo quiero ganarme el premio de la lotería para darme la buena vida y no tener que trabajar. I want to win the prize in the lottery so I can live it up and won't have to work.*

darse la mano to shake hands *L. Am., Sp* ◆ *Los tenistas se dieron la mano después del partido. The tennis players shook hands after the game.*

darse lija (to give oneself sandpaper) to be full of oneself, put on airs *Cuba, PR, CR* ◆ *Tito se da lija delante de la gente para disimular su timidez. Tito puts on airs in front of people to hide his shyness.*

darse paquete (to give oneself package) to be full of oneself, put on airs *Mex, G* ◆ *Lucy se da mucho paquete desde que se sacó la lotería. Lucy is really full of herself since she won the lottery.*

darse por vencido(-a) to give up, surrender *L. Am., Sp* ◆ *No te des por vencida; hay que seguir buscando. Don't give up; you (we) have to keep looking.*

darse prisa to be in a hurry, hurry up *L. Am., Sp* ◆ *Date prisa, Enrique, que ya son las nueve. Hurry up, Enrique, it's nine o'clock already.*

darse taco (to give oneself taco or plug) to be full of oneself, put on airs *Mex, Hond, CR* ◆ *Penélope se da mucho taco, como si ella mandara. Penélope is full of herself, as if she were in charge (giving orders).*

darse un atracón (to give oneself a big assault) to do something in excess, go over the top *Mex, DR, ES, Ch, Sp* ◆ *Después del bautizo, nos dimos un atracón en el restaurante. After the baptism, we went over the top at the restaurant.*

darse un cagazo (to take a big shit) to have a terrible fright (vulgar) *U, Arg* ◆ *Escuché un ruido en la sala y me dí un cagazo terrible. Pensé que había entrado un ladrón a la casa. I heard a noise in the living room, and it scared the shit out of me. I thought a thief had come into the house.*

darse un quemón (to burn oneself) to have a little surprise (usually visual, probably from **quemarse las pestañas**) *Mex* ◆ *Mira su página para darte un quemón. Look at his (web) page for a surprise.*

darse una clavada (to get hit by a nail) to have a bad or boring (crummy) time *Arg* ◆ *Fui a una fiesta aburridísima; me di una clavada tremenda. I went to a tremendously dull party; I was bored out of my mind.*

darse unas palizas (to beat oneself up with sticks) to get all worn out and sore (e.g., from walking) *U, Sp* ◆ *Se da unas palizas de caminar (trabajar). He (She) gets totally beat from walking (working).*

dársela a alguien con queso (to give it to someone with cheese) to deceive, make fun of *Sp* ◆ *Yo te conozco, y a mí no me la vas a dar con queso. I know you, and you're not going to fool me.*

dárselas de... (to give them to oneself as . . .) to pretend to be or act like . . . (also, **picarse de...**) *L. Am., Sp* ◆ *Se las da de culta, pero no lo es. She acts like she's well educated (cultured), but she isn't.*

decir a alguien (las) cuatro verdades (to tell someone the four truths) to tell someone exactly what one thinks is the truth; to get it off one's chest *ES, DR, PR, Ch, Sp* ◆ *Ana le dijo cuatro verdades para hacerle ver que no estaba en su derecho de seguir hiriendo a la gente. Ana gave him a piece of her mind to make him see that he had no right to keep hurting people.*

decir adiós con la mano (to say good-bye with the hand) to wave good-bye *L. Am., Sp* ◆ *El bebé decía adiós con la mano, contento de salir de la consulta. The baby waved good-bye, happy to leave the doctor's office.*

decir al pan pan y al vino vino (to call bread bread and wine wine) to tell something directly and without beating around the bush, tell it like it is *L. Am., Sp* ◆ *No le gustó mi idea, pero dije al pan pan y al vino vino. He didn't like my idea, but I told it like it is.*

decir amén a todo (to say amen to everything) to always agree, be a yes man *DR, ES, S. Cone, Sp* (RVar *Ch:* more common, **llevar el amén**) ◆ *A ella no le gustan los problemas: siempre dice amén a todo. She doesn't like problems: she always goes along with everything.*

decir cuatro cosas (to tell four things) to give (someone) a piece of one's mind, tell it like it is (often used in anger) *DR, PR, ES, Nic, Ec, Peru, Ch* (RVar *ES:* **decir tres o cuatro cosas**) ◆ *Estaba tan enojada que le dije cuatro cosas y la mandé al diablo. I was so mad that I gave her a piece of my mind and told her to go to the devil.*

decir madres (to say mothers) to bitch out, say crude or stupid things to or about, insult *Mex, Col* ◆ *Elena siempre dice madres de sus compañeras de trabajo. Elena always says really bad things about her coworkers.*

decir: ¡No me diga(s)! (Don't tell me!) You don't say! Really? *L. Am., Sp* ◆ *¿Me mintieron? ¡No me digas! They lied to me? Really?*

dedicarse: ¿A qué se dedica usted? What do you do for a living? *L. Am., Sp* ◆ *¿A qué te dedicas, mujer? —Soy contadora. What do you do for a living, my friend? — I'm an accountant.*

dedo →**hacer dedo; no mover un dedo; no tener dos dedos de frente**

defender a capa y espada (to defend with cape and sword) to always back someone up, take care of; to defend vehemently (e.g., a point of view) *L. Am., Sp* (see illustration, page 291) ◆ *Defendió esa opinión a capa y espada. He (She) defended that opinion to the hilt.*

defenderse (to defend oneself) to manage, get along *L. Am., Sp* ◆ *No te preocupes... me voy defendiendo. Don't worry . . . I'm managing.* ◆ *No hablo bien el japonés, pero me defiendo. I don't speak Japanese very well, but I get along.*

Deja de comer mierda. (Stop eating shit.) Cut the crap. Stop with your foolishness, trickery. (vulgar) *Mex, DR, Col* (RVar *Col:* also, stop letting people treat you badly) ◆ *Deja de comer mierda y habla en serio. Cut the crap and talk seriously.*

Deja de decir fanfarronadas. Stop tooting your own horn (bragging). (**tú** form) *Mex* ◆ *No te creo, Luis. Deja de decir fanfarronadas y pon los pies en la tierra. I don't believe you, Luis. Stop tooting your own horn and come down to earth.*

dejado(-a) (left behind) loser, has-been, unworthy or irresponsible *G, ES, Nic, Ch, U* ◆ *Emiliano es un dejado; no sé por qué Leticia sale con él. Emiliano is a loser; I don't know why Leticia is going out with him.*

dejar a alguien en cueros (to leave someone naked) to rob everything, take someone to the cleaners *Mex, U, Arg* ◆ *Me han dejado en cueros. They took me to the cleaners.*

dejar a alguien frío(-a) (helado[-a]) (to leave someone cold [frozen]) to shock, surprise *L. Am., Sp* (RVar *ES:* also, **fresco**; *Sp:* also, **Me trae al fresco.**) (see illustration, page 395) ◆ *La noticia de la muerte del pre-*

sidente me dejó fría. The news of the president's death left me in shock.

dejar a alguien sin camisa/quitarle hasta la camisa (to leave someone without a shirt/to take even someone's shirt) to ruin someone, take someone to the cleaners *Mex, U, Sp* ◆ *Las mujeres y las parrandas han dejado a mi primo sin camisa. Women and partying have ruined my cousin.*

dejar caer to let (something) fall, drop *L. Am., Sp* ◆ *Dejé caer la leche... ¡qué lío! I dropped the milk . . . what a mess!*

dejar colgado(-a) (to leave hung, suspended) to stand up, leave hanging, ditch *Mex, ES, U, Arg, Sp* ◆ *Mi novio me dejó colgada antes de la boda. My fiancé stood me up before the wedding.* ◆ *Me dejó colgado en la puerta del cine. She left me waiting at the door of the movie theater.* ◆ *Cerraron la puerta y me quedé fuera colgada. They closed the door and I was left hanging there outside.* ◆ *Estaba colgada al teléfono. (ES) She was stuck on the phone.*

dejar con los churquitos (colochos) hechos (to leave [someone] with their curls done) to stand up, leave waiting *C. Am., Caribbean* ◆ *¡Otra vez me dejó con los churquitos hechos! He (She) stood me up again!* ◆ *No me dejes con los colochos hechos. Don't stand me up.*

dejar de (hacer algo) to stop (doing something) *L. Am., Sp* ◆ *Deja de molestar, Juanito. Stop bothering people, Juanito.*

dejar el pellejo (to leave one's hide or skin) to kick the bucket, die *Mex, Sp* ◆ *Pobre. Dejó el pellejo en Guanajuato. Poor guy. He kicked the bucket in Guanajuato.*

dejar la escoba (to leave the broom) to spill the beans, disclose information that is shocking or embarrassing *Bol, Ch* (RVAR *Ch*: also, to mess something up) ◆ *Cristina se emborrachó en la fiesta y dejó la escoba. Ahora todos saben que ella sale con un hombre casado. Cristina got drunk at the party and spilled the beans. Now everyone knows that she's dating a married man.*

dejar planchado(-a) a alguien (to leave someone ironed) to knock someone for a loop, leave someone unable to respond to some unforeseen act or something said; to wear out *Sp* ◆ *El entrenador nos dejó plan-*

chados a todos. No podíamos ni hablar después del entreno. The coach wore us all out. We couldn't even speak after the training session.

dejar plantado(-a) (to leave [someone] planted) to stand up, ditch *L. Am., Sp* ◆ *No me dejes plantada. Don't stand me up.*

dejarle a alguien el tren (to have the train leave you) to lose out; often, to be left a spinster *DR, CR, Col, Ch* (RVAR *Mex:* **irse el tren**) ◆ *A María ya le ha dejado el tren; tiene más de cincuenta años y no ha podido encontrar el galán de su vida. María has lost out; she's more than fifty years old and hasn't found the love (literally, beau) of her life.*

dejarse caer (to let oneself fall) to drop by *Bol, Ch, Sp* ◆ *Si voy a Barcelona, me dejaré caer por tu casa. If I go to Barcelona, I'll drop by your house.*

dejarse de cuentos (de historias) (to leave off with stories) to stop telling stories, get to the point, cut to the chase *L. Am., Sp* ◆ *Déjate de cuentos. That's enough of your tall tales.* ◆ *Déjate de historias. ¿Qué pasó? Stop with the nonsense. What happened?*

Déjate de chiquilladas. (Stop the childish behavior.) Stop the foolishness. *ES, U, Arg, Sp* ◆ *Eres un hombre. ¡Déjate de chiquilladas! You're a man. Stop that childish behavior!*

delicia →**¡Qué delicia!**

demasié short for **demasiado**, too much *Sp* ◆ *Esa historia es demasié. No se la va a creer nadie. That story is too much. Nobody is going to believe it.*

del **demonio** (of the devil) super (good or bad), extraordinary, tremendous *Sp* ◆ *La maldita montaña del demonio se resistió a ser escalada hasta el tercer intento. The damned mountain wouldn't be climbed (literally, resisted being climbed) until the third attempt.*

el **demonio** →**llevarse (a alguien) el demonio; llevarse el demonio; mandar a alguien al demonio**

dentro →**por dentro y por fuera**

la **depre** (short for **depresión**) blues, depression *L. Am., Sp* ◆ *Tengo una depre que no me deja pensar en nada. I'm so depressed I can't think about anything.*

derecho(-a) →**hecho(-a) y derecho(-a)**

desbancar to push (someone) out of the way, take a job away from someone *U, Arg, Sp* ◆ *La chica minusválida desbancó a todo el resto de los concursantes. Es una persona extremadamente inteligente.* The disabled girl blew away all the rest of the contestants. She's an extremely intelligent person.

el/la **descarado(-a)** (the faceless one) scoundrel, creep *L. Am., Sp* ◆ *¡Qué descarado!* What a creep! (What a nasty person!)

la **descarga** (discharge, unloading) good time or jam session *PR, Cuba, Col* ◆ *Tremenda descarga la del conjunto.* Fantastic jam session by the band.

descargar (to discharge, unload) to let loose with emotion, let it all out *Mex, Cuba, PR, Col* (RVAR *Mex:* usually negative emotion, like **desahogarse**) ◆ *Llegó furiosa y descargó todo en su esposo. (Mex)* She was furious when she arrived and took it all out on her husband.

descaro →**¡Qué descaro!**

deschavetado(-a) (headless) stupid, dumb *Mex, ES, Ch* ◆ *Jorge todo el tiempo anda deschavetado, como en las nubes.* Jorge goes around all the time like an airhead, in the clouds.

descojonado(-a) (without testicles) said of someone when they have problems (vulgar); broke or not working (from **descojonar**) *Mex, DR, PR, Col* ◆ *¿Qué pasa con el televisor? —Está descojonado.* What's wrong with the television set? —It's screwed up.

descojonar (to de-testicle) to screw up, ruin, mess up *Mex, DR, PR, Col* ◆ *Por una estupidez, Mario descojonó la relación con sus suegros.* Over some stupid thing, Mario messed up his relationship with his in-laws.

descojonarse de risa (to de-testicle oneself with laughter) to laugh one's ass off, laugh uncontrollably (vulgar) *Sp* ◆ *Se descojonaron de risa cuando oyeron el chiste.* They laughed their asses off when they heard the joke.

descolgarse (to unhang oneself) to appear suddenly *Mex, ES* ◆ *Estaba lavando los platos cuando mi prima se descolgó.* I was washing the dishes when my cousin popped in.

desconectar (to disconnect) to avoid reality, relax, tune out *Mex, Cuba, DR, Col, U, Sp* ◆ *Cuando no me interesa la lección, desconecto.* When I'm not interested in the lesson, I tune out.

descubrirse el pastel (to discover the cake) to have the lid blown off a story, have a secret revealed *Mex, S. Cone, Sp* ◆ *Ayer se descubrió el pastel. Ahora todo el mundo lo sabe.* Yesterday the lid was blown off the story. Now everyone knows.

desde chico(-a) since childhood *L. Am., Sp* ◆ *Lo conozco desde chico.* I've known him since childhood.

desde el principio (from the first) all along, from the beginning *L. Am., Sp* ◆ *Lo sospechaba desde el principio; no me caía bien.* I suspected him all along; I didn't care for him.

desde entonces since then *L. Am., Sp* ◆ *Compraron un perro hace dos meses y desde entonces dan una vuelta todas las tardes.* They bought a dog two months ago and since then they take a stroll every afternoon.

desde ese día en adelante from that day on *L. Am., Sp* ◆ *Desde ese día en adelante somos buenos amigos.* From that day on we've been good friends.

desde hace mucho tiempo (muchos años) for a long time (many years) *L. Am., Sp* ◆ *Viven allí desde hace mucho tiempo.* They've lived there for a long time.

desde luego of course *L. Am., Sp* ◆ *¿No quieres ir a ver a tus padres? —Desde luego.* Don't you want to go see your parents? —Of course.

desde que el mundo es mundo since the world began *L. Am., Sp* ◆ *La ley del más fuerte existe desde que el mundo es mundo.* Survival of the fittest (literally, the law of the strongest) has existed since the world began.

el **desentendido(-a)** →**hacerse el/la desentendido(-a)**

desgracia →**por desgracia**

Desgraciado en el juego, afortunado en amores. (Unlucky in a game or gambling, lucky in loves.) Unlucky at cards, lucky with love, said to console someone who has lost a game or at gambling *Mex, ES, S. Cone, Sp* ◆ *Siempre le digo a Cristina que* *es desgraciada en el juego porque es afortunada en amores.* I always tell Cristina that she is unlucky with cards because she's lucky with love.

desgraciado(-a) →**más desgraciado(-a) que el Pupas**

Las **desgracias nunca vienen solas.** (Bad things never come alone.) It never rains but it pours. L. Am., Sp ◆ *Perdí el autobus, llegué tarde al trabajo, no pude terminar a tiempo mi informe y supe que mi novia me engaña. Las desgracias nunca vienen solas.* I missed the bus, arrived late to work, couldn't finish my report on time, and I found out my girlfriend was cheating on me. It never rains but it pours.

deshojando la margarita (taking off the petals from the daisy) worrying "Does he/she love me or not?" L. Am., Sp ◆ *Pilar está deshojando la margarita, y con el matrimonio a la vuelta de la esquina.* Pilar is worrying, "Does he love me or not?," and with the wedding right around the corner.

desmadrar 1. (to dismother) to beat up *Chicano, Mex, Col* ◆ *Me van a desmadrar en la escuela si me ven con esta camisa rosada.* They're going to give me a major beating at school if they see me with this pink shirt. **2.** (to dismother) to go too far, get a bit out of control *PR, ES, Sp* ◆ *Esa chica era muy tímida, pero se está desmadrando últimamente.* That girl was very shy, but she's getting out of control lately.

el **desmadre** (dismother) mess, confusion *Chicano, Mex, C. Am., Ec, Sp* ◆ *Había siempre un desmadre en esa casa.* There was always a mess in that house. ◆ *Fue un desmadre total.* It was a total disaster.

desnudar a un santo para vestir a otro (to strip one statue of a saint naked to dress another) to move something unnecessarily or take something from one person and give it to another when both need it, rob Peter to pay Paul *S. Cone* ◆ *Con la reestructuración del presupuesto de la provincia, el gobernador desnudó a un santo para vestir a otro.* With the restructuring of the province's budget, the governor robbed Peter to pay Paul.

la **despedida de soltero(-a)** (the sending off of the single person) stag party or bridal shower *L. Am., Sp* ◆ *El sábado le haremos* *una despedida de soltera a Betania.* Saturday we'll have a bridal shower for Betania. ◆ *Los amigos del novio le harán una despedida de soltero en el club.* The groom's friends will have a stag party for him at the club.

despegar la boca (to unstick the mouth) to talk, spit it out, open up *Mex, Sp* ◆ *Apúrate. Despega la boca y dinos la verdad.* Hurry up. Spit it out and tell us the truth.

despelotado(-a) disorganized, messy, messed up *S. Cone* ◆ *Eres muy despelotado, Javier. Por eso pierdes todo.* You are really messy, Javier. That's why you lose everything. ◆ *Esta oficina está totalmente despelotada. Comencemos a organizarla.* This office is totally messed up. Let's start organizing it.

despelotarse to take off one's clothes (vulgar) *PR, U, Arg, Sp* ◆ *Se despelotaron en la playa.* They took off their clothes at the beach.

el **despelote 1.** disorder, mess *L. Am., Sp* ◆ *No me gustan los conciertos rock por el despelote que se forma. (Sp)* I don't like rock concerts because of all the ruckus people make at them. **2.** nakedness, removal of clothes (vulgar) *PR, Sp* ◆ *En esa película hay mucho despelote.* There's a lot of undressing in that film.

ser el **despelote** (to be the nakedness) to be too much, unheard of, extraordinary (things) (vulgar) *Sp* ◆ *¡Esta discoteca es el despelote!* This discotecque is too much!

despintarse (to unpaint oneself) to take off, go away *Mex, PR* ◆ *Despíntate.* Clear out of here.

estar **despistado(-a)** to be lost, off the track, clueless, forgetful *L. Am., Sp* ◆ *Estoy totalmente despistado; no sé nada del asunto.* I'm completely clueless; I don't know anything about the matter.

despuesito a little later than now *Mex* ◆ *Despuesito llevaremos a los niños al parque.* In a little while we'll take the kids to the park.

destaparse (to uncork oneself) to open up, spit it out, tell something *L. Am.* ◆ *Destápate, cariño. ¿Qué pasó?* Open up, honey. What happened?

destripar a alguien el cuento (to remove the stuffing or guts of the story from someone) to steal someone's thunder (telling a story he or she began) *Sp* ◆ *Me estás destripando el cuento, mi amor. Déjame hablar.* You're stealing my thunder, honey. Let me talk.

el/la **desubicado(-a)** 1. (disoriented) confused *Mex, S. Cone* ◆ *¿Puedes ayudarme? Estoy un poco desubicada.* Can you help me? I'm a bit confused. 2. (disoriented) weirdo *S. Cone* ◆ *Mi jefe es un desubicado y hace comentarios inapropiados.* My boss is a weirdo and makes inappropriate comments.

devanarse los sesos (to wind up one's brain) to rack one's brain *Mex, Ch, U, Sp* ◆ *Nos devanamos los sesos, pero no encontramos la fórmula matemática.* We racked our brains, but we could not find the mathematical formula.

su **devoción** →**(no) ser santo de su devoción**

devolver la pelota a alguien (to return the ball to someone) to put the ball back into someone's court, counter someone with his or her own arguments or reasoning *Mex, DR, Sp* ◆ *Marta es un genio; cuando discute no hay quien le devuelva la pelota.* Marta's a genius; when she's debating something, no one gets the best of her (puts the ball back in her court).

el **día 30 de febrero** (the 30th of February) never, the twelfth of never *Mex, ES* ◆ *¿Cuándo te vas a casar conmigo? —El día 30 de febrero.* When are you going to marry me? —The twelfth of never.

el **día de arreglo de cuentas** (day of settling of accounts) day of reckoning *Mex, DR, PR, Ch, Arg, Sp* ◆ *El ataque de esta madrugada fue un arreglo de cuentas entre dos bandas de delincuentes.* The attack this morning at dawn was the day of reckoning between two gangs of delinquents.

un **día de estos** one of these days *L. Am., Sp* ◆ *¿Limpiar el garage? Lo haré un día de estos.* Clean out the garage? I'll do it one of these days.

el **día menos pensado** (the least thought-of day) at the least expected time, when you least expect it *L. Am., Sp* ◆ *El día menos pensado me llama y me invita a salir.* At the least expected time he calls and invites me out.

el **día sándwich** (sandwich day) day off between a weekend and a holiday *Bol, S. Cone*

◆ *Este mes tenemos un día sándwich. Iré a la playa.* This month we have a day off between the weekend and the holiday. I'll go to the beach.

diablo →**como todos los diablos; haber (armarse) una de todos los diablos; llevarse (a alguien) el diablo; llevarse el diablo; mil (todos los) diablos**

¡Diablo! (Devil!) Holy smoke! expression of surprise *Mex, DR, PR, Col* (RVar *Mex:* more common, **¡Diablos!**)

El **diablo anda suelto.** The devil is loose. Evil is afoot. *Mex* ◆ *¡Chispas! Ese tipo ganó las elecciones otra vez. El diablo anda suelto.* Good heavens! That guy won the election again. Back to the evil empire.

el **diablo vendiendo cruces** (the devil selling crosses) hypocrite, wolf in sheep's clothing *L. Am.* ◆ *El nuevo alcalde es más hipócrita que el diablo vendiendo cruces.* The new mayor is more hypocritical than a wolf in sheep's clothing.

de los **mil (todos los) diablos** (of a thousand [all the] devils) very bad, a heck of (plus noun), the pits *Mex, ES, Sp* ◆ *Ese niño se porta de lo peor. Tiene una conducta de los mil diablos.* That boy acts out in the worst way. His behavior is the pits.

¡Dianche!, ¡Diantre! (Devil!) Holy smoke!, used instead of **¡Diablo!, ¡Demonio!** to express surprise, dismay *Mex, DR, PR, Col* (RVar *DR:* **diache**; *Mex:* **diantres**) ◆ *¡Diantre! (¡Diache! ¡Diablo!) ¡Tú no sabes lo que te pierdes!* (DR) Holy smoke! You don't know what you're missing! ◆ *¡Diantre! (¡Diache!, ¡Diablo! ¡Diantres!), perdí mi autobús.* (Mex) Dang! Holey moley! I missed my bus.

días →**más días hay que longanizas**

¿Diay? But what can you do? (phrase of resignation) *CR* ◆ *Sí, hay muchos secuestros. ¿Diay?* Yes, there are a lot of kidnappings. But, what can you do?

dicha →**¡Qué dicha!**

Del **dicho al hecho hay mucho trecho.** (From what is said to what is done there is a big gap.) Easier said than done. *L. Am., Sp* ◆ *Esa es su historia; sin embargo, yo creo que del dicho al hecho hay mucho trecho.* That's his story; however, I think it's easier said than done.

Dichosos los ojos que te están viendo (que te ven). (Fortunate the eyes that are looking at you.) Great to see you. Also, **Dichosos los ojos.** *L. Am., Sp* ◆ *¡Hola, Susana! Hace mucho que no nos vemos. Dichosos los ojos.* Hi, Susana! It's been a long time since we've seen each other. Great to see you!

diente →**dar diente con diente; tener buen diente**

a **diestra y siniestra** (right and left) helter-skelter, every which way, all over the place *L. Am., Sp* ◆ *Tenemos problemas a diestra y siniestra.* We have problems all over the place. ◆ *Estaban repartiendo regalos a diestra y siniestra.* They were handing out presents right and left.

a **dieta** (on a diet) going without sex *Mex, Cuba, G, ES, Sp* ◆ *Estoy a dieta hasta que regrese Luis de su viaje.* I'm celibate until Luis comes back from his trip.

Diga. Dígame. (Tell. Tell me.) Hello (answering the telephone). *Sp*

dilatar(se) to dilly-dally, linger, take a long time *Mex, PR, ES, CR* ◆ *¡Cómo se dilata mi amiga!* How long my friend is taking!

en **dimes y diretes** squabbling, bickering *L. Am., Sp* ◆ *No quiero entrar en dimes y diretes con nadie.* I don't want to be squabbling with anyone.

dinero contante y sonante hard cash *L. Am., Sp* ◆ *Me pagaron con dinero contante y sonante.* They paid me in hard cash.

Dios →**como Dios manda; no servir a Dios ni al diablo; por Dios**

¡Dios guarde! ¡Dios libre! God forbid! *Mex, DR, PR, ES, CRCol* (RVar *Sp:* **Dios nos guarde (nos libre);** *PR and DR:* **Dios nos libre** only) ◆ *¿El bebé enfermo? Ay, ¡Dios guarde!* The baby sick? God forbid!

¡Dios mío! (My God!) Holy smoke! My God! (not sacreligious) *L. Am., Sp* ◆ *¡Dios mío!, recibí buenas noticias de mi familia.* My God! I received good news from my family.

¡Dios santo! (Holy God!) My goodness! My God! (not sacreligous) *L. Am., Sp* ◆ *¡Dios santo! No quiero ver más televisión con las atrocidades de la guerra.* My goodness! I don't want to see any more television with the atrocities of the war.

el qué **dirán** what people will say *L. Am., Sp* ◆ *Me importa un pepino el qué dirán.* I don't give a darn about what people will say.

el/la **dire** short for **director** or **directora**, director or principal *Mex, Cuba, Sp* ◆ *¿Cómo se llama el dire?* What's the name of the principal?

dirigir el cotarro (to direct the **cotarro**, a bank of a ravine or a shelter for vagrants) to be in charge *Sp* ◆ *Quien realmente dirige el cotarro es María, aunque no lo parezca. Las demás no mandan.* The person who's really in charge is María, although it may not look like it. The others don't give orders.

un **disgusto** →**tener un disgusto**

el **disparate** (shot off the mark) nonsense *L. Am., Sp* ◆ *¡Qué disparate! ¡Puros disparates!* What nonsense! Pure nonsense!

estar **dispuesto(-a) a** (to be disposed to) to be willing to *L. Am., Sp* ◆ *Están dispuestos a luchar por sus derechos.* They're willing to fight for their rights.

divertirse a sus anchas (to enjoy oneself to one's widths) to have a great time, enjoy oneself as much as possible *L. Am., Sp* ◆ *En las vacaciones se divirtieron a sus anchas.* On vacation, they enjoyed themselves as much as possible.

divis-divis divine, marvelous (an exaggeratedly feminine expression that may be said ironically or in jest, like "Simply divine, dahling!") *Mex* ◆ *Esa blusa te queda divis-divis.* That blouse looks divine on you.

doblar el lomo (to fold or bend the back) to work like a dog, do heavy work *Mex, DR, PR, Col, U, Arg* ◆ *Cuando inmigramos a Canadá, doblamos el lomo.* When we immigrated to Canada, we worked like dogs.

doblar el pico (to fold up the beak) to put a lid on it, keep quiet, shut up *Mex, ES* ◆ *No le gustó lo que le dije y rápido dobló el pico.* He (She) didn't like what I said and quickly shut up. ◆

el **doctor** →**Estás como lo recetó el doctor!**

dolerle hasta los huesos to be worn to the bone, ache all over with tiredness *L. Am., Sp* ◆ *He trabajado mucho y ahora me duelen hasta los huesos.* I've worked a lot and now I'm worn to the bone (dog tired).

la dolorosa: Le trajeron la dolorosa.
They brought him the bill.

los **dolores** (pains) used for **dólares** *Cuba, DR, ES* ◆ *Ahora yo no tengo dolores. Right now I don't have any greenbacks.*

la **dolorosa** (the painful one) the check, bill, damages *U, Sp* ◆ *Camarero, tráigame la dolorosa. Waiter, bring me the bill.*

el **don Juan** Don Juan, wolf, womanizer *L. Am., Sp* ◆ *Sabemos que es un Don Juan, pero es encantador. We know he's a Don Juan, but he's charming.*

don nadie (Sir Nobody) a nobody, unimportant person, with little influence or power *L. Am., Sp* ◆ *Ese tipo es un don nadie; pretende ser lo que no es. That guy is a nobody; he pretends to be more (important) than he is (literally, something he's not).*

la **dona** doughnut (from English) *Mex, DR, C. Am.* ◆ *A Homero le gustan mucho las donas. Homero really likes doughnuts.*

donde (where) in the home of, where someone is *L. Am.* ◆ *Fuimos donde Laura. We went to Laura's house.*

donde Cristo perdió el gorro (la sandalia) (where Christ lost his cap [sandal]) in a godforsaken spot, far away *Sp* ◆ *Viven allá en el norte, donde Cristo perdió la sandalia. They live up there in the north, in some godforsaken spot.*

donde el diablo dio las tres voces (where the devil gave the three words) in the middle of nowhere, far away *Sp* ◆ *Nuestra casa de verano está en donde el diablo dio las tres voces. Our summer house is in the middle of nowhere.*

donde el diablo perdió el poncho (where the devil lost his poncho) in a godforsaken spot, in a far or out-of-the-way place *S. Cone, Sp* ◆ *Nadie fue a la reunión porque llovía mucho y la oficina estaba por donde el diablo perdió el poncho. Nobody went to the meeting because it was raining hard and the office was way the heck out there.*

estar **donde las papas queman** (to be where the potatoes get burned) to be where the action is, in the eye of the storm, where it's at *Ch, U* ◆ *Enrique siempre está donde* *las papas queman. Enrique is always where the action is.*

donde te dicen hijito sin conocerte (where they call you my son without knowing you) house of ill repute, bordello, cathouse *parts of L. Am., Sp* ◆ *¿Adónde fuiste anoche? —Adonde te dicen hijito sin conocerte. Where did you go last night? — To the bordello.*

¿Dónde va Vicente? Donde va (toda) la gente. (Where is Vicente going? Wherever everyone else goes.) He's a sheep, someone who follows the crowd or plays the game. (phrase expressing the lack of initiative of someone or saying that he or she is just a follower) *Mex, DR, ES, Col, Ch, Sp* ◆ *Ese candidato ha cambiado de partido tres veces. ¿Dónde va Vicente? Donde va la gente. That candidate has changed parties three times. He's just a crowd follower.*

dorar la píldora (to make the pill golden) to sugarcoat something *L. Am., Sp* ◆ *No tienes que dorar la píldora; sé que ya no me quieres. You don't have to sugarcoat this; I know you don't love me any more.*

el **dormilón, la dormilona** describing someone who sleeps a lot, sleepyhead *L. Am., Sp* ◆ *¿Son las diez de la mañana ya? ¡Qué dormilón! It's already ten o'clock in the morning? What a long time I slept (literally, what a big sleeper)!*

dormir a alguien (to put someone to sleep) to pull the wool over someone's eyes, deceive someone *Mex, Cuba, DR, G* ◆ *Nos durmió a todos y se llevó su buena lana. He pulled the wool over all our eyes and took away a good bit of money.*

dormir a cuerpo de rey to sleep like a king (literally, like the body of a king) *most of L. Am., Sp* ◆ *En ese hotel, se duerme a cuerpo de rey. In that hotel, you sleep like a king.*

dormir a pierna suelta (to sleep with one's leg thrown out) to sleep like a log *L. Am., Sp* ◆ *Anoche dormí a pierna suelta; estoy muy a gusto aquí. Last night I slept like a log; I'm very comfortable here.*

dormir como un lirón (to sleep like a dormouse) to sleep like a log *Mex, DR, S. Cone, Sp* ◆ *Después de una ducha, dormiré como un lirón. After a shower, I'll sleep like a log.*

dormir como un tronco to sleep like a log (literally, trunk) *Mex, S. Cone, Sp* (RVAR *Sp:* also, less commonly, **como una leña**) ◆ *Había mucho ruido en la casa; sin embargo, Marisa durmió como un tronco. There was a lot of noise in the house; still, Marisa slept like a log.*

dormir con los ángeles (to sleep with the angels) to have sweet dreams, sleep well *Mex, ES, S. Cone* (RVAR *ES:* also, **soñar con los angelitos**) ◆ *Que duermas con los angelitos. Sweet dreams.*

dormir la juma to sleep it (the drunkenness) off *Cuba, ES, CR, Pan, Ven, Peru* ◆ *Voy a acostarme para dormir la juma. I'm going to lie down to sleep it off.*

dormir la mona (to sleep the monkey) to sleep it off *Cuba, Mex, G, Col, Peru, S. Cone, Sp* ◆ *Vete a dormir la mona, que estás muy borracho. Go sleep it off; you are really drunk.*

dormir(se) sobre los laureles to rest on one's laurels *L. Am., Sp* ◆ *No hay que dormirse sobre los laureles. Hay que escribir algo nuevo. You can't rest on your laurels. You need to write something new.*

dos →**como dos y dos son cuatro**

de **dos caras** two-faced *Mex, ES, U, Arg, Sp* ◆ *Javier parece honesto pero tiene dos caras y podría robarle hasta a su madre. Javier seems honest but he's two-faced and would even be capable of robbing his own mother.*

dos palabras (two words) short conversation, a word (with someone) *Mex, ES, S. Cone* ◆ *¿Puedo hablarte? Sólo van a ser dos palabras. Can I talk with you? Just a word (literally, it will only be two words).*

en **dos patadas** (in two kicks) in a jiffy, quickly *Mex, ES, CR, Col, Peru, S. Cone* ◆ *No se preocupen. En dos patadas el carro estará listo. Don't worry. The car will be ready in a jiffy.*

en un **dos por tres** (in a two by three) quickly, in a jiffy *L. Am.* ◆ *Mejor envíalo por fax que llega en un dos por tres. Send it by fax instead; it'll get there on the double.*

dos que tres (two that three) so-so, not all that great *Mex, G, ES* ◆ *Rogelio, ¿cómo fue el concierto? —Dos que tres. Rogelio, how was the concert? —So-so.*

un **download** →hacer un download (un backup)

el **dragón, la draga** (probably from **tragón**, big swallow) big eater, chowhound, glutton *DR, PR* ◆ *Tan flaca que es Luisa y eso que es una draga; siempre se sirve dos veces. As skinny as Luisa is, she happens to be a glutton and always takes two helpings.*

el **drama, el dramón** hassle, problem, difficult situation *S. Cone* ◆ *La partida de los hijos a España fue un drama para los padres. The kids' leaving for Spain was a hassle for the parents.*

el **drogo** short for **drogadicto**, druggie, junkie, addict *parts of L. Am.* ◆ *Rolando es un drogo; no da un buen ejemplo. Rolando is a druggie; he's not setting a good example.*

el/la **drogata** druggie, junkie, addict *Sp* ◆ *No salgas con él; es un drogata. Don't go out with him; he's a druggie.*

duende →tener duende

ser un **dulce (bombón)** (to be sweet [a bonbon]) to be a sweetie *Mex* ◆ *Esa niña es un dulce (bombón). That girl is a sweetheart.*

dulzura (sweetness) sweetie, honey *L. Am., Sp* ◆ *Dulzura, cada día te quiero más. Honey, each day I love you more.*

dundo(-a) dumb, foolish *C. Am.* ◆ *Esa niña es bien dunda. That girl is really dumb.*

a **duras penas** (at hard pains) with a lot of effort, great difficulty *Mex, DR, PR, S. Cone, Sp* ◆ *Luis pagó sus deudas a duras penas, pues no tiene trabajo desde hace tres meses. Luis paid his debts with great difficulty since he hasn't had any work for three months.*
◆ *A duras penas pude entender lo que me explicaba ese herido antes de llevarlo al hospital. With great effort I was able to understand what the injured person told me before I brought him to the hospital.*

el **duro** five pesetas *Sp* ◆ *No tengo ni un duro para comprar un café. I don't have even two cents to buy a coffee.*

al **duro y sin guante** (hard and without a glove, a term from baseball) pitilessly, without mercy, rough or tough *Mex, Cuba* ◆ *Me hablaron al duro y sin guante. They spoke to me really harshly.*

duro(-a) 1. (hard) hard to convince, pig-headed *Mex, G, Ch* ◆ *Intenté hablar con ella varias veces, pero es dura y no entiende razones. I tried to talk to her several times, but she's pig-headed and doesn't listen to reason (literally, understand reasons).* **2.** (hard) stingy *Cuba, ES, Pan, Peru* ◆ *El director es muy duro y no gastará dinero en nuevos proyectos este año. The director is very stingy and won't spend money on new projects this year.*

duro(-a) →más duro(-a) que el cemento

duro(-a) de pelar (hard to peel) pig-headed, difficult to convince or get *CR, U, Sp* (RVAR *CR*: also, someone who waits a long time before getting married) ◆ *Felipe es duro de pelar. Felipe is hard to convince (not easily influenced).*

E

ebrio(-a) →Ni ebrio(-a) ni dormido(-a).

¡Échale ganas! (Put in will!) Give it all you've got! (for instance, at a sports event) *Mex, ES* ◆ *¡Échale ganas! Así terminas tus tareas más temprano. Give it all you've got! That way you'll finish your homework earlier.*

¡Échale lo que hay que echarle! (Put in what has to be put in!) Give it all you've got! (for instance, at a sports event) *Sp* ◆ *Hijo, échale lo que hay que echarle para terminar este proyecto. Son, give it all you've got to finish this project.*

echar a alguien a escobazos to kick or throw someone out (with sweeps of a broom) *Mex, Sp* ◆ *Eché a escobazos a un vendedor que vino a la puerta porque fue muy insolente. I kicked out a salesman who came to the door because he was very insolent.*

echar a perder (to throw to lose) to ruin *L. Am., Sp* ◆ *El mal tiempo echó a perder la cosecha de maíz. The bad weather ruined the corn crop.*

echar agua al mar (to throw water into the sea) to take coals to Newcastle, do something useless *Sp* ◆ *Tratar de reformar el mundo es como echar agua al mar. Trying to reform the world is like taking coals to Newcastle (doing something useless).*

echar algo en cara (to throw something in face) to throw something up (to someone), bring up *L. Am., Sp* ◆ *Nos echaron en cara el dinero que les debemos. They brought up the money that we owe them.*

echar chispas (to throw off sparks) to show signs of anger or bad temper, to fume *Mex, DR, ES, Ch, Sp* ◆ *Esa mujer anda echando chispas de enojada. That woman walks around fuming with rage.* ◆ *Siempre echo chispas por la mañana. I'm always grouchy in the morning.*

echar de cabeza (to turn on one's head) to spill the beans, let the cat out of the bag, publicly reveal someone's secrets *Mex* ◆ *Lola me echó de cabeza con Irma de algo que yo le platiqué de mi trabajo. Lola let the cat out of the bag and told Irma something I told her about my work.*

echar de menos (to throw for less) to miss someone or something far away *L. Am., Sp* ◆ *Te vamos a echar de menos cuando te vayas. We're going to miss you when you go.*

echar el ojo (to throw the eye) to eye, have one's eye on *L. Am., Sp* ◆ *Mi tía le echaba el ojo a unos pantalones en el almacén. My aunt was eying some pants in the department store.* ◆ *Ya le echaste el ojo a ese muchacho, ¿no? You've already got your eye on that guy, right?*

echar en saco roto (to put into a broken or torn sack) to disregard completely (what someone says) *L. Am., Sp* ◆ *Echaron mis consejos en saco roto. They completely disregarded my advice.*

echar flores (to throw flowers) to pat on the back, compliment *L. Am., Sp* ◆ *¡Qué flores me está echando! What nice compliments you're giving me!*

echar fuego por los ojos (to be fiery-eyed) to show fury or anger *Mex, U, Sp* ◆ *No le hables; parece que echa fuego por los ojos porque tuvo un problema con la directora de la escuela. Don't talk to her; it seems she's all steamed up because she had a problem with the principal of the school.*

echar huevos a un asunto, echarle huevos (to throw eggs [testicles] to an issue) to work one's ass off, hustle, throw oneself into something, do something decisively or bravely (vulgar) *Mex, C. Am., Sp* (RVar Ven: **echarle bolas**; *Sp*: **echarle pelotas**; *Mex, Sp*: **echarle cojones**) ◆ *Le vamos a echar huevos a este trabajo para salir temprano. We're going to really hustle and work hard so we can leave early.*

echar humo (to throw off steam or smoke) to be furious *Mex, DR, ES, Sp* ◆ *No me hables, que vengo echando humo. Tuve un problema con la profesora de literatura.*

Don't talk to me because I'm hopping mad. I had a problem with the literature professor.

echar la bendición to give a blessing, bless *L. Am., Sp* ◆ *Cuando le dije a papá que me iba, me echó su bendición.* When I told Dad I was leaving, he gave me his blessing.

echar la culpa (to throw the blame) to blame *L. Am., Sp* ◆ *Robaron el dinero y me echaron la culpa.* They stole the money and blamed me.

echar leña al fuego to add fuel (literally, wood) to the fire *L. Am., Sp* ◆ *Es mejor callarse y no echar más leña al fuego.* It's better to keep quiet and not stir things up any more than they already are.

echar (lanzar) los perros (to throw on the dogs) to hit on, call out the cavalry, go all out to win; also, **lanzar los canes** *Mex, C. Am., Col, Ven* (RVAR *C. Am.:* **echar los perros** more common than **lanzar**; both are used in *Mex*) ◆ *Le eché los perros a esa chica.* I went all out for that girl (did everything possible to get or win her).

echar lumbre (to throw off fire) to fume, show signs of anger or bad temper *Mex, ES, Sp* ◆ *Anda tan enojada que hasta echa lumbre por los ojos.* She is so angry that she's giving everyone dirty looks.

echar madres (to throw mothers) to bitch out, curse, swear at *Chicano, Mex, Col* ◆ *Federico echaba madres porque estaba muy enojado con su hermano.* Federico was swearing because he was very angry at his brother.

echar mal de ojo (to throw the evil eye) to give someone the evil eye, wish ill to someone and try to cause him or her bad luck *Cuba, DR, PR, S. Cone* ◆ *Parecería que me han echado mal de ojo; todo me sale mal.* It would seem someone has given me the evil eye; everything is going badly for me.

echar pa'lante (to throw forward) to keep plugging away, move on, keep going after confronting a problem *DR, PR, Col, Ven, Ch* ◆ *La situación es muy difícil, pero hay que echar pa'lante.* The situation is very difficult, but we (you, they, etc.) have to keep plugging along (going forward). ◆ *Echemos pa'lante porque p'atrás no cunde.* Let's move forward because there's no going back.

echar para atrás to put off *Sp* ◆ *Ese olor a ajo me echa para atrás.* That garlic smell puts me off.

echar perlas a los puercos to cast pearls before swine, give something to someone who doesn't appreciate or deserve it *L. Am., Sp* ◆ *Nena, no te vistas tan elegante. Vamos a casa de Juan Carlos y él ni siquiera lo va a notar. Es como echarle perlas a los puercos.* Girl, don't dress so elegantly. We're going to Juan Carlos's house, and he won't even notice it. It's like casting pearls before swine.

echar raíces (to throw roots) to settle down *L. Am., Sp* ◆ *¿Cuándo te vas a casar y echar raíces, m'hijo?* When are you going to get married and settle down, dear?

echar rayos (to throw off lightning bolts) to show great anger *Mex, ES, Sp* (RVAR *Mex:* **rayos y centellas**, lightning bolts and sparks) ◆ *Después de hablar con él, salí echando rayos.* After talking with him, I left there flaming mad.

echar relajo (to throw off or make a rumpus) to have a blast *Mex, ES, Col* (RVAR *U, Arg:* **hacer relajo**) ◆ *Anoche echamos mucho relajo en la fiesta.* Last night we had a blast at the party.

echar un capote (echar la capa) (to throw a cape, as at a bullfight) to go to bat for, intervene on behalf of *Sp* ◆ *Gracias por echarme un capote porque yo no sabía qué decirle.* Thanks for helping me out because I didn't know what to say to him.

echar un casquete (to throw a cap) to have sex (a bit vulgar) *Sp* ◆ *Nos echamos un casquete fabuloso.* We had some great sex.

echar un fonazo to phone (someone) *Mex* ◆ *Te echo un fonazo esta noche.* I'll call you tonight.

echar un palo (to throw a stick) to have sex (vulgar; also, **palito**) *Mex, Cuba, G, ES* ◆ *Nomás se conocieron y se fueron a echar un palo.* As soon as they met they ran off to have sex.

echar un patín (to throw a skate) to hightail it, zip along, walk very fast *Mex, Cuba* ◆ *Echó un patín de una hora desde el mercado hasta el puerto.* He hightailed it in an hour from the market to the port.

echar rayos: Su papá echaba rayos cuando vio sus notas.
Her dad was flaming mad when he saw her grades.

echar un pie (to throw a foot) to dance, shake a leg (old expression) *Cuba, DR, PR* ◆ *A abuelito todavía le gusta echar un pie de vez en cuando. Grandpa still likes to shake a leg once in a while.*

echar un rollo (to throw a roll) to sling the bull, sweet-talk *Mex, ES, Col, Ven, Peru* ◆ *El presidente echó un rollo sobre el futuro de la economía. The president talked a lot of boloney about the future of the economy.*

echar un taco de ojo (to throw a taco of the eye) to look at but not obtain (e.g., to window-shop or referring to a good-looking person of the opposite sex) *Mex* ◆ *Vamos a entrar en esta tienda de ropa, ¿no? No tengo dinero, pero quiero echar un taco de ojo. Let's go into this clothing store, OK? I don't have any money, but I'd like to browse around (do some window-shopping).*

echar una bronca to bawl out, reprimand, chew out *parts of L. Am., Sp* ◆ *Me echaron una bronca espantosa por llegar tarde a casa. They gave me a terrible bawling out for getting home late.* ◆ *Vaya bronca le echó a*

Bárbara su padre por perder las llaves. *My goodness, how Barbara's father ripped her to shreds for losing the keys.*

echar una canita al aire (to throw a gray hair in the air) to have an affair; to let one's hair down *L. Am., Sp* ◆ *Los delegados al congreso echaron algunas canitas al aire. The conference delegates let their hair down.* ◆ *Voy a salir a bailar. Voy a echar una canita al aire. I'm going to go out dancing (said by someone who doesn't usually go dancing). I'm going to let my hair down.*

echar una mano (to put in a hand) *L. Am., Sp*

echar una mano (to put into a hand) to give (someone) a hand *L. Am., Sp* ◆ *Échanos una mano y terminaremos el trabajo más temprano. Lend us a hand and we'll finish the work sooner.*

echar una meadita (to throw a little pissing) to take a leak (vulgar) *L. Am., Sp* ◆ *Voy a echar una meadita, y ya regreso. I'm going to go take a leak, and then I'll come back.*

echar una pestaña (pestañeada) (to throw an eyelash) to catch forty winks, get some shut-eye *Mex, Ch* ◆ *Antes de su discurso el alcalde echó una pestaña.* Before his speech the mayor got some shut-eye.

echar vaina (to throw husk, sheath) to talk about nothing; to tease (somewhat vulgar but very common) *DR, Ven* ◆ *Encontré a Paco en el tren y me echó una vaina tremenda acerca de su divorcio.* I ran into Paco on the train and he told me a long story about his divorce.

echar(se) un polvo (to throw oneself powder or dust) to have sex (vulgar; also, **un polvito**) *L. Am., Sp* ◆ *Ése se echa un polvo cada día con una chica distinta.* That guy has sex every day with a different girl.

echar/tirar indirectas (to throw indirects) to make insinuations, drop hints *L. Am., Sp* ◆ *Ella tiraba muchas indirectas, pero nadie le hizo caso.* She was making a lot of insinuations, but no one paid any attention to her.

echar/tirar la casa por la ventana (to throw the house out the window) to spend lavishly, blow the works *L. Am., Sp* ◆ *Para los quince años de Rocío, doña Ana tiró la casa por la ventana. Fue una fiesta a todo dar.* For Rocío's fifteenth birthday, Doña Ana blew the works. It was a real bash.

echarle algo al buche (al pico) (to put something in one's craw [beak]) to feed one's face, eat *Mex, Cuba, DR, G, Col, U, Sp* (RVAR *Sp:* also, **llenar el buche**) ◆ *¿Qué le echamos al buche para la cena?* What should we eat for supper?

echarse a alguien 1. (to throw oneself to someone) to kill off, wipe out *Mex, Cuba, G* ◆ *Los mafiosos se lo echaron en pleno día.* The mafia wiped him out in broad daylight. **2.** (to throw oneself to someone) to flunk someone (e.g., on exams) *Mex, Cuba* ◆ *En física se echaron a la mitad de los estudiantes.* In physics they flunked half the students. **3.** (to throw oneself at someone) to have sex with someone *Mex, Cuba, G* ◆ *Se echó a su vecina.* He had sex with his neighbor.

echarse algo encima to bring down (something negative) upon oneself *L. Am., Sp* ◆ *El jefe, con su actitud negativa, se ha echado muchos enemigos encima.* The boss, with his negative attitude, has brought many enemies down upon himself.

echarse ese trompo a la uña (to put that top, the spinning toy, on one's fingernail) to perform an amazing feat *Mex, ES, Arg* ◆ *¿Reforma constitucional? A ver si se echan ese trompo a la uña.* Constitutional reform? We'll see if they manage that feat.

echarse flores (to throw flowers at oneself) to brag, praise oneself *L. Am., Sp* ◆ *Tomás se vende muy bien; siempre está echándose flores.* Tomás sells himself very well; he's always tooting his own horn.

echarse la soga al cuello (to put the rope around one's neck) to get into trouble or debt; in *L. Am.,* very commonly means to take the plunge, get married *Mex, DR, PR, G, CR, Col, Ch, Sp* ◆ *Mi hermana se echó la soga al cuello cuando menos lo esperábamos.* My sister took the plunge when we least expected it.

echarse un pollo (to throw a chicken at oneself) to take off, split *Ch* ◆ *¡Adiós! Son las once y tenemos que echarnos un pollo.* Good-bye! It's eleven o'clock and we have to make like the wind and blow.

echarse una mona encima (andar con la mona) (to throw a monkey on oneself [walk with the monkey]) to get drunk *Cuba, Ch, Arg* ◆ *Al festejar el partido de fútbol nos echamos una mona encima.* We got drunk celebrating the soccer game.

la **edad del pavo** (turkey age) teen years, change to adolescence, puberty *S. Cone, Sp* ◆ *No le hagas mucho caso a su comportamiento. Está en la edad del pavo.* Don't pay much attention to his behavior. He's at that difficult age (adolescence).

¡Éjele! used like **¡Oye!**, Listen! Hey! Are you kidding? *Mex, PR, Col* ◆ *¡Éjele! ¿Por qué quieren salir tan temprano?* What? (Are you kidding?) Why do you want to leave so soon?

El **muerto al hoyo y el vivo al bollo.** (The dead person in the hole and the opportunist at the bread roll.) What an opportunist! (vulgar in some places) *Mex, ES, CR, Ch, Sp* (RVAR *Ch:* **El muerto al pozo y el vivo al gozo.**) ◆ *¿Viste que la viuda de Jorge ya sale con Pedro? El muerto al hoyo y el vivo al bollo.* ¿Did you know that Jorge's widow is now dating Pedro? What an opportunist!

El que con lobos anda a aullar aprende. (The person who walks with wolves will learn to howl.) If you lie down with dogs, you get up with fleas. Keeping bad company will teach you bad ways. *Mex, Nic* ◆ *No salgas con esos borrachos. El que con lobos anda a aullar aprende. Don't go out with those drunks. If you lie down with dogs, you get up with fleas.*

El que con niños se acuesta... (The person who sleeps with children . . . ; the second part is understood: **... amanece mojado** wakes up wet). You made your bed, now lie in it. If you take risks, you may suffer the consequences. *Mex, DR, ES, Nic, S. Cone, Sp* ◆ *Ten cuidado con esos chicos. El que con niños se acuesta amanece mojado. Be careful with those guys. If you take risks, you may suffer the consequences.*

El que las hace las paga. (He who makes them pays for them.) You made your bed, now lie in it. You have to accept the consequences of an action. *Mex, DR, PR, ES, S. Cone* ◆ *Ulises perdió toda su fortuna. El que las hace las paga. Ulysses lost his entire fortune. He made his bed, now he has to lie in it.*

El que pestañea pierde. (The person who blinks loses.) He who hesitates is lost. If you snooze you lose. *L. Am., Sp* ◆ *Confía en ti mismo, porque el que pestañea pierde. Trust in yourself because if you snooze, you lose.*

El que pone el baile que pague la marimba. (Let the host of the dance pay for the music.) Deal with it. Let him (her) deal with it. The one who thinks up an idea should take care of implementing it. *ES, Nic* ◆ *No te podemos ayudar a resolver tu problema. El que pone el baile que pague la marimba. We can't help you solve your problem. Deal with it.*

El que quiere celeste que le cueste. (Whoever wants baby blue, it will cost him.) If you want a good life, you have to work for it. There's no free lunch. No bees, no honey; no work, no money. *ES, Nic, S. Cone* ◆ *¿Por qué trabajas tanto? —Porque el que quiere celeste que le cueste. Why do you work so much? —Because there's no free lunch.*

El que tiene plata platica. (Whoever has money makes conversation.) Money talks. *Nic* ◆ *Seguro que los conservadores vuelven a ganar. El que tiene plata platica. The conservatives are going to win again for sure. Money talks.*

El que va pa' viejo va pa' pendejo. (Whoever is getting old, is getting to be a fool.) (slightly vulgar) There's no fool like an old fool. *Mex, ES, Nic, Ven* (RVAR ES: also, **Más viejo, más pendejo.**) ◆ *¿Don Ramón tiene ochenta años y se casó con esa chica de veinte? El que va pa' viejo, va pa' pendejo. Don Ramón is eighty and he married that girl of twenty? There's no fool like an old fool.*

el **email** e-mail (pronounced with the sound of e-mail in English) *L. Am., Sp* (RVAR *Florida, Sp:* **emilio**) ◆ *Recibí muchos emails esta semana y no he podido contestarlos. I got a lot of e-mails this week and haven't been able to answer them.*

emailear to e-mail (pronounced with the sound of e-mail in English) *L. Am., Sp* ◆ *Te voy a emailear unos chistes. I'm going to e-mail you some jokes.*

la **embarrada** (mud plaster [for walls]) muddle, embarrassment, problem, dirty linen *Mex, CR, Col, Peru, S. Cone* ◆ *¡Qué embarrada! Se me olvidó mandar el cheque. (Col) How embarrassing! I forgot to mail the check.*

embarrado(-a) (plastered with mud [for walls]) tainted, stained (like having covered oneself with mud), involved in shady business, trouble *Mex, G, ES, CR, U, Arg* ◆ *Después del discurso del presidente, quedó la embarrada. (Ch) After the president's speech, the problem (embarrassing situation) remained.* ◆ *Ese señor está bien embarrado en malos negocios. That man is really tainted by shady business deals.*

embarrarla (to muddy it) to goof up, make a mistake *ES, Nic, Col, Peru, S. Cone* ◆ *La embarraste, hermano. Nunca debiste contar tus secretos. You messed up, brother. You should never have told your secrets.*

embotellarse (to bottle) to memorize, cram *DR, PR, Col* ◆ *Tengo que embotellarme todas las fórmulas para el examen de química. I have to cram all those formulas into my brain for the chemistry exam.*

el/la embustero(-a) fraud, cheat, liar *L. Am.,
Sp* ◆ *Tú eres un embustero. Eso no pasó así.
You're a big liar. That's not how that happened
at all.*

a la eme →mandar a alguien al cuerno, a la
eme

emoción →¡Qué emoción!

emocionado(-a) excited *L. Am., Sp* ◆ *El
equipo de fútbol está muy emocionado con
el triunfo en el campeonato. The soccer team
is very excited about winning the championship.*

una empanada →tener un cacao (una empanada) mental

emparparse en algo (to get wet in something) to bone up on something, inform
oneself about something *Mex, Cuba, DR, PR,
G, ES, Col, U, Arg* ◆ *Necesito empaparme
en el asunto. I need to bone up on the matter (immerse myself).*

emparrandarse to go out on the town, party
Mex, G, Col ◆ *Federico solía emparrandarse
cada fin de semana. Federico used to go out
on the town every weekend.*

estar empatados (to be tied) to be an item, a
couple *Mex, PR, Ven* ◆ *¿De veras? ¿Ofelia y
Pedro están empatados? Really? Ofelia and
Pedro are an item?*

empatar(se) to pair up, get together; to obtain or get *Mex, Cuba, CR, Col, Ven* ◆ *Silvia
y Pablo se empataron en febrero. Silvia and
Pedro got together (paired up) in February.*

emperrarse to persist doggedly *Ch,U, Sp* ◆
*Se emperró en que la solución era única-
mente la que él proponía. He persisted
doggedly that the only solution was the one he
proposed.*

empezar la casa por el tejado (to begin
the house with the roof, a traditional
proverb) to put the cart before the horse *Sp*
(RVar *U: ...por el techo*) ◆ *No te apures,
muchacho; tienes que aprender tu trabajo
bien. No se puede empezar la casa por el
tejado. Don't be in such a hurry, boy; you need
to learn your job well. Don't put the cart before the horse.*

empilcharse (to put on pieces of clothing)
to fix oneself up to go out, primp (from
pilcha, piece of clothing) *U, Arg* ◆ *Compramos a buen precio, y nos empilchamos
para todo el verano con pilchas de moda.
We bought stuff on sale, and we decked ourselves out for the whole summer with stylish
clothes.*

empinar el codo (to raise one's elbow) to
have a drink, wet one's whistle, have a swig
L. Am., Sp ◆ *Empinaron el codo toda la
tarde, y después no pudieron asistir al
concierto. They drank all afternoon, and afterwards they couldn't attend the concert.*

empollar to cram (from sitting for a long
time, like a hen on her chicks) *Sp* ◆ *Tenemos
que empollar. Mañana hay exámenes. We
have to cram. Tomorrow there are exams.*

el empollón, la empollona grind, student
who studies a lot *G, Sp* (RVar *G:* also, someone who works all the time) ◆ *Este chaval
es un empollón. Todo el día está estudiando
y no sale de casa. This boy is a grind. All
day he's studying and he doesn't go out of his
house.*

a empujones (at pushes) by force (a force
from outside) *Mex, S. Cone* ◆ *La gente fue
sacada a empujones. People were taken out
forcibly.* ◆ *Diego terminó su tesis a empujones. Diego finished his thesis because he had
to (he was pushed to do it).*

en las buenas y en las malas (in the
good and in the bad) in good times and bad
L. Am., Sp ◆ *Tengo un amigo que me apoya
en las buenas y en las malas. I have a friend
who supports me in good times and bad.*

enano(-a) (dwarf) short or small *Mex, G,
Col, Ch, U, Sp* ◆ *Esa enana es divertidísima;
nos hizo reír durante todo el viaje. That
short woman is loads of fun; she made us
laugh the whole trip.*

encabronado(-a) angry *Mex, PR, C. Am.,
many S. Am. countries, Sp* ◆ *No puedo
hablar ahora. Estoy encabronado con la
situación, y necesito pensar. I can't talk now.
I'm all worked up over the situation, and I
need to think.*

encabronar(se) to make (someone) angry,
furious (wild, like a goat); to become furious
Mex, C. Am., PR, many S. Am. countries ◆
*Ese chico se en abrona por nada. That guy
loses it over nothing.* ◆ *No me encabrones.
Don't get my goat.*

encajarse to mooch, sponge, take advantage
Mex ◆ *Cada vez que lo invito, se encaja y*

trae a varios amigos. Every time I invite him, he takes advantage and brings several friends. ◆ *Esos comerciantes se encajan con sus clientes.* Those businesspeople are taking advantage of their customers.

encamarse con (to get in bed with) to go to bed and make love with *S. Cone* ◆ *Pasamos el fin de semana encamados.* We spent the whole weekend in bed.

encantado(-a) de la vida (charmed or enchanted with life) happy as can be *L. Am., Sp* ◆ *Los niños van a la playa a pasear. Están encantados de la vida.* The children are going on an excursion to the beach. They're happy as can be.

encargarse de to take charge of *L. Am., Sp* ◆ *Me encargué de la cuenta bancaria.* I took charge of the bank account.

encendérsele el bombillo (to have the lightbulb turned on) to get a brilliant idea *Cuba, DR, PR, Col* ◆ *A Juana se le encendió el bombillo (el foco).* Juana had a brilliant idea.

enchicharse (also, **enchichado[-a]**) to get mad *Mex, Col, U* ◆ *Me tuvieron allí esperando hasta que me enchiché.* They had me waiting there until I lost it. ◆ *La mamá de Juliana sigue enchichada por lo que le rompimos el vidrio.* Juliana's mom is still hot under the collar because of our breaking her windowpane.

enchilado(-a) (sick from hot chilies) angry *Mex, G, Nic, CR* (RVar *CR:* also, curious or with interest piqued) ◆ *Rosa no permitió que José la besara y él se quedó enchilado.* Rosa didn't allow José to kiss her, and he got all hot under the collar. ◆ *Pepe está enchilado porque no puede averiguar cómo el mago hace sus trucos. (CR)* Pepe is piqued because he can't figure out how the magician does his tricks.

el/la **enchufado(-a)** (plugged in) teacher's pet; person with influence *Sp* ◆ *Es un enchufado; hizo peor el examen pero el profesor le puso mejor nota que a mí.* He's a teacher's pet; he did worse on the exam, but the professor gave him a better grade than me.

estar **enchufado(-a) 1.** (to be plugged in) to have connections *Mex, Sp* ◆ *Mi tío está enchufado en el gobierno.* My uncle has an "in" with the government. **2.** to be wrapped up *U* *Estás totalmente enchufado en tu trabajo.* You're totally wrapped up in your work.

enchufarse 1. (to plug into) to join in (conversation, etc.) *S. Cone* ◆ *Enchúfate Rodrigo; tenemos que terminar este trabajo.* Jump in any time, Rodrigo; we need to finish this job. ◆ *Estás pensativa. Enchúfate y danos tu opinion.* You're pensive. Join in and give us your opinion. **2.** (to plug in) to pay attention *Mex, U* ◆ *Enchúfate. Voy a explicarte el asunto.* Listen up. I'm going to explain the issue to you. **3.** (to connect, plug in) to get laid, get lucky, have sex *Mex, Col* ◆ *Rodrigo parece tímido pero se ha enchufado a sus dos vecinas.* Rodrigo looks shy, but he has gotten lucky with his two neighbors.

un **enchufe** →**tener un enchufe**

encima →**echarse algo encima**

encima de todo topping it all off, on top of everything (else) *L. Am., Sp* ◆ *Y encima de todo, Carolina ni se asomó.* And on top of everything else, Carolina didn't even show up.

encimoso(-a) insistent person who keeps coming back for something *Mex, ES* ◆ *Cerremos la puerta antes que regrese esa encimosa otra vez.* Let's close the door before that annoying woman comes back again.

encogerse de hombros to shrug one's shoulders *L. Am., Sp* ◆ *Se encogió de hombros como quien dice "No lo sé."* He shrugged his shoulders as if to say "I don't know."

encontrar la horma de su zapato (to find one's shoe size; **horma** means wooden model of foot) to meet one's match *Mex, DR, ES, S. Cone, Sp* ◆ *Cuando conocí a Jorge, supe que había encontrado la horma de mi zapato.* When I met Jorge, I knew I had met my match.

encontrar una mina (de oro) (to find a [gold] mine) to hit the jackpot, strike it rich, find a way to live without working much *Mex, ES, Ch, Sp* ◆ *Ese hombre encontró una mina de oro y se da la gran vida.* That man hit the jackpot, and he lives the high life.

encontrarse con to run across, meet *L. Am., Sp* ◆ *Me encontré con mi primo en el café.* I ran across my cousin at the café.

estar **endrogado(-a)** (to be drugged) to be heavily in debt *Mex* ◆ *Estamos endrogados* *con la compra de la casa.* We're heavily in debt with the purchase of our house.

energúmeno →**como energúmeno**

enfermo(-a) del mate (del chape) (sick from mate tea [from a kind of mollusk]) loose cannon, nut case *S. Cone* ◆ *¿Vas descalzo a la recepción del colegio? Estás enfermo del mate.* You're going barefoot to the school reception? You're a nut case.

enfogonarse to get angry *Mex, PR, Col* ◆ *No tienes que enfogonarte conmigo; yo estaba gufeando.* You don't have to lose your cool with me; I was just fooling around.

estar **enganchado(-a)** to be hooked up with, an "item" or together with *Mex, ES, CR, Col* ◆ *Camilo está enganchado con la computadora.* Camilo is married to the computer.

engancharse to hook up with, hook someone up with *Mex, ES, CR, Col* ◆ *Engánchame con aquélla.* Hook me up with her over there (introduce me). ◆ *Juan y María están enganchados.* Juan and María are an item (couple).

engrupido(-a) (grouped up) pretentious, a bit snobbish *U, Arg* ◆ *Con excepción de Ana Luisa, en esa familia todos son engrupidos.* With the exception of Ana Luisa, everyone in that family is stuck-up.

el/la **engrupidor(a)** (grouper) person who deceives you with wit or charm, smooth talker, con man *S. Cone* ◆ *Todos creímos que era una buena persona, y resultó ser una engrupidora.* We all thought she was a good person, and it turned out she was a con artist.

engrupir (to group up) to fool or trick with wit or charm, to con *S. Cone* ◆ *Nos engrupieron con el precio de la excursión; pagamos más de lo que valía.* They conned us with the price of the excursion; we paid more than it was worth.

la **enhorabuena** →**dar la enhorabuena**

enjaretar to force (on someone), stick (someone) with something *Mex, U, Arg* ◆ *Juan me enjaretó un trabajo horrible.* Juan stuck me with a horrible job.

enojón, enojona hostile, easily angered *L. Am., Sp* ◆ *Constanza es muy enojona.* Constanza is a real hothead.

enrollarse (to get rolled up) to sling the bull, talk at length, string along with talk or flat-

tery (like **dar cuerda**) *ES, Sp* ◆ *Miguel, ino te enrolles tanto! (Sp)* Miguel, don't sling the bull! ◆ *Felipe vio a una amiga y se enrolló con ella.* Felipe saw a friend and started a long conversation with her.

enrollarse con (to get rolled up with) to get mixed up or involved with *DR, ES, Sp* ◆ *Nos enrollamos con el equipo de fútbol.* We got involved with the soccer team.

entender →**dar a entender; no entender ni jota (ni papas)**

entendido(-a) →**no darse por entendido(-a)**

enterarse de to find out about *L. Am., Sp* ◆ *No me enteré de la boda hasta la semana pasada.* I didn't find out about the wedding until last week.

entero(-a) (complete) pretty; good *Mex, DR, PR, Col* ◆ *Con ésa sí me caso; es una chica entera. —Sí, completa y medio.* I'd marry that girl; she's a pretty babe. —Yes, a babe and a half (literally, complete and half).

enterrar a alguien (to bury someone) to write someone off, break off with someone for good *Mex, Cuba, DR, U, Arg* ◆ *No me hables más de Juan Carlos, que ya lo enterré con flores.* Don't talk to me anymore about Juan Carlos. I've put him out of my mind for good.

entierro →**como entierro de pobre**

entrada →**dar entrada**

entradito(-a) en años (a little bit entered into years) getting up there (euphemism) *most of L. Am., Sp* ◆ *¿Cuántos años tiene Facundo? —No lo sé, pero ya está entradito en años.* How old is Facundo? —I don't know, but he's getting up there.

entradito(-a) en carnes (a little bit entered into flesh) a little bit heavy, pleasingly plump (euphemism) *DR, S. Cone, Sp* ◆ *La verdad es que Manuel está bastante entradito en carnes. A ver si hace un poco de régimen.* The truth is that Manuel is a bit overweight. Let's see if he'll go on a little diet.

el/la **entrador(-a)** (enterer) charmer, people person, person who easily becomes part of a new group, gets everything easily *ES, CR, Col, S. Cone* (RVAR *ES, CR:* new love, someone brave and bold in romance) ◆ *Luis no tuvo problemas en la nueva escuela. Es muy* *entrador y en seguida hizo amigos. Luis didn't have any problems at his new school. He's a real people pleaser, and he made friends right away.*

entrar →**hacer entrar por el aro a alguien**

entrar (andar) como Pedro por su casa (to enter [walk around] like Pedro in his house) to make oneself at home *Mex, DR, Peru, Bol, Ch, Arg, Sp* (RVAR *Mex:* **Juan** instead of **Pedro**) ◆ *El vecino andaba aquí como Pedro por su casa. The neighbor made himself at home here.*

entrar bizco y salir cojo (to come in cross-eyed and leave crippled) to have things go from bad to worse *parts of L. Am.* ◆ *Entré bizco y salí cojo. Things went from bad to worse for me.*

entrarle una cosa por un oído y salirle por el otro to have something go in one ear and out the other *L. Am., Sp* ◆ *Por un oído le entra y por el otro le sale. It goes in one ear and out the other.*

entre algodones (within cottons) born with a silver spoon in one's mouth, spoiled or overprotected *L. Am., Sp* ◆ *Maribel fue criada entre algodones; es una fresa. Maribel was born with a silver spoon in her mouth; she's a princess (literally, a strawberry).*

estar **entre dos aguas** (to be between two waters) to be undecided *most of L. Am., Sp* ◆ *Estamos entre dos aguas: no sabemos si ir a Cuba o Costa Rica en nuestras vacaciones. We're undecided: we don't know whether to go to Cuba or Costa Rica for our vacation.*

entre la espada y la pared (between the sword and the wall) between a rock and a hard place, without the possibility of escape *L. Am., Sp* ◆ *No sé qué hacer. Estoy entre la espada y la pared. I don't know what to do. I'm between a rock and a hard place.*

entre paréntesis (between parentheses) by the way *L. Am., Sp* ◆ *Entre paréntesis, ¿has hablado con el gerente? By the way, have you spoken to the manager?*

entromparse 1. to get angry *Mex, ES, Col, Ec* ◆ *Los dos ex-novios se entromparon enfrente de ella. The two ex-fiancés tore into each other in front of her.* **2.** to get drunk *Sp* ◆ *Fue a una fiesta y se entrompó. He (She) went to a party and got bombed.*

entuturutar to mix up, confuse, brainwash *ES* (RVAR *Nic, CR:* **entotorotar**) ◆ *No dejes que Felipe te entuturute. Don't let Felipe mix you up.* ◆ *La novia de Esteban lo tiene bien entuturutado. Ya no quiere salir con nosotros. Esteban's girlfriend has him brainwashed. He no longer wants to go out with us.*

envolver en razones (to wrap in reasons) to confuse (someone) *Mex, ES, Sp* ◆ *No trates de envolverme en razones, que yo sé lo que pasó. Don't try to mix me up; I know what happened.*

¡Epa! Hey! Oops! *Caribbean* ◆ *¡Epa! Olvidaste el mapa. Hey! You forgot the map.*

¡Epa, Chepa! (Hey, Chepa!) Jeez Louise! interjection of surprise and disbelief *Nic* ◆ *¿Ya llegaron tus padres tan temprano? ¡Epa, Chepa! Your folks got here already? Jeez Louise!*

¡Epa, epa! Jeez Louise! interjection expressing surprise or shock *Caribbean* ◆ *¿No traes plata? ¡Epa, epa! You don't have any money with you? Jeez Louise!*

equivocarse de to be wrong about, get the wrong . . . , make a mistake *L. Am., Sp* ◆ *Se equivocaron de habitación. They got the wrong room.* ◆ *Me equivoqué. Lo siento. I made a mistake. Sorry.*

el **error garrafal** huge mistake, big mess-up *DR, PR, Nic, S. Cone, Sp* ◆ *Cometí un error garrafal en el examen. I goofed up big-time on the test.*

escala →**hacer escala**

escamado(-a) (scaled, like a fish) skittery, nervous, wary *Mex, PR, Col* ◆ *Estaba escamado por el abrazo que me dio. I was skittery (and a bit surprised) about the hug he gave me.*

escamar(se) (to be scaled, like a fish) to scare (be scared, wary) *Mex, PR, Col* ◆ *¡Me escamaste! Pensé que estaba solo. (Mex) You scared me! I thought I was alone.* ◆ *Me escama ese negocio. No quiero problemas. (Sp) I'm wary of that business (that business makes me skittery). I don't want any problems.*

escapar del trueno y dar con el relámpago (to escape the thunder and face or get hit by the lightning) to go from the frying pan into the fire *PR, Sp* ◆ *Después del huracán hubo una inundación. Escapamos del* *trueno y dimos con el relámpago.* After the hurricane there was a flood. We went from the frying pan into the fire.

una **escoba** →**no vender una escoba**

escobazos →**echar a alguien a escobazos**

el/la **escuintle(-a)** twerp, insignificant person or kid, from the Náhautl word for hairless dog (also spelled **escuincle**) *Mex, parts of C. Am.* ◆ *¿Por qué te da miedo? Es un escuincle.* Why are you afraid of him? He's just a little twerp.

escurrir el bulto (to drain the shape or package) to avoid work or responsibility, worm out, pass the buck *Ch, U, Sp* ◆ *Siempre escurre el bulto cuando hay que pagar.* He (She) always worms out of it when it's time to pay.

esfumarse to disappear into thin air *L. Am., Sp* ◆ *¿Dónde está tu hermanito? —No sé. Se ha esfumado.* Where is your little brother? — I don't know. He's disappeared into thin air.

esnob snobbish *L. Am., Sp* ◆ *Es un snob de primera clase.* He's a first-class snob.

eso →**por eso**

De **eso nada, monada!** (Of that nothing, monkey [cute] face!) mild expression of rejection, like No way! or Nothing doing! *Sp* ◆ *¿Me invitas con un trago? —¡De eso nada, monada!* Will you treat me to a drink? —No way, José!

el **espantapájaros** (scarecrow) ugly duckling, ugly or skinny person *L. Am., Sp* ◆ *Es un espantapájaros pero se cree buen mozo.* He's an ugly ducking, but he thinks he's really good-looking.

espantar la mula (to scare off the mule) to kick the bucket, die; to go away, leave *Mex, Cuba, DR, PR, CR,* ◆ *No quiero espantar la mula todavía.* I don't want to kick the bucket just yet.

espárragos →**mandar a alguien a freír espárragos**

especializarse en to major in; to specialize in *L. Am., Sp* ◆ *Me especializo en informática.* I'm majoring in computer science.

ser de **esperar** to be expected *L. Am., Sp* ◆ *¿Llegaron tarde otra vez? Bueno, era de esperar.* They got there (here) late again? Well, it was to be expected.

estar **espeso(-a)** (to be thick) to be slow, dull *Sp* ◆ *Estoy muy espeso hoy.* I'm very slow today.

espina →**darle mala espina**

las **esposas** (wives) handcuffs *L. Am., Sp* ◆ *La policía arrestó al ladrón y le puso las esposas.* The police arrested the thief and put handcuffs on him.

un **esquinazo** →**dar (un) esquinazo**

en la **estacada** (in the stockade) in danger, holding the bag (usually used with **dejar**) *Bol, Ch, Sp* ◆ *En los momentos difíciles nunca me dejó en la estacada.* At the most difficult times, he (she) never left me in the lurch.

en **estado** (in a state [of maternity]) expecting, pregnant *most of L. Am., Sp* ◆ *Me parece que Natalia está en estado. No quiere comer porque se siente mal del estómago, y está siempre cansada.* It seems to me that Natalia is expecting. She doesn't want to eat because her stomach bothers her, and she is always tired.

¡Estás como lo recetó el doctor! You're just what the doctor ordered! (can be a street compliment) *L. Am.* ◆ *¡Qué guapa, mujer! Estás como lo recetó el doctor.* How gorgeous you look, woman! You're just what the doctor ordered.

¡Estás como quieres! (You are like you want to be!) You look great! *Mex, DR, ES, Sp* ◆ *¿Te parece que estoy bien con este traje? —Sí, ¡estás como quieres!* Do you think I look good in this suit? —Yes, you look great!

el **estatequieto** (be quiet) blow or punch, hit *Mex, ES, Peru, U* ◆ *Su prima le dio un estatequieto a Lalo porque no dejaba de molestar.* His cousin gave Lalo a "reason to be quiet" (a spank) because he wouldn't let her alone.

Este... Uh . . . , Well . . . *L. Am., Sp* ◆ *Este... los ayudaremos por unas horas.* Uh . . . we'll help you for a few hours.

el **estilo** →**por el estilo**

estirado(-a) (stretched out) uptight, snobbish *ES, Nic, CR, Col, Peru, S. Cone, Sp* (*RVar Nic:* implies upper class or high society) ◆ *Desde que se graduó, Constantina se ha puesto muy estirada.* Since she graduated, Constantina has become very snobbish.

estirar la pata (to stretch out one's foot) to kick the bucket, die *L. Am., Sp* (RVᴀʀ *Nic:* also, take a walk) ◆ *El almacenero de mi barrio estiró la pata.* My neighborhood grocer kicked the bucket.

¡Esto es el colmo! (This is the limit, culmination!) This is the last straw! *L. Am., Sp* ◆ *No han lavado la ropa ni los platos por una semana. ¡Esto es el colmo!* You haven't washed the clothes or the dishes for a week. This is the last straw!

Esto resucita a un muerto. (This brings the dead back to life.) This livens, perks (a person, things) up. *U, Arg, Sp* ◆ *Esta música tan alegre resucita a un muerto.* This cheerful music livens a person (things) up.

Estoy a sus órdenes. I am at your service. *L. Am., Sp* ◆ *Estoy a sus órdenes si necesitan un guía por la ciudad.* I'm at your service if you need a guide around the city.

Estoy con ustedes. (I am with you.) I feel for you. (expressing sympathy for misfortune) *L. Am., Sp* ◆ *Señor Toledo, estoy con ustedes (en su dolor).* Mr. Toledo, I feel for you (in your suffering).

Estoy que me caigo. (I'm about to fall over.) I'm in bad shape (not well). I'm ready to drop. *U, Arg, Sp* ◆ *Esta semana trabajé ochenta horas. Estoy que me caigo.* This week I worked eighty hours. I'm ready to drop.

estrafalario(-a) outlandish, strange, weird (usually referring mainly to dress) *L. Am., Sp* ◆ *Esa chica siempre se ve muy estrafalaria.*

¡Qué vestido más estrafalario! That girl always looks weird. What a weird dress!

estrella ➞**tener estrella**

estrellado(-a) (seeing stars) star-crossed, unlucky *Mex, ES, S. Cone* ◆ *Unos nacen con estrella y otros estrellados.* Some people are born with a lucky star and some are born seeing stars (with bad luck).

la del **estribo** (the one of the stirrup) one for the road (usually referring to a drink) *Mex, ES, S. Cone* ◆ *¡Echemos la del estribo!* Let's have one for the road!

estrujarse el melón (to press one's melon, or head) to rack one's brain, think *Sp* ◆ *Tuvimos que estrujarnos el melón para poder satisfacer los requerimientos de nuestro cliente.* We had to rack our brains to be able to satisfy the client's requirements.

evaporarse (to evaporate) to disappear into thin air *Mex, Ch, Sp* ◆ *¿Dónde está Manuela? —¿Quién sabe? Se ha evaporado.* Where is Manuela? —Who knows? She's disappeared into thin air.

un **examen** ➞**dar un examen**

excelencia ➞**por excelencia**

el **excusado** (the excused place) bathroom (euphemism) *Mex, Col, Ch* ◆ *Leticia tuvo que usar la letrina porque no había excusado en esa área rural.* Leticia had to use the latrine because there was no bathroom in that rural area.

ey yeah *most of L. Am.* ◆ *¿Cansada? —Ey.* Tired? —Yeah.

F

la **facha** getup, ridiculous dress, outfit *L. Am., Sp* ◆ *Con esa facha no puedes entrar en la disco.* You can't go to the disco in that getup. ◆ *Cámbiate esa facha si quieres ir al cine conmigo.* Change that ridiculous outfit if you want to go to the movies with me.

fachoso(-a) badly dressed; affected, trying to appear elegant *Mex* ◆ *¿Así de fachosa vas a ir? Necesitas cambiar.* You're going dressed like that? You have to change.

fácil easy (woman) *L. Am., Sp* ◆ *Esa mujer es bastante fácil.* That woman is rather easy.

facilingo very easy *parts of L. Am.* ◆ *Este trabajo es facilingo. Podemos hacerlo en unas pocas horas.* This job is very easy. We can do it in a few hours.

fajar (to girdle, wrap) to make out *Mex* ◆ *Fajé con mi novio.* I made out with my steady boyfriend.

el **faldero** henpecked man, from **falda**, skirt *Mex, ES* ◆ *Aquí viene ese faldero con su mujer.* Here comes that wimpy (henpecked) man with his wife.

fallarle la azotea (to have one's roof failing) to have bats in the belfry, be crazy *Mex, DR, PR, S. Cone* ◆ *A Rolando le falla la azotea.* Rolando has bats in his belfry.

falta →**hacer falta; sin falta**

A **falta de pan, buenas son tortas.** (When there is no bread, cakes are fine.) One thing is as good as another. Beggars can't be choosers. *most of L. Am., Sp* ◆ *No me gusta la comida de Amanda, pero a falta de pan, buenas son tortas.* I don't like Amanda's food, but it will do just fine.

¡Lo que **faltaba para el duro!** (What was missing for the hard one!) That's all we needed! *Sp* ◆ *Tu embarazo es lo que faltaba para el duro en este momento.* Your pregnancy is all that we needed (the last straw) at this moment.

faltar a la palabra to not keep one's word *L. Am., Sp* ◆ *No confío en el negocio de Arturo; a menudo falta a la palabra.* I don't have confidence in Arturo's business; he often does not keep his word.

faltar el respeto a... (to lack respect) to disrespect, often used for a child who talks back or doesn't mind *L. Am., Sp* ◆ *No me faltes el respeto, niña.* Don't disrespect me, girl.

faltar: ¡No faltaba más! The very idea! (used to decline an offer of generosity) *L. Am., Sp* ◆ *Oh, no, ¡por favor! Yo pago la cena como eres mi invitada. ¡No faltaba más!* Oh, no, please! I'm paying for the dinner since you are my guest. The very idea!

faltarle a alguien un tornillo to have a screw loose (missing) *L. Am., Sp* ◆ *Rosario fue a la universidad con un vestido de fiesta. —Ya lo supe. Pobrecita; le falta un tornillo.* Rosario went to the university in a party dress. —I knew it. Poor thing; she's got a screw loose.

faltón, faltona irresponsible, describing someone who doesn't do what he (she) is supposed to do *most of L. Am., Sp* ◆ *¡Ojo con Rolando! Es un faltón.* Be careful of Rolando. He's unreliable.

fama →**tener fama**

fantasioso(-a) stuck-up *L. Am., Sp* ◆ *Serafina es muy fantasiosa.* Serafina is very stuck-up.

fantasma, fantasmón (fantasmona) (ghost) hypocritical, artificial *Sp* ◆ *Ya está bien de aparentar que tienes cuando no tienes. No te hagas más el fantasma.* Stop pretending you have things when you don't. Don't be so hypocritical.

el/la **fantoche(-a)** (puppet) presumptuous or ridiculous person; show-off *Mex, DR, ES, CR, Sp* (RVAR *CR*: person who is ridiculous, usually because of dress, not a show-off) ◆ *Ese joven es un fantoche; se cree la gran cosa.* That young guy is so stuck-up; he thinks he's hot stuff.

la **farmacia** →**tener la farmacia abierta (y el doctor dormido)** el **farolazo** drink (alcoholic) *Mex, ES, Nic, CR* ◆ *Echemos un farolazo. Let's have a drink.*

farra →**irse (andar) de farra**

la **farra** bash, party *Ec, S. Cone, Sp* ◆ *Salieron de farra anoche y tomaron demasiado.* They went out to party last night and drank too much.

fatal (fatal) awful, the pits, the bottom of the barrel, not well done or said *Mex, DR, PR, G, Col, Sp* ◆ *Esa película fue fatal.* That movie was the pits.

estar a **favor de** to be in favor of *L. Am., Sp* ◆ *Estuve a favor de la ley el año pasado, pero ahora he cambiado de opinión.* I was in favor of the law last year, but now I have changed my mind.

Favor que usted me hace. (Favor that you do me.) How nice of you to say so. (somewhat old-fashioned) *L. Am., Sp* ◆ *Has hecho un trabajo impecable; estamos muy satisfechos con los resultados. —Gracias, favor que usted me hace.* You've done an impeccable job; we are very satisfied with the results. —Thank you, how nice of you to say so.

el **fax** fax; fax machine *L. Am., Sp* ◆ *El fax se rompió.* The fax machine broke.

faxear to fax *L. Am., Sp* ◆ *Te lo puedo faxear si quieres.* I can fax it to you if you want.

la **fecha** →**hasta la fecha**

feliz como una lombriz (happy as a worm) happy as a lark *most of L. Am., Sp* ◆ *Adrianita estaba feliz como una lombriz jugando con otros niños en la playa.* Adrianita was happy as a lark playing with other kids on the beach.

fenomenal (phenomenal) great, super *S. Cone, Sp* ◆ *Pasamos un fin de semana fenomenal.* We had a great weekend.

feo(-a) →**más feo(-a) que carracuca**

feote (feota) super-ugly or run-down (**-ote**, augmentative) *L. Am., Sp* ◆ *Esa chica feota es carismática e inteligente.* That really ugly girl is charismatic and intelligent.

en **feria** →**irle a alguien como en feria**

la **feria** (fair or day off) dough, money *Mex, C. Am.* ◆ *No tengo feria.* I don't have any money.

la **festichola** bash, fantastic party *U, Arg* ◆ *Estamos preparando una festichola en la* casa nueva. We are preparing a big bash in the new house.

el **feto** (fetus) ugly person *Mex, U, Arg, Sp* ◆ *Hugo es un feto con un cerebro de Einstein.* Hugo is an ugly guy with brains like Einstein's.

al **fiado** on credit *L. Am., Sp* ◆ *Compramos un piano al fiado.* We bought a piano on credit.

fichado(-a) someone known by all; someone being watched carefully *L. Am.* ◆ *Me lo traiga bien fichadito. No quiero que salga.* Don't let him out of your sight. (Keep him under careful watch.) I don't want him to leave.

ser la **fiel estampa de alguien** (to be the faithful print of someone) to be the spitting image of someone *L. Am., Sp* ◆ *Tu hija es tu fiel estampa.* Your daughter is the spitting image of you.

una **fiera** →**como una fiera; ponerse como una fiera**

la **fiesta** →**Tengamos la fiesta en paz.**

fifí affected, overly concerned with dressing in style *Mex, U, Sp* (RVAR *Ch:* homosexual) ◆ *Esta chica es un poco fifí. ¿Has visto como se viste?* This girl is a little affected. Have you seen how she dresses?

un **figurín** →**estar hecho(-a) un figurín**

fijarse en to notice, look at *L. Am., Sp* ◆ *Fíjate en eso. Fíjate.* Look at that. Just imagine (think, look).

en **fila india** single file *L. Am., Sp* ◆ *Caminaron en fila india porque el sendero era muy estrecho.* They walked single file because the path was very narrow.

filete (fillet) very good, excellent *Mex, DR, PR, Ch* ◆ *Esta música es muy filete.* This music is great.

el **filo** (blade, file) hunger, appetite *Mex, ES, CR, Ven* ◆ *Gracias, pero ya no tengo filo.* Thanks, but I'm not hungry any more.

en **fin** in short *L. Am., Sp* ◆ *En fin, no podemos postergar la decisión ni un día más.* In short, we cannot postpone the decision even one more day.

a **fin de cuentas** (at the end of accounts) in the final analysis *L. Am., Sp* ◆ *A fin de cuentas, nunca sabremos la verdad.* In the final analysis, we'll never know the truth.

al **fin y al cabo** after all is (was) said and done *L. Am., Sp* ◆ *Al fin y al cabo, no tomaron* *ninguna decisión. After all was said and done, they didn't make any decisions.*

el **finde** short for **fin de semana**, weekend *Arg, Sp* ◆ *Hay una fiesta en casa de Julia el próximo finde. There's a party at Julia's house next weekend.*

a **fines de** toward the end of *L. Am., Sp* ◆ *Llegaré a fines de julio. I'll arrive at the end of July.*

fino(-a) como un coral (fine as a coral) astute, wise, sharp as a tack *Sp* ◆ *Su hija es fina como un coral. Her daughter is sharp as a tack.*

finolis exaggeratedly refined, uppity, finicky *Sp* ◆ *Este perro es muy finolis. No le gusta la carne que no esté muy cocida. This dog is very finnicky. He doesn't even like meat that isn't well done.*

estar en lo **firme** to be on solid ground, be in the right *L. Am., Sp* ◆ *No te eches para atrás, que estás en lo firme. Don't back down; you're on solid ground.*

firme como el roble (firm as the oak) solid as a rock, hard; strong *Mex, ES, S. Cone, Sp* ◆ *Esta mesa es firme como un roble. Puedes subir encima y no se rompe. This table is hard as rock. You can climb up on it and it won't break.*

flaco(-a) →**más flaco(-a) que un alfiler**

flaco(-a) (skinny) affectionate nickname *L. Am., Sp* ◆ *Flaca, ¡qué alegría de verte! Honey, what a pleasure to see you!*

flautas →**por pitos o por flautas**

¡Qué **flechazo!** (What a shot of the arrow!, referring to Cupid's arrow) It was love at first sight! *Mex, Col, DR, U, Arg, Sp*

flecharle (to strike with an arrow) to feel love at first sight *Mex, DR, ES, Col, S. Cone* ◆ *Me flechó. Estoy enamorada. It was love at first sight. I'm in love.*

la **flojera** laziness, lack of spirit *Mex, DR, PR, ES, Nic, CR, Col, Ch* ◆ *Tengo flojera; no voy a limpiar la casa hoy. I'm feeling lazy; I'm not going to clean the house today.*

flojo(-a) (loose, slack) lazy, slow, with no spirit; (n.) slacker, couch potato *Mex, DR, PR, ES, CR, Col, Ch* ◆ *Ese chico es muy flojo; nunca quiere hacer sus tareas. That boy is very lazy; he never wants to do his homework.*

flojos →**tener flojos los tornillos**

ser **flor de estufa** (to be a flower on the stove) to be a hothouse flower, overprotected, not allowed to grow or be independent *Sp* ◆ *Hasta que tuvo veinte años, Lucía no salió más de un día seguido de casa. Es una flor de estufa. Until she was twenty years old, Lucía didn't leave home for more than one day at a time. She's a hothouse flower.*

la **flor de la vida** (flower of life) the prime of life *L. Am., Sp* ◆ *Ese chico está en la flor de su vida. That boy is in the prime of his life.*

a **flor de labio(s)** (at the flower of the lip[s]) on the tip of one's tongue *L. Am., Sp* ◆ *Esa chica siempre tiene una respuesta a flor de labios. That girl always has an answer on the tip of her tongue.*

a **flor de piel** (at the flower of the skin) for all to see, obvious, readily present in a person's expression and nature *L. Am., Sp* ◆ *Ella tenía los nervios a flor de piel. Her nervousness was obvious.* ◆ *Edgar mostró su amor a flor de piel. Edgar wore his heart on his sleeve.*

la **flor y nata** (flower and cream) the cream of the crop, upper crust *L. Am., Sp* ◆ *En esa recepción estaba la flor y nata de la sociedad. The upper crust was at that reception.*

ser **florero** (to be a flower vase) to be the center of attention *Ch* ◆ *Aquí viene Isabel. Le encanta ser florero. Here comes Isabel. She loves being the center of attention.*

flores →**echar flores; echarse flores**

flotar (to float) to not be with it or in the world, not find out about things (said by young people) *Sp* ◆ *Estás flotando, hombre. You're out of it, man.*

flotar como el corcho en el agua (to float like cork in water) to come out on top, come out well despite adversity *Sp* ◆ *Sacrificó su vida personal para triunfar y ahora flota como el corcho en el agua. He sacrificed his personal life to get ahead and now he's come out on top.*

la **foca (vaca)** (seal [cow]) cow, fat person *U, Arg, Sp* ◆ *Silvia está hecha una foca, pero no le interesa hacer dieta. Silvia is a total cow, but she has no interest in going on a diet.*

follar to have sex, equivalent of the f-word (vulgar) *Sp* ◆ *Estábamos muy excitados y* *follamos en el jardín. We were very hot and we f-ed in the garden.*

el **follón** mess, confusion (a bit vulgar but very commonly used) *Sp* ◆ *¡Qué follón! What a mess!*

un **fonazo** →echar un fonazo

en el **fondo** (at the bottom) underneath it all, at heart *L. Am., Sp* ◆ *Aunque no lo parece, en el fondo Blanca es una persona muy altruista. Although it doesn't look like it, at heart Blanca is a very altruistic person.*

a **fondo** (to the bottom, in depth) completely, in depth, totally *L. Am., Sp* ◆ *No te cases sin conocer a fondo a tu pareja. Don't get married without knowing your partner completely.*

¡Fondo blanco! (White bottom [of glass]!) Bottoms up! *most of L. Am.* ◆ *El mejor brindis: ¡fondo blanco! The best toast: Bottoms up!*

formar un berrinche to have a fit, tantrum *PR, Col, Sp* ◆ *El niño de la vecina forma un berrinche cada vez que ella se va al trabajo. The neighbor's little boy has a tantrum every time she goes to work.*

forrado(-a) (lined, referring to lined pockets) moneybags, having money *Mex, Cuba, DR, PR, U, Arg, Sp* ◆ *El novio de Lourdes está forrado. Creo que su mamá es la vice presidenta del banco. Lourdes's boyfriend is loaded. I think his mom is vice president of the bank.*

forrarse 1. (to make a lining for oneself) to stuff oneself (with food) *ES, Nic, Sp* ◆ *Enrique se forró de pollo en salsa de mole en el almuerzo. Enrique stuffed himself with chicken in mole sauce at lunch.* 2. (to make a lining for oneself, referring to lined pockets) to feather one's nest, strike it rich *DR, Nic, Sp* ◆ *Se forró de dinero en la bolsa de valores. He (She) made a lot of money in the stock market.*

el **forro** 1. (lining) good-looking person, male or female *Mex* ◆ *Juanito es un forro. Juanito is a looker.* 2. condom *Ch, Arg, Sp* ◆ *¿Trajiste los forros, querido? Did you bring the condoms, dear?*

el **forro** →Ni por el forro

fosfatina →hacer fosfatina a alguien

fosforito (little match) quick-tempered, hotheaded *PR, Ven, U, Arg* (RVar ALSO, IN *PR,*

witty) ◆ *¡Cuidado con Iván! Es muy fosforito. Watch it with Iván! He has a short fuse.*

fotos →sacar fotos

el **fracatán** tons, many, large amount *DR, PR* ◆ *Tienes un fracatán de libros. You have tons of books.*

la **fregadera** 1. the act of continuously asking for something (slightly vulgar) *Chicano, Mex, G, ES, CR* ◆ *Sigues con la misma fregadera. You keep on with your same old nagging.* 2. thingamajig (slightly vulgar) *Chicano, Mex, G, ES, CR* ◆ *Alcánzame esa fregadera... allí está. Get (literally, reach) me that thingamajig . . . there it is.* 3. dirty trick (slightly vulgar) *Mex* ◆ *Nos hicieron una fregadera. They played a dirty trick on us.*

estar **fregado(-a)** (to be scrubbed) to be useless, messed up, ruined *most of L. Am. (not U, Arg)* ◆ *La situación de los agricultores está muy fregada este año. The situation of the farmers is really messed up this year.*

ser (un[a]) **fregado(-a)** (to be a scrubber) to be an annoying, demanding, or bossy person *Mex, Nic, CR, Peru, Ch* ◆ *El hijo de ellos es muy fregado; siempre quiere comprar ropa muy cara y gastar dinero con sus amigos. Their son is very demanding; he always wants to buy expensive clothing and spend money with his friends.*

fregar (to scrub, scour, rub [the wrong way]) to mess up, ruin, jerk around; to bug, bother with insistent requests *most of L. Am.* ◆ *Nos fregaron otra vez. They jerked us around again.* ◆ *Déjate de fregar. Get off my case.*

fregón, fregona (scrubber) annoying, badgering *Mex, G, CR, Col* ◆ *Pero si soy un fregón, luego lo agarre. But if I keep on badgering, eventually I'll get it.*

ser (un[a]) **fregón (fregona)** to be good, super (often at doing something) *Mex* ◆ *Mi hermano es un fregón para los deportes. My brother is really good at sports.* ◆ *Esa película es muy fregona. That film is terrific.*

freír →mandar a alguien a freír buñuelos; mandar a alguien a freír espárragos; mandar a alguien a freír papas

freno →poner freno a algo

la **frente** →dar frente a; traer/llevar algo escrito en la frente la **fresa** (strawberry) princess, young woman who is innocent but also a bit disdainful or spoiled, usually living with her parents *most of L. Am ◆ Verónica es una fresa; sus papás la miman mucho. Verónica is a princess; her parents spoil her a lot.*

fresco(-a) 1. (fresh) not worried, cool as a cucumber *Mex, Col, Ch, Sp ◆ Tiene un examen mañana, pero está tan fresca. She has a test tomorrow, but she's cool as a cucumber.* **2.** (fresh) shameless, unaffected by criticism *Ch, Sp ◆ Es una fresca. Le dejé un libro y aún no me lo ha devuelto. She's shameless. I left her a book and she still hasn't returned it. ◆ Es un fresco; se ha ido sin pagar. He's shameless; he's left without paying.*

fresco(-a) →**más (tan) fresco(-a) que una lechuga**

la **fría** (cold one) beer, brewsky *Cuba, PR, G, Col ◆ Tráeme una fría. Bring me a beer.*

friqueado(-a) (from English "freaked out") upset, freaked out *Mex, DR, PR, Ven ◆ Estaba friqueada cuando no llegaste a la hora. I was freaked out when you didn't get here on time.*

frito(-a) 1. (fried) dead as a doornail *PR, Col, U, Arg, Sp ◆ Se cayó de la ventana y se quedó frito en el suelo. (Sp) He (She) fell out the window and wound up dead as a doornail on the ground.* **2.** (fried) out like a light, asleep *U, Arg, Sp ◆ Se quedó frito en la playa. He fell asleep on the beach. ◆ Después de comer, siempre me quedo frito. After eating, I always fall asleep.*

frito(-a) →**tener (traer) a alguien frito(-a)**

estar **frito(-a)** (to be fried) to be toast, sunk, in trouble *L. Am., Sp ◆ Si no encuentras los papeles, estás frita. If you don't find the papers, you're toast.*

ser un(a) **fruncido(-a)** (to be a wrinkled-up person) to be very fussy, uptight, persnickety; to be a tightass *S. Cone ◆ Nadie le habla en la escuela porque ella es muy fruncida. Nobody talks to her at school because she's very uptight.*

fruncir (to pucker) to be a coward, wimp *Mex, Col ◆ ¡No te frunzas! Don't be a wimp!*

fruto →**dar fruto**

fu →**ni fu ni fa**

¡Fuchi! (¡Fúchila!) Yuck!, expression of disgust *Mex, ES, Col ◆ ¡Fúchila! ¡Qué asco! Yuck! How disgusting! ◆ No quiero ver a mi nuera con su cara de fuchi. I don't want to see my daughter-in-law with her yucky face.*

fuego →**echar fuego por los ojos**

a **fuego vivo (lento)** over a high (low) flame *L. Am., Sp ◆ Hay que cocinar esta salsa a fuego lento. You have to cook this sauce over a low flame.*

fuera →**por dentro y por fuera**

fuera de base (de órbita) 1. (off base [out of orbit]) out of it *Mex, Nic, Col, U ◆ No sé de qué hablan. Estoy totalmente fuera de base (órbita). I don't know what they're talking about. I'm totally out of it.* **2.** (off base [out of orbit]) stoned, in a state of hallucination *Mex, Col ◆ Patricio estuvo fuera de órbita por mucho tiempo después de consumir tanta cocaína. Patricio was wasted for a long time after using so much cocaine.*

Fuera de bromas. (Outside of jokes.) No joke. Seriously. *Mex, ES, S. Cone, Sp ◆ Ya fuera de bromas vamos a platicar de esto. Now let's talk about this seriously.*

fuera de onda out of it, totally unhip, old-fashioned *Mex, DR, ES, Col, U, Sp ◆ No se puede hablar con Antonieta. Está totalmente fuera de onda y no entiende nada. You can't talk to Antonieta. She's totally out of it and doesn't understand anything.*

fuera de serie (out of series) extraordinary, outstanding; (n.) outstanding person *L. Am., Sp ◆ Ese chico es un fuera de serie; siempre saca «excelentes» en todo. That guy is outstanding; he always gets "excellent" in everything.*

fuerte (strong) shocking, surprising; used as an intensifier *Mex, Sp ◆ ¿Lo arrestaron? ¡Qué fuerte! They arrested him? What a shock!*

la **fuerza** →**Ni a la fuerza.; sacar fuerzas de flaqueza**

a la **fuerza** (by force) against one's will *L. Am., Sp ◆ Ana no quería participar; lo hizo a la fuerza. Ana didn't want to participate; she did it against her will.*

fufurufo(-a) stuck-up *most of L. Am. (not Peru, Bol, Ch, U) ◆ Felipe es muy amable,* *pero su esposa es bien fufurufa. Felipe is very nice, but his wife is very stuck-up.*

el/la **fulano(-a), fulano(-a) de tal** so-and-so (to refer to someone you don't know, sometimes in a pejorative way), John or Jane Doe *L. Am., Sp* ◆ *La fulana que está a tu lado es la hermana del profesor. The (unknown) woman beside you is the professor's sister.* ◆ *Mira como esa fulana está flirteando con mi marido. Look at how that Susie Q. is flirting with my husband.*

Fulano, Mengano y Zutano so-and-so and his brothers; Tom, Dick, and Harry (expression used to name unknown people) *L. Am., Sp* ◆ *Invitaron a Pedro a cenar y resulta que vino con otro fulano, mengano y zutano. They invited Pedro to dinner and it turns out he came with another Tom, Dick, and Harry.*

fumar como (una) chimenea to smoke like a chimney *Mex, S. Cone, Sp* ◆ *Manuel Antonio fuma como una chimenea. Manuel Antonio smokes like a chimney.*

fumar como chacuaco (to smoke like a furnace or a cigarette butt) to smoke like a chimney *Mex* ◆ *En la calle vi a muchos jóvenes fumando como chacuacos. In the street I saw many young people smoking like chimneys.*

fumar como murciélago (to smoke like a bat) to smoke like a chimney *DR, PR, ES, S. Cone* ◆ *Su novio fuma como murciélago.*

Siempre tiene un cigarrillo en la mano. Her boyfriend smokes like a chimney. He always has a cigarette in his hand.

fumar como un carretero (to smoke like a trucker) to smoke like a chimney *Sp* ◆ *El bar estaba lleno de humo porque todo el mundo fumaba como carretero. The bar was full of smoke because everyone was smoking like a chimney.*

funcionar: No funciona. It's out of order, doesn't work. *L. Am., Sp* ◆ *No podemos ver la película porque la videocasetera no funciona. We can't watch the movie because the VCR is out of order.*

fundido(-a) (melted) wiped out, exhausted *G, Col, U, Arg* ◆ *Trabajé toda la noche. Estoy fundida. I worked all night. I'm wiped out.*

fundírsele a alguien los fusibles (to have one's fuses melt) to lose one's marbles, go crazy *Mex, DR, PR, ES, U, Sp* ◆ *Se me fundieron los fusibles. No sé en qué pensaba. I got temporarily disconnected. I don't know what I was thinking.*

fúrico(-a) furious *Mex* ◆ *Leandro está fúrico con su primo. Leandro is furious with his cousin.*

furor →**hacer furor**

furris bad, horrible *Mex, CR, Ven* (RVᴀʀ *Nic:* **furri**) ◆ *Su acción fue muy furris. What he did was really dumb (awful).*

G

gacho(-a) bad, unpleasant, of low quality or little worth *Mex, G, ES, CR* ◆ *Su novio es bien gacho. No sé porque ella sigue con él.* Her boyfriend is really a lowlife. I don't know why she keeps going out with him.

el **gafe** jinx *Sp* ◆ *Siempre que va Juan en el coche nos pasa algo. Es un gafe.* Every time Juan goes in the car with us something happens. He's a jinx. ◆ *Soy gafe.* I'm a jinx.

gafo(-a) silly, foolish *Ven* ◆ *Hugo siempre cuenta chistes gafos.* Hugo is always telling dumb jokes.

el/la **gafudo(-a)** (big glasses-wearer) person with glasses, four-eyes *Sp* (RVAR *Sp*: also, **gafas**) ◆ *El gafudo que recién llegó es el hermano del jefe.* The four-eyes that just arrived is the boss's brother.

los **gajes del oficio** (matters of the trade) part and parcel of the job, occupational hazards *Mex, DR, ES, Nic, S. Cone, Sp* ◆ *Roberto se rompió el brazo mientras escalaba. Ya se sabe, son gajes del oficio.* Roberto broke his arm while mountain climbing. It's understood that these are risks you have to take.

el **galanazo** good-looking guy, used instead of **galán** *Mex* ◆ *¿Quién es ese galanazo?* Who is that good-looking guy?

la **galleta** (cookie) traffic jam *Arg* ◆ *En la Avenida 9 de julio se forman galletas muy a menudo.* On 9th of July Avenue (a street named for an important date) there are usually traffic jams.

gallina →como gallina en corral ajeno

el **gallina** (hen) chicken, coward *Mex, Cuba, DR, PR, G, Nic, Col, Sp* ◆ *Valentín con las mujeres es muy agresivo, pero con los hombres se porta como un gallina.* Valentín is very aggressive with women, but with men he acts like a chicken.

el **gallinazo** womanizer; sleeping around *Mex, Col* ◆ *Pedro todavía sigue siendo un gallinazo a pesar de su avanzada edad.* Pedro still sleeps around in spite of his advanced age.

gallo →como gallo en patio ajeno

el **gallo 1.** (rooster) brave man, bulldog *Mex, C. Am., Sp* (RVAR *ES, Sp*: brave or angry) ◆ *Se puso como un gallo cuando le dijeron que bajara el volumen de su aparato de música. (Sp)* He became a bulldog when they told him to turn down the volume on his boom box. **2.** (rooster) dude, man, guy *Cuba, DR, PR, Peru, Ch* ◆ *Ese gallo allí vive en mi barrio.* That guy over there lives in my neighborhood.

la **gana** →darle a alguien la (real) gana, darle a alguien la regalada gana; tener ganas de (hacer algo)

ganarse la vida to earn a living *L. Am., Sp* ◆ *En este pueblo, ¿qué hace la gente para ganarse la vida?* In this town, what do people do to earn a living?

un **gancho** →hacer un gancho; tener gancho

el/la **gandalla** loser; opportunist, someone who takes or snatches things for himself or herself, grabby person *Mex, ES* ◆ *Entrégale el reloj; no seas gandalla.* Give him back his watch; don't be so grabby.

el **ganso** (goose) turkey, geek, introvert *PR, S. Cone* (RVAR *Ch*: also, **gansa** and **pavo[-a]**) ◆ *¡Qué ganso!* What a geek!

el **garabato** (scribbling, graffiti) swear word, bad word *Ch* ◆ *¡Basta de garabatos!* That's enough swear words!

al **garete** any which way, with no fixed direction or destination (**ir, andar al garete**) *Mex, DR, CR, Ch* ◆ *El muchacho andaba al garete.* The boy was going along with no fixed direction.

al **garete** →ir al garete

gárgaras →mandar a alguien a hacer gárgaras

el **garito** bar (usually small) *Sp* (RVAR *S. Cone*: a place to gamble illegally) ◆ *La policía llegó al garito y se llevó a todos los presentes.* The police arrived at the pub and took everyone there with them.

gato →dar (pasar) gato por liebre; como perros y gatos

Gato viejo, ratón tierno. (Old cat, young mouse.) phrase meaning that old geezers like sweet young things *Mex, ES, Ch* (RVar *Ch:* also, **Buey viejo, pasto tierno.** Old ox, fresh grass.) ◆ *Ese actor le lleva treinta años a su novia. Gato viejo, ratón tierno.* That actor is thirty years older than his girlfriend. No fool like an old fool.

una **gauchada** →hacer una gauchada

el **gavilán** (hawk) wolf, hustler, Don Juan *Mex, Col* ◆ *Hay muchas chicas en la piscina; por eso llegaron tantos gavilanes.* There are lots of girls at the swimming pool; that's why so many hustlers have arrived.

el **gazpacho** (cold vegetable soup) mess, mixup *Sp* ◆ *¡Qué tormenta! Habrá un gazpacho en el aeropuerto.* What a storm! There must be a mess at the airport.

lo **general** →por lo general

genio →tener mal genio

geniudo(-a) bad tempered, grouchy *Mex, Col* ◆ *Ese tipo es un geniudo. Es muy difícil trabajar con él.* That guy is a grouch. It's very hard to work with him.

ser **gente de medio pelo** (to be people by half a hair) to barely make ends meet, be barely middle-class *Mex, Nic, S. Cone, Sp* ◆ *Son gente de medio pelo, que trabaja por salarios mínimos.* They're barely middle class, people who work for the minimum wage.

el **gil (la gila, el gilberto)** chump, dupe, dope *Mex, Cuba, Col, Ec, Peru, S. Cone* ◆ *No te hagas el gil.* Don't act like a chump.

la **gilada** stupid action typical of a **gil**, or jerk; dirty trick *U, Arg* ◆ *Eso de sacarle el 10 por ciento de sueldo a los jugadores es una gilada.* Taking 10 percent of the players' salary is a dirty trick.

el/la **gilipollas** jerk, dope, asshole (vulgar, from **polla**) *Sp* ◆ *Conocí a ese gilipollas en enero en una disco.* I met that asshole in January at a disco.

las **gilipolleces** damn nonsense, stupidities (slightly vulgar) *Sp* ◆ *¡Qué gilipolleces! Yo nunca haría eso.* What damn nonsense! I would never do that.

¿En qué la **giras?** (In what do you spin it?) What do you do for a living? *Mex* ◆ *—¿En qué la giras, Miguel? —Soy diseñador de cocinas.* —What do you do for a living, Miguel? —I design kitchens.

un **giro** →tomar/dar un giro favorable

estar en la **gloria** (to be in one's glory) to be in seventh heaven, on cloud nine *L. Am., Sp* ◆ *Estoy en la gloria cuando hace fresco.* I'm in seventh heaven when it's cool out.

la **golfita** easy woman *Mex, Col* ◆ *En ese barrio hay muchas golfitas.* In that neighborhood there are many easy women.

golfo(-a) tramp, living a disorganized life or being dishonest sexually *Mex, ES, Sp* (RVar *ES:* feminine form only is used) ◆ *Sale por la noche cada día y con un chico distinto. Es bastante golfa. (Sp)* She goes out every night with a different guy. She's a bit of a tramp. ◆ *Vi a un par de golfos en la calle. (Mex)* I saw a couple of bums in the street.

el **gollete** →estar hasta el gollete

el **golpe** →dar el golpe; no dar un golpe

el **golpe bajo** low blow *L. Am., Sp* ◆ *¿Por qué me insultaste? Fue un golpe bajo.* Why did you insult me? It was a low blow.

el **golpe de teléfono** (hit with the telephone) phone call *U, Arg* ◆ *Dame un golpe de teléfono cuando estés lista para salir, y nos encontramos en el café.* Give me a call when you're ready to leave, and we'll meet in the café.

estar de **goma** (to be made of gum, rubber) to be hung over *C. Am.* ◆ *Tengo dolor de cabeza. Será que estoy de goma.* I have a headache. It could be that I'm hung over.

la **goma** →mandar a alguien a la goma

gorda →Ni gorda.

la **gorda** (fat one) ten-cent coin *Sp* ◆ *Está sin una gorda.* He (She) doesn't have a dime.

gordo(-a), gordito(-a) (fat, chubby) fat plum; darling, dear *L. Am., Sp* ◆ *Gordo, ¿dónde pusiste las llaves del coche?* Darling, where did you put the car keys?

el **gorila** gorilla, barbaric person, very big person *Mex, G* ◆ *Entró un gorila y empezó a gritarle al gerente.* A big guy came in and started yelling at the manager.

de **gorra** (by the cap) free, at someone else's expense *Mex, ES, CR, Sp* ◆ *Siempre como de gorra aquí.* I always mooch food here. ◆

Entró de gorra al cine. He (She) got into the movies free. ◆ *No quiero vivir de gorra. I don't want to live off other people.*

de **gorra, gorrón** →ir de gorra, de gorrón

gorrear to mooch, sponge, not pay for things *Mex, Col, Sp* (RVᴀʀ *Sp:* also, **gorronear**) ◆ *Siempre está gorreando tabaco a los amigos. Es un gorrón. He always bums tobacco from his friends. He's a sponge.* ◆ *Ella siempre me gorrea comida. She always hits me up for food.*

gorro →estar hasta el gorro; poner gorro a alguien; ponerse hasta el gorro

el **gorrón, la gorrona** mooch, freeloader *Mex, C. Am., Peru, Sp* (RVᴀʀ *Col:* **gorrero** [-a]) ◆ *Ernesto es un gorrón; nunca quiere pagar. Ernesto is a mooch; he never wants to pay.*

gota →como dos gotas de agua; ser la última gota; sudar la gota gorda

gotea →No llueve pero gotea.

gozar de buena salud to enjoy good health *L. Am., Sp* ◆ *Y tu mamá, ¿todavía goza de buena salud? Does your mom still enjoy good health?*

el **gozo en un pozo** (the enjoyment in a well or pit) It's all down the drain, What a bummer!, usually said when one's hopes for something have been dashed or something happens to ruin a good mood *Mex, Sp* ◆ *Salí de casa y vi que alguien me había robado la moto. Mi gozo en un pozo. I went outside and saw that someone had stolen my motorcycle. What a bummer.*

gracia →hacerle gracia a uno; tener (mucha) gracia

gran cosota big deal *Mex, C. Am.* ◆ *Para mí, el asunto del accidente es una gran cosota. To me, the accident is a big deal.*

grano →ir al grano

con un **grano de sal** with a grain of salt *L. Am., Sp* ◆ *Talia siempre lo critica todo; toma lo que dice con un grano de sal. Talia always criticizes everything; take what she says with a grain of salt.*

grasa (grease) low-class, common, rude *U, Arg* ◆ *No sé cómo puedes andar con ese tipo tan grasa. I don't know how you can go out with such a lowlife.*

greñudo(-a) longhaired, sloppy *Mex, DR, ES, Col* ◆ *Es un greñudo; nunca se peina. He's a slob; he never combs his hair.*

la **grifa** pot, marijuana *Chicano, Mex, CR, Ec* ◆ *¿Qué es eso? —Es una pipa para fumar grifa. What's that? —It's a pipe to smoke marijuana.*

grifo(-a) stoned on marijuana *Mex, CR, Ec* ◆ *No le hagas caso. Está grifo. Don't pay attention to him. He's stoned.*

Gringolandia Gringoland, the United States *L. Am.* ◆ *Los dos hermanos se fueron a trabajar a Gringolandia. The two brothers went to work in Gringoland.*

el **grito** →poner el grito en el cielo

a **grito pelado** (to the peeled shout) yelling loudly *most of L. Am., Sp* ◆ *Empezó a llamarme a grito pelado en medio de la fiesta. Todos se callaron. He started to call me at the top of his lungs in the middle of the party. Everybody stopped talking.*

groncho(-a) low-class, common, rude *U, Arg* ◆ *No salgas con él; es muy groncho. Don't go out with him; he's really crude.*

la **grosería** (gross thing, expression, etc.) vulgar or obscene word, swear word *L. Am., Sp* ◆ *Pablo le dijo una grosería, y ella se enfadó mucho. Pablo said something vulgar to her, and she got very angry.*

el/la **guacho(-a)** orphan, fatherless child; single thing left from a pair, as one glove or one earring; single person (e.g., at a party); can be a term of endearment *Ch, U, Arg* ◆ *Es guacho; su padre nunca se casó con su madre. He's a fatherless (illegitimate) child; his father never married his mother.* ◆ *Tengo un calcetín guacho después del lavado. I have a single sock after doing the wash.* ◆ *Guachita, hazme un gran favor. Honey, do me a big favor.*

la **guagua** baby *Ec, Peru, Bol, Ch* ◆ *¡Qué bonita guagua! How pretty the baby is!*

la **guagua** bus *Caribbean* ◆ *¿Cómo vas a la universidad? —En guagua. How do you go to the university? —By bus.*

el/la **guajiro(-a)** country person, simple person from rural area; (sometimes pejorative) hick *Cuba, Col* ◆ *Ese hombre habla como un guajiro. That man talks like a hick.*

el/la guajolote(-a) (turkey) turkey, stupid person *Mex* ◆ *Soy un guajolote; no pasé el examen.* I'm such a turkey; I didn't pass the test.

el guajolotero (turkey carrier) tightly packed bus or other vehicle *Mex* ◆ *Al día siguiente, tomamos un guajolotero a Monterrey.* The next day we took a really crowded bus to Monterrey.

el/la guanaco(-a) Salvadoran *DR, C. Am.* ◆ *Erminda es guanaca, su esposo es tico y sus hijos son canadienses.* Erminda is Salvadoran, her husband is Costa Rican, and their kids are Canadian.

el guapo (attractive, gorgeous) arrogant braggart, macho man *U, Arg* ◆ *Luis Felipe es el guapo de su grupo.* Luis Felipe is the arrogant braggart of his group.

guapo(-a) (attractive, gorgeous) brave *Mex, Cuba, DR, PR, S. Cone* ◆ *Adolfo es muy guapo; no tiene miedo de nada.* Adolfo is very brave; he's not afraid of anything.

guarango(-a) crude, with bad manners *U, Arg* ◆ *Fui al restaurante con Emilia y Angélica y me hicieron pasar vergüenza. Son muy guarangas.* I went to the restaurant with Emilia and Angélica and they embarrassed me. They're very crude.

guardar to keep in the clinker (jail), **guardado(-a)** *Mex, Cuba, DR, Col, U* ◆ *Todos creemos que Raúl y sus amigos están guardados, pero su familia no lo admite.* We all think that Raúl and his friends are in the clinker, but his family will not admit it.

guardar cama to stay in bed (especially when ill) *L. Am., Sp* ◆ *El doctor me recomienda guardar cama por tres días y tomar mucho líquido.* The doctor recommends that I stay in bed for three days and drink a lot of liquids.

guardar la línea to keep one's figure *L. Am., Sp* ◆ *¿Qué haces para guardar la línea? ¡Qué delgada te ves!* What do you do to keep your figure? You look so slim!

guardar rencor to hold a grudge *L. Am., Sp* ◆ *Perdóname, Paula. No guardes rencor.* Forgive me, Paula. Don't hold a grudge.

la guarra slut, loose woman *Sp* ◆ *La policía se llevó a las guarras que trabajan en esa calle.* The police took away the sluts who work in that street .

la guarrada dirty trick, crappy cheap shot (somewhat vulgar) *Sp* ◆ *Ya no es amigo mío porque me hizo una guarrada.* He's not my friend anymore because he played a dirty trick on me.

las guarrerías (pig things) junk, pieces of crap *Sp* ◆ *Pepito, no compres esas guarrerías en la tienda de golosinas. Sabes que no te sientan bien.* Pepito, don't buy that junk in the candy store. You know it isn't good for you.

el/la guarro(-a) (pig, swine) slob; person of loose morals *Sp* ◆ *No traigas más a esa panda de guarros a casa. Mira como lo han dejado todo después de la fiesta.* Don't bring that gang of slobs home again. Look how they left everything after the party.

la guata paunch, beer belly, potbelly *Peru, Bol, Ch* ◆ *Tienes mucha guata; necesitas una talla más grande.* You have a big paunch; you need a bigger size.

guay great, super, cool (same in the feminine as in the masculine); also, **guay del Paraguay** and **ir de guay** (to act cool) *Sp* ◆ *Adela es una chica muy guay. Es guay del Paraguay.* Adela is a real cool chick. She's the coolest.

la guayaba (guava) lie *most of L. Am.* (*not Ch, Arg*) ◆ *No voy a tragarme esa guayaba.* I'm not going to swallow that nonsense.

güero(-a) blond, fair *Mex, C. Am.* ◆ *Hola, güera, ¿qué tal?* Hi, (blondie), what's up?

el güey, buey (from "bovis": stupid, lazy [castrated] animal; somewhat vulgar) loser, dummy. Often used with affection among men, a mild insult like SOB *Chicano, Mex, PR, ES, Col* ◆ *Había puros güeyes, ni una pinche vieja.* There were only guys there, not a single broad. ◆ *Qué güey soy; olvidé el pasaporte.* How stupid I am; I forgot my passport. ◆ *Ey, güey, pásame el martillo.* Hey, pal, pass me the hammer.

gufear to joke or goof around, have a good time *PR* ◆ *Sólo estábamos gufeando.* We were just goofing around.

el gufeo something fun or amusing, good time *PR* ◆ *Esto no es gufeo.* This is no joke.

la **guial, guialcita** chick, babe, woman (from English girl) *Pan* ◆ *Conocí a una guial de Colombia.* I met a gal from Colombia.

el/la **guiri** foreigner *Sp* ◆ *¿Quién es ese tipo con la cámara? Parece guiri.* Who's that guy with the camera? He looks like a foreigner.

la **guita** dough, money *Ec, Peru, S. Cone, Sp* ◆ *No tenemos guita; nos quedaremos en casa este fin de semana.* We don't have any dough; we'll stay at home this weekend.

la **guita** →**tener la guita loca**

el **gurí, la gurisa** young boy, young girl *Par, U, Arg* ◆ *Ese gurí es muy trabajador y es-* *tudioso.* That young boy is very hard-working and studious.

gusto →**por gusto, de puro gusto**

estar a **gusto** to be at ease, comfortable, content *L. Am., Sp* ◆ *Como no sabe bailar, el canadiense no estaba muy a gusto en la fiesta.* Since he doesn't know how to dance, the Canadian guy wasn't very comfortable at the party.

gusto: ¡Qué gusto! What a pleasure! *L. Am., Sp* ◆ *Hace tiempo que no te veo, Adriana. ¡Qué gusto!* It's been a while since I last saw you, Adriana. What a pleasure!

H

haber (armarse) una de todos los diablos (to have [make] one of all the devils) to have a big problem, have a devil of a mess *L. Am., Sp* ◆ *Hubo (Se armó) una de todos los diablos cuando los obreros llegaron a la alcaldía.* There was a devil of a mess when the workers arrived at the mayor's office.

habla que te habla (talk that he or she talks to you) talking or chattering on, blah, blah, blah *DR, PR, Ch, U* ◆ *Esperé por largo rato mientras Estela, hable que te hable con sus amigas, sin preocuparse por mí.* I waited for a long time while Estela chattered on and on with her friends, without paying me any attention (literally, without worrying about me).

hablar →**Ni hablar.**

hablar como un carretero (to swear like a trucker) to swear like a trooper *U, Sp* ◆ *Benito habla como un carretero. Es desagradable escucharlo.* Benito swears like a trooper. It's unpleasant to listen to him.

hablar como un papagayo (un perico) to talk like a parrot, talk a lot (also: **hablar como un loro**) *DR, PR, Sp* ◆ *Miguelito es muy pequeño pero habla como un papagayo todo el día.* Miguelito is very small but he talks like a parrot all day.

hablar en cristiano (to talk in Christian) to speak plainly *L. Am., Sp* ◆ *Habla en cristiano, hombre, para que te entendamos.* Speak plainly, man, so we can understand you.

hablar entre dientes (to talk between the teeth) to mumble, murmur, grumble *L. Am., Sp* ◆ *Habla entre dientes, y no lo entiendo.* He swallows his words (mumbles), and I don't understand him.

hablar hasta por los codos (to talk even through one's elbows) to talk a blue streak, talk someone's ear off *L. Am., Sp* ◆ *La vecina vino a contarnos todo lo que pasó. Hablaba hasta por los codos.* The neighbor came to tell us what happened. She talked a blue streak.

hablar por hablar (to talk for to talk) to talk just for the sake of talking *L. Am., Sp* ◆ *Ese tipo está hablando por hablar; ni le importa el asunto.* That guy's just talking for the sake of talking; he doesn't even care about the issue.

Se hace a ciegas. (It's done blindly.) You can do it with your eyes closed. *Sp* ◆ *Ese trabajo es muy fácil. Se hace a ciegas.* That job is easy. You can do it with your eyes closed.

Se hace con la gorra. (It's done with the hat.) It's child's play, easy, a piece of cake. *Sp* ◆ *¿Hacer una videoconferencia? Se hace con la gorra.* Do a videoconference? It's a piece of cake.

hacer acto de presencia (to make an act of presence) to put in an appearance *L. Am., Sp* ◆ *Ni siquiera hizo acto de presencia en la boda de su hermano; su familia nunca lo va a perdonar.* He didn't even put in an appearance at his brother's wedding; his family will never forgive him.

hacer algo a lo bestia (to do something like a beast) to do something abruptly, do a bad job *Mex, PR, U, Arg, Sp* ◆ *Hizo sus maletas a lo bestia y se olvidó de cosas muy importantes.* He did a bad job packing his suitcases, and he forgot important things.

hacer algo con el culo (to do something with the ass) to do something in a half-assed way, badly (vulgar) *Mex, PR, Sp* ◆ *Rosalía, hiciste tu cama con el culo; tendrás que hacerla de nuevo.* Rosalía, you made your bed in a half-assed way; you'll need to do it over.

hacer algo volando to do something on the fly, quickly (literally, flying) *Mex, DR, G, ES, S. Cone, Sp* ◆ *Se lo voy a hacer volando. No se preocupe, señora, esta tarde tendrá sus zapatos arreglados.* I'll do it for you quickly. Don't worry, ma'am, you'll have your shoes fixed by this afternoon.

hacer algunas chapuzas to be working at odd jobs *Sp* ◆ *¿Tienes trabajo? —Hago al-*

gunas chapuzas. Do you have a job? —I'm doing some odd jobs.

hacer (viajar por) autostop to hitchhike *L. Am., Sp* ◆ *Viajamos de Madrid a Sevilla por autostop. We hitchhiked from Madrid to Seville.* ◆ *¿Cómo piensas ir sin dinero? —Haciendo autostop. How do you plan to go with no money? —Hitchhiking.*

hacer añicos (to break into pieces) to wear out, physically or mentally *Mex, ES, U, Arg, Sp* ◆ *La muerte de mis padres me hizo añicos. My parents' death wore me out emotionally.*

hacer brecha (to make an opening, breach) to break in, achieve fame or success *Mex, ES, U, Sp* ◆ *Los Beatles hicieron brecha en los sesenta, y aun hoy la gente los escucha. The Beatles made their big break in the sixties and even today people listen to them.*

hacer buenas migas (to make good crumbs) to hit it off, be good friends *L. Am., Sp* ◆ *Felipe y Raúl hacen buenas migas; sus esposas también se llevan muy bien. Felipe and Raúl hit it off (are good friends); their wives also get along well.*

hacer caso (to make case) to pay attention *L. Am., Sp* ◆ *Nunca me haces caso. You never pay attention to me.*

hacer caso omiso (to make omitted case) to not pay attention, disregard *L. Am., Sp* ◆ *Hicieron caso omiso de mis consejos. They didn't pay attention to my advice.*

hacer castillos de naipes (to build castles of cards) to make houses of cards, count on something one can't count on or do something in a foolish way *Sp* ◆ *Patricia se ha pasado haciendo castillos de naipes toda su vida. Patricia has spent her whole life building houses of cards.*

hacer castillos en el aire to build castles in the air *Mex, S. Cone, Sp* ◆ *Le encanta hacer castillos en el aire y soñar con cosas imposibles. He (She) loves to build castles in the air and dream of impossible things.*

hacer cerebro (to make brain) to rack one's brain, think (DR, PR: implies lust) *Nic, CR, Col* ◆ *Haremos cerebro y encontraremos la solución. We will rack our brains and find the solution.*

hacer clic to click (e.g., on a key or a mouse) *L. Am., Sp* ◆ *Haz clic en la letra A. Click on the letter A.*

hacer codos (to make elbows) to cram, study hard *Sp* ◆ *Si realmente quieres aprender ruso, hay que hacer codos. If you really want to learn Russian, you have to cram.*

hacer cola (to make tail or line) to stand in line *L. Am., Sp* ◆ *Fuimos al parque de atracciones pero pasamos el día entero haciendo cola. We went to the amusement park but we spent the whole day standing in line.*

hacer cuchi-cuchi to make out, have sex *Mex, Cuba, Col* (RVar *G:* to sleep) ◆ *Los padres de Florentina llegaron y la encontraron haciendo cuchi-cuchi con el novio. Florentina's parents came home and found her making out with her boyfriend.*

hacer de las suyas (to do your own) to do whatever one wants *Mex, DR, PR, ES, S. Cone* ◆ *Mi hermana siempre hace de las suyas. My sister always does whatever she wants.*

hacer de tripas corazón (to make heart of one's guts) to force oneself to overcome fear and adversity, pluck up courage *L. Am., Sp* ◆ *A pesar del problema que tenía, hice de tripas corazón y fui a la reunión. In spite of the problem I had, I pulled myself together and went to the meeting.*

hacer dedo (to make thumb) to hitchhike, thumb a ride *S. Cone, Sp* ◆ *Como no teníamos dinero, no tuvimos más opción que hacer dedo para ir a la playa. Since we had no money, we had no choice but to thumb a ride to get to the beach.*

hacer el cuatro (to make the four) to do the test for drunkenness, standing on one leg with arms spread out and bending the other leg at the knee in the form of a number 4 *Mex, DR, ES, Col, Ch* (RVar *Mex:* also, **poner el cuatro**) ◆ *Después de tratar de hacer el cuatro y no poder, fue arrestado por la policía porque estaba embriagado. After trying and failing to do the test for drunkenness, he was arrested by the police because he was smashed.*

hacer el oso (to do the bear) to do something embarrassing, embarrass oneself *Mex, Col* ◆ *Hice el oso de mi vida. Lo confundí con su hermano. I just did the most embar-*

rassing thing in my life. I confused him with his brother.

hacer el ridículo (to make the ridiculous) to act like a fool, look foolish *L. Am., Sp* ◆ *¡Córtala! Estás haciendo el ridículo. Cut it out! You're acting like a fool.*

hacer el viacrucis (to do the stations of the cross, a religious event) to go bar-hopping, go from bar to bar *Sp* ◆ *Hicimos el viacrucis en Madrid. We went bar-hopping in Madrid.*

hacer entrar por el aro a alguien (to make someone enter into the hoop) to make someone do something *L. Am., Sp* ◆ *No quería ir a la fiesta con ellos pero al final me hicieron entrar por el aro. I didn't want to go to the party with them but in the end they made me go.*

hacer escala to make a stop (e.g., a plane) *L. Am., Sp* ◆ *No es un vuelo directo; tenemos que hacer escala en Miami. It's not a direct flight; we have to make a stop in Miami.*

hacer falta (to make a lack) to be missing or lacking, to need (functions like **gustar**) *L. Am., Sp* ◆ *Mi hija me hace mucha falta. I miss my daughter a lot.*

hacer fosfatina a alguien (to make someone powder) to beat up, cause great harm *Sp* ◆ *Déjame en paz o te hago fosfatina. Leave me alone or I'll make mincemeat out of you.*

hacer furor (to make a furor) to be "in," be a hit or be in fashion *most of L. Am., Sp* ◆ *Su nuevo peinado hizo furor entre los presentes en la cena. Her new hairdo was a big hit with everyone at the dinner.*

hacer gárgaras →**mandar a alguien a hacer gárgaras**

hacer harina (to make flour) to break to pieces *DR, PR, U, Sp* ◆ *Se me cayeron los platos del estante y se hicieron harina. The plates fell off the shelf, and they broke all to pieces.*

hacer hincapié en to put special emphasis on, stress or emphasize *L. Am., Sp* ◆ *En ese colegio hacen hincapié en las bellas artes. In that school they put special emphasis on fine arts.*

hacer juego to go with, match *L. Am., Sp* ◆ *Esa falda hace juego con mi blusa; la voy*

a comprar. That skirt goes with (matches) my blouse; I'm going to buy it.

hacer la barba (to do the beard) to suck up *Mex* ◆ *Siempre le hace la barba al profe de ciencias. He's always sucking up to the science teacher.*

hacer la pelota (pelotilla) a alguien (to make the ball to someone) to flatter someone to obtain something, butter up *Sp* ◆ *Ese tío le hace la pelota al jefe. That guy is buttering up the boss.*

hacer la puñeta a alguien to bother, beg, annoy (slightly vulgar) *Sp* ◆ *El vendedor nos hizo a todos la puñeta. The salesman annoyed the hell out of all of us.*

hacer la rosca (to make the doughnut, e.g., rolled up like a doughnut) **1.** to crash, sleep anywhere, although it may not be comfortable *Sp* ◆ *Estábamos agotados e hicimos una rosca en el sendero a las montañas. We were exhausted and we curled up and slept on the path to the mountains.* **2.** to flatter, butter up ◆ *Julito le hacía la rosca a la maestra. Julito was buttering up the teacher.*

hacer la vista gorda (to do the fat look) to ignore, overlook *L. Am., Sp* ◆ *Ana llegó tarde, pero el jefe hizo la vista gorda. Ana came late, but the boss overlooked it.*

hacer las paces (to make peace) to bury the hatchet *L. Am., Sp* ◆ *Tengo ganas de hacer las paces con ellos. No podemos continuar así. I really want to make peace with them. We can't go on like this.*

hacer leña del árbol caído (to make firewood from the fallen tree) to kick someone when he or she is down *Ch, U* ◆ *Despúes de la bancarrota, todos trataron de hacer leña del árbol caído, y Gonzalo se enfermó seriamente. After the bankruptcy, everyone tried to kick him when he was down, and Gonzalo became seriously ill.*

hacer mal to harm *L. Am., Sp* ◆ *El principio más básico de la medicina es no hacer mal a nadie. The most basic principle of medicine is to do no harm to anybody.*

hacer migas a alguien (to make someone crumbs) to beat up, leave someone exhausted or overcome, cause stress or anxiety *Mex, ES, Sp* ◆ *Las discusiones con el abogado hicieron migas a Vicente. The discussions with the lawyer left Vicente exhausted.*

hacer mil maromas para...:
Ha hecho mil maromas para conseguir el helado; no quiere compartirlo.
He went to a lot of trouble to get the ice cream; he doesn't want to share it.

hacer mil maromas para... (to do a thousand acrobatic tricks in order to . . .) to go to a lot of trouble to . . . , spare no effort to . . . *most of L. Am., Sp* ◆ *He hecho mil maromas para verte.* I have gone to a lot of trouble to be able to see you.

hacer morder el polvo a alguien (to make someone bite the dust) to beat, beat up; to wear out *DR, Sp* ◆ *Nuestro entrenador de gimnasia nos hizo morder el polvo.* Our gymnastics coach wore us out.

hacer novillos (to make bell) to cut class *Sp* ◆ *Como hiciste novillos, ahora no tienes los apuntes de clase de aquel día.* Since you cut class, now you don't have the class notes from that day.

hacer ojitos (to make little eyes) to make (googoo) eyes at, flirt *L. Am., Sp* ◆ *Siempre te está haciendo ojitos en clase.* He's (She's) always making eyes at you in class.

hacer polvo a alguien o algo (to make someone or something dust) to beat up, cause serious damage, destroy, ruin *Mex, Cuba, DR, G, ES, Col, U, Sp* ◆ *Esa comida me dejó el estómago hecho polvo.* That food hit my stomach like a ton of bricks.

hacer puente (to make bridge) to take a long weekend by taking a day off before or after a holiday *Mex, DR, Sp* ◆ *Vamos a hacer el puente de pascua, ya que el martes es festivo y el lunes no iremos a trabajar.* We're going to have a long Easter weekend since Tuesday is a holiday and Monday we won't go to work.

hacer puré a alguien o algo (to make someone or something purée) to beat someone up, cause serious damage (physically or mentally) *Mex, DR, ES, U, Arg, Sp* ◆ *Me peleé con él y le dejé hecho puré.* I had a fight with him and I made mincemeat out of him.

hacer (un) serrucho to split a bill, make a kitty *DR, PR* ◆ *Hay que hacer un serrucho.* We have to take up a collection.

hacer su agosto (to make one's August) to make hay while the sun shines, take advantage of something, make a killing *L. Am., Sp* ◆ *Doña María hizo su agosto en la bolsa el año pasado. Doña María made a killing in the stock market last year.*

hacer su regalada gana (to do one's gifted desire) to do whatever one pleases, often describing a whim *Mex, ES* ◆ *Álvaro hizo su regalada gana cuando eligió la pintura para la casa sin consultar a su esposa. Álvaro did what he darn well pleased when he chose the paint for the house without consulting his wife.*

hacer sus necesidades (una necesidad) (to do one's necessities [a necessity]) to go to the bathroom *DR, C. Am., U* ◆ *Espera un segundo; tengo que hacer mis necesidades. Just a second; I have to go to the bathroom.*

hacer teatro (to make theater) to make a scene, act in a theatrical way *Mex, ES, Peru, S. Cone, Sp* ◆ *Deja de llorar; no estés haciendo teatro. Stop crying; don't act so melodramatic.* ◆

hacer tilín (to make a ringing sound, as of a bell) to be appealing; to like a little (functions like **gustar**) *Ch, Sp* ◆ *Juan me hace tilín. I kind of like Juan.*

hacer tortilla a una persona o cosa to beat up, crush or break (like eggs for an omelette, which is *tortilla* in Spain) *Mex, U, Sp* ◆ *El coche lo hizo tortilla. The car flattened him like a pancake.*

hacer trampas to cheat *L. Am., Sp* ◆ *Ramón siempre hace trampas cuando juega a las cartas; ten cuidado. Ramón always cheats when he plays cards; be careful.*

hacer un berrinche to have a tantrum *Mex, DR, Col, Sp* ◆ *Marta hizo un berrinche enorme cuando le dijeron que se fuera. Marta threw an enormous tantrum when they told her to leave.*

hacer un coraje to pick a fight; to get very angry *Mex, G* ◆ *Carmen hizo un coraje en el aeropuerto cuando le dijeron que sus maletas no estaban en el vuelo. Carmen got very angry at the airport when they told her that her suitcases were not on her flight.*

hacer un download (un backup) to download (back up) (a computer file) *L. Am., Sp* ◆ *Laura, necesito que me hagas un backup. Laura, I need you to make me a backup.*

hacer un gancho (to make a hook) to fix up with a blind date; also, to punch *S. Cone, Sp* ◆ *Mi hermano quiere que le haga un gancho con una de mis amigas. My brother wants me to fix him up with one of my friends.*

hacer un levante to pick (someone) up, make amorous conquests *Mex, DR, PR, G, Col* ◆ *Intenté hacer un levante en la playa. I tried to pick someone up at the beach.*

hacer un pancho to do something embarrassing *Mex* ◆ *Hice un pancho; se me olvidó saludar al jefe. I did something embarrassing; I forgot to say hello to the boss.*

hacer un papel to play a role or part *L. Am., Sp* ◆ *Esa actriz siempre hace el papel de la "segunda frente". That actress always plays the role of the "other woman."*

hacer un paro (to make a stop) to do (someone) a favor *Mex, parts of C. Am.* ◆ *Hazme un paro, mano. Do me a favor, bro'.*

hacer un sinpa (to do a no-pay, from **sin pagar**) to leave without paying *Sp* ◆ *Rolando hizo un sinpa en el bar. Rolando left the bar without paying.*

hacer un tango (to do a tango) to put on a show, cause a scene, have a fit *Mex, Col* ◆ *Hizo un tango porque no lo dejaron entrar en la discoteca porque no llevaba identificación. He made a scene because they wouldn't let him in the disco because he didn't have ID.* ◆ *El niño hizo un tango en McDonald's. The boy had a fit in McDonald's.*

hacer una gauchada (from **gaucho**, cowboy) to do an immense favor *S. Cone* ◆ *Gracias por la gauchada, che. Thanks for the big favor.*

hacer una vaca/vaquita (echar la vaca) (to make a cow [throw the cow]) to chip in, pool money for a common cause *G, Nic, Ven, S. Cone* (RVAR *Mex:* **hacer una vaquita**) ◆ *Vamos a hacer una vaquita para un regalo para los novios. Let's chip in for a present for the bride and groom.*

hacer zapping (to do zapping) to channel-surf, change the channel *Peru, S. Cone, Sp* ◆ *No me gusta mirar televisión con Gustavo porque hace zapping constantemente. I don't like watching television with Gustavo because he's always channel-surfing.*

hacerla de tos (de pedo) a alguien (to make someone of the cough [fart]) to give someone problems *Mex, ES* (**de pedo:** vulgar) ◆ *Cálmate. No la hagas de tos. Calm down. Don't cause problems.* ◆ *Con cualquier cosa me la hace de pedo. He (She) gives me a damn hard time with everything.*

hacerle a alguien de chivo los tamales (to make someone's tamales out of kid goat meat) to cheat on or deceive one's mate *Mex, ES* ◆ *Sara está segura que su marido le hace de chivo los tamales. Sara's sure that her husband is cheating on her.*

hacerle agua la boca (to make the mouth water) to have one's mouth watering *L. Am.* (RVar *Sp:* **hacerle la boca agua**) ◆ *¿Hiciste empanadas, mi amor? Se me hace agua la boca. (L. Am.) You made empanadas, my darling? My mouth is watering.* ◆ *Se me hace la boca agua. (Sp) My mouth is watering.*

hacerle gracia a uno to strike someone as funny *L. Am., Sp* ◆ *Ese comentario me hizo mucha gracia. That comment struck me as funny.*

hacerle la cama a alguien (to make the bed for someone) to get ahead of someone, take him or her by surprise, prevent someone from doing well, cut off at the pass *S. Cone* ◆ *Me distraje y ese tipo me hizo la cama. Perdí una buena oportunidad en el trabajo. I got distracted and that guy took me by surprise. I missed out on a good opportunity at work.*

hacerle la cruz a alguien (to make the cross to someone) to write someone off *S. Cone* ◆ *Supimos que Ramona es una chismosa y le hicimos la cruz. We found out that Ramona is a gossip, and we wrote her off.*

hacerle la vida un yogurt a alguien (to make someone's life a yogurt) to make someone's life sour *Cuba* ◆ *Mi suegro me hace la vida un yogurt. My father-in-law makes my life sour.*

hacerse bolas (to get balled up) to get confused or balled up in *Mex, C. Am.* ◆ *No te hagas bolas. Don't get all confused.* ◆ *Aquí siempre me hago bolas con el lenguaje. Here I always get confused with the language.*

hacerse camote (to make sweet potato) to get confused or balled up in *Mex* ◆ *Se hizo camote con el examen, y lo reprobaron. He*

got all confused on the exam, and they failed him.

hacerse cargo de to take charge of *L. Am., Sp* ◆ *Como era la mayor, Cecilia se hizo cargo de sus hermanos después de que sus padres murieron. Since she was the oldest, Cecilia took charge of her brothers and sisters after their parents died.*

hacerse de la vista choncha to ignore, overlook *Mex* ◆ *Estaban jugando, pero la maestra se hizo de la vista choncha. They were playing, but the teacher ignored them (overlooked it).*

hacerse de(l) rogar (to make oneself begged) to play hard to get, like to be begged *L. Am., Sp* (RVar *Mex, ES, Pan, Col:* **del;** *DR, Peru, Ch, Sp:* **de**) ◆ *A mi hermana le gusta hacerse de(l) rogar. My sister likes to play hard to get.*

hacerse el bocho to fixate on, obsess over something *U, Arg* ◆ *No se hagan el bocho porque no hay ningún peligro en esta situación. Don't obsess over it because there is no danger in this situation.*

hacerse el chivo loco (to make oneself the crazy kid goat) to play dumb, play the part of someone who didn't hear or see anything *Mex, DR* ◆ *Es más fácil aceptar las cosas y hacerse el chivo loco. It's easier to accept things and play dumb.*

hacerse el (la) desentendido(-a) (to make oneself the nonunderstanding one) to play dumb, pretend not to notice *L. Am., Sp* ◆ *No te hagas la desentendida. Sabes muy bien de lo que estoy hablando. Don't play dumb. You know very well what I'm talking about.*

hacerse el loco (tonto) (la loca [tonta]) (to make oneself the crazy one) to play dumb, pretend not to notice *L. Am., Sp* (RVar *Ch:* also, **hacerse el leso**) ◆ *No te hagas la loca; sabes bien que Ernesto es mi novio. Don't play dumb; you know very well that Ernesto is my boyfriend.*

hacerse el (la) vivo(-a) (to become the live one) to get ahead, be clever at taking advantage of others *L. Am., Sp* ◆ *No te hagas el vivo porque aquí te conocemos. Don't try to take advantage because we know you here.*

hacerse humo (to become steam or smoke) to disappear into thin air *L. Am., Sp* ◆ *Los* *ladrones se hicieron humo. The thieves took off in a puff of smoke.* ◆ *Hazte humo. ¿No sabes que ya caíste mal? Get the heck out of here. Don't you know you blew it (made a bad impression)?*

hacerse mala sangre (to make bad blood for oneself) to get upset, ticked off, rattled *L. Am., Sp* ◆ *No te hagas mala sangre. No es tan tremendo. Don't get ticked off. It's not so awful.*

hacerse pedazos (to make itself pieces) to break or smash to pieces *L. Am., Sp* ◆ *¿El florero? Se ha hecho pedazos. The vase? It broke all to pieces.*

hacerse rosca (to make oneself a doughnut) to refuse stubbornly (to do something), sometimes while acting sweet *Mex* ◆ *Cuando le pregunté sobre el dinero, se hizo rosca y no me lo dio. When I asked him about the money, he refused to give it to me.*

hacerse un ocho (to make oneself into an eight) to get balled up in difficulties *DR, PR, Col* ◆ *Porfa, ayúdame, que yo siempre me hago un ocho con esta computadora. Please help me; I always get all balled up with this computer.*

hacerse un ovillo (una pelota) (to make oneself a little egg [a ball]) to curl up; colloquially, to shrink with fear, pain, etc.; to get confused or balled up *Sp* ◆ *Se hizo un ovillo y no me quiso hablar. He curled up (with fear or pain) and didn't want to talk to me.*

hacerse un taco (to make oneself a plug) to get confused or balled up in difficulties *Sp* ◆ *Durante el examen me hice un taco. During the exam I got all balled up.*

hacerse una chaqueta to do a hand job, masturbate (males, vulgar) *Mex*

hacerse una paja (to make oneself a straw) to do a hand job, masturbate (vulgar); (*Col, Arg:* **hacerse la paja**) *L. Am., Sp*

hacerse: Eso no se hace. That's not allowed (done). *L. Am., Sp* ◆ *No pongas los pies sobre la mesa. Eso no se hace. Don't put your feet on the table. That's not done.*

hacérsele to have a hunch, think, imagine *most of L. Am., Sp* ◆ *Se me hace que el otro equipo va a ganar. I have a hunch that the other team is going to win.*

hache →por hache o por be
hambre →tener hambre de león
harina →hacer harina

Eso es **harina de otro costal.** (That's flour from another sack.) That's a horse of a different color, another kettle of fish. *L. Am., Sp* ◆ *Mi madre era muy cariñosa. Mi padre era harina de otro costal. My mother was very affectionate. My father was another kettle of fish.*

estar **harto(-a)** to be fed up *L. Am., Sp* ◆ *¡Estoy harta de limpiar y cocinar! Todos tienen que ayudar. I'm fed up with cooking and cleaning! Everybody has to help.*

hartón, hartona eating like a horse, gluttonous *Mex, C. Am.* ◆ *Tú comes a cualquier rato; eres bien hartón. You eat all the time; you're a chowhound.*

¡Hasta ahí podríamos llegar! (Even that far we could go!) phrase of indignation facing a possible abuse *Mex, Sp*

Hasta aquí llegó mi (el) amor. (My love lasted this far, up to here.) This was the last straw. *Florida, Mex, DR, G, Col, U, Arg* ◆ *Hasta aquí llegó mi amor; no voy a tolerar más errores. This was the last straw; I'm not going to tolerate any more mistakes.*

estar **hasta arriba** to be fed up, be up to here *Sp* ◆ *No puedo ir. Estoy hasta arriba de trabajo. I can't go. I'm up to here with work.*

estar **hasta atrás** (to be behind) to be smashed, very drunk *Mex, ES, Col* ◆ *Si ustedes se toman toda la botella, van a estar hasta atrás. If you guys drink the whole bottle, you're going to be smashed.*

hasta cierto punto (up to a certain point) up to a point, to some extent *L. Am., Sp* ◆ *Usted tiene razón hasta cierto punto, pero... You're right up to a certain point, but . . .*

estar **hasta el (mismísimo) coño** (to be up to the female organ, vulgar) to be fed up *Sp* ◆ *Estoy hasta el mismísimo coño de que vengas tarde todos los días. I'm damn fed up with your coming late every day.*

estar **hasta el cepillo** (to be up to the brush) to be smashed, very drunk *Mex* ◆ *Es obvio que don Ramón está hasta el cepillo. It's obvious that Ramón is smashed.*

estar **hasta el cogote** (to be up to the crest) to be fed up *Mex, PR, ES, Ch, Sp* ◆ *Estamos* *hasta el cogote con nuestro hijo mayor.* We're fed up with our oldest son.

estar **hasta el copete** 1. (to be up to the forelock, top of hair) to be very drunk *Mex, ES, Col, Sp* ◆ *Ese hombre está hasta el copete. That man is very drunk.* **2.** to be fed up *Mex, G, Nic, CR, Peru, Para, U* ◆ *Estamos hasta el copete con las exigencias de nuestro jefe. We're fed up with our boss's demands. He's very unfair.*

estar **hasta el gollete** (to be up to the gullet) to be fed up *Sp* ◆ *Estoy hasta el gollete de trabajo. I'm up to here with work.*

estar **hasta el gorro** (to be up to the cap) to be fed up *Mex, ES, Sp* ◆ *Estoy hasta el gorro con tus quejas. I'm sick and tired of your complaints.*

estar **hasta el moño** (to be up to the bun, roll of hair tied up in back) to be fed up *Sp* ◆ *Su mujer está hasta el moño de fútbol. His wife is fed up with soccer.*

estar **hasta el tope** (to be up to the top) to be fed up *Mex, DR, ES, Col, U* ◆ *Estamos hasta el tope con la política de ese partido; han arruinado al país. We're fed up with the politics of that party; they've ruined the country.*

estar **hasta la coronilla** (to be up to the top of the head, crown) to be fed up *L. Am., Sp* ◆ *¡Ya me tiene cansada hasta la coronilla! Now it's (you've, he's, she's) got me totally fed up, up to here!*

hasta la fecha (until the date) up to now, to date *L. Am., Sp* ◆ *Hasta la fecha mi computadora no me ha dado ningún problema. Up to now my computer hasn't given me any trouble.*

estar **hasta la madre** (to be up to the mother) to be up to here, fed up; to have had it *Mex, C. Am.* ◆ *Estoy hasta la madre de este tiempo. I'm up to here with this weather.*

estar **hasta las cejas** (to be up to the eyebrows) to be up to here, fed up; to have had it *Sp* ◆ *Estamos hasta las cejas de tus abusos. Debes cambiar. We've had as much as we can take of your abuse. You'd better change.*

estar **hasta las chanclas** (to be up to the sandals) to be smashed, very drunk *Mex, ES* ◆ *Paco está hasta las chanclas. Debes llevarlo*

a casa. Paco is smashed. You'd better take him home.

estar **hasta las manitas** (to be up to the little hands) to be very drunk *Mex, CR* ◆ *Pedro estaba hasta las manitas anoche y ahora tiene un dolor de cabeza terrible. Pedro was very drunk last night and now he has a terrible headache.*

estar **hasta las narices** to be fed up (to the nostrils) *Mex, Sp* ◆ *¡Estoy hasta las narices con los problemas de mi marido! I'm fed up with my husband's problems!*

hasta las piedras (even the stones) all, without exception *Sp* ◆ *Hasta las piedras escucharon las promesas de los políticos antes de las elecciones. Everyone without exception listened to the politicians' promises before the election.*

estar **hasta los ovarios** (to be up to the ovaries) to be fed up, used for a woman (like **estar hasta los cojones**) (vulgar) *L. Am., Sp* ◆ *Estoy hasta los ovarios con las obsesiones de mi novio. I'm sick and tired of my boyfriend's obsessions.*

estar **hasta los cojones** (to be up to the testicles) to be fed up (vulgar) *Mex, Sp* ◆ *Mi primo está hasta los cojones con los celos de su esposa. My cousin is fed up with his wife's jealousy.*

estar **hasta los huevos** (to be up to the eggs [testicles]) to be fed up (vulgar) *Sp*

estar **hasta los topes** to be fed up (to the top); to be very full, packed *CR, Sp* ◆ *El tren estaba hasta los topes. The train was packed.*

hasta los tuétanos down to the marrow, to the bone *L. Am., Sp* ◆ *Hacía mucho frío en el estadio, y nos enfriamos hasta los tuétanos. It was very cold in the stadium, and we were chilled to the bone.* ◆ *Soy puro puertorriqueño. Hasta los tuétanos. I'm pure Puerto Rican. Down to the marrow.*

hasta más no poder full-fledged; all possible *L. Am., Sp* ◆ *Es un naco hasta más no poder. He's a total jerk.*

Hasta que nos topemos. (Until we run into each other again.) See you next time (we meet). *Mex, G, ES, Col, Ec* ◆ *Un gusto de charlar contigo, Andrés. ¡Hasta que nos topemos! It's been great talking with you, Andrés. See you next time!*

en (**hasta) el quinto infierno** (in [as far as] the fifth hell) in a godforsaken spot, far away *Mex, DR, PR, ES, U, Arg* ◆ *Mi amiga se mudó y no la puedo ir a ver porque ahora vive en el quinto infierno.* My friend moved and I can't go see her because she lives way out in the boonies. ◆ *¡Diache! Ese bar queda en el quinto infierno. ¡Llevamos dos horas buscándolo! (DR)* Darn! That bar must be at the ends of the earth. We've been looking for it for two hours!

hasta/a tal punto to such an extent (point) *L. Am., Sp* ◆ *Insistían hasta tal punto que me cansé y me di por vencida.* They insisted to such an extent that I got tired and gave in.

¿Hay alguien que canté aquí? Porque hay uno que está tocando. Is there someone who sings here? Because there is someone who touches (plays a musical instrument). (Said, for example, on a crowded subway or bus when someone is touching someone else unnecessarily.) *ES*

Hay moros en la costa. (There are Moors on the coast.) The coast is not clear. The walls have ears, phrase warning that someone else may be listening *L. Am., Sp* ◆ *No podemos hablar ahora; hay moros en la costa.* We can't talk right now; the walls have ears.

Hay que joderse. 1. (You have to get screwed.) Deal with it. You have to put yourself out, put up with hard times. (vulgar) *Mex, ES, Sp* ◆ *En este país hay que joderse para ganarse la vida.* In this country you have to kill yourself to earn a living. **2.** expression of opposition, something like "screw you" but not as strong (vulgar) *DR, PR, U, Sp* ◆ *¡Hay que joderse! Yo no tengo la culpa.* Screw it! It's not my fault.

Hay ropa tendida. (There is clothing hung out to dry.) Be careful. The coast is not clear. *Mex, U, Ch, Sp* ◆ *Hay ropa tendida; no podemos hablar del asunto.* The coast is not clear; we can't talk about the issue.

de **hecho** in fact *L. Am., Sp* ◆ *Hay mucha gente mexicana en Estados Unidos; de hecho, dos de cada tres latinos son de ascendencia mexicana.* There are many Mexican people in the United States; in fact, two out of three Latinos are of Mexican descent.

hecho(-a) fosfatina (made into powder) worn out, exhausted *Sp* ◆ *Estaba hecho fosfatina después de correr tanto.* I (He) was worn out after running so much.

hecho(-a) (una) mierda (made into shit) tired as hell, worn down (vulgar) *Mex, DR, PR, U, Arg, Sp* ◆ *Estoy rendido, hecho mierda.* I'm wiped out, tired as hell.

hecho(-a) a mano made by hand *L. Am., Sp* ◆ *Mire, señora, el encaje está hecho a mano.* Look, ma'am, the lace is hand-made.

hecho(-a) la mocha (la raya) (made into the bow [the stripe]) like a shot, in a flash *Mex* ◆ *Me voy hecha la mocha.* I'm going in a flash.

hecho(-a) pedazos/añicos (in pieces) worn out, shattered *Mex, ES, U, Arg, Sp* ◆ *Estoy hecho pedazos con las malas noticias de la guerra.* I'm completely devastated with all this bad news about the war.

estar **hecho(-a) pelota** (to be made into a ball) to be all broken up and sad about something (a death or loss) *U, Arg* ◆ *Los muchachos están hechos pelota con la muerte de su madre.* The kids are all broken up about their mother's death.

hecho(-a) pinole (made into **pinole**, an aromatic powder that used to be used in making chocolate) worn out, ground down, exhausted *Mex* ◆ *La carrera me dejó hecho pinole.* The race left me dog tired.

hecho(-a) polvo (made into dust) worn out, exhausted *Mex, Cuba, DR, Sp* ◆ *¡Tanto trabajo! Estoy hecha polvo.* So much work! I'm beat.

estar **hecho(-a) un almíbar** (to be made a syrup) to act very friendly and affable, all sweetness and light *Sp* ◆ *Mi esposo está hecho un almíbar porque llegó tarde anoche.* My husband has become all sweetness and light because he got home late last night.

estar **hecho(-a) un asco** (to be made into something disgusting) to be dirty, revolting *ES, S. Cone, Sp* ◆ *Estoy hecho un asco luego de trabajar todo el día en la huerta. Tengo que bañarme antes de cenar.* I'm filthy after working all day in the garden. I have to take a bath before supper.

estar **hecho(-a) un cascajo** (to be made a piece of junk) to be decrepit *PR, Sp* ◆ *¿Has* visto a Manolo últimamente? Yo lo vi anoche, y está hecho un cascajo. *Have you seen Manolo lately? I saw him last night, and he's gotten really decrepit.*

estar **hecho(-a) un figurín** (to be made a figurine) to have a nice figure, look good physically; to cut a fine figure *DR, U, Arg, Sp* ◆ *La novia estaba hecha un figurín. Estaba preciosa. The bride cut a fine figure. She was gorgeous.*

estar **hecho(-a) un mulo** (to be made into a mule) to be strong as an ox *Sp* ◆ *Los ejercicios te han sentado; estás hecho un mulo. The exercises worked for you; you're strong as an ox.*

estar **hecho(-a) un pimpollo** (to be made a sprout, young thing) to look good, like a spring chicken *Mex, DR, ES, U, Sp* ◆ *Aunque tiene setenta años, está hecho un pimpollo. Es una maravilla lo bien que se conserva. Although he's seventy years old, he's like a spring chicken. It's amazing how well preserved he is.*

hecho(-a) un puré (made into a purée) worn out, exhausted *Mex, Sp* (RVar *Mex:* **hecho puré**) ◆ *El día que chocamos el coche quedó hecho puré. The day we crashed the car, he was worn to a frazzle.*

hecho(-a) una sopa (made a soup) sopping wet, drenched *L. Am., Sp* ◆ *Ven adentro, m'ija. Estás hecha una sopa. Come inside, dear. You're sopping wet.*

estar **hecho(-a) unos zorros** (to be made foxes) to be in bad shape or badly dressed *Sp* ◆ *Llegó de la fiesta hecha unos zorros. She came back from the party in bad shape.*

hecho(-a) y derecho(-a) (made and right) all grown up *L. Am., Sp* ◆ *Ya eres un hombre hecho y derecho. You're a grown man already.*

Eso está **hecho.** (That's done.) That's for certain. It's a sure thing. (used for promises) *Sp* ◆ *¿Quieres que te pinte la casa este verano? Eso está hecho. Do you want me to paint your house this summer? It's a sure thing.*

Lo que se **hereda no se roba (hurta).** (What is inherited is not robbed.) He (She) comes by it naturally. This person is just like his or her father (mother, grandfather, etc.). Here's a chip off the old block. *S. Cone, Sp*

◆ *No me critiques, mamá, por lo que hago. Lo que se hereda no se roba. Don't criticize me, mom, for what I do. I come by it naturally.*

el/la **hermano(-a) carnal(a)** (blood brother [sister]) close friend *Mex, DR, G* ◆ *Francisco es mi hermano carnal; siempre puedo contar con él. Francisco is my close friend; I can always count on him.*

Herodes →Como dijo Herodes, te jodes.

hielo →dar hielo

la **hierba** (grass) pot, grass, marijuana *Mex, Cuba, DR, G, Sp* ◆ *Deja de fumar hierba, hombre. Stop smoking pot, man.*

ser un **hígado** (to be a liver) to be a pain, jerk *Mex* ◆ *Chuy es un hígado, muy sangrón, y no voy a devolver su llamada. Chuy is a pain, really a drag, and I'm not going to return his (phone) call.*

de **higos a brevas** (from figs to early figs) once in a blue moon *Sp* ◆ *La última vez que lo vi fue en 1997; nos vemos únicamente de higos a brevas. The last time I saw him was in 1997; we only see each other once in a blue moon.*

estar en la **higuera** (to be in the fig tree) to be distracted, daydreaming *Sp* ◆ *Está en la higuera otra vez. Siempre le encuentro despistado, pensando en algo que no es del trabajo. He's daydreaming again. I always find him with his mind wandering, thinking of something not related to work.*

el/la **hijo(-a) de la chingada** (son [daughter] of the violated woman) son of a bitch (bitch) (vulgar) *Mex, C. Am.* ◆ *¿Qué te hizo el hijo de la chingada? What did the son of a bitch do to you?*

el/la **hijo(-a) de la gran puta** (son [daughter] of the big whore) son of a bitch (bitch) (vulgar) *L. Am., Sp* ◆ *El hijo de la gran puta nos robó el dinero de la caja fuerte. The son of a bitch stole the money from our safe.*

el/la **hijo(-a) de papá** (Daddy's child) rich kid, kid who has everything solved for him or her by the parents' influence *Mex, Cuba, DR, C. Am., Col, Peru, Sp* (RVar *U:* **nene de papá**) ◆ *Como siempre, sus argumentos son de un hijo de papá. Su único poder se lo da el dinero de su padre. As usual, his arguments are those of a spoiled rich kid. His only authority comes from his daddy's money.*

el/la **hijo(-a) de papi** →**hijo de papá** *Mex, G, ES, Col, Peru*

el/la **hijo(-a) de puta** (son [daughter] of a whore) son of a bitch (bitch) (vulgar) *L. Am., Sp* (RVAR *L. Am.*: also, **hijueputa;** *Sp:* also, **hijoputa**) ◆ *Pascual es un hijo de puta y trata mal a todo el mundo. Pascual is a son of a bitch and treats everyone badly.*

el/la **hijo(-a) de su** SOB (bitch) (somewhat vulgar, euphemism for **hijo[-a] de su puta madre**) *most of L. Am., Sp* ◆ *Ese tipo es un hijo de su... That guy is an SOB.*

Hijo(-a) de tigre, sale rayado(-a). (Son [Daughter] of the tiger turns out striped.) Like father, like son. *Mex, CR, S. Cone* ◆ *Ana Irene es madura y responsable, como su padre. —Hijo de tigre sale rayado. Ana Irene is mature and responsible, like her father. —Like father, like daughter.*

el/la **hijo(-a) natural** (natural child) illegitimate child *L. Am., Sp* ◆ *Rafael es hijo natural de don Claudio. Rafael is Don Claudio's illegitimate child.*

¡Híjole! Wow! Darn! expression of surprise *Mex, G, ES, Nic, Col* ◆ *¡Híjole! Me asustaste. No te vi. Wow! You scared me. I didn't see you.*

hijos de muchas madres (children of many mothers) all kinds of people, describing the diversity of a group *Sp* ◆ *En la guerra murieron hijos de muchas madres, no sólo soldados americanos. All kinds of people died in the war, not just American soldiers.*

al **hilo** →**ponerse al hilo (en onda)**

un **hilo** →**tener la vida en un hilo**

hincapié →**hacer hincapié en**

hincar los codos (to dig in one's elbows) to dig in and study, cram *Mex, Sp* ◆ *Tengo que hincar los codos si quiero pasar el examen. I have to really dig in if I want to pass the exam.*

el/la **hincha** (sports) fan *S. Am., Sp* ◆ *Los hinchas apoyaron a su equipo durante el campeonato. The fans supported their team during the championship.*

el/la **hincha (hinchapelotas)** (inflator [of balls]) irritating person, pest (vulgar) *U, Arg* ◆ *En mi viaje a Argentina, mi compañero de asiento era un hinchapelotas: habló durante toda la noche, y no pude dormir. On my trip to Argentina, the person sitting next to me was*
a pest: he talked the whole night, and I coudn't sleep.

hinchar las pelotas (to inflate the balls) to bother, bug, pester *Ch, U, Arg, Sp* (RVAR *Ch, Arg:* also used without **pelotas;** *Sp:* always used with either **pelotas** or **huevos** [vulgar]) ◆ *¡No me hinches (las pelotas) tanto! Don't give me such a damn hard time!*

el **hocico** →**meter el hocico en todo**

el **hocicón, la hocicona** (big mouth) loudmouth, gossip *Mex, C. Am., Col, Ch* ◆ *Mayte es la más hocicona del pueblo; todo lo cuenta y en todo está metida. Mayte is the biggest gossip in town; she tells everything and gets involved in everything.* ◆ *Ya deja de hablar de esas cosas; no seas hocicón. Stop talking about that stuff; don't be a gossip.*

hociconear (to snout) to shoot off one's mouth *Ch* ◆ *Pedro hociconeó toda la noche sobre sus conquistas amorosas. Pedro shot off his mouth the whole night about all the women he's had (literally, all his amorous conquests).*

el **hojaldra** (puff pastry) asshole (vulgar) *Mex* ◆ *Pancho es un hojaldra; me robó diez mil pesos. Pancho is an asshole; he stole ten thousand pesos from me.*

Hola. Hello (normal way of answering the telephone). *U, Arg* ◆ *Hola. ¿Con quién hablo? Hello. With whom am I speaking?*

hombre (man) term of address for either a man or a woman *L. Am., Sp* ◆ *Hola, hombre, ¿qué es de tu vida? Hi, how are things (in your life)?*

hombre de pelo en pecho real he-man *L. Am., Sp* ◆ *Clark Gable fue un hombre de pelo en pecho. Clark Gable was a real he-man.*

el **hombre del saco** (man of the jacket) bogeyman; homeless man *Ch, Sp* ◆ *Si no te portas bien, vendrá el hombre del saco a buscarte. If you don't behave, the bogeyman will come get you.*

el **hombro** →**poner el hombro**

la **home** digs, home (from English) *parts of L. Am. (not S. Cone)* ◆ *Olvidé mis libros en la home. I forgot my books at home.*

en **Honduras** →**meterse en Honduras**

de **hoquis** for free *Mex* ◆ *Parece que quieren que trabajemos de hoquis aquí.* It looks like they want us to work for free here.

la **hora** →**no dar ni la hora; no ver la hora (de)**

en **hora buena** luckily *L. Am., Sp* ◆ *En hora buena recibí mi cheque cuando ya se me acababa el dinero.* Luckily I got my check just when my money was almost gone.

la **hora pico** rush hour; peak hour of electricity use *Mex, DR, Nic* ◆ *Es imposible manejar en el centro a la hora pico.* It's impossible to drive downtown during rush hour.

la **hora punta** rush hour; peak hour of electricity use *Sp* ◆ *Voy temprano al trabajo para evitar la hora punta.* I leave early for work to avoid rush hour.

a estas **horas** at this time, at this hour *L. Am., Sp* ◆ *¿Y cómo te atreves a llegar a estas horas de la mañana?* And how do you dare to come home (here) at this hour of the morning?

hormigas →**tener hormigas en el culo**

una **hostia** →**Ni hostia.**

la **hostia** 1. (Host) blow, smack (vulgar) *Sp* ◆ *La verdad es que después de lo que te hizo, merece un par de hostias bien dadas.* The truth is that after what he did to you, he deserves a couple of well-placed smacks. ◆ *Alonso se dio una hostia al salir corriendo. No vio que la puerta de vidrio estaba cerrada.* Alonso hit himself damn hard as he was running out. He didn't see that the glass door was closed. 2. (Host) the damn limit, too much, a large quantity or exaggerated quality (good or bad) (vulgar) *Sp* ◆ *Esto es la hostia.* This is the damn limit. ◆ *Adela tiene un coche de la hostia; es estupendo.* Adela has a damn fine car; it's great. ◆ *Me tienen cansado con esa música de la hostia.* I'm tired of that damn music.

ser la **hostia** (to be the Host) to be too damn much, great, amazing (people or things) (vulgar, with religious reference) *Sp* (RVAR PR: to be annoying) ◆ *Ese tío es la hostia; le dije que me comprara cuatro entradas para el concierto y sólo me compró dos.* That guy is too much; I told him to buy me four tickets to the concert and he only bought me two. ◆ *Universal Studios es la hostia.* Universal Studios is the bomb (the greatest).

¡Hostia puta! (Host whore! religious reference) Goddamn it! (vulgar) *Sp* ◆ *¡Hostia puta! ¡Me han robado la cartera!* Goddamn it! They stole my wallet!

¡Hostia(s)! (Host[s]!) God damn it! a strong expletive implying religious sacrilege (vulgar) *Sp*

hostigar to annoy, badger, bug *most of L. Am., Sp* ◆ *¿Por qué hostigan tanto?* Why are they badgering (us) so much? ◆ *Que hostigas.* How you bug a person.

de **hoy en ocho (quince)** a week (two weeks) from now *L. Am., Sp* ◆ *¿Cuándo empiezan las vacaciones? ¿De hoy en ocho o de hoy en quince?* When does vacation begin? A week from now or two weeks from now?

hoy por hoy as of now, under the present circumstances *L. Am., Sp* ◆ *Hoy por hoy los conflictos en el Medio Oriente están sin resolver.* As of now the conflicts in the Middle East are still unresolved.

¡Huaca! (¡Huácala!) Yuck!, expression of distaste; also, **guaca, waca, ¡Guácala!** *Mex, ES, DR, G, Col* ◆ *¡Huácala! Esta carne está casi cruda.* Yuck! This meat is almost raw.

el **hueco** (hollow, hole) homosexual (vulgar, pejorative) *G, Ch*

hueco(-a) (hollow, empty) phony, superficial *Ch, U* ◆ *En ese grupo nadie habla de temas interesantes o informativos. Son todos muy huecos y superficiales.* In that group nobody talks about interesting or informative subjects. They're all very phony and superficial.

al **huerto** →**llevar a alguien al huerto**

hueso →**ser un hueso que roer; no poder alguien con sus huesos; sin hueso**

el **hueso** (bone) patronage job (for family or friends) *Mex, ES* ◆ *No quiere soltar ese hueso.* He (She) doesn't want to let go of that job.

ser un **hueso** (to be a bone) to be a stickler, very demanding (especially used for teachers or professors) *Sp* ◆ *El profesor Martínez es un hueso.* Professor Martínez is a tough nut.

ser un **hueso que roer** (to be a bone to gnaw on) to be a difficult person to deal with, be a difficult task or situation to be in *L. Am., Sp* ◆ *Ese profesor es un hueso que roer. Sus-*

pende a casi todos. That professor is impossible. *He flunks almost everyone.*

huevada →¡Qué huevada (güea)!

las **huevas** testicles (vulgar, variant of **huevos**) *Nic, Ch*

huevear (to egg around) to goof off, mess around (vulgar) *Ch* ◆ *Basta de huevear, colegas. ¡Manos a la obra!* That's enough goofing off, my friends. Time to get to work!

huevo →echar huevos a un asunto, echarle huevos; estar hasta los huevos; Ni a huevos.; no comer un huevo por no perder la cáscara; no tener huevos; tener huevos; tener los huevos bien puestos; tener los huevos de corbata

el **huevón, la huevona** 1. (big egg, meaning with large, heavy testicles) lazy, useless person, lazy bum (vulgar) *Mex, Cuba, C. Am. (not CR), Ven* ◆ *Rolando es un huevón; no le gusta trabajar.* Rolando is very lazy; he doesn't like to work. 2. (big egg) idiot, fool; also used affectionately between friends (vulgar) *PR, CR, Col, Ec, Ch* ◆ *Se comporta como un huevón con las chicas.* He acts like an idiot around girls.

los **huevos** (eggs) testicles (vulgar) *L. Am., Sp*

huevotes →¡Qué huevotes!

huir del fuego y caer en las brasas (to flee the fire and fall into the coals) to go from the frying pan into the fire *L. Am., Sp* ◆ *Antonio huyó del fuego y cayó en las brazas cuando se enamoró de la novia de su amigo.* Antonio went from the frying pan into the fire when he fell in love with his friend's girlfriend.

humo →echar humo; hacerse humo; irse todo en humo; tener la cabeza llena de humos; tener muchos humos

¡Huy! Wow! Darn! (expression of surprise) *L. Am., Sp* ◆ *Huy, ¡qué miedo! El bebé casi se cayó de la cama.* Wow, what a scare! The baby almost fell off the bed.

identificarse con to identify with *L. Am., Sp* ◆ *Me identifico con ella, que también perdió a sus papás de niña.* I identify with her; she also lost her parents when she was a girl.

las **íes** →**poner los puntos sobre las íes**

igual →**dar igual, dar lo mismo**

Igual Pascual. (Equal Pascual.) Me too. The same. *Ch* ◆ *Estoy cansado. —Igual Pascual.* I'm tired. —Same here.

Iguanas ranas. (Iguanas frogs; **iguanas** sounds like **igual**) Me too. The same. *Mex, Col* ◆ *No tengo ganas de trabajar. —Iguanas ranas.* I don't feel like working. —Me either.

imbancable (unbankable) unbearable, intolerable *U, Arg* ◆ *Esta comida es imbancable.* This food is disgusting. ◆ *¡No te pongas imbancable!* Don't be impossible!

No **importa.** It doesn't matter. *L. Am., Sp* ◆ *Es una fiesta informal, no importa como vayas vestida.* It's a casual party; it doesn't matter how you dress for it.

¿Qué **importancia tiene?** So what? *L. Am., Sp* ◆ *Si el regalo es caro o barato, ¿qué importancia tiene? Lo importante es el detalle.* If the gift is expensive or cheap, so what? It's the thought that counts (literally, "What is important is the detail").

importar un carajo (to not matter a male organ) to not give a damn (vulgar) *PR, U, Arg, Sp* ◆ *Todo les importa un carajo.* They don't give a damn about anything.

importarle madre →**valerle/importarle madre**

importarle tres cojones (to matter three testicles) to not give a damn, not matter (vulgar) *Sp* ◆ *Hablé con Alicia sobre el problema, pero me dijo que le importa tres cojones.* I spoke with Alicia about the problem, but she said she doesn't give a damn.

importarle un comino (to matter a cumin seed) to not give a darn, be unimportant *L. Am., Sp* ◆ *Nos importa un comino lo que di-*

gan tus amigos; tú tienes que seguir nuestras reglas en esta casa. We don't give a darn what your friends say; you need to follow our rules in this house.

importarle un pepino (to matter a cucumber) to not give a darn, be unimportant *L. Am., Sp* ◆ *Me importa un pepino lo que pueda pensar otra gente. Yo voy a hacer lo que pienso.* I don't give a darn what other people might think. I'm going to do what I think.

importarle un pimiento (to matter a pepper) to not give a darn, be unimportant *Sp* ◆ *Me importa un pimiento su opinión.* I don't give a darn about their opinion.

importarle un pito (un bledo) (to matter a whistle [a pigweed]) to not give a darn, be of no importance, not worth worrying about *Mex, DR, PR, Ch, U, Arg, Sp* (RVar *DR, PR:* **pito** only) ◆ *Como si el asunto les importara un bledo.* As if they gave a fig about the matter. ◆ *Me importa un pito que no me invites a tu fiesta.* I don't give a darn that you may not invite me to your party.

importarle un rábano (to matter a radish) to not give a darn, be unimportant *Mex, ES, Ch, U, Sp* ◆ *Me importa un rábano si te gusta o no te gusta.* I don't give a hoot whether you like it or not.

de **improviso** without notice, unexpectedly *L. Am., Sp* ◆ *Llegaron de improviso a la hora de la cena.* They arrived unexpectedly at dinner time.

inaugurar el pastel (to inaugurate the cake) to have sex with a virgin *Mex, Col* ◆ *Antes de casarnos, inauguramos el pastel.* Before getting married, we popped the cherry.

independizarse to become independent, self-sufficient *L. Am., Sp* ◆ *Mi hijo se independizó a los dieciocho años.* My son became self-sufficient at the age of eighteen.

la **indirecta muy directa** a very explicit hint meant not to be missed *Mex, Cuba, DR, U* ◆ *En el sermón, el padre dijo varias indi-*

rectas muy directas sobre el problema de los jóvenes. During the sermon, the priest gave several not-so-subtle hints about the problem of young people.

indirectas →echar/tirar **indirectas**

ínfulas →tener muchas **ínfulas**

las **ínfulas** airs *L. Am., Sp* ◆ *Hablaba con grandes ínfulas de su amistad con el presidente. Iba llena de ínfulas. (Se daba muchas ínfulas.)* She was putting on airs about her friendship with the president. She went around with a big head.

ingeniárselas para to manage to (see **arreglárselas**) *L. Am., Sp* ◆ *Daniela siempre se las ingenia para recibir una invitación al baile.* Daniela always manages to get an invitation to the dance.

el **insti** short for **instituto**, high school *Sp* ◆ *No quiero ir al insti hoy.* I don't want to go to school today.

con **intención** on purpose *L. Am., Sp* ◆ *¿Crees que lo hicieron con intención?* Do you think they did it on purpose?

ir (muy) lejos 1. to go (very) far *L. Am., Sp* ◆ *Porque ha luchado y trabajado mucho, Bernardo va a ir muy lejos.* Because he has struggled hard and worked a great deal, Bernardo will go very far. **2.** to be (very) far from what is said or done *L. Am., Sp* ◆ *Lo que dijo va muy lejos de la verdad.* What he (she) said leaves a lot to be desired (is very far from the truth).

ir (nadar) contra la corriente to go against the current *L. Am., Sp* ◆ *Berta nada contra la corriente solamente para molestar.* Berta goes against the current just to upset people.

ir a medias to go half and half *L. Am., Sp* ◆ *Fuimos a medias con los gastos.* We went half and half with the expenses.

ir a misa (to go to mass) to be correct, for real *Sp* ◆ *Lo que dice mi padre va a misa.* What my father says is for real.

ir a pie to go by or on foot *L. Am., Sp* ◆ *No tengo auto, pero iré a la fiesta a pie.* I don't have a car, but I'll go to the party on foot.

ir(se) abajo (to go down) to step down, lose a position, be demoted, come down in life *Cuba, G, Col* ◆ *Ese tipo se ha ido abajo por*

sus malos negocios. That guy has come down in life because of his bad business deals.

ir al garete to fail, go down the drain *Sp* ◆ *La relación fue al garete después de tres años.* The relationship failed after three years.

ir al grano (to go to the grain) to get to the point *L. Am., Sp* ◆ *No hables tanto. Ve al grano y dime la verdad.* Don't talk so much. Get to the point and tell me the truth.

ir al rollo (to go to the roll) to get to the point, the issue *Mex, ES* ◆ *Vamos al rollo.* Let's get down to brass tacks.

ir de compras to go shopping *L. Am., Sp* ◆ *¡Vamos de compras, amiga!* Let's go shopping, my dear!

ir de culo (to go ass) to have a hell of a time, have something be rushed, difficult, or complicated (vulgar) *Sp* ◆ *Esta semana entre los exámenes, las prácticas y el nuevo trabajo voy de culo. No puedo con tantas cosas.* This week with the exams, the apprenticeship, and the new job I'm having a hell of a time. I can't do so many things.

ir de gorra, de gorrón to go (somewhere) without having to pay, crash *Mex, ES* ◆ *Paco siempre dice que no tiene dinero y va de gorra todo el día.* Paco always says he doesn't have money and mooches all day.

ir de juerga to go out on the town, party *L. Am., Sp* ◆ *Anoche fui de juerga y ahora estoy muy cansada.* Last night I went out on the town and now I'm very tired.

ir de mal en peor to go from bad to worse *L. Am., Sp* ◆ *Desde que mi hija tiene novio, las cosas van de mal en peor.* Since my daughter has had a boyfriend, things have gone from bad to worse.

ir de miranda to guard, watch over, just watch *Sp* ◆ *Su mamá fue de miranda.* His (Her) mom went just to watch.

ir de parranda to go out on the town, party *L. Am., Sp* ◆ *Para festejar el triunfo, fuimos de parranda.* To celebrate the triumph, we went out partying.

ir de pegoste (to go as an add-on) to tag along, be superfluous, extra *Mex, ES, Nic* ◆ *Tu hermana vino de pegoste por culpa de tu mamá.* It was your mother's fault that we got stuck with your sister (literally, that she came along stuck on to us).

ir de pegote (to go as an add-on) to tag along, be superfluous, extra *Sp* ◆ *Iba al cine y mi hermanito fue de pegote. I was going to the movies and my little brother came along (stuck on to me).*

ir en el coche de San Fernando (to go in St. Ferdinand's car) to go on foot *DR, Sp* ◆ *Fuimos en el coche de San Fernando, un poco a pie y otro poco caminando. We went on foot (part way on foot and part way walking).*

ir hecho(-a) bala to go like a shot, rapidly (literally, as a bullet) *Mex, G, Ch* (RVAR *Mex:* also, **hecho la [una] bala;** *U, Arg:* **ir como bala**) ◆ *Me multaron por ir hecho la bala. They gave me a ticket for speeding (going like a bullet).*

ir para rato (to go for a while) to be a while *L. Am., Sp* ◆ *Ya va para rato que trabaja aquí. He (She) has been working here for a while.*

ir por lana y volver (salir) trasquilado (-a) (to go for wool and come back shorn) to have the tables turned on oneself *DR, S. Cone, Sp* ◆ *El ministro fue por lana y salió trasquilado cuando habló con los agricultores. The minister (secretary) had the tables turned on him when he spoke to the farmers.*

ir subiendo (to go ascending) to keep on going up *L. Am., Sp* ◆ *Los precios de la gasolina van subiendo tanto que pienso vender mi coche. Gas prices keep going up so much I'm thinking of selling my car.*

ir viento en popa (to go wind at the stern) to go full-speed ahead, make progress *L. Am., Sp* ◆ *El negocio me va viento en popa. My business is going full-speed ahead.*

ir volando to go like a shot, flying low (literally, flying) *Mex, C. Am., S. Cone, Sp* ◆ *Déjame dos minutos más y voy volando. Let me have two more minutes and I'll be off like a shot.*

ir y venir (going and coming) coming and going *L. Am., Sp* ◆ *En este edificio de apartamentos, he visto el ir y venir de mucha gente. In this apartment building, I've seen many people come and go.*

ir y venir en una cosa (to go and come in something) to run something into the ground, fixate on or insist on something *Sp* ◆ *Nadie entendió al profesor; vino y fue en el tema. No one understood the teacher; he ran the subject into the ground.*

ir/marchar/andar sobre ruedas (to go on wheels) to be going great *Mex, DR, PR, ES, Nic, Col, Ch, Sp* ◆ *Todo anda (marcha) sobre ruedas. Everything is going great.*

irle a alguien como en feria (to go as in a fair for someone) to have a hard time, have things go badly for someone *Mex, ES* ◆ *Mis exámenes en la universidad me fueron como en feria. I had a hard time with the exams at the university.*

irle a alguien como los perros en misa (to go like dogs in mass for someone) to have a hard time, have things go badly for someone *Sp* ◆ *A Apolonio le fue como perros en misa en su entrevista para el nuevo trabajo. Apolonio had a hard time with his interview for the new job.*

irle bien (mal) to look good (bad) on *L. Am., Sp* ◆ *Te va muy bien ese sombrero. That hat looks very good on you.*

irse (andar) de farra to go out on the town, party *Col, Ec, S. Cone, Sp* (RVAR *Para, U, Arg:* also, **farrear**) ◆ *Me voy de farra esta noche. I'm going out for a good time tonight.* ◆ *A Lucy le gusta farrear. Lucy likes to party.*

irse (salir) de marcha to go out on the town, party *Sp* ◆ *Vamos de marcha esta noche. ¿Te apuntas? We're going out on the town tonight. Want to join in?*

irse a la chingada (to go to the **chingada**, violated woman) to go to some godforsaken spot, far away (vulgar) *Mex, C. Am.* ◆ *Me voy a la chingada; no hay trabajo aquí. I'm going far away; there's no work here.*

irse a la cucha (to go to the doghouse) to hit the sack, drop into bed when you're tired *U, Arg* ◆ *Es hora de que los niños se vayan a la cucha. It's time for the kids to hit the sack.*

irse al (para el) carajo (to go to the **carajo**, male organ) to have a bad ending, go to hell in a handbasket (vulgar) *Mex, DR, PR, ES, U, Sp* ◆ *La empresa se fue al carajo un año después. The business went to hell in a handbasket a year later.*

irse al cuerno (to go to the horn) to come to nothing, go to the devil *Mex, Sp* ◆ *¡Vete al cuerno! No escucharé más tus excusas.*

Go to the devil! I won't listen to any more of your excuses.

irse con el viento que corre to go with the prevailing wind (opinions, ideas) *Mex, Sp* ◆ *Se dejan llevar por el viento que corre. No tienen criterio propio.* They go with the prevailing wind. They don't have any judgment of their own.

irse de cachondeo to go out on the town, party *Sp* (RVAR *Mex:* may imply to be on the prowl) ◆ *Se fueron de cachondeo y no llegaron hasta muy tarde.* They went out on the town and didn't get back until very late.

irse de pinta (to go away like spot) to play hooky *Mex* ◆ *Me fui de pinta el lunes.* I played hooky on Monday.

irse de rumba to go out on the town, party *Mex, Cuba* ◆ *Se fueron de rumba y no llegaron a su casa hasta las seis de la mañana.* They went out on the town and didn't get home until six in the morning.

irse para el (al) otro barrio (mundo) (to go to the other neighborhood [world]) to pass away *L. Am., Sp* ◆ *Su padre se fue al otro mundo a los 82 años.* His father went to a better place when he was 82 years old.

irse por las ramas (to go around the branches) to beat around the bush *Mex, S. Cone, Sp* ◆ *No te vayas por las ramas; dime exactamente lo que pasó.* Don't beat around the bush; tell me exactly what happened.

irse todo en humo to have everything go up in smoke *Sp* ◆ *Esperaba que volviera con ella, pero se fue todo en humo.* He was hoping to get back together with her, but everything went up in smoke.

írsele a alguien el santo al cielo (to have one's saint go to heaven) to forget something one was going to do or say (despite good intentions) *most of L. Am., Sp* ◆ *Iba a trabajar esta mañana, pero se me fue el santo al cielo.* I was going to work this morning, but my good intentions went all to heck.

írsele a alguien la lengua to make a slip of the tongue, speak without thinking *Mex, ES, U, Arg, Sp* ◆ *Ema, se te fue la lengua y dijiste cosas muy personales a tus compañeras de trabajo.* Ema, you spoke without thinking and told your coworkers very personal things.

írsele a alguien los ojos por algo o alguien (to have one's eyes go after something or someone) to desire or want something *Mex, DR, ES, U, Arg, Sp* ◆ *Cuando la vi, se me iban los ojos.* From the moment I saw her, I only had eyes for her.

írsele la mano (to have one's hand go off on one) to get carried away (and make a mistake, usually while doing something) *L. Am., Sp* ◆ *Se te fue la mano con los jalapeños; la salsa está muy picante.* You got carried away with the jalapeño peppers; the sauce is very hot.

írsele la olla (to have the pot fly off or go off on one) to lose it, fly off the handle *Sp* ◆ *Se le va la olla de vez en cuando, pero no es mal tío.* He flies off the handle every once in a while, but he's not a bad guy.

írsele por alto to go over one's head; to forget, overlook *Mex, ES, CR, U* ◆ *Se me fue por alto la reunión.* The meeting totally slipped my mind.

J

un **jabón** →tener un jabón

la **jaina** broad, gal, girlfriend *Chicano* ◆ *¿Quién es la jaina que canta?* Who's the gal who is singing?

la **jalada** (pull, jerk, stretch) dirty trick; nonsense, exaggeration (stretch) *Mex* ◆ *Pedro me hizo una jalada. Pedro played a dirty trick on me.* ◆ *Son puras jaladas. It's sheer nonsense (something like What a stretch!).*

jalarse los pelos (to pull one's hair out) to be upset, furious *Mex, ES, Sp* ◆ *Estoy que me jalo los pelos de rabia. I feel like tearing out my hair, I'm so mad.*

el **jaleo** tumult, fuss; lots of people *Mex, S. Cone, Sp* ◆ *Había un jaleo impresionante en la calle. There was quite a hoopla in the street.*

un **jalón** →dar (pedir) un jalón

a **jalones y estirones** (at pulls and stretches) kicking and screaming, with delays and difficulties, great effort *Mex* ◆ *A jalones y estirones la llevé a misa. I took her to mass kicking and screaming.*

la **jama** chow, food *Cuba, PR, CR, Ec, Peru* ◆ *¿Tienes jama? Tengo mucha hambre. Do you have any food? I'm hungry.*

jamar to chow down, eat *Cuba, CR, Ec* (RVAR *Peru:* **jamear;** *Nic:* **jambar**) ◆ *¿Ya jamaste? Did you eat already?*

la **jarana** bash, party *Mex, Peru, U, Arg, Sp* ◆ *Me voy de jarana esta noche. I'm going out partying tonight.*

jaranero(-a) party-loving, party animal *Sp* ◆ *Es un chico muy jaranero. He's a party-loving guy.*

estar en la **jaula** (to be in the cage) to be in the clinker (prison) *Chicano, Mex, Cuba, DR, Col* ◆ *Mateo vendía cocaína, pero ahora está en la jaula. Mateo was selling cocaine, but now he's in the clinker.*

los **jefazos, las jefazas** big shots, bosses *Mex, Col, Sp* ◆ *Nungún cambio dependía de ella, sino de sus jefazos. No changes de-*

pended on her, but rather on her superiors (bosses).

¡Jefe! (Boss!) Mac! Buddy! (to a stranger) *Cuba, DR, Col*

el/la **jefe(-a)** (boss) husband (wife) *L. Am., Sp* ◆ *Mi jefecita dice que no. The little woman (My wife) says no.*

los **jefes** (bosses) folks, parents *Mex, ES* ◆ *Mis jefes no están aquí. My parents aren't here.*

¡Jesús! Gesundheit!, said after a sneeze *L. Am., Sp*

¡Jesús, María y José! Gesundheit!, said after three sneezes *parts of L. Am., Sp*

jeta →tener mucha cara (mucho rostro, mucho morro, mucha jeta)

la **jeta** 1. mug, kisser (face) *Mex, Cuba, ES, Col, Sp* (RVAR *G, CR, U, Arg:* mouth) ◆ *Si te acercas, te rompo la jeta. If you come closer, I'll punch you in the kisser.* 2. (mug, face) mooch, sponge *Sp* ◆ *Es un jeta. Siempre dice que no tiene dinero para que lo inviten. He's a sponge. He always says he doesn't have money so that people will treat him.* 3. (mug, face) nerve, pushiness *Sp* ◆ *Esa chica tiene mucha jeta. That girl has a lot of nerve.*

estar **jetón, jetona** (to be big mouth) to be angry *Mex, G, ES* ◆ *Está jetón porque no puede salir. He's angry because he can't go out.*

la **jeva** girl, girlfriend, woman *Cuba, DR, PR, Nic, Ven, Ec* ◆ *¿Cómo se llama la jeva del vestido verde? What's the name of the chick (woman) in the green dress?*

el **jevo** boy; boyfriend *Cuba, DR, PR, Ec* ◆ *Tu jevo es una buena persona. Your boyfriend is a good guy.*

el/la **jíbaro(-a)** (country person) hick, ignorant person, someone afraid to speak *PR* ◆ *No seas jíbaro. Ve y habla con ella. Don't act like a country bumpkin. Go talk to her.*

los **jijos de la guayaba** (euphemism for **hijos de la chingada; guayaba** is guava) poor suckers *Mex, ES* ◆ *Esos jijos de la guayaba* *no saben nada. Those poor suckers don't know anything.*

joder 1. to screw *most of L. Am., Sp* ◆ *Son como unos tortolicos, esos dos. Pasan el día jodiendo. Those two are just like turtle doves. They spend the whole day screwing.* **2.** (to bug or bother) to bother, harm, beg (vulgar) *L. Am., Sp* ◆ *Le encanta joder a su hermana. He loves to bug his sister.* ◆ *No me jodas. Don't bother me.* **3.** to break (something) (vulgar in some places but inoffensive in others) *L. Am., Sp* ◆ *Se jodió el pie jugando al fútbol. He messed up his foot playing soccer.*

¡Joder! Damn! (vulgar) *Sp* ◆ *Joder, ¡qué hambre tengo! Damn, am I hungry!*

estar de la **jodida** to be very difficult, bad; to suck (somewhat vulgar) *Chicano, Mex, G, Col* ◆ *Esto está de la jodida. ¿Qué vamos a hacer? This sucks. What are we going to do?*

la **jodida** →**mandar a alguien a la jodida**

jodido(-a) (past participle of **joder**) screwed, messed up (vulgar) *L. Am., Sp* ◆ *Estoy jodida. Tengo muchos problemas económicos. I'm screwed. I have a lot of economic problems.*

jodienda →**¡Qué jodienda!**

Se **jodió el invento.** (The invention or TV broke.) It was a washout, expression used when something goes wrong or is not obtained *Sp*

jodón, jodona bothersome, annoying (vulgar) *Mex, DR, G, Col, U, Arg* ◆ *Mi tío es muy jodón. My uncle is really annoying.*

¡Joer! Darn!, euphemism for **joder** *Sp* ◆ *¡Joer! ¡Qué idiota! Darn! What an idiot!*

¡Jolines! Darn!, Holy smoke! euphemism for **joder** *Sp* ◆ *¡Jolines! No tenemos dinero. Holy smoke! We don't have any money.*

joroba →**¡Qué joroba!**

jorobar euphemism for **joder**, to bother (to screw) *Mex, Cuba, DR, PR, G, CR* (RVar *Sp:* also, **joder la marrana**) ◆ *Esta muela me está jorobando mucho. This molar is giving me a darn hard time.*

jorobarse →**hay que joderse (jorobarse)**

jota →**Ni jota.; sin faltar una coma (jota)**

joto(-a) gay, effeminate man, homosexual (vulgar, pejorative) (feminine form is used among Chicanos for lesbian) *Chicano, Mex, ES*

¡Joven! (Young person!) used to get the attention of a waiter, gas station attendant, security guard, etc., in some areas, even when the man being called is not young *Mex, Col, Sp* (where a bit old-fashioned) ◆ *Joven, ¿podría traerme un vaso de agua con hielo y limón? Waiter, could you get me a glass of water with ice and lime?*

ser una **joya** (to be a jewel) to be perfect, good, a gem *parts of L. Am.* ◆ *Esa iglesia es una joya del estilo colonial. That church is a colonial-style gem.*

juego →**hacer juego; no ser cosa de juego**

juegues →**No juegues.**

de **juerga** →**ir de juerga**

jueves →**no ser nada (cosa) del otro jueves; martes 13, jueves 13**

jugar a cartas vistas (to play with cards that can be seen) to do something above board *parts of L. Am., Sp* ◆ *En esta empresa jugamos a cartas vistas. In this company we do things above board.*

jugar a taca-taca (to play bang-bang) to play an electronic game *Peru, Bol, Ch* ◆ *Mi hermano pasó toda la tarde jugando a tacataca. My brother spent all afternoon playing video games.*

jugar al balero (to play cup and ball, a children's game) to fool around, have sex *Mex, Col* ◆ *Me gustó jugar al balero con un francés que conocí en la fiesta. I liked fooling around with a French guy I met at the party.*

jugar bien sus cartas to play one's cards right, do something with astuteness *Mex, DR, S. Cone, Sp* ◆ *Salimos bien en el negocio. Armando es astuto y jugó bien las cartas. We've had success with the business. Armando is bright and played his cards right.*

jugar con dos barajas (to play with two decks) to act with duplicity, cheat *most of L. Am., Sp* ◆ *No tienes escrúpulos; estás jugando con dos barajas. You don't have any scruples; you're cheating.*

jugar con fuego to play with fire *L. Am., Sp* ◆ *Pero ¿cómo se te ocurre salir con un hom-*

bre casado? Estás jugando con fuego. But how can you think of going out with a married man? You're playing with fire.

jugar en los dos bandos (to play in both bands or groups) to be bisexual, swing both ways *Mex, Cuba, DR, PR, Col, U* ◆ *Escuché que Lorenzo juega en los dos bandos. I heard that Lorenzo goes both ways.*

jugar la última carta (to play the last card) to go to the last resort, play one's last trick *Mex, U, Arg, Sp* ◆ *Jugamos la última carta para conseguir más dinero para las escuelas públicas. We've gone to the last resort to get more money for the public schools.* ◆ *El presidente del sindicato estaba listo para jugar su última carta. The president of the union was ready to play his last trick.*

jugar para el otro equipo (to play for the other team) to be gay, homosexual *L. Am.* ◆ *¡No me digas! ¿Jaime juega para el otro equipo? Don't tell me! Jaime is gay?*

jugarse el todo por el todo (to bet all for all) to bet everything at once, put all your eggs in one basket *L. Am., Sp* ◆ *Decidieron jugarse el todo por el todo cuando compraron el negocio. They decided to put all their eggs in one basket when they bought the business.*

jugarse la pasta to bet one's money *Sp* ◆ *Manuel se jugó toda la pasta en la ruleta, y después tuvo que pedir dinero prestado. Manuel bet all his money on roulette, and afterward he had to borrow money.*

jugársela (to bet it) to go for it, take a risk *Mex, DR, G, CR, S. Cone, Sp* ◆ *Te la jugaste fría, hombre. You took a big risk, man.*

jugárselo todo a una carta to bet everything on one card, put all your eggs in one basket *Mex, S. Cone, Sp* ◆ *Déjame pensar. No quiero jugármelo todo a una carta. Let me think. I don't want to bet everything on one card.*

el **jugo** →sacar el jugo

la **juma** drunkenness *ES, Nic, CR, Pan, Ven, Ec* ◆ *¡Qué juma tiene! How drunk he (she) is!*

el **junior** spoiled brat, playboy, son of the wealthy *Mex, Col* ◆ *El junior de la casa no tiene escrúpulos. The spoiled brat of the house has no scruples.*

juntos pero no revueltos (together but not mixed) just friends, together but not bosom buddies or romantically involved *L. Am., Sp* ◆ *Pablo y Silvia son sólo amigos, juntos pero no revueltos. Pablo and Silvia are just friends, not bosom buddies or romantically involved.*

jurar en arameo (to swear in Aramaic, the language of Christ) to swear because one is in a bad mood *Sp* ◆ *Cuando no me dieron el trabajo, empecé a jurar en arameo. When they didn't give me the job, I started using language that would make a sailor blush.*

Se lo **juro. (Te lo juro.)** (I swear it to you.) I swear. God's truth. *L. Am., Sp* ◆ *Es la verdad, papá, te lo juro. It's the truth, dad, I swear to you.*

L

el **laberinto** (labyrinth) mess *Peru* ◆ *No me metas en laberintos, por favor. Don't get me involved in any messes (problems), please.*

laburar to work *Para, U, Arg* ◆ *En el verano voy a laburar en la playa como salvavidas. In the summer I'm going to work at the beach as a lifeguard.*

el **laburo** work, job *Bol, Para, U, Arg* ◆ *Este hijo mío me da un laburo tremendo. This son of mine gives me a lot of work.*

la **ladilla** (leech) pain in the neck, insistent person *Mex, Cuba, DR, PR, G, Col, Ven, Peru* ◆ *¡Qué ladilla! What a pain in the neck!*

estar que **ladra** (to be barking) to be angry *Mex, Sp* ◆ *Ni le hables a Norma porque está que ladra. Don't even talk to Norma because she's ready to bite your head off.*

¿Ladrónde compraste eso? (used instead of **¿Dónde compraste eso?**, **ladrón** meaning thief) implies suspicions about the origin of something, often used in jest *Mex, DR, Col* ◆ *Oye, compadre, ¡qué lindo celular! ¿Ladrónde compraste eso? Hey, buddy, what a gorgeous cell phone! Where'd you steal that from?*

las **lagartijas** (lizards) push-ups *Mex, DR, G, ES, Col* ◆ *El instructor nos puso a hacer lagartijas. The instructor had us do push-ups.*

el **lambiscón, la lambiscona** kiss-up, flatterer, suck-up *Mex, G, ES, Arg* (RVAR *Arg:* **la lambiscona** only; *Sp:* **lamerón;** *PR:* **lambeojo** or **lameojo;** *Col:* **lambeón**) ◆ *No soy lambiscona, y no voy a hacer lo que quieren. I'm not a suck-up, and I'm not going to do what they want.*

lamer/lamber el culo (trasero) a alguien to kiss (lick) someone's ass (vulgar) *Mex, ES, S. Cone, Sp* (RVAR *Sp:* more common, **lamer**) ◆ *Sigue ahí, lamiéndole el culo a la profesora. He's (She's) still there, brownnosing the teacher (kissing the teacher's ass).*

la **lámina (lata)** wheels, car *Mex, Col* ◆ *Tenemos problemas con la lámina ahora. We have problems with the car right now.*

lana →**ir por lana y volver (salir) trasquilado(-a)**

la **lana** (wool) dough, money *Mex, Cuba, C. Am., Peru* ◆ *Esos señores tienen mucha lana. Son los dueños de unas boutiques exclusivas. Those people have a lot of dough. They own some exclusive boutiques.*

lanzado(-a) (thrown) opportunist, aggressive or bold person, operator *Mex, Col, Ch, Arg, Sp* ◆ *Ricardo y Esteban son hermanos, pero Ricardo es un lanzado y su hermano es tímido. Ricardo and Esteban are brothers, but Ricardo is an operator and his brother is shy.*

lanzar un rollo (to throw a roll) to start a long story *Mex, ES, Col, Peru* ◆ *Vi a mi amiga Elena en la tienda y empezó a lanzar el mismo rollo. I saw my friend Elena at the store and she started into the same long story.*

la **lapa** (barnacle) person who is hard to shake off, pest *Mex, DR, PR, Col, Ch, Sp* ◆ *¡Qué lapa! What a pest!*

a la **larga** in the long run *L. Am., Sp* ◆ *A la larga sacarás tus propias conclusiones. In the long run, you'll come to your own conclusions.*

a la **larga, a largo plazo** in the long run *L. Am., Sp* ◆ *No se ha estudiado los efectos de ese medicamento a largo plazo. They haven't studied the effects of that medication on a long-term basis.*

largar to send to the devil, blow off *U, Arg* ◆ *Me parece que voy a largar a esta mina. I'm thinking I'm going to send this dame to the devil.*

largarse to go away, move off *most of L. Am., Sp* ◆ *¡Lárgate, niño! ¿No ves que doña Carmen está muy cansada? Scram, kid! Don't you see that Doña Carmen is very tired?*

largo(-a) →**más largo(-a) que la esperanza del pobre**

lástima →**darle lástima a alguien; ¡Qué lástima!**

¡Qué lástima! What a shame! *L. Am., Sp* ◆ *¿Estás enferma de nuevo? ¡Qué lástima! ¿Are you sick again? What a shame!*

lata →dar lata

ser una **lata** (to be a tin can) to be a pain, drag, bore, annoyance *L. Am., Sp* (RVAR ALSO, **pura lata** in *G, ES, Sp*) ◆ *Ese chico es pura lata. That guy is a total drag.* ◆ *Levantarse todos los días para ir a trabajar es una lata. Getting up every morning to go to work is a pain.*

latir (to beat) to like *Mex* ◆ *Me late mucho ese programa. I really like that show.*

latirle to have a hunch, foresee, have a feeling about *Mex, DR, PR, ES, CR, Col, Ch* ◆ *Me late que no le va a ir nada bien. I have a feeling that it's not going to go well for him (her).* ◆ *Me late que va a chocar. I have a feeling that he's (she's) going to crash.*

latoso(-a) boring, bothersome, a pain *Mex, DR, ES, Col, Ec, Ch* ◆ *Esa muchacha es bien latosa. That girl is a big pain.*

lazo →poner a alguien como lazo de cochino/percha de perico

leche →¡Qué leche!; tener cara de mala leche; tener leche; tener mala leche

ser la **leche** (to be the milk) to be too much, be surprising (good or bad, people or things), unheard of *Sp* ◆ *Fernando es la leche. Siempre consigue lo que quiere. Fernando's too much. He always gets what he wants.* ◆ *Esa novela es la leche. That novel is really something.*

lechero(-a) lucky, as in **tener leche** *ES, Nic, CR, Col, Peru* (RVAR *ES:* **lechudo** is more common; *Ec:* **lechoso[-a]**) ◆ *¡Qué lechudo! Le dieron el trabajo. Tiene leche. What a lucky stiff! They gave him the job. He's lucky.*

leer entre líneas/entre renglones to read between the lines *L. Am., Sp* ◆ *Presta atención a lo que se dice realmente; aprende a leer entre líneas. Pay attention to what is really being said; learn to read between the lines.*

leerle a alguien la cartilla (to read the primer to someone) to set someone straight, read the riot act, lay down the law *Mex, DR, ES, Ch, Sp* ◆ *Le pedí permiso para salir con su hija y me leyó la cartilla. I asked him for permission to date his daughter and he laid down the law.*

legal (legal) good, correct, right; good person *Mex, DR, G, CR, Col, Ec, Ch, Sp* ◆ *Lo que dice Juan está legal. What Juan says is right.*

a **leguas** a mile away *L. Am., Sp* ◆ *A leguas se nota que es mentira. You can tell it's a lie from a mile away.*

lejos →ir (muy) lejos; tener buen lejos

lelo(-a) dumb, foolish, stupid *Chicano, Mex, DR, G, Col, U, Arg* ◆ *No entiendo de que me habla ese lelo. I don't understand what that stupid person is talking about.*

la **lengua** →írsele a alguien la lengua

el/la **lengua larga** (long tongue) blabbermouth, someone who reveals too much *L. Am., Sp* ◆ *No le cuentes eso, que éste es un lengua larga. Don't tell him that because he has a big mouth.*

el/la **lentejo(-a)** (sounds like **lenteja**, lentil, or a combination of **lento**, slow, and **pendejo**, stupid) dope, idiot, fool *Mex, Col, Peru* ◆ *Esa lenteja siempre habla demasiado. That dope always talks too much.*

lento(-a) →más lento(-a) que un suero de brea; más lento(-a) que una caravana de cojos

lento(-a) pero tardado(-a) (slow but late) very slow (ironic) *Mex, ES* ◆ *Voy a llegar pronto. Soy lenta pero tardada. I'm going to get there soon. I'm slow but late.*

leña →dar leña; echar leña al fuego; hacer leña del árbol caído; llevar leña al monte

un **león** →estar como un león (de bravo)

la **leperada** low-class action or vulgar expression *Mex, C. Am.* ◆ *Esta idea es muy absurda; parece de leperada. That idea is really absurd; it's so low-class.*

lépero(-a) low-class, rude *Mex, C. Am.* ◆ *No digas cochinadas; no seas lépero. Don't use dirty language; don't be crass.*

ser **levanta muertos** (to be a raiser of the dead) to perk or liven things (or someone) up *Mex, Nic, U, Arg* ◆ *Esta sopa es levanta muertos. This soup perks me right up.*

levantar (to pick up) to rob, steal, lift *Cuba, PR, G, Col, Ec* ◆ *¡Caramba! Me levantaron la bicicleta. Darn! They swiped my bicycle.*

el/la lengua larga: No le digas nada a ese lengua larga.
Don't say anything to that blabbermouth.

levantar (el) vuelo to take flight; to raise spirits or imagination *Mex, ES, S. Cone, Sp* ◆ *El negocio está levantando vuelo. The business is taking off.*

levantar la antena (to raise the antenna) to prick up one's ears, pay attention *Mex, ES, Col* ◆ *Cuando mencionaron el postre, Miguelito levantó la antena. When they mentioned dessert, Miguelito pricked up his ears.*

levantarle el ánimo to lift somone's spirits, encourage *L. Am., Sp* ◆ *Siempre me levantas el ánimo, Cecilia. You always lift my spirits, Cecilia.*

levantarse a alguien to pick someone up, make amorous conquests *Mex, DR, PR, G, ES, Col, U, Arg* ◆ *Ese tipo sí tiene suerte. Acaba de llegar a la fiesta y ya se levantó a esa rubia. That guy is really lucky. He just got to the party and he already picked up that blonde.* ◆ *Me voy a levantar a ese muchacho. I'm going to pick up that guy.*

levantarse con el pie izquierdo (to get up with the left foot) to get up on the wrong side of the bed (have a day of bad luck or be in a bad mood) *L. Am., Sp* ◆ *Hoy me levanté con el pie izquierdo. Primero perdí las llaves y después peleé con mi esposa. Today I got up on the wrong side of the bed. First I lost my keys and then I had a fight with my wife.*

levantarse del lado izquierdo to get up on the wrong side of the bed (literally, "on the left side") *L. Am., Sp* ◆ *Todo me sale mal hoy, me levanté del lado izquierdo. Everything is going wrong today; I got up on the wrong side of the bed.*

el **levante** pickup, date *Mex, DR, PR, G, Col* (RVar *G*: short-term lover) ◆ *Marcelo hizo un levante en la cantina. Marcelo picked someone up at the bar.*

un **levante** →hacer un levante

liar el petate (to roll up the **petate**, sleeping mat, but now in Spain referring to a green bag used for military service) to pack it in, die; also, to take off, leave *Sp* ◆ *Después de cenar, lié el petate y me fui de allí. After having dinner, I took off.*

127

liar los bártulos (to bundle up the household goods) to pack it in, die; also, to take off, leave *Sp* ◆ *Algún día todos tendremos que liar los bártulos. Some day we'll all have to pack it in.*

libar (to have a libation) to drink *Mex, ES, Col* ◆ *Después del partido, los jugadores libaron mucha cerveza. After the game, the players drank lots of beer.*

mi **lic** short for **mi licenciado**, a term of respect used in jest *Mex* ◆ *¿Qué onda, mi lic? What's up, doc?*

ligar (to link) to pick up, make amorous conquests; to obtain, get *L. Am., Sp* ◆ *Se la ligó durante las fiestas. He hooked up with her during the holidays.* ◆ *Ligué un avión a México. I got a plane to Mexico.* ◆ *El maestro se la pasa ligando con las estudiantes. The teacher keeps picking up female students.* ◆ *Ésos ya ligaron.* ◆ *Those two are an item (linked together).*

ligero(-a) de cascos (light of head) frivolous, foolish; also, **liviano(-a) de cascos** *L. Am., Sp* (RVAR *Mex:* easy woman in feminine form) ◆ *Es irresponsable y ligero de cascos. He's irresponsible and foolish.*

el **ligón** (big linker) pickup, date; stud, guy who flirts and is successful with women *Col, Sp* ◆ *Es un ligón. Cada semana sale con una chica distinta. (Sp) He's a hustler. Every week he goes out with a different girl.*

un **ligue** →**tener un ligue**

lija →**darse lija**

limpiarse el culo con algo (to wipe one's ass with something) to wipe one's feet on something, disdain (vulgar) *Mex, PR* ◆ *Ese político se limpia el culo con la gente del pueblo. That politician wipes his feet on the people in the town.*

linchar to kill, lynch (often figurative); in *Mex, CR, Ch,* also, to punish, in a threat *Mex, Cuba, DR, PR, G, ES, Col, Ch, U, Sp* ◆ *Expresó sus ideas y lo lincharon. He expressed his ideas and they lynched him (verbally).*

el **lío** (bundle) mess *L. Am., Sp* ◆ *Esto es un lío. Hay que ordenarlo rápidamente. This is a mess. It needs to be cleaned up quickly.*

la **lira** (lyre) guitar *Mex, Col* ◆ *Carolina toca muy bien la lira. Caroline plays the guitar well.*

liso y llano (smooth and flat, as a road) a piece of cake, easy, without difficulty *Sp* ◆ *La explicación fue lisa y llana. Quien no la entiende es que no puede comprender nada. The explanation was a piece of cake. If you can't understand it, you can't understand anything (literally, He who doesn't understand it can't understand anything).*

listo(-a) →**más listo(-a) que el hambre; más listo(-a) que un rayo (el relámpago)**

el **listón, la listona** (big clever) a real smartie *Mex, Col* ◆ *Juan es un listón. Juan is a real smartie.*

la **lisura** (smoothness; sincerity) obscene word, swear word *Peru* ◆ *A muchos adolescentes les gusta decir lisuras; es un signo de inmadurez. Many adolescents like to swear; it's a sign of immaturity.*

llamar la atención to call or attract attention (to oneself) *L. Am., Sp* ◆ *Con ese traje anaranjado, realmente llama la atención. She's really calling attention to herself with that orange outfit.*

la **llave** (key) pal, friend, connection *Col, Ven* (RVAR *DR:* **enllave**) ◆ *Hola, mi llave, ¿qué tal? Hi, old buddy (for men)/my dear (for women), how's it going?*

¡Llégale! Go for it! *Mex, ES, Col*

¡Llégale a la papa! (Go to the potato!) Eat! Soup's on! *Mex, Col* ◆ *¡A comer, muchachos! ¡Lléguenle a la papa! Time to eat, guys! Soup's on!*

llegar →**¡Hasta ahí podríamos llegar!**

llegar a ser (to arrive or come to be) to become *L. Am., Sp* ◆ *Empezó de secretaria y llegó a ser vicepresidenta de la empresa. She started out as a secretary and became vice president of the company.*

llegar y besar (el santo) (to arrive and kiss [the saint]) phrase describing how quickly something was obtained *Cuba, Sp* ◆ *Fui al consulado a pedir mi visa. Llegué, besé y salí con el documento. I went to the consulate to request my visa. In a split second I left with my document.*

estar que me (lo, la, etc.) **lleva el diablo** to be beside oneself (ready for the devil to take), in a very bad mood *Mex, DR, G, ES, CR* (RVAR *CR:* **que me llevan los diablos**) ◆ *Y anda que se la lleva el diablo. She's in a ter-*

rible mood. ◆ *Estoy que me lleva el diablo.* I'm in a very crummy mood.

Me **lleva la chingada.** (The **chingada**, violated woman, is taking me.) I'm screwed. (vulgar) Euphemism: **Me lleva el chile.** *Mex, C. Am.* ◆ *Me lleva la chingada; se me fregó el carro.* I'm screwed; my car is messed up.

llevar [time period] to have been (doing something) for [time period] *L. Am., Sp* ◆ *Llevo un mes en la clase de guitarra. Llevo un año estudiando música.* I've been in the guitar class for a month. I've been studying music for a year.

llevar a alguien al huerto (to take someone to the garden) to take someone down the garden path, deceive someone making them think they are favored when they are not; to convince someone to have sex *Mex, Sp* (RVAR *Mex:* also, **llevar al baile**) ◆ *El vendedor cree que me va a llevar al huerto. (Sp)* The salesman thinks he's going to lead me down the garden path.

llevar a cabo to carry out, complete *L. Am., Sp* ◆ *¿Cómo llevan a cabo las investigaciones?* How are they carrying out the research?

llevar bien puestos los pantalones (to wear the pants well placed) to impose one's authority, especially in a home setting, throw one's weight around *Mex, DR, PR, ES, U, Sp* ◆ *Gerardo lleva bien puestos los pantalones y logró organizar el presupuesto familiar.* Gerardo is throwing his weight around and managed to organize the family budget.

llevar contra la pared (la tabla) (to take against the wall [board]) to put in a tight spot, act cruelly (toward someone) or ask too much (of him or her) *Mex, Cuba, G, Ch, U* (RVAR *G:* **pared** only; *Ch, U:* **poner contra la pared**) ◆ *Mi novia me puso contra la pared y tuve que decirle que aún no me quiero casar.* My girlfriend put me in a tight spot and I had to tell her I still don't want to get married.

llevar en palmas (palmitas) (to carry with palm leaves) to treat like a king, pamper *Sp* ◆ *Sus padres le llevan en palmas; nunca será una persona adulta.* His parents treat him like a king; he's never going to grow up.

llevar la batuta (to carry the baton) to call the shots, be in charge, lead; to be the main person *L. Am., Sp* ◆ *En esa familia, Alfonso lleva la batuta.* In that family, Alfonso calls the shots.

llevar la contraria (contra) (to take the contrary) to contradict, oppose *L. Am., Sp* (RVAR *Ec:* **ser un contreras**) ◆ *Te encanta llevarme la contraria. ¿Por qué lo haces? Tu actitud me disgusta mucho.* You love to contradict me. Why do you do it? Your attitude really upsets me.

llevar la voz cantante (to carry the melody) to be in charge in a meeting, business, etc.; to call the shots *L. Am., Sp* ◆ *En mi oficina, el secretario lleva la voz cantante, y el gerente lo acepta.* In my office, the secretary calls the shots, and the manager accepts it.

llevar leña al monte (to take wood [logs] to the woods or brush) to take coals to Newcastle (old saying) *L. Am., Sp* ◆ *¿Una computadora a Juan? ¿Para qué si ya tiene tres? Es como llevar leña al monte.* A computer for Juan? Why if he already has three of them? It's like taking coals to Newcastle.

llevar puesto(-a) to have on, be wearing *L. Am., Sp* ◆ *Llevo puesta una chaqueta roja, para que me encuentres en el aeropuerto.* I have a red jacket on, so you can find me at the airport.

llevar una vida feliz (triste) to have a happy (sad) life *L. Am., Sp* ◆ *Mi abuelo llevó una vida feliz.* My grandfather had a happy life.

llevarla suave to take it easy, calmly *ES, CR, Col, U* (RVAR *Cuba, Pan:* cogerlo suave) ◆ *Llévala suave, que no hay prisa. (ES)* Take it easy; there's no hurry. ◆ *Cógelo suave, que no vale la pena. (Cuba)* Keep your cool; it's not worth worrying about.

llevarle el apunte (llevar de apunte) (to keep track of the score) to pay attention to someone or something *S. Cone* ◆ *El jefe grita mucho en esta oficina, pero no le lleves el apunte.* The boss shouts a lot in this office, but don't pay him any mind.

llevarle la carga (to carry the cargo for someone) to make a pass at, hit on, be coming on to someone sexually *U, Arg* ◆ *Ese muchacho siempre le lleva la carga a la* *más bonita.* That guy always puts the moves on the prettiest girl.

llevarse (a alguien) el demonio (to be taken by the devil or demon) to be angry or very irritated *Mex, Sp* ◆ *Estoy que me lleva el demonio.* I'm hopping mad *(mad as the devil).*

llevarse (a alguien) el diablo (to be taken by the devil) to be angry or very irritated *Mex, S. Cone* (RVAR *Mex:* also, **llevarse la trompada, la tostada, la trampa**) ◆ *El jefe estaba que se lo llevaba el diablo cuando vio que no terminé el trabajo.* The boss was as angry as heck when he saw that I hadn't finished my work.

llevarse bien (con alguien) to get along well (with someone) *L. Am., Sp* ◆ *Juana y yo nos llevamos muy bien. Somos amigas del alma. Juana and I get along very well. We are bosom buddies.* ◆ *Me llevo muy bien con mis suegros.* I get along very well with my in-laws. ◆ *Mercedes se lleva bien con sus compañeros de trabajo. Mercedes gets along well with her fellow workers.*

llevarse el demonio (to be taken by the demon) to go to the devil, fail *Mex, Sp* ◆ *Si no trabajamos en serio, a este negocio se lo va a llevar el demonio.* If we don't work seriously, this business is going to go to hell in a handbasket.

llevarse el diablo (to be taken by the devil) to go to the devil, fail *Mex, DR* ◆ *¿El proyecto que tenía? Se lo llevó el diablo. The plan I had? It went all to heck.*

llevarse la palma (to carry away the palm, meaning the honors) to take the cake, surpass; to get ahead or go first in a line *Ch, Sp* ◆ *Dices que tu hijo saca malas notas, pero el mío se lleva la palma. Ha suspendido siete asignaturas esta evaluación. You say that your son gets bad grades, but mine takes the cake. He's failed seven subjects this term.*

llevarse todo por delante (to carry away everything in front of you) to sweep everything away; also *(S. Cone)* to win at everything, to take on all comers *L. Am., Sp* ◆ *El agua se llevó todo por delante. The water swept everything away.* ◆ *Rodrigo García se llevó todo por delante, y su equipo ganó el campeonato. Rodrigo García took on all comers, and his team won the championship.*

llorar a mares to cry a sea (of tears), cry buckets *L. Am., Sp* ◆ *Cada vez que me despido de mi familia en el aeropuerto, lloro a mares. Every time I say good-bye to my family at the airport, I cry buckets.*

llorar a moco tendido (to cry with a lot of mucus) to cry like a baby *L. Am., Sp* ◆ *Silvia y su madre se encontraron después de muchos años; hablaron y lloraron a moco tendido, hasta desahogarse. Silvia and her mother met after many years; they talked and cried like babies until they had recovered emotionally.*

llorar lágrimas de cocodrilo to cry crocodile tears, feign sadness *L. Am., Sp* ◆ *Deja de llorar lágrimas de cocodrilo. Stop crying crocodile (fake) tears.*

llorón, llorona crybaby, whiner *L. Am., Sp* ◆ *Mi primo es un llorón. Nunca está contento. My cousin is a whiner. He's never happy.*

llover a cántaros (to rain pitchers) to rain buckets *L. Am., Sp* ◆ *Llovió a cántaros toda la semana. It was raining buckets all week.*

llover sobre mojado (to rain over the wetness) to have one bad thing happen after another; also, to be repetitive or superfluous *L. Am., Sp* ◆ *Llueve sobre mojado: otra vez subieron los precios. It never rains but it pours: they raised the prices again.*

ser **lo máximo** to be fantastic, the greatest, the best (the maximum) *L. Am.* ◆ *¡Esta música es lo máximo! This music is the best!*

Lo siento muchísimo. (I feel it very, very much.) I am very, very sorry. *L. Am., Sp* ◆ *Lo siento muchísimo que su esposo haya sufrido un ataque al corazón. I'm so very sorry that your husband has suffered a heart attack.*

el **lobo** (wolf) wolf, womanizer *Chicano, Mex, PR* ◆ *Nadie diría que don José es un lobo; parece tan respetable. Nobody would guess that José is a womanizer; he seems so respectable.*

loca (crazy) effeminate, sissyish, gay *Cuba, DR, CR, Col, Ch*

la **loca** (crazy person) floozie, woman who likes sex *Mex, DR, Col, Ec, U, Arg* ◆ *Cerca del puerto siempre hay muchas locas. Near the port there are always a lot of floozies.*

a lo **loco** (crazily) like crazy, without thinking *Mex, DR, PR, ES, U, Arg, Sp* (RVar *Ch:* **a la loca**) ◆ *Por estar hablando a lo loco, le conté a Ana de la fiesta sorpresa. Because I was talking without thinking (like crazy), I told Ana about the surprise party.*

el/la **loco (tonto)** →**hacerse el loco (tonto)**

loco(-a) →**más loco(-a) que una cabra; Ni loco(-a).**

el/la **loco(-a)** (crazy person) guy (girl) *Col, Ven, Ec* ◆ *¿Quién es esa loca allí? Who's that gal over there?*

el/la **loco(-a) (tonto[-a]) perdido(-a)** (lost fool) hopeless case, idiot *L. Am., Sp* ◆ *Felipe es un loco perdido. No sabe comportarse en sociedad. Felipe is a hopeless case. He doesn't know how to behave around other people.*

estar **loco(-a) de contento** (to be crazy happy) to be very happy *L. Am., Sp* ◆ *Estoy loca de contenta con mi viaje a Uruguay. I'm out of my mind with happiness about my trip to Uruguay.*

estar al **loro** (to be at the parrot) to pay attention, be attentive, be up to date *Sp* ◆ *No estás al loro. Esta canción es de la temporada pasada. You're out of it. This song is from last year (literally, the past season).*

el **lote** →**darse el lote**

la **luca** pesos or units of money *Ec, Peru, Bol, S. Cone* ◆ *Me dieron cien lucas. They gave me one hundred pesos (dollars, etc).*

lucir (to shine) to suit, wear, or fit well *DR, PR, ES, Nic, CR, Col, Sp* ◆ *A Rosa le lucen pantalones rojos y un collar grueso. Anda luciendo zapatos nuevos (un buen vestido). Red pants and a heavy necklace look good on Rosa. She's wearing new shoes (a good dress).*

lucirse (to shine) to stand out, do something unusual *Mex, Peru, U* ◆ *Te luciste. You were outstanding.* ◆ *Se lució con la comida. He (She) did a fabulous job with the dinner.*

luego luego right away *L. Am., Sp* ◆ *Busca tus llaves luego luego, Paco, que no tenemos mucho tiempo. Look for your keys right away, Paco; we don't have much time.*

lugar →**tener lugar**

en **lugar de** instead of *L. Am., Sp* ◆ *Y luego, en lugar de devolverme el dinero, me pidió otro préstamo. And then, instead of giving the money back to me, he (she) asked for another loan.*

de **lujo** fancy, deluxe *L. Am., Sp* ◆ *Es un hotel de lujo. It's a fancy hotel.*

lumbre →**echar lumbre**

estar en la **luna (de Valencia)** (to be in the moon [of Valencia]) to be distracted *L. Am., Sp* ◆ *Sería buen astronauta, ¿verdad? Porque siempre estoy en la luna. I'd be a good astronaut, wouldn't I? Because I always have my head in the clouds (I'm always daydreaming).*

luz →**dar a luz; sacar a luz**

la **luz** (light) dough, money (also: **morlacos, ojos**) *Mex* ◆ *¿Conseguiste la luz para comprar la moto? Did you get the dough to buy the motorcycle?*

La **luz d'alante (de adelante) es la que alumbra.** (The light in front of you is what shines.) A bird in the hand is worth two in the bush. Take what's right in front of you when you have the chance. (said by someone who offers you something to eat or drink, for instance, or when a job presents itself) *PR* ◆ *No seas tímida, amiga. Hice estas galletas hoy. La luz d'alante es la que alumbra. Don't be shy, dear. I made these cookies today. Take what you can get when you have the chance.*

ser la **luz de los (sus) ojos** to be the light of one's life (eyes) or the apple of one's eye *Mex, ES, S. Cone* ◆ *El hijo de Eduardo es la luz de sus ojos. Eduardo's son is the apple of his eye.*

luz de mi vida light of my life, dear *L. Am., Sp* ◆ *Te amo. Eres la luz de mi vida. I love you. You are the light of my life.*

m'ijo, m'ija (short for **mi hijo, mi hija**) my son, my daughter; used to show affection even to people who are not related *L. Am.*, *Sp* ◆ *M'ija, ten cuidado. No bebas mucho. My dear, be careful. Don't drink too much.* ◆ *Gracias, m'ijo. Thank you, dear.*

la **macana 1.** (weapon used by the Indians, and also possibly from Sr. Macana, a famous Argentine liar) whopper, big lie *Mex, Bol, S. Cone* ◆ *No creas lo que dicen los diarios; son macanas. Don't believe what the newspapers say; they're lies.* **2.** foolishness, stupid act *Bol, U, Arg* ◆ *Lo despidieron del hotel porque hizo muchas macanas. They fired him from the hotel because he did lots of stupid things.*

macanear to put someone on, say crazy or wild things that make no sense; also, to tease or make fun of *U, Arg* ◆ *No me macanées. Me estás macaneando. Don't put me on. You're putting me on.*

macanudo(-a) (probably from the Dominican cigar or from the Argentine liar, Sr. Macana) awesome, super *Nic, S. Cone* ◆ *Tus padres son macanudos, y nos ayudaron muchísimo. Your parents are awesome, and they really helped us.*

macarra vulgar, in bad taste *Sp* ◆ *Llevaba una camisa macarra, un pantalón macarra. He was wearing a cheap-looking shirt, a chintzy-looking pair of pants.*

el/la **macarra** troublemaker, person with bad manners and/or violent tendencies *Sp* ◆ *Entró un hombre con aspecto de macarra; se sentó cerca de nosotros. A man who looked like a troublemaker came in; he sat down near us.*

la **maceta 1.** (flower pot) head, noggin *Mex, G, Nic* ◆ *Me duele la maceta de tanto ver televisión. My head aches from watching television so much.* **2.** (flower pot) tightwad *PR* ◆ *Raúl es un maceta. No invita ni a su novia; siempre hay que hacer serrucho. Raúl is a cheapskate. He never even treats his girlfriend; they always have to go dutch.*

machetear (to machete) to not spend much, be a miser *S. Cone* ◆ *Este hombre machetea hasta para comprar comida. Siempre machetea y come cuando otros pagan. This guy scrimps even to buy food. He saves money and eats when other people are paying.*

macho term of endearment among males *CR, Sp* ◆ *Venga, macho, invítame a una copa. (Sp) Hey, guy! Come here and invite me for a drink.*

el **machote** macho man, male chauvinist pig *Mex, ES, Col* ◆ *Se porta así porque se cree muy machote. He acts like that because he thinks he's a macho man.*

macizo(-a) well-built, muscular *L. Am., Sp* (RVar *ES, Col*: also, **el macizo**, big boss or big man) ◆ *Luis Rodrigo sólo tiene quince años pero es bien macizo. Luis Rodrigo is only fifteen years old but he's very muscular.*

madera →**tener madera**

la **mano derecha** →**no saber dónde se tiene la mano derecha**

madre →**dar en la madre (romper/partir la madre); echar madres; estar hasta la madre; Ni madre.; no tener madre**

la **madre del cordero** (the mother of the lamb) the heart of the matter, the real reason for something *Peru, S. Cone, Sp* ◆ *Has encontrado la madre del cordero. Realmente ésta es la parte importante del problema. You've gotten to the heart of the matter. That's really the important part of the problem.*

¡La **madre que te parió!** (The mother who gave birth to you!) You son of a bitch! You bitch! (expression of anger, indignation; vulgar) *Mex, DR, PR, ES, Arg, Sp* ◆ *La madre que te parió, Francisco. ¿Cuándo dejarás de maltratar a tu mujer? You son of a bitch, Francisco. When will you stop mistreating your wife?*

madrear to hit, beat up *Mex, ES* ◆ *Si me sigues molestando, te voy a madrear. If you keep bothering me, I'm going to beat you up.*

madrugar (to get up early) to get ahead of someone, cut off at the pass, beat to the punch *L. Am., Sp* ◆ *Si no madrugas a ese señor, él te madruga a ti. If you don't get the better of that man, he's going to get the better of you.*

el **maestro** (teacher, master) dude, middle-aged or older man, guy *L. Am., Sp* ◆ *Pregúntale a ese maestro por dónde se va esta calle. Ask that guy where this street goes.*

el **maestro Ciruela, que no sabe leer y pone escuela** (Master Ciruela, who can't read and has a school) said to censure someone who is talking about something he or she doesn't know much about *L. Am., Sp* ◆ *No me des consejos de como criar a mis hijos. Escucha, Rafaela, tú eres cómo el maestro Ciruela, que no sabe leer y pone escuela. Don't give me advice on how to raise my kids. Listen, Rafaela, you shouldn't give advice on something you know nothing about.*

mafufo(-a) yucky, gross, weird (originally used to mean marijuana) *Mex* ◆ *Esa película mafufa no me gustó para nada. I didn't like that gross movie at all.*

maíz →**Ni maíz.**

el **maíz** (corn) dough, money *Cuba* ◆ *No tengo maíz para comprar una casa. I don't have the dough to buy a house.*

majá (majado[-a]) lazy *Cuba* ◆ *Qué majá me ha salido tu hermano. How lazy your brother has turned out.*

majadero(-a) 1. ill-mannered (person), fuss-budget *Mex, Cuba, U* ◆ *Con lo que dijiste, eres un majadero. Judging from what you just said, you're a rude boor.* ◆ *El niño no había comido y se puso majadero. The child hadn't eaten and got very fussy.* **2.** fraud, liar *Sp* ◆ *Manolo me vendió un coche que dijo que era casi nuevo y era mentira. Es un majadero. Manolo sold me a car he said was practically new and it was a lie. He's a fraud.*

maje 1. dumb, stupid *parts of Mex, G, Hond, ES, CR* ◆ *No te hagas el maje. Don't act like a dope.* **2.** (pronounced **ma'e**) fool, dummy, but commonly used as a term of address for friends *CR* ◆ *Hola, maje, ¿cómo te va? Hi, pal, how's it going?*

mal →**echar mal de ojo; hacer mal (a alguien, a nadie); ir de mal en peor**

estar **mal de la azotea** (to be bad in the roof) to be off one's rocker, crazy *DR, S. Cone, Sp* ◆ *Esa pobre señora está mal de la azotea. That poor woman's upstairs isn't fully furnished. (She's got bats in the belfry.)*

estar **mal de la cholla** (to be bad in the head) to be off one's rocker, crazy *Mex, PR, ES, Sp* ◆ *¿Ir caminando al centro? ¿Estás mal de la cholla? Walk downtown? Are you off your rocker?*

mal educado(-a) badly brought up, rude, spoiled *L. Am., Sp* ◆ *Carlos nunca contesta el saludo. —No le hagas caso; es un mal educado. Carlos never responds to a greeting. —Don't mind him; he's rude.*

estar de **mal humor** to be in a bad mood *L. Am., Sp* ◆ *No me hables. Estoy de mal humor. Don't talk to me. I'm in a bad mood.*

mal nacido(-a) (badly born, meaning bastard) jerk, SOB (vulgar) *L. Am., Sp* ◆ *Es una mal nacida. No cuida ni se preocupa de su madre, que es vieja y está enferma. She's a lowlife. She doesn't take care of her mother, who is old and sick.*

mal pensado(-a) thinking bad thoughts, especially thinking the worst of others *L. Am., Sp* ◆ *No seas mal pensada, Irene. Estoy segura que tu tío no quiso ofendernos. Don't be a negative thinker, Irene. I'm sure that your uncle didn't mean to offend us.*

mal que bien (badly as good, well) in any way possible, no matter what, any old way *Mex, DR, ES, Peru, Sp* ◆ *Mal que bien, hizo su trabajo; se lo aceptamos porque es la hija del director. She did her work any old way (not well); we accepted it because she's the daughter of the director.*

estar de **mal talante** to be in a bad mood *U, Arg, Sp* ◆ *Mi colega siempre está de mal talante cuando tenemos mucho trabajo. My colleague is always in a bad mood when we have a lot of work.*

mala (buena) noticia bad (good) news *L. Am., Sp* ◆ *¡Qué mala noticia! What bad news!*

estar de **mala leche** (to be of bad milk) to be in a bad mood (vulgar) *Mex, Sp* ◆ *¿Por qué estás de mala leche? Why are you in a bad mood?*

de **mala muerte** (of bad death) of little worth, poor quality *L. Am., Sp* ◆ *No quiero ir a ese bar de mala muerte. I don't want to go to that crummy bar.*

mala nota (bad note) unpleasant thing or person, bad news, bad reputation *most of L. Am.* ◆ *Esa escuela es (de) muy mala nota. That school has a bad reputation.*

la **mala pasada** dirty trick *L. Am., Sp* (RVAR *Ch:* **una mala jugada**) ◆ *A Salvador le hicieron una mala pasada y no le dieron su cheque. They gave Salvador a dirty deal and didn't give him his check.* ◆ *Nos jugaron una mala pasada con la devaluación. They played a rotten trick on us with the devaluation.*

estar de **mala uva** (to be of bad grape) to be in a bad mood *Sp* ◆ *El otro día Javier estaba de muy mala uva. No sé qué le pasaba pero no había manera de hablar normalmente con él. The other day Javier was in a very bad mood. I don't know what was happening to him but there was no way to talk normally with him.*

estar/andar de **malas** to be in a bad mood *L. Am., Sp* ◆ *Después de tres días de lluvia, todo el mundo anda de malas. After three days of rain, everyone is in a bad mood.*

las **malas** →**por las buenas o por las malas**

las **malas lenguas** (bad tongues) rumor-mongers, gossipers *L. Am., Sp* ◆ *Dicen las malas lenguas que ella maltrataba a sus empleados. According to the rumor mill, she mistreated her employees.*

a **malas penas** with a lot of effort, great difficulty *Sp* ◆ *A malas penas, los alpinistas llegaron a la cima de la montaña. With great effort, the mountain climbers arrived at the summit of the mountain.*

estar de **malas pulgas** (to be of bad fleas) to be in a bad mood; also, **andar de** or **tener** *ES, CR, Col, Ch, U, Sp* ◆ *Hoy está de malas pulgas. Today he (she) is in a really lousy mood.*

maldito(-a) damn(ed) *L. Am., Sp* ◆ *¡Maldita guerra! Han muerto muchos inocentes. Damned war! Many innocent people have died.*

¡Maldito(-a) sea! (May it be cursed!) Damn it! exclamation of anger *Mex, DR, PR, G, Col,* *U, Sp* ◆ *Malditos sean los políticos actuales; han destruído la economía del país. Damn the current politicians; they've destoyed the country's economy.*

malhablado(-a) crude in speaking habits, foul-mouthed, using bad language *L. Am., Sp* ◆ *No parece un profesional. Es muy mal-hablado. He doesn't seem like a professional. He's very foul-mouthed.*

mamacita (little mama) term of address derived from **mamá**, used with affection to a girl or woman; also, sometimes used as a come-on by a man to a good-looking woman *L. Am.* ◆ *Mamacita, termina tus tareas. Es hora de ir a la escuela. My darling girl, finish your homework. It's time to go to school.* ◆ *Buenas tardes, mamacita, estás divina con ese traje de baño. Good afternoon, gorgeous, you look divine in that bathing suit.*

la **mamada** (sucking, nursing) hogwash, nonsense, lie, fib (vulgar) *Mex, ES, Col* ◆ *Es un buen hombre. —¡Mamadas! He's a good man. —Baloney!*

estar **mamado(-a)** (to be breast-fed) to be drunk *U, Arg* ◆ *Deja de tomar vino; ya estás mamada. Stop drinking wine; you're already drunk.*

mamar (to suckle) to have oral sex (vulgar) *L. Am., Sp*

mamar una cosa con la leche (en la leche) (to suckle something along with mother's milk) to learn something at a very young age *L. Am., Sp* ◆ *Esta chica mamó la inteligencia de su madre con la leche. That girl was intelligent from a young age.*

la **mamasota** good-looking woman, cheesecake (sometimes used as a term to get a woman's attention; a bit vulgar) *Mex, ES, DR, G, PR, Col* ◆ *Estás bien buena, mamasota. You're a good-looking woman, mama.*

mambo →**tener mambo en la cabeza**

mames →**No mames.**

mamey (a fruit) good, of quality *Mex, Cuba, Col* ◆ *La rubia ésa está mamey. That blond is classy.*

ser un **mamey** (to be a mamey, a fruit) to be a piece of cake, easy *PR, Col* ◆ *Ese trabajo es un mamey. Lo podré terminar pronto. That* *job is a piece of cake. I'll be able to finish it quickly.*

mami, mamita term of affection for girl or woman, even a young girl; term used to get a woman's attention *L. Am.* ◆ *Pórtate bien, mami. Behave yourself, dear. (to a young girl)* ◆ *Mamita, mírame. Estás divina. Hey, hot stuff, look at me. You're gorgeous.*

el **mamón, la mamona 1.** (sucker, like a suckling baby) mooch, person who takes advantage of others *Sp* ◆ *Vaya mamón, se ha ido sin pagar. What a mooch; he left without paying.* **2.** (sucker, like a suckling baby) tiresome, annoying, or ridiculous (person) *Chicano, Mex, ES, Col, Peru, Sp* ◆ *¿Por qué toleras a esa mamona? Why do you put up with that annoying woman?*

ser un **manazas** to be a klutz *Sp* ◆ *Felipe intentó arreglar el asunto y lo estropeó más. Es un manazas. Felipe tried to fix things and messed them up more. He's a klutz.*

la **mancha de plátano** (banana stain) quality of being a real native of Puerto Rico *PR, Sp* ◆ *Mucha gente cree que soy de México, pero soy puertorriqueño. ¿Tú no me ves la mancha de plátano? Many people think I'm from Mexico, but I'm Puerto Rican. Can't you see my Puerto Ricanness?*

¡Manda huevos! Damn! used to indicate impossibility, opposition, surprise, the height of something (vulgar) *ES, CR, Col, Sp* (RVAR *Sp:* also, **manda cojones**) ◆ *¡Manda huevos! Las fotos no salieron bien. Damn! The photos didn't come out well.*

mandar a alguien a bañarse (to send someone to take a bath) to tell someone to get lost *ES, Nic, Peru, Bol, Ch, U* ◆ *Toleré muchas cosas de mi novio. Finalmente lo mandé a bañarse. I put up with a lot of things from my boyfriend. Finally, I sent him packing.*

mandar a alguien a buscar berros (to send someone to find watercress) to tell someone to get lost *Sp* ◆ *A Ignacio le mandaron a buscar berros; no quieren que vuelva aquí. They told Ignacio to get lost; they don't want him to come back here again.*

mandar a alguien a freír buñuelos (to send someone to fry doughnuts) to tell someone to get lost *Mex, Sp* ◆ *Mandó a sus amigos a freír buñuelos porque no lo deja-*

ban estudiar. He told his friends to get lost because they didn't let him study.

mandar a alguien a freír espárragos (to send someone to fry asparagus) to tell someone to get lost *Mex, PR, ES, Ch, Sp* ◆ *Cuando Estela le pidió un aumento de sueldo a su jefe, éste la mandó a freír espárragos. When Estela asked her boss for a raise, he told her to get lost.*

mandar a alguien a freír papas (to send someone to fry potatoes) to tell someone to get lost *PR* ◆ *Felipe la mandó a freír papas. Estaba cansado de esperarla. Felipe told her to get lost. He was tired of waiting for her.*

mandar a alguien a hacer gárgaras (to send someone to gargle) to tell someone to get lost *Sp* ◆ *El abogado no resolvió nada en dos meses, y lo mandé a hacer gárgaras. The lawyer didn't resolve anything in two months, and I told him to get lost.*

mandar a alguien a la chingada (to send someone to the **chingada**, a violated woman, vulgar) to tell someone to go to hell *Mex, C. Am.* ◆ *Le mandé a mi cuñada a la chingada porque se mete en mi vida. I told my sister-in-law to go to hell because she interferes in my life.*

mandar a alguien a la goma (to send someone to the rubber, as far as rubber expands) to tell someone to get lost *Mex* ◆ *Horacio nos mintió, y lo mandamos a la goma. Horacio lied to us, and we told him to get lost.*

mandar a alguien a la jodida (to send someone to the **jodida**, used like **a la chingada** but only slightly vulgar) to tell someone to go to the devil *Chicano, Mex, G* ◆ *Cuando traté de explicarle la situación, no quiso escuchar. Me mandó a la jodida. When I tried to explain the situation, he refused to listen. He told me to go to the devil.*

mandar a alguien a la mierda (to send someone to shit, vulgar) to tell someone to go to hell *L. Am., Sp* ◆ *Si sigue así, mándalo a la mierda. If he keeps this up, tell him to go to hell.*

mandar a alguien a la porra (to send someone to the stick) to tell someone to go to the devil *L. Am., Sp* ◆ *Su comportamiento era tan malo que Leticia lo mandó a la porra. His behavior was so bad that Leticia told him to go to the devil.*

mandar a alguien a la verga (to send someone to the male organ, vulgar) to tell someone to go to hell *ES, Nic, Ven* ◆ *Mi jefe me mandó a la verga.* My boss told me to go to hell.

mandar a alguien a paseo (to send someone to take a walk) to tell someone to get lost *Col, Sp* ◆ *La señora Bosco mandó de paseo a su cocinera porque llegaba tarde muy a menudo.* Mrs. Bosco told her cook to get lost because she often arrived late.

mandar a alguien al carajo (to send someone to the male organ, vulgar) to tell someone to go to hell *L. Am., Sp* ◆ *Estábamos celebrando el cumpleaños de Alcira, y su padre nos mandó al carajo porque la música estaba muy alta.* We were celebrating Alcira's birthday, and her dad told us to go to hell because the music was too loud.

mandar a alguien al cuerno, a la eme (to send someone to the horn; to the "m," which stands for **mierda**, shit) to tell someone to go to the devil *Mex, DR, PR, ES, Peru, S. Cone, Sp* ◆ *Si no quieren seguir las reglas de los instructores, mándalos al cuerno.* If they don't want to follow the instructors' rules, tell them to go to the devil.

mandar a alguien al demonio (to send someone to the devil) to tell someone to get lost, go to the devil *Mex, G, ES, Col* ◆ *A Quique lo mandaron al demonio.* They told Quique to get lost.

mandar a alguien por un tubo (to send someone through a pipe) to tell someone to get lost, get rid of someone; to dump (a friend or sweetheart) *Mex, ES, Col* ◆ *¿Cómo estás, Juan? —Mal. Mi novia me mandó por un tubo.* How are you, Juan? —Bad. My girlfriend dumped me.

mandar de paseo to send packing *L. Am., Sp* ◆ *El jefe lo mandó de paseo porque llegó tarde tres días seguidos.* The boss sent him packing because he arrived late three days in a row.

mandarse un discurso (to send a speech) to lecture at, preach, deliver a sermon *L. Am.* ◆ *El patrón se mandó un discurso de una hora.* The boss lectured for an hour.

¿Mande? Excuse me? What (did you say)? *Mex* ◆ *¿Mande? No te oí.* What? I didn't hear you.

el **mandilón** (big commander, said in an ironic way) henpecked man, meek husband whose wife orders him around *Mex, ES* ◆ *Hola, mandilón. ¿Cómo está tu mujercita?* Hi, you henpecked husband, you. How's your little lady?

mandón, mandona describing someone who likes to give orders, bossy *L. Am., Sp* ◆ *Mi hermana es muy mandona.* My sister is very bossy.

mandujano so-and-so; extension of **fulano, mengano, zutano** *Mex* ◆ *Además de fulano, mengano y zutano, llegaron mandujano y su familia.* In addition to Tom, Dick, and Harry, a whole other group of people that we didn't know came.

mangar (to "sleeve") to steal, lift *Cuba, PR, Sp* ◆ *Me mangaron la billetera.* They lifted my wallet.

el **mango** (mango) money, dough *U, Arg* ◆ *No tengo un mango hasta fin de mes.* I don't have a red cent until the end of the month.

el **mango** →**tener la sartén por el mango**

el **mango, manguito** ([little] mango) a good-looking person *most of L. Am.* ◆ *Está hecho(-a) un mango.* He's (She's) looking really good.

la **mani, manifa** (short for **manifestación**) demonstration *Sp* ◆ *Había cientos de estudiantes en la mani.* There were hundreds of students at the demonstration.

manija →**dar(se) manija**

las **manitas** →**estar hasta las manitas**

ser un **manitas** to be good at doing things, handy *Sp* ◆ *Andreu realmente es un manitas. Siempre consigue arreglarlo todo.* Andreu is really handy. He always manages to fix everything.

mano →**dar una mano; darle la mano a alguien; darse la mano; hecho(-a) a mano; írsele la mano; meter la mano hasta el codo en algo; meter las manos al fuego por alguien; meter mano; meterle mano; pasársele la mano; tener buena mano para; tener mano; tener mano de monja; tener manos de hacha**

estar a **mano** (to be at hand) to be even (with each other) *Mex, ES, S. Cone* ◆ *Te pagué la plata y ahora estamos a mano, amigo.* I paid you the money and now we're even, pal.

la **mano de santo** (saint's hand) charm, effective remedy *Sp* ◆ *Mi tía tiene una mano de santo para curar el mal de estómago. My aunt has a charm for curing stomach ache.*

el/la **mano(-a), manito(-a)** forms of **hermano(-a)**, brother (sister), used for a close friend *Mex, DR, C. Am., Col* ◆ *Hola, mana, ¿qué has hecho? Hi (dear). What have you been up to?*

una **manopla** →**echar una manopla**

Manos a la obra. Let's get to work. *L. Am., Sp* ◆ *Manos a la obra, muchachos. Tenemos que terminar el trabajo antes de las cinco. Let's get to work, boys. We have to finish the job before five o'clock.*

con las **manos en la masa** (with one's hands in the dough) caught in the act, red-handed *L. Am., Sp* (see illustration, page 387) ◆ *Lo agarraron con las manos en la masa. They caught him red-handed.*

el **manotazo** blow with the hand, slap *L. Am., Sp* ◆ *Mi madre me dio un manotazo porque le contesté de mala manera. My mother slapped me because I spoke back rudely.*

mantenerse en sus trece (to keep in one's thirteen) to stick to one's guns, keep doing the same thing, persist in an opinion or in doing something *L. Am., Sp* ◆ *Se mantuvo en sus trece a pesar de las circunstancias. He stuck to his guns despite the circumstances.*

Manuela (pun on **mano** meaning hand) handjob, masturbation (vulgar); e.g., **usar Manuela, hacer el amor con Manuela** *Mex, Cuba, DR, PR, G, Col, Ch*

manyar to chow down, eat (from Italian); also, in some places, to understand or realize *Peru, S. Cone* ◆ *¿Cuándo vamos a manyar? When are we going to eat?*

la **maña** (skill) bad habit *Mex, DR, C. Am., Ch, U* ◆ *Marilú tiene la maña de chuparse el dedo. Marilú has the bad habit of sucking her thumb.*

el **mapa** →**no estar en el mapa**

la **máquina** machine; car *Cuba* ◆ *Tengo mis maletas en la máquina. I've got my suitcases in the car.*

la **mar de** (the sea of) no end of, huge number of *L. Am., Sp* ◆ *¿No notaste la mar de errores en ese informe? Didn't you notice the huge number of errors in that report?*

la **maraca** whore; bitch, demanding, unpleasant woman (synonym: **maricona**) *Ch*

ser una **maraca sin palo** (to be a maraca, the musical instrument, without a handle or stick) to be a klutz, ding-a-ling, incompetent person *Col* ◆ *En la clase de química soy una maraca sin palo, el más cafre de todos. In chemistry class I'm a real ding-a-ling, the most klutzy of them all.*

marcando ocupado (dialing the busy signal—and just not connecting) out of it, not understanding anything *Ch, U* ◆ *Este chico no sabe nada. Está marcando ocupado. That guy doesn't know anything. He's on another planet.*

marcha →**dar marcha; dar marcha atrás; irse (salir) de marcha; ponerse en marcha**

marchar requete bien to be going great (in *Sp*, a bit old-fashioned) *Mex, G, Para, U, Arg, Sp* ◆ *¿Cómo te va la vida? —Me marcha requete bien. How's life going for you? —It's going very well (for me).*

marchar/andar/ir sobre ruedas (to go on wheels) to be going great *Mex, DR, PR, ES, Nic, Col, Ch, Sp* ◆ *Todo anda (marcha) sobre ruedas. Everything is going great.*

el **marica** sissy; euphemism for **maricón** *L. Am., Sp*

el **maricón** gay, homosexual (pejorative) *L. Am., Sp*

la **mariconada 1.** attitude or act of being effeminate or gay (pejorative) *L. Am., Sp* ◆ *Hicieron una mariconada al no pedir explicaciones concretas a los organizadores del congreso. They wimped out (did something wimpy) by not asking the organizers of the conference for an explanation.* **2.** dirty trick *Ch, Sp* ◆ *Mi jefe me hizo una mariconada al despedirme. (Ch) My boss played a dirty trick on me by firing me.*

la **marimacho, la marimacha** lesbian, dike; tomboy (pejorative, **marimacho** is used in *PR, G, Ch;* elsewhere **marimacha**) *Mex, DR, PR, G, ES, CR, Col, Ch, Sp* (RVar *Mex, Col:* **marimacha** means tomboy)

el **mariposa** (butterfly) gay, homosexual *Mex, ES, Nic, Pan, Col, U, Sp*

el **mariposo, el mariposón** (big or male butterfly) gay, homosexual (pejorative) *Chicano, Mex, DR, Col, Ch, Sp* ◆ *Mi modisto,* *que es mariposón, tiene un excelente gusto y es muy dedicado a su trabajo.* My designer, who is gay, has excellent taste and is very dedicated to his work.

el **mariquita** sissy; also, euphemism for **maricón** *Chicano, Mex, Cuba, DR, PR, Col, Ch, Sp* ◆ *No seas mariquita.* Don't be a sissy.

maromas →hacer mil maromas para...

el **marrano** pig (dirty or fat); undesirable person *Mex, G, Col, Sp* ◆ *¡Qué marrano! Mira cómo come. Parece que nunca le enseñaron buenos modales.* What a pig! Look how he (she) eats. It looks like they never taught him (her) good manners.

el **marrón** (chestnut) mess, bad situation, embarrassing situation *Sp* ◆ *El jefe me pasó un marrón y tuve que quedarme hasta las diez de la noche en la oficina.* The boss gave me a mess to handle and I had to stay in the office until ten o'clock at night.

martes 13, jueves 13 Tuesday the 13th, Thursday the 13th (considered unlucky days in Spanish-speaking countries, like Friday the 13th) *L. Am., Sp* ◆ *No voy a empezar a hacer nada nuevo hoy porque es martes 13.* I'm not going to start anything new today because it is Tuesday the 13th.

martillar (to hammer) to work *Mex, Col* ◆ *¿Qué tal, 'mano? —Por aquí, martillando.* What's up, bro'? —I'm just here working.

el **martilleo** (hammering) salt mines, work *Mex, Col* ◆ *Renuncié al martilleo.* I quit at the salt mines (my job).

maruja homebody, describing someone who likes to stay home and take care of the house (clean, etc.); same in the masculine as in the feminine *Sp* ◆ *Mi esposo y yo somos muy marujas; los fines de semana nos quedamos en casa.* My husband and I are homebodies; we stay home on weekends.

es **más** what's more, and furthermore *L. Am., Sp* ◆ *Joaquín es irresponsable; es más, es mentiroso.* Joaquín is irresponsible; what's more, he's a liar.

más adelante 1. farther ahead *L. Am., Sp* ◆ *Cuando los exploradores preguntaron por El Dorado, los indígenas les decían "Más adelante".* When the explorers asked for El Dorado, the Indians told them "Farther ahead." **2.** later on *L. Am., Sp* ◆ *Más adelante*

hablaremos de los detalles. We'll talk about the details later on.

más bien rather, somewhat; instead *L. Am., Sp* ◆ *Creo que nos hace falta un consejero, más bien, un buen psicólogo.* I think we need a counselor, or rather, a good psychologist.

ser **más bueno que el pan** (to be better than bread) to be as good as gold *most of L. Am., Sp* ◆ *Ese niño es más bueno que el pan.* That boy is as good as gold.

más cerrado(-a) que un huevo de gallina (un tubo de radio) (more closed than a hen's egg [a radio tube]) dumb as a post, total idiot *Mex, PR* (RVAR *CR:* **que un bombillo** [a lightbulb]) ◆ *Mi suegro es más cerrado que un huevo de gallina.* My father-in-law is dumb as a post.

ser **más corto(-a) que las mangas de un chaleco** (to be shorter than the sleeves of a vest) to be short on brains *Sp* ◆ *No me extraña su actitud; es más corta que las mangas de un chaleco.* Her attitude doesn't surprise me; she's short on brains.

más de la cuenta too much *L. Am., Sp* ◆ *Ay, comí más de la cuenta.* Oh dear, I ate too much.

ser **más del campo que las amapolas** (to be more from the country than poppies) to be a hick *Sp* ◆ *Nico es más del campo que las amapolas; nunca ha estado en un supermercado.* Nico is a hick (a real country boy); he's never been in a supermarket.

estar **más despistado(-a) que un pulpo en un garaje** (to be more lost than an octopus in a garage) to be lost, off the track *Sp* ◆ *Estoy más despistada que un pulpo en un garaje. ¿Dónde diablos estamos?* I'm totally lost. Where in the heck are we?

más días hay que longanizas (there are more days than pork sausages) there's no rush *Sp* ◆ *¿Cuál es la prisa? Más días hay que longanizas.* What's the hurry? There's no rush.

más duro(-a) que el cemento (harder than cement) stingy *PR* (RVAR *Col:* **duro[-a] como cemento**) ◆ *Elena es más dura que el cemento. No comparte nada con nadie.* Elena is as stingy as can be. She doesn't share anything with anyone.

más feo(-a) que carracuca (uglier than carracuca) ugly as hell (vulgar) *CR* ◆ *Soy más feo que carracuca, ¿verdad? —¡No digas eso, mi amor!* I'm ugly as hell, aren't I? —Don't say that, honey!

más flaco(-a) que un alfiler (thinner than a straight pin) as thin as a matchstick *L. Am., Sp* ◆ *El nuevo régimen de Lalo ha tenido éxito. Está más flaco que un alfiler.* Lalo's new diet has been a success. He's as thin as a matchstick.

ser **más (tan) fresco(-a) que una lechuga** (to be more [as] fresh as a lettuce) to be very brazen, bold, cool as a cucumber, fresh as a daisy *L. Am., Sp* ◆ *Esta mujer es más fresca que una lechuga.* This woman is very brazen.

Era **más grande (pequeño) el difunto.** (The dead person was bigger [smaller].) said to someone when they are wearing a large (small) article of clothing *Mex, DR, ES, S. Cone, Sp* ◆ *¿Era más grande el difunto? Ese abrigo es demasiado grande para ti.* Was the dead guy bigger? That coat is too big for you.

más largo(-a) que la esperanza del pobre (longer than the hope of the poor person) very tall, string bean *PR* ◆ *Tengo problemas para encontrar ropa para Juvenal. Es más largo que la esperanza del pobre.* I have trouble finding clothes for Juvenal. He's a string bean.

más lento(-a) que un suero de brea (slower than tar plasma) slower than molasses in January *PR* ◆ *La reunión fue más lenta que un suero de brea.* The meeting was slower than molasses in January.

más lento(-a) que una caravana de cojos (slower than a caravan of limping people) as slow as a snail *PR, Col* ◆ *¡Apúrate, niña! Eres más lenta que una caravana de cojos.* Hurry up, girl! You're a real slowpoke.

estar **liado(-a)** (to be linked) to be busy *Sp* ◆ *Estamos muy liados esta semana.* We're very busy this week.

estar **más liado(-a) que la pata de un romano (de una momia)** (to be more entangled than the foot of a Roman [of a mummy]) to be very busy; to be a messy or tangled situation, a can of worms *Sp* ◆ *Mi vida está más liada que la pata de un romano.* My life is a real can of worms. ◆ *Estás más liado que la pata de un romano.* You're so busy you don't have time to sneeze.

más listo(-a) que el hambre (more clever than hunger) bright as a dollar, quick-witted *Sp* ◆ *Estos perros son más listos que el hambre. Sólo les falta aprender a leer y escribir.* These dogs are quick-witted. The next thing you know they'll be learning to read and write.

más loco(-a) que una cabra (crazier than a she-goat) mad as a hatter *Mex, CR, S. Cone, Sp* ◆ *Gustavo escribió una carta de amor a la profesora de literatura. Está más loco que una cabra.* Gustavo wrote a love letter to the literature professor. He's as mad as a hatter.

en lo **más mínimo** in the least *L. Am., Sp* ◆ *¿Jorge? Sus problemas no me interesan en lo más mínimo.* Jorge? His problems don't interest me in the least.

Más o menos. (More or less.) OK *L. Am., Sp* ◆ *¿Cómo están tus padres? Más o menos.* How are your parents? OK.

más pesado(-a) que cargar un elefante (heavier than carrying an elephant) a drag, unpleasant (person) *Mex, PR* ◆ *¿Vas a ir a la fiesta con Mario? Es más pesado que cargar un elefante.* You're going to the party with Mario? He's a real drag.

lo **más pronto posible** (the soonest possible) as soon as possible *L. Am., Sp* ◆ *Mándeme el archivo lo más pronto posible.* Send me the file as soon as possible.

ser **más puta que las gallinas** (to be more of a slut than the hens are) to be a real slut (vulgar) *Mex, PR, ES, S. Cone, Sp* ◆ *¿Cómo te enamoraste de esa mujer? Es más puta que las gallinas.* How could you have fallen in love with that woman? She's such a slut.

más rápido(-a) que ligero(-a) (more quick than fast) like a shot, hurriedly, in a rush *Mex, PR, G* ◆ *Prepararon la comida más rápido que ligero.* They prepared the food in a rush.

más rápido(-a) que un rayo (faster than lightning) lightning fast *L. Am., Sp* ◆ *¿Ya terminaste el trabajo? Eres más rápido que un rayo.* You already finished the work? You're lightning fast.

estar **más serio(-a) que un burro en lancha** (to be more serious than a donkey in a rowboat) to look uptight, worried *CR* ◆ *¿Qué te pasa? Estás más seria que un burro en lancha.* What's up with you? You look worried.

ser **más sordo(-a) que una tapia** (to be more deaf than a wall) to be deaf as a post *L. Am., Sp* ◆ *Mi abuela era más sorda que una tapia.* My grandmother was as deaf as a post.

a **más tardar** at the latest *L. Am., Sp* ◆ *Terminaré el trabajo el jueves a más tardar.* I'll finish the work on Thursday at the latest.

Más ven cuatro ojos que dos. Four eyes are (see) better than two. *L. Am., Sp* ◆ *Acompáñame a ver la nueva casa. Más ven cuatro ojos que dos.* Come with me to see the new house. Four eyes are better than two.

más viejo(-a) que Matusalén older than Methuselah *L. Am., Sp* ◆ *Me siento más viejo que Matusalén.* I feel older than Methuselah.

el **mataburros** (donkey killers) dictionary *Mex, DR, PR, CR, Peru, U, Arg* ◆ *Matías y Gabriela compraron el mejor mataburros que pudieron encontrar.* Matías and Gabriela bought the best dictionary they could find.

matado(-a) 1. (killed) exhausting *Mex, G* ◆ *Es un trabajo matado.* It's an exhausting job. **2.** (killed) awful; bad; graceless; boring *Florida, Cuba, DR, PR, CR, Col* ◆ *Esa profesora está matada.* That teacher is lousy. ◆ *Es un lugar matado.* It's a crummy place.

matador(-a) 1. ugly as sin (often women), bad, too much *Mex, Cuba, G, Col, Peru, S. Cone* ◆ *¡Qué trabajo matador!* What a bad (exhausting) job! **2.** fabulous, wonderful, to die for *Mex, Col, Peru, U* ◆ *Tiene un sentido de humor matador.* He has a sense of humor to die for.

el/la **mátalas callando** (kill-them-being-quiet) discreet womanizer who appears faithful or woman who acts sweet and obedient but isn't *Mex, ES, DR, Col* ◆ *Esa mujer se ve muy buena, muy dulce, pero es mátalas callando.* That woman looks very good, very sweet, but she's not.

matar (to kill) to finish off or up *Mex, Cuba* ◆ *¿Matemos la ensalada?* Shall we kill (finish off) the salad?

matar al oso (to kill the bear) to masturbate (males, vulgar) *Mex, Col*

matar dos pájaros de un tiro (to kill two birds with one shot) to accomplish two goals at once, kill two birds with one stone *L. Am., Sp* ◆ *Invitando a mamá a vivir aquí, mato dos pájaros de un tiro porque ella estará más feliz y yo tendré a alguien que cuide a los chiquitines.* By inviting mom to live here, I'll kill two birds with one stone because she'll be happier and I'll have someone to watch the kids. ◆ *Fui a Montreal, y maté dos pájaros de un tiro: asistí a un congreso y visité a mi prima Susana.* I went to Montreal, and I killed two birds with one stone: I attended a conference and I visited my cousin Susana.

matar la gallina de los huevos de oro to kill the goose that lays the golden eggs *L. Am., Sp* ◆ *No despidas al cantante porque esto sería matar la gallina de los huevos de oro.* Don't fire the singer because that would be like killing the goose that lays the golden eggs.

matarse to kill oneself (for/to . . .) (figuratively) *L. Am., Sp* ◆ *Los García se mataron para dar educación a sus hijos.* The Garcías killed themselves to educate their children.

el/la **matasanos** (healthy people-killer) quack doctor *most of L. Am., Sp* ◆ *El matasanos recomendó un remedio muy inefectivo.* The quack doctor recommended a very ineffective cure.

mate →**darle mate**

las **mates** short for **matemáticas**, math *most of L. Am., Sp* ◆ *A Juan no le van las mates. Siempre suspende los exámenes.* Juan can't do math. He always fails the exams.

ser **mayor (menor) de edad** to be of age (a minor) *L. Am., Sp* ◆ *Cuando seas mayor de edad, Memito, te daré las llaves del coche... ¡quizás!* When you're older, Billy, I'll give you the keys to the car . . . maybe!

con la **mayor brevedad** (with the most briefness) quickly, fast or soon *L. Am., Sp* ◆ *Responda con la mayor brevedad posible.* Respond as soon as possible.

mayúsculo(-a) (capital letter) major, mega *L. Am.* ◆ *Es un problema mayúsculo. It's a mega problem.*

mazo tons, many, large amount *Sp* ◆ *Fernando tenía un mazo de dinero pero se lo gastó en el casino. Fernando had tons of money but he wasted it at the casino.*

mear fuera del tiesto (to pee outside the pot) to screw up, make a mistake (vulgar) *Sp* (RVar *U, Arg:* **tarro** instead of **tiesto**) ◆ *Ya measte fuera del tarro; ahora tienes que disculparte. You've messed up; now you have to apologize.*

mear(se) to pee, urinate *L. Am., Sp* ◆ *Apúrate. Déjame el baño porque me meo. Hurry up. Let me use the bathroom because I'm peeing in my pants.*

mearse de (la) risa to wet one's pants with laughter (also, **meado de la risa**) *Mex, DR, S. Cone, Sp* ◆ *Cuando vi ese programa, estaba meado de la risa. When I saw that show, I wet my pants laughing.*

mechudo(-a) hairy, with hair uncombed or very long (pejorative) *Mex, ES, Nic, CR, Col* ◆ *Qué mechudo anda ese cipote. (ES) How long (messy) that kid's hair is.*

media cosita (half a little thing) any little thing *Mex, C. Am.* ◆ *Si me dice media cosita, lo voy a mandar a freír espárragos. If he says the slightest thing to me, I'm going to tell him to get lost.*

la **media naranja** (half orange) better half, spouse, sweetheart (male or female), soul mate *L. Am., Sp* ◆ *¿Dónde está tu media naranja? Where's your better half?*

a **mediados de** about the middle of *L. Am., Sp* ◆ *Estaremos en Costa Rica a mediados de agosto. We'll be in Costa Rica about the middle of August.*

a **medias** →**ir a medias**

estar a **medio camino** (to be in mid road) to be halfway there *Mex, DR, PR, Ch, Sp* ◆ *Estás a medio camino; te falta sólo un año para recibirte. You're halfway there; you've got only one more year until you graduate.*

a **medio hacer** half-way done; unfinished *L. Am., Sp* ◆ *El proyecto está a medio hacer. The project is half finished.*

medio mundo (half the world) a lot of people, everybody and his uncle *L. Am., Sp* ◆ *Esa noticia la sabe medio mundo. Everybody and his uncle knows that news.*

a **medio palo** (to the half stick) half done; inconclusive, up in the air *DR, Hond, Nic, CR, Col* ◆ *No dejemos las cosas a medio palo. Let's not leave things half done.*

medio raro (sort of unusual) kind of weird; possibly gay *Mex, DR, ES, S. Cone, Sp* ◆ *Creo que ese chico es medio raro. Tiene un comportamiento extraño. I think that guy is kind of weird. He acts a little funny.*

medir calles (to measure streets) to hang out in the street *ES, CR, Col* ◆ *Pablito es tan vago; siempre está midiendo calles. Pablo is so lazy; he's always hanging out in the street.*

a lo **mejor** likely as not, probably *L. Am., Sp* ◆ *A lo mejor los invitados traen una botella de vino. Likely as not, the guests will bring a bottle of wine.*

mejor dicho rather, that is to say *L. Am., Sp* ◆ *Ellos viven en una casa muy linda, mejor dicho, en la casa más hermosa del barrio. They live in a very pretty house, that is to say, in the most beautiful house in the neighborhood.*

el **melón, la melona** (melon) idiot, fool *Sp* ◆ *No seas tan melón y piensa un poco. Don't be so foolish and think a bit.* ◆ *Me quedé como un melón. I sat (stood) there like a dolt.*

los **melones** (melons) woman's breasts *Cuba, Col, Sp* ◆ *¡Qué melones tiene esa mujer! What a pair of knockers that woman has!*

la **memez (las memeces)** stupid thing or idea, idiocy *Sp* ◆ *¡Qué memez! Eso no es cierto. What a piece of nonsense! That's not true.*

el/la **memo(-a)** fool, dope *DR, PR, Sp* ◆ *Sólo un memo diría eso. Only a fool would say that.*

de **memoria** (from memory) by heart *L. Am., Sp* ◆ *La niña recitó el poema de memoria. The girl recited the poem by heart.*

el/la **menda** so-and-so (to refer to someone you don't know) *Sp* ◆ *La menda de la que hablé vendrá a la reunión esta noche. That so-and-so I talked about will come to the get-together tonight.*

mi (el/la) **menda** I, me, yours truly (used in third person to refer to oneself) *Sp* ◆ *El*

menear el bote: Le gusta menear el bote.
She likes to boogie.

*(La/Mi) menda no va a fregar los platos. (=
Yo no voy a fregar los platos.)* I'm not going
to wash the dishes.

menear el bote (to rock or move the boat)
to boogie, dance *most of L. Am.* ◆ *¿No
quieres menear el bote? Don't you want to
dance?*

menear el esqueleto (to rock or move the
skeleton) to boogie, dance *L. Am., Sp* ◆ *¿Vamos a menear el esqueleto, Silvia? Are we
going to shake a leg, Silvia?*

menearse to get moving, get a move on *L.
Am., Sp* ◆ *Menéate, que no quiero llegar
tarde. Get a move on because I don't want to
be late.*

menos →echar de menos; por lo menos;
tener a menos

Menos da una piedra. (A stone gives less.)
Take what you can get, phrase urging someone to accept what little has been obtained
Sp ◆ *¿Me darás sólo 150 euros para mis
gastos personales? —Exactamente. Menos
da una piedra. You'll only give me 150 euros*

for my personal expenses? —Exactly. Take
what you can get.

en **menos (de lo) que canta un gallo** (in
less than a cock crows) in very little time, in
a jiffy *L. Am., Sp* ◆ *Voy a terminar mis tareas en menos de lo que canta un gallo. I'm
going to finish my work in a jiffy.*

Menos lobos (Caperucita). (Fewer wolves
[Red Riding Hood].) Don't exaggerate so
much. *Sp* ◆ *¿Que todos en el foro de discusión te insultaron? Menos lobos Caperucita. Everyone in the chat group insulted
you? Don't exaggerate.*

menos mal just as well, it's a good thing *L.
Am., Sp* ◆ *¿No fuiste al concierto? Menos
mal. No valió la pena. You didn't go to the
concert? Just as well. It wasn't worth it.*

el **mensaje de texto** text message *L. Am.*
(RVar *Sp:* **el s.m.s.**) ◆ *Me mandaron un
mensaje de texto que no van a poder
recogernos. They sent me a text message that
they won't be able to pick us up.*

mensear to act like a fool; to put someone on,
confuse someone with silly talk *Mex* ◆

Ramón chocó porque iba menseando en el carro. Ramón crashed because he was acting like a fool in the car. ◆ *No lo mensées más.* Don't confuse him more.

menso(-a) stupid, foolish *Chicano, Mex, DR, PR, C. Am., Col, Ch* ◆ *Llegó el señor Hernández con la mensa de su mujer. Mr. Hernández arrived with that fool of a wife of his.*

mentar la madre (to mention the mother) to insult someone by suggesting the moral impurity of his or her mother (usually this means calling someone an **hijo de puta**), bitch out *Mex, C. Am., Col* (RVAR *Ch:* **sacar la madre;** *Sp:* **mentar a la madre**) ◆ *Mentar la madre es muy peligroso. Esto puede causar peleas y a veces muertes.* Calling someone an SOB is very dangerous. This can cause fights and sometimes deaths.

la **mente** →**tener la mente en blanco**

a **menudo** often *L. Am., Sp* ◆ *Pienso en ellos a menudo.* I think about them often.

el **menudo número** (diminutive number, or show) quite a scene, quite a fine state of affairs, pretty picture (ironic) *Sp* ◆ *Menudo número montaste anoche. Los de la habitación de al lado no pudieron dormir.* Quite a scene you made last night. The people in the room next door couldn't sleep.

el/la **mequetrefe** just anyone, mediocre person, pretentious person who won't amount to much *Mex, DR, PR, G, ES, Nic, S. Cone, Sp* ◆ *¿Qué quiere ese mequetrefe?* What does that loser want?

el **merequetengue** disorder, uproar, confusion, mess *Mex, G, Col* ◆ *Había mucha gente en la calle. ¡Qué merequetengue!* There were a lot of people in the street. What a mess!

el **merluzo** (from **merluza,** hake, a kind of fish) dope, idiot *Sp* ◆ *¿Aún no sabe las tablas de multiplicar? Es un merluzo.* He (She) still doesn't know the multiplication tables? He's (She's) a dope.

el **mero jodón** big boss, head honcho (no feminine form is normally used; somewhat vulgar) *Chicano, Mex, ES* ◆ *¿Dónde está el mero jodón? Necesito hablarle.* Where's the head honcho? I need to talk to him.

el **mero mero (la mera mera); el mero mero petatero** boss; chief or most important one; main seller of **petates,** or mats *Chicano, Mex, G, ES* ◆ *Aquí soy yo el mero mero (petatero).* Here I'm the top dog.

mero(-a) (mere) exact, this or that very (one) *Mex, G* ◆ *ese mero* that exact one ◆ *en el mero momento* at the very moment ◆ *en la mera esquina* right at the corner

Ya **mero. Ya merito.** Almost. It's (I'm, etc.) on the way, almost ready. *Mex, G, ES, Nic* ◆ *¿Ya preparaste la comida? —Ya mero.* Did you prepare the food (fix the meal) yet? —Almost.

mes →**por semana (por mes)**

la **mesa** →**poner los puntos sobre la mesa; por debajo de la mesa**

la **mescolanza** confusion, mess *most of L. Am.* ◆ *Esta mezcolanza creará problemas. Tenemos que solucionarla.* This mess will create problems. We need to solve it.

el **metelón, la metelona** busybody *Mex, Col* ◆ *César es un metelón. En todas partes se le encuentra.* César is a busybody. You see (literally, meet) him everywhere.

el/la **metepatas** (stick-your-foot-in) busybody *Sp* (RVAR *U, Arg:* **metedor[a] de patas**) ◆ *Ester es una metedora de patas, y por eso tiene problemas en la oficina.* Ester is a busybody, and that's why she has problems at the office.

meter (to put in) to swallow, eat or drink, wolf down *Sp* ◆ *Me metí cuatro cañas y dos bocadillos en quince minutos.* I wolfed down four beers and two sandwiches in fifteen minutes.

meter a alguien con cuchara una cosa to spoon-feed something to someone *Mex, Sp* ◆ *Le metimos con cuchara la información que teníamos.* We spoon-fed the information we had to him.

meter baza (to play a card trick) to butt into someone's conversation, put in one's two cents *Ch, Sp* ◆ *Siempre mete baza en todas partes. No sé cómo lo hace para estar en todas las conversaciones.* He's always putting in his two cents. I don't know how he manages to take part in all the conversations.

meter cabeza (to put head) to pay attention, put mental energy into something *Mex, PR,*

CR, Col (RVar CR, Col: to persist in getting something) ◆ *Eliza está metiendo cabeza en ese problema tan complicado de matemáticas. Eliza is putting a lot of mental energy into that complicated math problem.*

meter cuarta (to put in fourth [gear]) to step on it, step on the gas *Mex, Col* ◆ *Mete cuarta o llegaremos tarde. Step on it or we'll get there late.*

meter el cazo (to put in one's dipper) to be wrong, like **meter la pata** *Sp* ◆ *Metiste el cazo. Esta habitación no es tuya. You blew it. This isn't your room.*

meter (el) coco (to put coconut, head) to rack one's brain, concentrate on something *Mex, Cuba, Col* ◆ *Metimos coco para resolver el problema de física. We racked our brains to solve the physics problem.*

meter el hocico en todo to stick one's nose (literally, snout) into everything *Mex, ES, DR, Sp* ◆ *No entiendo por qué metes el hocico en todo. I don't know why you stick your nose into everything.*

meter el pie (to stick one's foot in) to get one's foot in the door, get into a house, business *Mex, Sp* ◆ *Ya metí el pie en la comunidad. Trabajaré duro para que me conozcan. I've already gotten my foot in the door in the community. I'll work hard so that they will get to know me.*

meter/tener en un puño a alguien (to put/have someone in one's fist) to have someone under one's thumb, intimidate or oppress someone *Mex, U, Sp* ◆ *Marciano nos tiene a todos en un puño porque tiene el 55 por ciento de las acciones en la empresa. Marciano has us under his thumb because he has 55 percent of the company's stock.*

meter la cuchara (to put in the spoon) to put in one's two cents, butt into someone else's business or a conversation *L. Am., Sp* (see illustration, page 278)◆ *Y ¿quién es usted para meter la cuchara? And who are you to butt in?* ◆ *Metí la cuchara para decirles la verdad. I butt in to tell them the truth.*

meter la mano hasta el codo en algo (to put one's hand up to the elbow in something) to get very involved in something, do something with great dedication (sometimes implies overreaching and taking something for oneself that one should not) *most of L. Am., Sp* ◆ *El trabajo de Marina en la compañía es impecable; metió la mano hasta el codo para triunfar. Marina's work at the company is impeccable; she's given her all to get ahead.* ◆ *Mi sobrino metió la mano hasta el codo en mis negocios y perdí mucho dinero. My nephew got too involved in my business, and I lost a lot of money.*

meter la mula (to put in the mule) to betray, deceive, do a bad turn *S. Cone* ◆ *Ten cuidado que en ese negocio no te vayan a meter la mula. Be careful in that business so that they don't pull the wool over your eyes.*

meter la pata (to put one's foot in) to make a mistake; to put one's foot in one's mouth *L. Am., Sp* ◆ *Hablaste demasiado; metiste la pata. You've said too much; you put your foot in your mouth.*

meter las manos al fuego por alguien (to put one's hands in the fire for someone) to vouch for someone, stake one's life on someone *Mex, DR, ES, Peru, S. Cone* ◆ *Yolanda es una buena amiga. Meto las manos al fuego por ella. Yolanda is a good friend. I vouch for her.*

meter las narices en todo to stick one's nose into everything *L. Am., Sp* ◆ *Estoy harta de doña Amelia porque mete las narices en todo. I'm sick of Doña Amelia because she sticks her nose into everything.*

meter mano (to put hand) to feel up, touch someone with sexual intentions *Mex, PR, U, Sp* ◆ *Intentó meterme mano en el cine. He tried to feel me up in the movie theater.*

meter un paquete (to put in a package) to fine *Sp* ◆ *Le metieron un paquete de cien euros por no llevar el casco de la moto. He (She) was fined one hundred euros for not wearing a motorcycle helmet.*

meter/poner en cintura (to put/place on waist) to reign in or control, make (someone) toe the line *L. Am., Sp* ◆ *Metieron en cintura a sus rivales. They made their opponents toe the line.*

meterle (to put it) to step on it, step on the gas *Mex, ES, Col* ◆ *¡Métele! Step on it!* ◆ *Métele velocidad. Speed it up.*

meterle caña (to put cane) to study hard, put out some effort *Mex* ◆ *Si quieres aprobar el examen de biología, hay que meterle* *caña. If you want to pass the biology exam, you have to put your nose to the grindstone.*

meterle la chancla al pedal (to put the sandal on the pedal) to step on it, step on the gas *Mex, Col* ◆ *Manejas muy despacio. Métele la chancla al pedal. You're driving very slowly. Put the pedal to the metal.*

meterle mano (to put in hand) to take, undertake *Mex, Cuba, DR, PR, G, Col* ◆ *Señores, vamos a meterle mano al proyecto, que hay que entregarlo mañana. Gentlemen, let's get going on the project since we have to hand it in tomorrow.*

meterle velocidad (to put in speed) to step on it, speed it up *Mex* ◆ *No le metas velocidad en las zonas de escuelas. Don't speed in school zones.*

meterse algo en la cabeza (to put something in one's head) to fixate or obsess on something, get an idea and cling to it *ES, Ch, Sp* ◆ *Jaime es un tozudo. Cuando se le mete algo en la cabeza, siempre acaba haciéndolo. Jaime is very stubborn. When he gets something in his head, he always ends up doing it.*

meterse algo entre ceja y ceja (to put something between eyebrow and eyebrow) to fixate or obsess on something, get an idea and cling to it *most of L. Am., Sp* (see illustration, page 303) ◆ *No cambiará de idea porque la tiene metida entre ceja y ceja. He won't change his mind because he's fixated on his idea.*

meterse dónde no lo (la) llaman to get involved in things that are none of one's business *L. Am., Sp* ◆ *Pablo siempre se mete dónde no lo llaman. Pablo always gets involved in things that are none of his business.*

meterse en camisa de once varas (to put oneself in a shirt of eleven rods) to bite off more than one can chew; to get mixed up in and over one's head in a mess *L. Am., Sp* ◆ *Los Abarcón compraron una casa carísima en la playa y un auto esport. Se han metido en camisa de once varas. The Abarcón family bought a very expensive house on the beach and a sports car. They have bitten off more than they can chew.*

meterse en el sobre (to put oneself in one's envelope) to hit the sack, go to bed *Ec, S. Cone, Sp* (see illustration, page 331) ◆ *Es-* *toy supercansado. Me voy a meter en el sobre pronto y no me despertaré hasta de aquí a veinte horas. I'm super-tired. I'm going to hit the sack pretty soon and I won't wake up for about twenty hours.*

meterse en Honduras (to put oneself into Honduras, meaning the country and also "the depths," literal meaning of Honduras) to get into hot water, deep trouble *Mex, Ch* ◆ *Nos metimos en Honduras cuando intentamos ayudar a nuestro yerno a establecer un negocio. We got into hot water when we tried to help our son-in-law set up a business.*

meterse en la boca del lobo (to put oneself in the wolf's mouth) to go into the lion's den, expose oneself to unnecessary danger *Mex, DR, ES, S. Cone, Sp* ◆ *Estás loco si vas allí. ¿Te quieres meter en la boca del lobo? You're crazy if you go there. Do you want to go into the lion's den (get into a dangerous position)?*

¡Métetelo donde te quepa (por el culo)! (Put it where it fits [up your ass]!) Up yours! (vulgar) *Mex, DR, PR, ES, Ch, Sp* (RVAR *U, Arg:* **donde no te da el sol**, where the sun doesn't shine) ◆ *Necesito ir al hospital. ¿Me prestas tu coche? —¡No! Tengo poca gasolina. —¡Métetelo donde no te da el sol! I need to go to the hospital. Will you lend me your car? —No, I don't have much gas left. —Up yours!*

metiche nosy; busybody, buttinsky *Mex, DR, PR, G, Nic, CR, Col* ◆ *Alejandra es tan metiche que sus compañeros de trabajo no la invitan a ninguna parte. Alejandra is such a busybody that her coworkers don't invite her anywhere.*

la **metida (metedura) de pata** (insertion of foot) gaffe, mistake *Mex, DR, G, S. Cone, Sp* (RVAR *DR:* **metida** only; *Sp:* **metedura** only) ◆ *La metida de pata fue obvia. Tuvimos que disculparnos frente a los presentes. The mistake was obvious. We had to apologize in front of those present.*

el/la **metido(-a)** busybody (**entrometido**) *Mex, DR, PR, C. Am., Col, U, Arg* ◆ *Por favor, no seas metida. No necesito tu opinión. Please, don't be a busybody. I don't need your opinion.* ◆ *Guillermo es un entrometido y opina aunque nadie se lo pregunte.*

Guillermo is a busybody and gives his opinion even though no one asks him for it.

estar **metido(-a) en un rollo** (to be put in a roll) to be in a bind, involved or stuck in a problem *Mex, G, Nic, Col, Ven, Ec, Peru, Sp* ◆ *Tengo un gran problema. De veras, estoy metida en un rollo. I have a big problem. I'm in a real bind.*

estar **metido(-a) hasta los codos en algo** to be up to one's elbows in something *Mex* ◆ *Estoy metida hasta los codos en este proyecto. I've got my hands full with this project.*

México es un pañuelo. (Mexico is a handkerchief.) Mexico is a small world; used with any country: it's a small world. *Mex* ◆ *¿Ustedes conocen a mis primos? ¡México es un pañuelo! You know my cousins? What a small world Mexico is!*

mezclar la velocidad con el tocino (to mix speed with bacon) to mix things that are very different, apples and oranges *Sp* ◆ *¡Vaya! Estás mezclando la velocidad con el tocino. Aw, come on! You're mixing apples with oranges.*

de **miedo** (scary, frightening) awesome, super *Ch, Sp* ◆ *Me lo pasé de miedo en tu fiesta. I had a fantastic time at your party.*

miel sobre hojuelas (honey on pastries) so much the better, perfect; expression meaning that one thing goes very well with another, adding to its attractiveness *Mex, DR, Sp* ◆ *Si este producto se vende en otros países también, pues miel sobre hojuelas. If this product sells in other countries also, well, so much the better.*

¡Miércoles! (Wednesday!) Heck! euphemism for **¡Mierda!** *L. Am., Sp* ◆ *¿Qué miércoles te pasa ahora? ¿Otra vez necesitas dinero? What the heck is going on with you now? You need money again?*

de **mierda** (of shit) crappy, shitty (vulgar) *L. Am.* ◆ *¿Cómo se puede mantener con esa pensión de mierda? How can he (she) survive with that crappy pension?*

una **mierda** →**hecho(-a) (una) mierda; mandar a alguien a la mierda; Ni mierda.**

¡Mierda! Shit! (vulgar) *L. Am., Sp* ◆ *¡Mierda! Se me olvidó la llave. Shit! I forgot the key.*

migas →**hacer buenas migas; hacer migas a alguien**

la **migra** (short for **inmigración**) U.S. INS, immigration *Chicano, Mex, G, ES* ◆ *La migra los trató muy mal.* The (U.S.) immigration officials treated them very badly.

Miguel(ito)/Tiburcio me/you (**para Miguel/para Tiburcio**, meaning **para mí/para ti**, for or to me, in my opinion/for or to you, in your opinion) *Mex, ES, Col* ◆ *Estos dulces son para Miguel y Tiburcio. These sweets are for me and you.*

de **mil amores** (of a thousand loves) with pleasure *Mex, DR, ES, S. Cone, Sp* ◆ *Haré lo que me pides de mil amores. I'll do what you ask with pleasure.*

de **mil (todos los) diablos** (of a thousand [all the] devils) very bad, a heck of a (used to exaggerate something bad or uncomfortable) *Mex, ES, Sp* ◆ *Armaron una discusión de todos los diablos y no pudieron hacer nada. They had a heck of an argument and couldn't do anything.*

a las **mil maravillas** (to the thousand marvels) wonderful(ly), very good, excellent, perfectly *L. Am., Sp* ◆ *Nuria se sabía su papel a las mil maravillas. Hizo un espectáculo precioso. Nuria knew her role perfectly. She put on a wonderful show.*

la **mili** short for **servicio militar** *Sp* ◆ *La mili ya no es obligatoria. Military service is no longer obligatory.*

el **milico** soldier (pejorative) *Ec, S. Cone* (RVᴀʀ U: also, a policeman) ◆ *No hagan tanto ruido. Si los milicos nos oyen, nos joden. Don't make so much noise. If the soldiers hear us, they'll give us a damn hard time.*

el/la **millonetis** moneybags, millionaire *Sp* ◆ *Mi sueño es ir a Las Vegas para regresar a mi casa hecho un millonetis. My dream is to go to Las Vegas and come back home a millionaire.*

la **mina** (mine; from Lunfardo, Buenos Aires slang) girl, woman, chick *S. Am., especially Col, Ec, S. Cone* (RVᴀʀ Ch: **el mino** is also used for a hunk) ◆ *¿Quién es esa mina? — Se llama Laura. Who's that chick? —Her name is Laura.*

la **minga** thank-you party for workers *Ch* ◆ *Después del inventario general, la com-*

pañía nos dio una minga. *After the general inventory, the company gave us a thank-you party.*

el **ministerio de guerra** (war department) my wife (said by a man ironically) *Mex* ◆ *Antes de decidir, tengo que consultar con el ministerio de guerra. Before making a decision, I need to consult with the boss (i.e., my wife).*

la **mira en** →**poner la mira en**

lo que **mira (ve) la suegra** (what the mother-in-law sees) superficial part of house to be cleaned *Mex, ES, S. Cone, Sp* ◆ *No tengo mucho tiempo. Limpiaré sólo por lo que mira la suegra. I don't have much time. I'll just clean the most obvious things.*

¡Mira quién habla! Look who's talking! *L. Am., Sp* ◆ *Tienes que estudiar más, Emilia. —¡Mira quién habla! Tú jamás estudias. You need to study more, Emilia. —Look who's talking! You never study.*

Mírame esta cara. (Look at this face.) Who do you think I am?, phrase implying that the other person is unaware of one's merits *Mex, Sp* ◆ *Mírame esta cara. ¿Me crees capaz de mentirte? Who do you think I am? Do you think I'm capable of lying to you?*

mírame y no me toques (look at me and don't touch me) describing a very fussy person or things that break easily *Mex, DR, PR, ES, Ch, U, Sp* (RVAR *Nic:* **veme y no me toques**) ◆ *Esa chica es de las mírame y no me toques. That girl is very standoffish.*

de **miranda** →**ir de miranda**

mirar (ver) los toros desde la barrera (to look at [see] the bulls from behind the barrier) to remain on the sidelines, stay out of harm's way, participate in or witness something but avoid exposing oneself to danger *most of L. Am., Sp* ◆ *Durante la Segunda Guerra Mundial, estuvimos viendo los toros desde la barrera. During the Second World War, we stayed out of harm's way (remained on the sidelines).*

mirar a alguien por encima del hombro (to look over one's shoulder at someone) to look down one's nose at someone *L. Am., Sp* ◆ *Elvira y su esposo son muy arrogantes y miran a todos por encima del hombro. Elvira and her husband are very arrogant and look down their noses at everyone.*

mirar de reojo to look out of the corner of one's eye *L. Am., Sp* ◆ *Como iba manejando, no pude ver mucho, pero miré de reojo y me quedé muy impresionada de las casas de ese barrio. Since I was driving, I couldn't see much, but I looked out of the corner of my eye and was very impressed with the houses in that neighborhood.*

mirarse en alguien como en un espejo (to see oneself in another as in a mirror) to have great love for someone and be pleased with their actions or good qualities; to look like someone *Mex, Sp* ◆ *Me miro en ella como en un espejo. I love her like my own daughter.*

Mírate en ese espejo. (Look at yourself in that mirror.) Let that be a lesson for you. *Mex, DR, ES, U, Arg* ◆ *A causa del accidente en su moto, Juan está paralizado. Mírate en ese espejo, hija. Because of the accident on his motorcycle, Juan is paralyzed. Let that be a lesson for you, my girl.*

a **misa** →**ir a misa**

ser de la **misma madera** (to be of the same wood) to be a chip off the old block, be alike *Mex* ◆ *Manuela no es de la misma madera que sus papás. Manuela isn't like her parents.*

ser el **mismísimo demonio** to be the devil himself, very perverse or cunning *Mex, DR, PR, U, Arg, Sp* ◆ *Ese hombre es el mismísimo demonio. Ni le hables. That man is the devil himself. Don't even talk to him.*

lo **mismo** →**dar igual, dar lo mismo; por lo mismo**

el **mismo (la misma) que viste y calza** (the same who dresses and is shod) yours truly *L. Am., Sp* ◆ *¿Quién es Sebastián Vicente Rojas Romero, entre los presentes? —Soy yo, el mismo que viste y calza. Who among those present is Sebastián Vicente Rojas Romero? —It's me, yours truly.*

lo **mismo de siempre** the same as always *L. Am., Sp* ◆ *¿Qué va a desayunar usted, lo mismo de siempre? What will you have for breakfast, the same as always?*

Lo **mismo es Chana que Juana.** (Chana is the same as Juana.) It's six of one, half dozen of the other. There's no choice. Two of the same. Also used in the negative to mean two things are not the same: **No es lo mismo Chana que Juana.** *Mex, ES, Nic* ◆ *Miren, te-*

nemos tiempo para ir a la playa o para ir a las montañas. Lo mismo es Chana que Juana. *Look, we have time to go to the beach or to the mountains. It's six of one and half dozen of the other.*

a **mitad de** half, halfway *L. Am., Sp* ◆ *Estos libros están a mitad de precio. These books are half price.*

miti-miti (half-half) halves on a bill, dutch treat *S. Cone (RVAR Ch:* also, **miti-mota;** *ES:* **mita' mita';** *Nic:* **mitimita**) ◆ *Vamos miti-miti con la cuenta. Let's split the bill (like the old expression "go halfsies").*

el **mitote** (big myth) spontaneous party; mess *Chicano, Mex* ◆ *¡Qué mitote! Hay mucha gente aquí. What a huge party! There are a lot of people here.*

la **mocha** →hecho(-a) la mocha (la raya)

mocho →Ni mocho.

el/la **mocho(-a)** holier than thou, overly religious in appearances, always in church *Mex* ◆ *Tú eres una mocha. You're a real church lady.*

el/la **mocoso(-a)** (with a runny nose) kid *L. Am., Sp* ◆ *Facundo es un mocoso muy inteligente. Facundo is a very intelligent kid.*

estar de **moda** (to be in fashion) to be fashionable, to be "in" *L. Am., Sp* ◆ *Este año el negro está de moda. This year black is in fashion.*

moda: pasarse de moda to go out of style *L. Am., Sp* ◆ *Creo que mi falda azul ya se pasó de moda. I think my blue skirt has already gone out of style.*

moda: ponerse de moda to become fashionable *L. Am., Sp* ◆ *¿En qué año se puso de moda la minifalda? What year did the miniskirt come into fashion?*

módulo →Ni módulo (como dijo el astronauta).

el **mogollón** tons, gobs; mess (of) *Sp* ◆ *Había un mogollón de gente en la fiesta. There were zillions of people at the party.* ◆ *Me alucina mogollón. I like him (her) a lot.*

mojado(-a) (wet) wetback, illegal(ly) (pejorative, meaning wet from crossing the Rio Grande) *Chicano, Mex, G, ES, Col* ◆ *Don Fernando se vino mojado hace treinta años. Don Fernando came illegally thirty years ago.*

mojarse →no mojarse

el **mojón** (turd) insignificant person *PR, Ven, Ec, Ch* ◆ *¿Quién se habría imaginado que ese mojón llegaría a ministro? Who would have imagined that that little drip would wind up a government minister?*

molar (functions like **gustar**) to please, be pleasing; **molar cantidad**, to be very pleasing to; to rock *Sp* ◆ *Juan me mola. Nos mola cantidad tocar música juntos. I like Juan. We really like to play music together.* ◆ *Esta canción mola cantidad. This song really rocks.*

molido(-a) (ground down) worn out, exhausted *Mex, PR, ES, Ch, U, Sp* ◆ *Tenemos que descansar. Estamos molidos. We need to rest. We're worn out.*

la **mollera** →tener ya dura la mollera

molón, molona 1. bothersome, annoying *Mex* ◆ *Esa chica además de ser muy molona es una sinvergüenza. In addition to being really annoying, that girl is shameless.* 2. elegant, attractive *Sp* ◆ *Tu página web es muy molona. Your web page is really attractive.*

el **molote** tumult; crowd *Cuba, DR, G, ES, Nic, CR* ◆ *Vamos a salir del partido un poco antes para evitar el molote. Let's leave the game a little early to avoid the crowd.*

Un **momentico.** Just a moment. *CR, Col, Ven* ◆ *Estaré lista en un momentico. I'll be ready in just a moment.*

la **momia** (mummy) geezer, old fogy *Mex, Col* ◆ *Esa momia es insoportable. That old geezer is unbearable.*

la **momiza** geriatric set, fogies; opposite of **la chaviza,** young people *Mex* ◆ *Su abuela es una momiza. His (Her) grandmother is an old fogie.*

mona →echarse una mona encima (andar con la mona); estar como la mona

ser una **monada** (to be a monkey face) to be cute, pretty, sweet (often used by women to describe children) *Mex, S. Cone, Sp* ◆ *Estos niños son una monada. Han estudiado y terminado sus tareas antes de ir a jugar con sus amigos. These children are real cuties. They've studied and finished their homework before going to play with their friends.*

ser la **monda** to be too much, extraordinary (good or bad, said of things) *Sp* ◆ *Estos tu-*

ristas son la monda. *These tourists are too much.*

estar con el **mono** (to be with the monkey) to be in a state of abstinence from drugs or alcohol, have withdrawal symptoms *Sp* ◆ *Hoy estoy con el mono. Me siento fatal. Today I'm having withdrawal symptoms. I feel terrible.*

mono(-a) (monkey) cute *L. Am., Sp* ◆ *¿Quién es esa chica tan mona? Who is that cute girl?*

monos ➝*¿Tengo monos en la cara?*

montar un cirio (to put on a candle) to raise a fuss, do something that gets attention *Sp* ◆ *Felipe nos montó un cirio en plena calle porque pensaba que nosotros éramos los culpables de la situación. Felipe made a scene in the middle of the street because he thought that we were to blame for the situation.*

montar un número (numerito) (to put on a [little] number) to make a scene; to have a fit *Mex, Cuba, DR, ES, Sp* ◆ *Qué vergüenza que pasé con tu madre ayer. Montó un numerito en la recepción del hotel. What an embarrassing time I had with your mother yesterday. She made a scene at the hotel desk.*

el **montón** (heap) a lot (of), heaps or tons (also, **montones**) *L. Am., Sp* ◆ *Hicimos un montón de comida para la fiesta. We made a ton of food for the party.*

ser del **montón** (to be of the heap) to be no great shakes, common or mediocre *L. Am., Sp* ◆ *Esa maestra es del montón. That teacher is no great shakes.*

a **montones** (in heaps) tons, abundantly, in big quantities *Mex, DR, PR, Ch, Sp* ◆ *Había comida a montones. There was a ton of food.*

el **moño** ➝*estar hasta el moño*

moquiar to cry, snivel *Mex, ES, U, Arg* (RVᴀʀ Peru: **moquear**) ◆ *La niña ya está moquiando otra vez. The girl's sniveling again.*

morderse la lengua to bite one's tongue, avoid saying something *L. Am., Sp* ◆ *Me mordí la lengua para no decir a mi suegro lo que pienso de él. I bit my tongue so as not to tell my father-in-law what I thought of him.*

la **mordida** bribe *Mex, G, Nic, Pan* ◆ *Lamentablemente aquí todo se arregla con la mor-* dida. *Unfortunately here anything can be fixed with a bribe.*

moreno(-a) (dark-haired, dark skinned) black (person), of African descent *Chicano, Mex, Cuba, DR, G, ES, Col* ◆ *¿Quién es la mujer morena? Who's the black woman?*

morir con las botas puestas (to die with one's boots on) to keep on working up to the end of one's life *Mex, Nic, U, Arg, Sp* ◆ *Don Diego murió con las botas puestas, luchando por sus principios hasta el último momento. Diego worked to the end of his life, fighting for his principles until the last moment.*

morir vestido(-a) (to die dressed) to die violently, die with one's boots on *Mex, Sp* ◆ *El general Custer murió vestido. General Custer died with his boots on.*

morirse de la risa to die of laughter *L. Am., Sp* ◆ *Cada vez que escucho a Emilio contar cuentos, me muero de la risa. Every time I hear Emilio tell stories, I die laughing.*

morocho(-a) brunette *U, Arg* ◆ *Esa morocha es preciosa. That brunette is gorgeous.*

morro ➝*tener mucha cara (mucho rostro, mucho morro, mucha jeta)*

el **morro/el rostro** (face) brazenness, nerve *Sp* ◆ *¡Qué morro! Mirabel no te ha llamado para invitarte a su fiesta. What nerve! Mirabel hasn't called you to invite you to her party.*

morrocotudo(-a) great, fantastic *Mex, DR* ◆ *¿La música de Juan Luis Guerra? Es morrocotuda. Juan Luis Guerra's music? It's fantastic.*

mortal (mortal, deadly) super, good, great *Cuba, Col, S. Cone* ◆ *Estuvimos en un concierto mortal. We were at a great concert.* ◆ *Esa mujer está mortal. That woman is gorgeous.*

ser **mortal** (to be mortal, deadly) to be difficult, deadly *Mex, DR, Col, U, Arg* ◆ *Este crucigrama es mortal. Sólo he completado dos palabras. This crossword puzzle is deadly. I've only finished two words.*

la **mosca** ➝*ponerles la mosca detrás de las orejas; por si las moscas*

mosquear (to be like a fly) to bother, pester *Ch, Sp* ◆ *Me mosquea que aún no me haya llamado. It bothers me that he (she) still* *hasn't called me.* ◆ *No me mosquées. Don't pester me.*

la **mosquita (mosca) muerta** (dead fly) person who appears to be dim or dull but who doesn't miss the chance to take advantage of someone, hypocrite *L. Am., Sp* (RVAR *Sp*: **mosquita** only) ◆ *Te haces la mosquita muerta frente a tus padres, pero bien sabemos lo que eres.* *You play innocent in front of your parents, but we know perfectly well just what you are.*

mosquito →**tener cerebro de mosquito**

mostrar/enseñar los dientes (to show or bare one's teeth) to show one's true colors, threaten; also, to smile *L. Am., Sp* ◆ *El nuevo supervisor no demoró en mostrar los dientes.* *The new supervisor didn't take long to show his true colors.*

la **mota** pot, marijuana *Chicano, Mex, PR, G* ◆ *Horacio fumó toda la mota que encontró.* *Horacio smoked all the marijuana he found.*

motearse to smoke pot, marijuana *Mex, PR* ◆ *Cuando llegué a su casa, todos estaban moteándose, así que me fui.* *When I got to their house, everyone was smoking pot, so I left.*

la **moto** (short for **motocicleta**) motorcycle *L. Am., Sp* ◆ *El año pasado tuvo un accidente con la moto.* *Last year he had an accident on his motorcycle.*

el **mouse** mouse (computer, from English) parts of *L. Am.* ◆ *Los niños rompieron el mouse, y no puedo trabajar en la compu.* *The kids broke the mouse, and I can't work on the computer.*

mover cielo y tierra to move heaven and earth *L. Am., Sp* ◆ *Tanya tuvo que mover cielo y tierra para conseguir las entradas.* *Tanya had to move heaven and earth to get the tickets.*

mover el esqueleto 1. (to move one's skeleton) to boogie, dance *L. Am., Sp* ◆ *Vayamos a mover el esqueleto a la discoteca.* *Let's go shake a leg at the disco.* 2. (to move one's skeleton) to get going, get a move on *Mex, Ch, U, Sp* ◆ *¡Muevan el esqueleto! Es hora de irnos.* *Get a move on! (Shake a leg!) It's time to go.*

la **movida** 1. the action, the scene, fun *most of L. Am., Sp* ◆ *Ariel siempre está en la movida.* *Ariel is always in the center of the fun (where the action is).* 2. unlawful business, shenanigans *Mex, G, ES, Ch* ◆ *Ese ratero siempre anda en la movida.* *That thief is always mixed up in some kind of shenanigans.*

en la **movida, en la onda, a la moda, actualizado(-a)** "with it" *Mex, PR, Col, Sp* ◆ *No estás en la onda, amiga. Hay que estar en la movida.* *You're not with it, girlfriend. You have to be where the action is.*

mu →**no decir ni mu**

la **muchachada** group of young people *Mex, DR, ES, CR, U* ◆ *Allí está toda la muchachada.* *There's the whole gang (of kids).* ◆ *Durante las ferias ganaderas la muchachada bailó toda la noche.* *During the livestock festival the young people danced all night.*

Con **mucho gusto.** (With great pleasure.) You're welcome. *CR* ◆ *Gracias. —Con mucho gusto.* *Thank you. —You're welcome.*

Mucho ojo, que la vista engaña. (Much eye; the sight deceives.) Be careful because appearances are deceptive. *Mex, ES, U, Arg, Sp* ◆ *Esta mujer parece buena persona. —Mucho ojo, que la vista engaña.* *This woman looks like a good person. —Appearances can be deceiving.*

mucho ruido y pocas nueces (a lot of noise and few nuts) said when something yields very little despite appearances or expectations *Mex, Ch, U, Sp* ◆ *Tengo la impresión que este proyecto es de mucho ruido y pocas nueces.* *I get the impression that this project looks much better than it really is.*

la **muela** (molar, tooth) sweet-talk, chat, often with idea of persuading or sweet-talking *Cuba, DR, Col* (RVAR *DR*: **dar muela, muelear**; *Cuba*: **bajar una muela**) ◆ *Deja de darle muela a esa muchacha, que tiene novio. (DR)* *Stop sweet-talking that girl; she has a boyfriend.* ◆ *Yo no quería ir a la recepción pero Lourdes me bajó una muela y terminé diciendo que iría. (Cuba)* *I didn't want to go to the reception, but Lourdes convinced me and I ended up saying I would go.* ◆ *Tienes buena muela. (Cuba)* *You're a good talker.*

ser un **muermo** to be a drag, a snooze *Sp* ◆ *Ese programa es un muermo. That program is a snooze.*

un **muermo** →tener un muermo, estar amormado(-a)

estar de **muerte** (to be of death) to be very attractive (a woman) *Nic, U, Sp* ◆ *¿Conoces a la entrenadora del equipo? Está de muerte. Do you know the team's coach? She's a babe.*

la **muerte** (death) excellent, incredible, super *S. Cone* ◆ *Esas chicas son la muerte. Those girls are incredible.*

ser la **muerte en bicicleta** (to be death on a bicycle) to be as slow as a snail or a slow death *Florida, Nic, Sp* ◆ *Esta conexión es la muerte en bicicleta. This connection is as slow as a snail.* ◆ *Aquí no hay vida nocturna. Es la muerte en bicicleta. There's no nightlife here. It's slow death.*

un **muerto** →Esto resucita a un muerto.; no tener donde caerse muerto

muerto(-a) (dead) empty, boring *Mex, G, Ch* ◆ *Este club está muerto. Vámonos. This club is dead. Let's go.*

muerto(-a) de hambre (dead of hunger) starving to death *L. Am., Sp* ◆ *¿Cuándo vamos a comer? Estoy muerta de hambre. When are we going to eat? I'm starving to death.*

muerto(-a) de miedo (dead of fear) scared stiff *L. Am., Sp* ◆ *Miriam estaba muerta de miedo cuando oyó las noticias. Miriam was scared stiff when she heard the news.*

estar **muerto(-a) de la risa** to be dying of laughter *L. Am., Sp* ◆ *¡Qué chistoso! ¡Estaba muerta de la risa! How funny! I was dying of laughter!*

la **mujer de mal vivir** (woman who lives badly) woman of the streets, hooker *L. Am., Sp* (RVAR *Sp:* **mujer de mala vida**) ◆ *La muerta era una mujer de mal vivir. The dead woman was a hooker.*

la **mujer fatal** femme fatale *U, Sp* ◆ *Jacinta se cree una mujer fatal; en realidad, es ridícula. En cambio, su hermana sí, es una mujer fatal. Jacinta thinks she's a femme fatale; in reality, she's ridiculous. On the other hand, her sister really is a femme fatale.*

el **mujeriego (mujerero)** womanizer *L. Am., Sp* ◆ *En mi familia hay varios mujeriegos. In my family there are a number of womanizers.*

la **mula** →meter la mula

un **mulo** →estar hecho(-a) un mulo

multiplicarse por cero (to multiply oneself by zero) to put a lid on it, keep quiet *Sp* ◆ *Si no te gusta, multiplícate por cero. If you don't like it, shut up.*

el **mundo** →irse para el (al) otro barrio (mundo); no ser nada del otro mundo

la **muñeca** 1. (doll) pretty girl *Mex, Col, Para, U, Arg* ◆ *Esa niña es una muñeca. That girl is a doll.* 2. (wrist) connections, pull (from being able to move hands to get things) *Peru, S. Cone* ◆ *Tienen buena muñeca en el gobierno. They have pull (influence) in the government.*

muñeco(-a) (doll) term of affection *Mex, Cuba, G, Col,* ◆ *Gracias, muñeca. Thanks, doll.*

el **muñeco** (doll) good-looking man *Mex, G, ES* ◆ *Jaime Ernesto es un muñeco. ¡Qué guapo! Jaime Ernesto is a doll. How handsome he is!*

muñeco viejo (old doll) old hat (something already commented on) *DR, Col* ◆ *El plan del alcalde es muñeco viejo. The mayor's plan is old hat.*

muñequear (to wrist) to use connections, pull *Peru, S. Cone* ◆ *Hay que muñequear para conseguir una visa rápidamente. You have to use connections to get a visa quickly.*

la **música sacudida** (shaken music) lively music *Mex, Col, Ec* ◆ *Es un bar bacán con música sacudida. It's a great bar with lively music.*

ser **muy cabrón (cabrona) para algo** to be a damn whiz at, very good at something (vulgar) *Chicano, Mex, G, Col* ◆ *Sergio es muy cabrón para el ajedrez. Sergio is a damn whiz at chess.*

el/la **muy condenado(-a)** (the very condemned) that darn guy (girl, man, woman, etc.) *Florida, Mex, DR, G, CR, Col, Ch, U* ◆ *La muy condenada ganó un viaje a Hawai como premio. That darn chick won a trip to Hawaii as a prize.*

estar muy potable: Esa chica está muy potable.
That girl looks good enough to eat.

muy especial (very special) expression sometimes used ironically to mean difficult *L. Am., Sp* ◆ *Esta situación es muy especial, y tenemos que hacer algo inmediatamente. This situation is very difficult, and we have to do something immediately.* ◆ *Horacio es muy especial. Horacio is very difficult.*

estar **muy metido(-a) en** to be very involved in *L. Am., Sp* ◆ *Mi mamá está muy metida en la política; trabaja en varias campañas locales. My mom is very involved in politics; she's working in several local campaigns.*

estar **muy potable** (to be very drinkable) to look good physically *Mex, S. Cone, Sp* ◆ *Fíjate qué potables están esos muchachos amigos de mi primo. Get a load of my cousin's friends; they look good enough to eat.*

estar **muy verde** (to be very green) to be innocent, immature, not socially active, a greenhorn *S. Cone, Sp* ◆ *María Eugenia está muy verde para asistir a estas reuniones. María Eugenia is too naïve to come to these get-togethers.*

ser **muy vivo(-a)** (to be very clever) to be a go-getter, very good at getting ahead *L. Am., Sp* ◆ *Estos inmigrantes han sido muy vivos; tienen su casa propia y varias propiedades que alquilan. These immigrants have been real go-getters; they have their own house and various properties that they rent out.*

N

nacer con el pie derecho (to be born with the right foot) to be born lucky *Mex, ES, S. Cone* ◆ *Parece que Julián nació con el pie derecho y está trabajando muy bien.* It seems Julián was born lucky and is working very well.

nacer de pie (to be born standing) to be born lucky *DR, U, Ch, Sp* ◆ *Naciste de pie, Gabriela. Tienes una vida muy feliz.* You were born lucky, Gabriela. You have a very happy life.

naco(-a) (from **totonaco**, an Indian tribe, formerly with a racist meaning) jerk, uneducated or rude person (of any social class) *Mex* ◆ *¿Quién es ese naco allí?* Who is that jerk over there?

nada →**como si nada**

nada de (en) particular nothing special *L. Am., Sp* ◆ *¿Qué vas a hacer el viernes? —Nada de particular.* What are you going to do on Friday? —Nothing in particular.

Nada de eso. (None of that.) Not at all. Nothing like that. *L. Am., Sp* ◆ *¿Tienes algún problema? —No, nada de eso.* Do you have a problem? —No, not at all.

nada menos (nothing less) no less *L. Am., Sp* ◆ *Esta tormenta es nada menos que un huracán.* This storm is nothing less than a hurricane.

Nada, pescadito mojado. (Swim, little wet fish, with a pun on **nada** meaning both *nothing* and *swim.*) Zero, nothing, zip. *Mex, Col* ◆ *¿Qué tengo en el banco? Nada, pescadito mojado.* What do I have in the bank? Not a darn thing, zip.

nadar contra la corriente →**ir (nadar) contra la corriente**

¡Nadie lo (la) salva! (No one saves him [her, it]!) Nothing can be done. It's a hopeless case. *Mex, U* ◆ *Con esa actitud, nadie lo salva.* With that attitude, nothing can be done.

nalga →**como nalga de lavandera**

¡Naranjas de la China! (Oranges from China!) Nothing doing! *Sp*

Naranjas. (Oranges.) No. No way. *Chicano, Mex, G, ES, Col, Sp* ◆ *¿Me prestas mil pesos? —Naranjas. No tengo nada.* Will you lend me a thousand pesos? —No way. I don't have anything.

el/la **narco** nark, short for **narcotraficante** *L. Am., Sp* ◆ *Ese barrio es un paraíso para los narcos.* That neighborhood is a paradise for drug dealers.

narices (nostrils) dickens, often a euphemism for cojones *Sp* ◆ *¿Qué narices ha pasado?* What the dickens happened?

narices →**estar hasta las narices; meter las narices en todo; No hay más narices (cojones).; no ver más allá de sus narices; tener narices**

la **nave** (ship) boat in the sense of large car *Mex, DR, PR, G, Hond, CR, Col, Ven* ◆ *La nave de mi padre gasta mucho combustible.* My dad's "boat" burns a lot of gas.

navegar con bandera de inocente (tonto) (to sail with the flag of an innocent [a fool]) to play dumb, pretend to be innocent or foolish but have a motive for it *Mex* ◆ *Navegaban con bandera de inocentes esos diablos.* Those devils were pretending to be so innocent.

sus **necesidades** →**hacer sus necesidades (una necesidad)**

negociar con to do business with *L. Am., Sp* ◆ *No negociamos con criminales.* We don't do business with criminals.

los **negocios chuecos** (crooked deals) monkey business *Mex, DR, ES, Col, Ch* ◆ *Se metieron en negocios chuecos y ahora están preocupados.* They got involved in some monkey business and now they're worried.

negrito(-a) (black one) term of affection like sweetheart, used for people of any skin color *L. Am.* ◆ *Hola, negrito. ¡Qué alegría de verte, después de tanto tiempo!* Hi, sweety. It's great to see you after so much time!

estar **negro(-a)** (to be black) to be fed up, sick of something *Sp* ♦ *Estoy negra con toda esa publicidad que me echan en el buzón. I've had it with all that advertising they stick in my mailbox.*

Nel. Nel, pastel. (No. No, cake.) No. No way, José. *Chicano, Mex, G, ES, Nic* ♦ *Paco, ¿me prestas dinero para ir al cine? —¡Nel, pastel! No tengo ni cinco. Paco, will you lend me money to go to the movies? —No way, José. I don't have a dime.*

el/la **nene(-a)** used instead of **niño(-a)** *Mex, PR, G, Col, Para, U, Arg, Sp* ♦ *El nene mayor de mi amiga se llama Pedro Martín. My friend's oldest child is named Pedro Martín.*

el **nerdo** nerd *parts of L. Am.* ♦ *Hugo es un nerdo, muy inteligente y estudioso. El pobre casi nunca sale de la biblioteca. Hugo's a nerd, very intelligent and studious. The poor guy almost never leaves the library.*

los **nervios** →**poner a alguien los nervios de punta; ponerse de los nervios; tener los nervios de punta**

la **neta** the real truth of the matter *Mex* ♦ *Te platiqué la neta. I told you the real truth of the matter.*

ni corto(-a) ni perezoso(-a) (neither short nor lazy) right away, not losing any time; describes someone who acts quickly *L. Am., Sp* ♦ *A Néstor no le gusta perder tiempo. Lo llamaron para un trabajo y, ni corto ni perezoso, llegó en seguida. Nestor doesn't like to waste time. They called him for a job and he got there right away.*

Ni a huevos. (Not even by eggs, meaning testicles.) No damn way. (vulgar) *Mex, ES* ♦ *No me hacen ir ni a huevos. No damn way they can make me go.*

Ni a la de tres. (Not even by that of three.) No way. *Sp* ♦ *No hay manera de que nos tomen en serio ni a la de tres. No way they'll take us seriously.* ♦ *Aquí no llueve ni a la de tres. It doesn't rain here at all.*

Ni a la fuerza. (Not even by force.) Not on your life, no way. *L. Am.* ♦ *Ni a la fuerza votaré por un candidato que apoye la guerra. No way I'll vote for a candidate who supports war.*

Ni a palos. (Not even with blows of a stick.) No way. *L. Am., Sp* ♦ *Ni a palos lo iba a soltar. No way was he (she) going to let go of it.*

Ni a tiros. (Not even by gunshots.) Not a chance. *Mex, U, Sp* ♦ *Ni a tiros apoyaremos la reducción de programas sociales. Not a chance we'll support a reduction in social programs.*

Ni cagando. (Not even shitting.) Not on your life. No damn way. (vulgar) *Col, S. Cone* ♦ *Antonio dijo que ni cagando volvía a trabajar a la Antártida. Antonio said that no damn way was he going back to work in Antarctica.*

Ni chicles. (Not even chewing gum.) No. No way. *Mex* ♦ *No te compro nada más. Ni chicles. I'm not buying you anything else. Not a bloomin' thing.*

Ni de coña. (Not even as a joke.) No damn way. (vulgar) *Sp* ♦ *Ni de coña lo voy a hacer. No damn way I'm going to do it.*

Ni de vaina. (Not even as a husk.) No. No way. *Nic, Col, Ven, Peru* ♦ *¿Me presentas a tu hermana? —Ni de vaina. Will you introduce me to your sister? —No way.*

Ni ebrio(-a) ni dormido(-a). (Neither drunk nor asleep.) No way. *Mex, Col* ♦ *¿Vas a la fiesta de Martín? —Ni ebria ni dormida. Are you going to Martín's party? —No way. Not for love or money.*

Ni en sueños. (Not even dreaming.) No way. Not even in your dreams. *L. Am., Sp* ♦ *¿Qué tal si Enrique te invita a pasar el día en la playa? —¡Ni en sueños lo haría! What if Enrique invites you to spend the day on the beach? —Not even in his dreams!*

ni fu ni fa so-so, neither good nor bad, expression of indifference *L. Am., Sp* ♦ *¿Te gustó el concierto de Luis Miguel? —Ni fu ni fa, fue idéntico al del año pasado. Did you like the Luis Miguel concert? —It was no great shakes, since it was the same as last year.* ♦ *¿Qué tal? ¿Cómo estás? —Ni fu ni fa. What's up? How are you? —So-so. OK.*

Ni gorda. (Not even a fat one [coin of little value].) Nothing, not at all. *Sp* ♦ *A mí no me apetece ni gorda ir allí. I don't feel like going there at all.*

Ni hablar. Don't even think (talk) about it. No way. Out of the question! *L. Am., Sp* ♦ *¿Vas a salir con Inés? —Ni hablar. No lo haré.*

Are you going to go out with Inés? —Don't even think about it. I won't do it.

Ni hablar del peluquín. (Don't even talk about the toupée.) Enough said. *ES, Peru, Ch, Sp* ◆ *¿Ir a la playa? Buena idea. Ni hablar del peluquín. Go to the beach? Good idea. No buts about it.*

Ni hostia. (Not even Host, religious reference.) No, nothing. No damn way. (vulgar) *Cuba, Sp* ◆ *No sé ni hostia de ordenadores. I don't know a damn thing about computers.*

ni ir ni venirle (without it coming or going) to be neither here nor there, without it mattering (to anyone) *Mex, S. Cone, Sp* ◆ *El asunto de la campaña electoral ni me va ni me viene. To me, the whole matter of the election campaign is neither here nor there.*

Ni jota. (Not a jot.) No, nothing. *L. Am., Sp* ◆ *De biología no entiendo ni jota. I don't understand beans about biology.*

Ni loco(-a). (Not even crazy.) No way. *L. Am., Sp* ◆ *¿Me prestas tu carro? —Ni loca. Will you loan me your car? —No way.* ◆ *Ni loco que fuera lo haría. No way I'd do it.*

Ni madre(s). (Not even mother[s].) No. No damn way. (vulgar) *Mex, C. Am., Col* ◆ *No lo voy a hacer. Ni madre. I'm not going to do it. No damn way.*

Ni maíz. (Not even corn.) Nothing. *Mex* ◆ *No entendí ni maíz. I didn't understand beans.*

Ni mierda. (Not even shit.) No, nothing, not a damn thing. (vulgar) *L. Am.* ◆ *No me dieron ni mierda por la bicicleta. They didn't give me a damn thing for the bicycle.*

Ni mocho. No, no way (used instead of **Ni modo**). *Mex, ES* ◆ *Entonces, tengo que irme. Ni mocho. Then I have to leave. There's no other way.*

Ni módulo (como dijo el astronauta). (No module [as the astronaut said]. **Módulo** sounds like **modo**, way.) No way, José. *Mex* ◆ *Tenemos que aceptar la propuesta porque no hay otra. Ni módulo (como dijo el astronauta). We have to accept the offer because there's no other way. No way, José.*

ni muy muy ni tan tan (not very very nor so-so) so-so, mediocre, blah *Mex, DR, ES, Nic, Col, U, Arg* ◆ *¿Te gusta la nueva colección para la moda de invierno? —Ni muy muy ni tan tan. Do you like the new winter fashion collection? —So-so.*

Ni papa(s). (Not even potato[es].) No, nothing. *Mex, C. Am., Col* ◆ *¿Entendiste lo que dijo el profesor? —Ni papas. Did you understand what the professor said? —Not a thing.*

ni para vestir santos (not even to dress saints) good for nothing, useless, worthless *Mex, PR, Col, Arg, Sp* ◆ *Este chico no sirve ni para vestir santos. This boy is useless.*

Ni pensarlo. Don't even think about it. *L. Am., Sp* ◆ *¿Podemos cambiar de carro este año? —No, ni pensarlo. Can we get a new car this year? —No, don't even think about it.*

ni pinchar ni cortar (to not pinch or cut) to be useless, of no influence or importance, have no say in *U, Arg, Sp* ◆ *En la venta de la casa no pincho ni corto. I have no say about the selling of the house. El ex-presidente ni pincha ni corta en ese asunto. The ex-president has no influence in that matter.*

ni pizca de (not even a pinch of) not even a shred of *Mex, DR, C. Am., Col, Ch, Arg* ◆ *No tiene ni pizca de educación. He (She) has no manners whatsoever.*

Ni por asomo. (Not even by conjecture.) No way, not by a longshot. *DR, S. Cone, Sp* ◆ *¿Yo hacer semejante cosa? No, hombre, ni por asomo. Me do such a thing? No, man, not by a longshot.*

Ni por el forro. (Not even by the lining.) Nothing, not at all. *U, Sp* ◆ *Hugo no entendía de números ni por el forro; nunca había pasado ningún examen de matemáticas. Hugo didn't understand diddly about numbers; he'd never passed any math test.*

Ni que decir tiene(s). (You don't have to say it.) It's a done deal, understood. *Mex, Peru, Sp* ◆ *Ni que decir tienes; lo haremos inmediatamente. It's understood; we'll do it right away.*

ni siquiera not even *L. Am., Sp* ◆ *No voy a comer nada dulce, ni siquiera el pastel de cumpleaños. I'm not going to eat anything sweet, not even the birthday cake.*

Ni soñarlo. Don't even dream about it. In your dreams. *L. Am., Sp* ◆ *¿Puedo fumar aquí en la sala? —No, ni soñarlo. Can I smoke here in the living room? —In your dreams.*

Ni tanto ni tan poco. (Not so much nor so few.) Don't exaggerate. All things in moderation. *Mex, DR, PR, S. Cone, Sp* ◆ *No puedo comprar un café porque estoy ahorrando. —Pero, amigo, es demasiado. Ni tanto ni tan poco.* I can't buy a coffee because I'm on a budget. —But, my friend, that's too extreme. All things in moderation.

Ni torta. (Not even cake.) Nothing. *Sp* ◆ *Con estas gafas no veo ni torta.* I can't see squat with these glasses.

el/la **nica** Nicaraguan, short for **nicaragüense** *L. Am.* ◆ *Los López son nicas, pero vivieron muchos años en Costa Rica.* The Lopez's are Nicaraguan, but they lived for many years in Costa Rica.

De **ninguna manguera (como dijo el bombero).** (No hose [as the fireman said]. **Manguera** sounds like **manera**, way.) No way, José. Absolutely not. *Mex , ES* ◆ *Desgraciadamente, no podemos ayudarte en este momento. Ni manguera (como dijo el bombero).* Unfortunately, we can't help you at this time. No way, José.

ningunear to treat (someone) badly, like dirt, make them feel like a nobody *L. Am., Sp* ◆ *Lo acusaron de ningunearlos.* They accused him of treating them like dirt (like nobodies).

ser la **niña de los (sus) ojos** to be the apple (pupil) of one's eye *Mex, DR, ES, Sp* ◆ *Mi único hijo es la niña de mis ojos.* My only son is the apple of my eye.

la **niña fresa** princess, naive, conservative girl (virgin) *Mex* ◆ *Es una niña fresa; sus papás le compran todo.* She's a princess; her parents buy her everything.

ser una **niña pija** (to be a young, innocent upper-class or spoiled girl, not vulgar but pejorative) to be born with a silver spoon *Sp* ◆ *Dolores es una niña pija, pero quiere trabajar con los pobres.* Dolores is a girl born with a silver spoon in her mouth, but she wants to work with the poor.

niño →**como niño con juguete nuevo; como niño con zapatos nuevos**

el **niño (la niña) bien** rich kid, well-brought-up (upper-class) boy (girl), usually snobbish or spoiled *L. Am., Sp* ◆ *Son niños bien, hijos de papá.* They're rich kids, children whose parents do everything for them.

los **niños popis** (upper-class kids) rich brats *Mex* ◆ *Los (niños) popis arruinaron la fiesta del colegio.* The rich brats ruined the school party.

nítido(-a) (clear, bright) great, perfect, correct, very acceptable *Pan, Caribbean* ◆ *¿Hay una fiesta mañana en tu casa? ¡Nítido!* There's a party tomorrow at your house? Great!

el **nivel de vida** standard of living *L. Am., Sp* ◆ *Aquí somos muy afortunados y gozamos de un alto nivel de vida.* Here we are very fortunate and we enjoy a high standard of living.

no agarrar la onda (to not seize the sound wave) to not get it or get with it *Mex, G, ES, U, Arg* ◆ *El capataz nos explicó el trabajo pero no agarramos la onda.* The foreman explained the job to us, but we didn't get it.

no aguantar pulgas (to not tolerate fleas) to not tolerate problems, not put up with much *Mex, Sp* ◆ *Cuidado con Héctor. No aguanta pulgas; es muy delicado.* Be careful of Héctor. He doesn't put up with much; he's very fussy.

no atreverse a decir «esta boca es mía» (to not dare to say "this mouth is mine") to not dare open one's mouth *L. Am., Sp* ◆ *Cuando vino la policía, no me atreví a decir «esta boca es mía».* When the police came, I didn't dare open my mouth.

no bancarle a alguien to not be able to stand, dislike (used like **gustar**) *U, Arg* ◆ *No (me) banco a esas muchachas tan creídas. Ellas no me bancan.* I can't stand those stuck-up girls. They can't stand me.

no caber duda (to not fit doubt) to not be in doubt *L. Am., Sp* ◆ *No cabe duda que Tomás es el padre del bebé.* There's no doubt that Tomás is the baby's father.

no caber en sí de contento to not be able to contain oneself with happiness *Mex, ES, Peru, U, Arg, Sp* ◆ *Don Alonso no cabía en sí de contento con el título de su hijo.* Don Alonso could scarcely contain his excitement about his son getting his degree.

no caber una cosa en el pecho (a thing won't fit in one's chest) to have something weighing on one's mind; to be about to burst *Mex, DR, ES, Sp* ◆ *Tenía tanta rabia que no* *me cabía en el pecho. I was about to burst with anger.*

no calentar el asiento (to not warm the seat) to not last long (e.g., in a job) *Mex, ES, U, Arg, Sp* ◆ *No calenté el asiento allí. (Sp) I didn't last long there.* ◆ *Pablo no duró mucho en ese trabajo; sólo llegó a calentar el asiento. (ES) Pablo didn't last long in that job; he just barely warmed the seat.*

no casarse con nadie (to not marry anyone) to keep one's own opinions or attitudes independently, not take sides *L. Am., Sp* ◆ *Escuché la opinión de todos, pero no me casé con nadie. Primero tengo que pensar. I listened to everyone's opinions, but I didn't take sides. First I need to think.*

no cerrar la puerta (to not close the door) to not cut down on choices or options, not burn one's bridges *Ch, U* ◆ *No cierres las puertas a las nuevas oportunidades de trabajo. Don't close the door on new job opportunities.*

no chuparse el dedo (to not suck one's thumb) to not be born yesterday, not be naive or easily deceived *Mex, DR, PR, ES, S. Cone, Sp* ◆ *Yo no me chupo el dedo. Eso es pura mentira. I wasn't born yesterday. That's a lie.*

no comer plátano por no tirar la cáscara (to not eat a banana so as not to throw out the peel) to be stingy or miserly, especially with food *Mex* ◆ *Tus suegros no comen plátano en su casa, por no tirar la cáscara. Your in-laws are stingy.*

no comer un huevo por no perder la cáscara (to not eat an egg so as not to lose or waste the shell) to be stingy or miserly, especially with food *Mex, ES, Peru, U, Arg* ◆ *Don Pedro es muy amarrete y no come huevos por no tirar la cáscara. Don Pedro is very stingy.*

no comerse una rosca (to not eat a doughnut) to strike out with the opposite sex, not find anyone to pick up *Sp* ◆ *Fui a la discoteca pero no me comí una rosca. I went to the disco but I wasn't able to hook up with any girls (guys).*

no dar calce (to not give wedge) to not give an opportunity or opening (entree) to *U, Arg* ◆ *Quise hablar, pero Enrique no me dio calce; siguió hablando. I tried to speak up,* but *Enrique didn't give me a chance; he kept on talking.* ◆ *La invité a una fiesta pero no me dio calce. I invited her to a party but she didn't give me a chance.*

no dar con ello to not get it *Sp* ◆ *No doy con ello; es muy difícil. I don't get it; it's very difficult.*

no dar cuartel (to give no quarters) to be ruthless, show no mercy *L. Am., Sp* ◆ *No les vamos a dar cuartel a los narcotraficantes. We'll be ruthless with drug dealers.*

no dar el brazo a torcer (to not give one's arm to twist) to be stubborn or persistent and not give in *L. Am., Sp* ◆ *En esa cuestión, yo no quería dar mi brazo a torcer. On that point, I didn't want to give in.*

no dar ni la hora to not even give (someone) the time of day *Mex, ES, S. Cone, Sp* ◆ *Vi a Marcelo en la universidad, pero no me dio ni la hora. I saw Marcelo at the university, but he didn't even give me the time of day.*

no dar ni los «Buenos días» (to not even give a "Good day") to not even give (someone) the time of day *Mex, DR, PR, ES, U, Arg, Sp* ◆ *El jefe estaba enojado; entró en la oficina y no dio ni los «Buenos días». The boss was angry; he came into the office and wouldn't even give us the time of day.*

no dar pie con bola (to not hit the ball with one's foot) to not be correct; to make a mess of things, not do things right *Mex, DR, PR, U, Sp* ◆ *Es la tercera vez que se me quedan las llaves dentro del carro. Estoy que no doy pie con bola. This is the third time I've left the keys in the car. I can't seem to do anything right.*

no dar un golpe (to not give a hit) to be lazy, do nothing *Mex, DR, Sp* (RVar *Sp: no dar golpe*) ◆ *El esposo de Alejandra no da un golpe. Ella lo hace todo en esa casa. Alejandra's husband doesn't lift a finger to do anything. She does everything in that house.*

no dar una (to not give one) to goof up constantly *Mex, U, Sp* (RVar *DR, PR:* **no pegar una**) ◆ *No doy una. I can't do anything right.*

no darle a alguien vela (no tener vela) en el entierro (to not give someone [not have] a candle at a funeral) to not give someone a say or a reason to participate (to not have a reason to participate) *Mex, DR, S. Cone, Sp* ◆ *Mejor no opines, que nadie te* *dio vela en este entierro. Better not give your opinion; nobody gave you any say in this matter.* ◆ *Ni hables porque no tienes vela en el entierro. Don't even talk because you don't have any say here.*

no darle a uno la(s) gana(s) (to not give one the desire) to not feel like something *L. Am., Sp* ◆ *No me da la gana. I just don't feel like it.*

no darse por entendido(-a) to pretend not to understand, play dumb *L. Am., Sp* ◆ *Juan quería invitarla a salir, pero Marta no se dio por entendida. Juan wanted to invite her to go out, but Marta pretended not to understand.*

no darse por enterado(-a) (to not show yourself as aware or informed of something) to pretend that you don't know, play dumb *DR, PR, S. Cone, Sp* ◆ *Todos sabíamos lo que Marcos quería hacer, pero cuando le hablamos en grupo no se dio por enterado. We all knew what Marcos wanted to do, but when we spoke to him as a group he acted like he wasn't informed.*

no decir «esta boca es mía» (to not say "this mouth is mine") to not say a word *L. Am., Sp* ◆ *Escuché los comentarios, pero no dije «esta boca es mía». I heard the comments, but I didn't say a word.*

no decir ni mu (to not even say **mu**) to not say a word *U, Arg, Sp* ◆ *De esto ni mu, ¿entiendes? —Calladita como una tumba. Don't say a word about this, understand? —Mum's the word (Quiet as a tomb).*

no decir ni pío (to not even say **pío**, peep) to not say a word *Mex, DR, PR, Ch, Sp* ◆ *Todos escucharon el sermón sin decir pío. They all listened to the sermon without a peep.*

no dejar a alguien sentar el pie en el suelo to not let someone rest (put his or her foot on the floor) *Sp* ◆ *Aunque ayer fue día de fiesta, mamá no nos dejó sentar el pie en el suelo. Although yesterday was a holiday, Mom didn't let us rest a minute.*

no dejar (ni) a sol ni a sombra a alguien 1. (to not leave someone in the sun or the shade) to hound, not let someone out of one's sight *L. Am., Sp* ◆ *Esta mujer no deja ni a sol ni a sombra a su marido; es muy celosa. That woman doesn't let her husband out of her sight for a minute; she's really*

jealous. **2.** (to not leave someone in the sun or the shade) to demand constant attention *L. Am., Sp* ◆ *Este bebé no deja ni a sol ni a sombra a su madre. Ella está agotada. This baby demands attention from his mother day and night. She's exhausted.*

no dejar piedra sobre piedra (to not leave stone upon stone) to leave nothing standing, destroy completely *Mex, DR, U, Sp* ◆ *Los investigadores del crimen no dejaron piedra sobre piedra. The crime scene investigators destroyed everything completely.*

no dejar títere con cabeza (to not leave a puppet with a head) to destroy, blow someone away with insults, screaming *S. Cone* ◆ *Voy a revisar todo el trabajo y si está mal, no voy a dejar títere con cabeza. I'm going to look over the whole job and if it isn't good, heads will roll.*

no entender ni jota (ni papa) (to not understand a jot [potato]) to not understand beans, anything *L. Am., Sp* ◆ *No entiendo ni jota de lo que dice el profesor de matemáticas. I don't understand beans about what the mathematics professor is saying.*

No es para tanto. (It's not for so much.) It's not as bad as all that. *L. Am., Sp* ◆ *No te enojes, Alfonsina, no es para tanto. Don't get mad, Alfonsina. It's not all that bad.*

no es soplar y hacer botellas (it's not blowing and making bottles) it's not that easy, not a walk in the park *Cuba, Hond, ES, Nic, Col, Ven, Ec, U, Arg, Sp* ◆ *Conducir este tipo de coches especiales no es soplar y hacer botellas. Necesitas una buena preparación. Driving this type of special car isn't a walk in the park. You need to be specially trained.*

No está en na'a (nada). (He [she] is not in anything.) He (she) is out of it. *most of L. Am.* ◆ *Sus hermanos hablaron con ella sobre la herencia de los padres, pero es obvio que ella no está en nada. No quiso escuchar. Her brothers and sisters spoke to her about the inheritance from their parents, but it's obvious that she's out of it. She refused to listen.*

no estar en el mapa (to not be on the map) to be off the charts, be unusual, not ordinary *DR, ES* ◆ *Esto no estaba en el mapa. This is off the wall. We couldn't have predicted this.*

no estar para bromas to not be in a joking mood *L. Am., Sp* ◆ *Habla en serio; la situación es difícil, y no estoy para bromas.* *Talk seriously; the situation is difficult, and I'm not in a joking mood.*

no haber roto un plato (to not have broken a plate) to act like someone who's never made a mistake (although, of course, they have) *Mex, Sp* ◆ *Luis nunca ha roto un plato. Luis acts like he's never made a mistake.*

¡No habla(s) en serio! You're not serious (talking seriously)! *L. Am., Sp* ◆ *Pero no podemos viajar de noche. ¡No hablas en serio! But we can't travel at night. You can't be serious!*

No hay bronca. (There's no dispute.) No problem. *Mex, ES* ◆ *No hay bronca. Hablemos de otra cosa. No problem. Let's talk about something else.*

No hay de qué. Don't mention it. You're welcome. *L. Am., Sp* ◆ *No hay de qué, amiga. Estoy encantada de ayudarte. You're welcome, dear friend. I'm delighted to help you.*

No hay más narices (cojones). (There are no other noses [testicles].) There's no (damn) choice (alternative). (vulgar with **cojones**) *Sp*

No hay pena. No need to be embarrassed. *L. Am., Sp* ◆ *Mire, no hay pena. Usted no puede recordar el nombre de todos sus clientes. Look, no need to be embarrassed. You can't remember the names of all your customers.*

No hay pero que valga. (There's no but that's of value.) No buts about it. *L. Am., Sp* ◆ *Tienes que aceptar esta oferta y no hay pero que valga. You have to accept this offer and there's no buts about it.*

No hay que darle vueltas. (There's no need to turn it around.) It's just as it looks; it's obvious. *Mex, DR, ES, S. Cone, Sp* ◆ *Terminemos esta plática... no hay que darle vueltas al asunto. Let's finish this conversation . . . there's no need to dwell on the matter.*

No hay tos. (There's no cough.) No problem. *Mex, ES* ◆ *No hay tos, hermano, lo comprendo. No problem, brother, I understand.*

No hay vuelta de hoja. (There's no turning of the page.) There's no turning back. There's no doubt about it. *Mex, ES, Nic, U, Arg, Sp* ◆ *Así se va a hacer y no hay vuelta de hoja. That's the way it'll be done and there's no backing out of it (second guessing).* ◆ *Ya no hablemos; no hay vuelta de hoja. Let's not talk any more about it; there's no turning back.*

No juegues. Don't play around. *Caribbean* ◆ *No juegues. Eso no puede ser. Don't play around. That's impossible.*

No la chifles que va cantada. (Don't whistle it; it's being sung.) euphemism for **No la chingues.** Don't mess it up. *Mex* ◆ *Estamos para firmar el contrato. No la chifles que va cantada. We're right on the verge of signing the contract. Don't mess it up.*

No llueve pero gotea. (It's not raining but it's dripping.) Things could be worse. *Ch* ◆ *¿Qué tal el trabajo? —No llueve pero gotea. How's the work going? —Little by little. Things could be worse.*

No mames. (Don't suckle.) That's enough. Don't be so tiresome. Don't talk nonsense. (used like **No seas cansón.**) *Mex, ES, Col* ◆ *No mames con ese tema, Tonio. Es suficiente. Don't be so tiresome with that topic, Tonio. That's enough.*

No me busques. (Don't look for me.) Don't get on my bad side. Don't go there. (also, **No le busques.**) *Mex, DR, PR, Col, U* ◆ *Ando cabreadísima, así que no me busques, ¡que me encuentras! I'm really angry, so don't get on my bad side because you won't like it! (literally, because you'll find it!)*

No me cargues. (Don't load me up.) Don't bother (bug) me. *U, Arg* ◆ *No me cargues con esas bromas. Ya sabes que no tengo mucha paciencia. Don't bother me with those jokes. You know I don't have a lot of patience.*

No me cuentes tu vida. Don't tell me your life story. *Mex, Sp* ◆ *Estoy recansado. No me cuentes tu vida. I'm really tired. Don't tell me the story of your life.*

No me jodas. (Don't screw me.) Don't bother me. *most of L. Am., Sp*

No me vuelve loco(-a). (It doesn't drive me crazy.) It doesn't do a thing for me. *Ch* ◆ *La verdad es que este restaurante no me* *vuelve loco.* The truth is that this restaurant doesn't do a thing for me.

no medirse (to not measure oneself) to be really something; to outdo oneself *Mex, Col, U* ◆ *Realmente no te mides en tus esfuerzos para triunfar.* You're really something in your efforts to win. ◆ *No se mide para comer (hablar).* No one can eat (talk) like you can (you outdo yourself).

no mojarse (to not get oneself wet) to not go out on a limb, not take any risk *Sp* ◆ *Juan no se moja para nada.* Juan never goes out on a limb for anything.

no mover un dedo to not lift (literally, move) a finger *L. Am., Sp* ◆ *Ni siquiera movió un dedo para ayudarme con la computadora.* He (She) didn't even lift a finger to help me with the computer.

no obstante in spite of, nevertheless, however *L. Am., Sp* ◆ *Estoy muy ocupada; no obstante te acompaño a la cita.* I am very busy; nevertheless I'll go with you to the appointment.

no oler bien una cosa, oler mal (to not smell good, to smell bad) to seem suspicious *Mex, S. Cone, Sp* ◆ *Esto me huele mal.* This seems fishy to me.

no pasar a alguien (to not pass someone) to not like someone, be unable to stand someone *Mex, DR, ES, S. Cone* ◆ *La empleada de esa tienda no me pasa.* I don't like the clerk in that store.

no pegar los ojos en toda la noche to not sleep a wink (literally, glue the eyes) the whole night *L. Am., Sp* (RVAR *Sp:* **no pegar ojo**) ◆ *Tengo un problema en la oficina. No pegué los ojos en toda la noche.* I have a problem at the office. I didn't sleep a wink all night.

no pintar nada (to not paint anything) to not have any say, be of no importance *Sp* ◆ *Yo no pinto nada en la fiesta de Juan porque casi no lo conozco. Yo ahí no pinto nada.* I don't have any say in Juan's party because I hardly know him. I'm of no importance there.

no poder alguien con sus huesos (to not be able with one's bones) to be bone tired, very tired *Mex, U, Sp* ◆ *Después de tanto trabajar, no podía con mis huesos.* After working so much, I was bone weary.

no poder más to not be able to take any more, be fed up *L. Am., Sp* ◆ *Esta situación es insoportable. No puedo más.* This situation is unbearable. I can't take it any longer.

no poder ver a alguien ni en pintura (to not be able to see someone even in a painting) to not be able to stand the sight of someone *Mex, DR, PR, ES, Ch, U, Sp* (RVAR *CR, Arg, Sp:* also, **ni pintado**) ◆ *Matilde es tan orgullosa. No puedo verla ni en pintura.* Matilde is so conceited. I can't stand the sight of her.

no quedar títere con cara (cabeza) (to not have a puppet with a face [head] remaining) to be totally destroyed, often because of verbal abuse *Mex, S. Cone, Sp* ◆ *El jefe dio su discurso y no quedó títere con cabeza.* The boss gave his talk and no one was left standing.

no saber a qué carta quedarse (to not know what card to keep) to not know what to do, be undecided *Sp* ◆ *Ernesto no supo a qué carta quedarse hasta el final. Su tardanza en la decisión le costó el puesto.* Ernesto didn't know what to do until the end. His slowness in the decision cost him the job.

no saber de la misa la mitad (to not know half the mass) to not know half the story, not know beans *U, Sp* ◆ *Quedamos perplejos con la noticia del fraude, pues nosotros no sabíamos de la misa la mitad.* We were perplexed with the news of the fraud; we didn't know half the story.

no saber dónde meterse (to not know where to put oneself) to not know where to turn (out of embarrassment) *L. Am., Sp* ◆ *¡Qué vergüenza! Me salí sin pagar la cuenta y cuando me llamaron, no sabía dónde meterme.* How embarrassing! I left without paying the bill and when they called me back, I didn't know what to do with myself.

no saber dónde se tiene la mano derecha (to not know where one's right hand is) to be inept, of little talent *Sp* (RVAR *U: ... se tiene la nariz*) ◆ *No saben donde tienen la mano derecha en esta sección. No tienen ni idea de qué se trata el trabajo.* They are inept in this department. They have no idea what the job is about.

(no) saber en lo que se mete to (not) know what one is getting into *L. Am., Sp* ◆

No quiero firmar los papeles hasta que sepamos en lo que nos metemos. I don't want to sign the papers until we know what we're getting into.

no saber ni jota (to not know even a jot) to not know anything *L. Am., Sp* ◆ *Mi tío no sabe ni jota del negocio.* My uncle doesn't know anything about the business.

no saber ni papa (to not know potato) to not know beans, know nothing *Mex, DR, PR, ES, U, Ch, Sp* ◆ *Ojalá no me pregunten en la clase de historia porque no sé ni papa de la Revolución Mexicana.* I hope they don't ask me any questions in history class because I don't know beans about the Mexican Revolution.

no saber qué hacerse del mal genio to be in such a bad mood one doesn't know what to do *L. Am., Sp* ◆ *Cuando nuestros vecinos vieron cómo su auto se había destruido, no sabían qué hacer del mal genio.* When our neighbors saw that their car had been destroyed, they were in such a bad mood they didn't know what to do.

no salirle a alguien la(s) cuenta(s) (to not have the accounts come out for someone) to not turn out right for someone, said of a miscalculation that led to damages *Mex, Sp* ◆ *No me salen las cuentas.* Things are not working for me (not coming out right).

No se entienden ni se enteran. (They don't understand each other or find out anything.) They don't get along. *Col, Sp*

No se lo sacarán ni con pinzas. They won't get it out of him (her, them) even with tweezers. (referring to information from someone who is reserved or who clams up) *Mex, DR, S. Cone, Sp* ◆ *Confío en Alejandrina. Sé que no le sacarán ni con pinzas lo que sabe de sus amigos.* I trust Alejandrina. I know they won't ever get out of her what she knows about her friends.

No se puede contigo (con él, ella, etc.). Things are impossible with you (him, her, etc.). *L. Am., Sp* ◆ *No se puede con ustedes, muchachos. Son irresponsables y no cumplen con sus tareas.* Things are impossible with you. You're irresponsible and you don't do your work.

no ser carne ni pescado (to be neither meat nor fish) to be blah, undefined, insipid, neither fish nor fowl *Sp* ◆ *Esta opción es la que mejor va a todo el mundo, aunque no es ni carne ni pescado.* This choice is the one that best suits everyone, although it's neither fish nor fowl.

no ser cojo(-a) ni manco(-a) (to be neither lame nor one-handed) to be competent and experienced *Mex, DR, PR, Ch, Sp* ◆ *Mamá, no puedo hacer esta tarea. —¿Y por qué, si no eres ni cojo ni manco?* Mom, I can't do this chore. —And why not, if you've got your head screwed on?

no ser cosa de juego (to not be a thing of play) to be no laughing matter *L. Am., Sp* ◆ *Estas elecciones no son cosa de juego.* These elections are no laughing matter.

no ser de piedra (to not be of stone) to not be made of stone, be vulnerable to temptation *L. Am., Sp* ◆ *¡Qué vergüenza! Traicionaste a tu esposa por una aventura fácil. —Bueno, me tenté. No soy de piedra.* You should be ashamed! You betrayed your wife for an easy affair. —Well, I was tempted. I'm not made of stone.

no ser el primero (to not be the first) phrase used to excuse an action because there are other examples *Mex, DR, PR, ES, S. Cone* ◆ *No soy el primero ni el último.* I'm not the first nor the last (to make this mistake).

no ser nada (cosa) del otro jueves (to not be a thing of next Thursday) to be no great shakes, not be extraordinary *Sp* ◆ *Es guapo, pero no es cosa del otro jueves.* He's good-looking, but nothing to write home about.

no ser nada del otro mundo (to not be something from the other world) to be nothing to write home about, not rare *Mex, DR, PR, ES, S. Cone, Sp* ◆ *¿Es interesante el curso que estás siguiendo? —No es nada del otro mundo.* Is the course you're taking interesting? —It's nothing to write home about.

no ser ni chicha ni limonada (to be neither corn liquor nor lemonade) to be run of the mill, useless, superfluous, blah *most of L. Am., Sp* ◆ *El nuevo director no me impresiona mucho. No es ni chicha ni limona'.* The new director doesn't impress me much. He's mediocre.

no ser ni la sombra de lo que era (to not be even the shadow of what one was) to be a shadow of one's former self *L. Am., Sp* ◆ *Elsa era muy inteligente, pero después del accidente no es ni la sombra de lo que era. Elsa was very smart, but after the accident she's a shadow of her former self.*

no ser perita en dulce (to not be a pear in sugar) to be difficult, disagreeable, not sweetness and light *Mex, ES* ◆ *Uno de los niños que cuido me da problemas casi todos los días. Digamos que no es perita en dulce. One of the children I take care of gives me problems almost every day. Let's just say he's not sweetness and light.*

no servir a Dios ni al diablo (to serve neither God nor the devil) to be good for nothing, useless or inept *Mex, Ch* ◆ *Estos nuevos reglamentos no sirven ni a Dios ni al diablo. These new regulations are good for nothing.*

No te azotes, que hay chayotes. (Don't flog yourself; there are **chayotes**, a kind of squash.) Buck up! It's not that bad. Hang in there. *Mex, Col* ◆ *Ya verás que las cosas se van a mejorar. No te azotes, que hay chayotes. You'll see that things will get better. Buck up! Every cloud has a silver lining.*

No te comas un cable. (Don't eat a cable.) Don't worry. Don't have a cow. *PR, Col*

No te pongas cerril. (Don't put wax on yourself.) Don't get rigid, uptight. Chill out. *Sp* ◆ *No te pongas cerril con los chicos. Don't be so uptight with the guys.*

No te rompas la cabeza. (Don't break your head.) Don't worry about it. Don't think too much about it. *L. Am., Sp* ◆ *No se rompan la cabeza, que la explicación es sencilla. Don't worry about it; the explanation is simple.*

no tener alternativa to have no choice *L. Am., Sp* ◆ *Ustedes pagarán la cuenta porque no tienen alternativa. You will pay the bill because you have no choice.*

no tener arte ni parte (to have neither art nor part) to have no part in, nothing to do with *L. Am., Sp* ◆ *Comenzaremos un nuevo proyecto, pero la administración no tendrá arte ni parte. We'll start a new project, but the administration will have no part in it.*

no tener blanca (to not have a white one, coin) to be broke *Sp* ◆ *Tuve gastos extras este mes y no tengo blanca. I had extra expenses this month, and I am broke.*

no tener cara (to have no face) to have no shame, be shameless *Mex, Col, ES* ◆ *Esta gente no tiene cara y sigue robando a los más necesitados. These people have no shame and they keep robbing the poor (literally, the neediest).*

no tener chiste (to not have any joke) to be blah, unappetizing; to be senseless or useless, a waste *Mex, ES, Col, Ec, Peru* ◆ *No tiene chiste que hayamos salido a pasear; está lloviendo. It's a waste that we have come out to take a walk; it's raining.* ◆ *¿Qué chiste tiene que mi esposo venga por mí si tú me vas a llevar a la casa? What sense does it make for my husband to come get me if you're going to take me home?* ◆ *Esa novela no tiene chiste. That novel is mediocre.*

no tener donde caerse muerto (to not even have a place to fall dead in, not vulgar) to not have a pot to pee in, be very poor *L. Am., Sp* ◆ *Préstame dinero, Rafael; no tengo donde caerme muerto. Lend me money, Rafael; I don't have a pot to pee in.*

no tener dos dedos de frente (to not have two fingers' length of forehead) to not have the sense God gave a goose, be brainless *L. Am., Sp* ◆ *¡Caramba! Parece que mi hijo no tiene dos dedos de frente. Jeez! Seems my son doesn't have the sense God gave a goose.*

no tener huevos (to not have eggs, testicles) to not have the balls (to do something), be a coward (vulgar) *Mex, DR, Sp* ◆ *¿A que no tienes huevos de ir a un cementerio de noche? So, want to bet you don't have the balls to go to the cemetery at night?*

no tener madre (to have no mother) to be unheard of, the best (worst) *Mex, ES* ◆ *Tienes que leer este libro; no tiene madre. You have to read this book; it's the best.*

no tener ni cinco (to not have even five [cents]) to be broke, not have a plug nickel *Mex, DR, ES, Sp* ◆ *No tengo ni cinco para comprar comida. I don't have a plug nickel to buy food.*

no tener ni papa(s) (to not have even potato[es]) to be broke *Mex, ES* ◆ *¿Me prestas dinero? No tengo ni papas. Will you lend me some money? I don't have a dime.*

no tener ni para pipas (to not have even for [pumpkin] seeds) to be broke *Sp* ◆ *Ca-*

No tiene agua para beber y quiere bañarse.
She has nothing but dreams and pretentions.

mina al trabajo todos los días porque no tiene ni para pipas. He walks to work every day because he is broke.

no tener nombre (to have no name) to be unspeakable *L. Am., Sp* ◆ *El crimen de ese hombre no tiene nombre. That man's crime is unspeakable.*

no tener pelos en la lengua (to not have hair on the tongue [hair implies animals, or more primitive forms, that do not have language]) to talk clearly, without mincing words *L. Am., Sp* ◆ *Les expliqué la situación con todos los detalles y sin pelos en la lengua. I explained the situation to them with all the details and without mincing words.*

no tener pies ni cabeza (to have neither feet nor head) to have no rhyme or reason, no order or logic *L. Am., Sp* ◆ *El argumento de esa película no tiene ni pies ni cabeza. The plotline of that movie has no rhyme or reason.*

no tener por donde agarrarlo (to have no place to hang onto) to be hard to get a handle on, difficult to comprehend *Mex, DR, PR, U, Ch, Sp* ◆ *Este problema es difícil; no sé por dónde agarrarlo. This problem is difficult; I don't know how to get a handle on it.*

no tener remedio (to have no remedy) to be hopeless, beyond help *L. Am., Sp* ◆ *¡Qué*

caso! No tiene remedio. What a case! It's hopeless.

no tener sal en la mollera (to not have salt on the crown of the head) to not be very bright, not the brightest penny in the jar *L. Am., Sp* ◆ *Me parece que este tipo no tiene sal en la mollera. It seems to me that this guy isn't the brightest penny in the jar.*

no tener tiempo ni para rascarse (to not have time even to scratch oneself) to not even have time to sneeze, be very busy *Mex, DR, ES, U, Sp* ◆ *¿Por qué no vienes a visitarnos? —No puedo. Estoy preparando exámenes, y no tengo tiempo ni para rascarme. Why don't you come visit us? —I can't. I'm studying for exams, and I don't even have time to sneeze.*

no tener un cuarto (to not have a fourth) to not have a dime, be broke *Sp* ◆ *No tenemos un cuarto para comprar comida. We don't have a dime to buy food.*

no tener un quinto (to not have a fifth) to be broke *Mex, ES* ◆ *Al final del viaje, no teníamos un quinto. At the end of the trip, we were broke.*

No tiene agua para beber y quiere bañarse. (He [she] doesn't have water to drink and wants to take a bath.) said of someone who wants to be more than he or

163

she can be *Mex* ◆ *Tus cuñados no tienen agua para beber y quieren bañarse.* Your brother and sister-in-law have nothing but dreams.

No tiene(s) que jurarlo. (You don't have to swear it.) It goes without saying. (said when something is agreed, obvious) *Mex, Col* ◆ *Por supuesto que llegaré temprano. No tienes que jurarlo.* Of course I'll get there early. That goes without saying.

no tragar (to not swallow) to not stand *Mex, DR, G, ES, S. Cone, Sp* ◆ *No trago a esos chicos.* I can't stand those guys. ◆ *A Carlos lo masco pero no lo trago.* I deal with (literally, chew) Carlos but I don't want him as a friend.

No va pa'l baile. (He [She] is not going to the dance.) He (She) is a loser, not wanted. *Ven* ◆ *Rodrigo es buena persona, pero no va pa'l baile.* Rodrigo is a nice person but he's not gonna get anywhere.

no valer ni cacahuetes (to not be worth a peanut) to be worthless *Mex, ES* ◆ *Ese carro no vale ni cacahuetes.* That car isn't worth peanuts.

no valer un bledo (to not be worth a pigweed) to be worthless, to not be worth a plug nickel *Mex, ES, U, Arg, Sp* ◆ *Sus opiniones no valen un bledo.* His opinions aren't worth a red cent.

no valer un carajo to not be worth a damn (literally, a male organ) (vulgar) *Mex, U, Arg, Sp* ◆ *Ese tipo no vale un carajo.* That guy is not worth a damn.

No van por ahí los tiros. (The shots aren't going that way.) You're off the track, cold. *DR, Ch, Sp* ◆ *Patricio está visitando mucho la casa de los Benavides. Creo que le gusta Josefina. — Amiga mía, no van por ahí los tiros. Es Rosmarí que le interesa.* Patricio is visiting the Benavides family a lot. I think he likes Josefina. —No, my dear, you're on the wrong track. It's Rosmarí he's interested in.

no vender una escoba (to not sell a broom) to wash out, fail, not accomplish what was intended *Sp* ◆ *Son las doce del mediodía y aún no hemos vendido ni una escoba. No hemos hecho nada de nuestro trabajo, y nuestro jefe se va a enfadar.* It's twelve noon and we still haven't done anything

we were supposed to. We haven't done any of our work, and our boss is going to get angry.

no ver la hora (to not see the hour) to not be able to wait, to look forward to *L. Am., Sp* ◆ *No veo la hora que llegue mi amiga Brenda.* I can't wait until my friend Brenda gets here. ◆ *No veo la hora de salir con él.* I can't wait to go out with him.

no ver más allá de sus narices to not (be able to) see past the end of one's nose *L. Am., Sp* ◆ *Muchos de los empleados no hacen nada. Nuestro jefe no ve más allá de sus narices.* Many of the employees don't do anything. Our boss can't see past the end of his nose.

no ver ni tres en un burro (to not even see three on a burro) to not see anything *Sp* ◆ *No veía ni tres en un burro hasta que le pusieron las gafas. Pobre niño.* He couldn't see a thing until they put on his glasses. Poor kid.

no vérsele a alguien el pelo to not see (hide nor hair of) someone *Mex, Sp* ◆ *Juan trabaja día y noche; no le vemos el pelo. (Sp)* Juan works day and night; we don't see hide nor hair of him. ◆ *Pasó tan rápido que ni el pelo se le vio. (Mex)* He went by so fast that we didn't even see him.

No voy a tragar carros y carretas. I'm not going to swallow that nonsense (cars and carts). *Mex, Sp*

No voy a tragarme esa guayaba. I'm not going to swallow that nonsense (guava). *L, Am. (except Ch, Arg)* ◆ *No trates de convencerme; no me voy a tragar esa guayaba.* Don't try to convince me; I'm not swallowing that nonsense.

no... en absoluto not (not any) . . . at all *L. Am., Sp* ◆ *No me causa problemas en absoluto.* It doesn't cause me any problems at all.

de la **noche a la mañana** (from night to morning) from one day to the next, overnight *L. Am., Sp* ◆ *No se puede cambiar el sistema de la noche a la mañana.* You can't change the system from one day to the next.

En la **noche todos los gatos son pardos (negros).** (At night all cats are dark-colored.) Who can tell? It's hard to see any difference between some things. *L. Am., Sp* ◆ *¿Quieres ir al cine? —No, no me he maquillado aun. —¿Qué importa? En la noche* *todos los gatos son negros. Do you want to go to the movies? —No, I haven't even put on my make-up. —What difference does it make? Who can tell?*

la **noche toledana** (Toledo night) sleepless night, night of insomnia *Sp* ◆ *Pasé una noche toledana; no me sentía bien. I had a sleepless night; I didn't feel well.*

nombre →**no tener nombre**

¡Nones para los preguntones! Nothing for those who ask too many questions! *Mex* ◆ *Basta de preguntas, niña. ¡Nones para los preguntones! That's enough questions, my little dear. Ask me no questions, I'll tell you no lies!*

¡Nones! No! *Mex, Col* ◆ *La invitó a salir, pero la chica le dijo que nones. He invited her to go out, but the girl said "Nope."*

Al **nopal lo van a ver sólo cuando tiene tunas.** (They only go to see the nopal cactus when it has **tunas**, fruits.) Laugh and the world laughs with you (weep and you weep alone). He's (She's) a fair-weather friend. (saying that means people will call on others only when they are prosperous or doing well) *Mex* ◆ *Así que veniste a verme porque necesitas plata, hija. Al nopal lo van a ver sólo cuando tiene tunas. So you came to see me because you need money, dear (daughter). You're kind of like a fair-weather friend.*

norteado(-a) (northed) disoriented, confused *Mex, ES* ◆ *Ando norteada. I'm feeling all confused.*

Nos wachamos. (We'll see each other.) See you. (from the English "to watch") *Chicano*

nota →**dar la nota; dar la nota alta; mala nota; ¡Qué nota!; ¿Qué notas me cuentas?; sacar buenas (malas) notas**

en **nota** high, inebriated *Mex, Cuba, DR, PR* ◆ *¿No ves que Raúl está en nota? Don't you see that Raúl is high?*

la(s) **nota(s)** news *L. Am.* ◆ *¿Qué notas me cuentas? What's new (what news are you telling me)?*

novedad →**sin novedad**

estar en las **nubes** (to be in the clouds) to be daydreaming, have one's head in the clouds *L. Am., Sp* ◆ *No recuerdo lo que dijo Carmela; yo estaba en las nubes cuando ella habló. I don't remember what Carmela said; I was daydreaming when she spoke.*

de **nuevo** again *L. Am., Sp* ◆ *¿Tienen su casa en venta de nuevo? Do they have their house for sale again?*

de **nuez** again (sounds like **de nuevo**; **nuez** means nut) *Mex* ◆ *¿La misma pregunta de nuez? Ya te lo dije veinte veces. The same question again? I already told you twenty times.*

nunca →**estar como nunca**

Nunca falta un pelo en la sopa. (There's always a hair in the soup.) There's always a hitch, problem. *L. Am.* ◆ *¿Otra vez renunciaste a tu empleo? Nunca falta un pelo en la sopa. You've quit your job again? There's always some hitch.*

Ñ

las **ñáñaras** heebie-jeebies, nervousness, willies *Mex, ES* ◆ *Cuando estoy sola me dan ñáñaras. When I'm alone I get the heebie-jeebies.*

O

O sea... That is . . . *L. Am., Sp* ◆ *O sea, que no vas a terminar tu carrera.* That is, you're not going to finish your studies.

O somos o no somos. (We are or we aren't.) phrase used to mean that because we are who we are, we can or should act in a certain way or do a certain thing (e.g., get in the door at a fancy place), often used jokingly (also: **¿Somos o no somos?** Are you with me or not? Are we on or not?) *L. Am., Sp* ◆ *Tenemos que apoyar a los obreros. Es el momento de demostrar que somos o no somos.* We need to support the workers. It's time to demonstrate what team we're on (whether we're with them or not with them).

a la **obra** ➙**ponerse a la obra**

ser una **obra maestra** (to be a masterpiece) to be great, wonderful, a work of art *L. Am., Sp* ◆ *Teresa, ¡el vestido que me hiciste es una obra maestra!* Teresa, the dress you made for me is fantastic!

obstante ➙**no obstante**

un **ocho** ➙**hacerse un ocho**

ser la **octava maravilla** to be the eighth wonder (of the world), said of things, often used in the negative *Mex, Peru, Bol, S. Cone, Sp* ◆ *Josefina se cree la octava maravilla y trata a sus colegas con arrogancia.* Josefina thinks she's the eighth wonder of the world, and she treats her colleagues arrogantly.

ocurrencia ➙**¡Qué ocurrencia!; tener la ocurrencia de**

¡Oiga! (**usted** command form of **oír**; Listen!) Excuse me, may I speak with you? (used to get attention of passerby, waiter, etc.) *parts of L. Am., Sp* ◆ *¡Oiga señor! ¿Dónde está la casa de cambio?* Excuse me, sir. Where is the currency exchange?

Ojalá que... I wish that . . . , I hope that . . . *L. Am., Sp* ◆ *¡Ojalá que nos veamos pronto!* I hope that we see each other soon!

el **ojete** (eyelet, hole) asshole (vulgar) *Mex* ◆ *Ese ojete me mentó la madre.* That asshole

insulted my mother (usually this means calling someone an SOB).

ojitos ➙**hacer ojitos**

ojo ➙**echar el ojo; echar mal de ojo; írsele a alguien los ojos por algo o alguien; Más ven cuatro ojos que dos.; no pegar los ojos en toda la noche; tener buen ojo; tener mucho ojo con**

estar con **ojo** (to be with eye) to be warned, suspicious *Mex, Sp* (RVar *U:* **abrir el ojo**) ◆ *Tienes que estar con ojo, Amanda. Esa persona puede tener malas intenciones.* You have to watch out, Amanda. That person could have bad intentions.

estar **ojo al charqui** (to be eye on the beef jerky) to take special care with something *Ch* ◆ *Los niños están jugando en el jardín. Yo estaré ojo al charqui mientras ustedes preparen la comida.* The kids are playing in the garden. I'll keep an eye on them while you (two) prepare the food.

Okei. OK. (from the English expression) *L. Am.* ◆ *¿Entiendes lo que te dije? —Okei, okei.* Understand what I told you? —OK, OK.

oler ➙**no oler bien una cosa, oler mal**

estar en la **olla** (to be in the pot) to be in hot water, in trouble *parts of L. Am.* ◆ *Si no llego a la entrevista a las once, estaré en la olla.* If I don't get to the interview at 11:00, I'll be in hot water.

la **olla** ➙**írsele la olla**

estar de **onda** to be "in," cool, "with it" *Mex, ES, Col, U, Arg* (RVar *Ch:* **en onda**) ◆ *Ese baile está muy de onda.* That dance is very "in."

la **onda** ➙**no agarrar la onda; ¿Qué onda(s)?; sacar de onda**

la **onda gruesa** (thick sound wave) heavy (difficult, scary, dangerous) thing, situation *Mex, ES, Col* ◆ *Me parece que tu amiga anda en la onda gruesa.* Seems to me your friend is in deep water.

optar por (hacer algo) to choose to (do something) *L. Am., Sp* ◆ *Optemos por un nuevo candidato. Let's choose a new candidate.*

Oquey, maguey. (All right, maguey cactus.) Okey-dokey. *Mex, Col* ◆ *¿Nos encontramos a las ocho? —Oquey, maguey. Shall we meet at eight? —Okey, dokey.*

Órale. used to animate someone to do something or in accepting an invitation; all right; that's it; OK (used originally in Mex but young people now use it in C. Am. and Col; Mex: also, can be used to express surprise) *Mex, G, ES, Col* ◆ *Órale, vamos al cine. All right, then, let's go to the movies.* ◆ *Órale, ¡qué coche tan lujoso te compraste! My, my, what a fancy car you bought yourself!*

sus **órdenes** →**Estoy a sus órdenes.**

ordinario(-a) common, low-class, tacky *L. Am., Sp* ◆ *Nunca creímos que nuestros primos pudieran ser tan ordinarios. We never thought our cousins could be so low-class.*

el/la **oreja** (ear) spy, informer *Mex, ES, Nic* ◆ *No hablen. Aquí viene la oreja. Don't talk. Here comes the tattle-tale.*

¡La **osa!** Darn! exclamation of surprise, euphemism for **la hostia** *Ch, Sp*

oso →**hacer el oso; ¡Qué oso!**

¡Ostras! (Oysters!) euphemism for **¡Hostias!**, Darn! Holy smoke! *Sp* ◆ *¡Ostras! No sé dónde dejé nuestros pasajes. Darn! I don't know where I left our tickets.*

estar en **otra** (to be on another, with the idea of **onda** or **dimensión** understood) to feel spaced out, detached, have one's mind somewhere else *Mex, S. Cone* ◆ *¿Salimos de parranda hoy? —No, gracias, estoy en otra. Tengo muchas responsabilidades. Shall we go out on the town today? —No, thanks, my mind is somewhere else. I have a lot of responsibilities.*

ser de la **otra acera** (to be of the other sidewalk or row of houses on the other side) to be gay, homosexual *Mex, Sp* (RVar *Sp*: also, **de la acera de enfrente**)

de la **otra banqueta** (from the other sidewalk) gay, homosexual *Mex, G* ◆ *Algunas personas dicen que Arturo es de la otra banqueta. Some people say Arturo is gay.*

ser **otra canción (otro cantar)** (to be another song) to be another kettle of fish *L. Am., Sp* ◆ *Ahora entendemos lo que pasó; eso es otro cantar. Now we understand what happened; that's another kettle of fish.*

Otra cosa es con guitarra. (It's something else with a guitar.) That's a different thing, another kettle of fish. *S. Cone* (RVar *Ch*: also, it's easy to talk but harder to do something) ◆ *Marina cree que es fácil conseguir un buen puesto, pero ella no vive en un pueblo pequeño. Otra cosa es con guitarra. Marina thinks it's easy to find a good job, but she doesn't live in a small town. That's a whole different ball game.*

Otra cosa, mariposa. (Another thing, butterfly.) Not the same thing. It's a different kettle of fish. *Mex, DR, ES, Col, Sp* ◆ *No es lo mismo el fútbol que el fútbol americano. Otra cosa, mariposa. Soccer and American football are not the same thing. It's a different kettle of fish.*

A **otra cosa, mariposa.** (To another thing, butterfly.) That's that, forget it. (also, used for changing the topic) *Mex, DR, Sp* ◆ *A otra cosa mariposa. No me interesan los chismes de familia. Forget it. I'm not interested in family gossip.* ◆ *A otra cosa mariposa. Nadie quiere hablar de política ahora. On to a new topic. No one wants to talk about politics now.*

el (la) **otro(-a)** next (when referring to directions) *L. Am., Sp* ◆ *Dobla en la otra esquina. Turn at the next corner.*

Otro gallo me cantaría (cantara). (Another rooster would be singing for me.) Things would be different for me. *L. Am., Sp* ◆ *Si hubiera estudiado matemáticas, otro gallo me cantaría. Hubiera podido elegir la carrera. If I'd studied math, things would be different for me. I'd be able to choose my course of studies.*

del **otro lado (bando)** (from the other side [band]) gay, homosexual *Chicano, Mex, DR, G, ES, Col, U, Ch* ◆ *Carmen se la pasa invitando a Julio a salir; parece que no sabe que es del otro lado. Carmen keeps inviting Julio to go out; it looks like she doesn't know he's gay.*

del **otro Laredo** gay, homosexual (probably from **del otro lado**) *Mex, ES* ◆ *A ese bar* van hombres del otro Laredo; la música y los tragos son muy buenos. *Gay men go to that bar; the music and the drinks are very good.*

Ése es **otro rollo.** (That's another roll.) That's another kettle of fish. *Mex* ◆ *No me cambies la conversación, Juana. Ése es otro rollo.* *Don't change the topic on me, Juana. That's a horse of a different color.*

un **ovillo** ➞**hacerse un ovillo (una pelota)**

¡Óyeme manito! Hey, pal!, term of affection used to call a friend *Mex, G* ◆ *¡Óyeme, manito! Quiero hablar contigo.* *Hey, buddy! I want to talk to you.*

P

pa' (para) que sepas just so you know *L. Am., Sp* ◆ *¿Adónde vas, querida? —Para que sepas, voy al abogado a pedir el divorcio.* Where are you going, darling? —Just so you know, I'm going to the lawyer to ask for a divorce.

pa'lante →**echar pa'lante**

las **paces** →**hacer las paces**

la **pachanga, el pachangón** bash, party *Mex, Cuba, G, Hond, ES, Nic, CR, Ven, Para, U, Arg* (RVar *ES, CR:* also, **pachanguear**) ◆ *Este sábado habrá una pachanga en casa de Eduardo.* This Saturday there'll be a party at Eduardo's house.

la **pachocha** dough, money *Mex* (RVar *Cuba, Col:* slow, slowness) ◆ *Saqué la pachocha de mi billetera y se la di a mi hijo.* I took the money out of my billfold and gave it to my son.

los **pacos** police *Ven, Ec, Bol, Ch* ◆ *Los pacos estaban armados hasta los dientes.* The police were armed to the teeth.

de **pacotilla** of bad quality or little importance *DR, PR, S. Cone, Sp* ◆ *Es un cantante de pacotilla.* He (She) is a run-of-the-mill singer.

la **pacotilla** gang, crowd *G, ES, Nic, Ec* ◆ *Era una pacotilla de vagos la que llegó.* A bunch of slackers showed up.

padre →**¡Qué padre!; sin padre ni madre, ni perro que me ladre**

padre, padrísimo(-a) (father, very father) fantastic, super *Mex* ◆ *Su casa es padrísima.* Their house is fantastic.

padrote super, good *Mex* ◆ *¡Qué carro más padrote!* What a fantastic car!

el **padrote** pimp *Mex, G, ES, Col* ◆ *Pusieron preso al padrote.* They put the pimp in jail.

pagar con la misma moneda (to pay with the same currency) to give tit for tat *L. Am., Sp* ◆ *Ella se portó muy mal, y ahora le están pagando con la misma moneda.* She behaved very badly, and now they're giving her tit for tat.

pagar el pato (los patos) (to pay for the duck[s]) to pay for something unfairly (when someone else has done it), be left holding the bag, be the fall guy *Mex, Nic, S. Cone, Sp* ◆ *Dos o tres estudiantes armaron un lío y todos pagamos el pato.* Two or three students made a big mess and we were all left holding the bag.

pagar en especie to pay in kind *L. Am., Sp* ◆ *Vamos a pagarles en especie y no invitarlos a la fiesta.* Let's pay them in kind and not invite them to the party.

pagar los platos rotos (to pay for the broken plates) to pay for something unfairly (when someone else was responsible), be left holding the bag, be the fall guy *L. Am., Sp* (RVar *CR:* **pagar los elotes**) ◆ *Juan pagó los platos rotos. Le cayeron todas las culpas a él.* Juan was the fall guy. All the blame fell on him. *Ellos causaron el problema, pero yo pagué los platos rotos.* They caused the problem, but I was left holding the bag.

pagar por sustos (to pay in frights) to buy something on credit *ES* ◆ *Mi esposo compró el carro hace un año y todavía estamos pagando por sustos.* My husband bought the car a year ago and we're still paying on credit.

el/la **paisa** short for **paisano** *Mex, G, Col* ◆ *Mucho gusto, paisa. ¿Somos de la misma ciudad?* Glad to meet you (fellow countryman or countrywoman). Are we from the same city?

paja →**hacerse una paja; por un «quítame allá esas pajas»**

la **paja** (straw) lie, nonsense *Mex, C. Am., Col* ◆ *No me des paja.* Don't give me that baloney.

pajarear to observe, look at (from **pájaro**, bird); also, used to mean one is paying attention to something other than what is at hand, being distracted by something *Mex, ES, Nic, Col, Ch* ◆ *Estás pajareando. Hazme* *caso. You're getting distracted. Pay attention to me.*

el **pájaro 1.** (bird) male organ (vulgar) *Mex, G* **2.** (bird) gay, effeminate (pejorative) *Chicano, Cuba, DR, CR*

el/la **pajero(-a) 1.** liar or someone who talks a lot without making a point *Mex, C. Am., Col* (RVAR *ES, CR, Col:* also, **pajoso[-a]**) ◆ *Deja de hablar; no seas pajero. Stop talking; don't run off at the mouth.* **2.** jerk-off, masturbator *parts of S. Cone, Sp*

palabra →**sin cruzar palabra; tener la palabra**

la **palabrota** swear word, vulgar word *L. Am., Sp* ◆ *Jaimito siempre dice palabrotas en presencia de sus abuelos para disgustarlos. Jaimito always says swear words in front of his grandparents to upset them.*

la **palanca** (bar, lever) someone who helps someone, uses his or her influence to their benefit *Mex, Cuba, ES, Nic, CR, Col, Ven, Peru, U, Arg* ◆ *Tiene muy buenas palancas; por eso consiguió el trabajo. He has very influential friends; that's how he got the job.*

palancón, palancona very tall, string bean (from **palanca**, a lever or stick) *most of L. Am., Sp* ◆ *Pobre Vicenta es tan palancona que no encuentra pantalones que le queden bien. Poor Vicenta is such a string bean that she can't find pants that fit her.*

palanquear (to move levers) to push buttons to help *ES, Col, Peru, S. Cone* ◆ *Ernesto me palanqueó, y agarré el trabajo. Ernest pushed some buttons for me, and I got the job.*

ser **paleta** (to be a little shovel) to be backward (a hick) *Sp* ◆ *Miguel es muy paleta. No le invites a ese restaurante tan elegante. Miguel is backward. Don't take him to that elegant restaurant.*

la **paliza** (beating) boring time (**dar la paliza**, to bore to death); boring person *Sp* ◆ *María siempre nos da la paliza hablando de sus viajes. María always bores us to death talking about her trips.* ◆ *Ese tío es un paliza; no lo aguanto. That guy is a bore; I can't stand him.*

unas **palizas** →**darse unas palizas**

la **palma** →**llevar en palmas (palmitas); llevarse la palma**

palmarse to kick the bucket, die *ES, CR* (RVAR *Sp:* **palmarla**) ◆ *Ya se palmó. (CR) He (She) kicked the bucket.* ◆ *Juan la palmó a los setenta años. (Sp) Juan packed it all in at seventy years.*

palmo a palmo inch by inch *L. Am., Sp* ◆ *La policía buscó al ladrón palmo a palmo en la colonia sin encontrarlo. The police searched the neighborhood inch by inch for the thief without finding him.*

el **palo** (stick) male organ (vulgar) *Mex, Cuba, DR, G, ES, CR, Col*

ser un **palo** (to be a stick) to be boring, a drag (people or things) *DR, PR, Sp* ◆ *Esa clase es un palo. That class is a drag.*

el **palo de escoba** (broomstick) matchstick, person who is too skinny *L. Am.* ◆ *Es tan flaco el profesor. Parece un palo de escoba. The professor is so skinny. He looks like a matchstick.*

palo →**andar a palos; darle palo; echar un palo; maraca sin palo; medio palo; Ni a palos.; poner a alguien (quedar) como palo de gallinero; ser un palo/palo de escoba; serruchar el palo; tal palo, tal astilla**

la **paloma** (dove) male organ (vulgar) *C. Am., Col, Ven, Ec, Peru, Bol*

ser un **pan** (to be a loaf of bread) to be good-natured, kind, not selfish, a good egg *Mex, Cuba, DR* ◆ *Luz es un pan. Siempre me ayuda cuando tengo problemas. Luz is a good egg. She always helps me when I have problems.*

ser **pan comido** (to be eaten bread) to be very easy, a piece of cake (said of things) *Mex, DR, PR, S. Cone, Sp* ◆ *No te preocupes. Ese trabajo es pan comido. Don't worry. That job is a piece of cake.*

ser (un) **pan de Dios** (to be God's bread) to be good-natured, an angel *DR, ES, Ch, U* ◆ *El chofer del bus es un pan de Dios. Siempre espera que entre a la casa antes de irse. The bus driver is an angel. He always waits until I get in the house before leaving.*

el/la **pana** (male or female) friend, buddy, pal (from **panal**, honeycomb) *DR, PR, Col, Ven, Ec* ◆ *Oye, mi pana, ¿qui úbo? Hey, my friend, what's happening?*

el **panal** (honeycomb) long-term group of friends *DR, Ven* ◆ *¿Ves esta foto? Aquí es-*

toy con mi panal. See this photo? Here I am with my gang.

un **pancho** →**hacer un pancho**

la **panda, pandilla** band, gang *Col, Sp* (RVᴀʀ *Sp*: **panda, pandilla**, a bit old-fashioned; *Mex*: **pandilla or banda**, *U*: **pandilla**) ♦ *Una pandilla atacó una casa de cambio. A gang attacked the currency exchange.* ♦ *Es una panda de gilipollas. (Sp) They're a bunch of idiots.*

la **panocha** (kind of candy) female organ (vulgar) *Chicano, Mex, ES, CR, Col*

los **pantalones** →**llevar bien puestos los pantalones; ponerse los pantalones**

estar en **pañales 1.** (to be in diapers) to be in knee pants, have little or no knowledge of something *L. Am., Sp* (see illustration, page 424) ♦ *Ahora me doy cuenta que estaba en pañales antes de leer el informe. Now I realize I was in the dark (had little information on the subject) before reading the report.* **2.** (to be in diapers) to be small fry, young *L. Am., Sp* ♦ *No tienes experiencia; estás en pañales aún. You don't have experience; you're still in knee pants.*

papa →**mandar a alguien a freír papas; Ni papa(s).; no tener ni papa(s)**

la **papa** (potato) chow, food, especially used for children *Mex, Cuba, DR, Col, Ch, U* ♦ *¡Vamos a la papa! Let's chow down!* ♦ *¿Comieron la papa? Did you eat the food?*

papacito (little daddy) term of affection for a man *Mex, DR, PR, G, ES* ♦ *Ese papacito me trae loca. That sweetie is driving me crazy.*

estar **papando (cachando) moscas** (to be swallowing [catching] flies) to be fooling around, acting silly, goofing off *Mex, U* ♦ *Están papando moscas en lugar de estudiar para los exámenes. They're goofing off instead of studying for their exams.*

¡Papas! (Potatoes!) Great! You're on! Agreed! *Mex, ES, Col* ♦ *¿Vienes con nosotros al río? —¡Papas! Will you come to the river with us? —Sure thing!*

la **papaya** (papaya) female organ (vulgar) *Mex, Cuba, Nic, Col* ♦ *Estando en Nicaragua pedí un jugo de papaya en el restaurante y el mesero me miró muy raro, casi ofendido. In Nicaragua I ordered papaya juice in*

a restaurant and the waiter looked at me funny, almost offended.

papazote big daddy *Mex, DR, PR, G, Col* ♦ *Me gusta ese papazote. I like that hunk.*

papear (to potato) to chow down, eat *Mex, Cuba, DR, PR, C. Am., Ven, Peru, Sp* ♦ *Ya es hora de ir a papear. It's time to go eat.*

un **papel** →**hacer un papel**

papel mojado (wet paper) useless document or, in general, something useless or of little importance, not worth the paper it's printed on *most of L. Am., Sp* ♦ *El famoso principio de que todos los hombres son iguales es papel mojado. Mira la situación de los indígenas. The famous principle that all men are equal is worthless. Look at the situation of the Native Americans.*

el **papeo** (potato) chow, food *Mex, Cuba, DR, PR, Peru, Sp* ♦ *Es la hora del papeo. ¿Qué quieren comer? It's chow time. What do you want to eat?*

papi (dad) term of affection used by women to men; also **papito** *Mex, Cuba, DR, PR, G, ES, Pan, Col* ♦ *Ay, papi, te amo mucho. Oh, big daddy, I love you so much.*

el **papito** handsome guy *DR, PR, Col*

papucho daddy-o, big daddy (for boyfriends, not dads) *Mex, ES, CR, Col* ♦ *Papucho, vamos a tomar un café. Hey you hunk, let's go get a coffee.*

paquete →**darse paquete; meter un paquete**

de **paquete** (as a package) referring to someone riding behind in a two-wheeled vehicle *Sp* ♦ *Yo no tengo moto; siempre voy de paquete. I don't have a motorcycle; I always ride on the back.*

ser un **paquete 1.** (to be a package) to be very attractive, chic *Col* ♦ *Esa mujer es un paquete. That woman is chic.* **2.** (to be a package) to be a dolt, dumb *Sp* ♦ *Ese niño es un paquete. Por mucho que se lo explique no lo entiende. That child is a dolt. No matter how much it's explained to him he doesn't understand it.*

paquete (paqueta) (package) elegant, nicely turned out (people or things) *U, Arg* ♦ *Esa mujer es repaqueta. That woman is super chic.* ♦ *Tu ropa es de muy buen gusto,* *y te ves muy paqueta.* Your clothing is in very good taste, and you look very elegant.

el/la **paquetero(-a)** fraud; liar *Cuba, PR, Col* ◆ *Mi vecino es un paquetero. Ayer me dijo que mi hijo le robó dinero.* My neighbor is a liar. Yesterday he told me that my son stole money from him.

par →sin par

para acabarla de joder (to finish screwing it up) to screw it up even more, to screw up matters worse (vulgar) *Chicano, Mex, DR, PR, G, ES, Col, Sp* ◆ *Para acabarla de joder, antes de comenzar el concierto, empezó a llover y el escenario se desarmó.* To make matters worse, before the concert began, it started to rain and the stage fell apart.

ser **para chuparse los dedos** (to be to suck one's fingers) to be delicious, finger-lickin' good *L. Am., Sp* ◆ *Este postre es para chuparse los dedos.* This dessert is finger-lickin' good.

para colmo; para colmo de desgracias (de males) (for the culmination of misfortunes) to top it all off, on top of everything else *L. Am., Sp* ◆ *El negocio no salió y, para colmo, mi socio me dejó con todas las deudas.* The business didn't work out and, to top it all off, my partner left me with all the debts.

estar **para comérselo** (to be as if to eat) to be very attractive *Florida, Mex, Cuba, DR, ES, U, Arg, Sp* ◆ *Carlos Vives es un papazote. Está pa'comérselo.* Carlos Vives is one handsome guy. He's gorgeous. ◆ *Adrián está para comérselo.* Adrián is cute as a button.

para dar y regalar (to give and give as a present) to burn, in abundance *Mex, Ch, U, Sp* ◆ *En la huerta tenemos verduras para dar y regalar.* In the garden we have vegetables in abundance.

para dar y tomar (to give and take) to burn, in abundance *Mex, Sp* ◆ *Tienen tanto dinero como para dar y tomar.* They have money to burn.

¡Para los (las) que amamos! For those whom we love! (a toast) *most of L. Am.* ◆ *Vamos a brindar: ¡Para las que amamos!* Let's make a toast: To the ladies that we love!

Para luego es tarde. (For **luego**, then, it's late.) Don't wait until it's too late, phrase to get someone else to act quickly and not wait *Mex, DR, ES* ◆ *Vete ahora y háblale. Para luego es tarde.* Go now and talk to him (her). Don't wait until it's too late.

para parar un tren (to stop a train) in large quantities, tons of *Mex, ES, Sp* ◆ *Hay comida para parar un tren. Te has pasado calculando lo necesario para esta fiesta.* There's food here to feed an army. You've gone overboard in your calculations of how much we need for this party.

para puro paladar curtido (only for the finest palate) for gourmets *Mex* ◆ *Esta cena será para puro paladar curtido.* This dinner will be solely for gourmets.

¿Para qué? (For what?) You're welcome. *Mex* ◆ *Gracias por su ayuda. —¿Para qué?* Thanks for your help. —You're welcome.

para servirle (to serve you) at your service *L. Am., Sp* ◆ *Soy Alfonso Rodríguez Pizarro para servirle, señorita.* I am Alfonso Rodríguez Pizarro at your service, miss.

estar **para sopita(s) y buen vino** (to be for light soup and good wine) to be old, on his (her) last legs *Sp* ◆ *Lupita está para sopita y buen vino.* Lupita is on her last legs.

para tirar pá (para) arriba (to throw up in the air) to burn, in abundance, tons *S. Cone* ◆ *Prepararon comida para tirar para arriba.* They prepared tons of food.

el/la **paracaidista** (parachutist) freeloader, party crasher (also, less common, someone who jumps into a discussion but doesn't know anything about the topic) *DR, Nic, CR, Ec, Peru, S. Cone* ◆ *No hablemos de la fiesta delante de Ramón; es un paracaidista y seguro viene con sus amigos.* Let's not talk about the party in front of Ramón; he's a freeloader and it's a sure thing he'll come with all his friends.

parar bolas (to stop balls) to pay attention *Nic, Ven, Ec, U* ◆ *Nadie le para bolas al ministro porque saben que no cumplirá con su palabra. Son sólo promesas huecas.* No one pays attention to the minister because they know he won't keep his word. They're just empty promises.

parar en seco (to stop someone dry) to stop someone cold *Mex, ES, Col, Ch, U* ◆ *Arturo intentó gritarme, y lo paré en seco.* Arturo tried to shout at me, and I stopped him cold.

parar oreja (parar las orejas, parar la oreja) to prick up one's ears, listen carefully *L. Am., Sp* ◆ *Para la oreja: escucha bien lo que te voy a decir. Es muy importante.* Prick up your ears: listen carefully to what I'm going to tell you. It's very important.

pararle el carro a (to stop his or her cart) to firmly prevent someone from doing something, put one's foot down *S. Cone, Sp* ◆ *Habló de vender el negocio, pero yo le paré el carro.* He (She) talked about selling the business, but I put my foot down.

pararse en seco (to stop oneself dry) to stop in one's tracks *Mex, ES, Col, Ch, U* ◆ *Cuando Yoli me vio, se paró en seco.* When Yoli saw me, she stopped in her tracks.

parchar (to put a patch on) to have sex (vulgar) *Mex, ES* ◆ *No me gusta parchar con mujeres fáciles.* I don't like to have sex with easy women.

Parece Volkswagen con las puertas abiertas. (He [she] looks like a Volkswagen with the doors open.) big-eared, having very large ears *parts of L. Am.* ◆ *Leonardo parece un Volkswagen con las puertas abiertas y está acomplejado.* Leonardo is a real Dumbo (i.e., big-eared) and has a complex about it.

al **parecer** apparently *L. Am., Sp* ◆ *Al parecer, este restaurante es caro.* Apparently, this restaurant is expensive.

parecer araña fumigada (to seem like a fumigated spider) to be suffering from the effects of too much partying or drinking *Mex, ES* ◆ *Fui a una pachanga anoche y hoy parezco araña fumigada.* I went to a big party last night and today I'm like a toxic waste zone.

parecer chiva loca (to seem like a crazy goat) to be running around like crazy, like a chicken with its head cut off *Mex* ◆ *Niña, siéntate. Pareces chiva loca.* Sit down, girl. You're running around like a chicken with its head cut off.

parecer que alguien está empollando huevos (to seem like someone is nesting eggs) to be a homebody *Sp* ◆ *Dorotea parece que está empollando huevos; no sale a ninguna parte.* Dorotea is a real homebody; she doesn't go anywhere.

parecer que se ha tragado un palo de escoba (to look like one has swallowed a broomstick) to be stuck-up, hard to deal with, uppity, or arrogant *Mex, Sp* ◆ *La recepcionista que trabaja allí parece que se ha tragado un palo de escoba. ¡Qué arrogante!* The receptionist who works there looks very stuck-up. How arrogant!

parecer siete pisos to look ten feet tall, seem or look very tall (seven stories) *Florida, Col* ◆ *Guadalupe y Lurdes parecen siete pisos y juegan en el equipo de básquetbol del colegio.* Guadalupe and Lurdes look ten feet tall, and they play on the college basketball team.

parecer un pato mareado (to seem like a dizzy duck) to seem mixed up, inept, uncoordinated physically *Sp* ◆ *No es muy hábil con los ejercicios físicos. Tú ves a mi hermano bailar y parece un pato mareado.* He's not very good at physical exercises. You see my brother dance and he looks really uncoordinated.

parecerse una cosa a otra como un huevo a una castaña (to be as similar as an egg to a chestnut) to be like apples and oranges, very different *Sp* ◆ *Este cepillo con el peine, se parecen como un huevo a una castaña. ¡No combinan en nada! ¿Cómo es que los compraste como si de un conjunto se tratara?* This brush and comb are like apples and oranges. They don't go together at all! Why did you buy them as if they were a set?

la **pared** → **llevar contra la pared (la tabla)**

parejo → **poner parejo**

parir chayotes (to give birth to chayotes, a vegetable with prickly skin) to be like pulling teeth, do something very difficult *Mex* ◆ *Programar esta computadora es como parir chayotes.* Programming this computer is like pulling teeth.

parla lingo, way of speaking *Mex, Cuba, CR* ◆ *Muchas expresiones comunes vienen de la parla deportiva, como "fuera de base" o "en tres y dos". (Cuba)* Many common expressions come from sports lingo, like "off base" or "in three and two" (meaning a difficult situation, from baseball).

parlar (from Italian and French) to talk *Mex, ES, Col* ◆ *Tenemos que parlar. ¿Con quién* *estuviste anoche? We have to talk. Who were you with last night?*

un **paro** →**hacer un paro**

en **paro** (in stop) out of work, unemployed *L. Am., Sp* ◆ *¿Cuánto tiempo hace que estás en paro? How long have you been out of work?*

en un **parpadeo** in the blink of an eye *Mex, ES, Nic, U* ◆ *Me lo robó en un parpadeo. He (She) stole it from me in the blink of an eye.*

la **parrafada** (paragraph) long monologue, spiel *Sp* ◆ *Un político cuando le dan el micrófono, no hay manera de que acabe hasta terminar de soltar su parrafada. When they give a politician the microphone, there's no way he'll stop until he finishes his spiel.*

párrafo aparte (paragraph apart) not to change the subject *L. Am., Sp* ◆ *Párrafo aparte, me encantaría ver el jardín. Not to change the subject, but I would love to see the garden.*

de **parranda** →**ir de parranda**

el/la **parrandista, fiestero(-a)** party lover, partier *Mex, Col* ◆ *Marcos es un parrandista incansable. Marcos is a tireless partier.*

parte →**por otra parte; por todas partes (todos lados)**

partes (parts) euphemism meaning private parts *most of L. Am., Sp* ◆ *Martina le dijo a la doctora que le duelen sus partes. Martina told the doctor that her private parts are hurting her.*

partido →**sacar partido**

a **partir de** starting with (at) *L. Am., Sp* ◆ *A partir del próximo miércoles, no te llevo a la escuela. Starting next Wednesday, I won't be taking you to school.*

partirle/romperle a alguien la cara (to break someone's face) to beat someone up *most of L. Am., Sp* ◆ *En la manifestación, la policía le partió la cara a varios manifestantes. At the demonstration, the police beat up several demonstrators.*

partirle el alma a alguien to break someone's heart (literally soul) *L. Am., Sp* ◆ *Me parte el alma que en los hospitales de ese país no haya medicamentos para los enfermos. It breaks my heart that in the hospitals in that country there is no medicine for the sick.*

partirse de la risa to break up with laughter *DR, PR, Sp* ◆ *La película era muy cómica; nos partimos de la risa. The movie was really funny; we cracked up laughing.*

partirse los cojones (to break one's testicles) to work very hard, work one's ass off (vulgar) *Sp* ◆ *Estaban partiéndose los cojones todos. They were all working their asses off.*

el/la **pasa rato** (pastime) boyfriend or girlfriend who's just OK for now; also, in the feminine, slut *Mex, DR, ES, Col* ◆ *No son novios; es un pasa rato. They're not boyfriend/girlfriend; they're just together for now (until they find someone better).*

pasable (passable) tolerable, so-so *Mex, S. Cone* ◆ *La película de anoche era pasable. The movie last night was so-so.*

de **pasada** on the fly, fast and while doing something else *Mex, ES, Col, Ch* ◆ *De pasada al colegio, hablé con Beatriz. I spoke with Beatriz on the fly at school.*

ser una **pasada** (to be a past) to be too much, amazing *Sp* ◆ *Esta chica es una pasada. Qué rápida e inteligente es. This girl is too much. How quick and intelligent she is. ◆ El concierto fue una pasada. The concert was amazing.*

pasado mañana the day after tomorrow *L. Am., Sp* ◆ *Salimos para la ciudad pasado mañana. We leave for the city the day after tomorrow.*

pasadón, pasadona (way in the past) out of date, old-fashioned *Mex* ◆ *Tienen algunas ideas pasadonas. They have some old-fashioned ideas.*

los **pasa-palos** (drink-passers) munchies, appetizers, food taken with drinks (**palos**) *Ven* ◆ *Antes de comer, vamos a servir los pasa-palos. Before we eat, we'll serve the appetizers.*

pasaporte →**dar pasaporte a alguien**

pasar 1. to pass (on something), decline *Mex, S. Cone* ◆ *¿Te casarías con mi hermana? —No, yo paso. Would you marry my sister? —No, I pass.* **2.** (to pass) to be indifferent, not suffer or change because of something *Sp* ◆ *Yo paso de todo. I don't care about anything.*

pasar →**no pasar a alguien**

pasar (sacar) en limpio to make a clean copy *L. Am., Sp* ◆ *Mi jefe me pidió que pasara el informe en limpio para mañana.* My boss asked me to make a clean copy of the report by tomorrow.

pasar a mejor vida (to go to a better life) to pass away, die *L. Am., Sp* ◆ *Julia pasó a mejor vida anoche, después de sufrir mucho.* Julia passed on to a better place last night, after a great deal of suffering.

pasar de castaño oscuro (to get darker than chestnut) to be really bleak, get too serious or troublesome (things) *DR, PR, S. Cone, Sp* ◆ *Tus problemas han pasado de castaño oscuro.* Your problems have gotten very serious.

pasar de un extremo a otro to go from one extreme to the other *L. Am., Sp* ◆ *El año pasado su hija era conservadora y este año es socialista; pasa de un extremo a otro.* Last year her daughter was a conservative and this year she is a socialist; she goes from one extreme to the other.

pasar la bola 1. (to pass the ball) to give the floor (in conversation) *Cuba, ES* ◆ *Le pasé la bola a Felipe porque no sabía qué decir.* I passed the buck to Felipe because I didn't know what to say. **2.** (to pass the ball) to spread a rumor *Cuba, DR, G, ES, CR, U, Arg* ◆ *Alfredo vio a Silvia y Rodolfo abrazados y pasó la bola a todos sus amigos.* Alfredo saw Silvia and Rodolfo hugging and spread the rumor to all their friends.

pasar la noche contando estrellas (cabritos) (to spend the night counting stars [little goats]) to spend a night counting sheep *Mex, ES* ◆ *No pude dormir; pasé la noche contando estrellas.* I couldn't sleep; I spent the night counting sheep.

pasar la noche en blanco (claro) (to spend the night blank [clear]) to spend a sleepless night *Mex, DR, PR, S. Cone, Sp* ◆ *Los investigadores policiales pasaron la noche en blanco planeando la estrategia para el día siguiente.* The police investigators spent a sleepless night planning the strategy for the next day.

pasar la noche en vela (to spend the night on watch) to spend a sleepless night *L. Am., Sp* ◆ *Pasamos la noche en vela cuidando al bebé.* We spent a sleepless night taking care of the baby.

pasar la voz (to pass the voice) to spread the word, let (someone) know *parts of L. Am.* ◆ *Pásame la voz cuando lleguen.* Let me know when they get here.

pasar las de Caín (to spend those of Cain) to have a rough time, often financially *Mex, DR, PR, CR, S. Cone, Sp* ◆ *Pasamos las de Caín anoche, pues mamá se enfermó y tuvimos que llevarla al hospital.* We had a tough time last night because Mom got sick and we had to take her to the hospital.

pasar muchas navidades y sin nochebuena (to have a lot of Christmases with no Christmas Eve celebrations) to be a sourpuss, Scrooge, describing a bitter person *PR, Col* ◆ *Pobre Ramona. Ha pasado muchas navidades y sin nochebuena.* Poor Ramona. She's such a sourpuss.

pasar por alto to go over one's head; to not realize, overlook; to miss *Mex, DR, PR, ES, S. Cone, Sp* ◆ *Esta vez voy a pasar por alto tus insultos, pero que sea la última vez.* This time I'm going to let your insults go, but don't let it happen again.

pasarla de peluche (to spend it like a stuffed toy) to have a great time *Mex, ES* ◆ *¿Cómo te fue en la fiesta? —La pasamos de peluche.* How'd it go at the party? —We had a great time.

pasarlas negras (canutas) (to spend them blacks [tubes]) to have a rough time *Mex, S. Cone, Sp* (RVar *Mex, U, Arg:* **negras** only) ◆ *Las pasé negras con todos los niños allí a la vez.* I had a tough time with all the kids there at once.

pasarlas putas (to spend them prostitutes) to have a hell of a time (vulgar) *Mex, Sp* ◆ *Las pasamos putas en la finca este fin de semana.* We had a hell of a time on the farm this weekend.

pasarlo(-a) bien to have a good time *L. Am., Sp* ◆ *¿Cómo te fue en las vacaciones? —Lo pasé rebien.* How was your vacation? —I had a great time. (The prefex *re-* is often added to an adjective or adverb to augment or increase its meaning, e.g., *rebien* very good *remal* very bad.)

pasarlo bomba (to spend it bomb) to have a blast *Ch, Arg, Sp* ◆ *Siempre lo pasamos bomba aquí. We always have a blast here.*

pasarlo chancho (to spend it pig) to have a blast *Ch, Arg* ◆ *Vamos a pasarlo chancho y olvidarnos de nuestros problemas. We're going to have a blast and forget our problems.*

pasarlo en grande (to pass or spend it big) to have a great time *U, Arg, Sp* (RVAR *U, Arg:* **pasarlo a lo grande**) ◆ *Lo vamos a pasar en grande. ¿Te has enterado que vienen todos nuestros amigos? We're going to have a great time. Did you know that all our friends are coming?*

pasarlo piola (to pass it string, from "piola" in Italian, string or cord) to take it easy, keep cool or mellow about a problem *S. Cone* ◆ *Fuimos al lago el fin de semana y lo pasamos piola. We went to the lake on the weekend and we took it easy.*

pasarlo pipa (to spend it pipe) to have a great time *Sp* ◆ *Lo pasamos pipa en tu fiesta. Gracias por invitarnos. We had a great time at your party. Thank you for inviting us.*

pasarse (to pass oneself) to go too far, go overboard, overdo it *Mex, DR, ES, S. Cone* ◆ *Yo soy feo, pero tú te pasaste. I'm ugly, but you've gone beyond the limit.* ◆ *¡Ya te pasaste! You've gone too far!*

pasarse de la raya (to go over the line) to go too far, go overboard *L. Am., Sp* ◆ *Jacinta los echó de su casa porque se pasaron de la raya. Jacinta threw them out of her house because they went too far.*

pasarse de listo(-a) (vivo[-a]) (to pass oneself as clever, be overly clever) to be a smartass, outsmart oneself, try to show oneself (erroneously) to be smarter than others *L. Am., Sp* (RVAR *Mex:* also, **pasarse de víbora**, instead of **vivo**) ◆ *¡Te pasaste de listo! You thought you were clever (but weren't so clever after all)!*

pasarse de rosca (to pass oneself as doughnut) to go too far, go overboard *Mex, Sp* ◆ *El maestro se pasó de rosca conmigo al darme un 6 de calificación en el examen. The teacher went too far giving me a 6 as a grade on the test.* ◆ *Mi papá se pasó de rosca al no darme permiso para ir a la fiesta. My dad went too far by not giving me permission to go to the party.* ◆ *No te pases de rosca con la repartición del pastel. Don't go overboard when you serve the cake (literally, with the giving out of the cake).*

pasársele con el tiempo (to pass by one with time) to get over it in time *L. Am., Sp* ◆ *Rompió con su novio, pero se le va a pasar con el tiempo. She broke up with her boyfriend, but she'll get over it in time.*

pasársele la mano (to have your hand slip on you) to go too far, overdo it *L. Am., Sp* ◆ *Lo siento. Se me pasó la mano. I'm sorry. I went too far.*

unas **pascuas** →**estar como unas pascuas**

de **Pascuas a Ramos** (from Easter to Palm Sunday) once in a blue moon *most of L. Am., Sp* ◆ *De Pascuas a Ramos salimos a comer. Once in a blue moon we eat out.*

Pasemos a otro patín. (Let's go to another skate.) Let's change the subject. *Mex, G, Ec* ◆ *Cambien de patín, muchachas; es hora de hablar sobre la financiación del viaje. Let's change the subject, girls; it's time to talk about the financing of our trip.*

paseo →**dar un paseo; mandar a alguien a paseo**

pasión →**¿Qué pasión?**

la **pasma** police *Sp* ◆ *Le pilló la pasma antes de que pudiera escapar. The police caught him before he could escape.*

pasmado(-a) foolish, stupid *Mex, C. Am., U* ◆ *Es una buena chica, pero es pasmada. She's a good girl, but she's foolish.*

pasmar to dumbfound or surprise; also, to scold *Mex, Col, Sp* ◆ *La noticia me pasmó. The news dumbfounded me.*

un **paso** →**dar un paso**

a **paso de tortuga** (at a turtle's pace) at a snail's pace *L. Am., Sp* ◆ *La construcción del nuevo hotel marcha a paso de tortuga; dudo que lo inauguren a fin de año. The construction of the new hotel is going at a snail's pace; I doubt if they'll dedicate it by the end of the year.*

Pasó un ángel. (An angel passed by.) said when there is silence in a conversation (also, **pasa un ángel**) *S. Cone, Sp* ◆ *Los invitados hablaban ruidosamente. Cuando entró la rubia con su marido, pasó un ángel. The guests were speaking noisily. When the blonde* *came in with her husband, there was a break in the conversation.*

el/la **pasota** someone who doesn't care about anything, slacker *Sp* ◆ *Juan es un pasota, como muchos de sus amigos. Juan is a slacker, like a lot of his friends.*

la **pasta** (pasta, dough) dough, money *Cuba, Sp* ◆ *Ese tipo está lleno de pasta. That guy is loaded.*

la **pasta gansa** (goose pasta, dough) a lot of money, fortune *Sp* ◆ *Ganó una pasta gansa en aquel concurso. He (She) won a fortune in that contest.*

pastelear (to cake) to make out, hug and kiss (boyfriend and girlfriend) *Mex* ◆ *Vimos a tu novio pasteleando con otra chica. We saw your boyfriend making out with another girl.*

pata →**estirar la pata; meter la pata; tener mala pata; tener patas**

a **pata** (by foot of an animal) on foot, walking *Mex, C. Am., S. Cone, Sp* ◆ *Nos fuimos a pata a la clínica porque había huelga del transporte público. We went to the clinic on foot because there was a public transportation strike.*

el/la **pata de perro (pata'eperro)** (dog foot) gadabout, wanderer, person on the go, out and about *Mex, DR, Nic, Peru, Bol, Ch, Arg* ◆ *Francisca es una pata de perro; nunca está en casa. Francisca is a gadabout; she's never home.*

a **pata pelada** (with a peeled paw) barefoot *Ch* ◆ *Perdóname por recibirte a pata pelada. Excuse me for greeting you barefooted.*

estar de la **patada** (to be of the kick) to be in a bad way *Mex, G, ES, Col, Peru* ◆ *He amanecido mal. Estoy de la patada hoy. I got up feeling bad. I'm in a bad way today.*

una **patada** →**dar una patada**

la **pataleta** (kicking fit) fit, tantrum *L. Am., Sp* (RVar *DR, Col:* also, **patalear**) ◆ *El niño hizo una pataleta. The boy had a tantrum.*

el **patán** lowlife *Mex, Nic, Col, U, Arg* ◆ *El dueño de ese negocio es un patán. The owner of that business is a lowlife.*

las **patas** (paws) feet, tootsies *L. Am., Sp* ◆ *Caminamos todo el día en las montañas, y a mí me duelen las patas. We walked all day in the mountains, and my tootsies hurt.*

patas pa'arriba, patas arriba (paws up in the air) topsy-turvy, disorganized *ES, Nic, DR, PR, S. Cone, Sp* ◆ *El terremoto puso el mundo patas arriba. The earthquake turned the world upside down.*

la **patata caliente** (hot potato) hot potato, very delicate matter *Mex, Sp* ◆ *No intervengas en su problema; es una patata caliente y te vas a quemar. Don't intervene in his problem; it's a hot potato and you'll get burned.*

patatín →**que si patatín que si patatán**

el **patatús** tantrum, (fainting) fit *Mex, DR, PR, ES, CR, Col, Ch, U, Sp* ◆ *A Josefa le dio un patatús cuando supo que su novio había salido con Regina. Josefa had a fit when she found out her boyfriend had gone out with Regina.*

patear to go a long way on foot, walk a lot *U, Sp* ◆ *Después del partido pateamos cinco kilómetros porque no pudimos encontrar un taxi. After the game we walked five kilometers because we couldn't find a taxi.*

a **patín** (from **a pata**, by foot of an animal) on foot, walking *Chicano, Mex, G* ◆ *Fui al centro a patín. I went downtown on foot.*

un **patín** →**echar un patín**

¿En qué **patín andas?** (What skate are you on?) How are things? What's up? *Mex, G, Ec* ◆ *¿Qué tal, Mauricio? ¿En qué patín andas? How are you, Mauricio? What's up with you?*

patinarle a alguien el coco (to have one's head [coconut] skate) to be crazy, having a slipped gear mentally *Mex, DR, ES, CR, Col, Ch* ◆ *A Rafael le patina el coco. Rafael has gone crazy.*

patinarle a alguien el embrague (to have one's clutch [of the car] skate) to be crazy, have a slipped gear mentally *Ch, U, Sp* ◆ *A mi tía le patina el embrague; se pelea con todos los vecinos. My aunt is off her rocker; she fights with all the neighbors.*

de **patitas** →**poner de patitas en la calle**

el **pato** (duck) sissy; gay, homosexual (pejorative) *Cuba, PR, Nic*

estar **pato(-a)** (to be duck) to be broke *Peru, S. Cone* ◆ *Alicia canceló su viaje porque está pata. Alicia canceled her trip because she's broke.*

el/la **patojo(-a)** guy (girl), kid *G, Col* ◆ *Los patojos no fueron a la escuela hoy. The kids didn't go to school today.*

los **patos malos** (bad ducks) bad guys *Ch* ◆ *En las películas antiguas nunca ganaban los patos malos. In the old-time movies, the bad guys never won.*

la **patota** (great big foot) bunch of people *S. Cone* ◆ *Una patota rompió las ventanas de los edificios del centro. A mob broke the windows of the downtown buildings.*

las **patrullas** (patrols) feet, tootsies (girl chasers) *Mex* ◆ *Caminé al centro y me duelen mucho las patrullas. I walked downtown and my feet hurt.*

el/la **patudo(-a)** ([ugly] bigfoot) pushy or nervy person *Ch* ◆ *Lorena es una patuda y logró hacer su voluntad. Lorena is a pushy person and managed to get her way.*

la **pava** (turkey hen) girl, woman, chick *Col, Ven* ◆ *Esa pava es superbuena. That chick is terrific.*

la **payasada** (clown action) clowning around, silly thing or action *L. Am., Sp* ◆ *La charla con el profesor fue una payasada. The talk with the professor was silly.*

de **pe a pa** entirely; from beginning to end *Mex, DR, ES, CR, S. Cone, Sp* ◆ *Felicia tiene buena memoria. Se sabe de pe a pa todos los hechos históricos durante la colonización española y las fechas correctas. Felicia has a good memory. She knows all the historical facts during the Spanish colonization and their correct dates from beginning to end.*

el **pe'o** (from **pedo**, fart) drunkenness (vulgar) *Cuba, Col, Sp* ◆ *Fidel llegó con un pe'o tremendo. Tiene un pe'o. Fidel arrived drunk as a skunk. He's smashed.*

la **pechocha** (big-breasted) well-endowed female, with a large bust *Mex, ES, Col* ◆ *¿Dónde está mi pechocha? Where's my busty gal?*

la **pechugona** (from **pechuga**, the breast of a fowl) big-breasted (woman) *Mex, DR, Col, Ch, Sp* ◆ *Estaba enamorado de una pechugona de Cali. He was in love with a big-breasted woman from Cali.*

el **pedazo de alcornoque** (piece of cork oak) blockhead, fool *Mex, DR, G, Col, Ch, U, Sp* ◆ *Eres un pedazo de alcornoque. Es-cucha lo que te dicen tus padres. You're a blockhead. Listen to what your parents tell you.*

ser un **pedazo de pan** (to be a piece of bread) to be affable, good-natured *DR, PR, U, Arg, Sp* ◆ *Don Rogelio es un pedazo de pan; siempre ayuda a los niños del barrio. Don Rogelio is good-natured; he always helps the neighborhood children.*

pedazo de... (piece of . . .) used to intensify an insult *Mex, Peru, S. Cone, Sp* ◆ *Dile a ese pedazo de imbécil (tonto) que deje de molestar. Tell that moron to stop bothering us.*

pedazos →hacerse pedazos; hecho(-a) pedazos, añicos

pedir (tomar) prestado(-a) to borrow *L. Am., Sp* ◆ *¿Mi nuevo auto? Anoche me lo pidió prestado Angelina. My new car? Angelina borrowed it last night.*

a **pedir de boca** (at the mouth's asking) just so or right, exactly as one wishes *L. Am., Sp* ◆ *¡Qué bien! Nos ha salido a pedir de boca. How nice! It came out exactly as we wanted.*

pedir la luna (to ask for the moon) to ask for the moon, the impossible *L. Am., Sp* (see illustration, page 267) ◆ *Necesito un auto, papá. —Hijo, estás pidiendo la luna; sabes que no tenemos dinero. I need a car, Dad. —Son, you're asking for the moon; you know we don't have any money.*

En **pedir no hay engaño.** (There is no deceit in asking.) No harm in asking. *Ch* ◆ *Vamos a firmar la petición. En pedir no hay engaño. Let's sign the petition. No harm in asking.*

pedir peras al olmo (to ask the elm tree for pears) to ask for something in vain *L. Am., Sp* ◆ *¿A Juan le pediste dinero? Es como pedir peras al olmo, que él nunca tiene nada. You asked Juan for money? That's like asking for blood from a turnip; he never has anything.*

pedirle cobija al frío (to ask the cold for a blanket) to ask for the impossible *Mex, ES* ◆ *Los agricultores pidieron ayuda al ministro; es como pedir cobija al frío. The farmers asked the minister (secretary) for aid; it's asking for the impossible.*

pedirle comida al hambre (to ask hunger for food) to ask for the impossible *Mex, ES*

◆ *Los obreros pidieron aumento de sueldo. ¡Qúe ingenuos! Es como pedirle comida al hambre.* The workers asked for a raise. How naive! That's like asking for blood from a turnip.

pedirle cuentas a alguien to ask someone for an explanation *L. Am., Sp* ◆ *Después del desastre, es preciso pedirle cuentas a alguien.* After the disaster, it's necessary to ask someone for an explanation.

el **pedo** (fart) stink, problem (vulgar) *Chicano, Mex, G, Hond, ES, Ven* ◆ *Después del partido, se armó un gran pedo.* After the game, there was a big stink. ◆ *Yo no tengo la culpa. Ése no es mi pedo.* It's not my fault. That's not my problem.

estar **pedo(-a)** (to be fart) to be drunk (vulgar) *Mex, C. Am., U, Arg, Sp* (RVAR *U, Arg:* also, **estar en pedo;** *Sp:* **llevar un pedo**) ◆ *Está pedo.* He's drunk.

pegado(-a) a las faldas (glued to the skirts) clinging to the skirt *Sp* ◆ *Es un hombre sumiso, siempre pegado a las faldas de su mujer.* He's a submissive man, always clinging to his wife's skirt.

pegajoso(-a) (sticky) always at your side, saying silly things or overly attentive; also, something that sticks in your mind *Mex, Col, Ch, U* ◆ *Ese chico es muy pegajoso.* That boy is very pesky. ◆ *Es una canción pegajosa.* It's a catchy song.

pegar el grito (to stick the shout) to protest, cry out, raise a hue and cry *DR, ES, CR, Col, U* ◆ *El cocinero pegó un grito cuando comenzó el fuego en la cocina, y todos salieron corriendo.* The cook raised a ruckus when the fire started in the kitchen, and everyone ran out.

pegar una cosa como guitarra en un entierro (to stick like a guitar at a funeral) to be out of whack, out of time or place *Sp* ◆ *Ese vestido con ese bolso le pegan como guitarra en un entierro.* That dress and that purse are out of whack.

pegarse la vida padre (to stick or fasten to oneself the father life) to live it up *Sp* ◆ *Ese hombre se está pegando la vida padre desde que heredó la fortuna de su tía.* That man is living it up ever since he inherited his aunt's fortune.

pegársele a alguien la silla (el asiento) (to have the seat stuck to one) to stay somewhere for a long time *U, Sp* ◆ *Ayúdame con la limpieza de la casa. ¿Acaso se te ha pegado el asiento?* Help me with the housecleaning. Are you stuck to your seat or what?

pegársele a alguien las sábanas (to have the sheets stick to one) to oversleep *L. Am., Sp* (see illustration, page 374) ◆ *Se me pegaron las sábanas y llegué tarde al aeropuerto.* I overslept and got to the airport late.

de **pegoste** →**ir de pegoste**

de **pegote** →**ir de pegote, tirarse de pegote**

el **pegue** appeal (sometimes sex appeal) *Mex, ES, Col* ◆ *Ese chico tiene pegue.* That guy has sex appeal. ◆ *Esa música tiene pegue.* That music is catchy.

la **pela** money, short for **peseta** *Sp* ◆ *Los billetes me costaron muchas pelas.* The tickets cost me a lot of money.

la **pelada** (balding) haircut, cut *DR, ES, CR* ◆ *¡Qué pelado me dio esta señora! Me dejó sin pelo.* What a haircut this lady gave me! She left me without any hair.

pelado(-a) 1. (peeled) broke, penniless *Cuba, DR, PR, C. Am., Col, Sp* ◆ *¿Me prestas dinero? Estoy pelado.* Will you loan me money? I'm broke. **2.** (peeled, bald) shameless, rude (person) *Mex* ◆ *No invité a Paco porque es un pelado.* I didn't invite Paco because he's a lowlife.

el/la **pelagatos** (cat skinner) jerk, usually poor and uneducated person *PR, ES, Ch, U* ◆ *No voy a permitir que cualquier pelagatos se case con mi hija.* I'm not going to let any old jerk marry my daughter.

pelar los dientes (to peel the teeth) to smile or make smile *Mex, ES, Nic, CR, Col, Ec* ◆ *Vos sólo pelando los dientes pasas. (ES)* (In El Salvador and some other Latin American countries, **vos** is used instead of **tú** for speaking to a close friend.) You're always smiling. ◆ *Tus palabras me pelan los dientes. (Mex)* Your words make me smile.

pelársela (to peel it) to not give a damn, be indifferent (vulgar, **la** refers to **la verga**, male organ) *Mex, G, ES* ◆ *(CR: to fail, end up badly or look ridiculous)* ◆ *Me pela lo que digas. Me la pela.* I don't give a damn about what you say. I don't give a damn.

peleados(-as) mad (angry) at each other, treating each other as enemies *L. Am., Sp* ◆ *María y José están peleados; ya no se hablan.* María and José are angry at each other after a fight; they aren't speaking to each other anymore.

la **peli** flick, short for **película** *Mex, DR, Sp* ◆ *¿Fueron al cine? ¿Qué peli vieron?* Did you go to the movies? What flick did you see?

de **película** (like in a movie) great, fantastic, like a dream *Mex, DR, PR, C. Am., S. Cone, Sp* ◆ *Hola, Marisa. ¿Qué onda con los chavos? –De película.* Hi, Marisa. How's it going with the guys? —Like a dream!

la **película** →**tener clara la película**

la **película verde** erotic (green) movie *U, Arg, Sp* ◆ *¡No vas a ver esa película verde!* You're not going to see that erotic film!

el **pellejo** (skin) old geezer *Mex* ◆ *Don Mario es un pellejo muy inteligente.* Don Mario is a smart old geezer.

estar en el **pellejo de otro** to be in someone else's shoes (literally, skin), to be in someone else's circumstances or situation *L. Am., Sp* ◆ *No puedes entender su situación porque no estás en su pellejo.* You can't understand his situation because you're not in his shoes.

el **pellizco** (pinch) pinch, small adjustment, tweaking *L. Am., Sp* ◆ *Necesito un pellizco de azúcar para el café.* I need a pinch of sugar for the coffee.

el **pelma (pelmazo)** (mass of undigested food) idiot, boring person *Sp* ◆ *No seas pelmazo/pelma.* Don't be a pain (bore).

el **pelo chino(-a)** curly hair *Mex, C. Am.* ◆ *Me gusta el pelo chino.* I like curly hair.

el **pelo, pelito** (hair) little bit *L. Am., Sp* ◆ *Sólo un pelito.* Just a tad.

al **pelo** (to the hair) exactly, as one wishes *Mex, DR, G, ES, Ven, S. Cone* ◆ *La bici le cae al pelo.* The bike is just right for him (her).

el **pelo** →**no vérsele a alguien el pelo; no tener pelos en la lengua; poner a alguien los pelos de punta; por un pelo**

la **pelona** (the bald one) death, Grim Reaper *Mex, C. Am.* ◆ *¿Cómo está, don César? –No muy bien. Me está llevando la pelona.* How are you, Don César? —Not so good. The Grim Reaper is taking me off (said in jest).

de **pelos** (of hairs) great, fantastic, good (like **de película**) *Mex* ◆ *Lo vamos a pasar de pelos.* We're going to have a great time.

con **pelos y señales** (with hairs and gestures) in great detail *L. Am., Sp* ◆ *Lo expliqué con pelos y señales.* I explained it in great detail.

pelota →**hacer la pelota (pelotilla) a alguien; hacerse un ovillo (una pelota); por pelotas (cojones); tener pelotas**

en **pelota** (in ball) bare-assed, naked (vulgar) *G, Nic, DR, PR, S. Cone* ◆ *Hizo mucho calor este verano; dormí todas las noches en pelota.* It was really hot this summer; I slept every night in the buff.

en **pelotas** (in balls) bare-assed, naked (vulgar) *Mex, DR, PR, Col, Peru, S. Cone, Sp* ◆ *Toca la puerta antes de entrar, que a don Bartolo le gusta andar en pelotas por la casa.* Knock on the door before you go in; Don Bartolo likes to go around the house naked.

pelotear to bounce (someone) around (e.g., from office to office) *Cuba, Col, U, Arg* ◆ *¡Qué burocracia! Me pelotearon de una oficina a otra hasta que por fin alguien me ayudó.* What bureaucracy! They bounced me around from one office to another until finally someone helped me.

una **pelotera** →**tener una pelotera**

pelotudo(-a) (big-balled) jerk (bitch), schmuck (often accompanied by a gesture with hands up as though holding two balls; similar to **huevón** in *Mex, Ch* or **Le pesan** in Nic, vulgar) *S. Cone* ◆ *Pelotudo, ¡maneja con más cuidado!* Drive more carefully, you jerk!

la **pelu** (short for **peluquería**) beauty shop, barber shop *Mex, Sp* ◆ *La pelu está cerrada los fines de semana.* The beauty shop is closed on weekends.

de **peluche** (used instead of **de película**; **peluche** means plush, like the fabric of stuffed toys) fantastic *Mex, DR, ES, Col* ◆ *Lo pasamos de peluche en casa de Yolanda.* We had a great time at Yolanda's house.

peluquín →**Ni hablar del peluquín.**

la **pelusa** (fuzz) riffraff, the masses, hordes *Chicano, Mex* ◆ *No quiero compartir la playa con la pelusa; vamos al hotel Miramar.* I don't want to share the beach with riffraff; let's go to the Miramar Hotel.

pena →No hay pena.; tener pena

la **pendejada** damn nonsense, silly or stupid thing to do; trick (vulgar) *Mex, C. Am.* ◆ *No hagan más pendejadas. Don't (you all) do any more damn stupid tricks.*

pendejear to act like a damn fool, dick around, behave in a foolish or stupid way (vulgar) *Mex, C. Am.* ◆ *Deja de pendejear. Stop dicking around.*

pendejo(-a) 1. (pubic hair) asshole, jerk, idiot; adj. damn stupid (vulgar) *Mex, DR, PR, C. Am., Col, Ven* ◆ *No quiero escucharte; eres un pendejo. I don't want to listen to you; you're a damn jerk.* **2.** (pubic hair, vulgar and offensive in many places) kid, child *Ch, U, Arg* ◆ *Estos pendejos no respetan a sus padres. These kids don't respect their parents.*

pender de un hilo to hang from a thread *L. Am., Sp* ◆ *Su trabajo pende de un hilo. Si sigue así, lo van a despedir. His job is hanging from a thread. If he keeps on this way, they're going to fire him.*

el/la **pensante** dope, idiot *Mex, Col* ◆ *¡Eres un pensante! You're an idiot!*

pensar →Ni pensarlo.

pensar para sus adentros to think to one-self *L. Am., Sp* ◆ *Durante la boda, la novia pensaba para sus adentros que no conocía muy bien al hombre que sería su marido. During the wedding, the bride thought to herself that she didn't really know the man who would be her husband.*

la **peña** (cliff) group of friends *Sp* ◆ *Estuve con toda la peña tomando cerveza. I was with the whole gang drinking beer.*

Peor es chile y agua lejos. (Worse is chili and water far away.) Things could be worse. *Mex* ◆ *Pues aunque la webcam no funciona por lo menos tenemos conexión a la Red. Peor es chile y agua lejos. Well, although the webcam isn't working at least we have an Internet connection. Things could be worse.*

Peor es nada. (Worse is nothing.) Be happy with what you've got, phrase meaning one should be satisfied with what one has. It's better than nothing. *L. Am., Sp* ◆ *Tengo sólo un pantalón nuevo. —Es suficiente. Peor es nada. I only have one new pair of pants. —That's enough. It's better than nothing.*

el/la **peoresnada** (worse is nothing) phrase used to describe a boyfriend or girlfriend (sometimes chosen because there was no one better, said in jest) *Mex, ES, Col, Peru, Bol, S. Cone* ◆ *Me voy a ver a mi peoresnada. I'm going to see my better half (literally, better than nothing).*

peque short for **pequeño(-a)** most of *L. Am. (not U, Arg), Sp* (where a bit old-fashioned) ◆ *Cuando era peque, me gustaba mucho la película «La sirenita». When I was little, I really liked the movie The Little Mermaid.*

ser la **pera** (to be the pear) to be too much, the limit *Sp* ◆ *¡Eres la pera! You take the cake!*

los **percances del oficio** (chances of the trade) part and parcel of the job, occupational hazards *ES, Nic, Sp* ◆ *Por percances del oficio, a José le falta un dedo. Es carpintero. Because of occupational hazards, José's missing a finger. He's a carpenter.*

percha →poner a alguien como lazo de cochino/percha de perico

perder →echar a perder

perder (el) tiempo to waste time *L. Am., Sp* ◆ *Nuestro proyecto es urgente, y no debemos perder el tiempo. Our project is urgent, and we shouldn't waste time.*

perder(se) de vista (to lose from view) to not see again, lose sight of *L. Am., Sp* ◆ *Perdimos de vista por mucho tiempo a nuestros parientes. We lost contact with our relatives for a long time.* ◆ *No debe perderse de vista la importancia de esta idea. You shouldn't lose sight of the importance of this idea.*

perder el culo (to lose one's ass) to bust a gut, do the impossible (for someone) (vulgar) *Sp* ◆ *Jaime perdió el culo por esa chica y dejó los estudios. Jaime busted a gut for that girl and gave up (left) his studies.*

perder el hilo to lose the thread (e.g., of a conversation) *L. Am., Sp* ◆ *Perdón, perdí el hilo de la conversación. ¿Puede repetir lo último que dijo? Sorry, I've lost the thread of the conversation. Can you repeat what you just said?*

perder el norte (to lose the north) to be disoriented in what one says or does *Sp* ◆ *Perdimos el norte con todos los problemas que* *tuvimos. We got completely disoriented with all the problems we had.*

perder el (último) tren (to miss the [last] train) to miss the boat, lose out *Mex, DR, ES, Ch, U, Arg, Sp* ◆ *Tomás perdió el tren cuando no aceptó el empleo en la nueva compañía. Tomás missed the boat when he didn't accept the job at the new company.*

perder hasta la camisa to lose (even) one's shirt *L. Am., Sp* ◆ *Si sigues jugando en los casinos, vas a perder hasta la camisa. If you keep gambling in the casinos, you're going to lose your shirt.*

perder la cabeza to lose one's head *L. Am., Sp* ◆ *Agustín se enoja y pierde la cabeza fácilmente. Agustín gets angry and loses his head easily.*

perder la chaveta (to lose one's head) to lose one's head, go crazy, be off one's rocker *Mex, DR, ES, Sp* ◆ *¿Qué le pasa a Tito? ¿Perdió la chaveta? Lo vi salir de su casa con un vestido rosado. What's wrong with Tito? Did he go off his rocker? I saw him leaving his house with a pink dress on.*

perder los estribos (to lose the stirrups) to lose patience, lose your cool *L. Am., Sp* ◆ *Si no dejas de molestar, voy a perder los estribos. If you don't stop bugging me, I'm going to lose my cool.*

perderse: ¡No se puede perder! You can't miss it (get lost)! *L. Am., Sp* ◆ *Sigue derecho tres cuadras y ahí está. ¡No se puede perder! Go straight for three blocks and there it is. You can't miss it!*

el/la **perdonavidas** (forgiver or pardoner of lives) bully *L. Am., Sp* ◆ *Pepito es el perdonavidas de la escuela. Pepito is the school bully.*

de **perillas** (of little pears) timely or opportune (often used with **venir** or **caer**) *S. Cone, Sp* ◆ *Ese libro me vino de perillas. That book came to me at a very good time.* ◆ *El dinero me cae de perillas. The money is really opportune.*

perita →**no ser perita en dulce**

ser una **perla** (to be a pearl) to be perfect, good, a gem or jewel *ES, Sp* ◆ *Esta chica es una perla; cocina muy bien. This girl is a jewel; she cooks very well.*

perlas →**echar perlas a los puercos**

de **perlas** (of pearls) perfectly, at a good time, great; often used with **caer** or **venir** *most of L. Am., Sp* ◆ *Este dinero me vino de perlas. This money came to me at a great time.* ◆ *Esa blusa te cae de perlas. That blouse suits you to a "T."*

con **permiso** excuse me (for interrupting, stepping ahead, etc.) *L. Am., Sp* ◆ *Con permiso, necesito pasar por delante. Excuse me. I have to go ahead (move forward).*

pero →**No hay pero que valga.**

Pero bendito... (But blessed one . . .) But please . . . *PR, Col* ◆ *¡Pero bendito! Déjame ir contigo. But please! Let me go with you.*

la **perra 1.** (female dog) bitchy woman *Chicano, G, Col, Sp* ◆ *Dicen que su novia es una perra. They say his girlfriend is a bitch.* **2.** (female dog) ten-cent coin *Sp* ◆ *No tiene ni una perra. He (She) doesn't have a dime.*

el **perrillo de todas bodas** (little dog of all weddings) gadabout, person who likes to be at all social events and parties *Mex, Sp* (RVAR *Mex*, also, **mole de todas bodas**) ◆ *Rodrigo es un perrillo de todas bodas. Lo veo por todas partes. Rodrigo is a gadabout. I see him everywhere.*

perro →**como perro en canoa; como perros y gatos; echar (lanzar) los perros; irle a alguien como los perros en misa**

perro(-a) (dog) rotten, mean, a bitch, a bitch of (plus noun), exaggerated, tremendous, difficult *Mex, Cuba, G, ES, Col* ◆ *Este trabajo está perro. This job is a bitch.* ◆ *Recibí una noticia perra. I got a lousy piece of news.* ◆ *¡Qué perra vida! What a dog's life!*

de **perros** (of dogs) very disagreeable, a bitch of (plus noun) *Mex, ES, Sp* ◆ *¡Qué tiempo de perros! What crummy weather!* ◆ *Hoy estoy de un humor de perros. Today I'm in a bitch of a mood.*

los **perros** (dogs) cops, police *Chicano, Mex, PR, ES, Col* ◆ *Cuando venía para la casa, me siguieron los perros. When I was coming home, the cops followed me.*

pesado(-a) →**más pesado(-a) que cargar un elefante**

ser **pesado(-a)** (to be weighty) to be a pain, a drag, boring, or unpleasant *L. Am., Sp* ◆ *La visita a los Magallanes fue muy pesada. Sólo hablaron de sus riquezas y sus hijos* *maravillosos. The visit with the Magallanes was a drag. All they talked about was their wealth and their marvelous kids.* ◆ *No lo invites a la fiesta; es un pesado. Don't invite him to the party; he's a bore.*

el **pésame** →dar el pésame

a **pesar de los pesares** (in spite of the sorrows) in spite of everything *L. Am., Sp* ◆ *A pesar de los pesares, todavía tenemos esperanza. In spite of everything, we still have hope.*

pescar (un marido, etc.) (to fish) to catch or trap (a husband, etc.) *L. Am., Sp* ◆ *Hace tiempo que Rosalía asiste a las reuniones sólo para pescar un marido. Rosalía has been coming to get-togethers for some time now just in order to catch a husband.*

pescar en río revuelto (to fish in a turbulent river) to get while the getting is good, make hay while the sun shines, take advantage of confusion or disorder and profit from it *Mex, DR, Sp* ◆ *Este partido político ha pescado en río revuelto. Si no hubiera sido por los atentados, no hubiera ganado las elecciones. That political party made hay while the sun shone. If it hadn't been for the attacks, they wouldn't have won the elections.*

pescar un resfriado to catch (literally, fish for) a cold (also, **resfrío**) *Mex, G, Ch, U, Sp* ◆ *Frederico se pescó un resfrío terrible. Frederico caught a terrible cold.*

pese a quien pese (weigh whatever it may weigh) at whatever (the) cost, no matter what *L. Am., Sp* ◆ *Pese a quien pese, pidieron una investigación. At whatever the cost, they requested an investigation.*

un **peso** →sacarse/quitarse un peso de encima

una **pestaña (pestañeada)** →echar una pestaña (pestañeada)

ser un **petardo** (to be a detonator, firecracker) to be of bad quality, boring, or ugly *Sp* ◆ *Esa película (Esa chica) es un petardo. That movie (That babe) is a dud.*

petizo(-a) short, small *S. Cone* ◆ *Alex es el único petizo de su familia. Alex is the only short one in his family.*

pez →estar como pez en el agua

el **pez gordo** (fat fish) big shot, big cheese, honcho *L. Am., Sp* ◆ *Ese señor es un pez*

gordo en el gobierno. That gentleman is a big shot in the government.

el/la **pibe(-a)** kid, young person *Col, Ven, U, Arg* ◆ *Ese pibe juega muy bien al fútbol. That kid plays soccer well.*

Pica, lica y califica. (Poke, look, and judge.) Look before you leap (examine something before you buy it, or think carefully before deciding on something or someone). *Mex, Col* ◆ *No compres la primera casa que veas. Pica, lica y califica. Don't buy the first house you see. Look before you leap.*

las **picadas** (pickings) munchies, appetizers *Arg* ◆ *Elisa preparó picadas exquisitas. Elisa prepared exquisite appetizers.*

picado(-a) **1.** (piqued, stung) annoyed, resentful *Mex, G, CR, Col, Ven, Bol, Ch, Sp* ◆ *El perro no te obedece y ya estás picado. (CR) The dog won't obey you and now you're annoyed.* **2.** (piqued, stung) caught up with, enthusiastic or curious *Mex, parts of C. Am.* ◆ *Fue tan bueno el partido que todos estábamos picados viéndolo. (Mex) The game was so good that we all got carried away watching it.*

picado(-a) de la curiosidad burning (literally, "itching") with curiosity *L. Am., Sp* ◆ *Tienes que decirme qué pasó porque me dejaste picada de la curiosidad. You have to tell me what happened because you left me burning with curiosity.*

el **picaflor** (hummingbird) playboy *Nic, CR, Col, Ch, Arg* ◆ *José Manuel es un picaflor; todas las semanas sale con una mujer diferente. José Manuel is a playboy; each week he goes out with a different woman.*

picante (spicy) tacky, low-class, in bad taste *Mex, DR, Peru, Ch* (RVAr *Peru:* also, ill-mannered person) ◆ *Octavio me mandó un chiste picante. Octavio sent me a joke that was in bad taste.*

picar a alguien (to bite, sting someone) to upset someone *Mex, DR, PR, G, Peru, Sp* ◆ *¿Qué le picó a ese muchacho? What's got into that boy?* ◆ *¿Qué te pica? What's bugging you?*

picarle (to poke at it) to step on it, get a move on *Mex, ES, Col* ◆ *¡Pícale! Hay que picarle duro para que terminemos ligero. Hurry up! We have to get a move on so we can finish quickly.*

picarle a alguien una mosca (to have a fly biting or stinging someone) to be bothered, have something be the matter *L. Am., Sp* ◆ *¿Qué mosca te ha (habrá) picado? What could have been the matter?* ◆ *El niño hizo una pataleta. The boy had a tantrum.*

picarse 1. (to become piqued) to get angry, be annoyed *PR, Col, Ch, Sp* ◆ *No te piques, que no es para tanto. Don't get steamed up because it's not a big deal.* 2. (to become piqued) to get drunk *Mex, PR, G, Nic* ◆ *Toma sólo una cerveza; no te piques con más. (Mex) Drink just one beer; don't go getting blasted by drinking more.* 3. (to become piqued) to get caught up with; be interested, enthusiastic, or curious *Mex* ◆ *Nos picamos con tu plática tan interesante. We got caught up with your talk because it was so interesting.* ◆ *Estaba tan rica la sopa que nos picamos comiendo más y más. The soup was so tasty that we got carried away and ate more and more of it.*

la **pichicata** shot, may imply heroin or illegal drug *S. Cone* ◆ *Le dieron una pichicata. They gave him (her) a shot.*

pichicato(-a) (from the Italian "pizzicato," pinch) stingy *Mex, Nic* ◆ *Es tacaño el señor, bien pichicato. The man is stingy, a real penny-pincher.*

el/la **pichiruche** unimportant person who fusses about small details, lower civil servant; Peru, also: useless thing or person *Nic, Peru, S. Cone* ◆ *Ese tipo es un pichiruche del gobierno; no tiene ni voz ni voto. That guy works in the low level of the government; he has no say.* ◆ *Es un pichiruche; no tiene valor. It's nothing; it's useless.*

mi **pichón** (my pigeon; *Mex:* **pichoncito**) my turtledove, love *parts of L. Am.* ◆ *Ay, mi pichoncito dorado. —Oh, no seas cursi. Ah, my darling little turtledove. —Oh, don't be corny.*

el **pico** 1. (beak) mouth, kisser *L. Am., Sp* ◆ *Al principio, nadie abrió el pico. At first, no one opened his mouth.* 2. (beak) kiss *most of L. Am., Sp* ◆ *Gloria me dio un pico en la boca. Gloria gave me a peck (kiss) on the mouth.* 3. (beak) male organ (vulgar) *G, ES, CR, Ch*

un **pico** ➞**tener un pico de oro**

picones ➞**dar picones**

picudo(-a) sharp as a tack, well connected and clever *Mex, ES* ◆ *Juan es muy picudo, por eso le promovieron. Juan is very well connected and clever; that's why they promoted him.*

un **pie** ➞**echar un pie; ir a pie; meter el pie; no dar pie con bola; no dejar a alguien sentar el pie en el suelo; poner pies en polvorosa; sacar con los pies adelante**

al **pie de la letra** (to the foot of the letter) just so, exactly, to the letter *L. Am., Sp* ◆ *Vamos a hacer todo al pie de la letra. We're going to do everything just so.*

estar al **pie del cañón** (to be at the foot of the cannon) to be always at one's post, ready and waiting, on one's toes *Mex, ES, S. Cone, Sp* ◆ *Si necesitas algo, llámame. Aquí estaré al pie del cañón. If you need something, call me. I'll be here ready and waiting.*

con el **pie derecho** (with the right foot) in the right way, well *L. Am., Sp* ◆ *Queremos empezar con el pie derecho. We want to start off on the right foot.*

estar con un (el) **pie en el estribo** 1. (to have one [the] foot in the stirrup) to be ready to die *Mex, ES, Ch, Arg, Sp* ◆ *Ese pobre señor tiene un pie en el estribo. That poor man is on his way out (ready to die).* 2. (to have one [the] foot in the stirrup) to be on the way out, ready to take a trip *Mex, ES, S. Cone, Sp* ◆ *Te volveré a llamar, tía; ahorita estoy con un pie en el estribo. I'll call you back (Aunt); right now I'm going out the door.*

con un **pie en el hoyo** (with one foot in the hole) with one foot in the grave, near death *Mex, DR, PR, Sp* ◆ *Pobrecito don Danilo anda con un pie en el hoyo. —Bueno, pero ya tiene noventa y siete años. Poor old Don Danilo has one foot in the grave. —Well, right, but he's ninety-seven years old.*

con un **pie en el otro mundo** (with one foot in the other world) with one foot in the grave, near death *Sp* ◆ *Su padre está con un pie en el otro mundo; sin embargo sigue dando órdenes. His father has one foot in the grave; however, he's still giving orders.*

piedra ➞**hasta las piedras; no dejar piedra sobre piedra; no ser de piedra**

la **piel** ➞**sacarle la piel a tiras**

estar con un pie en el estribo: Saldrá pronto. Está con un pie en el estribo.
He'll leave soon. He's on his way out.

ser la **piel del diablo** (to be the devil's skin) to be very mischievous, a little dickens *most of L. Am., Sp* ◆ *No descuides a ese niño; es la piel del diablo. Don't let that boy out of your sight; he's a little devil.*

¡Piérdete! (Lose yourself!) Go away! Get lost! Scram! *Sp*

piernón →**¡Qué piernón!**

de (los) **pies a (la) cabeza** (from [the] feet to [the] head) from head to toe, entirely *L. Am., Sp* ◆ *Estaba vestida de negro de los pies a la cabeza. She was dressed in black from head to foot.*

Pies, ¿para qué os quiero? (Feet, why do I love you?) said when one is about to flee from danger *Mex, S. Cone, Sp* (RVAR *Mex, S. Cone:* **Patitas, ¿pa' qué te [las] quiero?**) ◆ *Empezó el incendio y Juan salió ¿patitas pa' qué te quiero? The fire started and Juan got the heck out of there.*

la **pija** male organ (vulgar) *Hond, Nic, U, Arg*

las **pilas** →**ponerse las pilas; tener bien puestas las pilas, estar con las pilas puestas**

pillar (to plunder) to catch, get *Mex, Col, Ch, Sp* ◆ *En el super pillaron a un ratero. They caught a shoplifter in the supermarket.*

pillo(-a) sharp, on the ball, clever *Mex, Hond, CR, Col, Peru, S. Cone, Sp* ◆ *Esta chica es muy pilla y a todos cae muy simpática. This girl is very clever and everyone thinks she's really nice.*

un **pimpollo** →**estar hecho(-a) un pimpollo**

a **pincel** (by paintbrush) on foot, walking (like **a pata**) *Mex, Hond, Nic, CR* ◆ *A pincel, llegamos hasta la universidad. Walking, we made it to the university.*

la **pincelada** →**dar la última pincelada**

los **pinceles** (paintbrushes) feet, tootsies *Mex, ES* ◆ *¿Cómo viniste? —A puros pinceles. (A pincel.) How did you come? — On foot.*

pinchar →**ni pinchar ni cortar**

pinche blasted, damn *Mex* ◆ *La pinche máquina no funciona. The blasted machine isn't working.*

el **pinche buey** (damn) jerk, loser *Mex* ◆ *¡No me digas que ese pinche buey es el hermano de Miguel! Don't tell me that damn jerk is Miguel's brother!*

pinche cabrón rotten bastard (vulgar) *Mex* ◆ *¡Pinche cabrón! ¿Por qué me robaste la cartera? You rotten bastard! Why did you steal my wallet?*

la **pinga** male organ (vulgar) *Cuba, DR, PR, G, CR, Col*

de **pinga, de pinguísima** (of the male organ) damn fantastic, great, exciting (vulgar) *DR, Ven* ◆ *Lo pasamos de pinga. We had a damn good time.* ◆ *Esos pantalones te quedan de pinga. Those pants fit great.*

pinole →**hecho(-a) pinole**

de **pinta** →**irse de pinta; por la (su) pinta; tener pinta (de)**

pintar →**no pintar nada**

pintar monos (to paint monkeys) to show off, call attention to oneself *Ch* ◆ *Allí está tu amigo Esteban, pintando monos como siempre. There's your friend Esteban, acting out like usual.*

pintar su calaverita (to paint one's little skull) to take off, disappear *Mex* ◆ *Luis pintó su calaverita y no lo vimos más. Luis took off and we never saw him again.*

pintarlo (de) color de rosa (to paint it pink) to make it sound and look great, gild the lily *Mex, DR, PR, ES, Col, Ch, U, Sp* ◆ *Sara todo lo pinta color de rosa; nunca habla de los problemas que tienen. Sara really gilds the lily about how everything is going; she never talks about the problems they have.*

pintarse (to paint yourself) to take off, go away, leave *Mex, ES, CR* ◆ *Se pintó de colores. (Mex) He (She) got out of there like a house on fire.*

pintarse solo(-a) (to paint oneself alone) to take the cake *Mex, U* (see illustration, page 427) ◆ *Te pintas sola, m'hija. You're really something (my daughter).*

pintarse solo(-a) para una cosa (to paint oneself alone for something) to be very apt or skillful at something *Mex, U, Arg, Sp* ◆ *Mi hija se pinta sola en la cocina. For my daughter, cooking is right up her alley.* ◆ *Mi esposo se pinta solo tocando el piano. My husband is outstanding at playing piano.*

pintárselo bonito to gild the lily, present a pretty picture or make things look good (usually better than they really are) *Mex, DR, PR, ES, Col* ◆ *Tengo que pintárselo bonito para que salga conmigo. I have to present a pretty picture so he (she) will go out with me.*

Píntate (de colores). (Paint yourself [in color].) Go away. Get lost. *Mex, ES* ◆ *No quiero verte más. Píntate de colores. I don't want to see you anymore. Make like the wind and blow.*

en **pintura** →**no poder ver a alguien ni en pintura**

con **pinzas** →**No se lo sacarán ni con pinzas.**

la **piña** (pineapple) clique, select group, two or more people who act as one *Cuba, CR, Sp* ◆ *Tengo un problema en el trabajo. Se formaron piñas allí. I have a problem at work. There are cliques there.* ◆ *Los trabajadores hicieron piña para exigir sus derechos. The workers got together in a group to demand their rights.* ◆ *Están hechos una piña. They've become very close (formed a pair or group).*

pío →**no decir ni pío**

de **pipa y guante** (with pipe and glove) all dressed up, dressed to the nines *Chicano, Mex* ◆ *Me sugirió que viniera de pipa y guante a la fiesta. He (She) suggested that I come all dressed up to the party.*

pipas →**no tener ni para pipas**

pipiris nais highfalutin, chic (**nais** is from the English "nice") *Mex, ES* ◆ *A esa no la invites; se cree pipiris nais. Don't invite her (that one); she's thinks she's highfalutin.*

el **piquete** shot of alcohol put in coffee *Mex, ES* ◆ *Prepárame, por favor, un café con piquete. Please make me a coffee with a shot of alcohol.*

estar **pirado(-a)** to be off one's rocker, crazy *Sp* ◆ *Este tío está pirado. Quería saltar de un balcón a otro sin utilizar una escalera como hacen todos los empleados que mantienen la red telefónica. This guy is off his rocker. He wanted to jump from one balcony to another without using a ladder like* *all the other employees who maintain the phone lines.*

el/la **piraña** (piranha) shark; astute in business, taking advantage of others *ES, CR, Col* RVAR *Mex: vulture, chowhound)* ◆ *No le compres a ése, que es muy piraña. Don't buy from him; he's a shark.*

pirar to take off, disappear (probably from **pira**, funeral pyre) *Mex* ◆ *Pablo piró cuando oyó que los papás de Adela habían llegado. Pablo took off when he heard that Adela's parents had arrived.*

pirarse to take off, leave, go away, beat it *Cuba, Arg, Sp* ◆ *Se piraron cuando vino la policía. They took off when the police came.*

estar **piripi** to be drunk *Sp* ◆ *Después de beber tanto, estaban todos piripis. After drinking so much, they were all drunk.*

el **piro** →darse el piro

piropear to compliment *L. Am., Sp* ◆ *En España y América Latina los hombres piropean a las mujeres más a menudo. In Spain and Latin America men compliment women more frequently.*

pisado(-a), pisa'o(-a) (stepped on) dominated *DR* ◆ *La mujer de Ernesto lo tiene pisa'o. Ella es la que manda en esa casa. Ernesto's wife has him under her thumb. She's the one who rules in that house.*

pisar (to step on) to have sex (vulgar) *Mex, Cuba, G, ES, Nic, CR* ◆ *Sólo piso cuando encuentro alguna mujer especial. I only have sex when I find a special woman.*

pisarle los callos a alguien (to step on someone's callouses) to bother someone without rhyme or reason, be all over someone *ES, Peru, Ch* ◆ *Mi suegra siempre me está pisando los callos; no me deja en paz. My mother-in-law is always all over me; she doesn't leave me alone.*

Pisémonos. (Let's step on ourselves.) Let's beat it. *Col, Ec*

el **pisto** dough, money *G, ES, Nic, CR* ◆ *Martina necesita pisto para comprar zapatos. Martina needs money to buy shoes.*

el **pitillo** 1. joint, marijuana cigarette *Mex, G, Col* ◆ *Fernando me ofreció un pitillo, pero no lo quería. Fernando offered me a joint, but I didn't want it.* 2. coffin nail, cigarette *Ch,*

U, Arg, Sp ◆ *Fumo sólo dos pitillos por día. I smoke only two cigarettes a day.*

pito →por pitos o por flautas; que si pito que si flauta

el **pito** 1. (whistle, fife) joint (marijuana) *Mex, Cuba, G, Nic, Ch* ◆ *Salió y fumó un pito. He went out and smoked a joint.* 2. (whistle, fife) male organ (vulgar) *Mex, Cuba, G, ES, CR, U, Arg, Sp*

la **pitopausia** male menopause *Mex, Sp* ◆ *Creo que Eduardo tiene síntomas de la pitopausia; ya está volviéndose viejo. I think Eduardo has symptoms of male menopause; he's already getting old.*

pituco(-a) affected, snobbish *S. Cone* (RVAR *Peru: wealthy)* ◆ *A ese club solamente van los pitucos de la ciudad. Only the snobbish people in the city go to that club.*

pizca →ni pizca de

planchar la oreja (to iron one's ear) to get some shut-eye, sleep *Mex, PR, CR, Col, Ven, Ec, Sp* (see illustration, page 310) ◆ *Tan pronto como termine este informe, plancharé la oreja. As soon as I finish this report, I'll get some shut-eye.*

de **plano** (flatly) for sure *Mex, C. Am.* ◆ *De plano que sí. De plano que voy. Absolutely yes. I'm going for sure.*

plantar cara a alguien (to plant one's face at someone) to stand up to, make a stand against, or resist someone *DR, PR, Sp* ◆ *La señora mayor logró plantar cara al carterista de manera que no le robó el bolso. The older woman managed to stand up to the pickpocket so that he did not steal her purse.*

estar de **plantón** (to be planted) to be stuck somewhere for a while, stood up *Mex, ES, Ch, U, Sp* ◆ *Estuve de plantón por dos horas en la biblioteca esperando a Eva y Natalia. I was stuck for two hours in the library waiting for Eva and Natalia.*

un **plantón** →dar (un) plantón

plástico(-a) (plastic) hypocritical, shallow, or superficial; sometimes used as **hijo de papi** *DR, PR, G, Col, Ch* ◆ *Raquel es una plástica. Lo único que le interesa es la ropa, los carros y el dinero. Raquel is very shallow. The only things that interest her are clothing, cars, and money.* ◆ *Es una persona plástica. She's an airhead.*

la **plata** (silver) dough, money *L. Am.* ♦ *¿Tienes plata para prestarme?* *Do you have money to lend me?*

el **platal** fortune, a lot of money (**plata**), big bucks *ES, CR, Col* ♦ *Aquella casa costó un platal.* *That house cost big bucks.*

plátano ➜**no comer plátano por no tirar la cáscara**

ser **plato** ➜**(no) ser plato del gusto de alguien**

ser un **plato** (to be a dish) to be funny, amusing, a real character *S. Cone* ♦ *Ese tipo es un plato.* *That guy is a real character.*

un **plato** ➜**no haber roto un plato**

ser **plato de segunda mesa** (to be a plate of a second table) to be or feel put off or not treated with consideration, be a second-class citizen, play second fiddle *Mex, DR, PR, ES, Sp* (RVAR *Mex:* used mainly for women who are with married men) ♦ *Yo no soy plato de segunda mesa.* *I am not a second-class citizen. (I don't play second fiddle to anyone.)*

platudo(-a) moneybags, rich *L. Am.* ♦ *Doña Catalina era platuda e hizo muchas obras de beneficencia en la ciudad.* *Doña Catalina was rich and did many good works in the city.*

a **plazos** in installments *L. Am., Sp* ♦ *Tuvimos que pagar la videocasetera a plazos.* *We had to pay for the VCR in installments.*

en **plena forma** (in full form) in good shape, fit as a fiddle *L. Am., Sp* ♦ *Mi abuelo está en plena forma aunque tiene sus setenta años.* *My grandfather is in good shape although he's seventy years old.*

en **pleno día** (in full day) in broad daylight *L. Am., Sp* ♦ *Me robaron la cartera en pleno día.* *They stole my wallet in broad daylight.*

en **pleno vuelo** (in full flight) high on drugs or alcohol *Mex, Col, Ec* ♦ *El muchacho estaba en pleno vuelo cuando llegó al colegio.* *The boy was flying high when he got to school.*

pleno(-a) (full, complete) good, great, good-looking; also, high on drugs *Col, Ec, Para* ♦ *Se siente bien pleno.* *He feels great.*

el **plomazo** (hit with lead) lead balloon, a drag (dull, boring thing or person) *DR, U, Arg* ♦ *Eres un plomazo; déjame tranquila.* *You're a drag; leave me alone.*

ser un **plomo** (to be lead) to be boring *DR, PR, S. Cone, Sp* ♦ *Ese tipo es un plomo. Siempre cuenta las mismas historias.* *That guy is a real bore. He always tells the same stories.*

de un **plumazo** with the stroke of a pen (**pluma**), quickly *L. Am., Sp* ♦ *De un plumazo dio las órdenes a los secretarios.* *Quickly he (she) gave the orders to the secretaries.*

po' short for **pues**, added at end of phrases *Ch* ♦ *Sí, po'. Right you are.* ♦ *Ya po'. All right already.*

las **poblaciones callampas** (mushroom populations) slums *Ch* ♦ *Las poblaciones callampas alrededor de la capital han aumentado en los últimos años.* *The slums surrounding the capital have increased in the last few years.*

pobre como una rata poor as a (church)mouse *Mex, ES, Pan, S. Cone, Sp* (RVAR *Sp:* also, **más pobre que las ratas;** *Pan:* **más pobre que una rata**) ♦ *En esta zona viven personas que son más pobres que las ratas.* *The people who live in this area are poor as churchmice.*

Pobre pero caballero. Poor but dignified (a gentleman). *L. Am.* ♦ *Me ha tocado la lotería con Casimiro: pobre pero caballero.* *I won the lottery with Casimiro: he's not rich, but he's a gentleman.*

¡Pobrecito(-a)! Poor (little) thing! *L. Am., Sp* ♦ *Pobrecita la niña. Está muy enferma.* *The poor little girl. She is very sick.*

ser de **pocas pulgas** (to be of few fleas) to be bad-tempered, have a short fuse *Mex, ES, CR, Col, U, Arg* (RVAR *U, Arg:* also, **tener pocas pulgas;** *Sp:* **tener malas pulgas**) ♦ *La secretaria es de muy pocas pulgas y se enoja por cualquier cosa.* *The secretary has a short fuse and gets angry over any little thing.*

el/la **pocho(-a)** someone of Mexican descent, usually those living in the United States (from the Ópata Indian **potzico**, to cut or pull up grass; the Sonoran community called those who left **pochis**, uprooted grass; can be slightly pejorative) *Chicano, Mex, ES* ♦ *No habla bien el español; es pocho. He doesn't speak Spanish well; he's of Mexican descent (but not born in Mexico).*

poco ➜**por poco**

Un **poco de respeto.** (A little respect.) Let's show a little respect; polite way of criticizing someone *L. Am., Sp* ◆ *Un poco de respeto, señor. No me grite. Show some respect, sir. Don't shout at me.*

poco espléndido(-a) (not very splendid) tightfisted, stingy *DR, ES, Ven, Sp* ◆ *Debes llevarla a un restaurante de mejor calidad; eres poco espléndido. You should take her to a better-quality restaurant; you're tightfisted.*

a **poco que se descuide** if one isn't careful *L. Am., Sp* ◆ *Al hornear estas galletas hay que tener cuidado. A poco que se descuide, se queman. When you bake these cookies you have to be careful. If you're not careful, they burn.*

al **poco rato** in a little while *L. Am., Sp* ◆ *Se fue enojado, pero al poco rato regresó ya tranquilo. He left angry, but in a little while he came back calmed down.*

a **pocos pasos** (at a few steps) right at hand, close by; without much effort *Mex, S. Cone, Sp* ◆ *A pocos pasos encontramos la solución del problema. We found the solution to the problem close at hand.*

poder ➝hasta más no poder; no poder más

Poderoso caballero es don Dinero. (A powerful gentleman is Sir Money.) Money talks. *L. Am., Sp* ◆ *Por supuesto que ganaron las elecciones. Poderoso caballero es don Dinero. Of course they won the election. Money talks.*

estar **podrido(-a) de dinero** (to be rotten with money) to be filthy rich *Mex, DR, ES, CR, U, Arg, Sp* ◆ *Están podridos de dinero y no saben disfrutarlo. They're filthy rich and they don't know how to enjoy it (their money).*

la **polilla** ➝sacarse la polilla

la **polilla de biblioteca** (library moth) bookworm *most of L. Am., Sp* ◆ *Todo el mundo la considera polilla de biblioteca porque se mantiene allí día y noche, estudiando. Everyone considers her to be a bookworm because she's there in the library day and night, studying.*

la **poli** policemen, coppers *Sp* ◆ *La poli los persiguió hasta dar con ellos en una casa escondida. The police chased them until they found them in a hidden-away house.*

la **polla** (young female chicken, pullet) male organ (vulgar) *Sp*

ser la **polla** (to be the male organ) to be too damn much, unheard of, extraordinary (people or things) (vulgar) *Sp* ◆ *Esta canción es la polla. This song is damn fantastic.*

un **pollo** ➝echarse un pollo

el/la **pololo(-a)** (bumblebee) sweetheart, steady boyfriend (girlfriend) *Ch* ◆ *¿De dónde es el pololo de tu hija? Where is your daughter's sweetheart from?*

un **polvo** ➝echar(se) un polvo; hacer morder el polvo a alguien; hacer polvo a alguien o algo; hecho(-a) polvo

el **polvo blanco (polvo de ángel)** (white powder [angel dust]) cocaine *Sp* ◆ *Les vendió dos gramos de polvo blanco. He (She) sold them two grams of cocaine.*

las **pompis** rear end, derriere *Mex, Col, Ven, Ec, Sp* (RVar *Mex:* also, **pompas**) ◆ *Juan tiene buenas pompis. Juan has a nice derriere.*

pon ➝dar (pedir) pon

Pon los pies sobre la tierra. (Put your feet on the ground.) Come down to earth; said to someone who is too proud or too idealistic *Mex, DR, ES, S. Cone, Sp* ◆ *Pon los pies sobre la tierra, Antonia; tienes que trabajar si quieres viajar. Come down to earth, Antonia; you have to work if you want to travel.*

ponchar to flunk (an exam) *Mex, Cuba, DR, G* (RVar *Mex, C. Am.:* also, to puncture, as a tire) ◆ *El maestro me ponchó en el examen con un 4 de calificación. The teacher failed me on the test with a grade of D (4 in the usual Hispanic system). ◆ Ponché el examen. I failed the exam. ◆ Me poncharon en biología. They flunked me in biology.*

poner a alguien (quedar) como palo de gallinero (to make someone [end up] like a perch in a chicken coop, i.e., covered with droppings) to ream out, rip apart with insults *Mex, Ch, U* ◆ *El padre de Esteban lo puso como palo de gallinero cuando supo que chocó el coche. Esteban's father ripped him to shreds when he found out he crashed the car.*

poner a alguien a cien (to put someone to the hundred) to excite or exasperate someone *Sp* ◆ *Tus comentarios lograron ponerlo* *a cien. Creo que no te va a hablar más. Your comments brought him to the point of no return. I don't think he'll speak to you anymore.*

poner a alguien como lazo de cochino/percha de perico (to make someone like a pig's rope/parakeet's perch) to ream out, rip apart with insults *Mex* ◆ *Fernando me puso como lazo de cochino. No quiero volver a verlo. Fernando ripped me apart with insults. I never want to see him again.*

poner a alguien como un trapo (viejo) (to make someone like a rag [like an old rag]) to chew someone out, bawl someone out with offensive and angry words *Mex, PR, U, Arg, Sp* (RVar *U, Arg:* **dejar** instead of **poner**) ◆ *Me insultó y me dejó como un trapo, sin ningún motivo. He (She) insulted me and chewed me out, for no reason.*

poner a alguien de vuelta y media (to put someone to a turn and a half) to chew someone out, treat someone badly, heap insults on him or her *DR, Ch, Sp* ◆ *Mira este lío. Cuando venga mamá, te va a poner de vuelta y media. Look at this mess. When Mom comes, she's going to chew you out.*

poner a alguien en su sitio (lugar) to put someone in his or her place *L. Am., Sp* ◆ *Mi novio quería controlarme y prohibirme salir con mis amigas. Al final, lo puse en su lugar. My boyfriend wanted to control me and prevent me from going out with my girlfriends. In the end, I put him in his place.*

poner a alguien los nervios de punta (to make someone's nerves stand up) to put someone's nerves on edge *L. Am., Sp* ◆ *El mensaje me puso los nervios de punta. The message put my nerves on edge.*

poner a alguien los pelos de punta to make someone's hair stand on end, give him or her the creeps (from fear) *L. Am., Sp* (RVar *Sp:* also, **parar los pelos de punta**) ◆ *Jorge me contó lo que le había pasado y se me pusieron los pelos de punta. Jorge told me what had happened to him and it made my hair stand on end.*

poner a caldo (to put to broth, perhaps implying someone is being scalded) to chew out, criticize, rake over the coals *Sp* ◆ *Sus adversarios políticos lo pusieron a caldo una vez que acabó su turno en el parla-*

mento. His political enemies raked him over the coals once he finished his term in parliament.

poner a prueba to put to the test *L. Am., Sp* ◆ *Pongamos a prueba el nuevo plan y veremos. Let's put the new plan to the test and we shall see.*

poner a raya (to put a stripe, line) to put in his or her place, draw the line when someone is trying to take advantage *Mex, Ch, Sp* ◆ *Me presionaba mucho, pero por fin lo puse a raya. He (She) was pressuring me a lot, but I finally drew the line.*

poner al corriente de (to put at the running total of) to bring up to date on *L. Am., Sp* ◆ *Tú siempre me pones al corriente de lo que pasa en este pueblo. You always bring me up to date on what happens in this town.*

poner como camote a alguien (to make someone like a sweet potato [purple and swollen]) to give someone his or her due (dressing down, beating) *Mex, ES* ◆ *Si me sigues provocando, te voy a poner como camote. If you keep provoking me, I'm going to beat you to a pulp.*

poner como dado (to put like a die—from a pair of dice—square and with spots) to scold, chew out, beat up *Mex* ◆ *Mi papá me puso como dado cuando reprobé el año. My dad made mincemeat out of me when I flunked out (failed the school year).*

poner de patitas en la calle (to put to the street on little paws) to throw (someone) out *L. Am., Sp* ◆ *Estaba muy borracho y se portó tan mal que lo pusieron de patitas en la calle. He was very drunk and behaved so badly that they threw him out.*

poner el cascabel al gato (to bell the cat) to do something difficult or dangerous *L. Am., Sp* ◆ *¿Quién le pone el cascabel al gato y le dice a la profesora que no terminaremos el proyecto hoy? Who's going to take the risk and tell the professor that we won't finish the project today?*

poner el grito en el cielo (to put the cry to the heavens) to raise a hue and cry, complain loudly *L. Am., Sp* ◆ *Cuando vea tu madre lo que has hecho en la cocina, va a poner el grito en el cielo. When your mother sees what you've done in the kitchen, she will raise the roof.*

poner el hombro (to put the shoulder) to get down to work, put one's shoulder to the wheel *S. Cone* ◆ *Todos pusimos el hombro para conseguir nuestros propósitos.* We all put our shoulders to the wheel to achieve our goals.

poner en claro to clear up, make clear *L. Am., Sp* ◆ *Una cosa que tenemos que poner en claro es que el roble está en nuestro terreno.* One thing we have to make clear is that the oak tree is on our property.

poner en el cielo a alguien (to put someone in the sky) to praise someone to the skies *Mex, DR, U, Arg, Sp* ◆ *La suegra de Yolanda la pone en el cielo cada vez que habla de ella.* Yolanda's mother-in-law praises her to the skies every time she talks about her.

poner freno a algo (to put the brake on something) to put a stop to something *most of L. Am., Sp* ◆ *Mi hija quería casarse a los diecisiete años, pero yo le puse freno a esa locura.* My daughter wanted to get married at seventeen, but I put a stop to that nonsense.

poner gorro a alguien (to put the cap on someone) to treat someone like a fifth wheel, said of lovers who make out in someone else's presence *Mex, DR* ◆ *No me gusta salir con Rosa y Pepe porque me ponen gorro. Siempre andan besuqueándose.* I don't like to go out with Rosa and Pepe because they treat me like a fifth wheel. They're always smooching.

poner la antena (to put up one's antenna) to prick up one's ears, listen *Mex, Sp* (RVAR *U, Arg:* **parar la antena**) ◆ *Cuando escuché a Álvaro, puse la antena para entender sus argumentos.* When I heard Álvaro, I pricked up my ears to understand his arguments.

poner la mira en to set one's sights on *L. Am., Sp* ◆ *Desde el principio, Gabriel puso su mira en Marilú.* From the first, Gabriel set his sights on Marilú.

poner las cartas sobre la mesa (to put one's cards on the table) to lay things out clearly, put one's cards on the table without concealing anything *L. Am., Sp* ◆ *Le pusimos las cartas sobre la mesa al abogado contrincante.* We put our cards out on the table for the opposition's lawyer.

poner los puntos sobre la mesa (to put one's points on the table) to lay things out clearly *Mex, G* ◆ *Pongamos los puntos sobre la mesa. Creo que hay muchas cosas que ustedes no saben.* Let's put our cards on the table. I think there are a lot of things that you don't know.

poner los puntos sobre las íes to dot the "i"s (and cross the "t"s) *L. Am., Sp* ◆ *Hablé con los estudiantes claramente y les puse los puntos sobre las íes.* I talked clearly to the students and explained things in detail.

poner parejo (to put even) to flatten, beat to a pulp *Mex, ES, Col* ◆ *Déjamelo a mí; yo lo pongo parejo.* Leave him to me; I'll beat him to a pulp.

poner pies en polvorosa (to put one's feet in the dustiness) to hit the trail, run away *L. Am., Sp* ◆ *Los traficantes de drogas pusieron los pies en polvorosa cuando vieron a la policía.* The drug traffickers hit the trail when they saw the police.

poner sobre los cuernos de la luna (to put on the horns of the moon) to praise (someone or something) to the skies *most of L. Am., Sp* ◆ *En la recepción de la oficina, el director puso en los cuernos de la luna a los empleados que se jubilaron este año.* At the office reception, the director praised to the skies the employees who had retired this year.

poner toda la carne en el asador (to put all the meat on the spit) to put all one's eggs in one basket *Mex, Sp* ◆ *En este momento hay que diversificar las inversiones; no se puede poner toda la carne en el asador.* Nowadays you need to diversify your investments; you can't put all your eggs in one basket.

poner un candado a la boca (to put a lock on one's mouth) to keep one's lips sealed, keep a secret or keep quiet *Mex, DR, U, Arg, Sp* ◆ *Ponte un candado a la boca.* Keep your lips sealed.

poner un zíper en la boca to zip up one's mouth, button one's lip, keep quiet *Mex, ES* (RVAR *U:* **poner un cierre**) ◆ *Para que no hables malas palabras, te voy a poner un zíper en la boca.* So you don't say bad words (swear), I'm going to zip up your mouth.

poner una vela a San Miguel (a Dios) y otra al diablo (to light one candle for Saint Michael [for God] and one for the devil) to try to keep one's options open to profit from either of two people or groups *DR, PR, Sp* ◆ *Intentando entrar en esas dos empresas es como poner una vela a San Miguel y otra al diablo. Ya sabes que no es posible.* Trying to get into those two companies is keeping your options too open. You know it's not possible.

poner verde (to make green) to chew out, heap insults or censure (on someone) *Mex, Sp* ◆ *Estaba muy enojada con él y lo puso verde.* She was very angry with him and called him every name under the sun.

ponerle algo en (una) charola de plata (to put something on a silver platter for someone) to give someone something on a silver platter, give them a great opportunity *Mex, ES, Bol, S. Cone* (RVar *S. Cone*: **en bandeja de plata**) ◆ *A Rogelio le puso en bandeja de plata una propuesta de trabajo en el exterior.* They gave Rogelio an offer for international work on a silver platter.

ponerle los cachos a alguien (to put the horns on someone) to cheat on, be unfaithful to someone (a significant other) *C. Am., Col, Ec* ◆ *Tu vecina le pone los cachos a su marido.* Your neighbor is cheating on her husband.

ponerle los cuernos a alguien (to put the horns on someone) to cheat on one's significant other *L. Am., Sp* ◆ *Ese señor le pone los cuernos a su esposa.* That man is cheating on his wife.

ponerles la mosca detrás de las orejas (to put the fly behind their ears) to tell people something with the intent of changing their minds or moving them to action, put a bug in their ears *Sp* ◆ *Nuestro profesor de ciencias políticas nos ponía la mosca detrás de las orejas para desafiarnos a analizar el asunto.* Our political science professor put a bug in our ears to challenge us to analyze the situation.

ponerse a la obra to get to work *L. Am., Sp* ◆ *Amigos, debemos ponernos a la obra cuanto antes.* Friends, we should get down to work as soon as possible.

ponerse águila (to put oneself eagle) to be on the lookout, keep one's eyes peeled *Mex, C. Am.* ◆ *Ponte águila; viene el maestro.* Keep your eyes peeled; the teacher is coming.

ponerse al hilo (en onda) to get with it, become aware *Mex, C. Am., Col* ◆ *Pongámonos al hilo. Let's get with it.*

ponerse al rojo vivo to get red hot (a situation), heat up *Mex, DR, PR, ES, Col* ◆ *La situación se puso al rojo vivo porque el ministro anunció que mandarían tropas a la guerra.* The situation got red hot because the minister announced that they would send troops to the war.

ponerse al tiro (to put oneself to the shot) to face the music (duel), prepare for a fight or struggle *Mex, ES, Col* ◆ *Se puso al tiro para pasar el examen.* He (She) had to face the music and study to pass the exam.

ponerse borde to be rude and crude *Sp* ◆ *Se puso borde en la fiesta y empezó a gritar.* He was very vulgar at the party and began to yell.

ponerse buzo (to become a diver) to be alert (often to avoid something); to be suspicious *Mex, G, ES* ◆ *¡Ponte buzo! Aquí tratan de venderte cualquier cosa.* Be on the alert! Here they try to sell you any old thing.

ponerse como un tomate (to become like a tomato) to turn red as a beet, blush *Mex, DR, PR, S. Cone, Sp* ◆ *Cuando Graciela tuvo que hablar delante de tantas personas, se puso como un tomate.* When Graciela had to talk in front of so many people, she turned red as a beet.

ponerse como una fiera (to become like a wild animal) to get very angry *ES, Ch, U, Sp* ◆ *Se puso como una fiera cuando no lo dejaron hablar con el director de la empresa.* He was furious when they wouldn't let him talk with the director of the company.

ponerse de los nervios (to become of the nerves) to get nervous *ES, Sp* ◆ *Me puse de los nervios cuando vi que aún no había llegado a casa.* I got nervous when I saw that he (she) had still not gotten home.

ponerse (estar) en curda, tener una curda to be (get) drunk *Cuba, U, Arg* ◆ *Siempre está curda. (Cuba)* He's (She's) always bombed (drunk). ◆ *Tiene una curda. (Arg)* He's (She's) bombed (drunk).

ponerse en marcha to get going, get underway *L. Am., Sp* ◆ *Si todos están listos, ¡pongámonos en marcha!* If you're all ready, let's get going!

ponerse hasta el gorro (to put on even the cap) to pig out, eat and drink oneself silly *Mex, Sp* ◆ *Pablo se puso hasta el gorro en la fiesta.* Pablo pigged out to the max at the party. ◆ *Con esta botella de tequila se pusieron hasta el gorro.* With this bottle of tequila they drank themselves silly.

ponerse la cara como un chile (to have the face like a chili pepper) to turn red as a beet, blush *CR, Col* ◆ *Estaba tan avergonzado que se le puso la cara como un chile.* He was so embarrassed his face turned red as a beet.

ponerse las botas (to put on one's boots) to pig out, indulge in something (food, sex, etc.) or partake of it; to feather one's nest, make a killing (financially, sometimes to others' detriment) *Ch, U, Sp* (RVAR *Ch:* second meaning only) ◆ *Me puse las botas en esa cena. Comí de todo.* I really pigged out (indulged myself) at that dinner. I ate some of everything.

ponerse las pilas (to put in one's batteries) to get with it, get going, get a move on *L. Am., Sp* ◆ *Se puso las pilas y logró que la trasladaran a América del Sur.* She got a move on and got her transfer to South America.

ponerse los pantalones (to put on one's pants) to take charge of a situation *DR, PR, S. Cone* ◆ *Finalmente Alcira se puso los pantalones y controló a sus hijos, que no obedecían a nadie.* Finally Alcira took charge of the situation and took control of her kids, who wouldn't obey anybody.

estar o **ponerse mosca** (to be or become fly, an insect with large eyes) to be suspicious and alert to avoid something *Mex, Ven, Peru, Sp* ◆ *Ponte mosca. ¿Ves el dire allí? Hay que estar mosca.* Get with the program! Do you see the director there? You have to be alert.

ponerse trucha (to make oneself trout) to be aware, alert *Mex, ES* ◆ *¡Ponte trucha! Sharpen up! (Pay attention!)*

ponérsele to have a hunch, suppose, think *ES, CR, Ch* ◆ *A Fernando se le puso que iban a cancelar la reunión.* (CR) Fernando had a feeling (suspicion) that they were going to cancel the meeting. ◆ *Se me pone que va a llover ahora.* I think it's going to rain now.

popa →ir viento en popa

popis swanky, high-class (adj.) *Mex, Col* ◆ *Es un hotel popis.* It's a posh hotel.

popoff (popis) posh, upper-class, snooty (sometimes said with gesture of index finger under the nose and moving up) *Mex, DR* ◆ *Ese chico es muy popoff y no me gusta salir con él.* That guy is very snooty and I don't like to go out with him.

a **poquitos** bit by bit *Mex* ◆ *Me dices a poquitos las cosas. Dime, ¿qué pasó?* You're telling me things bit by bit. Tell me, what happened?

Por aquí (trabajando, estudiando). ([I'm] Just here [working, studying].) Nothing new. Same as usual. *L. Am., Sp* ◆ *¿Cómo anda, don Felipe? —Por aquí, visitando a mis hijos.* How are you, Felipe? —Nothing new, visiting my kids.

Por aquí pasó mi suegra. (My mother-in-law passed by here.) expression telling that one is working hard, from the idea of cleaning up *Mex, Col*

Por aquí, vagando. (Just here, wandering.) Just goofing around. *C. Am.* ◆ *¿Cómo están los muchachos? —Por aquí, vagando.* How are the kids? —Just goofing around.

por arte de birlibirloque as if by magic, through extraordinary or unnatural means (also, **...magia**) *DR, PR, Ch, Sp* ◆ *Por arte de birlibirloque y sin saber muy bien cómo, Gabriel nos convenció a todos de su posición.* As if by magic and without really knowing how he did it, Gabriel convinced us all of his point of view.

por chiripa (by a fluke, from a term in billiards) by luck, by chance *DR, Hond, Nic, CR, Col, Ch, Sp* (RVAR *DR, G, ES, Ven, U, Arg:* **de chiripa**) ◆ *Por chiripa encontramos dos entradas para el concierto de esta noche.* By chance we found two tickets for the concert tonight.

por de pronto, por lo pronto meanwhile, provisionally *L. Am., Sp* (RVAR *Ch, Sp:* **por lo pronto** only) ◆ *Vendimos nuestra casa en el campo. Por lo pronto alquilaremos un apartamento en la ciudad.* We sold our house in the country. In the meantime we'll rent an apartment in the city.

por debajo de cuerda (bajo cuerda) (under cord) under the table, through hidden means, on the sly *Mex, S. Cone, Sp*

(RVAR *Arg:* **bajo la cuerda;** *Ch, U:* **bajo cuerda**) ◆ *Josefa no tiene visa; está trabajando por debajo de cuerda. Josefa doesn't have a visa; she is working on the sly.*

por debajo de la mesa (under the table) in a corrupt way *most of L. Am.* ◆ *Todo lo hacen por debajo de la mesa. They do everything under the table.*

por debajo del agua (underwater) under the table *Mex* ◆ *Por debajo del agua di el dinero al policía. I gave the money to the police under the table (on the QT).*

por dentro y por fuera inside and out, through and through *L. Am., Sp* ◆ *Nuestro profe conoce el libro de texto por dentro y por fuera. Our prof knows the textbook inside and out.*

por desgracia (through bad luck) unfortunately *L. Am., Sp* ◆ *Marta no regresará nunca, por desgracia. Marta will never come back again, unfortunately.*

por Dios (for God) for goodness sake, wow *L. Am., Sp* ◆ *¡Por Dios, te ves bien, amigo! Wow, you are looking good, my friend!*

por el contrario on the contrary, however *L. Am., Sp* ◆ *¿Perezoso? Por el contrario, Eduardo es el mejor trabajador del taller. Lazy? On the contrary, Eduardo is the best worker in the shop.*

por el estilo (through the style) like that *L. Am., Sp* ◆ *Dijo algo por el estilo. He (She) said something like that.*

por eso for that reason *L. Am., Sp* ◆ *Margarita es sincera y responsable; por eso confío en ella. Margarita is sincere and responsible; that's why I trust her.*

por excelencia par excellence *L. Am., Sp* ◆ *Armando es un atleta por excelencia. Armando is an athlete par excellence.*

por favorciano pretty please (**por favorciano, mi amorciano**) *Mex* ◆ *Llévame contigo, por favorciano, mi amorciano. Take me with you, pretty please with sugar on it.*

por gusto, de puro gusto for the fun of it, as a whim *L. Am., Sp* ◆ *Por puro gusto me fui a las montañas por tres días. Just for the fun of it, I went to the mountains for three days.*

por hache o por be (by "h" or by "b") for one reason or another *DR, U, Arg, Sp* ◆ *Por hache o por be no conocimos a su novia cuando estuvimos en Córdoba. For one reason or another we didn't meet his girlfriend when we were in Córdoba.*

por la (su) pinta (by the[ir] spot) because of their appearance (e.g., because of some signal or because of family resemblance) *L. Am., Sp* (RVAR *Sp:* also, **sacar a alguien por la pinta**) ◆ *Descubrí que era tu hermano por la pinta. I discovered that he was your brother because of family resemblance.* ◆ *Por su pinta se conoce. You can recognize him (her) by his (her) appearance.*

por la tremenda (by the tremendous) violently or without respect *Sp* ◆ *Impusieron su voluntad por la tremenda, sin respetar la opinión de ninguno de los demás. They imposed their will forcefully, without respecting anyone else's opinion.*

por las buenas o por las malas (for the good or for the bad) one way or another, by force or voluntarily *L. Am., Sp* (RVAR *Pan:* **a la buena o a la mala**) ◆ *Vas a acompañarme al concierto por las buenas o por las malas. You're going with me to the concert whether you want to or not.*

estar **por las nubes** (to be in the clouds) to be sky-high, very expensive *Mex, DR, ES, S. Cone, Sp* ◆ *¡Caramba! La gasolina está por las nubes ahora. Wow! Gasoline prices are sky-high now.*

por lo bajini (bajo) (by the low) in secret, under wraps, on the sly *Sp* ◆ *Se enteró por lo bajini. Y no por ningún conducto oficial. He found out on the sly. Not by any official channel.*

por lo general as a general rule, generally *L. Am., Sp* ◆ *Llegan a las tres, por lo general. They get here at three, as a general rule.*

por lo menos at least *L. Am., Sp* ◆ *Por lo menos dime dónde estabas anoche. At least tell me where you were last night.*

por lo mismo just for that reason, for that very reason *L. Am., Sp* ◆ *Por lo mismo creemos que sería mejor esperar. For that very reason we think it would be better to wait.*

por lo regular as a rule *L. Am., Sp* ◆ *Abuelita no fuma en la casa, por lo regular. Grandma doesn't smoke in the house, as a rule.*

por lo tanto therefore *L. Am., Sp* ◆ *Me dijeron que iban a venir; por lo tanto, debemos esperarlos.* They told me that they were coming; therefore, we should wait for them.

por lo visto (by what is seen) evidently *L. Am., Sp* ◆ *Por lo visto, nuestros vecinos no se llevan bien.* Evidently, our neighbors don't get along very well.

estar **por los suelos** (to be on the floor) to be dirt cheap (things) *ES, Ch, Sp* ◆ *En esa tienda todo está por los suelos ahora.* In that store everything is dirt cheap now.

al **por mayor** wholesale *L. Am., Sp* ◆ *¿Los azulejos? Los compramos al por mayor.* The tiles? We bought them wholesale.

por otra parte on the other hand *L. Am., Sp* ◆ *Me encantaría acompañarlo a usted pero, por otra parte, no quiero perder mi programa favorito.* I'd love to go with you but, on the other hand, I don't want to miss my favorite program.

por pelotas (cojones) (by balls) with a hell of a lot of effort; just because of a whim (vulgar) *Sp* ◆ *Tuvo que hacerlo por pelotas.* He (She) had to do it no matter what.

por pitos o por flautas (for fifes or for flutes) for one reason or another *Mex, Ch, Sp* ◆ *Pensábamos reunirnos con nuestros amigos en verano, pero por pitos o por flautas, no lo hicimos.* We thought about getting together with our friends in the summer, but for one reason or another we didn't do it.

por poco (by little) by a miracle, by a hair *L. Am., Sp* ◆ *Choqué el carro. Por poco me mato.* I crashed the car. It was a miracle I wasn't killed. (I was nearly killed.)

por primera vez for the first time *L. Am., Sp* ◆ *Por primera vez me siento como un carpintero hecho y derecho.* For the first time, I feel like a tried and true carpenter.

por pura casualidad by pure chance *L. Am., Sp* ◆ *Se encontraron por pura casualidad en el centro.* They bumped into each other by pure chance downtown.

por real decreto (by royal decree) because that's how it is, it's not to be appealed, because I (or someone) said so *most of L. Am., Sp* ◆ *Por el real decreto de sus padres, Marcelina tuvo que cambiar la fecha de la boda.* Because her parents said so, Marcelina had to change the date of the wedding.

por regla general as a general rule *L. Am., Sp* ◆ *Por regla general no hago tantas preguntas.* As a general rule, I don't ask so many questions.

por semana (por mes) weekly (monthly) *L. Am., Sp* ◆ *¿Me van a pagar por semana?* Are they going to pay me weekly?

de **por sí** used like **de todas formas**, anyhow *Mex, ES, CR, Col, Peru, Bol, U, Arg* ◆ *¿Dónde estabas? De por sí te estaba esperando hace días.* Where were you? Anyhow, I've been waiting for you for days. ◆ *No es muy inteligente ese chico; de por sí que no lo quiero para una tesis.* That fellow isn't very bright; at any rate I don't want him for a thesis.

por si acaso just in case *L. Am., Sp* ◆ *Dame tu teléfono, por si acaso.* Give me your phone number, just in case.

por si las moscas (because if the flies) just in case *most of L. Am., Sp* ◆ *Cerramos la puerta con llave por si las moscas.* Let's lock the door just in case.

por su cara bonita (because of his or her pretty face) for no good reason, usually meaning that something may come about undeservedly *Mex, ES, Ch, Sp* ◆ *¿Crees que por tu cara bonita vas a aprobar el examen?* Do you think you're going to pass the test because of your good looks?

por su (propia) cuenta on one's own; for oneself *L. Am., Sp* ◆ *Estoy trabajando por mi propia cuenta ahora.* I'm working on my own (for myself) now.

por su linda cara (because of his or her handsome face) for no good reason, usually meaning that something may come about undeservedly *Mex, DR, S. Cone, Sp* ◆ *Por la linda cara de María y su novio, tuvimos que cambiar todos nuestros planes.* Just because of María and her boyfriend, we had to change all our plans.

por suerte (through luck) luckily *L. Am., Sp* ◆ *Por suerte, no me pillaron.* Luckily, they didn't catch me.

por supuesto of course *L. Am., Sp* ◆ *Por supuesto te puedes quedar en mi casa.*

¡Claro que sí! Of course you can stay at my house. Naturally!

por término medio (by the median term) on (the) average *L. Am., Sp* ◆ *Por término medio ganamos un buen sueldo en la compañía. On average we make a good salary at the company.*

por todas partes (todos lados) everywhere *L. Am., Sp* ◆ *En este barrio se ven flores por todas partes. In this neighborhood you see flowers everywhere.*

por un pelo (by a hair) by a little bit *DR, PR, S. Cone, Sp* ◆ *Evitamos un accidente por un pelo. We avoided an accident by a hair.*

por un «quítame allá esas pajas» (for a "take away from me those straws") just for the heck of it, for nothing, for no reason at all *Mex, Nic, Ch, Sp* ◆ *Por un quítame esas pajas, cambió su decisión y no pudimos hacer nada. Just for the heck of it, he changed his decision and we couldn't do anything.*

por un tubo (through a pipe) tons, abundantly *DR, Sp* ◆ *Gracias, pero ya no quiero más. Comí torta por un tubo. Thanks, but I don't want any more. I ate a ton of cake.*

de **por vida, de toda la vida** for life, lifelong *L. Am., Sp* ◆ *Somos amigos de por vida. We're lifelong friends.*

porfa (short for **por favor**) please *most of L. Am., Sp* ◆ *Acompáñame al médico, porfa. Come with me to the doctor, please.*

la **porno** short for **pornografía** *L. Am., Sp* ◆ *Es una pretensión de elevar la porno a la categoría de arte. It's a pretense of raising porno to the category of art.* ◆ *Encontré unas revistas porno en el cuarto de Pablito. I found some porno magazines in Pablito's room.*

porque la abuela fuma (because his [her, your, my, etc.] grandmother smokes) just for the heck of it, for no good reason, meaning that someone is inventing an excuse for something *Sp* ◆ *Le pegó la depresión porque la abuela fuma. He's depressed for no good reason.*

porque voló la mosca (because the fly flew away) just for the heck of it, for no reason at all *Mex, Col* ◆ *¿Por qué cambiaste de opinión tan rápidamente? —Porque voló la mosca. Why did you change your mind so quickly? Just for the heck of it.*

la(s) **porquería(s)** (pig stuff) junk, trash; junk food *L. Am., Sp* ◆ *¿Cómo puedes comer esas porquerías? How can you eat that junk food?* ◆ *Por favor, no compres más porquerías. Please don't buy more junk.*

la **porra** → **mandar a alguien a la porra**

¡Porras! exclamation of disgust or anger *Sp*

el **porro** marijuana joint *U, Arg, Sp* ◆ *Se lió un porro dentro del metro y fue obligado a bajarse. He rolled a joint in the metro and was made to get off.*

portarse bien (mal) to behave oneself (behave badly), be good (bad) *L. Am., Sp* ◆ *Pórtate bien, mami, y hazle caso a tu papá. Behave yourself, dear, and mind your dad.*

en **pos de** in pursuit of *L. Am., Sp* ◆ *Los periodistas deberían ir siempre en pos de la verdad. Journalists should always be in pursuit of the truth.*

ser un **poste** (to be a post) to be deaf; to be slow, dim-witted *Sp* ◆ *Margarita es un poste; sin embargo, lo disimula bien. Margarita is a bit deaf; however, she covers it up pretty well.*

a la **postre** (at the dessert) last, at the end *Mex, DR, Sp* ◆ *A la postre me vas a agradecer que te haya obligado a ir a la escuela. In the end you're going to thank (literally, be thankful to) me for making you go to school.*

el **poto** base, bottom, rear end (for things or people) *Ch* ◆ *Cálmate, Pepito. Si sigues corriendo, te vas a caer en el poto. Calm down, Pepito. If you keep running around, you'll fall on your rear end.*

la **potranca** (female horse) pretty girl, filly *Mex, DR, Col* ◆ *Mi potranca y yo fuimos de compras a la tienda. My filly and I went to the store to shop.*

a **precio cómodo** (at a comfortable price) cheap(ly) *ES, Nic, Peru, U* ◆ *Compré regalos para todos mis amigos a precios cómodos. I bought presents for all my friends cheaply.*

estar **precioso** (to be precious, humorous play on **preso**, meaning prisoner) to go to the clinker (jail) *Ch* ◆ *Ana se siente triste porque otra vez su hermano está precioso.*

Ana feels sad because her brother's in the clinker again.

prender to turn on *Mex* ◆ *Ese tipo me prende. That guy turns me on.*

prendérsele el foco (to have the lightbulb turned on) to get a brilliant idea *Mex, ES* ◆ *No sabían qué hacer, y a Matilde se le prendió el foco y encontró la solución. They didn't know what to do, and Matilde got a brilliant idea and found the solution.*

prendérsele la lamparita (to have the lightbulb turned on) to get a brilliant idea *U, Arg* ◆ *Al entrenador se le prendió la lamparita, cambió varios jugadores y ganaron el partido. The coach got a brilliant idea, changed a few players, and they won the game.*

estar **prendido(-a) con alfileres** (to be fastened with pins, like clothing that hasn't been sewn together yet) to be thrown together, hastily put together *L. Am., Sp* ◆ *Era un proyecto prendido con alfileres. It was a hastily put together project.*

Le **prendió la vacuna.** (The vaccination "took.") She got pregnant. *Mex, U, Arg* ◆ *A mi prima le prendió la vacuna después de cinco años de casada. Está feliz. My cousin finally got pregnant after five years of marriage. She's happy.*

prensa →**tener buena (mala) prensa**

la **preocupabilidad** worry about guilt (**preocupar** and **culpabilidad**) *Mex, ES, Col* ◆ *Su problema es la preocupabilidad. His problem is worrying about guilt.*

presentar armas (to present arms) to have a hard-on (vulgar) *L. Am., Sp* ◆ *Ay, mi amor, ¿tan pronto me presentas armas? Oh, my love, you already have a hard-on for me?*

prestarle a alguien la guitarra (to lend someone the guitar) to let someone get a word in *ES* (RVAR *U*: **pasarle el micrófono**) ◆ *Préstame la guitarra. Let me get a word in.* ◆ *Pásale el micrófono a tu mujer; ella también quiere hablar. (U) Let your wife get a word in; she wants to talk too.*

prestar atención to pay attention *L. Am., Sp* ◆ *No prestes atención a sus indirectas. Don't pay any attention to his insinuations.*

prestar pa' la orquesta (to loan for the orchestra) to chip in for some cooperative

event; to borrow temporarily *Mex, Col* ◆ *Mi primo necesita dinero para pagar la hipoteca. Vamos a prestar pa' la orquesta. My cousin needs money to pay his mortgage. Let's all chip in.*

prieto(-a) black or dark (person) (can also be a nickname of endearment) *Mex, Cuba, DR, PR, G, ES* ◆ *Llegaste prieta de la playa. Ten cuidado con el sol. You came back from the beach very brown. Be careful of the sun.*

al **primer envite** at once, right off the bat, from the beginning, right away *Sp* ◆ *Es un tipo blando que se viene abajo al primer envite. He's a softie who gives up right away.*

de **primera** (of first) first-class *L. Am.* ◆ *Ese muchacho ha resultado de primera. That boy has turned out first-class.* ◆ *Es un cabrón de primera. He's a first-class SOB.* ◆ *Marisa tiene una cámara digital de primera. Marisa has a first-class digital camera.*

primera vez →**por primera vez**

a **primera vista** at first sight (glance), right from the start *L. Am., Sp* ◆ *A primera vista comprendí que el director era una persona difícil. At first glance I understood that the principal was a difficult person.*

el **primero** →**no ser el primero**

Primero Dios. (First God.) God willing. (often used when an action is proposed or some statement of optimism is made) *Mex, C. Am.* ◆ *¿Vienes al concierto con nosotros?— Primero Dios. Will you come to the concert with us? —God willing.*

el/la **primo(-a)** (cousin) naive person, hick *Mex, Sp* ◆ *Pobre Martín. Es un primo y siempre lo estafan. Poor Martín. He's a poor hick and they always cheat him.*

el **príncipe azul** (blue prince) prince charming, ideal man *L. Am., Sp* ◆ *Estela está encantada con su príncipe azul. Estela is enchanted with her prince charming.*

a **principios de, al principio** at the beginning *L. Am., Sp* ◆ *Al principio, me trataron bien. At first, they treated me well.*

el/la **pringado(-a)** (soaked in grease) drudge, flunkie, someone who is overworked or who always gets stuck with everything *Sp* ◆ *Pepe es el pringado de la empresa. Pepe is the flunkie of the company.*

pringar (to dip or soak in grease; to stab) to do the dirty work, work more than others, be a pushover (vulgar) *Sp* ◆ *En esa empresa sólo hay uno que pringa. In that company there's only one person who works like a dog.*

pringarla (to soak it in grease; to stab it) to make a mistake, blow it (like **cagarla**) (vulgar) *Sp* ◆ *La pringó cuando se casó con ese idiota. She really goofed when she married that idiot.*

prisa →**darse prisa**

de **prisa** in a hurry, quickly *L. Am., Sp* ◆ *Hice el reportaje muy de prisa. I did the report in a big hurry.*

el **privado** (private) the john, head, bathroom *Mex, Col* ◆ *¿Dónde está el privado? Where's the john?*

ser un **problema mayúsculo** to be a major (literally, capital letter) problem *L. Am.* ◆ *Aquí el tráfico es un problema mayúsculo. The traffic here is a mega problem.*

La **procesión va por dentro.** (The procession goes on the inside.) He's (She's) bottling it all up. (said when one feels pain or sadness but covers it up) *Mex, S. Cone, Sp* (RVAR *Mex:* also, **Las penas se llevan por dentro.**) ◆ *Todos tratan de disimular su dolor, pero la procesión va por dentro. Everyone is trying to hide their pain, but it's there, bottled up.*

el/la **profe** short for **profesor** or **profesora**, prof *L. Am., Sp* ◆ *La profe es muy exigente. The prof is really demanding.*

el/la **profe** smart person (said in jest, short for **profesor[a])** *Chicano, Mex* ◆ *El profe nos dio buenos consejos. Mr. Smart Guy here gave us some really good advice.*

de **pronto** →**por de pronto, por lo pronto**

de **pronto** suddenly, soon *Mex, C. Am., Col, Ch, Arg, Sp* ◆ *De pronto el viento invadió toda la habitación y se rompió la ventana. Suddenly the wind filled the whole room and the window broke.*

pronunciar (dar) un discurso to make a speech *L. Am., Sp* ◆ *¿Va a pronunciar un discurso esta noche el ministro? Will the minister be making a speech tonight?*

a **propósito** by the way; on purpose *L. Am., Sp* ◆ *A propósito, voy a estar en Madrid la semana que viene. By the way, I'm going to*

be in Madrid next week. ◆ *Lo hizo a propósito. He (She) did it on purpose.*

a **propósito de...** talking about . . . *L. Am., Sp* ◆ *A propósito de la casa, ¿todavía piensa venderla? Talking about the house, are you still planning to sell it?*

provecho: Buen provecho. Enjoy your meal. Bon appetit. *L. Am., Sp* ◆ *Perdonen la interrupción, amigos míos; no sabía que estaban comiendo. Buen provecho. Excuse me for interrupting you, my friends; I didn't know that you were eating. Bon appetit.*

provocarle algo a alguien (to provoke something in someone) to feel like having something *Col* ◆ *¿Te provoca un tinto (café)? Do you feel like having a coffee?*

a **prueba** →**poner a prueba**

¡Puah! Yuck! Bah! (expression of disgust) *Sp* ◆ *¡Puah! ¡Qué asco! Yuck! How disgusting!*

¡Pucha! ¡La pucha! (softened form of **¡La puta!**, the whore) equivalent to Darn it! Holy smoke! *L. Am.* ◆ *¡La pucha! Olvidé mi pasaporte en el hotel. Darn it! I forgot my passport at the hotel.* ◆ *¡La pucha! Se me descompuso el auto y llegaré tarde. Darn! My car broke down and I'm going to be late.*

¡Púchica! Holy smoke!, euphemism for **puta** *C. Am.* ◆ *¡Púchica! Sus propias hijas le han robado el dinero. Holy smoke! Her own daughters stole the money from her.*

puede que it's possible *L. Am., Sp* ◆ *Puede que llegue a tu casa más tarde. Maybe I'll go to (arrive at) your house later.*

puente →**hacer puente**

pueque (reduced form of **puede ser que**) maybe *Mex* ◆ *Pueque encuentre los videos allí. Maybe I'll find the videos there.*

puerta →**dar a alguien con la puerta en las narices; darle con la puerta en las narices; no cerrar la puerta**

a las **puertas de la muerte** at death's door *Mex, DR, Ch, Sp* ◆ *Mi hermana estuvo en las puertas de la muerte, pero gracias a Dios está mejor. My sister was at death's door, but thank God she's better now.*

Pues... Uh . . . , Well . . . *L. Am., Sp* ◆ *Pues... no sé. Well . . . I don't know.*

puesto(-a) →**llevar puesto(-a)**

estar **puesto(-a)** **1.** (to be put, turned on) to be savvy, have a lot of knowledge (about something) or a talent for it *Mex, Sp,* ◆ *Contraté a Jimena porque está puesta. I hired Jimena because she is with it (up-to-date).* **2.** (to be put, turned on) to be ready and waiting, on one's toes *Mex, U* ◆ *Estoy bien puesta para irme a Hawai mañana. I'm really ready to go to Hawaii tomorrow.*

pulento(-a) flashy, extraordinary; good, great *Peru, Ch, Arg* (RVAR *Peru, Arg:* **pulenta**, invariable) ◆ *Néstor es una persona bien pulenta. Néstor is a great person.*

pulgas →**no aguantar pulgas**

el **pulpo** (octopus) wolf, someone who's "all hands," guy who likes to touch women inappropriately *Mex, DR, Col, Sp* ◆ *Yo no bailo con ese hombre porque es un pulpo. I'm not dancing with that man because he's all hands.*

punta →**sacar punta a una cosa; tener algo en la punta de la lengua**

estar de **punta uno con otro** (to be at point with another) to be at odds or on bad terms with someone *Mex, Ch, U* ◆ *Los socios siempre estuvieron de punta, y el negocio no anduvo. The partners were always at odds with each other, and the business didn't work out.*

la **puntada** wisecrack, clever or barbed remark; kick, hoot, something unusual and amusing that someone does *Mex, ES* ◆ *Qué gran puntada la de cantar en la fiesta. What a hoot it was to do that singing at the party.*

la **puntilla** →**dar la puntilla**

de **puntillas** on tiptoe *L. Am., Sp* ◆ *Entré de puntillas para no despertar a mi marido. I came in on tiptoe so as not to wake up my husband.*

punto →**darle a alguien el punto; hasta cierto punto; hasta/a tal punto; poner los puntos sobre la mesa; poner los puntos sobre las íes**

en **punto** on the dot *L. Am., Sp* ◆ *Son las cinco en punto. It's five o'clock on the dot.*

Punto acabado. (Punto final.) (Finished, period.) Absolutely not, period. *Mex, U, Arg* ◆ *Punto final. No hablemos más del tema. Absolutely not, period. Let's not talk about that subject any more.*

a **punto de** on the point of, about to *L. Am., Sp* ◆ *Estaba a punto de llamar a la policía cuando se calmó. I was about to call the police when he (she) calmed down.*

ser **punto y aparte** (to be point and apart, new paragraph) to be dead set against (something) *Mex* ◆ *Con el problema de la droga, yo soy punto y aparte. Regarding the problem of drugs, I'm dead set against them.*

con **puntos y comas** (with periods and commas) just so, meticulously *Mex, DR, U, Arg, Sp* ◆ *A mi tía le gusta hacer las cosas con puntos y comas. My aunt likes to do things just so.*

una **puñalada** →**dar una puñalada por la espalda**

la **puñeta** hand job, masturbation (vulgar) *Chicano, Mex, U*

la **puñeta** →**hacer la puñeta a alguien**

puñeta(s) (masturbation) devil, dickens (vulgar) *PR, Sp* ◆ *¡Puñeta! No traje mi cartera. Damn! I didn't bring my wallet.* ◆ *¿Dónde puñetas estabas? Where the devil were you?*

un **puño** →**meter/tener en un puño a alguien**

el **Pupas** (the pupas) unlucky person; also, **ser más desgraciado(-a) que el Pupas** *Sp* ◆ *Lo llamamos el Pupas porque tiene muchas desgracias. We call him "the unlucky one" because he has a lot of bad luck.*

de **pura cepa** (of pure stock) the real thing, genuine (said of people) *most of L. Am., Sp* ◆ *Jacinto es una persona de pura cepa. Jacinto is the real thing, very genuine.*

¡Pura leche! (Pure milk!) Baloney! Nonsense! *Mex, Col* ◆ *Sus ideas sobre la política me parecen muy raras. ¡Pura leche! Their ideas on politics seem really weird to me. A lot of baloney!*

ser **pura mierda (una mierda)** (to be pure shit [to be shitty]) to be very bad, worthless (vulgar) *Mex, DR, PR, ES, Ch, Sp* ◆ *Ese tipo es pura mierda. No ayuda a nadie. That guy is a real shithead. He doesn't help anyone.*

¡Pura paja! (Pure straw!) Baloney! Nonsense! *Mex, C. Am., Col, Ec* ◆ *Dicen que van a bajar el precio de la gasolina. −¡Pura paja! They say they're going to lower the price of gas. —What baloney!*

Pura verdad. (Pure truth.) True. Right you are. *L. Am., Sp* ◆ *Tú y yo tenemos mucha suerte. —Pura verdad, mi querido. You and I are very lucky. —Right you are, my dear.*

pura vida (pure life) great, nice, fantastic *CR* ◆ *¡Pura vida! Riding the wave! Great! (used as a positive response in many kinds of situations)* ◆ *Esa mujer es pura vida. That woman is the best.*

puras madres (pure mothers) junk, things of little value *Mex, C. Am.* ◆ *Todas estas cosas son puras madres. All these things are pure junk.*

¡Puras vainas! (Pure husks!) Baloney! Nonsense! *CR, parts of S. Am.* ◆ *Dice que su novia es de una familia aristocrática. —¡Puras vainas! He says his girlfriend is from an aristocratic family. —What a crock! ◆ Ella no hace sino echar puras vainas. All she does is make insinuations.*

puré → hacer puré a alguien o algo; hecho(-a) un puré

puritito(-a) pure, sheer *Mex, G, ES* ◆ *Era puritita mentira. That was pure lies.*

¡Puro cuento! (Pure story!) What a whopper! What a fib! *Mex, ES, Col, U* ◆ *¡Puro cuento! No lo creas. What a fib! Don't believe it.*

a **puro pulmón** (at pure lung) with a lot of effort, by working as hard as possible *L. Am., Sp* ◆ *Lo hice a puro pulmón. I did it by sheer force of will.*

a (**puro) huevo** (at [pure] egg, testicle) with a hell of a lot of effort (vulgar); also, **a huevos** *Mex, C. Am.* ◆ *Julia no quería ir, pero la hice ir a puro huevo. Julia didn't want to go, but I forced her to go.*

puta → más puta que las gallinas

la **puta** (prostitute) bitch; slut *L. Am., Sp* ◆ *Lamentablemente, es mi pariente, pero es una puta, y no quiero verla. Unfortunately, she's my relative, but she's a bitch, and I don't want to see her.*

¡Puta la huevada (güea)! (Whore the bunch of testicles!) Goddamn it to hell! (vulgar but common, like *Mex:* **hijo de la gran chingada**) *Ch* ◆ *¡Puta la huevada! Nos quitaron los asientos. Goddamn it to hell! They took our seats.*

¡Puta madre! 1. (Mother whore!) expression of surprise or anger (vulgar) *Mex, C. Am., S. Cone* ◆ *Vete a la puta madre con tus comentarios sarcásticos. Go to hell with your sarcastic comments.* ◆ *¡Puta madre! Me olvidé de mi portafolios en el subte. Damn! I left my wallet on the subway.* 2. (mother whore) damn fantastic, great (vulgar) *Sp* ◆ *Esta comida es de puta madre. This is one hell of a good meal.* ◆ *Esos pantalones te sientan de puta madre. Those slacks look damn good on you.* ◆ *Todo va de puta madre. Everything is going damn well.*

¡La **puta que te parió!** (The whore who gave birth to you!) You son of a bitch! You bitch! (vulgar) *S. Cone, Sp* ◆ *La puta que te parió. ¿Cuándo asumirás responsabilidades en tu familia? You son of a bitch, when will you start taking some responsibility in your family?*

¡Puta! (Whore!) Damn! (vulgar) *L. Am., Sp* ◆ *¡Puta! Me han robado mi coche. Damn! Someone's stolen my car.* ◆ *¡Puta! Perdí las llaves de la oficina. Damn! I lost the keys to the office.*

la **putada** (whore thing or action) dirty trick; piece of crap *L. Am., Sp* ◆ *Estoy muy enojada con José. —Sí, ¡fue una putada lo que te hizo! I'm very angry at José. —Yeah, what he did to you was a piece of crap! ◆ Le hace muchas putadas a su hermana menor. He plays a lot of dirty tricks on his little sister.*

ser el **putas** (to be the whores) to be really good at something (vulgar) *Col* ◆ *Eduardo es el putas del tenis en este club. Eduardo is the tennis ace at this club.*

putear to bother, annoy, harass *Sp* (RVAR *Sp:* usually used for actions rather than words [vulgar]; *L. Am.:* usually verbal) ◆ *Ese chico siempre me está puteando en la escuela. That boy is always giving me a hell of a time at school.* ◆ *La profesora me puteó al suspenderme el examen. Ahora tengo que repetir el curso entero. The teacher screwed me by flunking me on the exam. Now I have to repeat the whole course.*

putear, echar puteadas to bitch out, insult with offensive names (vulgar) *L. Am.* ◆ *Ayer fui a un partido de fútbol con Jesús. Primera y última vez, porque estaba puteando al ár-*

bitro y yo me sentía mal. Yesterday I went to a soccer game with Jesús. First and last time because he was swearing at the referee and I felt bad.

el **puto** 1. homosexual (vulgar, pejorative) *Mex, U, Arg* 2. pimp; damn womanizer (vulgar) *parts of L. Am.* ◆ *Anda de puto; tiene muchas mujeres. He's a damn womanizer; he has a lot of women.*

puto(-a) (pimp or whore) blasted, damn (vulgar) *L. Am., Sp* ◆ *Esta puta máquina no funciona. This damn machine doesn't work.* ◆ *No me hizo ni puto caso. He didn't pay a damn bit of attention to me.* ◆ *¿Dónde está un puto taxi? Where's a blasted taxi?*

puyar (to jab) to give (someone) a hard time, pressure *C. Am., Col* ◆ *Sólo andas puyando. You're only being a nuisance.*

¡Qué amoroso(-a)! How sweet! How charmingly cute! (used by women) *S. Cone* ◆ *Tus padres acaban de invitarme a su casa. ¡Qué amorosos!* Your parents just invited me to their home. How sweet of them!

¡Qué barbaridad! (What barbarity!) Good grief! How awful! *L. Am., Sp* ◆ *¡Qué barbaridad! Nunca imaginé que su esposo sería capaz de pegarle.* How awful! I'd never have thought her husband would be capable of hitting her. ◆ *¡Qué barbaridad! No peleen más.* Good grief! Don't fight anymore.

¡Qué bárbaro! (How barbarous!) Good grief! How awful! *L. Am., Sp* ◆ *¡Qué bárbaro! No hables de esa manera a los niños.* How awful! Don't speak that way to the children. ◆ *¡Qué bárbaro! No creas todo lo que lees en el periódico.* Good grief! Don't believe everything you read in the newspaper.

¿Qué bicho te ha picado? (What insect has bitten you?) What's bothering (bugging) you? *Mex, DR, G, S. Cone, Sp* ◆ *¿Por qué gritas de esa manera? ¿Qué bicho te ha picado, muchacho?* Why are you shouting like that? What's got your goat?

¿Qué bolá? What's up? *Cuba* ◆ *Hola, Felipe, ¿qué bolá?* Hi, Felipe, what's up?

¡Qué bombón y yo con diabetes! (What a bonbon and me with diabetes!) street compliment *L. Am., Sp*

¿Qué crees? (What do you think?) Guess what. *L. Am., Sp* ◆

¡Qué cruz! (What a cross!) What a drag (burden, cross to bear)! *Mex, DR, PR, Col, U, Sp* ◆ *¡Qué cruz tener un marido borracho!* What a drag to have a drunk for a husband! ◆ *¿Ser tímido hoy en día? ¡Qué cruz! Being shy these days? What a drag!

¡Qué cuento! (What a story!) Yeah, right! Baloney! (expression of opposition) *CR, Col* ◆ *No puedo ir. —¡Qué cuento! Vamos.* I can't go. —Yeah, right! Let's get going.

Qué curvas y yo sin freno. (What curves and me without brakes.) street compliment *L. Am., Sp*

¡Qué delicia! (What a delight!) How delicious! *most of L. Am.* ◆ *Qué delicia el postre que has preparado.* How delicious this dessert you've prepared is.

¡Qué descaro! What nerve (brazenness)! *L. Am., Sp* ◆ *¡Qué descaro! ¿Cómo te atreves a hablar con esas palabras a tus padres?* What nerve! How dare you speak with your parents using those words?

¡Qué dicha! (What bliss!) What luck! *G, Nic, CR* ◆ *¡Qué dicha volverte a ver después de tantos años!* What luck to see you again after so many years!

que digamos to speak of, so to speak, let's just say *L. Am., Sp* ◆ *No es muy generoso, que digamos.* Let's just say he's not very generous.

¡Qué emoción! (What emotion!) expression of amazement, similar to How wonderful! *Mex, DR, PR, Col, S. Cone* ◆ *¡Qué emoción verte!* How wonderful to see you!

¡Qué gran cagada! (What a pile of shit!) What a piece of shit! What a dirty trick! (usually refers to a lie or betrayal, although in Sp it's often used to imply a big mistake) *ES, S. Cone, Sp* ◆ *La gran cagada de mi vida fue casarme con Luis. (Sp)* The big screwup of my life was marrying Luis.

¿Qué habré hecho yo para merecer tal preciosura? What could I have done to deserve such beauty (such preciousness)? A phrase sometimes used as **piropo**, a street compliment given to a good-looking woman as she passes by. *L. Am., Sp*

¡Qué huevada (güea)! (What a bunch of testicles!) Oh, shit! (vulgar) *Ch* ◆ *¡Qué huevada! Olvidé el cumpleaños de mi madrina.* Oh, shit! I forgot my godmother's birthday.

¡Qué huevotes! (What big eggs, or testicles!) What damn nerve! (vulgar) *Mex, ES* (RVAR *G:* **¡Qué huevos!**) ◆ *¡Chispas! Ése del carro* *gris me quitó el lugar. ¡Qué huevotes!* Darn! *That guy in the gray car stole my parking place. What nerve!*

¡Qué jodienda! What a nuisance/pain! (vulgar, from **joder**) *Cuba, DR, PR, Col, Ven, Para, U, Sp* ◆ *Qué jodienda tener que lavar tantos platos después de la cena. What a pain to have to wash so many plates after supper.*

¡Qué joroba! What a pain! How annoying (people or things)! *Mex, DR, PR, Col, U* ◆ *¡Qué joroba tener que trabajar los fines de semana! What a pain to have to work on weekends!*

¿Qué jue? What's up? *Mex, Col*

¡Qué lástima! What a shame! *L. Am., Sp* ◆ *¡Qué lástima! No podré ver a mi amiga cuando vaya a Boston. What I shame! I won't be able to see my friend when I go to Boston.*

¿Qué le pongo? What shall I serve (put before) you? *Sp*

¡Qué leche! (What milk!) What luck! *Mex, PR, G, Col, Sp* (RVar a bit vulgar in *Sp*) ◆ *Qué leche que tienes. ¿Te tocó la lotería y es la primera vez que jugabas? What luck you have. You won the lottery and it's the first time you played?*

Que lo haga Rita. Let George (literally Rita, meaning someone else) do it. *Sp* ◆ *¿Por qué no has lavado los platos todavía? —Que lo haga Rita. Why haven't you washed the dishes today? —Let George (i.e., someone else) do it.*

Que lo pase(s) bien. (May you spend it well.) Have a good day (time). Have a good one. (said to someone who is leaving or about to leave) *L. Am., Sp* ◆ *Muchas gracias por habernos visitado. ¡Que lo pasen bien! Thank you very much for visiting us. Have a good day!*

¿Qué más da? (What more does it give?) Who cares? Whatever. *L. Am. (not S. Cone), Sp* ◆ *Mamá, rompí el plato. —¿Qué más da? Mom, I broke the plate. —Who cares? ◆ ¿Vamos al cine? —¿Qué más da? Shall we go to the movies? —Whatever.*

el **que más y el que menos** (he who most and he who least) everybody (under the sun) *Ch, U, Sp* ◆ *El que más y el que menos trajo el material necesario para la clase. Everybody brought the necessary materials to class.*

¿Qué me cuentas? (What do you tell me?) What's happening? *L. Am., Sp* ◆ *¿Qué me cuentas de tu relación con Alfonso? What's happening in your relationship with Alfonso?*

¡Que no te enteras, Contreras! (So you don't find out, Contreras!) phrase reproaching someone for being distracted and not listening *Sp*

¡Qué nota! (What a note!) How nice! *Mex, Col*

¿Qué notas me cuentas? (What notes are you telling me?) What's new? *most of L. Am.* ◆ *Hola, Graciela. ¿Qué notas me cuentas? Hi, Graciela. What's up?*

¡Qué ocurrencia! (What an occurrence! What a thing to occur to you!) The very idea! How thoughtful! Yeah, right! (sometimes used to react to a compliment in a modest way) *L. Am., Sp* ◆ *¡Qué ocurrencia! Nunca debiste gastar tanto dinero en el regalo para Miguelito. How thoughtful! You shouldn't have spent so much money on the gift for Miguelito. ◆ ¡Qué bonita te ves! —¡Qué ocurrencia! How pretty you look! —Yeah, right!*

¿Qué onda(s)? (What sound wave[s]?) What's happening? What's up? *L. Am.* ◆ *Hola, Enriqueta. ¿Qué onda? Hi, Enriqueta. What's up?*

¡Qué oso! (What a bear!) How embarrassing! *Mex, Col* ◆ *¡Qué oso! Empezaba a presentarla a mi profesor de inglés y no pude acordarme de su nombre. How embarrassing! I began to introduce her to my English professor and I couldn't remember her name.*

¡Qué padre! How terrific! *Mex* ◆ *¡Qué padre te ves aquí con tus nietas! How great you look here with your granddaughters!*

¿Qué pasión? variant of ¿Qué pasó? *Mex*

¡Qué piernón! (What big leg or legginess!) What shapely legs! *Mex, Col* ◆ *Pero, mujer, ¡qué piernón tienes! ¿Andas mucho de bicicleta? My dear, what gorgeous legs you have! Do you ride your bike a lot?*

¡Qué remedio! (What a remedy!) What an option that is! What choice do I have?, phrase of resignation meaning there is no alternative *L. Am., Sp* ◆ *¿Te gusta la ópera? —¡Qué remedio! La entrada valió un dineral.*

Do you like the opera? —What choice do I have? The ticket cost a fortune.

a lo **que salga** (with whatever comes up) taking what comes, without knowing or caring about the result *Mex, DR, PR, ES, U, Arg, Sp* ◆ *Yo prefiero los viajes organizados pero a Víctor le encanta la aventura, así que nos vamos a México a lo que salga. I prefer organized tours but Víctor likes adventure, so we're going to Mexico and we'll take what comes.*

¿Qué se teje? (What's being knitted?) How's it going? What's up? *Ch*

que si patatín que si patatán and so on and so on; blah, blah, blah; excuses for someone who doesn't want to talk directly about something *Mex, DR, PR, Sp* ◆ *Ramón me estuvo contando de su viaje a Chile, que visitó Santiago, que si patatín que si patatán, pero no me dijo nada del accidente. Ramón was telling me about his trip to Chile, that he went to Santiago, that blah, blah, blah, and so on and so forth, but he didn't tell me anything about the accident.*

que si pito que si flauta (that if fife that if flute) yada, yada, yada; one thing and then another *PR* ◆ *Y siguió hablando, que si pito que si flauta... And he (she) kept talking, yada, yada, yada . . .*

¡Que si quieres arroz, Catalina! (So you want rice, Catalina!) Life's not a bed of roses; sarcastic remark said when someone hasn't gotten something expected (for example, a promise has been broken) *Sp* ◆ *¿La has llamado muchas veces por teléfono y no te ha devuelto las llamadas? ¡Que si quieres arroz, Catalina! You've phoned her many times and she hasn't returned your calls? Tough luck, but life isn't a bed of roses! (You don't always get what you want!)*

¿Qué tal? How are things? *L. Am., Sp* ◆ *¿Qué tal? ¿Cómo andas? How are things? How are you doing?*

¿Qué tal andas? How are things? *Mex, Sp* ◆ *Hola, chamaca, ¿qué tal andas? Hi, kiddo, how're you doing?*

Que te (le, les) vaya bien. May all go well with you. Have a nice day (time, trip, etc.). (to someone who is leaving) *L. Am., Sp* ◆ *Adiós, muchachos. Que les vaya bien en las montañas. 'Bye, guys. Have a good time in the mountains.*

que te cagas (that you defecate) too much, as hell, expression denoting something unusual or expensive (vulgar) *Mex, Sp* ◆ *Hace un sol que te cagas. It's hot as hell.* ◆ *Tiene una casa que te cagas. He (She) has a hell of a nice house.*

¿Qué te parece (si...)? How does it seem to you (if . . .)? How about (if . . .)? How do you like . . . ? *L. Am., Sp* ◆ *¿Qué te parece la música? How do you like the music?*

¡Qué tontería(s)! What nonsense! *L. Am., Sp* ◆ *¡Qué tonterías dices! Jamás gastaría dinero en un abrigo de piel. What nonsense! I'd never spend money on a fur coat.*

¡Qué uvas! (What grapes!) Hi! (sounds like **¡Qui úbo!**) *Mex, Ec*

¡Qué va! Oh, come on! *parts of L. Am., Sp* ◆ *¡Qué va! No me interesa escuchar más quejas. Oh, come on! I'm not interested in hearing more complaints.*

¡Qué vaina! (What a husk, sheath!) Darn! expression of surprise, unpleasantness, anger, annoyance, disagreement *DR, G, Nic, CR, Col, Ven, Peru* ◆ *¡Qué vaina! Con las lluvias, el sótano se inundó y perdimos todo lo que teníamos allí. Darn! With the rain, the basement flooded and we lost everything we had there.* ◆ *¡Qué vaina! Han arrestado a varios manifestantes. Darn! They've arrested several demonstrators.*

¿Qué vaina (mierda) es ésta? (What screwup [thing, shit] is this?) What the hell is happening? What's going on? *ES, Ven, U.* ◆ *¿Qué mierda es ésta? No puedes irte sin explicar tu decisión. What the hell is going on? You can't go off without explaining your decision.*

A **que...** I bet . . . *L. Am., Sp* ◆ *A que eres de Argentina, ¿no? I bet you're from Argentina.*

la **quedada** get-together *Sp* ◆ *Van a organizar una quedada el fin de semana. Por fin todos los amigos del grupo de Internet se van a conocer personalmente. They're going to organize a get-together this weekend. Finally all the friends from the Internet group are going to get to know each other personally.*

el/la **quedado(-a)** (one who's been left behind) loser, has-been, fool *DR, CR, Col, Ven* ◆ *Enrique es un quedado; le falta ambición.* Enrique is a loser; he lacks ambition.

quedar (to remain) to leave it, agree, decide *L. Am.* ◆ *Así quedamos.* So that's the way we'll leave it. ◆ *Quedamos en eso.* Then it's agreed upon. ◆ *¿En qué quedamos? ¿Nos vemos a las siete o a las ocho?* So, what did we decide? We're getting together at seven or at eight?

quedar bien (mal) con (to remain good [bad] with) to be on the good (bad) side of *L. Am., Sp* ◆ *Mario siempre sabía quedar bien conmigo.* Mario always knew how to get on my good side.

quedar bien (mal) parado(-a) (to end up standing well [badly]) to have good (bad) luck in something, come out well (badly); (with **bien**) to land on one's feet or come out in good standing *L. Am., Sp* ◆ *Después de terminar la publicación, Nicolás quedó muy bien parado en la compañía.* After finishing the publication, Nicolás came out in good standing in the company.

quedar en la calle (to end up in the street) to be homeless, left with nothing *Mex, C. Am., S. Cone* ◆ *Quedaron en la calle después del incendio de la fábrica.* They were left with nothing after the fire at the factory.

quedar en la página dos (to remain on page two) to break, get ruined or eliminated, not make the cut; to die *Cuba* ◆ *El plato quedó en la página dos.* The plate got broken.

quedar flechado(-a) (to remain hit with the shot of an arrow, referring to Cupid's arrow) to fall in love with, feel love at first sight, be in love *Mex, DR, G, Col, S. Cone, Sp* ◆ *La estudiante de intercambio quedó flechada con Rodolfo y no quiso regresar a su país.* The exchange student fell hard for Rodolfo and didn't want to return to her country. ◆ *Cuando vi a Isabel, quedé flechado.* When I saw Isabel, it was love at first sight.

quedar grande (pequeño) to be big (small) *L. Am., Sp* ◆ *Le quedó grande el vestido.* The dress was too big for her.

quedar limpio(-a) (to be left clean) to be cleaned out, without money *Mex, DR, U, Arg, Sp* ◆ *Después del robo, me quedé limpio. No sé qué hacer.* After the robbery, I was cleaned out. I don't know what to do.

quedar pintado(-a) (to remain painted) to fit like a glove, very well; to be skin tight *Mex, Cuba, DR, Col, Peru, S. Cone, Sp* ◆ *¡Este vestido te queda pintado!* This dress fits you like a glove!

quedarse/estar a dos velas **1.** (to remain [be] at two sails) to be broke *Mex, Sp* ◆ *Me quedé a dos velas, esperando a fin de mes para poder comprar más comida.* I was left totally broke, waiting until the end of the month to be able to buy more food. **2.** (to remain [be] at two sails) to not understand something *Mex, Sp* ◆ *Llegamos tarde a la función y nos quedamos a dos velas.* We arrived late to the show, and we we were lost.

quedarse a oscuras (to be left in the dark) to be in the dark, not understand *Mex, Ch, Sp* ◆ *El padre de Eduardo está completamente a oscuras de sus planes.* Eduardo's father is completely in the dark about his plans.

quedarse como en misa (to be left as in mass) to put a lid on it, be quiet *CR, Col, U* ◆ *Después de la reprimenda, los niños se quedaron como en misa.* After the reprimand, the children were quiet as little mice.

quedarse con la boca abierta (to be left with one's mouth open) to be flabbergasted *L. Am., Sp* ◆ *Cuando le dijo que estaba embarazada, su novio se quedó con la boca abierta.* When she told him she was expecting, her boyfriend was flabbergasted.

quedarse con la cara cuadrada (to be left with the square face) to be flabbergasted, very surprised *Mex* ◆ *Juan se quedó con la cara cuadrada cuando me vio llegar en mi carro nuevo.* Juan was stunned when he saw me arrive in my new car.

quedarse con la copla (to remain or end up with the verse, stanza) to get it, realize what someone was trying to do secretively, find out *Sp* ◆ *Al principio las cosas no estaban muy claras, pero al final me quedé con la copla.* At first things were not very clear, but finally I got it. ◆ *Después de varios fracasos, se quedó con la copla.* After several failures, he (she) figured it out.

quedarse con los crespos hechos (to be left with one's curls made) to be stood up, left hanging *ES, Peru, Bol, Ch* ◆ *Íbamos a* salir con una pareja de amigos, pero nos quedamos con los crespos hechos. We were going to go out with a couple of friends, but we were stood up.

quedarse en la estacada (to end up in the stockade) to be left in the lurch, in hot water, come out of a business badly; to have been gotten the better of in a dispute *Ch, U, Sp* ◆ *En los momentos difíciles nunca me dejó en la estacada.* At the most difficult times, he (she) never left me in the lurch.

quedarse frío(-a) (helado[-a]) (to end up cold [frozen]) to be flabbergasted, surprised, stunned; said when something turns out contrary to what one wanted or expected *Mex, ES, CR, Ec, S. Cone, Sp* ◆ *Me quedé frío de lo que me dijo.* I was dumbfounded by what he (she) told me. ◆ *Me quedé helada cuando me dijeron que su hijo había muerto.* I was shocked when they told me that their son had died.

quedarse para vestir santos (to stay behind to dress [statues of] saints) to lose out, be left behind, usually meaning to be an old maid (also, less commonly, **vestir imágenes**) *L. Am., Sp* ◆ *Ramona cumplió cuarenta y dos años el jueves. —¿Y todavía soltera? —Bueno, ésa se quedó para vestir santos.* Ramona turned forty-two years old on Thursday. —And still single? —Well, she was left an old maid.

quedarse pasmado(-a) to be dumbfounded, surprised *Mex, Col, Peru, S. Cone, Sp* ◆ *Me quedé pasmada cuando me dijeron que se habían divorciado.* I was flabbergasted when they told me that they'd gotten a divorce.

quedarse patidifuso(-a) (y perplejo[-a]) to be (end up) confused (and perplexed) *DR, Col, Ch, Sp* ◆ *Nos quedamos patidifusos con las propuestas del nuevo director.* We were confused by the proposals of the new director.

quedarse sopa (to remain soup) to be out like a light, asleep; to be stunned *Sp* ◆ *Se me caían los ojos de sueño; después me quedé sopa.* My eyelids were heavy; then I was out like a light.

quedarse tieso(-a) (to be left stiff) to die, kick the bucket *Mex, Sp* ◆ *Se quedó tieso*

después de estar enfermo durante unos días. He died after being sick for several days.

quedarse tirado(-a) (to be left cast off) to be left (somewhere); to be stood up by someone; to lose everything *Mex, U, Arg, Sp* ◆ *Me dejaron tirado en la carretera, esperándolos, por varias horas.* They left me on the highway, waiting for them, for several hours. ◆ *Cuando nos divorciamos, quedé tirado porque ella y los niños se llevaron todo.* When we divorced, I lost everything because she and the kids took it all.

quedarse/estar en blanco (to remain [be] blank) to draw a blank, not know the answer to a question *L. Am., Sp* ◆ *Me sabía muy bien la lección pero cuando me la preguntó el profesor, me puse tan nervioso que me quedé en blanco.* I knew the lesson well but when the teacher asked me about it, I got so nervous I drew a blank.

a **quema ropa** (at burning of clothing) directly, straight out, point-blank *L. Am., Sp* ◆ *Cuando lo vi, le di las noticias a quema ropa.* When I saw him, I gave him the news straight out. ◆ *La policía lo baleó a quema ropa.* The police shot him point-blank.

la **quemada** (burn) put-down, disparaging remark *Chicano, Mex, U* ◆ *Toni se dio una buena quemada al escribir esa carta llena de errores y mandarla al jefe.* Toni got her comeuppance in spades when she wrote that letter full of errors and sent it to the boss. ◆ *¿Te dijo eso? ¡Qué quemada!* He (She) said that to you? What a put-down!

quemado(-a) 1. (burned) wiped out, exhausted *Mex, DR, G, CR, Col, Sp* (RVAR *Sp:* also, burned out) ◆ *El corredor estaba quemado antes de llegar a la meta.* The runner was burned out before reaching the finish line. 2. (burned) burned, damaged (usually in reputation) *L. Am., Sp* (RVAR *Ch:* also, having bad luck) ◆ *Está totalmente quemado como presidente de la asociación. Deberá ser sustituido pronto.* He's completely ruined as president of the association. He should be replaced soon.

quemar el último cartucho (to burn the last cartridge) to go to the last resort, play one's last trick *L. Am., Sp* ◆ *Nadie se atrevió a quemar el último cartucho y el* *proyecto fracasó. No one dared to go to the last resort and the project failed.*

quemar las naves to burn one's bridges (ships) *L. Am., Sp* ◆ *No voy a quemar mis naves con la compañía. Hablaré nuevamente con el gerente. I'm not going to burn my bridges with the company. I'll speak with the manager again.*

quemarse (to be burned, burn oneself) to get involved in a problem; blow it; discredit oneself *L. Am.* (RVAR *G, Cuba:* also, to reveal one's true self) ◆ *Ese hombre llegaba a las reuniones de infiltrado, pero se quemó. (Cuba) That man came to the meetings as an infiltrator (spy), but he revealed his true identity.* ◆ *Te quemaste. You blew it.* ◆ *¡Pobre Ramón! Se quemó ante todos sus amigos. Poor Ramón! He discredited himself in front of all his friends.*

quemarse (estrujarse) los sesos (to burn out [press] one's brain) to rack one's brain, think about something over and over *S. Cone, Sp* ◆ *El problema era fácil pero nadie quiso quemarse los sesos para resolverlo. The problem was easy but no one wanted to rack his or her brain to solve it.*

quemarse las pestañas (cejas) (to burn one's eyelashes [eyebrows]) to study hard, burn the midnight oil, cram *L. Am., Sp* ◆ *Me quemé las pestañas para pasar el examen de historia. I burned the midnight oil to pass the history exam.*

un **quemón** →**darse un quemón**

querer →**Estás como quieres!**

querer decir to mean *L. Am., Sp* ◆ *¿Qué quiere decir eso? What does that mean?*

el **queso** →**darse en el queso; dársela a alguien con queso**

¡Qui úbole!, ¡Qui úbo! Hi!, a greeting, like **¡Hola!** *most of L. Am.* ◆ *¡Qui úbole, Manuel! ¿Cómo estás? Hi, Manuel! How are you?*

de **quicio** →**sacarle de quicio**

¿Quién es? (Who is it?) Hello (answering the phone). *Col, Sp*

¡Quién lo diría! (Who would say it!) Oh, come on! Who would have thought it? *Mex, DR, S. Cone, Sp* ◆ *¿Los hermanos Barrio son traficantes de drogas? ¿Quién lo diría? Parecían buenas personas. The Barrio*

brothers are drug traffickers? Who would have thought it? They seemed like good people.

¿Quién quita que...? (Who takes away that . . . ?) expression used to indicate the probability or chance of something happening *Mex, DR, C. Am., Col, Ven, Peru* ◆ *¿Quién quita que mañana llegue de sorpresa? Who can say that tomorrow he (she) won't show up by surprise?* ◆ *Quien quita que venga mi prima. You never can tell when my cousin might show up.*

¿Quién te mete, Juan Bonete? (Who brings you into this, Juan Bonete?) This isn't your affair. None of your business! *Mex, Nic* (RVAR *U:* **Juan Copete**) ◆ *Deja a tu novio. Es un mujeriego. —¿Y a ti quién te mete, Juan Bonete? Leave your boyfriend. He's a womanizer. —And what business is it of yours?*

el **quilombo** (bordello) mess *U, Arg* ◆ *¡Qué quilombo! Todo nos salió mal. What a mess! Everything turned out badly for us.*

en la **quinta puñeta** in a godforsaken spot, far away (vulgar) *PR, Sp* ◆ *Acho, 'mano, y ¿dónde es que tú vives, en la quinta puñeta? Man alive, bro', where is it you live, in goddamn Timbuktu?*

un **quinto** →**no tener un quinto**

en el **quinto coño (carajo)** (in the fifth female [male] organ) in a godforsaken spot, far away (vulgar) *DR, PR, Sp* ◆ *Está allá en el sur, en el quinto carajo. It's there in the South, in some damn godforsaken spot.*

el **quinto pino** (the fifth pine) in a godforsaken spot, far away *PR, Sp* ◆ *Tuve que ir al quinto pino para comprar esa lavadora. I had to go to the ends of the earth to buy that washing machine.*

estar en el **quinto sueño** (to be in the fifth sleep) to be fast asleep *Mex, DR, ES, U* ◆ *Estábamos en el quinto sueño cuando sonó el teléfono. We were fast asleep when the telephone rang.*

estar de **quitar el hipo** (to be such as to take away hiccups) to be amazing, breathtaking *Mex, Sp* ◆ *Es tan bonita que quita el hipo. She's so pretty she takes your breath away.*

quitar hierro (to take away iron) to smooth over, downplay, take away the importance of something that one thinks was exaggerated

Sp ◆ *He intentado hablar con él para quitar hierro al problema que os había surgido.* I've tried to talk to him to smooth over the problem that had come up (for you).

quitar lo bailado to take away what has been enjoyed (danced) *L. Am., Sp* ◆ *No se puede quitar lo bailado.* The fun we have today nobody can take away from us. ◆ *Mañana tengo un examen y estoy aquí con este chico tan guapo. Bueno, ¡que me quiten lo bailado!* Tomorrow I have an exam and here I am with this super handsome guy. Well, let them try to take what I'm enjoying away from me!

quitarle la paciencia to wear down, try one's patience *L. Am., Sp* ◆ *Ese niño me quita la paciencia.* That child wears me down (takes aways my patience).

quitarse de en medio to get out of the way *L. Am., Sp* ◆ *Esperen tantito, señores, y me voy a quitar de en medio.* Wait a minute, gentlemen, and I'll get out of your way.

quitarse la careta (to take off one's mask) to stop acting or making a show, show one's true colors *Mex, ES, S. Cone* ◆ *Quítate la careta, ya.* Take off your mask. (Stop acting and be yourself.)

quitarse un peso de encima →sacarse/ **quitarse un peso de encima**

los **quiubos** (the what-happeneds) the explanation, truth *Ch* ◆ *Vamos a hablar de los quiubos. Es la hora de los quiubos.* Let's talk about what happened. It's the moment of truth.

R

¡Un **rábano!** (A radish!) No way!, expression of rejecting or declining something *Mex, Sp* ◆ *¡Un rábano! No pienso hacerlo. No way! I'm not planning to do it.*

rabieta →**darse (agarrarse) una rabieta**

con el **rabo entre las piernas 1.** with one's tail between one's legs, in a humiliated way *L. Am., Sp* ◆ *Fue a casa de los vecinos para quejarse del ruido, pero regresó con el rabo entre las piernas cuando vio que su hijo estaba allí. He went to the neighbors' house to complain about the noise, but he came back with his tail between his legs when he saw that his son was there.* ◆ *El profesor lo encontró copiando el examen, y tuvo que salir de la clase con el rabo entre las piernas. The professor caught him copying the exam, and he had to leave the class with his tail between his legs.*

el **rabo verde** (green tail) letch, dirty old man *Mex, C. Am., Peru,* ◆ *Manolo es un rabo verde; siempre sale con mujeres mucho menores que él. Manolo is a dirty old man; he always goes out with women much younger than he is.*

la **racha** period of time, streak, run *L. Am., Sp* ◆ *Hemos pasado una mala racha, pero creo que hoy vamos a ganar el partido. We've had a bad streak, but I think today we're going to win the game.*

el **radio macuto** rumormill, grapevine, nonexistent radio station from which rumors or falsehoods are supposedly broadcast *Sp* ◆ *Me he enterado por radio macuto de que van a despedir al director. I found out through the grapevine that they are going to fire the director.*

raíces →**echar raíces**

rajado(-a) (split) wimpy, describing someone who has chickened out, given up or backed down, taken back his or her words *Mex, Cuba, DR, ES, Col, Sp* ◆ *Es un rajado; promete y nunca cumple. He's a person who* backs down a lot; he makes promises and doesn't keep his word.

rajar 1. (to split) to flunk (as on an exam) *Mex, DR, Col, Ch* ◆ *Me rajaron en química. They failed me in chemistry.* **2.** (to split) to put down, speak badly of, talk about behind (someone's) back *Col, Peru, Bol, U, Arg* ◆ *Su mejor amiga la rajó todo el día. Her best friend put her down behind her back all day long.*

rajarse 1. (to split) to back down, chicken out, give up, take back one's words *Mex, Cuba, DR, ES, Col, Peru, U, Sp* ◆ *Dijiste que vendrías al cine; no te rajes ahora. You said you'd come to the movies, so don't back out now.* ◆ *Mauricio quería hacer bonjee en Costa Rica pero al final se rajó. Mauricio wanted to go bungee jumping in Costa Rica but he chickened out at the last minute.* ◆ *Ay, Jalisco, ¡no te rajes! Oh, Jalisco, don't let me down!* **2.** to treat, pay the check *Hond, CR, Pan* ◆ *Fuimos a cenar y el jefe se rajó. We went out to dinner and the boss treated us.*

a **rajatabla** (to board breaking) at any cost, no matter what, fanatical, strictly *L. Am., Sp* ◆ *Es vegetariano a rajatabla. He's a strict vegetarian.* ◆ *El plan saldrá bien si siguen las normas a rajatabla. The plan will turn out well if they follow the rules no matter what.*

el **rajón, la rajona** chicken, someone who backs down or doesn't do something promised, wimp *Mex, Cuba, DR, ES, Nic, Col, Sp* ◆ *Ramón nunca sale con sus amigos desde que se casó. No lo invitemos más; es bien rajón. Ramón never goes out with his friends since he got married. Let's not invite him anymore; he's a wimp (he promised to go out and didn't do it).*

las **ramas** →**irse por las ramas**

la **ranfla** car *Chicano, Mex* ◆ *Vendí la ranfla. I sold the car.*

rapidingo like a shot, very quick *parts of L. Am.* ◆ *Rapidingo, rapidingo, tienes una lla-*

rajarse: Contábamos con ella, pero se rajó. ¡Qué lástima!
We were counting on her, but she backed out. What a shame!

mada de larga distancia. Quick, quick, you have a long-distance phone call.

rápido(-a) →**más rápido(-a) que ligero(-a)**

estar **rascado(-a)** (to be scraped) to be drunk *Nic, CR, Col, Ven* ◆ *Está rascado. Llévalo a su casa.* He's drunk. Take him home.

rascarse (to scratch oneself) to get drunk *CR, Col, Ven* ◆ *Carlos se rasca todos los fines de semana y llega a su casa sin un peso.* Carlos gets drunk every weekend and comes (arrives) home without a dime.

rascarse el bolsillo (to scratch the pocket) to dig deep into one's pockets, fork up money, spend money against one's will (also, old-fashioned, **rascarse la faltriquera**) *Sp* ◆ *Finalmente el abuelo de Sergio se rascó el bolsillo y le pagó los libros de la universidad.* Finally Sergio's grandfather forked up the money and paid for his university books.

rasgarle el alma a alguien (to scratch someone's soul) to break someone's heart, hurt badly, cause pain *Mex, ES* ◆ *Recorrimos las colonias más humildes, y se nos rasgó el alma al ver cómo vive la gente allí.* We went through the poorest neighbourhoods, and it

broke our hearts to see how the people there lived.

raspa cum laude describing a big failure *PR, Col* ◆ *Miguelito se graduó raspa cum laude.* Miguelito graduated with the loser's degree (didn't really graduate).

a **rastras** by force, against one's will, kicking and screaming *Mex, U, Sp* ◆ *A rastras llevé a los niños al dentista.* I took the kids to the dentist kicking and screaming.

el/la **ratero(-a)** thief *L. Am.* ◆ *El ratero entró por la ventana y se llevó todas las alhajas.* The thief came in through the window and took all the jewelry.

en un **ratito** in a little while *L. Am., Sp* ◆ *El médico te verá en un ratito, Pablito.* The doctor will see you in a little while, Pablito.

rato →**ir para rato**

el **ratón de biblioteca** (library mouse) bookworm *L. Am., Sp* ◆ *Es un ratón de biblioteca, y su cuarto está lleno de libros.* He's a bookworm (always in the library), and his room is full of books.

ratón y queso (mouse and cheese) used instead of **rato** *Cuba* ◆ *¡Hola, socio! Hace*

211

ratón y queso que no nos vemos. Hi, pal! We haven't seen each other for ages.

los **ratos libres** (free times) free time *L. Am., Sp* ◆ *¿Qué haces en tus ratos libres? What do you do in your free time?*

los **ratos perdidos** (lost times) times when you do not have any obligatory thing to do and so do other chores or tasks, as opposed to **ratos libres**, free time *Mex, Sp* ◆ *Puedes trabajar en este proyecto en tus ratos perdidos. You can work on this project in your time that would otherwise be wasted.*

la **raya** →**hecho(-a) la mocha (la raya); poner a raya**

rayado(-a) (striped) lucky *Mex, G, ES* ◆ *¡Qué rayada esa muchacha! Sus papás le compraron un Mercedes. How lucky that girl is! Her parents bought her a Mercedes.*

rayarse 1. to luck out, often by getting something good *Chicano, Mex, G, ES, Peru* ◆ *Te rayaste con la grabadora, hombre. You lucked out with the cassette player, man.* **2.** to lose one's marbles, go crazy *Ec, Peru, S. Cone* ◆ *Después de perder su empleo, Horacio se rayó y quemó todos los documentos de la oficina. After losing his job, Horacio lost his marbles and burned all the documents in his office.*

rayársela to bitch out, used like **mentar la madre** *Mex, ES* ◆ *Me la rayaron. They insulted me big-time.*

un **rayo** →**como un rayo; echar rayos**

¡Rayos! (Lightning bolts!) Holy smoke! Good grief! (a bit old-fashioned, used to express surprise or when there is a problem) *most of L. Am., Sp* ◆ *¿Qué rayos pasa? What in blazes is going on?*

con **razón** (with reason) no wonder *L. Am., Sp* ◆ *Este niño es casi sordo. Con razón no entiende nada en la clase. This boy is almost deaf. No wonder he doesn't understand anything in class.*

real decreto →**por real decreto**

realidad as a matter of fact, really *L. Am., Sp* ◆ *En realidad, eso no tiene nada que ver. As a matter of fact, that has nothing to do with it.*

en **rebaja** (in a reduced state) on sale *L. Am., Sp* ◆ *Hoy los libros de cocina están en rebaja. Today the cookbooks are on sale.*

rebotar (to repel, bounce) to annoy, upset *Mex, Sp* ◆ *Lo que me rebotó es que escogieran a ese inepto y no a ti. What really upset me was that they chose that idiot and not you.*

rebuscarse (to relook for oneself) to hustle to get (e.g., work or money), get with it *ES, Pan, U* ◆ *Mi marido se quedó sin trabajo y esta semana tiene que rebuscarse. My husband found himself without work and this week he has to hustle (to find work).*

el **recalentado** (reheated) leftovers *Mex, ES, Col* ◆ *A Miriam le encantan los recalentados. Miriam loves leftovers.*

recoger el guante (to pick up the glove) to accept or rise to a challenge *Mex, Peru, S. Cone, Sp* ◆ *Recogí el guante y acepté el proyecto del departamento de arquitectura. I rose to the challenge and accepted the project from the architecture department.*

Recógete. Keep in your place. Behave yourself. *Mex, PR, Col* ◆ *Recógete, hijo, y ponte a estudiar. Pull yourself together, son, and concentrate on your studies.*

recopado(-a)/copado(-a) (cupped, trophied) overwhelmed (usually with joy or a positive emotion), happy, fantastic *Arg* ◆ *¿Cómo estás, Naldo? —¡Recopado! How are you, Naldo? —Fantastic!*

recorrer la Red to surf or navigate the Net *L. Am., Sp* ◆ *Su pasatiempo favorito es recorrer la Red. Their favorite pastime is surfing the Net.*

redondo(-a) (round) complete, perfect *U, Arg, Sp* ◆ *El viaje salió redondo. The trip turned out like a perfect dream.*

en **redondo** (in round, in a circle) out and out, clearly, categorically *Mex, Sp* ◆ *Se negaron en redondo. They out and out refused.*

referir: en lo que se refiere a... as far as . . . is concerned *L. Am., Sp* ◆ *En lo que se refiere al testamento de tu abuelo, no sé nada. As far as your grandfather's will is concerned, I don't know anything.*

el/la **refri** (short for **refrigerador[a]**) fridge, refrigerator *Mex, G, ES* (RVAR **el** in *Mex*, **la** in *G, ES*) ◆ *La refri está vacía. The fridge is empty.*

la **refriega** (rescrubbing) fight, blowup *U, Arg, Sp* ◆ *Hubo una refriega entre dos bandas* *rivales de la ciudad, pero al final todo acabó bien.* There was a rumble between two rival city gangs, but in the end everything turned out all right.

refrito(-a) (refried) reruns of TV programs, rehashed stories *Mex, Ven* ◆ *Hay refritos en todos los canales, especialmente en verano.* There are reruns on all the channels, especially in the summer.

una **regadera** ➝**estar como una regadera**

regalada ➝**hacer su regalada gana**

el **regalón, la regalona** (big gift-getter) pet, favorite, pampered one *Ch* ◆ *Esta niña es la regalona de sus abuelos.* That girl is her grandparents' pet.

a **regañadientes** gritting one's teeth, grudgingly, grinning and bearing it *L. Am., Sp* ◆ *Papá me dio el dinero a regañadientes.* Dad gave me the money gritting his teeth.

regarla (to spread it) to make a big mistake, do or say something that causes a problem, blow it (original meaning was vulgar—**la** refers to **mierda**—but is a very common expression) *Mex, ES, Nic, Col* ◆ *Todos la regamos de vez en cuando.* Everybody goofs up once in a while.

regio(-a) (regal, royal) great, beautiful, super *Nic, Col, Ec, S. Cone* ◆ *¿Quieres ir al museo de bellas artes? —Regio. ¿A qué hora?* Do you want to go to the fine arts museum? —Super. What time?

A mí que me **registren!** Search me! Check me out! (I'm innocent.) *Mex, S. Cone, Sp* ◆ *¡A mí que me registren! No sé nada del problema entre ustedes.* Search me! I don't know anything about the problem between you.

regla ➝**por regla general**

el **reguero** (stream, sprinkle) mess, disorder *Mex, DR, PR, Col* ◆ *Por favor, no veas el reguero que tiene el cuarto.* Please, don't look at the mess in the room.

el **reguero de gente** (stream of people) crowd *Mex, DR, PR* ◆ *Cuando llegó la policía, había un reguero de gente en el lugar del accidente.* When the police arrived, there was a crowd at the site of the accident.

lo **regular** ➝**por lo regular**

una **reina** ➝**estar como una reina**

reírse de los peces de colores (to laugh at colored fish) to not worry about something, not take seriously the consequences of one's or another's action, let it roll off like water off a duck's back *Cuba, CR, S. Cone* ◆ *Pase lo que pase, me río de los peces de colores.* Whatever happens, I let it roll off my back.

relajo ➝**echar relajo**

el **relajo** uproarious fun, joke, diversion; uproar or confusion *Mex, DR, PR, G, ES, Nic, Col, U, Sp* ◆ *En los bailes de carnaval hubo grandes relajos, pero todo el mundo se divirtió.* In the Mardi Gras dancing there was a lot of hullabaloo, but everyone had a good time.

la **reliquia** (relic) geezer, old person *L. Am.* ◆ *Nilda es una reliquia; estoy segura que tiene ochenta años.* Nilda is an old bag; I'm sure that she's eighty.

de **remate** (terminally) hopelessly, completely *L. Am., Sp* ◆ *Es loco de remate.* He is completely crazy.

remedio ➝**no tener remedio; ¡Qué remedio!**

ser una **rémora** to be retro, a reactionary, a drag or obstacle to progress or advancement *Peru, Sp* ◆ *Es una rémora social.* He's (She's) a drag on society. *Paco es una rémora en el equipo.* Paco's a hindrance to the team.

rendido(-a) (rendered) wiped out, exhausted *L. Am., Sp* ◆ *Trabajé siete días seguidos y estoy rendido.* I worked seven days straight and I'm wiped out.

ser la **repanocha** to be too much, the height (of something) *Sp* ◆ *¡Esa película sobre Che Guevara fue la repanocha!* That film about Che Guevara was too much!

reparar en migajas (pelillos) (to notice crumbs [small hairs]) to split hairs, pay attention to unimportant things instead of the bigger issue *Sp* ◆ *El director reparó en migajas, sin prestar atención a cosas más importantes.* The director split hairs, without paying any attention to more important things.

repatear (to rekick) to suck, repel; to dislike *Mex, Sp* ◆ *Me repatea esta música.* This music sucks (bothers me).

repelón, repelona describing someone who refuses to do things, is always negative *Mex* ◆ *Gloria nunca quiere hacer nada. ¡Qué repelona! Gloria never wants to do anything. What a negative Nelly!*

de **repente** suddenly *L. Am., Sp* ◆ *De repente se abrió la puerta y entró un señor muy alto. Suddenly the door opened and a very tall man came in.*

repetirlo hasta el cansancio (hasta el agotamiento) (to repeat it until tiredness [exhaustion]) to keep saying something again and again, go on and on, repeat ad nauseam *DR, PR, S. Cone, Sp* (RVar *DR, PR, Ch:* **cansancio** only) ◆ *Le repetimos hasta el cansancio que llegara a casa temprano. We repeated ad nauseam that he needed to get home early.*

re-que-te intensifiers used before adjectives, adverbs, and even verbs, meaning "very" *L. Am., Sp* ◆ *rebien; retesimpático; requeteinteresante; very good; very nice; very, very interesting* ◆ *¡Te reodio! I really hate you!* ◆ *Los reamo. I love you all very much.*

resaca →**tener resaca**

la **resaca** (undertow) hangover *Peru, S. Cone, Sp* ◆ *Anoche no pude dormir por la resaca. Last night I couldn't sleep because of my hangover.*

resbalarle algo a alguien (to slide off someone) to be indifferent, to roll off one's back *Mex, DR, PR, Sp* ◆ *¿Pedro? Le resbala totalmente el resultado. No tenía ningún interés por hacerlo bien. Pedro? The outcome (result) just rolls off his back. He had no interest in doing it well.*

respirar hondo to breathe deeply *L. Am., Sp* ◆ *¡Qué agradable el olor a pino! Debemos respirar hondo. How pleasant the smell of pine is! We should breathe deeply.*

respondón, respondona uppity, sassy, describing someone who talks back unjustifiably when reprimanded *Mex, Col, Sp* ◆ *"No seas respondón", le dijo su papá a Juanito. "Don't be sassy," Juanito's dad said to him.*

resultar que to turn out that *L. Am., Sp* ◆ *Resulta que mi prima compró un solo boleto y le tocó la lotería. It turned out that my cousin bought one single ticket and won the lottery.*

en **resumen** in short *L. Am., Sp* ◆ *Ni come ni duerme; en resumen, está enamorada otra vez. She neither eats nor sleeps; in short, she's in love again.*

Retaca la buchaca. (Stuff your craw.) Eat your fill. *Mex* ◆ *Esta noche nos sobra la comida. Retaca la buchaca. Tonight we have more than enough food. Chow down.*

retar (a un niño, a un subordinado) (to challenge [a child, subordinate]) to chew out, scold *S. Cone* ◆ *Debes retar a esos niños. Son muy desobedientes. You should scold those children. They are very disobedient.*

retirarse de to withdraw from or leave, retire from *L. Am., Sp* ◆ *Voy a retirarme ahora, señores. Buenas noches. I'm going to leave now, people. Good night.*

retorcer el hígado (to twist one's liver) to get angry *Mex* (RVar *CR:* **tener un ataque de hígado**) ◆ *Se me retorció el hígado de coraje cuando lo vi. I had an attack of anger when I saw him.*

reunirse con to meet, join (up with) *L. Am., Sp* ◆ *Se reunió con sus compañeros en el café. He met up with his friends at the café.*

reventado(-a) (burst, blown apart) wiped out, exhausted *Mex, Cuba, PR, Col, S. Cone, Sp* ◆ *Trabajamos muchas horas preparando la conferencia. Estamos reventados. We worked many hours preparing the lecture. We're wiped out.*

reventar de risa to crack up with laughter *DR, U, Sp* ◆ *Reventamos de risa escuchando los comentarios ridículos de Tito. We cracked up with laughter hearing Tito's ridiculous remarks.*

el **reventón (de primera)** (a blowout [of first]) a (first-class) bash *Mex, C. Am.* ◆ *Fuimos a un reventón de primera el viernes. We went to a first-class bash on Friday.*

reverso de la medalla flip side of the coin, just the opposite *L. Am., Sp* ◆ *Sí, este barrio es muy lujoso, pero si seguimos un poco más, veremos el reverso de la medalla. Yes, this neighborhood is very fancy, but if we go a little farther, we'll see just the opposite.*

al **revés** the other way around, backwards, the opposite *L. Am., Sp* ◆ *No, tiene que estar al revés. No, it has to be the other way around.*

◆ *Siempre hace todo al revés.* He always does everything backwards.

el **revoltijo** disorder, mess *Mex, S. Cone* ◆ *No podemos vivir en este revoltijo. Ahora mismo vamos a ordenarlo.* We can't live in this disorder. We need to tidy it up right away.

el **revolú** disorder, mess, brawl *DR, PR, Col* ◆ *Se formó un revolú porque ninguno de los dos equipos aceptaron la decisión del árbitro.* There was a brawl because neither of the teams accepted the referee's decision.

revolver a alguien las tripas (el estómago) (to have one's intestines [stomach] turn) to make one's stomach turn, cause disgust *L. Am., Sp* ◆ *Las noticias de la guerra nos revolvió las tripas.* The news of the war made our stomachs turn.

mi **rey (reina)** (my king [queen]) my dear, sweetheart *L. Am., Sp* ◆ *Te extraño mucho, mi reina.* I miss you very much, my darling.

el **ricachón, la ricachona** moneybags, rich person *L. Am., Sp* ◆ *Se casó con un ricachón que trabaja en una empresa.* She married a moneybags who works in a big company.

el **ricardo** (richard) rich guy *Mex* ◆ *¿Vas a salir con tu amigo ricardo?* Are you going to go out with your friend, Mr. Rich Guy?

rico(-a) (rich) delicious (food); hot, sexy *L. Am., Sp* (RVar *Ch:* **¡Qué rico!** is used for agreement) ◆ *Estuvo muy rica la comida.* The food was delicious. ◆ *Me dio un beso muy rico.* He (She) gave me a hot kiss.

el **ridículo** →hacer el ridículo

el **ridículum vitae** ironic for CV, curriculum vitae *Mex, ES, DR, Col* ◆ *Tengo que hacer un ridículum vitae. Voy a empezar a buscar trabajo.* I have to do a CV. I'm going to start looking for work.

a **rienda suelta** with free rein, freely or quickly *Mex, DR, PR, S. Cone, Sp* ◆ *Nos divertimos a rienda suelta.* We enjoyed ourselves freely.

Riendo se va aprendiendo. (By laughing a person goes along learning.) Humor helps learning. *Ch, Arg*

rifarse to fight *Mex, DR, G, ES* ◆ *Alberto se rifa con cualquiera.* Alberto will pick a fight with anybody.

rizar el rizo (to curl the curl) to make a mountain out of a molehill, take coals to Newcastle, complicate something unnecessarily *Sp* ◆ *Están rizando el rizo sin necesidad.* They're making a mountain out of a molehill for nothing.

robar el show (to steal the show) to steal the show, said when someone steals someone's thunder *Mex, ES, S. Cone* (RVar *Ch:* also, **robar la película**) ◆ *Con este producto nuevo, vamos a robar el show.* With this new product, we're going to steal the show. ◆ *Tú siempre quieres robarme el show.* You always want to steal my thunder.

de **rodillas** on one's knees *L. Am., Sp* ◆ *Abuelita estaba de rodillas buscando su lente de contacto.* Grandma was on her knees looking for her contact lense.

de(l) **rogar** →hacerse de(l) rogar

al **rojo vivo** →ponerse al rojo vivo

al **rojo vivo** red hot (passions) *Mex, Sp* ◆ *Esta mujer me tiene al rojo vivo.* That woman has me red hot.

el **rollo** (roll) long story or tale; bull; problem, complicated situation; also, way of being *Mex, C. Am., Col, Ven, Peru, Ch, Sp* ◆ *Vaya rollo que tiene.* Oh, my, what a story he (she) has. ◆ *Esa película es un rollo.* That movie is a bore. ◆ *No me va el rollo de tus amigos (no me gustan).* I don't care for your friends. ◆ *Déjate de tanto rollo.* Stop giving me such a crock. ◆ *Ese chico está metido en un rollo raro.* That guy is mixed up in some strange monkey business. ◆ *Yo no abro la puerta a nadie porque los vendedores a domicilio tienen un rollo bárbaro.* I don't open the door to anybody because door-to-door salesmen have such incredible spiels.

un **rollo** →echar un rollo; ir al rollo; tener mal rollo (con alguien); tener mucho rollo; tener un rollo con alguien

el **rollo macabeo (patatero)** (Maccabean [potato-seller's] roll) a lie, deception, baloney *Sp* ◆ *Esa novela fue un rollo macabeo interminable.* That novel was an interminable bunch of baloney.

de **rompe y rasga** (of break and tear) strong-willed, determined and forceful *parts of L. Am., Sp* ◆ *Esa mujer es de rompe y rasga. ¡Qué decidida!* That woman is really forceful. How decisive she is!

romper a llorar to burst into tears *L. Am., Sp* ◆ *Los niños rompieron a llorar porque no les compramos un juguete.* The children burst into tears because we didn't buy them a toy.

romper con alguien to break up with someone *L. Am., Sp* ◆ *¿Por qué rompiste con Felipe?* Why did you break up with Felipe?

romper el hielo to break the ice *L. Am., Sp* ◆ *Para romper el hielo entre los participantes del taller, cada persona se presentó y habló de su agencia.* To break the ice among the workshop participants, each person introduced himself or herself and spoke about his or her agency.

romper una lanza (to break a spear) to defend another person absolutely, to the hilt *Peru, Ch, Sp* (*Ch:* **romper lanzas**) ◆ *Rompió una lanza por su amigo. Le dio todo su apoyo frente a los que dudaban de su palabra.* He defended his friend to the hilt. He gave him all his support in front of those who doubted his word.

romperle los huevos a alguien (to break someone's eggs, meaning testicles) to bug, pester, get someone very upset (vulgar) *U, Arg* ◆ *Por favor, no me rompas los huevos.* Please stop giving me such a damn hard time.

romperse la cabeza (los cascos) (to break the head [skulls]) to think a lot about something, beat one's brains out *Mex, DR, Peru, U, Arg, Sp* ◆ *Me rompí la cabeza estudiando para el examen para nada. Al final, suspendí.* I beat my brains out studying for the test for nothing. In the end, I flunked.

romperse los codos (to break one's elbows) to cram, study diligently *Sp* ◆ *Pedro se está rompiendo los codos para estudiar. Pero como ha empezado en el último momento, no sabemos si conseguirá aprobar el examen.* Pedro is cramming hard. But since he began at the last minute, we don't know if he'll manage to pass the test.

romperse los cuernos (to break the horns) to beat one's brains out, work very hard *U, Sp* ◆ *Se rompió los cuernos trabajando para ti todo el fin de semana. Está muy cansado ahora.* He beat his brains out working for you all weekend. He's very tired now.

rondar los cincuenta (cuarenta, etc.) (to round the fifty [forty, etc.]) to be pushing fifty (forty, etc.) years old *ES, S. Cone, Sp* ◆ *¿Cuántos años tendrá tu prima? —No estoy seguro. Debe rondar los cuarenta, como yo.* How old is your cousin? —I'm not sure. She must be pushing forty, like me.

ropa →Hay ropa tendida.

La **ropa sucia se lava en casa.** (Dirty clothes are washed at home.) Let's not air dirty laundry in public. *Mex, ES, S. Cone, Sp* ◆ *Por favor no hables así de tu hermano; la ropa sucia se lava en casa.* Please don't talk that way about your brother; let's not air dirty laundry in public.

rosca →hacer la rosca; hacerse rosca; no comerse una rosca

la **rosca** (doughnut) clique, circle, closed group *Col, U, Arg* ◆ *Si no estás en esa rosca, para ellos no estás en na'a.* If you're not in that clique, to them you're nobody.

el **rostro** →el morro/el rostro; tener mucha cara (mucho rostro, mucho morro, mucha jeta)

el/la **roto(-a)** (broken) low-class person; jerk *Ch* ◆ *Son unos rotos con plata.* They're nouveaux riches (jerks with money).

la **ruca 1.** girl, woman, broad *L. Am. (not S. Cone)* (RVAR *Mex, G:* often an older and unattractive woman) ◆ *Pobre ruca. Nadie quiere bailar con ella. (Mex)* Poor old girl. No one wants to dance with her. **2.** digs, house, home (from the Mapuche language) *Ec, Ch* ◆ *Vamos a la ruca, que mi madre preparó almuerzo para todos.* Let's go home; my mother prepared lunch for everyone.

el **ruco, rucailo** geezer, old guy *Mex, G, ES, Nic* (RVAR *CR:* **roco** or **rocolo**) ◆ *¿Cómo se llama ese ruco? Parece que lo he visto en alguna parte.* What's that old guy's name? Seems like I've seen him somewhere.

los **rucos** old folks, fogies *Mex, ES, Col* ◆ *Mis rucos se van para Venezuela.* My folks are leaving for Venezuela.

de **rumba** →irse de rumba

el **rumbón** (augmentative of **rumba**) spontaneous party *PR, Col* ◆ *Anoche hubo un rumbón en la plaza principal.* Last night there was a party in the main square.

saber de letras (to know letters) to be an egghead, intellectual *Mex, DR, Col* ◆ *Esta señorita sabe de letras realmente.* This young woman is a real egghead.

Sabe Dios. God knows. *most of L. Am., Sp*

saber →**no saber de la misa la mitad; no saber dónde meterse**

saber a gloria (to taste like glory) to be very pleasant *Mex, DR, ES, CR, Sp* ◆ *El triunfo le supo a gloria. Está muy pero muy contento.* The win was great. He was very, very happy.

saber al dedillo (to know to the little finger) to know to a "T," have knowledge at one's fingertips *Mex, U, Sp* ◆ *Rosa se sabía el papel al dedillo. Por eso se lo dieron.* Rosa knew her part to a T. That's why they gave it to her.

saber de buena fuente (to know from a good source) to have it on good authority *Mex, Peru, Bol, S. Cone* ◆ *Puedes estar segura de que esta información es correcta. Lo sé de buena fuente.* You can be sure this information is correct. I have it on good authority.

saber de buena tinta una cosa (to know something from good ink) to know something from a reliable source, have it on good authority *L. Am., Sp* ◆ *¿Estás seguro que lo van a despedir? —Sí, lo sé de buena tinta.* Are you sure they're going to fire him? —Yes, I have it on good authority.

saber de qué pie cojea (to know what foot someone is limping on) to know what's going on with someone or some situation, know how the cookie crumbles, know what someone's weak point or Achilles heel is *L. Am., Sp* ◆ *Saben de qué pie cojea la gerencia. Por eso van a esperar para pedir aumento de sueldo hasta antes de Navidad.* They know management's weak point. That's why they're going to wait to ask for a raise until just before Christmas.

saber dónde le aprieta el zapato (to know where the shoe is too tight) to know one's limits, know what is suitable or appropriate for one *L. Am., Sp* ◆ *El contratista sabía dónde le apretaba el zapato y no aceptó el contrato.* The contractor knew his limits and didn't accept the contract.

A **saber.** (To be known.) Who knows? *parts of L. Am., Sp* ◆ *¿Es cierto que asaltaron el banco cerca de casa? —A saber.* Is it true that they robbed the bank near our house? —Who knows?

saber: ¿Qué sé yo? What do I know? *L. Am., Sp* ◆ *¿Por qué trabajo tan duro? ¿Qué sé yo?* Why do I work so hard? What do I know?

sabiondo(-a) (sabihondo[-a]) know-it-all *L. Am.* ◆ *Ella se cree que tiene todas las respuestas. Se las da de sabihonda.* She thinks she has all the answers. She acts like a know-it-all.

el **sablazo** (blow with a saber) loan *Mex, Ch* (RVar *Ch*: bad loan scam) ◆ *No tengo dinero. Voy a tirarle un sablazo a mi hermano.* I don't have any money. I'm going to hit on my brother for a loan.

sacar a alguien de sus casillas (de quicio) (to take someone out of their pigeon holes [out of doorjamb]) to change someone's way of doing things or drive them crazy, rattle their cage *L. Am., Sp* ◆ *Mi primo me sacó de mis casillas con sus preguntas.* My cousin drove me nuts with his questions.

sacar a luz to publish *L. Am., Sp* ◆ *El periódico ha sacado a luz las sucias maniobras de nuestro alcalde.* The newspaper has published the dirty manipulations of our mayor.

sacar agua de las piedras (to get water from stones) to get something from an improbable source, get blood from a turnip *Mex, Sp* ◆ *Los primeros españoles en las Américas sacaron agua de las piedras, trabajando sin descanso hasta vivir en forma confortable.* The first Spaniards in the Americas got blood from a turnip, working with-

out rest until they were able to live comfortably.

sacar buenas (malas) notas to get good (bad) grades *L. Am., Sp* ◆ *Mis hijos siempre sacan buenas notas en historia. My children always get good grades in history.*

sacar canas verdes (to bring out green **canas**, gray hairs) to do in, give someone gray hair, make them despair *L. Am.* ◆ *Esos niños me sacan canas verdes. Those kids are giving me gray hair.*

sacar con los pies adelante (to take out feet first) to take out, kill *Mex, DR, PR, Sp* (RVAR *Sp:* **sacar con los pies por delante**) ◆ *Cuídate; esa gente es peligrosa. En cualquier momento te sacan con los pies adelante. Be careful; those people are dangerous. At any minute they'll do you in.*

sacar de onda to knock out of kilter, throw off *L. Am.* ◆ *Lo siento. Es que me sacaste de onda. I'm sorry. It's just that you knocked me for a loop.*

sacar el jugo (to take out the juice) to make the most of, take maximum advantage, get the best (from) *L. Am., Sp* ◆ *Ese patrón te saca el jugo. That boss will take you for everything you've got.* ◆ *Hernán le sacó el jugo a sus vacaciones. Hernán took maximum advantage of his vacation.*

sacar en claro to come to a conclusion *L. Am., Sp* ◆ *Después de nuestra discusión, saqué en claro que tenemos que buscar más dinero. After our discussion, I came to the conclusion that we have to look for more money.*

sacar fotos to take photos *L. Am., Sp* ◆ *No te olvides de sacar muchas fotos de tu viaje. Don't forget to take a lot of pictures of your trip.*

sacar fuerzas de flaqueza (to take forces from thinness) to gather one's courage *L. Am., Sp* ◆ *Compañeros, ya que se murió el director, tenemos que sacar fuerzas de flaqueza y seguir adelante. My friends, since the principal has died, we must gather our courage and move ahead.*

sacar la cara por alguien (to bring or take out one's face for someone) to go to bat for someone, defend that person openly *Mex, S. Cone, Sp* ◆ *El único que sacó la cara por mí cuando me peleé con mi jefe fue Tomás; los demás no dijeron nada. The only one who went to bat for me when I had a fight with my boss was Tomás; the others didn't say anything.*

sacar las castañas del fuego (to take the chestnuts out of the fire) to help someone else out at one's own expense, save someone's bacon *U, Arg, Sp* ◆ *Siempre tienen que sacarle las castañas del fuego. Si no fuera por sus amigos, ya estaría suspendido. Someone always has to save his bacon. If it weren't for his friends, he would already have flunked out.*

sacar las uñas (to take out one's nails) to show one's true colors *Mex, DR, S. Cone, Sp* (RVAR *Ec, Peru:* **mostrar las uñas**) ◆ *Ramón sacó las uñas como gato, defendiendo su postura hasta el final. Ramón showed his true colors, defending his position to the end.*

sacar los trapos al sol (to take the rags or clothes out into the sun) to give someone the lowdown, air the dirty laundry *L. Am., Sp* ◆ *Saca los trapos al sol, Matilde. ¿Qué pasó entre Juan y Julia? Out with it, Matilde. What went on between Juan and Julia?*

sacar partido (to take out game) to take maximum advantage, get or make the most of *S. Cone, Sp* ◆ *Le sacó partido a este juguete. (Sp) He (She) enjoyed this toy to the max.* ◆ *Tenemos que sacarle partido a lo poco que tenemos. We have to make the most of what little we have.*

sacar punta a una cosa (to sharpen something, make pointed) to attribute malice or something bad to something wrongly, twist (e.g., a comment) and interpret maliciously; to use something for a purpose that wasn't intended *DR, PR, Sp* ◆ *¡Cómo te gusta sacarle punta a todo lo que te digo! How you like to twist around everything I say!*

sacar una copia to make a copy *L. Am., Sp* ◆ *Saque una copia de este documento, Enrique. Make a copy of this document, Enrique.*

sacarle a alguien de un apuro to get someone out of a jam *L. Am., Sp* ◆ *Me sacaste de un apuro ayer. ¡Gracias! You got me out of a jam yesterday. Thanks!*

sacarle de quicio (to take someone from doorjamb) to drive someone crazy, throw off or out of kilter *L. Am., Sp* ◆ *Las quejas constantes de mi compañera de cuarto me* *sacan de quicio.* The constant complaints of my roommate are driving me nuts.

sacarle el cuero a alguien (to take the leather out of someone) to rip someone to shreds with gossip, bad comments *S. Cone* (RVAR *DR:* **sacarle las tiras del cuero**) ◆ *Nadie hizo un comentario positivo en la reunión. Solamente les sacaron el cuero a las personas que no asistieron.* Nobody made any positive comments at the meeting. They just ripped the people who didn't attend to shreds.

sacarle la piel a tiras (to take off the skin in strips) to rip someone apart, speak badly of *PR, Sp* ◆ *Los gremialistas le sacaron la piel a tiras a la patronal.* The trade unionists tore the management to shreds.

sacarse la polilla (to get the moths off) to boogie, dance *Mex* ◆ *¿Te gusta esta música? Vamos a sacarnos la polilla, ¿no?* Do you like this music? Let's cut a rug, OK?

sacarse/quitarse un peso de encima (to take a weight off oneself) to take a load off; to sit down *Mex, DR, PR, S. Cone, Sp* ◆ *Te sacaste un peso de encima cuando terminaste tu libro.* You took a load off when you finished your book.

saco →**echar en saco roto**

sacudir el polvo a alguien (to shake the dust off someone) to rip someone apart, hit or tell off *Sp* ◆ *Fernanda le sacudió el polvo a Rosario cuando supo que le había sacado dinero de su bolsa.* Fernanda tore into Rosario when she found out she had taken money from her purse.

sae (sa, tusa, tusabe) used like **tú sabes**, for emphasis *PR* ◆ *A mí no me interesan las cosas materiales, sae. Lo mío es lo espiritual.* I'm not interested in material things, you know. My thing is spirituality.

sal →**no tener sal en la mollera**

salado(-a) 1. (salty) unlucky *Mex, Cuba, DR, PR, C. Am., Col, Ven, Peru, Bol, U* ◆ *¡Qué hombre más salado! Primero perdió su empleo y después le robaron el carro.* What an unlucky man! First he lost his job and then they stole his car. **2.** (salty) pricey *S. Cone* ◆ *En aquella tienda los precios son muy salados.* In that store over there the prices are really high. **3.** (salty) witty, funny, kind *Sp*

◆ *La profesora de arte es muy salada.* The art professor is very funny.

salarse (to be salted) to be down on one's luck, be unlucky *Mex, Cuba, DR, G, ES, CR, Col* ◆ *Ya me he salado: primero se me jodió la computadora y perdí todos los archivos. Después se canceló una reunión importante.* I've been really unlucky: first the computer broke down and I lost all my files. Then an important meeting was canceled.

Sale y vale. (It goes/turns out and it's worth it.) It's a deal. *Mex, C. Am., Col* (RVAR *Mex, ES:* sometimes shortened to **Sale**) ◆ *¿Cinco mil pesos? —Okei, sale y vale.* Five thousand pesos? —OK, it's a done deal.

salir a escote to go dutch (each person pays for himself or herself) *Sp* ◆ *Saldremos a escote esta noche.* We'll go dutch tonight.

salir a la americana (to go out American style) to go dutch *Mex* ◆ *Siempre salimos a la americana.* We always go dutch.

salir a la inglesa (to go out English style) to go dutch *Peru, Bol, Ch, Arg* ◆ *Saldremos esta noche a la inglesa; de lo contrario es muy caro.* Let's go out dutch tonight; otherwise it's too expensive.

salir adelante to get ahead, make progress *L. Am., Sp* ◆ *Si aprendes bien el español, saldrás adelante en tu trabajo.* If you learn Spanish well, you will get ahead in your work. ◆ *Con muchos sacrificios, logramos salir adelante.* With many sacrifices, we managed to get ahead.

salir bien (mal) parado(-a) (to come out standing well [badly]) to come out well (badly), be lucky (unlucky) *L. Am., Sp* ◆ *Los sindicalistas salieron mal parados después de la huelga.* The union members came out badly after the strike.

salir como bala (to leave like a bullet) to leave quickly, to leave like a shot *L. Am., Sp* ◆ *Cuando vio a su ex-esposa, salió como bala.* When he saw his ex-wife, he left like a shot.

salir como bólido (to take off like a fireball) to leave or take off quickly *Mex, G, CR, Cuba, DR, Col, U, Ch, Sp* ◆ *Salió como bólido cuando escuchó la sirena de la policía.* He left like a bat out of hell after he heard the police sirens.

salir como cohete to take off like a rocket *Mex, DR, ES, U, Arg, Sp* ◆ *Salimos como cohete al aeropuerto para alcanzar nuestro vuelo, pero no llegamos a tiempo.* We took off like a rocket for the airport to catch our flight, but we didn't make it on time.

salir con su domingo siete (to turn out with his or her Sunday the 7th) to have bad luck, often meaning to be pregnant; Sunday the 7th is an unlucky day *Mex, ES, S. Cone* (RVar *CR, U, Arg:* to say stupid things; *Ch:* both meanings) ◆ *¿Has oído la noticia? Esperanza salió con su domingo siete. Y su novio se ha esfumado. (ES)* Have you heard the news? Esperanza got pregnant. And her boyfriend has disappeared into thin air. ◆ *Ernesto salió con su domingo siete cuando empezó a contar chistes colorados en el velorio. (S. Cone)* Ernesto lost it and said a bunch of nonsense when he started telling dirty jokes at the wake.

salir de Guatemala para entrar en Guatepeor to go from the frying pan (from Guate**mala** [meaning "bad"]) into the fire (Guate**peor** [meaning "worse"]) *L. Am., Sp* ◆ *Salimos de Guatemala para entrar en Guatepeor al pedir un nuevo préstamo al banco.* We went from the frying pan into the fire when we asked the bank for another loan.

salir de marcha →**irse (salir) de marcha**

salir del paso to make it through, to get through (some problem) *L. Am., Sp* ◆ *Tuve un gran conflicto con mi jefe pero salí del paso.* I had a big fight with my boss, but I got through it.

salir del sistema to log off *L. Am., Sp* ◆ *Son las tres de la mañana, Pepe. ¡Es hora de salir del sistema!* It's three in the morning, Pepe. It's time to log off!

salir el tiro por la culata (to have the shot go out the butt of the rifle) to backfire, have an opposite result from what was expected *L. Am., Sp* ◆ *Estaban seguros que ganarían las elecciones fácilmente; sin embargo les salió el tiro por la culata, y fueron derrotados.* They were sure they would win the election easily, but things backfired on them, and they were defeated.

salir hasta en la sopa (to come up even in the soup) to pop up everywhere, get around *L. Am., Sp* ◆ *Felipe, ¿otra vez nos encontramos? Me sales hasta en la sopa.* Felipe, we bump into each other again? You seem to be everywhere.

salir pitando 1. (to leave honking the horn or blowing a whistle) to take off quickly *Mex, Sp* ◆ *Metimos todo en el coche y salimos pitando.* We put everything in the car and we took off. **2.** to come out swinging, show anger or vehemence in a conversation ◆ *No te preocupes; no voy a salir pitando como antes.* Don't worry; I'm not going to come out swinging like I did before.

salir por la ventana (to take off through the window) to sneak out the back door, get out of a place or business in a disgraceful way *Sp* ◆ *Como sigan comportándose así, van a salir por la ventana.* Because you keep acting like that, you will end up leaving in disgrace.

(no) salirle a alguien algo de los cojones (huevos) (to [not] come from one's testicles) to [not] be in the mood, [not] feel like (vulgar) *PR, Sp* (RVar *Sp:* also, **de las narices**, not vulgar) ◆ *No me sale de los cojones cortarme el pelo y no lo haré.* I don't freaking feel like cutting my hair and I won't do it. ◆ *¿Por qué no quieres preparar el café? —Porque no me sale de los huevos.* Why don't you want to make the coffee? —Because I don't freaking feel like it.

salirse con la suya to get one's way *L. Am., Sp* ◆ *Sara se salió con la suya y se fue con sus amigas a la playa sin terminar sus exámenes.* Sara got her way and went with her friends to the beach without finishing her exams.

salirse de las casillas (to go out of one's boxes) to go overboard, go too far, do something abnormal, flip out *L. Am., Sp* ◆ *Agustín se enojó, se salió de las casillas y se puso a gritar a la gente.* Agustín got angry, flipped out, and started yelling at people.

salirse de madre en algo (to go out of the mother in something) to go overboard, do something not normal, flip out *Mex, Sp* ◆ *Te estás saliendo de madre.* You're overdoing it.

salirse del guacal (to go out of one's container or gourd) to go overboard, go too far, do something not normal, flip out *Mex, ES* ◆ *Mi hijo se me salió del guacal... se portó* *muy mal. My son went beyond the limit . . . he behaved very badly.*

salirse por el cuello de la camisa (to go out by the neck of the shirt) to be skin and bones, very skinny *Sp* ◆ *Ayer vi a Ómar. Está tan delgado que parece que va a salirse por el cuello de la camisa. Yesterday I saw Ómar. He's so thin he's just skin and bones.*

salirse por la tangente (to go off on a tangent) to sidestep or avoid *Mex, CR, S. Cone, Sp* ◆ *Cada vez que le pregunto algo y espero una respuesta concreta, me sale por la tangente. No hay quien consiga hablar con él de este tema. Every time I ask him something and expect a concrete response, he sidesteps the issue. Nobody can get him to talk on that subject.*

el **salmón** (salmon) idiot, fool *PR*

saltos →**dar saltos de alegría**

¡Salud! (Health!) To your health! Gesundheit!, said as a toast or after a sneeze *L. Am., Sp* (*Mex:* also, **¡Salucitas!**) ◆ *Brindemos por la familia y los amigos. ¡Salud! Let's make a toast to family and friends. Cheers!*

salvar el pellejo to save one's skin *L. Am., Sp* ◆ *Salvaron el pellejo de milagro. Fueron los últimos en cruzar el puente antes que el río se lo llevara. They were saved (saved their skins) by a miracle. They were the last to cross the bridge before the river washed it away.*

salvarse por un pelo (to be saved by a hair) to be saved by the bell, escape by a hair *L. Am., Sp* (RVAR *Peru:* **salvarse por los pelos**) ◆ *Dos personas murieron en el accidente. Yo me salvé por un pelo. Two people died in the accident. I was saved by a hair.*

sanano(-a) stupid, foolish *PR* ◆ *El perrito de la esquina es bien sanano; corre delante de los carros. Un día lo van a matar. The little dog on the corner is really stupid; he runs in front of cars. One day he's going to get killed (they're going to kill him).*

sancocharse to be steaming hot (people) *Mex, DR, PR, Col, Ch* ◆ *Me estoy sancochando del calor. ¡Abran las ventanas! I'm roasting hot. Open the windows.*

las **sandeces** nonsense *L. Am., Sp* ◆ *No digas sandeces. Don't talk nonsense.*

sangre →**hacerse mala sangre; tener mala sangre**

ser de **sangre azul** to be a blue blood, from an aristocratic family *L. Am., Sp* ◆ *Julio es de sangre azul pero no le gusta mencionarlo. Julio is a blue blood, but he doesn't like to mention it.*

a **sangre y fuego** (by blood and fire) violently or vehemently, to the hilt *Mex, Sp* ◆ *Defendió su postura a sangre y fuego, hasta que al final le dieron la razón. He defended his position to the hilt, until finally they agreed that he was right.*

sangrón, sangrona bad tempered, unpleasant, annoying; jerk, a pain *Mex, Cuba, G, ES, CR, Col* (RVAR *CR:* usually someone who humiliates or mistreats people smaller or weaker) ◆ *Ese tipo es tan sangrón que nadie lo quiere. That guy is such a pain that nobody likes him.*

sano(-a) como una manzana (healthy as an apple) very well, healthy, fit as a fiddle *Sp* ◆ *Hola, Verónica. ¿Cómo estás? —Sana como una manzana. Hi, Verónica. How are you? —Fit as a fiddle.*

sano(-a) y salvo(-a) (healthy and safe) safe and sound *L. Am., Sp* ◆ *Luisita volvió de su viaje sana y salva, gracias a Dios. Luisita came back from her trip safe and sound, thank goodness.*

Sanseacabó. (Saint it's over.) That's that; phrase used to end a discussion *Mex, DR, PR, G, ES, S. Cone, Sp* ◆ *Esto no tiene sentido. ¡Sanseacabó! This doesn't make any sense. That's enough talk about it!*

la **Santa Inquisición** (the Holy Inquisition) your, my, etc. (inquiring) wife *Mex, Col* ◆ *Aquí viene la Santa Inquisición. Todo lo quiere saber. Here comes my (inquiring) wife. She wants to know everything.*

Santas pascuas. (Holy Easter or Passover) And that's the end of it; phrase to end a discussion or said when one is forced to resign oneself to something *Mex, Ch, Sp* ◆ *Tú te quedas con la casa y yo con el Mercedes, y santas pascuas. You get the house and I get the Mercedes, and that's that.* ◆ *No podemos hacer el viaje y santas pascuas. We can't go on the trip and that's the end of it.*

en un **santiamén** (in the time it takes to say **santiamén**) in a jiffy, an instant *L. Am., Sp*

◆ *Lo puedo hacer en un santiamén.* I can do it in a jiffy.

¡Santísima Trinidad! (Holy Trinity!) Good heavens!, Holy smoke! expression of surprise or fright, especially used by women *Mex, ES, CR, Col* ◆ *¡Santísima Trinidad! Han muerto cientos de personas en el terremoto.* Good heavens! Hundreds of people have died in the earthquake.

el **santito** (little saint) good boy, little angel (sometimes said sarcastically) *DR, ES, Col, U, Arg* ◆ *Tus hijos son unos santitos; se comportan muy bien. —Sí, gracias, sobre todo cuando duermen.* Your children are good kids; they behave so well. —Yes, thanks, especially when they're asleep.

santo →**írsele a alguien el santo al cielo; tener el santo de cabeza; tener el santo de cara; tener el santo de espaldas; tener santos en la corte**

un **santo cristo** →**como a un santo cristo un par de pistolas**

Santo que no me quiere, basta con no rezarle. (Saint that doesn't like me, it's enough not to pray to him.) I'll keep my distance. Who cares about that person? There's no need to bother with someone who doesn't care about me. *parts of L. Am.* ◆ *Verónica no quiere verte más. —Santo que no me quiere, basta con no rezarle.* Veronica doesn't want to see you anymore. —Well, I don't want to bother with someone who doesn't care about me.

santo(-a) y bueno(-a) (holy and good) good-natured, great *Mex, PR, Col* ◆ *Carmelita es una persona tan santa y tan buena que se va a ir derechito al cielo cuando se muera.* Carmelita is such a good-natured person that she's going to go straight to heaven when she dies.

el **santurrón, la santurrona** goody-two-shoes, goody-goody *L. Am.* (RVAR *parts of the Americas:* **santulón, santulona**) ◆ *¿Qué quiere ese santurrón de tu primo?* What's that goody-goody of a cousin of yours want?

sapear to tell on someone, squeal *CR, Col, Ven* (RVAR *Peru, Ch:* to spy on) ◆ *No me vayas a sapear a la maestra.* Don't tell the teacher on me.

el **sapo** (frog, toad) informer, stool pigeon, fink (used like **soplón**) *Nic, CR, Col, Ven, Ec,*

Peru, Ch (RVAR *Col:* also, **rana;** *Peru:* **ranear**) ◆ *Es un sapo. Todo lo cuenta.* He's a fink. He tells everything.

sardina →**como sardina en lata**

la **sartén** →**tener la sartén por el mango**

el **sastre de campillo, que cosía de balde y ponía el hilo** (the country tailor who sewed for free and paid for the thread) said of someone who works for free and suffers a cost *Sp*

sato(-a) stupid, foolish (also, a mixed breed animal) *PR* ◆ *¡Qué nena más sata! Ahora se las da de Madonna.* What a silly girl! Now she's acting like she's Madonna. ◆ *Ese perrito parece un labrador pero es sato.* That little dog looks like a Labrador but he's a mongrel.

Se caen los patos asados. (Ducks are falling already roasted.) It's a scorcher. *Ch* ◆ *Este verano se caen los patos asados.* This summer is a scorcher.

a **secas** (dry) only (that); alone, and that's it *Mex, Ch, Sp* ◆ *La carta no llegó porque no llevaba la dirección. Llevaba un nombre a secas.* The letter didn't arrive because it didn't have an address. It had a name and that's it.

estar **seco(-a)** (to be dry) to be broke, without money *U, Arg* ◆ *Estoy seco hasta el próximo día de pago.* I'm broke until the next payday.

en **seguida** right away *L. Am., Sp* ◆ *En seguida le traigo el café, señor.* I'll bring your coffee right away, sir.

seguir adelante/seguir derecho to go or proceed straight ahead *L. Am., Sp* ◆ *Para llegar a la gasolinera, siga derecho tres cuadras.* To get to the gas station, go straight ahead three blocks.

seguir en sus trece (to keep in one's thirteen) to stick to one's guns, keep doing the same thing, persist in an opinion or in doing something *Ch, Sp* ◆ *A pesar de todos los consejos, María Herminia sigue en sus trece y sale con Julián.* Despite all advice, María Herminia sticks to her guns and keeps going out with Julián.

seguir las huellas de alguien to follow in someone's footsteps *Mex, Ch, Sp* ◆ *El hijo sigue las huellas del padre; va a ser banquero.* The son is following in his father's footsteps; he's going to be a banker.

seguir un curso to take a course *L. Am., Sp* ◆ *¿Cuántos cursos sigues este semestre, Andrés?* How many courses are you taking this semester, Andrés?

seguirle a alguien la corriente (to follow someone's current) to follow someone and agree with him or her, go along (sometimes just to humor someone) *Mex, DR, ES, Nic, S. Cone, Sp* ◆ *Esta chica está loca. Es mejor seguirle la corriente y no discutir con ella.* This girl is crazy. It's better to humor her and not argue.

seguirle el rastro to track down *L. Am., Sp* ◆ *¡Vamos, muchachos, tenemos que seguirle el rastro a ese ladrón!* Come on, guys, let's track down that thief!

según dicen (so) people say, (so) they say *L. Am., Sp* ◆ *Se ha casado cinco veces en los últimos diez años, según dicen.* He (She) has gotten married five times in the last ten years, people say.

según el caso as the case may be *L. Am., Sp* ◆ *Más tarde te sentirás muy enojada o muy aliviada, según el caso.* Later on you'll feel very angry or very relieved, as the case may be.

de **segunda mano** second-hand *L. Am., Sp* ◆ *Es un coche de segunda mano, pero parece casi nuevo.* It's a second-hand car, but it looks almost new.

el **segundo frente** (second front) mistress, lover of a married man *Mex, ES, Ven* ◆ *Recién vimos a tu tío con su segundo frente.* Recently we saw your uncle with his mistress.

el **semáforo de medianoche** (traffic light at midnight) person no one respects and whom everyone takes advantage of, pushover *Ven* ◆ *¿Vas a invitar a tu primo a la fiesta? —No, es semáforo de medianoche.* Are you going to invite your cousin to the party? —No, he's such a dud.

semana →**por semana (por mes)**

la **senda de elefantes** (elephant path) area where there are a lot of bars (from **trompa,** which means *elephant's trunk* or *drunk*) (trunk or drunk) *Sp* ◆ *Fuimos a un bar en la senda de elefantes.* We went to a bar in the area of town where there are a lot of watering holes.

sendo(-a) big, great *Mex, C. Am.* ◆ *Se sirvieron sendos platos de menudo.* They served themselves great plates of tripe soup.

sentar cabeza (to seat head) to settle down most of *L. Am., Sp* ◆ *Por fin mi hijo se casó y sentó cabeza.* Finally my son got married and settled down.

sentir (que) to be sorry (that) *L. Am., Sp* ◆ *¡Cuánto lo siento!* I'm so sorry! (literally, How much I feel it!)

sentir un nudo en la garganta (to feel a knot in one's throat) to have a lump in one's throat *L. Am., Sp* ◆ *Cuando me describió las hermosas ceremonias planeadas para el homenaje, sentí un nudo en la garganta.* When she described to me the beautiful ceremonies planned for the memorial service, I felt a lump in my throat.

sentirse cortado(-a) →**cortarse**

sentirse en plena forma (to feel in full form) to feel your best, in great condition *Mex, Sp* ◆ *Me siento en plena forma. Estoy mejor que nunca. Y todo gracias al gimnasio.* I feel in great shape. I'm better than ever. And all thanks to the gym.

señalar a alguien con el dedo; poner el dedo a alguien to point the finger at someone, single out *Mex, ES, Peru, Ch, Sp* ◆ *Le puso el dedo al narcotraficante.* He (She) singled out the drug dealer.

seño short for **señorita** or **señora** parts of *L. Am.* ◆ *¿Cóma está, seño?* How are you, ma'am?

Sepa Chepa. (Chepa probably knows.) Who knows? *Chicano, Nic*

sepetecientos(-as) gazillion, many, an uncountable number *Mex, DR, PR, Col* ◆ *Te lo he dicho sepetecientas veces: ¡No voy!* I've told you a zillion times: I'm not going!

(no) ser plato del gusto de alguien to (not) be one's cup of tea (literally, preferred dish) *Sp* ◆ *Estas ideas no son plato del gusto de Javier. Seguro que no va a aceptar la propuesta.* These ideas are not Javier's cup of tea. It's a sure bet he won't accept the proposal.

(no) ser santo de su devoción (to [not] be the saint of one's devotion) to (not) be someone looked up to, to (not) be an idol; often used in the negative to mean to not be one's cup of tea *ES, Nic, S. Cone, Sp* ◆ *Jennifer López* *nunca fue santo de mi devoción, pero la tolero.* Jennifer López was never really my cup of tea, but I can put up with her.

en **serio** →**¡No habla(s) en serio!**

serrucharle el piso a alguien (to saw off the floor under someone) to undermine someone, often by saying bad things about him or her to others behind his or her back, pull the chair out from under someone or cook someone's goose *Hond, Nic, CR, Col, Ec, Peru, S. Cone* (RVar *DR:* **serruchar el palo;** *U, Arg,* also, **serruchar las patas**) ◆ *Mireya me serruchó el piso con mi jefe cuando fui de vacaciones.* Mireya cooked my goose with the boss by telling him lies when I went on vacation.

serrucho →**hacer un serrucho**

el **serrucho** kitty, pool of money to buy something collectively *DR, PR* ◆ *Señores, es un serrucho: cada uno pone quince pesos.* People, it's a collective effort; everyone puts fifteen pesos (in the kitty).

los **servicios públicos/los baños públicos** public washrooms *L. Am., Sp* ◆ *Los baños públicos allí están muy sucios.* The public washrooms (bathrooms) there are very dirty.

servir de to serve the purpose of *L. Am., Sp* ◆ *¿De qué sirve estar deprimido? —En realidad, no me sirve de nada.* What purpose does getting depressed serve? —Actually, it doesn't serve me any purpose.

servir lo mismo para un fregado que para un barrido (to serve the same for a scrubbing as for a sweeping) to be all-purpose; to serve for contrary uses *Cuba, Sp* ◆ *Este chico es estupendo; tanto sirve para un fregado como para un barrido.* This boy is wonderful; he can do anything.

servir para (to serve for) to be for, serve as *L. Am., Sp* ◆ *¿Para qué sirve ese aparato?* What's that gadget for?

servir: ¿En qué puedo servirle(s)? How can I help you? *L. Am., Sp* ◆ *¿En qué puedo servirle, señor? —Sólo estoy mirando.* How can I help you, sir? —I'm just looking.

servir: No sirve. It's no good. *L. Am., Sp* ◆ *Este televisor no sirve; lo voy a devolver.* This television is no good; I'm going to take it back.

Si Dios quiere. (If God wants.) God willing. (often used when an action is proposed or some statement of optimism is made) *L. Am., Sp* ◆ *Vamos a comprar una casa más grande, si Dios quiere.* We're going to buy a bigger house, if all goes well (if God wills it).

Si no lo veo, ¡no lo creo! (If I don't see it, I don't believe it!) I can't believe my eyes! Incredible! *Mex, ES, S. Cone, Sp* ◆ *Salvador se enojó con su mujer y le pegó. Si no lo veo, ¡no lo creo!* Salvador got mad and hit his wife. I can't believe my eyes!

Si se quema la casa, no pierde nada. If the house burns down, he or she won't lose anything (referring to someone who is overdressed, wearing lots of jewelry, etc.). *PR*

Siempre pa'lante. (Always forward.) Plugging along. *DR, PR, Col, Ven* ◆ *¿Cómo anda, doña Tomasa? —Siempre pa'lante, m'hija.* How are you, Tomasa? —Just plugging along, my dear.

de **siete suelas** (of seven soles/bases) true, for real (usually used for something bad) *Mex, Ch, U, Sp* ◆ *Es un pícaro de siete suelas.* He's a real rascal.

simón used instead of *sí most of L. Am.* ◆ *¿Has visto a Paco? —Simón.* Have you seen Paco? —Yup.

sin aliento out of breath *L. Am., Sp* ◆ *Llegamos a la cumbre, contentos y sin aliento.* We got to the top, happy and out of breath.

sin blanca (without a white one, meaning a coin) broke *Sp* ◆ *Despúes del concierto, me quedé sin blanca. No pude ni comprar una bebida.* After the concert, I was broke. I couldn't even buy a drink.

sin cachondeo(s) with no joking around *Sp* ◆ *Sin cachondeos hablamos con nuestros hijos.* We talked to our children with no joking around.

sin chiste (without joke) so-so, blah, unappetizing *Mex, Col, Peru, Bol* ◆ *Me parece muy sin chiste su vestido.* Her dress looks very blah to me.

estar **sin cinco** (to be without five) to not have a plug nickel *Mex, ES, Sp* ◆ *Le presté dinero a Javier porque estaba sin cinco.* I lent money to Javier because he didn't have a plug nickel.

sin co short for **sin comentarios**, without comment *Mex, Col* ◆ *¿Tienes algo más que decir? —No, sin co.* Do you have anything else to say? —No, no comment.

sin cruzar palabra (without crossing word) without speaking, without saying a word *L. Am., Sp* ◆ *Estuvimos tres horas en la misma mesa sin cruzar palabra.* We spent three hours at the same table without saying a word to each other.

sin embargo however *L. Am., Sp* ◆ *Decidimos no regalar la mesa; sin embargo, Graciela realmente la merece.* We decided not to give away the table; however, Graciela really deserves it.

sin falta without fail *L. Am., Sp* ◆ *Lo hago sin falta, amigo.* I will do it without fail, my friend.

sin faltar una coma (jota) (without missing a comma [jot]) just so, with accuracy *Mex, DR, Sp* ◆ *Está todo terminado, sin faltar una coma.* Everything is finished, just right.

la **sin hueso** (the boneless one) tongue *Ch, U, Sp* ◆ *Movimos la sin hueso toda la tarde con Elisa; hablamos de todas nuestras frustraciones.* We chatted all afternoon with Elisa; we spoke about all our frustrations.

sin ir más lejos (without going farther) for instance *L. Am., Sp* ◆ *Mucha gente votó por él. Mi hermano, sin ir más lejos.* Many people voted for him. My brother, for instance.

sin más ni más just like that, with no further ado *L. Am., Sp* ◆ *¿Así que me vas a dejar, Humberto, sin más ni más?* So, Humberto, you are going to leave me just like that?

sin novedad same as always, just as usual (often at the end of a letter) *L. Am., Sp* ◆ *Aquí nos encontramos bien, sin novedad.* Here we are all fine, same as always.

sin padre ni madre, ni perro que me ladre (without father or mother or dog that barks for me) all by one's lonesome, alone, independent, or without support *Mex, PR, Ch, Arg, Sp* ◆ *¿Tienes amigos en esta ciudad? —No, estoy sin padre ni madre, ni perro que me ladre.* Do you have friends in this city? —No, I'm all by my lonesome.

sin par (without equal) peerless, incomparable *L. Am., Sp* ◆ *Este ron de Venezuela es sin par.* This rum from Venezuela is incomparable.

sin ton ni son (without tone or sound) without rhyme or reason *L. Am., Sp* ◆ *Esa novela es absurda. Sin ton ni son.* That novel is absurd. Without rhyme or reason.

sincho of course, natch *Chicano, Mex, Col* ◆ *¿Vas al cine con nosotros? —¡Sincho!* Are you going to the movies with us? —Natch!

un **sinnúmero** (without number) countless, a number beyond measure *L. Am., Sp* ◆ *Luz tiene un sinnúmero de amigos.* Luz has countless friends.

un **sinpa** →hacer un sinpa

siquiera →ni siquiera

el **sistema jodicial** (screwed-up system, corruption of **judicial; jodicial** is from **joder**, to screw up) police and legal system *Mex, Col* ◆ *Es un experto en el sistema jodicial de su país.* He's an expert in the screwed-up legal system of his country.

en su **sitio** →poner a alguien en su sitio (lugar)

siútico(-a) stuck-up, affected, pretentious *Ch* ◆ *Ese tipo es tan siútico que siempre utiliza palabras en francés mal pronunciadas.* That guy is so pretentious that he always uses badly pronounced French words.

sobar (to massage) to get some shut-eye, sleep *Sp* ◆ *Me pasé el día sobando.* I spent the day snoozing.

sobrado(-a) (more than enough, excessive) stuck-up *Peru, Ch* ◆ *No te metas con ella; es una sobrada.* Don't get involved with her; she's stuck-up.

sobrar (haber) tela que cortar (to have extra material to cut) to have no lack of material, plenty of material to deal with an issue *Mex, DR, PR* ◆ *Todavía hay mucha tela que cortar sobre esta materia, según la maestra.* There's still a lot of material to deal with on this topic, according to the teacher.

en el **sobre** →meterse en el sobre

la **sobremesa** after-dinner conversation at the table *L. Am., Sp* ◆ *Después de la cena estuvimos de sobremesa charlando y haciendo bromas hasta las dos de la mañana.* After supper we stayed at the table talking and telling jokes until two in the morning. ◆ *Los domingos nos reuníamos todos en la casa* *de los abuelos, y la sobremesa duraba tres o cuatro horas. Sundays we would all get together in my grandparents' house, and our time chatting around the table would last three or four hours.*

Sobres. Right. *Mex, ES* ◆ *Llegaremos esta noche a tu casa. —Sobres. We'll go to your house tonight. —All righty.*

el/la **socio(-a)** (associate, member) friend, pal, often used in direct address *Mex, Cuba, Col, Peru, Ch* (RVAR *Cuba:* masculine form only) ◆ *Hola, socio, ¿qué tal? Hi, pal, how's it going?*

la **soda** (soda) café that sells reasonably priced food *CR* ◆ *Hay una buena soda en mi barrio. There's a good café in my neighborhood.*

ser una **soda** (to be a soda) to be super, terrific *Col* ◆ *¡Qué lugar más simpático! —De veras, es una soda. What a charming place! —It's really terrific.*

sofocarse (to get suffocated) to get upset, worked up *L Am., Sp* ◆ *No te sofoques. Don't hit the ceiling.*

la **soga** →echarse la soga al cuello

con la **soga al cuello** (with the noose at the neck) in hot water, at risk, in a bad position or in bad straits *L. Am., Sp* ◆ *La separación de mi mujer me ha dejado con la soga al cuello. The separation from my wife has left me in bad straits.*

a **sol** →no dejar (ni) a sol ni a sombra a alguien

de **sol a sol** (from sun to sun) from sunup to sundown *L. Am., Sp* ◆ *Trabajaron de sol a sol. They worked from sunup to sundown.*

solano(-a) alone, all by one's lonesome, used instead of **solo(-a)** *Chicano, Mex, Cuba, Col, U, Arg* ◆ *¿Ya no sales con Carmen? Siempre te veo solano. You're not going out with Carmen anymore? I always see you all by your lonesome.*

sólo por donde pasa/ve la suegra (just where the mother-in-law will pass by or see things) expression telling that one is working fast to keep up appearances *Mex, Col* ◆ *No te fijes en la casa, porfa. Limpié sólo por donde ve la suegra. Don't look too closely at the house, please. I gave it only a lick and a polish.*

soltar el rollo (to let loose the roll) to talk at length, let out a long tale or tell all that one knows *parts of L. Am., Sp* (RVAR *Arg:* **largar el rollo**) ◆ *Suelta el rollo, Ana. ¿Qué pasó? Tell all, Ana. What happened?*

soltar la cuerda (to let go of or loosen the cord) to let the cat out of the bag, spill the beans, confess, implicate someone in something *Mex, Sp* ◆ *El detenido soltó la cuerda, y la policía encontró el resto de los delincuentes. The guy they arrested spilled the beans, and the police found the rest of the criminals.*

soltar la lengua (to loosen the tongue) to open up, spill the beans *DR, S. Cone* ◆ *Suelta la lengua, muchacha. Dinos que pasó. Spill the beans, girl. Tell us what happened.*

estar a la **sombra** (to be in the shade) to be in the clinker (jail) *Mex, Cuba, G, Peru, S. Cone, Sp* ◆ *Hace cinco años que el ladrón del banco está a la sombra. The bank robber has been behind bars for five years.*

la **sombra** →no ser ni la sombra de lo que era; tener buena sombra; tener mala sombra

el **sombrero (el gorro)** (hat [cap]) condom, rubber *DR, PR, G, ES, Col* ◆ *Por favor, ino arriesguen sus vidas! Si van a salir con mujeres, lleven sombreros. Please don't risk your lives! If you're going to go out with women, take along some condoms.* ◆ *¡Tengan cuidado, muchachas! No se acuesten con hombres que no usen gorros. Be careful, girls! Don't go to bed with men who don't use condoms.*

¿A **son de qué?** How come? For what reason? *Mex, DR, Ch, U, Sp* (RVAR *Mex, U:* **¿Al son...?**) ◆ *¿A son de qué tenías que contarle que viste a su novio en la playa? For what reason did you have to tell her that you saw her boyfriend at the beach?*

Son habas contadas. (They're counted beans.) They're a sure thing. They're few and far between (scarce and with a fixed number). *Sp* ◆ *No hay muchos contratistas que puedan hacer esa clase de trabajo. Son habas contadas. There aren't many contractors who can do that kind of work. They're few and far between.*

soltar el rollo: Cuando ella suelta el rollo, hay que escucharla.
When she lets out a long tale, you have to listen to her.

Son palabras mayores. (They are major words.) It's a serious matter. There's something very serious or difficult that has to be talked about. *Mex, DR, ES, Nic, Peru, S. Cone* ◆ *Vamos a hablar más sobre tu decisión de casarte. El casamiento... ya son palabras mayores.* We're going to talk some more about your decision to get married. Marriage . . . it's a serious matter.

sonado(-a) (sounded, rung) in hot water, big trouble *S. Cone* ◆ *Alberto está sonado. Su novia lo vio con otra chica.* Alberto is in big trouble. His girlfriend saw him with another girl.

sonar (como tarro) (to ring [like a tin can]) to try and fail at something, really blow it, fall (flat) on your face *Ch, U* ◆ *Soné como tarro viejo en el examen de sociología. I really blew it on the sociology exam.*

sonsacar to distract someone or get them to go out instead of doing their work *Mex, DR, PR G, ES* ◆ *Ella es muy tranquila. Lo que pasa es que su hermana la sonsaca para que vaya a las discotecas. She is very quiet.* What happens is that her sister gets her to go out dancing. ◆ *Iba a estudiar, pero pasaron unas amigas y me sonsacaron. I was going to study, but some friends came by and dragged me out for some fun.*

soñar →**Ni soñarlo.**

soñar con pájaros preñados (to dream of pregnant birds) to be dreaming (of the impossible) *parts of L. Am.* ◆ *Si crees que te voy a comprar ese carro, estás soñando con pájaros preñados. If you think I'm going to buy you that car, you're dreaming.*

sopa →**hecho(-a) una sopa; Nunca falta un pelo en la sopa.**

la **sopa boba** (crazy or foolish soup) life on Easy Street, life lived at others' expense, without working *Sp* ◆ *Estos chicos viven la sopa boba. ¿Cuándo van a trabajar? These kids live life on Easy Street. When will they go to work?*

la **sopa de letras** (alphabet soup, referring to something spoken or written) confusion *Mex, Col, Peru* ◆ *Este poema es una sopa* *de letras. No lo entiendo. This poem is like alphabet soup. I don't understand it.*

el **sopapo** blow or punch *L. Am., Sp* ◆ *Si no te callas, te doy un sopapo. If you don't quiet down, I'll give you a smack.*

soplar (to blow) to squeal, tell or inform on someone, tattle; to whisper the answer to someone taking a test *L. Am., Sp* ◆ *Juan sopló a la policía, y ahora sus compañeros están en la cárcel. Juan squealed to the police, and now his pals are in jail.* ◆ *Lolita le sopló la respuesta a su novio en el examen de historia. Lolita whispered the answer to her boyfriend on the history test.*

el **soplón, la soplona** informer, tattletale, rat; someone who whispers the answer to someone taking a test *L. Am., Sp* ◆ *Fue expulsada por soplona. She was expelled for cheating (being a cheater).*

sordo(-a) →**más sordo(-a) que una tapia**

en **su propia salsa** (in his or her sauce) in your (his, her) element *Mex, Peru, S. Cone, Sp* ◆ *Con este nuevo grupo de amigos, Mario se encuentra como en su propia salsa. With this new group of friends, Mario is in his element.*

suave (soft) good, easy-going, pleasant (people and things) *Mex, Cuba, Col* ◆ *Adelia es una persona muy suave. Adelia is a very easy-going person.*

suave →**llevarla suave**

Suave. (Smooth, soft.) Chill out. Take it easy. *DR, Ven, Ch* ◆ *Suave, suave. No escuches esos comentarios absurdos. Take it easy. Don't listen to those absurd comments.*

Súbete al micro. (Step up to the microphone.) Join in the conversation. *Ch* ◆ *Súbete al micro, Miguel; la conversación es muy interesante. Join in, Miguel; the conversation is very interesting.*

subido(-a) de tono (heightened in tone, with a louder tone) strong language, implying vulgar expressions *DR, ES, Peru, Bol, Ch, U, Sp* ◆ *La conversación degeneró, y subió excesivamente de tono. Tuvimos que parar para no herir la sensibilidad de los clientes. The conversation degenerated and got louder and a bit offensive. We had to stop so as not to hurt the clients' feelings.*

subiendo →**ir subiendo**

subir al poder to rise to power *L. Am., Sp* ◆ *Por lo general, los dictadores suben al poder por la violencia. As a general rule, dictators rise to power through violence.*

subirse los humos a la cabeza (to have the vapors go to one's head) to get a swollen head *L. Am., Sp* ◆ *Se casó con una millonaria y se le han subido los humos a la cabeza. He married a millionaire, and he's gotten a swollen head.*

subirse por las paredes to be climbing (up) the walls (with annoyance) *U, Sp* ◆ *Cuando lo vi, estaba que se subía por las paredes. ¡Vaya qué enfado! When I saw him, he was climbing the walls. He was really mad! (literally, What anger!)*

subírsele a alguien el humo a las narices (a la cabeza) (to have smoke rising up to one's nostrils [to one's head]) to be very annoyed, steamed *CR, Sp* (RVar *CR:* **a la cabeza** instead of **a las narices;** *Ch:* **írsele el humo a la cabeza**) ◆ *A Sergio se le subió el humo a las narices cuando supo que su hija le había mentido. Sergio got all steamed up when he found out his daughter had lied to him.*

subírsele a alguien los huevos (to have one's eggs, or testicles, rise) to get a hell of a scare, be scared shitless, lose one's courage (vulgar) *Mex* ◆ *Cuando me di cuenta de que había un ladrón en la casa, se me subieron los huevos hasta la garganta. When I realized there was a robber in the house, I got a hell of a scare.*

subírsele la mostaza (to have the mustard rise up) to get angry *Peru, Sp* ◆ *Perdona que se me subiera la mostaza ayer. Excuse me for blowing my top yesterday.*

Me la **suda.** I don't give a damn. (vulgar) *Mex, Sp* ◆ *Me la suda lo que piensen. Voy de vacaciones. I don't give a damn what they think. I'm going on vacation.*

sudar frío (to sweat cold) to break out in a cold sweat, to be fearful *DR, CR, Col, U, Arg* ◆ *Los estudiantes sudaron frío porque el director los llamó a su oficina. The students broke out in a cold sweat because the principal called them to his office.*

sudar la gota gorda (to sweat the fat drop) to sweat bullets, sweat it out *L. Am., Sp* ◆ *Yo aquí sudando la gota gorda y ella no hace* *nada. I'm here sweating it out and she isn't doing anything.*

Está por el **suelo.** (It's down on the floor.) It's the pits, in a bad way. *L. Am.* ◆ *La situación económica está por el suelo.* The economic situation is at rock bottom.

el **sueño dorado** (golden dream) heart's desire, dream *L. Am., Sp* ◆ *Mi sueño dorado es vivir en un país tropical ocho meses al año.* My heart's desire is to live in a tropical country eight months of the year.

en **sueños** ➞**Ni en sueños.**

suerte ➞**por suerte**

a la **suerte de la olla** (to the luck of the pot) whatever is found in the fridge or wherever, potluck *Ch* ◆ *Te invitamos a comer a la suerte de la olla.* We invite you over to eat potluck.

sufrir un ataque de cuernos (to suffer an attack of horns) to go into a jealous rage, be jealous and react violently *Ch, Sp* ◆ *Jaime sufrió un ataque de cuernos cuando vio a Cristina y Pedro en el cine.* Jaime had an attack of jealousy when he saw Cristina and Pedro at the movies.

sulfurarse to get steamed up (sulfured) *L. Am., Sp* ◆ *Es una persona muy sensible; en seguida se sulfura.* He's an overly sensitive person; he gets all steamed up really quickly.

supuesto ➞**por supuesto**

surfear la Red (la Internet) to surf the Internet *parts of L. Am.* ◆ *Surfeamos la Red para conseguir la información que necesitábamos.* We surfed the Net to get the information we needed.

sus más y sus menos hassles, difficulties or complications that a matter gives; pros and cons *Mex, Sp* ◆ *El director tuvo sus más y sus menos con esa actriz, pero es una película excelente.* The director had his hassles with that actress, but it's an excellent film.

a **sus órdenes** (at your orders) at your service *L. Am., Sp* ◆ *Estoy a sus órdenes.* I am at your service.

suspender (to suspend) to flunk *L. Am., Sp* ◆ *La maestra me suspendió.* The teacher flunked me. ◆ *Tres alumnos suspendieron el examen.* Three students failed the exam.

las **suyas** ➞**hacer de las suyas**

¿'Tá la vaina? (How's the thing?) How's everything? What's up? *Ven* ◆ *Hola, mi amigo. ¿Tá la vaina? Hi, my friend. How's it all going?*

la **tabla** →**llevar contra la pared (la tabla)**

tablas →**tener tablas**

taco →**armar un taco; darse taco; echar un taco de ojo; hacerse un taco**

el **taco 1.** bad word, swear word *Sp* ◆ *No me gustan los tacos. Esa película tiene muchos tacos. I don't like bad words. That picture is loaded with swear words.* **2.** year, year old *Sp* ◆ *Tengo veinte tacos. I'm twenty years old.* **3.** mess *Sp* (see: **armar un taco, hacerse un taco**)

el **tajo** short for **trabajo**, work *Sp* ◆ *Este tajo es agotador. This job is exhausting.*

tal →**¿Qué tal?**

De **tal palo, tal astilla.** (From such a tree or stick, such a splinter.) A chip off the old block, like father like son. *L. Am., Sp* ◆ *Mario y su papá se parecen mucho, ¿no? De tal palo, tal astilla. Mario and his dad look a lot alike, don't they? He's a chip off the old block.*

tal para cual made for each other, birds of a feather *L. Am., Sp* ◆ *Esta pareja es tal para cual. That couple is made for each other.*

el/la **tal por cual** (such for which) nobody, son of a gun, word sometimes used instead of an insult; also, (adj.) out-and-out, dyed-in-the-wool *L. Am.* ◆ *Lorenzo es un tal por cual. Lorenzo is a son of a gun.* ◆ *Ese tal por cual se mete mucho en mi vida. That son of a gun is meddling in my life.*

tamales →**hacerle a alguien de chivo los tamales**

estar en el **tambo** to be in the clinker (jail) *Mex, ES, Col* ◆ *Después de haber cometido semejante crimen, estuvo en el tambo por muchos años. After having committed such a crime, he was in the clinker for many years.*

tango →**hacer un tango**

un **tanque** →**estar como un tanque (estar como un tren)**

las **tantas** the wee hours, an undetermined hour, late at night or in the day *Mex, DR, Sp* ◆ *Claudio llegó a las tantas de la madrugada. Claudio arrived in the wee hours of the morning.*

lo **tanto** →**por lo tanto**

tanto mejor (peor) so much the better (the worse) *L. Am., Sp* ◆ *¿El pueblo votó por ese fanfarrón mentiroso? ¡Tanto peor para ellos! The people voted for that lying braggart? So much the worse for them!*

tapando el sol con un dedo (covering the sun with a finger) covering things up, trying to keep up appearances *Mex, ES, Nic, Pan, Ven, Col, Peru, Ch* (see illustration, page 418) ◆ *Deben plantearle el problema a sus padres; no pueden seguir tapando el sol con un dedo. They should talk about the problem to their parents; they can't keep trying to cover things up.*

taquillero(-a) (box office; [adj.] sometimes meaning good box office) cool, "in" *S. Cone* ◆ *Es un actor taquillero. He's a hot (popular) actor.* ◆ *Es la cosa taquillera. It's the "in" thing.*

la **tarabilla** windbag, hot-air artist, nonstop talker *Mex, ES, Nic* ◆ *No invitemos a la vecina, que es una tarabilla. Let's not invite the neighbor; she's a windbag.*

tarado(-a) foolish, stupid (from **tara**, mental deficiency) *L. Am., Sp* ◆ *¿Cómo puedes estar enamorada de ese tarado? How can you be in love with that fool?*

el **tarambana** undisciplined (person, kid) *Cuba, Ch, U, Sp* ◆ *Su hermano no había cambiado; seguía siendo el mismo tarambana. His (Her) brother hadn't changed a bit; he was still the same brat.*

tardar en (hacer algo) to take (to do something) *L. Am., Sp* ◆ *¿Cuánto tardaste en escribir el reportaje? How long did it take you to write the report?*

el **tarro** (jar) head, noggin (CR: face) *Sp* ♦ *¿Estás mal del tarro? ¿Cómo se te ocurre eso?* *Are you crazy? How can you think of that?*

la **tartamuda** (stutterer) machine gun, automatic weapon *Mex, ES, U* ♦ *Los asaltantes atacaron con tartamudas.* *The robbers attacked with machine guns.*

tarugo(-a) stupid *Chicano, Mex, DR, Col, Sp* ♦ *Es un tarugo. De veras, no sabe nada.* *He's an idiot. Really, he doesn't know anything.*

tarumba crazy *Sp* (*Ch:* **turumba**) ♦ *Creo que me voy a volver tarumba aquí.* *I think I'm going to go crazy here.*

el **tata** dad, father (variant in some rural areas of *DR, Col, Ven, Ch:* **taita**); also, grandpa *L. Am.* ♦ *Mi tata está muy viejo para trabajar en el campo.* *My old man is too old to be working in the field.*

los **tatas** folks, parents, father and mother; also, grandparents *most of L. Am.* ♦ *¿De dónde vinieron tus tatas?* *Where did your grandparents (or parents) come from?*

Te conozco, bacalao, aunque vengas disfraza'o (disfrazado). (I know you, codfish, although you come in disguise.) I see you coming. I see what you're up to. *Sp* ♦ *No trates de convencerme. Te conozco, bacalao, aunque vengas disfraza'o.* *Don't try to convince me. I see what you're up to.*

Te conozco, mosco. (I know you, fly.) You can't trick me. I see what you're up to. *ES, Nic, Peru, Ch, Arg* ♦ *Te conozco, mosco. No te compraré ese coche.* *You can't trick me. I won't buy that car from you.*

Te dan pon y ya quieres guiar. They give you a ride and you already want to steer (meaning take over). *PR* ♦ *¡Cállate, hija, y no sigas pidiendo favores! Te dan pon y ya quieres guiar.* *Be quite, daughter, and stop asking for favors. They give you a ride and you want to drive the car.*

Te pasaste. (You passed yourself.) You overdid it. You blew it, did something wrong. *Mex, DR, PR, G, Col, S. Cone, Sp* (RVAR *Ch, U:* also, you did something well, outdid yourself) ♦ *Te pasaste con tus comentarios agresivos.* *You overdid it with your aggressive comments.* ♦ *La cena estuvo estupenda; te pasaste.* *The dinner was great. You outdid yourself.*

Te veo venir. (I see you coming.) I see what you're up to. *Mex, Peru, U, Arg, Sp* ♦ *Te veo venir. ¿Qué andas buscando?* *I see what you're up to. What are you looking for?*

teatro →**hacer teatro**

el **tejemaneje** (knack) shenanigans, problem, bad business, scheme (also, **tequemanejes**) *L. Am., Sp* ♦ *No sé qué tequemanejes te traes ni quiero saberlos.* *(Sp)* *I don't know what shenanigans you're up to (bringing here) nor do I want to know.*

tejos →**tirar/echar los tejos**

la **tele** (short for **televisión**) TV *L. Am., Sp* ♦ *Mi esposo prende la tele y empieza a hacer zapping.* *My husband turns on the TV and starts changing the channels.*

la **teleculebra** (tele-snake) TV soap opera, used like **telenovela** *Mex, ES, Ven* ♦ *Hay personas que miran varias teleculebras todos los días.* *There are people who watch several soap operas every day.*

teléfono →**tener una cara de teléfono ocupado**

temático(-a) (thematical) obsessive, single-minded, monomaniacal, crazy *ES, Nic, Peru, Bol* ♦ *No se puede hablar con ese hombre; es bien temático.* *You can't talk with that man; he keeps obsessing about the same thing.*

tener (andar con) cables pelados (to have or go around with frayed wires) to be on edge, strung out *ES, Nic, S. Cone* (RVAR *ES:* also, **tener los alambres pelados**) ♦ *Se le pelan los alambres (cables). Tiene los cables (alambres) pelados.* *(ES)* *He (She) is a nervous wreck.*

tener (mucha) gracia to be (very) funny *L. Am., Sp* ♦ *Esta tira cómica tiene mucha gracia.* *This comic strip is very funny.*

tener (traer) a alguien frito(-a) (to have [bring] someone fried) to tire someone out, bothering them *Mex, DR, Sp* ♦ *Daniela me tiene frita con su conducta.* *Daniela has got me at my wits' end with her behavior.*

tener a alguien en el alma (to have someone in one's soul) to feel for someone who is having problems, wanting to help *Mex, Sp* ♦ *Supe de tu tragedia y te tengo en mi alma.* *I found out about your tragedy, and I feel for you.*

tener a menos (to hold for less) to look down on, disdain *Arg, Sp* ♦ *En esa tienda tienen a menos a los inmigrantes. In that store they look down on immigrants.*

tener abriles (to have Aprils) to have a certain age *L. Am., Sp* ♦ *Tiene sus abriles, pero es bonita. She has a few years on her, but she's pretty.*

tener agallas (to have galls) to have guts, nerve *L. Am., Sp* ♦ *Ese tipo tiene muchas agallas. That guy has a lot of nerve.* ♦ *No tuvo agallas para hacerlo. He didn't have the guts to do it.*

tener algo en la punta de la lengua to have something on the tip of one's tongue *L. Am., Sp* ♦ *Ay, no puedo recordar su nombre, pero lo tengo en la punta de la lengua. Oh, I can't remember his (her, their) name, but I have it on the tip of my tongue.*

tener algo entre ceja y ceja (to have something between eyebrow and eyebrow) to have in mind, be set on *L. Am., Sp* ♦ *Tengo el proyecto entre ceja y ceja. I have the project firmly in mind.*

tener algo (no tener nada) que ver con to have something (to have nothing) to do with *L. Am., Sp* ♦ *¿Por qué mencionas esos factores que no tienen nada que ver con nuestro negocio? Why do you mention those factors that have nothing to do with our business?*

tener alma de acero (to have a soul of steel) to have a heart of stone, be without feelings, cold *Mex, ES, Sp* ♦ *Juan tiene un alma de acero; esto tortura a las mujeres. Juan has a heart of stone; this tortures women.*

tener ángel (to have angel) to have that special something (charm) *Mex, ES, Col* (RVAR *ES:* to be a good person) ♦ *Esa señora tiene ángel; te das cuenta con sólo escucharla hablar. That woman has a special something; just hearing her speak you realize it.*

tener banca to have influence, power, worth *U, Arg, Sp* ♦ *Gracias a la banca que tiene su padre, Ignacio y Rafael comenzaron a trabajar en la contaduría de la nación. Thanks to their father's influence, Ignacio and Rafael began to work in the national accounting office.*

tener bien puestas las pilas, estar con las pilas puestas (to have one's batteries well placed) to have one's act together, be on the ball *DR, Ven, Ch, U* ♦ *Ese chico es muy listo; tiene las pilas bien puestas. That guy is very clever; he's really got his act together.*

tener bien puestos los calzones (to have one's underwear well placed) to be gutsy, worthy, have character or valor *Mex, C. Am., Col, Ch* (RVAR *Ch:* **pantalones**, not **calzones**) ♦ *El padre de Arturo tiene bien puestos los calzones. Arturo's father has a lot of character (a strong personality).*

tener bolas (to have balls) to be brave (vulgar) *U, Arg* ♦ *No creo que Sebastián le hable a Valentina; no tiene bolas para eso. I don't think Sebastián will speak to Valentina; he doesn't have the balls to.* ♦ *Mario tiene bolas, y se va a presentar en las elecciones para presidente. Mario has balls, and he's going to run for president in the election.*

tener bolsillos alegres (to have cheerful pockets) to be rolling in dough *Mex* ♦ *Saqué la lotería; tengo los bolsillos alegres. I won the lottery; I am rolling in dough.*

tener buen carácter to have a good disposition, be good-tempered *L. Am., Sp* ♦ *Me encanta trabajar con Tere porque tiene muy buen carácter. I love working with Tere because she has a very good disposition.*

tener buen diente (to have good tooth) to have a hollow leg, be a big eater *Mex, DR, PR, ES, S. Cone, Sp* ♦ *Ricardo tiene buen diente. Se comió dos hamburguesas doble carne y un batido de fresa. Ricardo has a hollow leg. He had two double-patty hamburgers and a strawberry shake.*

tener buen lejos (to have a good far away) to be good only from a distance (ironic way of saying someone is not too much fun to have around) *Ch* ♦ *No pienso invitar a Jaime. Ese hombre tiene buen lejos. I'm not thinking of inviting Jaime. That man is not much fun to be with.*

tener buen ojo to have a good eye *L. Am., Sp* ♦ *El doctor Ramírez tiene muy buen ojo para detectar tumores. Dr. Ramírez has a good eye for detecting tumors.*

tener buena (mala) prensa (to have good [bad] press) to have a good (bad) reputation *most of L. Am., Sp* ♦ *Juan Manuel tiene buena prensa con las chicas. Juan Manuel has a good reputation with the ladies (girls).*

tener clara la película: Ahora tienes clara la película, hija mía.
Now you get the picture, my dear.

tener buena mano para (to have a good hand for) to have the skill for something, have the knack, the right touch *DR, PR, S. Cone, Sp* ◆ *Ana tiene buena mano para las plantas. Ana has a green thumb.*

tener buena sombra (to have good shade) to be pleasant, a good influence; to be lucky *ES, Sp* ◆ *Mi tío tiene muy buena sombra. My uncle is very lucky.*

tener buena vibración (to have good vibration) to give good vibes, inspire confidence *Mex, Sp* ◆ *Me encanta platicar con Elenita. Tiene buenas vibraciones. I adore talking with Elenita. She has good vibes.*

tener cancha (to have court, field for sports) to be on one's home court *CR, Col, Peru, S. Cone* ◆ *Juan tiene cancha. Juan is on his home court (feels at ease in the present circumstances).*

tener cerebro de mosquito (to have a gnat's brain) to be brainless, a birdbrain *U, Arg, Sp* ◆ *No esperamos un razonamiento lógico de ella; tiene cerebro de mosquito. We don't expect logical reasoning from her; she's a birdbrain.*

tener cara de «yo no fui» (to have the face of "it wasn't me") humble or innocent-looking face, contrary to truth *Mex, ES, CR, U* ◆ *¡Qué sorpresa me dio Joaquín! Es un pícaro y con esa carita de «yo no fui». What*

a surprise Joaquín gave me! He's a rascal and with that expression on his face of "Who, me?"

tener cara de cemento armado (to have the face of fixed cement) to have a lot of nerve, brazenness *Sp* (RVAR *U:* **cara de piedra**) ◆ *Con cara de cemento armado, le dijo al director que nadie trabajaría el día puente. Brazenly, he told the director that nobody would work on the long weekend holiday.*

tener cara de chiste (to have the face of a joke) to look like a fool *Mex, Sp* ◆ *A pesar de que el contador es inteligente, tiene cara de chiste. Even though the accountant is intelligent, he looks like a fool.*

tener cara de mala leche (to have the face of bad milk) to look like one is in a bad mood *Sp* ◆ *Ese señor tiene cara de muy mala leche, ¿no crees? That man looks like he's ready to bite your head off, don't you think?*

tener cara de pocos amigos (to have the face of few friends) to look like a sourpuss, hostile, unwelcoming, or unfriendly *Mex, Ch, U* ◆ *No compro nada en esa tienda porque los dependientes tienen cara de pocos amigos. I don't buy anything at that store because the clerks look like sourpusses.*

tener clara la película (to have the movie or film clear) to get the picture, have a clear idea of some situation *Peru, S. Cone, Sp* ◆

233

Ahora tenemos clara la película sobre la situación política en este país. We now have a clear picture of the political situation in this country.

tener colmillo (to have eyetooth) to be sharp or astute (in business) *Mex, ES, CR* ◆ *Jaime Ernesto tiene colmillo; su jefe lo va a subir.* Jaime Ernesto is good in business; his boss is going to promote him. ◆ *Roberto Rodríguez tiene colmillo para la taquilla.* Roberto Rodríguez is sharp in the movie (box office) business.

tener/estar con el alma en un hilo (to have [be with] the soul in a thread) to be a bundle of nerves, on edge, nervous as a cat *L. Am.* ◆ *¿Qué pasa, Verónica? —Estoy con el alma en un hilo. Mi hijo está en el hospital.* What's wrong, Verónica? —I'm a bundle of nerves. My son is in the hospital.

tener/estar con las antenas puestas (to have [be with] one's antennas up) to have one's ears pricked up, be listening (and ready for gossip) *Mex, DR, ES, U, Arg, Sp* ◆ *Habla bajito. Por ahí viene Elena, que siempre tiene las antenas puestas.* Pipe down. Here comes Elena, and she always has her ears pricked up (for the latest gossip).

tener conexiones to have friends in high places, have pull, connections *L. Am., Sp* ◆ *Ese comerciante es muy poderoso; tiene conexiones en el gobierno.* That businessman is very powerful; he has connections in the government.

tener crudo algo (to have something raw) to have it tough, be difficult to do or get *Sp* ◆ *Lo tienes crudo, amigo.* You have it tough, friend.

tener cuernos (to have horns) to be a cuckold, said when a person's spouse or sweetheart is cheating on him or her *S. Cone* (RVAR *CR:* **tener cachones**) ◆ *Pobre Chabela tiene cuernos más grandes que las pinturas de Frida.* Poor Chabela is a real cuckold (literally, she has horns bigger than Frida [Kahlo's] paintings).

tener duende (to have elf) to be charming, enchanting (said of people or places that generate their own special attractive atmosphere) *Peru, Sp* ◆ *Parece que Ana tuviera duende. Todo le sale bien; es una persona encantadora que atrae a la gente.* It seems

as if Ana had a special charm. Everything turns out well for her; she's a charming person who attracts people.

tener el billete largo (to have the long bill) to be loaded, rolling in dough *Ch* ◆ *Tu novio tiene el billete largo.* Your boyfriend is loaded.

tener el santo de cabeza (to have the saint on its head) to ask for something until you get it *Mex* ◆ *Tuve el santo de cabeza por mucho tiempo. Por fin me dieron lo que pedía.* I was insistent for a long time. Finally they gave me what I was asking for.

tener el santo de cara (to have one's saint facing one) to have good luck *ES, Peru, Sp* ◆ *Ricardo tiene el santo de cara; tiene mucho éxito en su negocio.* Ricardo has good luck; he has great success with his business.

tener el santo de espaldas (to have one's saint turning his back on one) to have bad luck *Mex, ES, Sp* (see illustration, page 325) ◆ *Todo me sale mal. Hace días que tengo el santo de espaldas.* Everything is turning out badly for me. For days I've had only bad luck.

tener en cuenta (to have in account) to keep in mind *L. Am., Sp* ◆ *Tengan en cuenta, chicos, que mañana son las competencias regionales.* Bear in mind, boys, that the regional sports competitions are tomorrow.

tener en el bolsillo a alguien to have someone in one's pocket, be able to count on that person *Mex, DR, PR, ES, U, Arg, Sp* ◆ *Juan tiene a la novia en el bolsillo.* Juan has his girlfriend at his beck and call. ◆ *A ésos los tengo en el bolsillo; seguro que votan por mí en las elecciones.* I've got those guys under my thumb; they'll vote for me for sure in the election.

tener en el bote (to have in the boat) to sweet-talk or pick up, to convince *Sp* ◆ *Un par de argumentos más y ya tenemos a todo el comité en el bote. Me alegro de haberlos convencido.* A couple of arguments more and we'll have the whole committee in our pockets. I'm glad we convinced them.

tener en poco a una persona o cosa (to hold someone or something in small) to look down on, have little regard for someone or something *Sp* ◆ *En la otra empresa tenían a menos a Ramón. Suerte que ha cambiado* *y ahora puede brillar en su trabajo. In the other company they looked down on Ramón. Luckily he's changed (jobs) and now he can shine in his work.*

tener entre algodones (to have within cottons) to handle with kid gloves *L. Am., Sp* ◆ *Miguel tiene a su esposa entre algodones. Miguel handles his wife with kid gloves* ◆ *A los yernos entre algodones, y así ¡no son sangrones! Treat sons-in-law with kid gloves, and that way they won't be nasty! (Mexican saying)*

tener estrella (to have a star) to be born under a lucky star, be lucky and easily accepted by people *Mex, Sp* ◆ *Estos chicos tienen estrella. Han viajado por todo el mundo. These kids were born under a lucky star. They have traveled all over the world.*

tener fama (to have fame) to be known for, be famous for, have a reputation for *L. Am., Sp* ◆ *Tiene fama de intelectual. He (She) has a reputation for being an intellectual.* ◆ *Tiene fama de ser una ciudad cara. It's famous for being an expensive city.*

tener flojos los tornillos to have a screw (screws) loose *Mex, ES, U, Sp* ◆ *Estoy segura que mi profesor de filosofía tiene los tornillos flojos; dice cosas totalmente ridículas. I'm sure that my philosophy professor has a screw loose; he says completely ridiculous things.*

tener ganas de (hacer algo) to feel like (doing something) *L. Am., Sp* ◆ *Tengo ganas de viajar a Costa Rica este enero. I feel like traveling to Costa Rica this January.*

tener gancho (to have hook) to fascinate, seduce, captivate *Ch, Sp* ◆ *Este chico tiene gancho. Jamás se quedará solo. This guy is captivating. He'll never end up alone.*

tener hambre de león (to be hungry as a lion) to be hungry as a bear *Mex* ◆ *¿Qué hay que comer? Los niños tienen hambre de león. What is there to eat? The kids are hungry as bears.*

tener hormigas en el culo (to have ants in your ass) to be impatient, have ants in your pants (vulgar) *ES, U, Arg* ◆ *Estos niños nunca están quietos; parece que tienen hormigas en el culo. These kids are never still; it's as if they had ants in their pants.*

tener huevos (to have eggs, testicles) to have balls, be bold, brave *L. Am., Sp* ◆ *Hay que tener huevos para enfrentar a ese grupo de delincuentes. You need to have balls to stand up to that group of delinquents.*

tener la bondad de to be so kind as to, please *L. Am., Sp* ◆ *¿Tendría usted la bondad de llamar un taxi para nosotras? Would you be so kind as to call us a taxi?*

tener la cabeza hueca (to have the head hollow) to be brainless, an airhead *Mex, U, Arg, Sp* ◆ *No tienes la cabeza hueca. Entonces piensa cómo vas a resolver este problema. You're not an airhead. So think about how you're going to solve this problem.*

tener la cabeza llena de humos (to have the head full of smoke/vapors) to be full of oneself, have one's head swollen *Florida, Mex, DR, ES, Col, U, Arg* ◆ *Después de terminar su carrera, a Alejandro se le ha llenado la cabeza de humo. After finishing his degree, Alejandro is really full of himself.*

tener la culpa to be guilty *L. Am., Sp* ◆ *Sí, llegamos tarde, pero yo no tengo la culpa. Yes, we arrived late, but it's not my fault.*

tener la farmacia abierta (y el doctor dormido) (to have the pharmacy open [and the doctor asleep]) to have the barn door open, pants with an open fly *ES, Sp* ◆ *La farmacia está abierta y el doctor dormido. The barn door is open. (Your fly is unzipped.)*

tener la guita loca (to have crazy money) to be loaded *U, Arg* ◆ *Hace unos años los Flores tenían la guita loca. A few years ago, the Flores were loaded.*

tener la mente en blanco to be daydreaming, have one's mind blank *Mex, DR, G, Col, U, Arg* (RVar *ES, Ch, Sp:* **quedarse/estar con la mente en blanco**) ◆ *Las preguntas del profesor eran fáciles, pero yo tenía la mente en blanco y no pude contestar. The professor's questions were easy, but my mind was blank, and I couldn't answer.*

tener la ocurrencia de to have the bright idea to *L. Am., Sp* ◆ *Luego mi buen marido tuvo la ocurrencia de ir en el periférico. Then my dear husband had the bright idea of taking the freeway.*

tener la palabra (to have the word) to have the floor *L. Am., Sp* ◆ *Silencio, por favor. El* *señor Chávez tiene la palabra. Silence, please. Mr. Chávez has the floor.*

tener la sartén por el mango (to have the frying pan by the handle) to be in charge of a situation, have the upper hand *L. Am., Sp* ◆ *No sé si te das cuenta, pero tenemos la sartén por el mango. Podemos hacer lo que queramos. I don't know if you realize it, but we have the upper hand. We can do whatever we want.*

tener la vida en un hilo (to have one's life by a thread) to have one's life hanging by a thread, be in great danger *Mex, DR, ES, S. Cone, Sp* ◆ *Los mineros fueron atrapados por un deslizamiento y tuvieron sus vidas en un hilo hasta que los rescataron tres días más tarde. The miners were trapped by a landslide, and their lives were hanging by a thread until they were rescued three days later.*

tener las bolas bien puestas (to have one's balls well placed) to have balls, be brave (vulgar) *S. Cone* ◆ *Nuestra secretaria tenía las bolas bien puestas cuando presentó su queja contra el jefe. Our secretary had the balls to bring a complaint against the boss.*

tener las bolas llenas (to have your balls full) to be fed up (vulgar) *U, Arg* ◆ *Naldo tiene las bolas llenas con ese contador. Naldo is royally pissed off at that accountant.`*

tener leche (to have milk) to be lucky (RVAR A BIT VULGAR IN *Sp*) *PR, G, Col, Ec, Ch, Sp* ◆ *A Hugo le salieron en el examen sólo los temas que había estudiado. ¡Tiene una leche estupenda! Only the topics Hugo had studied came up on the exam. He has great luck!*

tener los codos pelados (to have the elbows peeled) to be tired from cramming, studying *Sp* ◆ *Tengo los codos pelados de tanto estudiar. I'm studied out (tired of studying).*

tener los cojones bien puestos (to have one's testicles well placed) to have balls, be bold, brave (vulgar) *DR, Sp* ◆ *Los manifestantes tenían los cojones bien puestos y no se movieron cuando llegó la policía. The demonstrators had balls and didn't move when the police came.*

tener los cojones por corbata (to have one's testicles as a tie) to be scared shitless, fearful, timid (vulgar); also, **tenerlos por**

corbata *Sp* (RVAR *see:* **tener los huevos de corbata**)

tener los huevos bien puestos (to have one's eggs, meaning testicles, well placed) to have balls, be bold, brave (vulgar) *Mex, ES, U, Arg, Sp* ◆ *Ellos dijeron que tenían los huevos bien puestos y que enfrentarían a los delincuentes para terminar con los fraudes. They said they had balls and would stand up to the delinquents to end the fraud.*

tener los huevos de corbata (to have one's testicles as a tie) to be scared shitless, fearful, timid (vulgar); also, tenerlos por corbata *ES, Sp* ◆ *Cuando fui con Ricardo a la capital, manejó tan rápido que yo tenía los huevos de corbata. When I went with Ricardo to the capital, he drove so fast that it scared the hell out of me.*

tener los nervios de punta (to have one's nerves standing) to have one's nerves on edge *L. Am., Sp* ◆ *Ella no ha tenido noticias de su familia, y tiene los nervios de punta. She hasn't had news of her family, and her nerves are on edge.*

tener los ovarios bien puestos (to have the ovaries well placed) to have balls, used for a woman, like **tener los huevos (cojones, etc.) bien puestos** (vulgar) *L. Am., Sp* ◆ *Reina tiene los ovarios bien puestos. Ayer le pidió un aumento a nuestro jefe. Reina has balls. Yesterday she asked our boss for a raise.*

tener lugar (to have place) to take place *L. Am., Sp* ◆ *La película tiene lugar en la República Dominicana. The film takes place in the Dominican Republic.*

tener madera 1. (to have wood) to have strength, aptitude, have what it takes (to do something) *Mex, Col, Ven, Ch, U, Sp* ◆ *Tienes madera de músico. You have a talent for music.* **2.** (to have wood) to have the right stuff, have what it takes, a good or strong character *Mex, Col, Sp* ◆ *Elizabeth tiene mucha madera. Elizabeth has the right stuff.*

tener mal carácter (to have bad character) to be a grouch *L. Am., Sp* ◆ *¡Que mal carácter tiene tu tío! What a grouch your uncle is!*

tener mal genio to have a bad disposition, be bad-tempered *L. Am., Sp* ◆ *No me gusta trabajar con Esmeralda porque tiene muy* *mal genio.* I don't like working with Esmeralda because she has a very bad disposition.

tener mal rollo (con alguien) to lead a bad life (with someone) *Sp* ◆ *Tiene mal rollo con su mujer. He has a bad life with his wife.*

tener mala leche (to have bad milk) to be bad tempered, disagreeable, grouchy, or to have bad intentions (vulgar in *Sp*, where **leches** is a euphemism for semen) *Mex, ES, S. Cone, Sp* ◆ *Se les veía la mala leche desde que llegaron. You could see their bad intentions ever since they got here.* ◆ *Sara reaccionó con toda mala leche. ¡Qué genio! Sara reacted like a real grouch. What a temperament!*

tener mala leche (to have bad milk) to be unlucky *G, ES, Col, Ven, Peru* ◆ *Tengo muy mala leche. ¿Por qué me escogieron a mí? I have very bad luck. Why did they choose me?*

tener mala pata (to have bad foot) to have bad luck *Mex, DR, PR, G, ES, CR, Ven, S. Cone, Sp* ◆ *¡Qué mala pata (tiene)! Todo le sale mal. What bad luck (he or she has)! Everything turns out badly for him (her).* ◆ *Dicen que perdieron las elecciones porque tuvieron mala pata. They say they lost the election because they had bad luck.*

tener mala sangre (to have bad blood) to be bad tempered, disagreeable *Mex, ES* ◆ *¡Qué mala sangre tiene el dueño de la gasolinera! How grouchy the owner of the gas station is!*

tener mala sombra (to have bad shade) to be unpleasant, a bad influence; to be unlucky *L. Am., Sp* ◆ *Tiene mala sombra que vayan a construir allí. I have a bad feeling about them starting to build there.*

tener mala uva (to have bad grape) to have a gruff or severe demeanor *Chicano, Sp* ◆ *Tiene muy mala uva y se enoja por cualquier cosa. He's (She's) a real grouch and gets upset over any little thing.*

tener mambo en la cabeza (to have mambo in the head) to be confused, disoriented, perhaps hung over *Arg* ◆ *¡Qué ruido! Tengo mambo en la cabeza. How noisy (it is)! My mind is soup.*

tener mano (to have hand) to be competent *DR, PR, U, Sp* ◆ *Elena tiene mano para la pintura. Elena has a knack for painting.*

tener mano de monja (to have a nun's hand) to be a good cook, have the gourmet touch *Ch* ◆ *Luci, eres una excelente cocinera. ¡Tienes mano de monja! Luci, you are an excellent cook. You have the magic touch!*

tener manos de hacha (to have hachet hands) to be clumsy, a klutz; describing someone who breaks everything like a bull in a china shop *Ch* ◆ *No dejes que entre Umberto en el comedor. Tiene manos de hacha. Don't let Umberto into the dining room. He's like a bull in a china shop.*

tener más cojones que nadie (to have more testicles than anyone) to have balls, be very brave (vulgar) *Sp* ◆ *Margarita tiene más cojones que nadie en la familia y aceptó hacerse cargo de la administración de la compañía. Margarita has more balls than anyone in the family, and she agreed to be in charge of the company's management.*

tener más vidas que un gato to have more lives than a cat *Mex, ES, Ch, U, Sp* ◆ *Flavio ha tenido accidentes graves, pero está muy bien. Es que tiene más vidas que un gato. Flavio has had serious accidents, but he is all right. He has nine lives.*

tener mucha cara (mucho rostro, mucho morro, mucha jeta) to have a lot of nerve (literally, face), be an opportunist *Sp* ◆ *Carmen tiene un morro que se lo pisa. —Sí, tiene mucha cara. Carmen has so much nerve (literally, so much face she steps on it). —Yes, she has a lot of chutzpah.* ◆ *Juan tiene mucho rostro. Habla mal de Rosa pero sale con ella. Juan has a lot of nerve. He speaks badly of Rosa but goes out with her.*

tener mucha cuerda (to have a lot of cord) to look very healthy, have a lot of life left *Mex, Sp* ◆ *Mi papá tiene 68 años, pero todavía tiene mucha cuerda. My father is 68 years old, but he still has a lot of life left.*

tener muchas ínfulas (to have many airs) to be full of oneself *L. Am., Sp* ◆ *Magdalena tiene muchas ínfulas. Magdalena is full of herself.*

tener buen (mucho) coco (to have a good [a lot of] coconut) to have a good head on one's shoulders, be smart *Sp* ◆ *Anita tiene mucho coco. Anita is very smart.*

tener mucho ojo con (to have a lot of eye with) to be very careful with *L. Am., Sp* ◆

Hay que tener mucho ojo con el nuevo empleado. You have to be very careful with the new employee.

tener mucho rollo (to have a lot of roll) to talk a lot without saying much *Mex, Sp* ♦ *Esa persona tiene mucho rollo; habla mucho pero no dice nada interesante. That person is a real windbag; he talks a lot but doesn't say anything interesting.*

tener muchos humos (to have a lot of smoke/vapors) to be full of oneself *L. Am., Sp* ♦ *Olguita tiene muchos humos, y sus primas no la toleran. Olguita is full of herself and her cousins cannot stand her.*

tener narices (to have nostrils, euphemism for **cojones**) to have guts, be brave *Sp* ♦ *Martín tiene narices. Martín has guts.*

tener patas (to have paws) to have guts, be brash or bold *Ch* ♦ *Tiene patas mi amiga. Dice lo que piensa. My friend has guts. She says what she thinks.*

tener pelotas (to have balls) to have balls, be brave, bold (vulgar) *U, Arg, Sp* ♦ *Faustino no tiene pelotas para aceptar el empleo porque teme el desafío. Faustino doesn't have the balls to accept the job because he's afraid of a challenge.*

tener pena (to have sorrow) to be shy, embarrassed *most of L. Am. (not S. Cone)* ♦ *No tengas pena, hijo. Don't be shy, son.*

tener pinta (de) (to have spot [of]) to look (like) *L. Am., Sp* ♦ *Ese cocido tiene buena pinta. (Sp) That stew looks good.* ♦ *Ese fulano tiene pinta de narcotraficante. That guy looks like a drug dealer.*

tener resaca (to have undertow) to be hung over *Peru, S. Cone, Sp* ♦ *Me siento mal. Tengo resaca del fin de semana. I feel bad. I have a hangover from the weekend.*

tener santos en la corte (to have saints at court) to have connections, friends in high places *Ch, parts of Sp* ♦ *Rosa recibe sus papeles pronto porque tiene santos en la corte. Rosa gets her papers quickly because she has friends in high places.*

tener siete vidas como los gatos (como el gato) to have nine lives like a cat *L. Am., Sp* ♦ *Doña Dolores parece tener siete vidas como los gatos. A menudo está grave y se recupera muy bien. Doña Dolores seems to* have nine lives like a cat. Often she is seriously ill and then she recovers just fine.

tener tablas (to have boards) to have a lot of experience at doing something; to lose one's timidity in public or to get oneself out of a jam *Arg, Sp* ♦ *Ese conferenciante tiene muchas tablas. That speaker has what it takes.* ♦ *Tienen unas tablas increíbles. They have incredible poise.*

tener un cacao (una empanada) mental (to have a mental cacao tree or bean [meat pie]) to be mixed up, have a confusion of ideas in one's head *Sp* ♦ *De tanto estudiar, Verónica tiene un cacao mental. From studying so long, Verónica is all mixed up.*

tener un careto (to have a white-faced mask) to look like death warmed over, look bad because of worry or lack of sleep *Sp* ♦ *Después de estar toda la noche de fiesta, llegué a la oficina con todo un careto. After partying all night, I got to the office looking like death warmed over.*

tener un corazón de oro to have a heart of gold *L. Am., Sp* ♦ *El doctor Campos tiene un corazón de oro y se dedica a sus pacientes. Doctor Campos has a heart of gold and is dedicated to his patients.*

tener un corazón de piedra to have a heart of stone *Mex, DR, ES, S. Cone* ♦ *No intentes convencer a Pedro que nos ayude. Tiene un corazón de piedra. Don't try to convince Pedro to help us. He has a heart of stone.*

tener un disgusto to have a falling out, disagreement, or hard feelings *L. Am., Sp* ♦ *Tuve un disgusto con mi hermana. I had a falling out with my sister.*

tener un enchufe (to have a plug) to have a connection, influential friend or acquaintance *DR, PR, Col, Sp* ♦ *Tiene un enchufe en esa empresa; seguro que le dan el trabajo. He has a connection at that company; they'll give him the job for sure.* ♦ *Mi abogado es mi enchufe con mi ex-esposa. My lawyer is my connection with my ex-wife.*

tener un jabón (to have a soap) to be shaken up, scared *U, Arg* ♦ *Tenía un jabón tremendo cuando aterrizó el avión. I was all shaken up when the airplane landed.*

tener un ligue to have a fling (or date) *Mex, Cuba, ES, U, Sp* ♦ *Mi prima tuvo un ligue* *con su abogado. My cousin had a fling with her lawyer.*

tener un muermo, estar amormado(-a) (to have glanders, viral disease of animals) to be droopy, drowsy, sleepy *Sp* ◆ *Tengo un muermo. Estoy amormado(-a). I'm sleepy.*

tener un pico de oro (to have a golden beak) to have the gift of gab, be a good talker, gifted speaker *most of L. Am., Sp* ◆ *El director de la empresa tiene un pico de oro y convenció al resto del directorio de que el aumento de sueldo fuera del cinco por ciento. The director has the gift of the gab and convinced the rest of the board of directors that the salary increase should be five percent.*

tener un rollo con alguien to have an affair (literally, roll) with someone *Sp* (RVAR *ES:* to have a disagreement) ◆ *Tuve un rollo con mi terapista. I had a fling with my therapist.*

tener una calentura (to have a fever) to be really excited sexually, be turned on, hot *U, Arg* ◆ *Estos adolescentes tienen una calentura tremenda; por eso están nerviosos. These adolescents are really turned on (sexually); that's why they're nervous.*

tener una cara de teléfono ocupado (to have a face like a busy telephone) to be angry, annoyed *PR* ◆ *Niña, tienes una cara de teléfono ocupado. Little girl, you have a very angry face.*

tener una pelotera to have a fight, blowup, brawl *S. Cone, Sp* ◆ *Anoche los borrachos tuvieron una pelotera en la calle. Last night the drunks had a brawl in the street.*

tener vergüenza (to have shame) to be ashamed *L. Am., Sp* ◆ *Maite, tengo vergüenza de haberme olvidado de tu cumpleaños. Maite, I'm a bit ashamed about having forgotten your birthday.*

tener ya dura la mollera (to have the crown of the head already hard) to no longer be able to learn (also, **tener mucha/poca mollera**, to be bright/stupid) *U, Sp* ◆ *Ya no aprenderé inglés; tengo ya dura la mollera. I won't learn English now; I'm no longer able to learn.*

tenerle una bronca a alguien to be upset with someone *U, Arg* ◆ *No me hables de ese tipo. Le tengo una bronca. Es un men-*

tiroso. Don't talk to me about that guy. I'm upset with him. He's a liar.

Tengamos la fiesta en paz. (Let's have the party in peace.) Let's have some peace. Don't cause trouble. Give it a rest. *L. Am., Sp* (RVAR *ES:* **Llevemos la fiesta en paz.**) ◆ *No discutamos más. Tengamos la fiesta en paz. Let's not talk about this anymore. Give it a rest.*

¿Tengo monos en la cara? (Do I have monkeys on my face?) Why are you staring at me? *Mex, Ch, U, Sp* ◆ *¿Por qué me miras tanto? ¿Tengo monos en la cara? Why are you looking at me so long? Why are you staring at me?*

el **tenorio** womanizer, Don Juan (old expression) *Mex (provinces), parts of L. Am.* ◆ *Pablo es todo un tenorio. Pablo is a real Don Juan.*

el **tentempié (tente en pie)** (keep you on your feet) midmorning snack *Mex, DR, Col* (RVAR *Cuba:* usually a coffee with milk) ◆ *Oigan, paremos de trabajar un rato. Es hora de un tentempié. Listen, let's stop working awhile. It's time to have a snack.*

término →**por término medio**

(mi) **tesoro** (my treasure) my dear *L. Am., Sp* ◆ *Tesoro, apúrate o llegaremos tarde. Sweetheart, hurry up or we'll be late.*

las **tetas** tits (vulgar) *L. Am., Sp* ◆ *Andaba en la playa con las tetas al aire. She was walking down the beach with her tits in plain view.*

tetona, tetuda big-breasted, busty (woman) (vulgar) *DR, PR, Col, S. Cone, Sp* ◆ *Patricia es muy tetona. Patricia is very busty.*

Tiburcio →**Miguel(ito)/Tiburcio**

el **tiburón** (shark) wolf, womanizer *PR, Col, U* ◆ *Salgamos con Carlos. Es un tiburón y seguro que nos presentará a sus amigas. Let's go out with Carlos. He's a wolf and for sure he'll introduce us to his women friends.*

el/la **tico(-a)** Costa Rican *L. Am.* ◆ *Mi peluquero es tico. My hairdresser is Costa Rican.*

tiempo →**dar tiempo al tiempo; no tener tiempo ni para rascarse**

¡Tiene huevos (narices) la cosa! (The thing has eggs, meaning testicles [nostrils]!) How bizarre! It's unheard of! (vulgar with **huevos**) *Sp* ◆ *Esos comentarios tienen* *narices (huevos). Those comments are bizarre.*

los **tiesos** (stiffs) the dead *Mex, Col, Ec* ◆ *Los tiesos no hablan. Stiffs don't talk.*

el **tigre** (tiger) shark, aggressive person (RVAR *DR:* also, stud or streetwise guy) *Mex, DR, G, ES, Col* ◆ *Fernando es un tigre y se hizo conocer por su actitud. Fernando is a shark and made himself known by his attitude.*

tijerear a alguien (to cut someone with scissors) to cut (with words), criticize *Mex, ES* ◆ *No estoy de acuerdo que tijereen a la secretaria sin escuchar su propia versión sobre el problema. I don't think they should criticize the secretary without hearing her version of the problem.*

los **tiliches** trinkets, things, stuff *Mex, C. Am.* ◆ *Cerca de la oficina venden tiliches muy baratos. Near the office they sell cheap trinkets.*

tilín →**hacer tilín**

el/la **timador(a)** rip-off artist, con artist *Mex, Ch, Sp* ◆ *Es un timador. No le compres nada. He's a con artist. Don't buy anything from him.*

el **tío, la tía** (uncle [aunt]) guy, fellow (gal, woman) *Ch, Sp* ◆ *Esa tía gasta mucho dinero en ropa barata. That woman spends lots of money on cheap clothes.*

el **tipazo** handsome guy *Mex, DR, ES, Col* ◆ *Jaime es un tipazo muy bueno. Jaime is a super gorgeous guy.*

el **tipo** (type) guy, fellow, dude *L. Am.* ◆ *Ese tipo es buen mozo y amable. That guy is handsome and kind.*

el/la **tiquis miquis** snob, fussy or high-class person, not easily pleased *PR, Sp* ◆ *A la prima de Roberto no le gusta nada de lo que hacemos. Es una tiquis-miquis. Roberto's cousin doesn't like anything we do. She's a snob.*

la **tira** police, cops (from **tirana**) *Mex, G* ◆ *¡Córrele! Viene la tira. Run! The cops are coming.*

tira y afloja (pull and give slack) push and pull, give and take, back and forth negotiations between two people or groups having trouble arriving at a solution *Mex, Peru, S. Cone, Sp* ◆ *El divorcio de Ana y Leandro fue muy triste. Por años se pasaron en tira y afloja sin resolver nada. Ana and Leandro's divorce was very sad. They spent years in negotiations back and forth without resolving anything.*

tirado(-a) (thrown away) cheap, a steal (at such a good price), used with **ser** or **estar** *U, Arg, Sp* ◆ *Compra estos suéteres de pura lana; están tirados. Buy these pure wool sweaters; they're a steal.*

estar **tirado(-a)** (to be pulled) to be a piece of cake, easy *Sp* ◆ *Este juego está tirado. This game is a piece of cake.*

Tirando. (Pulling.) Hanging in, getting along. *U, Arg, Sp* ◆ *¿Cómo andas? —Tirando, como siempre. How are you doing? —Hanging in there, as usual.*

tirar/jalar (de) la cuerda a alguien (to pull someone by the cord) to pull someone back, control (RVAR *Mex:* **jalar [de] la cuerda**) *Mex, Sp* ◆ *¿Tienes que irte? ¿Te jalan la cuerda? You have to leave? Is someone pulling your strings (controlling you)?*

tirar (salírsele) la baba (por litros) (to throw out saliva [by the liter]) to have one's tongue hanging out (e.g., when a man has seen a beautiful woman); to drool over or go wild for *Mex, Col* ◆ *Se te salió la baba cuando viste a Cindy Crawford. Your tongue was hanging out when you saw Cindy Crawford.*

tirar a los leones (to throw to the lions) to do in, rip to shreds, leave in a tight spot *Pan, Ch, Arg, Sp* ◆ *Parece que me quieren tirar a los leones; no sé por qué están tan enojados. It looks like they want to rip me to shreds; I don't know why they're so angry.*

tirar arroz (to throw rice) to put down, criticize *Peru* ◆ *No me gusta tirar arroz a nadie, pero ese hombre se cree mucho. I don't like to put anybody down, but that man has an inflated opinion of himself.*

tirar bomba (to throw a bomb) to stand (someone) up, ditch *Caribbean* ◆ *No vuelvo a hacer planes con Víctor. Es la segunda vez que me tira bomba y me quedo sin hacer nada. I'm not going to make plans with Víctor again. This is the second time he's stood me up and left me (literally, I'm left) with nothing to do.*

tirar de manoletina to masturbate (males, vulgar) *Sp*

tirar la esponja (to throw the sponge) to throw in the towel *S. Cone* ◆ *Tiramos la esponja después de muchos años de sacrificios sin lograr ningún resultado.* We threw in the towel after many years of sacrifice without achieving any results.

tirar la piedra y esconder la mano (to throw the stone and hide one's hand) to hurt someone but cover up one's action, propose an action but later deny having a part in it, be a hypocrite *L. Am., Sp* ◆ *Es una persona de las que tira la piedra y esconde la mano. No te puedes fiar de ella.* She's a hypocrite. You can't trust her.

tirar la toalla to throw in the towel, give up *L. Am., Sp* ◆ *Voy a tener que tirar la toalla. Me doy por vencido.* I'm going to have to throw in the towel. I give up.

tirar piedras (to throw stones) to put down, criticize, make disparaging comments *Mex, ES, CR, Col* (RVAR *Mex:* more common, **echar pedradas**) ◆ *Me voy de acá porque están tirando piedras.* I'm leaving here because they're putting people down. ◆ *No quiero que me echen piedras.* I don't want them to put me down.

tirar pinta (to throw spot) to dress to impress *Ch* ◆ *¡Esta noche tiramos pinta, hermana!* Tonight, we get all dressed up, Sis!

tirar/echar los tejos (to throw the disks) to hit on, seduce, make passes *U, Sp* ◆ *Seguro que le gustas a Alberto porque siempre te está tirando los tejos.* Alberto must like you because he's always making passes at you.

tirarse a alguien (to throw oneself at someone) to have sex (vulgar) *Mex, DR, PR, C. Am., Col, Ven, Ec, Peru, Ch, Arg, Sp* ◆ *Pablo se tiró a tres mujeres de su colonia.* Pablo had sex with three women from his neighborhood.

tirarse de los pelos (to pull one's hair out) to be upset, furious *S. Cone, Sp* ◆ *Viendo cómo perdió la oportunidad, se tiró de los pelos.* Seeing how he missed the opportunity (his chance), he was tearing out his hair.

tirarse el lance (to throw oneself the spear) to try something without being sure of succeeding, take a stab or shot at *S. Cone* ◆ *Me voy a tirar el lance al declararle mi amor (pedirle un aumento).* I'm going to take a shot in the dark and confess my love for him (her)

(ask him [her] for a raise). ◆ *La compañía se tiró el lance cuando contrató a Elvira. Por suerte todo salió muy bien.* The company took a shot in the dark when they hired Elvira. Luckily, everything turned out well.

tirarse el pegote (to throw oneself the sticky mess or awful thing) to lie, brag, toot one's own horn *Sp* ◆ *Siempre se tira el pegote. Le gusta dárselas de rico.* He's always tooting his own horn. He likes to act like he's rich.

tirarse el rollo (to throw the roll) to lie, brag *Sp* ◆ *Mirella se tiró el rollo de que sabía cantar muy bien, y tiene una voz espantosa.* Mirella was slinging the bull about how well she can sing, and she has a horrendous voice.

al **tiro** →**Ni a tiros.; No van por ahí los tiros.; ponerse al tiro**

el **tiro al aire** (shot in the air) unreliable or unpredictable person, loose cannon; slacker type who doesn't commit *S. Cone* ◆ *No confío en la información de Juvenal porque es un tiro al aire.* I don't trust what Juvenal says because he's a loose cannon.

el **tiro de gracia** (gunshot of pity) fatal blow, coup de grace *L. Am., Sp* ◆ *Le dieron el tiro de gracia al insultar a su familia.* They gave him the fatal blow when they insulted his family.

de un **tirón** (at one pull) in one fell swoop, at once, all at one time *L. Am., Sp* ◆ *Terminé el trabajo de un tirón.* I finished the work in one fell swoop.

To'el tiempo pa'lante. (All the time forward.) Onward and upward. *Caribbean*

tocado(-a) de la cabeza touched in the head, a bit crazy *Mex, G, ES, Col, U, Arg, Sp* (RVAR *Mex:* also, just **tocado**) ◆ *Anselmo está tocado de la cabeza. Dice que va a pintar toda su casa de negro.* Anselmo is touched in the head. He says he's going to paint his whole house black.

tocar de oído to play (a musical instrument) by ear *L. Am., Sp* ◆ *Laura toca piano de oído.* Laura plays piano by ear.

tocar el violín (to play the violin) to go out with a couple and have the feeling they really want to be alone, be a fifth wheel *Ch, U* (RVAR *Ec:* **violinista**, fifth wheel) ◆ *Me fui más temprano de la discoteca porque es-*

taba tocando el violín. I left the disco early because I was the fifth wheel.

tocar en lo vivo to touch to the quick *L. Am., Sp* ◆ *Su comentario tan sarcástico me tocó en lo vivo.* Her sarcastic comment touched me to the quick.

tocar fondo to touch bottom, hit rock bottom; to get to the bottom of something *L. Am., Sp* ◆ *Parece que la economía ha tocado fondo.* It looks like the economy has hit rock bottom. ◆ *Tenemos que investigar la situación hasta tocar fondo.* We have to investigate the situation until we get to the bottom of it.

tocar las narices (los cojones/los huevos) a alguien (to touch someone's nostrils [testicles]) to bother someone continually (vulgar with **cojones/huevos**) *Sp* ◆ *Sigue tocándome las narices.* He keeps bugging me. ◆ *¡Tócame las narices!* Get lost! Screw off!

tocar madera to touch (knock on) wood (used as in English, so that something that was said shouldn't happen) *L. Am., Sp* ◆ *¿Estás enferma? —No, toco madera.* Are you sick? —No, knock on wood.

tocar muchas teclas (to touch many keys) to push a lot of buttons, go to everyone or do everything to solve a problem *U, Arg, Sp* ◆ *Tuve que tocar muchas teclas para conseguir el permiso.* I had to push a lot of buttons to get the permit.

tocarle a alguien la lotería (to win the lottery) to have a windfall, luck out, hit the jackpot (also, **caerle, sacar**) *Mex, Cuba, S. Cone, Sp* ◆ *Le tocó la lotería de tener un nombre único, interesante.* He (She) lucked out having a unique, interesting name.

tocarle a uno hacer algo to be one's turn to do something *L. Am., Sp* ◆ *Beto, ya te toca a ti hablar.* Beto, it's your turn to talk now.

tocarse las narices (los cojones/los huevos) (to touch one's nostrils [testicles]) to screw around, goof off, not do anything (vulgar with **cojones/huevos**) *Sp* ◆ *Ese empleado es muy haragán; está todos los días tocándose las narices.* That employee is very lazy; he's screwing around doing nothing all day. ◆ *¡Tócate las narices!* expression of anger or surprise, like Get lost!

a **tocateja** in hard cash *Sp* ◆ *Tuvo que pagar el coche a tocateja. No aceptaban cheques.* He (She) had to buy the car with hard cash. They didn't accept checks.

de **tocho morocho** at any rate (used instead of **de todos modos**) *Mex, ES* ◆ *De tocho morocho, no me importa si van o si no van.* At any rate, I don't care if they go or not.

a **toda hostia** (at all Host) like a bat out of hell, fast, quickly (vulgar, with religious reference) *Sp* ◆ *El coche iba a toda hostia cuando ocurrió el accidente.* The car was going like a bat out of hell when the accident occurred.

a **toda leche** (at all milk) like a bat out of hell, fast, quickly (vulgar) *Sp* ◆ *El ciclista iba a toda leche y chocó con un árbol.* The cyclist was going at full blast and hit a tree.

a **toda madre** (at all mother) full blast *Mex, G, ES, Col* ◆ *Salió a toda madre para agarrar el vuelo.* He (She) left at full speed to catch the flight.

a **toda máquina** (at all machine) full blast, quickly, fast *Chicano, Mex, DR, G, Ch, Sp* ◆ *Están trabajando a toda máquina para terminar el puente.* They're working full blast to finish the bridge.

a **toda marcha** (at all march) very quickly, full blast *Mex, Sp* ◆ *Están trabajando a toda marcha para terminar la carretera a la playa antes del verano.* They're working at full speed to finish the highway to the beach before summertime.

a **toda mecha** (at all wick) very quickly, full blast *Mex, Sp* ◆ *Tienen que terminar a toda mecha el escenario para el concierto.* They have to finish the stage quickly for the concert.

a **toda pastilla** (at all pill) quickly, full blast, used like **a toda prisa** *Sp*

a **toda prisa** in a hurry, in a big rush *L. Am., Sp* ◆ *Terminaron el trabajo a toda prisa.* They finished the work in a hurry.

todititito(-a) everything, every little bit (variant of **todo**) *Mex, ES, Nic* ◆ *Ya se nos arruinó todititito.* Everything was wrecked for us. ◆ *Se me arruinó todititita la comida.* Every last bit of my dinner was ruined.

en **todo caso** (in all case) in any event, in any case *L. Am., Sp* ◆ *En todo caso no tenemos el dinero, así que ¿para qué hablar de com-*

prar una casa? In any event we don't have the money, so why talk about buying a house?

a **todo dar** (at all giving) fast, full blast; great *Mex, ES* ◆ *Sonó la alarma de fuego en el cine, y la gente salió a todo dar. The fire alarm in the movie theater went off, and the people rushed out.* ◆ *El viaje estuvo a todo dar. The trip was great.*

todo el santo día the whole live-long (literally, holy) day *L. Am., Sp* ◆ *Esperé su llamada todo el santo día. I waited for her call all the live-long day.*

a **todo esto** by the way, used like **a propósito**; meanwhile *L. Am.* ◆ *A todo esto, los vecinos hablaban mucho de ella. In the meantime, the neighbors were talking a lot about her.*

a **todo gas** (at all gas) fast, full blast *Mex, Sp* ◆ *La campaña política para las elecciones está a todo gas. The political campaign for the election is at full speed.*

todo lo contrario (all the contrary) just the opposite *L. Am., Sp* ◆ *¿No te gusta la comida caribeña? —Todo lo contrario, me encanta, pero no me siento bien hoy. Don't you like Caribbean food? —On the contrary, I love it, but I don't feel so good today.*

a **todo lo que da** (at all that it gives) going great guns, like a house on fire *Mex, S. Cone* ◆ *El partido está a todo lo que da. The game is going full blast.* ◆ *Salimos a todo lo que da y llegamos en el momento que cerraban el portón. We left at top speed and arrived just as they were closing the gate.*

Todo me sale torcido (al revés). (Everything turns out twisted [backwards] for me.) Everything turns out badly for me. I can't do anything right. *ES, Nic, CR, Sp* (RVAR *S. Cone:* **al revés** only) ◆ *A pesar de haber planeado cada detalle de la entrevista, todo me salió al revés. Despite having planned every detail of the interview, I couldn't do anything right.*

a **todo meter** (at all putting) fast, full blast *Mex, DR, PR, Sp* ◆ *Salió de la clínica a todo meter. He (She) went out of the clinic at full speed.*

ser **todo oídos** to be all ears *L. Am., Sp* ◆ *Cuéntame los chismes, amiga. ¡Soy todo oídos! Tell me the gossip, girl. I'm all ears!*

todo quisque everyone, used like **todo el mundo** *Sp* ◆ *Todo quisque tiene su opinión sobre los medios de comunicación. Everyone has his or her opinion about the media.*

a **todo trapo** (at full rag) dressed to the nines, with style or class *S. Cone* ◆ *Se vistieron para la fiesta a todo trapo; estaban muy elegantes. They were dressed to the nines for the party; they were very elegant.*

a **todo vapor** (at all steam) fast, full blast *ES, Peru, U, Arg* ◆ *Corrí a todo vapor para tomar el autobús. I ran at top speed to catch the bus.*

estar **todo(-a) derretido(-a)** (to be all melted) to be completely under the spell, spellbound *most of L. Am.* ◆ *Carmen está toda derretida con la visita de sus nietos. Carmen is spellbound with the visit of her grandchildren.*

de **todos modos** (of all ways) anyhow *L. Am., Sp* ◆ *De todos modos, nunca me haces caso. Anyway you never pay attention to me.*

¡Toma! (Take!) Take that!, So there! (as punishment, for instance) So what?, interjection implying that something is unimportant or not new *Sp* ◆ *¡Toma! Te lo dije, tu padre tenía razón. So there! I told you, your father was right.*

¡Toma castaña! (¡Toma del frasco, Carrasco!) (Take chestnut! [Take from the flask, Carrasco!]) Take that! (in a discussion) So what? So there! (when something has happened that doesn't affect one directly) *Sp* ◆ *¿Perdieron otra vez en las elecciones? ¡Toma castaña! They lost the elections again? So what?*

estar **tomado(-a)** to be drunk *L. Am.* ◆ *Todos admitieron que estaban tomados. They all admitted that they were drunk.*

tomar a coña algo (to take something at **coña**, a word referring to the female organ) to not give a damn, not take something seriously (vulgar) *Sp* ◆ *Se tomó a coña lo que le dijimos. No pensó que podía ser cierto, y ahora paga las consecuencias. He didn't take what we said seriously. He didn't think it could be true, and now he's paying the consequences.*

tomar a pecho to take to heart *L. Am., Sp* ◆ *No tomes a pecho lo que dijo mi abuelo, que no se sentía muy bien hoy. Don't take* what my grandfather said to heart; he wasn't feeling very well today.

tomar algo con soda (to take something with soda) to take something with a grain of salt, calmly *Ch, U* ◆ *Esas cosas, hay que tomarlas con soda.* You have to take those things calmly.

tomar algo con un grano de sal to take something with a grain of salt *Mex, DR, PR, CR, Ch, Sp* ◆ *Todo lo que dice Tomás hay que tomarlo con un grano de sal porque es un chismoso.* Everything that Tomás says has to be taken with a grain of salt because he's such a gossip.

tomar el pelo a alguien to pull someone's leg (hair), tease *L. Am., Sp* ◆ *El alumno le tomaba el pelo a la maestra.* The student was pulling the teacher's leg.

tomar el poder to take power *L. Am., Sp* ◆ *Los militares tomaron el poder y acto seguido acabaron con la democracia.* The military took power and immediately put an end to democracy.

tomar el portante (to take the big door) to disappear fast, get the heck out (sometimes because of anger or bad feeling) *Peru, Sp* ◆ *Como todo el mundo la criticaba, tomó el portante y se largó.* Since everyone was criticizing her, she took off and went on her way.

tomar en cuenta to take into account *L. Am., Sp* ◆ *Hay que tomar en cuenta que tu sueldo es más alto que el suyo.* You have to take into account that your salary is higher than his.

tomar las de Villadiego (to take those of Villadiego) to take to one's heels, beat it *L. Am., Sp* ◆ *Cuando Carlos vio que la relación iba en serio, tomó las de Villadiego y ya no lo vimos más.* When Carlos saw that the relationship was getting serious, he flew the coop and we didn't see him anymore.

tomar once (to take eleven) to have tea, a snack in the afternoon *Ch* ◆ *¿Vienen tus primos a tomar once?* Are your cousins coming for afternoon tea?

tomar partido to take sides, take a stand *L. Am., Sp* ◆ *Tomemos partido en este asunto tan importante.* Let's take a stand on this very important issue.

tomar sobre sí to take upon oneself *L. Am., Sp* ◆ *Tu hermano tomó sobre sí la dirección de todo el proyecto.* Your brother took upon himself the administration of the entire project.

tomar una copa (copita) (to have a wine glass [small wine glass]) to have a drink *L. Am., Sp* ◆ *Tomamos una copa en la Torre Latinoamericana.* We're having a drink at the Torre Latinoamericana. ◆ *Salgamos, chico, y tomemos una copita.* Let's go out, dear, and have a little drink.

tomar una decisión to make a decision *L. Am., Sp* ◆ *¿Cuándo van a tomar una decisión los socios?* When are the members going to make a decision?

tomar vuelo (to take flight) to take off, make progress (things) *Mex, DR, U, Arg* ◆ *El negocio tomó vuelo cuando llegó el nuevo gerente.* The business took off when the new manager arrived.

tomar/dar un giro favorable to take a turn for the better *L. Am., Sp* ◆ *La condición de mi tía dio un giro favorable.* My aunt's condition took a turn for the better.

tomarle la palabra a alguien to take someone's word (for something), take someone at their word *L. Am., Sp* ◆ *Les tomé la palabra, pero me fallaron.* I took their word for it, but they let me down.

tomarlo a mal to take it the wrong way *L. Am., Sp* ◆ *No hay que tomarlo a mal; sólo fue un chiste.* There's no need to take it the wrong way; it was only a joke.

tomarse las cosas a la tremenda (to take things to the tremendous) to take things too hard, give things too much importance *U, Arg, Sp* ◆ *Suspender un examen no es tan grave; no te lo tomes a la tremenda.* Failing a test is not so serious; don't take it so hard.

un **tomate** →**ponerse como un tomate**

los **tombos** police, cops *CR, Col, Ven, Ec, Peru* ◆ *Cuídate de los tombos.* Be careful of the cops.

ton →**sin ton ni son**

a **tontas y a locas** recklessly, like crazy, without thought *most of L. Am., Sp* ◆ *César hablaba a tontas y a locas de su jefe.* César *was talking like crazy (without thinking) about his boss.*

tontear to act like a fool, behave in a foolish or stupid way *L. Am., Sp* (RVAR *Sp:* also, to flirt) ◆ *Iba tonteando durante media hora, pero por fin encontré la casa. (ES)* I *was putzing around (going along stupidly) for a half hour, but I finally found the house.* ◆ *Luisa siempre está tonteando con los chicos del barrio. (Sp)* Luisa *is always flirting with the guys in the neighborhood.*

tontería →**¡Qué tontería(s)!**

a lo **tonto** like crazy, without thinking (also, **a lo tarugo, a lo pendejo**) *Chicano, Mex, ES* ◆ *Escribió una carta en pocos minutos a lo tonto.* He *(She) wrote a letter in a few minutes without thinking.*

el/la **tonto** →**hacerse el loco (tonto)**

tonto(-a) de capirote (idiot chief) stupid to the nth degree, dope of dopes *Mex, Peru, Sp* ◆ *Ese inquilino que tienes es un tonto de capirote.* That *tenant you have is stupid to the nth degree.*

toparse →**Hasta que nos topemos.**

toparse con to bump into, run across *L. Am., Sp* ◆ *¡Nunca adivinará con quién me topé en el mercado!* You'll *never guess who I bumped into at the market!* ◆ *Hoy me topé con Hugo en el mercado.* I *bumped into Hugo today at the market.*

al **tope** totally, with all one's energy, fast *Mex, Sp, U* ◆ *Aproveche al tope este sitio de la Red.* Take *advantage of this website to the max.*

el **tope** →**estar hasta el tope; estar hasta los topes; Hasta que nos topemos.**

el **toque 1.** (touch) sec(ond), short time *CR, Col, Sp* ◆ *Fue un toque de unos minutos, no más.* It *was a short time, a couple of minutes, no more.* **2.** (touch) hit (marijuana) (also, **el toquesín**) *Chicano, Mex, G, ES, Col* (RVAR *Mex:* also, **el guato, la goma**)

un **toque** →**dar un toque**

torear (to fight a bull) to provoke *L. Am., Sp* (RVAR *Mex, DR, Col, Ch, U, Sp:* also, to manage or manipulate people or a situation) ◆ *Antonio toreó a Juanito hasta que éste se cansó de las provocaciones y lo golpeó.* An- *tonio provoked Juanito until the latter got tired of his provocations and hit him.*

torpe dim-witted, slow *Mex, Cuba, DR, PR, C. Am., U* ◆ *Soy muy torpe. No puedo hacer este dibujo.* I'm *very slow. I can't do this drawing.*

torre →**dar en la torre**

torta →**Ni torta.**

la **torta** (cake) female organ (vulgar) *Mex, G, ES*

tortilla →**hacer tortilla a una persona o cosa**

la **tortillera** (tortilla maker) lesbian, dike (pejorative) *L. Am., Sp*

la **tortuga** (turtle) slowpoke, slow person *Mex, DR, ES, Col* ◆ *Siempre que salimos con Beatriz llegamos tarde porque es una tortuga.* Every *time we go out with Beatriz we're late because she's a slowpoke.*

tos →**hacerla de tos (de pedo) a alguien; No hay tos.**

total que after all, since in any case, so, in short *L. Am., Sp* ◆ *¿Para qué estudiar? Total que ya me reprobaron.* Why *study? After all, they already flunked me.*

trabajar como burro (to work like a donkey) to work like a dog *L. Am., Sp* ◆ *Olga trabajó como burra en invierno, y en verano viajará.* Olga *worked like a dog in the winter, and she'll travel in the summer.*

trabajar como enano (to work like a dwarf) to work like the devil *Ch, U, Sp* ◆ *Emilio trabaja como un enano. No para ni un segundo.* Emilio *works like the devil. He doesn't stop even for a second.*

el/la **trabajólico(-a)** workaholic, someone who works too hard or is addicted to work *parts of L. Am.* ◆ *Tenemos un hijo atorrante y una hija trabajólica.* We *have a good-for-nothing son and a workaholic daughter.*

la **tracalada** droves, bunch; crowd *Mex, ES, Ch, N. Arg* ◆ *¡Qué tracalada de tontos!* What *a bunch of idiots!*

el/la **tracalero(-a)** swindler, cheat *Mex* ◆ *¿Tan barato compraste el estéreo? Eres un tracalero.* You *bought that stereo as cheap as that? You're a con artist.*

traer a alguien de acá para allá (aquí para allí) (to bring someone from here to there) to keep someone busy, moving constantly, or confused or upset *Mex, DR, PR,*

U, Arg, Sp (RVAR *ES:* **allá para acá**) ◆ *Mi niño de un año me trae de acá para allá.* My one-year-old son keeps me on the run.

traer cola (coleta) (to bring a tail [pigtail]) to crop up again, come back to hit one in the face, bring serious consequences (used for things) *Mex, U, Arg, Sp* ◆ *No quiero intervenir en esta discusión porque sé que traerá cola.* I don't want to intervene in this discussion because I know it will come back to haunt me.

traer de culo a alguien (to bring someone by the ass) to upset someone, give someone a damn hard time (vulgar) *Sp* ◆ *Este niño me trae de culo.* This kid is giving me a damn hard time.

traer de un ala (to bring by a wing) to have (someone) helplessly in love *Mex* ◆ *Sergio la trae de un ala.* Sergio has her helplessly in love with him.

traer/llevar algo escrito en la frente (to bring [take] something written on the forehead) to have something written all over one's face *L. Am., Sp* ◆ *No me mientas, hombre, porque tienes tu deshonra escrita en la frente.* Don't lie to me, man, because dishonesty is written all over your face.

traerlo (tenerlo) entre ojos (to bring [have] it between the eyes) to have a grudge against someone, dislike *Mex, Ch, U* ◆ *Me trae entre ojos.* He (She) has a grudge against me. ◆ *Lo traigo entre ojos.* I have a grudge against him. ◆ *La tengo entre ojos porque no es honesta.* I dislike her because she's not honest.

el/la **tragaldabas** (door hinge gobbler) chowhound, glutton, guzzler *L. Am., Sp* ◆ *Ese chico es tragaldabas; todo se lo come.* That boy is a chowhound; he eats everything.

tragar (to swallow) to put up with, accept *DR, Nic, U, Arg, Sp* ◆ *No estoy de acuerdo con algunas cosas que dice el jefe, pero hay que tragárselas.* I don't agree with some of the things the boss says, but I have to put up with them.

tragar →no tragar

tragar camote (to swallow sweet potato) to put up with something quietly or to be unable to express oneself *Mex* ◆ *El jefe me re-*gañó y yo tragué camote. The boss bawled me out and I had to just keep quiet.

tragar el anzuelo (to swallow the hook) to swallow something hook, line, and sinker, fall for something *L. Am., Sp* ◆ *Mi amigo me habló, y tragué el anzuelo como una tonta.* My friend called me, and I took the bait hook, line, and sinker like an idiot.

tragar saliva (to swallow saliva) to be dumbfounded; to have to be silent and put up with something *L. Am., Sp* ◆ *Estefanía quería responder a los insultos, pero tuvo que tragar saliva.* Estefanía wanted to respond to the insults, but she had to bite her tongue and put up with it.

tragar(se) algo (to swallow something) to fall for something, believe something *L. Am., Sp* ◆ *No voy a tragar ese cuento. No me lo trago.* I'm not swallowing that story. I'm not swallowing it.

tragarle la tierra a alguien (to have the earth swallow one) used to express embarrassment, a wish to disappear from view *L. Am., Sp* ◆ *¡Trágame tierra! Aquí viene Eduardo, y yo con esta ropa tan fea.* I wish the earth would swallow me! Here comes Eduardo, and I'm wearing these ugly clothes.

tragarse la píldora (to swallow the pill) to believe a lie, fall for something *Mex, Ch, U, Sp* (RVAR *Sp:* also, **tragarse la bola**, to swallow the ball) ◆ *Me dijo que no tenía novia y me tragué la píldora.* He told me he didn't have a girlfriend and I fell for it.

tragárselo a alguien la tierra (to be swallowed by the earth) to disappear from the face of the earth, places one usually frequents *Mex, DR, PR, ES, S. Cone, Sp* ◆ *Nunca vemos a Juan; se lo tragó la tierra.* We never see Juan; it's like the earth swallowed him.

el **trago** (swallow) drink of any kind, but often refers to a cocktail, alcoholic drink *L. Am., Sp* ◆ *Estoy cansada. Necesito un trago.* I'm tired. I need a drink.

el **tragón, la tragona** chowhound, big eater *Mex, ES* ◆ *Nicole es tragona; le encanta comer.* Nicole is a big eater; she loves to eat.

el **trajín** a lot of work, things to do *L. Am., Sp* ◆ *¡Pobre Miriam! Vaya trajín se trae con la boda de su hija. (Sp)* Poor Miriam! What a lot of work her daughter's wedding is giving her. ◆ *Con tanto trajín, no he tenido tiempo de llamar a mis amigos.* With so much work, I haven't had time to call my friends.

trampas →**hacer trampas**

el/la **tramposo(-a)** con artist, cheat *L. Am., Sp* ◆ *¡No seas tramposo! No mires las cartas de los otros jugadores.* Don't be a cheat! Don't look at the other players' cards.

a **trancas y barrancas** (at beams and ravines [cliffs]) with a lot of effort, passing over all obstacles *Mex, Sp* ◆ *A trancas y barrancas, los médicos llegaron a las poblaciones más remotas.* With great effort, the doctors made it to the most remote populations.

Tranquilo(-a). (Tranquil.) No problem, relax. Chill out. (very common in *Col; Sp:* also, **tranqui** for short and **de tranqui,** calmly) *L. Am., Sp* ◆ *Tranquilo, tranquilo. No hay problema.* Keep your cool. (Relax.) There's no problem. ◆ *Tranqui. Relax. Chill out.* ◆ *Comimos de tranqui.* We ate in peace.

la **transa** ruse, trick, con *Mex, ES, Col* ◆ *¿Quién sabe qué transas se trae Juan?* Who knows what tricks Juan has up his sleeve?

transar to swindle, cheat *Mex, ES* ◆ *Este televisor no sirve. Me transaron.* This television set is no good. They conned me.

el/la **transista** con artist *Mex, Col: see* **transa**

estar en **tránsito** (to be in transit) to be under way (said of a project) *Mex, Col, Ch* ◆ *El informe está en tránsito.* The report is on its way.

un **trapo** →**poner a alguien como un trapo (viejo); sacar los trapos al sol**

los **trapos** (rags) duds, clothing *L. Am., Sp* ◆ *Se gasta un dineral en trapos.* You can spend a fortune on your duds. ◆ *Me compré algunos trapos.* I bought some rags (clothes).

traqueteado(-a) (clattered) old, used or worn out *Mex, ES, S. Cone* (RVar *CR:* tired or badly made) ◆ *Ese carro está traqueteado.* That car is worn out (ready for the junk yard).

el **traqueteo** (banging, creaking) intense activity, mess, transaction *Mex, DR, PR, G, ES, Col* (RVar *Col:* refers to drug dealing) ◆ *¿Cuál es el traqueteo que tienen esos dos? A mí me huele bien feo.* What's the deal with

those two? It looks (literally, smells) ugly to me. ◆ *Deja el traqueteo, que vamos a llegar tarde.* Stop messing around—we're going to be late. ◆ *¿Cuál es el traqueteo?* What's up? (greeting, but implies immoral activity in Caribbean and Col)

el **trasero** rear end *L. Am., Sp* ◆ *Le di una patada en el trasero y le dije que no volviera a mi casa.* I gave him a kick in the rear end and told him not to come back to my house.

trasnochar (to cross the night) to stay out or up late at night *L. Am., Sp* ◆ *Trasnoché toda la semana, pero hoy voy a acostarme temprano.* I stayed out late all week, but tonight I'm going to go to sleep early.

la **trastada** dirty trick *L. Am., Sp* ◆ *A mí también me han hecho algunas trastadas.* They've played some dirty tricks on me, too.

el **traste** rear end, backside *Ch, U* ◆ *Me duele el traste de estar sentada todo el día trabajando en la computadora.* My backside hurts from sitting all day working on the computer.

tratarse de to be a matter of *L. Am., Sp* ◆ *Ven tan pronto como puedas; se trata de un asunto urgente.* Come as soon as possible; it's a matter of great urgency.

Trato hecho. (Agreement made.) It's a deal. *L. Am., Sp* ◆ *Te compro el carro. Trato hecho.* I'll buy your car. It's a deal.

la **tremenda** →**por la tremenda**

tremendo(-a) too much, tremendous, exaggerated (often bad) *L. Am., Sp* ◆ *Los artículos de los diarios son tremendos.* The articles in the newspapers are exaggerated.

un **tren** →**estar como un tanque (estar como un tren)**

tres →**Ni a la de tres.**

de **tres al cuarto** (from three to fourth) so-so, run of the mill, phrase denoting the small value or esteem of something *Sp* ◆ *Es una tienda de tres al cuarto.* It's a run-of-the-mill store.

tripón, tripona potbellied, heavy *L. Am., Sp* ◆ *El tripón se llama David. Trabaja conmigo.* The potbellied guy is named David. He works with me.

la **troca** truck (from English) *Chicano, parts of Mex, ES* ◆ *Su troca es último modelo. His (Her) truck is the newest model.*

a **troche y moche (trochemoche)** willy-nilly, pell-mell *parts of L. Am., Sp* ◆ *Están gastando a troche y moche. No sé cómo van a poder recuperar la inversión. They're spending willy-nilly. I don't know how they're going to be able to get back their investment.*

la **trompa** (trunk of an elephant) mouth, kisser (often in reference to an angry person) *Mex, Nic, CR, Col* ◆ *Marisol es muy sangrona; todo el tiempo con su trompa de pato. Marisol is very unpleasant; always with her puckered (literally duck) mouth.*

estar **trompa** (also, **trompeta, tururú**) (to be trunk of an elephant) to be drunk *Sp* ◆ *Me parece que está un poco trompa. It seems to me he (she) is a little drunk.*

el **trompabulario** condescending term for bad language, sounds like **trompa**, meaning mouth or angry, and **vocabulario** *Mex, Col* ◆ *¡Qué trompabulario tiene José! What bad language José uses!*

la **trompada** hard blow *most of L. Am.* (RVAR *Sp:* **el trompazo**) ◆ *A la salida de la discoteca le dieron una trompada en la nariz. As he left the dance club someone punched him in the nose.*

trompo →**echarse ese trompo a la uña**

trompudo(-a) (with a big snout) loud-mouthed or big-mouthed; someone sounding off threats *Mex, C. Am., Col, U* ◆ *Cada vez que lo veo, está trompudo. Every time I see him, he's yelling and screaming.*

tronado(-a) (blasted) stoned *Mex* ◆ *Cuando Marta llegó a la disco, ya estaba tronada. When Marta got to the disco, she was already stoned.*

tronar (to thunder) to flunk (exam), to wash out *Mex, C. Am.* ◆ *Me tronaron. They washed me out.*

tronar como (un) ejote (to thunder or snap like a peapod) to wash out, end badly, fail *Mex* ◆ *Tronó como (un) ejote en el trabajo. He (She) messed up big-time at work.* ◆ *Tronó con su novia como (un) ejote. He was a washout with his girlfriend.*

el **trono, trono de los césares** (throne, throne of the Caesars) potty, toilet seat *Mex, Col* ◆ *¿Donde está Pepito? Está sentado en el trono. Where's little Pepe? He's on the potty.*

tropezar(se) con to bump into *L. Am., Sp* ◆ *Tropezamos con los Méndez en el centro. ¡Qué placer! We bumped into the Mendezes downtown. What a pleasure!*

a **tropezones** (with trips, falling down) with a lot of effort, with delays and difficulties, haltingly *Mex, DR, U, Sp* ◆ *Miguelito lee a tropezones. Miguelito reads haltingly.*

trucha →**ponerse trucha**

trucho(-a) (trout) fake, phony *U, Arg* ◆ *Esta maleta no es de cuero; es trucha. This suitcase isn't leather; it's imitation.* ◆ *Ese hombre es trucha; no lo escuches. That man is a fake; don't listen to him.*

¡Tu abuela! (¡Tu padre!) (Your grandmother! [Your father!]) You son of a bitch! You bitch! *DR, ES, Sp* ◆ *¿Fuiste tú quien sacó dinero de mi billetera? ¡Tu abuela! Was it you who took money out of my wallet? You SOB!*

¡Tu madre! (Your mother!) You son of a bitch! You bitch! (vulgar) insult impugning the honor of one's mother, often accompanied by a gesture with the fist of one hand raised and clenched *Mex, C. Am., Col*

tuanis great, nice, healthy, too nice; also, a greeting among young people *G, CR* ◆ *(ES, Nic: tuani) ¿Qué tal el viaje? —¡Tuanis! How was the trip? —Great!*

un **tubo** →**por un tubo; mandar a alguien por un tubo**

el **tuerca** (metal nut in mechanics) grease monkey; car lover *S. Cone* ◆ *Ricardo y sus amigos son tuercas y pasan los fines de semana arreglando sus coches. Ricardo and his friends are grease monkeys, and they spend the weekends fixing up their cars.*

los **tuétanos** →**hasta los tuétanos**

tumbar 1. (to fell, knock down) to mug, rob *PR, Col* ◆ *Yo no encuentro mi cartera desde ayer. Creo que me la tumbaron en la guagua. (PR) I can't find my wallet since yesterday. I think someone picked my pocket on the bus.* **2.** (to fell, knock down) to kill; to convince or persuade; to deceive *Mex, Cuba,*

Col ◆ *Me tumbaron al hacer ese negocio. They ripped me off when I made that business transaction.*

al **tuntún** helter-skelter, haphazardly, without thinking or knowing about a subject, without a plan *S. Cone, Sp* ◆ *Siempre hace las cosas al tuntún, sin pensar. He (She) always does things haphazardly, without thinking.*

tupirle (to compact it) to step on it, get a move on *Mex* ◆ *¡Túpele! Se nos atrasa. Speed it up! We're getting behind.*

el/la **turista (vacacionista)** (tourist [vacationist]) someone who rarely goes to class *Mex, Cuba, Col* ◆ *Carmen es la turista de la clase; casi nunca está aquí. Carmen is the tourist of the class; she's almost never here.*

turistear to play tourist, go on an outing *Mex, DR, ES, CR, Col* ◆ *En las últimas vacaciones turisteamos los parques nacionales. During our last vacation we visited (as tourists) the national parks.*

la **u** short for **universidad** *C. Am., Col, Ch (U of Chile only)* ◆ *Voy a la u. ¿Me quieres acompañar?* I'm going to the university. Want to come with me?

Ubícate. (Find yourself.) Straighten up. Get with the program. *Mex, DR, Col, Peru, S. Cone* ◆ *Ésta es una reunión muy importante para mí, así que ubícate y no te pongas a hablar de política. This is a very important meeting for me, so get with the program and don't start talking about politics.*

¡Úchala!/¡Úchale! Yuck!, expression of repugnance *Mex* ◆ *¡Úchala! Tengo que ir a recoger a los niños de la escuela. Yuck! I have to go get the kids from school.*

¡Újule! expression of surprise like **¡Híjole!**, sometimes indicates a put-down, often followed by a disparaging remark *Mex, ES* ◆ *¡Újule! ¡Qué trabajo más pesado! Jeez! What hard work!* ◆ *¡Újule! ¡Qué bárbaro lo que me dijo! Wow! What a nasty thing he (she) said to me!*

ser la **última gota** (to be the last drop, from the expression **La última gota es la que colma el vaso.** The last drop is the one that fills the glass.) to be the last straw *Sp* ◆ *La última gota fue cuando me pusieron a trabajar en la cocina. The last straw was when they put me to work in the kitchen.*

estar en las **últimas** (to be on the last) to be on one's last legs *L. Am., Sp* ◆ *Doña Jacinta tiene noventa años y está en las últimas. Doña Jacinta is ninety years old and on her last legs.*

ser el **último mono** (to be the last monkey) to be the low man on the totem pole, not count (people) *Sp* ◆ *Parece que soy el último mono de la oficina. It looks like I'm the low man on the totem pole in the office.*

el **último toque** finishing (last) touch *Mex, Ch, U, Sp* ◆ *Dale el último toque al artículo y lo publicaremos. Put the finishing touch on the article and we'll publish it.*

una y no más (santo Tomás) (once and no more [Saint Thomas]) once, but never again *Sp* ◆ *¿Le prestaste dinero a Teresa? —Una y no más. Did you lend money to Teresa? —Once, but never again.*

la **uni** short for universidad *Mex, DR, Sp* ◆ *Estaré estudiando todo el día en la uni. I'll be studying at the university all day.*

ser **uña y carne** (to be fingernail and flesh) to be very close, bosom buddies *L. Am., Sp* ◆ *Anita y Luz son uña y carne, y siempre andan juntas. Anita and Luz are bosom buddies, and they always go around together.*

ser **uña y mugre** (to be fingernail and dirt) to be tight (friends), bosom buddies *Mex, Col, Peru, Ch* ◆ *Miriam y yo somos como uña y mugre. Miriam and I are bosom buddies.*

las **uñas** →sacar las uñas

ustedes →Estoy con ustedes.

uva →tener mala uva

uvas →¡Qué uvas!

de **uvas a peras** (from grapes to pears) once in a blue moon *most of L. Am., Sp* ◆ *No comemos mucha carne. De uvas a peras compro un pollo. We don't eat a lot of meat. Once in a blue moon I buy a chicken.*

V

una **vaca** →hacer una vaca (echar la vaca)

estar de **vacaciones en el bote** (to be on vacation in the jar) to be in the clinker (jail) *Mex, Cuba* ♦ *¿Dónde está Gabriel? Hace mucho que no lo veo. —Está de vacaciones en el bote. Where's Gabriel? I haven't seen him for a long time. —He's "on vacation" in the clinker.*

la **vacilada 1.** deceit, con, trick *Mex, Col, Sp* ♦ *Es otra vacilada del gobierno. It's another government trick.* **2.** joke, humorous language *Mex* ♦ *Cantinflas fue famoso por sus vaciladas. Cantinflas was famous for his jokes (humorous language).*

el/la **vacilador(-a)** tease, goofoff, cutup, someone who enjoys life without working hard, someone who jokes or makes fun of others; also, someone who deceives others *Mex, Cuba, G, ES, Col* ♦ *No lo creas. ¡Qué vacilador! Don't believe him. What a nut!*

vacilar (to vacillate, go back and forth) to joke around, have a good time; to put someone on, tease *Mex, C. Am., Col, Ven, Ec, Peru, Sp* ♦ *Nunca sé cuando habla en serio; siempre está vacilando. I never know when he's serious about what he's saying; he's always kidding around.* ♦ *Niña, no vaciles tanto. Habla seriamente. Girl, don't tease so much. Talk seriously.* ♦ *¡Vamos a vacilar! Let's enjoy ourselves!*

vacilar a alguien to hit on someone, look at someone with lascivious intentions; to try to pick someone up *Cuba, ES, Col, Ec* ♦ *Estás vacilando a esa chama, ¿no? You're hitting on that girl, right?* ♦ *Vamos a vacilar a aquella chava. Let's go put the moves on that girl.*

vacilar con (alguien) to fool around with, have fun with (someone) *Mex, Cuba, DR, G, ES, Pan, Col* ♦ *Está vacilando con la novia. He's fooling around (having fun) with his girlfriend.*

el **vacilón** party, fun, diversion *Mex, DR, PR, ES, CR* ♦ *Tenemos que planear desde ahora*

el *vacilón para las navidades. We have to start planning the Christmas fun now.*

ser un **vacilón** to be a cutup, comic, entertaining person *Mex, ES, CR, DR, PR, Sp* ♦ *José es un vacilón, siempre contando chistes. José is a clown, always telling jokes.*

vacunar (to vaccinate) to deceive or cheat *S. Cone* ♦ *Ese grupiento me vacunó, vendiéndome un radio que no funciona. That ripoff artist conned me by selling me a radio that doesn't work.*

el/la **vago(-a)** slacker, drifter (also, drug addict or alcoholic) *L. Am.* ♦ *Benjamín es un vago, pero no es mala persona. Benjamín is a slacker, but he's not a bad person.*

la **vaina 1.** (husk) hassle, problem, mess (all-purpose word for any thing, situation, etc., slightly vulgar) *DR, PR, C. Am., Col, Ven, Peru* ♦ *¡Qué vaina! Dejamos los pasaportes en el hotel. What a pain! We left the passports in the hotel.* **2.** (husk) thing (all-purpose word for any thing, situation, etc., slightly vulgar) *C. Am., DR, PR, Col, Ven, Peru* ♦ *Dame esa vaina, por favor. Give me that thingamabob, please.*

vaina →echar vaina; Ni de vaina.; ¡Qué vaina!; ¿Qué vaina (mierda) es ésta?

el **vale** male friend, guy (probably short for **valedor,** defender) *Chicano, Mex, Ven* ♦ *Oye, vale, ¿entiendes esto? Hey, pal, do you understand this?*

Vale. (It is worth something.) All right. OK. *Col, Sp* ♦ *¿Vamos al cine con mis padres? Vale. Let's go to the movies with my parents. All right.*

Me **vale.** I don't give a damn. (slightly vulgar; used instead of **Me vale madre, pinga,** or **verga,** which are vulgar].) *Mex, ES* ♦ *Me vale no aprobar el examen. I don't give a damn about not passing the exam.*

el **valedor** (defender) casual drinking buddy *Mex, G, ES, Col, Ven* ♦ *Mi valedor Ramón nos va a acompañar al cine. My friend Ramón is going to go with us to the movies.*

el **valemadrismo** (from the expression **me vale madre**; *Es, Nic:* **valevergismo** [vulgar]) attitude of indifference, slacker attitude *Mex* ◆ *A pesar de su aparente actitud de valemadrismo, Hugo tiene buen corazón.* In spite of his slacker attitude, Hugo has a good heart.

valer la pena to be worthwhile *L. Am., Sp* ◆ *Valió la pena sacar mi título.* It was worthwhile getting my degree.

valer papas (to be worth potatoes) to be worthless, worth beans *Mex, ES* ◆ *Esta ropa usada vale papas.* This used clothing is worth beans.

valer su peso en oro (to be worth its weight in gold) to be worth a fortune *Mex, DR, U, Sp* ◆ *Esa muchacha vale su peso en oro.* That girl is worth her weight in gold.

valer un Potosí (un mundo, un imperio) (to be worth a Potosí, from the silver-mining area in Bolivia [a world, an empire]) to be worth a fortune *Mex, DR, Peru, Sp* (RVar *Peru:* also, **valer un Perú**) ◆ *Las alhajas de tu abuela valen un Potosí. Deberías tenerlas en la caja fuerte.* Your grandmother's jewelry is worth a fortune. You should keep it in the safe.

valer: más vale it's better *L. Am., Sp* ◆ *Más vale algo que nada.* It's better than nothing (literally, "Something is better than nothing").

valerle madre (to matter mother) to not give a damn, not matter (vulgar) (also: **importarle madre**) *Mex, parts of C. Am.* ◆ *Les vale madre lo que opinen los demás.* They don't give a damn what other people think.

¡Válgame Dios! Good grief! Good Lord! *L. Am., Sp* ◆ *¡Válgame Dios! ¿Pagaste dos mil pesos por un par de zapatos? Estás loca.* Good Lord! You paid two thousand pesos for a pair of shoes? You're crazy.

la **valona** favor *Mex, ES* ◆ *Necesito que me hagas una valona, 'mano.* I need you to do me a favor, bro.

en **vano** in vain, for nothing *L. Am., Sp* ◆ *Todo mi trabajo fue en vano. De nada sirvió.* All my work was for nothing. It didn't help.

estar en **varas dulces** (to be in sweet rods, pun with **en-varas** sounding like **em-baraz**) to be pregnant *Mex* ◆ *Juanita está en varas dulces desde febrero.* Juanita has been expecting since February.

el **vato (bato)** guy, dude *Chicano, Mex* ◆ *Oye, bato, ¿por qué no vamos a echar una copa? Hey, dude, why don't we go have us a drink? ◆ Luis es un vato loco; vive en San Diego, pero su corazón está en México. Luis is a crazy dude; he lives in San Diego, but his heart is in Mexico.*

¡Vaya! Good, great, agreed, understood. *Mex, DR, G, ES, Col* ◆ *¿Nos vemos a las ocho? — Vaya, pues.* Shall we meet at eight? —Agreed.

vaya: Que te (le) vaya bien. (May it go well for you.) Have a good time (day, trip). Good luck to you! (said to someone who is leaving) *L. Am., Sp* ◆ *Hasta pronto, Memo. Que te vaya bien.* See you soon, Memo. Good luck to you.

Vaya a contárselo a su tía (abuela). (Go tell it to your aunt [grandmother].) Oh, come on! Go figure! *Mex, ES, S. Cone, Sp* ◆ *No le creo eso. Vaya a contárselo a su tía.* I don't believe that. Come on!

Vaya a decírselo a su abuela. (Go tell it to your grandmother.) Oh, come on! Go figure! *Mex, ES, U, Arg* ◆ *Basta de cuentos. Vaya a decírselo a su abuela.* That's enough tall tales! Come on!

Vaya uno a saber. (Go to know.) Who knows? Go figure. *L. Am., Sp* ◆ *Vaya uno a saber lo que hacen ustedes.* Heaven only knows what you guys are up to.

Vaya usted (Vete) a saber. (Go to know.) Who knows? Go figure. *Peru, Bol, Sp* ◆ *¿Cuándo llegan los muchachos desde Buenos Aires? —Vaya usted a saber.* When do the kids arrive from Buenos Aires? —Who knows?

a **veces** at times *L. Am., Sp* ◆ *A veces pienso que no te importo nada.* Sometimes I think I don't matter at all to you.

estar de **veinticinco alfileres** (to be of twenty-five pins) to be all dressed or dolled up *L. Am., Sp* ◆ *Mati está de veinticinco alfileres; tendrá una cita con Pablo.* Mati is all dolled up; she must have a date with Pablo.

vejestorio(-a) geezer, fogy *DR, ES, Nic, S. Cone, Sp* ◆ *¿Conoces a ese vejestorio que llegó con la pintora a la cena? Nadie sabe quién es.* Do you know that old geezer who came to the dinner party with the painter? Nobody knows who he is.

el **vejete** old man *L. Am.* ◆ *Nicolás es un vejete; sin embargo todavía es buen mozo.* Nicolas is an old guy, but he's still good-looking.

una **vela** ➙**poner una vela a San Miguel (a Dios) y otra al diablo; quedarse/estar a dos velas**

velocidad ➙**meterle velocidad**

la **venada** fit *Sp* ◆ *A Hugo le dio una venada y rompió su examen.* Hugo threw a fit and ripped up his exam.

vencido(-a) ➙**darse por vencido(-a)**

vender la pomada (to sell the ointment) to do a hard sell, sell snake oil *Peru, Ch* ◆ *Nos vendieron la pomada de que los precios no subirían.* They sold us the story that the prices wouldn't go up.

venderse (to sell oneself) to sell out *L. Am., Sp* ◆ *El diputado se vendió sin importarle las consecuencias.* The representative sold himself out without caring about the consequences.

venderse como pan caliente (to sell like hot bread) to sell very well, sell like hot cakes *most of L. Am.* ◆ *Las sandalias que estaban en oferta se vendieron como pan caliente.* The sandals that were on sale sold like hot cakes.

vendido(-a) sellout, person who sells out *most of L. Am.* ◆ *Lo acusaron de ser un vendido cuando su equipo perdió el partido.* They accused him of being a sellout when his team lost the game.

estar **vendido(-a)** (to be sold) to be deep in debt *Mex* ◆ *Estoy vendida; no puedo usar mi tarjeta de crédito.* I'm deeply in debt; I can't use my credit card.

Venga. way of ending a conversation on the phone (just before saying good-bye), sometimes indicates that one is in a hurry or wants to finish up *Sp* ◆ *Venga. Adiós.* Okay. Good-bye.

venir ➙**ir y venir, ir y venir en una cosa**

venir a alguien en bandeja (to come to someone on a tray) to have something handed to one on a silver platter, come without effort *Ch, U, Sp* ◆ *¡Qué suerte! Este puesto me vino en bandeja.* What luck! This job was handed to me on a silver platter.

venir a menos (to come to less) to come down in the world, deteriorate *L. Am., Sp* ◆ *Ese hombre era rico pero ahora está venido a menos.* That man was rich but now he's come down in the world.

venir al caso to be to the point *L. Am., Sp* ◆ *Eso no viene al caso, amigos.* That's not to the point, my friends.

venir con cuentos (to come with stories) to tell tales *L. Am., Sp* ◆ *No me vengas con cuentos.* Don't come to me with your tall tales.

venir(se) to come sexually (vulgar) *Mex, Cuba, DR, PR* ◆ *¿Ya te viniste, querida? ¡Qué bien!* Did you come, my dear? That's great!

venirle grande (to come to him or her very big) to be excessive (for one's size or merit); to be too much (for someone) *Mex, Sp* (RVar *U, Arg:* **quedarle grande**) ◆ *Con la poca experiencia que Dolores tiene en negocios, ese trabajo le viene grande.* With the little bit of experience Dolores has in business, that job is too much for her.

venirse abajo to fall apart, collapse, go to pieces *L. Am., Sp* ◆ *La empresa para la cual trabajo se ha venido abajo.* The business I work for fell apart. ◆ *Después del accidente mi esposa se ha venido abajo.* After the accident my wife went to pieces.

ventajoso(-a) opportunistic (from **ventaja**, advantage) *Mex* ◆ *No seas ventajoso.* Don't take advantage.

a **ver** let's see *L. Am., Sp* ◆ *A ver si tengo el dinero... sí, aquí lo tengo.* Let's see if I have the money . . . yes, here it is (here I have it).

ver las estrellas to see stars *L. Am., Sp* ◆ *Me caí y vi las estrellas. ¡Qué dolor!* I fell and saw stars. What pain!

¿A **ver?** (To see?) Hello (answering the phone). *Hond, Nic, CR, Col*

la **verdad clara y desnuda** (the clear and naked truth) the clear, unadulterated truth *most of L. Am., Sp* ◆ *Hay que hablar de la verdad clara y desnuda.* We need to speak about the unadulterated truth.

la **verdad de la milanesa** (the truth of the Milanese chop) the real truth of the matter *Peru, S. Cone* ◆ *La verdad de la milanesa es que tenemos que ser más responsables.* The *real truth of the matter is that we need to be more responsible.*

verde (green) blue, dirty, referring to sex *parts of L. Am., Sp* ◆ *Contó un chiste verde. She told a dirty joke.*

verde ➞**poner verde**

la de la **verde** (of the green) pot, marijuana *Mex, Col* ◆ *Tengo de la verde; vamos a engrifarnos. I have some pot; let's get stoned.*

los **verdes** (the green ones) soldiers *U, Arg* ◆ *Cuidado con los verdes; no respetan a nadie. Be careful with the soldiers; they have no respect for anyone.*

la **verga** male organ (vulgar) *Mex, C. Am., Col, Ec, U, Arg, Sp*

la **verga** ➞**mandar a alguien a la verga**

la de la **vergüenza** (the one of shame) the last piece of food on a plate that no one dares to take *DR, Sp* ◆ *Se quedó en el plato la de la vergüenza. The last portion of food that no one dared take stayed on the plate.*

vergüenza ➞**tener vergüenza**

verla peluda (to see it hairy) to have a rough time, find oneself in a jam *Mex, ES, CR, Col* ◆ *En este momento la estoy viendo peluda. At this moment I'm having a rough time.*

verle la cara a alguien (to see someone's face) to deceive or take advantage of (implying verle la cara de tonto) *Mex, ES, Nic, S. Cone* ◆ *Ese hombre me vio la cara cuando me vendió un carro tan malo. That man saw me coming and played me for a fool when he sold me such a bad car.*

verlo todo de color rosa to see life through rose-colored glasses, always look on the bright side *L. Am., Sp* ◆ *Eres optimista y siempre lo ves todo de color rosa. You're an optimist and always see everything through rose-colored glasses.*

vérselas negras (to see them black) to have a rough time, problem, trouble *L. Am., Sp* ◆ *Me las vi negras con el jefe porque no le gustó el trabajo que hice. I had a devil of a time with the boss because he didn't like the work I did.*

vestido(-a) y calzado(-a) dressed and shod, having satisfied the main things necessary for interaction with others *L. Am., Sp* ◆ *Patricia, ya nos vamos. —Sí, aquí estoy,*

vestida y calzada. Patricia, we're leaving. — Yes, here I am, ready to go.

vestir santos ➞**ni para vestir santos**

los **veteranos** (veterans) folks, parents *U, Arg* ◆ *¿Cómo están tus veteranos? How are your folks?*

a la **vez** at the same time *L. Am., Sp* ◆ *No puedo hacer dos cosas a la vez. I can't do two things at once.*

de **vez en cuando** (of time in when) from time to time *L. Am., Sp* ◆ *De vez en cuando comemos en casa de mi tío. From time to time we eat at my uncle's house.*

el **viacrucis** ➞**hacer el viacrucis**

vibración ➞**tener buena vibración**

vida ➞**darse la buena (gran) vida; llevar una vida feliz (triste); tener la vida en un hilo; tener más vidas que un gato; tener siete vidas como los gatos (como el gato)**

mi **vida** (my life) sweetheart, darling *L. Am., Sp* ◆ *¿A qué hora regresas, mi vida? What time will you get back, darling?*

¡La **vida me sonríe!** (Life is smiling on me!) What a stroke of luck! *L. Am., Sp* ◆ *Tengo salud, una familia estupenda, trabajo y mucho amor: la vida me sonríe. I have health, a great family, work, and a great deal of love: life is smiling on me!*

el/la **viejo(-a) 1.** (old one) husband (wife), old man (woman), partner *L. Am., Sp* ◆ *Hola, vieja, has llegado temprano del trabajo hoy. Hi, Wifey, you came home early from work today.* ◆ *Momento. Déjame preguntarle a mi viejo. Just a minute. Let me ask my hubby (common and not as pejorative as "old man").* **2.** (old one) father (mother); also, term of endearment *L. Am., Sp* ◆ *Mis viejos no me permiten salir de noche. My folks won't let me go out at night.*

el **viejo verde (viejo caliente)** (green old man [hot old man]) old man who is still involved in romantic relationships *L. Am., Sp,* ◆ *Es un viejo verde, y como tiene dinero las chicas jóvenes salen con él. He's an old letch, and since he has money the young women go out with him.*

viejo(-a) ➞**más viejo(-a) que Matusalén**

viene: el mes (año) que viene (the month [year] that is coming) next month (year) *L. Am., Sp* ◆ *Estaremos en Argentina* *el mes que viene.* We'll be in Argentina next month.

el **viento** →**irse con el viento que corre**

en **vigor** (in vigor) in practice or effect, in force (referring to a law or rule) *L. Am., Sp* ◆ *La ley del divorcio todavía no estaba en vigor en Chile en 2003.* The divorce law was still not in effect in Chile in 2003.

¡Virgen santísima! (Holy Virgin!) Good heavens! (old-fashioned) *L. Am., Sp* ◆ *¡Virgen santísima! ¡Qué tormenta!* Good heavens! What a storm!

visitar al señor Roca (to visit Mr. Rock) to go to the john, restroom *Sp* ◆ *Hay que dejar tiempo para visitar al señor Roca.* You have to leave time to go to the john.

la **vista** →**hacer la vista gorda; hacerse de la vista choncha**

¿Viste? (Did you see?) See? *L. Am.* ◆ *¿Viste? Ya sabía que tenía razón.* See? I knew I was right.

lo **visto** →**por lo visto**

la **viuda verde (mujer rabo verde)** (green widow [woman with a green tail]) dirty old woman *Chicano, Mex* ◆ *Esa señora es una viuda verde.* That lady is a dirty old woman.

ser la **viva (fiel) imagen de alguien** (to be the live [faithful] image of someone) to be the spitting image of someone *L. Am., Sp* ◆ *Nelson es la viva imagen de su abuelo.* Nelson is the spitting image of his grandfather.

vivaracho(-a) sharp, astute; fresh *S. Cone, Sp* ◆ *Este perro es muy vivaracho. Corre y come mucho más que los otros.* This dog is really lively and sharp. He runs and eats much more than the others.

vivir como escopeta de hacienda (to live like an old farm rifle) to be always pregnant (like an old farm rifle, always loaded and left in the corner) *Nic* ◆ *Pobre Matilde está embarazada otra vez. Vive como escopeta de hacienda.* Poor Matilde is pregnant again. She's like an old farm rifle (loaded and left in the corner).

vivito(-a) y coleando (alive and wagging its tail) living and breathing, alive and well *L. Am., Sp* ◆ *¿Has visto a Daniela? —No, pero sé que está vivita y coleando.* Have you seen Daniela? —No, but I know she's alive and well.

el **vivo** →**hacerse el vivo**

ser el **vivo retrato de alguien** to be the spitting image (literally, living portrait) of someone *L. Am., Sp* ◆ *Enrique es el vivo retrato de su tío abuelo.* Enrique is the spitting image of his great-uncle.

de **volada** on the fly or run *Mex, ES, Col* ◆ *Eso se hace de volada.* That can be done very quickly.

volado(-a) 1. (blown up high or flown away) on the fly, in a flash *Mex, Nic, Col* ◆ *Llegó volado al hospital.* He got to the hospital in a flash. **2.** (blown up high or flown away) daydreaming *Mex* ◆ *Está en las nubes, bien volado por la chava.* He's in the clouds, daydreaming about the girl. **3.** (blown up high or flown away) stoned, high; spaced out *Ch*

el/la **volador(a)** (flyer, swinger) someone who is disorganized and forgetful, scatterbrained person, used like despistado *U, Arg* ◆ *¿Por qué no está lista la cena? —Ya conoces a Alba; es una voladora y se olvidó de la mayoría de los ingredientes.* Why isn't dinner ready? —You know Alba; she's a scatterbrain and she forgot most of the ingredients.

volando →**hacer algo volando; ir volando**

volar 1. (to fly) to rob, lift; to be robbed *Mex, Col* ◆ *Mi bolsa voló.* My purse was lifted. ◆ *Me volaron la bolsa. (Col)* They snatched my purse. **2.** (to blow up, to make fly) to flunk, fail *Mex* ◆ *Me volaron en historia.* They flunked me in history. ◆ *Volé el examen.* I flunked the exam.

volar con las propias alas (to fly with one's own wings) to stand on one's own (two) feet *L. Am., Sp* ◆ *Quiero que mis hijos vuelen con sus propias alas.* I want my children to stand on their own two feet.

volarle (to fly it) to step on it, take off *Mex, Col* ◆ *¡Vuélale!* Step on it!

volarse la barda (to blow up the fence) to do something very impressive, usually good *Mex* ◆ *Te volaste la barda con este examen.* You really outdid yourself on this exam.

Voló la paloma. (The dove flew off.) We missed the boat. It was almost in the bag, said when something escapes unexpectedly from one's grasp *Mex, ES* ◆ *Me parece que ya voló la paloma.* I think we (you, etc.) missed the boat.

de **volón pinpón** on the fly, fast or while do-ing something else *Mex, ES* ◆ *Esta semana se ha ido de volón pinpón. This week has flown by.*

volver tarumba a alguien to mix someone up *Sp* (RVar *Ch:* **volver o hacer turumba**) ◆ *Los vendedores me volvieron tarumba. Ahora no sé qué hacer. The salespeople mixed me up. Now I don't know what to do.*

volver a hacer algo to do something again *L. Am., Sp* ◆ *Volveré a llamarla. I'll call her again.*

volver a las andadas (to return to one's walkings, tracks) to go back to one's old habits, tricks *L. Am., Sp* ◆ *Alfonso volvió a sus andadas. Alfonso went back to his old tricks.*

volver sobre sus pasos to retrace one's steps *L. Am., Sp* ◆ *Para hallar tus anteojos,* *tienes que volver sobre tus pasos. To find your glasses, you have to retrace your steps.*

volverse loco(-a) to go crazy *L. Am., Sp* ◆ *Me vuelvo loca con tanto ruido. I'm going crazy with so much noise.*

¡Vóytelas! Wow! interjection of surprise *Mex* ◆ *¡Vóytelas! ¿Qué te pasó? Wow! What hap-pened to you?*

la **voz** →**llevar la voz cantante**

la **vuelta** →**dar la vuelta a la tortilla; dar una vuelta; No hay que darle vueltas.; No hay vuelta de hoja.; poner a alguien de vuelta y media**

a **vuelta de ruedas** (at wheels' turning) slow(ly) *Mex, Hond, ES* (RVar *Ch:* **a la vuelta de la rueda**) ◆ *El tráfico está a vuelta de ruedas. The traffic is moving very slowly.*

wach(e)ar to watch, look (from English) *Chicano, ES* ◆ *¡Wacha eso! Look at that!*

Y

y así sucesivamente and so on *L. Am., Sp* ◆ *Luego das otro paso a la izquierda, y así sucesivamente. Then you take another step to the left, and so on.*

Y dale la burra al trigo. (And let the donkey keep at the wheat.) Same old story, said when someone keeps repeating the same thing. *Mex, ES, Col* ◆ *Y dale la burra al trigo. Siempre con lo mismo. Same old story. Always the same thing.*

Y de la vida, ¿qué más? (And of life, what more?) What else is happening in your life? *Caribbean*

y en paz (and in peace) that's that; phrase said to end a matter *Mex, ES, Sp* ◆ *Yo recojo mis cosas y tú las tuyas, ¡y en paz! I'll take my things and you take yours, and that's that!*

y eso que despite the fact that *L. Am., Sp* ◆ *Lo eligieron presidente del comité y eso que ni siquiera había asistido a las reuniones. They elected him president of the committee, despite the fact that he hadn't even attended the meetings.*

¿Y eso? (And that?) What does that mean? What's that all about? *L. Am., Sp* ◆ *¿Y eso? ¿De dónde sacaste esas ideas tan extrañas, Manuelita? What's that all about? Where did you come up with such strange ideas, Manuelita?* ◆ *Mira lo que traje. —¿Y eso? Look what I brought. —What's up with that?*

y pico and a bit, small amount *L. Am., Sp* ◆ *Son las tres y pico. It's a bit after three.*

y por si eso fuera poco and as if that weren't enough *L. Am., Sp* ◆ *Y por si eso fuera poco, no me dieron ni las gracias. And as if that weren't enough, they didn't even thank me.*

¿Y qué? So what? *L. Am., Sp* ◆ *¿No te dijo que estaba casado? —¿Y qué? A mí no me importa. Didn't he tell you that he was married? —So what? I don't care.*

Ya está bien de cuentos. Enough stories. *most of L. Am., Sp* ◆ *Ya está bien de cuen-tos; no hables más. That's enough stories (fibs); don't say anything more.*

Ya le han caído cincuenta castañas (tacos). (Fifty chestnuts [bad words] have fallen on him or her.) He (She) is fifty. *Sp* ◆ *Nadie lo cree pero a Albertina le han caído cincuenta castañas este año. Nobody believes it, but Albertina's hit the half century mark this year.*

Ya lo creo. (I already believe it.) I should say so. I believe it. *L. Am., Sp* ◆ *¿Estás seguro que terminarás el proyecto para la próxima semana? —Ya lo creo. Are you sure you'll finish the project by next week. —I believe so.* ◆ *Nunca fui a una cantina. —¡Ya lo creo! I've never been to a bar. —I believe it!*

Ya pasó. It's over, meaning something like "you may as well forget it." *L. Am., Sp* ◆ *No llores tanto, querida. Ya pasó. Don't keep on crying, dear. It's all over.*

Ya sábanas (sabadabas). Ya sabes. *Mex, Col* ◆ *Ya sábanas; paquetes de hilo. (Ya sabes, ¿p'a qué te digo?) You know what I mean; why should I tell you?*

Ya se ve. (It's already seen.) I see, expression of agreement. *L. Am., Sp* ◆ *Ya se ve que te has dedicado a cuidar a tus padres. I see you've devoted yourself to taking care of your parents.*

ya tener una pata allí (to now have a paw in there) to have earned a place somewhere, have a foot in the door *Mex* ◆ *Laura trabajó tres meses en esa empresa y no le pagaron nada, pero ya tiene una pata allí. Laura worked three months in that company and they didn't pay her anything, but now she has her foot in the door.*

ya tú sabe' you know (already) *Caribbean* ◆ *Ya tú sabe' que no es verdad lo que ella dice. You know what she says is not true.*

Ya vas, Barrabás. All right. Agreed. *Mex, Col* (RVar *ES*: usually ironic, meaning There you go again! Same old story!) ◆ *He vuelto* con Manuela. —¡Ya vas, Barrabás! *I'm back with Manuela again. —Same old story!*

de **yapa** for free *S. Cone* ◆ *La comida en el restaurante era barata y de yapa siempre comíamos postre.* The food in the restaurant was cheap and we always ate dessert for free.

la **yapa** freebie; free gift *S. Cone* ◆ *Gracielita compró flores para su mamá y de yapa le dieron bombones.* Gracielita bought flowers for her mom, and as a freebie they gave her candy.

« **yo no fui**» →tener cara de «yo no fui»

yo que tú (I that you) if I were you *L. Am., Sp* ◆ *Yo que tú, no lo compraría.* If I were you, I wouldn't buy it.

Yo soy como (Juan) Orozco; cuando como no conozco. (I'm like [Juan] Orozco; when I'm eating I don't recognize people.) said of someone who is too absorbed in eating *Mex, ES* ◆ *Perdona mi falta de atención. Yo soy como Juan Orozco; cuando como no conozco.* Excuse me for not paying attention to you. When I eat, I only think of eating.

un **yogurt** →hacerle la vida un yogurt a alguien

mi **yunta** (my yoke, as of oxen) my best friend *Mex, Cuba, Ec, Peru, Ch* ◆ *Tenía que traer a mi yunta para divertirme.* I had to bring my best bud to have a good time.

259

Z

¡Zafa! Get out of here! *PR* ◆ *¿Yo? ¿Novia de Hugo? ¡Zafa! Ese tipo es un sanano.* Me Hugo's girlfriend? Get out of here! That guy is a dope.

zafado(-a) **1.** crazy *Chicano, Mex, C. Am., Col, Peru, Ch* ◆ *Creo que esa cantante está bien zafada.* I think that singer is off the wall. **2.** sassy, fresh, disrespectful *PR, Col* ◆ *Ten cuidado con lo que dices, que andas zafadito hoy.* Be careful what you say; you're a little sassy today.

zafarse (de) to excuse oneself, back or get out of, avoid; to get rid of *L. Am.* ◆ *Záfate de Fernando, que no te conviene ese tipo.* Stay clear of Fernando. He's not good for you. ◆ *¡Zafo! (Mex)* I'm out (I won't do it)!

¡Záfate! Go away! *Mex, G, ES, Col*

ser un **zafio** to be a blunderer, klutz *Sp* ◆ *Aunque el protagonista de la película es un zafio, logra conquistar a una chica bella e inteligente.* Although the protagonist of the film is a klutz, he manages to win a beautiful and intelligent girl.

Ésa se te **zafó.** (That one got away from you.) You blew it. *Mex* ◆ *Un vendedor no debe hablar tanto. Esa venta se te zafó.* A salesman shouldn't talk so much. You blew it on that sale.

el **zambrote** (Moorish party) mess *CR*

el/la **zanahorio(-a)** (carrot) geek, young person who is innocent, not socially active or "with it" ; health nut *Col, Ven, Ec* ◆ *Pedro es tan sano que todo el mundo lo considera un zanahorio.* Pedro is so healthy that everyone considers him a health nut.

zángano(-a) foolish, silly *DR, PR, Col* ◆ *No seas zángano. ¡Pídele el teléfono!* Don't be foolish. Ask her for her telephone number!

el/la **zángano(-a)** (drone) lazybones, slacker *Mex, most of C. Am., Col, Peru, S. Cone, Sp* ◆ *Fernandina es una zángana. No hace nada y espera que los demás hagan su tra-* bajo. Fernandina is a lazybones. She doesn't do anything, and she waits for someone else to do her work.

Zapatero a tus zapatos. (Shoemaker to your shoes.) Mind your own business. (This is not usually said with the sharp tone that often accompanies the phrase in English.) Let's stick to what we know best. *L. Am., Sp* ◆ *Yo de la mecánica no entiendo mada pero me parece que te han arreglado mal el motor de tu auto. —Zapatero a tus zapatos, amigo.* I dont' konw anything about auto mechanics, but I think they did a bad job on fixing the motor of your car. —Stick to what you know best, my friend.

¡Zape! Shoo! Go away! *DR, PR, Col* ◆ *¡Zape, gato! Señora, llévese a este gato, por favor, que soy alérgico.* Shoo, kitty! Ma'am, take this cat out of here please. I'm allergic.

el **zaperoco** mess, mixup *PR, Ven* ◆ *¡Qué zaperoco tenemos!* What a mess we have!

zapping →**hacer zapping**

zarrapastroso(-a) (from **zarrapastra**, meaning both mud and claw, implying dirty and torn) badly dressed, dirty, having a bad appearance or looking like a slob *L. Am., Sp* (RVar *Mex, G:* also, **salapastroso, chaparrastroso;** *S. Cone:* also, **zaparrastroso**) ◆ *¿Y cómo se atreve a ir a una quinceañera así de zarrapastroso?* And how dare he go to a sweet-fifteen coming-out party in a sloppy getup like that?

en un **zas** in a jiffy, quickly *Mex, ES* ◆ *¿El postre? Lo hago en un zas.* The dessert? I'll make it in a jiffy.

un **zíper** →**poner un zíper en la boca**

zonzo(-a) silly, stupid *most of L. Am.* (not *Ch*) ◆ *Esta chica es muy zonza y su amiga toma ventaja.* That girl is very silly and her friend takes advantage of it.

zoquete (zoqueta) stupid, foolish *Chicano, Mex, DR, Col, Sp* ◆ *¡Qué muchacha más zo-*

queta! ¡No quiso salir en el show de don Francisco! What a foolish girl! She refused to go on Don Francisco's show!

la **zorra** (female fox) bitch, nasty woman *Sp* ◆ *Es una zorra; se quedó con mi dinero y se largó. She's a real bitch; she took my money and ran.*

zorro(-a) (fox) sly, clever like a fox *L. Am., Sp* (RVAR *Ch:* masculine form only) ◆ *Agustina es muy zorra y ha engañado a sus padres por muchos años. Agustina is smart as a fox and has been fooling her parents for many years.*

unos **zorros** →**estar hecho(-a) unos zorros**

English–Spanish Dictionary

to be **about to burst** no caber una cosa en el pecho (a thing won't fit in one's chest) *Mex, DR, ES, Sp* ◆ *I was about to burst with anger.* Tenía tanta rabia que no me cabía en el pecho.

Absolutely not, period. (→see also: No way.) Punto acabado. (Punto final.) (Finished, period.) *Mex, U, Arg* ◆ *Absolutely not, period. Let's not talk about that subject any more.* Punto final. No hablemos más del tema.

to **act innocent but not be** (hurt someone but cover up one's action) tirar la piedra y esconder la mano (to throw the stone and hide one's hand) *L. Am., Sp* ◆ *She acts innocent, but isn't. You can't trust her.* Es una persona de las que tira la piedra y esconde la mano. No te puedes fiar de ella.

to **act like . . .** (pretend to be like) dárselas de... (to give them to oneself as . . .) *L. Am., Sp*; picarse de... (to peck oneself as . . .) *L. Am., Sp* ◆ *She acts like she's well educated (cultured), but she isn't.* Se las da de culta, pero no lo es.

to **act like a fool** tontear *L. Am., Sp* (RVar *Sp:* also, to flirt); mensear *Mex* ◆ *Ramón crashed because he was acting like a fool in the car.* Ramón chocó porque iba menseando en el carro.

to **act like someone who's never made a mistake** no haber roto un plato (to not have broken a plate) *Mex, Sp* ◆ *Luis acts like he's never made a mistake.* Luis nunca ha roto un plato.

to **act sheepish** aparecer avergonzado(-a) *L. Am., Sp*; chivearse *Mex, ES* ◆ *When they asked him to sing, he acted sheepish.* Cuando le pidieron que cantara, se chiveó.

to **act sweet** (all sweetness and light) estar hecho(-a) un almíbar (to be made a syrup) *Sp* ◆ *My husband has become all sweetness and light because he got home late last night.* Mi esposo está hecho un almíbar porque llegó tarde anoche.

action (fun) la movida *most of L. Am., Sp* ◆ *Ariel is always where the action is (in the center of fun).* Ariel siempre está en la movida.

Actions speak louder than words. En la cancha se ven los gallos. (It's in the ring that we see the roosters.) *Ch* ◆ *The new boss says he knows how to increase productivity, but actions speak louder than words.* El nuevo jefe dice que sabe aumentar la productividad, pero en la cancha se ven los gallos.

to **add fuel to the fire** echar leña al fuego *L. Am., Sp* ◆ *It's better to keep quiet and not add fuel (lit., wood) to the fire.* Es mejor callarse y no echar leña al fuego.

against one's will (because one has to; →see also: by force, grudgingly) a la fuerza (by force) *L. Am., Sp*; a la brava (at the brave) *Chicano, Mex, DR, PR, DR, CR,Col, Sp*; a rastras *Mex, U, Sp*; a chaleco (at vest) *Mex* ◆ *I finished the work, but I did it against my will (because I had to).* Terminé el trabajo, pero lo hice a la brava.

Age before beauty. (said to someone who goes first or names himself or herself first) El burro delante, (para que no se espante). (The burro first[, so he isn't frightened, doesn't get startled].) *Mex, DR, ES, Ch, Arg, Sp*

ages ago (a long time ago) cuando Franco era cabo (corneta) (when Franco was a corporal [a trumpet player]) *Sp*; en el año catapún (in the year catapún) *Sp*; en el año de la pera (in the year of the pear) *Ven, Peru, Ch, Sp* ◆ *See this picture from school? It's from ages ago.* ¿Ves esta foto del colegio? Es del año de la pera.

to **air dirty laundry** (→see also: to give someone the lowdown) sacar los trapos al sol (to take the rags or clothes out into the sun) *L. Am., Sp* ◆ *Adela is airing dirty laundry, but I'm not interested in her gossip.* Adela está sacando los trapos al sol, pero no me interesan sus chismes.

airhead →see: space cadet

to be an **airhead** tener la cabeza hueca (to have the head hollow) *Mex, U, Arg, Sp* ◆ *You're not an airhead. So think about how you're going to solve this problem.* No tienes la cabeza hueca. Entonces piensa cómo vas a resolver este problema.

alive and kicking vivito(-a) y coleando (alive and wagging its tail) *L. Am., Sp* ◆ *Have you seen Daniela? —No, but I know she's alive and kicking.* ¿Has visto a Daniela? –No, pero sé que está vivita y coleando.

to be **all broken up about something** (a death or loss) quedarse hecho(-a) polvo (to be made into dust) *L. Am., Sp;* estar hecho(-a) pelota (to be made into a ball) *U, Arg* ◆ *The kids are all broken up about their mother's death.* Los muchachos están hechos pelota con la muerte de su madre.

all by my lonesome (alone, independent, or without support) sin padre ni madre, ni perro que me ladre (without father or mother or dog that barks for me) *Mex, PR, Ch, Arg, Sp* ◆ *Do you have friends in this city? —No, I'm all by my lonesome.* ¿Tienes amigos en esta ciudad? –No, estoy sin padre ni madre, ni perro que me ladre.

all by oneself (with no help, alone; slang) solano(-a) (used instead of solo[-a]) *Chicano, Mex, Cuba, Col, U, Arg* ◆ *You're not going out with Carmen anymore? I always see you all by yourself.* ¿Ya no sales con Carmen? Siempre te veo solano.

all kinds of people hijos de muchas madres (children of many mothers) *Sp* ◆ *All kinds of people died in the war, not just American soldiers.* En la guerra murieron hijos de muchas madres, no sólo soldados americanos.

all of a sudden (soon) de pronto *Mex, C. Am., Col, Ch, Arg, Sp* ◆ *All of a sudden the wind filled the whole room and the window broke.* De pronto el viento invadió toda la habitación y la ventana se rompió.

to be **all over someone** (annoy; →see also: to give someone a hard time) pisarle los callos a alguien (to step on someone's callouses) *ES, Peru, Ch* ◆ *My mother-in-law is always all over me; she doesn't leave me alone.* Mi suegra siempre me está pisando los callos; no me deja en paz.

All right. (That's it. OK.) Órale. (used to animate someone to do something or in accepting an invitation) *Mex, C. Am., Col* (RVar used originally in *Mex*, but young people now use it in *C. Am., Col* also, can be used to express surprise) ◆ *All right, then, let's go to the movies.* Órale, vamos al cine.

All right, agreed. It's a deal. Está bien. De acuerdo. *L. Am., Sp;* Vaya. *Mex, G, ES, DR, Col;* Vale. (It is worth something.) *Sp* ◆ *Let's go to the movies with my parents. —All right.* Vamos al cine con mis padres. –Vale.

All righty. Sobres. *Mex, ES* ◆ *We'll go to your house tonight. —All righty.* Llegaremos esta noche a tu casa. –Sobres.

to be **all the same (to someone)** dar igual, dar lo mismo (to give the same) *L. Am., Sp* ◆ *Going to the party or not is all the same to me.* Me da igual (lo mismo) ir a la fiesta que no ir.

all the time (frequently) a cada rato (at each little time) *L. Am., Sp* ◆ *You keep asking me what time it is all the time. Why don't you wear a watch?* Me pides la hora a cada rato. ¿Por qué no llevas reloj?

All things in moderation. De lo bueno, poco. (Of the good, a little.) *L. Am., Sp;* Ni tanto ni tan poco. (Not so much nor so few.) *Mex, DR, PR, S. Cone, Sp;* Ni tanto que queme al santo, ni tan poco que no lo alumbre. (Not so much as to burn the saint nor so much as not to illuminate it.) *Mex, DR;* Ni tan pelado, ni tan peludo. (Neither so bald, nor so hairy.) *S. Cone* ◆ *Can I serve you more dessert? —No, thank you. All good things in moderation.* ¿Te sirvo más postre? –No, gracias. De lo bueno, poco. ◆ *I can't buy a coffee because I'm on a budget. —But, my friend, that's too extreme. All things in moderation.* No puedo gastar en un café porque estoy ahorrando. –Pero, amigo, es demasiado. Ni tanto ni tan poco.

to be **all-purpose** (serve for contrary uses) servir lo mismo para un fregado que para un barrido (to serve for a scrubbing as for a sweeping) *Cuba, Sp* ◆ *This boy is wonderful; he's all purpose and can do anything.* Este chico es estupendo; tanto sirve para un fregado como para un barrido.

Almost. It's (I'm, etc.) on the way. (almost ready) Ya casi. *L. Am., Sp;* mero: Ya mero. Ya merito. *Mex, G, ES, Nic* ◆ *Did you prepare the food (fix the meal) yet? —Almost.* ¿Ya preparaste la comida? –Ya mero.

and a bit (small amount) y pico *most of L. Am., Sp* ◆ *It's a bit after three.* Son las tres y pico.

and so on and so on (so forth) →see: blah, blah, blah

and that's it (only that; alone) a secas (dry) *Mex, Ch, Sp* ◆ *The letter didn't arrive because it didn't have an address. It had a name and that's it.* La carta no llegó porque no llevaba la dirección. Llevaba un nombre a secas.

to be an **angel** (→see also: good-natured) ser (un) pan de Dios (to be God's bread) *DR, ES, Ch, U* ◆ *The bus driver is an angel. He always waits until I get in the house before leaving.* El chofer del bus es un pan de Dios. Siempre espera que entre a la casa antes de irse.

to be **another kettle of fish** →see also: That's another (a different) kettle of fish. ser otra canción (otro cantar) (to be another song) *L. Am., Sp;* ser capítulo aparte (to be a separate chapter) *Mex, DR, S. Cone, Sp* ◆ *Now we understand what happened; that's another kettle of fish.* Ahora entendemos lo que pasó; eso es otro cantar.

anxiety attack el ataque de ansiedad *L. Am., Sp;* el calambre (cramp) *Mex, Col* ◆ *He had an anxiety attack at the office.* Le dio un calambre en la oficina.

any old way (in any possible way) mal que bien (badly as well) *Mex, DR, ES, Peru, Sp* ◆ *She did her work any old way (not well); we accepted it because she's the daughter of the director.* Mal que bien, hizo su trabajo; se lo aceptamos porque es la hija del director.

appetizers →see: munchies

to be the **apple of one's eye** ser la niña de los (sus) ojos (to be the pupil of one's eyes) *Mex, DR, ES, Sp* ◆ *My only son is the apple of my eye.* Mi único hijo es la niña de mis ojos.

Are you with me or not? ¿Somos o no somos? (Are we or aren't we?) *L. Am., Sp*

armed to the teeth armado(-a) hasta los dientes *L. Am., Sp* ◆ *She came to the meeting armed to the teeth with all her arguments prepared and convinced the board of directors.* Vino a la reunión armada hasta los dientes

con todos sus argumentos preparados y convenció al directorio.

to be **as good as gold** ser más bueno que el pan (to be better than bread) *most of L. Am., Sp* ◆ *That boy is as good as gold.* Ese niño es más bueno que el pan.

as if by magic (through extraordinary or unnatural means) por arte de birlibirloque (also, por arte de magia) *DR, PR, Ch, Sp* ◆ *As if by magic and without really knowing how he did it, Gabriel convinced us all of his point of view.* Por arte de birlibirloque y sin saber muy bien cómo, Garbriel nos convenció a todos de su posición.

as if he (she, etc.) didn't have a care in the world (just like that) como si nada (as if nothing) *L. Am., Sp* ◆ *He heard the bad news as if he didn't have a care in the world.* Escuchó las malas noticias como si nada.

as if to say como quien dice (as someone says) *L. Am., Sp* ◆ *He made a face as if to say "Yuck!"* Hizo un gesto como quien dice "¡Huácala!"

as slow as molasses in January (as a snail) ser la muerte en bicicleta (to be death on a bicycle) *Florida;* más lento(-a) que una caravana de cojos (slower than a caravan of limping people) *PR, Col;* más lento(-a) que un suero de brea (slower than tar plasma) *PR* ◆ *Hurry up, girl! You're slow as molasses in January.* ¡Apúrate, niña! Eres más lenta que una caravana de cojos.

as sure as we're standing here (as shootin') como dos y dos son cuatro (like two and two are four) *L. Am., Sp* ◆ *Are you sure of what you're saying? —As sure as we're standing here.* ¿Estás segura de lo que dices? —Por supuesto, como dos y dos son cuatro.

As (If) you like. Como quiera(s). (Whatever you want.) *L. Am., Sp* *Shall we eat at that restaurant? —If you like.* ◆ *¿Comamos en aquel restaurán? —Como quieras.*

to **ask for a lift** →see: to ask for a ride

to **ask for a ride** pedir un aventón *Mex, ES, Nic;* pedir un jalón *G, ES, CR, Peru;* pedir pon *PR, Col, Sp* ◆ *The car's in the shop again. I have to ask the neighbor for a ride.* Otra vez he tenido que llevar el coche al taller. Tengo que pedirle pon al vecino.

to ask for the moon: *You're asking for the moon, angel.*
Estás pidiendo la luna, mi ángel.

to **ask for the moon (the impossible)**
pedir la luna *L. Am., Sp;* pedir peras al olmo
(to ask the elm tree for pears) *L. Am., Sp;*
pedirle cobija al frío (to ask the cold for a
blanket) *Mex, ES;* pedirle comida al hambre
(to ask hunger for food) *Mex, ES* ◆ *I need a
car, Dad. —Son, you're asking for the moon;
you know we don't have any money. Necesito
un auto, papá. –Hijo, estás pidiendo la luna;
sabes que no tenemos dinero.*

asshole (lazy, uncooperative person, person
who takes no initiative, vulgar) el/la
culero(-a) (commonly used in masculine;
may also refer to pedofile or gay, pejorative)
Chicano, Mex, C. Am. ◆ *Those assholes did
nothing to help us. Esos culeros no hicieron
nada para ayudarnos.*

asshole el/la pendejo(-a) (pubic hair, vulgar)
Mex, DR, PR, C. Am., Col, Ven; el hojaldra
(puff pastry) *Mex;* el ojete (eyelet, hole)
Mex; el cerote (turd, vulgar) *C. Am.;* el/la
cara de culo (ass face, vulgar) *ES, Arg, Sp;*
el/la gilipollas (vulgar, from **polla**) *Sp* ◆ *I*

*don't want to listen to you; you're an asshole.
No quiero escucharte; eres un pendejo.*

at a snail's pace a paso de tortuga (at a turtle's pace) *L. Am., Sp;* a vuelta de ruedas (at
wheels' turning) *Mex, Hond, ES* ◆ *The construction of the new hotel is going at a snail's
pace; I doubt if they'll open it by the end of the
year. La construcción del nuevo hotel marcha a paso de tortuga; dudo que lo inauguren a fin de año.*

at any cost →see: no matter what

to be **at blows** (always fighting; →see also:
to have a blowup) andar a palos *Mex, Sp* ◆
*Germán and Dora hardly speak to each other
because they're always fighting. Germán y
Dora casi no se hablan porque andan a palos constantemente.*

at breakneck speed →see: full blast, like
a bat out of hell, like a shot, on the fly, quick
as lightning

at death's door a las puertas de la muerte
Mex, DR, Ch, Sp ◆ *My sister was at death's
door, but thank God she's better now. Mi her-*

mana estuvo a las puertas de la muerte, pero gracias a Dios está mejor.

at first sight →see: right away, right from the start

at full speed, at full blast →see: full blast

to be **at odds with someone** (on bad terms) estar de punta uno con otro (to be at point with another) *Mex, U, Ch* ◆ *The partners were always at odds with each other, and the business didn't work out.* Los socios siempre estuvieron de punta, y el negocio no anduvo.

at once (all at one time; →see also: right away) de un tirón (at one pull) *L. Am., Sp* ◆ *I finished the work at once.* Terminé el trabajo de un tirón.

to be **at one's post** (on one's toes) estar al pie del cañón (to be at the foot of the cannon) *Mex, ES, S. Cone, Sp* ◆ *If you need something, call me. I'll be here at my post (on my toes).* Si necesitas algo, llámame. Aquí estaré al pie del cañón.

at random →see: helter-skelter

to be **at the boiling point** (because of anger or passion; →see also: to be hot, to be steamed) estar como agua para chocolate (to be like water for chocolate) *Mex, CR* ◆ *When Miguel got home, his wife was at the boiling point.* Cuando Miguel llegó a la casa, su esposa estaba como agua para chocolate.

at the end (in the end, at last) al final *L. Am., Sp;* a la postre (at the dessert, slang) *Mex, DR, Sp* ◆ *In the end you're going to thank (lit.,*

be thankful to) me for making you go to school. A la postre me vas a agradecer que te haya obligado a ir a la escuela.

at the ends of the earth →see: in a god-forsaken spot

at the top of one's lungs a grito pelado (to the peeled shout) *most of L. Am., Sp* ◆ *He started to call me at the top of his lungs in the middle of the party. Everybody stopped talking.* Empezó a llamarme a grito pelado en medio de la fiesta. Todos se callaron.

at this point; at this stage a estas alturas (at these heights) *L. Am., Sp* ◆ *You want to change the plan at this point (in time)? I don't believe it!* ¿Quieres cambiar el plan a estas alturas? ¡No lo creo!

at top speed →see: full blast, like a bat out of hell, like a shot, on the fly, quick as lightning

at whatever (the) cost →see: no matter what

At your service. A sus órdenes. *L. Am., Sp* ◆ *I am at your service.* Estoy a sus órdenes.

awesome →see also: cool, super (amazing; good or bad, unusual, exceptional) bestial *Mex, DR, PR, Col, Peru, U, Arg, Sp* (RVar: more likely bad in *Mex*); macanudo(-a) (probably from the Dominican cigar or from the Argentine liar, Sr. Macana) *Nic, S. Cone;* de miedo (scary, frightening) *Ch, Sp* bárbaro(-a) (barbarous) *L. Am., Sp* ◆ *It was an awesome film.* Fue una película bestial. ◆ *Let's get together at the beach. —Awesome!* Reunámosnos en la playa. —¡Bárbaro!

B

babe 1. (good-looking woman, woman with a good figure; →see also: to be hot, chick, hot number) la buenona *Chicano, Mex, Cuba, C. Am., Col, Ec, Para, Ch, Sp;* la mamasota (sometimes used as a term to get a woman's attention; also, a bit vulgar) *Mex, DR, PR, G, ES, Col;* el cuero (skin, leather; also used for men) *Mex* ◆ *My neighbor is a babe. Mi vecina es una buenona.* 2. (pretty girl, filly; →see also: broad, chick, woman) la potranca (female horse) *Mex, DR, Col* ◆ *My babe and I went to the store to shop. Mi potranca y yo fuimos de compras a la tienda.*

back and forth (negotiations between two people or groups having trouble arriving at a solution) tira y afloja (pull and give slack) *Mex, Peru, S. Cone, Sp* ◆ *Ana and Leandro's divorce was very sad. They spent years in negotiations back and forth without resolving anything. El divorcio de Ana y Leandro fue muy triste. Por años se pasaron en tira y afloja sin resolver nada.*

to **back down** (give in; →see also: to give in, to give up) echarse atrás *L. Am., Sp;* bajarse del burro (to get off the donkey) *Mex, Col, Ec, Peru;* apearse del burro (to get off the donkey) *Sp;* bajar las orejas (to lower the ears) *Sp* ◆ *When he saw that everyone was against him, he backed down. Cuando vio que todos estaban en su contra, bajó las orejas.*

to **back out** (chicken out, give up) rajarse (to split) *Mex, Cuba, DR, ES, Col, Peru, U, Sp;* apendejarse *Mex, Cuba, PR, DR, Col;* amilanarse *G, S. Cone, Sp;* achicarse (to get small) *S. Cone, Sp* ◆ *You said you'd come to the movies, so don't back out now. Dijiste que vendrías al cine; no te rajes ahora.*

to **backfire** (have an opposite result from what was expected) salir el tiro por la culata (to have the shot go out the butt of the rifle) *L. Am., Sp* ◆ *They were sure they would win the election easily, but things backfired on them. Estaban seguros que ganarían las elecciones fácilmente; sin embargo les salió el tiro por la culata.*

bad guy (→see also: con artist, creep, troublemaker) el malvado/la malvada *L. Am., Sp;* el pato malo (bad duck) *Ch;* el/la macarra *Sp* ◆ *A man who looked like a troublemaker came in and sat down near us. Entró un hombre con aspecto de macarra y se sentó cerca de nosotros.*

bad intentions mala leche (vulgar) *S. Cone, Sp* ◆ *You could see their bad intentions ever since they got here. Se les veía la mala leche desde que llegaron.*

bad rap or rep mala nota (bad note) *most of L. Am.* ◆ *That school has a bad rep. Esa escuela es (de) muy mala nota.*

bad words →see also: swear word (swear words; slightly vulgar) la chingadera *Chicano, Mex, G, ES* ◆ *Don't say bad words (like that). No digas chingaderas.*

to **badger someone** →see: to bug, to give someone a hard time

badgering →see: pain in the neck

bad-tempered →see: to be a grouch, to be grouchy

balled up →see: mixed up

balls (testicles) los huevos (eggs, vulgar) *L. Am., Sp;* los cojones (vulgar) *parts of L. Am., Sp;* los coyoles (fruits of a kind of palm tree, vulgar) *C. Am.;* las huevas (testicles, variant of huevos) *Nic, Ch;* las bolas (balls, vulgar) *S. Cone*

ballsy (brave) cojonudo(-a) (from cojones, testicles; vulgar) *Mex, Cuba, Col, Sp* ◆ *You're a ballsy woman. Eres una mujer cojonuda.*

to be **ballsy** (have balls) tener los huevos bien puestos (to have one's eggs, meaning testicles, well placed; vulgar) *L. Am., Sp* ◆ *They said they had balls and would stand up to the delinquents. Ellos dijeron que tenían los huevos bien puestos y que enfrentarían a los delincuentes.*

baloney 1. (bunch of nonsense) el disparate (shot off the mark) *L. Am., Sp;* las sandeces *L. Am., Sp;* la babosada *L. Am.;* la mamada (sucking, nursing; vulgar) *Mex, ES, Col*; el cuento chino (Chinese story) *Mex, Nic, U, Arg, Sp*; el rollo macabeo (patatero) (Maccabean [potato-seller's] roll) *Sp*; las chorradas *Sp*; las gilipolleces (slightly vulgar) *Sp*; las pamplinas (from the name of a plant) *Sp* ◆ *He's a good man. —Baloney!* Es un buen hombre. –¡Qué disparate! **2.** (false arguments) la paja (straw) *Mex, C. Am., Col*; la casaca (priest's coat) *G, ES* ◆ *Don't give me that baloney.* No me des casaca.

Baloney! (Nonsense!) ¡Puro cuento! (Pure story!) *Mex, ES, Col, U*; ¡Pura paja! (Pure straw!) *Mex, C. Am., Col*; ¡Pura leche! (Pure milk!) *Mex, Col*; ¡Puras jaladas! (Pure stretches!) *Mex*; ¡Puras vainas! (Pure husks!) *CR, parts of S. Am.* ◆ *He says his girlfriend is from an aristocratic family. —Baloney!* Dice que su novia es de una familia aristocrática. –¡Puras vainas!

bananas →see: nuts

bare naked (→see also: in the raw) en pelota (in ball, somewhat vulgar) *DR, PR, G, Nic, S. Cone*; en pelotas (in balls, somewhat vulgar) *Mex, DR, PR, Col, Peru, S. Cone, Sp* ◆ *It was really hot this summer; I slept bare naked every night.* Hizo mucho calor este verano; dormí todas las noches en pelota.

to **barely make ends meet** (be barely middle-class) ser gente de medio pelo (to be people by half a hair) *Mex, Nic, S. Cone, Sp* ◆ *They barely make ends meet; they work for the minimum wage.* Son gente de medio pelo, que trabaja por salarios mínimos.

barking up the wrong tree (→see also: to blow it) No van por ahí los tiros. (The shots aren't going that way.) *DR, Ch, Sp* ◆ *Patricio is visiting the Benavides family a lot. I think he likes Josefina. —You're barking up the wrong tree. It's Ana he likes.* Patricio está visitando mucho la casa de los Benavides. Creo que le gusta Josefina. –No van por ahí los tiros. Es Ana que le interesa.

bash 1. (party) la pachanga, el pachangón *most of L. Am.*; el mitote (big myth) *Chicano, Mex*; el reventón (blowout) *Mex, C. Am.*; el bonche (also, mess or disorder) *Mex, DR, ES, Nic, Ven, Bol*; la jarana *Mex, Peru, U, Arg, Sp*; el bembé *Caribbean*; la farra *Ec, S. Cone, Sp*; la festichola *U, Arg* ◆ *We went to a first-class bash on Friday.* Fuimos a un reventón de

primera el viernes. **2.** (dance) la charanga *ES, CR, Col*; la bachata (a type of music) *DR, Col*; el bailongo *U, Arg* ◆ *Let's go to the bash now!* ¡Vamos ya al bailongo! **3.** (fun time, street dance) el carnaval (Mardi Gras) *Mex, ES, CR, Col* ◆ *Once the party began, it turned into a real bash.* Una vez que la fiesta comenzó, ésta se convirtió en carnaval. **4.** (fun, diversion) el vacilón *Mex, DR, PR, ES, CR* ◆ *We have to start planning the Christmas bash now.* Tenemos que planear desde ahora el vacilón para las navidades.

bauble →see: trinkets

to **bawl out** →to chew out

Be careful! →see: Watch out!

to **be like a homebody** parecer que alguien está empollando huevos (to seem like someone is nesting eggs) *Sp* ◆ *Dorotea is a real homebody; she doesn't go anywhere.* Dorotea parece que está empollando huevos; no sale a ninguna parte.

to **be on the lookout, look out for** (→see also: to pay attention) aguaitar, estar al aguaite *Pan, Ec, Peru, Ch* ◆ *Juan is looking out for the house, which is empty.* Juan está al aguaite de la casa, que se queda sola. **1.** (be suspicious and alert to avoid something) estar o ponerse mosca (to be or become fly, an insect with large eyes) *Mex, Ven, Peru, Sp*; ponerse buzo (to become a diver) *Mex, G, ES* ; ponerse trucha (to become trout) *Mex, ES*; ponerse águila (to put oneself eagle) *Mex, G, ES* estar con ojo (to be with eye) *Mex, Sp*; andar con ojo (to go with eye) *Sp*; estar con cien (diez) ojos (to be with one hundred [ten] eyes) *Sp* ◆ *Be on the lookout! Do you see the director there? You have to be alert.* Ponte mosca. ¿Ves el dire allí? Hay que estar mosca. **2.** (take special care with something, keep an eye on) estar ojo al charqui (to be eye on the beef jerky) *Ch, U* ◆ *The kids are playing in the garden. I'll look out for them while you guys prepare the food.* Los niños están jugando en el jardín. Yo estaré ojo al charqui mientras ustedes preparen la comida.

beat →see: wiped out

to **beat around the bush** andarse con rodeos (to go around and around) *L. Am., Sp*; andarse por las ramas (to go around the branches) *L. Am., Sp*; irse por las ramas (to go around the branches) *Mex* ♦ *This guy doesn't beat around the bush. He says exactly what he thinks and doesn't hold back. Este muchacho no se anda por las ramas. Dice directamente lo que piensa y no se entretiene.*

to **beat it** →see: to take off

to **beat one's brains out** (→see also: to work like a dog) romperse la cabeza (los cascos) (to break the head [skulls]) *Mex, DR, Sp;* romperse los cuernos (to break the horns) *U, Sp* ♦ *I beat my brains out studying for the test for nothing. In the end, I flunked. Me rompí la cabeza estudiando para el examen para nada. Al final, suspendí.*

to **beat someone to a pulp** →see: to beat someone up

to **beat someone to the punch** (get ahead of someone) madrugar a alguien (to get up early on someone) *L. Am., Sp;* hacerle la cama a alguien (to make the bed for someone) *S. Cone* ♦ *I got distracted and that guy beat me to the punch. I missed out on a good opportunity at work. Me distraje y ese tipo me madrugó. Perdí una buena oportunidad en el trabajo.*

to **beat someone up** (lit. or fig.; fix someone's wagon) partirle/romperle a alguien la cara (to break someone's face) *most of L. Am., Sp;* desmadrar a alguien (to dismother someone) *Chicano, Mex, Col;* hacer polvo a alguien (to make someone dust) *Mex, Cuba, DR, G, ES, Col, Sp;* hacer puré a alguien (to make someone a purée) *Mex, DR, ES, U, Arg, Sp;* poner parejo a alguien *Mex, ES, Col;* hacer migas a alguien (to make someone crumbs) *Mex, ES, Sp;* madrear a alguien *Mex, ES;* poner como camote a alguien (to make someone like a sweet potato) *Mex, ES;* hacer tortilla a alguien *Mex, U, Sp;* poner como dado a alguien (to put someone like a die—from a pair of dice—square and with spots) *Mex;* darle leña a alguien (to give someone wood) *Cuba, DR, PR, Sp;* hacer morder el polvo a alguien (to make someone bite the dust) *DR, Sp;* hacer fosfatina a alguien (to make someone powder) *Sp* ♦ *At the demonstration, the police beat up several demonstrators. En la manifestación, la policía le partió la cara a varios manifestantes.* ♦ *If you keep provoking me, I'm going to beat you*

up. *Si me sigues provocando, te voy a poner como camote.*

because he (she, etc.) damn well has to (→see also: against one's will) a puro huevo (also, a huevos) (at pure egg, testicle; vulgar) *Mex, C. Am.;* por pelotas (cojones) (by balls, vulgar) *Sp* ♦ *Juan damn well had to do it. Juan tuvo que hacerlo por pelotas.*

because of his (her, etc.) good looks (usually meaning that something may come about undeservedly) por su cara bonita (because of his or her pretty face) *Mex, ES, Ch, Sp;* por su linda cara (because of his or her handsome face) *Mex, DR, S. Cone, Sp* ♦ *Do you think you're going to pass the test because of your good looks? ¿Crees que por tu cara bonita vas a aprobar el examen?*

to **become an item** (get together) empatarse *Mex, Cuba, CR, Col, Ven;* estar empatados (to be tied) *Mex, PR, Ven* ♦ *Silvia and Pedro became an item in February. Silvia y Pablo se empataron en febrero.*

beer →see: brewsky

Beggars can't be choosers. Comer y callar. (Eat and be quiet, said when someone is benefiting from someone else and should not speak against them.) *most of L. Am., Sp* ♦ *Who cares that this cabin is small? Beggars can't be choosers. ¿Qué importa que esta cabaña sea chica? Comer y callar.*

to be **behind** (in work, payments, etc.) estar atrasado(-a) *L. Am., Sp;* estar atrás *Mex, Cuba, DR, Col;* colgarse (to hang, be suspended) *Mex, Col* ♦ *I'm behind in my work. Estoy atrasado en el trabajo.* ♦ *Rosario got behind in her rent payments. Rosario se colgó en el pago del alquiler.*

to be **behind bars** →see: to be in the clinker

to **bell the cat** (do something difficult or dangerous; →see also: to be like pulling teeth) poner el cascabel al gato *L. Am., Sp* ♦ *Who's going to bell the cat and tell the professor that we won't finish the project today? ¿Quién le pone el cascabel al gato y le dice a la profesora que no terminaremos el proyecto hoy?*

to be **beside oneself** (in a very bad mood) estar que me (lo, la, etc.) lleva el diablo (to be ready for the devil to take) *Mex, DR, C. Am.;* estar como todos los diablos (to be like all the devils) *Mex, G, CR* ♦ *It's difficult to work with you today; you're beside yourself. Es difícil trabajar contigo hoy; estás como todos los diablos.*

the **best** →see: super

better half (spouse, sweetheart; male or female) la media naranja (half orange) *L. Am., Sp* ♦ *Where's your better half? ¿Dónde está tu media naranja?*

It's better than nothing. Peor es nada. (Worse is nothing.) *L. Am., Sp* ♦ *I only have one new pair of pants. —That's enough. It's better than nothing. Tengo sólo un pantalón nuevo. —Es suficiente. Peor es nada.*

Better watch it →see: Watch out!

between a rock and a hard place (without the possibility of escape) entre la espada y la pared (between the sword and the wall) *L. Am., Sp* ♦ *I don't know what to do. I'm between a rock and a hard place. No sé qué hacer. Estoy entre la espada y la pared.*

big bucks (a lot of money; →see also: dough) el dineral *L. Am., Sp;* el platal *ES, CR, Col;* la pasta gansa (goose pasta, dough) *Sp* ♦ *She won big bucks in that contest. Ganó una pasta gansa en aquel concurso.*

big cheese →see: big shot

big daddy (boyfriend) papazote *Mex, DR, PR, G, Col;* papucho *Mex, ES, CR, Col* ♦ *Oh, big daddy! How handsome you are. ¡Ay, papucho! Qué guapo eres.*

big deal gran cosota *Mex, C. Am;* cosa grandotota (great big thing) *Mex, ES, Nic, U, Arg* ♦ *To me, the accident is a big deal. Para mí, el asunto del accidente es una gran cosota.*

big kahuna →see: big shot, top banana

big shot el pez gordo (fat fish) *L. Am., Sp* ♦ *That gentleman is a big shot in the government. Ese señor es un pez gordo en el gobierno.*

big shots (people in charge) los jefazos, las jefazas *Mex, Col, Sp;* los amos del cotarro (the masters of the cotarro, the bank of a ravine or a shelter for vagrants) *Sp* ♦ *No changes depended on her, but rather on the big shots. Ningún cambio dependía de ella, sino de los jefazos.*

bigwig →see: big shot

bike la bici (short for bicicleta) *L. Am., Sp* ♦ *They stole her bike at school. Le robaron la bici en la escuela.*

birdbrain (→see also: fool, idiot) el/la cabeza de chorlito (head of golden plover, a small bird) *L. Am., Sp* ♦ *That guy is a birdbrain. How could he even think of doing something like that? Este tipo es una cabeza de chorlito. ¿Cómo se le puede ocurrir hacer algo así?*

birds of a feather →see: made for each other

bit by bit a poquitos (used for poco a poco) *Mex* ♦ *You're telling me things bit by bit. Tell me, what happened? Me dices a poquitos las cosas. Dime, ¿qué pasó?*

bitch la puta (prostitute) *L. Am., Sp;* la perra (female dog) *Chicano, G, Col, Sp;* la cabrona (female goat) *Mex, Cuba, PR, C. Am., Bol, Ch, Sp;* la maraca *Ch;* la zorra (female fox) *Sp* ♦ *Let's not speak to that bitch. No le hablemos a esa cabrona.*

to be a **bitch** (awful, tremendous, difficult) estar perro(-a) (to be dog) *Mex, Cuba, G, ES, Col* ♦ *This job is a bitch. Este trabajo está perro.*

a **bitch of a** 1. (god-awful) de perros (of dogs) *Mex, ES, Sp* ♦ *Today I'm in a bitch of a mood. Hoy estoy de un humor de perros.* 2. (vulgar) cabrón, cabrona (big goat) *Mex, Cuba, PR, C. Am., Col, Bol, Ch, Sp* ♦ *What a bitch of an illness! ¡Qué enfermedad más cabrona!*

to **bitch out** 1. (insult with offensive names, vulgar) putear, echar puteadas *L. Am.;* rayársela *Mex, ES* ♦ *They bitched me out. Me la rayaron.* 2. (insult someone by suggesting the moral impurity of his or her mother, usually by calling someone an hijo de puta) mentar la madre (to mention the mother) *Mex, C. Am., Col* (RVar *Sp:* mentar a la madre) ♦ *Bitching out someone by calling him or her an SOB is very dangerous. This can cause fights and sometimes deaths. Mentar la madre es muy peligroso. Esto puede causar peleas y a veces muertes.* 3. (swear at) echar madres (to throw mothers) *Chicano, Mex, Col;* decir madres (to say mothers) *Mex, Col* ♦ *Elena always bitches out her coworkers. Elena siempre dice madres a sus compañeras de trabajo.*

to **bite off more than one can chew** (get mixed up in something unnecessarily) meterse en camisa de once varas (to put oneself in a shirt of eleven rods) *L. Am., Sp* ♦ *The Abarcón family bought a very expensive house on the beach and a sports car. They have bitten off more than they can chew.* Los Abarcón compraron una casa carísima en la playa y un auto esport. Se han metido en camisa de once varas.

to **bite one's tongue** (avoid saying something) morderse la lengua *L. Am., Sp* ♦ *I bit my tongue so as not to tell my father-in-law what I thought of him.* Me mordí la lengua para no decir a mi suegro lo que pienso de él.

a **bite to eat** (midmorning snack) el tentempié (tente en pie) (keep you on your feet) *Mex, DR, Col* ♦ *Listen, let's stop working awhile. It's time for a bite to eat.* Oigan, paremos de trabajar un rato. Es hora de un tentempié.

to **blab** →see: to chatter away, to spill the beans

blabbermouth (big mouth; →see also: busybody, gossip) el hocicón, la hocicona (big animal mouth) *Mex, C. Am., Col, Ch;* el/la lengua larga (long tongue) *most of L. Am., Sp;* el bocón, la bocona *Mex, PR, ES, Nic, CR, Col, Arg;* trompudo(-a) *Mex, G, ES, CR, Col, U;* bocachón, bocachona (big mouth) *U, Arg;* el/la bocazas *Sp* ♦ *You're a blabbermouth. Why did you tell my father that I'm going out with Mónica?* Eres un bocón. ¿Por qué le dijiste a mi padre que salgo con Mónica?

black (dark person) prieto(-a), moreno(-a) (dark, can also be a nickname of endearment) *Mex, Cuba, DR, PR, G, ES* ♦ *Who's the black woman?* ¿Quién es la mujer morena?

to be **blah** (unappetizing) no tener chiste (to not have any joke) *Mex, ES, Col, Ec, Peru* ♦ *That movie is blah.* Esa película no tiene chiste.

blah, blah, blah (and so on and so forth) que si patatín, que si patatán *Mex, DR, PR, Sp;* habla que te habla (talk that he or she talks to you) *DR, PR, Ch, U;* que si pito que si flauta (that if fife then flute) *PR* ♦ *Ramón was telling me about his trip to Chile, that he went to Santiago, that blah, blah, blah, and so*

on and so forth, but he didn't tell me anything about the accident. Ramón me estuvo contando de su viaje a Chile, que visitó Santiago, que si patatín que si patatán, pero no me dijo nada del accidente.

Blast! →see: Good grief! Darn!

to **blast** →see: to put down

blasted (→see also: blessed, damn) pinche *Mex* ♦ *The blasted machine isn't working.* La pinche máquina no funciona.

Bless my soul! (expression of sympathy) ¡Ay, bendito! (Blessed one!) *PR* ♦ *Bless my soul! What are you going to do?* ¡Ay, bendito! ¿Qué vas a hacer?

Bless you! 1. (said after a sneeze) ¡Salud! (Health!) *L. Am., Sp;* ¡Jesús! *L. Am., Sp* 2. (said after three sneezes) ¡Jesús, María y José! *parts of L. Am., Sp*

blessed bendito(-a) (blessed, sometimes used ironically for the opposite) *L. Am.* ♦ *That blessed car!* ¡Ese bendito coche!

blind (as a bat) (wearing glasses) chicato(-a) *Peru, U, Arg* ♦ *Nelda is blind as a bat, and although she uses glasses, she sees very little.* Nelda es chicata, y a pesar de usar lentes, ve poco.

to be **blind as a bat** (→see also: to not see a thing) ser más ciego que un topo (to be blind as a mole) *L. Am., Sp*

blockhead (→see also: fool, idiot) el pedazo de alcornoque (piece of cork oak) *Mex, DR, G, Col, Ch, Sp* ♦ *You're a blockhead. Listen to what your parents tell you.* Eres un pedazo de alcornoque. Escucha lo que te dicen tus padres.

to **blow a gasket** →see: to lose it

to **blow it** 1. (make a gaffe, mistake; →see also: to screw up) cometer una burrada (to commit a drove of donkeys) *L. Am., Sp;* quemarse (to be burned, burn oneself) *L. Am.;* regarla (to spread it; original meaning was vulgar—la refers to mierda—but is a very common expression) *Mex, ES, Nic, Col;* embarrarla (to muddy it) *ES, Nic, Col, Peru, S. Cone;* dejar la escoba (to leave the broom) *Ch;* pringarla (to soak it in grease, to stab it; vulgar) *Sp* ♦ *We blew it in not clearly explaining our position on this issue.* ♦ *Cometimos una burrada al no explicar claramente nuestra posición en este asunto.* 2. (get flustered and make mistakes) **abatatarse** (to get sweet potatoed) *Para, U, Arg* ◆ *There were a lot of people at the interview and I blew it and didn't answer the question correctly.* **Había mucha gente en la entrevista y me abataté y no contesté la pregunta correctamente.**

to **blow it constantly** no dar una (to not give one) *Mex, U, Sp* ◆ *I'm constantly blowing it (I can't do anything right).* **No doy una.**

to **blow off** correr *L. Am., Sp;* mandar por un tubo (to send through a pipe) *Mex, ES, Col;* largar *U, Arg* ◆ *I'm thinking of blowing this chick off.* **Me parece que voy a largar a esta mina.**

to **blow off some steam** →see: to have a fit, to lose it

to **blow one's top** →see: to lose it

to **blow the works** (spend lavishly) echar/tirar la casa por la ventana (to throw the house out the window) *L. Am., Sp* ◆ *For Rocío's fifteenth birthday, Doña Ana blew the works. It was a real bash.* **Para los quince años de Rocío, doña Ana tiró la casa por la ventana. Fue una fiesta a todo dar.**

blowup (noisy dispute among several people) el bochinche *most of L. Am. (not Mex);* la refriega (rescrubbing) *Arg, U, Sp* ◆ *There was a blowup in the street last night!* **Se armó un bochinche en la calle anoche.**

to be a **blue blood** (from an aristocratic family) ser de sangre azul *L. Am., Sp* **Julio es de sangre azul pero no le gusta mencionarlo.** ◆ *Julio is a blue blood, but he doesn't like to mention it.*

blues (depression) la depre (short for depresión) *L. Am., Sp* ◆ *I've got the blues and I can't think about anything.* **Tengo una depre que no me deja pensar en nada.**

bogeyman el hombre del saco (man of the jacket) *Ch, Sp* el coco *Sp* ◆ *If you don't behave, the bogeyman will come get you.* **Si no te portas bien, vendrá el hombre del saco a buscarte.**

to **bomb** (fail; →see also: to wash out) tronar (to thunder) *Mex,C. Am.* ◆ *The film bombed at the box office.* **La película tronó en la taquilla.**

to be **bombed** →see: to be plastered, to be wasted

bone tired →see: wiped out

to **bone up on** (inform oneself about something) empaparse en algo (to get wet in something, immerse oneself) *most of L. Am.* ◆ *I need to bone up on the matter.* **Necesito empaparme en el asunto.**

bone-headed →see: stupid

bonkers →see: nuts

boob tube (TV) la caja tonta (idiot box) *Mex, Sp* ◆ *I don't spend much time in front of the boob tube.* **No paso mucho tiempo frente a la caja tonta.**

boobs (breasts; →see also: tits) los chichis (from Náhuatl for "to suckle") *Mex, Col;* los chicharrones *Mex;* los melones (melons) *Cuba, Col, Sp*

to **boogie** menear el esqueleto (to rock or move the skeleton) *L. Am., Sp;* mover el esqueleto (to move one's skeleton) *L. Am., Sp;* menear el bote (to rock or move the boat) *most of L. Am.;* chanclear *Chicano;* dar un chanclazo (give a hit with a chancleta, sandal) *Chicano;* sacarse la polilla (to get the moths off) *Mex* ◆ *Are we going to boogie, Silvia?* **¿Vamos a menear el esqueleto, Silvia?**

bookworm el ratón de biblioteca (library mouse) *L. Am., Sp;* la polilla de biblioteca (library moth) *most of L. Am., Sp;* el comelibros (book eater) *most of L. Am., Sp* ◆ *He's a bookworm (always in the library), and his room is full of books.* **Es un ratón de biblioteca, y su cuarto está lleno de libros.**

boor →see: to be a boor, jerk, lowlife

to be a **boor** (rude) ser bestia (to be a beast, animal) *L. Am.* ◆ *Don't be a boor.* **No seas bestia.**

bootlicker →see: suck-up

to **booze it up** (drink booze, alcohol) chupar (to suck) *L. Am., Sp* (RVAR *C.Am.:* slightly vulgar); pistear *Mex* (mainly northern) ◆ *They invited me to go boozing it up (with them) Saturday.* **Me invitaron a pistear el sábado.**

bore (boring person) el pelma (pelmazo) (mass of undigested food) *Sp* ◆ *Don't be a bore.* **No seas pelmazo/pelma.**

to **bore to death** (→see also: to be a drag) dar la paliza (to give the beating) *Sp* ◆ *María always bores us to death talking about her trips.* **María siempre nos da la paliza hablando de sus viajes.**

to be **bored stiff** aburrirse como una ostra (to be bored as an oyster) *Mex, DR, Ven, Peru, Ch, Arg, Sp;* darse una clavada (to get hit by a nail) *Arg* ◆ *That party was a disaster. We were bored stiff.* **Esta fiesta fue un desastre. Nos aburrimos como una ostra.**

to be **born lucky** nacer con el pie derecho (to be born with the right foot) *Mex, ES, S. Cone;* nacer de pie (to be born standing) *DR, Ch, U, Sp* ◆ *You were born lucky, Gabriela. You have a very happy life.* **Naciste de pie, Gabriela. Tienes una vida muy feliz.**

to be **born under a lucky star** (be easily accepted by people) tener estrella (to have a star) *Mex, Sp* ◆ *These kids were born under a lucky star. They have traveled all over the world.* **Estos chicos tienen estrella. Han viajado por todo el mundo.**

to be **born with a silver spoon** →see: rich kid

bosom buddies (→see also: pal) los amigos (las amigas) del alma (friends of the soul) *L. Am., Sp;* amigotes(-tas) *L. Am., Sp* ◆ *All her bosom buddies were with Martina at her graduation.* **Todos los amigos del alma estuvieron junto a Martina en su graduación.**

to be **bosom buddies** (very close friends) ser uña y carne (to be fingernail and flesh) *L. Am., Sp;* comer en el mismo plato (to eat out of the same plate) *Mex, G, ES, Ch;* ser uña y mugre (to be fingernail and dirt) *Mex, Col, Ch* ◆ *Myriam and Luz are bosom buddies, and they always go around together.* **Myriam y Luz son uña y carne, y siempre andan juntas.**

bossy mandón, mandona *L. Am., Sp* ◆ *My sister is very bossy.* **Mi hermana es muy mandona.**

He's (She's) **bottling it all up.** (said when one feels pain or sadness but covers it up) La procesión va por dentro. (The procession goes on the inside.) *Mex, S. Cone, Sp* ◆ *Everyone is trying to hide their pain; they're bottling it up.* **Todos tratan de disimular su dolor; la procesión va por dentro.**

the **bottom of the barrel** →see: the pits

Bottoms up! ¡Fondo blanco! (White bottom [of glass]!) *most of L. Am.* ◆ *The best toast: Bottoms up!* **El mejor brindis: ¡Fondo blanco!**

to be a **brain** (smart) ser (un) coco (to be [a] coconut; feminine is also coco) *L. Am. (not S. Cone);* tener mucho coco (to have a lot of coconut) *Sp* ◆ *Marisa is a brain.* **Marisa es bien coco (es un coco).**

to be **brainless** (→see also: to be stupid) no tener dos dedos de frente (to not have two fingers' length of forehead) *L. Am., Sp;* tener la cabeza hueca (to have the head hollow) *Mex, U, Arg, Sp;* tener cerebro de mosquito (to have a gnat's brain) *U, Arg, Sp;* ser más corto(-a) que las mangas de un chaleco (to be shorter than the sleeves of a vest, be short on brains) *Sp* ◆ *We don't expect logical reasoning from her; she's brainless.* **No esperamos un razonamiento lógico de ella; tiene cerebro de mosquito.**

to **brainwash someone** lavar el cerebro de alguien *L. Am., Sp;* comer el coco a alguien (to eat someone's coconut, meaning head) *DR, PR, Sp* ◆ *They brainwashed Paula and she joined that cult.* **Le comieron el coco a Paula e ingresó en esa secta.**

brat el/la malcriado(-a) *L. Am., Sp* el tarambana *Cuba, Ch, U, Sp;* el/la bicho(-a) *Sp* ◆ *His brother hadn't changed a bit; he was still the same brat.* **Su hermano no había cambiado; seguía siendo el mismo tarambana.**

brawl el revolú *DR, PR, Col* la pelotera *S. Cone, Sp* ◆ *There was a brawl because neither of the teams accepted the referee's decision.* **Se formó un revolú porque ninguno de los dos equipos aceptaron la decisión del árbitro**

to **break out in a cold sweat** (be fearful) sudar frío (to sweat cold) *DR, CR, Col, U, Arg, Sp* ◆ *The students broke out in a cold sweat because the principal called them to his office.* **Los estudiantes sudaron frío porque el director los llamó a su oficina.**

to **break someone's heart** (cause great pain) partirle el alma a alguien (to break someone's soul) *L. Am., Sp;* arrancarle a alguien el alma (to tear out one's soul) *Mex, ES, Sp;* arrancarle a alguien la vida (to tear out one's life) *Mex, ES;* rasgarle el alma a alguien (to scratch someone's soul) *Mex, ES* ◆ *It broke my heart to see those children working.* **Me arrancó el alma ver a esos niños trabajando.**

to **break the ice** romper el hielo *L. Am., Sp* ◆ *To break the ice among the workshop partic-*

ipants, each person introduced himself or herself and spoke about his or her agency. **Para romper el hielo entre los participantes del taller, cada persona se presentó y habló de su agencia.**

to **break to pieces** hacer pedazos *L. Am., Sp;* hacer polvo (to make dust or powder) *Mex, Cuba, G, ES;* hacer migas (to make crumbs) *Mex, ES, Sp;* hacer tortilla *Mex, U, Sp;* hacer harina (to make flour) *DR, PR, U, Sp* ◆ *The vase? They broke it to pieces.* **¿El florero? Lo han hecho pedazos.**

to **break up** (with someone) romper (con alguien) *L. Am., Sp* abrirse (to open, also used for business or social relationships) *S. Cone* ◆ *Why did you break up with Felipe?* **¿Por qué rompiste con Felipe?** ◆ *After the death of their son, they broke up.* **Después de la muerte de su hijo, se abrieron.**

to **break up with laughter** (→see also: to crack up with laughter) partirse de la risa *DR, PR, Sp* ◆ *The movie was really funny; we broke up with laughter.* **La película era muy cómica; nos partimos de la risa.**

breasts →see: boobs, tits

brewsky (beer) la birria *Mex, PR, G, Nic;* la cheve *Mex, G, ES;* la fría (cold one) *Cuba, PR, G, Col;* la caña (cane) *Sp* ◆ *Give me a brewsky.* **Dame una birria.**

bribe (grease for the palm; slang) la mordida (the bite) *Mex, G, Nic, Pan;* el chayote (vegetable with prickly skin) *Mex;* la coima *Peru, S. Cone;* el acomodo *Arg* ◆ *Unfortunately here anything can be fixed with a bribe.* **Lamentablemente aquí todo se arregla con la mordida.**

bridal shower la despedida de soltera (sending off of the single woman) *L. Am., Sp* ◆ *Saturday we'll have a bridal shower for Betania.* **El sábado le haremos una despedida de soltera a Betania.**

to **bring home the bacon** →see: to call the shots, to wear the pants

to **bring it on oneself** buscárselo (to look for it oneself) *L. Am., Sp* ◆ *She's bringing it on herself going around with that idiot.* **Ella se lo busca andando con ese idiota.**

to **bring out the champagne** (brag about or rejoice in a triumph) cantar victoria (to sing victory) *L. Am., Sp* ◆ *Let's not bring out*

the champagne yet. **No cantemos victoria todavía.**

to **bring up to date on** poner al corriente de (to put to the running total of) *L. Am., Sp* ◆ *You always bring me up to date on what happens in this town.* **Tú siempre me pones al corriente de lo que pasa en este pueblo.**

broad (girl, woman; →see also: babe, chick, woman) la ruca *L. Am. (not S. Cone)* ◆ *Poor broad. No one wants to dance with her.* **Pobre ruca. Nadie quiere bailar con ella.**

to be **broke** (→see also: to not have a plug nickel) estar pelado(-a) (to be peeled) *PR, Cuba, DR, C. Am., Col, Sp;* no tener ni papa(s) (to not have even potato[s]) *Mex, ES;* no tener un quinto (to not have a fifth) *Mex, ES;* estar (quedarse) a dos velas (to be [remain] at two sails) *Mex, Sp;* estar asfixiado(-a) (to be asphyxiated) *Mex, Sp;* andar quebrado(-a) (to go broken) *Mex;* estar arrancado(-a) (to be torn out) *Cuba, DR, Nic, Col;* estar pato (to be duck) *Peru, S. Cone;* estar seco(-a) (to be dry) *U, Arg;* no tener blanca (to not have a white one, coin) *Sp;* no tener ni para pipas (to not have even for [pumpkin] seeds) *Sp;* no tener un cuarto (to not have a fourth) *Sp;* estar sin blanca (to be without a white one, meaning a coin) *Sp* ◆ *I was left totally broke, waiting until the end of the month to be able to buy more food.* **Me quedé a dos velas, esperando a fin de mes para poder comprar más comida.**

brought up in a barn criado(-a) a lo bruto (raised in a brutish way) *L. Am., Sp;* criado(-a) a puro machete (raised by pure machete) *Mex, ES* ◆ *How rude that kid is. It looks like he was brought up in a barn.* **Qué mal educado ese chavo. Parece que fue criado a puro machete.**

brownnoser →see: suck-up

bruise (black and blue mark) el batacazo *U, Arg, Sp* ◆ *He got bruised (a black and blue mark).* **Se dio un batacazo.**

buck →see bucks

Buck up! (It's not that bad.) ¡Ánimo! (Spirit!) *L. Am., Sp;* No te azotes, que hay chayotes. (Don't flog yourself; there are chayotes, a kind of squash.) *Mex, Col* ◆ *You'll see that things will get better. Buck up! It's not that bad.* **Ya verás que las cosas se van a mejorar. No te azotes, que hay chayotes.**

to **buckle down to study** (→see also: to cram) clavarse (to be nailed) *Mex, Col* ♦ *Luis buckled down to study day and night and for that reason he was able to graduate.* Luis se clavaba estudiando día y noche y por eso pudo graduarse.

bucks (→see also: dough) los dolores (pains, used for dólares) *Cuba, DR, ES;* los mangos (mangos) *U, Arg* ♦ *It's tough to earn the bucks.* Está duro ganarse los dolores.

buddy →see pal

to **bug** (bother, pester; screw, trick someone; to screw up or break [something]) joder *L. Am., Sp* (RVAR vulgar in some places but inoffensive in others); fregar (to scrub, scour, rub [the wrong way]) *most of L. Am.;* mosquear (to be like a fly) *Ch, Sp* ♦ *He loves to bug his sister.* Le encanta fregar a su hermana.

to be **bugged** (bothered, have something be the matter; →see also: to be upset with someone) picarle a alguien una mosca (to have a fly biting or stinging someone) *L. Am., Sp* ♦ *What's got you bugged (upset)?* ¿Qué mosca te ha (habrá) picado?

to **build castles in the air** hacer castillos en el aire *Mex, S. Cone, Sp* ♦ *He loves to build castles in the air and dream of impossible things.* Le encanta hacer castillos en el aire y soñar con cosas imposibles.

bull →see: Baloney!, crock

bulldog (angry man) el gallo (rooster) *Mex, C. Am., Sp* ♦ *He became a bulldog when they told him to turn down the volume on his boom box.* Se puso como un gallo cuando le dijeron que bajara el volumen de su aparato de música.

bum el/la vago(-a) *L. Am.;* el/la atorrante *Peru, S. Cone;* el hombre del saco (man of the jacket) *Ch, Sp* ♦ *He doesn't have money because he's a bum.* No tiene dinero porque es un atorrante.

to **bum** →see: to mooch

to be **bummed out** (depressed; →see also: down, to be down) achicopalarse *Mex, ES, Nic;* agüitarse *Mex, C. Am.;* estar bajoneado(-a) *S. Cone* ♦ *Hang in there! Don't let yourself get bummed out, pal.* ¡Ánimo! No te achicopales, 'mano.

bummer (bad feeling) el bajón (big down) *Mex, DR, PR, ES, S. Cone, Sp* ♦ *What a bummer to have to work all weekend.* Qué bajón tener que trabajar todo el fin de semana.

to **bump off** →see: to wipe out

bumpkin →see: hick

bunch (crowd; →see also: gang) la tracalada *Mex, ES, Ch, Arg;* la bola (ball) *Mex, ES;* el bonche (from English) *Mex, PR* ♦ *What a bunch of idiots!* ¡Qué tracalada de tontos!

bunches →see: tons

to be a **bundle of nerves** (very upset because of problems or danger; →see also: to be on edge) estar con (tener) el alma en un hilo (to be with [have] the soul on a thread) *L. Am.* ♦ *What's wrong, Verónica? —I'm a bundle of nerves. My son is in the hospital.* ¿Qué pasa, Verónica? —Estoy con el alma en un hilo. Mi hijo está en el hospital.

to **burn one's bridges** quemar las naves (to burn one's ships) *L. Am., Sp* ♦ *I'm not going to burn my bridges with the company. I'll speak with the manager again.* No voy a quemar mis naves con la compañía. Hablaré nuevamente con el gerente.

to **burn out** agotarse (to exhaust onself) *L. Am., Sp;* quemarse (to be burned) *Sp* ♦ *The runner burned out before reaching the finish line.* El corredor se quemó antes de llegar a la meta.

to **burn the midnight oil** (→see also: to cram) quemarse las pestañas (cejas) (to burn one's eyelashes [eyebrows]) *L. Am., Sp* ♦ *I burned the midnight oil to pass the history exam.* Me quemé las pestañas para pasar el examen de historia.

to **bury the hatchet** hacer las paces (to make peace) *L. Am., Sp* ♦ *I want to bury the hatchet now. We can't go on like this.* Tengo ganas de hacer las paces ahora. No podemos continuar así.

to **bust one's butt (for someone)** (do the impossible) perder el culo (to lose one's ass, vulgar) *Sp* ♦ *Jaime busted his butt for that girl and gave up (left) his studies.* Jaime perdió el culo por esa chica y dejó los estudios.

busty gal (with a large breast; →see also: hot number) la pechocha (big-breasted) *Mex, ES, Col;* la pechugona (from pechuga, the breast of a fowl) *Mex, DR, Col, Ch, Sp;* la te-

to butt in: *I'm going to butt in to tell you the truth.*
Voy a meter la cuchara para decirles la verdad.

tona, tetuda (vulgar) *DR, PR, S. Cone, Sp* ◆ *He was in love with a busty gal from Cali. Estaba enamorado de una pechugona de Cali.*

busybody (→see also: blabbermouth, gossip) el/la metido(-a) (from entrometido) Mex, DR, PR, C. Am., Col, U, Arg; el metelón, la metelona *Mex*; el/la metepatas (stick-your-foot-in) *Sp* ◆ *Please, don't be a busybody. I don't need your opinion. Por favor, no seas metida. No necesito tu opinión.*

to **butt in (to someone's conversation)** meter la cuchara (to put in the spoon) *L. Am., Sp;* meter baza (to play a card trick) *Ch, Sp* ◆ *And who are you to butt in? Y ¿quién es usted para meter la cuchara?*

to **butter up** →see: to sweet-talk

buttinsky →see: busybody

to **button one's lip** poner un zíper en la boca (to put a zipper on one's mouth) *Mex, ES* (RVAR *U:* poner un cierre...) ◆ *Button your lip. Ponte un zíper en la boca.*

by a fluke →see: by a stroke of luck

by a hair por poco (by little) *L. Am., Sp;* por un pelo (by a hair) *DR, PR, S. Cone, Sp* ◆ *We avoided an accident by a hair. Evitamos un accidente por un pelo.*

by a stroke of luck de carambola (by a fluke, billiard term) *DR, ES, Nic, Ch, U;* de chepa *DR, PR, CR, Col;* de chiripa (by a fluke, billiard term) *DR, G, ES, Ven, U, Arg;* por chiripa (by a fluke, billiard term) *DR, Hond, Nic, CR, Col, Ch, Sp* ◆ *By a stroke of luck we found Alicia in the airport before she left. De carambola encontramos a Alicia en el aeropuerto antes de que saliera.*

by fits and starts (haltingly) a tropezones (with trips, falling down) *Mex, DR, U, Sp* ◆ *Miguelito reads by fits and starts. Miguelito lee a tropezones.*

by foot →see: hoofing it

by force 1. (with a lot of effort; →see also: against one's will) a la fuerza *L. Am., Sp;* a la brava *Chicano, Mex, DR, PR, ES, CR, Col, Sp;* a rastras *Mex, Sp;* a jalones y estirones (at pulls and stretches) *Mex;* a chaleco (at vest) *Mex* ◆ *Julia didn't want to go, but I made* her go *by force. Julia no quería ir, pero la hice ir la fuerza* (a la brava). **2.** (with a lot of effort, because he [she] damn well has to) **a (puro) huevo** (also, **a huevos**) (at [pure] egg, testicle; vulgar) *Mex, C. Am.;* **por pelotas (cojones)** (by balls, vulgar) *Sp* ◆ *Tuvieron que hacerlo por pelotas. They damn well had to do it.* **3.** (sloppily) **a la brava** (also, **a la mala**) *Mex, G, ES, Sp* ◆ *José opened the door without using the key; he opened it by force. José abrió la puerta sin utilizar la llave; la abrió a la brava.*

by (pure) luck →see: by a stroke of luck

by no means (under no circumstances, no way) **de ninguna manera** *L. Am., Sp*

by the seat of one's pants **a la buena de Dios** (at the good [will] of God) *DR, ES, Nic,*

CR, S. Cone, Sp ◆ *I'm going to Chile by the seat of my pants.* ◆ *Voy a viajar a Chile a la buena de Dios.*

by the truckload **a montones** (in heaps) *Mex, DR, PR, Ch, Sp;* **para dar y regalar** (to give and give as a present) *Mex, Ch, U, Sp;* **para dar y tomar** (to give and take) *Mex, Sp;* **por un tubo** (through a pipe) *DR, Sp;* **para tirar pá (para) arriba** (to throw up in the air) *S. Cone* ◆ *Thanks, but I don't want any more. I ate cake by the truckload. Gracias, pero ya no quiero más. Comí torta por un tubo.*

Bye. **Chau, chau.** (from the Italian "ciao") *S. Cone;* **Venga.** (way of ending a conversation on the phone; also, often used instead of **vale**) *Sp* ◆ *Bye. Good-bye. Venga. Adiós.* ◆ *See you tonight. Bye-bye. Nos vemos esta noche. Chau, chau.*

C

cakewalk →see: piece of cake

call girl →see: hooker, slut

to **call someone on the carpet** →see: to chew out

to **call the shots** llevar la batuta (to carry the baton) *L. Am., Sp;* llevar la voz cantante (to carry the melody) *L. Am., Sp;* dirigir el cotarro (to direct the cotarro, a bank of a ravine or a shelter for vagrants) *Sp* ◆ *In that family, Alfonso calls the shots. En esa familia, Alfonso lleva la batuta.*

can →see: restroom

to be a **can of worms** (a messy situation) (→see also: mess) estar más liado(-a) que la pata de un romano (de una momia) (to be more entangled than the foot of a Roman [of a mummy]) *Sp* ◆ *My life is a real can of worms. Mi vida está más liada que la pata de un romano.*

caper →see: trick

car →see: wheels

car lover →see: grease monkey

carefree as the wind (without preparation) a la buena de Dios (at the good [will] of God) *DR, ES, Nic, CR, S. Cone, Sp* ◆ *Those folks are really poor; they live carefree as the wind (without plans or money). Ésos son pobres; viven a la buena de Dios (sin planes ni dinero).*

cash: in (hard) cash en efectivo *L. Am., Sp;* al contado *L. Am., Sp;* con dinero contante y sonante *L. Am., Sp* a tocateja *Sp* ◆ *She had to buy the car with hard cash. They didn't accept checks. Tuvo que pagar el coche a tocateja. No aceptaban cheques.*

to **cash in one's chips** (die) →see: to kick the bucket

to **cast pearls before swine** (give something to someone who doesn't appreciate or deserve it) echar perlas a los puercos *L. Am., Sp* ◆ *Girl, don't dress so elegantly. We're going to Juan Carlos's house, and he won't even notice it. It's like casting pearls before swine. Nena,*

no te vistas tan elegante. Vamos a casa de Juan Carlos y él ni siquiera lo va a notar. Es cómo echarle perlas a los puercos.

to **catch** (a husband, etc.) pescar (to fish) *L. Am., Sp* ◆ *Rosalía has been coming to get-togethers for some time now just in order to catch a husband. Hace tiempo que Rosalía asiste a las reuniones sólo para pescar un marido.*

to **catch (in the act)** agarrar (to catch, grab) *L. Am.;* pillar (to plunder) *Mex, Col, Ch, Sp* ◆ *They caught a shoplifter in the supermarket. En el super pillaron a un ratero.*

to **catch a cold** resfriarse *L. Am., Sp;* pescarse un resfriado (also, resfrío; slang) (to fish for a cold) *Mex, G, Ch, Sp* ◆ *Frederico caught a terrible cold. Frederico se pescó un resfrío terrible.*

to **catch forty winks** →see: to get some shut-eye

to **catch some Zs** →see: to get some shut-eye

to **catch the drift** cachar (to catch) *most of L. Am.* (RVar *Peru, Ch:* also, to have sex) ◆ *Did you catch the drift? ¿Cachaste?*

catchy (sticking in your mind) pegajoso(-a) (sticky) *Mex, Col, Ch* ◆ *It's a catchy song.* ◆ *Es una canción pegajosa.*

to be **catchy** tener pegue *Mex, ES, Col* ◆ *That music is catchy. Esa música tiene pegue.*

cathouse →see: house of ill repute

caught in the act; caught red-handed con las manos en la masa (with one's hands in the dough) *L. Am., Sp* ◆ *They caught him red-handed. Lo agarraron con las manos en la masa.*

caught up with (something) (enthusiastic or curious) picado(-a) (piqued, stung) *Mex, parts of C. Am.* ◆ *The game was so good that we all got caught up watching it. Estaba tan bueno el partido que todos estábamos picados viéndolo.*

to **cause a commotion** →see: to make a scene

to **cause a fuss** →see: to make a scene

to **cause a scene** →see: to make a scene

to **cave in** (→see also: to give in, to throw in the towel) aflojar (to loosen up) *L. Am., Sp* ◆ *Don't cave in; hang tough.* No aflojes; dale duro.

to be the **center of attention** ser florero (to be a flower vase; slang) *Ch*

a **certain someone** (used jokingly to avoid naming a person) ciertas hierbas (certain herbs) *Col* ◆ *A certain someone didn't clean up his (her) room.* Ciertas hierbas no limpió su cuarto.

chance la chanza (from the English "chance") *Chicano, Mex, Col* ◆ *Give me a chance. I want to explain it to you.* Dame chanza. Quiero explicártelo.

to **change activity/pace/subject** →see: to shift gears

to **change one's mindset (way of thinking)** cambiar el chip (to change one's [computer] chip) *Mex, Sp* ◆ *You have to change your mindset if you want to succeed.* Ustedes tienen que cambiar el chip si quieren tener éxito.

to **channel-surf** (change the channel) hacer zapping (to do zapping) *Peru, Ch, Arg, Sp* ◆ *I don't like watching television with Gustavo because he's always channel-surfing.* No me gusta mirar televisión con Gustavo porque hace zapping constantemente.

to be a **character** (be amusing; →see also: to be a cutup) ser todo un carácter *L. Am., Sp;* ser un plato (to be a dish) *S. Cone* ◆ *That guy is a real character.* Ese tipo es un plato.

charmer (people person) el/la entrador(-a) (enterer) *CR, ES, Col, S. Cone* ◆ *Luis didn't have any problems at his new school. He's a real charmer, and he made friends right away.* Luis no tuvo problemas en la nueva escuela. Es muy entrador y en seguida hizo amigos.

chat (→see also: gab session) la cháchara *Mex, DR, Sp* ◆ *I got here (there) late because in the office we had a very entertaining chat.* Llegué tarde porque en la oficina teníamos una cháchara muy entretenida.

to **chat on the Internet** chatear *parts of L. Am., Sp* ◆ *Every Saturday at noon, I chat with my sister on the Internet.* Todos los sábados a mediodía chateo con mi hermana.

chat room el cuarto de discusión *L. Am., Sp;* el chat *Mex* ◆ *If you're interested in that topic, you should go in the chat room.* Si te interesa ese tema, debes entrar en el cuarto de discusión.

to **chatter away** cotorrear *Mex, DR, PR, G, Col, U, Arg, Sp;* hablar como un papagayo (un perico, una cotorra) (to talk like a parrot) *DR, PR, Sp* ◆ *Miguelito is very small but he chatters aways all day.* Miguelito es muy pequeño pero habla como un papagayo todo el día.

cheap →see: steal; tacky

cheap shot la mala pasada *L. Am., Sp;* la trastada *L. Am., Sp* la canallada *most of L. Am.;* la cabronada *Mex, PR, G, Col, Sp;* la jalada (fregadera) (pull or jerk) *Mex* ◆ *What a cheap shot!* ¡Qué mala pasada!

cheapskate →see: tightwad

cheat 1. (someone who whispers the answer to someone taking a test) el soplón, la soplona *L. Am., Sp* ◆ *She was expelled for cheating (being a cheat).* Fue expulsada por soplona. 2. (→see also: con artist) el/la tramposo(-a) (tricky) *L. Am., Sp* ◆ *Don't be a cheat! Don't look at the other players' cards.* ¡No seas tramposo! No mires las cartas de los otros jugadores.

to **cheat** hacer trampas *L. Am., Sp;* soplar (to blow [whisper the answer to someone taking a test]) *L. Am., Sp* ◆ *Lolita cheated by whispering the answer to her boyfriend on the history test.* Lolita le sopló la respuesta a su novio en el examen de historia.

to **cheat on someone** (a significant other) ponerle los cuernos a alguien (to put the horns on someone) *L. Am., Sp;* hacerle a alguien de chivo los tamales (to make tamales for someone out of kid goat meat) *Mex, ES;* ponerle los cachos a alguien (to put the horns on someone) *C. Am., Col, Ec* ◆ *That man is cheating on his wife.* Ese señor le pone los cuernos a su esposa.

to **check** (→see also: to pay attention) chequear, chequar (slang, from English) *Mex, DR, PR, C. Am., Ven, Ch, Sp* ◆ *Let's check the schedule.* Vamos a chequear el horario. Let's check the schedule.

Check me out! (I'm innocent.) ¡A mí que me registren! *Mex, S. Cone, Sp* ◆ *Check me out! I don't have it.* ¡A mí que me registren! No lo tengo.

Cheers! ¡Salud! (Health!) *L. Am., Sp;* ¡Chin chin! (imitating the sound of glass clinking) *parts of L. Am., Sp* ◆ *Cheers and may you be very happy!* ¡Chin chin y que seas muy feliz!

cheesecake →see: babe; to be an eyeful, hot number

to **chew out** (bawl out; →see also: to rake over the coals) echar una bronca *parts of L. Am., Sp;* poner a alguien como un trapo (viejo) (to make someone like a rag [like an old rag]) *Mex, PR, U, Arg, Sp;* poner como camote a alguien (to make someone like a sweet potato) *Mex, ES;* poner a alguien como palo de gallinero (to make someone [end up] like a perch in a chicken coop, i.e., covered with droppings) *Mex, U, Ch;* poner verde (to make green) *Mex, Sp;* poner a alguien como lazo de cochino/percha de perico (to make someone like a pig's rope/parakeet's perch) *Mex;* poner como dado a alguien (to put someone like a die—from a pair of dice—square and with spots) *Mex;* poner a alguien de vuelta y media (to put someone to a turn and a half) *DR, Ch, Sp;* dar una achurada (to eviscerate) *Arg;* poner a caldo (to put to broth, perhaps implying someone is being scalded) *Sp;* darle dos hostias a alguien (to give someone two Hosts [vulgar]) *Sp* ◆ *Esteban's father chewed him out when he found out he crashed the car.* El padre de Esteban lo puso como un trapo cuando supo que chocó el coche.

to **chew the fat** →see: to chatter away

chic (elegant; →see also: decked out) chic *L. Am., Sp;* catrín *Mex, C. Am.;* paquete(-a) *U, Arg* (RVar *Col:* ser un paquete [to be a package]) ◆ *How chic you look!* ¡Qué catrín te ves! ◆ *That woman is chic.* Esa mujer es un paquete.

chick 1. (girl) la chavala *Mex, C. Am., Sp;* la jeva *Cuba, DR, PR, Nic, Ven, Ec;* la guial, la guialcita *Pan;* la pava (turkey hen) *Col, Ven;* la mina (mine, from Lunfardo, Buenos Aires slang) *S. Am., esp. Col, Ec, S. Cone* ◆ *Who's that chick? —Her name is Laura.* ¿Quién es esa mina? —Se llama Laura. 2. (woman, pretty woman; →see also: babe, broad, hot number) el cuero (skin, leather; a bit vulgar, especially in *Ch*, where it can be a come-on) *ES, Col, Ec, Peru, Ch* ◆ *Did you see that chick?* ¿Ya viste ese cuero?

chicken 1. (coward) el gallina (hen) *Mex, Cuba, DR, PR, G, Nic, Col, Sp* ◆ *Valentín is very aggressive with women, but with men he acts like a chicken.* Valentín con las mujeres es muy agresivo, pero con los hombres se porta como un gallina. 2. (someone who backs down or doesn't do something promised; →see also: wimp) el rajón, la rajona *Mex, Cuba, DR, ES, Nic, Col, Sp* ◆ *Let's not invite him to go bungee jumping; he's a chicken.* No lo invitemos a hacer bonjee; es bien rajón.

to be a **chicken** (wimp) fruncir (to pucker) *Mex, Col* ◆ *Don't be a chicken!* ¡No te frunzas!

to **chicken out** →see: to back down or out

to be **child's play** (a cinch; →see also: to be a piece of cake) ser pan comido (to be eaten bread) *Mex, DR, PR, S. Cone, Sp;* ser coser y cantar (to be sew and sing) *Sp* ◆ *For you who knows so much, this job will be child's play.* Para ti que sabes tanto, este trabajo será coser y cantar.

Chill out. (→see also: take it easy) Tranquilo(-a). (Tranquil.) *Mex, DR, Col, Ven, S. Cone, Sp;* No hay bronca. (There's no dispute.) *Mex, ES;* No hay tos. (There's no cough.) *Mex, ES;* Suave. (Smooth, soft.) *DR, Ch, Ven;* Tranqui. *Sp* ◆ *Chill out. Let's talk about something else.* No hay bronca. Hablemos de otra cosa.

to **chill out** bajar el volumen (to lower the volume) *Mex, Col* ◆ *Chill out, darling. Let's find (lit., look for) a solution to the problem.* Baja el volumen, querida. Busquemos una solución al problema.

chintzy →see: cheap, tacky

to **chip in** (pool money for a common cause) prestar pa' la orquesta (to loan for the orchestra) *Mex, Col;* hacer una vaquita (to make a little cow) *Mex;* hacer una vaca (echar la vaca) (to make a cow [throw the cow]) *G, Nic, Ven, S. Cone* ◆ *My cousin needs money to pay his mortgage. Let's all chip in.* Mi primo necesita dinero para pagar la hipoteca. Vamos a prestar pa' la orquesta.

chip off the old block (very similar) cortado(-a) por la misma tijera (cut by the same scissors) *Mex, DR, PR, ES, S. Cone, Sp;* cortado(-a) por (con) el mismo patrón (cut by [with] the same pattern) *Mex, Sp;* ser de la misma madera (to be of the same wood)

Mex ◆ *Obviously he's from the family; he's a chip off the old block.* Sin duda es de la familia; está cortado con el mismo patrón.

A **chip off the old block.** De tal palo, tal astilla. (From such a tree or stick, such a splinter.) *L. Am., Sp;* Hijo de tigre sale rayado. (The tiger's son turns out with stripes.) *Mex, CR, S. Cone;* Lo que se hereda no se roba (hurta). (What is inherited is not robbed.) *S. Cone, Sp* ◆ *Mario and his dad look a lot alike, don't they? He's a chip off the old block.* Mario y su papá se parecen mucho, ¿no? De tal palo, tal astilla.

chow (food) el papeo (from papa, potato) *Mex, Cuba, DR, PR, Peru, Sp;* la jama *Cuba, CR, PR, Ec, Peru;* la papa (potato) *Mex, Cuba, DR, Col, Ch* ◆ *It's chow time. What do you want to eat?* Es la hora del papeo. ¿Qué quieren comer?

to **chow down** (eat) papear (to potato) *Mex, Cuba, DR, PR, C. Am., Ven, Peru, Sp;* jamar *Cuba, CR, Ec;* manyar *(from Italian) Peru, S. Cone* ◆ *It's time to go chow down.* Ya es hora de ir a papear.

chowhound (glutton, guzzler) el/la tragaldabas (door hinge gobbler) *L. Am., Sp;* la piraña (piranha, fish that devours its prey) *Mex, Col;* el tragón, la tragona *Mex;* el dragón, la draga (probably from tragón) *DR, PR* ◆ *That boy is a chowhound; he eats everything.* Ese chico es tragaldabas; todo se lo come.

chum →see: pal

chump (→see also: fool, idiot) el gil (la gila, el gilberto) *Mex, Cuba, Col, Ec, Peru, S. Cone* ◆ *Don't act like a chump.* No te hagas el gil.

chutzpah →see: nerve

cinch →see: piece of cake

circle →see: clique

to **clam up** →see: to put a lid on it

claptrap →see: junk, trinkets

to **clean out** (take everything, one's own and others') alzarse con el santo y la limosna (to make off with the saint and the alms) *DR, PR CR* ◆ *Cristián left yesterday and cleaned us all out.* Cristián se nos fue ayer y se alzó con el santo y la limosna.

to **clean up** (take advantage of something; →see also: to hit the jackpot) hacer su agosto (to make one's August) *L. Am., Sp* ◆

Doña María cleaned up in the stock market last year. Doña María hizo su agosto en la bolsa el año pasado.

the **clear, unadulterated truth** la verdad clara y desnuda (the clear and naked truth) *most of L. Am., Sp* ◆ *We need to speak about the clear, unadulterated truth.* Hay que hablar de la verdad clara y desnuda.

clever (smart) like a fox (sly) zorro(-a) (fox) *L. Am., Sp* ◆ *Agustina is smart as a fox and has been fooling her parents for many years.* Agustina es muy zorra y ha engañado a sus padres por muchos años.

to **click** (computer) hacer clic *L. Am., Sp;* cliquear *parts of L. Am.* ◆ *Click on the letter A.* Haz clic en la letra A.

to be **climbing (up) the walls** (with annoyance; →see also: to be upset with someone) subirse por las paredes *U, Sp* ◆ *When I saw him, he was climbing the walls. He was really mad! (lit., What anger!)* Cuando lo vi, estaba que se subía por las paredes. ¡Vaya qué enfado!

to **cling to someone's skirts** agarrarse a los faldones de alguien *Mex, Sp* ◆ *He always clings to his mother's skirts. This kid will never be successful.* Siempre se agarra a los faldones de su madre. Este chico nunca prosperará.

clingy (clinging to the skirts of someone) pegado(-a) a las faldas (glued to the skirts) *Sp* ◆ *He's a submissive man, always clinging to his wife's skirt.* Es un hombre sumiso, siempre pegado a las faldas de su mujer.

clique (select or closed group) la piña (pineapple) *CR, Cuba, Sp;* la rosca (doughnut) *Col, U, Arg* ◆ *If you're not in that clique, to them you're nobody.* Si no estás en esa rosca, para ellos no estás en na'a.

closed-minded cerrado(-a) (closed) *L. Am., Sp* ◆ *I don't like to talk to Felipe about those topics because he's very closed-minded and we end up not speaking to each other (lit., having fought).* No me gusta hablar de esos temas con Felipe porque es muy cerrado y terminamos peleados.

close-mouthed taciturno(-a) *L. Am., Sp;* cerrado(-a) (closed) *G, Col, U, Arg, Sp* ◆ *Marilú is very close-mouthed and never spoke to us during the excursion.* Marilú es muy cerrada y nunca nos habló durante la excursión.

to **clown around** (→see also: to joke around) hacer payasadas *L. Am., Sp* ◆ *My friend at work is always clowning around.* Mi compañero en el trabajo siempre anda haciendo payasadas.

clowning around 1. (silly thing or action, a joke) la payasada (clown action) *L. Am., Sp* ◆ *The talk with the professor was just clowning around (a joke).* La charla con el profesor fue una payasada. 2. (fooling around) el bufeo *Mex, DR;* el gufeo *PR* ◆ *Jorgito, stop clowning around because I'm serious about what I'm saying.* Jorgito, deja el bufeo que estoy hablando en serio. 3. (uproarious fun, joke, diversion) el relajo *Mex, DR, PR, G, ES, Nic, Col, U, Sp* ◆ *In the Mardi Gras dancing there was a lot of clowning around, but everyone had a good time.* En los bailes de carnaval hubo grandes relajos, pero todo el mundo se divirtió.

clueless 1. (dopey or easily taken advantage of) caído(-a) del nido (fallen out of the nest) *L. Am.;* caído(-a) de la cuna (fallen from the cradle) *U, Arg* ◆ *Do you think I was born yesterday, and that I'll believe your lies?* ¿Piensas que soy una caída de la cuna, para creer tus mentiras? 2. (naive) →see: to be off track, out of it, to wise up

to **clutch at straws** agarrarse a un clavo ardiendo (to cling to a burning nail) *L. Am., Sp* ◆ *They're so desperate from hunger that they're clutching at straws. They do whatever you ask them.* Están tan desesperados por el hambre que se agarran a un clavo ardiendo. Hacen lo que les pidas.

The **coast is not clear.** →see: The walls have ears.

cock-and-bull story →see: baloney, crock, fib

coffin nail (cigarette) pitillo *Ch, U, Arg, Sp* ◆ *I smoke only two coffin nails a day.* Fumo sólo dos pitillos por día.

coke (cocaine) la coca *L. Am., Sp;* la nieve *L. Am., Sp;* el polvo blanco (polvo de ángel) (white powder [angel dust]) *parts of L. Am., Sp;* el perico *L. Am.* ◆ *She sold them two grams of coke.* Les vendió dos gramos de polvo blanco.

cold as a witch's tit como nalga de lavandera (like a washerwoman's buttock) *Nic* ◆ *After many falls in the snow, Patricia felt cold as a witch's tit. Después de muchas caídas en la nieve, Patricia se sentía como nalga de lavandera.*

to **come at a good time** (come in handy) caer (venir) de perillas (to fall or come with little pears) *S. Cone, Sp* ◆ *That book came to me at a very good time. Ese libro me vino de perillas.*

to **come back to haunt someone** (bring serious consequences; used for things) traer cola (coleta) (to bring a tail [pigtail]) *Mex, U, Arg, Sp* ◆ *I don't want to intervene in this discussion because I know it will come back to haunt me. No quiero intervenir en esta discusión porque sé que traerá cola.*

to **come by it naturally** →see: He (She) comes by it naturally.

to **come down in the world (in life)** venir a menos (to come to less) *L. Am., Sp;* ir(se) abajo (to go down) *Cuba, G, Col* ◆ *That man was rich but now he's come down in the world. Ese hombre era rico pero ahora está venido a menos.* ◆ *That guy has come down in life because of his bad business deals. Ese tipo se ha ido abajo por sus malos negocios.*

Come down to earth. (said to someone who is too proud or too idealistic) Pon los pies sobre la tierra. (Put your feet on the ground.) *Mex, DR, ES, S. Cone, Sp* ◆ *Come down to earth, Antonia; you have to work if you want to travel. Pon los pies sobre la tierra, Antonia; tienes que trabajar si quieres viajar.*

come hell or high water contra viento y marea (against wind and tides) *L. Am., Sp;* aunque truene y relampaguée (even if it thunders and lightnings) *Mex, ES, S. Cone* ◆ *Come hell or high water water, we're going to travel. Aunque truene y relampaguée, vamos a viajar.*

Come off it. →see: Get off it.

to **come on to** →see: to hit on

to **come out on top** (come out well, despite adversity) flotar como el corcho en el agua (to float like cork in water) *Sp* ◆ *He sacrificed his personal life to get ahead and now he's come out on top. Sacrificó su vida personal para triunfar y ahora flota como el corcho en el agua.*

to **come out swinging** (show anger or vehemence in a conversation) salir pitando (to leave honking the horn or blowing a whistle) *Mex, Sp* ◆ *Don't worry; I'm not going to come out swinging like I did before.* No te preocupes; no voy a salir pitando como antes.

to **come out well [badly]** quedar bien [mal] parado(-a) (to end up standing well [badly]) *L. Am., Sp*; salir bien [mal] parado (-a) (to come out standing well [badly]) *L. Am., Sp* ◆ *The union members came out badly after the strike.* Los sindicalistas salieron mal parados después de la huelga.

to **come sexually** (vulgar) acabar (to finish) *Mex, C. Am., S. Cone*; venir(se) *Mex, Cuba, DR, PR*; correrse (vulgar) *Sp* ◆ *You inspired me, dear. I came three times.* Me inspiraste, chica. Acabé tres veces.

come what may →see: no matter what

He (She) **comes by it naturally.** Lo que se hereda no se roba (hurta). (What is inherited is not robbed, meaning that this person is just like his or her father, mother, grandfather, etc.) *S. Cone, Sp* ◆ *Don't criticize me, mom, for what I do. I come by it naturally.* No me critiques, mamá, por lo que hago. Lo que se hereda no se roba.

complainer →see: crybaby

to **con** →see: to rip off

con artist el/la estafador(a) *L. Am., Sp*; el/la embustero(-a) *L. Am., Sp*; el/la timador(a) *Mex, Ch, Sp*; el/la tracalero(-a) *Mex*; el/la paquetero(-a) *Cuba, PR, Col*; el/la engrupidor(-a) (grouper) *S. Cone*; el/la afanador(a) *U, Arg*; el/la majadero(-a) *Sp* ◆ *We all thought she was a good person, and it turned out she was a con artist.* Todos creímos que era una buena persona, y resultó ser una estafadora.

confusion →see: mess

connection (social, political) la palanca (bar, lever) *Mex, Cuba, ES, Nic, CR, Col, Ven, Peru, U, Arg*; el conecte *Mex, ES, Nic*; el enchufe (plug) *DR, PR, Col, Sp*; la cuña (prop, wedge) *S. Cone*; el acomodo *U, Arg* ◆ *I have a connection in the government. I'll call him now.* Tengo un conecte en el gobierno. Ahorita lo llamo. ◆ *He has a connection at that company; they'll give him the job for sure.* Tiene un enchufe en esa empresa; seguro que le dan el trabajo.

connections (social, political; pull) la muñeca (doll, wrist) *Peru, S. Cone* ◆ *They have connections in the government.* Tienen buena muñeca en el gobierno.

to be **conspicuous by its absence** brillar por su ausencia (to shine by its absence) *L. Am., Sp* ◆ *We were all waiting for an explanation from the manager, but he was conspicuous by his absence, and we left the meeting feeling cheated.* Todos esperábamos las explicaciones del gerente, pero éste brilló por su ausencia, y salimos de la reunión muy defraudados.

to **cook someone's goose** (often by saying bad things to others behind his or her back) serrucharle el piso a alguien (to saw off the floor under someone) *Hond, Nic, CR, Col, Ec, Peru, S. Cone* ◆ *Mireya cooked my goose with the boss by telling him lies when I went on vacation.* Mireya me serruchó el piso con mi jefe cuando fui de vacaciones.

cool 1. (great; →see also: super) chido(-a) (perhaps from chingón or from chic) *Chicano, Mex, ES*; mamey (a fruit) *Mex, Cuba, Col*; a todo dar (at all giving) *Mex, ES*; padrote *Mex*; bacán *Cuba, Col, Ec, Peru, S. Cone*; mortal (mortal, deadly) *Cuba, Col, S. Cone*; pulento(-a) *Peru, Ch, Arg* ◆ *You saw Antonio Banderas? Cool!* ¿Viste a Antonio Banderas? ¡Bacán! 2. (great; same in the feminine as in the masculine) guay (also, guay del Paraguay) *Sp*; alucinante *Sp* ◆ *Adela is a real cool chick. She's the coolest.* Adela es una chica muy guay. Es guay del Paraguay. 3. (good, easy-going, pleasant; people and things) suave (soft) *Mex, Cuba, Col* ◆ *Adelia is a very cool person.* Adelia es una persona muy suave.

to be **cool** ("with it"; →see also: super) estar de onda *Mex, ES, Col, U, Arg*; ser cul *Mex, DR*; ser buena nota (to be good note) *CR, Ven*; ser guay (same in the feminine as in the masculine; also, guay del Paraguay and ir de guay, to act cool) *Sp* ◆ *That dance is very cool.* Ese baile está muy de onda.

cool as a cucumber 1. (not worried) fresco(-a) (fresh) *Mex, Col, Ch, Sp* ◆ *She has a test tomorrow, but she's cool as a cucumber.* Tiene un examen mañana, pero está tan fresca. 2. (brazen, bold) ser más (tan) fresco(-a) que una lechuga (to be more [as] fresh as a lettuce) *L. Am., Sp* ◆ *The thief left* cool as a cucumber. *El ladrón salió más fresco que una lechuga.*

to **cop out** →see: to back down, to back out

cops (police) los perros (dogs) *Chicano, Mex, PR, ES, Col;* la tira (from tirana) *Mex, G;* los tombos *CR, Col, Ven, Ec, Peru;* los pacos *Ven, Ec, Bol, Ch;* la pasma *Sp;* la poli *Sp* ♦ *When I was coming home, the cops followed me.* **Cuando venía para la casa, me siguieron los perros.**

corny (overly sweet, sentimental, or cute [language, dress, etc.]) cursi *L. Am., Sp* ♦ *Divine treasure of my soul and heart, do you want to go out for dinner? —Please don't be so corny.* **Tesoro divino de mi alma y corazón, ¿quieres ir a cenar? —Por favor, no seas tan cursi.**

to **cost a fortune** costar una fortuna *L. Am., Sp;* costar más que un hijo tonto (to cost more than a foolish son) *Mex, U, Sp* (RVar *Arg:* bobo); costar un pastón (augmentative of pasta, meaning money) *Sp* ♦ *This motorcycle cost me a fortune.* **Esta moto me costó un pastón.**

to **cost an arm and a leg** costar un ojo de la cara (to cost an eye of the face) *L. Am., Sp;* costar un huevo (y la mitad de otro) (to cost an egg, meaning testicle [and a half]; vulgar) *L. Am., Sp* ♦ *You can't buy that coat. It's pretty, but it costs an arm and a leg.* **No puedes comprar ese abrigo. Es muy bonito, pero cuesta un ojo de la cara.**

couch potato →see: laid back, slacker

to **count (someone) in** apuntarse *most of L. Am., Sp* ♦ *Count us in.* **Nos apuntamos.**

coup de grace (fatal blow) el tiro de gracia (gunshot of pity) *L. Am., Sp* ♦ *They gave him the coup de grace when they insulted his family.* **Le dieron el tiro de gracia al insultar a su familia.**

cow (fat person) la ballena (whale) *Mex, G, ES, Col;* la foca (vaca) (seal [cow]) *U, Arg, Sp* ♦ *Silvia is a total cow, but she has no interest in going on a diet.* **Silvia está hecha una foca, pero no le interesa hacer dieta.**

coyote el coyote (coyote, someone who takes people across the US border) *Mex, C. Am.* ♦ *My son-in-law is a coyote.* **Mi yerno es coyote.**

crab (having a hostile, crabby appearance) el/la cara de perro (dog face) *Mex, PR, Sp* ♦ *I didn't dare talk to the police officer because he looked like a real crab.* **No me atreví a hablarle al policía porque tenía una cara de perro terrible.**

to **crack up with laughter** (→see also: to break up with laughter) reventar de risa *DR, U, Sp* ♦ *We cracked up with laughter hearing Tito's ridiculous remarks.* **Reventamos de risa escuchando los comentarios ridículos de Tito.**

crackpot →see: nuts, to be nuts

cradle robber (someone who goes out with someone much younger) el asaltacunas (cradle assaulter) *Mex, Sp* ♦ *Rolando was very much in love with Silvia, although his friends said he was a cradle robber.* **Rolando estaba muy enamorado de Silvia, aunque sus amigos le decían asaltacunas.**

to **cram** (study hard) clavarse (to be nailed) *Mex, Col;* hincar los codos (to dig in one's elbows) *Mex, Sp;* darse un quemón (to burn oneself) *Mex;* embotellarse (to bottle) *DR, PR, Col;* empollar *Sp;* romperse los codos (to break one's elbows) *Sp;* hacer codos (to make elbows) *Sp* ♦ *If you really want to learn Russian, you have to cram.* **Si realmente quieres aprender ruso, hay que hacer codos.**

Crap! →see: Damn!, Darn!

crap (something of poor quality or someone not trustworthy, often used in negation; →see also: baloney, crock, crummy, tacky) la caca de la vaca (cow dung, vulgar) *Sp* ♦ *About buying another car, what crap! And let's not talk about it any more.* **Sobre la compra de otro coche, ¡caca de la vaca! Y no hablemos más de eso.**

crappy (vulgar; →see also: crummy, tacky) de mierda (of shit) *L. Am., Sp* ♦ *How can she survive with that crappy pension?* **¿Cómo se puede mantener con esa pensión de mierda?**

to be **crappy** (worthless, vulgar) ser pura mierda (ser una mierda) (to be pure shit [to be shitty]) *Mex, DR, PR, ES, Ch, Sp* ♦ *What they did is crappy.* **Lo que hicieron es pura mierda.**

to **crash 1.** (sleep) →see also: to go out like a light, to go somewhere without having to pay, to hit the sack) caer muerto(-a) de sueño (to fall dead tired) *L. Am., Sp;* hacer la rosca (to make the doughnut, i.e., rolled up like a doughnut, meaning to sleep anywhere although it may not be comfortable) *Sp* ◆ *We were exhausted and we curled up and slept on the path to the mountains.* **Estábamos agotados e hicimos una rosca en el sendero a las montañas. 2.** (party, gate; uninvited) colarse (to be filtered or strained) *L. Am., Sp* ◆ *I crashed the party.* **Me colé en la fiesta.**

to be **crazy** ➞see: mad as a hatter, to be nuts, to be off one's rocker, to have a screw loose, to lose one's marbles

to be **crazy about** (love) estar loco(-a) por *L. Am., Sp;* chiflar *Mex, Sp* ◆ *I'm crazy about dancing.* **Me chifla bailar.**

crazy to the nth degree (completely mad) loco de remate (terminally) *L. Am., Sp* ◆ *He is crazy to the nth degree.* **Es loco de remate.**

the **cream of the crop** la flor y nata (flower and cream) *L. Am., Sp* ◆ *The cream of the crop was at that reception.* **En esa recepción estaba la flor y nata de la sociedad.**

to **create a ruckus** ➞see: to make a scene

creep (scoundrel; ➞see also: bad guy, troublemaker, con artist) el/la canalla (from canine, dog) *L. Am., Sp;* el/la descarado(-a) (faceless one) *L. Am., Sp* ◆ *He acted like a total creep. What a loser!* **Se comportó como un canalla. ¡Qué sinvergüenza!**

crib ➞see: digs

crib sheet el acordeón (accordion [because it's folded]) *Mex, Cuba, G, U;* la chuleta (chop, cut of meat) *Sp* ◆ *He took a crib sheet to math class.* **Llevó un acordeón a la clase de matemáticas.**

to **criticize** ➞to chew out

to **croak** (die) ➞see: to kick the bucket

crock (➞see also: baloney, spiel) el rollo (roll) *Mex, C. Am., Col, Ven, Peru, Ch, Sp* ◆ *Stop giving me such a crock.* **Déjate de tanto rollo.**

crooked chueco(-a) *Mex, DR, ES, Col, Ch* ◆ *They play crooked.* **Juegan chueco.**

to **cross the line** (➞see also: to go too far) pasarse de la raya (to go over the line) *Mex, DR, PR, ES, S. Cone, Sp* ◆ *Jacinta threw them out of her house because they crossed the line.* **Jacinta los echó de su casa porque se pasaron de la raya.**

to **cross your fingers** (hope for the best) cruzar los dedos *L. Am;* hacer changuitos (to make little monkeys) *Mex* ◆ *Let's cross our fingers and hope it works.* **Hay que cruzar los dedos y esperar que funcione.**

crowd ➞see: gang, mob

crummy 1. (bad, inappropriate, deteriorated) chungo(-a) *Mex, Sp* ◆ *I have a crummy job.* **Tengo un trabajo muy chungo. 2.** (lousy, bad, horrible) furris *Mex, CR, Ven* ◆ *What he did was really crummy.* **Su acción fue muy furris. 3.** (of bad quality or little importance, run of the mill) de pacotilla *DR, PR, S. Cone, Sp* ◆ *He is a crummy singer.* **Es un cantante de pacotilla. 4.** (of little worth) de mala muerte (of bad death, usually refers to places) *L. Am., Sp* ◆ *I don't want to go to that crummy bar.* **No quiero ir a ese bar de mala muerte. 5.** ➞see also: tacky

to **cry a sea (of tears), cry buckets** llorar a mares *Mex, ES, S. Cone, Sp* ◆ *Every time I say good-bye to my family at the airport, I cry buckets.* **Cada vez que me despido de mi familia en el aeropuerto, lloro a mares.**

to **cry crocodile tears** (feign sadness) llorar lágrimas de cocodrilo *L. Am., Sp* ◆ *Stop crying crocodile (fake) tears.* **Deja de llorar lágrimas de cocodrilo.**

to **cry like a baby** llorar a moco tendido (to cry with a lot of mucus) *L Am., Sp* ◆ *Silvia and her mother met after many years; they talked and cried like babies until they had recovered emotionally.* **Silvia y su madre se encontraron después de muchos años; hablaron y lloraron a moco tendido, hasta deshogarse.**

crybaby (complainer) llorón, llorona *L. Am., Sp;* chillón, chillona *Chicano, Mex, G, ES, Col, Sp* ◆ *My cousin is a crybaby (whiner). He's never happy.* **Mi primo es un llorón. Nunca está contento.**

cunt (female organ) ➞see: pussy

to (not) be one's **cup of tea** (no) ser lo suyo (to not be one's own) *L. Am., Sp;* (no) ser plato del gusto de alguien (to not be one's preferred dish) *Sp* ◆ *These ideas are not Javier's cup of tea. It's a sure bet he won't accept the proposal.* **Estas ideas no son plato del gusto de Javier. Seguro que no va a aceptar la propuesta.**

to **cuss** ➞see: swear word

to **cut (classes)** faltar a clase *L. Am., Sp;* cortar (clases) *Mex, PR;* hacer campana (to make bell) *Sp* hacer novillos *Mex., Sp;* irse de pinta *Mex* ◆ *Since you cut class, now you don't have the class notes from that day.* Como que hiciste campana, ahora no tienes los apuntes de clase de aquel día.

to **cut a fine figure** (look good physically) estar hecho(-a) un figurín (to be made a figurine) *DR, U, Arg, Sp* ◆ *The bride cut a fine figure.* La novia estaba hecha un figurín.

to **cut a rug** →see: to boogie

cut from the same cloth (very similar; →see also: chip off the old block) cortado (-a) por la misma tijera (cut by the same scissors) *Mex, DR, PR, ES, S. Cone, Sp;* cortado(-a) por (con) el mismo patrón (cut by [with] the same pattern) *Mex, Sp* ◆ *You really notice that they're relatives. They look the same.* Realmente se nota que son familiares. Están cortados por la misma tijera.

Cut it out. Basta ya. (That's enough already.) *L. Am., Sp;* Córtala. (Cut it.) *S. Cone* ◆ *Cut it out. Nobody wants to hear any more from you.* Córtala. Nadie quiere escucharte más.

to **cut off 1.** (interrupt a conversation or other thing) cortar el hilo (to cut the thread) *Mex, DR, S. Cone* ◆ *Don't cut me off because I'll forget (lose) the story. It's very complicated.* No me cortes el hilo porque me pierdo la historia. Es muy complicada. **2.** (a relationship) cortar (to cut) *Mex, G, U, Sp* ◆ *I cut Mario off. I was sick and tired of hearing about his problems.* Corté a Mario. Me tenía cansado con sus problemas.

to **cut off at the pass** (get ahead of) madrugar (to get up early) *L. Am., Sp;* hacerle la cama a alguien (to make the bed for someone) *S. Cone* ◆ *If you don't cut that man off at the pass, he's going to cut you off.* Si no madrugas a ese señor, él te madruga a ti.

to **cut someone down to size** (in a sharp reply) dar un cortón a alguien *Mex* ◆ *Julio cut him down to size in an ugly way.* Julio le dio un cortón muy feo.

Cut the crap. (Stop with your foolishness/trickery.) Deja de joder. (Stop screwing around.; slightly vulgar) *L. Am., Sp;* Deja de comer mierda. (Stop eating shit.; vulgar) *Mex, DR, Col*

to **cut the jive** cortar el rollo (to cut the roll) *Mex, Sp* ◆ *Cut the jive and pay me what you owe me.* Corta el rollo y págame lo que me debes.

to **cut to pieces** →see: to chew out, to do in, to put down, to rip apart

to **cut to the chase** (→see also: to get to the point) ir al grano (to go to the grain) *L. Am., Sp;* dejarse de cuentos (historias) (to leave off with stories) *L. Am., Sp* ◆ *Cut to the chase.* Déjate de cuentos.

cute mono(-a) (monkey) *L. Am., Sp;* chulo(-a) *Florida, Mex, DR, PR, G, Sp* ◆ *I adore Sandra's dress. It's super cute!* Me encanta el vestido de Sandra. ¡Está superchulo!

to be **cute (as a button)** estar para comérselo (to be as if to eat) *Florida, Mex, Cuba, DR, ES, U, Arg, Sp* ◆ *That child is cute as a button.* Ese niño es para comérselo.

to be a **cutie** (pretty, sweet; often used by women to describe children) ser una monada (to be a monkey face) *Mex, S. Cone, Sp* ◆ *These children are real cuties. They've studied and finished their homework before going to play with their friends.* Estos niños son una monada. Han estudiado y terminado sus tareas antes de ir a jugar con sus amigos.

cutup (tease) el/la vacilador(-a) *Mex, Cuba, G, ES, Col* ◆ *Don't believe him. What a cutup!* No lo creas. ¡Qué vacilador!

to be a **cutup 1.** (silly or amusing) ser como payaso de circo (to be like a circus clown) *Mex, ES* ◆ *Roberto is a cutup; he makes us all laugh.* Roberto es como payaso de circo; nos hace reír a todos. **2.** (comic, entertaining person; →see also: to be a character) ser un vacilón *Mex, DR, PR, ES, CR, Sp* ◆ *José is a cutup, always telling jokes.* José es un vacilón, siempre contando chistes.

D

dad el tata *L. Am.* ◆ *My dad doesn't love me. Mi tata no me quiere.*

the **damages** (check, bill) la dolorosa (the painful one) *U, Sp* ◆ *Waiter, bring me the damages. Camarero, tráigame la dolorosa.*

damn (vulgar) puto(-a) (pimp or whore, vulgar) *L. Am., Sp;* cabrón, cabrona (big goat) *Mex, Cuba, PR, C. Am., Col, Bol, Ch, Sp;* de los cojones (of the testicles) *Mex, Sp;* pinche *Mex* ◆ *Where is that damn music coming from? ¿De dónde viene esa musiquita de los cojones?*

Damn! (expression of anger, surprise) ¡Puta! (Whore!; vulgar) *L. Am., Sp;* ¡Carajo! (male organ, vulgar) *L. Am., Sp;* ¡Coño! (reference to female organ; vulgar, especially in L. Am.) *Mex, Caribbean, Col, Sp;* ¡Manda huevo! (vulgar) *ES, CR, Col, Sp;* ¡Cojones! (Testicles!; vulgar) *Cuba, Sp;* ¡Hostia(s)! (Host[s]!; vulgar) *Sp;* ¡Joer! (from joder) *Sp;* ¡Anda la hostia (leche, osa, puta)! (Go the Host [milk, bear, whore]!; vulgar) *Sp;* ¡Coña! (vulgar) *Sp* ◆ *Damn! Someone's stolen my computer. ¡Cojones! Me han robado la computadora.*

damn fantastic (great; →see also: super) del carajo (of the male organ, vulgar) *DR, PR, Col, Ven;* de pinga, de pinguísima (of the male organ, vulgar) *DR, Ven;* de puta madre (mother whore, vulgar) *Sp;* cojonudo(-a) (vulgar) *Sp* Those slacks look damn fantastic on you. ◆ *Esos pantalones te sientan de puta madre.*

damn god-awful (→see also: a bitch of a, crappy) de los cojones (of the testicles, vulgar) *Mex, Sp* ◆ *Where is that damn god-awful music coming from? ¿De dónde viene esa musiquita de los cojones?*

damn hard time el coñazo (blow, from coño; vulgar) *Sp* ◆ *What a damn hard time (I had)! ¡Qué coñazo!*

Damn it! ¡Maldito(-a) sea! (May it be cursed!) *Mex, DR, PR, G, Col, U, Sp* ◆ *Damn the current politicians; they've destoyed the country's economy. Malditos sean los políticos actuales; han destruido la economía del país.*

to be a **damn whiz (at something)** ser un(a) chingón (chingona) (vulgar) *Chicano, Mex, C. Am.;* ser muy cabrón (cabrona) para algo (vulgar) *Chicano, Mex, G, Col* ◆ *Juan is a damn whiz at music. Juan es un chingón para la música.*

damn(ed) maldito(-a) *L. Am., Sp* ◆ *Damned war! Many innocent people have died. ¡Maldita guerra! Han muerto muchos inocentes.*

darling →see: dear, my love, sweetie

daredevil atrevido(-a) *L. Am., Sp;* aventado (-a) (thrown out) *Mex, G, ES, Nic, Col, Peru* ◆ *Aurelio is a daredevil and accepted his friends' challenge (dare). Aurelio es aventado y aceptó el desafío de sus amigos.*

Darn! (→see also: Holy smoke! Wow!) ¡Caramba! (euphemism for ¡Carajo!) *L. Am., Sp;* ¡Caracoles! (snails; euphemism for ¡Carajo!) *Mex, DR, Col, U, Arg, Sp;* ¡Pucha! ¡La pucha! (euphemism for ¡La puta! r}) *L. Am.;* ¡Caray! (euphemism for ¡Carajo!) *Mex, Cuba, DR, PR, Col, Sp;* ¡Qué vaina! (What a husk, sheath!) *DR, most of C. Am., Col, Ven;* ¡Chis! *Mex, G, ES;* ¡Chin! ¡Chihuahua! ¡Chispas! (euphemisms for chinga'o, screwed) *Mex;* ¡Chuchas! (female organ; very common, vulgar) *Ch;* ¡Joer! (from joder) *Sp;* ¡Jolines! *Sp;* ¡La osa! (euphemism for la hostia) *Sp;* ¡Ostras! (Oysters!; euphemism for ¡Hostias!) *Sp;* ¡Porras! *Sp* ◆ *Darn it! I don't remember where I put the documents from the lawyer. ¡Caramba! No recuerdo dónde puse los documentos del abogado.*

darned bendito(-a) (blessed, sometimes used ironically for the opposite) *L. Am.* ◆ *This darned car won't start. Este bendito carro no me arranca.*

to **dawn on** (→see also: to get it) caer en la cuenta (to fall into the account) *Mex, DR, PR, U, Arg, Sp* ◆ *When I saw his photo, it dawned on me (I figured out) that I had known*

289

him for many years. Cuando vi su foto, caí en la cuenta de que lo conocía desde hacía muchos años.

day of reckoning el día de arreglo de cuentas (day of settling of accounts) *L. Am., Sp* ♦ *The attack this morning at dawn was the day of reckoning between two gangs of delinquents. El ataque de esta madrugada fue un arreglo de cuentas entre dos bandas de delincuentes.*

daydreaming (→see also: to be daydreaming, to tune out) volado(-a) (blown up high or flown away) *Mex, Col* ♦ *He's in the clouds, daydreaming about the girl. Está en las nubes, bien volado por la chava.*

to be **daydreaming** estar en la luna (de Valencia) (to be in the moon [of Valencia]) *L. Am., Sp;* estar en las nubes (to be in the clouds) *L. Am., Sp;* estar en la higuera (to be in the fig tree) *Sp* ♦ *I don't remember what Carmela said; I was daydreaming when she spoke. No recuerdo lo que dijo Carmela; yo estaba en las nubes cuando ella habló.*

dead (empty, boring; →see also: to be a drag) muerto(-a) (dead) *Mex, G, Ch* ♦ *This disco is dead. Let's go. Esta discoteca está muerta. Vámonos.*

dead as a doornail frito(-a) (fried) *PR, Col, U, Arg, Sp* ♦ *He fell out the window and wound up dead as a doornail on the ground. Se cayó de la ventana y se quedó frito en el suelo.*

to be **dead set against (something)** ser punto y aparte (to be period and apart, new paragraph) *Mex* ♦ *Regarding the problem of drugs, I'm dead set against them. Con el problema de la droga, yo soy punto y aparte.*

dead tired →see: wiped out

dead-end situation el callejón sin salida *L. Am., Sp* ♦ *I don't know what to do; I'm in a dead-end situation. No sé qué hacer; estoy en un callejón sin salida.*

deadhead →see: idiot

to be **deadly** (difficult) ser mortal (to be mortal, deadly) *Mex, DR, Col, U, Arg* ♦ *This crossword puzzle is deadly. Este crucigrama es mortal.*

to be **deadly dull** (people; →see also: to be a drag) ser capaz de dormir a un muerto (to be capable of putting a dead person to sleep) *Mex, Sp* ♦ *My chemistry teacher is deadly dull.*

Mi profesora de química es capaz de dormir a un muerto.

to be **deaf as a post** ser más sordo(-a) que una tapia (to be more deaf than a wall) *L. Am., Sp* ♦ *My grandmother was as deaf as a post. Mi abuela era más sorda que una tapia.*

deal (transaction, intense activity; slang) el traqueteo (banging, creaking) *Mex, DR, PR, G, ES, Col* (RVAR *Col:* usually refers to drug dealing) ♦ *What's the deal with those two? It looks bad (lit., smells ugly) to me. ¿Cuál es el traqueteo que tienen esos dos? A mí me huele bien feo.*

Deal with it. (Let him [her] deal with it.) El que pone el baile que pague la marimba. (Let the host of the dance pay for the music—the one who thinks up an idea should take care of implementing it.) *ES, Nic* ♦ *We can't help you solve your problem. Deal with it. No te podemos ayudar a resolver tu problema. El que pone el baile que pague la marimba.*

dear (→see also: my love, sweetie) mi vida (my life) *L. Am., Sp;* (mi) cielo ([my] heaven) *L. Am., Sp;* (mi) tesoro ([my] treasure) *L. Am., Sp;* corazón (heart) *L. Am., Sp;* gordito (-a) (chubby) *L. Am., Sp;* m'ijo, m'ija (short for mi hijo, mi hija, lit. my son, my daughter; used to show affection even to people who are not related) *L. Am., Sp;* negrito(-ita) (black one; term of affection, used for people of any skin color) *L. Am.;* mamacita (little mama; term of address derived from mamá, used with affection to a girl or woman; also, sometimes used as a come-on by a man to a good-looking woman) *L. Am.;* mi alma (my soul) *L. Am.;* mami, mamita (term of affection for girl or woman, even a young girl *Mex, Cuba, DR, PR, G, CR, Col, S. Cone;* papacito (term of affection for a man) *Mex, DR, PR, G, ES;* papi, papito (dad, term of affection used by women to men) *Mex, Cuba, DR, PR, G, ES, Pan, Col;* muñeco(-a) (doll) *Mex, Cuba, G, Col;* chulis (used between women) *Mex, ES* ♦ *Come here, my dear. Ven acá, mi vida (corazón, mi alma, m'ijo, negrita).*

death →see: Grim Reaper

decked out vestido(-a) de punta en blanco (dressed all in white) *L. Am., Sp;* de pipa y

to defend to the hilt: *He defends his opinion to the hilt.*
Defiende su opinión a capa y espada.

guante (with pipe and glove) *Chicano, Mex;* a todo trapo (at full rag) *S. Cone* ◆ *They were all decked out for the party; they were very elegant.* Se vistieron para la fiesta a todo trapo; estaban muy elegantes.

to **defend to the hilt** (back up) defender a capa y espada (to defend with cape and sword) *L. Am., Sp;* romper una lanza (to break a spear) *Peru, Ch, Sp* ◆ *He defended that opinion to the hilt.* Defendió esa opinión a capa y espada.

to be **demanding** (annoying or bossy person) ser un(a) fregado(-a) (to be a scrubber) *Mex, Nic, CR, Peru, Ch* ◆ *Their son is very demanding; he always wants to buy expensive clothes and spend money with his friends.* El hijo de ellos es muy fregado; siempre quiere comprar ropa muy cara y gastar dinero con sus amigos.

derriere → see: rear end

to be **devastated** (by grief or disappointment) quedarse hecho(-a) polvo (to be made into dust) *L. Am., Sp* ◆ *When I heard the news, I was devastated.* Al oír la noticia, me quedé hecho polvo.

to be the **devil himself** (very perverse or cunning) ser el mismísimo demonio *Mex, DR, PR, U, Arg, Sp* ◆ *That man is the devil himself. Don't even talk to him.* Ese hombre es el mismísimo demonio. Ni le hables.

dick (cock; male organ) el pito (whistle, fife; vulgar) *Mex, Cuba, G, ES, CR, U, Arg, Sp;* la verga (vulgar) *Mex, C. Am., Col, Ec, U, Arg, Sp;* el palo (stick, vulgar) *Mex, Cuba, DR, G, ES, CR, Col;* el chorizo (sausage, vulgar) *Mex, Cuba, G, ES, U;* el cuero (hide, leather, vulgar) *Chicano, Cuba, Col;* el pájaro (bird, vulgar) *Mex, G;* el chile (chili pepper, vulgar) *Mex, ES;* el pico (beak, vulgar) *G, ES, CR, Ch;* la pinga (vulgar) *Cuba, DR, PR, G, CR, Col;* la pija (vulgar) *Hond, Nic, U, Arg;* la polla (young female chicken, pullet; vulgar) *Sp;* el carajo *Sp*

to **dick around** (act like a fool) pendejear (vulgar) *Mex, C. Am* ◆ *Stop dicking around.* Deja de pendejear.

291

dickens diablos (devils) *L. Am., Sp;* narices (noses, often a euphemism for **cojones**) *Sp* ◆ *What the dickens am I doing here? ¿Qué diablos hago aquí?* ◆ *What the dickens happened? ¿Qué narices ha pasado?*

Diddly (squat) (nothing at all; →see also: zip) Ni jota. (Not a jot) *L. Am., Sp;* Ni chicles. (Not even chewing gum.) *Mex;* Ni por el forro. (Not even by the lining.) *U, Sp* ◆ *Hugo didn't understand diddly about numbers; he'd never passed any math test. Hugo no entendía de números ni por el forro; nunca había pasado ningún examen de matemáticas.*

to be to **die for** (delicious) ser para chuparse los dedos (to be to suck one's fingers) *L. Am., Sp* ◆ *This dessert is to die for. Este postre es para chuparse los dedos.*

to **die of laughter** morirse de la risa *L. Am., Sp* ◆ *Every time I hear Emilio tell stories, I die of laughter. Cada vez que escucho a Emilio contar cuentos, me muero de la risa.*

to **die with one's boots on** morir con las botas puestas (to die with one's boots on) *Mex, Nic, U, Arg, Sp;* morir vestido(-a) (to die dressed) *Mex, Sp* ◆ *General Custer died with his boots on. El general Custer murió vestido.*

to be **difficult** (person, thing, or situation; →see also: to be a pain, drag, grouch, pain in the neck) ser un hueso que roer to be a bone to gnaw on *L. Am., Sp* ◆ *That professor is really difficult to deal with. He flunks almost everyone. Ese profesor es un hueso que roer. Suspende a casi todos.*

to **dig in and study** (→see also: to cram) hincar los codos (to dig in one's elbows) *Mex, Sp* ◆ *I have to really dig in if I want to pass the exam. Tengo que hincar los codos si quiero pasar el examen.*

digs (home) la home (from English) *parts of L. Am. (not S. Cone);* la choza (hut) *Mex, G, ES, CR, Col, Para, U, Arg;* el chante (chanti) *Mex, ES, Nic, CR, Pan;* la cueva (cave) *Mex, Col;* la ruca (from the Mapuche language) *Ec, Ch* ◆ *I'm going to my digs now. Voy a mi choza ahora.*

to **dilly-dally** (linger) vacilar *L. Am., Sp;* dilatar(se) *Mex, PR, ES, CR* ◆ *The child is dilly-dallying. El niño se dilata.*

dime: without a dime (→see also: to be broke, to not have a plug nickel) sin una gorda (without a fat one) *Sp* ◆ *She doesn't have a dime. Está sin una gorda.*

dimwit →see: idiot, birdbrain, fool

dim-witted (→see also: stupid, fool) lelo (-a) *Chicano, Mex, DR, G, Col, U, Arg;* menso(-a) *Chicano, Mex, DR, PR, C. Am., Col, Ch;* pasmado(-a) *Mex, C. Am., U;* zoquete (zoqueta) *Chicano, Mex, DR, Col, Sp;* dundo(-a) *C. Am.* ◆ *What a dim-witted girl! ¡Qué muchacha más zoqueta! ¡No quiso salir en el show de don Francisco!*

to be a **ding-a-ling** (be an incompetent person; →see also: to be a klutz, to be klutzy) ser una maraca sin palo (to be a maraca, the musical instrument, without a handle or stick) *Col* ◆ *In chemistry class I'm a real ding-a-ling, the most klutzy of them all. En la clase de química soy una maraca sin palo, el más cafre de todos.*

to be **dirt cheap** (things; →see also: a steal) estar por los suelos (to be on the floor) *ES, Ch, Sp* ◆ *In that store everything is dirt cheap now. En esa tienda todo está por los suelos ahora.*

dirty (obsessed with sex) cochambroso(-a) *Mex, DR, PR, ES, Col, Sp* ◆ *My friend has a very dirty mind. Mi amiga tiene la mente bien cochambrosa.*

dirty old man el viejo verde (viejo caliente) (green old man [hot old man]; not necessarily pejorative) *L. Am., Sp;* el rabo verde (green tail) *Mex, C. Am., Peru;* el birriondo *Mex, G, ES;* el coscolino *Mex, ES* ◆ *Don't talk to that dirty old man. No le hables a ese viejo verde.*

dirty old woman la viuda verde (mujer rabo verde) (green widow [woman with a green tail]) *Chicano, Mex;* la birrionda *Mex, G, ES* ◆ *That lady is a dirty old woman. Esa señora es una viuda verde.*

dirty trick la mala pasada (bad pass) *L. Am., Sp;* la trastada *L. Am., Sp;* la cochinada (pig action) *L. Am., Sp;* la canallada *most of L. Am.;* la cabronada (slightly vulgar) *Mex, PR, G, Col, Sp;* la fregadera (scrubbing) *Mex;* la jalada (pull or jerk) *Mex;* la cagada (shit, vulgar) *S. Cone;* la putada (whore thing or action, vulgar) *S. Cone, Sp;* la gilada *U, Arg;* la mariconada (gayness, slightly vulgar) *Ch, Sp;* la guarrada (pig action, somewhat vulgar) *Sp* ◆ *They've played some dirty tricks on me, too.* **A mí también me han hecho algunas trastadas.** ◆ *Ana played a hell of a dirty trick on me; she tried to go out with my boyfriend.* **Ana me hizo una gran cagada; trató de salir con mi novio.**

to **disappear from the face of the earth** (from places one usually frequents; →see also: to take off) tragárselo a alguien la tierra (to be swallowed by the earth) *L. Am., Sp* ◆ *We never see Juan; it's like he's disappeared from the face of the earth.* **Nunca vemos a Juan; se lo tragó la tierra.**

to **disappear into thin air** (→see also: to take off) esfumarse *L. Am., Sp;* hacerse humo (to become steam or smoke) *L. Am., Sp;* evaporarse (to evaporate) *Mex, Ch, Sp* ◆ *Where is your little brother? —I don't know. He's disappeared into thin air.* **¿Dónde está tu hermanito? –No sé. Se ha esfumado.**

to **disregard completely** (what someone says) echar en saco roto (to put into a broken or torn sack) *L. Am., Sp* ◆ *They completely disregarded my advice.* **Echaron mis consejos en saco roto.**

to **disrespect** faltar el respeto a... (to lack respect) *L. Am., Sp* ◆ *Don't disrespect me, girl.* **No me faltes el respeto, niña.**

to **ditch** →see: to stand up

ditzy →see: mixed up

dive (seedy bar or club; →see also: joint) el antro *Mex, U, Arg, Sp;* el boliche *U, Arg* ◆ *Shall we have a drink here? —Not in that dive; I don't like that place.* **¿Vamos a tomar un trago aquí? –No en ese antro; no me gusta ese lugar.**

divine divis-divis (an exaggeratedly feminine expression that may be said ironically or in jest, like "Simply divine, dahling!") *Mex* ◆ *That blouse looks divine on you.* **Esa blusa te queda divis-divis.**

to **do a bad job (at something)** hacer algo a lo bestia (to do something like a beast) *Mex, PR, U, Arg, Sp* ◆ *He did a bad job packing his suitcases, and he forgot important things.* **Hizo sus maletas a lo bestia y se olvidó de cosas muy importantes.**

to **do (someone) a favor** hacer un favor *L. Am., Sp;* hacer un paro (to make a stop) *Mex, parts of C. Am.;* hacer una segunda (to do a

second) *Ven;* hacer una gauchada (from gaucho, cowboy) *S. Cone* ◆ *Do me a favor, bro'.* **Hazme un paro, mano.**

Do I know you? (Since when are we bosom buddies? Said when someone acts in an overfamiliar way.) ¿Cuándo hemos comido en el mismo plato? (When have we eaten from the same plate?) *Mex, G, ES*

to **do in** (kill figuratively, finish off or be the ruin of) linchar (to lynch) *Mex, Cuba, DR, PR, ES, G, Col, Ch, Sp;* sacar a alguien con los pies adelante (to take someone out feet first; also, lit., to kill) *Mex, DR, PR, Sp;* capar (to neuter, castrate) *Mex, Col, Arg, U;* darle mate (to give kill) *Mex;* tirar a los leones (to throw to the lions) *Ch, Sp;* dar la puntilla (to give the dagger) *Sp* ◆ *His insults to the manager were what did him in (finished him off). He's fired.* **Sus insultos al gerente fue lo que le acabó de dar la puntilla. Está despedido.** ◆ *They're going to do me in (kill me) at home if I don't pass the exam.* **Me van a capar en la casa si no paso el examen.**

to **do something in a half-assed way** (badly) hacer algo con el culo (to do something with the ass, vulgar) *Mex, PR, Sp* ◆ *Rosalia, you made your bed in a half-assed way; you'll need to do it over.* **Rosalía, hiciste tu cama con el culo; tendrás que hacerla de nuevo.**

to **do something on the fly** (quickly) hacer algo volando (to do something flying) *Mex, DR, G, ES, S. Cone, Sp* ◆ *I did it on the fly.* **Lo hice volando.**

to **do the dirty work** cargar con el mochuelo (to carry the bird [a nocturnal bird of prey]) *L. Am., Sp;* cargar con el muerto (to carry the dead person) *Ch, Sp;* pringar (to dip or soak in grease; to stab; vulgar) *Sp* ◆ *In that company there's only one person who does the dirty work.* **En esa empresa sólo hay uno que pringa.**

to **do things above board** (openly) jugar a cartas vistas (to play with cards that can be seen; can also mean to do something with knowledge that others don't have, referring to cards out on the table but sometimes also to cards in one's hand) *Sp* ◆ *In this company we do things above board.* **En esta empresa jugamos a cartas vistas.**

to **do whatever one pleases** (often describing a whim) hacer de las suyas (to do your own) *Mex, DR, PR, ES, S. Cone;* hacer su regalada gana (to do one's gifted desire) *Mex, ES* ◆ *Álvaro did what he darn well pleased when he chose the paint for the house without consulting his wife.* **Álvaro hizo su regalada gana cuando eligió la pintura para la casa sin consultar a su esposa.**

doc (said in jest, short for mi licenciado[-a]) mi lic *Chicano, Mex* ◆ *What's up, doc?* **¿Qué onda, mi lic?**

dog tired →see: wiped out

doll (pretty girl; →see also: babe, chick, hot number) la muñeca (doll) *Mex, Col, Para, U, Arg* ◆ *That girl is a doll.* **Esa niña es una muñeca.**

dolt →see: idiot

Don Juan →see: womanizer

Done deal. →see: It's a deal.

Don't even think about it. (→see also: No way.) Ni pensarlo. *L. Am., Sp;* Ni hablar. Don't even think (lit., talk) about it. *L. Am., Sp* ◆ *Can we get a new car this year? —No, don't even think about it.* **¿Podemos cambiar de carro este año? —No, ni pensarlo.**

Don't exaggerate so much. Ni tanto ni tan poco. (Not so much nor so few.) *Mex, DR, PR, S. Cone, Sp;* Menos lobos (Caperucita). (Fewer wolves [Red Riding Hood].) *Sp*

Don't get on my bad side. No me busques. (also, No le busques.) (Don't look for me.) Mex, DR, PR, Col, U ◆ *I'm really angry, so don't get on my bad side because you won't like it! (lit., because you'll find it!)* **Ando cabreadísima, así que no me busques, ¡que me encuentras!**

Don't get uptight →see: Chill out.

Don't go there. Ese tema no lo toques. (Don't touch that topic.) *L. Am., Sp;* No me busques. (also, No le busques.) (Don't look for me.) *Mex, DR, PR, Col, U*

Don't have a cow →see: Chill out.

do-nothing →see: slacker

doohickey →see: thingamajig

dope →see: fool, idiot

dork →see: loser

to **dot the "i"s (and cross the "t"s)** poner los puntos sobre las íes *Mex, DR, G, S. Cone* ◆ *I talked clearly to the students, dotting the "i"s and crossing the "t"s for them.* **Hablé con los estudiantes claramente y les puse los puntos sobre las íes.**

dough 1. (money; →see also: bucks, big bucks) la plata (silver) *L. Am.;* la lana (wool) *Mex, Cuba, C. Am., Peru;* la feria (fair or day off) *Mex, C. Am.;* la pachocha (paper money) *Mex;* el pisto *G, ES, Nic, CR;* la harina (wheat) *CR, Ec;* el chen chen *Pan;* la pasta (pasta, dough) *Cuba, Sp;* la guita *Ec, Peru, S. Cone, Sp;* la pela (short for peseta) *Sp* ◆ *Do you have any dough to lend me?* **¿Tienes plata para prestarme?** 2. (coin, penny) el chele *DR, Sp;* el chavo *Cuba, PR* ◆ *Do you have any dough? I left my wallet at home.* **¿Tú tienes chavos? Se me quedó la cartera en casa.**

down 1. (sad) deprimido(-a) *L. Am., Sp;* con/en la depre *L. Am., Sp;* bajoneado(-a) *S. Cone* ◆ *How are you? I'm down (depressed).* **¿Cómo estás? Estoy con (en) la depre.** ◆ *The boy is down (sad) today.* **El chico anda bajoneado hoy.** 2. (tired or low; →see also: wiped out) agüitado(-a) *Mex, C. Am.;* aguado(-a) (watery, watered-down) *Mex, DR, G, ES, CR, Col, Para;* achicopalado(-a) *Mex, ES, Nic* ◆ *Poor Carlos. Someone stole his girlfriend (took her away) and he's down.* **Pobre Carlos. Le quitaron la novia y anda agüitado.**

to be **down** 1. (depressed) deprimirse *L. Am., Sp;* tener una depre *L. Am., Sp;* achicopalarse *Mex, ES, Nic* ◆ *Hang in there! Don't let yourself get down, pal.* **¡Ánimo! No te achicopales, 'mano.** 2. (tired or low; →see also: wiped out) agüitarse *Mex, C. Am.* ◆ *Don't let yourself get down. We'll get the money.* **No te agüites. Vamos a conseguir el dinero.**

down at the heel chungo(-a) *Mex, Sp* ◆ *These shoes are a little down at the heel.* **Estos zapatos están un poco chungos.**

down in the dumps →see: down, to be down

to be **down on one's luck** →see: to be unlucky, to have bad luck

Down the hatch! (toast said before drinking) ¡(Arriba, abajo,) al centro y p'adentro! (Up, down, to the center, and inside!) *L. Am.,*

downer: *You have to overcome that existential downer!*
¡Tienes que superar ese bajón existencial!

Sp ◆ *Let's make a toast. Down the hatch with great dispatch!* **Vamos a brindar. ¡Arriba, abajo, al centro y p'adentro!**

down to the marrow hasta los tuétanos *L. Am., Sp* ◆ *I'm pure Puerto Rican. Down to the marrow.* ◆ *Soy puro puertorriqueño. Hasta los tuétanos.*

to be **down to your bottom dollar** →see: to be broke

downer (including one caused by drugs) el bajón (big down) *Mex, DR, PR, ES, S. Cone, Sp* ◆ *What a downer! I failed my final exams.* **¡Qué bajón! Fracasé en mis exámenes finales.**

to **download (back up) a computer file** descargar *L. Am., Sp;* hacer un download (un backup) *L. Am., Sp* ◆ *I downloaded the file.* **Descargué el archivo.** ◆ *Laura, I need you to make me a backup.* **Laura, necesito que me hagas un backup.**

draft (beer) de barril (from the barrel) *L. Am.;* la caña *Sp* ◆ *A beer, please. Draft.* **Una cerveza, por favor. De barril.**

drag (annoying, boring) mamón, mamona (sucker, like a suckling baby, somewhat vulgar) *Chicano, Mex, Col, Peru, ES;* fregón, fregona (scrubber) *Mex, G, Col;* sangrón, sangrona *Mex, Cuba, G, ES, CR, Col* ◆ *That woman is a drag. Why do you put up with her?* **Esa mujer es sangrona. ¿Por qué la toleras?**

a **drag** 1. (boring person) el pelma (pelmazo) (mass of undigested food) *Sp* ◆ *Don't be a drag.* **No seas pelmazo/pelma. 2.** (→see also: hassle, pain) el clavo (nail) *G, Nic, ES, CR, S. Cone* ◆ *The movie was a drag.* **La película fue un clavo.**

to be a **drag** (people or things; →see also: to be a pain, pain in the neck) ser pesado(-a) (to be heavy) *L. Am., Sp;* ser una lata (to be a tin can) *L. Am., Sp* (RVar *G, ES, Sp:* also pura lata); ser matado(-a) (to be killed) *Florida, Cuba, DR, PR, CR, Col;* ser un plomo (to be lead) *DR, PR, S. Cone, Sp;* ser un palo (to be a stick) *DR, PR, Sp;* ser un bodrio *S. Cone, Sp;* ser una paliza (to be a beating) *Sp;* ser un petardo (to be a detonator, firecracker) *Sp;* ser un pestiño (to be a fritter) *Sp*; ser un muermo *Sp* ◆ *That guy is a drag. He always tells the same stories.* **Ese tipo es pesado. Siempre cuenta las mismas historias.** ◆ *That class is a drag.* **Esa clase es un palo.**

dragging along arrastrando la cobija (dragging the blanket) *Mex, ES, Col* ◆ *How are you today? —Dragging along.* **¿Cómo estás hoy? —Arrastrando la cobija.**

to **draw a blank** estar (quedarse) en blanco (to be [remain] blank) *L. Am., Sp*; trancarse (to be blocked, as with a bar) *DR, Col, Ch* ◆ *I knew the lesson well but when the teacher asked me about it, I got so nervous I drew a blank.* **Me sabía muy bien la lección pero cuando me la preguntó el profesor, me puse tan nervioso que me quedé en blanco.**

to **draw the line** fijar los límites (to fix the limits) *L. Am., Sp*; poner a raya (to put a stripe, when someone is trying to take advantage) *Mex, Ch, Sp* ◆ *She was pressuring me a lot, but I finally drew the line.* **Me presionaba mucho, pero por fin lo puse a raya.**

dreamer (unreliable person) el/la cantamañanas *Sp* ◆ *That guy is a dreamer. He never gets anything done.* **Ese tipo es un cantamañanas. Es realmente un incumplidor.**

to be **dreaming** (of the impossible) soñar con pájaros preñados (to dream of pregnant birds) *parts of L. Am.* ◆ *If you think I'm going to buy you that car, you're dreaming.* **Si crees que te voy a comprar ese carro, estás soñando con pájaros preñados.**

dressed to impress →see: decked out

dressed to the nines (all dressed up) →see: decked out

to **drink booze** (→see also: to have a drink) chupar (to suck) *L. Am., Sp* (R*Var C.Am.*: slightly vulgar); pistear *Mex (mainly northern)* ◆ *That guy likes to drink booze.* **A ese tipo le gusta chupar.**

to **drink like a sponge** beber como una esponja *U, Sp* ◆ *Manolo drinks like a sponge and has health problems.* **Manolo bebe como una esponja y tiene problemas de salud.**

to **drive someone crazy** (change someone's way of doing things or upset someone) volverle loco(-a) a alguien *L. Am., Sp*; sacar a alguien de sus casillas (de quicio) (to take someone out of their pigeon holes [out

of doorjamb]) *L. Am., Sp* ◆ *My daughter drives me crazy.* **Mi hija me saca de mis casillas.**

to be **drooling with admiration** caérsele a alguien la baba (to have drool falling) *Mex, ES, S. Cone* ◆ *He was drooling with admiration when she came out in that miniskirt.* **Se le cayó la baba cuando ella salió en esa minifalda.**

to **drop: see to dump, to write off**

to **drop by** descolgarse (to unhang oneself) *Mex, ES*; dejarse caer (to let oneself fall) *Bol, Ch, Sp* ◆ *If I go to Barcelona, I'll drop by your house.* **Si voy a Barcelona, me dejaré caer por tu casa.**

to be **drowsy** (sleepy) tener sueño *L. Am., Sp*; tener un muermo, estar amormado(-a) (to have glanders, a viral disease of animals) *Sp* ◆ *I'm sleepy.* **Tengo un muermo. Estoy amormado.**

drudge (someone who is overworked or who always gets stuck with everything) el/la chupatintas (ink sucker) *Mex, Ch, Sp*; el/la pringado(-a) (soaked in grease) *Sp* ◆ *Pepe is the drudge of the company.* **Pepe es el chupatintas de la empresa.**

druggie (addict) el drogo (short for drogadicto, drug addict) *parts of L. Am.*; el/la drogata *Sp* ◆ *Don't go out with him; he's a druggie.* **No salgas con él; es un drogata.**

to be **drunk** (→see also: to be plastered, to be wasted) estar tomado(-a) *L. Am, Sp* ◆ *They all admitted that they were drunk.* **Todos admitieron que estaban tomados.**

drunkard (→see also: to be plastered, to be wasted) el/la briago(-a) *Mex, C. Am.* ◆ *Poor Leonor; her husband is a drunkard.* **Pobre Leonor; su esposo es un briago.**

drunkenness (slang) la juma *Cuba, ES, Nic, CR, Pan, Ven, Ec, Peru*; el/la curda *Cuba, Ven, U, Arg*; el pe'o (from pedo, fart; vulgar) *Cuba, Col, Sp*; el colocón *Sp* ◆ *Fidel has to sleep it (his drunkenness) off.* **Fidel tiene que dormir la juma.**

to be a **dud** (bad quality, boring, or ugly; →see also: to be a drag) ser un petardo (to be a detonator, firecracker) *Sp* ◆ *That movie (That babe) is a dud.* **Esa película (Esa chica) es un petardo.**

dude 1. (guy; →see also: guy) el chavalo *Chicano, Mex, C. Am.;* el vato (bato) *Chicano, Mex;* el gallo (rooster) *Cuba, DR, PR, Peru, Ch* Luis is a crazy dude; he lives in San Diego, but his heart is in Mexico. ◆ *Luis es un vato loco; vive en San Diego, pero su corazón está en México.* **2.** (middle-aged or older man, guy) el maestro (teacher, master) *L. Am., Sp* ◆ *Ask that dude where this street goes. Pregúntale a ese maestro por dónde se va esta calle.*

duds (clothing) los trapos (rags) *L. Am., Sp* ◆ *You can spend a fortune on your duds. Se puede gastar un dineral en trapos.*

dumb (stupid) tarado(-a) (from tara, mental deficiency) *L. Am, Sp;* baboso(-a) (drooling) *most of L. Am.;* tarugo(-a) *Chicano, Mex, DR, Col, Sp;* deschavetado(-a) (headless) *Mex, ES, Ch;* maje *parts of Mex, C. Am.;* aguacatón, aguacatudo(-a) (avocado) *PR, G, ES, CR, Col;* memo(-a) *DR, PR, Sp;* bambalán, bambalana *PR* ◆ *How dumb my brother is! ¡Qué baboso mi hermano!*

dumb as a post (→see also: brainless, stupid) más cerrado(-a) que un huevo de gallina (un tubo de radio) (more closed than a hen's egg [a radio tube]) *Mex, PR* ◆ *Mi suegro es más cerrado que un huevo de gallina. My father-in-law is dumb as a post.*

to **dumbfound** (to surprise) pasmar *Mex, Col, Sp* ◆ *The news dumbfounded me. La noticia me pasmó.*

to be **dumbfounded** →see: to be flabbergasted

dummy →see: dim-witted, dumb, fool, idiot, stupid

to **dump someone** (friend, sweetheart, etc.; →see also: to write off) correr *L. Am., Sp;* largar *U, Arg;* mandar por un tubo (to send through a pipe) *Mex, ES, Col* ◆ *How are you, Juan? —Bad. My girlfriend dumped me. ¿Cómo estás, Juan? —Mal. Mi novia me mandó por un tubo.*

dupe →see: chump

dyed-in-the-wool tal por cual (such for which) *L. Am.* ◆ *He's a dyed-in-the-wool liar. Es un mentiroso tal por cual.*

to be **dying of laughter** estar muerto(-a) de la risa *L. Am., Sp* ◆ *How funny! I was dying of laughter. ¡Qué chistoso! ¡Estaba muerta de la risa!*

dyke (lesbian, tomboy; pejorative) la tortillera (tortilla maker) *L. Am., Sp;* la marimacha *Mex, DR, ES, Col, Sp;* la marimacho *PR, G, Ch,;* la cachapera (from cachapa, corn bread) *PR, Ven*

E

Easier said than done. Del dicho al hecho hay mucho trecho. (From what is said to what is done there is a big gap.) *L. Am., Sp* ◆ *That's his story; however, I think it's easier said than done. Ésa es su historia; sin embargo, yo creo que del dicho al hecho hay mucho trecho.*

easy as pie →see: to be piece of cake

Easy does it. (→see also: Chill out.) Tranquilo(-a). (Tranquil.) *Mex, DR, Col, Ven, S. Cone, Sp* ◆ *Easy does it. No problem. Tranquilo, tranquilo. No hay problema.*

easy woman (→see also: slut) mujer fácil *L. Am., Sp* ◆ *That woman is rather easy. Esa mujer es bastante fácil.*

to **eat** →see: to chow down

Eat and run. Comida hecha, amistad deshecha. (Meal finished, friendship ended, said in jest) *most of L. Am., Sp* ◆ *Unfortunately we have to go now. Eat and run. Desgraciadamente tenemos que ir ahora. Comida hecha, amistad deshecha.*

to **eat like a pig** comer como cerdo (to eat like a pig) *L. Am., Sp* (RVAR *ES, Nic, S. Cone:* also, comer como chancho) ◆ *We ate like pigs on our vacation. Comimos como cerdos en nuestras vacaciones.*

eating like a horse (gluttonous; →see also: chowhound) comilón, comilona *L. Am., Sp;* hartón, hartona *Mex, C. Am.* ◆ *Tomás eats like a horse! ¡Tomás es tan comilón!*

to be an **egghead** (intellectual) saber de letras (to know letters) *Mex, DR, Col* ◆ *This young woman is a real egghead. Esta señorita sabe de letras realmente.*

to be **embarrassed** estar avergonzado(-a) *L. Am., Sp;* estar abochornado(-a) (to be suffocating from heat) *L. Am., Sp;* tener pena (to have sorrow) *most of L. Am. (not S. Cone);* dar corte (to give cut, slang) *DR, PR, Sp;* cortarse, sentirse cortado(-a) (to cut oneself off, feel cut off, slang) *S. Cone, Sp* I

felt embarrassed when she asked me that very personal question. ◆ *Me corté (Me quedé cortada) cuando me hizo esa pregunta tan personal.*

to **end badly** →see: to wash out

to be **engaged** andar de novios (to go as [be] boyfriend and girlfriend) *L. Am., Sp* ◆ *Felipe and Carmen are engaged. Felipe y Carmen andan de novios.*

Enough already. →see: That's enough.

Enough said. Ni hablar del peluquín. (Don't even talk about the toupee.) *ES, Peru, Ch, Sp* ◆ *Go to the beach? Good idea. Enough said. ¿Ir a la playa? Buena idea. Ni hablar del peluquín.*

to **escape by a hair** salvarse por un pelo (to be saved by a hair) *L. Am., Sp* ◆ *Two people died in the accident. I escaped by a hair. Dos personas murieron en el accidente. Yo me salvé por un pelo.*

to be **even** (with each other) estar a mano (to be at hand) *Mex, ES, S. Cone* ◆ *I paid you the money and now we're even, pal. Te pagué la plata y ahora estamos a mano, amigo.*

every last bit (all) todititito(-a) (variant of todo) *Mex, ES, Nic* ◆ *Every last bit of my dinner was ruined. Se me arruinó todititita la comida.*

every mother's son →see: everybody and his uncle

every Tom, Dick and Harry →see: everybody and his uncle

everybody and his uncle 1. (a lot of people) medio mundo (half the world) *L. Am., Sp* ◆ *Everybody and his uncle knows that news. Esa noticia la sabe medio mundo.* 2. (all, without exception) cada hijo de vecino (any neighbor's son) *Mex, Sp;* el que más y el que menos (he who most and he who least) *Ch, Sp;* todo quisque *Sp;* hasta las piedras (even the stones) *Sp* ◆ *Everybody and his uncle should help protect the environment. Cada hijo* *de vecino debería ayudar a proteger el medio ambiente.*

everybody under the sun →see: everybody and his uncle

Everyone for himself or herself. (being alone or without support). Cada quien se rasque con sus propias uñas. (Each person should scratch himself or herself with his or her own fingernails.) *Mex, ES, Ch* ◆ *There's no transportation to the conference. They told us everyone for himself or herself.* No hay transporte al congreso. Nos han dicho que cada quien se rasque con sus propias uñas.

Evil is afoot. El diablo anda suelto. (The devil is loose.) *Mex*

to **eye** (have one's eye on; →see also: to pay attention) echar el ojo (to throw the eye) *L. Am., Sp;* echar un taco de ojo (to throw a taco of the eye) *Mex* ◆ *You've already got your eye on that guy, right?* ◆ *Ya le echaste el ojo a ese muchacho, ¿no?*

to be an **eyeful** (be good-looking) estar para comérselo (to be as if to eat) *Florida, Mex, Cuba, DR, ES, U, Arg, Sp;* ser un muñeco (to be a doll; for men) *Mex, G;* estar muy potable (to be very drinkable) *Mex, S. Cone, Sp;* estar hecho(-a) un figurín (to be made a figurine) *DR, U, Arg, Sp;* estar de bandera (to be of flag) *Sp* ◆ *Carlos Vives is one handsome guy. He's an eyeful.* Carlos Vives es un papazote. Está pa'comérselo.

F

to **face the music** (prepare for a struggle; →see also: to wait it out) ponerse al tiro (to put oneself to the shot) *Mex, ES, Col* ◆ *He had to face the music and study to pass the exam. Se puso al tiro para pasar el examen.*

to **fail** →see: to wash out

He's (She's) a **fair-weather friend.** Al nopal lo van a ver sólo cuando tiene tunas. (They only go to see the nopal cactus when it has tunas, fruits—people will call on others only when they are prosperous or doing well.) *Mex* ◆ *So you came to see me because you need money, dear (daughter). You're kind of like a fairweather friend. Así que veniste a verme porque necesitas plata, hija. Al nopal lo van a ver sólo cuando tiene tunas.*

fake (phony) falso(-a) *L. Am., Sp*; trucho(-a) (trout) *U, Arg* ◆ *This suitcase isn't leather; it's fake. Esta maleta no es de cuero; es trucha.*

to **fall (flat) on your face** →see: to wash out

to **fall for (something)** 1. (be tricked, duped) caer como un gil (como un angelito) (to fall like a fool [like a little angel]) *Bol, S. Cone* 2. (to believe something) tragar(se) algo (to swallow something) *L. Am., Sp*; tragar el anzuelo (to swallow the hook) *Mex, DR, ES, S. Cone, Sp* ◆ *I'm not swallowing that story. I'm not swallowing it. No voy a tragar ese cuento. No me lo trago.*

to be the **fall guy** (→see also: to be left holding the bag) pagar los platos rotos (to pay for the broken plates) *L. Am., Sp*; pagar los vidrios rotos (to pay for the broken windows) *Mex, Sp*; pagar el pato (los patos) (to pay for the duck[s]) *Mex, Nic, S. Cone, Sp* ◆ *They caused the problem, but I was the fall guy. Ellos causaron el problema, pero yo pagué los platos rotos.*

to **fall hard** (be in love, hit by Cupid's arrow) quedar flechado(-a) *Mex, DR, G, S. Cone* ◆ *The exchange student fell hard for Rodolfo and didn't want to return to her country. La estu-diante de intercambio quedó flechada con Rodolfo y no quiso regresar a su país.*

to **fall into the trap** (the net) caer en la trampa (en la red) *Mex, DR, ES, S. Cone, Sp* ◆ *They fell into the trap and bought a stolen car. Cayeron en la trampa y compraron un auto robado.*

fan (sports) el/la aficionado(-a) *L. Am., Sp*; el/la hincha *S. Am., Sp* ◆ *The fans supported their team during the championship. Los hinchas apoyaron a su equipo durante el campeonato.*

fanny →see: rear end

fast (sexually; →see also: hot) acelerado *Mex, G, ES, Sp* ◆ *I went out with Fernando for the first and last time. He's so fast! Salí con Fernando por primera y última vez. ¡Qué acelerado!*

fast and furious →see: full blast, like a bat out of hell

to be **fast asleep** estar bien dormido(-a) *L. Am., Sp*; estar en el quinto sueño (to be in the fifth sleep) *Mex, DR, ES, U* ◆ *We were fast asleep when the telephone rang. Estábamos en el quinto sueño cuando sonó el teléfono.*

fast food la(s) porquería(s) (pig stuff) *L. Am., Sp*; la comida chatarra (scrap-metal food) *Mex, Col, Ch* ◆ *I filled up on fast food and now I'm not hungry. Me llené con puras porquerías y ahora no tengo hambre.*

fat cat →see: moneybags

to **feather one's nest** (→see also: to clean up, to hit the jackpot) forrarse (to make a lining for oneself, referring to lined pockets) *DR, Nic, Sp* ◆ *He feathered his nest with the stock market. Se forró de dinero en la bolsa de valores.*

to be **fed up** estar hasta la coronilla (to be up to the top of the head, crown) *L. Am., Sp*; no poder más (to be able no more) *L. Am., Sp*; estar hasta los cojones (to be up to the testicles; vulgar) *Mex, Sp*; estar hasta los ovarios (to be up to the ovaries, used for a woman; vulgar) *L. Am., Sp*; estar hasta la

madre (to be up to the mother) *Mex, C. Am.;* estar hasta las narices (to be up to the nose) *Mex, Sp;* estar hasta los topes (to be up to the top) *CR, Col, Sp;* estar hasta las cejas (to be up to the eyebrows) *Sp;* estar negro(-a) (to be black) *Sp* ◆ *Now it's (you've, he's, she's) got me totally fed up, up to here!* ¡Ya me tiene cansada hasta la coronilla!

to **feed one's face** echarle algo al buche (al pico) (to put something in one's craw [beak]) *Mex, Cuba, DR, G, Col, U, Sp* ◆ *I'm hungry. I need to feed my face.* Tengo hambre. Necesito echarle algo al buche.

to **feed someone a line** →see: to sweet-talk

to **feel for someone** (who is having problems) tener a alguien en el alma (to have someone in one's soul) *Mex, Sp* ◆ *I found out about your tragedy, and I feel for you.* Supe de tu tragedia y te tengo en mi alma.

to **feel in great shape** sentirse en plena forma (to feel in full form) *Mex, Sp* ◆ *I feel in great shape. And all thanks to the gym.* Me siento en plena forma. Y todo gracias al gimnasio.

to **feel in the mood (to do something)** tener ganas de (to have the desire to) *L. Am., Sp;* darle a alguien el punto (to give oneself the point, get in a mood, slang) *Sp* ◆ *The other day I felt in the mood and told my boss to go jump in the lake.* El otro día me dio el punto y mandé a mi jefe a freír espárragos.

to **feel like** apetecerle (provoke a desire or yearning, be appealing or appetizing) *Sp* ◆ *I feel like dancing.* Me apetece bailar.

to **feel like (be) a second-class citizen** (not treated with consideration) ser plato de segunda mesa (to be a plate of a second table) *Mex, DR, PR, ES, Sp* (RVAR *Mex:* used mainly for women who are with married men) ◆ *I am not a second-class citizen. (I don't play second fiddle to anyone.)* Yo no soy plato de segunda mesa.

to **feel like having something** provocarle algo a alguien (to have something provoke a desire in someone) *Col* ◆ *Do you feel like having a coffee?* ¿Te provoca un tinto (café)?

to **feel like (be) love at first sight** flecharle (to strike with an arrow) *Mex, DR, ES, Col, S. Cone* ◆ *It felt like love at first sight. I'm in love.* Me flechó. Estoy enamorada.

to **feel someone up** (to touch someone with sexual intentions) meter mano (to put hand) *Mex, PR, U, Sp* ◆ *He tried to feel me up in the movie theater.* Intentó meterme mano en el cine.

femme fatale (→see also: hot number) la mujer fatal *U, Sp* ◆ *Jacinta thinks she's a femme fatale; in reality, she's ridiculous.* Jacinta se cree una mujer fatal; en realidad, es ridícula.

fib (→see also: baloney, whopper) la guayaba (guava) *most of L. Am. (not Arg, Ch)* ◆ *I'm not going to fall for that fib.* No voy a tragarme esa guayaba.

to be a **fifth wheel** (to go along with a couple on a date) cargar el arpa (to carry the harp) *Mex, Ec;* tocar el violín (to play the violin) *U, Ch* ◆ *Please don't bring your sister along as a fifth wheel when we go out tomorrow.* Por favor no traigas a tu hermana a cargar el arpa cuando salgamos mañana.

fiftyish cincuentón, cincuentona (the -ón is an augmentative, emphasizing age) *L. Am., Sp* ◆ *Agustina is fiftyish, but she looks much younger, and she's always very active.* Agustina es cincuentona, pero parece mucho más joven, y siempre está muy activa.

fight →see: blowup

to **fight like cats and dogs** (→see also: to be at odds with someone, to be like oil and water, to have a blowup) pelear (andar, ser) como perro y gato (to fight [walk, be] like dog and cat) *Mex, DR, ES, U, Ch, Sp* ◆ *These kids fight like cats and dogs.* Estos niños pelean como perro y gato.

to **filch** →see: to lift

to be **filthy rich** estar podrido(-a) de dinero (to be rotten with money) *Mex, DR, ES, CR, U, Arg, Sp* ◆ *They're filthy rich and they don't know how to enjoy it (their money).* Están podridos de dinero y no saben disfrutarlo.

to be **fine** (of great worth) ser canela fina (to be fine cinnamon) *Mex, G, ES, Peru, Sp* ◆ *This music is fine.* Esta música es canela fina.

fine kettle of fish →see: drag, hassle, pain

to be **finger-licking good** (delicious) ser para chuparse los dedos (to be to suck one's fingers) *L. Am., Sp* ◆ *This dessert is finger-lickin' good.* Este postre es para chuparse los dedos.

to **finish off** 1. (finish up) matar (to kill) *Mex, Cuba* ♦ *Shall we finish off the salad? ¿Matemos la ensalada?* 2. →see: to do in

finishing touch el último toque (last touch) *Mex, Ch, U, Sp* ♦ *Put the finishing touch on the article and we'll publish it. Dale el último toque al artículo y lo publicaremos.*

fink (stool pigeon, one who rats on another) el chivato *Mex, Cuba, DR, Sp* (RVar *Cuba, DR:* also; chiva); el sapo (frog, toad, used like soplón) *Nic, CR, Col, Ven, Ec, Peru, Ch* ♦ *If my brother finds out I'm coming late, I'm toast. He's a fink, and for sure he'll fink on me to Dad. Si mi hermano se entera de que llegue tarde, estoy frita. Es un chivato y seguro me chivatea con papi.*

to **fire** (someone; kick out or run off) despedir *L. Am., Sp;* correr (to run) *Mex, C. Am., U, Arg* ♦ *They fired him because he wasn't working well. Lo corrieron porque no trabajaba bien.*

fired up (describing a real fan or enthusiast) con la camiseta puesta (with the T-shirt on) *S. Cone* ♦ *All fired up, Ernesto worked day and night for the candidate of his political party. Con la camiseta puesta, Ernesto trabajó día y noche para el candidato de su partido político.*

fit (tantrum) →see: to have a fit

fit as a fiddle sano(-a) como una manzana (healthy as an apple) *Sp* ♦ *Hi, Verónica. How are you? —Fit as a fiddle. Hola, Verónica. ¿Cómo estás? —Sana como una manzana.*

to **fit like a glove** (fit very well) quedar pintado(-a) (to remain painted) *Mex, Cuba, DR, Col, Peru, S. Cone, Sp* ♦ *This dress fits you like a glove! ¡Este vestido te queda pintado!*

to be **fit to be tied** →see: to be steamed, to lose it

to **fit well** (look good on) lucir (to shine) *DR, PR, ES, Nic, CR, Col, Sp* ♦ *Those red pants fit Rosa well. A Rosa le lucen esos pantalones rojos.*

to **fix someone's wagon** →see: to beat someone up, to do in, to hit where it hurts

to **fix up with a blind date** hacer un gancho (to make a hook) *S. Cone, Sp;* enganchar (to hook) *ES* ♦ *My brother wants me to fix him up with one of my friends. Mi hermano quiere que le haga un gancho con una de mis amigas.*

to **fixate on** (worry or be preoccupied) comerse el coco (to eat the head) *Mex, Sp* (RVar *Sp:* also; comerse el tarro, comerse la olla) ♦ *Don't fixate on it; we're going to get the money. No te comas el coco; vamos a conseguir el dinero.*

to **fixate on something** (have something fixed in one's head; →see also: to obsess over something) meterse algo entre ceja y ceja (to put something between eyebrow and eyebrow) *most of L. Am., Sp;* meterse algo en la cabeza (to put something in one's head) *ES, Ch, Sp;* ir y venir en una cosa (to go and come in something) *Sp* ♦ *She won't change her mind because she's fixated on her idea. No cambiará de idea porque la tiene metida entre ceja y ceja.*

to be **flabbergasted** 1. (astounded) quedarse boquiabierto(-a) (to be left open-mouthed) *L. Am., Sp;* quedarse frío(-a) (helado[-a]) (to end up cold [frozen]) *L. Am., Sp;* quedarse con la cara cuadrada (to be left with the face square) *Mex;* alucinar (en colores) (to hallucinate [in color]) *Sp* ♦ *Susana was flabbergasted when I told her I'd gotten married. Susana se quedó boquiabierta cuando le dije que me había casado.* 2. (often by something attractive, be drooling with admiration) caérsele a alguien la baba (to have drool falling) *Mex, ES, S. Cone* ♦ *I was flabbergasted when I saw that actress. Se me cayó la baba cuando vi a esa actriz.*

flake 1. (unreliable person) faltón, faltona *most of L. Am., Sp;* el tiro al aire (shot in the air) *S. Cone;* el/la cantamañanas *Sp* ♦ *That guy is a flake. Ese tipo es un faltón.* 2. →see: out of it

to **flatten like a pancake** →see: to beat up

flick la peli (short for película) *Mex, DR, Sp* ♦ *Did you go to the movies? What flick did you see? ¿Fueron al cine? ¿Qué peli vieron?*

fling (affair; →see also: to have a fling) la aventura (adventure) *L. Am., Sp* ♦ *I had a great fling in Sevilla. Tuve una aventura fantástica en Sevilla.*

to **flip out** (do something abnormal; →see also: to go overboard, to go too far) salirse de las casillas (to go out of the little boxes or pigeon holes) *L. Am., Sp;* salirse del guacal

to fixate on something: *She is fixated on the idea of being a supermodel.*
Ella tiene metida entre ceja y ceja la idea de ser supermodelo.

(to go out of one's container) *Mex, ES*; salirse de madre en algo (to go out of the mother in something) *Mex, Sp* ◆ *Agustín got angry, flipped out, and started yelling at people. Agustín se enojó, se salió de las casillas y se puso a gritar a la gente.*

to **flirt** coquetear *L. Am., Sp*; flirtear *L. Am.*; dar entrada (to give entrance, slang) *Mex* ◆ *Lilián was flirting with her friend's boyfriend. Lilián le daba entrada al novio de su amiga.*

to **floor it** →see: to step on it

floozie 1. (easy woman, woman who likes sex; →see also: slut) la loca (crazy person) *Mex, DR, Col, Ec, U, Arg*; la pasa rato (pastime) *Mex, DR, Col, ES*; la golfita *Mex, Col*; la coscolina *Mex*; la guarra *Sp* ◆ *Near the port there are always a lot of floozies. Cerca del puerto siempre hay muchas locas.* 2. (one who wears scanty or cheap-looking clothing) la bataclana *S. Cone* ◆ *Look at that badly dressed girl; she looks like a floozie. Mirá esa mina mal vestida; parece una bataclana.*

to **flunk, to be flunked** (→see also: to wash out) suspender (to suspend) *L. Am., Sp*; tronar (to thunder) *Mex, C. Am.*; rajar (to split) *Mex, DR, Col, Ch*; ponchar (to puncture) *Mex, Cuba, DR, G*; volar (to blow up, to make fly) *Mex*; catear (to search) *Sp* ◆ *They flunked me in chemistry. I flunked the chemistry exam. Me suspendieron (tronaron, volaron, etc.) en química. Suspendí (troné, volé, etc.) el examen de química.*

flunkie →see: drudge

to **fly off the handle** →see: to lose it

fogy (fogie) →see: geezer

folks 1. (parents) los viejos (old ones; also, term of endearment) *L. Am., Sp*; los jefes (bosses) *parts of L. Am., incl. Mex, S. Cone*; los rucos *Mex, ES, Col*; los veteranos (veterans) *U, Arg* ◆ *My folks aren't here. Mis jefes no están aquí.* 2. (parents, father and mother; also, grandparents) los tatas *most of L. Am.* ◆ *Where did your folks (parents or grandparents) come from? ¿De dónde vinieron tus tatas?*

to **follow in someone's footsteps** seguir las huellas de alguien *Mex, Ch, Sp* ◆ *The son is following in his father's footsteps; he's going* *to be a banker. El hijo sigue las huellas del padre; va a ser banquero.*

to **follow the crowd** 1. (always agree) decir amén a todo (to say amen to everything) *DR, ES, S. Cone, Sp* ◆ *She doesn't like problems: she always follows the crowd. A ella no le gustan los problemas: siempre dice amén a todo.* 2. (do whatever is appropriate) bailar al son que le tocan (to dance to the sound that is played) *L. Am., Sp* ◆ *Esteban always follows the crowd. Esteban siempre baila al son que le tocan.*

He (She) **follows the crowd.** (is like a sheep, plays the game) ¿Dónde va Vicente? Donde va (toda) la gente. (Where is Vicente going? He follows the crowd [where everyone else goes].) *Mex, ES, DR, Col, Ch, Sp* ◆ *That candidate has changed parties three times. He just follows the crowd. Ese candidato ha cambiado de partido tres veces. ¿Dónde va Vicente? Donde va la gente.*

food →see: chow

fool 1. (dope; →see also: idiot) el/la tonto (-a) *L. Am., Sp*; el gil (la gila, el gilberto) *Mex, Cuba, Col, Ec, Peru, S. Cone*; el/la pensante *Mex, Col*; el/la guajolote(-a) (turkey) *Mex*; aguacate (avocado) *PR, G, ES, CR, Col*; el/la memo(-a) *DR, PR, Sp*; el/la batata (sweet potato) *Para, Arg*; el melón, la melona (melon) *Sp*; el merluzo (hake, type of fish) *Sp* ◆ *Only a fool would say that. Sólo un memo diría eso.* 2. (simpleton) el/la buenas peras (good pears) *Bol, Ch*

to **fool around** 1. (flirt) jugar al balero (to play cup and ball, a children's game) *Mex, Col* ◆ *I like fooling around with a French guy I met at the party. Me gusta jugar al balero con un francés que conocí en la fiesta.* 2. (clown or goof around; →see also: to joke around) vacilar *Mex, ES, Col, Sp* ◆ *Girl, don't fool around so much. Talk seriously. Niña, no vaciles tanto. Habla seriamente.*

foolish: →see: dim-witted

for ages (for a while) hace mucho tiempo, hace ratos *L. Am., Sp*; hace ratón y queso (it makes rat and cheese; slang) *Cuba* ◆ *Hi, pal! We haven't seen each other for ages. ¡Hola, socio! Hace ratón y queso que no nos vemos.*

for all to see (obvious, readily present in a person's expression and nature) a flor de

piel (at the flower of the skin) *L. Am., Sp* ◆ *Her nervousness was obvious. Ella tenía los nervios a flor de piel.*

for free (free of charge) de balde *L. Am., Sp*; de hoquis *Mex*; de yapa *S. Cone* ◆ *It looks like they want us to work for free here. Parece que quieren que trabajemos de balde aquí.*

for life (lifelong) de por vida, de toda la vida *L. Am., Sp* ◆ *We're friends for life. Somos amigos de por vida.*

for no good reason (→see also: because of his [her] good looks) por un «quítame allá esas pajas» (for a "take away from me those straws") *Mex, Nic, Ch, Sp*; porque voló la mosca (because the fly flew away) *Mex, Col*; porque la abuela fuma (because Grandma smokes) *Sp* ◆ *For no good reason, he changed his mind and we couldn't do anything. Por un quítame esas pajas, cambió su decisión y no pudimos hacer nada.*

for nothing en balde (in bucket) *L. Am., Sp* ◆ *We did the work for nothing. En balde hicimos el trabajo.*

for one reason or another por pitos o por flautas (for fifes or for flutes; colloquial) *Mex, Ch, Sp*; por hache o por be (by "h" or by "b"; colloquial) *DR, U, Sp* ◆ *We thought about getting together with our friends in the summer, but for one reason or another we didn't do it. Pensábamos reunirnos con nuestros amigos en verano, pero por pitos o por flautas, no lo hicimos.*

to be **for real** (correct) ir a misa (to go to mass, slang) *Sp*; ser la neta *Mex* ◆ *What my father says is for real. Lo que dice mi padre va a misa.*

for sure a ciencia cierta (for certain knowledge) *L. Am., Sp*; de plano (flatly) *Mex, ES, Nic* ◆ *No doubt about it. We know it for sure. No hay duda. Lo sabemos a ciencia cierta.*

for the real gourmet para puro paladar curtivo (only for the finest palate) *Mex* ◆ *This dinner will be solely for the real gourmet. Esta cena será para puro paladar curtido.*

foreplay el cachondeo (horning around) *Mex, ES, Sp* ◆ *What's love, my darling, without a little foreplay? ¿Qué es el amor, mi cielo, sin un poquito de cachondeo?*

Forget it. A otra cosa, mariposa. (To another thing, butterfly.) *Mex, DR, Sp* ◆ *Forget it. I'm* not interested in family gossip. *A otra cosa mariposa. No me interesan los chismes de familia.*

to **fork up money** (spend it against one's will, dig deep into one's pockets; →see also: to loosen the purse strings) rascarse el bolsillo (to scratch the pocket) *Sp* ◆ *Finally Sergio's grandfather forked up the money and paid for his university books. Finalmente el abuelo de Sergio se rascó el bolsillo y le pagó los libros de la universidad.*

fossil →see: geezer

foul-mouthed (using strong language) malhablado(-a) (badly spoken) *L. Am., Sp;* deslenguado(-a) (untongued) *Mex, Ch, Sp* ◆ *He doesn't seem like a professional. He's very foul-mouthed. No parece un profesional. Es muy malhablado.*

four-eyes (person with glasses) el/la cuatrojos (four-eyes) *L. Am.;* el/la gafudo(-a) (big glasses-wearer) *Sp* ◆ *I put on contact lenses so they wouldn't call me four-eyes. Me puse lentes de contacto para que no me dijeran cuatrojos.*

four-eyes (wearing glasses, blind as a bat) chicato(-a) *Peru, U, Arg* ◆ *Nelda is a four-eyes (blind as a bat), and although she uses glasses, she sees very little. Nelda es chicata, y a pesar de usar lentes, ve poco.*

Four eyes are better than two. Más ven cuatro ojos que dos. (Four eyes see better than two.) *L. Am., Sp* ◆ *Come with me to see the new house. Four eyes are better than two. Acompáñame a ver la nueva casa. Más ven cuatro ojos que dos.*

to be **four sheets to the wind** →see: to be plastered, to be wasted

fox →see: babe, to be an eyeful, hot number

frankly and sincerely con el corazón en la mano (with one's heart in one's hand) *L. Am., Sp* ◆ *Frankly and sincerely, I told them what I knew of their father. Con el corazón en la mano, les dije lo que sabía de su padre.*

freaked out (upset) friqueado(-a) (from English "freaked out") *Mex, DR, PR, Ven* ◆ *I was freaked out when you didn't get here on time. Estaba friqueada cuando no llegaste a la hora.*

to be a **free thinker** (keep one's own opinions or attitudes independently) no casarse con nadie (to not marry anyone) *L. Am., Sp* ◆ *I listened to everyone's opinions, but I'm a free thinker. Escuché la opinión de todos, pero no me casé con nadie.*

free time los ratos libres (free time periods) *L. Am., Sp* ◆ *What do you do in your free time? ¿Qué haces en tus ratos libres?*

freebie (free gift) la yapa *S. Cone* ◆ *Gracielita bought flowers for her mom, and as a freebie they gave her candy. Gracielita compró flores para su mamá y de yapa le dieron bombones.*

freeloader →see: mooch, operator

french kiss el beso de lengua (kiss with the tongue) *L. Am., Sp*

to **french-kiss** besar con la lengua (to kiss with the tongue) *L. Am., Sp* ◆ *Fernando tried to french-kiss me, and I didn't like it. Fernando trató de besarme con la lengua, y no me gustó.*

Friday the 13th martes 13, jueves 13 (Tuesday the 13th, Thursday the 13th, which are considered unlucky days in Spanish-speaking countries) *L. Am., Sp* ◆ *I'm not going to start anything new today because it is Tuesday the 13th. No voy a empezar a hacer nada nuevo hoy porque es martes 13.*

fridge (refrigerator) el/la refri (short for refrigerador[a]) *Mex, G, ES* (RVar el in *Mex,* la in *G, ES*) ◆ *The fridge is empty. La refri está vacía.*

friend →see: pal

from beginning to end (completely) de pe a pa *Mex, DR, ES, S. Cone, Sp;* de cabo a rabo *Mex, S. Cone, Sp* ◆ *Felicia knows all the historical facts during the Spanish colonization and their correct dates from beginning to end. Felicia se sabe de pe a pa todos los hechos históricos durante la colonización española y las fechas correctas.*

from head to toe (entirely) de (los) pies a (la) cabeza (from [the] feet to [the] head) *L. Am., Sp* ◆ *She was dressed in black from head to toe. Estaba vestida de negro de los pies a la cabeza.*

from pillar to post de la Ceca a la Meca (from Ceca to Mecca) *Mex, DR, PR, ES, Ch,*

Sp ◆ *They sent me from pillar to post.* **Me mandaron de la Ceca a la Mecca.**

from sunup to sundown de sol a sol (from sun to sun) *L. Am., Sp* ◆ *They worked from sunup to sundown.* **Trabajaron de sol a sol.**

from the Stone Age →see: ages ago

from top to bottom de cabo a rabo *Mex, S. Cone, Sp* She knows everything about it, from top to bottom. ◆ *Se lo sabe todo, de cabo a rabo.*

fruitcake →see: nut case, nuts

Fuck! →see: Damn!, God damn it (to hell)!

full blast (at full speed, going great guns) a toda máquina (at all machine) *Chicano, Mex, DR, G, Ch, Sp;* a toda madre (at all mother) *Mex, G, ES, Col;* a todo dar (at all giving) *Mex, ES;* a todo meter (at all putting) *Mex, DR, PR, Sp;* a todo lo que da (at all that it gives) *Mex, S. Cone;* a toda marcha (at all march) *Mex, Sp;* a toda mecha (at all wick) *Mex, Sp;* a todo gas (at all gas) *Mex, Sp;* a todo vapor (at all steam) *ES, Peru, U, Arg;* a todo ful *Nic, CR, Col, Ch;* a toda pastilla (at all pill) *Sp* ◆ *The game is going full blast.* **El partido está a todo lo que da.**

to be **full of hot air** tener mucho rollo (to have a lot of roll) *Mex, Sp* ◆ *That person is full of hot air; he talks a lot but doesn't say anything interesting.* **Esa persona tiene mucho rollo; habla mucho pero no dice nada interesante.**

to be **full of life** (look very healthy) tener mucha cuerda (to have a lot of cord) *Mex, Sp* ◆ *My father is 68 years old, but he is still full of life.* **Mi papá tiene 68 años, pero todavía tiene mucha cuerda.**

to be **full of oneself** 1. (brag) darse paquete (to give oneself package) *Mex, G;* darse coba (to give oneself flattery) *Mex, DR, CR, Sp;* darse taco (to give oneself taco or plug) *Mex, Hond, CR;* darse lija (to give oneself sandpaper) *Cuba, PR, CR* ◆ *Nora is full of herself.* **Nora se da mucha coba. 2.** (have a swollen head) tener muchos humos (to have many smokes/vapors) *L. Am., Sp;* tener muchas ínfulas (to have a lot of airs) *L. Am., Sp;* tener la cabeza llena de humos (to have the head full of smoke/vapors) *Florida, Mex, DR, ES, Col, U, Arg* ◆ *Olguita is full of herself and her cousins cannot stand her.* **Olguita tiene muchos humos, y sus primas no la toleran.**

full-fledged (complete) hasta más no poder *L. Am., Sp* ◆ *He's a full-fledged jerk.* **Es un naco hasta más no poder.**

to **fume** →see: to be steamed

funk →see: bummer

fuss →see: mess

to be a **fussbudget 1.** (fussy person) ser un(a) fruncido(-a) (to be a wrinkled-up person) *S. Cone* ◆ *Nobody talks to her at school because she's a fussbudget.* **Nadie le habla en la escuela porque ella es muy fruncida. 2.** (not tolerate problems) ser de pocas pulgas (to be of few fleas) *Mex, ES, CR, Col, U, Arg;* no aguantar pulgas (to not tolerate fleas) *Mex, Sp* ◆ *Be careful of Héctor. He's a fussbudget.* **Cuidado con Héctor. No aguanta pulgas. 3.** (fussy or high-class person, not easily pleased) ser un(a) tiquis miquis *PR, Sp* ◆ *Roberto's cousin doesn't like anything we do. She's a fussbudget.* **A la prima de Roberto no le gusta nada de lo que hacemos. Es una tiquis-miquis.**

fussy 1. delicado(-a) (delicate) ◆ *That man is very fussy; he doesn't like just anything.* ◆ *Ese señor es muy delicado; no le gusta cualquier cosa.* **2.** (bad-mannered) majadero(-a) *Mex, Cuba, U* ◆ *The child hadn't eaten and got very fussy.* ◆ *El niño no había comido y se puso majadero.*

G

gab session el cotorreo *Mex, DR, ES, Col* ◆ *They were in a constant gab session last night and didn't let anyone sleep. Estuvieron en un constante cotorreo anoche y no dejaron dormir a nadie.*

gadabout 1. (person on the go, out and about) el/la pata de perro (pata'eperro) (dog foot) *Mex, DR, Nic, Peru, Bol, Arg, Ch* ◆ *Francisca is a gadabout; she's never home. Francisca es una pata de perro; nunca está en casa.* 2. (person who likes to be at all social events and parties el perrillo de todas bodas (little dog of all weddings) *Mex, Sp* ◆ *Rodrigo is a gadabout. I see him everywhere. Rodrigo es un perrillo de todas bodas. Lo veo por todas partes.*

gag →see: trick

gaga (doting, proud) chocho(-a) *Mex, DR, PR, CR, Col, S. Cone* ◆ *He's gaga over his granddaughter. Está chocho con su nieta.*

gang 1. (group; →see also: mob) la pandilla, la banda *Mex, ES, U;* la pacotilla *G, ES, Nic, Ec;* la panda, pandilla *Col, Sp* ◆ *A gang of slackers showed up. Era una pacotilla de vagos la que llegó.* 2. (group of friends) el panal (honeycomb) *DR, Ven;* la barra (bar) *U, Arg;* la basca, basquilla *Sp;* la peña (cliff) *Sp* ◆ *I was with the whole gang drinking beer. Estuve con toda la peña tomando cerveza.* 3. (group of young people) la muchachada *Mex, DR, ES, CR, U;* la chamacada *Mex* ◆ *There was a gang of kids in the street. Había una chamacada en la calle.*

gate crasher (someone who shows up uninvited or gets in somewhere) el/la colado (-a) (passed through a sieve) *L. Am., Sp* ◆ *Do you know those people? —No, they must be gate (party) crashers. ¿Conoces a esa gente? —No, serán unos colados.*

gay (homosexual; pejorative) el maricón *L. Am., Sp;* el gay *L. Am., Sp;* el pájaro (bird) *Chicano, Cuba, DR CR;* el mariposo, el mariposón (big or male butterfly) *Chicano, Mex, DR, Col, Ch, Sp;* el chuparosa, flor (hummingbird, flower) *Chicano, Mex;* el mariposa (butterfly) *Mex, ES, Nic, Pan, Col, U, Sp*

to be **gay** (homosexual) jugar para el otro equipo (to play for the other team) *L. Am.;* ser del otro lado (bando) (to be from the other side [band]) *Chicano, Mex, DR, G, ES, Col, U, Ch;* ser de la otra banqueta (to be from the other sidewalk) *Mex, G;* ser de la otra acera (to be of the other sidewalk or row of houses on the other side) *Mex, Sp;* ser de la acera de enfrente (to be of the sidewalk in front) *Sp* ◆ *Don't tell me! Jaime is gay? ¡No me digas! ¿Jaime juega para el otro equipo?*

gazillion →see: tons

geek (turkey, introvert; →see also: bookworm, grind) el ganso (goose) *PR, S. Cone* (RVAR *Ch:* also, gansa and pavo[-a]) ◆ *What a geek! ¡Qué ganso!*

geezer (→see also: getting up there) el vejete (used for a man) *L. Am.;* la momia (mummy, male or female) *L. Am.;* el/la ruco(-a) *Mex, G, ES, Nic;* el cascarón, la cascarona (thick rind or bark) *Mex, PR;* la reliquia (relic; male or female) *Mex, Col;* la momiza (male or female) *Mex;* el pellejo (skin) *Mex;* el/la vejestorio(-a) *DR, ES, Nic, S. Cone, Sp* ◆ *That old geezer is unbearable. Esa momia es insoportable.*

to be a **gem** ser una joya (to be a jewel) *parts of L. Am.;* ser una perla (to be a pearl) *ES, Sp* ◆ *This girl is a gem; she cooks very well. Esta chica es una perla; cocina muy bien.*

geriatric set →see: geezer

Gesundheit! 1. (said after a sneeze) ¡Jesús! *L. Am., Sp;* ¡Salud! (Health!) *L. Am., Sp* 2. (said after three sneezes) ¡Jesús, María y José! *parts of L. Am., Sp*

to **get a bright idea** encendérsele el foco (to have the lightbulb turned on) *Mex, ES;* encendérsele el bombillo (to have the lightbulb turned on) *Cuba, DR, PR, Col;* encendérsele la lamparita to have the little lamp turned on *U, Arg* ◆ *Juana got a bright* *idea. A Juana se le encendió el bombillo (el foco).*

Get a hold of yourself. Tranquilo(-a). *L. Am., Sp*

to **get a move on** →see: to get moving

to **get ahead** salir adelante *L. Am., Sp* ◆ *If you learn Spanish well, you will get ahead in your work.* Si aprendes bien el español, saldrás adelante en tu trabajo.

to **get ahead (of others)** (take advantage) hacerse el vivo (to become the live one) *L. Am., Sp* ◆ *Don't try to get ahead of us (take advantage).* No te hagas el vivo.

to **get all messed up** (to get mixed up, to turn out badly) estropear *L. Am., Sp* cuatrapear *Mex* ◆ *Everything got all messed up (on me).* Todo se me estropeó.

to **get along okay** defenderse (to defend oneself) *L. Am., Sp* ◆ *I don't speak Japanese very well, but I get along okay.* No hablo bien el japonés, pero me defiendo.

to **get along well (with someone)** llevarse bien (con alguien) *L. Am., Sp* ◆ *Juana and I get along very well. We are bosom buddies.* Juana y yo nos llevamos muy bien. Somos amigas del alma.

to **get angry** (→see also: to get steamed, to get ticked off) enojarse *L. Am., Sp* ◆ *Don't get angry.* No te enojes.

to **get around** (seem to be everywhere) salir hasta en la sopa (to come up even in the soup) *L. Am., Sp;* ser como arroz blanco (to be like white rice) *most of L. Am.* ◆ *Felipe, we bump into each other again? You get around (seem to be everywhere).* Felipe, ¿otra vez nos encontramos? Me sales hasta en la sopa.

to **get balled up** →see: to get mixed up

to **get beaten down** (by troubles) aplatanarse (also, aplatanado[-a]) *Mex, Col* ◆ *Marcos has gotten beaten down and he no longer does anything.* Marcos se ha aplantanado y ya no hace nada.

to **get blasted** →see: to get wasted

to **get blood from a turnip** (get something from an improbable source) sacar agua de las piedras (to get water from stones) *Mex, Sp* ◆ *You can't get blood from a turnip.* No se puede sacar agua de las piedras.

to **get bombed** →see: to get wasted

to **get by on a shoestring** comerse un cable (to eat a cable) *Cuba, DR, PR, Pan* ◆ *I've been out of work for three months, so we're getting by on a shoestring.* Llevo tres meses sin trabajo, así que andamos comiéndonos un cable.

to **get carried away** (→see also: to go overboard, to go too far) dejarse llevar *L. Am., Sp;* agarrar viento en la camiseta (to grab wind in the T-shirt) *U, Arg;* darse manija (to give oneself a crank, pull with a string) *U, Arg* ◆ *We gave her permission to go out with her friends to dance, but she got carried away and didn't come home the whole weekend.* Le dimos permiso para salir con sus amigos a bailar, pero ella agarró viento en la camiseta y no regresó a casa en todo el fin de semana.

to **get caught up with** (be interested, enthusiastic, or curious) picarse (to become piqued) *Mex* ◆ *We got caught up with your talk because it was so interesting.* Nos picamos con tu plática tan interesante.

to **get distracted** distraerse *L. Am., Sp;* pajarear (from pájaro, bird; slang) *Mex, ES, Nic, Col, Ch* ◆ *You're getting distracted. Pay attention to me.* Estás pajareando. Hazme caso.

to **get down to brass tacks** →see: to get to the point

to **get down to business** →see: to get to the point

to **get drunk** →see: to get wasted

to **get going** →see: to get moving

to **get high** (→see also: to get wasted) colocarse (con) (to place oneself) *Mex, Sp* ◆ *I got high on two beers.* Me coloqué con dos cervezas.

to **get hot** (become heated; with anger or sexual desire) calentarse *L. Am., Sp* ◆ *Don't get hot (under the collar). Don't get turned on.* No te calientes.

to **get in a mood** (feel like doing something) darle a alguien el punto (to give someone the point) *Sp* ◆ *The other day I got in a mood and told my boss to go jump in the lake.* El otro día me dio el punto y mandé a mi jefe a freír espárragos.

to **get into a bind** (→see also: to get into hot water) meterse en un camote (to put oneself in a sweet potato) *Mex;* estar metido(-a) en un rollo (to be put in a roll) *Mex, G, Nic, Col, Ven, Ec, Peru, Sp* ◆ *I didn't have the papers that I needed and I got into a bind.* No tenía los papeles que necesitaba y me metí en un camote.

to **get into hot water** (trouble) echarse la soga al cuello (to put the rope around one's neck) *Mex, DR, PR, G, CR, Col, Ch, Sp;* meterse en Honduras (to put oneself into Honduras, meaning the country and also "the depths," literal meaning of Honduras) *Mex, Ch* ◆ *We got into hot water when we tried to help our son-in-law set up a business.* Nos metimos en Honduras cuando intentamos ayudar a nuestro yerno a establecer un negocio.

to **get it** 1. (figure out, become aware of something; →see also: to wise up) cachar (to catch) *most of L. Am.* (RVAR *Ch, Peru: also, to have sex);* caer en la cuenta (to fall into the account) *Mex, DR, PR, U, Arg, Sp;* caer en el chiste (to fall into the joke) *Mex, Sp;* caerle el veinte (to have the twenty [meaning twenty-cent coin] fall to one, as into a pay phone) *Mex* ◆ *Now I get it.* Ya me cayó el veinte. Ya caí en la cuenta. 2. (understand) agarrar la onda (to grasp the sound wave) *Mex, G, ES, Col, Ch;* agarrar el hilo (to grasp the thread) *Mex, ES, Col, Ch;* captar la onda (to capture the sound wave) *Mex, DR* ◆ *I got what Marita was implying, but I didn't answer her.* Capté la onda de lo que decía Marita, pero no le contesté.

to **get laid** →see: to have sex

Get lost! ¡Váyase (Vete) a freír espárragos! (Go fry asparagus!) *Mex, PR, ES, Ch, Sp;* ¡Váyase (Vete) a freír buñuelos! (Go fry doughnuts!) *Mex, Sp;* ¡Váyase (Vete) a la goma! (Go to the rubber, as far as rubber expands!) *Mex;* ¡Váyase a bañarse! (¡Vete a bañarte!) (Go take a bath!) *ES, Nic, Peru, Bol, Ch;* ¡Váyase (Vete) a hacer puñetas! (Go masturbate!; vulgar) PR, Sp (RVAR not considered very vulgar in *Sp*); ¡Váyase (Vete) a paseo! (Go take a walk!) *Col, Sp;* ¡Váyase (Vete) a hacer gárgaras! (Go gargle!) *Sp;* ¡Váyase (Vete) a buscar berros! (Go find watercress!) *Sp;* ¡Záfate! *Mex, G, ES, Col;* Píntate (de colores). (Paint yourself [in color].) *Mex, ES;* ¡Piérdete! (Lose yourself!) *Sp*

to **get mad** →see: to get pissed off, to get steamed, to lose it

to **get mixed up** (get confused) hacerse bolas (to get balled up) *Mex, C. Am.;* hacerse camote (to make sweet potato) *Mex;* hacerse un ocho (to make oneself into an eight) *DR, PR, Col;* hacerse un taco (to make oneself a plug) *Sp* ◆ *Here I always get mixed up with the language.* ◆ *Aquí siempre me hago bolas con el lenguaje.*

to **get mixed up with** (get involved with) enredarse con (to get tangled up with) *L. Am., Sp* enrollarse con (to get rolled up with) *DR, ES, Sp* ◆ *We got mixed up with some kids from another neighborhood.* Nos enrollamos con unos chicos de otro barrio.

to **get moving** menearse *L. Am., Sp;* ponerse las pilas (to put in one's batteries) *L. Am., Sp;* meterle mano (to put in hand) *Mex, Cuba, DR, PR, G, Col;* mover el esqueleto (to move one's skeleton) *Mex, U, Ch, Sp* ◆ *Get moving because I don't want to be late.* Menéate (Ponte las pilas), que no quiero llegar tarde.

to **get nailed** (involved in a bad situation or problem; →see also: to get into hot water) clavarse (to be nailed) *Mex, PR, U* ◆ *I trusted a friend, and I got nailed.* Confié en una amiga, y me clavé.

to **get nervous** (→see also: to be on edge) ponerse nervioso(-a) *L. Am., Sp;* ponerse de los nervios (to become of the nerves) *ES, Sp* ◆ *I got nervous when I saw that he had still not gotten home.* Me puse de los nervios cuando vi que aún no había llegado a casa.

Get off it. (Come off it. Don't exaggerate.) Bájale de crema a tus tacos. (Lower or decrease the cream in your tacos.) *Mex, Col;* Bájale de huevos a tu licuado. (Lower or decrease the eggs in your blended drink.) *Mex, ES, Col;* Bájale. (Lower it.) *Mex, ES, Col* ◆ *You don't like anything in this store? Get off it.* ¿No te gusta nada en esta tienda? Bájale de crema a tus tacos.

to **get off someone's case** dejarse de fregar (to stop scrubbing) *most of L. Am.* ◆ *Get off my (his, her, etc.) case.* Déjate de fregar.

to **get (be) on someone's back** →see: to bug, to chew out

to get some shut-eye: *He needs to get some shut-eye.*
Necesita planchar la oreja.

to **get one's foot in the door** (get into a house or business) meter el pie (to stick one's foot in) *Mex, Sp* ◆ *I've already gotten my foot in the door in the community. I'll work hard so that they will get to know me. Ya metí el pie en la comunidad. Trabajaré duro para que me conozcan.*

to **get one's way** salirse con la suya *L. Am., Sp* ◆ *Sara got her way and went with her friends to the beach without finishing her exams. Sara se salió con la suya y se fue con sus amigas a la playa sin terminar sus exámenes.*

Get out of here! (→see also: Baloney!, Get lost!) ¡Zafa! *PR* ◆ *Me Hugo's girlfriend? Get out of here! That guy is a dope. ¿Yo? ¿Novia de Hugo? ¡Zafa! Ese tipo es un sanano.*

to **get pissed off** (→see also: to get steamed, to lose it) encabronarse *Mex, PR, C. Am., many S. Am. countries, Sp;* cabrearse (to act like a goat, vulgar) *CR, Ec, Ch, Arg, Sp* ◆ *That guy gets pissed off over nothing. Ese chico se cabrea por nada.*

to **get (be) rattled** →see: to be upset with someone, to get ticked off

to **get really into something** (do something with great dedication) meter la mano hasta el codo en algo (to put one's hand up to the elbow in something) *most of L. Am., Sp* ◆ *Marina's work on that project is impeccable; she really got into it in order to get ahead. El trabajo de Marina en ese proyecto es impecable; metió la mano hasta el codo para triunfar.*

to **get red hot** (a situation; heat up) ponerse al rojo vivo *Mex, DR, PR, ES, Col* ◆ *The situation got red hot because the minister announced that they would send troops to the war. La situación se puso al rojo vivo porque el ministro anunció que mandarían tropas a la guerra.*

to **get rid of** (avoid) zafarse de *L. Am.* ◆ *Get rid of that guy. He's a real idiot. Záfate de ese tipo. Es un tonto perdido.*

to **get some shut-eye** (sleep, nap) planchar la oreja (to iron one's ear) *Mex, PR, CR, Col, Ven, Ec, Sp;* echar una pestaña (pestañeada) (to throw an eyelash [a wink]) *Mex, Ch;* aplastar la oreja (to flatten the ear) *Mex;* apolillar (from polilla, moth) *U, Arg;* sobar (to massage) *Sp* ♦ *As soon as I finish this report, I'll get some shut-eye.* Tan pronto como termine este informe, plancharé la oreja.

to **get someone into trouble** ponerle la soga al cuello (to put the rope around someone's neck) *Ch, Sp* ♦ *Who got you into trouble?* ¿Quién te puso la soga al cuello?

to **get someone out of a jam** 1. (help someone) sacarle a alguien de un apuro *L. Am., Sp* ♦ *You got me out of a jam yesterday. Thanks!* Me sacaste de un apuro ayer. ¡Gracias! 2. (help someone else out at one's own expense) sacar las castañas del fuego (to take the chestnuts out of the fire) *U, Arg, Sp* ♦ *Someone always has to get him out of a jam. If it weren't for his friends, he would already have flunked out.* Siempre tienen que sacarle las castañas del fuego. Si no fuera por sus amigos, ya estaría suspendido.

to **get someone's goat** encabronar *Mex, PR, C. Am., many S. Am. countries;* cabrear (to "goat," vulgar) *CR, Ec, Ch, Arg, Sp* ♦ *Don't get my goat.* ♦ No me cabrées.

to **get something off one's chest** →see: to tell it like it is

to **get steamed** (angry; →see also: to get pissed off, to get ticked off, to lose it) sofocarse (to get suffocated) *L. Am., Sp;* retorcer el hígado (to have one's liver twist) *Mex;* picarse (to become piqued) *PR, Col, Ch, Sp* ♦ *Don't get steamed.* No te sofoques.

to **get taken to the cleaners** (left somewhere; to lose everything) quedarse tirado (-a) (to be left cast off) *Mex, U, Arg, Sp* ♦ *When we divorced, I got taken to the cleaners because she and the kids took it all.* ♦ Cuando nos divorciamos, quedé tirado porque ella y los niños se llevaron todo.

to **get the best (from)** (take maximum advantage) sacar el jugo (to take out the juice) *L. Am., Sp* ♦ *Hernán got the best from his vacation.* ♦ Hernán le sacó el jugo a sus vacaciones.

to **get the heck out** →see: to take off

to **get the picture** (have a clear understanding of some situation) tener clara la película (to have the movie or film clear) *Peru, S. Cone, Sp* ♦ *Now we get the picture* about the political situation in this country. Ahora tenemos clara la película sobre la situación política en este país.

to **get (be) ticked off** (→see also: to get pissed off, to get steamed, to lose it) hacerse mala sangre (to make bad blood for oneself) *L. Am., Sp;* agitarse *Mex, DR, G, ES, Col* ♦ *Don't get ticked off. It's not so awful.* No te hagas mala sangre. No es tan tremendo.

to **get to the bottom of something** tocar fondo (to touch bottom) *L. Am., Sp* ♦ *We have to investigate the situation until we get to the bottom of it.* ♦ *Tenemos que investigar la situación hasta tocar fondo.*

to **get to the point** ir al grano (to go to the grain) *L. Am., Sp;* dejarse de cuentos (to leave off with the stories) *L. Am., Sp;* ir al rollo (to go to the roll) *Mex, ES* ♦ *Don't talk so much. Get to the point and tell me the truth.* No hables tanto. Ve al grano y dime la verdad.

to **get tripped up** (hit the pavement) besar el diablo (to kiss the devil) *Mex, ES* ♦ *Watch where you're walking, or you're going to get tripped up.* Ten cuidado cómo andas, o vas a besar el diablo.

to **get up on the wrong side of the bed** (have a day of bad luck or be in a bad mood) levantarse con el pie izquierdo (to get up with the left foot) *L. Am., Sp* ♦ *Today I got up on the wrong side of the bed. First I lost my keys and then I had a fight with my wife.* Hoy me levanté con el pie izquierdo. Primero perdí las llaves y después peleé con mi esposa.

to **get wasted** (drunk) picarse (to become piqued) *Mex, PR, G, Nic;* rascarse (to scratch oneself) *CR, Col, Ven;* ajumarse *Cuba, DR, PR;* echarse una mona encima (andar con la mona) (to throw a monkey on oneself [walk with the monkey]) *Cuba, Ch, Arg;* coger una trompa (to grab an elephant's trunk) *Sp;* entromparse *Sp* ♦ *Drink just one beer; don't get wasted by drinking more.* Toma sólo una cerveza; no te piques con más.

to **get while the getting is good** (take advantage of confusion or disorder and profit from it) pescar en río revuelto (to fish in a turbulent river) *Mex, DR, Sp* ♦ *They decided to get while the getting was good.* Decidieron pescar en río revuelto.

to **get with it** 1. (get going, get a move on) ponerse las pilas (to put in one's batteries) *L. Am., Sp* ◆ *She got with it and got her transfer to South America.* Se puso las pilas y logró que la trasladaran a América del Sur. 2. (become aware) agarrar la onda (to grasp the sound wave) *Mex, G, ES, Col, Ch*; ponerse al hilo (en onda) (to put oneself on the thread [sound wave]) *Mex, Hond, ES, CR, Col* ◆ *Let's get with it.* Pongámonos al hilo.

Get with the program. (Get a hold of yourself.; said when someone is acting inappropriately for the circumstances) Ubícate. (Find yourself.) *Mex, DR, Col, Peru, S. Cone*; Recógete. (Pick yourself up.) *Mex, PR, Col*

to **get with the program** →see: to get with it, to pay attention

to **get (be) worked up** →see: to be steamed, to get steamed, to lose it, upset

to be getting up there 1. (old in years; →see also: geezer, over the hill) estar entrado(-a) en años (to be entered into years, euphemism) *L. Am., Sp*; tener abriles (to have Aprils) *L. Am., Sp* ◆ *How old is Facundo? —I don't know, but he's getting up there.* ¿Cuántos años tiene Facundo? —No lo sé, pero ya está entrado en años. ◆ *She's getting up there, but she's pretty.* Tiene sus abriles, pero es bonita. 2. (old-fashioned; →see also: old-fashioned) ser una carroza (to be a carriage, a bit of a fogie; describing someone middle-aged who tries to be young) *Mex, Sp* ◆ *Felipe is getting up there (a bit of a fogie).* Felipe es una carroza.

get-together (→see also: bash) la quedada *Sp* ◆ *They're going to organize a get-together this weekend.* Van a organizar una quedada el fin de semana.

getup (ridiculous dress, outfit) la facha *L. Am., Sp* ◆ *You can't go to the disco in that getup.* Con esa facha no puedes entrar en la disco.

gibberish →see: baloney, hot air

gigolo (man who lives off women; →see also: playboy, womanizer) el chulo *DR, PR, Pan, Col, Ven, Sp* ◆ *Felipe is a gigolo; he never works.* Felipe es un chulo; nunca trabaja.

to **gild the lily** →see: to present a pretty picture

to **give (someone) a hand** echar una mano (also, dar una mano) *L. Am., Sp*; echar una manopla (to put in a big helping hand) *Mex, Col* ◆ *Give us a hand and we'll finish the work sooner.* Échanos una manopla y terminaremos el trabajo más temprano.

to **give a lift** (to someone's mood; →see also: give a ride [lift]) levantar el ánimo (to raise the spirit) *L. Am., Sp*; dar marcha (to give march) *Sp* ◆ *That music gives me a real lift.* Esa música me da mucha marcha.

to **give a ride** (from one place to another) llevar (a alguien a alguna parte) *L. Am., Sp*; dar un aventón *Mex, ES, Nic*; dar un jalón *G, ES, CR, Peru*; dar pon *PR, Col, Sp* ◆ *They took me (gave me a ride) to the store.* Me llevaron a la tienda. ◆ *I gave them a ride.* Les di un aventón.

to **give a ticket** (fine) multar *L. Am., Sp*; meter un paquete (to put in a package, slang) *Sp* ◆ *They gave her a ticket for one hundred euros for not wearing a motorcycle helmet.* Le metieron un paquete de cien euros por no llevar el casco de la moto.

give and take (back and forth negotiations) tira y afloja (pull and give slack) *Mex, Peru, S. Cone, Sp* ◆ *Ana and Leandro's divorce was very sad. They spent years in negotiations back and forth without resolving anything.* El divorcio de Ana y Leandro fue muy triste. Por años se pasaron en tira y afloja sin resolver nada.

to **give birth** dar a luz (to give to light) *L. Am., Sp* ◆ *My wife gave birth today at three in the morning.* Mi esposa dio a luz hoy a las tres de la mañana.

to **give condolences** (express one's sympathy) dar el pésame (to give the "it weighs on me") *L. Am., Sp* ◆ *We have to go give our condolences to Mrs. García and her family.* Tenemos que ir a dar el pésame a la señora García y su familia.

to **give hell to** (→see also: to give someone a damn hard time) armarle una de todos los diablos (to make one of all the devils) *L. Am., Sp*; armarle un sanquentín (to make one a Saint Quentin) *Mex* ◆ *The bride's father gave the groom hell.* El papá de la novia le armó un sanquintín al novio.

Give him (her) an inch and he'll (she'll) take a mile. Le da el pie y le toma hasta la mano. *(You give him your foot and he takes even your hand.)* L. Am., Sp; **Le da la mano y se agarra hasta el codo.** (You give him or her your hand and he or she takes even your elbow.) *ES, S. Cone, Sp*

to **give in (give up)** darse por vencido(-a) *L. Am., Sp;* **aflojar** (to loosen up) *L. Am., Sp;* **rajarse** (to split, slang) *Mex, Cuba, DR, ES, Col, Peru, U, Sp;* **amilanarse** (slang) *G, S. Cone, Sp;* **achicarse** (to get small, slang) *S. Cone, Sp;* **arrugarse** (to wrinkle up, get wrinkled, slang) *Sp* ◆ *I give in.* **Me doy por vencida.** ◆ *Don't give up.* **No te rajes.**

to **give in to (something)** (go along with something) alcahuetear (to procure, pimp) *Mex, DR, ES, Col, Ch* ◆ *That boy is a spoiled brat because his parents give in to him on everything.* **Ese niño es un malcriado porque sus padres le alcahuetean todo.**

Give it a rest. Let's have some peace. Tengamos la fiesta en paz. (Let's have the party in peace.) *DR, ES, Sp* ◆ *Let's not talk about this anymore. Give it a rest.* **No discutamos más. Tengamos la fiesta en paz.**

Give it all you've got! (for instance, at a sports event) ¡Échale ganas! (Put in will!) *Mex, ES;* **¡Échale lo que hay que echarle!** (Put in what has to be put in!) *Sp* ◆ *Give it all you've got! That way you'll finish your homework earlier.* **¡Échale ganas! Así terminas tus tareas más temprano.**

to **give it one's all** (apply oneself; →see also: to work like a dog) darle (duro) (to give to it [hard]) *Mex, DR, C. Am., S. Cone* Give it your all! ◆ *¡Dale duro!*

to **give it (some) time** (to be patient, wait for an opportunity) dar tiempo al tiempo (to give time to time) *Mex, DR, PR, ES, Ch* ◆ *Give it some time and you'll see that things will work out.* **Dale tiempo al tiempo y verás cómo se resuelven las cosas.**

Give me five (fingers). Dame. Dame cinco dedos. *Mex*

Give me five! Put it here! (said in greeting before a handshake) ¡Chócala! (Hit it!) *Mex, DR, PR, Col, U, Sp* ◆ *Give me five, bro'! How're you doing?* **¡Chócala, mi hermano! ¿Cómo estás?**

to **give notice** avisar *L. Am., Sp;* dar un toque (to give touch) *Sp* ◆ *They gave us notice that we should evacuate the building.* **Nos dieron un toque de que debíamos evacuar el edificio.**

to **give someone a damn hard time** joderle a alguien (to screw or bother someone, vulgar) *L. Am., Sp;* hacerla de pedo a alguien (to make someone of the fart, vulgar) *Mex, ES;* hincharle las pelotas a alguien (to inflate somone's balls, vulgar) *Ch, Arg, U, Sp;* romperle los huevos a alguien (to break someone's eggs [testicles], vulgar) *U, Arg;* traer de culo a alguien (to bring someone by the ass, vulgar) *Sp;* tocar los cojones (huevos) a alguien (to touch someone's testicles, vulgar) *Sp;* hacer la puñeta a alguien (vulgar) *Sp;* putearle a alguien *Sp* ◆ *Don't give me such a damn hard time.* **No me jodas.** *(No me rompas los huevos.)*

to **give someone a dressing down** →see: to chew out, rip apart

to **give someone a hard time** (→see also: to bug, to rile up, to upset someone) darle lata a alguien (to give someone tin can) *L. Am., Sp;* hostigarle a alguien *most of L. Am., Sp;* jorobarle a alguien (to screw around with someone, euphemism for **joder**) *Mex, Cuba, DR, PR, G, CR;* buscarle las pulgas a alguien (to look for someone's fleas) *Mex, Cuba, Sp;* hacerla de tos a alguien (to make someone of the cough) *Mex, ES;* puyarle a alguien (to jab someone) *C.Am, Col;* tocar las narices a alguien (to touch someone's noses) *Sp* ◆ *These neighbors never stop giving us a hard time.* **Estos vecinos no paran de darnos lata.**

to **give someone a lemon** (deceive someone, giving them something inferior) dar (pasar) gato por liebre (to give [pass] cat for rabbit) *L. Am., Sp* ◆ *The camera I bought Monday is already broken; I think I got a lemon.* **La cámara que compré el lunes ya se estropeó; creo que me dieron gato por liebre.**

to **give someone a pat on the back** →see: to pat on the back

to **give someone a piece of one's mind** (say what one really thinks, often used in anger; →see also: to set someone straight, to tell it like it is) decir cuatro cosas (to tell four things) *DR, PR, ES, Nic, Ec, Peru, Ch;* decir a alguien (las) cuatro verdades (to tell someone the four truths) *DR, PR, ES, Ch, Sp;* cantar a alguien las cuarenta (to sing the forty to someone) *Ec, Peru, Ch, Arg, Sp;* can-

to give someone a lemon: *When he bought the hat, they gave him a lemon.*
Cuando compró el sombrero, le dieron gato por liebre.

tar la justa (la pura) (to sing the just [the pure]) *U, Arg* ◆ *I was so mad that I gave her a piece of my mind and told her to go to the devil.* Estaba tan enojada que le dije cuatro cosas y la mandé al diablo.

to **give someone gray hair** (make them despair) sacar canas verdes (to bring out green canas, gray hairs) *L. Am.* ◆ *Those kids are giving me gray hair.* Esos niños me sacan canas verdes.

to **give someone his (her) walking papers** (to break off with someone) dar pasaporte a alguien (to give someone passport) *Mex, ES, Sp;* dar el boleto a alguien (to give someone the ticket) *Mex, ES* ◆ *We gave the secretary her walking papers because she wasn't doing her job.* Le dimos pasaporte a la secretaria porque no estaba haciendo su trabajo.

to **give someone lip** (talk back unjustifiably when reprimanded) ser respondón, respondona *Mex, Sp* ◆ *"Don't give me any lip,"* Juanito's dad said to him. "No seas respondón", le dijo su papá a Juanito.

to **give someone something on a silver platter** ponerle algo en (una) charola de plata (to put something on a silver platter for someone) *Mex, ES, Bol, S. Cone* (RVᴀʀ *S. Cone:* en bandeja de plata) ◆ *They gave Rogelio an offer for international work on a silver platter.* A Rogelio le pusieron en bandeja de plata una propuesta de trabajo en el exterior.

to **give someone the cold shoulder** (go out of one's way to avoid someone) darle (un) esquinazo a alguien (to hit someone with a corner) *Arg, Sp;* darle hielo a alguien (to give someone ice) *Mex, Cuba, DR, Ch* ◆ *I saw that jerk of a professor walking down the street, but I gave him the cold shoulder.* Vi a ese profesor tan pesado en la calle, pero le di esquinazo. ◆ *I went up to greet him very nicely and the guy gave me the cold shoulder. I don't know what I did to him.* Yo fui a saludarlo muy simpática y el tipo me hizo un hielo. No sé qué le hice.

to **give someone the creeps** (from fear) poner a alguien los pelos de punta (to put someone's hairs on end) *L. Am., Sp* (RVar *Sp:* also, **parar los pelos de punta**) ♦ *Jorge told me what had happened to him and it gave me the creeps. Jorge me contó lo que le había pasado y se me pusieron los pelos de punta.*

to **give someone the lowdown** (→see also: to air dirty laundry) **sacar los trapos al sol** (to take the rags or clothes out into the sun) *L. Am., Sp* ♦ *Give me the lowdown, Matilde. What went on between Juan and Julia? Saca los trapos al sol, Matilde. ¿Qué pasó entre Juan y Julia?*

to **give (someone) the shaft** →see: to do in, to screw

to **give tit for tat** **pagar con la misma moneda** (to pay with the same currency) *L. Am., Sp* ♦ *She behaved very badly, and now they're giving her tit for tat. Ella se portó muy mal, y ahora le están pagando con la misma moneda.*

to **give up** (→see: to back down, to give in, to throw in the towel)

to **give up the ghost** →see: to kick the bucket, to pass away

Give you an inch and you take a mile. **Te dan pon y ya quieres guiar.** (They give you a ride and you already want to steer, meaning take over.) *PR*

glamour boy (→see also: playboy) **el bacán** (controller of a woman who earns money for him, from Lunfardo, Buenos Aires slang) *S. Cone* ♦ *Look at that shallow glamour boy; he has the newest model Mercedes Benz. Mirá que hombre tan bacán; tiene un Mercedes Benz último modelo.*

gluttonous →see:eating like a horse

Go! (at a sports event) **¡Aupa!** *Sp* ♦ *Go, Armstrong! Let's see if you win the race. ¡Aupa, Armstrong! A ver si ganas la carrera.*

to **go all out** (try everything in times of trouble) **bajar a todos los santos** (to get all the saints down, as if to pray to all of them at once) *Mex, ES* ♦ *What a big problem! We're going to go all out to try to solve it. ¡Qué problema más grande! Vamos a bajar a todos los santos para tratar de resolverlo.*

to **go all the way with something** →see: to get really into something

to **go all to to hell** (to fail; →see also: to go to the devil, to wash out) **irse al (para el)** **carajo** (to go to the **carajo**, male organ; vulgar) *Mex, DR, PR, ES, U, Sp* ♦ *The business went all to hell a year later. La empresa se fue al carajo un año después.*

to **go along with others** (do whatever is appropriate) **bailar al son que le tocan** (to dance to the sound that is played) *L. Am., Sp* ♦ *Esteban always goes along with others. Esteban siempre baila al son que le tocan.*

to **go along with everything** (always agree) **decir amén a todo** (to say amen to everything) *DR, ES, S. Cone, Sp* ♦ *She doesn't like problems: she always goes along with everything. A ella no le gustan los problemas: siempre dice amén a todo.*

to **go along with someone** (agree with) **seguirle a alguien la corriente** (to follow someone's current) *Mex, DR, ES, Nic, S. Cone, Sp* ♦ *This girl is crazy. It's better to go along with her and not argue. Esta chica está loca. Es mejor seguirle la corriente y no discutir con ella.*

Go away! →see: Get lost!

to **go ballistic** →see: to lose it

to **go bananas** →see: to lose it

to **go bar-hopping** **hacer el viacrucis** (to do the stations of the cross, a religious event) *Sp* ♦ *We went bar-hopping in Madrid. Hicimos el viacrucis en Madrid.*

to **go berzerk** →see: to flip out

to **go beyond the limit** →see: to go overboard, to go too far

to **go dutch** **salir a la americana** (to go out American style) *Mex;* **hacer (un) serrucho** *DR, PR;* **salir a la inglesa** (to go out English style) *Peru, Bol, Ch, Arg;* **ir miti-miti** (to go half-half, like the old expression to "go halfsies") *S. Cone;* **salir a escote** *Sp* ♦ *We always go dutch. Siempre salimos a la americana.*

Go figure. **Vaya uno a saber.** (Go to know.) *L. Am., Sp;* **Vaya usted (Vete) a saber.** (Go to know.) *Peru, Bol, Sp*

Go for it! **¡Córrele!** *Mex, ES, Col;* **¡Llégale!** (Get to it!) *Mex, ES, Col*

to **go from bad to worse** (→see also: to go from the frying pan to the fire) **ir de mal en peor** *L. Am., Sp;* **salir de Guatemala para entrar en Guatepeor** (to go from Guatemala [meaning "bad"] to Guatepeor [meaning "worse"]) *L. Am., Sp;* **entrar bizco y salir cojo** (to come in cross-eyed and leave crippled) *parts of L. Am.* ◆ *Since my daughter has had a boyfriend, things have gone from bad to worse.* **Desde que mi hija tiene novio, las cosas van de mal en peor.**

to **go from the frying pan to the fire** (→see also: to go from bad to worse) huir del fuego y caer en las brasas (to flee the fire and fall into the coals) *L. Am., Sp;* escapar del trueno y dar con el relámpago (to escape the thunder and face or get hit by the lightning) *PR, Sp* ◆ *Antonio went from the frying pan into the fire when he fell in love with his friend's girlfriend.* **Antonio huyó del fuego y cayó en las brazas cuando se enamoró de la novia de su amigo.**

to **go full-speed ahead** ir viento en popa (to go wind at the stern) *L. Am., Sp* ◆ *My business is going full-speed ahead.* **El negocio me va viento en popa.**

to **go flying off** (go quickly) ir volando *Mex, G, ES, S. Cone, Sp* ◆ *Let me have me two more minutes and I'll go flying off to pick you up.* **Déjame dos minutos más y voy volando a recogerte.**

to **go halfsies** (→see also: to go dutch) ir miti-miti (to go half-half) *S. Cone* ◆ *Let's split the bill (like the old expression "go halfsies").* **Vamos miti-miti con la cuenta.**

to **go into the lion's den** meterse en la boca del lobo (to put oneself in the wolf's mouth) *L. Am., Sp* ◆ *You're crazy if you go there. Do you want to go into the lion's den?* **Estás loco si vas allí. ¿Te quieres meter en la boca del lobo?**

to **go like a shot** ir hecho(-a) bala (to go made into a bullet) *Mex, G, Ch;* irse como bala (to go like a bullet) *Para, U, Arg* ◆ *I went like a shot to the hospital.* **Me fui como bala al hospital.**

to **go off one's rocker** →see: to flip out, to go too far

to **go off the deep end** →see: to go too far

to **go on a bender** →see: to get wasted

to **go on a (drug/alcohol) trip** agarrar el avión (to grab the plane) *Mex, ES;* estar en pleno vuelo (to be in full flight) *Mex, Col, Ec* ◆ *You heard about Julián; he went on another drug (alcohol) trip.* **Ya supiste de Julián; volvió a agarrar el avión.**

to **go on and on** (repeat ad nauseam) repetirlo hasta el cansancio (to repeat it until tiredness) *DR, PR, S. Cone, Sp* ◆ *He went on and on about how I should get home early.* **Me repitió hasta el cansancio que llegara a casa temprano.**

to **go out like a light** (fall asleep; →see also: to crash, to hit the sack) clavar el pico (to nail the beak) *Mex, CR, Col, U;* quedarse frito(-a) (to be fried) *U, Arg, Sp;* quedarse sopa (to be soup) *Sp* ◆ *The child went to his room and immediately went out like a light.* **El niño fue a su cuarto y clavó el pico de inmediato.** ◆ *After eating, I always go out like a light.* ◆ *Después de comer, siempre me quedo frito.*

to **go out on a limb** aventarse (to throw oneself) *Mex, DR, ES, Nic, Peru* ◆ *Don't go out on a limb . . . It's not worth it to take a risk.* **No te aventes... no vale la pena arriesgarte.**

to **go out on the town** (→see also: to have a blast, to have a good time, to live it up, to party) ir de juerga *L. Am., Sp;* ir de parranda *L. Am., Sp;* emparrandarse *Mex, G, Col;* irse (andar) de farra *Col, Ec, S. Cone, Sp* ◆ *Last night I went out on the town and now I'm very tired.* **Anoche fui de juerga y ahora estoy muy cansada.**

to **go over the top** →see: to go too far

to **go overboard** (do something abnormal; →see also: to go too far) salirse de las casillas (to go out of one's boxes) *L. Am., Sp;* salirse de madre en algo (to go out of the mother in something) *Mex, Sp;* salirse del guacal (to go out of one's container) *Mex, ES* ◆ *You're going overboard.* **Te estás saliendo de madre.**

to **go (somewhere) without having to pay** ir de gorra, ir de gorrón *Mex, ES* ◆ *Paco always says he doesn't have money and goes places without paying.* **Paco siempre dice que no tiene dinero y va de gorra.**

to **go steady** andar de novios (to go as [be] boyfriend and girlfriend) *L. Am., Sp* ◆ *Felipe and Carmen are going steady.* **Felipe y Carmen andan de novios.**

to **go (swim) against the current** ir (nadar) contra la corriente *L. Am., Sp* ◆ *Berta goes against the current just to upset people.* **Berta nada contra la corriente solamente para molestar.**

to **go the way of all flesh** →see: to pass away

to **go to a lot of trouble to...** hacer mil maromas para... (to do a thousand acrobatic tricks in order to . . .) *most of L. Am., Sp* ♦ *I have gone to a lot of trouble to be able to see you.* He hecho mil maromas para verte.

to **go to bat for** (intervene on behalf of) echar un capote (echar la capa) (to throw a cape, as at a bullfight) *Sp* ♦ *Thanks for going to bat for me because I didn't know what to say to him.* Gracias por echarme un capote porque yo no sabía qué decirle.

to **go to bat for someone** (defend someone openly) sacar la cara por alguien (to bring or take out one's face for someone) *Mex, S. Cone, Sp* ♦ *The only one who went to bat for me when I had a fight with my boss was Tomás; the others didn't say a thing.* El único que sacó la cara por mí cuando me peleé con mi jefe fue Tomás; los demás no dijeron nada.

Go to hell! (all vulgar:) ¡Váyase (Vete) a la porra! (Go to the pot!) *L. Am., Sp;* ¡Váyase (Vete) al carajo! (Go to the male organ!) *L. Am., Sp;* ¡Váyase (Vete) a la mierda! (Go to shit!) *L. Am., Sp;* ¡Váyase (Vete) a la jodida! *Chicano, Mex, G;* ¡Váyase (Vete) a la chingada! (Go to the chingada, a violated woman) *Mex, C. Am.;* ¡Váyase (Vete) a la verga! (Go to the male organ!) *ES, Nic, Ven*

to **go to hell in a handbasket (or handcart)** →see: to go all to hell, to go to the devil, to wash out

to **go to one's reward** →see: to pass away

to **go to some damn godforsaken spot** (far away, vulgar) irse a la chingada (to go to the chingada, violated woman) *Mex, C. Am.* ♦ *Ernesto? He went to some damn godforsaken spot.* ¿Ernesto? Se fue a la chingada.

Go to the devil! ¡Váyase (Vete) al cuerno, a la eme! (Go to the horn, to the "m," which stands for mierda, shit!) *Mex, DR, PR, ES, Peru, S. Cone, Sp;* ¡Váyase (Vete) al demonio! (Go to the devil!) *Mex, G, Col, ES*

to **go to the devil** (fail; →see also: to come to nothing, to go all to hell, to wash up) llevarse el demonio (to be taken by the devil) *Mex, Sp;* llevarse el diablo (to be taken by the devil) *Mex, DR* ♦ *If we don't work seriously, this business is going to go to the devil.*

Si no trabajamos en serio, a este negocio se lo va a llevar el demonio.

to **go to the john** (go to the bathroom; →see also: to make a pit stop) hacer sus necesidades (una necesidad) (to do one's necessities [a necessity], euphemism) *DR, C. Am., U* ♦ *Just a second; I have to go to the john.* Espera un segundo; tengo que hacer mis necesidades.

to **go to the last resort** quemar el último cartucho (to burn the last cartridge) *L. Am., Sp;* jugar la última carta (to play the last card) *Mex, Arg, U, Sp* ♦ *No one dared to go to the last resort and the project failed.* Nadie se atrevió a quemar el último cartucho y el proyecto fracasó.

to **go too far 1.** (do or say something extraordinary or ridiculous) botar la bola (pelota), botarla (to throw away the ball) *Mex, Cuba, DR, PR;* ponerse borde *Sp* ♦ *Martín is a fool, but Rafaelito really went too far!* Martín es un tonto, ¡pero Rafaelito botó la bola! **2.** (get a bit out of control) darse un atracón (to give oneself a big assault) *Mex, DR, ES, Ch, Sp;* desmadrar (to dismother) *PR, ES, Sp* ♦ *That girl was very shy, but she's going too far lately.* Esa chica era muy tímida, pero se está desmadrando últimamente. **3.** (→see also: to go overboard) pasarse de la raya (to go over the line) *Mex, DR, PR, ES, S. Cone, Sp;* pasarse de rosca (to pass oneself as doughnut) *Mex, Sp* ♦ *My dad went too far by not giving me permission to go to the party.* Mi papá se pasó de rosca al no darme permiso para ir a la fiesta. **4.** (overdo it) pasársele la mano (to have your hand slip on you) *L. Am., Sp* ♦ *I'm sorry. I went too far.* Lo siento. Se me pasó la mano.

to **go (very) far** ir (muy) lejos *L. Am., Sp* ♦ *Because he has struggled hard and worked a great deal, Bernardo will go very far.* Porque ha luchado y trabajado mucho, Bernardo va a ir muy lejos.

to **go with the prevailing wind** (opinions, ideas) irse con el viento que corre (dejarse llevar por el viento que corre) *Mex, Sp* ♦ *They go with the prevailing wind. They don't have any judgment of their own.* Se dejan llevar por el viento que corre. No tienen criterio propio.

to **go with the winner** (serve and flatter the most powerful) arrimarse al sol que más calienta (to put oneself by the sun that heats the most) *Mex, Sp* ◆ *Elena is very opportunistic; she always goes with the winner.* **Elena es muy oportunista; siempre se arrima al sol que más calienta.**

to **go without saying** (to be obvious) caer de cajón (also, ser de cajón) (to fall like a drawer) *Mex, Hond, Nic, Ven, Ec, Peru, S. Cone, Sp* ◆ *It goes without saying that Gloria is in love with Hector.* **Cae de cajón que Gloria está enamorada de Héctor.**

goat →to get someone's goat

gobs →see: tons

God damn it (to hell)! (all vulgar:) ¡Puta madre! (Mother whore!) *Mex, C. Am., S. Cone;* ¡Puta la huevada (güea)! (Whore the bunch of testicles!) *Ch;* ¡Hostia(s)! (Host[s]!, religious reference) *Sp;* ¡Hostia puta! (Host whore!, religious reference) *Sp;* ¡Me cago en la puta (diez, leche)! (I shit on the whore [ten, milk]!, very vulgar) *Sp;* ¡Me cago en Dios! (I shit on God!, very strong) *Sp* ◆ *God damn it! They stole my wallet!* ¡Hostia puta! ¡Me han robado la billetera!

God forbid! ¡Dios guarde! ¡Dios libre! *Mex, DR, PR, CR, ES, Col* ◆ *The baby sick? God forbid!* ¿El bebé enfermo? Ay, ¡Dios guarde!

God knows. Sabe Dios. *most of L. Am., Sp*

God willing. Si Dios quiere. (If God wants. Often used when an action is proposed or some statement of optimism is made.) *L. Am., Sp;* Primero Dios. (First God.) *Mex, C. Am.* ◆ *We're going to buy a bigger house, God willing.* Vamos a comprar una casa más grande, si Dios quiere.

to be a **go-getter** (getting ahead) ser muy vivo(-a) (to be very clever) *L. Am., Sp* ◆ *These immigrants have been real go-getters; they have their own house and various properties that they rent out.* Estos inmigrantes han sido muy vivos; tienen su propia casa y varias propiedades que alquilan.

to be **going around in circles** (any which way) andar como bola sin manija (to go around like a ball without a string) *Para, U, Arg,* ◆ *Tomorrow I leave for Spain, so today I'm going around in circles.* Mañana salgo para España, así que hoy ando como bola sin manija.

to be **going great** marchar requete bien *Mex, G, Para, U, Arg, Sp;* ir/marchar sobre ruedas (to go on wheels) *Mex, DR, PR, ES, Nic, Col, Ch, Sp* ◆ *Everything is going great.* Todo anda (marcha) sobre ruedas.

going great guns →see: full blast, like a shot, on the fly, quick as lightning

to be **good at** →see: to be a whiz at something

good deal 1. (lucky break, stroke of luck) el chollo *Sp* ◆ *Look what a good deal this girl has had; she just finished her studies and she's already found a job.* Mira qué chollo ha tenido esta chica; acaba de terminar la carrera y ya ha encontrado un trabajo. **2.** (thing, idea) buena onda (good sound wave) *L. Am., Sp* ◆ *That business is a good deal.* Ese negocio es muy buena onda.

good egg (person) buena gente (good people) *L. Am., Sp;* buena onda (good sound wave) *L. Am., Sp;* un chile de todos los moles (a chili pepper for all sauces) *Mex* ◆ *Miriam is a good egg; we can always count on her.* Miriam es un chile de todos los moles; siempre podemos contar con ella.

good-for-nothing →see: to be useless, loser, slacker

to be **good for nothing** →see: to be useless, to be worthless

Good grief! (→see also: Darn!, Holy smoke!, Wow!) ¡Qué barbaridad! (What barbarity!) *L. Am., Sp;* ¡Qué bárbaro! (How barbarous!) *L. Am., Sp;* ¡Rayos! (Lightning rays!; a bit old-fashioned) *L. Am., Sp;* ¡Válgame Dios! *L. Am., Sp* ◆ *Good grief! We missed the plane!* ¡Qué barbaridad! ¡Perdimos el avión!

good looking →see: to be an eyeful, cute

to be a **good match** (for marriage) ser un buen partido *L. Am., Sp* ◆ *You should marry Julián. He's a good match.* Debes casarte con Julián. Es un buen partido.

to be **good-natured** ser un pan (to be a loaf of bread) *Mex, Cuba, DR;* ser un pedazo de pan (to be a piece of bread) *DR, PR, U, Arg, Sp;* ser (un) pan de Dios (to be God's bread) *DR, ES, U, Ch* ◆ *Luz is good-natured. She always helps me when I have problems.* Luz es un pan. Siempre me ayuda cuando tengo problemas.

Good riddance! (for people or things) ¡Buen viaje! (Have a good trip!) *Mex, U, Arg, Sp* ◆ *So she doesn't want to go to the club with us? Good riddance! ¿Que no quiere ir al club con nosotras? ¡Buen viaje!*

goody-goody →see: goody two-shoes

goody two-shoes el santurrón, la santurrona *L. Am.* (RVAR *parts of the Americas:* santulón, santulona); el santito (little saint) *DR, ES, Col, U, Arg* ◆ *What's that goody two-shoes of a cousin of yours want? ¿Qué quiere ese santurrón de tu primo?*

to **goof around** →see: to joke around

goof-off →see: slacker

to **goof off** →see: to not lift a finger

goof-up →see: screw-up

to **goof up** →see: to blow it, to screw up

goofball →see: fool, idiot, stupid

to be **goofing off** (fooling around or acting silly) estar papando (cachando) moscas (to be swallowing [catching] flies) *Mex, U* ◆ *They're goofing off instead of studying for their exams. Están papando moscas en lugar de estudiar para los exámenes.*

gorilla (barbaric or very big person) el gorila *Mex, G* ◆ *A gorilla came in and started yelling at the manager. Entró un gorila y empezó a gritarle al gerente.*

gossip (person who gossips; →see also: blabbermouth, busybody) el/la chismoso(-a) *L. Am., Sp;* chambroso(-a) (slang) *Mex, ES;* el/la copuchento(-a) (slang) *Bol, Ch;* el/la cotilla (slang) *Sp* ◆ *You're a real gossip. How can you look in my purse and then tell your friends about it? Eres realmente un cotilla. ¿Cómo puedes estar mirando dentro de mi bolso y después contarlo a tus amigos?*

to **gossip** chismear *L. Am., Sp;* copuchar (to puff up cheeks, slang) *Bol, Ch* ◆ *You guys were there gossiping the whole afternoon. Estaban allí copuchando toda la tarde.*

gossips las malas lenguas (bad tongues) *L. Am., Sp* ◆ *The gossips say she stole money from her parents. Dicen las malas lenguas que ella robó dinero de sus padres.*

gourmand (person who loves food) el/la boquisabroso(-a) (slang) *Mex, Col* ◆ *I'm a gourmand. I love trying exotic foods. Yo soy un* boquisabroso. *Me encanta probar comidas exóticas.*

grabby (person) el/la gandalla *Mex, ES* ◆ *Give him back his watch; don't be so grabby. Entrégale el reloj; no seas gandalla.*

grapevine →see: rumormill

grass (marijuana; →see also: joint) la grifa *Chicano, Mex, CR, Ec;* la mota *Chicano, Mex, PR, G;* de la verde (of the green) *Mex, Col;* la hierba (grass) *Mex, Cuba, DR, G, Sp* ◆ *Stop smoking grass, man. Deja de fumar hierba, hombre.*

grease monkey (car lover) el tuerca (metal nut in mechanics) *S. Cone* ◆ *Ricardo and his friends are grease monkeys, and they spend the weekends fixing up their cars. Ricardo y sus amigos son tuercas y pasan los fines de semana arreglando sus coches.*

great →see: super

Great to see you. Dichosos los ojos que te están viendo (que te ven). (Also, Dichosos los ojos.) (Fortunate the eyes that are looking at you.) *L. Am., Sp* ◆ *Hi, Susana! It's been a long time since we've seen each other. Great to see you. ¡Hola, Susana! Hace mucho que no nos vemos. Dichosos los ojos.*

the **greatest** →see: super

to be the **greatest** (the best) ser lo máximo (to be the maximum) *L. Am.* ◆ *This music is the greatest! ¡Esta música es lo máximo!*

to be **Greek** (incomprehensible) estar en chino (to be in Chinese) *Mex, DR, CR, Col, Peru, Bol, Ch, Arg, Sp* ◆ *This book looks like it's in Greek. I don't understand squat. Este libro parece que está en chino. No entiendo ni jota.*

to be a **greenhorn** (innocent or immature, not socially active) estar muy verde (to be very green) *S. Cone, Sp* ◆ *María Eugenia is a greenhorn and doesn't want to come to these get-togethers. María Eugenia está muy verde y no quiere asistir a estas reuniones.*

the **Grim Reaper** (death) la pelona (the bald one) *Mex, C. Am.;* la calaca *Mex, ES;* la calva (the bald one) *Cuba, G, ES, Col* ◆ *If you don't take care of your health, the Grim Reaper will take you. Se no se cuida la salud, se lo va a llevar la calaca.*

Grin and bear it. Como dijo Herodes... (As Herod said . . . [last part is vulgar: te jodes, meaning "You're screwed.") *Mex, DR, Sp;* Ajo y agua. (Garlic and water. [short for **A joder y aguantar.** You're screwed and you have to put up with it, vulgar.) *Sp* (RVar *S. Cone:* Agua y ajo.) ◆ *I can go back to my country, but you all: Grin and bear it.* Yo puedo volver a mi país, pero ustedes: Ajo y agua.

grind (serious student who studies a lot) el/la cuadernícola (from cuaderno, notebook) *most of L. Am.;* el empollón, la empollona *G, Sp* ◆ *It's another joke about a grind.* Es otro chiste sobre un cuadernícola.

Gringoland (the United States) Gringolandia *L. Am.* ◆ *The two brothers went to work in Gringoland.* Los dos hermanos se fueron a trabajar a Gringolandia.

gross →see: yucky

to be **gross** (be disgusting, worthless) ser un asco *Mex, U, Arg, Sp* ◆ *This food (program) is gross.* Esta comida (Este programa) es un asco.

grouch (having a hostile appearance) el/la cara de perro (dog face) *Mex, PR, Sp* ◆ *I didn't dare talk to the police officer because he looked like a grouch.* No me atreví a hablarle al policía porque tenía una cara de perro terrible.

to be a **grouch** (to be bad tempered; →see also: to be a grouch, pain, pain in the neck, sourpuss) tener mala uva (to have bad grape) *Chicano, Sp;* tener mala leche (to have bad milk) *Mex, ES, Sp;* tener mala sangre (to have bad blood) *Mex, ES;* ser un geniudo(-a) *Mex, Col* ◆ *What a grouch the owner of the gas station is!* ¡Qué mala sangre tiene el dueño de la gasolinera! ◆ *That guy is a grouch. It's very hard to work with him.* Ese tipo es un geniudo. Es muy difícil trabajar con él.

to be **grouchy** echar chispas (to throw off sparks) *Mex, DR, ES, Ch, Sp* ◆ *I'm always grouchy in the morning.* ◆ Siempre echo chispas por la mañana.

grudgingly (against one's will) de mala gana *L. Am., Sp;* a contrapelo (against the natural direction, the way the hair or fur grows) *DR, Ch, U, Sp* ◆ *They're doing that favor for you grudgingly. For sure they'll want a payback.* Te están haciendo ese favor a contrapelo. Seguro que van a querer una contraprestación.

Guess what. ¿Qué crees? (What do you think?) *L. Am., Sp*

to **gun it** →see: to step on it

gutsy (brave, daring) guapo(-a) (attractive, gorgeous) *Mex, Cuba, DR, PR, S. Cone;* choro(-a) *Bol, Ch, U* ◆ *Adolfo is very gutsy; he's not afraid of anything.* Adolfo es muy guapo; no tiene miedo de nada.

to be **gutsy** (worthy, have character or valor; →see also: to be ballsy, to have balls, to have guts) tener bien puestos los calzones (to have one's underwear well placed) *Mex, C. Am., Ch* ◆ *Arturo's father is a gutsy guy.* El padre de Arturo tiene bien puestos los calzones.

guy 1. (gal; →see also: kid) el tío; la tía (uncle; aunt) *Ch, Sp;* el/la loco(-a) (crazy person) *Col, Ven, Ec;* el/la chamo(-a) *Col, Ven;* el/la patojo(-a) *G* ◆ *Who's that gal over there?* ¿Quién es esa loca allí? ◆ *That guy spends lots of money on cheap clothes.* Ese tío gasta mucho dinero en ropa barata. **2.** (boy, dude) el chavalo *Chicano, Mex, C. Am.;* el buay *Pan* ◆ *My guy never gets home before six.* Mi chavalo nunca viene a la casa antes de las seis. **3.** (fellow, dude) el tipo (type) *L. Am.;* el vato (bato) *Chicano, Mex;* el gallo (rooster) *Cuba, DR, PR, Peru, Ch* ◆ *That guy is handsome and kind.* Ese tipo es buen mozo y amable. **4.** (middle-aged or older man) el maestro (teacher, master) *L. Am., Sp* ◆ *Ask that guy where this street goes.* Pregúntale a ese maestro por dónde se va esta calle.

gyp →see: rip-off

H

half done (inconclusive, up in the air) a medio palo (to the half stick) *DR, Hond, Nic, CR, Col* ◆ *Let's not leave things half done. No dejemos las cosas a medio palo.*

to be **half-blasted** →see: to be plastered, to be wasted

to be **half-starved** (not have eaten) estar en blanco (to be blank) *Mex, Cuba, G,* (RVAR *Mex:* also, to have not slept) ◆ *We're half-starved, not having eaten a bite. Andamos en blanco, sin probar bocado.*

halfway done (unfinished) a medio hacer *L. Am., Sp* ◆ *The project is halfway done. El proyecto está a medio hacer.*

to be **halfway there** estar a medio camino (to be in mid road) *Mex, DR, PR, Ch, Sp* ◆ *You're halfway there; you've got only one more year until you graduate. Estás a medio camino; te falta sólo un año para recibirte.*

halfwit →see: birdbrain, fool, idiot

to be **handy** (→see also: to be a whiz) tener mano (to have hand) *DR, PR, U, Sp;* ser un manitas *Sp* ◆ *Andreu is really handy. He always manages to fix everything. Andreu realmente es un manitas. Siempre consigue arreglarlo todo.*

to **hang from a thread** pender de un hilo *L. Am., Sp* ◆ *His job is hanging from a thread. If he keeps on this way, they're going to fire him. Su trabajo pende de un hilo. Si sigue así, lo van a despedir.*

Hang in there! 1. (Don't give up.) Ánimo. (Spirit.) *L. Am., Sp;* Adelante con la cruz. (Forward with the cross.) *most of L. Am., Sp* ◆ *Hang in there if you want to finish your studies (get your degree) this year. Adelante con la cruz si quieres terminar tu carrera este año.* 2. (It's not that bad.) No te azotes, que hay chayotes. (Don't flog yourself; there are chayotes, a kind of squash.) *Mex, Col*

to **hang on** (get ready for a shock or surprise) agarrarse (to hang on) *Mex, DR, PR, ES, S. Cone, Sp* ◆ *Hang on. Guess who called*

me last night? Agárrate. ¿Adivina quién me llamó anoche?

to **hang out in the street** medir calles (to measure streets) *ES, CR, Col* ◆ *Pablo is such a slacker; he's always hanging out in the street. Pablito es tan vago; siempre está midiendo calles.*

to **hang up (the phone)** colgar (to hang) *L. Am., Sp;* cortar (to cut) *L. Am., Sp* ◆ *I have to hang up. Mom wants to use the phone. Tengo que cortar. Mamá quiere usar el teléfono.*

Hanging in there. (getting along; →see also: Just getting by.) Tirando. (Pulling.) *U, Arg, Sp* ◆ *How are you doing? —Hanging in there, as usual. ¿Cómo andas? —Tirando, como siempre.*

hangover la cruda (rawness) *Mex, C. Am.;* la resaca (undertow) *Peru, S. Cone, Sp* ◆ *The day after the party I had a horrible hangover and couldn't work. Al día siguiente de la fiesta tenía una cruda tremenda y no pude trabajar.*

hanky-panky →see: shenanigans

happy as a clam →see: happy as a lark

to be **happy as a lark** estar feliz como una lombriz (happy as a worm) *most of L. Am., Sp;* estar (alegre) como unas castañuelas (to be happy as castanets) *Mex, Sp;* estar como unas pascuas (to be like Easter) *Sp* ◆ *Adrianita was happy as a lark playing with other kids on the beach. Adrianita estaba feliz como una lombriz jugando con otros niños en la playa.*

happy as can be encantado(-a) de la vida (charmed or enchanted with life) *L. Am., Sp* ◆ *The children are going on an excursion to the beach. They're happy as can be. Los niños van a la playa a pasear. Están encantados de la vida.*

hard cash el dinero contante y sonante *L. Am., Sp* ◆ *They paid me in hard cash. Me pagaron con dinero contante y sonante.*

to be **hard to get a handle on** (be difficult to comprehend) no tener por dónde

agarrarlo (to have no place to hang onto) *Mex, DR, PR, Ch, U, Sp* ◆ *This problem is difficult; it's hard to get a handle on.* **Este problema es difícil; no tiene por dónde agarrarlo.**

to be **hard up** →see: to be broke

hardheaded 1. (bonehead) cabezón, cabezona (bighead) *Florida, Mex, DR, PR, G, Col, Peru, S. Cone, Sp* ◆ *Don't be so hardheaded. Listen to what your doctor tells you.* **No seas cabezón. Escucha lo que te dice tu médico.** 2. (stubborn) terco(-a) *L. Am., Sp;* cabezota (bigheaded) *Sp* ◆ *If you persist in being so hardheaded, you'll come to a bad end.* **Si sigues siendo tan cabezota, acabarás mal.**

hassle 1. (disappointment, obstacle to success) el bache (pothole) *Mex, DR, ES* ◆ *I wasn't able to finished my studies; stress was a big hassle.* **No pude terminar mi carrera; la tensión fue un bache grande.** 2. (problem, difficult situation; →see also: drag, pain) el clavo (nail) *G, Nic, ES, CR, S. Cone;* el drama, el dramón *S. Cone* ◆ *The kids' leaving for Spain was a hassle for the parents.* **La partida de los hijos a España fue un drama para los padres.** 3. (mess; all-purpose word for any thing, situation, etc.; slightly vulgar) la vaina (husk) *C. Am, DR, PR, Col, Ven* ◆ *What a hassle! We left the passports in the hotel.* **¡Qué vaina! Dejamos los pasaportes en el hotel.**

hassles (obstacles or problems that one puts up with patiently) carros y carretas (cars and carts) *Mex, Sp* ◆ *Néstor has had to put up with hassles in his job because he has three kids and needs the money.* **Néstor ha tenido que aguantar carros y carretas en su trabajo porque tiene tres niños y necesita el dinero.**

to **have a ball** →see: to have a blast

to **have a big mess** →see: to have all hell break loose

to **have a big scene** (make a big scene) armarse la gorda (to make the fat one) *L. Am., Sp* ◆ *When she found out that her boyfriend was going out with her best friend, there was a big scene (a big scene was made).* **Cuando supo que su novio salía con su mejor amiga, se armó la gorda.**

to **have a blast** (→see also: to go out on the town, to have a good time, to live it up) echar relajo (to throw off or make a rumpus) *Mex, ES, Col* (RVar *U, Arg*: also, hacer relajo); pasarla de peluche (to spend it like a stuffed toy) *Mex, ES;* pasarlo bomba (to spend it bomb) *Ch, Arg, Sp;* pasarlo en grande (to spend it big) *U, Arg, Sp;* pasarlo chancho (to spend it pig) *Ch, Arg;* pasarlo pipa (to spend it pipe) *Sp* ◆ *We always have a blast here.* **Siempre lo pasamos bomba aquí.**

to **have a blowup, have a brawl** armar o tener una bronca *L. Am., Sp;* rifarse *Mex, DR, G, ES;* bronquear(se) *Mex, Col, Peru, U, Arg;* tener una pelotera *S. Cone, Sp* ◆ *They had such a big blowup that their voices were heard out in the street.* **Tuvieron tal bronca que las voces se oían desde la calle.**

to **have a crush** (be in love) estar colgado (-a) (to be hung, suspended) *Mex, G, Sp* ◆ *Marta has a crush on a guy from Córdoba.* **Marta está colgada por un chico de Córdoba.**

to **have a devil of a mess** haber (armarse) una de todos los diablos (to have [make] one of all the devils) *L. Am., Sp* ◆ *There was a devil of a mess when the workers arrived at the mayor's office.* **Hubo (Se armó) una de todos los diablos cuando los obreros llegaron a la alcaldía.**

to **have a drink** tomar una copa (to have a wine glass) *L. Am., Sp* ◆ *Let's go out, dear, and have a little drink.* **Salgamos, querido, y tomemos una copita.**

to **have a feeling** →see: to have a hunch

to **have a few years on one** (→see also: to be getting up there) tener abriles (to have Aprils) *L. Am., Sp* ◆ *She has a few years on her, but she's pretty.* **Tiene sus abriles, pero es bonita.**

to **have a fight** →see: to be at odds with someone, to be like oil and water, to beat up, to have a blowup, to hit where it hurts

to **have a fit** (→see also: to make a scene) darse (agarrarse) una rabieta *L. Am., Sp;* hacer una pataleta (to have a kicking fit) *L. Am., Sp;* hacer un patatús *Mex, DR, PR, ES, CR, Col, Ch;* hacer un berrinche *Mex, DR, Col, Sp;* formar un berrinche *PR, Col, Sp;* hacer un coraje *Mex, G;* tener un ataque de caspa (to have a dandruff attack) S. Cone; coger o tener un cabreo Sp; dar una venada Sp ◆ The neighbor's little boy has a fit every time she goes to work. El niño de la vecina forma un berrinche cada vez que ella se va al trabajo.

to **have a fling** echar una canita al aire (to throw a gray hair in the air) L. Am., Sp tener un ligue (also, to have a date) Mex, Cuba, ES, Sp; tener un rollo con alguien (to have a roll with someone) Sp ◆ My cousin had a fling with her lawyer. Mi prima tuvo un ligue con su abogado.

to **have a foot in the door** (have earned a place somewhere) ya tener una pata allí (to now have a paw in there) Mex ◆ Laura worked three months in that company and they didn't pay her anything, but now she has a foot in the door. Laura trabajó tres meses en esa empresa y no le pagaron nada, pero ya tiene una pata allí.

Have a good day (time). Have a good one. Que lo pase(s) bien. (May you spend it well, said to someone who is leaving or about to leave.) L. Am., Sp ◆ Thank you very much for visiting us. Have a good day! Muchas gracias por habernos visitado. ¡Que lo pasen bien!

to **have a good head on one's shoulders** (→see also: to be a brain) tener buen coco (to have a good coconut, head) Mex, Ch (RVAR Mex: more common, ser coco) ◆ My sister has a good head on her shoulders. Mi hermana tiene buen coco.

to **have a good (bad) reputation** tener buena (mala) prensa (to have good [bad] press) most of L. Am., Sp ◆ Juan Manuel has a good reputation with the ladies (girls). Juan Manuel tiene buena prensa con las chicas.

to **have a good (great) time** (→see also: to go out on the town, to have a blast, to live it up) pasarlo(-a) bien L. Am., Sp; divertirse a sus anchas (to enjoy oneself to one's widths) L. Am., Sp ◆ How was your vacation? —I had a good time. ¿Cómo te fue en las vacaciones? —Lo pasé bien.

to **have a green thumb** tener buena mano para las plantas (to have a good hand for plants) DR, PR, S. Cone, Sp ◆ Ana has a green thumb. Ana tiene buena mano para las plantas.

to **have a grudge against** guardar rencor (to hold bitterness) L. Am., Sp; traer (tener) entre ojos (to bring between the eyes, meaning also to dislike) Mex, Ch, U ◆ I have a grudge against him. Lo traigo entre ojos.

to **have a hard time** (have things go badly) irle a alguien como en feria (to go as in a fair for someone) Mex, ES; irle a alguien como los perros en misa (to go like dogs in mass for someone) Sp ◆ I had a hard time with the exams at the university. Mis exámenes en la universidad me fueron como en feria.

to **have a hard-on** presentar armas (to present arms, vulgar) L. Am., Sp ◆ Oh, my love, you already have a hard-on for me? Ay, mi amor, ¿tan pronto me presentas armas?

to **have a heart of gold** tener un corazón de oro L. Am., Sp ◆ Dr. Campos has a heart of gold and is dedicated to his profession. El doctor Campos tiene un corazón de oro y está dedicado a su profesión.

to **have a heart of stone** tener un corazón de piedra Mex, DR, ES, S. Cone; tener alma de acero (to have a soul of steel) Mex, ES, Sp ◆ Don't try to convince Pedro to help us. He has a heart of stone. No intentes convencer a Pedro que nos ayude. Tiene un corazón de piedra.

to **have a hell of a time** (→see also: to have a rough time) 1. (have a riot) pasarlas putas (to spend them [like] sluts, vulgar) Mex, Sp ◆ We had a hell of a time on the farm this weekend. Las pasamos putas en la finca este fin de semana. 2. (have something be rushed, difficult, or complicated; vulgar) ir de culo (to go ass) Sp ◆ This week with the exams, the apprenticeship, and the new job I'm having a hell of a time. I can't do so many things. Esta semana entre los exámenes, las prácticas y el nuevo trabajo voy de culo. No puedo con tantas cosas.

to **have a hell of an accident** darse una hostia (to give oneself the Host; vulgar, with religious reference) Sp ◆ Alonso had a hell of an accident as he was running out. He didn't see that the glass door was closed. Alonso se dio una hostia al salir corriendo. No vio que la puerta de vidrio estaba cerrada.

to **have a hollow leg** (be a big eater; →see also: chowhound) tener buen diente (to have good tooth) *Mex, DR, PR, ES, S. Cone, Sp* ◆ *Ricardo has a hollow leg. He had two double-patty hamburgers and a strawberry shake. Ricardo tiene buen diente. Se comió dos hamburguesas doble carne y un batido de fresa.*

to **have a hunch** (have a feeling about) hacérsele *most of L. Am., Sp;* latirle *Mex, DR, PR, ES, CR, Col, Ch;* ponérsele *ES, CR, Ch* ◆ *I have a hunch that the other team is going to win. Se me hace que el otro equipo va a ganar.*

to **have a knack for something** tener buena mano para algo (to have a good hand for something) *DR, PR, S. Cone, Sp* ◆ *You have a knack for cooking. Tienes buena mano para la cocina (para cocinar).*

to **have a lightbulb go on** →see: to get a bright idea

to **have a lot of influence** (→see also: big shot, to call the shots) llevar la batuta (to carry the baton) *L. Am., Sp;* tener banca *U, Arg, Sp* ◆ *Thanks to the influence that their father has, Ignacio and Rafael began to work in the national accounting office. Gracias a la banca que tiene su padre, Ignacio y Rafael comenzaron a trabajar en la contaduría de la nación.*

to **have a lot of material** sobrar (haber) tela que cortar (to have extra material to cut) *Mex, DR, PR* ◆ *There's still a lot of material to deal with on this topic, according to the teacher. Todavía hay mucha tela que cortar sobre esta materia, según la maestra.*

to **have a lot of nerve** tener mucha cara (mucho rostro, mucho morro, mucha jeta) (to have a lot of face) *Sp;* tener mucha concha (shell) *Mex, Nic, Pan, Ec, Peru;* tener cara de cemento armado (to have the face of fixed cement) *Sp* ◆ *Juan has a lot of nerve. He speaks badly of Rosa but goes out with her. Juan tiene mucho rostro. Habla mal de Rosa pero sale con ella.*

to **have a nice build** (of a man; be muscular) estar cuadrado (square) *Mex, G, ES, Sp* ◆ *He plays a lot of sports; he has a nice build. Hace mucho deporte; está cuadrado.*

Have a nice/good day (time). (Have a safe trip.) Que te (le, les) vaya bien. (May all go well with you, said to someone who is leaving.) *L. Am., Sp* ◆ *'Bye, guys. Have a*

good time in the mountains. *Adiós, muchachos. Que les vaya bien en las montañas.*

to **have a rough time** (→see also: in hot water, to be in a bind, to have a hell of a time) verla peluda (to see it hairy) *Mex, ES, CR, Col;* pasar las de Caín (to spend those of Cain) *Mex, DR, PR, CR, S. Cone, Sp;* vérselas negras (to see them black) *Mex, ES, S. Cone;* pasarlas negras (to spend them blacks) *Mex, S. Cone, Sp;* pasarlas canutas (to spend them tubes) *Ch, Sp* ◆ *At this moment I'm having a rough time. En este momento la estoy viendo peluda.*

Have a safe trip. (Have a nice day/time.) Que te (le, les) vaya bien. (May all go well with you, said to someone who is leaving.) *L. Am., Sp* ◆ *Have a safe trip, dear. Que te vaya bien, querido.*

to **have a screw loose** (be off one's rocker; →see also: to be nuts) faltarle a alguien un tornillo (to be missing a screw) *L. Am., Sp;* caérsele un tornillo (to have a screw fall out) *Mex, CR, ES, Col, Sp;* tener flojos los tornillos (to have screws loose) *Mex, ES, U, Sp* ◆ *Rosario went to the university in a party dress. —I knew it. Poor thing; she has a screw loose. Rosario fue a la universidad con un vestido de fiesta. —Ya lo supe. Pobrecita; le falta un tornillo.*

to **have a short fuse** →see: hothead

to **have a shotgun wedding** casarse de penalti (to get married as a penalty) *Mex, Col, Sp;* casarse por el sindicato de las prisas (to get married by the syndicate of haste) *Sp* ◆ *He had a shotgun wedding with his girlfriend at the age of seventeen. Se casó de penalti con su novia a la edad de diecisiete años.*

to **have a swollen head** →see: to be full of oneself

to **have a windfall** (luck out) tocarle a alguien la lotería (also caerle or sacar la lotería) (to win the lottery) *Mex, Cuba, S. Cone, Sp* ◆ *Alejandro had a windfall. His uncle left him a million pesos. A Alejandro le tocó la lotería. Su tío le dejó un millón de pesos.*

to **have all hell break loose** (→see also: to make a scene) armarse la gorda (to make the fat one) *L. Am., Sp;* haber (armarse) una de todos los diablos (to have [make] one of all the devils) *L. Am., Sp* ◆ *When she found out that her boyfriend was going out with her*

to have bad luck: *I'm having bad luck.*
Tengo el santo de espaldas.

best friend, all hell broke loose. *Cuando supo que su novio salía con su mejor amiga, se armó la gorda.*

to **have ants in your pants** tener hormigas en el culo (to have ants in your ass, vulgar) *ES, U, Arg* ◆ *These kids are never quiet; it's like they have ants in their pants. Estos niños nunca están quietos; parece que tienen hormigas en el culo.*

to **have bad luck** 1. tener mala pata (to have bad foot) *Mex, DR, PR, G, ES, CR, Ven, S. Cone, Sp;* tener mala leche (to have bad milk) *G, ES, Col, Ven, Peru* ◆ *I have very bad luck. Why did they choose me? Tengo muy mala leche. ¿Por qué me escogieron a mí?* 2. (be out of luck) tener el santo de espaldas (to have one's saint turning his back on one) *Mex, ES, Sp* ◆ *Everything is turning out badly for me. For days I've had only bad luck. Todo me sale mal. Hace días que tengo el santo de espaldas.* 3. (often meaning to be pregnant) salir con su domingo siete (to turn out with his or her Sunday the 7th, considered an unlucky day) *Mex, ES, Ch* ◆ *Have*

you heard the news? Esperanza had bad luck (got pregnant). And her boyfriend has disappeared into thin air. ¿Has oído la noticia? Esperanza salió con su domingo siete. Y su novio se ha esfumado.*

to **have balls** (be brave) tener huevos (to have eggs, testicles) *L. Am., Sp;* tener los cojones bien puestos (to have one's testicles well placed) *DR, Sp;* tener pelotas (to have balls) *U, Arg, Sp;* tener bolas (to have balls) *U, Arg;* tener las bolas bien puestas (to have one's balls well placed) *S. Cone;* tener más cojones que nadie (to have more testicles than anyone) *Sp* ◆ *You need to have balls to stand up to that group of delinquents. Hay que tener huevos para enfrentar a ese grupo de delincuentes.*

to **have bats in the belfry** (→see also: to be nuts, to be off one's rocker, to have a screw loose) fallarle la azotea (to have one's roof failing) *Mex, DR, PR, S. Cone* ◆ *Rolando has bats in his belfry. A Rolando le falla la azotea.*

to **have character** (strength, aptitude) tener madera (to have wood) *Mex, Col, Ven, Ch, U, Sp* ◆ *Silvia has character. Silvia tiene madera.*

to **have charisma** (charm) →see: to have that special something

to **have connections** →see also: connection[s]) estar enchufado(-a) (to be plugged in) *Mex, Sp;* tener santos en la corte (to have saints at court) *Ch, parts of Sp* ◆ *My uncle has connections in the government. Mi tío está enchufado en el gobierno.*

to **have everything go up in smoke** irse todo en humo *Sp* ◆ *He was hoping to get back together with her, but everything went up in smoke. Esperaba que volviera con ella, pero se fue todo en humo.*

to **have friends in high places** →see: to have connections

to **have good intentions go all to heck** írsele a alguien el santo al cielo (to have one's saint go to heaven) *most of L. Am., Sp* ◆ *I was going to work this morning, but my good intentions went all to heck. Iba a trabajar esta mañana, pero se me fue el santo al cielo.*

to **have good luck** 1. (be in luck) tener el santo de cara (to have one's saint facing one) *ES, Peru, Sp* ◆ *Ricardo has good luck; he has great success with his business. Ricardo tiene el santo de cara; tiene mucho éxito en su negocio.* 2. (to get out of a bad situation with no harmful consequences) caer parado(-a) (to fall standing up, landing on one's feet) *DR, ES, S. Cone* ◆ *After six months without work, Julio went to an interview and fortunately had good luck. Después de seis meses sin trabajo, Julio fue a una entrevista y suerte fue que cayó parado.*

to **have good (bad) luck in something** quedar bien (mal) parado(-a) (to end up standing well [badly]) *L. Am., Sp* ◆ *How did it go with your new job? —I had good luck. ¿Cómo te fue en tu nuevo trabajo? –Quedé bien parado.*

to **have guts** (nerve; →see also: ballsy, to be ballsy, to be gutsy, guts) tener agallas (to have galls) *L. Am., Sp;* tener narices (to have noses, euphemism for cojones) *Sp* ◆ *Martín has guts. Martín tiene agallas (narices).*

to **have had a falling out** estar peleados (-as) (to be fought) *L. Am., Sp* ◆ *María and José have had a falling out; they aren't speaking to each other anymore. María y José están peleados; ya no se hablan.*

to **have had enough of something** →see: to be fed up

to **have had it** →see: to be fed up

to **have (something) handed to one on a silver platter** (come without effort) venir a alguien en bandeja (to come to someone on a tray) *U, Ch, Sp* ◆ *What luck! This job was handed to me on a silver platter. ¡Qué suerte! Este puesto me vino en bandeja.*

to **have heads roll** no dejar títere con cabeza (to not leave a puppet with a head) *S. Cone* ◆ *I'm going to look over all the work and if it isn't good, heads will roll. Voy a revisar todo el trabajo y si está mal, no voy a dejar títere con cabeza.*

to **have it on good authority** (from the horse's mouth) saber de buena tinta una cosa (to know something from good ink) *L. Am., Sp;* saber de buena fuente (to know from a good source) *Mex, Peru, Bol, S. Cone* ◆ *You can be sure that information is correct. I have it on good authority. Puedes estar segura de que esta información es correcta. Lo sé de buena fuente.*

to **have it tough** tenerlo crudo (to have it raw) *Sp* ◆ *You have it tough, friend. Lo tienes crudo, amigo.*

to **have nine lives** tener siete vidas como los gatos (como el gato) (to have seven lives like cats [like the cat]) *L. Am., Sp;* tener más vidas que un gato (to have more lives than a cat) *Mex, ES, U, Ch, Sp* ◆ *Doña Dolores seems to have nine lives. Often she is seriously ill and then she recovers just fine. Doña Dolores parece tener siete vidas como los gatos. A menudo está grave y se recupera muy bien.*

to **have no one left standing** (be totally destroyed, often because of verbal abuse) no quedar títere con cara (cabeza) (to not have a puppet with a face [head] remaining) *Mex, S. Cone, Sp* ◆ *The boss gave his talk and no one was left standing. El jefe dio su discurso y no quedó títere con cabeza.*

to **have no part in** (have nothing to do with) no tener arte ni parte (to have neither art nor part) *L. Am., Sp* ◆ *We'll start a new project, but the administration will have no part in it.* Comenzaremos un nuevo proyecto, pero la administración no tendrá arte ni parte.

to **have no rhyme or reason** (no order or logic) no tener (ni) pies ni cabeza (to have neither feet nor head) *L. Am., Sp* ◆ *The plotline of that movie has no rhyme or reason.* El argumento de esa película no tiene ni pies ni cabeza.

to **have no say** (in a matter) ni pinchar ni cortar (to not pinch or cut) *Arg, U, Sp;* no tener vela en el entierro (to not have a candle at a funeral) *Mex, DR, S. Cone, Sp* ◆ *I have no say about the selling of the house.* En la venta de la casa no pincho ni corto.◆ *Don't even talk because you don't have any say in the matter.* Ni hables porque no tienes vela en el entierro.

to **have no shame** (be shameless; →see also: pushy person) no tener cara (to have no face) *Mex, Col, ES* ◆ *These people have no shame and they keep robbing the poor (lit., the neediest).* Esta gente no tiene cara y sigue robando a los más necesitados.

to **have nothing to do with** →see: to have no part in, to have something (nothing) to do with

to **have one door close and another open** cerrarle una puerta y abrirle otra *L. Am., Sp* ◆ *The economic circumstances closed one door for him but opened another interesting one.* Las circunstancias económicas le cerraron una puerta, pero le abrieron otra muy interesante.

to **have one foot in the grave** estar con un (el) pie en el estribo (to have one [the] foot in the stirrup) *Mex, ES, S. Cone, Sp* ◆ *That poor man has one foot in the grave.* Ese pobre señor tiene un pie en el estribo.

to **have one's act together** tener bien puestas las pilas, estar con las pilas puestas (to have one's batteries well placed) *DR, Ven, U, Ch* ◆ *That guy is very clever; he's really got his act together.* Ese chico es muy listo; tiene las pilas bien puestas.

to **have one's ears pricked up** (ready for gossip; →see also: to gossip) estar con (tener) las antenas puestas (to be with [have] one's antennas up) *Mex, DR, ES, U,* *Arg, Sp* ◆ *Pipe down. Here comes Elena, and she always has her ears pricked up (for the latest gossip).* Habla bajito. Por ahí viene Elena, que siempre tiene las antenas puestas.

to **have one's hands full with something** estar muy ocupado(-a) con algo *L. Am., Sp;* estar metido(-a) hasta los codos en algo *Mex* ◆ *I've got my hands full with this project.* Estoy metida hasta los codos en este proyecto.

to **have one's head in the clouds** (be daydreaming) estar en las nubes (to be in the clouds) *L. Am., Sp* ◆ *Carlos always has his head in the clouds.* Carlos siempre está en las nubes.

to **have one's life hanging by a thread** (be in great danger) tener la vida en un hilo (to have one's life by a thread) *Mex, DR, ES, S. Cone, Sp* ◆ *The miners were trapped by a landslide, and their lives were hanging by a thread until they were rescued a few days later.* Los mineros fueron atrapados por un deslizamiento y tuvieron sus vidas en un hilo hasta que los rescataron unos días más tarde.

to **have one's mind a soup** →see: mixed up

to **have one's mind blank** tener la mente en blanco *Mex, DR, G, Col, U, Arg* (RVar *ES, Ch, Sp:* estar con la mente en blanco) ◆ *The professor's questions were easy, but my mind was blank, and I couldn't answer.* Las preguntas del profesor eran fáciles, pero yo tenía la mente en blanco y no pude contestar.

to **have one's mind like a sieve** (forget things) estar como una regadera (to be like a watering can) *Sp* ◆ *This woman has a mind like a sieve. Don't waste time arguing with her.* Esta mujer está como una regadera. No pierdas el tiempo discutiendo con ella.

to **have one's mind somewhere else** estar en otra (to be on another, with the idea of onda or dimensión understood) *Mex, S. Cone* ◆ *Shall we go out on the town today? — No, thanks, my mind is somewhere else. I have a lot of to do.* ¿Salimos de parranda hoy? – No, gracias, estoy en otra. Tengo mucho que hacer.

to **have one's mouth watering** hacerle agua la boca (to make the mouth water) *L. Am.;* hacerle la boca agua (to make the mouth water) *Sp* ◆ *You made empanadas, my darling? My mouth is watering.* ¿Hiciste empanadas, mi amor? Se me hace agua la boca.

to **have one's nerves on edge** (→see also: to be on edge, to be stressed out, nervous as a cat) tener los nervios de punta (to have one's nerves standing) *L. Am., Sp* ◆ *She hasn't had news of her family, and her nerves are on edge.* Ella no ha tenido noticias de su familia, y tiene los nervios de punta.

to **have one's tongue hanging out** (with admiration, etc.) tirar/salírsele la baba (por litros) (to throw out saliva [by the liter]) *Mex, Col;* caerse la baba (to have saliva fall) *L. Am., Sp* ◆ *Your tongue was hanging out when you saw Esmeralda.* Se te salió la baba cuando viste a Esmeralda.

to **have oral sex** (vulgar) mamar (to suckle) *L. Am., Sp*

to **have senior moments** chochear *Mex, S. Cone, Sp* ◆ *Don't pay attention to what Don Santiago says. He has senior moments and doesn't know what he's saying.* No preste atención a lo que diga don Santiago. Chochea y no sabe lo que dice.

to **have sex** (screw around with; all vulgar:) echar(se) un polvo/un polvito (to throw [oneself] powder or dust) *L. Am., Sp;* tirarse a alguien (to throw oneself at someone) *L. Am., Sp;* coger (to take, catch, grab) *most of L. Am.;* chingar (to rip, tear; equivalent of the F-word) *Mex, Cuba, PR, C. Am., Col;* pisar (to step on) *Mex, Cuba, G, ES, Nic, CR;* echar un palo/un palito (to throw a stick) *Mex, Cuba, G, ES;* echarse a alguien (to throw oneself at someone) *Mex, Cuba, G;;* clavar (to nail) *Mex, Cuba, PR, G, ES, Col, U;* parchar (to put a patch on) *Mex, ES;* apañar (to seize) *Mex;* follar (equivalent of the F-word) *Sp;* joder *L. Am., Sp* ◆ *After the movie we had sex in the car.* Después del cine cogimos en el auto. ◆ *He had sex with his neighbor.* Se tiró a su vecina.

to **have (sex) appeal** (fascinate, captivate) tener pegue (to have glue) *Mex;* tener gancho (to have hook) *Ch, Sp* ◆ *This guy has appeal (is captivating). He'll never end up alone.* Este chico tiene gancho. Jamás se quedará solo.

to **have someone at one's beck and call** (→see also: to call the shots, to have someone under one's thumb) tener en el bolsillo a alguien (to have someone in one's pocket) *Mex, DR, PR, ES, U, Arg, Sp;* tirar/jalar (de) la cuerda a alguien (to pull someone by the cord) *Mex, Sp;* tener en el bote a alguien (to have someone in the boat) *Sp* ◆ *Juan has his girlfriend at his beck and call.* Juan tiene a la novia en el bolsillo.

to **have someone at wits' end** (→see also: to bug, to rile up, to upset someone) tener (traer) a alguien frito(-a) (to have [bring] someone fried) *Mex, DR, Sp* ◆ *Daniela has got me at my wits' end with her behavior.* Daniela me tiene frita con su conducta.

to **have someone eating out of one's hand** →see: to have someone at one's beck and call

to **have someone under one's thumb** (intimidate or oppress someone; →see also: to have someone at one's beck and call) meter en un puño a alguien (to put someone in one's fist) *Mex, U, Sp* ◆ *Marciano has us under his thumb because he has 55 percent of the company's stock.* Marciano nos tiene a todos en un puño porque tiene el 55 por ciento de las acciones en la empresa.

to **have something go in one ear and out the other** entrarle una cosa por un oído y salirle por el otro *L. Am., Sp* ◆ *It goes in one ear and out the other.* Por un oído le entra y por el otro le sale.

to **have something special** (sport something) ostentar *L. Am., Sp;* botarse *Mex* ◆ *What a gorgeous bride Miguel has.* Qué cuero de novia se bota Miguel.

to **have something (nothing) to do with** tener algo (no tener nada) que ver con (to have something [not have anything] to do with) *L. Am., Sp* ◆ *Why do you mention those factors that have nothing to do with our business?* ¿Por qué mencionas esos factores que no tienen nada que ver con nuestro negocio?

to **have sweet dreams** dormir con los ángeles (to sleep with the angels) *Mex, ES, S. Cone* ◆ *(Have) Sweet dreams.* Que duermas con los angelitos.

to **have teeth chattering** (be very cold or be afraid) dar diente con diente (to give tooth with tooth) *L. Am., Sp* ◆ *I saw a shadow in the window, and my teeth chattered with fear. It turned out to be my cat.* Vi una sombra a través de la ventana, y di diente con diente del susto. Resultó que era mi gato.

to **have that special something** (charm) tener ángel (to have angel) *Mex, ES, Col;* tener duende (to have elf) *Peru, Sp* ◆ *That woman has a special something; just hearing her speak you realize it.* Esa señora tiene ángel; te das cuenta con sólo escucharla hablar.

to **have the barn door open** (an unzipped fly) tener la farmacia abierta (y el doctor dormido) (to have the pharmacy open [and the doctor asleep]) *ES, Sp* ◆ *The barn door is open. (Your fly is unzipped.)* La farmacia está abierta y el doctor dormido.

to **have the gift of gab** tener un pico de oro (to have a golden beak) *most of L. Am., Sp* ◆ *The director of the company has the gift of the gab and convinced the rest of the board of directors that the salary increase should be five percent.* El director de la empresa tiene un pico de oro y convenció al resto del directorio de que el aumento de sueldo fuera del cinco por ciento.

to **have the gourmet touch** tener mano de monja (to have a nun's hand) *Ch, U;* tener buena mano para la cocina (to have a good hand for cooking) *DR, PR, S. Cone, Sp* ◆ *Lucy, you are an excellent cook. You have the gourmet touch!* Lucy, eres una excelente cocinera. ¡Tienes mano de monja!

to **have the lid blown off a story** descubrirse el pastel (to discover the cake) *Mex, S. Cone, Sp* ◆ *Yesterday the lid was blown off the story. Now everyone knows.* Ayer se descubrió el pastel. Ahora todo el mundo lo sabe.

to **have the right stuff** (good character) tener (mucha) madera (to have [a lot of] wood) *Mex, Col, Sp* ◆ *Elizabeth has the right stuff.* Elizabeth tiene mucha madera.

to **have the right touch** tener buena mano (to have a good hand) *DR, PR, S. Cone, Sp* ◆ *Pilar draws really well. She has the right touch.* Pilar dibuja muy bien. Tiene buena mano.

to **have the tables turned on oneself** ir por lana y volver (salir) trasquilado(-a) (to

go for wool and come back shorn) *DR, S. Cone, Sp* ◆ *The minister (secretary) had the tables turned on him when he spoke to the farmers.* El ministro fue por lana y salió trasquilado cuando habló con los agricultores.

to **have the upper hand** (→see also: to call the shots, to have someone at one's beck and call, wear the pants) tener la sartén por el mango (to have the frying pan by the handle) *L. Am., Sp* ◆ *I don't know if you realize it, but we have the upper hand. We can do whatever we want.* No sé si te das cuenta, pero tenemos la sartén por el mango. Podemos hacer lo que queramos.

to **have the world crumbling around one** caérsele a alguien el mundo encima (to have the world fall on one) *Mex, DR, PR, ES, S. Cone, Sp;* caérsele a alguien la casa encima (to have the house fall on one) *Mex, DR, S. Cone, Sp* ◆ *With all their family and economic problems, the world is crumbling around them.* Con todos los problemas familiares y económicos, se les ha caído la casa encima.

to **have too many irons in the fire** (trying to do too many things at once, trying to please more than one person) bailar en la cuerda floja (to dance on the the tightrope) *L. Am., Sp* ◆ *He has too many irons in the fire. It's very possible that they'll fire him.* Está bailando en la cuerda floja. Es muy posible que lo despidan.

to **have what it takes** (strong character; be competent) tener madera (to have wood) *Mex, Col, Ven, Ch, U, Sp;* tener tablas (to have boards) *Arg, Sp* ◆ *You have what it takes to be a musician.* Tienes madera de músico.

head →see: noggin

head honcho el jefazo (la jefaza) →see also: big shot) el mero jodón (boss; no feminine form is normally used, slightly vulgar) *Chicano, Mex* ◆ *Where's the head honcho? I need to talk to him.* ¿Dónde está el mero jodón? Necesito hablarle.

Heads up! →see: Watch out!

health nut (someone who doesn't smoke, drink, etc.) el/la zanahorio(-a) (carrot) *Ven, Ec* ◆ *Pedro is so healthy that everyone considers him a health nut.* Pedro es tan sano que todo el mundo lo considera un zanahorio.

heaps →see: tons

hearsay →see: piece of gossip

the **heart of the matter** (the real reason for something) la madre del cordero (the mother of the lamb) *Peru, S. Cone, Sp ◆ You've gotten to the heart of the matter. That's really the important part of the problem. Has encontrado la madre del cordero. Realmente ésta es la parte importante del problema.*

heart's desire (dream) el sueño dorado (golden dream) *L. Am., Sp ◆ My heart's desire is to live in a tropical country eight months of the year. Mi sueño dorado es vivir en un país tropical ocho meses del año.*

Heck! →see: Darn!, Shoot!

a **heck of a** (+ noun) de mil (todos los) diablos (of a thousand [all the] devils, used to exaggerate something bad or uncomfortable) *Mex, ES, Sp ◆ They had a heck of an argument and couldn't do anything. Armaron una discusión de todos los diablos y no pudieron hacer nada.*

heebie-jeebies (nervousness) las ñáñaras *Mex, ES ◆ When I'm alone I get the heebie-jeebies. Cuando estoy sola me dan ñáñaras.*

to be the **height (of something)** →see: to be too much

to **heist** →see: to lift

Hello (on the phone). Aló. (Hello.) *most of L. Am.;* Bueno. (Good.) *Mex;* ¿A ver? (To see?) *Hond, Nic, CR, Hond, Col;* Oigo. (I'm hearing.) *Cuba;* ¿Quién es? (Who is it?) *Col, Sp;* ¡Hola! (Hello.) *U, Arg;* Diga., Dígame. (Tell., Tell me.) *Sp ◆ Hello, [this is] the Rosales family. Aló, familia Rosales.*

a **helluva** que te cagas (that you defecate; vulgar expression denoting something unusual or expensive) *Mex, Sp ◆ That's a helluva sun. Hace un sol que te cagas.*

helter-skelter (haphazardly, without a plan) a troche y moche (trochemoche) *parts of L. Am., Sp;* al tuntún *S. Cone, Sp ◆ They're spending helter-skelter. I don't know how they're going to be able to get back their investment. Están gastando a troche y moche. No sé cómo van a poder recuperar la inversión.*

henpecked man (whose wife orders him around) el mandilón (big commander, said in an ironic way) *Mex, ES;* el faldero (from falda, skirt) *Mex, ES;* el calzonudo (oversized pants) *Mex, ES, Peru, Ch, Arg;* el calzonazos (oversized pants) *Ch, Sp ◆ Hi, you henpecked husband, you. How's your little lady? Hola, mandilón. ¿Cómo está tu mujercita?*

He who hesitates is lost. El que pestañea pierde. (The person who blinks loses.) *L. Am., Sp*

Hey there! ¡Oiga! ¡Oye! (used to get attention of passerby, waiter, etc. command forms of oír; Listen!) *L. Am., Sp;* ¡Amigo! (Friend!) *Mex, DR, G, ES;* ¡Éjele! *Mex, PR, Col ◆ Hey there, I want to talk to you. Oye, quiero hablar contigo.*

Hi! ¡Hola! *L. Am.,Sp;* ¡Qui úbole!, ¡Qui úbo! (slang) *most of L. Am.;* ¡Qué uvas! (What grapes!, slang) *Mex, Ec ◆ Hi, Manuel! How are you? ¡Qui úbole, Manuel! ¿Cómo estás?*

hick 1. (country person, simple person from rural area, not always pejorative) el/la guajiro(-a) *Cuba ◆ That man talks like a hick. Ese hombre habla como un guajiro.* **2.** (naive person) el/la primo(-a) (cousin) *Mex, Sp ◆ Poor Martín. He's a poor hick and they always cheat him. Pobre Martín. Es un primo y siempre lo estafan.* **3.** (timid person) el/la jíbaro(-a) *PR ◆ Don't act like a hick. Go talk to her. No seas jíbaro. Ve y habla con ella.*

to be a **hick** ser más del campo que las amapolas (to be more from the country than poppies) *Sp ◆ Nico is a hick (a real country boy); he's never been in a supermarket. Nico es más del campo que las amapolas; nunca ha estado en un supermercado.*

high (on alcohol or drugs; →see also: stoned) acelerado(-a) (sped up) *Mex, PR, G, Col, Ch, Sp;* en nota (in note) *Mex, Cuba, DR, PR;* en pleno vuelo (in full flight) *Mex, Col, Ec;* cruzado(-a) (crossed) *Mex;* arrebatado(-a) (carried away) *Cuba, DR, PR, G;* colgado(-a) (hung, suspended) *Sp ◆ That dude seems high. Ese loco parece acelerado.*

highfalutin (chic; →see also: stuck-up) pipiris nais (nais is from the English "nice") *Mex, ES ◆ Don't invite her (that one); she thinks she's highfalutin. A esa no la invites; se cree pipiris nais.*

to **hightail it** →see: to get moving, to scoot, to take off

to the **hilt** (violently) a sangre y fuego (by blood and fire) *Mex, Sp ◆ He defended his po-*

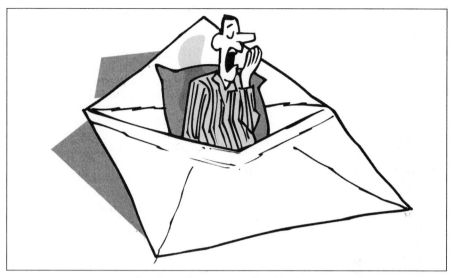

to hit the sack: *He was tired and hit the sack.*
Estuvo cansado y se metió en el sobre.

sition to the hilt, until finally they agreed that he was right. Defendió su postura a sangre y fuego, hasta que al final le dieron la razón.

hit 1. (marijuana) el toque (also, el toquesín) (touch) *Chicano, Mex, G, ES, Col* 2. →see also: smack

to **hit** (+ an age) caerle cincuenta castañas (tacos) (to have [+ number] chestnuts [bad words] fallen on one) *Sp* ◆ *He or she has hit fifty.* ◆ *Ya le han caído cincuenta castañas (tacos).*

to **hit like a ton of bricks** caerle como piedra (plomo) (to fall on someone like stone [lead]) *S. Cone* ◆ *What we read in the newspaper hit us like a ton of bricks. Lo que leimos en el periódico nos cayó como piedra.*

to **hit on** 1. (try to pick up) vacilar *Cuba, ES, Col, Ec;* llevarle la carga (to carry the cargo for someone) *U, Arg* ◆ *You're hitting on that girl, right? Estás vacilando a esa chama, ¿no?* 2. (call out the cavalry, go all out to win) echar (lanzar) los perros (also lanzar los canes) (to throw on the dogs) *Mex, C. Am., Col, Ven* (RVAR; *C. Am.:* echar los perros more common than lanzar; both are used in *Mex*); tirar/echar los tejos (to throw the disks) *U, Sp* ◆ *I hit on (went all out for) that girl but she doesn't pay attention to me. Le eché*

los perros a esa chica pero no me hace caso.

to **hit rock bottom** tocar fondo *L. Am., Sp* ◆ *It looks like the economy has hit rock bottom. Parece que la economía ha tocado fondo.*

to **hit someone like a bombshell** (arrive as a surprise, generally unpleasant) caerle a alguien como bomba *Mex, DR, PR, G, ES, S. Cone, Sp* ◆ *The news (The food) hit me like a bombshell. La noticia (La comida) me cayó como bomba.*

to **hit the ceiling** →see: to be steamed, to be upset with someone, to lose it

to **hit the jackpot** tocarle a alguien la lotería (to win the lottery; also caerle or sacar la lotería) *Mex, Cuba, S. Cone, Sp* ; encontrar una mina (de oro) (to find a [gold]mine, a way to live or get rich without working much) *Mex, ES, Ch, Sp Ese hombre encontró una mina de oro y se da la gran vida.* ◆ *That man hit the jackpot, and he lives the high life.*

to **hit the nail on the head** (figure out or be right about something) dar en el clavo *L. Am., Sp* ◆ *That's right! You hit the nail on the head. ¡Eso es! Diste en el clavo.*

to **hit the roof** →see: to lose it

to **hit the sack** (go to bed) meterse en el sobre (to put oneself in the envelope) *Ec, S. Cone, Sp;* irse a la cucha (to go to the doghouse) *U, Arg* ◆ *I'm super-tired. I'm going to hit the sack pretty soon and I won't wake up for about twenty hours.* **Estoy supercansado. Me voy a meter en el sobre pronto y no me despertaré hasta de aquí veinte horas.**

to **hit the target** dar en el blanco *L. Am., Sp* ◆ *I hit the target!* **¡Di en el blanco!**

to **hit the trail (road)** →see: to take off

to **hit up for a loan** tirarle un sablazo (to throw a blow with a saber) *Mex, Ch* ◆ *I don't have any money. I'm going to hit up my brother for a loan.* **No tengo dinero. Voy a tirarle un sablazo a mi hermano.**

to **hit where it hurts** dar en la madre (romper/partir la madre) (to give in the mother [to break the mother]) *Chicano, Mex, C. Am., Col;* dar en la torre (to give in the tower) *Mex, C. Am.* ◆ *They hit him (her) where it hurts.* **Le dieron en la madre.**

hitched (married) amarrado(-a) (tied) *Chicano, Mex, DR, G, ES, Col* ◆ *He's very young to be hitched already.* **Es muy joven para estar amarrado.**

to **hitchhike** →see: to thumb a ride

hogwash →see: baloney

holier-than-thou (person) el/la mocho(-a) *Mex* ◆ *My aunt is holier-than-thou (a real church lady).* **Mi tía es una mocha.**

Holy cow! →see: Holy smoke! Wow!

Holy smoke! 1. (a bit old-fashioned, used to express surprise or when there is a problem) ¡Rayos! (Lightning rays!) *most of L. Am., Sp;* ¡Diablo! (Devil!) *Mex, DR, PR, Col;* ¡Diablos! (Devils!) *Mex, DR, PR, Col;* ¡Dianche!, ¡Diantre! (used instead of ¡Diablo!) *Mex, DR, PR, Col;* ¡Virgen santísima! (Holy Virgin!) *L. Am., Sp;* ¡Ave María! *Mex, PR, G, CR, Col, Sp;* ¡Santísima Trinidad! (Holy Trinity!) *Mex, ES, CR, Col* ◆ *Holy smoke! Hundreds of people have died in the earthquake.* **¡Virgen santísima! Han muerto cientos de personas en el terremoto.** 2. (Good grief!; →see also: Darn! Wow!) ¡Qué barbaridad! (What barbarity!) *L. Am., Sp;* ¡Qué bárbaro! (How barbarous!) *L. Am., Sp* ◆ *Holy smoke! (How awful!) I'd never have thought her husband was*

capable of hitting her. *¡Qué barbaridad! Nunca imaginé que su esposo sería capaz de pegarle.* 3. (Holy cow!, euphemism for puta) ¡Pucha! ¡La pucha! *L. Am.;* ¡Púchica! *C. Am.* ◆ *Holy smoke! Her own daughters stole the money from her. ¡Púchica! Sus propias hijas le han robado el dinero.* 4. (used to express surprise, Jeeze Louise! Will wonders never cease!) ¡Chicles, muéganos y palomitas! (Chewing gum, caramel-covered candies, and popcorn!) *Mex, Col;* ¡Epa, Chepa! (Hey, Chepa!) *Nic;* ¡Cielo verde! (Green sky!) *PR* ◆ *Holy smoke! What are the Garcías doing here? ¡Cielo verde! ¿Qué hacen los García aquí?*

Holy smoke! My God! (not sacreligious) ¡Dios mío! (My God!) *L. Am., Sp;* ¡Dios santo! (Holy God!) *L. Am., Sp* ◆ *Holy smoke! I received good news from my family. ¡Dios mío! Recibí buenas noticias de mi familia.*

homebody (describing someone who likes to stay home and take care of the house; same in the masculine as in the feminine) maruja *Sp* ◆ *My husband and I are homebodies; we stay home on weekends. Mi esposo y yo somos muy marujas; los fines de semana nos quedamos en casa.*

to be **homeless** no tener donde caerse muerto (to not even have a place to fall dead in) *L. Am., Sp;* quedar en la calle (to be left in the street) *Mex, C. Am., S. Cone* ◆ *That poor man is homeless. Ese pobre señor no tiene donde caerse muerto.*

homosexual →see: gay

honcho →see: big shot, head honcho

honey →see: babe, broad, chick, dear, hot number, my love, sweetie

hoofing it (on foot) a patín (by skate, from a pata) *Chicano, Mex, G;* a pata (by foot of an animal) *Mex, C. Am., S. Cone, Sp;* a pincel (by paintbrush) *Mex, Hond, Nic, CR* ◆ *We went hoofing it to the clinic because there was a public transportation strike. Nos fuimos a pata a la clínica porque había huelga del transporte público.*

to **hook (someone) up with** enganchar(se) *Mex, ES, CR, Col;* hacer un gancho (to make a hook) *S. Cone, Sp* ◆ *Hook me up with her over there (introduce me). Engánchame con aquélla.*

hooker (prostitute; →see also: slut) la puta *L. Am., Sp* ◆ *She's a hooker and I don't want to see her.* **Es una puta y no la quiero ver.**

hoopla →see: mess

hoot (amusing thing someone does or clever or cutting remark) la puntada *Mex, ES* ◆ *What a hoot it was to do that singing at the party.* **Qué gran puntada la de cantar en la fiesta.**

to be **hopeless** (beyond help) no tener remedio (to have no remedy) *L. Am., Sp* ◆ *What a case! It's hopeless.* **¡Qué caso! No tiene remedio.**

hopeless case (someone very stupid) el/la loco(-a) (tonto[-a]) perdido(-a) (lost fool) *L. Am., Sp* ◆ *Felipe is a hopeless case. He doesn't know how to behave around other people.* **Felipe es un loco perdido. No sabe comportarse en sociedad.**

to be **hopping mad** estar mordido(-a) (to be bitten) *Mex, G, CR;* estar jetón, jetona (to be big mouth) *Mex, G, ES;* estar como un león (de bravo) (to be [mad as] a lion) *Mex, G, U;* estar que ladra (to be barking) *Mex, Sp* ◆ *He's hopping mad because he can't go out.* **Está jetón porque no puede salir.**

horny (→see also: hot) cachondo(-a) (vulgar; also, poner a alguien cachondo) *Mex, ES, Sp;* cabreado(-a) (vulgar) *Mex, CR, Col, Sp;* alzado(-a) (raised up, vulgar) *Mex, U, Arg* ◆ *You always make me horny (hot).* **Me pones siempre muy cachondo.**

to **horse around** →see: to joke around

horse of a different color →see: another kettle of fish

hot, to make (someone) hot (often with anger or sexual desire) calentar *L. Am., Sp* ◆ *Her look makes me hot.* **Su mirada me calienta.**

to be **hot** 1. (a woman) estar de muerte (to be of death) *Nic, U, Sp;* estar bomba (to be bomb) *DR, Sp;* ser una bomba (to be a bomb) *U, Arg* ◆ *Do you know the team's coach? She's hot.* **¿Conoces a la entrenadora del equipo? Está de muerte.** 2. (sexually turned on (→see also: fast, horny) estar caliente (to be hot) *L. Am., Sp;* estar excitado(-a) *L. Am., Sp;* estar como agua pa' chocolate (to be like water for chocolate, referring to anger or passion) *Mex;* tener una calentura (to have a fever) *U, Arg* ◆ *Let's make love, doll; I'm hot for you.* **Vamos a hacer el amor, muñeca; estoy caliente.** 3. (good in bed; said about women) estar/ser buenota (adj. or n.) *Chicano, Mex, ES, Pan, Ec, Para;* estar buenísima (to be very good) *Mex, DR, PR, ES, Ven, Ch* ◆ *That girl is hot (a hot number).* **Esa chica está buenísima (buenota).**

hot air (doubletalk; referring to Mexican actor Cantinflas in his satirical movies) la cantinflada (Cantinflas thing) *L. Am.* ◆ *It's all hot air.* **Son puras cantinfladas.**

hot chick (piece of ass) el culito (small ass, vulgar) *Mex, G, Ven*

hot number 1. (good-looking woman; →see also: babe) la mamasota (big mama, often used to get a woman's attention, a bit vulgar) *Mex, DR, PR, G, ES, Col;* la candela (candle) *Cuba, DR, PR* ◆ *Margarita is a hot number.* **Margarita es candela.** 2. (good-looking person, male or female; →see also: babe) el mango, manguito ([little] mango) *most of L. Am.;* el bizcocho (also, bizcochito) (biscuit, usually a woman) *Mex, PR, Col;* el forro (lining) *Mex;* el/la castigador(a) (punisher) *DR, PR, Col* ◆ *Manuel's a hot number.* **Manuel es un mango.**

hot potato (very delicate matter) la patata caliente (hot potato) *Mex, Sp* ◆ *Don't intervene in his problem; it's a hot potato and you'll get burned.* **No intervengas en su problema; es una patata caliente y te vas a quemar.**

hot under the collar (→see also: steamed) enchilado(-a) (sick from hot chilies) *Mex, G, Nic;* ardido(-a) (burned) *Mex, G, CR* ◆ *Rosa didn't allow José to kiss her and he got all hot under the collar.* **Rosa no permitió que José la besara y él se quedó enchilado.** ◆ *She's got me hot under the collar after what she said about me.* **Ella me tiene ardida después de lo que dijo de mí.**

hot-air artist →see: windbag

to **hotfoot it** →see: to take off

hothead enojón, enojona *L. Am., Sp;* fosforito (little match) *PR, Ven, U, Arg;* el/la chinchudo(-a) (big ugly bedbug) *U, Arg;* acalorado(-a) (heated up) *U, Arg, Sp* ◆ *Constanza is a real hothead.* **Constanza es muy enojona.**

to be a **hothouse flower** (overprotected, not allowed to grow or be independent) ser flor

de estufa (to be a flower on the stove) *Sp* ◆ *Until she was twenty years old, Lucía didn't leave home for more than one day at a time. She's a hothouse flower.* **Hasta que tuvo veinte años, Lucía no salió más de un día seguido de casa. Es una flor de estufa.**

to **hound** (pursue someone at all hours and in all places) no dejar (ni) a sol ni a sombra a alguien (to not leave someone in the sun or the shade) *L. Am., Sp* ◆ *That woman hounds her daughter; she's very dominating.* **Esta mujer no deja ni a sol ni a sombra a su hija; es muy dominadora.**

house of ill repute (bordello) donde te dicen hijito sin conocerte (where they call you my son without knowing you) *parts of L. Am., Sp* ◆ *Where did you go last night? —To a house of ill repute.* **¿Adónde fuiste anoche? —Adonde te dicen hijito sin conocerte.**

How about (if . . .)?; How do you like . . . ? ¿Qué le (te) parece (si...)? *L. Am., Sp* ◆ *How about if we go dancing?* **¿Qué te parece si vamos a bailar?** ◆ *How do you like the music?* **¿Qué te parece la música?**

How are things? (→see also: What's up?) ¿Qué tal? *L. Am., Sp;* ¿Cómo lo llevas? (How do you carry it?) *Mex, Sp* ◆ *How are things? How are you doing?* **¿Qué tal? ¿Cómo andas?**

How awful! (Good grief!) ¡Qué barbaridad! (What barbarity!) *L. Am., Sp;* ¡Qué bárbaro! (How barbarous!) *L. Am., Sp;* ¡Que horror! (What horror!) *L. Am., Sp* ◆ *How awful! I'd never have thought her husband would be capable of hitting her.* **¡Qué barbaridad! Nunca imaginé que su esposo sería capaz de pegarle.**

How can you think that? (disclaimer after a compliment) ¿Cómo cree(s)? *L. Am., Sp* ◆ *How young you look! —How can you think that?* **Te ves tan jovencita. —¿Cómo crees?**

How come? (For what reason?) ¿Por qué? *L. Am., Sp;* ¿A son de qué? *Mex, DR, Ch, U, Sp* (RVar *Mex, U:* ¿Al son de qué?) ◆ *How come you had to tell her that you saw her boyfriend at the beach?* **¿A son de qué tenías que contarle que viste a su novio en la playa?**

How delicious! ! ¡Qué rico (sabroso, delicioso)! *L. Am., Sp;* ¡Qué delicia! (What a delight!) *most of L. Am.* ◆ *How delicious this dessert you've prepared is.* **Qué delicia el postre que has preparado.**

How embarrassing! ¡Qué vergüenza! *L. Am., Sp;* ¡Qué bochorno! (What embarrassment!, What a heat wave!) *L. Am., Sp;* ¡Qué oso! (What a bear!) *Mex, Col* ◆ *How embarrassing! I began to introduce her to my English professor and I couldn't remember her name.* **¡Qué oso! Empezaba a presentarla a mi profesor de inglés y no pude acordarme de su nombre.**

How exciting! ¡Qué emoción! (What emotion!) *Mex, DR, PR, Col, S. Cone* ◆ *How exciting to see him!* **¡Qué emoción verlo!**

How nice of you to say so. Favor que usted me hace. (Favor that you [usted] do me.) *L. Am., Sp* ◆ *You've done an impeccable job; we are very satisfied with the results. —Thank you, how nice of you to say so.* **Ha hecho un trabajo impecable; estamos muy satisfechos con los resultados. —Gracias, favor que usted me hace.**

How should I put it (say this)? ¿Cómo (lo) diría? *L. Am., Sp;* ¿Cómo diré? *most of L. Am. (not S. Cone)* ◆ *What do you think of my decision? —Well, how should I put it? I think you are too young to get married.* **¿Qué piensas de mi decisión? —Bueno, ¿cómo lo diría? Pienso que eres muy joven para casarte.**

How thoughtful (of you)! ¡Qué ocurrencia! (What an occurrence! What a thing to occur to you!) *L. Am., Sp* ◆ *How thoughtful! You shouldn't have spent so much money on the gift for Miguelito.* **¡Qué ocurrencia! Nunca debiste gastar tanto dinero en el regalo para Miguelito.**

How wonderful! ¡Qué emoción! (What emotion!) *Mex, DR, PR, Col, S. Cone* ◆ *How wonderful to see you!* **¡Qué emoción verte!**

How's it going? (What's up?) ¿Cómo te ha ido? (How has it gone for you?) *L. Am., Sp;* ¿Cómo te va? (How's it going for you?) *L. Am., Sp;* ¿En qué patín andas? (What skate are you on?) *Mex, G, Ec;* ¿Cómo lo llevas? (How do you carry it?) *Mex, Sp* ◆ *How's it going? When did you get back from the country?* **¿Cómo te ha ido? ¿Cuándo llegaste del campo?**

How's the action? (→see also: What's up?) ¿Cómo está la movida? *parts of L. Am.*

hullabaloo (hoopla; →see also: mess) el jaleo *Mex, S. Cone, Sp;* el barullo *CR, U, Arg, Sp;* el cirio (candle) *Sp* ◆ *There was quite a hullabaloo in the street.* Había un jaleo impresionante en la calle.

humongous (great big) gigantesco(-a) *L. Am., Sp* sendo(-a) *Mex, C. Am.* ◆ *They served themselves humongous plates of tripe soup.* Se sirvieron sendos platos de menudo.

to **humor someone** seguirle a alguien la corriente (to follow someone's current) *Mex, DR, ES, Nic, S. Cone, Sp* ◆ *This girl is crazy. It's better to humor her and not argue.* Esta chica está loca. Es mejor seguirle la corriente y no discutir con ella.

to be **hung over** estar crudo(-a) (to be raw) *Mex, C. Am.;* parecer araña fumigada (to seem like a fumigated spider) *Mex, ES;* estar de goma (to be made of gum, rubber) *C. Am.;* tener resaca (to have undertow) *Peru, S. Cone, Sp* ◆ *I feel bad. I'm hung over from the weekend.* Me siento mal. Tengo resaca del fin de semana.

to be **hung up** colgarse (to hang, be suspended) *Mex, ES* ◆ *He was hung up on the telephone for an hour.* Se colgó una hora en el teléfono.

to be **hungry as a bear** tener hambre de león (to be hungry as a lion) *Mex;* tener un hambre de caballo (to be hungry as a horse) *Sp* ◆ *What is there to eat? The kids are hungry as bears.* ¿Qué hay que comer? Los niños tienen hambre de león.

hunk (good-looking guy; →see also: stud, hot) el tipazo *Mex, DR, ES, Col;* el cuero (skin, leather; also used for women) *Mex;* el galanazo (used instead of galán) *Mex;* el churro (long doughnut or fritter) *Peru, S. Cone* ◆ *Jaime is a real hunk.* Jaime es un tipazo muy bueno.

to be a **hunk** (strong and attractive) estar como un tanque (como un tren) (to be like a tank [like a train]) *Mex, Sp* ◆ *Elvira says that her boyfriend is a hunk.* Elvira dice que su novio está como un tanque.

to **hurry up** →see: to step on it

to **hush** →see: to put a lid on it

hussy →see: slut

to **hustle** (throw oneself into something, do something decisively; →see also: to get moving) echar huevos a un asunto, echarle huevos (to throw eggs or testicles to an issue, vulgar) *Mex, C. Am., Sp;* echarle ganas (to throw desires at it; not vulgar) *Mex* ◆ *We're going to really hustle and work hard so we can leave early.* Le vamos a echar huevos a este trabajo para salir temprano.

to **hustle to get (work, money, etc.)** (get with it) rebuscarse (to relook for oneself) *ES, Pan, U* ◆ *My husband found himself without work and this week he has to hustle (to find work).* Mi marido se quedó sin trabajo y esta semana tiene que rebuscarse.

hustler el gavilán (hawk) *Mex, Col;* el compadrito (little pal) *Arg;* el ligón (big linker, referring to a womanizer) *Col, Sp* ◆ *There are lots of girls at the swimming pool; that's why so many hustlers have arrived.* Hay muchas chicas en la piscina; por eso llegaron tantos gavilanes. ◆ *He's a hustler. Every week he goes out with a different girl.* Es un ligón. Cada semana sale con una chica distinta.

I believe so. (I should say so.) Ya lo creo. (I already believe it.) *L. Am., Sp* ◆ *Are you sure you'll finish the project by next week? —I believe so. ¿Estás seguro que terminarás el proyecto para la próxima semana? —Ya lo creo.*

I can't believe my eyes! Incredible! Si no lo veo, ¡no lo creo! (If I don't see it, I don't believe it!) *Mex, ES, S. Cone, Sp* ◆ *Salvador got mad and hit his wife. I can't believe my eyes! Salvador se enojó con su mujer y le pegó. Si no lo veo, ¡no lo creo!*

I don't give a damn. (vulgar; →see also: to not give a damn) Me vale. (used instead of Me vale madre or verga [vulgar].) *Mex, ES, Col;* Me la suda. *Mex, Sp;* Me importa un carajo. *PR, U, Arg* ◆ *I don't give a damn what they think. I'm going on vacation. Me la suda lo que piensen. Voy de vacaciones.*

I don't want to hear your life story. No me cuentes tu vida. *Mex, Sp* ◆ *I'm really tired. I don't want to hear your life story. Estoy recansado. No me cuentes tu vida.*

I feel for you. (I feel your pain.) Lo (La/Le) acompaño en su dolor (en sus sentimientos). Te acompaño en tu dolor. (I accompany you in your pain.) *L. Am., Sp;* Estoy con ustedes. (I am with you.) *L. Am., Sp* ◆ *Elena, they told me that your father passed away. I feel for you. Elena, me dijeron que falleció tu padre. Te acompaño en tu dolor.*

I see. Ya se ve. (It's already seen; can be an expression of agreement.) *L. Am., Sp* ◆ *I see you've devoted yourself to taking care of your parents. Ya se ve que te has dedicado a cuidar a tus padres.*

I see what you're up to. Te veo venir. (I see you coming.) *Mex, Peru, U, Arg, Sp;* Te conozco, bacalao, aunque vengas disfraza'o (disfrazado). (I know you, codfish, although you come in disguise.) *Sp* ◆ *I see what you're up to. What are you looking for? Te veo venir. ¿Qué andas buscando?*

I see you coming →see: I see what you're up to.

I swear (it) to you. Se (Te) lo juro. *L. Am., Sp* ◆ *It's the truth, dad, I swear to you. Es la verdad, papá, te lo juro.*

I'll keep my distance. (Who cares about that person?) Santo que no me quiere, basta con no rezarle. (Saint that doesn't like me, it's enough not to pray to him.) *parts of L. Am.* ◆ *Verónica doesn't want to see you anymore. —Well, I'll keep my distance (I don't want to bother with someone who doesn't care about me). Verónica no quiere verte más. —Santo que no me quiere, basta con no rezarle.*

I'm ready to drop. Estoy que me caigo. (I'm about to fall over.) *U, Arg, Sp* ◆ *This week I worked eighty hours. I'm ready to drop. Esta semana trabajé ochenta horas. Estoy que me caigo.*

I'm screwed. (vulgar) Estoy jodido(-a). *L. Am., Sp* Me lleva la chingada. (The chingada, violated woman, is taking me. Euphemism: Me lleva el chile.) *Mex, C. Am.* ◆ *I'm screwed; my car is messed up. Me lleva la chingada; se me fregó el carro.*

idiot 1. (→see also: fool) el/la tonto(-a) (perdido[-a]) *L. Am., Sp;* el/la imbécil *L. Am., Sp;* el/la cretino(-a) (cretin) *L. Am., Sp;* el/la lentejo(-a) (sounds like lenteja, lentil, or a combination of lento, slow, and pendejo, stupid) *Mex, Col, Peru;* el/la pensante *Mex, Col;* el/la guajolote(-a) (turkey) *Mex;* aguacate (aguacatón) (avocado) *PR, G, ES, CR, Col;* el/la batata (sweet potato) *Para, Arg;* el melón, la melona (melon) *Sp;* el merluzo (from merluza, hake, a kind of fish) *Sp;* el paquete (package) *Sp* ◆ *Don't get involved with him; he's an idiot. No te metas con él, que es aguacatón (es un imbécil).* **2.** (dummy) el buey, güey (from "bovis": stupid, lazy [castrated] animal, often used with affection among men, a mild insult like SOB) *Chicano, Mex, PR, ES, Col* ◆ *What an idiot I am; I forgot my passport.* ◆ *Qué güey* soy; olvidé el pasaporte. **3.** (asshole; →see also: fool) (all vulgar) **pendejo(-a)** (pubic hair) *Mex, DR, PR, C. Am., Col, Ven;* **el/la boludo(-a)** (big balled) *Nic, CR, S. Cone;* **pelotudo(-a)** (big-balled) *S. Cone;* **el/la gilipollas** *Sp* ♦ *The governor is a damn idiot who doesn't know how to do anything.* **El gobernador es un boludo que no sabe hacer nada. 4.** (used affectionately between friends; vulgar; can also mean lazy) **el huevón, la huevona** (big egg) *CR, PR, Col, Ec, Ch* ♦ *He acts like an idiot around girls.* **Se comporta como un huevón con las chicas.**

if I were you yo que tú (I that you) *L. Am., Sp* ♦ *If I were you, I wouldn't buy it.* **Yo que tú, no lo compraría.**

If you lie down with dogs, you get up with fleas. (Keeping bad company will teach you bad ways.) El que con lobos anda a aullar aprende. (The person who walks with wolves will learn to howl.) *Mex, Nic* ♦ *Don't go out with those drunks. If you lie down with dogs, you get up with fleas.* **No salgas con esos borrachos. El que con lobos anda a aullar aprende.**

If you snooze you lose. El que pestañea pierde. (The person who blinks loses.) *L. Am., Sp* ♦ *Trust in yourself because if you snooze you lose.* **Confía en ti mismo, porque el que pestañea pierde.**

If you want. Como quiera(s). *L. Am., Sp* ♦ *Shall we eat at that restaurant? —If you want.* **¿Comemos en aquel restaurán? —Como quieras.**

the **impossible** (overcomplication of something) la cuadratura del círculo (the squareness of the circle) *Mex, Sp* ♦ *They want to demonstrate the impossible.* **Quieren demostrar la cuadratura del círculo.**

in →see: connection (social, political, etc.), cool, to have connections, with it

to be **in a bind 1.** →see also: to have a rough time, in hot water) estar metido(-a) en un rollo (to be put in a roll) *Mex, G, Nic, Col, Ven, Ec, Peru, Sp* ♦ *I have a big problem. I'm in a real bind.* **Tengo un gran problema. De veras, estoy metida en un rollo. 2.** (usually economic; →see also: in hot water) colgado(-a) del cuello (hung by the neck) *Mex, ES* ♦ *The drought has left us in a bind.* **La sequía nos ha dejado colgados del cuello.**

in a damn godforsaken spot (→see also: in a godforsaken spot; vulgar) en el culo del mundo (in the world's ass) *PR, Nic, Ven, U, Arg, Sp;* en el quinto coño (carajo) (in the fifth female [male] organ) *DR, PR, Sp;* en la quinta puñeta *PR, Sp* ♦ *Marcelino lives in some damn godforsaken spot (in goddamn Timbuktu); we have to take several buses to get there.* **Marcelino vive en el culo del mundo; para llegar allí tenemos que tomar varios autobuses.**

to be **in a dither** →see: to be mixed up

to be **in a fix** →see: to be in a bind, messed up

in a flash (in a hurry; →see also: full blast, like a shot, on the fly, quick as lightning) volado(-a) (blown up high or flown away) *Mex, Nic, Col* ♦ *He got to the hospital in a flash.* **Llegó volado al hospital.**

in a godforsaken spot (far away) en (hasta) el quinto infierno (in [as far as] the fifth hell) *Mex, DR, PR, ES, U, Arg;* en el quinto pino (in the fifth pine) *PR, Sp;* donde el diablo perdió el poncho (where the devil lost his poncho) *S. Cone, Sp;* donde Cristo perdió el gorro (la sandalia) (where Christ lost his cap [sandal]) *Sp;* donde el diablo dio las tres voces (where the devil gave the three words) *Sp* ♦ *My friend moved and I can't go see her because she lives out in some godforsaken spot.* **Mi amiga se mudó y no la puedo ir a ver porque ahora vive en el quinto infierno.**

to be **in a good mood** estar de buen humor *L. Am., Sp;* estar/andar de buenas (to be/walk good) *L. Am., Sp;* estar de/andar de/tener buenas pulgas (to be of/walk/have good fleas) *ES, CR, Col, Ch, Arg, Sp* ♦ *Today he is in a good mood.* **Hoy anda de buenas pulgas.**

to be **in a jam** →see: to be in a bind, in hot water

in a jiffy (in an instant; →see also: in the blink of an eye) en un santiamén (in the time it takes to say **santiamén**) *L. Am., Sp;* en una avemaría (in the time it takes to say Ave María) *L. Am., Sp;* en menos que canta un gallo (in less than a cock crows) *L. Am., Sp;* en un dos por tres (in a two by three) *L. Am.;* en dos patadas (in two kicks) *Mex, ES, CR, Col, Peru, S. Cone;* en un zas *Mex, ES* ♦

I can do it in a jiffy. Lo puedo hacer en un santiamén.

to be **in a league (class) of its own** (the best or worst; →see also: to be too much) no tener madre (to have no mother) *Mex, ES* ◆ *You have to read this book; it's in a league of its own. Tienes que leer este libro; no tiene madre.*

in a little while al rato *L. Am., Sp;* al ratón *Mex, Col* ◆ *See you in a while. Nos vemos al ratón.*

to be **in a pinch** →see: to be in a bind, in hot water

in a ridiculous outfit fachoso(-a) *Mex* ◆ *You're going in that ridiculous outfit? You have to change. ¿Así de fachosa vas a ir? Necesitas cambiar.*

in a sloppy getup (badly dressed, dirty, looking like a slob) zarrapastroso(-a) (from zarrapastra, meaning both mud and claw, implying dirty and torn) *L. Am., Sp* ◆ *And how dare he go to a sweet-fifteen coming-out party in a sloppy getup like that? ¿Y cómo se atreve a ir a una quinceañera así de zarrapastroso?*

to be **in a tight spot** (economically; →see also: to be in a bind) comerse un cable (to eat a cable) *Cuba, DR, PR, Pan* ◆ *I've been out of work for three months, so we're in a tight spot financially. Llevo tres meses sin trabajo, así que andamos comiéndonos un cable.*

to be **in a (very) bad mood** estar de muy mal humor *L. Am., Sp;* andar/estar de malas (to go/be bad) *L. Am., Sp;* estar que me (lo, la, etc.) lleva el diablo (to be ready for the devil to take) *Mex, DR, G, ES, CR;* estar como todos los diablos (to be like all the devils) *Mex, G, CR* ◆ *She's in a very bad mood. Y anda que se la lleva el diablo.*

to be **in bad shape** 1. (badly dressed) estar hecho(-a) unos zorros (to be made foxes) *Sp* ◆ *She came back from the party in bad shape. Llegó de la fiesta hecha unos zorros.* 2. (disgusting mess) estar hecho(-a) un asco (to be made into something disgusting) *ES, S. Cone, Sp* ◆ *I'm in bad shape after working all day in the garden. I have to take a bath before supper. Estoy hecho un asco luego de trabajar todo el día en la huerta. Tengo que bañarme antes de cenar.*

to be **in charge** →see: to call the shots

in droves →see: tons

in (good) shape en (buena) forma *L. Am., Sp* ◆ *Don César is in good shape for his age. Don César está en buena forma para su edad.*

in great detail con pelos y señales (with hairs and gestures) *L. Am., Sp* ◆ *I explained it in great detail. Lo expliqué con pelos y señales.*

in hot water (in a bad position or situation; →see also: to be in a bind) con la soga al cuello (with the noose at the neck) *L. Am., Sp;* estar en la olla (to be in the pot) *parts of L. Am.;* en las astas del toro (usually used with dejar) (at the horns of the bull) *Mex, Sp;* en la estacada (usually used with dejar) (in the stockade) *Bol, Ch, U, Sp;* sonado(-a) (sounded, rung) *S. Cone* ◆ *They left us in hot water. Nos dejaron en las astas del toro.*

to be **in jail** →see: to be in the clinker

to be **in knee pants** (to be green, have little or no knowledge of something; →see also: to be a greenhorn) estar en pañales (to be in diapers) *L. Am., Sp* ◆ *You don't have experience; you're still in knee pants. No tienes experiencia; estás en pañales aún.*

in one fell swoop →see: at once

in one's birthday suit →see: in the raw

to be **in one's element** (enjoy comforts and conveniences) estar como pez en el agua (to be like a fish in water) *L. Am., Sp* ◆ *I feel very happy; I'm really in my element here. Me siento muy contento; aquí estoy como pez en el agua.*

in poor taste →see: tacky

to be **in seventh heaven** (→see also: to be happy as a lark) estar en la gloria (to be in one's glory) *L. Am., Sp* ◆ *I'm in seventh heaven when it's cool out. Estoy en la gloria cuando hace fresco.*

to be **in someone else's shoes** (be in someone else's circumstances or situation) estar en el pellejo de otro (to be in someone else's skin) *L. Am., Sp* ◆ *You can't understand his situation because you're not in his shoes. No puedes entender su situación porque no estás en su pellejo.*

in the blink of an eye (→see also: in a jiffy) en un abrir y cerrar de ojos (in an opening and closing of the eyes) *L. Am., Sp;*

en un parpadeo (in the blink of an eye) *Mex, ES, Nic* ◆ *They made the decisions in the blink of an eye. Se tomaron las decisiones en un abrir y cerrar de ojos.*

in the boonies (far away, on the outskirts; →see also: in a godforsaken spot) en las chimbambas *DR, PR, Sp* ◆ *They have a house out in the boonies. Tienen una casa en las chimbamas.*

in the buff →see: in the raw

to be **in the clinker** (in jail) estar en la jaula (to be in the cage) *Chicano, Mex, Cuba, DR, Col;* estar en chirona *Mex, most of C. Am., Peru, Sp;* estar a la sombra (to be in the shade) *Mex, Cuba, G, Peru, S. Cone, Sp;* estar en el bote (to be in the jar, container) *Mex, Cuba, C. Am.;* estar de vacaciones en el bote (to be on vacation in the jar) *Mex, Cuba;* estar en el tambo *Mex, ES;* estar en la cana (to be in a small space) *Cuba, Ec, Peru, Ch, Arg;* estar precioso (to be precious, humorous play on estar preso, meaning to be a prisoner) *Ch, U* ◆ *Mateo was selling cocaine, but now he's in the clinker. Mateo vendía cocaína, pero ahora está en la jaula (en chirona).*

to be **in the clover** →see: loaded, to be loaded, moneybags

to be **in the dark** quedarse a oscuras (to be left in the dark) *Mex, Ch, Sp;* estar en ayunas (to be fasting) *Mex, S. Cone, Sp* ◆ *Eduardo's father is completely in the dark about his plans. El padre de Eduardo está completamente a oscuras de sus planes.*

to be **in the eye of the storm** →see: to be in a bind

to be **in the hole** (deep in debt; →see also: to be broke) estar cargado(-a) de deudas (to be loaded with debts) *Mex;* estar vendido(-a) (to be sold) *Mex;* estar endrogado(-a) (to be drugged) *Mex, ES* ◆ *Estoy vendida; no puedo usar mi tarjeta de crédito. I'm in the hole (deeply in debt); I can't use my credit card.*

to be **in the know** estar en el ajo (to be in the garlic) *Mex, Sp* ◆ *They know what's happening. They're in the know. Bien saben lo que está pasando. Están en el ajo.*

in the long run a largo plazo *L. Am., Sp;* a la larga *L. Am., Sp* ◆ *They haven't studied the effects of that medication in the long run. No se ha estudiado los efectos de ese medicamento a largo plazo.*

in the meantime por lo pronto, por de pronto *L. Am., Sp* ◆ *We sold our house in the country. In the meantime we'll rent an apartment in the city. Vendimos nuestra casa en el campo. Por lo pronto alquilaremos un apartamento en la ciudad.*

in the proper way (perfectly, as it should be; →see also: on the up and up, super) como Dios manda (as God commands) *L. Am., Sp* ◆ *We're going to do it in the proper way (good and proper). Lo vamos a hacer como Dios manda.*

in the raw (naked) en cueros (in skins) *Mex, DR, G, Sp;* en carnes (in flesh) *Sp* ◆ *The bathroom door was open; I went in and Jacinto was in the raw, shaving. La puerta del baño estaba abierta; entré y Jacinto estaba en carnes, afeitándose.*

in Timbuktu →see: in a godforsaken spot

in vain en balde (in bucket) *L. Am., Sp* ◆ *After the fire, they tried to recover the photos in vain. Después del incendio, en balde trataron de recuperar las fotos.*

In your dreams. (sarcastic; →see also: No way.) Ni soñarlo. *L. Am., Sp* ◆ *Can I smoke here in the living room? —In your dreams. ¿Puedo fumar aquí en la sala? —No, ni soñarlo.*

in your (his, her) element en su propia salsa (in his or her sauce) *Mex, Peru, S. Cone, Sp* ◆ *With this new group of friends, Mario is in his element. Con este nuevo grupo de amigos, Mario se encuentra como en su propia salsa.*

It beats me. →see: to not get it

It dawned on me (him, etc.). Caí (Cayó) en la cuenta. (I [He] fell into the account.) *Mex, DR, PR, U, Arg, Sp* ◆ *When I saw his photo, it dawned on me (I figured out) that I had known him for many years. Cuando vi su foto, caí en la cuenta de que lo conocía desde hacía muchos años.*

It doesn't do a thing for me. No me vuelve loco(-a). (It doesn't drive me crazy.) *Ch* ◆ *The truth is that this restaurant doesn't do a thing for me. La verdad es que este restaurante no me vuelve loco.*

It never rains but it pours. Las desgracias nunca vienen solas. (Bad things never come alone or one at a time.) *L. Am., Sp* ♦ *I missed the bus, arrived late to work, couldn't finish my report on time, and I found out my girlfriend is cheating on me. It never rains but it pours. Perdí el autobus, llegué tarde al trabajo, no pude terminar a tiempo mi informe y supe que mi novia me engaña. Las desgracias nunca vienen solas.*

It was a washout. (→see also: to wash out, to blow it) Se jodió el invento. (The invention or TV broke, said when when something goes wrong or is not obtained, slightly vulgar) *Sp;* Tronó como un ejote (It snapped like a peapod.) *Mex*

It was almost in the bag. Voló la paloma. (The dove flew off.) *Mex, ES*

It was love at first sight! Huy, ¡qué flechazo! (Oh, what a shot of the [Cupid's] arrow!) *Mex, DR, Col, U, Arg, Sp*

It will do just fine. (One thing is as good as another.) A falta de pan, buenas son tortas. (Where there is no bread, cakes are fine.) *L. Am., Sp* ♦ *I don't like Amanda's food, but it will do just fine. No me gusta la comida de Amanda, pero a falta de pan, buenas son tortas.*

It would be a different story (for me). Otro gallo (me) cantaría (cantara). (Another rooster would be singing for me.) *L. Am., Sp* ♦ *If I'd studied math, it would be a different story for me. I'd be able to choose my course of studies. Si hubiera estudiado matemáticas, otro gallo me cantaría. Hubiera podido elegir la carrera.*

It's a bitch (of a situation). Está cabrón. (vulgar) *most of L. Am.* ♦ *You're impossible. (Nothing can be done with you.) It's a bitch of a situation. ♦ No se puede contigo. Está cabrón.*

It's a deal. Trato hecho. (Agreement made.) *L. Am., Sp;* Sale y vale. (It goes/turns out and it's worth it; also, just Sale.) *Mex, C. Am., Col;* ¡Juega! (Play!) *Mex, ES, Col;* Vale. (It is worth something.) *Col, Sp* ♦ *I'll buy your car. —It's a deal. Te compro el carro. —Trato hecho.*

It's a hopeless case. No tiene remedio. (It has no cure.) *L. Am., Sp;* ¡Nadie lo (la) salva! (No one saves him [her, it]!) *Mex, U* ♦ *What a case! It's hopeless. ¡Qué caso! No tiene remedio.*

It's a lost cause. No tiene remedio. (It has no cure.) (L. Am., Sp); . Es como arar en el mar. (It's like ploughing the sea.) *Mex, DR, PR;* ¡Nadie lo (la) salva! (No one saves him [her, it]!) *Mex, U* ♦ *This is the third time I've cleaned the kitchen today. It's a lost cause. Es la tercera vez hoy que limpio la cocina. Es como arar en el mar.*

It's a piece of cake (easy). →see: to be a piece of cake

It's a scorcher. Se caen los patos asados. (Ducks are falling already roasted.) *Ch* ♦ *This summer is a scorcher. Este verano se caen los patos asados.*

It's a serious matter. (There's something very serious or difficult that has to be talked about.) Son palabras mayores. (They are major words.) *Mex, DR, ES, Nic, Peru, S. Cone* ♦ *We're going to talk some more about your decision to get married. Marriage . . . it's a serious matter. Vamos a hablar más sobre tu decisión de casarte. El matrimonio... ya son palabras mayores.*

It's a sure thing. (used for promises) Eso está hecho. (That's done.) *Sp* ♦ *Do you want me to paint your house this summer? It's a sure thing. ¿Quieres que te pinte la casa este verano? Eso está hecho.*

It's all down the drain. (said when one's hopes for something have been destroyed) El gozo en un pozo. (The enjoyment in a well or pit.) *Mex, Sp*

It's an ugly business. Está el asunto feo. *L. Am., Sp* ♦ *What do you think of all the environmental changes in the last twenty years? —It's an ugly business. ¿Qué piensas de todos los cambios ambientales de los últimos veinte años? —Está el asunto feo.*

It's at fever pitch (and getting worse). Está que arde. (It's burning.) *L. Am., Sp* ♦ *The situation in my house is at fever pitch. My parents don't speak to each other. La situación en mi casa está que arde. Mis padres no se hablan.*

It's at rock bottom. Está por el suelo. (It's down on the floor.) *L. Am.* ♦ *The economic situation is at rock bottom. La situación económica está por el suelo.*

It's common knowledge. (It's understood.) Ni que decir tiene(s). (You don't have to say it.) *Mex, Peru, Sp* ◆ *It's common knowledge; we already know.* Ni que decir tienes; ya lo sabemos.

It's his (her) hobbyhorse. Cada loco con su tema. (Every crazy person with his or her subject, usually said when someone is very insistent about something.) *L. Am., Sp* ◆ *Let's let him talk; it's his hobbyhorse.* Dejémoslo que hable; cada loco con su tema.

It's in the bag (said when something has been obtained or done). *Ese arroz ya se coció.* (That rice has already been cooked.) *Mex, ES* ◆ *What you planned is going well. It's in the bag.* Lo que planeaste va por buen camino. Ese arroz ya se coció.

It's like a broken record. (same thing over and over) Este disco tiene raya. (Este disco está rayado.) (This record has a scratch [is scratched].) *Mex, DR, ES, Nic, Ch*

It's no picnic. (It's not that easy; →see also: to be like pulling teeth) No es soplar y hacer botellas. (It's not blowing and making bottles.) *Cuba, Hond, ES, Nic, Col, Ven,* *Ec, U, Arg, Sp* ◆ *Driving this type of special car is no picnic. You need to be specially trained.* Conducir este tipo de coches especiales no es soplar y hacer botellas. Necesitas una buena preparación.

It's not all that bad. No es para tanto. (It's not for so much.) *L. Am., Sp* ◆ *Don't get mad, Alfonsina. It's not all that bad.* No te enojes, Alfonsina, no es para tanto.

It's the damn pits (unbearable). Está cabrón. (vulgar) *most of L. Am.* ◆ *I can't live with that woman any longer. It's the damn pits.* Ya no puedo vivir con esa mujer. Está cabrón.

It's the pits (in a bad way). Está por el suelo. (It's down on the floor.) *L. Am.* ◆ *How's the situation at work? —It's the pits.* ¿Qué tal la situación en el trabajo? –Está por el suelo.

to be an **item (a couple)** estar enganchados (to be hooked up with) *Mex, ES, CR, Col;* estar empatados (to be tied) *Mex, PR, Ven* ◆ *Really? Ofelia and Pedro are an item?* ¿De veras? ¿Ofelia y Pedro están empatados?

J

to **jabber (away)** →see: to chatter (away)

to **jack (steal)** →see: to lift

jalopy (old car) el cacharro *Mex, DR, PR, Col, U, Arg, Sp;* la carcacha *Mex, DR, G, ES, Col* ◆ *It's time for you to trade in that jalopy for a new car.* Ya es hora de que cambies esa carcacha por un carro nuevo.

jam session la descarga (discharge, unloading) *Cuba, PR, Col,* ◆ *Fantastic jam session by the band.* Tremenda descarga la del conjunto.

Jeez! →see: Darn! Holy smoke! Wow!

Jeez Louise! →see: Holy smoke!

to **jerk around** (→see also: to bug [pester], to screw up) fregar (to scrub, scour, rub [the wrong way]) *most of L. Am.* ◆ *They jerked us around again.* Nos fregaron otra vez.

to **jerk off** (masturbate) hacerse una paja (to make oneself a straw, vulgar) *L. Am., Sp;* usar Manuela, hacer el amor con Manuela *Mex, Cuba, DR, PR, G, Col, Ch*

jerk 1. (→see also: loser) el cero a la izquierda (zero to the left) *L. Am., Sp;* el/la mequetrefe *Mex, DR, PR, G, ES, Nic, S. Cone, Sp;* naco (-a) (from totonaco, an Indian tribe, formerly with a racist meaning but now of any social class) *Mex;* el/la pelado(-a) (peeled, bald) *Mex;* el/la pelagatos (cat skinner) *PR, ES, Ch;* el bacán (controller of a woman who earns money for him, from Lunfardo, Buenos Aires slang; often someone with money) *S. Cone* ◆ *I'm not going to allow any old jerk to marry my daughter.* No voy a permitir que cualquier pelagatos se case con mi hija. **2.** (damn jerk, damn idiot) el cabrón, la cabrona (big goat; vulgar; masculine form used with affection among males to friends jokingly) *Mex, Cuba, PR, C. Am., Col, Bol, Ch, Sp;* el pinche buey (slightly vulgar) *Mex, Col;* el/la boludo(-a) (big balled, vulgar) *Nic, CR, S. Cone;* pelotudo(-a) (big-balled, vulgar) *S. Cone;* el/la gilipollas (vulgar, from polla) *Sp* ◆ *Don't tell me that damn jerk is*

Miguel's brother! *¡No me digas que ese pinche buey es el hermano de Miguel!*

jerk 3. (shithead, proud or stupid person, snob, fake; vulgar) el/la comemierda (eat shit) *Mex, Cuba, DR, PR, G, ES, Nic, Col* ◆ *I can't stand Lucy's cousin. He's a damn jerk (shithead); he thinks he's better than everyone else.* No soporto al primo de Lucy. Es un tremendo comemierda; se cree mejor que todo el mundo.

jerk 4. (damn jerk, SOB) mal nacido(-a) (badly born, meaning bastard; vulgar) *L. Am., Sp* ◆ *She's a damn jerk. She doesn't take care of her mother, who is old and sick.* Es una mal nacida. No cuida ni se preocupa de su madre, que es vieja y está enferma.

jerk-off (masturbator) el/la pajero(-a) *parts of S. Cone, Sp*

jerking off (masturbation, vulgar) la puñeta *Chicano, Mex, U;* Manuela (pun on mano, meaning hand, as in usar Manuela) *Mex, Cuba, DR, PR, G, Col, Ch;* la paja *L. Am., Sp*

to **jilt** (→see also: to dump, to write off) dar calabazas (ayotes) (to give pumpkins [squash]) *C. Am.* ◆ *Poor Martín. His girlfriend jilted him.* Pobre Martín. Su novia le dio calabazas.

jinx el gafe *Sp* ◆ *Every time Juan goes in the car with us something happens. He's a jinx.* Siempre que va Juan en el coche nos pasa algo. Es un gafe.

jittery (nervous from caffeine; →see also: to be on edge) nervioso(-a) (nervous) *L. Am., Sp;* acelerado(-a) (sped up) *Mex, PR, G, Col, Ch, Sp* ◆ *I had three coffees and now I'm jittery.* Tomé tres cafés y ahora estoy acelerada.

to **jive-talk (feed a line)** cotorrear *Chicano, Mex, Col* ◆ *He was jive-talking me, but I didn't pay him any attention.* Me estaba cotorreando, pero no le hice caso.

job (work, slang) la chamba *Mex, C. Am., Col, Ven, Ec, Peru;* el camello (camel) *Mex, ES, Col, Ec;* el chance (chance) *Mex, G;* el martilleo (hammering) *Mex, Col*; el curro *Sp* ◆ *Gerardo got a good job.* **Gerardo consiguió una buena chamba.**

john →see: restroom

John (Jane) Doe →see: so-and-so

joint 1. (bar, usually small; →see also: dive) el garito *Sp* ◆ *The police arrived at the joint and took everyone there with them.* **La policía llegó al garito y se llevó a todos los presentes. 2.** (marijuana cigarette) el pito (whistle, fife) *Mex, Cuba, G, Nic, Ch*; el pitillo *Mex, G, Col*; el canuto *Mex, Sp*; el porro *U, Arg, Sp*; el churro (long doughnut or fritter) *Mex* ◆ *He went out and smoked a joint.* **Salió y fumó un pito.**

to **joke around (fool or goof around)** vacilar (con alguien) *Mex, Cuba, DR, G, Pan, Col*; bachatear *Cuba, PR*; gufear *PR* ◆ *He's joking around (having fun) with his friend.* **Está vacilando con su amiga.**

joking →see: clowning around, to joke around

to **josh** →see: to joke around, to put someone on

to **jump for joy** dar saltos de alegría (to give jumps of happiness) *L. Am., Sp* ◆ *With the news they gave her about her daughter, Susana was jumping for joy.* **Con la noticia que le dieron sobre su hija, Susana daba saltos de alegría.**

to **jump the gun (enjoy something before it should be enjoyed, usually with a sexual overtone)** comer la torta antes de la fiesta (to eat the cake before the party) *ES*; comer el sanduche antes del recreo (to eat the sandwich before recess) *PR* ◆ *The bride is pregnant. Looks like they jumped the gun.* **La novia está embarazada. Parece que comieron la torta antes de la fiesta.**

junk 1. (piece of junk, trash) el cacharro *Mex, DR, PR, Col, U, Arg, Sp*; la cafrería *Mex, PR* ◆ *This piece of junk (car) is going to leave us out in the middle of the highway some day.* **Este cacharro cualquier día nos deja tirados en medio de la carretera. 2.** (pieces of crap) la(s) porquería(s) (pig stuff) *L. Am., Sp*; puras madres (pure mothers, vulgar) *Mex, C. Am.*; las guarrerías (pig things) *Sp* ◆ *All these things are pure junk.* **Todas estas cosas son puras madres. 3.** (piece of crap, trick; vulgar) la chingadera *Chicano, Mex, G, ES*

◆ *What's that piece of crap?* **Esa chingadera, ¿qué es? 4.** (thing[s] of little value) las baratijas *L. Am., Sp*; los cachivaches *L. Am., Sp* ◆ *In that store they sell only junk (trinkets, odds and ends).* **En esa tienda sólo se venden cachivaches.**

junk food la(s) porquería(s) (pig stuff) *L. Am., Sp*; la comida chatarra (scrap-metal food) *Mex, Col, Ch*; la chuchería (from chuches, candy) *DR, PR, ES, Sp* ◆ *Over the weekend, I didn't cook; we just ate junk food.* **Durante el fin de semana no cociné; solo comimos comida chatarra.**

junkie →see: druggie

junky →see: tacky

Just a moment. Un momentico. *CR, Col, Ven* ◆ *I'll be ready in just a moment.* **Estaré lista en un momentico.**

to be **just around the corner (about to happen)** estar al caer (to be to fall) *Sp* ◆ *My birthday is just around the corner.* **Mi cumpleaños está al caer.**

just because (because that's how it is, it's not to be appealed) por real decreto (by royal decree) *most of L. Am., Sp* ◆ *Just because her parents said so, Marcelina had to change the date of the wedding.* **Por el real decreto de sus padres, Marcelina tuvo que cambiar la fecha de la boda.**

just because I feel like it (→see also; just for the heck of it) porque me da la gana (because the desire gives me) *L. Am., Sp* ◆ *Why are you running? —Just because I feel like it.* **¿Por qué estás corriendo? —Porque me da la gana.**

just for the fun of it (on a whim) por gusto, de puro gusto *L. Am., Sp* ◆ *Just for the fun of it, I went to the mountains for three days.* **Por puro gusto, me fui a las montañas por tres días.**

just for the heck of it por un «quítame allá esas pajas» (for a "take away from me those straws") *Mex, Nic, Ch, Sp*; porque voló la mosca (because the fly flew away) *Mex, Col*; porque la abuela fuma (because Grandma smokes) *Sp* ◆ *Just for the heck of it, he changed his decision and we couldn't do anything.* **Por un quítame allá esas pajas, cambió su decisión y no pudimos hacer nada.**

just friends (together but not bosom buddies or romantically involved)
juntos pero no revueltos (together but not mixed) *L. Am., Sp* ◆ *Pablo and Silvia are just friends, not bosom buddies or romantically involved.* Pablo y Silvia son sólo amigos, juntos pero no revueltos.

Just getting by (so-so). Aquí pasándola. (Por aquí pasándola.) (Passing it here.) *Mex, ES, Col, U, Arg;* Arrastrando la cobija. (Dragging the blanket.) *Mex, ES, Col;* Tirando. (Pulling.) *U, Arg, Sp* ◆ *How are you? —Just getting by.* ¿Cómo estás? –Aquí pasándola.

Just goofing around. Por aquí, vagando. (Just here, wandering.) *C. Am.* ◆ *How are the kids? —Just goofing around.* ¿Cómo están los muchachos? –Por aquí, vagando.

Just imagine. (Think about it.) Fíjese (usted). Fíjate (tú). *L. Am., Sp*

just in case por si acaso *L. Am., Sp;* por si las moscas (because if the flies, slang) *most of L. Am., Sp* ◆ *Give me your phone number, just in case.* Dame tu teléfono, por si acaso.

just like that 1. así como así *L. Am., Sp* ◆ *I can't decide just like that.* No puedo decidirme así como así. **2.** (without giving the matter any importance) como si nada (as if nothing) *L. Am., Sp* ◆ *He listened to the bad news just like that (without giving the matter any importance).* Escuchó las malas noticias como si nada.

just like the doctor ordered →see: just so

just right (exactly as one wishes) a pedir de boca (at the mouth's asking) *L. Am., Sp;* al pelo (to the hair) *Mex, DR, G, ES, Ven, S. Cone* ◆ *How nice! It came out just right, exactly as we wanted.* ¡Qué bien! Nos ha salido a pedir de boca.

just so (exactly, to the letter) al pie de la letra (to the foot of the letter) *L. Am., Sp;* con puntos y comas (with periods and commas) *Mex, DR, U, Arg, Sp;* sin faltar una coma (jota) (without missing a comma [jot]) *Mex, DR, Sp* ◆ *We're going to do everything just so.* Vamos a hacer todo al pie de la letra. ◆ *My aunt likes to do things just so.* A mi tía le gusta hacer las cosas con puntos y comas.

just so you know pa' (para) que sepas *L. Am., Sp* ◆ *Where are you going, darling? —Just so you know, I'm going to the lawyer to ask for a divorce.* ¿Adónde vas, querida? –Para que sepas, voy al abogado a pedir el divorcio.

just the opposite todo lo contrario (all the contrary) *L. Am., Sp* ◆ *You don't like Caribbean food? —Just the opposite, I love it, but I don't feel so good today.* ¿No te gusta la comida caribeña? –Todo lo contrario, me encanta, pero no me siento bien hoy.

to be **just what I need, just what the doctor ordered** →see: to be opportune

K

to **keep doing the same thing** (persist in an opinion or in doing something) seguir/mantenerse en sus trece (to keep in one's thirteen) *L. Am, Sp* ◆ *He kept doing the same thing despite the circumstances. Se mantuvo en sus trece a pesar de las circunstancias.*

to **keep it under wraps** →see: to put a lid on it

to **keep mum** →see: to not say a word

to **keep one's eyes peeled** →see: to be on the lookout, to pay attention

to **keep one's lips sealed** (keep a secret or keep quiet; →see also: to button one's lip, to not say a word, to put a lid on it) poner un candado a la boca (to put a lock on one's mouth) *Mex, DR, U, Arg, Sp* ◆ *Keep your lips sealed. Ponte un candado a la boca.*

to **keep one's nose to the grindstone** →see: to work like a dog

to **keep plugging along** (move on, keep going after confronting a problem) echar pa'lante (to throw forward) *DR, PR, Col, Ven, Ch* ◆ *The situation is very difficult, but we (you, they, etc.) have to keep plugging along (going forward). La situación es muy difícil, pero hay que echar pa'lante.*

to **keep someone on the run** (busy or upset) traer a alguien de acá para allá (aquí para allí) (to bring someone from here to there) *Mex, DR, PR, U, Arg, Sp* ◆ *My one-year-old son keeps me on the run. Mi niño de un año me trae de acá para allá.*

to **keep tabs on** →see: to pay attention

to **keep under wraps** (in secret) mantener en secreto (to keep in secret) *L. Am., Sp* ◆ *She kept the document under wraps. Mantuvo el documento en secreto.*

kick (amusing thing someone does or clever or cutting remark) la puntada *Mex, ES* ◆ *What a kick it was to do that singing at the party. Qué gran puntada la de cantar en la fiesta.*

to **kick (someone) out** echar *L. Am., Sp;* correr (to run) *Mex, C. Am., U, Arg;* echar a escobazos (to throw out with sweeps of a broom, slang) *Mex, Sp* ◆ *I kicked out a salesman who came to the door because he was very insolent. Eché a escobazos a un vendedor que vino a la puerta porque fue muy insolente.*

to **kick someone when he or she is down** hacer leña del árbol caído (to make firewood from the fallen tree) *Ch* ◆ *After the bankruptcy, everyone tried to kick him when he was down, and Gonzalo became seriously ill. Despúes de la bancarrota, todos trataron de hacer leña del árbol caído, y Gonzalo se enfermó seriamente.*

to **kick the bucket** 1. (die) estirar la pata (to stretch out one's foot) *L. Am., Sp;* colgar los tenis (to hang up one's tennis shoes) *Mex, DR, C. Am., Peru;* espantar la mula (to scare off the mule) *Mex, Cuba, DR, PR, CR;* dejar el pellejo (to leave one's hide or skin) *Mex, Sp;* colgar los guantes (to hang up the gloves) *ES, Nic, Sp;* cerrar el paraguas (to close the umbrella) *CR;* palmarla *Sp* ◆ *Caty's little dog kicked the bucket. El perrito de Caty colgó los tenis.* 2. (pack it in) liar el petate (to roll up the **petate**, sleeping mat, but in Spain referring to a green bag used for military service) *Sp;* liar los bártulos (to bundle up the household goods) *Sp* ◆ *Some day we'll all have to kick the bucket (pack it in). Algún día todos tendremos que liar los bártulos.*

kicking and screaming (with great effort) a jalones y estirones (at pulls and stretches) *Mex* ◆ *I took her to mass kicking and screaming. A jalones y estirones la llevé a misa.*

kid 1. (→see also: guy [girl]) el/la mocoso(-a) (with a runny nose, somewhat pejorative) *L. Am., Sp;* el chiquitín, la chiquitina *most of L. Am., Sp;* el/la chamaco(-a) (also, chamaquito[-a]) *Chicano, Mex, Cuba, PR, ES, CR;* el/la chavito(-a) (diminutive of chavo(-a)) *Chicano, Mex, G, ES;* el/la chavo(-a) *Chi-*

to kick the bucket: *What a surprise! He was so young and he kicked the bucket.*
¡Qué sorpresa! Era tan joven y colgó los tenis.

cano, Mex, G, ES, Col; el/la buqui *Chicano;* el/la escuintle(-a) (from the Náhautl word for hairless dog; also spelled escuincle, pejorative) *Mex, parts of C. Am.;* el/la chilpayate(-a) *Mex;* el/la bicho(-a) (bug, beast) *ES, Sp* (RVar *Sp:* brat, implies naughtiness; *ES:* also, can be pejorative); el/la carajillo(-a) (diminutive of carajo; vulgar) *Nic, CR;* el/la cipote(-a) *G, Hond, ES, Nic;* el/la carajito(-a) (diminutive of carajo; vulgar) *DR, Ven;* el/la pibe(-a) *Col, Ven, U, Arg;* el/la cabrito(-a) (little goat) *Peru, Ch;* el/la chibolo(-a) (ball) *Peru;* el chiquilín, la chiquilina *U, Arg;* el/la pendejo(-a) (pubic hair; vulgar and offensive in many places) *Arg* ◆ *Let's take the kids to the park.* Vamos a llevar a los chiquitines al parque. **2.** (child) el/la nene(-a), used instead of niño(-a) *Mex, PR,G, Col, Para, U, Arg, Sp* ◆ *My friend's oldest kid is named Pedro Martín.* El nene mayor de mi amiga se llama Pedro Martín. **3.** (young boy) el guri *U, northern Arg* ◆ *That kid (young boy) is very hard-working and studious.* Ese gurí es muy trabajador y estudioso.

to **kid around** →see: to joke around

to **kill** →see: to do in

to **kill oneself 1.** (for/to; figurative) matarse *L. Am., Sp* ◆ *The Garcías killed themselves to educate their children.* Los Garcías se mataron para dar educación a sus hijos. **2.** (suffer like hell, vulgar) chingarse (to get screwed) *Mex, ES, Col* ◆ *I kill myself (suffer like hell) working night and day.* Yo me chingo trabajando día y noche.

to **kill two birds with one stone** (achieve two goals at once) matar dos pájaros de un tiro (to kill two birds with one shot) *L. Am., Sp* ◆ *By inviting mom to live here, I'll kill two birds with one stone because she'll be happier and I'll have someone to watch the kids.* Invitando a mamá a vivir aquí, mato dos pájaros de un tiro porque ella estará más feliz y yo tendré a alguien que cuide a los chiquitines.

kind of weird (possibly gay) medio raro (sort of unusual) *Mex, DR, ES, S. Cone, Sp* ◆ *I think that guy is kind of weird. He acts a little funny.* Creo que ese chico es medio raro. Tiene un comportamiento extraño.

to **kiss someone's ass** lamer/lamber el culo (trasero) a alguien (to kiss someone's ass [rear], vulgar) *Mex, ES, S. Cone, Sp* ◆ *He's (She's) still there, kissing the teacher's ass. Sigue ahí, lamiéndole el culo a la profesora.*

to **kiss up** →see: to suck up

kiss-ass →see: suck-up

kisser (mouth, face; →see also: trap, yap) la jeta *most of L. Am., Sp* ◆ *If you come closer, I'll punch you in the kisser. Si te acercas, te rompo la jeta.*

kitty (pool of money to buy something collectively) la coperacha *Mex, G, ES;* la vaca (cow) *Mex, Ch;* el serrucho (saw) *DR, PR* ◆ *People, it's a collective effort; everyone puts fifteen pesos (in the kitty). Señores, es un serrucho: cada uno pone quince pesos.*

to be a **klutz** tener manos de hacha (to have hachet hands) *Ch;* ser un manazas *Sp;* ser un zafio *Sp* ◆ *Felipe tried to fix things and messed them up more. He's a klutz. Felipe intentó arreglar el asunto y lo estropeó más. Es un manazas.*

to be **klutzy** ser paleta (to be a little shovel) *Sp* ◆ *I'm a bit klutzy at peeling the orange with a fork and knife. Soy un poco paleta para pelar la naranja con tenedor y cuchillo.*

knickknack →see: trinkets

to **knock** →see: to put down

to **knock off** (kill) →see: to do in, to wipe out

to **knock out of kilter** (rattle) sacar de onda (to take from the sound wave) *L. Am.* ◆ *I'm sorry. It's just that you knocked me out of kilter. Lo siento. Es que me sacaste de onda.*

to **knock someone for a loop** (leave someone unable to respond) dejar planchado(-a) a alguien (to leave someone ironed) *Sp* ◆ *The coach knocked us for a loop. We couldn't even speak. El entrenador nos dejó planchados a todos. No podíamos ni hablar.*

to **knock someone's block off** (fix someone good) dar en la torre (to give in the tower) *Mex, C. Am.* ◆ *They knocked my block off. Me dieron en la torre.*

knock-down-drag-out →see: blowup

knockers →see: boobs, tits

to **know like the back of one's hand** conocer como la palma de la mano *L. Am., Sp* ◆ *I know the capital like the back of my hand. Conozco la capital como la palma de la mano.*

to **know someone since he or she was in knee pants** conocer a alguien desde su (la) cuna (to know someone from the cradle) *most of L. Am., Sp* ◆ *I've known Carlos and Beto since they were in knee pants. Conozco a Carlos y Beto desde la cuna.*

to **know (some)one's limits** (know what is suitable or appropriate for one) saber dónde le aprieta el zapato (to know where the shoe is too tight) *L. Am., Sp* ◆ *The contractor knew his limits and didn't accept the contract. El contratista sabía dónde le apretaba el zapato y no aceptó el contrato.*

to **know the score** estar en el ajo (to be in the garlic) *Mex, Sp* ◆ *They know what's happening. They know the score. Bien saben lo que está pasando. Están en el ajo.*

to **know to a "T"** (have knowledge at one's fingertips) saber al dedillo (to know to the little finger) *Mex, U, Sp* ◆ *Rosa knew her part to a T. That's why they gave it to her. Rosa se sabía el papel al dedillo. Por eso se lo dieron.*

to **know what someone's Achilles heel (weak point) is** saber de qué pie cojea alguien (to know what foot someone is limping on) *L. Am., Sp* ◆ *They know management's Achilles heel. That's why they're going to wait to ask for a raise until just before Christmas. Saben de qué pie cojea la gerencia. Por eso van a esperar para pedir aumento de sueldo hasta antes de Navidad.*

know-it-all sabiondo(-a) (sabihondo[-a]) *L. Am.* ◆ *She thinks she has all the answers. She acts like a know-it-all. Ella se cree que tiene todas las respuestas. Se las da de sabihonda.*

to **konk out** →see: to crash

lackadaisical →see: laid back, slacker

ladies room →see: restroom

lady of the evening →see: hooker, slut

lady-killer (guy who is or thinks he is attractive to women) el castigador (punisher) *Chicano, Mex, DR, PR, Col* ◆ *Juan is a lady-killer; he has me going crazy.* **Juan es un castigador; me tiene loca.**

laid back (letting others do things) atenido (-a) *Mex, ES, CR* ◆ *That kid is very laid back; he doesn't like to do anything.* **Ese chico es muy atenido; no le gusta hacer nada.**

to be **laid back** (unworried, not take seriously the consequences of one's or another's action; →see also: slacker) reírse de los peces de colores (to laugh at colored fish) *Cuba, CR, S. Cone* ◆ *He's very laid back.* **Se ríe de los peces de colores.**

lame: (→see crummy, old-fashioned, out of it, stupid)

to **land on one's feet** quedar bien parado (-a) (to end up standing well) *L. Am., Sp;* caer parado(-a) (to fall standing up) *DR, ES, S. Cone* ◆ *At work Mario made a big mistake but managed to solve the problem. What luck! He landed on his feet.* **En la oficina Mario metió la pata pero pudo solucionar el problema. ¡Qué suerte! Cayó parado.**

to be the **last straw** ser el colmo (to be the culmination) *L. Am., Sp;* ser la última gota (to be the last drop) *Sp* ◆ *The last straw was when they put me to work in the kitchen.* **La última gota fue cuando me pusieron a trabajar en la cocina.**

to be the **limit** →see: to be too much

Laugh and the world laughs with you (weep and you weep alone). Al nopal lo van a ver sólo cuando tiene tunas. (They only go to see the nopal cactus when it has tunas, fruits—people will call on others only when they are prosperous or doing well.) *Mex*

to **laugh one's ass off** cagarse de la risa, estar cagado(-a) de la risa (to shit from laughter, vulgar) *Mex, ES, Ven, S. Cone* ◆ *We laughed our asses off hearing his stories.* **Nos cagamos de la risa escuchando sus historias.**

to **lay down the law** →see: to set someone straight, to tell it like it is

to **lay into** →see: to chew out, to rip apart

to **lay it on thick** →see: to praise to the skies

to **lay it out** (explain) barajar (to shuffle) *Mex, DR, PR, Hond, G, ES, Col* ◆ *I don't understand; lay it out for me (lay it out more slowly for me).* **No entiendo; barájame eso (barájemela más despacio).**

to **lay things out clearly** (→see also: to put one's cards on the table) poner los puntos sobre la mesa (to put one's points on the table) *Mex, G* ◆ *Let's lay things out clearly. I think there are a lot of things that you don't know.* **Pongamos los puntos sobre la mesa. Creo que hay muchas cosas que ustedes no saben.**

lazy bastard (uncooperative person who takes no initiative; very vulgar, can also mean pedophile or homosexual, commonly used in masculine) el/la culero(-a) *Chicano, Mex, C. Am.* ◆ *Those lazy bastards did nothing to help us.* **Esos culeros no hicieron nada para ayudarnos.**

lazy bum (useless person, vulgar) el huevón, la huevona (big egg, meaning with large, heavy testicles) *Mex, Cuba, C. Am. (not CR), Ven (RVAR CR, S. Cone: this word means "idiot")* ◆ *Rolando is a lazy bum; he doesn't like to work.* **Rolando es un huevón; no le gusta trabajar.**

lazybones el/la zángano(-a) (drone) *Mex, most of C. Am., Col, Peru, S. Cone, Sp* ◆ *Fernandina is a lazybones. She doesn't do anything, and she waits for someone else to do her job.* **Fernandina es una zángana. No hace nada y espera que los demás hagan su trabajo.**

lead balloon (boring thing or person; →see also: to be a drag) el plomazo (hit with lead) *DR, U, Arg* ◆ *You're a lead balloon; leave me alone.* Eres un plomazo; déjame tranquila.

to **lead someone on** (encourage) darle alas a alguien (to give someone wings) *Mex, DR, S. Cone, Sp* ◆ *Don't keep leading Marcelo on.* No le sigas dando alas a Marcelo.

to **learn from someone else's experience** aprender en cabeza ajena (to learn in another's head, often used in the negative) *Mex, DR, Ch, U, Sp* ◆ *Nobody learns from someone else's experience.* Nadie aprende en cabeza ajena.

to **leave hanging** →see: to stand up

to **leave in the lurch** (come out of a business badly; to have been gotten the better of in a dispute) (→see also: in hot water, in a bind) dejar en la estacada (to leave in the stockade) *Bol, Ch, U, Sp* ◆ *At the most difficult times, she never left me in the lurch.* En los momentos difíciles nunca me dejó en la estacada.

to **leave nothing standing** (destroy completely) no dejar piedra sobre piedra (to not leave stone upon stone) *Mex, DR, U, Sp* ◆ *The crime scene investigators left nothing standing.* Los investigadores del crimen no dejaron piedra sobre piedra.

to **lecture at** (preach to) mandarse un discurso (to give a speech) *L. Am.*; dar una cantaleta *Mex, DR, C. Am., Col, Peru* ◆ *The boss lectured for an hour.* El patrón se mandó un discurso de una hora.

to be **left hanging** →see: to be stood up

to be **left holding the bag** pagar los platos rotos (to pay for the broken plates) *L. Am., Sp*; pagar el pato (los patos) (to pay for the duck[s]) *Mex, Nic, S. Cone, Sp*; pagar los vidrios rotos (to pay for the broken windows) *Mex, Sp* ◆ *They caused the problem, but I was left holding the bag.* Ellos causaron el problema, pero yo pagué los platos rotos.

to be **left in the lurch** quedarse en la estacada (to end up in the stockade) *Bol, Ch, U, Sp* ◆ *The investors were left in the lurch, without their money.* Los inversionistas se quedaron en la estacada, sin su dinero.

to be **left with nothing** quedar en la calle (to end up on the street) *Mex, C. Am., S.* Cone ◆ *They were left with nothing after the fire at the factory.* Quedaron en la calle después del incendio de la fábrica.

leftovers el recalentado (reheated) *Mex, ES, Col* ◆ *Miriam loves leftovers.* A Miriam le encantan los recalentados.

to **let (someone) have it** →see: to chew out, to rip apart

to **let bygones be bygones** dar vuelta a la página (to turn the page) *ES, CR, S. Cone, Sp* ◆ *It's better to forget that affair and let bygones be bygones (put the whole thing behind us).* Es mejor olvidarse de ese asunto y dar vuelta a la página.

Let George do it. (Let someone else do it.) Que lo haga Rita. (Let Rita do it.) *Sp* ◆ *Why haven't you washed the dishes today? —Let George (i.e., someone else) do it.* ¿Por qué no has lavado los platos todavía? –Que lo haga Rita.

to **let go** (ignore) pasar por alto *Mex, DR, PR, ES, S. Cone, Sp*; írsele por alto *Mex, ES, CR, U* ◆ *This time I'm going to let your insults go, but don't let it happen again.* Esta vez voy a pasar por alto tus insultos, pero que sea la última vez.

to **let it roll off** (like water off a duck's back) (not worry about something, not take seriously the consequences of one's or another's action) reírse de los peces de colores (to laugh at colored fish) *Cuba, CR, S. Cone* ◆ *Whatever happens, I let it roll off like water off a duck's back.* Pase lo que pase, me río de los peces de colores.

Let me get a word in. Préstame la guitarra. (Lend me the guitar.) *ES*; Pasáme el mate. (Pass me the mate tea.) *Arg*; Pásame el micrófono. (Give me the microphone.) *U*

to **let one's hair down** echar una canita al aire (to throw a gray hair in the air) *Mex, DR, PR, ES, S. Cone, Sp* ◆ *The conference delegates let their hair down.* Los delegados al congreso echaron algunas canitas al aire.

Let that be a lesson for you. Mírate en ese espejo. (Look at yourself in that mirror.) *Mex, DR, ES, U, Arg* ◆ *Because of the accident on his motorcycle, Juan is paralyzed. Let that be a lesson for you, my girl.* A causa del accidente en su moto, Juan está paralizado. Mírate en ese espejo, hija.

to **let the cat out of the bag** levantar la liebre (to raise up the hare) *parts of L. Am., Sp;* soltar la cuerda (to let go of or loosen the cord) *Mex, Sp;* echar de cabeza (to turn upside down) *Mex* ◆ *The guy they arrested let the cat out of the bag, and the police found the rest of the criminals.* El detenido soltó la cuerda, y la policía encontró al resto de los delincuentes.

Let's beat it! (said when something comes to an end or something crazy or scandalous happens) Apaga y vámonos. (Turn off and let's go.) *L. Am., Sp* ◆ *Guess who came. Felipe, drunk! —Let's beat it because he's always a drag when he's like that.* Adivina quien llegó. ¡Felipe, borracho! —Apaga y vámonos que siempre se pone pesado cuando está así.

Let's change the subject. Sanseacabó. (Saint it's over; phrase used to end a discussion.) *Mex, DR, PR, G, ES, S. Cone, Sp;* A otra cosa, mariposa. (To another thing, butterfly.) *Mex, DR, Sp;* Santas pascuas. (Holy Easter; phrase to end a discussion or said when one is forced to resign oneself to something.) *Mex, Ch, Sp* ◆ *Let's change the subject. I'm not interested in family gossip.* A otra cosa mariposa. No me interesan los chismes de familia.

Let's chill out. (Don't cause trouble.) Tengamos la fiesta en paz. (Let's have the party in peace.) *DR, ES, Sp* ◆ *Let's not talk about this anymore. Let's chill out.* No discutamos más. Tengamos la fiesta en paz.

Let's get down to business. (Let's go to it.) Al agua, patos. (To the water, ducks.) *Mex, DR, ES, S. Cone, Sp* ◆ *Let's not lose any more time. (Time's a-wastin'!) Let's get down to business.* No perdamos más tiempo. ¡Al agua, patos!

Let's not air dirty laundry in public. La ropa sucia se lava en casa. (Dirty clothes are washed at home.) *Mex, ES, S. Cone, Sp* ◆ *Please don't talk that way about your brother; let's not air dirty laundry in public.* Por favor no hables así de tu hermano; la ropa sucia se lava en casa.

Let's show a little respect. (polite way of criticizing someone) Un poco de respeto. (A little respect.) *L. Am., Sp* ◆ *Let's show a little respect, sir. Don't shout at me.* Un poco de respeto, señor. No me grite.

Let's stick to what we know best. Zapatero a tus zapatos. (Shoemaker to your shoes.) *L. Am., Sp*

letch el rabo verde (green tail) *Mex, C. Am., Peru* ◆ *Manolo is a letch; he always goes out with women much younger than he is.* Manolo es un rabo verde; siempre sale con mujeres mucho menores que él.

to the **letter** →see: just so

to **lick someone's boots** →see: to suck up

lie →see: baloney, fib

life on Easy Street (lived at others' expense, without working) la vida loca (crazy life) *parts of L. Am.;* la sopa boba (crazy or foolish soup) *Sp* ◆ *These kids live life on Easy Street. When will they go to work?* Estos chicos viven la sopa boba. ¿Cuándo van a trabajar?

Life's not a bed of roses. (sarcastic remark said when someone hasn't gotten something expected) ¡Que si quieres arroz, Catalina! (So you want rice, Catalina!) *Sp* ◆ *You've phoned her many times and she hasn't returned your calls? Tough luck, but life isn't a bed of roses! (You don't always get what you want!)* ¿La has llamado muchas veces por teléfono y no te ha devuelto las llamadas? ¡Que si quieres arroz, Catalina!

to **lift** (steal) levantar (to pick up) *Cuba, PR, G, Col, Ec;* mangar (to "sleeve") *Cuba, PR, Sp;* afanar (from Lunfardo, Buenos Aires slang; to take advantage of someone) *Cuba, Peru, U, Arg, Sp* ◆ *They lifted my wallet.* Me mangaron (afanaron) la billetera.

to **lift purses or wallets** (pick pockets) bolsear (to purse) *Mex, C. Am.* ◆ *They just get on buses to lift wallets (pick people's pockets).* Sólo se suben a los buses a bolsear a las personas.

to be the **light of one's life** (→see also: dear, my love, sweetie) ser la luz de mi (su, etc.) vida *L. Am., Sp* ser la luz de los (sus) ojos (to be the light of one's eyes) *Mex, ES, S. Cone* ◆ *I love you. You are the light of my life.* Eres la luz de mi vida. *Eduardo's son is the light of his life.* El hijo de Eduardo es la luz de sus ojos.

lightning fast más rápido(-a) que un rayo *L. Am., Sp* ◆ *You already finished the work?*

You're lightning fast. ¿Ya terminaste el trabajo? Eres más rápido que un rayo.

like a bat out of hell (fast; →see also: full blast, like a shot, on the fly, quick as lightning) como alma que lleva el diablo (like a soul that the devil takes) *Mex, DR, ES, CR, S. Cone, Sp;* a toda hostia (at all Host, with religious reference; vulgar) *Sp;* a toda leche (at all milk, vulgar) *Sp ♦ The cyclist was going like a bat out of hell and hit a tree. El ciclista iba a toda leche y chocó con un árbol.*

to be like a bull in a china shop tener manos de hacha (to have hachet hands) *Ch ♦ Don't let Umberto into the dining room. He's like a bull in a china shop. No dejes que entre Umberto en el comedor. Tiene manos de hacha.*

like a dream →see: super

like a fish out of water como gallo en patio ajeno (like a rooster in someone else's or a different patio) *ES, Nic, CR, Pan;* como gallina en corral ajeno (like a hen in someone else's or a different pen) *Col, Peru, Ch ♦ I saw Maruja in the parliament, and she was like a fish out of water. Vi a Maruja en el parlamento, y estaba como gallina en corral ajeno.*

like a house afire →see: full blast, like a shot, on the fly, quick as lightning

like a kid in a candy store como niño con zapatos nuevos (like a kid with new shoes) *Mex, DR, ES, Ch, U, Sp;* como niño con juguete nuevo (like a kid with a new toy) *Mex, ES, U, Arg ♦ Alejandro bought a pickup truck, and he's like a kid in a candy store. Alejandro compró una camioneta y está como niño con juguete nuevo.*

like a shot (very fast; →see also: full blast, like a bat out of hell, on the fly, quick as lightning) rapidingo *parts of L. Am.;* más rápido(-a) que ligero(-a) (more quick than fast) *Mex, PR, G;* cayendo el muerto y soltando el llanto (the dead person falling and the scream being let out) *Mex, ES;* hecho(-a) la mocha (la raya) (made into the bow [the stripe]) *Mex;* como entierro de pobre (like a poor person's funeral) *ES, CR, Col ♦ This year went by like a shot. Este año se fue como entierro de pobre.*

to be like a wildman/wildwoman (hysterical) estar como energúmeno (to be like one possessed) *Mex, ES, Ch ♦ No one enjoyed the conversation; Adela was like a wildwoman and kept interrupting all the time. Nadie disfrutó de la conversación; Adela estaba como energúmena e interrumpía todo el tiempo.*

to be like apples and oranges (very different) parecerse una cosa a otra como un huevo a una castaña (to be as similar as an egg to a chestnut) *Sp ♦ This brush and comb are like apples and oranges. They don't go together at all! Why did you buy them as if they were a set? Este cepillo con el peine, se parecen como un huevo a una castaña. ¡No combinan en nada! ¿Cómo es que los compraste como si de un conjunto se tratara?*

like cats and dogs (enemies) como perros y gatos (like dogs and cats) *Mex, ES, Peru, Ch ♦ The newlyweds were fighting like cats and dogs day and night. Los recién casados se peleaban como perros y gatos día y noche.*

like crazy (without thinking) a tontas y a locas *most of L. Am., Sp;* a lo tonto (also, a lo tarugo, a lo pendejo) *Chicano, Mex, ES;* a lo loco (crazily) *Mex, DR, PR, ES, U, Arg, Sp ♦ César was talking like crazy (without thinking) about his boss. César hablaba a tontas y a locas de su jefe.*

Like father, like son. De tal palo, tal astilla. (From such a tree or stick, such a splinter.) *L. Am., Sp;* Hijo(-a) de tigre, sale rayado(-a). (Son [Daughter] of the tiger turns out striped.) *Mex, CR, S. Cone ♦ Ana Irene is mature and responsible, like her father. —Like father, like daughter. Ana Irene es madura y responsable, como su padre. —Hija de tigre sale rayada.*

like hell como un (el) culo (like an [the] ass, vulgar) *Cuba, Col, S. Cone* That skirt looks like hell on her. *♦ Esa falda le queda como un culo.*

like mad →see: full blast, like a shot, like crazy, on the fly, quick as lightning

to be like oil and water (→see also, to be at odds) como el aceite y el vinagre (like oil and vinegar) *Mex, Caribbean, Col, U, Arg;* como el agua y el aceite (like water and oil) *Mex, G, ES, Ch ♦ Those two groups are like oil and water; they don't mix and they always fight. Estos dos grupos son como el aceite y* *el vinagre; no se mezclan y siempre se pe-lean.*

to be **like pulling teeth** (difficult) como parir chayotes (like giving birth to chayotes, a vegetable with prickly skin) *Mex* ◆ *Programming this computer is like pulling teeth.* *Programar esta computadora es como parir chayotes.*

like sardines in a can (crowded or packed) como sardina en lata *L. Am., Sp*; como una lata de sardinas *Sp* ◆ *This bus is very full. We're like sardines in a can.* ◆ *Este autobús está muy lleno. Estamos como sardina en lata.*

like two peas in a pod como dos gotas de agua (like two drops of water) *L. Am., Sp* ◆ *Paco and his friend Miguelito are like two peas in a pod.* *Paco y su amigo Miguelito son como dos gotas de agua.*

limp-wristed (sissyish, effeminate) loca (crazy) *Cuba, DR, CR, Col, Ch*; partido (split, broken) *Cuba, DR, PR*

lingo (way of speaking, conversation) parla *Mex, Cuba, CR* ◆ *Many common expressions come from sports lingo, like "off base" or "in three and two" (meaning a difficult situation, from baseball).* *Muchas expresiones comunes vienen de la parla deportiva, como "fuera de base" o "en tres y dos".*

to **listen up** →see: to pay attention

little bit (slang) el pellizco (pinch) *L. Am., Sp*; el pelo, pelito (hair) *L. Am., Sp*; el cachito (little catch) *Mex, G, ES, S. Cone, Sp* ◆ *Give me a little bit of cinnamon, please.* *Dame un cachito de canela, porfa.*

to be a **little dickens** (very mischievous) ser la piel del diablo (to be the devil's skin) *most of L. Am., Sp* ◆ *Don't let that boy out of your sight; he's a little dickens.* *No descuides a ese niño; es la piel del diablo.*

to **live high on the hog** →see: moneybags, to be loaded

to **live it up** (enjoy oneself; →see also: to go out on the town, to have a blast, to have a good time) darse la buena (gran) vida (to give oneself the good [great] life) *Mex, DR, PR, S. Cone*; pegarse la vida padre (to stick or fasten to oneself the father life) *Sp* ◆ *I want to win the prize in the lottery so I can live it up and won't have to work. Yo quiero ga-*narme el premio de la lotería para darme la buena vida y no tener que trabajar.*

to **live together as if married** casarse por detrás de la iglesia (to get married behind the church) *U* ◆ *After going out for a number of years they decided to live together without getting married.* *Después de andar de novios por varios años decidieron casarse por detrás de la iglesia.*

to **liven things (or someone) up** ser levanta muertos (to be a raiser of the dead) *Mex, Nic, U, Arg* ◆ *This soup livens me right up. Esta sopa es levanta muertos.*

loaded (having money) platudo(-a) *L. Am.*; forrado(-a) (lined, as in pockets being lined) *Mex, Cuba, DR, PR, U, Arg, Sp* ◆ *Lourdes's boyfriend is loaded. I think his mom is vice president of the bank. El novio de Lourdes está forrado. Creo que su mamá es la vicepresidenta del banco.*

to be **loaded** (→see also: moneybags, to be filthy rich) tener bolsillos alegres (to have cheerful pockets) *Mex*; tener la guita loca (to have crazy money) *U, Arg* ◆ *A few years ago, the Flores were loaded. Hace unos años los Flores tenían la guita loca.*

to **loaf around** →see: slack off

loafer →see: slacker

local yokel (person who seems to be from the neighborhood) el/la baquiano(-a) *S. Cone* ◆ *Ask that local yokel for the address. He must be from around here. Pregúntale a ese baquiano la dirección. Debe ser de estos lugares.*

to **log on** registrarse *L. Am., Sp* ◆ *I've logged on. Now what do I do? Me he registrado. Ahora ¿qué hago?*

long face (sad appearance) la cara larga (long face) *Mex, DR, ES, Col, Ch, U, Sp* ◆ *Sonia came into the room and saw that her mother had a long face. Sonia entró a la habitación y vio que su madre tenía la cara larga.*

to **look (like)** tener pinta (de) (to have spot [of]) *L. Am., Sp* ◆ *That guy looks like a drug dealer. Ese fulano tiene pinta de narcotraficante.*

to look at (pay attention to, notice) fijarse en (to fix oneself on) *L. Am., Sp* ◆ *Look at that. Fíjate en eso.*

Look before you leap. (Examine something before you buy it, or think carefully before deciding on something or someone.) Pica, lica y califica. (Poke, look, and judge.) *Mex, Col* ◆ *Don't buy the first house you see. Look before you leap.* No compres la primera casa que veas. Pica, lica y califica.

to **look better than ever** estar como nunca (to be like never) *L. Am., Sp* ◆ *You look better than ever, Marisol.* Estás como nunca, Marisol.

to **look damn good on** (fit well, vulgar) estar de coña *Sp* ◆ *This dress looks damn good on you.* Este vestido te está de coña.

to **look down on** (disdain) tener a menos (to hold for less) *Arg, Sp;* tener en poco a una persona o cosa (to hold someone or something in small) *Sp* ◆ *In that store they look down on immigrants.* En esa tienda tienen a menos a los inmigrantes.

to **look down one's nose at someone** mirar a alguien por encima del hombro (to look over one's shoulder at someone) *L. Am., Sp* ◆ *Elvira and her husband are very arrogant and look down their noses at everyone.* Elvira y su esposo son muy arrogantes y miran a todos por encima del hombro.

to **look for a needle in a haystack** buscar una aguja en un pajar *L. Am., Sp* ◆ *Don't persist with that. Finding your ring in the stadium where there are more than a hundred thousand people is like looking for a needle in a haystack.* No insistas. Encontrar tu anillo en el estadio donde hay cien mil personas es como buscar una aguja en un pajar.

to (not) **look for problems** (no) verle pelos a la sopa (to [not] see hairs in the soup) *Mex* ◆ *Don't look for problems (make excuses). You have to finish that work.* No le busques pelos a la sopa. Tienes que terminar ese trabajo.

to **look for trouble** (go looking for trouble; to get involved in something that can be harmful or senseless) buscarle tres (cinco) pies al gato (to look for three [five] feet on the cat) *L. Am., Sp;* buscar chichis a las culebras (to look for breasts on a snake) *Mex* ◆ *Why look for trouble?* ¿Para qué buscarle tres (cinco) pies al gato?

to **look forward to** esperar con ansia (to wait with eagerness, →see also: to not be able to wait) *L. Am., Sp* ◆ *I'm looking forward to my friend María's visit.* Espero con ansia la visita de mi amiga María.

to **look good** (→see also: to look damn good on) lucir (to shine) *DR, PR, ES, Nic, CR, Col, Sp* ◆ *Red pants and a heavy necklace look good on Rosa.* A Rosa le lucen pantalones rojos y un collar grueso.

to **look like a fool** tener cara de chiste (to have the face of a joke) *Mex, Sp* ◆ *Even though the accountant is intelligent, he looks like a fool.* A pesar de que el contador es inteligente, tiene cara de chiste.

to **look like a queen** estar como una reina (to be like a queen) *L. Am., Sp* ◆ *You look like a queen.* Está (usted) como una reina.

to **look like a sourpuss** (hostile, unwelcoming, or unfriendly) tener cara de pocos amigos (to have a face of few friends) *Mex, Ch, U* ◆ *I don't buy anything at that store because the clerks look like sourpusses.* No compro nada en esa tienda porque los dependientes tienen cara de pocos amigos.

to **look like a spring chicken** (look good) estar hecho(-a) un pimpollo (to be made into a sprout, young thing) *Mex, DR, ES, U, Sp* ◆ *Although he's seventy years old, he looks like a spring chicken. It's amazing how well preserved he is.* Aunque tiene setenta años, está hecho un pimpollo. Es una maravilla lo bien que se conserva.

to **look like one is in a bad mood** tener cara de mala leche (to have the face of bad milk) *Sp* ◆ *That man looks like he's in a bad mood, don't you think?* Ese señor tiene cara de muy mala leche, ¿no crees?

to **look ten feet tall** parecer siete pisos (to look like seven stories) *Florida, Col* ◆ *Guadalupe and Lurdes look ten feet tall, and they play on the college basketball team.* Guadalupe y Lurdes parecen siete pisos y juegan en el equipo de básquetbol del colegio.

to **look uptight** (worried) estar más serio(-a) que un burro en lancha (to be more serious than a donkey in a rowboat) *CR* ◆ *What's up with you? You look uptight.* ¿Qué te pasa? Estás más seria que un burro en lancha.

Look who's talking! ¡Mira quién habla! *L. Am., Sp* ◆ *You need to study more, Emilia.* —*Look who's talking! You never study.* **Tienes que estudiar más, Emilia. –¡Mira quién habla! Tú jamás estudias.**

looking like a slob (badly dressed, dirty) zarrapastroso(-a) (from zarrapastra, meaning both mud and claw, implying dirty and torn) *L. Am., Sp* ◆ *And how dare he go to a sweet-fifteen coming-out party looking like a slob like that?* **¿Y cómo se atreve a ir a una quinceañera así de zarrapastroso?**

loony →see: nuts

loose cannon (unreliable person, slacker type who doesn't commit) el tiro al aire (shot in the air) *S. Cone* ◆ *I don't trust Juvenal because he's a loose cannon.* **No confío en Juvenal porque es un tiro al aire.**

Loose lips sink ships. (Talking can get you into trouble.) En boca cerrada no entran moscas. (In a closed mouth flies don't enter.) *L. Am., Sp* ◆ *Think before talking. Loose lips sink ships.* **Piensa antes de hablar. En boca cerrada no entran moscas.**

loose woman →see: easy woman, slut

to **loosen the purse strings** aflojar el billete (to loosen the bill) *Mex, Ch;* aflojar la bolsa *Mex, Sp* ◆ *Loosen the purse strings, Dad; we want to go dancing with the girls.* **Afloja el bolsillo, viejo; queremos ir a bailar con las chicas.**

to **loosen up (discipline)** aflojar las riendas (to loosen the reins) *Mex, DR, U, Sp* ◆ *Monica's parents won't loosen up with her because they don't trust her.* **Los padres de Mónica no le aflojan las riendas porque no confían en ella.**

to **lose heart** (have one's heart sink) caérsele a alguien el alma a los pies (to have one's soul fall to one's feet) *DR, Ch, U, Sp* ◆ *We lost heart seeing them so sad.* **Se nos cayó el alma a los pies al verlos tan tristes.**

to **lose it** (get mad; →see also: to get pissed off, to get steamed) encabronarse *Mex, C. Am., PR, much of S. Am.;* enfogonarse *Mex, PR, Col;* entromparse *Mex, ES, Col, Ec;* enchicharse *Mex, Col, U;* arrecharse (to get horns like an animal) *Nic, Ven, Ec;* ponerse como una fiera (to become like a wild animal) *ES, Ch, U, Sp;* agarrarse una chinche

(to grab oneself a bedbug) *U, Arg;* írsele la olla (to have the pot fly off or go off on one) *Sp* ◆ *They had me waiting there until I lost it.* **Me tuvieron allí esperando hasta que me enchiché.**

to **lose one's head** (→see also: to be nuts, to lose one's marbles) perder la cabeza *L. Am., Sp;* perder la chaveta (to lose one's head) *Mex, DR, ES, Sp* ◆ *What's wrong with Tito? Did he lose his head? I saw him leaving his house with a pink dress on.* **¿Qué le pasa a Tito? ¿Perdió la chaveta? Lo vi salir de su casa con un vestido rosado.**

to **lose one's marbles** (→see also: to be nuts, to have a screw loose) fundírsele a alguien los fusibles (to have one's fuses melt) *Mex, DR, PR, ES, U, Sp;* botar la canica (la bola) (to throw the marble [ball]) *Mex;* rayarse *Ec, Peru, S. Cone* ◆ *Antonio lost his marbles and began to sing at the funeral.* **Antonio se botó la canica y empezó a cantar en el entierro.**

to **lose one's nerve** →see: to back down or out

to **lose one's shirt** perder hasta la camisa *L. Am., Sp* ◆ *If you keep gambling in the casinos, you're going to lose your shirt.* **Si sigues jugando en los casinos, vas a perder hasta la camisa.**

to **lose out 1.** (be left behind, usually meaning to be a spinster) quedarse para vestir santos (also, less commonly, vestir imágenes) (to stay behind to dress [statues of] saints) *L. Am., Sp;* dejarle a alguien el tren (to have the train leave you) *DR, CR, Col, Ch* (RVAR *Mex:* irse el tren) ◆ *Ramona turned forty-two years old on Thursday. —And still single? —Well, she was left an old maid.* **Ramona cumplió cuarenta y dos años el jueves. –¿Y todavía soltera? –Bueno, ésa se quedó para vestir santos. 2.** (miss the boat, →see also: We (you, etc.) missed the boat.) perder el (último) tren (to miss the [last] train) *Mex, DR, ES, Ch, U, Arg, Sp* ◆ *Tomás lost out when he didn't accept the job at the new company.* **Tomás perdió el tren cuando no aceptó el empleo en la nueva compañía.**

to **lose sight of** perder(se) de vista (to lose from view) *L. Am., Sp* ◆ *You shouldn't lose sight of the importance of this idea.* **No debe** *perderse de vista la importancia de esta idea.*

to **lose the thread** (of a conversation, etc.) perder el hilo *L. Am., Sp* ◆ *Sorry, I've lost the thread of the conversation. Can you repeat what you just said?* **Perdón, perdí el hilo de la conversación. ¿Puede repetir lo último que dijo?**

to **lose your cool** (→see also: to lose it) perder los estribos (to lose the stirrups) *L. Am., Sp* ◆ *If you don't stop bugging me, I'm going to lose my cool.* **Si no dejas de molestar, voy a perder los estribos.**

loser el cero a la izquierda (zero to the left) *L. Am., Sp;* el buey, güey (from "bovis": stupid, lazy [castrated] animal, often used with affection among men, a mild insult like SOB) *Chicano, Mex, PR, ES, Col;* dejado(-a) (left behind) *G, ES, Nic, Ch;* el/la achantado(-a) (hidden, lying low, submitting) *Hond, Nic, CR, Ven;* el/la quedado(-a) (one who's been left behind) *DR, CR, Col, Ven;* el/la batata (sweet potato) *Para, U, Arg* ◆ *What a playboy! That guy is a total loser.* **¡Qué mujeriego! Ese chico es un cero a la izquierda.**

He (She) is a **loser.** (not wanted) No va pa'l baile. (He/She is not going to the dance.) *Ven* ◆ *Rodrigo is a nice person, but he's a loser.* **Rodrigo es buena persona, pero no va pa'l baile.**

lost (confused) →see: mixed up

to be a **lost cause** ser como arar en el mar (to be like ploughing in the sea) *Mex, DR, PR;* buscar chichis a las culebras (to look for breasts on a snake) *Mex;* echar agua en el mar (to throw water into the sea) *Sp;* rizar el rizo (to curl the curl) *Sp* ◆ *This is the third time I've cleaned the kitchen today. It's a lost cause.* **Es la tercera vez hoy que limpio la cocina. Es como arar en el mar.**

loudmouth (big mouth) el bocón, la bocona *Mex, PR, ES, Nic, CR, Col, Arg* ◆ *Don't be a loudmouth.* **No seas bocón.**

lousy →see: crummy, the pits

love affair la aventura (adventure) *L. Am., Sp* ◆ *I had a fantastic love affair in Sevilla.* **Tuve una aventura fantástica en Sevilla.**

to **love someone like one's own son or daughter** (have great love for someone and be pleased with their actions or good qualities) mirarse en alguien como en un espejo (to see oneself in another as in a mirror) *Sp* ◆ *I love her like my own daughter.* **Me miro en ella como en un espejo.**

low blow (→see also: smack) el golpe bajo *L. Am., Sp* ◆ *Why did you insult me? It was a low blow.* **¿Por qué me insultaste? Fue un golpe bajo.**

to be the **low man on the totem pole** (not count) ser una bacteria en el horizonte (to be a bacterium on the horizon) *Sp;* ser el último mono (to be the last monkey) *Sp* ◆ *Don't hire that singer; he's the low man on the totem pole.* **No contraten a ese cantante; es una bacteria en el horizonte.**

low-class **1.** (cheap, low quality, for person or thing; →see also: crummy) ordinario(-a) *L. Am., Sp;* gacho(-a) *Mex, G, ES;* trililís *PR;* berreta (used to describe things or people) *Arg;* el/la roto(-a) (broken) *Ch;* cutre *Sp* ◆ *Her boyfriend is really low-class. I don't know why she keeps going out with him.* **Su novio es bien gacho. No sé porque ella sigue con él.** **2.** (pretentious and in poor taste, person or thing) el cache *Arg* ◆ *My cousin's house struck me as very low-class.* **La casa de mi prima me pareció un cache.**

lowlife **1.** (ignorant person and proud of it) analfabestia (used instead of analfabeta, illiterate; bestia means beast) *Mex, Col* ◆ *Some lowlifes went by in a truck.* **Pasaron unos analfabestias en una caminoneta.** **2.** (rude, crude) lépero(-a) *Mex, C. Am.;* burdo(-a) (coarse) *Mex, CR, Col;* cafre *G, Sp;* balurdo(-a) *Ven* (RVar *Nic, Ec:* balurde); guarango(-a) *U, Arg;* macarra *Sp;* basto(-a) *Sp* ◆ *I went to the restaurant with Emilia and Angélica and they embarrassed me. They're lowlifes.* **Fui al restaurante con Emilia y Angélica y me hicieron pasar vergüenza. Son muy guarangas.**

to be a **lowlife** (→see also: jerk) ser bestia (to be a beast, animal) *L. Am.;* ser un gorila (to be a large or barbaric person) *Mex, G;* ser un patán *Mex, Nic, Col, U, Arg;* ser una corriente (feminine only) *Mex;* ser un barbaján (masculine only) *Mex, Cuba* ◆ *The owner of that business is a lowlife.* **El dueño de ese negocio es un patán.**

to **luck out** (often by getting something good) rayarse *Chicano, Mex, G, ES, Peru;* tocarle a alguien la lotería (to win the lottery; also caerle or sacar la lotería) *Mex, Cuba, S. Cone, Sp* ◆ *You lucked out with the cassette player, man.* Te rayaste con la grabadora, hombre.

lucky (duck) rayado(-a) (striped) *Mex, G, ES;* lechero(-a) *ES, Nic, CR, Col, Peru;* lechudo (-a) *ES, Ven* ◆ *What a lucky duck! They gave him the job. He's lucky.* ¡Qué lechudo! Le dieron el trabajo. Tiene leche.

to be **lucky** tener leche (to have milk) *PR, G, Col, Ec, Ch, Sp* (RVar *Sp:* a bit vulgar) ◆ *Only the topics Hugo had studied came up on the exam. He's really lucky!* A Hugo le salieron en el examen sólo los temas que había estudiado. ¡Tiene una leche estupenda!

lucky stiff →see: lucky duck

M

macho man (male chauvinist pig) el machote *Mex, ES, Col* ◆ *He acts like that because he thinks he's a macho man.* Se porta así porque se cree muy machote.

mad as a hatter (→see also: nuts) más loco(-a) que una cabra (crazier than a she-goat) *Mex, CR, S. Cone, Sp* ◆ *Gustavo wrote a love letter to the literature professor. He's as mad as a hatter.* Gustavo escribió una carta de amor a la profesora de literatura. Está más loco que una cabra.

mad at (angry with, treating each other as enemies; →see also: hopping mad, steamed) peleados(-as) *L. Am., Sp* ◆ *María and José are mad at each other after a fight; they aren't speaking to each other anymore.* María y José están peleados; ya no se hablan.

made for each other (birds of a feather) tal para cual *L. Am., Sp* ◆ *That couple is made for each other.* Esa pareja es tal para cual.

to be **made of steel** (tough, strong) ser de acero (bronce) (to be of steel [bronze]) *Mex, U, Arg, Sp* ◆ *Claudia seems to be made of steel. She doesn't get perturbed under any circumstances.* Claudia parece ser de acero. No se inmuta bajo ninguna circunstancia.

main squeeze (boyfriend or girlfriend; →see also: dear, sweetheart) el/la jevo(-a) *Cuba, DR, PR, Ven, Ec* ◆ *Eduardo is here with his main squeeze.* Eduardo está aquí con su jeva.

to be a **major problem** ser un problema mayúsculo (to be a capital letter problem) *L. Am.* ◆ *The traffic here is a major problem.* Aquí el tráfico es un problema mayúsculo.

to **make a big break** (break in, achieve fame or success) hacer brecha (to make an opening, breach) *Mex, ES, U, Sp* ◆ *The Beatles made their big break in the sixties and even today people listen to them.* Los Beatles hicieron brecha en los '60, y aun hoy la gente los escucha.

to **make a commotion** →see: to make a scene

to **make a deal with someone** llegar a un acuerdo con alguien *L. Am., Sp;* cuadrar con alguien *Mex, Cuba, Col* ◆ *We made a deal with the boss to leave early today.* Cuadramos con el jefe para salir temprano hoy.

to **make a fast getaway** →see: to take off

to **make a fool of oneself** (→see also: to act like a fool) hacer el ridículo (to make the ridiculous) *L. Am., Sp* ◆ *Cut it out! You're making a fool of yourself.* ¡Córtala! Estás haciendo el ridículo.

to **make a fuss** →see: to make a scene

to **make a gaffe** →see: to blow it

to **make a hit** (steal or rob; →see also: to lift, to mug, to take someone to the cleaners) dar el golpe (to give the hit) *Mex, ES, Sp* ◆ *Two robbers made a hit on the bank and got away with a great deal of money.* Dos asaltantes dieron un golpe en el banco y se llevaron mucho dinero.

to **make a killing** (take advantage of) hacer su agosto (to make one's August) *L. Am., Sp;* ponerse las botas (to put on one's boots) *Ch, U, Sp* ◆ *Doña María made a killing on the stock market last year.* Doña María hizo su agosto en la bolsa el año pasado.

to **make a mess of things** (not do things right) no dar pie con bola (to not hit the ball with one's foot) *Mex, DR, PR, U, Sp* ◆ *This is the third time I've left the keys in the car. I'm making a mess of things.* Es la tercera vez que se me quedan las llaves dentro del carro. Estoy que no doy pie con bola.

to **make a mountain out of a molehill** (complicate something unnecessarily) rizar el rizo (to curl the curl) *Sp* ◆ *They're making a mountain out of a molehill for nothing.* Están rizando el rizo sin necesidad.

to **make a pit stop** (to urinate; euphemism) cambiar el agua a los peces (al acuario) (to change the fishes' water) *Cuba, DR, PR, Col, U, Arg;* visitar al señor Roca (to visit Mr. Rock) *Sp* ◆ *You have to leave time to make a* *pit stop. Hay que dejar tiempo para visitar al señor Roca.*

to **make a scene** **1.** (commotion) armar un escándalo (to make a scandal) *L. Am., Sp;* armar un jaleo *Mex, Sp;* armar un molote (to set up a bunch) *DR, ES, Nic;* armar mitote (to make a big myth) *Mex;* armar un sanquentín (to make a Saint Quentín) *Mex;* armar gresca (to make a din or brawl) *S. Cone, Sp;* armar un revuelo *U, Arg, Sp;* armar la de San Quentín (to make that of Saint Quentín) *Ch, Sp;* armar un cristo (to make a Christ) *Sp;* armar el taco (to make the swear word) *Sp* ◆ *The girl made a scene at the clinic and didn't allow the doctor to examine her. La niña armó un escándalo en la clínica y no permitió que el doctor la examinara.* ◆ *Some drunks made a scene at the disco. Unos borrachos armaron un jaleo en la discoteca.* **2.** (do something to get attention) montar un número (numerito) (to put on a number) *Mex, Cuba, DR, ES, Sp;* hacer teatro (to make theater) *Mex, ES, Peru, S. Cone, Sp;* hacer un tango (to do a tango) *Mex, Col;* montar un cirio (to put on a candle) *Sp;* ◆ *What an embarrassing time I had with your mother yesterday. She made a scene at the hotel desk. Qué vergüenza que pasé con tu madre ayer. Montó un numerito en la recepción del hotel.* **3.** (to show off, call attention to oneself) pintar monos (to paint monkeys) *Ch* ◆ *There's your friend Esteban, making a scene as usual. Allí está tu amigo Esteban, pintando monos como siempre.*

to **make a slip of the tongue** (speak without thinking) írsele a alguien la lengua *Mex, ES, U, Arg, Sp* ◆ *Emma, you made a slip of the tongue and told your coworkers very personal things. Ema, se te fue la lengua y dijiste cosas muy personales a tus compañeras de trabajo.*

to **make eyes at** (flirt, ogle) hacer ojitos (to make little eyes) *L. Am., Sp* ◆ *He's (She's) always making eyes at you in class. Siempre te está haciendo ojitos en clase.*

to **make fun of** (tease, make someone look ridiculous) burlarse de *L. Am, Sp;* chotear *Mex, Cuba, CR;* cargar (to load) *U, Arg;* cachondearse (de alguien) *Sp;* dársela a alguien con queso (to give it to someone with cheese) *Sp* ◆ *Felipe made fun of me. Felipe me choteó.*

to **make hay while the sun shines** **1.** hacer su agosto (to make one's August) *L. Am., Sp* ◆ *Doña María made hay while the sun was shining in the stock market last year. Doña María hizo su agosto en la bolsa el año pasado.* **2.** (take advantage of confusion or disorder and profit from it) pescar en río revuelto (to fish in a turbulent river) *Mex, DR, Sp* ◆ *That political party made hay while the sun shone. If it hadn't been for the attacks, they wouldn't have won the election. Este partido político ha pescado en río revuelto. Si no hubiera sido por los atentados, no hubiera ganado las elecciones.*

to **make houses of cards** (count on something one can't count on, do something in a foolish way) hacer castillos de naipes (to build castles of cards) *Sp* ◆ *Patricia has spent her whole life making houses of cards. Patricia se ha pasado haciendo castillos de naipes toda su vida.*

to **make it snappy** →see: to step on it

to **make mincemeat out of** →see: to beat someone up

to **make off with it all** (take everything, one's own and others') alzarse con el santo y la limosna (to make off with the saint and the alms) *DR, PR, CR* ◆ *Cristián left yesterday and made off with it all. Cristián se nos fue ayer y se alzó con el santo y la limosna.*

to **make one's stomach turn** (cause disgust) revolver a alguien las tripas (el estómago) (to have one's intestines [stomach] turn) *L. Am., Sp* ◆ *The news of the war made our stomachs turn. Las noticias de la guerra nos revolvieron las tripas.*

to **make oneself at home** entrar (andar) como Pedro por su casa (to enter [walk around] like Pedro in his house) *Mex, DR, Peru, Bol, Ch, Arg, Sp* (RVAR *Mex:* Juan instead of Pedro) ◆ *The neighbor made himself at home here. El vecino andaba aquí como Pedro por su casa.*

to **make oneself scarce** ser el as de la baraja (to be the ace of the deck) *most of L. Am.* ◆ *Where is Felipe? He's made himself scarce. ¿Dónde está Felipe? Es el as de la baraja.*

to **make out** hacer cuchi-cuchi *Mex, Cuba, Col;* cachondear *Mex, ES ;* pastelear (to cake) *Mex;* fajar (to girdle, wrap) *Mex;* darse el lote (to give each other the lot) *Sp* ◆ *Florentina's parents came home and found her making out with her boyfriend.* Los padres de Florentina llegaron y la encontraron haciendo cuchi-cuchi con el novio.

to **make room** dar cabida (to give space) *L. Am., Sp* ◆ *We're going to make room for them; don't worry.* Vamos a darles cabida; no te preocupes.

to **make someone feel like a nobody** (treat badly) ningunear *Mex, ES, Nic* ◆ *They accused him of making them feel like nobodies (like dirt).* Lo acusaron de ningunearlos.

to **make someone mad** darle coraje (a alguien) (to give someone courage) *parts of L. Am., Sp* ◆ *It makes me mad to hear his complaints.* Me da coraje escuchar sus quejas.

to **make someone's hair stand on end** (from fear) poner a alguien los pelos de punta *L. Am., Sp* ◆ *Jorge told me what had happened to him and it made my hair stand on end.* Jorge me contó lo que le había pasado y se me pusieron los pelos de punta.

to **make the most (of)** (take maximum advantage, get the best from) sacar el jugo (to take out the juice) *L. Am., Sp;* sacar partido (to take out game) *S. Cone, Sp* ◆ *Hernán made the most of his vacation.* Hernán le sacó el jugo a sus vacaciones.

to **make tracks** →see: to go like a shot, to step on it

Make yourself at home. Estás en tu casa. (You're in your house.) *L. Am., Sp;* La casa es chica, el corazón grande. (The house is small, the heart large.) *S. Cone* ◆ *Come in, my friends. Make yourselves at home.* Entren, amigos míos. Están en su casa.

making out →see foreplay, smooching

mama's boy (milktoast, man who is pushed around by his wife or girlfriend or is overly attached to his mother; →see also: pushover, wimp) el calzonudo (oversized pants) *Mex, ES, Peru, Arg, Ch;* el calzonazos (oversized pants) *Ch, Sp* ◆ *It doesn't surprise me that he married that bossy woman; he's always been a mama's boy.* No me extraña que se haya casado con esa sargenta; siempre ha sido un calzonudo.

man (term of address for either a man or a woman) hombre (man) *L. Am., Sp* ◆ *Man,*

you've had a lot of problems this week, haven't you? Hombre, has tenido muchos problemas esta semana, ¿no?

to **manage** (get along) defenderse (to defend oneself) *L. Am., Sp* ◆ *Don't worry . . . I'm managing.* No te preocupes... me voy defendiendo.

to **manage to do something** (often something tricky) arreglárselas (to arrange them for yourself) *L. Am., Sp* ◆ *I managed to convince her.* Me las arreglé para convencerla.

maniac drivers los cafres del volante (jerks at the wheel) *Mex, Col* ◆ *Some maniac drivers caused an accident downtown.* Unos cafres del volante causaron un accidente en el centro.

matchstick →see: string bean

the **max** →see: super

to the **max** a brazo partido (to a broken arm) *L. Am., Sp;* hasta más no poder *L. Am., Sp;* al tope *Mex, U, Sp* ◆ *We worked to the max for our party's candidate.* Trabajamos a brazo partido para el candidato de nuestro partido.

Me too.; Me either. Iguanas ranas. (Iguanas frogs; iguanas sounds like igual) *Mex, Col;* Igual Pascual. (Equal Pascual.) *Ch* ◆ *I don't feel like working. —Me either.* No tengo ganas de trabajar. –Iguanas ranas.

to be **mediocre** (superfluous) no ser ni chicha ni limonada (to be neither corn liquor nor lemonade) *most of L. Am., Sp* ◆ *The new director doesn't impress me much. He's mediocre.* El nuevo director no me impresiona mucho. No es ni chicha ni limoná.

to **meet one's match** encontrar la horma de su zapato (to find one's shoe size; horma means wooden model of foot) *Mex, DR, ES, S. Cone, Sp* ◆ *When I met Jorge, I knew I had met my match.* Cuando conocí a Jorge, supe que había encontrado la horma de mi zapato.

mega mayúsculo(-a) (capital letter) *L. Am.* ◆ *That's a mega problem.* Eso es un problema mayúsculo.

mess 1. (disorder) el lío (bundle) *L. Am., Sp* ; el despelote *L. Am., Sp;* la mescolanza *most of L. Am.;* el desmadre (dismother) *Chicano, Mex, C. Am., Ec, Sp;* el arroz con bicicleta (rice with bicycle) *Florida, PR, Col;* el berenjenal (eggplant patch) *Mex, PR, S. Cone, Sp*; el reguero (stream, sprinkle) *Mex, DR, PR, Col*; el revoltijo *Mex, S. Cone*; la sopa de letras (alphabet soup, referring to something spoken or written) *Mex, Col, Peru*; la burundanga *Mex, Cuba, PR*; el zaperoco *PR, Ven*; el merequetengue *Col*; el burdel (bordello) *U, Arg*; el laberinto (labyrinth) *Peru*; el gazpacho (cold vegetable soup) *Sp*; el follón (a bit vulgar but very commonly used) *Sp* ◆ *This is a mess. It needs to be cleaned up quickly.* **Esto es un lío. Hay que ordenarlo rápidamente.** ◆ *There was always a mess in that house.* **Había siempre un desmadre en esa casa. 2.** (quagmire) el atolladero *ES, CR, Ch, Sp* ◆ *I don't know how we're going to get out of this mess that Juan has gotten us into.* **No sé cómo vamos a salir de este atolladero en que nos ha metido Juan. 3.** (bad situation, embarrassing situation) el marrón (chestnut) *Sp* ◆ *The boss gave me a mess to handle and I had to stay in the office until ten o'clock at night.* **El jefe me pasó un marrón y tuve que quedarme hasta las diez de la noche en la oficina. 4.** (mess, problem, complicated situation; also, way of being) el rollo (roll) *Mex, C. Am., Col, Ven, Peru, Ch, Sp* ◆ *Oh, my, what a mess you have.* **Vaya rollo que tienes.**

to **mess up** (ruin the plan;→see also: to blow it)arruinar el estofado (to spoil the stew) *U, Arg* ◆ *I had everything all set up and that woman messed it up.* **Yo lo tenía todo arreglado y esa mujer me arruinó el estofado.**

messed up (→see also: screwed [up]) **1.** (mixed up) despelotado(-a) *S. Cone* ◆ *This office is totally messed up. Let's start organizing it.* **Esta oficina está totalmente despelotada. Comencemos a organizarla. 2.** (ruined) amolado(-a) (ground, sharpened) *Mex, C. Am.*; fregado(-a) (scrubbed) *most of L. Am.* ◆ *They left you totally messed up.* **Te dejaron bien amolado(-a).** *The situation of the farmers is really messed up this year.* **La situación de los agricultores está muy fregada este año.**

messing around (fooling around) el traqueteo (banging, creaking) *Mex, DR, PR, G, ES* Stop messing around—we're going to be late. ◆ **Deja el traqueteo, que vamos a llegar tarde.**

milktoast →see: mama's boy, pushover, wimp

mindless →see: stupid

miser →see: tightwad

to **miss the boat 1.** (miss opportunity) perder el (último) tren (to miss the [last] train) *Mex, DR, ES, Ch, Arg, Sp Ven*; quedarse en el aparato (to be left on the phone receiver) ◆ *Tomás missed the boat when he didn't accept the job at the new company.* **Tomás perdió el tren cuando no aceptó el empleo en la nueva compañía. 2.** (be left behind, left a spinster) dejarle a alguien el tren (to have the train leave you) *DR, CR, Col, Ch* (RVar *Mex:* irse el tren) ◆ *María has missed the boat; she's more than fifty years old and hasn't found the love (lit., beau) of her life.* **A María ya le ha dejado el tren; tiene más de cincuenta años y no ha podido encontrar el galán de su vida.**

to **mix apples and oranges** (two very different things) confundir la gimnasia con la magnesia (to confuse gymnastics with magnesia) *Mex, Sp*; mezclar la velocidad con el tocino (to mix speed with bacon) *Sp* ◆ *You're mixing apples and oranges. You can't compare a house in Madrid with a house in the country.* **Estás confundiendo la gimnasia con la magnesia. No se puede comparar una casa en Madrid con una casa en el campo.**

to **mix someone up 1.** (talk with double meaning, confuse in a teasing way) alburear *Mex, ES, CR* ◆ *He mixed me up with double meanings and in the end I didn't understand anything.* **Me albureó y al final no entendí nada. 2.** to confuse envolver en razones (to wrap in reasons) *Mex, ES, Sp*; entuturutar *ES*; volver a alguien tarumba *Sp* (RVar *Ch:* turumba) ◆ *Don't try to mix me up; I know what happened.* **No trates de envolverme en razones, que yo sé lo que pasó.**

mixed bag (describing the diversity of a group or community) hijos de muchas madres (children of many mothers) *Sp* ◆ *A mixed bag of people died in the war, not just American soldiers.* **En la guerra murieron hijos de muchas madres, no sólo soldados americanos.**

to be **mixed up** (confused, disoriented) estar norteado(-a) (to be northed) *Mex, ES*; quedarse patidifuso(-a) (y perplejo[-a]) (to end up confused [and perplexed]) *DR, Col, Ch, U, Sp*; estar azurumbado(-a) *Nic, CR, Col*

(RVar *ES, Nic:* zurumbo[-a]); tener mambo en la cabeza (to have mambo in the head) *Arg;* perder el norte (to lose the north) *Sp;* tener un cacao mental (to have a mental cacao tree or bean) *Sp;* tener una empanada mental (to have a mental empanada, a pastry filled with meat and/or other things) *Sp* ◆ *We were mixed up by the proposals of the new director.* Nos quedamos patidifusos con las propuestas del nuevo director. ◆ *I'm feeling all mixed up.* Estoy norteada.

mixup →see: mess

mob (crowd; →see also: gang) el reguero de gente (stream of people) *Mex, DR, PR;* el molote *Cuba, DR, G, ES, Nic, CR;* la patota (great big foot) *S. Cone* ◆ *When the police arrived, there was a mob at the site of the accident.* Cuando llegó la policía, había un reguero de gente en el lugar del accidente.

the **moment of truth** (the time for explanation) la hora de los quiubos (the time of the what-happeneds) *Ch* ◆ *Let's talk about what happened. It's the moment of truth.* Vamos a hablar de lo que pasó. Es la hora de los quiubos.

Money talks. (Money is power.) Poderoso caballero es don Dinero. (A powerful gentleman is Sir Money.) *L. Am., Sp;* El que tiene plata platica. (Whoever has money makes conversation.) *Nic* ◆ *Of course they won the election. Money talks.* Por supuesto que ganaron las elecciones. Poderoso caballero es don Dinero.

moneybags (rich person; →see also: loaded, to be loaded) el ricachón, la ricachona *L. Am., Sp;* el ricardo (richard) *Mex;* el/la millonetis *Sp* ◆ *My dream is to go to Las Vegas and come back home a moneybags.* Mi sueño es ir a Las Vegas para regresar a mi casa hecho un millonetis.

to **monkey around** →see: to joke around

monkey business los negocios chuecos (crooked deals) *Mex, DR, ES, Col, Ch* ◆ *They got involved in some monkey business and now they're worried.* Se metieron en negocios chuecos y ahora están preocupados.

mooch 1. (→see also: operator) aprovechado(-a) *L. Am., Sp* (RVar *S. Cone:* aprovechador[-a]); el gorrón, la gorrona *Mex, C. Am., Peru, Sp;* arrimado(-a) (put near, from arrimarse al sol que más calienta) *Mex,* *Cuba, DR, PR, G, Nic, Col, Peru;* el/la abusivo(-a) (abusive) *Mex, C. Am.;* el abusón, la abusona *Mex, Sp;* el/la jeta (face) *Sp* ◆ *He's a mooch; he's always eating at my house and he never brings anything.* Es un aprovechado; siempre está comiendo en mi casa y nunca trae nada. **2.** (person who takes advantage of others) el/la abusador(-a) (abuser) *S. Cone;* el mamón, la mamona (sucker, like a suckling baby) *Sp* ◆ *Elena is a mooch, and she has abused her husband's good will.* Elena es una abusadora, y ha aprovechado de la bondad de su esposo.

to **mooch** (not pay for things) gorrear *Mex, Col, Sp;* encajarse *Mex* ◆ *She always mooches food off me.* Ella siempre me gorrea comida.

moolah →see: dough

moron →see: idiot

mouthing off (yelling and screaming) trompudo(-a) (with a big snout or mouth; sounding off threats) *Mex, C. Am., Col* ◆ *Every time I see him, he's mouthing off.* Cada vez que lo veo, está trompudo.

mouthy (describing someone who talks back unjustifiably when reprimanded) respondón, respondona *Mex, Sp* ◆ *Memo lost his job by being mouthy.* Memo perdió su trabajo por respondón.

Moving right along (to a new topic) . . . (Forget it.) A otra cosa, mariposa. (To another thing, butterfly.) *Mex, DR, Sp;* Pasemos a otro patín. (Let's go to another skate.) *Mex, G, Ec* ◆ *Moving right along to a new topic. No one wants to talk about politics now.* ◆ A otra cosa mariposa. Nadie quiere hablar de política ahora.

to be **much ado about nothing** ser más el ruido que las nueces (to have more noise than nuts) *L. Am., Sp;* ser de mucho ruido y pocas nueces (to be) a lot of noise and few nuts; said when something yields very little despite expectations) *Mex, Ch, U, Sp* ◆ *I get the impression that this project is much ado about nothing.* Tengo la impresión que este proyecto es de mucho ruido y pocas nueces.

muddle (embarrassment, problem) la embarrada (mud plaster [for walls]) *Mex, Col, Peru, S. Cone* ◆ *What a muddle! I forgot to mail the check.* ¡Qué embarrada! Se me olvidó mandar el cheque.

muddled →see: mixed up

mug (face) →see: kisser

to **mug** (rob; →see also: to lift, to make a hit, to take someone to the cleaners) tumbar (to fell, knock down) *PR, Col, Ven* ◆ *I can't find my wallet since yesterday. I think someone mugged me on the bus.* Yo no encuentro mi billetera desde ayer. Creo que me la tumbaron en la guagua.

to **mumble** (murmur, grumble) hablar entre dientes (to talk between the teeth) *L. Am., Sp* ◆ *He mumbles (swallows his words), and I don't understand him.* Habla entre dientes, y no lo entiendo.

munchies (appetizers, hors d'oeuvres) la botana *Mex;* los pasa-palos (drink-passers) *Ven;* las picadas (pickings) *Arg;* las cosas para picar (things to pick at) *Ch, U, Sp* ◆ *Elisa prepared the munchies.* Elisa preparó las cosas para picar.

My goodness! →see: Holy smoke! Wow!

My humble home is yours. La casa es chica, el corazón grande. (The house is small, the heart large.) *S. Cone* ◆ *Stay with us. My humble home is yours.* Quédense con nosotros. La casa es chica, el corazón grande.

my love (→see also: dear, sweetie) mi amor *L. Am., Sp;* mi amorcito (my little love) *L. Am., Sp;* mi rey (reina) (my king [queen]) *L. Am., Sp;* mi pichón (my pigeon) *parts of L. Am.;* (RVar *Mex:* pichoncito) ◆ *What time will you be back, my love?* ¿A qué horas regresas, mi amor?

N

nag (badgering, bossy person) fregón, fregona (scrubber) *Mex, G, Col*; molón, molona *Mex* ◆ *But if I keep on being a nag, eventually I'll get it.* Pero si soy un fregón, luego luego lo voy a agarrar.

nagging (continuously asking for something) la fregadera (slightly vulgar) *Chicano, Mex, G, ES, CR* ◆ *You keep on with your same old nagging.* Sigues con la misma fregadera.

nark el/la narco (short for narcotraficante) *L. Am., Sp* ◆ *That neighborhood is a paradise for narks.* Ese barrio es un paraíso para los narcos.

natch (of course) sincho *Chicano, Mex, Col* ◆ *Are you going to the movies with us? —Natch!* ¿Vas al cine con nosotros? —¡Sincho!

nattering on (→see also: blah, blah, blah) habla que te habla (talk that he or she talks to you) *DR, PR, Ch, U* ◆ *I waited for a long time while Estela nattered on and on with her friends, without paying any attention to me (lit., without worrying about me).* Esperé largo rato mientras Estela, hable que te hable con sus amigas, sin preocuparse por mí.

necking →see: foreplay, smooching

to **needle** →see: to bug, to give (someone) a hard time, to rile up

ne'er-do-well →see: slacker

to be **neither deaf nor dumb** (be competent and experienced) no ser cojo(-a) ni manco(-a) (to be neither lame nor one-handed) *L. Am., Sp*; no ser ni tonto(-a) ni perezoso(-a) (to be neither stupid nor lazy) *L. Am., Sp* ◆ *Mom, I can't do this chore. —And why not, if you aren't deaf or dumb?* Mamá, no puedo hacer esta tarea. –¿Y por qué, si no eres ni cojo ni manco?

to be **neither fish nor fowl** (undefined, insipid) no ser ni carne ni pescado (to be neither meat nor fish) *Sp* ◆ *This choice is the one that best suits everyone, although it's neither fish nor fowl.* Esta opción es la que mejor va a todo el mundo, aunque no es ni carne ni pescado.

to be **neither here nor there** (without it mattering to anyone) ni ir ni venirle (without it coming or going) *Mex, S. Cone, Sp* ◆ *To me, the whole matter of the election campaign is neither here nor there.* El asunto de la campaña electoral ni me va ni me viene.

nerd (→see also: bookworm, grind) el nerdo *parts of L. Am.* ◆ *Hugo's a nerd, very intelligent and studious. The poor guy almost never leaves the library.* Hugo es un nerdo, muy inteligente y estudioso. El pobre casi nunca sale de la biblioteca.

nerve (brazenness) la concha (shell) *Mex, Nic, Pan, Ec, Peru*; el morro/el rostro (face) *Sp*; la jeta/la cara (face) *Sp* ◆ *That girl has a lot of nerve.* Esa chica tiene mucha concha.

nervous as a cat (uptight →see also: to be on edge) como cocodrilo en fábrica de carteras (like a crocodile in a wallet factory) *PR*; como perro en canoa (like a dog in a canoe) *PR* ◆ *I have a job interview and I'm nervous as a cat.* Tengo una entrevista de trabajo y me siento como cocodrilo en fábrica de carteras.

nervy →see: pushy person

never again una y no más (santo Tomás) (once and no more [Saint Thomas]) *Sp* ◆ *Did you lend money to Teresa? —Once, but never again.* ¿Le prestaste dinero a Teresa? –Una y no más, santo Tomás.

to **never rain but to pour** (have one bad thing happen after another; to be repetitive or superfluous) llover sobre mojado (to rain over the wetness) *L. Am., Sp* ◆ *It never rains but it pours: they raised the prices again.* Llueve sobre mojado: otra vez subieron los precios.

news flash (surprising piece of news) la bomba, el bombazo (bomb) *Mex, DR, G, ES, Sp* ◆ *Hang on—I've got a news flash. Guess who got pregnant.* Agárrate, que tengo un bombazo. Adivina quién salió embarazada.

No big deal.; No biggie. No es para tanto. (It's not for so much.) *L. Am., Sp* ◆ *Don't get* *mad, Alfonsina, it's no big deal.* **No te enojes, Alfonsina, no es para tanto.**

No buts about it. No hay pero que valga. (There's no but that's of value.) *L. Am., Sp* ♦ *You have to accept this offer and no buts about it.* **Tienes que aceptar esta oferta y no hay pero que valga.**

No damn way. (all vulgar:) Ni madre. (Not even mother.) *Mex, C. Am., Col;* Ni mierda. (Not even shit.) *Mex, G, ES, Nic, S. Cone;* Ni a huevos. (Not even by eggs, meaning testicles.) *Mex, ES* ♦ *I'm not going to do it. No damn way.* **No lo voy a hacer. Ni madre.**

No go. (Absolutely not, period. →see also: No way.) Ahí muere. (It dies there.) *Mex, ES* ♦ *I'm not going to the meeting; I'm staying at home, and no go.* **No voy a la reunión; me quedo en casa. Ahí muere.**

to be **no good for anything** →see: to be useless

to be **no great shakes** (→see also: to be nothing to write home about; so-so) ser del montón (to be of the heap) *L. Am., Sp;* no ser nada del otro mundo (to not be something from the other world) *Mex, DR, PR, ES, S. Cone, Sp;* no ser nada (cosa) del otro jueves (to not be a thing of next Thursday) *Sp* ♦ *That teacher is no great shakes.* **Esa maestra es del montón.**

No harm in asking. En pedir no hay engaño. (There is no deceit in asking.) *Ch* ♦ *Let's sign the petition. No harm in asking.* **Vamos a firmar la petición. En pedir no hay engaño.**

No joke. (Seriously.) Fuera de bromas. (Outside of jokes.) *Mex, ES, S. Cone, Sp* ♦ *Now let's talk about this, no joke.* **Ya fuera de bromas vamos a platicar de esto.**

no matter what 1. (whatever happens; →see also: come hell or high water) contra viento y marea (against wind and tide) *L. Am., Sp;* pese a quien pese (weigh whatever it may weigh) *L. Am., Sp;* cueste lo que cueste (cost whatever it may cost) *L. Am., Sp;* aunque truene y relampaguée (even if it thunders and there is lightning) *Mex, ES, S. Cone* ♦ *No matter what, we're going to travel.* **Aunque truene y relampaguée, vamos a viajar.** 2. (fanatically, strictly) a rajatabla (to board breaking) *L. Am., Sp* ♦ *The plan will turn out well if they follow the rules no matter what.* ♦

El plan saldrá bien si siguen las normas a rajatabla.

No more baloney (enough stories; stop with the fibs). Ya está bien de cuentos. *most of L. Am., Sp* ♦ *No more baloney; don't say anything more.* **Ya está bien de cuentos; no hable más.**

No problem, relax. (→see also: to chill out) Tranquilo(-a). (Tranquil.) *Mex, DR, Col, Ven, S. Cone, Sp* ♦ *No problem, relax. Everything's OK.* **Tranquilo, tranquilo. Todo va bien.**

No way. 1. (→see also: Don't even think about it. Not even in your dreams.) Ni a palos. (Not even with blows of a stick.) *L. Am., Sp;* Ni loco(-a). (Not even crazy.) *L. Am., Sp;* Ni ebrio(-a) ni dormido(-a). (Neither drunk nor asleep.) *Mex, Col;* Ni de vaina. (Not even as a husk.) *Nic, Col, Ven;* Ni a la de tres. (Not even by that of three.) *Sp* ♦ *No way was she going to let go of it.* **Ni a palos lo iba a soltar.** 2. (Nothing doing!; expression of rejecting or declining something) Naranjas. (Oranges.) *Chicano, Mex, G, ES, Col, Sp;* ¡Un rábano! (A radish!) *Mex, Sp;* ¡Naranjas de la China! (Oranges from China!) *Sp* ♦ *Will you lend me a thousand pesos? —No way. I don't have anything.* **¿Me prestas mil pesos? —Naranjas. No tengo nada.**

No way. Absolutely not, period. Ahí muere. (It dies there.) *Mex, ES* ♦ *I'm not going to the meeting; I'm staying at home. No way.* **No voy a la reunión; me quedo en casa. Ahí muere.**

No way, José. De ninguna manguera (como dijo el bombero). (No hose [as the fireman said]. **Manguera** sounds like **manera**, way.) *Mex, ES;* Nel. Nel, pastel. (No. No, cake.) *Chicano, Mex, G, ES, Nic;* Ni módulo (como dijo el astronauta). (No module [as the astronaut said]. **Módulo** sounds like **modo**, way.) *Mex;* ¡De eso nada, monada! (Of that nothing, monkey [cute] face!) *Sp* ♦ *Paco, will you lend me money to go to the movies? —No way, José. I don't have a dime.* **Paco, ¿me prestas dinero para ir al cine? —¡Nel, pastel! No tengo ni cinco.**

no wonder con razón (with reason) *L. Am., Sp* ♦ *This boy is almost deaf. No wonder he doesn't understand anything in class.* **Este niño**

es casi sordo. Con razón no entiende nada en la clase.

a **nobody** (unimportant person, with little influence or power) don Nadie (Sir Nobody) *L. Am., Sp* ◆ *That guy is a nobody; he pretends to be more (important) than he is. Ese tipo es un don Nadie; pretende ser lo que no es.*

noggin (head) el coco (coconut) *L. Am., Sp;* la chaveta *Mex, DR, PR, ES;* la maceta (flower pot) *Mex, G, Nic;* la chirimoya (type of fruit) *Mex, ES, CR;* el tarro (jar) *Sp* ◆ *Tito fell out of a tree and hurt his noggin. Tito se cayó de un árbol y se lastimó la chirimoya.*

None of your business. (This isn't your affair.) ¿Quién te mete, Juan Bonete? (Who brings you into this, Juan Bonete?) *Mex, Nic* ◆ *Leave your boyfriend. He's a womanizer.— It's none of your business. Deja a tu novio. Es un mujeriego. —¿Y a ti quién te mete, Juan Bonete?*

none whatsoever (not even a shred of) ni pizca de (not even a pinch of) *Mex, DR, C. Am., Col, Ch, Arg* ◆ *He has no manners, none whatsoever. No tiene ni pizca de educación.*

nonsense (→see also: baloney) las tonterías stupidities *L. Am., Sp;* las memeces *Sp* ◆ *What a piece of nonsense! That's not true. ¡Qué memez! Eso no es cierto.*

noodle (head; →see: noggin)

Nope. Nel. *Chicano, Mex, G, ES, Nic;* Chale. *Chicano, Mex;* ¡Nones! *Mex, Col* ◆ *Nope! I don't believe you. ¡Chale! No te creo.*

nosy (→see also: busybody) metiche *Mex, DR, PR, G, Nic, CR, Col;* chute *Mex, ES* ◆ *Alejandra is so nosy that her coworkers don't invite her anywhere. Alejandra es tan metiche que sus compañeros de trabajo no la invitan a ninguna parte.*

Not a chance. →see: No way.

not a pretty picture (ironic, meaning not very nice or well done) menudo número (diminutive number or show; ironic) *Sp* ◆ *Not a pretty picture what you did last night. The people in the room next door couldn't sleep. Menudo número montaste anoche. Los de la habitación de al lado no pudieron dormir.*

to **not amount to a hill of beans** →see: to be worthless, to wash out (fail)

Not at all. Nada de eso. (None of that.) *L. Am., Sp* ◆ *Do you have a problem? —No, not at all. ¿Tienes algún problema? —No, nada de eso.*

to **not be a bowl of cherries** →see: to be a drag, to be a pain

to **not be able to contain oneself with happiness** no caber en sí de contento *Mex, ES, Peru, U, Arg, Sp* ◆ *Don Alonso couldn't contain himself with happiness about his son getting his degree. Don Alonso no cabía en sí de contento con el título de su hijo.*

to **not be able to do anything right** no dar pie con bola (to not hit the ball with one's foot) *Mex, DR, PR, U, Sp;* salirle al revés (to turn out backwards for someone) *C. Am., S. Cone, Sp;* no dar una (to not give one) *Mex, U, Sp;* no dar ni una (to not hit even one) *Mex;* Todo me sale al revés. Everything turns out badly for me. I can't do anything right. *L. Am., Sp* ◆ *This is the third time I've left the keys in the car. I can't do anything right. Es la tercera vez que se me quedan las llaves dentro del carro. Estoy que no doy pie con bola.*

to **not be able to make up one's mind** (be undecided) estar entre dos aguas (to be between two waters) *most of L. Am., Sp* ◆ *We're unable to make up our mind whether to go to Cuba or Costa Rica for our vacation. Estamos entre dos aguas: no sabemos si ir a Cuba o a Costa Rica en nuestras vacaciones.*

to **not be able to stand someone** (dislike) no pasar a alguien (to not pass someone; used like gustar) *Mex, DR, ES, S. Cone;* no bancar *U, Arg* ◆ *I can't stand the clerk in that store. La empleada de esa tienda no me pasa.*

to **not be able to stand the sight of someone** no poder ver a alguien ni en pintura (to not be able to see someone even in a painting) *Mex, DR, PR, ES, Ch, U, Sp;* no poder ver a alguien ni pintado (to not be able to see someone even painted) *CR, Arg, Sp* ◆ *Matilde is so conceited. I can't stand the sight of her. Matilde es tan orgullosa. No puedo verla ni en pintura.*

to **not be able to take any more** →see: to be fed up

to **not be able to wait** no ver la hora (de) (to not see the hour) *L. Am., Sp* ◆ *I can't wait until my friend Brenda gets here. No veo la* *hora que llegue mi amiga Brenda.* ◆ *I can't wait to go.* No veo la hora de ir.

to **not be all sweetness and light** (→see also: to be a drag, to be a grouch, sourpuss) no ser perita en dulce (to not be a pear in sugar water) *Mex, ES* ◆ *One of the children I take care of gives me problems almost every day. Let's just say he's not all sweetness and light.* Uno de los niños que cuido me da problemas casi todos los días. Digamos que no es perita en dulce.

to **not be born yesterday** no acabar de caerse del nido (to still be falling out of the nest) *LA;* no chuparse el dedo (to not suck one's thumb) *Mex, DR, PR, ES, S. Cone, Sp* ◆ *I wasn't born yesterday. That's a lie.* Yo no me chupo el dedo. Eso es pura mentira.

to **not be in a joking mood** no estar para bromas *L. Am., Sp* ◆ *Talk seriously; the situation is difficult, and I'm not in a joking mood.* Habla en serio; la situación es difícil, y no estoy para bromas.

to **not be made of stone** (be vulnerable to sexual provocation) no ser de piedra (to not be of stone) *L. Am., Sp* ◆ *You should be ashamed! You betrayed your wife for an easy affair. —Well, I was tempted. I'm not made of stone.* ¡Qué vergüenza! Traicionaste a tu esposa por una aventura fácil. —Bueno, me tenté. No soy de piedra.

to **not be one's cup of tea** (not be to one's liking) no ser santo de su devoción (to not be the saint of one's devotion; said of people) *ES, Nic, S. Cone, Sp* ◆ *Jennifer López was never really my cup of tea, but I can put up with her.* Jennifer López nunca fue santo de mi devoción, pero la tolero.

to **not be playing with a full deck** →see: to be off one's rocker, to have a screw loose

to **not be the first** (nor the last; phrase used to excuse an action because there are other examples) no ser el primero ni el último (to not be the first nor the last) *Mex, DR, PR, ES, S. Cone* ◆ *I'm not the first nor the last (to make this mistake).* No soy el primero ni el último.

to **not be too damn likely** (be difficult) ser carajo(-a) (to be male organ, vulgar) *Mex* ◆ *It's not too damn likely that our team'll make it to the championship.* Es muy carajo que nuestro equipo llegue al campeonato.

to **not be worth a damn** no valer un carajo (to not be worth a male organ, vulgar) *Mex, U, Arg, Sp;* no valer ni mierda (to not be worth shit; vulgar) *L. Am., Sp* ◆ *That guy is not worth a damn.* Ese tipo no vale un carajo.

to **not be worth a plug nickel** →see: to be worthless

to **not burn one's bridges** (not cut down on options) →see: burn one's bridges no cerrar la puerta (to not close the door) *Ch* ◆ *Don't burn your bridges for new job opportunities.* No cierres las puertas a las nuevas oportunidades de trabajo.

Not by a longshot. (→see also: No way.) Ni por asomo. (Not even by conjecture.) *DR, S. Cone, Sp* ◆ *Me do such a thing? No, man, not by a longshot.* ¿Yo hacer semejante cosa? No, hombre, ni por asomo.

to **not care** (be indifferent, not suffer or change because of something) pasar (to pass) *Sp* ◆ *I don't care about anything.* Yo paso de todo.

to **not care a fig** →see: to not give a darn

to **not dare open one's mouth** no atreverse a decir «esta boca es mía» (to not dare to say "this mouth is mine") *L. Am., Sp* ◆ *When the police came, I didn't dare open my mouth.* Cuando vino la policía, no me atreví a decir «esta boca es mía».

to **not even give (someone) the time of day** no dar ni los «Buenos días» (to not even give a "Good day") *Mex, DR, PR, ES, U, Arg, Sp;* no dar ni la hora *Mex, ES, S. Cone, Sp* ◆ *The boss was angry; he came into the office and wouldn't even give us the time of day.* El jefe estaba enojado; entró en la oficina y no dio ni los "Buenos días".

to **not even have time to sneeze** (be very busy) no tener tiempo ni para rascarse (to not have time even to scratch oneself) *Mex, DR, ES, U, Sp* ◆ *Why don't you come visit us? —I can't. I'm studying for exams, and I don't even have time to sneeze.* ¿Por qué no vienes a visitarnos? —No puedo. Estoy preparando exámenes, y no tengo tiempo ni para rascarme.

Not even in your (his, her, etc.) dreams. (Not a chance. →see also: No way.) Ni a palos. (Not even with blows of a stick.) *L. Am., Sp;* Ni en sueños. (Not even dreaming.) *L. Am., Sp;* Ni a tiros. (Not even by gunshots.) *Mex, Sp* ◆ *What if Enrique invites you to spend the day on the beach? —Not even in his dreams! ¿Qué tal si Enrique te invita a pasar el día en la playa? –¡Ni en sueños lo haría!*

to **not fall for something** no tragarse esa guayaba (to not swallow that guava) *L. Am., except Arg., Ch;* no tragar carros y carretas (to not swallow cars and carts) *Mex, Sp* ◆ *I'm not going to fall for that baloney (nonsense). No voy a tragarme esa guayaba.*

to **not get involved** no involucrarse *L. Am., Sp;* no pintar nada (to not paint anything) *Sp* ◆ *I'm not getting involved in Juan's party because I hardly know him. Yo no pinto nada en la fiesta de Juan porque casi no lo conozco.*

to **not get it** no agarrar la onda (to not seize the sound wave) *Mex, G, ES, U, Arg;* no dar con ello *Sp;* estar (quedarse) a dos velas (to be [remain] at two sails) *Mex, Sp* ◆ *The foreman explained the job to us, but we didn't get it. El capataz nos explicó el trabajo pero no agarramos la onda.* ◆ *We arrived late to the show and didn't get it. Llegamos tarde a la función y nos quedamos a dos velas.*

to **not give a damn** (not matter; all vulgar) importarle/valerle madre (to matter mother) *Mex, most of C. Am.;* importar un carajo (to not matter a male organ) *PR, U, Arg;* importarle tres cojones (to matter three testicles) *Sp;* tomar a coña algo (to take something at coña, a word referring to the female organ) *Sp* ◆ *They don't give a damn what other people think. Les vale madre lo que opinen los demás.*

to **not give a darn** (not matter) importarle un pepino (to matter a cucumber) *L. Am., Sp;* ni me (te, le, etc.) va ni me (te, le, etc.) viene (it doesn't go or come to me [you, him, etc.]) *L. Am., Sp;* importarle un comino (to matter a cumin seed) *L. Am., Sp;* importarle un rábano (to matter a radish) *Mex, ES, Ch, U, Sp;* importarle un pito (to matter a whistle) *Mex, DR, PR, S. Cone;* importarle un bledo (to matter a pigweed) *Mex, S. Cone, Sp;* importarle un pimiento (to matter a pepper) *Sp* ◆ *I don't give a darn what other people might think. Me importa un pepino lo que pueda pensar otra gente.* ◆ *I don't give a darn about the election campaign. El asunto*

de la campaña electoral ni me va ni me viene.

to **not give a hoot** →see: to not give a darn

to **not give in** (be stubborn or persistent) no dar el brazo a torcer (to not give one's arm to twist) *L. Am., Sp* ◆ *That's just the way Vicente is. He never gives in. Así es Vicente. No se da el brazo a torcer.*

to **not go out on a limb** (not take any risk) no aventurarse (to not venture, not risk) *L. Am., Sp;* no mojarse (to not get oneself wet) *Sp* ◆ *Juan never goes out on a limb for anything. Juan no se moja para nada.*

to **not have a dime** →see: to be broke

to **not have a plug nickel** (→see also: to be broke) no tener ni cinco (to not have even five [cents]) *Mex, DR, ES, Sp;* estar sin cinco (to be without five) *Mex, ES, Sp* ◆ *I don't have a plug nickel to buy food. No tengo ni cinco para comprar comida.*

to **not have a pot to pee in** no tener dónde caerse muerto (to not even have a place to fall dead in; not vulgar) *L. Am., Sp* ◆ *Lend me money, Rafael; I don't have a pot to pee in. Préstame dinero, Rafael; no tengo dónde caerme muerto.*

to **not have any say in a matter** no tener vela en el entierro (to not have a candle at a funeral) *Mex, DR, S. Cone, Sp* ◆ *Better not give your opinion; you don't have any say in this matter. Mejor no opines, que no tienes vela en este entierro.*

to **not have balls** (→see also: to back down, to back out; all vulgar) no tener huevos (to not have eggs, testicles) *L. Am., Sp;* no tener bolas *S. Cone;* ser (un) acojonado (to be without testicles) *PR, Sp* ◆ *So, want to bet you don't have the balls to go to the cemetery at night? ¿A que no tienes huevos de ir a un cementerio de noche?*

to **not have the sense God gave a goose** →see: stupid, to be brainless

to **not have too much upstairs** (not be very bright; →see also: stupid, to be brainless) no tener sal en la mollera (to not have salt on the crown of the head) *L. Am., Sp* ◆ *It seems to me that this guy doesn't have too much upstairs. Me parece que este tipo no tiene sal en la mollera.*

to **not keep one's word** faltar a la palabra *L. Am., Sp* ◆ *I don't have confidence in Arturo's business; he often does not keep his word.* **No confío en el negocio de Arturo; a menudo falta a la palabra.**

to **not know beans about** no saber ni papa de (to not know potato about) *Mex, DR, PR, ES, Ch, U, Sp* ◆ *I hope they don't ask me any questions in history class because I don't know beans about the Mexican Revolution.* **Ojalá no me pregunten en la clase de historia porque no sé ni papa de la Revolución Mexicana.**

to **not know half the story** (not know the half of it) no saber de la misa la mitad (to not know half the mass) *U, Sp* ◆ *We were perplexed with the news of the fraud; we didn't know half the story.* **Quedamos perplejos con la noticia del fraude, pues nosotros no sabíamos de la misa la mitad.**

to **not know right from left (up from down)** no saber dónde se tiene la mano derecha (to not know where one's right hand is) *Sp* ◆ *They don't know right from left in this department. They have no idea what the job is about.* **No saben dónde tienen la mano derecha en esta sección. No tienen ni idea de qué se trata el trabajo.**

to **not know what move to make** (what to do; be undecided) no saber a qué carta quedarse (to not know what card to keep) *Sp* ◆ *Ernesto didn't know what move to make until the end. His slowness in the decision cost him the job.* **Ernesto no supo a qué carta quedarse hasta el final. Su tardanza en la decisión le costó el puesto.**

to **not last long** (in a job, etc.) no calentar el asiento (to not warm the seat) *Mex, ES, U, Arg, Sp* ◆ *Pablo didn't last long in that job.* **Pablo no calentó el asiento en ese trabajo.**

to **not let someone out of one's sight** no dejar (ni) a sol ni a sombra a alguien (to not leave someone in the sun or the shade) *L. Am., Sp* ◆ *That woman doesn't let her husband out of her sight for a minute; she's really jealous.* **Esa mujer no deja ni a sol ni a sombra a su marido; es muy celosa.**

to **not let someone rest** 1. (keep busy) no dejar a alguien sentar el pie en el suelo (to not let someone put his or her foot on the floor) *Sp* ◆ *Although yesterday was a holiday, Mom didn't let us rest a minute.* **Aunque ayer fue día de fiesta, mamá no nos dejó sentar el pie en el suelo. 2.** (pursue someone at all hours and in all places) no dejar (ni) a sol ni a sombra a alguien (to not leave someone in the sun or the shade) *L. Am., Sp* ◆ *This baby doesn't let his mother rest. She's exhausted.* **Este bebé no deja ni a sol ni a sombra a su madre. Ella está agotada.**

to **not lift a finger** (be lazy, do nothing) no mover un dedo (to not move a finger) *L. Am., Sp;* no dar un golpe (to not give a hit) *Mex, DR, Sp* ◆ *She didn't even lift a finger to help me with the computer.* **Ni siquiera movió un dedo para ayudarme con la computadora.**

to **not matter to someone** →see: to not give a darn

to **not mince words** no tener pelos en la lengua (to not have hair on the tongue; hair implies animals, or more primitive forms, that do not have language) *L. Am., Sp* ◆ *I explained the situation to them with all the details and I didn't mince words.* **Les expliqué la situación con todos los detalles y no tenía pelos en la lengua.**

Not on your life. →see: No way.

to **not pay any attention to someone** no hacerle caso a alguien (to not make a case for someone) *L. Am., Sp;* no prestarle atención a alguien (to not lend attention to someone) *L. Am., Sp;* no dar bola a alguien (to not give someone the ball) *S. Cone* ◆ *I tried to explain the situation, but they didn't pay me any attention.* **Traté de explicar la situación, pero no me dieron bola.**

to **not put up with much** no aguantar pulgas (to not tolerate fleas) *Mex, Sp* ◆ *Be careful of Héctor. He doesn't put up with much; he's very fussy.* **Cuidado con Héctor. No aguanta pulgas; es muy delicado.**

not quite right (in the head) →see: nuts

to **not say a word** (→see also: to button one's lip, to keep one's lips sealed, to put a lid on it) no decir «esta boca es mía» (to not say "this mouth is mine") *L. Am., Sp;* no decir ni pío (to not even say pío, peep) *Mex, DR, PR, Ch, Sp;* no decir ni mu (to not even say mu) *U, Arg, Sp* ◆ *I heard the commentaries, but I didn't say a word.* **Escuché los comentarios, pero no dije "esta boca es mía".**

to **not see a thing** no ver ni tres en un burro (to not even see three on a burro) *Sp* ◆ *He couldn't see a thing until they put on his glasses. Poor kid.* No veía ni tres en un burro hasta que le pusieron las gafas. Pobre niño.

to **not see hide nor hair of someone** no vérsele a alguien el pelo *Mex, Sp* ◆ *Juan works day and night; we don't see hide nor hair of him.* Juan trabaja día y noche; no le vemos el pelo.

to **not sleep a wink all night** (→see also: to spend a sleepless night) no pegar los ojos en toda la noche (to not glue the eyes the whole night) *L. Am., Sp* (RVAR *Sp:* no pegar ojo); pasar una noche toledana (spend a Toledo night) *Sp* ◆ *I have a problem at the office. I didn't sleep a wink all night.* Tengo un problema en la oficina. No pegué los ojos en toda la noche.

to **not stand** (→see also: to be a pain, to not be able to stand [the sight of someone], to put off) no soportar *L. Am, Sp;* no tragar (to not swallow) *Mex, DR, G, ES, S. Cone, Sp* ◆ *I can't stand those guys.* No trago a esos chicos.

to **not take sides** (keep one's own opinions or attitudes independently) no casarse con nadie (to not marry anyone) *L. Am., Sp* ◆ *I listened to everyone's opinions, but I didn't take sides. First I need to think.* Escuché la opinión de todos, pero no me casé con nadie. Primero tengo que pensar.

to **not turn out right for someone** (said of a miscalculation that led to damages) no salirle a alguien la(s) cuenta(s) (to not have the accounts come out for someone) *Mex, Sp* ◆ *Things are not turning out right for me.* No me salen las cuentas.

to **not understand beans (anything)** no entender ni jota (ni papa) (to not understand a jot [potato]) *L. Am., Sp* ◆ *I don't understand beans about what the mathematics professor is saying.* No entiendo ni jota de lo que dice el profesor de matemáticas.

not worth the paper it's printed on (useless document) papel mojado (wet paper) *most of L. Am., Sp* ◆ *The famous principle that all men are equal is not worth the paper it's printed on. Look at the situation of the Native Americans.* El famoso principio de que todos los hombres son iguales es papel mojado. Mira la situación de los indígenas.

Nothing doing. →see: No way.

Nothing new. →see: Same as usual.

to be **nothing special** →see: to be no great shakes, to be nothing to write home about

to be **nothing to write home about** (not be extraordinary) no ser nada del otro mundo (to not be something from the other world) *L. Am., Sp;* ser del montón (to be of the heap) *L. Am., Sp;* no ser nada (cosa) del otro jueves (to not be a thing of next Thursday) *Sp* ◆ *Is the course you're taking interesting? —It's nothing to write home about.* ¿Es interesante el curso que estás siguiendo? –No es nada del otro mundo.

Now I get it. Ahora caigo. *L. Am., Sp* ◆ *Now I get it. You want to break up with me.* Ahora caigo. Quieres romper conmigo.

numbskull →see: birdbrain, fool, idiot

nut case →see: nuts

nuts (crazy, bats in the belfry; →see also: to be off one's rocker, to have a screw loose, to lose one's marbles, mad as a hatter, off the wall) alocado(-a) (turned crazy) *L. Am., Sp;* chiflado(-a) *L. Am., Sp;* atravesado(-a) (crossed) *Mex, Nic, CR, Col;* arrebatado(-a) (carried away) *Cuba, DR, PR, G;* arrevesado(-a) *DR, ES, CR;* ◆ *Nobody trusts him because he's nuts.* Nadie confía en él porque es muy alocado.

to be **nuts** (→see also: to be off one's rocker, to have a screw loose, to lose one's marbles) estar mal de la cholla (to be bad in the head) *Mex, ES, PR, Sp;* estar mal de la azotea (to be bad in the roof) *DR, S. Cone, Sp;* estar enfermo(-a) del mate (del chape) (to be sick from mate tea [from a kind of mollusk]) *S. Cone* estar pirado(-a) *Sp* ◆ *Walk downtown? Are you nuts?* ¿Ir caminando al centro? ¿Estás mal de la cholla?

O

oaf, oafish →see: lowlife, stupid

to **obsess over something** (→see also: to fixate on) estar obsesionado(-a) con algo *L. Am.*; hacerse el bocho *U, Arg* ◆ *Don't obsess over it because there is no danger in this situation.* **No se hagan el bocho porque no hay ningún peligro en esta situación.** ◆ *She's obsessed with yoga and practices it night and day.* **Está obsesionada con el yoga y lo practica día y noche.**

to be an **oddball** ser un bicho raro (to be a strange bug, beast) *Mex, S. Cone, Sp* ◆ *That person is an oddball.* **Esa persona es un bicho raro.**

odds and ends →see: trinkets, junk

to be **of no importance to** →see: to not give a darn

to **off** (kill) →see: to wipe out

off base →see: all wet, to blow it

to be **off one's rocker** (→see also: to be nuts, to have a screw loose) cruzarse los cables (to have one's cables crossed) *L. Am., Sp*; patinarle a alguien el coco (to have one's head [coconut] skate) *Mex, DR, ES, CR, Col, Ch*; patinarle a alguien el embrague (to have one's clutch [of the car] skate) *Ch, U, Sp* ◆ *What's this about you buying another computer? Are you off your rocker?* **¿Cómo que vas a comprar otra computadora? ¿Se te cruzaron los cables?**

off the wall (→see also: nuts) zafado(-a) *Chicano, Mex, C. Am., Col, Ch* ◆ *I think that singer is off the wall.* **Creo que esa cantante está bien zafada.**

to be **off the wall** (unusual, not ordinary) no estar en el mapa (to not be on the map) *DR, ES* *This is off the wall. We couldn't have predicted this.* **Esto no estaba en el mapa.**

to be **off track** estar despistado(-a) (to be off the track) *L. Am., Sp* ◆ *You're completely off track.* **Estás totalmente despistado.**

off-color joke el chiste colorado (rojo) (red joke) *L. Am., Sp* (RVAR *Mex, ES, Ch:* more common than chiste verde); el chiste verde (green joke) *L. Am., Sp;* el chiste pelado (peeled joke) *Mex* ◆ *He tells good jokes although some are off-color and not appropriate when children are around.* **Cuenta buenos chistes aunque algunos son verdes y no son apropiados cuando hay niños.**

Oh, come on! ¡Qué va! *parts of L. Am., Sp;* ¡Quién lo diría! (Who would say it!) *Mex, DR, S. Cone, Sp;* Vaya a decírselo a su abuela. (Go tell it to your grandmother.) *Mex, ES, U, Arg;* Vaya a contárselo a su tía (abuela). (Go tell it to your aunt [grandmother].) *Mex, S. Cone, Sp* ◆ *The Barrio brothers are drug traffickers? Oh, come on! They seemed like good people.* **¿Los hermanos Barrio son traficantes de drogas? ¡Qué va! Parecían buenas personas.**

OK. Más o menos. (More or less.) *L. Am., Sp;* Okei. (from the English expression) *L. Am.* ◆ *How are your parents? —OK.* **¿Cómo están tus padres? —Más o menos.**

Okey-dokey. Oquey, maguey. (All right, maguey cactus.) *Mex, Col* ◆ *Shall we meet at eight? —Okey, dokey.* **¿Nos encontramos a las ocho? —Oquey, maguey.**

old and worn out (→see also: geezer, over the hill) traqueteado(-a) ◆ *That car is worn out (ready for the junk yard).* **Ese carro está traqueteado.**

old bag (used for women) →see: geezer

old fogey →see: geezer

old goat →see: geezer

old hat 1. (something already commented on) muñeco viejo (old doll) ◆ *The mayor's plan is old hat.* **El plan del alcalde es muñeco viejo.** 2. (out of date) pasado(-a) de moda (passed from fashion) *L. Am., Sp;* pasadón, pasadona (way in the past) *Mex* ◆ *Those ideas are old hat.* **Esas ideas son pasadas de moda.**

out of style 1. (out of date) pasado(-a) de moda (passed from fashion) *L. Am., Sp* ◆ *Those boots are out of style.* **Esas botas son**

pasadas de moda. **2.** (old-fashioned) pasadón, pasadona (way in the past) *Mex*

old man (meaning spouse, partner; →see also: geezer) el/la viejo(-a) (old one; not as pejorative as "old man") *L. Am., Sp* ◆ *Just a minute. Let me ask my old man.* **Momento. Déjame preguntarle a mi viejo.**

the **old one-two** →see: smack

old tricks las andadas (walkings, tracks) *L. Am., Sp* ◆ *My cousin has gone back to his old tricks. Too bad!* **Mi primo ha vuelto a sus andadas. ¡Qué lástima!**

old wives' tale el cuento de viejas *most of L. Am., Sp* ◆ *Tuesday (for English speakers, Friday) the thirteenth is a day of bad luck? No, no, those are old wives' tales.* **¿Que el martes 13 es día de mala suerte? No, no, son cuentos de viejas.**

older than Methuselah (→see also: geezer) más viejo(-a) que Matusalén *L. Am., Sp* ◆ *I feel older than Methuselah.* **Me siento más viejo que Matusalén.**

old-fashioned 1. (with old values) chapado(-a) a la antigua *L. Am., Sp* ◆ *He's an old-fashioned kind of man.* **Es un hombre chapado a la antigua. 2.** (lame, out of it) fuera de onda *Mex, DR, ES, Col, U, Sp*; charro(-a) (relating to cowboys or country people) *Mex, PR, Col* ; ser un atraso a la cultura (to be a setback for the culture) *Col* ◆ *You can't talk to Antonieta. She's totally old fashioned.* **No se puede hablar con Antonieta. Está totalmente fuera de onda.**

on a whim →see: just for the fun of it

on and on (over and over again) dale que dale *L. Am., Sp* ◆ *I'm tired of you always playing on and on at the piano.* **Ya me cansé de que siempre estés dale que dale al piano.**

to be **on cloud nine** (→see also: happy as a lark, in seventh heaven) estar en la gloria (to be in one's glory) *L. Am., Sp* ◆ *I'm on cloud nine when it's cool out.* **Estoy en la gloria cuando hace fresco.**

to be **on edge 1.** estar en ascuas (to be on embers) *L. Am., Sp* ◆ *I was on edge until they gave me the news.* **Estaba en ascuas hasta que me dieron la noticia. 2.** (strung out, nervous) tenerlos cables pelados (to have frayed wires) *ES, Nic, S. Cone* ◆ *She is on edge.* **Tiene los cables pelados.**

on foot →see: hoofing it

to be **on one's home court** tener cancha (to have court, field for sports) *CR, Col, Peru, S. Cone* ◆ *Juan is on his home court (feels at ease in the present circumstances).* **Juan tiene cancha.**

to be **on one's last legs** (→see also: geezer) estar en las últimas (to be on the last) *L. Am., Sp*; estar hecho(-a) un cascajo (to be made a piece of junk) *PR, Sp*; estar para sopitas y buen vino (to be for light soup and good wine) *Sp* ◆ *Doña Jacinta is ninety years old and on her last legs.* **Doña Jacinta tiene noventa años y está en las últimas.**

on one's own →see: all by my lonesome, all by oneself

to be **on pins and needles** (anxiously awaiting something) estar en ascuas (to be on embers) *Mex, ES, Nic, S. Cone, Sp* ◆ *I was on pins and needles until they gave me the news.* **Estaba en ascuas hasta que me dieron la noticia.**

on the ball avispado(-a) (wasped) *L. Am., Sp*; pillo(-a) *Mex, Hond, CR, Col, Peru, S. Cone, Sp*; buzo (diver) *Mex, G, Hond, ES* ◆ *Ivana is on the ball.* **Ivana es muy avispada.**

to be **on the ball** tener bien puestas las pilas, estar con las pilas puestas (to have one's batteries well placed) *DR, Ven, Ch, U* ◆ *That guy is very clever; he's really on the ball.* **Ese chico es muy listo; tiene las pilas bien puestas.**

on the double →see: in a jiffy

on the fly 1. (quickly; →see also: in a flash) de volada (of flown away) *Mex, ES, Col*; de volón pinpón *Mex, ES*; de boleto (of ticket) *Mex* ◆ *That can be done on the fly.* **Eso se hace de volada. 2.** (fast and while doing something else) de pasada (of passed) *Mex, ES, Col, Ch* ◆ *I spoke with Beatriz on the fly at school while we were looking for the library.* **De pasada en el colegio, hablé con Beatriz mientras buscábamos la biblioteca.**

to be **on the prowl** (out to get [a lover]) andar tras sus huesos (to go after his or her bones) *Mex, ES* ◆ *That girl is very stuck-up. She thinks all the guys are on the prowl after her.* **Esa chava es muy creída. Piensa que todos los chicos andan tras sus huesos.**

on the right foot 1. (in the right way) con el pie derecho (with the right foot) *L. Am., Sp* ◆ *We want to start off on the right foot.* Queremos empezar con el pie derecho. 2. (happily, with good fortune) con buen pie (with good foot) *L.Am., Sp* ◆ *Today I started the day on the right foot. I'm happy.* Hoy me levanté con buen pie. Estoy contento.

on the sly (in secret) por lo bajini (bajo) (by the low) *Sp* ◆ *He found out on the sly. Not by any official channel.* Se enteró por lo bajini. Y no por ningún conducto oficial.

on the spur of the moment (suddenly) de buenas a primeras (from good ones to first ones) L. Am., Sp. ◆ *On the spur of the moment we decided to go to Costa Rica.* De buenas a primeras decidimos ir a Costa Rica.

on the tip of one's tongue a flor de labio(s) (at the flower of the lip[s]) *L. Am., Sp* ◆ *That girl always has an answer on the tip of her tongue.* Esa chica siempre tiene una respuesta a flor de labios.

on the up and up (proper, correct, reliable person) legal (legal) *Mex, DR, G, CR, Col, Ec, Ch, Sp* ◆ *That Internet site is on the up and up.* Ese sitio Web está legal.

to be **on the way out** (ready to leave) estar con un (el) pie en el estribo (to have one [the] foot in the stirrup) *Mex, ES, S. Cone, Sp*; estar con las botas puestas (to have one's boots on) *Mex, Sp* ◆ *I'll call you back; right now I'm on the way out.* Te volveré a llamar; ahorita estoy con un pie en el estribo.

on top of everything else →see: to top it all off

once in a blue moon de uvas a peras (from grapes to pears) *most of L. Am., Sp*; de Pascuas a Ramos (from Easter to Palm Sunday) *most of L. Am., Sp*; cada muerte de un obispo (each death of a bishop) *Col, Peru, S. Cone*; de higos a brevas (from figs to early figs) *Sp* ◆ *We don't eat a lot of meat. Once in a blue moon I buy a chicken* No comemos mucha carne. De uvas a peras compro un pollo.

one for the road (usually referring to a drink) la del estribo (the one of the stirrup) *Mex, ES, S. Cone* ◆ *Let's have one for the road!* ¡Echemos la del estribo!

one way or another (by force or voluntarily) por las buenas o por las malas (for the good or for the bad) *L. Am., Sp* ◆ *You're going with me to the concert one way or another.* Vas a acompañarme al concierto por las buenas o por las malas.

to **only have eyes for something or someone** (desire or want) írsele a alguien los ojos por algo o alguien (to have one's eyes go after something or someone) *Mex, DR, ES, U, Arg, Sp* ◆ *They showed me a lot of coats, but I only had eyes for this blue jacket.* Me mostraron muchos abrigos, pero se me fueron los ojos por esta chaqueta azul.

Onward and upward. To'el tiempo pa'lante. (All the time forward.) *Caribbean* ◆ *Onward and upward, my friends, because going backwards brings us nothing.* ◆ *¡To'el tiempo pa'lante, amigos míos, porque p'atrás no cunde!*

Oops! ¡Uf! *Mex, Col*

to **open one's heart to someone** abrir su corazón a alguien *Mex, DR, U, Arg, Sp* ◆ *Finally Ana opened her heart to him.* Finalmente Ana le abrió su corazón.

to **open up** destaparse (to uncork oneself) L. Am.; despegar la boca (to unstick the mouth) *Mex, Sp*; soltar la lengua (to loosen the tongue) *DR, S. Cone*; cantar. (to sing) *Sp* ◆ *Open up, honey. What happened?* Destápate, cariño. ¿Qué pasó?

openly (frankly) a calzón quitado (with underwear removed) *L. Am.* ◆ *I told him frankly that I didn't want to see him again in my home.* A calzón quitado le dije que no lo quería ver más en mi casa.

operator 1. (opportunist; →see also: mooch) aprovechado(-a) *L. Am., Sp* (*RVar S. Cone:* aprovechador[-a]); el buitre (vulture) *Mex, PR, Col, Ven, U, Arg, Sp*; el buscón, la buscona (searcher) *Mex, DR, PR, Col, Sp*; ventajoso(-a) (from ventaja, advantage) *Mex* ◆ *Let's not give that operator any information; he'll use it for his own gain.* No le demos información a ese buitre; la usará para su propio beneficio. 2. (aggressive or bold person) lanzado(-a) (thrown) *Mex, Col, Ch, Arg, Sp* ◆ *Ricardo and Esteban are brothers, but Ricardo is an operator and his brother is timid.* Ricardo y Esteban son hermanos, pero Ricardo es un lanzado y su hermano es *tímido.* **3.** (person who wants something) el/la antojado(-a) *Mex, PR, G, Col* ♦ *These kids are operators, and they always want candy.* Estos niños son muy antojados y siempre quieren golosinas.

to be opportune caer de perlas (to fall like pearls) *L. Am., Sp;* caer de perillas (to fall like little pears) *S. Cone, Sp* ♦ *The money is really opportune.* ♦ *El dinero me cae de perillas.*

out and out (clearly, categorically) en redondo (in round, in a circle) *Mex, Sp* ♦ *They out and out refused.* Se negaron en redondo.

out like a light (asleep) →see: to go out like a light

out of date →see: old hat, old-fashioned

out of it 1. (not understanding anything) marcando ocupado (dialing the busy signal, and just not connecting) *Ch, U* ♦ *That guy doesn't know anything. He's out of it.* Este chico no sabe nada. Está marcando ocupado. **2.** (totally unhip) fuera de onda *Mex, DR, ES, Col, U, Sp* ♦ *You can't talk to Antonieta. She's totally out of it and doesn't understand anything.* No se puede hablar con Antonieta. Está totalmente fuera de onda y no entiende nada.

to be **out of it 1.** (not on the same page) no estar en na'a (nada) (to not be in anything) *most of L. Am.;* estar fuera de base (de órbita) (to be off base [out of orbit]) *Mex, Nic, Col, U* ♦ *Her brothers and sisters spoke to her about the inheritance from their parents, but it's obvious that she's out of it. She refused to listen.* Sus hermanos hablaron con ella sobre la herencia de los padres, pero es obvio que ella no está en nada. No quiso escuchar. **2.** (lost, clueless, forgetful) estar despistado(-a) (to be off the track) *L. Am., Sp* ♦ *I'm completely out of it; I don't know anything about the matter.* Estoy totalmente despistado; no sé nada del asunto. **3.** (not be with it or in the world, not find out about things, said by young people) flotar (to float) *Sp* ♦ *You're out of it, man.* Estás flotando, hombre. **4.** (spaced out, detached) estar en otra (to be on another, with the idea of onda or dimensión understood) *Mex, S. Cone*

out of luck (→see also: to be down on one's luck, to have bad luck) salado(-a) (salty; note that in Spain this means nice or kind) *most of L. Am. (not Arg);* estrellado(-a) (see-

ing stars) *Mex, ES, S. Cone* ♦ *That man is really out of luck! First he lost his job and then they stole his car.* ¡Qué hombre más salado! Primero perdió su empleo y después le robaron el carro.

out of style →see: old-fashioned, old hat

out of the blue 1. (unexpected) como caído(-a) de las nubes (like fallen from the clouds) *Mex, Sp* ♦ *Your visit comes out of the blue. I needed to talk to someone.* Tu visita es como caída de las nubes. Necesitaba hablar con alguien. **2.** (describing a windfall, boon) caído(-a) del cielo (fallen from the sky) *Mex, ES, S. Cone* ♦ *The money was a real windfall. It came out of the blue.* El dinero me vino como caído del cielo. Me cayó del cielo.

out of the ordinary (outstanding; outstanding person) fuera de serie (out of series) *L. Am., Sp* ♦ *That guy is out of the ordinary; he always gets "excellent" in everything.* Ese chico es un fuera de serie; siempre saca «excelente» en todo.

Out of the question! (→see also: No way) Ni hablar. *L. Am., Sp* ♦ *Are you going to go out with Inés? —Out of the question! I won't do it.* ¿Vas a salir con Inés? —¡Ni hablar! No lo haré.

to be **out of whack** (out of time or place) pegar una cosa como guitarra en un entierro (to stick like a guitar at a funeral) *Sp* ♦ *That dress and that purse are out of whack.* Ese vestido con ese bolso le pegan como guitarra en un entierro.

out to lunch →see: mixed up

to **outdo oneself 1.** (do something very impressive, →see also: to take the cake) volarse la barda (to blow up the fence) *Mex* ♦ *You outdid yourself with this test.* Te volaste la barda con este examen. **2.** (dressing well, doing things well, looking good) botarse *DR, PR* ♦ *You outdid yourself.* Te botas. **3.** (do something unusual) lucirse (to shine) *Mex, Peru, U* ♦ *He outdid himself with the dinner.* ♦ *Se lució con la comida.*

outlandish (weird, usually referring mainly to dress) estrafalario(-a) *L. Am., Sp* ♦ *That girl always looks outlandish. What an outlandish dress!* Esa chica siempre se ve muy estrafalaria. ¡Qué vestido más estrafalario!

to **outsmart oneself** (try to show oneself [erroneously] to be smarter than others)

to oversleep: *It looks like she overslept again.*
Parece que se le pegaron las sábanas otra vez.

pasarse de listo(-a) (vivo[-a]) (to pass one-self as clever, be overly clever) *L. Am., Sp* ◆ *You outsmarted yourself! ¡Te pasaste de listo!*

over and over again (on and on) dale que dale *L. Am., Sp* ◆ *Here I am, cooking over and over again. Aquí estoy, dale que dale a la cocina.*

over the hill (→see also: geezer) entradi-to(-a) en años (a little bit entered into years, euphemism) *most of L. Am., Sp* ◆ *How old is Facundo? —I don't know, but he's over the hill. ¿Cuántos años tiene Facundo? —No lo sé, pero ya está entradito en años.*

to **overdo it** →see: to go too far

to **overlook** (ignore) hacer la vista gorda (to do the fat look) *L. Am., Sp;* hacerse de la vista choncha *Mex* ◆ *Ana came late, but the boss overlooked it. Ana llegó tarde, pero el jefe hizo la vista gorda.*

to **oversleep** pegársele a alguien las sábanas (to have the sheets stick to one) *L. Am., Sp;* quedarse dormido(-a) (to stay asleep) *L. Am., Sp* ◆ *I overslept and got to the airport late. Se me pegaron las sábanas y llegué tarde al aeropuerto.*

overwhelmed with emotion (→see also: happy as a lark, in seventh heaven) abru-mado(-a) *L. Am., Sp;* copado(-a), recopa-do(-a) (cupped, trophied, usually with pos-itive emotion or joy) *Arg* ◆ *What a lovely gift! I'm overwhelmed. ¡Qué lindo regalo! Estoy copada.*

P

to **pack it in** (die) →see: to kick the bucket

pain (boring, bothersome) latoso(-a) *Mex, DR, ES, Col, Ec, Ch* *That girl is a big pain. Esa muchacha es bien latosa.*

to be a **pain** (→see also: to be a drag, to be a grouch, to be a sourpuss, to not [be able to] stand someone, pain in the neck) ser pesado(-a) (to be weighty) *L. Am., Sp;* ser un hígado (to be a liver) *Mex;* ser un(-a) desubicado(-a) (disoriented one) *S. Cone;* ser una lata (to be a tin can) *Florida, Mex, DR, G, ES, Col, Ch, Sp;* no ser perita en dulce (to not be a pear in sugar water) *Mex, ES;* ◆ *Don't invite him to the party; he's a pain.* ◆ *No lo invites a la fiesta; es un pesado.* ◆ *Chuy is a pain, really a drag, and I'm not going to return his (phone) call. Chuy es un hígado, muy sangrón, y no voy a devolver su llamada.* ◆ *Getting up every morning to go to work is a pain. Levantarse todos los días para ir a trabajar es una lata.* **2.** (be intolerable to) caerle pesado[-a]) (to fall heavy on someone) *L. Am., Sp;* caerle gordo(-a) (to fall fat on someone) *L. Am., Sp;* caerle de la patada (pedrada) (to fall on someone like the kick [blow with a stone]) *Mex, Ch;* caerle en el hígado (also, caerle en los huevos; vulgar) (to fall to one's liver) *Mex, ES;* caerle como piedra (plomo) (to fall on someone like stone [lead]) *S. Cone* ◆ *That man is a pain. (I can't stand that man.) Ese hombre me cae gordo.*

pain in the ass (annoying or bothersome; all vulgar) chingón, chingona *Chicano, Mex, C. Am.;* jodón, jodona *Mex, DR, G, Col;* la jodedera *PR, ES, CR, Col;* la jodienda *DR, Sp* el coñazo (blow, from coño) *Sp* ◆ *Valentín doesn't want to do business with pain in the ass clients. Valentín no quiere hacer negocios con los clientes chingones.* ◆ *What a pain in the ass! ¡Qué jodienda!*

pain in the neck (insistent person, pest; →see also: troublemaker) la lapa (barnacle) *Mex, DR, PR, Col, Ch, Sp;* la ladilla (leech) *Mex, Cuba, DR, PR, G, Col, Ven, Peru;* enci-moso(-a) *Mex, ES* ◆ *What a pain in the neck! ¡Qué ladilla!*

pal 1. (male; guy) el compinche (accomplice) *L. Am.;* el vale (probably short for valedor, defender) *Chicano, Mex, Ven;* el valedor (defender) *Mex, G, ES, Col, Ven;* el compi (short for compinche) *Mex, Peru, Sp;* el compa (from compadre) *Florida, Mex, C. Am.;* bróder (from English "brother") *ES, Nic, Ven* ◆ *My pal Ramón is going to go with us to the movies. Mi valedor Ramón nos va a acompañar al cine.* **2.** (best bud, male or female) el/la mano(-a), manito(-a) (forms of hermano[-a] brother [sister]) *Mex, DR, C. Am., Col;* el/la cuate(-a) *Mex, C. Am.;* el/la hermano(-a) carnal(a) (blood brother [sister]) *Mex, DR, G;* mi yunta (my yoke, as of oxen) *Mex, Cuba, Ec, Peru, Ch;* el/la socio(-a) (associate, member) *Mex, Cuba, Col, Peru, Ch;* el/la pana (from panal, honeycomb) *DR, PR, Col, Ven, Ec;* chico(-a) (guy, girl; used in direct address) *Caribbean;* che (used in direct address) *U, Arg* ◆ *I had to bring my pal to have a good time. Tenía que traer a mi yunta para divertirme.* **3.** (friend, connection) la llave (key) *Col, Ven* ◆ *Hi, pal, how's it going? Hola, mi llave, ¿qué tal?*

paper-pusher el/la chupatintas (ink sucker) *Mex, Ch, Sp* ◆ *Ever since they promoted her, she's a paper-pusher. Desde que la ascendieron, es una chupatintas.*

part and parcel of the job (occupational hazards) los gajes del oficio (matters of the trade) *Mex, DR, ES, Nic, S. Cone, Sp;* los percances del oficio (chances of the trade) *ES, Nic, Sp* ◆ *Roberto broke his arm while mountain climbing. It's understood that these are part and parcel of the job. Roberto se rompió el brazo mientras escalaba. Ya se sabe, son gajes del oficio.*

party →see bash

to **party** (→see also: to go out on the town, to have a blast, to have a good time, to live it up) ir de parranda *L. Am., Sp;* irse de rumba *Mex, Cuba;* irse de cachondeo *Sp;*

irse (salir) de marcha *Sp* ◆ *To celebrate the triumph, we went out partying.* **Para festejar el triunfo, fuimos de parranda.**

party animal el/la parrandero *L. Am.*; el/la parrandista, fiestero(-a) *Mex, Col*; jaranero (-a) *Sp* ◆ *Marcos is a tireless party animal.* **Marcos es un parrandista incansable.**

party crasher (gate crasher; also, less common, someone who jumps into a discussion but doesn't know anything about the topic) el/la colado(-a) (passed through a sieve) *L. Am., Sp*; el/la paracaidista (parachutist) *DR, Nic, CR, Ec, Peru, S. Cone* ◆ *Let's not talk about the party in front of Ramón; he's a party crasher and it's a sure thing he'll come with all his friends.* **No hablemos de la fiesta delante de Ramón; es un paracaidista y seguro viene con sus amigos.**

party pooper (→see also: to be a drag, wet blanket) el aguafiestas, el/una aguafiestas (party water, maybe implying someone who pours water over something to ruin it) *L. Am., Sp* ◆ *Since I didn't want to be a party pooper, I went with them.* **Como no quería ser aguafiestas, fui con ellos.**

The party's over! Time to go! ¡Calabaza! (Pumpkin!, from the phrase ¡Calabaza, calabaza, cada uno [or cada quien] para su casa!) *Ch, ES*

party-loving parrandero(-a) *L. Am.*; jaranero(-a) *Sp* ◆ *He's a party-loving guy.* **Es un chico muy jaranero.**

to **pass (on something)** (decline) pasar *Mex, S. Cone* ◆ *Would you marry my sister? —No, I pass.* **¿Te casarías con mi hermana? —No, yo paso.**

to **pass away** (go to one's reward; →see also: to kick the bucket) fallecer *L. Am., Sp*; pasar a mejor vida (to go to a better life) *L. Am., Sp*; irse para el (al) otro barrio (mundo) (to go to the other neighborhood [world]) *L. Am., Sp* ◆ *Julia passed away last night, after a great deal of suffering.* **Julia pasó a mejor vida anoche, después de sufrir mucho.**

to **pass the buck** (avoid work or responsibility) pasar la pelota (to pass the ball) *parts of L. Am., Sp*; escurrir el bulto (to drain the shape or package) *Mex, Ch, U, Sp* ◆ *He always passes the buck when it's time to pay.* **Siempre escurre el bulto cuando hay que pagar.**

to **pat on the back** (compliment, praise) echar flores (to throw flowers) *L. Am., Sp* ◆ *What a pat on the back you're giving me!* **¡Qué flores me está echando!**

to **patch things up** hacer las paces (to make peace) *L. Am., Sp*; arreglar el pastel (to fix the cake) *S. Cone* ◆ *I really want to patch things up with them. We can't go on like this.* **Tengo ganas de hacer las paces con ellos. No podemos continuar así.**

paunch (beer belly, potbelly) la panza *L. Am., Sp*; la guata *Peru, Bol, Ch* ◆ *You have a big paunch; you need a bigger size.* **Tienes mucha panza; necesitas una talla más grande.**

to **pay attention** (listen up) enchufarse (to plug in; also, less commonly, to have sex, as in Me enchufé a esa chica.) *Mex, U* ◆ *Pay attention. I'm going to explain the issue to you.* **Enchúfate. Voy a explicarte el asunto.**

to **pay attention to (someone)** hacerle caso (to make a case to him or her) *L. Am., Sp*; prestarle atención (to lend attention to him or her) *L. Am., Sp*; pelarle (to peel him or her) *Mex, ES*; llevarle el apunte (llevar de apunte) (to keep track of the score) *S. Cone*; darle bola (to give the ball) *S. Cone*; pararle bola (to stop the ball) *Ven* ◆ *I tried to explain the situation, but they didn't pay attention to me.* **Traté de explicar la situación, pero no me dieron bola.**

to **pee** mear(se) *L. Am., Sp* ◆ *Hurry up. Let me use the bathroom because I'm peeing in my pants.* **Apúrate. Déjame el baño porque me meo.**

to **pee one's pants laughing** mearse de (la) risa (also, estar meado(-a) de la risa) *Mex, DR, S. Cone, Sp* ◆ *When I saw that show, I peed in my pants laughing.* **Cuando vi ese programa, estaba meado de la risa.**

to **peel out** →see: to go like a shot

pell-mell →see: helter-skelter

to be a **people person** tener don de gentes (to have the gift of peoples) *L. Am., Sp*; ser una persona carismática *L. Am., Sp*; ser entrador(-a) (enterer) *Col, S. Cone* ◆ *Dr. Alvarez is very popular as a conference speaker because she is a people person.* **La doctora Alvarez es muy buscada para conferenciante porque tiene don de gentes.**

to **perk things (or someone) up** ser levanta muertos (to be a raiser of the dead) *Mex, Nic, U, Arg* ♦ *This soup perks me right up.* Esta sopa es levanta muertos.

persnickety →see: to be a fussbudget

pervert (who likes to touch women inappropriately) el pulpo (octopus) *Mex, DR, Col, Sp* ♦ *I'm not dancing with that man because he's a pervert.* Yo no bailo con ese hombre porque es un pulpo.

pest (irritating person; →see drag, pain in the ass, pain in the neck) el chicle (chewing gum) *Mex, Cuba, DR, PR, G*; la ladilla (leech) *Mex, Cuba, DR, PR, G, Col, Ven, Peru*; pegajoso(-a) (sticky) *Mex, Col, Ch*; chayote (vegetable with prickly skin) *Mex, PR*; el/la hincha (hinchapelotas) (inflator [of balls], vulgar) *U, Arg* ♦ *Let's get out of here because Tomás has already arrived. —Oh, that pest! If he sees us, he'll stick to us like glue.* Vámonos de aquí que ya llegó Tomás. –Ay, ¡ese chicle! Si nos ve, no se nos despega.

pet (favorite) el/la mimado(-a) (pampered one) *L. Am., Sp*; el/la consentido(-a) (one who is given into) *L. Am., Sp* el regalón, la regalona (big gift-getter) *Ch* ♦ *That girl is her grandparents' pet.* Esta niña es la regalona de sus abuelos.

to **pet** →see: to make out

petting →see: foreplay, smooching

phony 1. (artificial, superficial) plástico(-a) (plastic, sometimes used as hijo de papi) *DR, PR, G, Col, Ch*; hueco(-a) (hollow, empty) *Ch, U*; fantasma, fantasmón (fantasmona) (ghost) *Sp* ♦ *Raquel is very phony. The only things that interest her are clothing, cars, and money.* Raquel es una plástica. Lo único que le interesa es la ropa, los carros y el dinero. 2. hypocrite el diablo vendiendo cruces (the devil selling crosses) *L. Am.* ♦ *The new mayor is a real phony.* El nuevo alcalde es el diablo vendiendo cruces.

to **pick a fight** (→see also: to have a blowup) armar una bronca *L. Am., Sp*; hacer un coraje *Mex, G* ♦ *Carmen picked a fight at the airport when they told her that her suitcases were not on her flight.* Carmen hizo un coraje en el aeropuerto cuando le dijeron que sus maletas no estaban en el vuelo.

to **pick someone out** (tell who they are by their appearance) sacar a alguien por la pinta (to take someone out because of their spot) *Sp* ♦ *I picked out your brother because of family resemblance.* Saqué a tu hermano por la pinta.

to **pick up** (e.g., someone of the opposite sex) ligar (to link) *L. Am., Sp*; levantarse (a alguien) *Mex, DR, PR, G, ES, Col, U, Arg*; hacer un levante *Mex, DR, PR, G, Col* ♦ *He picked her up during the holidays.* Se la ligó durante las fiestas. ♦ *Marcelo picked someone up at the bar.* Marcelo hizo un levante en la cantina.

to **pick up** (someone) in your car (to take them somewhere) pasar por (to pass by for) *L. Am., Sp* ♦ *I'll pick you up at 8:00 sharp.* Paso por ti a las ocho en punto.

piece of ass (girl, woman) el culito (small ass, vulgar) *Mex, G, Ven*

to be a **piece of cake** (easy; said of things) ser facilingo *parts of L. Am.*; ser pan comido (to be eaten bread) *Mex, DR, PR, S. Cone, Sp*; ser un mamey (to be a mamey, a fruit) *PR, Col*; estar chupado(-a) (to be sucked) *Sp*; estar tirado(-a) (to be pulled) *Sp* ser coser y cantar (to be sew and sing) *Sp*; ser liso y llano (to be smooth and flat, as a road) *Sp*; hacerse con la gorra (to be done with the hat) *Sp* ♦ *Don't worry. That job is a piece of cake.* No te preocupes. Ese trabajo es pan comido. ♦ *Do a videoconference? It's a piece of cake.* ¿Hacer una videoconferencia? Se hace con la gorra.

piece of gossip el chisme *L.Am., Sp*; los chismorreos *most of L. Am., Sp*; el chambre *ES*; la copucha *Ch*; la bola (ball) *Cuba, DR, G, ES, CR, U, Arg* ♦ *You really believe that she said that? It's probably just a piece of gossip.* ¿Tú crees de verdad que ella dijo eso? A lo mejor es una bola. ♦ *Any gossip? What can you tell me?* ¿Hay chismes? ¿Qué me cuentas?

piece of junk (→see also: junk) la porquería *L. Am., Sp*; la chafa (low-quality or fake item) *Mex, G, ES* ♦ *This a Rolex? No, it's a fake.* ¿Esto un Rolex? No, es una chafa.

Piece of shit! ¡Una mierda! *L. Am., Sp*; ¡Chorro de mierda! (Squirt of shit!; vulgar) *DR, PR, ES*

pig (dirty or fat; undesirable person) el cochino *L. Am., Sp*; el marrano *Mex, G, Col, Sp*; el/la cerdo(-a) (pig) *Sp*; el/la guarro(-a) (pig, swine) *Sp* ♦ *What a pig! Look how she* eats. *It looks like they never taught her good manners.* ¡Qué marrano! Mira cómo come. Parece que nunca le enseñaron buenos modales.

to **pig out** (eat and drink oneself silly; ➡see also: to stuff oneself) ponerse hasta el gorro (to put oneself up to one's cap) *Mex, Sp;* ponerse las botas (to put on one's boots) *U, Sp* ◆ *They pigged out at the party.* Se pusieron hasta el gorro en la fiesta.

pig-headed (difficult to convince or get; ➡see also: hardheaded) terco(-a) (stubborn) *L. Am., Sp;* duro(-a) (hard) *Mex, G, Ch;* duro(-a) de pelar (hard to peel) *U, Sp* ◆ *I tried to talk to her several times, but she's pig-headed and doesn't listen to reason.* Intenté hablar con ella varias veces, pero es dura y no entiende razones.

pimp el puto (vulgar) *parts of L. Am.;* el padrote *Mex, G, ES, Col;* el chulo *DR, PR, Pan, Col, Ven, Sp* (RVar *Ch:* lout); el chivo (kid goat) *C. Am., Col;* el cafiche *S. Cone* ◆ *Felipe is a pimp; he never works.* Felipe es un chulo; nunca trabaja.

pinch (small adjustment, tweaking; ➡see also: little bit) el pellizco (pinch) *L. Am., Sp* ◆ *I need a pinch of sugar for the coffee.* Necesito un pellizco de azúcar para el café.

to be **pissed off** (➡see also: to be steamed, to be fed up) estar hasta los cojones (to be up to the testicles, vulgar) *Mex, Sp;* tener las bolas llenas (to have your balls full, vulgar) *U, Arg;* estar hasta los huevos (to be up to the eggs [testicles], vulgar) *Sp;* estar hasta el (mismísimo) coño (to be up to the female organ, vulgar) *Sp* ◆ *My cousin is pissed off with his wife's jealousy.* Mi primo está hasta los cojones con los celos de su esposa.

the **pits** (awful; ➡see also: a bitch of a, crappy, damn) matado(-a) (killed) *Florida, Cuba, DR, PR, CR, Col;* de mil (todos los) diablos (of a thousand [all the] devils, used to exaggerate something bad or uncomfortable) *Mex, ES, Sp;* fatal (fatal) *Mex, DR, PR, G, Col, Sp;* perro(-a) (dog) *Mex, Cuba, G, Col* ◆ *That boy acts out in the worst way. His behavior is the pits.* Ese niño se porta de lo peor. Tiene una conducta de los mil diablos.

to be **plastered** (drunk; ➡see also: to be wasted) estar pedo(-a) (to be fart, vulgar)

Mex, C. Am., U, Arg, Sp (RVar *U, Arg:* also, estar en pedo; *Sp:* llevar un pedo); estar hasta las manitas (to be up to the little hands) *Mex, CR;* estar rascado(-a) (to be scratched) *Nic, CR, Col, Ven;* estar mamado(-a) (to be breast-fed) *U, Arg;* ponerse (estar) en curda, tener una curda *U, Arg;* estar trompa (also, trompeta, tururú) (to be trunk of an elephant) *Sp;* estar piripi *Sp* ◆ *Pedro was plastered last night and now he has a terrible headache.* Pedro estaba hasta las manitas anoche y ahora tiene un dolor de cabeza terrible.

to **play dumb** 1. (look innocent, contrary to truth) tener cara de «yo no fui» (to have the face of "it wasn't me") *Mex, ES, CR, U* ◆ *What a surprise Joaquín gave me! He's a rascal and then plays dumb.* ¡Qué sorpresa me dio Joaquín! Es un pícaro y tiene esa carita de «yo no fui». 2. (pretend not to notice) hacerse el (la) desentendido(-a) (to make oneself the nonunderstanding one) *L. Am., Sp;* hacerse el loco (tonto) (la loca [tonta]) (to make oneself the crazy one) *L. Am., Sp;* hacerse el chivo loco (to make oneself the crazy kid goat) *Mex, DR* ◆ *Don't play dumb. You know very well what I'm talking about.* No te hagas la desentendida. Sabes muy bien de lo que estoy hablando. 3. (pretend to be innocent or foolish) navegar con bandera de inocente (tonto) (to sail with the flag of an innocent [a fool]) *Mex;* no darse por enterado(-a) (entendido[-a]) (to not show yourself as understanding something) *DR, PR, S. Cone, Sp* ◆ *Those devils were playing dumb.* Navegaban con bandera de inocentes esos diablos. 4. (person who appears to be dim or dull but who doesn't miss the chance to take advantage of someone) hacerse la mosquita (mosca) muerta (to make oneself the dead fly) *L. Am., Sp* ◆ *You play dumb in front of your parents, but we know perfectly well just what you are.* Te haces la mosquita muerta frente a tus padres, pero bien sabemos lo que eres.

to **play hard to get** (like to be begged) hacerse de(l) rogar (to make oneself begged) *L. Am., Sp* (RVar *Mex, ES, Pan, Col:* del; *DR, Peru, Ch, Sp:* de) ◆ *My sister likes to play hard to get.* A mi hermana le gusta hacerse de rogar.

to **play hooky** (→see: to cut class)

to **play one's cards right** (do something with astuteness) jugar bien sus cartas *Mex, DR, S. Cone, Sp* ◆ *We've had success with the business. Armando is bright and played his cards right. Salimos bien en el negocio. Armando es astuto y jugó bien las cartas.*

to **play one's last trick** quemar el último cartucho (to burn the last cartridge) *L. Am., Sp;* jugar la última carta (to play the last card) *Mex, U, Arg, Sp* ◆ *They didn't dare play their last trick and the project failed. No se atrevieron a quemar el último cartucho y el proyecto fracasó.*

to **play second fiddle** (not be treated with consideration) ser plato de segunda mesa (to be a plate of a second table) *Mex, DR, PR, ES, Sp* (RVAR *Mex:* used mainly for women who are with married men) ◆ *I am not playing second fiddle. (I don't play second fiddle to anyone.) Yo no soy plato de segunda mesa.*

to **play the game** (do whatever is appropriate; →see also: to follow the crowd, to go along with) bailar al son que le tocan (to dance to the sound that is played) *L. Am., Sp* ◆ *Esteban always goes along with the others and plays the game. Esteban siempre baila al son que le tocan.*

to **play tourist** (go on an outing) turistear *Mex, DR, ES, CR, Col* ◆ *During our last vacation we played tourist at the national parks. En las últimas vacaciones turisteamos los parques nacionales.*

playboy 1. (→see also: womanizer) el calavera (skull) *L. Am., Sp;* el mujeriego (womanizer) *L. Am., Sp;* el picaflor (hummingbird) *Nic, CR, Col, Ch, Arg* ◆ *José Manuel is a playboy; each week he goes out with a different woman. José Manuel es un picaflor; todas las semanas sale con una mujer diferente.* 2. (spoiled rich boy) el junior *Mex, Col* ◆ *The spoiled playboy of the house has no scruples. El junior de la casa no tiene escrúpulos.*

player (successful player, achiever) el bacán (controller of a woman who earns money for him, from Lunfardo, Buenos Aires slang) *S. Cone* ◆ *That guy is a successful player; he gets everything he wants. Ese hombre es un bacán; consigue todo lo que quiere.*

Please accept my condolences. Lo (La/Le) acompaño en su dolor (en sus sentimientos). Te acompaño en tu dolor. (I accompany you in your pain.) *L. Am., Sp* ◆ *Elena, they told me that your father passed away. Please accept my condolences. Elena, me dijeron que falleció tu padre. Te acompaño en tu dolor.*

pleasingly plump (a little bit heavy) entradito(-a) en carnes (a little bit entered into flesh; euphemism) *DR, S. Cone, Sp* ◆ *Manuel is pleasingly plump. Manuel está entradito en carnes.*

to **pluck up one's courage** hacer de tripas corazón (to make heart of one's guts) *L. Am., Sp;* sacar fuerzas de flaquezas (to take force from weakness) *L. Am., Sp* ◆ *In spite of the problem I had, I plucked up my courage and went to the meeting. A pesar del problema que tenía, hice de tripas corazón y fui a la reunión.*

to **plug away** →see: to work like a dog

Plugging along. Siempre pa'lante. (Always forward.) *DR, PR, Col, Ven* ◆ *How are you, Doña Tomasa? —Just plugging along, my dear. ¿Cómo anda, doña Tomasa? —Siempre pa'lante, m'hija.*

to **point the finger at someone** (single out) señalar a alguien con el dedo; poner el dedo a alguien *Mex, ES, Peru, Ch, Sp* ◆ *He pointed the finger at the drug dealer. Le puso el dedo al narcotraficante.*

point-blank (directly, straight out) a quema ropa (at burning of clothing) *L. Am., Sp* ◆ *When I saw him, I gave him the news point-blank. Cuando lo vi, le di las noticias a quema ropa.*

police →see: cops

pooch (dog) el chucho *Mex, ES* ◆ *The robber came in the window, and the pooch attacked him. El ladrón entró por la ventana, y el chucho lo atacó.*

to **pool money for a common cause** →see: to chip in

poor as a (church)mouse pobre como una rata *Mex, ES, Pan, S. Cone, Sp;* en la quinta chilla (in the fifth balcony of a theater) *Mex* ◆ *The people who live in that area* *are poor as churchmice.* **En esa zona viven personas que son más pobres que las ratas.**

Poor (little) thing! ¡Pobrecito(-a)! *L. Am., Sp* ◆ *The poor little thing. She is very sick.* **Pobrecita la niña. Está muy enferma.**

to **pop someone's cherry** (have sex with a virgin) inaugurar el pastel (to inaugurate the cake) *Mex, Col* ◆ *Before getting married, we popped the cherry.* **Antes de casarnos, inauguramos el pastel.**

to **pop up everywhere** salir hasta en la sopa (to come up even in the soup) *L. Am., Sp* ◆ *Felipe, we bump into each other again? You seem to pop up everywhere.* **Felipe, ¿otra vez nos encontramos? Me sales hasta en la sopa.**

porn la porno (short for pornografía) *L. Am., Sp* ◆ *I found some porno magazines in Pablito's room.* **Encontré unas revistas porno en el cuarto de Pablito.**

posh (high-class; adj.) popis *Mex, Col* ◆ *It's a posh hotel.* **Es un hotel popis.**

pot →see: grass

the **pot calling the kettle black** (meaning that both are alike but one puts the other down) El comal le dijo a la olla: ¡Mira qué tiznada estás! (The comal [a flat pan for cooking tortillas] said to the pot: Look how charred you are!) *Mex, ES* ◆ *You think that I'm spending too much money? Ha, the pot's calling the kettle black!* **¿Crees que yo estoy gastando demasiada plata? El comal le dijo a la olla: ¡Mira qué tiznada estás!**

potbellied barrigón, barrigona *L. Am., Sp;* tripón, tripona *L. Am., Sp;* guatón, guatona *Ch* ◆ *Roberta is potbellied because she's pregnant.* **Roberta está barrigona porque está embarazada.**

pothead →see: druggie

potty (→see also: restroom) el trono, trono de los césares (throne, throne of the Caesars) *Mex, Col* ◆ *Where's little Pepe? He's on the potty.* **¿Donde está Pepito? Está sentado en el trono.**

to **praise (someone) to the skies** poner en las nubes (to put in the clouds) *L. Am., Sp;* poner sobre los cuernos de la luna (to put on the horns of the moon) *most of L. Am., Sp;* dar bombo a alguien (to give some-

one a fanfare) *Mex, DR, U;* poner en el cielo (to put in the sky) *Mex, DR, Sp* ◆ *At the office reception, the director praised to the skies the employees who had retired this year.* **En la recepción de la oficina, el director puso sobre los cuernos de la luna a los empleados que se jubilaron este año.**

prank →see: trick

to **preach to** →see: to lecture at

to **present a pretty picture** (to gild the lily) pintarlo (de) color de rosa (to paint it pink) *Mex, PR, ES, CR, Col, Ch, U, Sp;* pintárselo bonito (to paint it pretty) *Mex, DR, PR, ES, Col* ◆ *I have to present a pretty picture so she will go out with me.* **Tengo que pintárselo bonito para que salga conmigo.**

pretty please porfa (short for por favor) *most of L. Am., Sp;* por favorciano (mi amorciano) *Mex, Col* ◆ *Come with me to the doctor, pretty please.* **Acompáñame al médico, porfa.**

pricey salado(-a) (salty) *S. Cone* ◆ *In that store over there things are really pricey.* **En aquella tienda los precios son muy salados.**

to **prick up one's ears** (→see also: to pay attention) parar oreja (parar las orejas, parar la oreja) (to put up one's ear or ears) *L. Am., Sp;* poner la antena (to put up one's antenna) *Mex, Sp;* levantar la antena (to raise one's antenna) *Mex, Col;* parar bolas (to put up one's balls) *Nic, Ven, Ec, U* ◆ *Prick up your ears: listen carefully to what I'm going to tell you. It's very important.* **Para la oreja: escucha bien lo que te voy a decir. Es muy importante.**

prime of life la flor de la vida (flower of life) *L. Am., Sp* ◆ *That boy is in the prime of his life.* **Ese chico está en la flor de su vida.**

to **primp** (fix oneself up to go out, deck oneself out) empilcharse (from pilcha, piece of clothing) (to put on pieces of clothing) *U, Arg* ◆ *We bought stuff on sale, and primped to go out on the town.* **Compramos a buen precio, y nos empilchamos para salir de parranda.**

prince charming (ideal man) el príncipe azul (blue prince) *L. Am., Sp* ◆ *Estela is enchanted with her prince charming.* **Estela está encantada con su príncipe azul.**

princess 1. (high-maintenance young woman who is innocent but also a bit spoiled) la fresa (strawberry) *most of L. Am., Sp* ◆ *Verónica is a princess; her parents spoil her a lot.* **Verónica es una fresa; sus papás la miman mucho.** **2.** (naive, conservative girl; virgin) la niña fresa *Mex* ◆ *She's a princess; her parents buy her everything.* **Es una niña fresa; sus papás le compran todo.**

private parts las partes (parts, euphemism) *most of L. Am., Sp* ◆ *Martina told the doctor that her private parts are hurting her.* **Martina le dijo a la doctora que le duelen sus partes.**

prof el/la profe (short for profesor, profesora) *L. Am., Sp* ◆ *The prof is really demanding.* **La profe es muy exigente.**

pull →see: connection (social, political, etc.), to have connections

to **pull a fast one** →see: to pull the wool over someone's eyes, to rip off

to **pull oneself together** (to do something) hacer de tripas corazón (to make heart of one's guts) *L. Am., Sp;* sacar fuerzas de flaquezas (to take force from weakness) *L. Am., Sp* ◆ *In spite of the problem I had, I pulled myself together and went to the meeting.* **A pesar del problema que tenía, hice de tripas corazón y fui a la reunión.**

to **pull someone's leg** (→see also: to make fun of) tomar el pelo a alguien (to pull someone's hair) *L. Am., Sp;* dársela a alguien con queso (to give it to someone with cheese) *Sp* ◆ *The student was pulling the teacher's leg.* **El alumno le tomaba el pelo a la maestra.**

to **pull strings** (go to everyone or do everything to solve a problem) palanquear (to move levers) *ES, Col, Peru, S. Cone;* tocar muchas teclas (to touch many keys) *U, Arg, Sp;* muñequear (to wrist) *Peru, S. Cone* ◆ *Ernest pulled some strings for me, and I got the job.* **Ernesto me palanqueó, y conseguí el trabajo.**

to **pull the chair out from under someone** (cook someone's goose, often by saying bad things to others behind his or her back) serrucharle el piso a alguien (to saw off the floor under someone) *Hond, Nic, CR, Col, Ec, Peru, S. Cone* ◆ *Mireya pulled the chair out from under me with the boss by telling* him lies when I went on vacation. **Mireya me serruchó el piso con mi jefe cuando fui de vacaciones.**

to **pull the wool over someone's eyes** (fool; →see also: to rip off) dormir a alguien (to put someone to sleep) *Mex, Cuba, DR, G;* dar atole con el dedo a alguien (to give someone atole [a cornmeal drink] with the finger) *Mex, CR* ◆ *He pulled the wool over our eyes and got away with a good bit of money.* **Nos durmió a todos y se llevó su buena lana.**

Pull yourself together. →see: Get with the program.

punch →see: smack

pure gravy miel sobre hojuelas (honey on pastries) *Mex, DR, Sp* ◆ *If this product sells in other countries also, well, it'll be pure gravy.* **Si este producto se vende en otros países también, pues miel sobre hojuelas.**

to **push someone's buttons** →see: to give (someone) a hard time

to **push up daisies** (be dead; see also: to kick the bucket) criar margaritas (to grow daisies) *Mex, Sp* ◆ *If it weren't for you, I'd be pushing up daisies now.* **Si no fuera por ti, estaría criando margaritas ahora.**

pushiness →see: nerve

to be **pushing fifty (forty, etc.) years old** rondar los cincuenta (cuarenta, etc.) (to round the fifty, [forty], etc.) *ES, S. Cone, Sp* ◆ *How old is your cousin? —I'm not sure. She must be pushing forty, like me.* **¿Cuántos años tendrá tu prima? —No estoy seguro. Debe rondar los cuarenta, como yo.**

pushover (softie; person everyone takes advantage of) el/la blandengue (soft and squishy) *Mex, DR, Arg, Sp;* el barco, el barcazo (ship; e.g., parent who never says no or professor who passes everyone or always gives good grades) *Mex, Hond;* el/la agachado(-a) (bent over) *Mex;* el semáforo de medianoche (traffic light at midnight) *Ven* ◆ *I don't study much because my professors are pushovers.* **No estudio mucho porque mis profesores son barcos.**

push-ups las lagartijas (lizards) *Mex, DR, G, ES, Col* ◆ *The instructor had us do push-ups.* **El instructor nos puso a hacer lagartijas.**

pushy (person) (insensitive to others) con-chudo(-a) (hard-shelled) *Mex, C. Am., Ven, Col, Ec, Bol, Peru;* el/la patudo(-a) ([ugly] bigfoot) *S. Cone;* el/la cara dura (hard face) *ES, PR, S. Cone* ◆ *Trinidad is so pushy that even though they reject her, she comes back. Trinidad es tan conchuda que aunque la rechazan, ella regresa.*

pussy (female organ, all vulgar) la panocha (kind of candy) *Chicano, Mex, ES, CR, Col;* el bizcocho (biscuit) *Chicano, Mex;* la papaya (papaya) *Mex, Cuba, Nic, Col;* la torta (cake) *Mex, G, ES;* el chocho (round sweet) *Mex, Cuba, Nic, Sp* (RVar *PR:* la chocha); la cuca (sedge; a sweet) *DR, G, ES, Col, Ven;* el bollo (bread roll) *Cuba, PR, ES, Nic, Col;* el bicho (bug) *PR;* la chucha *Ch;* la concha (shell) *S. Cone*

to **put a bug in someone's ear** (tell people something with the intent of changing their minds or moving them to action) ponerles la mosca detrás de las orejas (to put the fly behind their ears) *Sp* ◆ *Our political science professor put a bug in our ears about government corruption to challenge us to analyze the situation. Nuestro profesor de ciencias políticas nos ponía la mosca detrás de las orejas sobre la corrupción del gobierno para desafiarnos a analizar la situación.*

to **put a hex on someone** (try to cause him or her bad luck) echar mal de ojo (to throw the evil eye) *Cuba, DR, PR, S. Cone* ◆ *It would seem someone has put a hex on me; everything is going badly. Parecería que me han echado mal de ojo; todo me sale mal.*

to **put a lid on it** (shut one's trap or yap, be quiet; →see also: to button one's lip, to keep one's lips sealed, to not say a word) cerrar el pico (to close the beak) *Mex, DR, PR, U, Arg, Sp;* doblar el pico (to fold up the beak) *Mex, ES;* quedarse como en misa (to be left as in mass) *CR, Col, U;* multiplicarse por cero (to multiply oneself by zero) *Sp;* achantarse *Sp* ◆ *Put a lid on it; the children are listening. Cierra el pico, que los niños están escuchando.*

to **put a stop to something** poner freno a algo (to put the brake on something) *most of L. Am., Sp* ◆ *My daughter wanted to get married at seventeen, but I put a stop to that non-*

sense. Mi hija quería casarse a los diecisiete años, pero yo le puse freno a esa locura.

to **put all one's eggs in one basket** (bet everything at once) jugarse el todo por el todo (to bet all for all) *L. Am., Sp;* jugárselo todo a una carta *Mex, S. Cone, Sp;* poner toda la carne en el asador (to put all the meat on the spit) *Mex, Sp* ◆ *They decided to put all their eggs in one basket when they bought the business. Decidieron jugarse el todo por el todo cuando compraron el negocio.*

to **put down 1.** (criticize; →see also: to chew out, to rip apart) tirar piedras (to throw stones) *Mex, ES, CR, Col;* tirar arroz (to throw rice) *Mex, ES, Nic, Peru;* rajar (to split) *Col, Peru, Bol, U, Arg* ◆ *I'm leaving here because they're putting people down. Me voy de acá porque están tirando piedras.* **2.** (with a sharp reply) dar un cortón a alguien *Mex* ◆ *Julio put him down in an ugly way. Julio le dio un cortón muy feo.* **3.** (often by saying bad things to others behind their backs) serrucharle el piso a alguien (to saw off the floor under someone) *Hond, Nic, CR, Col, Ec, Peru, S. Cone* ◆ *Mireya put me down with the boss by telling him lies when I went on vacation. Mireya me serruchó el piso con mi jefe cuando fui de vacaciones.*

to **put in a tight spot** (act cruelly toward someone or ask too much of someone) llevar contra la pared (la tabla) (to take against the wall [board]) *Mex, Cuba, G, Ch, U* ◆ *My girlfriend put me in a tight spot and I had to tell her I still don't want to get married. Mi novia me llevó contra la pared y tuve que decirle que aún no me quiero casar.*

to **put in one's two cents** (→see also: to butt into [someone's conversation]) meter la cuchara (to put in the spoon) *L. Am., Sp;* meter baza (to play a card trick) *Ch, Sp* ◆ *I put in my two cents to tell them the truth.* ◆ *Metí la cuchara para decirles la verdad.*

to **put off** (repel, bother) repatear (to rekick) *Mex, Sp;* echarle para atrás *Sp* ◆ *This music puts me off. Me repatea esta música.*

to **put on airs** →see: to be full of oneself

to **put on the finishing touch** (to perfect) dar la última pincelada (to give the last brush stroke) *Sp* ◆ *Last night we put the finishing* *touch on the project; tomorrow we present it in public. Anoche dimos la última pincelada al proyecto; mañana lo presentamos en público.*

to **put one's cards on the table** (be direct about a situation, explain it without concealing anything) poner las cartas sobre la mesa (to put one's cards on the table) *L. Am., Sp* ◆ *We put our cards out on the table for the lawyer of the opposition. Le pusimos las cartas sobre la mesa al abogado contrincante.*

to **put one's foot down** (put a stop to something; →see also: to call the shots, to wear the pants) poner freno a algo (to put the brake on something) *most of L. Am., Sp;* pararle el carro a alguien (to stop someone's cart) *S. Cone, Sp* ◆ *My daughter wanted to get married at seventeen, but I put my foot down on that nonsense. Mi hija quería casarse a los diecisiete años, pero yo le puse freno a esa locura.*

to **put one's foot in one's mouth** (make a mistake; →see also: to blow it) meter la pata (to put one's foot in) *L. Am., Sp* ◆ *You've said too much; you put your foot in your mouth. Hablaste demasiado; metiste la pata.*

to **put one's nose to the grindstone** (→see also: to cram, to work one's fingers to the bone) meterle caña (to put cane) *Mex* ◆ *If you want to pass the biology exam, you have to put your nose to the grindstone. Si quieres aprobar el examen de biología, hay que meterle caña.*

to **put one's shoulder to the wheel** (get down to work; →see also: to get moving, to hustle, to work like a dog, to work one's fingers to the bone) poner el hombro (to put the shoulder) *S. Cone* ◆ *We all put our shoulders to the wheel to achieve our goals. Todos pusimos el hombro para conseguir nuestros propósitos.*

to **put someone in his or her place** hacer entrar al aro a alguien (to make someone enter into the hoop) *L. Am., Sp;* poner a alguien en su sitio (lugar) *L. Am., Sp;* bajarle a alguien los humos (to lower someone's smoke) *Mex, DR, PR, S. Cone, Sp;* poner a raya (to put a stripe, line) *Mex, Ch, Sp;* bajarle el copete (to take down his or her crest or hairpiece) *S. Cone* ◆ *The lady put that rude bu-*

reaucrat in his place. La señora le bajó los humos al funcionario mal educado.

to **put someone on** (say crazy or wild things that make no sense, tease) vacilar (to vacillate, go back and forth) *Mex, C. Am., Col, Ven, Ec, Peru, Sp* mensear *Mex;* macanear *U, Arg* ◆ *I never know when he's serious about what he's saying; he's always putting us on. Nunca sé cuando habla en serio; siempre está vacilando.*

to **put someone on the spot** (by asking an indiscreet question or getting the person to do something embarrassing) avergonzar (to embarrass) *L. Am., Sp;* balconear a alguien (to balcony someone) *Mex, ES* ◆ *The reporter put the man on the spot in front of his colleagues. La reportera balconeó al señor delante de sus colegas.*

to **put someone's nerves on edge** poner a alguien los nervios de punta (to make someone's nerves stand up) *L. Am., Sp* ◆ *The message put my nerves on edge. El mensaje me puso los nervios de punta.*

to **put the ball back in someone's court** (get the best of someone, counter someone with their own arguments or reasoning) devolver la pelota a alguien (to return the ball to someone) *Mex, DR, Sp* ◆ *Marta's a genius; when she's debating something, no one can put the ball back in her court. Marta es un genio; cuando discute no hay quien le devuelva la pelota.*

to **put the cart before the horse** empezar la casa por el tejado (to begin the house with the roof) *Sp* ◆ *Don't be in such a hurry, boy; you need to learn your job well. Don't put the cart before the horse. No te apures, muchacho; tienes que aprender tu trabajo bien. No se puede empezar la casa por el tejado.*

to **put the whole thing behind one (you, us, etc.)** dar vuelta a la página (to turn the page) *ES, CR, S. Cone, Sp* ◆ *It's better to forget that affair and put the whole thing behind us. Es mejor olvidarnos de ese asunto y dar vuelta a la página.*

to **put through the wringer** →see: to beat someone up, to put in a tight spot

to **put to sleep** (bore; →see also: to be a drag, to bore to death) amuermar *Sp* ◆ *That* *guy puts anyone to sleep. Ese tipo amuerma a cualquiera.*

to **put two and two together** atar cabos (to tie ends) *L. Am., Sp* ◆ *Putting two and two together, I guessed they were cousins. Atando cabos, adiviné que eran primos.*

to **put up with** (accept) tragar camote (to swallow sweet potato) *Mex;* tragar (to swallow) *DR, Nic, U, Arg, Sp;* arrugarse (to wrinkle up, get wrinkled) *U, Arg;* bancar(se) *U, Arg;* arremangarse *Arg* ◆ *I had to put up with*

it; I had to accept it. Me la tuve que tragar; tuve que arrugarme.

put-down (disparaging remark) la quemada (burn) *Chicano, Mex, U;* el cortón *Mex;* el corte (cut) *Sp* ◆ *She said that to you? What a put-down!* ◆ *¿Te dijo eso? ¡Qué quemada!*

to **putz around** tontear *L. Am., Sp* ◆ *I was putzing around (going along stupidly) for a half hour, but I finally found the house. Iba tonteando durante media hora, pero por fin encontré la casa.*

quack doctor el/la matasanos (healthy people-killer) *most of L. Am., Sp* ◆ *The quack doctor recommended a very ineffective cure. El matasanos recomendó un remedio muy inefectivo.*

quick as lightning (lightning fast; →see also: full blast, like a bat out of hell, like a shot) como un rayo (like a lightning bolt) *ES, Nic, CR, Ch, U, Sp* ◆ *He's quick as lightning. Es rápido como un rayo.*

R

to **rack one's brain** meter (el) coco (to put coconut, head) *Mex, Cuba, Col;* dar cráneo (cabeza) (to give cranium, skull [head]) *Mex, PR;* devanarse los sesos (to wind up one's brain) *Mex, Ch, Sp;* darle al coco (to give to the coconut, head) *Mex, Sp;* cranear *G, Col, Ec, Ch;* quemarse (estrujarse) los sesos (to burn out [press] one's brain) *S. Cone, Sp;* estrujarse el melón (to press one's melon [head]) *Sp* ◆ *We racked our brains, but we could not find the mathematical formula.* **Nos devanamos los sesos, pero no encontramos la fórmula matemática.**

to be a **ragamuffin** (dressed in rags or rag-tag) andar con las hilachas colgando (to go with threads hanging) *S. Cone* ◆ *I don't know what kind of problems my nephews and nieces have. They're dressed like ragamuffins.* **No entiendo qué problemas tienen mis sobrinos. Andan con las hilachas colgando.**

to **rain buckets, to rain cats and dogs** llover a cántaros (to rain pitchers) *L. Am., Sp* ◆ *We came back early because it was raining buckets.* **Regresamos pronto porque llovía a cántaros.**

to **raise a fuss** (→see also: to make a scene) armarla (to arm it) *Mex, Sp* ◆ *Daniel raised a fuss with me.* **Daniel me la armó.**

to **raise a hue and cry** (complain loudly) poner el grito en el cielo (to put the cry to the heavens) *L. Am., Sp;* pegar el grito (to stick the shout) *DR, CR, ES, Col, U* ◆ *When your mother sees what you've done in the kitchen, she will raise a hue and a cry.* **Cuando vea tu madre lo que has hecho en la cocina, va a poner el grito en el cielo.**

to **raise someone's spirits** (inspire, encourage) darle alas a alguien (to give someone wings) *Mex, DR, S. Cone, Sp;* levantar el ánimo (to raise the spirit) *L. Am., Sp* ◆ *My brother's visit raised my spirits.* **La visita de mi hermano me dio alas.**

to **rake over the coals** (criticize; →see also: to chew out) comer vivo(-a) (to eat live) *most of L. Am., Sp;* poner a caldo (to put to broth, perhaps implying someone is being scalded) *Sp* ◆ *His political enemies raked him over the coals once he finished his term in parliament.* **Sus adversarios políticos lo pusieron a caldo una vez que acabó su turno en el parlamento.**

rat (person who rats on others) el soplón, la soplona *L. Am., Sp;* el sapo (toad) *Nic, CR, Col, Ven, ES, Peru;* el chivato *Mex, Cuba, DR, Sp* ◆ *He's a rat. He tells everything.* **Es un sapo. Todo lo cuenta.**

rat race (hullabaloo) el corre-corre (run-run) *Mex, DR, PR* ◆ *I don't like the rat race in the city.* **No me gusta el corre-corre de la ciudad.**

to **rattle someone's cage** →see: to upset someone

raunchy →see: tacky

to **read the riot act** →see: to set someone straight, to tell it like it is

to be **ready to bite someone's head off** →see: to be in a very bad mood, to be steamed

to be **ready to tear one's hair out** estar para jalarse los pelos (to be ready to pull one's hair out) *Mex, ES, Sp* ◆ *I'm ready to tear out my hair, I'm so mad.* **Estoy que me jalo los pelos de coraje.**

to be **ready, willing and able** (→see also: to be on one's toes) estar al pie del cañón (to be at the foot of the cannon) *Mex, ES, S. Cone, Sp;* estar puesto(-a) (to be put, turned on) *Mex, U;* tener bien puestas las pilas, estar con las pilas puestas (to have one's batteries well placed) *DR, Ven, Ch, U* ◆ *If you need something, call me. I'll be here ready, willing, and able.* **Si necesitas algo, llámame. Aquí estaré al pie del cañón.** ◆ *That guy is very clever; he's ready, willing, and able.* **Ese chico es muy listo; tiene las pilas bien puestas.**

to be a **real slut** ser más puta que las gallinas (to be more of a slut than the hens are, vulgar) *Mex, PR, ES, S. Cone, Sp* ◆ *How could*

red-handed: *There you have him, red-handed!*
Ahí lo tienen, icon las manos en la masa!

you have fallen in love with that woman? She's a real *slut*. ¿*Cómo te enamoraste de esa mujer? Es más puta que las gallinas.*

a **real smartie** el listón, la listona (big clever) *Mex, Col* ◆ *Juan is a real smartie. Juan es un listón.*

the **real thing** (genuine; said of people) de pura cepa (of pure stock) *most of L. Am., Sp* ◆ *Jacinto is the real thing (very genuine). Jacinto es una persona de pura cepa.*

the **real truth of the matter** la neta *Mex;* la verdad de la milanesa (the truth of the Milanese chop; slang) *Peru, S. Cone* ◆ *I told you the real truth of the matter. Te platiqué la neta.*

rear end (backside) el trasero *L. Am., Sp;* el traste *S.Cone;* los pompis *Mex, Col, Ven, Ec, Sp* ◆ *I gave him a kick in the rear end and told him not to come back to my house. Le di una patada en el trasero y le dije que no volviera a mi casa.*

red hot (passions) al rojo vivo *Mex, Sp* ◆ *This woman has me red hot. Esta mujer me tiene al rojo vivo.*

red-handed con las manos en la masa (with one's hands in the dough) *L. Am., Sp* ◆ *They caught him red-handed. Lo agarraron con las manos en la masa.*

regular guy, regular Joe (everyday, common) común y corriente *L. Am., Sp;* corriente y moliente *Mex, Sp* ◆ *Even though he's a famous actor, he's just a regular guy. Aunque es un actor famoso, es una persona corriente y moliente.*

to **remain on the sidelines** (participate in or witness something but avoid exposing oneself to danger) mirar (ver) los toros desde la barrera (to look at [see] the bulls from behind the barrier) *most of L. Am., Sp* ◆ *During the Second World War, we remained on the sidelines. Durante la Segunda Guerra Mundial, estuvimos viendo los toros desde la barrera.*

to **repeat something ad nauseam** dar una cantaleta *Mex, DR, C. Am., Col, Peru;* repetirlo hasta el cansancio (to repeat it until tiredness) *DR, PR, S. Cone, Sp* ◆ *The boss repeated her lecture to us ad nauseam and we* *knew she was right. La jefa nos dio una cantaleta y sabíamos que tenía razón.*

to **reprimand** →see: to chew out, to rip apart

reruns (of TV programs; rehashed stories) refritos (refried) *Mex, Ven* ◆ *There are reruns on all the channels, especially in the summer. Hay refritos en todos los canales, especialmente en verano.*

restroom (public washrooms) el baño *L. Am., Sp;* los servicios públicos (public services) *L. Am., Sp;* el excusado (the excused place; euphemism) *Mex, Col, Ch;* el privado (private; euphemism) *Mex, Col* ◆ *The public restrooms there are very dirty. Los baños públicos allí están muy sucios.*

to be **rich** →see: to be filthy rich

rich brats los (niños) popis (stuck-up kids) *Mex* ◆ *The rich brats ruined the school party. Los (niños) popis arruinaron la fiesta del colegio.*

rich kid 1. (kid who has everything solved for him or her by the parents' influence) el/la hijo(-a) de papá (Daddy's child) *Mex, Cuba, DR, C. Am., Col, Peru, Sp;* el/la hijo(-a) de papi (Daddy's child) *Mex, G, ES, Col, Peru;* el junior *Mex, Col* ◆ *As usual, his arguments are those of a spoiled rich kid. Como siempre, sus argumentos son de un hijo de papá.* **2.** (well-brought-up [upper-class] boy or girl) el niño (la niña) bien *L. Am., Sp;* el/la chico(-a) bien *L. Am., Sp;* la niña pija (young, innocent upper-class or spoiled girl, not vulgar but pejorative) *Sp* ◆ *Dolores is a rich kid, but she wants to work with the poor. Dolores es una niña pija, pero quiere trabajar con los pobres.* ◆ *They're rich kids and have good manners. Son niños bien y tienen buenos modales.*

to be **riding high** estar en la cresta de la ola (to be on the crest of the wave) *Sp* ◆ *This singer is riding high at the moment. Esta cantante está en la cresta de la ola en este momento.*

riffraff la chuzma *L. Am., Sp;* la pelusa (fuzz) *Chicano, Mex* ◆ *I don't want to share the beach with riffraff; let's go to the Miramar Hotel. No quiero compartir la playa con la pelusa; vamos al hotel Miramar.*

to be **right** (get [something] right) dar en el blanco (to hit the target) *L. Am., Sp* ◆ *You got*

that right, my friend: I need a loan. Diste en el blanco, amigo: necesito un préstamo.

to be **right for** (to suit) cuadrar (to square) *L. Am.* ◆ *The color of this dress isn't right for me. No me cuadra el color de este vestido.*

right and left (all over the place) a diestra y siniestra (right and left) *L. Am., Sp* ◆ *On the highway there were restaurants right and left. En la carretera había restaurantes a diestra y siniestra.*

right at hand (close by; without much effort) a pocos pasos (at a few steps) *Mex, S. Cone, Sp* ◆ *We found the solution to the problem right at hand. A pocos pasos encontramos la solución del problema.*

right away 1. (immediately) ahora mismo (now same) *L. Am., Sp;* en seguida *L. Am., Sp En seguida le traigo el café, señor.* ◆ *I'll bring your coffee right away, sir.*

right from the start (the beginning) de buenas a primeras (from good ones to first ones) *L. Am., Sp;* al primer envite *Sp* ◆ *Right from the start we became friends. De buenas a primeras nos hicimos amigas.*

right now ahorita (diminutive of ahora) *L. Am. (not Cuba, S. Cone);* ahora mismo (now same) *L. Am., Sp* ◆ *I'm going to clean the kitchen right now. Ahorita voy a limpiar la cocina.*

right off the bat (right from the start, at once; →see also: right away) de buenas a primeras (from good ones to first ones) *L. Am., Sp;* al primer envite *Sp* ◆ *He's a softie who gives up right off the bat. Es un tipo blando que se viene abajo al primer envite.*

Right (you are)! Pura verdad. (Pure truth.) *L. Am., Sp;* ¡Ándale! (¡Ándate!) *Chicano, Mex, Col* ◆ *Right you are! That's how you play the marimba. Ándale, pues. Así se toca la marimba.*

to **rile up** (needle, excite; →see also: to bug, to give someone a hard time, to upset) torear (to fight a bull) *L. Am., Sp;* dar picones (to give scratches) *Mex, ES;* poner a alguien a cien (to put someone to the hundred) *Sp* ◆ *Antonio riled up Juanito until the latter got tired of his provocations and hit him. Antonio toreó a Juanito hasta que éste se cansó de las provocaciones y lo golpeó.*

to **rip apart** 1. (beat up, chew out) poner como dado (to put like a die—from a pair of dice—square and with spots) *Mex;* sacudir el polvo a alguien (to shake the dust off someone) *Sp;* comer vivo(-a) a alguien (to eat someone alive) *Mex, DR, ES, S. Cone, Sp* ◆ *My dad ripped me apart when I flunked out (failed the school year).* Mi papá me puso como dado cuando reprobé el año. ◆ *I've had it with that job. My boss ripped me apart just because I forgot and left some documents at home.* Ya estoy harto de ese trabajo. Mi jefe me comió vivo solamente porque olvidé unos documentos en casa. 2. (destroy, blow someone away with insults) no dejar títere con cabeza (to not leave a puppet with a head) *S. Cone* ◆ *I'm going to look over the whole job and if it isn't good, I'll rip you apart (heads will roll).* Voy a revisar todo el trabajo y si está mal, no voy a dejar títere con cabeza. 3. (rip to shreds, speak badly [of someone]) tijerear a alguien (to cut someone with scissors) *Mex, ES;* sacarle la piel a tiras (to take off the skin in strips) *PR, Sp* ◆ *The trade unionists ripped the management apart.* Los gremialistas le sacaron la piel a tiras a la patronal.

to **rip into** →see: to chew out, to rip apart

to **rip off** 1. (overcharge, swindle; →see also: to cheat) estafar *L. Am., Sp;* clavar (to nail) *Mex, Cuba, DR, G, CR, S. Cone, Sp;* atracar (to hold up, waylay) *Mex, DR, CR;* tranzar *Mex, ES;* afanar *Cuba, Peru, U, Arg, Sp;* dar una clavada (to give a nailing) *DR, Arg, Sp;* bajar la caña (to lower the reed, cane) *U, Arg* ◆ *I'm sure the taxi driver ripped us off.* Estoy segura que el taxista nos estafó. ◆ *They ripped off (conned) those tourists with a Taino statue; they think it's an original work of art!* A esos turistas los clavaron con una estatua taína; ¡creen que es una pieza original! 2. (deceive someone) →see also: to pull the wool over someone's eyes) timar *parts of L. Am., Sp;* bailar a alguien (to dance someone) *Mex, G, ES;* vacunar (to vaccinate) *S. Cone;* engrupir (to group up) *S. Cone;* meter la mula (to put in the mule) *S. Cone* ◆ *They ripped me off with that product because it was another brand name.* Me bailaron con ese producto porque era de otra marca.

rip-off (faked or rigged deal, rigged elections, or jacked-up prices) el chanchullo (piggish) *Mex, DR, PR, CR, Peru, Bol, Ch;* el afano total *Arg* ◆ *He is investigating a big money rip-off.* Está investigando un gran chanchullo de dinero.

rip-off artist →see: con artist

to **rise to a challenge** recoger el guante (to pick up the glove) *Mex, Peru, S. Cone, Sp* ◆ *I rose to the challenge and accepted the project from the architecture department.* Recogí el guante y acepté el proyecto del departamento de arquitectura.

to **rise to power** subir al poder *L. Am., Sp* ◆ *As a general rule, dictators rise to power through violence.* Por lo general, los dictadores suben al poder por la violencia.

to be **roasting hot** (people) sancocharse *Mex, DR, PR, Col, Ch* ◆ *I'm roasting hot. Open the windows!* Me estoy sancochando del calor. ¡Abran las ventanas!

to **rob Peter to pay Paul** desnudar a un santo para vestir a otro (to strip one statue of a saint naked to dress another) *S. Cone* ◆ *With the restructuring of the province's budget, the governor robbed Peter to pay Paul.* Con la reestructuración del presupuesto de la provincia, el gobernador desnudó a un santo para vestir a otro.

to **rock** (be pleasing to) molar, molar cantidad (functions like gustar) *Sp* ◆ *Juan rocks. It really rocks for us to play music together.* Juan me mola. Nos mola cantidad tocar música juntos.

to **roll off one's back** (not affect or cause concern) resbalarle algo a alguien (to slide off someone) *Mex, DR, PR, Sp* ◆ *Pedro? The outcome (result) just rolls off his back. He has no interest in doing it well.* ¿Pedro? Le resbala totalmente el resultado. No tiene ningún interés por hacerlo bien.

rolling in money/dough →see: moneybags, to be loaded

rotten →see: crummy, the pits

rotten bastard (→see also: son of a bitch) pinche cabrón (vulgar) *Mex* ◆ *You rotten bastard! Why did you steal my wallet?* ¡Pinche cabrón! ¿Por qué me robaste la cartera?

rubber (condom) el sombrero (el gorro, gorrito) (hat [cap]) *Mex, DR, PR, G, ES, Col* ◆ *Please don't risk your lives! If you're going to go out with women, take along some rubbers.*

Por favor, ¡no arriesguen sus vidas! Si van a salir con mujeres, lleven sombreros (gorritos).

ruckus →see: mess

to be the **ruin of** →see: to do in

rumormill (nonexistent radio station from which rumors or falsehoods are supposedly broadcast) el radio macuto *Sp* ♦ *I found out through the rumormill (grapevine) that they are going to fire the director.* Me he enterado por radio macuto de que van a despedir al director.

rumormongers →see: gossips

run (streak, period of time) la racha *L. Am., Sp* ♦ *We've had a bad run, but I think today we're going to win the game.* Hemos pasado una mala racha, pero creo que hoy vamos a ganar el partido.

to be **run of the mill** (mediocre) no ser ni chicha ni limonada (to be neither corn liquor nor lemonade) *most of L. Am., Sp* ♦ *The new director doesn't impress me much. He's run of the mill.* El nuevo director no me impresiona mucho. No es ni chicha ni limoná.

to **run off at the mouth** →see: to talk a blue streak

to **run (someone) off** correr (to run) *Mex, C. Am., U, Arg* ♦ *They ran us off from the party.* Nos corrieron de la fiesta.

to **run something into the ground** (insist on something) ir y venir en una cosa (to go and come in something) *Sp* ♦ *No one understood the teacher; he ran the subject into the ground.* Nadie entendió al profesor; vino y fue en el tema.

run-down (ugly) feote (feota) (-ote, augmentative) *L. Am., Sp* ♦ *What a run-down house!* ¡Qué casa más feota!

to be **running around like a chicken with its head cut off** parecer chiva loca (to seem like a crazy goat) *Mex* ♦ *Sit down, girl. You're running around like a chicken with its head cut off.* Niña, siéntate. Pareces chiva loca.

He (She) is **running it into the ground.** Cada loco con su tema. (Every crazy person with his or her subject, usually said when someone is excessively insistent about something.) *L. Am., Sp* ♦ *María doesn't stop talking about politics. She's running it into the ground.* María no deja de hablar de política. Cada loco con su tema.

rush hour (peak hour of traffic or electricity use) la(s) hora(s) pico *Mex, DR, Nic;* la(s) hora(s) punta *Ch, Sp* ♦ *It's impossible to drive downtown during rush hour.* Es imposible manejar en el centro a la hora pico.

salt mines (work; →see also: job) el camello (camel) *Mex, ES, Col, Ec*; el martilleo (hammering) *Mex, Col* ♦ *I quit at the salt mines (my job).* Renuncié al martilleo.

Same as usual. Nothing new. Por aquí (trabajando, estudiando, etc.). ([I'm] Just here [working, studying].) *L. Am., Sp*; Aquí nomás. ([I'm] Just here.) *Mex, C. Am.*; Aquí pasándola. (Por aquí pasándola.) (Passing it here.) *Mex, ES, Col, U, Arg* ♦ *How are you, Felipe? —Same as usual, visiting my kids.* ¿Cómo anda, don Felipe? —Por aquí, visitando a mis hijos.

Same here. Igual Pascual. (Equal Pascual.) *Ch*; Iguanas ranas. (Iguanas frogs; iguanas sounds like igual) *Mex, Col* ♦ *I'm tired. —Same here.* Estoy cansado. –Igual Pascual.

Same old same old →see: Same as usual.

Same old story. Este disco tiene raya. (Este disco está rayado.) (This record has a scratch [is scratched].) *Mex, DR, ES, Nic, Ch*; Y dale la burra al trigo. (And let the donkey keep at the wheat, said when someone keeps repeating the same thing.) *Mex, ES, Col* ♦ *Same old story. Always with the same thing.* Y dale la burra al trigo. Siempre con lo mismo.

sappy →see: corny

sassy (describing someone who talks back unjustifiably when reprimanded) respondón, respondona *Mex, Sp* ♦ *"Don't be sassy,"* Juanito's dad said to him. "No seas respondón", le dijo su papá a Juanito.

to **save one's skin** salvar el pellejo *L. Am., Sp* ♦ *They saved their skins by a miracle. They were the last to cross the bridge before the river washed it away.* Salvaron el pellejo de milagro. Fueron los últimos en cruzar el puente antes que el río se lo llevara.

to **save someone's bacon** (help someone else out at one's own expense) sacar las castañas del fuego (to take the chestnuts out of the fire) *U, Arg, Sp* ♦ *Someone always has to save his bacon. If it weren't for his friends, he would already have flunked out.* Siempre tienen que sacarle las castañas del fuego. Si no fuera por sus amigos, ya estaría suspendido.

to be saved by the skin of one's teeth salvarse por un pelo (to be saved by a hair) *Mex, ES, Peru, S. Cone, Sp* ♦ *Two people died in the accident. I was saved by the skin of my teeth.* Dos personas murieron en el accidente. Yo me salvé por un pelo.

to be **savvy** (have a lot of knowledge [about something] or a talent for it; →see also: smarts) estar puesto(-a) (to be put, turned on) *Mex, Sp* ♦ *I hired Jimena because she is savvy.* Contraté a Jimena porque está puesta.

scam →see: rip-off

to **scare** (frighten) achantar *Nic, Sp*; asustar *L.Am., Sp* ♦ *Your blackmail threats don't scare me.* A mí tus chantajes no me achantan.

to be **scared** estar asustado(-a) *L. Am., Sp*; quedarse chiquito(-a) (to be left small) *CR, Col*

to be **scared shitless** (fearful, timid; all vulgar) subírsele a alguien los huevos (to have one's eggs, or testicles, rise) *Mex*; tener los huevos de corbata, tenerlos por corbata (to have one's testicles as a tie) *ES, Sp*; estar cagado(-a) (to be pooped) *S. Cone, Sp*; tener los cojones por corbata or tenerlos por corbata (to have one's testicles as a tie) *Sp* ♦ *When I realized there was a robber in the house, I was scared shitless.* Cuando me di cuenta de que había un ladrón en la casa, se me subieron los huevos hasta la garganta.

to be **scared stiff** estar muerto(-a) de miedo (to be dead of fear) *L. Am., Sp*; estar achuchado(-a) *Para, U, Arg* ♦ *Miriam was scared stiff when she heard the news.* Miriam estaba muerta de miedo cuando oyó las noticias.

scaredy-cat (easily frightened; →see also: chicken) asustón, asustona *Chicano, Mex* ♦ *Claudia is afraid of everything. What a* *scaredy-cat! Claudia tiene miedo de todo. ¡Qué asustona!*

scatterbrained (clueless; →see also: birdbrain, fool) despistado(-a) (off the path) *L. Am., Sp* ◆ *I'm completely scatterbrained (clueless); I don't know anything about the matter.* Estoy totalmente despistado; no sé nada del asunto.

schmaltzy (overly sweet, sentimental, or cute [language, dress, etc.]) cursi *L. Am., Sp* ◆ *Divine treasure of my soul and heart, do you want to go out for dinner? —Please don't be so schmaltzy.* Tesoro divino de mi alma y corazón, ¿quieres ir a cenar? —Por favor, no seas tan cursi.

to **schmooze** →see: to sweet-talk

schmuck (moron) →see: idiot

to **scoot** (walk very fast; →see also: to get moving, to take off) echar un patín (to throw a skate) *Mex, Cuba* ◆ *He scooted (hightailed it) in an hour from the market to the port.* Echó un patín de una hora desde el mercado hasta el puerto.

to **score** (get, pick up; colloquial) ligar *L. Am., Sp* ◆ *I scored a plane to Mexico.* Ligué un avión a México.

scourge of the neighborhood (local troublemaker or criminal) el azote del barrio (whip of the neighborhood) *Mex, Ven* ◆ *The community collaborated to identify a group that was the scourge of the neighborhood.* La comunidad colaboró para identificar a un grupo que era el azote del barrio.

Scram! →see: Get lost!

to **screw** →see: to have sex

to **screw 1.** (equivalent of the f-word; screw up, mess with; vulgar) chingar (to rip, tear) (vulgar) *Mex, Cuba, PR, C. Am., Col;* joder (vulgar in some places but inoffensive in others) *L. Am., Sp;* cagar (to shit on, vulgar) *S. Cone;* descojonar (to de-testicle, vulgar) *Mex, DR, PR, Col* ◆ *Don't f-ing screw with me; I need money.* No me chingues; necesito dinero. **2.** (bother, trick, or bug someone; to wreck or screw up something) joder (vulgar in some places but inoffensive in others) *L. Am., Sp;* jorobar (euphemism for joder) *Mex, Cuba, DR, PR, G, CR;* fregar (to scrub, scour, rub [the wrong way]) *most of L. Am.;* ◆ *Don't*

screw around with me. ◆ *No me jodas (friegues).*

to **screw around** (goof off, not do anything) tocarse las narices (los huevos, los cojones) (to touch one's nose [testicles]; vulgar with huevos/cojones) *Sp* ◆ *That employee is very lazy; he's screwing around doing nothing all day.* Ese empleado es muy haragán; está todos los días tocándose las narices.

to **screw it up even more** para acabarla de joder (to finish screwing it up, vulgar) *Chicano, Mex, DR, PR, G, ES, Col, Sp* ◆ *To screw it up more, before the concert began, it started to rain and the stage fell apart.* Para acabarla de joder, antes de comenzar el concierto, empezó a llover y el escenario se desarmó.

to **screw oneself** (dishonor oneself) cubrirse de mierda (to cover oneself with shit, vulgar) *Mex, Sp* ◆ *Gerónimo is very dishonest and he's screwed himself.* Gerónimo es muy deshonesto y se ha cubierto de mierda.

to **screw up 1.** (make a mistake) meter el cazo (to put in one's dipper) *Sp* ◆ *You screwed it up. This isn't your room.* Metiste el cazo. Esta habitación no es tuya. **2.** ("f" up, make a mistake; vulgar but common; →see also: to blow it) cagarla (to shit on it) (sometimes used without la) *L. Am., Sp;* mear fuera del tiesto (to pee outside the pot) *Sp* (RVar *U, Arg:* tarro instead of tiesto) ◆ *I screwed up by inviting him to the party because he was just as much of a jerk as always.* La cagué invitándolo a la fiesta porque estuvo tan pesado como siempre. **3.** (do something embarrassing, embarrass oneself, goof) hacer el oso (to do the bear) *Mex, Col; Ch;* hacer un pancho *Mex* ◆ *I screwed up and was embarrassed; I forgot to say hello to the boss.* Hice un pancho; se me olvidó saludar al jefe.

screwed (messed up, all vulgar) jodido(-a) (past participle of joder) *L. Am., Sp;* chingado(-a) (chinga'o[-a]) (ripped, torn, broken) *Mex, Cuba, PR, C. Am., Col;* descojonado(-a) (without testicles) *Mex, DR, PR, Col, Sp;* estar cagado(-a) (to be pooped) *S. Cone* ◆ *I'm screwed. I have a lot of money problems.* Estoy jodida. Tengo muchos problemas económicos.

screw-up (major goof-up) la metida (metedura) de pata (the insertion of foot) *Mex,*

DR, G, S. Cone, Sp; la barrabasada Mex, DR, Col, Ch, Arg, Sp; el error garrafal DR, PR, Nic, S. Cone, Sp ◆ The screw-up was obvious. We had to apologize in front of those present. La metida de pata fue obvia. Tuvimos que disculparnos frente a los presentes.

screwy →see: nuts

to be a **Scrooge** (describing a bitter person) pasar muchas navidades y sin nochebuena (to have a lot of Christmases with no Christmas Eve celebrations) PR, Col ◆ Poor Ramona. She's such a Scrooge (sourpuss). Pobre Ramona. Ha pasado muchas navidades y sin nochebuena.

scrumptious (delicious) rico(-a) (rich) L. Am., Sp; para chuparse los dedos (for licking your fingers) L. Am., Sp ◆ The food was scrumptious. Estuvo muy rica la comida.

scumbag →see: asshole, jerk, lowlife

scuttlebutt →see: piece of gossip

Search me! ¡A mí que me registren! Mex, S. Cone, Sp ◆ Search me! I don't know anything about the problem between you. ¡A mí que me registren! No sé nada del problema entre ustedes.

to be a **second-class citizen** →see: to feel like/be a second-class citizen

See? ¿Viste? (Did you see?) L. Am. ◆ See? I knew I was right. ¿Viste? Ya sabía que tenía razón.

to **see the light** →to wise up

See you. Nos wachamos. (We'll see each other.; from the English "to watch") Chicano; Ahí nos vidrios. (colloquial, We'll see each other there; but vidrios, pieces of glass, instead of vemos.) Mex, C. Am., Ven, Ec, Peru

See you later, alligator. Chao, pesca'o. (Bye, fish.) Ven

See you next time (we meet). Hasta que nos topemos. (Until we run into each other again.) Mex, G, ES, Col, Ec ◆ It's been great talking with you, Andrés. See you next time! Un gusto de charlar contigo, Andrés. ¡Hasta que nos topemos!

seedy →see: tacky, crummy

to **seem fishy** (be suspicious) no oler bien una cosa, oler mal (to not smell good, to smell bad) Mex, S. Cone, Sp ◆ This seems fishy to me. Esto me huele mal.

to **seem inept** (uncoordinated, clumsy) parecer un pato mareado (to seem like a dizzy duck) Sp ◆ He's not very good at physical exercises. You see my brother dance and he seems really inept. No es muy hábil con los ejercicios físicos. Tú ves a mi hermano bailar y parece un pato mareado.

to **sell like hot cakes** venderse como pan caliente (to sell like hot bread) most of L. Am. ◆ The sandals that were on sale sold like hot cakes. Las sandalias que estaban en oferta se vendieron como pan caliente.

to **sell out** venderse L. Am., Sp ◆ The representative sold himself out without caring about the consequences. El diputado se vendió sin importarle las consecuencias.

sellout (person who sells out) vendido(-a) L. Am. ◆ They accused him of being a sellout when his team lost the game. Lo acusaron de ser un vendido cuando su equipo perdió el partido.

to **send to the devil** (→see also: to blow off) correr L. Am., Sp; mandar por un tubo Mex, ES, Col; largar U, Arg ◆ I'm thinking of sending this dame to the devil. Me parece que voy a largar a esta mina.

to be **senseless or useless** no tener chiste (to not have any joke) Mex, ES, Col, Peru, Bol ◆ It's senseless that we have come out to take a walk; it's raining. No tiene chiste que hayamos salido a pasear; está lloviendo.

to **serve two masters** (work for two, often opposing, people or ideas) comer a dos carrillos (to eat with two cheeks) U, Sp ◆ You can't serve two masters; you have to choose. No se puede comer a dos carrillos; tienes que escoger.

to **set someone straight** (read the riot act, lay down the law) leerle a alguien la cartilla (to read the primer to someone) Mex, DR, ES, Ch, Sp; cantarle a alguien la cartilla (el salmo) (to sing someone the primer [psalm]) Mex, Ch, Sp ◆ Josefina set her lover straight. Josefina le cantó la cartilla a su amante.

to **settle down** sentar cabeza (to seat head) most of L. Am., Sp ◆ Finally my son got married and settled down. Por fin mi hijo se casó y sentó cabeza.

to **settle in** (stay in one place without moving) apoltronarse L. Am., Sp; apalancarse Sp

♦ *I settled in at their house and we didn't go out in the evening.* Me apalanqué en su casa y no salimos por la noche.

to **settle it** (agree on something, decide) quedar (to remain) *L. Am.* ♦ *Then we settled it.* Quedamos en eso.

sex appeal el pegue *Mex, ES, Col* ♦ *That guy has sex appeal.* Ese chico tiene pegue.

to be a **sex maniac** (obsessed with sex, vulgar) ser un cachondo mental *Sp* ♦ *I'm a sex maniac and I have a good time.* Soy un cachondo mental y lo paso muy bien.

to be a **shadow of one's former self** no ser ni la sombra de lo que era (to not be even the shadow of what one was) *L. Am., Sp* ♦ *Elsa was very smart, but after the accident she's a shadow of her former self.* Elsa era muy inteligente, pero después del accidente no es ni la sombra de lo que era.

to **shake a leg** →see: to boogie

to be **shaken up** →see: to be on edge, nervous as a cat, to be scared (stiff)

shallow →see: to be an airhead, phony

shallow glamour boy (jerk, also implies someone with money) el bacán (controller of a woman who earns money for him, from Lunfardo, Buenos Aires slang) *S. Cone* ♦ *Look at that shallow glamour boy; he has the newest model Mercedes Benz.* Mira que hombre tan bacán; tiene un Mercedes Benz último modelo.

shark 1. (aggressive person) el tigre (tiger) *Mex, DR, G, ES, Col* ♦ *Fernando is a shark and gave himself away through his attitude.* Fernando es un tigre y se hizo conocer por su actitud. **2.** (astute in business, taking advantage of others) el/la piraña (piranha) *ES, CR, Col* ♦ *Don't buy from him; he's a shark.* No le compres a ése, que es muy piraña.

sharp (astute; fresh) vivaracho(-a) *S. Cone, Sp* ♦ *This dog is really lively and sharp. He runs and eats much more than the others.* Este perro es muy vivaracho. Corre y come mucho más que los otros.

sharp as a tack 1. (quick-witted) avispado(-a) (wasped) *L. Am., Sp;* buzo (diver) *Mex, G, Hond, ES;* pillo(-a) *Mex, Hond, CR, Col, Peru, S. Cone, Sp;* abusado(-a) (abused) *Mex;* fino(-a) como un coral (fine as a coral) *Sp;* más listo(-a) que el hambre (more clever

than hunger) *Sp* ♦ *Paco is very clever, sharp as a tack.* Paco es muy avispado. **2.** (well connected and clever) picudo(-a) *Mex, ES* ♦ *Juan is sharp as a tack; that's why they promoted him.* Juan es muy picudo, por eso lo ascendieron.

to **sharpen up** →see: to pay attention

sheepish (embarrassed, inhibited) avergonzado(-a) *L. Am., Sp;* chiveado(-a) *Mex, ES* ♦ *What's wrong with your brother? —He's sheepish and doesn't want to talk because there's the boss over there.* ¿Qué pasa con tu hermano? —Está chiveado y no quiere hablar porque allí está el patrón.

shenanigans (bad business, scheme) el tejemaneje (knack) *L. Am., Sp;* la movida *Mex, G, ES, Ch* ♦ *I don't know what shenanigans you're up to (bringing here) nor do I want to know.* No sé qué tejemanejes te traes ni quiero saberlos.

to **shift gears** (change pace) cambiar de canal (to change the channel) *Mex, DR, ES, Col* ♦ *The minister (secretary) shifted gears so as not to talk about the subject of taxes.* El ministro cambió de canal para no hablar del tema de los impuestos.

shiftless →see: lazy bastard, lazy bum, lazybones, slacker

shindig (party; →see also: bash) la pachanga, el pachangón *most of L. Am.* ♦ *What a huge shindig! There are a lot of people here.* ¡Qué pachanga! Hay mucha gente aquí.

Shit! (→see Damn!) ¡Mierda! (vulgar) *L. Am., Sp*

shithead (vulgar) el/la comemierda (shit eater) *Mex, Cuba, DR, PR, G, ES, Nic, Col* ♦ *I can't stand Lucy's cousin. He's a shithead; he thinks he's better than everyone else.* No soporto al primo de Lucy. Es un tremendo comemierda; se cree mejor que los demás.

to be a **shithead** (vulgar) ser pura mierda (ser una mierda) (to be pure shit [to be shitty]) *Mex, DR, PR, ES, Ch, Sp* ♦ *That guy is a real shithead. He doesn't help anyone.* Ese tipo es pura mierda. No ayuda a nadie.

shitty (vulgar) de mierda (of shit) *L. Am., Sp* ♦ *How can he survive with that shitty (crappy) pension?* ¿Cómo se puede mantener con esa pensión de mierda?

to shock: *I see that the news has shocked you.*
Veo que las noticias te han dejado frío.

to **shock** (surprise) dejar a alguien frío(-a) (helado[-a]) (to leave someone cold [frozen]) *L. Am., Sp* ◆ *The news of the president's death shocked me. La noticia de la muerte del presidente me dejó fría.*

to be **shocked** (stunned; surprised) quedarse frío(-a) (helado[-a]) (to end up cold [frozen]) *L. Am., Sp*; quedarse pasmado(-a) *Mex, Col, Peru, S. Cone, Sp* ◆ *I was shocked when they told me that their son had died.* ◆ *Me quedé helada cuando me dijeron que su hijo había muerto.*

shocking (surprising; used as an intensifier) fuerte (strong) *Mex, Sp* ◆ *They arrested him? How shocking! ¿Lo arrestaron? ¡Qué fuerte!*

Shoo! (Go away!) ¡Zape! *DR, PR, Col* ◆ *Shoo, kitty! Ma'am, take this cat out of here please. I'm allergic. ¡Zape, gato! Señora, llévese a este gato, por favor, que soy alérgico.*

Shoot! (→see also: Darn!) ¡Miércoles! (Wednesday!, euphemism for ¡Mierda!) *L. Am., Sp* ◆ *Shoot! You need money again? ¡Miércoles! ¿Otra vez necesitas dinero?*

to **shoot down** →see: to put down.

shoplifter el/la ratero(-a) (thief) *L. Am.* ◆ *The shoplifter took the jewelry. El ratero se llevó las alhajas.*

short (abrupt, giving short answers only) cortante (cutting) *L. Am., Sp* ◆ *That doctor is very short with his patients. Ese médico es bien cortante con sus pacientes.*

short on looks →see: ugly as hell, (to be) ugly as sin

to **show no mercy** (be ruthless) no dar cuartel (to not give any barracks) *L. Am., Sp;* ◆ *We'll show no mercy to drug dealers. No les vamos a dar cuartel a los narcotraficantes.*

to **show off in front of less fortunate people** comer delante de los pobres (to eat in front of the poor) *Ch, U* ◆ *When Pedro came back from his date, he talked about his girlfriend until I said to him, "Don't show off in front of the less fortunate." Cuando Pedro regresó de su cita, nos hablaba de su novia hasta que le dije, "Deja de comer delante de los pobres."*

to **show one's true colors** (in a negative way) mostrar los dientes (to bare one's teeth) *L. Am., Sp;* quitarse la careta (to take off one's mask) *Mex, ES, S. Cone;* sacar las uñas *Mex, DR, S. Cone, Sp* (RVar *Ec, Peru:* mostrar las uñas) ◆ *The new supervisor didn't take long to show his true colors. El nuevo supervisor no demoró en mostrar los dientes.*

to **show up** asomarse *L. Am.;* descolgarse (to unhang oneself) *Mex, ES;* dejarse caer (to let oneself fall) *Bol, Ch, Sp* ◆ *The architect showed up at the construction site to make sure that all of us were working. El arquitecto se asomó en el lugar de construcción para estar seguro que todos estábamos trabajando.*

to **shrink with fear** (pain, etc.) hacerse un ovillo (una pelota) (to make oneself a little egg [a ball]) *Sp* ◆ *He shrank with fear and didn't want to talk to me. Se hizo un ovillo y no me quiso hablar.*

to **shush** →see: to put a lid on it

Shut up! (Put a lid on it!) ¡Corta! ¡Corta! (Cut! Cut!) *Mex, PR;* ¡Córtala! (Cut it!) *Mex, ES, S. Cone* ◆ *Shut up. Nobody wants to hear any more from you. Córtala. Nadie quiere escucharte más.*

to **shut up** →see: to put a lid on it

to be **shy** (embarrassed) tener pena (to have sorrow) *most of L. Am. (not S. Cone);* cortarse, sentirse cortado(-a) (to cut oneself off, to feel cut off) *S. Cone, Sp* ◆ *Don't be shy, son. No tengas pena, hijo.*

to be **sick and tired** →see: to be fed up

to **sidestep** (avoid; →see also: to steer clear of) salirse por la tangente (to go off on a tangent) *Mex, S. Cone, Sp* ◆ *Every time I ask him something and expect a concrete response, he sidesteps the issue. Cada vez que le pregunto algo y espero una respuesta concreta, me sale por la tangente.*

silly (feather-brained, foolish; →see also: dim-witted) bobo(-a) *most of L. Am., Sp;* casquivano(-a) *L. Am., Sp;* ligero(-a) de cascos (light of head; also, liviano[-a] de cascos) *L. Am., Sp;* gafo(-a) *Ven* ◆ *Don't be silly! Think about what you're going to do. ¡No seas boba! Piensa en lo que vas a hacer.*

simpleton →see: fool

to **sing someone's praises** →see: to praise to the skies

single-minded (obsessive; →see also: nuts) temático(-a) (thematical) *ES, Nic, Peru, Bol* ◆ *You can't talk with that man; he's so single-minded. No se puede hablar con ese hombre; es bien temático.*

sissy el marica (euphemism for maricón) *L. Am., Sp;* el mariquita *Chicano, Mex, Cuba, DR, PR, Col, Ch, Sp* ◆ *Don't be a sissy. No seas mariquita.*

sitter (babysitter) el/la canguro (kangaroo) *Sp* ◆ *I'm the sitter; the lady of the house isn't home. Soy la canguro; la señora no está en casa.*

Six to one, half-dozen to the other. (Both the same.) Lo mismo es Chana que Juana. (Chana is the same as Juana.) *Mex, ES, Nic;* Tanto monta. (So much it adds up.) *Sp* ◆ *Look, we have time to go to the beach or to the mountains. It's six to one and half dozen to the other. Miren, tenemos tiempo para ir a la playa o para ir a las montañas. Lo mismo es Chana que Juana.*

to be **skin and bones** (very skinny; →see also: string bean) salirse por el cuello de la camisa (to go out by the neck of the shirt) *Sp* ◆ *Yesterday I saw Ómar. He's so thin he's just skin and bones. Ayer vi a Ómar. Está tan delgado que parece que va a salirse por el cuello de la camisa.*

to be **skin tight** (fit very well) quedar pintado(-a) (to remain painted) *Mex, Cuba, DR, Col, Peru, S. Cone, Sp* ◆ *This dress fits you skin tight! ¡Este vestido te queda que ni pintado!*

to **skip out on the bill** hacer un sinpa (to do a no-pay, from sin pagar) *Sp* ◆ *Rolando skipped out on the bill at the bar. Rolando hizo un sinpa en el bar.*

skittery (wary) escamado(-a) (scaled, like a fish) *Mex, PR, Col* ◆ *I was skittery (and a bit surprised) about the hugs he gave me. Estaba escamado por el abrazo que me dio.*

to be **sky-high** (very expensive; →see also: to cost an arm and a leg) estar por las nubes (to be in the clouds) *Mex, DR, ES, S. Cone, Sp* ◆ *Wow! Gasoline prices are sky-high now. ¡Caramba! La gasolina está por las nubes ahora.*

to **slack off** achancharse (to become like a pig) *Arg* ◆ *Raquel has slacked off since her divorce. Raquel está totalmente achanchada después de su divorcio.*

slacker 1. (couch potato) flojo(-a) (loose, slack) *Mex, DR, PR, ES, CR, Col, Ch;* aplatanado(-a) *Mex, DR, PR, Sp* (RVAR *Sp:* means sleepy); calzonudo(-a) (in oversized pants) *CR, Col, Ch* ◆ *That boy is a slacker; he never wants to do his homework.* **Ese chico es muy flojo; nunca quiere hacer sus tareas.** **2.** (lazybones) el/la zángano(-a) (drone) *L. Am., Sp;* el/la achanchado(-a) (pigged out) *Arg* ◆ *Fernandina is a slacker. She doesn't do anything, and she waits for someone else to do her job.* **Fernandina es una zángana. No hace nada y espera que los demás hagan su trabajo.** **3.** (lazy bum, useless person; vulgar) el huevón, la huevona (big egg, meaning with large, heavy testicles) (note: in many countries, such as the S. Cone and CR, this word means idiot) *Mex, Cuba, C. Am. (not CR), Ven* ◆ *Rolando is a slacker; he doesn't like to work.* **Rolando es un huevón; no le gusta trabajar.** **4.** (unreliable person) el faltón, la faltona *most of L. Am., Sp;* el/la vago(-a) (drifter) *L. Am. Sp;* el/la pasota (big passer-upper) *Sp* ◆ *Benjamín is a slacker, but he's not a bad person.* **Benjamín es un vago, pero no es mala persona.**

slacker attitude (attitude of indifference) el pasotismo (from the expression Yo paso de todo); el valemadrismo (from the expression me vale madre) *ES, Nic;* valevergismo [vulgar]) *Mex, Col* ◆ *In spite of his slacker attitude, Hugo has a good heart.* **A pesar de su aparente actitud de valemadrismo, Hugo tiene buen corazón.**

to **slam** →see: to put down

to **slam the door on someone** (refuse someone something) dar a alguien con la puerta en las narices (to slam the door on someone's nose) *Mex, ES, S. Cone, Sp* ◆ *I went to the consulate to ask for the documents, but they slammed the door on me.* **Fui al consulado para pedir los documentos, pero me dieron con la puerta en las narices.**

to **slave away** →see: to work like a dog

to **sleep** →see: to crash, to go out like a light, to hit the sack,

to **sleep it off** dormir la mona (to sleep the monkey) *Mex, Cuba, G, Col, Peru, S. Cone, Sp;* dormir la juma *Cuba, ES, CR, Pan, Ven, Peru* ◆ *Go sleep it off; you are really drunk.*

Vete a dormir la mona, que estás muy borracho.

to **sleep like a king** dormir a cuerpo de rey (to sleep like the body of a king) *most of L. Am., Sp* ◆ *In that hotel, you sleep like a king.* **En ese hotel, se duerme a cuerpo de rey.**

to **sleep like a log** dormir como un tronco (to sleep like a trunk) *Mex, S. Cone, Sp;* dormir como un lirón (to sleep like a dormouse) *Mex, DR, S. Cone, Sp* ◆ *After a shower, I'll sleep like a log.* **Después de una ducha, dormiré como un lirón.**

to **sleep on it** (wait and think things over) consultar con la almohada (to consult with the pillow) *L. Am., Sp* ◆ *Before making a decision, I'm going to sleep on it.* **Antes de tomar una decisión, voy a consultar con la almohada.**

sleepless night (→see also: to spend a sleepless night) la noche toledana (Toledo night) *Sp* ◆ *I had a sleepless night; I didn't feel well.* **Pasé una noche toledana; no me sentía bien.**

sleepyhead el dormilón, la dormilona *L. Am., Sp* ◆ *It's already ten o'clock in the morning? What a sleepyhead I am!* **¿Son las diez de la mañana ya? ¡Qué dormilón!**

slew →see: tons

to **sling the bull** (launch into a spiel, start a long story) lanzar un rollo (to throw a roll) *Mex, ES, Col, Peru;* echar vaina (to throw husk, sheath) *DR, Ven* ◆ *I saw my friend Elena at the store and she started to sling the bull.* **Vi a mi amiga Elena en la tienda y empezó a lanzar el mismo rollo.**

to **slip up** →see: to blow it

slob 1. (slovenly person) el/la greñudo(-a) *Mex, DR, ES, Col* ◆ *He's a slob; he never combs his hair.* **Es un greñudo; nunca se peina.** **2.** (person who is dirty or has loose morals) el/la guarro(-a) (pig, swine) *Sp;* el/la cochino(-a) (pig, swine) *L. Am., Sp* ◆ *Don't bring that gang of slobs home again. Look how they left everything after the party.* **No traigas más a esa panda de guarros a casa. Mira cómo lo han dejado todo después de la fiesta.**

sloppy →see: messed up

slouch →see: slacker

to be **slow** (dim-witted) ser un poste (to be a post) *Sp* ♦ *Margarita is a bit slow; however, she covers it up pretty well.* **Margarita es un poste; sin embargo, lo disimula bien.**

to be **slow** (dull) estar espeso(-a) (to be thick) *Sp* ♦ *I'm very slow today.* **Estoy muy espeso hoy.**

slowpoke (slow person) la tortuga (turtle) *Mex, DR, ES, Col* ♦ *Every time we go out with Beatriz we're late because she's a slowpoke.* **Siempre que salimos con Beatriz llegamos tarde porque es una tortuga.**

to **slug it out** →see: to beat someone up, to have a blowup, to hit where it hurts

slums (slang) las poblaciones callampas (mushroom populations) *Ch* ♦ *The slums surrounding the capital have increased in the last few years.* **Las poblaciones callampas alrededor de la capital han aumentado en los últimos años.**

slut (vulgar; →see also: floozie) la puta (whore) *Cuba, DR, PR, Col*; el cuero (skin, leather) *Cuba, DR, PR, Col*; la furcia *Sp* ♦ *At school Martica has a reputation for being a slut.* **En la escuela Martica tiene fama de cuero.**

smack **1.** (hard hit) la trompada *most of L. Am.*; el trompazo *most of L. Am., Sp*; la hostia (Host; vulgar with religious reference) *Sp* ♦ *As he left the dance club someone gave him a smack.* **A la salida de la discoteca le dieron una trompada. 2.** (blow with the hand) el manotazo *L. Am., Sp* ♦ *My mother smacked me because I spoke back rudely.* **Mi madre me dio un manotazo porque le contesté de mala manera. 3.** (hit on the head) el cachimbazo *G, ES, Nic, CR*; el cocotazo (the coco, coconut) *Chicano, Cuba, DR, PR, Col* ♦ *Emilio climbed up the ladder and smacked himself on the head.* **Emilio se subió a la escalera y se dio un cachimbazo. 4.** (punch; smackeroo) el sopapo *L. Am., Sp*; el estatequieto (be quiet) *Mex, ES, Peru;* el boyo *Arg, U* ♦ *His cousin gave Lalo a smack ("a reason to be quiet") because he wouldn't leave her alone.* **Su prima le dio un estatequieto a Lalo porque no dejaba de molestarla.**

smart aleck →see: know-it-all

a smart cookie (→see also: to be a whiz) el listón, la listona (big clever) *Mex, Col* ♦ *Juan is a real smart cookie.* **Juan es un listón.**

to be a **smartass** (outsmart oneself, try unsucessfully to show oneself to be smarter than others) pasarse de listo(-a) (vivo[-a]) (to pass oneself as clever, be overly clever) *L. Am., Sp* ♦ *You were a real smartass!* **¡Te pasaste de listo!**

Smarten up. (Behave yourself.) Recógete. (Pick yourself up.) *Mex, PR, Col;* Ubícate. (Find yourself.) *Mex, DR, Col, Peru, S. Cone* ♦ *Smarten up, son, and concentrate on your studies.* **Recógete, hijo, y ponte a estudiar.**

smarts (intelligence) la chispa (spark) *Mex, DR, ES, CR, Col* ♦ *Julio has the smarts (for business).* **Julio tiene chispa (para los negocios).**

smashed →see: to be wasted

to **smoke like a chimney** fumar como (una) chimenea *Mex, S. Cone, Sp;* fumar como chacuaco (to smoke like a furnace or a cigarette butt) *Mex;* fumar como murciélago (to smoke like a bat) *ES, DR, PR, S. Cone;* fumar como un carretero (to smoke like a trucker) *Sp* ♦ *Manuel Antonio smokes like a chimney.* **Manuel Antonio fuma como una chimenea.**

to **smoke pot** (marijuana, grass, weed; →see also: grass, joint) motearse *Mex, PR* ♦ *When I got to their house, everyone was smoking pot.* **Cuando llegué a su casa, todos estaban moteándose.**

to **smooch** (→see also: to make out) besuquearse *C. Am., DR, PR, S. Cone, Sp* ♦ *My boyfriend and I love to smooch.* **A mi novio y yo nos encanta besuquearnos.**

smooches los besotes (big sloppy kisses) *Mex, C. Am.* ♦ *I don't like my aunt's smooches.* **No me gustan los besotes de mi tía.**

smooching (repeated kissing) el besuqueo *L. Am., Sp* ♦ *Elisa was smooching with her boyfriend when her father came in.* **Elisa estaba a los besuqueos con su novio cuando llegó su padre.**

to **smooth over** (take away the importance of something that one thinks was exaggerated) quitar hierro (to take away iron) *Sp* ♦ *I've tried to talk to him to smooth over the problem that had come up (for you).* **He intentado hablar con él para quitar hierro al problema que os había surgido.**

snafu →see: screw-up

to be a **snake in the grass** tirar la piedra y esconder la mano (to throw the stone and hide one's hand) *L. Am., Sp* ♦ *She's a snake in the grass. You can't trust her.* Es una persona de las que tira la piedra y esconde la mano. No te puedes fiar de ella.

snap →see: to be a piece of cake

to **snap** →see: to lose it

to **sneak out the back door** (get out of a place or business in a disgraceful way) salir por la ventana (to take off through the window) *Sp* ♦ *Because you keep acting like that, you will end up sneaking out the back door.* Como sigan comportándose así, van a salir por la ventana.

to **snivel** lloriquear *L. Am., Sp;* moquiar *Mex, ES, U, Arg* ♦ *The girl's sniveling again.* La niña ya está moquiando otra vez.

snob (→see also: stuck-up) **1.** (stuck-up person with a big ego) el/la esnob *L. Am., Sp* el/la alzado(-a) (raised up) *Mex, U, Arg;* el/la agrandado(-a) (made larger) *ES, U, Arg;* el/la acartonado(-a) (cardboard-like) *Arg* ♦ *Esmeralda is a snob; she doesn't like anybody.* Esmeralda es una alzada; no le viene nadie bien. **2.** (ridiculous person; show-off) el/la fantoche(-a) (puppet) *Mex, DR, ES, CR, Sp* ♦ *That young guy is so stuck-up; he thinks he's hot stuff.* Ese joven es un fantoche; se cree la gran cosa.

snobbish →see: stuck-up

snooty →see: stuck-up

to be a **snooze** →see: to be a drag

to be **so busy you don't have time to sneeze** estar tan ocupada que no tiene tiempo ni para rascarse (to not have time even to scratch oneself) *Mex, DR, ES, U, Sp;* estar más liado(-a) que la pata de un romano (de una momia) (to be more entangled than the foot of a Roman [of a mummy]) *Sp* ♦ *Why don't you come visit us? —I can't. I'm studying for exams, and I'm so busy that I don't even have time to sneeze.* ¿Por qué no vienes a visitarnos? –No puedo. Estoy preparando exámenes, y estoy tan ocupada que no tengo tiempo ni para rascarme.

so much the better miel sobre hojuelas (honey on pastries, expression meaning that one thing goes very well with another,

adding to its attractiveness) *Mex, DR, Sp* ♦ *If this product sells in other countries also, well, so much the better.* Si este producto se vende en otros países también, pues miel sobre hojuelas.

So there! (in a discussion) ¡Toma! *Sp* ♦ *So there! I told you, your father was right.* ¡Toma! Te lo dije, tu padre tenía razón.

so-and-so 1. (to refer to someone you don't know), John or Jane Doe el/la fulano(-a), fulano(-a) de tal *L. Am., Sp;* el/la menda *Sp* ♦ *The (unknown) woman beside you is the professor's sister.* La fulana que está a tu lado es la hermana del profesor. **2.** (unknown person; pejorative) el/la carajo(-a) (male organ) *DR, ES, Nic, CR, Col* (RVar *ES*: used like tonto but can be used for unknown person without being too strong) ♦ *Who's that guy (girl) going that way?* ¿Quién es ese carajo (esa caraja) que va por allá? **3.** (extension of fulano, mengano, zutano) mandujano *Mex* ♦ *In addition to Tom, Dick, and Harry, a whole other group of so-and-sos we didn't know came.* Además de fulano, mengano y zutano, llegaron mandujano y su familia.

so-and-so and his brothers (Tom, Dick, and Harry; expression used to name unknown people) fulano, mengano y zutano *L. Am., Sp* ♦ *They invited Pedro to dinner and it turns out he came with so-and-so and his brothers.* Invitaron a Pedro a cenar y resulta que vino con otro fulano, mengano y zutano.

soap opera la telenovela (television novel, slang) *L. Am.;* la teleculebra (tele-snake, slang) *Mex, ES, Ven;* el culebrón (big snake, slang) *CR, Ven, Bol, Ch, Arg, Sp* ♦ *I am completely hooked on the Mexican soap opera at four o'clock in the afternoon.* Estoy totalmente enganchado al culebrón mexicano de las cuatro de la tarde.

SOB (→see also: son of a bitch) mal nacido(-a) (badly born, meaning bastard) *L. Am., Sp;* el/la hijo(-a) de su (somewhat vulgar, euphemism for hijo[-a] de su puta madre) *most of L. Am., Sp;* cabrón, cabrona (big goat, vulgar) *Mex, Cuba, PR, C. Am., Col, Bol, Ch, Sp* ♦ *That guy is an SOB.* Ese tipo es un hijo de su.

softie (→see also: pushover) blandengue (soft and squishy) *Mex, DR, Arg, Sp* ♦ *You can't be such a softie when you want to defend your position; one must remain firm.* No se puede ser tan blandengue cuando se defiende una postura; uno debe mantenerse firme.

solid as a rock (strong) firme como el roble (firm as the oak) *Mex, S. Cone, Sp* ♦ *This table is solid as a rock. You can climb on it and it won't break.* Esta mesa es firme como un roble. Puedes subir encima y no se rompe.

son of a bitch (bitch; all vulgar →see also: SOB) el/la hijo(-a) de la gran puta (son [daughter] of the big whore) *L. Am., Sp*; el/la hijo(-a) de puta (son [daughter] of a whore) *L. Am., Sp* (RVar *L. Am.*: also, hijueputa; *Sp*: also, hijoputa; vulgar); el cabrón, la cabrona (big goat) *most of L. Am. (not S. Cone)*; el/la hijo(-a) de la chingada (son [daughter] of the violated woman) *Mex, C. Am.*; la concha de su madre (your mother's shell, referring to female organ; vulgar, as an insult or term of endearment to friend or foe) *S. Cone* ♦ *Let's not speak to that son of a bitch.* No le hablemos a ese cabrón.

son of a gun tal por cual (such for which) *L. Am.*; hijo de su (son of his "immoral" mother) *L. Am* ♦ *Lorenzo is a son of a gun.* Lorenzo es un tal por cual.

sooner or later (slang) a la corta o a la larga (in the short or the long) *L. Am., Sp* ♦ *Sooner or later they will know the truth.* A la corta o a la larga sabrán la verdad.

sopping wet (drenched) hecho(-a) una sopa (made a soup) *L. Am., Sp* ♦ *Come inside, dear. You're sopping wet.* Ven adentro, m'ija. Estás hecha una sopa.

so-so 1. (blah, no great shakes, mediocre) ni muy muy ni tan tan (not very very nor so so) *Mex, DR, ES, Nic, Col, U, Arg*; sin chiste (without joke) *Mex, Col, Peru, Bol*; ni fu ni fa *L. Am., Sp*; pasable (passable) *Mex, S. Cone* ♦ *Did you like the Luis Miguel concert? —It was so-so—the same as last year.* ¿Te gustó el concierto de Luis Miguel? —Ni fu ni fa, fue idéntico al del año pasado. **2.** (not all that great) dos que tres (two that three) *Mex, G, ES*; de tres al cuarto (from three to fourth) *Sp* ♦ *Rogelio, how was the concert? —So-so.*

Rogelio, ¿cómo fue el concierto? —Dos que tres.

to be so-so (blah, unappetizing) no tener chiste (to not have any joke) *Mex, ES, Col, Peru, Bol* ♦ *That novel is just so-so.* ♦ *Esa novela no tiene chiste.*

soul mate (spouse, sweetheart [male or female]) la media naranja (half orange) *L. Am., Sp* ♦ *Where's your soul mate?* ¿Dónde está tu media naranja?

to **sound someone or something out** catar el melón (to inspect the melon) *Sp* ♦ *I hope there will be time to sound things out.* Ojalá haya tiempo suficiente para catar el melón.

Soup's on! (Dig in! Eat!) ¡Llégale a la papa! (Go to the potato!) *Mex, Col* ♦ *Time to eat, guys! Soup's on!* ¡A comer, muchachos! ¡Lléguenle a la papa!

sourpuss 1. (disagreeable [person]) ácido(-a) (acidic) *PR, G, Col, Sp* ♦ *What a sourpuss you are!* ¡Qué ácida eres! **2.** (unpleasant or annoyed appearance) el/la cara de limón (lemon face) *Mex, ES* ♦ *Marieta always looks like a sourpuss.* Marieta siempre anda con cara de limón.

to be a sourpuss (bitter or disagreeable person; with an annoyed appearance) pasar muchas navidades y sin nochebuena (to have a lot of Christmases with no Christmas Eve celebrations) *PR, Col* ♦ *Poor Ramona. She's such a sourpuss.* Pobre Ramona. Ha pasado muchas navidades y sin nochebuena.

space cadet (airhead, someone disorganized and forgetful; unreliable person →see also: to be an airhead, to be spaced out, flake) el/la volador(a) (flyer, swinger) *U, Arg*; el/la cantamañanas *Sp* ♦ *Why isn't dinner ready? —You know Alba. She's a space cadet and forgot most of the ingredients.* ¿Por qué no está lista la cena? —Ya conoces a Alba. Es una voladora y se olvidó de la mayoría de los ingredientes.

spaced out →see: to be spaced out, mixed up, out of it

to be **spaced out** (detached) estar en otra (to be on another, with the idea of onda or dimensión understood) *Mex, S. Cone* ♦ *Shall we go out on the town today? —No, thanks, I'm a little spaced out. I have a lot to do.* ¿Salimos *de parranda hoy? —No, gracias, estoy en otra. Tengo mucho que hacer.*

to **spare no effort in order to** hacer mil maromas para... (to do a thousand acrobatic tricks in order to . . .) *most of L. Am., Sp* ◆ *I have spared no effort to be able to see you.* He hecho mil maromas para verte.

to **speak plainly** hablar en cristiano (to talk in Christian) *L. Am., Sp* ◆ *Speak plainly, man, so we can understand you.* Habla en cristiano, hombre, para que te entendamos.

to **speed it up** →see: to step on it

to be **spellbound** estar embelesado(-a) (to be enthralled) *L. Am., Sp;* star todo(-a) derretido(-a) (to be all melted) *most of L. Am.* ◆ *Carmen is spellbound with the visit of her grandchildren.* Carmen está toda derretida con la visita de sus nietos.

to **spend a night counting sheep** pasar la noche contando estrellas (cabritos) (to spend the night counting stars [little goats]) *Mex, ES* ◆ *I couldn't sleep; I spent the night counting sheep.* No pude dormir; pasé la noche contando estrellas.

to **spend a sleepless night** (→see also: to not sleep a wink) pasar la noche en vela (to spend the night on watch) *L. Am., Sp;* pasar la noche en blanco (claro) (to spend the night blank [clear]) *Mex, DR, PR, S. Cone, Sp;* pasar una noche toledana (to spend a Toledo night) *Sp* ◆ *We spent a sleepless night taking care of the baby.* Pasamos la noche en vela cuidando al bebé.

to **spend money like a drunken sailor** →see: to blow the works

spiel (long story, monologue, tale [of woe]) el rollo (roll) *Mex, C. Am., Col, Ven, Peru, Ch, Sp;* la parrafada (paragraph) *Sp* ◆ *I don't open the door to anybody because door-to-door salesmen have such incredible spiels.* Yo no abro la puerta a nadie porque los vendedores a domicilio tienen un rollo bárbaro.

to **spill the beans** 1. (to reveal; →see also: Open up., to spit it out, to squeal) destaparse (to uncork oneself) *L. Am.;* echar de cabeza (to turn upside down) *Mex;* soltar la lengua (to loosen the tongue) *DR, S. Cone* ◆ *Spill the beans, honey. What happened?* Destápate, cariño. ¿Qué pasó? 2. (implicate someone in something; →see also: to squeal) soltar la cuerda (to let go of or

loosen the cord) *Mex, Sp* ◆ *The guy they arrested spilled the beans, and the police found the rest of the criminals.* El detenido soltó la cuerda, y la policía encontró el resto de los delincuentes.

to **spit it out** (→see also: to spill the beans) destaparse (to uncork oneself) *L. Am;* despegar la boca (to unstick the mouth) *Mex, Sp;* desembuchar (to disgorge, like desahogar) *Mex, ES, Ch* ◆ *Hurry up. Spit it out and tell us the truth.* Apúrate. Despega la boca y dinos la verdad.

to be the **spitting image of someone** ser el vivo retrato de alguien (to be the living portrait of someone) *L. Am., Sp;* ser la fiel estampa de alguien (to be the faithful print of someone) *L. Am., Sp;* ser la viva (fiel) imagen de alguien (to be the live [faithful] image of someone) *L. Am., Sp* ◆ *Enrique is the spitting image of his great-uncle.* Enrique es el vivo retrato de su tío abuelo.

to **split** →see: to take off

to **split hairs** (pay attention to unimportant things instead of the bigger issue) reparar en migajas (pelillos) (to notice crumbs [small hairs]) *Sp* ◆ *The director split hairs, without paying any attention to more important things.* El director reparó en migajas, sin prestar atención a cosas más importantes.

spoiled brat (playboy; →see also: rich kid) el junior *Mex, Col* ◆ *The spoiled brat of the house has no scruples.* El junior de la casa no tiene escrúpulos.

sponge →see: mooch

to **sponge** →see: to mooch

to **spoof** →see: to joke around, to put someone on

to **spoon-feed something to someone** meter a alguien con cuchara una cosa *Mex, Sp* ◆ *We spoon-fed the information we had to him.* Le metimos con cuchara la información que teníamos.

to **spread a rumor** contar un chisme *L. Am., Sp;* pasar la bola (to pass the ball) *Cuba, DR, G, ES, CR, U, Arg* ◆ *Alfredo saw Silvia and Rodolfo hugging and spread the rumor to all their friends.* Alfredo vio a Silvia y Rodolfo abrazados y pasó la bola a todos sus amigos.

spy (informer) el/la oreja (ear) *Mex, ES, Nic* ◆ *Don't talk. Here comes the spy (tattle-tale).* No hablen. Aquí viene la oreja.

to **squabble** →see: to be at odds, to be like oil and water, to have a blowup

to **square things with someone** cuadrar con alguien *Mex, Cuba, Col* ◆ *We squared things with the boss to leave early today.* Cuadramos con el jefe para salir temprano hoy.

squat →see: Diddly squat, Zip.

to **squeal** (inform; →see also: to spill the beans) cantar (to sing) *L. Am., Sp;* soplar (to blow) *L. Am., Sp ;* chillar *Chicano, Mex, G, Col, U* ◆ *No matter how much they beat him, he didn't squeal.* Por más que lo golpearon no cantó.

stacked (woman) →see: babe, busty gal, hot, hot number

stag party la despedida de soltero (sending off of the single man) *L. Am., Sp* ◆ *The groom's friends will have a stag party for him at the club.* Los amigos del novio le harán una despedida de soltero en el club.

to **stake one's life on someone** (vouch for someone) meter las manos al fuego por alguien (to put one's hands in the fire for someone) *L. Am., Sp* ◆ *Yolanda is a good friend. I stake my life on her.* Yolanda es una buena amiga. Meto las manos al fuego por ella.

to **stand out** (do something unusual; →see also: to outdo oneself, to stick out like a sore thumb, to take the cake) destacarse *L. Am., Sp;* lucirse (to shine) *Mex, Peru, U* ◆ *You stood out (were outstanding).* Te luciste.

to **stand out from the crowd** →see: to be a whiz

to **stand (someone) up** (ditch, jilt) dejar plantado(-a) (to leave [someone] planted) *L. Am., Sp ;* dar (un) plantón (also, plante) (to give [a] planting) *L. Am., Sp;* dar calabazas (ayotes) (to give pumpkins [squash]) *L. Am., Sp;* dejar colgado(-a) (to leave hung, suspended) *Mex, ES, U, Arg, Sp ;* dejar con los churquitos (colochos) hechos (to leave [someone] with their curls done) *C. Am., Caribbean;* tirar bomba (to throw a bomb) *Caribbean* ◆ *Don't stand me up.* No me dejes plantada.

to **stand up to** (stand one's ground, oppose, defy, resist) plantar cara a alguien (to plant one's face at someone) *DR, PR, Sp* ◆ *The older woman managed to stand up to the pickpocket so that he did not steal her purse.* La señora mayor logró plantar cara al carterista de manera que no le robó el bolso.

standoffish →see: stuck-up

star-crossed (out of luck, with bad luck; →see also: to be out of luck, to be unlucky) estrellado(-a) (seeing stars) *Mex, ES, S. Cone* ◆ *Some people are born with a lucky star and some are born star-crossed (with bad luck).* Unos nacen con estrella y otros estrellados.

stark raving mad →see: mad as a hatter

starving to death muerto(-a) de hambre (dead of hunger) *L. Am., Sp* ◆ *When are we going to eat? I'm starving to death.* ¿Cuándo vamos a comer? Estoy muerta de hambre.

to **stay out (or up) late at night** trasnochar (to cross the night) *L. Am., Sp* ◆ *I stayed out late all week, but tonight I'm going to go to sleep early.* Trasnoché toda la semana, pero hoy voy a acostarme temprano.

to **stay out of harm's way** (participate in or witness something but avoid exposing oneself to danger) mirar (ver) los toros desde la barrera (to look at [see] the bulls from behind the barrier) *most of L. Am., Sp* ◆ *During the Second World War, we stayed out of harm's way (remained on the sidelines).* Durante la Segunda Guerra Mundial, estuvimos viendo los toros desde la barrera.

a **steal** (cheap) casi regalado(-a) *L. Am., Sp;* tirado(-a) (thrown away, used with ser or estar) *U, Arg, Sp* ◆ *Buy these pure wool sweaters; they're a steal.* Compra estos suéteres de pura lana; están tirados.

to **steal** →see: to lift, to make a hit, to swipe, to take someone to the cleaners

to **steal someone's thunder** 1. (taking the limelight) robar el show (to steal the show) *Mex, ES, S. Cone* ◆ *You always want to steal my thunder.* Tú siempre quieres robarme el show. 2. (telling a story another began) destripar a alguien el cuento (to remove the stuffing or guts of the story from someone) *Sp* ◆ *You're stealing my thunder, honey. Let me talk.* Me estás destripando el cuento, mi amor. Déjame hablar.

steamed (mad) bravo(-a) *L. Am., Sp;* cabreado(-a) *Mex, CR, Col, Sp;* encabronado(-a) *Mex, PR, C. Am., many S. Am. countries;* enchichado(-a) *Mex, Col, U;* fúrico(-a) *Mex* ◆ *Why are you so steamed?* ◆ *¿Por qué andas tan brava?*

to be **steamed** (→see also: to be hopping mad, to get pissed off; hot under the collar, to lose it) sulfurarse (to get sulfured) *L. Am., Sp;* llevarse (a alguien) el diablo (to be taken by the devil) *Mex, S. Cone;* echar chispas (to throw off sparks) *Mex, DR, ES, Ch, Sp;* echar humo (to throw off steam or smoke) *Mex, DR, ES, Sp;* echar lumbre (to throw off fire) *Mex, ES, Sp;* echar rayos (to throw off lightning rays) *Mex, ES, Sp;* echar fuego por los ojos (to be fiery-eyed) *Mex, U, Sp;* llevarse (a alguien) el demonio (to be taken by the devil or demon) *Mex, Sp;* subírsele a alguien el humo a las narices (a la cabeza) (to have smoke rising up to one's nostrils [head]) *CR, Sp;* subírsele la mostaza (to have the mustard rise up) *Peru, Sp* ◆ *I was steamed when I found out the truth. Estaba echando chispas cuando supe la verdad.*

to be **steaming hot** (people) sancocharse *Mex, DR, PR, Col, Ch* ◆ *I'm steaming hot. Open the windows! Me estoy sancochando del calor. ¡Abran las ventanas!*

to **steer clear of** (excuse oneself, avoid or get out of; get rid of) zafarse de *L. Am.;* darle (un) esquinazo a alguien (to hit someone with a corner) *Arg, Sp* ◆ *Steer clear of Fernando. It's not good for you to get mixed up with that guy. Záfate de Fernando, que no te conviene ese tipo.*

to **step on it** 1. (get a move on) picarle (to poke at it) *Mex, ES, Col;* volarle (to fly it) *Mex, Col;* tupirle (to compact it) *Mex* ◆ *Step on it! We have to get a move on so we can finish quickly. ¡Pícale! Hay que picarle duro para que terminemos ligero.* 2. (step on the gas) meterle *Mex, ES, Col;* meter cuarta (to put fourth [gear]) *Mex, Col;* meterle la chancla al pedal (to put the sandal on the pedal) *Mex, Col;* meterle velocidad (to put in speed) *Mex* ◆ *Step on it or we'll get there late. Mete cuarta o llegaremos tarde.*

to **stick one's nose into everything** (→see also: busybody) meter las narices (el hocico) en todo (to stick your nose [snout] into everything) *L. Am., Sp* ◆ *I don't know why you stick your nose into everything. No entiendo por qué metes las naricas en todo.*

to **stick out like a sore thumb** (call attention to oneself and look ridiculous) dar la nota alta (to give the high note) *DR, Nic, Ch;* dar la nota (to give the note) *Bol, U, Arg, Sp;* cantar como una almeja (to sing like a clam) *Sp;* dar el cante (to give flamenco singing) *Sp* ◆ *She stuck out like a sore thumb with that outlandish dress. Cantaba como una almeja con ese vestido estrafalario.*

to **stick someone with something** (force on someone) enjaretar *Mex, U, Arg* ◆ *Juan stuck me with a horrible job. Juan me enjaretó un trabajo horrible.*

to **stick to one's guns** (persist in an opinion or in doing something) seguir/mantenerse en sus trece (to keep in one's thirteen) *L. Am, Sp* ◆ *Despite all advice, María Herminia sticks to her guns and keeps going out with Julián. A pesar de todos los consejos, María Herminia sigue en sus trece y sale con Julián.*

stiffs (the dead) los tiesos (stiffs) *Mex, ES, Col, Ec* ◆ *Stiffs don't talk. Los tiesos no hablan.*

to **stifle it** →see: to put a lid on it

stingy (tight-fisted) agarrado(-a) (holding on [to money]) *most of L. Am., Sp;* codo(-a) (elbow) *Chicano, Mex, DR, PR, G, Hond, ES, Nic;* pichicato(-a) (from the Italian "pizzicato," pinch) *Mex, Nic;* poco espléndido(-a) (not very splendid) *DR, ES, Ven, Sp;* más duro(-a) que el cemento (harder than cement) *PR;* duro(-a) (hard) *Cuba, ES, Pan, Peru* ◆ *He refused to take me to dinner because he's very stingy. No me quiso llevar a cenar porque es bien agarrado.*

to be **stingy** (miserly, especially with food) no comer un huevo por no perder la cáscara (to not eat an egg so as not to lose or waste the shell) *Mex, ES, Peru, U, Arg ;* no comer plátano por no tirar la cáscara (to not eat a banana so as not to throw out the peel) *Mex* ◆ *Your in-laws are stingy. Tus suegros no comen plátano en su casa, por no tirar la cáscara.*

stink (problem) el pedo (fart, vulgar) *Chicano, Mex, G, Hond, ES, Ven* ◆ *After the game, there was a big stink. Después del partido, se armó un gran pedo.*

to **stir up trouble** →see: to upset the applecart

stogie (cigar) la breva *Mex, Cuba, Pan, Peru* ◆ *Did you buy a stogie? ¿Compraste una breva?*

stomping grounds →see: digs

to be **stone deaf** ser un poste (to be a post) *Sp* ◆ *Margarita is stone deaf; however, she covers it up pretty well. Margarita es un poste; sin embargo, lo disimula bien.*

stoned (→see also: to be plastered, to be spaced out, to be wasted; high) fuera de base (de órbita) (off base [out of orbit]) *Mex, Col;* tronado(-a) (blasted) *Mex;* volado(-a) (blown up high or flown away) *Ch* ◆ *Patricio was stoned for a long time after using so much cocaine. Patricio estuvo fuera de órbita por mucho tiempo después de consumir tanta cocaína.*

stoned on marijuana grifo(-a) *Mex, CR, Ec* ◆ *Don't pay attention to him. He's stoned (on marijuana). No le hagas caso. Está grifo.*

to be **stood up** (stuck somewhere for a while) estar de plantón (to be planted) *Mex, ES, Ch, U, Sp;* estar colgado(-a) (to be hung, suspended) *Mex, ES, U, Arg, Sp;* quedarse con los crespos hechos (to be left with one's curls made) *ES, Peru, Bol, Ch;* quedar como semáforo (to wind up like a traffic light) *Nic* ◆ *Last night I was stood up. Last night me quedé con los crespos hechos.*

stool pigeon (→see also: fink) el sapo (frog, toad; used like soplón) *Nic, CR, Col, Ven, Peru, Ec, Ch* ◆ *He's a stool pigeon. He tells everything. Es un sapo. Todo lo cuenta.*

to **stop in one's tracks** pararse en seco (to stop oneself dry) *Mex, ES, Col, Ch, U* ◆ *When Yoli saw me, she stopped in her tracks. Cuando Yoli me vio, se paró en seco.*

to **stop someone cold** parar en seco (to stop someone dry) *Mex, ES, Col, Ch, U* ◆ *Arturo tried to shout at me, and I stopped him cold. Arturo intentó gritarme, y lo paré en seco.*

to **stop telling stories** (cut the nonsense) dejarse de cuentos (to leave off with the stories) *L. Am., Sp* ◆ *Stop telling stories (tall tales). Déjate de cuentos.*

Stop the foolishness. Déjate de chiquilladas. (Stop the childish behavior.) *ES, U, Arg, Sp* ◆ *Stop the foolishness. Déjate de cuentos.*

Stop tooting your own horn. (Stop bragging.) Deja de decir fanfarronadas. *Mex*

straight out (point-blank, directly) a quema ropa (at burning of clothing) *L. Am., Sp* ◆ *When I saw him, I gave him the news straight out. Cuando lo vi, le di las noticias a quema ropa.*

to **strain the noggin** →see: to rack one's brain

streak (run, period of time) la racha *L. Am., Sp* ◆ *We've had a bad streak, but I think today we're going to win the game. Hemos pasado una mala racha, pero creo que hoy vamos a ganar el partido.*

streetwalker →see: hooker, slut

to **stress someone out** poner a alguien los nervios de punta (to make someone's nerves stand up) *L. Am., Sp* ◆ *The message stressed me out. El mensaje me puso los nervios de punta.*

to be **stressed out** (have one's nerves on edge; →see also: to be on edge) tener los nervios de punta (to have one's nerves standing) *L. Am., Sp;* estar con el corazón en un puño (to be with one's heart in a fist) *most of L. Am., Sp* ◆ *She hasn't had news of her family, and she's all stressed out. Ella no ha tenido noticias de su familia, y tiene los nervios de punta.*

stretch (exaggeration) la jalada (stretch, pull) *Mex* ◆ *What a stretch! Son puras jaladas.*

to **strike it rich** (→see also: to make a killing) encontrar una mina (de oro) (to find a [gold]mine, a way to live or get rich without working much) *Mex, ES, Ch, Sp;* forrarse (to make a lining for oneself, referring to lined pockets) *DR, Nic, Sp* ◆ *That man struck it rich, and he lives the high life. Ese hombre encontró una mina de oro y se da la gran vida.*

to **strike out with the opposite sex** (not find anyone to pick up) no comerse una rosca (to not eat a doughnut) *Sp* ◆ *I went to the disco but I struck out. Fui a la discoteca pero no me comí una rosca.*

string bean 1. (skinny person) el palo de escoba (broomstick) *L. Am.;* el bacalao (codfish) *Florida, PR, Col, U* ◆ *The professor is so skinny. He's a string bean.* **Es tan flaco el profesor. Es un palo de escoba.** 2. (very tall) palancón, palancona (from palanca, a lever or stick) *most of L. Am., Sp;* más largo(-a) que la esperanza del pobre (longer than the hope of the poor person) *PR* ◆ *Poor Vicenta is such a string bean that she can't find pants that fit her.* **Pobre Vicenta es tan palancona que no encuentra pantalones que le queden bien.**

to **string someone along** dar carrete a alguien (to give someone a reel, coil) *Sp* ◆ *She strings him along and keeps talking to him, but he says he has to go to work.* **Ella le da carrete y le sigue hablando, pero él le dice que tiene que ir a trabajar.**

to be **strong as an ox** estar hecho(-a) un mulo (to be made into a mule) *Sp* ◆ *The exercises worked for you; you're strong as an ox.* **Los ejercicios te han sentado; estás hecho un mulo.**

strong-willed (determined and forceful) de rompe y rasga (of break and tear) *parts of L. Am., Sp* ◆ *That woman is really strong-willed. How decisive she is!* **Esa mujer es de rompe y rasga. ¡Qué decidida!**

strung out →see: to be on edge, nervous as a cat

to **strut one's stuff** balconearse (to balcony oneself, used mainly for women) *Mex* ◆ *That chick put on a miniskirt because she loves to strut her stuff.* **Esa chica se puso una minifalda porque le gusta balconearse.**

stuck pegado(-a) (glued) *L.Am.;* clavado(-a) (nailed) *Mex, Col, U, Arg* ◆ *I'm stuck here, cooking.* **Estoy clavada aquí, cocinando.**

to be **stuck to your seat** (stay somewhere for a long time; →see also: to settle in) pegársele a alguien la silla (el asiento) (to have the seat stuck to one) *U, Sp* ◆ *Help me with the housecleaning. Are you stuck to your seat or what?* **Ayúdame con la limpieza de la casa. ¿Acaso se te ha pegado el asiento?**

stuck-up 1. (snobbish, snooty) creído(-a) (believed) *L. Am., Sp;* fantasioso(-a) *L. Am., Sp;* esnob *L. Am., Sp;* fufurufo(-a) *most of L. Am. (not Peru, Bol, Ch, U);* burguesito(-a) (bourgeois) *Mex, G, Col, U, Arg;* estirado(-a) (stretched out) *ES, Nic, CR, Col, Peru, S. Cone, Sp;* copetudo(-a) (crested, referring to the copete, crest or crown) *ES, S. Cone;* sobrado(-a) (more than enough, excessive) *Peru, Ch;* pituco(-a) *S. Cone;* engrupido(-a) (grouped up) *U, Arg* ◆ *Your sister is very stuck-up, and she doesn't even speak to me at school.* **Tu hermana es muy creída, y ni siquiera me habla en el colegio.** 2. (affected, pretentious) popoff (popis) *Mex, DR;* siútico(-a) *Ch;* finolis *Sp* ◆ *That guy is very stuck-up and I don't like to go out with him.* **Ese chico es muy popoff y no me gusta salir con él.**

to be **stuck-up** 1. (feel superior [without reason], be proud or pretentious) creerse (to believe oneself) *L. Am., Sp* ◆ *Amalia se cree mucho y por eso no me cae bien.* **Amalia is stuck-up and that's why I don't like her.** 2. (hard to deal with, uppity, or arrogant) parecer que se ha tragado un palo de escoba (to look like one has swallowed a broomstick) *Mex, Sp* ◆ *The receptionist who works there looks very stuck-up. How arrogant!* **La recepcionista que trabaja allí parece que se ha tragado un palo de escoba. ¡Qué arrogante!**

stud (guy who flirts and is successful with women; →see also: hot number, hunk) el castigador (punisher) *Chicano, Mex, DR, PR, Col;* el ligón *Col, Sp* ◆ *Juan is a stud; he has me going crazy.* **Juan es un castigador; me tiene loca.**

to **study hard** →see: to cram

stuff →see: junk, trinkets

to **stuff one's face** →see: to feed one's face, to pig out, to stuff oneself, to wolf down

to **stuff oneself** (with food; →see also: to pig out) forrarse (to make a lining for oneself) *ES, Nic, Sp* ◆ *Enrique stuffed himself with chicken in mole sauce at lunch.* **Enrique se forró de pollo en salsa de mole en el almuerzo.**

to be **stunned** →see: to be flabbergasted

stupid 1. (silly; not right in the head; →see also: dim-witted, dumb, dumb as a post, fool, idiot) zonzo(-a) *most of L. Am. (not Ch);* torpe *Mex, Cuba, DR, PR, C. Am.;* cerrado(-a) (closed) *Mex, PR, CR, Col;* zángano(-a) *DR, PR, Col;* caído(-a) de la cuna (fallen from the cradle) *U, Arg* ◆ *That* girl is very stupid and her friend takes advantage of it. *Esa chica es muy zonza y su amiga toma ventaja.* **2.** (stupid and rude) bruto(-a); (brutish, ill-mannered) *L. Am., Sp;* borde *Sp* ◆ *Nobody can stand her because she's so stupid.* *Nadie la tolera porque es una bruta.*

to be **stupid** (no longer be able to learn) tener ya dura la mollera (to have the crown of the head already hard) *U, Sp* ◆ *I won't learn English now; I'm stupid (no longer able to learn).* *Ya no aprenderé inglés; tengo ya dura la mollera.*

stupid jerk (incompetent, →see also: fool, idiot) el/la imbécil *L. Am., Sp;* el/la cafre *Mex, Cuba, PR, Col;* el/la boludo(-a) (with heavy balls) *S.Cone* ◆ *He drives the car like a stupid jerk (maniac).* *Maneja el coche como imbécil.*

stupid to the nth degree (dope of dopes) tonto(-a) de capirote (idiot chief) *Mex, Peru, Sp* ◆ *That tenant you have is stupid to the nth degree.* *Ese inquilino que tienes es un tonto de capirote.*

stupid trick (vulgar; →see also: dirty trick) la pendejada *Mex, C. Am.* ◆ *Don't (you all) do any more damn stupid tricks.* *No hagan más pendejadas.*

stupidity (→see also: baloney) la estupidez *L. Am., Sp;* la babosada *L. Am.;* la memez *Sp* ◆ *It's stupidity. Is there anyone so stupid as to believe that? Es una babosada. ¿Hay alguien tan idiota que vaya a creer eso?*

to **suck 1.** (to be screwed up, useless; vulgar) estar fregado(-a) (to be scrubbed; slightly vulgar) *most of L. Am.;* estar de la jodida *Chicano, Mex, G, Col;* estar de la chingada (to be of the chingada, violated woman; vulgar) *Mex, G, ES, Col;* estar de la fregada *Mex;* estar cagado(-a) (to be pooped, vulgar) *S. Cone, Sp* ◆ *The situation of the farmers really sucks this year. La situación de los agricultores está muy fregada este año.* ◆ *This sucks. What are we going to do? Esto está de la jodida. ¿Qué vamos a hacer?* **2.** (put off, repel, bother) repatear (to rekick) *Mex, Sp;*

to **suck up** (do anything to please people in authority, →see also: to sweet-talk) hacerle el barbero (to be the barber to him or her) *Mex;* chupar media (to suck stocking) *Bol, Peru, S. Cone;* hacerle la pelota (to play

someone the ball) *Sp* ◆ *I passed the chemistry exam by sucking up to the teacher. Pasé el examen de química por hacerle el barbero a la maestra.* ◆ *Agustín really sucks up to the director. Agustín le chupa las medias al director.*

suck-up (brown nose) el lambiscón, la lambiscona *Mex, G, ES, Arg* (RVar *Sp:* lamerón; *PR:* lambeojo or lameojo; *Col:* lambeón; *Arg:* la lambiscona only); el/la chupamedia(s) (stocking sucker) *Peru, Bol, S. Cone* ◆ *Agustín is a real suck-up (brown nose). Agustín es un lambiscón total.* pelotillero(-a) *Sp*

sucker →see: loser, jerk

suckers los hijos de la guayaba (euphemism for hijos de la chingada; guayaba is guava) *Mex, ES;* los hijos de sayula (euphemism for hijos de la chingada) *Mex* ◆ *Those poor suckers don't know anything. Esos hijos de la guayaba no saben nada.*

to **suit** (agree with) cuadrar (to square) *L. Am.* ◆ *The color of this dress doesn't suit me. No me cuadra el color de este vestido.*

to **suit to a T** caer de perlas (to fall of pearls) *most of L. Am., Sp* ◆ *That blouse suits you to a T.* ◆ *Esa blusa te cae de perlas.*

to be **sunk** →see: to be in a bind, in hot water

super 1. (good, nice, great; →see also: awesome, cool) como anillo al dedo (like a ring on the finger) *L. Am., Sp;* de perlas (of pearls, often used with caer or venir) *most of L. Am., Sp;* chévere *most of L. Am.; most common in Caribbean, Col, Ven;* de peluche (used instead of de película; peluche means plush, like the fabric of stuffed toys) *Mex, DR, ES, Col;* a todas margaritas (at all daisies) *Mex, ES;* de película (like in a movie) *Mex, DR, PR, C. Am., S. Cone, Sp;* filete (fillet) *Mex, DR, PR;* morrocotudo(-a) *Mex, DR;* chicho(-a) *Mex;* padre, padrísimo (-a) (father, very father) *Mex;* de pelos (of hairs, used like de película) *Mex;* regio(-a) (regal, royal) *Nic, Col, Ec, S. Cone;* nítido(-a) (clear, bright) *Pan, Caribbean;* pura vida (pure life) *CR;* bacano(-a) *DR, Col;* fenomenal (phenomenal) *S. Cone, Sp;* redondo (-a) (round) *U, Arg, Sp;* chachi *Sp;* de cine (used like de película) *Sp;* tuanis *G, CR* ◆ *How was the trip? —Super! ¿Qué tal el viaje? —¡Tuanis!* ◆ *When I go out with Casimiro, we* *always have a super time.* **Cuando salgo con Casimiro, siempre lo pasamos de película.** **2.** (good or bad; abnormal, unusual, exceptional; badly done) bárbaro(-a) (barbarous) *L. Am., Sp;* bestial *Mex, DR, PR, Col, Peru, U, Arg, Sp;* matador(-a) *Mex, Col, Peru, U;* del demonio (of the devil) *Sp* ◆ *Let's get together at the beach. —Super!* **Nos reunamos en la playa. –¡Bárbaro!**

to be **super 1.** (a gem, perfect) ser una joya (to be a jewel) *parts of L. Am.;* ser una perla (to be a pearl) *ES, Sp* ◆ *Barcelona is super.* **Barcelona es una joya. 2.** (wonderful, great) ser una obra maestra (to be a masterpiece) *L. Am., Sp;* ser la octava maravilla (to be the eighth wonder [of the world], said of things) *Mex, Peru, Bol, S. Cone, Sp;* ser una soda (to be a soda) *Col* ◆ *Teresa, the dress you made for me is super!* **Teresa, ¡el vestido que me hiciste es una obra maestra! 3.** (the greatest, the best) ser lo máximo (to be the maximum) *L. Am.* ◆ *This music is super!* **¡Esta música es lo máximo!**

sure →see: natch, uh-huh, yeah

sure cure (charm, effective remedy) la mano de santo (saint's hand) *Sp* ◆ *My aunt has a sure cure for a stomachache.* **Mi tía tiene una mano de santo para curar el mal de estómago.**

Sure thing. (→see also: All right., It's a deal.) ¡Claro! (Clearly!) *L .Am., Sp;* ¡Papas! (Potatoes!) *Mex, ES, Col* ◆ *Will you come to the river with us? —Sure thing!* **¿Vienes con nosotros al río? –¡Papas!**

to **surf the Internet** surfear la Red (la Internet) *parts of L. Am.* ◆ *We surfed the Net to get the information we needed.* **Surfeamos la Red para conseguir la información que necesitábamos.**

to **swallow something** (believe a story, fall for something) tragar(se) algo *L. Am., Sp;* tragarse la píldora (to swallow the pill) *Mex, Ch, U, Sp* ◆ *I'm not swallowing that story. I'm not swallowing it.* **No voy a tragar ese cuento. No me lo trago.**

to **swallow something hook, line, and sinker** tragar el anzuelo (to swallow the hook) *Mex, DR, ES, S. Cone, Sp* ◆ *My friend told me the story, and I swallowed it hook, line, and sinker like an idiot.* **Mi amigo me contó**

la historia, y tragué el anzuelo como una tonta.

swanky (high-class, posh; adj.) popis *Mex, Col* ◆ *It's a swanky hotel.* **Es un hotel popis.**

to **swear like a trooper (or a trucker)** hablar como un carretero (to talk like a trucker) *U, Sp;* jurar en arameo (to swear in Aramaic, the language of Christ) *Sp* ◆ *Benito swears like a trooper. It's unpleasant to listen to him.* **Benito habla como un carretero. Es desagradable escucharlo.**

swear word la grosería (gross thing) *L. Am., Sp;* la palabrota (big word) *L. Am., Sp;* la lisura (smoothness) *Peru;* el garabato (graffiti) *Ch;* el taco *Sp* ◆ *Jaimito always says swear words in front of his grandparents to upset them.* **Jaimito siempre dice palabrotas en presencia de sus abuelos para disgustarlos.**

to **sweat bullets** sudar la gota gorda (to sweat the fat drop) *L. Am., Sp* ◆ *I'm here sweating bullets and she isn't doing anything.* **Yo aquí sudando la gota gorda y ella no hace nada.**

to **sweat it out** →see: to sweat bullets

to **sweat the small stuff 1.** (worry about something unimportant) ahogarse en un vaso de agua (to drown in a glass of water) *L. Am., Sp* ◆ *Don't worry. Don't sweat the small stuff.* **No te preocupes. No te ahogues en un vaso de agua. 2.** (get involved in something that can be harmful or senseless) buscarle tres (cinco) pies al gato (to look for three [five] feet on the cat) *L. Am., Sp* ◆ *Why sweat the small stuff?* **¿Para qué buscarle tres pies al gato si tiene cuatro?**

to **sweep everything away** llevarse todo por delante (to carry away everything) *L. Am., Sp* ◆ *The water swept everything away.* **El agua se llevó todo por delante.**

sweetheart (steady boyfriend or girlfriend; →see also: dear, my love, sweetie) el/la novio(-a) *L. Am., Sp.;* el/la pololo(-a) (bumblebee) *Ch* ◆ *Where is your daughter's sweetheart from?* **¿De dónde es el pololo de tu hija?**

sweetie (→see also: dear, my love) dulzura (sweetness) *L. Am., Sp* ◆ *Sweetie, each day I love you more.* **Dulzura, cada día te quiero más.**

to sweet-talk: *She gives him a lot of sweet-talk.*
Ella le da mucha cuerda.

to be a **sweetie** (nice, kind person) ser un caramelo (to be a caramel) *Mex, Cuba, G, Col;* ser un dulce (un bombón) (to be sweet [a bonbon]) *Mex* ◆ *Hernando's new girlfriend is a real sweetie. La nueva novia de Hernando es un caramelito.*

sweet-talk (chat, often with idea of persuading) la muela (molar [tooth]) *Cuba, DR, Col* ◆ *Stop sweet-talking that girl; she has a boyfriend. Deja de darle muela a esa muchacha, que tiene novio.*

to **sweet-talk** 1. (butter up, often in a provocative or annoying way) dar cuerda (to give string) *L. Am., Sp;* dar coba (to give flattery, tales) *most of L. Am., Sp;* cuentiar *Mex, G, ES, CR, Col* (RVar CR: cuentear) ◆ *They made Rolando vice president of the bank, and all he knows how to do is sweet-talk the president. A Rolando lo nombraron vicepresidente del banco y lo único que sabe hacer es dar coba al presidente.* 2. (talk at length trying to persuade) comer el coco a alguien (to eat someone's coconut, meaning head) *DR, PR, Sp;* chamullar *Peru, Ch, Arg* ◆ *I*

sweet-talked the salesman so he would lower the price for me. Le chamullé al vendedor para que me bajara el precio. 3. (flatter someone to obtain something, butter up) hacer la rosca a alguien (to make the doughnut to someone) *Sp;* hacer la pelota (pelotilla) a alguien (to make the ball to someone) *Sp* 4. (sling the bull) soltar el rollo (to let loose the roll) *parts of L. Am., Sp;* echar el rollo (to throw the roll) *Mex, parts of L. Am., Sp.;* enrollarse (to get rolled up) *ES, Sp* ◆ *The president sweet-talked us about the future of the economy. El presidente echó el rollo sobre el futuro de la economía.*

swine →see: pig

to **swing both ways** (be bisexual) jugar en los dos bandos (to play in both bands or groups) *Mex, Cuba, DR, PR, Col, U* ◆ *I heard that Lorenzo swings both ways. Escuché que Lorenzo juega en los dos bandos.*

to **swipe** (snatch, filch, lift) agandallar *Mex* ◆ *He saw the wallet and swiped it. Vio la cartera y la agandalló.*

T

tacky ordinario(-a) *L. Am., Sp;* balurdo(-a) *Ven;* berreta *U, Arg;* basto(-a) *Sp* ◆ *These shoes are very tacky.* Estos zapatos son muy bastos.

tacky action (or vulgar expression) la leperada *Mex, C. Am.* ◆ *That idea is really absurd; it's so tacky.* Esta idea es muy absurda; parece de leperada.

to **tag along** (be superfluous or extra) ir de pegoste (to go as an add-on) *Mex, ES, Nic;* ir de pegote (to go as an add-on) *Sp* ◆ *It was your mother's fault that your sister tagged along with us (lit., that she came along stuck on to us).* Tu hermana vino de pegoste por culpa de tu mamá.

tainted (stained, muddied, involved in shady business or trouble) embarrado(-a) (mud plaster for walls) *Mex, G, ES, CR, U, Arg* ◆ *That man is really tainted by shady business deals.* Ese señor está bien embarrado en malos negocios.

to **take a leak** (vulgar) echar una meadita (to throw a little pissing) *L. Am., Sp* ◆ *I'm going to go take a leak, and then I'll come back.* Voy a echar una meadita, y ya regreso.

to **take a long weekend** (by taking a day off before or after a holiday) hacer puente (to make bridge) *Mex, DR, Sp* ◆ *We're going to take a long Easter weekend since Tuesday is a holiday and Monday we won't go to work.* Vamos a hacer el puente de pascua, ya que el martes es festivo y el lunes no iremos a trabajar.

to **take a look** wach(e)ar (from English) *Chicano, ES* ◆ *Take a look at that!* ¡Wacha eso!

to **take a shot in the dark** tirarse el lance (to throw oneself the spear) *S. Cone* ◆ *The company took a shot in the dark when they hired Elvira. Luckily, everything turned out well.* La compañía se tiró el lance cuando contrató a Elvira. Por suerte todo salió muy bien.

to **take advantage** (be clever at taking advantage of others) hacerse el (la) vivo(-a) (to become the live one) *L. Am., Sp* ◆ *Don't try to take advantage because we know you here.* No te hagas el vivo porque aquí te conocemos.

to **take charge of a situation** (→see also: to call the shots, to wear the pants) ponerse los pantalones (to put on one's pants) *DR, PR, S. Cone* ◆ *Finally Alcira took charge of the situation and took control of her kids, who wouldn't obey anybody.* Finalmente Alcira se puso los pantalones y controló a sus hijos, que no obedecían a nadie.

to **take (or bring) coals to Newcastle** llevar leña al monte (to take wood [logs] to the woods or brush) *L. Am., Sp* ◆ *A computer for Juan? Why if he already has three of them? It's like taking coals to Newcastle.* ¿Una computadora a Juan? ¿Para qué si ya tiene tres? Es cómo llevar leña al monte.

to **take it all out** descargar en (to discharge, unload on) *Mex, Cuba, PR, Col* ◆ *She was furious when she arrived and took it all out on her husband.* Llegó furiosa y descargó todo en su esposo.

to **take it easy** 1. (keep cool or mellow about a problem; →see also: Chill out.) llevarla suave *ES, CR, Col, U* (RVar *Cuba, Pan:* cogerlo suave); pasarlo piola (to pass it string, from "piola" in Italian, string or cord) *S. Cone* ◆ *We went to the lake on the weekend and we took it easy.* Fuimos al lago el fin de semana y lo pasamos piola. 2. (loosen up discipline) aflojar la cuerda (to slacken the cord) *Mex, Sp* ◆ *The coach had to take it easy because the players were angry about the discipline.* El entrenador tuvo que aflojar la cuerda porque los jugadores estaban furiosos con el régimen de disciplina.

Take it easy. Suave. (Smooth, soft.) *DR, Ven, Ch* ◆ *Take it easy. Don't listen to those absurd comments.* Suave, suave. No escuches esos comentarios absurdos.

to **take it one day at a time** tomarlo día por día *L. Am., Sp* ◆ *Take it one day at a time.* Tómalo día por día.

Take it or leave it. (phrase urging someone to accept what little they have obtained) Menos da una piedra. (A stone gives less.) *Sp* ◆ *You'll only give me 150 euros for my personal expenses? —Exactly. Take it or leave it.* ¿Me darás sólo 150 euros para mis gastos personales? –Exactamente. Menos da una piedra.

to **take off** (get out; →see also: to hit the road) largarse *most of L. Am., Sp;* espantar la mula (to scare off the mule) *Mex, Cuba, DR, PR, CR;* borrarse, borrarse del mapa (to wipe oneself off the map) *Mex, ES, S. Cone, Sp;* despintarse (to unpaint oneself) *Mex, PR;* agarrar su patín (to grab his [her] skate) *Mex, Cuba;* pintarse (to paint yourself out) *Mex, ES;* pintar su calaverita (to paint one's little skull) *Mex;* pirar (probably from pira, funeral pyre) *Mex;* abrirse (to open) *CR, S. Cone, Sp;* pirarse *Cuba, Arg, Sp;* liar el petate (to roll up the petate, sleeping mat or green bag used for military service) *Sp;* liar los bártulos (to bundle up the household goods) *Sp* ◆ *I don't want to take off yet.* No quiero espantar la mula todavía. ◆ *They took off when the police came.* Se piraron cuando vino la policía.

to **take off** (improve, make progress) levantarle (el) vuelo *Mex, ES, S. Cone, Sp;* alzar vuelo (to take flight) *Mex, DR, PR ES;* tomar vuelo (to take flight) *Mex, DR, U, Arg* ◆ *The business is taking off.* El negocio está levantando vuelo.

to **take off** (escape) poner pies en polvorosa (to put one's feet in the dustiness) *L. Am., Sp;* tomar el portante (to take the big door) *Peru, Sp;* darse el piro (like pirotécnica, fireworks) *Sp;* aplicar (la) retirada (to apply [the] retreat) *U, Arg* ◆ *The drug traffickers took off when they saw the police.* Los traficantes de drogas pusieron los pies en polvorosa cuando vieron a la policía.

to **take off** (take to one's heels; →see also: to fly the coop) tomar las de Villadiego (to take those of Villadiego) *Nic, Ch, Sp* ◆ *When Carlos saw that the relationship was getting serious, he took off and we didn't see him anymore.* Cuando Carlos vio que la relación iba en serio, tomó las de Villadiego y ya no lo vimos más.

to **take off like a rocket** salir como cohete *Mex, DR, ES, U, Arg, Sp;* salir como bólido (to take off like a fireball) *Mex, Cuba, DR, G, CR, Col, Ch, U, Sp;* chillar goma(s), chillarla (to screech rubber) *Mex, PR;* salir pitando (to leave honking the horn or blowing a whistle) *Mex, Sp* ◆ *We took off like a rocket for the airport to catch our flight, but we didn't make it on time.* Salimos como cohete al aeropuerto para alcanzar nuestro vuelo, pero no llegamos a tiempo.

to **take on all comers** (win at everything) llevarse todo por delante (to carry away everything in front of you) *S. Cone, Sp* ◆ *Rodrigo García took on all comers, and his team won the championship.* Rodrigo García se llevó todo por delante, y su equipo ganó el campeonato.

to **take one's medicine** (→see also: to wait it out) aguantar el chaparrón (to put up with the rain shower) *S. Cone, Sp* ◆ *They took their medicine from their boss in a very professional manner.* Aguantaron el chaparrón que les cayó de su jefe de forma muy profesional.

to **take someone down a peg or two** →see: to put someone in his or her place

to **take someone down the garden path** (deceive someone; convince someone to have sex) llevar a alguien al huerto (to take someone to the garden) *Mex, Sp* ◆ *The salesman thinks he's going to lead me down the garden path.* El vendedor cree que me va a llevar al huerto.

to **take someone for a fool** (to deceive or take advantage of someone) verle la cara a alguien (implying verle la cara de tonto) (to see someone's face) *Mex, ES, Nic, S. Cone* ◆ *The clerk took me for a fool and tried to sell me those cheap shoes for sixty dollars.* El dependiente me vio la cara y trató de venderme esos zapatos baratos por sesenta dólares.

to **take (someone) for everything they've got** sacar el jugo (to take out the juice) *Mex, DR, PR, ES, CR, Col, Ch, Arg, Sp* ◆ *The boss will take you for everything you've got.* El patrón te saca el jugo.

to **take someone off a high horse** →see: to put someone in his or her place

to **take someone to task** →see: to chew out, to set someone straight, to tell it like it is

to **take someone to the cleaners** (ruin someone; →see also: to lift, to make a hit, to mug) dejar a alguien sin camisa/quitarle hasta la camisa (to leave someone without a shirt/to take even someone's shirt) *Mex, Sp;* dejar a alguien en cueros (to leave someone naked) *Mex* ◆ *They took my cousin to the cleaners.* Dejaron a mi primo sin camisa.

to **take something calmly** (→see also: Chill out.) tomar algo con calma *L. Am., Sp* (RVᴀʀ tomar algo con soda) (to take something with soda) *Ch* ◆ *You have to take those things calmly.* Esas cosas, hay que tomarlas con soda.

to **take something hard** (give things too much importance) tomarse las cosas a la tremenda (to take things to the tremendous) *U, Arg, Sp* ◆ *Failing a test is not so serious; don't take it so hard.* Suspender un examen no es tan grave; no te lo tomes a la tremenda.

to **take something upon oneself** tomar sobre sí una cosa *Sp* ◆ *Your brother took upon himself the administration of the entire project.* Tu hermano tomó sobre sí la dirección de todo el proyecto.

to **take something with a grain of salt** tomar algo con un grano de sal *Mex, DR, PR, CR, Ch, Sp* ◆ *Everything that Tomás says has to be taken with a grain of salt because he's such a gossip.* Todo lo que dice Tomás hay que tomarlo con un grano de sal porque es un chismoso.

to **take the ball and chain** (get married) echarse la soga al cuello (to put the rope around one's neck) *Mex, DR, PR, G, CR, Col, Ch, Sp;* ahorcarse (to hang oneself, like echarse la soga al cuello) *Mex, CR, U* ◆ *Adela and Beto decided to take the ball and chain next summer.* Adela y Beto decidieron ahorcarse el próximo verano.

to **take the cake** (to outdo oneself) no medirse (to not measure oneself) *Mex, Col, U;* pintarse solo(-a) (to paint oneself alone) *Mex, U;* ganar el premio (to win the prize, ironic; refers to bad habits such as always arriving late, etc.) *Arg, Ch;* llevarse la palma (to carry away the palm, meaning the honors) *Ch, Sp* ◆ *You really take the cake in your efforts to win.* Realmente no te mides en tus esfuerzos para triunfar.

to **take the other side** (contradict) llevar la contraria (contra) (to take the contrary) *L.*

Am., Sp ◆ *You love to take the other side. Why do you do it? Your attitude really upsets me.* Te encanta llevarme la contraria. ¿Por qué lo haces? Tu actitud me disgusta mucho.

Take the plunge. Al agua, patos. (To the water, ducks.) *Mex, DR, ES, S. Cone, Sp* ◆ *Let's not lose any more time. (Time's a-wastin'!) Take the plunge!* No perdamos más tiempo. ¡Al agua, patos!

to **take to one's heels** →see: to take off

to **take your breath away** (be amazing) estar de quitar el hipo (to be such as to take away hiccups) *Mex, Sp* ◆ *She's so pretty she takes your breath away.* Es tan bonita que quita el hipo.

to be **taken in** (duped; →see also: to fall for) caer como un gil (como un angelito) (to fall like a fool [like a little angel]) *Bol, S. Cone* ◆ *That fellow gilded the lily for me so well that I was taken in.* Ese muchacho me doró tan bien la píldora que caí como un gil.

to be **taken to the cleaners** (cleaned out) quedar limpio(-a) (to be left clean) *Mex, DR, U, Arg, Sp* ◆ *I was taken to the cleaners. I don't know what to do.* Me quedé limpio. No sé qué hacer.

to **talk a blue streak** hablar hasta por los codos (to talk even through one's elbows) *L. Am., Sp* ◆ *The neighbor came to tell us what happened. She talked a blue streak.* La vecina vino a contarnos todo lo que pasó. Hablaba hasta por los codos.

to **talk a good game** (promise something and not fulfill it) cacarear y no poner huevo (to cackle and not lay an egg) *Mex, ES, Sp* ◆ *That politician talks a good game but doesn't deliver.* Ese diputado cacarea y no pone huevo.

to **talk someone's ear off** hablar hasta por los codos (to talk even through one's elbows) *L. Am., Sp* ◆ *The neighbor came to tell us what happened. She talked our ears off.* La vecina vino a contarnos todo lo que pasó. Hablaba hasta por los codos.

tall tale →see: baloney, whopper

tantrum →see: to have a fit

to **tattle** (inform, snitch on) cantar (to sing) *L. Am., Sp;* soplar (to blow) *L. Am., Sp;* sapear *CR, Col, Ven* ◆ *Juan tattled to the police, and now his pals are in jail.* Juan sopló a la *policía, y ahora sus compañeros están en la cárcel.*

tattle-tale el soplón, la soplona *L. Am., Sp* ◆ *He's a tattle-tale. He tells everything.* **Es un saplón. Todo lo cuenta.**

teacher's pet (also, someone with influence) el/la enchufado(-a) (plugged in) *Sp* ◆ *He's a teacher's pet; he did worse on the exam but the professor gave him a better grade than me.* **Es un enchufado; hizo peor el examen pero el profesor le puso mejor nota que a mí.**

to **tear someone up** →see: to break someone's heart

tease (someone who makes fun of or deceives others, someone who enjoys life without working hard) el payaso *L. Am., Sp*; el/la vacilador(-a) *Mex, Cuba, G, ES, Col* ◆ *Don't believe him. What a tease!* **No lo creas. ¡Qué vacilador!**

to **tease** (→see also: to make fun of, to put someone on) tomarle el pelo a alguien (to pull someone's hair) *L .Am., Sp;* burlarse de (to make fun of) *L. Am., Sp;* vacilar (to fool around) *Mex, ES;* cargar (to load) *Arg, U* ◆ *You must be teasing!* **¡Me estás cargando!**

teen years (change to adolescence, puberty) la edad del pavo (turkey age) *S. Cone, Sp* ◆ *Don't pay much attention to his behavior. He's in those teen years (adolescence).* **No le hagas mucho caso a su comportamiento. Está en la edad del pavo.**

teenie weenie (very small; a shrimp) chiquitito(-a) *L. Am., Sp;* chiquitico(-a) *CR, Col, Ven* ◆ *Sofía has teenie weenie hands and feet.* **Sofía tiene manos y pies chiquiticos.**

to **tell it all** (let out a long tale) soltar el rollo (to let loose the roll) *L. Am., Sp* ◆ *Tell all, Ana. What happened?* **Suelta el rollo, Ana. ¿Qué pasó?**

to **tell it like it is** (not mince words) no tener pelos en la lengua (to not have hair on the tongue [hair implies animals, or more primitive forms, that do not have language]) *L. Am., Sp;* decir al pan pan y al vino vino (to call bread bread and wine wine) *L. Am., Sp* ◆ *He explained the situation to them with all the detail. He tells it like it is.* **Les explicó la situación con todos los detalles. No tiene pelos en la lengua.**

to **tell someone to get lost** (→see also: to dump someone, to write someone off) mandar a alguien a freír espárragos (to send someone to fry asparagus) *Mex, PR, ES, Ch, Sp;* mandar a alguien por un tubo (to send someone through a pipe) *Mex, ES, Col;* mandar a alguien a bañarse (to send someone to take a bath) *ES, Nic, Peru, Bol, Ch* ◆ *When Estela asked her boss for a raise, he told her to get lost.* **Cuando Estela le pidió un aumento de sueldo a su jefe, éste la mandó a freír espárragos.**

to **tell someone to go to hell** mandar a alguien al carajo, a la mierda (to send someone to the male organ, to shit; vulgar) *L. Am., Sp* ◆ *We were celebrating Alcira's birthday, and her dad told us to go to hell because the music was too loud.* **Estábamos celebrando el cumpleaños de Alcira, y su padre nos mandó al carajo porque la música estaba muy alta.**

to **tell "war stories"** (stories of one's life) contar batallitas (to recount small battles) *Sp* ◆ *Your grandpa is always telling us his war stories (stories of his youth).* **Tu abuelo siempre nos está contando batallitas de su juventud.**

to be a **tempest in a teapot** ser más el ruido que las nueces (to be more the noise than the nuts) *L. Am., Sp* ◆ *I'm not worried about this fight between Marta and Rodrigo. It's a tempest in a teapot.* **No me preocupa la pelea entre Marta y Rodrigo. Es más el ruido que las nueces.**

text message el mensaje de texto *L. Am.;* el s.m.s. *Sp* ◆ *They sent me a text message.* **Me mandaron un mensaje de texto.**

Thanks a bunch. Chasgracias. (short for Muchas gracias.) *L. Am., Sp* ◆ *Thanks a bunch, brother.* **Chasgracias, hermano.**

that darn guy (girl, man, woman, etc.) el/la muy condenado(-a) (the very condemned) *Florida, Mex, DR, G, CR, Col, Ch, U* ◆ *That darn chick won a trip to Hawaii as a prize.* **La muy condenada ganó un viaje a Hawai como premio.**

That goes without saying. No tiene(s) que jurarlo. (You don't have to swear it.) *Mex, Col* ◆ *Of course. That goes without saying. I believe you.* **Por supuesto que sí. No tienes que jurarlo. Ya te creo.**

That is . . . O sea... *L. Am., Sp* ◆ *That is, you're not going to finish your studies.* O sea, que no vas a terminar tu carrera.

That's all we needed! ¡Lo que faltaba para el duro! (What was missing [to make] a five-cent coin) *Sp* ◆ *Your pregnancy . . . that's all we needed (the last straw) at this moment.* Tu embarazo es lo que faltaba para el duro en este momento.

That's another (or different) kettle of fish. (Not the same thing.) Eso es harina de otro costal. (That's flour from another sack.) *L. Am., Sp;* Otra cosa, mariposa. (Another thing, butterfly.) *Mex, DR, ES, Col, Sp;* Ése es otro rollo. (That's another roll.) *Mex;* Otra cosa es con guitarra. (It's something else with a guitar.) *S. Cone;* No es lo mismo Chana que Juana. (Chana is not the same as Juana.) *Mex, ES, Nic* ◆ *My mother was very affectionate. My father . . . that was another kettle of fish.* Mi madre era muy cariñosa. Mi padre era harina de otro costal.

That's enough. ¡Basta ya! *L. Am., Sp;* Y en paz. (And in peace.; phrase said to end a matter) *Mex, ES, Sp;* Tengamos la fiesta en paz. (Let's have the party in peace.) *DR, ES, Sp* ◆ *I'll take my things and you take yours. That's enough!* Yo recojo mis cosas y tú las tuyas. ¡Y en paz!

That's for sure. (You betcha. →see also: Yeah, right!) Ya lo creo. (I already believe it; sometimes ironic: Yeah, right.) *L. Am., Sp* ◆ *He has no money. —That's for sure!* No tiene dinero. —¡Ya lo creo!

That's it! Right! Así es. (That's how it is.) *L. Am., Sp;* ¡Ándale! (¡Ándate!) *Chicano, Mex, Col* ◆ *That's it. That's how you play the marimba.* Ándale, pues. Así se toca la marimba.

That's the point! ¡Allí está el detalle! (There's the detail!) (a saying popularized by the actor Cantinflas) *Mex, DR, S. Cone* ◆ *I don't know why you're mad. —That's the point: you don't understand my problems.* No sé porque estás enojada. —Ahí está el detalle: no entiendes mis problemas.

There's always a hitch (problem). Nunca falta un pelo en la sopa. (There's always a hair in the soup.) *L. Am.* ◆ *You've quit your job again? There's always a hitch.* ¿Otra vez renunciaste a tu empleo? Nunca falta un pelo en la sopa.

There's no choice (alternative). No hay opción. *L. Am., Sp;* Ni modo. (Not even a way.) *Mex;* No hay más narices (cojones). (There are no other noses [testicles].; vulgar with cojones) *Sp*

There's no free lunch. No bees, no honey; no work, no money. El que quiere celeste que le cueste. (Whoever wants baby blue, it will cost him.) *Mex, ES, Nic, S. Cone* ◆ *Why do you work so much? —Because there's no free lunch.* ¿Por qué trabajas tanto? —Porque el que quiere celeste que le cueste.

There's no need to dwell on the matter. (It's just as it looks, obvious.) No hay que darle vueltas. (There's no need to turn it around.) *Mex, DR, ES, S. Cone, Sp* ◆ *Let's finish this conversation . . . there's no need to dwell on the matter.* Terminemos esta plática... no hay que darle vueltas al asunto.

There's no other way. (Nothing else can be done about it.) No hay alternativa. *L. Am., Sp;* Ni mocho. *Mex* ◆ *Then I have to leave. There's no other way.* Entonces, tengo que irme. Ni mocho.

There's no rush. No hay prisa. *L. Am., Sp;* Más días hay que longanizas. (There are more days than pork sausages.) *Sp* ◆ *What's the hurry? There's no rush.* ¿Cuál es la prisa? Más días hay que longanizas.

There's no turning back. There's no backing out. No hay vuelta de hoja. (There's no turning of the page.) *Mex, ES, Nic, U, Arg, Sp* ◆ *Let's not talk any more about it; there's no turning back.* Ya no hablemos; no hay vuelta de hoja.

There's something here for everyone. Hay de todo como en botica. (There's everything like in a pharmacy.) *Mex, DR* ◆ *What is there in that store? —There's something for everyone.* ¿Qué hay en esta tienda? —Hay de todo como en botica.

They don't get along. No se entienden ni se enteran. (They don't understand each other or find out anything.) *Col, Sp* ◆ *They are sisters but they don't get along.* Son hermanas pero no se entienden ni se enteran.

They're few and far between. Son habas contadas. (They're counted beans; i.e., scarce and with a fixed number.) *Sp* ♦ *No hay muchos contratistas que puedan hacer esa clase de trabajo. Son habas contadas.* There aren't many contractors who can do that kind of work. They're few and far between.

thin (as a rail) →see: to be skin and bones, string bean

thingamabob →see: thingamajig

thingamajig la fregadera (slightly vulgar) *Chicano, Mex, G, ES, CR;* el chirimbolo *Mex, Cuba, Col, U, Arg;* la vaina (husk, pod) *DR, PR, C. Am., Col, Ven;* el chunche *C. Am.;* la cuestión (issue, theme) *DR, ES, Nic, Ch, U* ♦ *Why are there so many thingamajigs in this house? ¿Por qué hay tantos chirimbolos en esta casa?* ♦ *Give me that thingamajig, please.* Dame esa vaina, por favor.

thingie →see: thingamajig

Things could be worse. Peor es chile y agua lejos. (Worse is chili and water far away.) *Mex;* No llueve pero gotea. (It's not raining but it's dripping.) *Ch* ♦ *Well, although the webcam isn't working at least we have a connection to the Net. Things could be worse.* Pues aunque la webcam no funciona por lo menos tenemos conexión a la Red. Peor es chile y agua lejos.

to **think one is God's gift** →see: to think one is hot stuff

to **think one is hot shit** creerse la gran caca (to think one is the great poop, vulgar) *Chicano, Mex, G, Col* ♦ *That foreigner thinks he's hot shit and expects us to admire him.* Ese extranjero se cree la gran caca y espera que lo admiremos.

to **think one is hot stuff** creerse la divina pomada (to think one is the divine cream) *L. Am.;* creerse la divina garza (to think one is the divine heron) *most of L. Am.;* creerse el (la) muy muy (to think one is the very very) *Mex, C. Am., Col;* creerse la última Coca-Cola en el desierto (to think one is the last Coca-Cola in the desert) *Mex, DR, PR, ES, Nic, Pan, Col;* creerse la gran cosa (also, cosota) (to think one is the big thing) *Mex, DR, G, U, Arg, Sp;* creerse la última chupada del mango (to think one is the last suck on the mango) *Mex;* creerse la última chupada del mate (to think one is the last sip of the mate, strong tea) *S. Cone;* creerse el hoyo del queque (to think one is the hole in the cen-

ter of the cake) *Ch;* creerse el ombligo del mundo (to think one is the belly button of the world) *Sp* ♦ *We spoke with Alicia at the art exhibit. She thinks she's hot stuff.* Hablamos con Alicia en la exposición de arte. Se cree la muy muy.

to **think that money grows on trees** creer que el dinero se encuentra debajo de las piedras (to believe that money is found underneath rocks) *U, Sp* ♦ *Isabel's family always asks her for lots of money. They think money grows on trees here in North America.* La familia de Isabel siempre le pide mucho dinero. Ellos creen que el dinero se encuentra debajo de las piedras aquí en Norteamérica.

This is the last straw! ¡Esto es el colmo! (This is the limit, culmination!) *L. Am., Sp;* Es la última gota. (It's the last drop.) *Sp* ♦ *You haven't washed the clothes or the dishes for a week. This is the last straw!* No han lavado la ropa ni los platos por una semana. ¡Esto es el colmo!

This is too damn much. (→see: to be too damn much, to suck)

This livens (perks) things up. Esto resucita a un muerto. (This brings the dead back to life.) *U, Arg, Sp* ♦ *This cheerful music livens a person (things) up.* Esta música tan alegre resucita a un muerto.

This was the last straw. Hasta aquí llegó mi (el) amor. (My love lasted this far, up to here.) *Florida, Mex, DR, G, Col, U, Arg* ♦ *This was the last straw; I'm not going to tolerate any more mistakes.* Hasta aquí llegó mi amor; no voy a tolerar más errores.

through the grapevine →see: to travel by word of mouth

to **throw a fit** →see: to have a fit, to make a scene

to **throw in the towel** (→see also: to give in [give up]) tirar la toalla *L. Am., Sp;* colgar la toalla (to hang up the towel) *Mex, U, Arg;* tirar la esponja (to throw the sponge) *S. Cone* ♦ *I'm going to have to throw in the towel. I give up.* Voy a tener que tirar la toalla. Me doy por vencido.

to **throw off** (knock out of kilter; →see also: to knock someone for a loop) sacar de onda (to take from the sound wave) *L. Am* ♦ *I'm* *sorry. It's just that you threw me off. Lo siento. Es que me sacaste de onda.*

to **throw oneself (into something)** aventarse (to throw oneself) *Mex, DR, ES, Nic, Peru* ◆ *When the party began, she threw herself onto the dance floor. Cuando empezó la fiesta, se aventó a bailar.*

to **throw one's weight around** llevar bien puestos los pantalones (to wear the pants well placed) *Mex, DR, PR, ES, Sp* ◆ *Gerardo is throwing his weight around and managed to organize the family budget. Gerardo lleva bien puestos los pantalones y logró organizar el presupuesto familiar.*

to **thumb a ride** hacer (viajar por) autostop *L. Am., Sp;* hacer dedo (to make thumb) *S. Cone, Sp* ◆ *We thumbed a ride from Madrid to Seville. Viajamos de Madrid a Sevilla por autostop.*

to **tick off** (make angry; get one's goat) encabronar *Mex, PR, C. Am., many S. Am. countries* ◆ *Don't tick me off. No me encabronées.*

ticked off (→see also: steamed, to be pissed off) encabronado(-a) *Mex, PR, C. Am., many S. Am. countries;* cabreado(-a) *Mex, CR, Col, Sp* ◆ *I can't talk now. I'm all ticked off about the situation, and I need to think. No puedo hablar ahora. Estoy encabronado con la situación, y necesito pensar.*

to **tie one on** →see: to get wasted

to be **tied up** estar ocupado(-a) (to be occupied, busy) *L. Am., Sp;* estar liado(-a) (to be linked) *Sp* ◆ *We're tied up this week. Estamos muy liados esta semana.*

to be **tight** (friends) →see: to be bosom buddies

tight-assed (proud, prissy; woman) apretada (tight) *Mex, ES, Col* ◆ *Silvia always plays hard to get; she's very tight-assed (not vulgar in Spanish). Silvia siempre se hace del rogar; es bien apretada.*

to **tighten one's belt** (economically) apretarse el cinturón *Mex, DR, PR, ES, S. Cone, Sp* ◆ *We had to tighten our belts when my husband lost his job. Tuvimos que apretarnos el cinturón cuando mi marido perdió su trabajo.*

tight-fisted →see: stingy

tightly (strong) a cal y canto (at lime and stone, stone masonry) *Mex, Sp* ◆ *The store was closed tightly. La tienda estaba cerrada a cal y canto.*

tightwad (stingy person; →see also: stingy) el/la tacaño(-a) *L. Am., Sp;* el/la agarrado (-a) (grabbed) *most of L. Am., Sp;* el/la maceta (flower pot) *PR;* el amarrete (one who ties things up) *Bol, S. Cone* ◆ *Raúl is a tightwad. He never even treats his girlfriend; they always have to go dutch. Raúl es un maceta. No invita ni a su novia; siempre hay que hacer serrucho.*

Time to eat. (Let's eat.) A comer se ha dicho. (To eat it has been said.) *L. Am., Sp* ◆ *The food is ready. Time to eat. La comida está lista. A comer se ha dicho.*

tired →see: wiped out

tired as hell (→see also: wiped out) hecho (-a) (una) mierda (made into shit, vulgar) *Mex, DR, PR, U, Arg, Sp* ◆ *I'm wiped out, tired as hell. Estoy rendido, hecho mierda.*

tiresome pesado(-a) (heavy) *L. Am., Sp;* mamón, mamona (sucker, like a suckling baby, very annoying or ridiculous) *Chicano, Mex, ES, Col, Peru;* sangrón, sangrona *Mex, Cuba, G, ES, CR, Col* ◆ *Why do you put up with that extremely tiresome woman? ¿Por qué toleras a esa mamona?*

tits (→see also: boobs) las tetas (vulgar) *L. Am., Sp* ◆ *She was walking down the beach with her tits in the air. Andaba en la playa con las tetas al aire.*

to be **toast** (in trouble; →see also: to be in a bind, in hot water) estar frito(-a) (to be fried) *L. Am., Sp* ◆ *If you don't find the papers, you're toast. Si no encuentras los papeles, estás frita.*

To your health! (said as a toast) ¡Salud! (Health!) *L. Am., Sp;* ¡Salucitas! (Health!) *Mex* ◆ *Let's make a toast to family and friends. To your health! Brindemos por la familia y los amigos. ¡Salud!*

Tom, Dick, and Harry (expression used to name unknown people) fulano, mengano y zutano *L. Am., Sp* ◆ *They invited Pedro to dinner and it turns out he came with another Tom, Dick, and Harry. Invitaron a Pedro a cenar y resulta que vino con otro fulano, mengano y zutano.*

tomboy la marimacha *Mex, DR, ES, Col, Sp* la marimacho *PR, G, Ch* ◆ *That girl is a tomboy. All she wants to do is play baseball.* **Esa niña es marimacha. Lo único que quiere hacer es jugar al béisbol.**

tons 1. (a lot [of]) el montón (heap) (also, montones) *L. Am., Sp;* la barbaridad (barbarity) *L. Am., Sp;* el chingo (vulgar) *Mex, C. Am.;* el chorro (stream) *Mex, ES;* el fracatán *DR, PR;* mazo *Sp ;* el mogollón *Sp* ◆ *We made tons of food for the party.* **Hicimos un montón de comida para la fiesta. 2.** (an uncountable number) sepetecientos(-as) *Mex, DR, PR, Col;* chorrocientos(-as) *Mex, ES* ◆ *I've told you tons of times: I'm not going!* **Te lo he dicho sepetecientas veces: ¡No voy! 3.** (a lot of knowledge) la biblia en verso (the Bible in verse) *Sp* ◆ *Julia knows tons about that subject.* **De esa materia, Julia sabe la biblia en verso. 4.** (a lot of people) ciento y la madre (one hundred and the mother) *Sp* ◆ *There were tons of them; finally we stopped confronting them and left.* **Eran ciento y la madre; al final desistimos en enfrentarnos con ellos y nos fuimos.**

to be **too damn much** (great, awesome, amazing [people or things]; extreme) tener narices (algo) (to have noses, somewhat vulgar) *Sp;* tener huevos (to have eggs, meaning testicles; vulgar) *Sp;* ser la leche (to be the milk, somewhat vulgar) *Sp;* ser la hostia (to be the Host; vulgar, with religious reference) *Sp;* ser la polla (to be the male organ, vulgar) *Sp;* ser el despelote (to be the nakedness, vulgar) *Sp;* ser la coña (vulgar) *Sp* ◆ *Universal Studios is too damn much (the greatest).* **Universal Studios es la hostia.** ◆ *Those comments are too damn much.* **Esos comentarios tienen narices.**

too much 1. (amazing) demasié (short for demasiado) *Sp* ◆ *That story is too much. Nobody is going to believe it.* **Esa historia es demasié. No se la va a creer nadie. 2.** (exaggerated, phenomenal) tremendo(-a) *L. Am., Sp* ◆ *The articles in the newspapers are too much.* **Los artículos de los diarios son tremendos.**

to be **too much** (extreme, the height of something, either the best or the worst) ser la monda *Sp;* ser la repanocha *Sp;* ser la pera (to be the pear) *Sp;* ser una pasada (to be a past) *Sp;* no tener madre (to have no mother) *Mex, ES* ◆ *These tourists are too much.* **Estos turistas son la monda.** ◆ *That film about Che Guevara was too much!* **¡Esa película sobre Che Guevara fue la repanocha!** ◆ *You have to read this book; it's too much (the best).* **Tienes que leer este libro; no tiene madre.**

to be **too much for someone** (excessive for one's size or merit) venirle grande (to come to him or her very big) *Mex, Sp* ◆ *With the little bit of experience Dolores has in business, that job is too much for her.* **Con la poca experiencia que Dolores tiene en negocios, ese trabajo le viene grande.**

to **toot one's own horn** (brag; →see also: to be full of oneself) echarse flores (to throw flowers at oneself) *L. Am., Sp;* apantallar *Mex, DR, G, ES, Col;* cacarear (to cackle like a hen) *Arg;* tirarse el pegote (to throw oneself the sticky mess or awful thing) *Sp;* tirarse el rollo (to throw the roll at oneself) *Sp* ◆ *Tomás sells himself very well; he's always tooting his own horn.* **Tomás se vende muy bien; siempre está echándose flores.**

toothpick (skinny leg) la canilla (long bone of leg or arm) *Cuba, DR, G, Nic, CR, Col, Ch* ◆ *She goes around in miniskirts showing off those toothpicks as if she had legs.* **Ella anda en minifaldas exhibiendo las canillas como si tuviera piernas.**

tootsies (feet) las patas (paws) *L. Am., Sp;* las patrullas (patrols [girl chasers]) *Mex;* los pinceles (paintbrushes [they paint you out of the room]) *Mex* ◆ *We walked all day in the mountains, and my tootsies hurt.* **Caminamos todo el día en las montañas, y a mí me duelen las patas.**

top banana (→see also: big shot) el mero mero (la mera mera); el mero mero petatero (main seller of **petates**, or mats) *Chicano, Mex, G, ES;* el mero jodón (no feminine form is normally used; slightly vulgar) *Chicano, Mex, ES* ◆ *Here I'm the top banana.* **Aquí soy yo el mero mero (petatero).**

top dog →see : big shot, top banana

to **top it all off** para colmo; para colmo de desgracias (de males) (for the culmination of misfortunes) *L. Am., Sp* ◆ *The business didn't work out and, to top it all off, my partner left me with all the debts.* **El negocio no** *salió y, para colmo, mi socio me dejó con to-das las deudas.*

tops →see: super

to be **tops at** →see: to be a whiz

topsy-turvy (disorganized) patas pa'arriba, patas arriba (paws up in the air) *DR, PR, ES, Nic, S. Cone, Sp* ◆ *The earthquake turned the world topsy-turvy. El terremoto puso el mundo patas arriba.*

to **touch (knock on) wood** tocar madera (used as in English, so that something that was said shouldn't happen) *L. Am., Sp* ◆ *Are you sick? —No, let me touch wood. ¿Estás enferma? –No, déjame tocar madera.*

touched in the head (→see also: nuts) tocado(-a) de la cabeza *Mex, G, ES, Col, U, Arg, Sp* ◆ *Anselmo is touched in the head. He says he's going to paint his whole house black. Anselmo está tocado de la cabeza. Dice que va a pintar toda su casa de negro.*

to be a **tough nut** (very demanding, especially used for teachers or professors) ser un hueso (to be a bone; from ser un hueso duro de roer, to be a tough nut to crack) *Sp* ◆ *Professor Martínez is a tough nut. El profesor Martínez es un hueso.*

traffic jam el atasco *L. Am., Sp;* el embotellamiento (bottling up) *L. Am., Sp;* la galleta (cookie, slang) *Arg* ◆ *On 9th of July Avenue (a street named for an important date) there are usually traffic jams. En la Avenida 9 de julio se forman galletas muy a menudo.*

tramp 1. (living a disorganized life or being dishonest sexually; →see also: slut) golfo(-a) *Mex, ES, Sp* ◆ *She goes out every night with a different guy. She's a bit of a tramp. Sale por la noche cada día y con un chico distinto. Es bastante golfa.* 2. (bum) el/la vagabundo(-a) *L. Am., Sp.;* el/la atorrante *Peru, S. Cone* ◆ *He doesn't have money because he's a tramp. No tiene dinero porque es un atorrante.*

trap (mouth; →see also: kisser, yap) el buzón (mailbox) *Mex, Cuba* ◆ *Shut your trap. Cierra el buzón.*

to **trap a husband** →see: to catch (a husband)

trash →see: junk

to **trash** →see: to rip apart, to screw up

to **travel by word of mouth** (be common knowledge) andar de boca en boca (to go from mouth to mouth) *L. Am., Sp* ◆ *We heard the commentaries that travel by word of mouth about the election fraud. Escuchamos los comentarios que andan de boca en boca sobre el fraude en las elecciones.*

to **treat like a king (queen)** (pamper) llevar en palmas (palmitas) (to carry with palm leaves) *Sp* ◆ *His parents treat him like a king; he's never going to grow up. Sus padres le llevan en palmas; nunca será una persona adulta.*

to **treat like dirt** ningunear *Mex, ES, Nic* ◆ *They accused him of treating them like dirt (like nobodies). Lo acusaron de ningunearlos.*

to **treat someone like a fifth (or third) wheel** (make out in front of someone) poner gorro a alguien (to put the cap on someone, referring to lovers) *Mex, DR* ◆ *I don't like to go out with Rosa and Pepe because they treat me like a fifth wheel. They're always smooching. No me gusta salir con Rosa y Pepe porque me ponen gorro. Siempre andan besuqueándose.*

to **treat** (pay the check) rajarse (to split) *Hond, CR, Pan* ◆ *We went out to dinner and the boss treated us. Fuimos a cenar y el jefe se rajó.*

trick (caper, ruse; slang) la vacilada *Mex, Col, Sp;* la transa *Mex, ES, Col* ◆ *It's another government trick. Es otra vacilada del gobierno.*

trifle →see: trinkets

trinkets 1. (that don't cost much; →see also: thingamajig, junk) las baratijas *L. Am., Sp;* los cachivaches *L. Am.;* las chácharas *Mex;* las chivas *Mex;* las carambadas *ES, Nic, CR, Col* ◆ *In that store they sell only trinkets (odds and ends). En esa tienda sólo se venden cachivaches.* 2. (things of little value but cute) las chucherías (from chuches, candy) *DR, PR, Ch, U, Sp;* los tiliches *Mex, C. Am.;* los chiches *S. Cone* ◆ *I don't want to spend a lot of money for Claudia's birthday; I just want to buy her some trinkets. No me quiero gastar mucho dinero para el cumpleaños de Claudia; sólo le quiero comprar unas chucherías.*

troublemaker (→see also: pain in the neck) el/la buscapleitos *L. Am., Sp;* el/la alborotado(-a) (made upset) *Mex, DR, ES, Arg;*

trying to keep up appearances:
The boy doesn't know anything; his dad is trying to keep up appearances.
El niño no sabe nada; su papá le tapa el sol con un dedo.

el/la broncudo(-a) *Mex, ES;* el buscón, la buscona (searcher) *Mex, DR, PR;* el/la bochinchero(-a) (argumentative) *DR, PR, ES, Nic, Ven, Bol, Ch;* el camorrero *S. Cone;* el/la macarra *Sp* ◆ *Miguel is a troublemaker; he always bothers his co-workers.* Miguel es un alborotado; siempre molesta a sus compañeros en el trabajo ◆ *I've had it up to here with that troublemaker.* Ese buscapleitos me tiene hasta la coronilla.

True enough. Pura (Purita) verdad. (Pure truth.) *L. Am., Sp* ◆ *Guanajuato is one of a kind. —True enough, my dear.* Guanajuato is one of a kind. –Purita verdad, comadre.

to **try to keep one's options open** (to profit from either of two people or groups) poner una vela a San Miguel (a Dios) y otra al diablo (to light one candle for Saint Michael [for God] and another for the devil) *DR, PR, Sp* ◆ *Trying to get into those two companies is keeping your options open.* Intentando entrar en esas dos empresas es como poner una vela a San Miguel y otra al diablo.

trying to keep up appearances tapando el sol con un dedo (covering the sun with a finger) *Mex, ES, Nic, Pan, Ven, Col, Peru, Ch* ◆ *They should talk about the problem to their parents; they can't keep trying to keep up appearances.* Deben plantearle el problema a sus padres; no pueden seguir tapando el sol con un dedo.

tumult →see: mess, mob

to **tune out** tener la mente en blanco (to have the mind blank) *Mex, DR, G, Col, U, Arg* (RVar *ES, Ch, Sp:* estar con la mente en blanco); desconectar (to disconnect) *Mex, Cuba, DR, Col, Sp* ◆ *The professor's questions were easy, but I tuned out and couldn't answer.* Las preguntas del profesor eran fáciles, pero yo tenía la mente en blanco y no pude contestar.

turkey 1. (introvert; →see also: geek) el ganso (goose) *PR, S. Cone* (RVar *Ch:* also, gansa and pavo[-a]) ◆ *What a turkey!* ¡Qué ganso! **2.** (stupid person) el/la guajolote(-a) (turkey) *Mex* ◆ *I'm such a turkey; I didn't pass* *the test.* **Soy un guajolote; no pasé el examen.**

to **turn in** →see: to hit the sack, to crash

to **turn on** (be turned on, often has sexual overtones) calentar(se) *L. Am., Sp;* prender *Mex;* hacer tilín (to make a ringing sound, as of a bell, functions like gustar) *Ch, Sp* ♦ *That woman really turns me on.* **Esa mujer me calienta mucho.**

to **turn out badly** salir al revés (to turn out backwards) *C. Am., S. Cone, Sp;* cuatrapear *Mex* ♦ *Despite having planned every detail of the interview, everything turned out badly.* **A pesar de haber planeado cada detalle de la entrevista, todo me salió al revés.**

to **turn red as a beet** (blush) ponerse como un tomate (to become like a tomato) *Mex, DR, PR, S. Cone, Sp* ♦ *When Graciela had to talk in front of so many people, she turned red as a beet.* **Cuando Graciela tuvo que hablar delante de tantas personas, se puso como un tomate.**

to **turn something upside down** poner algo patas pa'rriba (to put something paws up in the air) *DR, PR, ES, Nic, S. Cone, Sp* ♦ *The hurricane turned everything upside down.* **El huracán puso todo patas pa'rriba.**

to **turn the tables** dar la vuelta a la tortilla (to turn over the omelette) *Ch, Sp* ♦ *Rosario has turned the tables and now she's the one who gives the orders in that house.* **Rosario ha dado la vuelta a la tortilla y ahora es ella la que manda en esa casa.**

to **turn up one's nose at** →see: to look down on, to look down one's nose at someone

to be a **turncoat** cambiar de casaca (to change jackets; i.e., leave a group, political party, etc., and go to a different one) *parts of L. Am., Sp* ♦ *That politician is a turncoat.* **Ese político ha cambiado de casaca.**

to be a **turnoff** (be disgusting; be worthless) ser un asco *Mex, U, Arg, Sp* ♦ *This movie is a turnoff.* **Esta película es un asco.**

TV la tele (short for televisión) *L. Am., Sp* ♦ *My husband turns on the TV and starts changing the channels.* **Mi esposo prende la tele y empieza a hacer zapping.**

the **twelfth of never** cuando la rana eche pelos (when the frog sprouts hair) *L. Am.;* el día 30 de febrero (the 30th of February) *Mex, ES;* el día del pago de los bomberos (day when the firemen get paid) *Ch* ♦ *Is Enrique going to call you? —Yes, on the twelfth of never.* **¿Enrique te va a llamar? —Sí, cuando la rana eche pelos.**

twerp (insignificant person or kid) el/la escuintle(-a) (from the Náhautl word for hairless dog; also spelled escuincle) *Mex, parts of C. Am.* ♦ *Why are you afraid of him? He's just a little twerp.* **¿Por qué te da miedo? Es un escuincle.**

twiddling one's thumbs (idle, doing nothing) con los brazos cruzados (also, de brazos cruzados) (with arms crossed) *L. Am., Sp* ♦ *Instead of helping me, Pablo's there twiddling his thumbs.* **En vez de ayudarme, Pablo se queda allí con los brazos cruzados.**

to **twist** (change the meaning of a comment and make it negative; use something for a purpose that wasn't intended) sacar punta a una cosa (to sharpen something, make something pointed) *DR, PR, Sp* ♦ *How you like to twist everything I say around!* **¡Cómo te gusta sacarle punta a todo lo que te digo!**

Two by two. (Everyone with a partner.) Cada oveja con su pareja. (Every sheep with its partner.) *L. Am., Sp* ♦ *We sailed in the Caribbean for three days, and all of us two by two.* **Navegamos en el Caribe por tres días, y cada oveja fue con su pareja.**

to be **two-faced** (act with duplicity) jugar con dos barajas (to play with two decks) *most of L. Am., Sp;* tener dos caras *Mex, ES, U, Arg, Sp;* comer a dos carrillos (to eat with two cheeks) *U, Sp* ♦ *He doesn't have any scruples; he's two-faced.* **No tiene escrúpulos; está jugando con dos barajas.**

two-timer →see: easy woman, slut, womanizer

U

ugly as hell (vulgar) más feo(-a) que carracuca (uglier than carracuca) *Sp* ◆ *I'm ugly as hell, aren't I? —Don't say that, honey!* **Soy más feo que carracuca, ¿verdad? –¡No digas eso, mi amor!**

to be **ugly as sin** ser un(-a) espantapájaros (to be a scarecrow) *L. Am., Sp;* ser un cardo borriquero (to be a cotton thistle) *Sp* ◆ *He's ugly as sin, but he thinks he's really good-looking.* **Es un espantapájaros pero se cree buen mozo.** ◆ *That kid is ugly as sin.* **Ese niño es un cardo borriquero.**

uh-huh ajá *L. Am., Sp* ◆ *Are you ready? Uh-huh, just about.* **¿Estás listo? –Ajá, casi casi.**

under careful watch fichado(-a) *L. Am., Sp* ◆ *Keep him under careful watch. I don't want him to go out.* **Me lo traiga bien fichadito. No quiero que salga.**

under the table (on the sly) por debajo de la mesa (under the table) *most of L. Am.;* por debajo de cuerda (bajo cuerda) (under cord) *Mex, S. Cone, Sp;* por debajo del agua (underwater) *Mex* ◆ *Josefa doesn't have a visa; she is working under the table.* **Josefa no tiene visa; está trabajando por debajo de cuerda.**

to be **under the weather** (feeling bad, physically or mentally) (estar) arrastrando la cobija ([to be] dragging the blanket) *Mex, ES, Col;* (estar) como la mona (to be like the she-monkey) *U, Ch* ◆ *Why are you so quiet? —I'm under the weather.* **¿Por qué estás tan callado? –Estoy como la mona.**

to be **under way** (said of a project) estar en tránsito (to be in transit) *Mex, Col, Ch* ◆ *The report is under way.* **El informe está en tránsito.**

to be **unheard of** →see: to be in a league of its own, to be too much

to be **unlucky** (slang) salarse (to be salted) *Mex, Cuba, DR, G, ES, CR, Col;* tener mala leche (to have bad milk) *G, ES, Col, Ven, Peru;* tener mala sombra (to have bad shade) *ES, Sp;* ser el Pupas, ser más desgraciado(-a) que el Pupas (to be Pupas, unluckier than

Pupas) *Sp* ◆ *I've been really unlucky: first the computer broke down and I lost all my files. Then an important meeting was canceled.* **Ya me he salado: primero se me jodió la computadora y perdí todos los archivos. Después se canceló una reunión importante.**

Unlucky at cards, lucky in love. (said to console someone who has lost a game or at gambling) Desgraciado en el juego, afortunado en amores. (Unlucky at gambling, lucky at love.) *Mex, ES, S. Cone, Sp* ◆ *I always tell Cristina that she is unlucky with cards because she's lucky with love.* **Siempre le digo a Cristina que es desgraciada en el juego porque es afortunada en amores.**

to be **up the creek (without a paddle)** →see: to be in a bind, in hot water

to be **up to date on** estar al corriente de (to be at the running total of) *L. Am., Sp;* estar al tanto de *L. Am., Sp;* estar actualizado *L. Am., Sp* ◆ *Do you need more information about the proposal? —No, thank you, I'm up to date.* **¿Necesitas más información sobre la propuesta? –No, gracias, estoy al corriente.**

to be **up to here** →see: to be fed up

to be **up to one's ears (in something)** (up to one's eyebrows [in something]) estar metido(-a) hasta los codos en algo *Mex* ◆ *I'm up to my ears with this project.* **Estoy metida hasta los codos en este proyecto.**

Up yours! ¡Métetelo donde te quepa! (Put it where it fits!) *Mex, DR, PR, ES, Ch, Sp;* ¡Métetelo donde no te da el sol! (Put it where the sun doesn't shine!) *Arg, U* ◆ *I feel like having a few beers. Will you lend me your car? —No way. —Up yours!* **Tengo ganas de tomar unas cervezas. ¿Me prestas tu coche? –¡Ni a palos! –¡Métetelo donde no te da el sol!**

to **update** 1. (an article, computer program, technology, etc.) actualizar *L. Am., Sp* ◆ *This program is out of date. —You're right; we have to update all our equipment.* **Este programa está desactualizado. –Tienes razón, tene-**

mos que actualizar todo nuestro equipo. **2.** (someone about a situation) poner (a alguien) al día *L. Am., Sp;* poner (a alguien) al tanto *L. Am., Sp;* poner (a alguien) al corriente *L. Am., Sp ◆ How is it in the office? Can you update me on what is going on with the new manager? ¿Qué tal en la oficina? ¿Puedes ponerme al tanto de lo que pasa con el nuevo gerente?*

the **upper crust** (highest social class) la flor y nata (flower and whipped cream) *L. Am., Sp;* la crema y nata (cream and whipped cream) *L. Am., Sp ◆ The upper crust was at that reception. En esa recepción estaba la flor y nata de la sociedad.*

uproar (confusion; →see also: mess) el relajo *Mex, DR, PR, G, ES, Nic, Col, U, Sp ◆ What an uproar, kids! Calm down because you are going to bother the neighbors. ¡Qué relajo, muchachos! Cálmense, porque van a molestar a los vecinos.*

ups and downs altibajos *L. Am., Sp;* sus más y sus menos *Mex, Sp ◆ The director had his ups and downs with that actress, but it's an excellent film. El director tuvo sus más y sus menos con esa actriz, pero es una película excelente.*

upset (annoyed, resentful; →see also: mad at, steamed) picado(-a) (piqued, stung) *Mex, G, CR, Col, Ven, Bol, Ch, Sp ◆ The dog won't obey you and now you're upset. El perro no te obedece y ya estás picado.*

to **upset someone** (→see also: to bug, to give someone a hard time, to rile up) sacar a alguien de sus casillas (de quicio) (to take someone out of their pigeon holes [out of doorjamb]) *L. Am., Sp;* picar a alguien (to bite, sting someone) *Mex, DR, PR, G, Peru, Sp ◆ What's upsetting you? ¿Qué te pica?*

to **upset the apple cart** (get people riled up) alborotar las avispas (el panal) (to stir up the wasps [honeycomb]) *Mex, ES, CR, Ch, Sp;* alborotar el gallinero (to stir up the henhouse) *Mex, Ch, Sp ◆ Juana is always upsetting the apple cart. Juana siempre anda alborotando las avispas.*

to be **upset with someone** (→see also: to be bugged, mad at, steamed) andar mosca (to go fly) *PR, Sp;* tenerle una bronca a alguien *U, Arg ◆ Don't talk to me about that guy. I'm upset with him. He's a liar. No me hables de ese tipo. Le tengo una bronca. Es un mentiroso.*

uptight →see: to be on edge, to be stressed out, nervous as a cat

to be **uptight** **1.** (a tightass) ser un(a) fruncido(-a) (to be a wrinkled-up person) *S. Cone ◆ Nobody talks to her at school because she's very uptight. Nadie le habla en la escuela porque ella es muy fruncida.* **2.** (worried) estar nervioso(-a) (to be nervous) *L. Am., Sp;* estar más serio(-a) que un burro en lancha (to be more serious than a donkey in a rowboat) *CR ◆ What's up with you? You look uptight. ¿Qué te pasa? Estás más seria que un burro en lancha.*

to **use connections to help** palanquear (to move levers) *ES, Col, Peru, S. Cone;* muñequear (to wrist) *Peru, S. Cone ◆ Ernest used some connections for me, and I got the job. Ernesto me palanqueó, y conseguí el trabajo.*

to be **useless** (inept; →see also: to be worthless) no servir para nada (to not serve for anything) *L. Am., Sp;* no tener chiste (to not have any joke) *Mex, ES, Col, Ec, Peru;* no servir ni a Dios ni al diablo (to serve neither God nor the devil) *Mex, Ch ◆ These new regulations are useless. Estos nuevos reglamentos no sirven ni a Dios ni al diablo.*

user →see: druggie

V

to **vent** (problems, etc.) desahogarse (to undrown oneself) *L. Am., Sp* ◆ *I needed to vent, so I took a walk.* Necesitaba desahogarme, así que hice una caminata.

very re-que-te (intensifiers used before adjectives, adverbs, and even verbs) *L. Am., Sp* ◆ *I love you all very much. Actually, very very very much!* Los reamo. De hecho, ¡los requeteamo!

very good →see: super

The **very idea!** →see: What a thing to say!

very similar: →chip off the old block

violently 1. (without respect) por la tremenda (by the tremendous) *Sp* ◆ *They imposed their will violently, without respecting anyone else's opinion.* Impusieron su voluntad por la tremenda, sin respetar la opinión de ninguno de los demás. 2. (to the hilt) a sangre y fuego (by blood and fire) *Mex, Sp* ◆ *He defended his position violently, until finally they agreed that he was right.* Defendió su postura a sangre y fuego, hasta que al final le dieron la razón.

vulgar →see: tacky, swear word

vulture →see: chowhound, eating like a horse

W

to **wait it out** (get through something difficult but necessary) aguantar el chaparrón (to put up with the rain shower) *S. Cone, Sp;* aguantar el nublado (el nubarrón) (to put up with the cloudiness) *Sp* ◆ *Beatriz waited out her parents' anger patiently because she knew they were right. Beatriz aguantó el nublado de sus padres porque sabía que tenían razón.*

The **walls have ears.** (The coast is not clear.) Hay moros en la costa. (There are Moors on the coast, phrase warning that someone else may be listening.) *L. Am., Sp* ◆ *We can't talk right now; the walls have ears. No podemos hablar ahora; hay moros en la costa.*

to be a **walk in the park** →see: to be a piece of cake, It's no picnic.

wary →see: skittery

to **wash one's hands of something or someone** (forget about) borrar algo (a alguien) del mapa (to wipe something [someone] off the map) *Mex, DR, ES, S. Cone, Sp* ◆ *Wash your hands of all that. Borra eso del mapa.*

to **wash (someone) out** (on an exam, a project, in love, etc.) tronar (to thunder) *Mex, C. Am.* ◆ *They washed me out. Me tronaron.*

to **wash out** (fail totally; →see also: to blow it, to flunk, to go to the devil) caerse con todo el equipo (to fall with the whole team or equipment) *Mex, Sp;* tronar como (un) ejote (to snap like a peapod) *Mex;* sonar (como tarro) (to ring [like a tin can]) *Ch, U;* ir al garete *Sp;* no vender una escoba (to not sell a broom) *Sp* ◆ *The con man washed up totally. Finally he was found out, and now he's in jail. El estafador se cayó con todo el equipo. Finalmente fue descubierto, y ahora está en la cárcel.*

to be **wasted** (dead drunk; →see also: to be plastered) estar hasta el copete (to be up to the forelock, top of hair) *Mex, ES, Col, Sp;* estar ahogado(-a) (to be drowned) *Mex, ES, Col;* estar hasta atrás (to be behind) *Mex, ES, Col;* estar hasta las chanclas (to be up to the sandals) *Mex, ES;* andar haciendo eses (to go around making "s"s) *Mex, S. Cone, Sp;* andar cacheteando la banqueta (to go along with one's cheek on the sidewalk) *Mex;* estar hasta el cepillo (to be up to the brush) *Mex;* estar bolo(-a) *C. Am.;* estar curdo(-a) (from Lunfardo, Buenos Aires slang) *Cuba, Ven, U, Arg;* estar como una cuba (to be like a cask) *U, Arg, Sp* ◆ *I saw your uncle yesterday coming out of the bar and he was wasted. Vi a tu tío ayer saliendo del bar y caminaba haciendo eses.*

to **watch out** (be warned, suspicious; →see also: to pay attention) estar con ojo (to be with eye) *Mex, Sp* ◆ *You have to watch out, Amanda. That person could have bad intentions. Tienes que estar con ojo, Amanda. Esa persona puede tener malas intenciones.*

Watch out! Hay moros en la costa. (There are Moors on the coast, phrase warning that someone else may be listening.) *L. Am., Sp;* Mucho ojo, que la vista engaña. (Much eye; the sight deceives.) *Mex, ES, U, Arg, Sp;* ¡Aguas! (Waters!) *Mex, G, ES, Col;* ¡Agua sucia! (Dirty water!) *Mex, Col;* Hay ropa tendida. (There is clothing hung out to dry.) *Mex, Ch, U, Sp* ◆ *Watch out! The foreman has arrived. ¡Aguas! Llegó el capataz.*

to **watch over** (guard) ir de miranda *Sp* ◆ *Her mom went just to watch (over her). Su mamá fue de miranda.*

Way to go! That's the way to do it! ¡Así se hace! *L. Am., Sp* ◆ *I'll finish my studies (degree) this year. —Congratulations, way to go! Terminaré mi carrera este año. —Te felicito, ¡así se hace!*

way too much para parar un tren (to stop a train) *Mex, ES, Sp* ◆ *There's way too much food here (enough to feed an army). You've gone overboard in your calculations of how much we need for this party. Hay comida para parar un*

to be wet behind the ears: *I think the new director is wet behind the ears.*
Creo que el nuevo director está en pañales.

tren. Te has pasado calculando lo necesario para esta fiesta.

We (you, etc.) missed the boat. (→see also: to miss the boat) Voló la paloma. (The dove flew off.) *Mex, ES;* Pasó la vieja. (The old lady went by.; said to mean that someone missed out on something by acting too slowly or forgetting it) *Ch* ◆ *I think we missed the boat. Me parece que ya voló la paloma.*

to **wear and look good in** lucir (to shine) *DR, PR, CR, ES, Nic, Col, Sp* ◆ *Red pants and a heavy necklace look good on Rosa. She's wearing new shoes (a good dress). A Rosa le lucen pantalones rojos y un collar grueso. Anda luciendo zapatos nuevos (un buen vestido).*

to **wear someone down** (by bothering them) tener (traer) a alguien frito(-a) (to have [bring] someone fried) *Mex, DR, Sp* ◆ *Daniela has worn me down with her behavior. Daniela me tiene frita con su conducta.*

to **wear the pants** (make one's authority felt) llevar bien puestos los pantalones (to wear the pants well placed) *Mex, DR, PR, ES, Sp;* amarrarse los pantalones (to tie up or tighten one's pants) *CR, ES, Ch* ◆ *In that house, Marcos wears the pants. En esa casa Marcos lleva bien puestos los pantalones.*

the **wee hours** (an undetermined hour, late at night or in the day) las tantas *Mex, DR, Sp* ◆ *Claudio arrived in the wee hours of the morning. Claudio llegó a las tantas de la madrugada.*

well built (muscular; →see also: to have a nice build) macizo(-a) *L. Am., Sp* ◆ *Luis Rodrigo is only fifteen years old but he's very well built. Luis Rodrigo sólo tiene quince años pero es bien macizo.*

wet behind the ears (naive; →see also: clueless) caído(-a) del nido (fallen out of the nest) *L. Am.* ◆ *I explained it to you a hundred times, but you didn't get it. You seem wet behind the ears. Te lo expliqué cien veces, pero ni cuenta te diste. Pareces como caído del nido.*

to be **wet behind the ears** (have little or no knowledge of something) estar en pañales (to be in diapers) *L. Am., Sp* ◆ *You don't have* *experience; you're still wet behind the ears.* **No tienes experiencia; estás en pañales aún.**

wet blanket (turn-off, someone who refuses to do things, is always negative; →see also: drag, party pooper, grouch, pain) repelón, repelona *Mex* ◆ *Gloria never wants to do anything. What a wet blanket!* **Gloria nunca quiere hacer nada. ¡Qué repelona!**

to **wet one's whistle** (have a swig or drink) empinar el codo (to raise one's elbow) *L. Am., Sp* ◆ *They wet their whistles all afternoon, and afterwards they couldn't attend the concert.* **Empinaron el codo toda la tarde, y después no pudieron asistir al concierto.**

wetback (illegal) mojado(-a) (wet; pejorative, meaning wet from crossing the Rio Grande) *Chicano, Mex, G, ES, Col* ◆ *Don Fernando came as a wetback thirty years ago.* **Don Fernando se vino mojado hace treinta años.**

whacko →see: nuts

What a bummer! El (Mi) gozo en un pozo. (The [My] enjoyment in a well.) *Mex, Sp* ◆ *I went outside and saw that someone had stolen my motorcycle. What a bummer.* **Salí de casa y vi que alguien me había robado la moto. Mi gozo en un pozo.**

What a damn pain! ¡Qué jodienda! (vulgar, from **joder**) *Cuba, DR, PR, Col, Ven, Para, U, Sp* ◆ *What a damn pain to have to wash so many plates after supper.* **Qué jodienda tener que lavar tantos platos después de la cena.**

What a drag! (→see also: What a pain [in the neck]!) ¡Qué cruz! (What a cross!) *Mex, DR, PR, Col, U, Sp* ◆ *What a drag to have a drunk for a husband!* **¡Qué cruz tener un marido borracho!**

What a gem! (ironic) ¡Buena alhaja! *L. Am., Sp* ◆ *Fernando is a total jerk. —Yes, he's a real gem!* **Fernando es un cero a la izquierda. —Sí, ¡buena alhaja!**

What a helluva dirty trick! ¡Qué gran cagada! (What a pile of shit!, usually refers to a lie or betrayal) *ES, S. Cone, Sp* (RVar *Sp:* often used to imply a big mistake)

What a pain (in the neck)! (→see also: What a drag!) ¡Qué lata! *L. Am., Sp;* ¡Qué joroba! *Mex, DR, PR, Col, U;* ¡Qué vaina! (What a husk, sheath!) *DR, most of C. Am., Col, Ven* ◆ *What a pain to have to work on*

weekends! **¡Qué joroba tener que trabajar los fines de semana!**

What a piece of shit! ¡Qué gran cagada! (What a pile of shit!; usually refers to a lie or betrayal) *ES, S. Cone, Sp* (RVar *Sp:* often used to imply a big mistake).

What a shame! ¡Qué lástima! *L. Am., Sp;* ¡Achará!, ¡Chará! *CR* ◆ *What I shame! I won't be able to see my friend when I go to Boston.* **¡Qué lástima! No podré ver a mi amiga cuando vaya a Boston.**

What a stretch! ¡Puras jaladas! (Pure stretches!) *Mex* ◆ *I don't believe those stories about your trip. What a stretch!* **No creo esas historias sobre tu viaje. ¡Son puras jaladas!**

What a stroke of luck! ¡La vida me sonríe! (Life is smiling on me!) *L. Am., Sp* ◆ *I just found out that they gave me the job. What a stroke of luck!* **Acabo de saber que me dieron el puesto. ¡La vida me sonríe!**

What a thing to say! (The very idea!; sometimes used to react to a compliment in a modest way) ¡Qué ocurrencia! (What an occurrence! What a thing to occur to you!) *L. Am., Sp* ◆ *How pretty you look! —What a thing to say!* **¡Qué bonita te ves! –¡Qué ocurrencia!**

What can you do? ¿Qué remedio? (What remedy?, phrase of resignation meaning there's no apparent solution) *L. Am., Sp* ◆ *Don't you like the opera? —What can you do? The tickets cost a fortune.* **¿Te gusta la ópera? –¡Qué remedio! La entrada valió un dineral.**

What do you do for a living? ¿A qué te dedica(a)? *L. Am., Sp;* ¿En qué la giras? (In what do you [tú] spin [it]?) *Mex, Col* ◆ *What do you do for a living, Miguel? —I design kitchens.* **¿En qué la giras, Miguel? –Soy diseñador de cocinas.**

What do you mean . . . ? ¿Cómo que... ? *parts of L. Am., Sp* ◆ *What do you mean you lost the money?* **¿Cómo que perdiste el dinero?**

What does that mean? →see: What's all that about?

What else is happening in your life? Y de la vida, ¿qué más? (And of life, what more?) *Caribbean*

What goes around comes around. (Someday we'll meet and we'll be in the same situation; reply after someone has criticized another, putting that person in his or her place) Arrieros somos que en el camino andamos. (We are mule drivers and we travel the roads.) *Mex, ES, Ch* ◆ *We worked much harder than Edgar on that project for the same pay, but what goes around comes around.* Trabajamos mucho más que Edgar en ese proyecto por la misma plata, pero arrieros somos y en el camino andamos.

What luck! ¡Qué suerte! *L. Am., Sp;* ¡Qué leche! (What milk!, a bit vulgar in Sp) *Mex, PR, G, Col, Sp;* ¡Qué dicha! (What bliss!) *G, Nic, CR* ◆ *What luck to see you again after so many years!* ¡Qué dicha volverte a ver después de tantos años!

What nerve (brazenness)! ¡Qué descaro! *L. Am., Sp* ◆ *What nerve! How dare you speak with your parents using those words?* ¡Qué descaro! ¿Cómo te atreves a hablar con esas palabras a tus padres?

What nonsense! (→see also: Baloney!) ¡Qué tontería(s)! *L. Am., Sp* ◆ *What nonsense! I'd never spend money on a fur coat.* ¡Qué tonterías dices! Jamás gastaría dinero en un abrigo de piel.

What the hell is going on? ¿Qué mierda pasa? (What shit is happening? vulgar) *L. Am., Sp;* ¿Qué vaina (mierda) es ésta? (What screw-up [thing, shit] is this?; vulgar) *ES, Ven* ◆ *What the hell is going on? You can't go off without explaining your decision.* ¿Qué mierda es ésta? No puedes irte sin explicar tu decisión.

What will become of us? ¿(A)dónde vamos a parar? (Where are we going to end up?) *Mex, DR, ES, S. Cone, Sp* ◆ *What are we going to do with this crisis? What will become of us?* ¿Qué vamos a hacer con esta crisis? ¿Adónde vamos a parar?

whatchamacallit →see: thingamajig

Whatever . . . Como quiera(s). (Whatever you want.) *L. Am., Sp;* Lo que sea. (Whatever may be.) *L. Am., Sp;* No me importa. (Whatever you want.) *L. Am., Sp;* Qué más da. (What more does it give.) *L. Am. (not S. Cone)* ◆ *What are you doing tonight? —Whatever . . .* ¿Qué vas a hacer esta noche? —Lo que sea.

whatever happens, happens (→see also: come hell or high water, no matter what) a lo que salga (with whatever comes up) *Mex, ES, DR, PR, U, Arg, Sp* ◆ *I prefer organized tours but Víctor likes adventure, so we're going to Mexico and whatever happens, happens.* Yo prefiero los viajes organizados pero a Víctor le encanta la aventura, así que nos vamos a México a lo que salga.

What's all that about? ¿Y eso? (And that?) *L. Am., Sp* ◆ *What's all that about? Where did you come up with such strange ideas, Manuelita?* ¿Y eso? ¿De dónde sacaste esas ideas tan extrañas, Manuelita?

What's bugging you? ¿Qué bicho te ha picado? (What insect has bitten you?) *Mex, DR, G, S. Cone, Sp* ◆ *Why are you shouting like that? What's bugging you?* ¿Por qué gritas de esa manera? ¿Qué bicho te ha picado?

What's happening? ¿Qué pasa? (What passes?) *L. Am., Sp*

What's happening with . . . ? (→see also: What's up?) ¿Qué me cuentas? (What do you tell me?) *L. Am., Sp* ◆ *What's happening in your relationship with Alfonso?* ¿Qué me cuentas de tu relación con Alfonso?

What's up? (→see also: How are things/ you?) ¿Qué onda(s)? (What sound wave[s]?) *L. Am.;* ¿Qué jue? *Mex, Col;* ¿Qué bolá? *Cuba;* ¿Tá la vaina? (How's the thing?) *Ven;* ¿Qué se teje? (What's being knitted?) *Ch;* ¿Qué notas me cuentas? (What notes are you telling me?) *most of L. Am.* ◆ *Hi, Graciela. What's up?* Hola, Graciela. ¿Qué notas me cuentas? (¿Qué ondas?)

to **wheel and deal** (be clever and try hard to get something) apiolarse *Mex, Arg* ◆ *Those businesspeople are really wheeling and dealing.* Esos comerciantes se están apiolando.

wheels 1. (car) la ranfla *Chicano, Mex;* el carro *Mex, C. Am., Peru, Arg;* la lámina (use of part for the whole) *Mex, Col;* la máquina (machine) *Cuba;* el buga *Sp* ◆ *Our car was in the shop, but a friend gave us a ride.* Nuestro carro estaba en el taller, pero un amigo nos dio un aventón. **2.** (nice big car) el carrazo *Mex, ES, Col* ◆ *Alejo bought some nice big wheels.* Alejo compró un carrazo.

to be a whiz at something: *That artist is a whiz at painting.*
Ese artista se pinta solo.

when hell freezes over →see: the twelfth of never

when you least expect it el día menos pensado (the least thought-of day) *L. Am., Sp* ◆ *When you least expect it, they call you and invite you out. El día menos pensado te llaman y te invitan a salir.*

to be a **while** ir para rato (to go for a while) *L. Am., Sp* ◆ *She has been working here for a while. Ya va para rato que trabaja aquí.*

to **whine** (complain) chillar *Chicano, Mex, G, ES, Col, U* ◆ *I went to the tax office and I whined and whined until they gave me back my money. Fui a la oficina de impuestos y chillé y chillé hasta que escucharon y me devolvieron mi dinero.*

whiner →see: crybaby

to be a **whiz** (competent) ser cachimbón, cachimbona *Mex, G, ES;* ser un fregón (una fregona) *Mex;* ser un crack (to be a crack) *Sp* ◆ *That guy is a whiz at working with wood. Ese chico es bien cachimbón para trabajar con madera.* ◆ *Diego is a whiz. They offered him*

three scholarships. *Diego es un crack. Le ofrecieron tres becas.*

to be a **whiz at something** pintarse solo(-a) para una cosa (to paint oneself alone for something) *Mex, U, Arg, Sp* ◆ *My husband is a whiz at playing the piano. Mi esposo se pinta solo tocando el piano.*

to be a **whiz in business** tener colmillo (to have eyetooth) *Mex, ES, CR*

Who cares? ¿Qué más da? (What more does it give?) *L. Am., not S. Cone, Sp* ◆ *Mom, I broke the plate. —Who cares? Mamá, rompí el plato. —¿Qué más da?*

Who do you think I am? (phrase implying that the other person is innocent or unaware of one's merits) Mírame esta cara. (Look at this face.) *Mex, Sp* ◆ *Who do you think I am? Do you think I'm capable of lying to you? Mírame esta cara. ¿Me crees capaz de mentirte?*

Who knows? Vaya uno a saber. (Go to know.) *L. Am., Sp;* A saber. (To be known.) *parts of L. Am., Sp;* Sepa Chepa. (Chepa probably knows.) *Chicano, Nic;* Chepa la

bola. *Mex;* Vaya usted (Vete) a saber. (Go
to know.) *Peru, Bol, Sp* ◆ *Who knows what
you guys are up to? Vaya uno a saber lo que
hacen ustedes.*

the **whole enchilada** (the whole nine yards,
the whole shooting match; all) todititito(-a),
(variant of todo) *Mex, ES, Nic* ◆ *The whole
enchilada was wrecked for us. Ya se nos
arruinó todititito.*

the **whole live-long day** todo el santo día
(all the holy day) *L. Am., Sp* ◆ *I waited for her
call the whole live-long day. Esperé su llamada
todo el santo día.*

a **whole lot** (a lot; used as an adverb in
slang) cantidad (quantity) *Mex, ES, Ch, Sp*
◆ *I've eaten a whole lot. He comido cantidad.*

to **whoop it up** →see: to have a blast, to
have a good time

Why are you staring at me? ¿Tengo
monos en la cara? (Do I have monkeys on
my face?) *Mex, Ch, U, Sp* ◆ *Why are you looking at me so long? Why are you staring at me?
¿Por qué me miras tanto? ¿Tengo monos en
la cara?*

**Why bother when no one will see the
difference?** En la noche todos los gatos
son pardos (negros). (At night all cats are
dark-colored; it's hard to see any difference
between some things.) *L. Am., Sp* ◆ *Do you
want to go to the movies? —No, I haven't even
put on my make-up. —Why bother when no
one will see the difference? ¿Quieres ir al cine?
—No, no me he maquillado aun. —¿Qué importa? En la noche todos los gatos son negros.*

wiener (penis; →see also: dick) la paloma
(dove) *C. Am., Col, Ven, Ec, Peru, Bol*

to **wig out** →see: to lose one's marbles

wigged out →see: nuts

to be **wildly happy, ecstatic** (→see also:
happy as a lark) estar loco(-a) de contento
(to be crazy with happiness) *DR, Sp*

Will wonders never cease! →see: Holy
smoke!

willies (nervousness; →see: heebie-jeebies)

willy-nilly →see: helter-skelter

wimp 1. (man who is pushed around by his
wife or girlfriend or overly attached to his
mother; →see also: chicken, henpecked

man, pushover) el calzonudo (oversized
pants) *Mex, ES, Peru, Ch, Arg;* el calzonazos
(oversized pants) *Ch, Sp* ◆ *It doesn't surprise
me that he married that bossy woman; he's always been a wimp. No me extraña que se
haya casado con esa sargenta; siempre ha
sido un calzonudo.* **2.** (timid) el/la corto(-a)
de genio (short of temper) *Peru, Ch* ◆ *My
son is a wimp and doesn't know how to defend
himself. Mi hijo es corto de genio y no sabe
defenderse.*

windbag (nonstop talker; →see also: to talk
a blue streak) la tarabilla *Mex, ES, Nic* ◆ *Let's
not invite the neighbor; she's a windbag. No invitemos a la vecina, que es una tarabilla.*

to be a **windbag** (talk a lot without saying
much) tener mucho rollo (to have a lot of
roll) *Mex, Sp* ◆ *Tomás is a real windbag; he
talks a lot but doesn't say anything interesting.
Tomás tiene mucho rollo; habla mucho pero
no dice nada interesante.*

to **window-shop** mirar las vitrinas *L. Am.;*
echar un taco de ojo (to throw a taco of the
eye, slang) *Mex* ◆ *Let's go window shopping
downtown! ¡Vamos al centro a echar un taco
de ojo!*

to **wipe out** **1.** (exhaust) hacer migas a alguien (to make someone crumbs) *Mex, ES,
Sp;* hacer morder el polvo a alguien (to make
someone bite the dust) *DR, Sp* ◆ *Our gymnastics coach wiped us out. Nuestro entrenador de gimnasia nos hizo morder el
polvo.* **2.** (kill) borrar (to erase) *Chicano,
Mex;* linchar (to lynch) *Mex, Cuba, DR, PR,
ES, G, Col, Ch, Sp;* dar pasaporte a alguien
(to give someone passport) *Mex, ES, Sp;*
tumbar (to fell, knock down) *Mex, Cuba,
Col;* echarse a alguien (to throw oneself to
someone) *Mex, Cuba, G* ◆ *Paco is dead? —
People say they wiped him out because he knew
too much about the murder. ¿Paco está
muerto? —Se dice que lo borraron porque
sabía demasiado del crimen.* **3.** (physically
or mentally) hacer añicos (pedazos) (to
break into pieces) *Mex, ES, U, Arg, Sp* ◆ *My
parents' death wiped me out emotionally. La
muerte de mis padres me hizo añicos.*

wiped out (exhausted) rendido(-a) (rendered) *L. Am., Sp;* amolado(-a) (ground,
sharpened) *Mex, C. Am.;* hecho(-a) pedazos,
(or añicos) (made into pieces) *Mex, ES, U,
Arg, Sp;* quemado(-a) (burned) *Mex, DR, G,*

CR, Col, Sp; molido(-a) (ground down) *Mex, PR, ES, Ch, U, Sp;* reventado(-a) (burst, blown apart) *Mex, Cuba, PR, Col, S. Cone, Sp;* hecho(-a) polvo (made into dust) *Mex, Cuba, DR, Sp;* hecho(-a) un puré (made into a purée) *Mex, Sp;* hecho(-a) pinole (made into pinole, an aromatic powder that used to be used in making chocolate) *Mex;* fundido (-a) (melted) *G, Col, U, Arg;* hecho(-a) fosfatina (made into powder) *Sp ◆ I worked seven days straight and I'm wiped out. Trabajé siete días seguidos y estoy rendido.*

to **wise up** (see the light; find out something everyone else already knows; →see also: to get it) caerse el veinte (to have the twenty-cent piece fall, as in a machine) *Mex;* caerse del mecate (to fall off the cord) *Mex;* caerse de la mata (to fall out of the bush or shrub) *Cuba, DR, PR, Col;* quedarse con la copla (to remain or end up with the verse, stanza) *Sp ◆ I finally wised up (saw the light). Por fin me cayó el veinte. ◆ ¿Te caíste de la mata? Did you (finally) wise up?*

wisecrack (barbed remark) la puntada *Mex, ES ◆ What a a great wisecrack Mario made at the party. Qué gran puntada la que hizo Mario en la fiesta.*

with a helluva lot of effort (slang) a (puro) huevo (also, a huevos) (at [pure] egg, testicle; vulgar) *Mex, C. Am. ◆ Julia finished the project in two weeks with a helluva lot of effort. Julia terminó el proyecto en dos semanas a puro huevo.*

with a lot of effort a duras penas (at hard pains) *Mex, DR, PR, S. Cone, Sp;* a puro pulmón (at pure lung) *L. Am., Sp;* a trancas y barrancas (at beams and ravines/cliffs, passing over all obstacles) *Mex, Sp;* a malas penas (at bad pains) *Sp ◆ With a lot of effort, the doctors made it to the most remote populations. A trancas y barrancas, los médicos llegaron a las poblaciones más remotas.*

with a lot of fanfare (news broadcast far and wide) a bombo y platillo (also, con bombos y platillos) (at drum and saucer) *Mex, DR, PR, Sp ◆ The news arrived from Spain to Mexico with a lot of fanfare. A bombo y platillo las noticias llegaron desde España hasta México.*

with great difficulty →see: with a lot of effort

with great pleasure de mil amores (of a thousand loves) *Mex, DR, ES, S. Cone, Sp ◆ I'll do what you ask with great pleasure. Haré lo que me pides de mil amores.*

with it ("in"; →see also: cool) en la movida, en la onda, a la moda, actualizado(-a) *Mex, PR, Col, Sp ◆ You're not with it, girlfriend. You have to be where the action is. No estás en la onda, amiga. Hay que estar en la movida.*

with no joking (fooling) around sin cachondeo(s) *Sp ◆ We talked to our children with no joking around. Sin cachondeos platicamos con nuestros hijos.*

with one foot in the grave (near death) con un pie en el hoyo (with one foot in the hole) *Mex, DR, PR, Sp;* con un pie en el otro mundo (with one foot in the other world) *Sp ◆ Poor old Danilo has one foot in the grave. — Well, right, but he's ninety-seven years old. Pobrecito don Danilo anda con un pie en el hoyo. —Bueno, pero ya tiene noventa y siete años.*

with one's heart on one's sleeve con el corazón en la mano (with one's heart in one's hand) *L. Am., Sp ◆ With my heart on my sleeve, I told them what I knew of their father. Con el corazón en la mano, les dije lo que sabía de su padre.*

with one's tail between one's legs (humiliated, embarrassed) con el rabo entre las piernas *DR, PR, S. Cone, Sp ◆ He went to the neighbors' house to complain about the noise, but he came back with his tail between his legs when he saw that his son was there. Fue a casa de los vecinos para quejarse del ruido, pero regresó con el rabo entre las piernas cuando vio que su hijo estaba allí.*

with the stroke of a pen (quickly) de un plumazo *L. Am., Sp ◆ With the stroke of a pen she gave the orders to the secretaries. De un plumazo dio las órdenes a los secretarios.*

without rhyme or reason sin ton ni son (without tone or sound) *L. Am., Sp ◆ That novel is absurd. Without rhyme or reason. Esa novela es absurda. Sin ton ni son.*

wolf →see: womanizer

to **wolf down** (gobble up) devorar (to devour) *L. Am., Sp;* meter (to put in) *Sp ◆ I wolfed down four beers and two sandwiches in fifteen minutes. Me metí cuatro cañas y dos bocadillos en quince minutos.*

wolf in sheep's clothing 1. el diablo vendiendo cruces (the devil selling crosses) *L. Am.* ◆ *The new mayor is more hypocritical than a wolf in sheep's clothing.* El nuevo alcalde es más hipócrita que el diablo vendiendo cruces. 2. (man who appears faithful but is really a Don Juan, or, very rarely, a woman who acts sweet and obedient but isn't) el/la mátalas callando (kill-them-being-quiet) *Mex, DR, ES, Col* ◆ *Geraldito seems like the perfect husband, but he's really a wolf in sheep's clothing.* Geraldito parece el marido perfecto, pero realmente es un mátalas callando.

woman →see: babe, broad, chick,

woman of ill repute →see: hooker, slut

woman of the streets (→see also: hooker, slut) la mujer de mal vivir (woman who lives badly) *L. Am., Sp;* la mujer de mala vida (woman of a bad life) *Sp* ◆ *In that neighborhood there are a lot of women of the streets.* En ese barrio hay muchas mujeres de mal vivir.

womanizer →see also: playboy) el mujeriego (mujerero) *L. Am., Sp;* el don Juan (Don Juan) *L. Am., Sp;* el tenorio (old expression) *L. Am., Sp;* el lobo (wolf) *Chicano, Mex, PR;* el buitre (vulture) *Mex, PR, Col, Ven, U, Sp;* el barbarazo *Mex, PR, Col;* el gallinazo *Mex, Col;* el gavilán (hawk) *Mex, Col;* el caimán (alligator) *Mex, Col;* el tiburón (shark) *PR, Col, U* ◆ *In my family there are a number of womanizers.* En mi familia hay varios mujeriegos.

to be a **wonder worker** →see: to be a whiz at something

wonderfully a las mil maravillas (to the thousand marvels) *L. Am., Sp* ◆ *Nuria knew her role wonderfully. She put on a terrific show.* Nuria se sabía su papel a las mil maravillas. Hizo un espectáculo precioso.

word of mouth →see: to travel by word of mouth

a **word (with you)** (a short conversation) dos palabras (two words) *Mex, ES, S. Cone* ◆ *Can I talk with you? Just a word.* ¿Puedo hablarte? Sólo van a ser dos palabras.

The **word is that . . .** Se corre que... (It's run that . . .) *L. Am, Sp* ◆ *The word is that (There's a rumor going around that) he has a girlfriend.* Se corre que tiene novia.

to **work like a dog** trabajar como burro (to work like a donkey) *L. Am., Sp;* trabajar como enano (to work like a dwarf) *Ch, U, Sp* ◆ *Olga worked like a dog in the winter, and she'll travel in the summer.* Olga trabajó como burra en invierno, y en verano viajará.

to **work one's ass off** (all vulgar; →see also: to work like a dog) echar huevos a un asunto, echarle huevos (to throw eggs or testicles to an issue) *Mex, C. Am., Sp;* partirse los cojones (to break one's testicles) *Sp;* pringar (to dip or soak in grease; to stab) *Sp* ◆ *They were all working their asses off.* Estaban partiéndose los cojones todos.

to **work one's fingers to the bone** (→see also: to work like a dog) bailar de coronilla (to dance on one's head) *L. Am., Sp;* doblar el lomo (to fold or bend the back) *Mex, DR, PR, Col, U, Arg;* dar el callo (to give callus) *Sp* ◆ *When we immigrated to Canada, we worked our fingers to the bone.* Cuando inmigramos a Canadá, doblamos el lomo.

to **work wonders** hacer maravillas *L. Am., Sp;* echarse ese trompo a la uña (to put that top, the spinning toy, on one's fingernail, perform an amazing feat) *Mex, ES* ◆ *Constitutional reform? We'll see if they can work that wonder.* ¿Reforma constitucional? A ver si se echan ese trompo a la uña.

workaholic el/la trabajólico(-a) *parts of L. Am.* ◆ *Poor Esmeralda! She never goes out on the weekend because her husband is a workaholic.* ¡Pobre Esmeralda! Nunca sale los fines de semana porque su marido es trabajólico.

to be **working at odd jobs** hacer algunas chapuzas *Sp* ◆ *Do you have a job? —I'm doing some odd jobs.* ¿Tienes trabajo? —Hago algunas chapuzas.

working guy/girl (rank and file) el/la currante *Sp* ◆ *I'm just a working guy; tell (it to) my boss.* Sólo soy un currante; díselo a mi jefe.

workover (a beating or sexual play) la calentadita (little heating up) *Mex, ES, Col, U* ◆ *They said they were looking for a guy to give him a little workover.* Dijeron que buscaban a un tipo para darle una calentadita.

to **worm out of** →see: to back out of, to pass the buck

worn down/out →see: wiped out

worn to a frazzle →see: wiped out

to be **worn to the bone** (→see also: to be wiped out) dolerle hasta los huesos (to have even the bones ache) *L. Am., Sp*; no poder alguien con sus huesos (to not be able with one's bones) *Mex, U, Sp* ♦ *After working so much, I was worn to the bone.* **Después de tanto trabajar, no podía con mis huesos.**

to be **worth a fortune** valer un Potosí (un mundo, un imperio) (to be worth a Potosí, from the silver-mining area of Bolivia [a world, an empire]) *Mex, DR, Peru, Sp* ♦ *Your grandmother's jewelry is worth a fortune. You should have it in the safe.* **Las alhajas de tu abuela valen un Potosí. Deberías tenerlas en la caja fuerte.**

to be **worth beans** →see: to be worthless

to be **worth its weight in gold** valer su peso en oro *Mex, DR, Sp* ♦ *That girl is worth her weight in gold.* **Esa muchacha vale su peso en oro.**

worthless (thing) papel mojado (wet paper) *most of L. Am., Sp* ♦ *The famous principle that all men are equal is worthless.* **El famoso principio de que todos los hombres son iguales es papel mojado.**

to be **worthless** (worth beans) no valer un bledo (to not be worth a pigweed) *Mex, ES, U, Arg, Sp*; no valer ni cacahuetes (to not be worth even peanuts) *Mex, ES*; valer papas (to be worth potatoes) *Mex*; valer gorro (to be worth cap) *Mex* ♦ *His opinions are worthless.* **Sus opiniones no valen un bledo.**

Wow! (surprise) ¡Caramba! *L. Am., Sp*; ¡Caray! *L. Am., Sp*; ¡Huy! *L. Am., Sp*; ¡Híjole! *Mex, G, ES, Nic, Col*; ¡Chanclas! (Old shoes!) *Mex, ES*; ¡Chispas! (Sparks!) *Mex, Col*; ¡Chanfle! *Mex, Col*; ¡Cámara!, ¡Camaronchas! *Mex*; ¡Vóytelas! *Mex*; ¡Chale! *Mex*; ¡Epa, epa! *Caribbean* ♦ *Wow! You scared me. I didn't see you.* **¡Híjole! Me asustaste. No te vi.**

to **wrangle** →see: to have a blowup, to be at odds

to **write someone off** (break off with someone for good; →see also: to dump someone) borrar (a alguien) del mapa (to erase someone from the map) *parts of L. Am.*; enterrar a alguien (to bury someone) *Mex, Cuba, DR, U, Arg*; hacerle la cruz a alguien (to make the cross to someone) *S. Cone* ♦ *Don't talk to me anymore about Juan Carlos. I've written him off for good.* **No me hables más de Juan Carlos, que ya lo enterré con flores.**

X

X-rated flick (erotic) la película verde (green movie) *U, Arg, Sp* ◆ *You're not going to see that X-rated flick!* ¡No vas a ver esa película verde!

Y

to **yack** →see: to chatter away

yackety yak →see: chat

yada, yada, yada →see: blah, blah, blah

yap (mouth; often in reference to an angry person; →see also: kisser, trap) la trompa (trunk of an elephant) *Mex, Nic, CR, Col* ♦ *Marisol is very unpleasant; always with her puckered (lit. duck) yap.* Marisol es muy sangrona; todo el tiempo con su trompa de pato.

to **yap** →see: to chatter away

yarn →see: baloney, fib

to be a **yawn** →see: to be a drag

yeah (→see also: natch, uh-huh) ey *most of L. Am.;* simón (used instead of sí) *most of L. Am.* ♦ *Tired? —Yeah.* ¿Cansada? –Ey.

Yeah, right! (sometimes used to react to a compliment in a modest way) ¡Qué ocurrencia! (What an occurrence! What a thing to occur to you!) *L. Am., Sp* ♦ *How pretty you look! —Yeah, right!* ¡Qué bonita te ves! –¡Qué ocurrencia!

Yeah, right, and that's likely. (sarcastic) Claro, y los chanchos vuelan. (Right, and pigs fly.) *parts of L. Am.* ♦ *You think we're going to win the contest? —Yeah, right, like that's really gonna happen.* ¿Te parece que vamos a ganar el concurso? –Claro, y los chanchos vuelan.

Yeah, right, if you say so. (disclaimer after a compliment) ¿Cómo cree(s)? (How do you believe [that]?) *L. Am., Sp* ♦ *How young you look! —Yeah, right, if you say so.* Te ves tan jovencita. –¿Cómo crees?

Yeah, right. Sure thing. Ya está bien de cuentos. *most of L. Am., Sp* ♦ *Yeah, right. Sure thing. Don't say anything more.* Ya está bien de cuentos; no hables más.

to be a **yes man** decir amén a todo (to say amen to everything) *DR, ES, S. Cone, Sp* ♦ *He doesn't like problems: he's a real yes man.* A él no le gustan los problemas: siempre dice amén a todo.

You blew it. (You were too smart for your own good. You goofed; →see also: to blow it) Te pasaste. (You passed yourself.) *Mex, DR, PR, G, Col, S. Cone, Sp;* Ésa se te zafó. (That one got away from you.) *Mex* ♦ *A salesman shouldn't talk too much. You blew it on that sale.* Un vendedor no debe hablar tanto. Esa venta se te zafó.

You can count on me. Cuenta conmigo. (Count with me.) *L. Am., Sp* ♦ *We need volunteers. —You can count on me.* Necesitamos voluntarios. –Cuenta conmigo.

You can do it with your eyes closed. Se hace a ciegas. (It's done blindly.) *Sp* ♦ *That job is easy. You can do it with your eyes closed.* Ese trabajo es muy fácil. Se hace a ciegas.

You can't trick me. (You can't make a fool outta me. →see also: I see what you're up to.) Te conozco, mosco. (I know you, fly.) *ES, Nic, Peru, Ch, Arg* ♦ *You can't trick me. I won't buy that car from you.* Te conozco, mosco. No te compraré ese coche.

You don't have to think twice. (It's just as it looks, obvious.) No hay que darle vueltas. (There's no need to turn it around.) *Mex, DR, ES, S. Cone, Sp* ♦ *Let's finish this conversation . . . you don't have to think twice.* Terminemos esta plática... no hay que darle vueltas al asunto.

You give him or her an inch and he or she takes a mile. Le da el pie y le toma la mano. (You give him or her your foot and he or she takes your hand.) *L. Am., Sp*

You got it! (Agreed! That's understood!) ¡Vaya! *Mex, DR, G, ES, Col;* ¡Vale! *Sp* ♦ *Shall we meet at eight? —You got it!* ¿Nos vemos a las ocho? –Vaya, pues.

You have to put yourself out (put up with damn hard times) Hay que joderse. (You have to screw yourself.; vulgar)*Mex, ES, Sp* ♦ *In this country you have to put yourself out to earn a living.* En este país hay que joderse para ganarse la vida.

you know very well what I mean Ya sábanas (sabadabas). (used instead of Ya sabes because of the sound) *Mex, Col*; ya tú sabe') *Caribbean* ◆ *You know what I mean; why should I tell you? Ya sábanas; paquetes de hilo. (Ya sabes, ¿p'a qué te digo?)*

You look great! ¡Estás como quieres! (You are like you want to be!) *Mex, DR, ES, Sp* ◆ *Do you think I look good in this suit? —Yes, you look great! ¿Te parece que estoy bien con este traje? –Sí, ¡estás como quieres!*

You made your bed, now lie in it. El que con niños se acuesta... amanece mojado. (The person who sleeps with children . . . wakes up wet; the second part is understood, not normally added. If you take risks, you suffer the consequences.) *Mex, DR, ES, Nic, S. Cone, Sp*; El que las hace las paga. (He who makes them pays for them.) *Mex, DR, PR, ES, S. Cone*

You never can tell when . . . (expression used to indicate the probability or chance of something happening) ¿Quién quita que... ? (Who takes away that . . . ?) *Mex, DR, C. Am., Col, Ven, Peru* ◆ *You never can tell when my cousin might show up. Quien quita que venga mi prima.*

You outdid yourself. (→see also: to outdo oneself) Te luciste. (You shone.) *Mex, Peru, U*; Te pasaste. (You passed yourself.) *Ch, U* ◆ *The dinner was great. You outdid yourself. La cena estuvo estupenda; te pasaste.*

You overdid it. Te pasaste. (You passed yourself.) *Mex, DR, PR, G, Col, S. Cone, Sp* ◆ *You overdid it with your aggressive comments. Te pasaste con tus comentarios agresivos.*

You son of a bitch! (You bitch!) ¡La madre que te parió! (The mother who gave birth to you!; vulgar) *Mex, DR, PR, ES, Arg, Sp*; ¡Tu madre! (Your mother!, often accompanied by a gesture with the fist of one hand raised and clenched; vulgar) *Mex, C. Am.*; ¡Tu abuela! (¡Tu padre!) (Your grandmother! [Your father!]) *DR, ES, Sp* ◆ *You son of a bitch, Francisco. When will you stop mistreating your wife? La madre que te parió, Francisco. ¿Cuándo dejarás de maltratar a tu mujer?*

You're hopeless. No se puede contigo. (One can't with you.) *L. Am., Sp* ◆ *You're hopeless, boys. You're irresponsible and you don't do your work. No se puede con ustedes, muchachos. Son irresponsables y no cumplen con sus tareas.*

You're impossible. (I want nothing to do with you.) Contigo ni el saludo. (With you not even the greeting. Used humorously after being refused when an invitation was made, meaning that the other person is being unfriendly.) *Mex, G, ES, Col* ◆ *Enough already. Don't insist. You're impossible. Ya basta. No insistas. Contigo ni el saludo.*

You're just what the doctor ordered! (can be a street compliment) ¡Estás como lo recetó el doctor!) *L. Am.* ◆ *How gorgeous you look, woman! You're just what the doctor ordered. ¡Qué guapa, mujer! Estás como lo recetó el doctor.*

You're not serious! ¡No habla(s) en serio! (You're not talking seriously!) *L. Am., Sp* ◆ *But we can't travel at night. —You're not serious! Pero no podemos viajar de noche. –¡No hablas en serio!*

You're off the track (cold). No van por ahí los tiros. (The shots aren't going that way.) *DR, Ch, Sp* ◆ *Patricio is visiting the Benavides family a lot. I think he likes Josefina. —No, my dear, you're off the track. It's Rosmarí he's interested in. Patricio está visitando mucho la casa de los Benavides. Creo que le gusta Josefina. —Amiga mía, no van por ahí los tiros. Es Rosmarí que le interesa.*

You're on! (Agreed!; →see also: It's a deal., You got it!) ¡Papas! (Potatoes!) *Mex, ES, Col*; ¡Vale! *Sp*; ¡Vaya, pues! *Mex, DR, G, ES, Col* ◆ *Will you come to the river with us? —You're on! Vienes con nosotros al río? –¡Papas!*

You're screwed. Como dijo Herodes, te jodes. (As Herod said, you're screwed.; vulgar phrase of resignation) *Mex, DR, Sp* ◆ *You're going to be working with the new boss? —You're screwed! ¿Estarás trabajando con el nuevo jefe? –Como dijo Herodes, ¡te jodes!*

You're welcome. De nada. (Of nothing.) *L. Am., Sp*; No hay de qué. (There isn't of that.) *L. Am., Sp*; ¿Para qué? (For what?) *Mex*; Con mucho gusto. (With great pleasure.) *CR* ◆

Thanks for your help. —You're welcome. Gracias por su ayuda. –¿Para qué?

young folks la chaviza (opposite of momiza, fogies) *Mex, Col* ◆ *The young folks are all upset because they closed the disco.* La chaviza anda toda alborotada porque les cerraron la disco.

yours truly (I, me) el mismo (la misma) que viste y calza (the same who dresses and is shod) *L. Am., Sp;* su servidor(a) *Mex;* mi (el/la) menda *Sp* ◆ *And when you arrive, yours truly will be at the airport to meet you.* Y cuando ustedes lleguen, su servidor estará en el aeropuerto para recibirlos.

Yuck! ¡Huaca! (¡Huácala!) (also, guaca, waca) *Mex, DR, G, ES, Col;* ¡Fuchi! (¡Fúchila!) *Mex, ES, Col;* ¡Úchala! *Mex;* ¡Puah! *Sp* ◆ *Yuck! How disgusting! ¡Puah! ¡Qué asco!*

Z

zero →see: Zip.

zilch →see: Zip.

zillions →see: tons

to **zip along** (walk very fast, hightail it) echar un patín (to throw a skate) *Mex, Cuba* ◆ *He zipped along in an hour from the market to the port. Echó un patín de una hora desde el mercado hasta el puerto.*

Zip. (Zilch. Nothing. Not even beans.) Ni jota. (Not a jot.) *L. Am., Sp;* Ni papa(s). (Not even potato[es].) *Mex, C. Am., Col;* Nada, pescadito mojado. (Swim, little wet fish, with a pun on nada meaning both "nothing" and "swim.") *Mex, Col;* Ni maíz. (Not even corn.) *Mex;* Ni hostia. (Not even Host.; religious reference, vulgar.) *Cuba, Sp;* Ni torta. (Not even cake.) *Sp;* Ni gorda. (Not even a fat one [coin of little value].) *Sp* ◆ *Did you understand what the professor said? —Zip. ¿Entendiste lo que dijo el profesor? —Ni papas.*